W9-AJU-193

Ninth Edition

PRINCIPLES AND METHODS OF ADAPTED PHYSICAL EDUCATION AND RECREATION

Ninth Edition

Principles and Methods of Adapted Physical Education and Recreation

David Auxter, Ed.D.
Senior Scientist
Research Institute for Independent Living
Edgewater, Maryland

Jean Pyfer, P.E.D.
Dean, College of Health Sciences
Texas Woman's University
Denton, Texas

Carol Huettig, Ph.D., CAPE
Coordinator, Project I.N.S.P.I.R.E.
Visiting Professor, Department of Kinesiology
Texas Woman's University
Denton, Texas

Boston   Burr Ridge, IL   Dubuque, IA   Madison, WI   New York   San Francisco   St. Louis
Bangkok   Bogotá   Caracas   Lisbon   London   Madrid
Mexico City   Milan   New Delhi   Seoul   Singapore   Sydney   Taipei   Toronto

McGraw-Hill Higher Education

A Division of The **McGraw-Hill** Companies

PRINCIPLES AND METHODS OF ADAPTED PHYSICAL EDUCATION AND RECREATION
NINTH EDITION

Vice president and editor-in-chief: *Kevin T. Kane*
Executive editor: *Vicki Malinee*
Senior developmental editor: *Michelle Turenne*
Senior marketing manager: *Pamela S. Cooper*
Project manager: *Joyce Watters*
Associate media producer: *Judi David*
Production supervisor: *Laura Fuller*
Coordinator of freelance design: *Rick D. Noel*
Cover designer: *Jamie O'Neal*
Interior designer: *Kathleen Theis*
Cover images provided by authors
Supplement coordinator: *Sandra M. Schnee*
Compositor: *Interactive Composition Corporation*
Typeface: *10/12 Minion*
Printer: *Quebecor Printing Book Group/Fairfield, PA*

Library of Congress Cataloging-in-Publication Data

Auxter, David.
    Principles and methods of adapted physical education and recreation / David Auxter,
Jean Pyfer, Carol Huettig.—9th ed.
        p.   cm.
    Includes index.
    ISBN 0-07-232926-2
    1. Physical education for handicapped children—Study and teaching—United States.
    2. Handicapped children—Recreation—United States.   I. Pyfer, Jean.   II.   Huettig, Carol.
III. Title.

GV445 .A94   2001   00–037990
371.9′04486—dc21   CIP

To our families, students, and friends who understand and support our need to enable individuals with disabilities to take their rightful place in the mainstream of society

BRIEF CONTENTS

CONTENTS

PART

III

Children and Youth at Risk 291

PREFACE

As we embrace the beginning of the twenty-first century and re-envision the future of physical education and physical activity for individuals with disabilities, we must acknowledge that the present is, at once, the "best of times" and the "worst of times."

- It is the "best of times" because the Reauthorization of the Individuals with Disabilities Education Act of 1999 retained physical education as a *mandated, direct education service.*
- It is the "worst of times" because congressional mandates for a specially designed, *individual education program* based on a comprehensive assessment (which have existed since the initial passage of P.L. 94-142 in 1975) are often virtually ignored, and learners with disabilities are routinely placed in inappropriate physical education programs that do not meet their unique physical, social, or emotional needs.
- It is the "best of times" because there are increasing numbers of physical educators with specialized training, at the undergraduate and graduate levels, to meet the needs of learners with disabilities in play, games, leisure, recreation, sports, and physical fitness activities.
- It is the "worst of times" because many school boards and school administrators continue to relegate physical education to the role of an "extra" experience instead of acknowledging its critical role in the educational curriculum for *all* learners. In the "worst case" scenario, administrators are choosing to replace physical education with recess or to eliminate physical activity from the daily schedule altogether.

- It is the "best of times" because educators know more about how students, with and without disabilities, learn effectively than ever before in our history.
- It is the "worst of times" because state education agency and school district policies continue to emphasize performance on standardized, often culturally, linguistically, and gender-biased, tests that force well-meaning building principals and teachers to adopt educational methodologies which are not consistent with how students learn and experience success.
- It is the "best of times" because medical and instructional technology can critically improve the quality of life of an individual with a disability.
- It is the "worst of times" because ethical and moral standards regarding the equitable distribution and use of this technology have not kept pace with the technological growth.
- It is the "best of times" because individuals with disabilities have access to an increasing number of quality play, leisure, recreation, sports, and physical fitness programs and experiences that are family- and community-based.
- It is the "worst of times" because an increasing number of our children are poor, hungry, abused, homeless, disenfranchised, frightened, unwanted, and unloved. An increasing number of adults in this society are also poor, hungry, abused, homeless, disenfranchised, frightened, unwanted, and unloved.
- It is the "best of times" because of the influence of such individuals as Christopher Reeve, Marlee Matlin, Rudy Garcia, Jason Wenning,

and other talented individuals with disabilities. Because of these individuals, our society is more accepting and cognizant of the potential contributions of individuals with disabilities.

- It is the "worst of times" because individuals with conduct, behavior, and emotional disorders and mental illness continue to be discriminated against in horrific ways.
- It is the "best of times" because early childhood intervention and preschool programs, including Head Start, have been shown to play a significant role in improving the future of at-risk children and infants, toddlers, and preschoolers with disabilities.
- It is the "worst of times" because early childhood intervention and preschool programs continue to be underfunded at a time when increased dollars are being used for youth detention centers, jails, and prisons.

We have tried to honestly and comprehensively address these issues, and others, because physical education for individuals with disabilities cannot be addressed or understood outside of the context of contemporary education within the larger society.

It is vital that professionals committed to quality, individually designed, developmentally appropriate physical education, play, leisure, recreation, and sports programs for children and adults with disabilities be vocal and active advocates for those we serve to ensure that they receive the education, leisure, and recreation services they deserve.

CONTENT FEATURES

Content throughout the book has, once again, been thoroughly researched, referenced, and updated. In addition, many new photographs have been added to enhance the text.

Part I: The Scope

In this section, we provide an overview of adapted physical education—the definition, its historical development, the benefits strong programs have to offer persons with disabilities, and the barriers we must overcome if we are to provide meaningful services in the future.

Part II: Key Techniques

The types of physical education services needed by learners are common; however, each individual has unique needs that must be addressed. The learner's specific needs must be identified, a program to address those needs must be designed, a teaching approach to facilitate learning must be developed, and learner progress must be monitored. We address each of these critical components in this section.

Part III: Children and Youth at Risk

Today, more than at any other time in our history, more children are entering our schools with significant physical, social, and psychological disadvantages. The challenges these learners represent to themselves, to the schools, and to society are addressed in this section. In addition, strategies the physical educator can use to help *all* children grow and reach their full potential are shared.

Part IV: Needs of Specific Populations

In this section, specific types of disabilities and suggestions for intervention strategies are described. While we recognize that each person has unique qualities and needs, for ease of communication we have grouped similar conditions together. Each condition is defined, characteristics are given, means of testing are suggested, and specific programming and teaching techniques are detailed.

Website Resources

The Instructor's Manual and Test Bank will now be provided entirely on-line, along with additional content on posture and body mechanics, stress-reduction techniques, and web links for selected sports organizations that serve individuals with disabilities. A web link is also provided to Project

I.N.S.P.I.R.E. at Texas Women's University that includes additional activities, web links, and teaching suggestions. Visit our website at http://www.mhhe.com/hper/physed/humanperformance for more information.

COVERAGE OF CONTEMPORARY ISSUES

We have addressed specific issues of critical importance to the general physical educator, adapted physical educator, and therapeutic recreation specialist, including

- The Reauthorization of IDEA, 1999, and its particular implications regarding the emphasis on the family and the education of learners with disabilities in the general program, using the general curriculum
- The emphasis in contemporary litigation on the inclusion of learners with disabilities in the general education program
- Practical strategies for educating learners with disabilities in the general physical education program
- Specific strategies for educating learners with conduct and behavior disorders
- Strategies for teaching effectively within a learning community comprised of students and professionals representing diverse cultures, abilities and disabilities, linguistic backgrounds, socioeconomic status, ethnicity, gender, and gender preferences
- Specific strategies for teaching a physical education class comprised of children who use English as a second language
- Techniques for interacting effectively with the families of learners within a diverse learning community
- Specific strategies for the adapted physical education consultant to enhance the physical education experience for children with disabilities
- Specific techniques for the general physical educator to effectively use the services of the adapted physical education consultant

- Methods for effective collaboration with other professionals
- Significant education reform efforts, including charter schools, school voucher systems, and total quality management systems

NEW TO THIS EDITION

- Chapter 1, "Adapted Physical Education," uses a "good news/bad news" format to address the potentialities and problems associated with physical education for learners with disabilities.
- Chapter 2, "Determining Educational Needs Through Assessment," is redesigned to provide the reader with a better understanding of authentic assessment strategies. Examples are given for curriculum-based, sport skills, functional skills, physical fitness, perceptual-motor skills, and sensorimotor skills tests.
- Chapter 4, "Teaching to Meet Learners' Needs," is reworked to give the reader a better understanding of practical, appropriate intervention strategies.
- Chapter 6 is retitled "Behavior Management" and simplified to make the information more applicable in practical settings. Also, a section on schoolwide behavior-management systems has been added.
- Chapter 8 has been expanded to include sports conditioning for athletes with disabilities.
- Chapter 12 has been reorganized to address the broad category of pervasive developmental delays and includes autism, Asperger's syndrome, Rett syndrome, childhood disintegrative disorder (CDD), and pervasive developmental disorders–not otherwise specified (PDD–NOS).
- Chapter 14 is retitled "Conduct, Behavior and Emotional Disorders." Specific strategies for teaching children with these problems in the physical education program are highlighted.
- Chapter 16 is retitled "Communicative Disorders" and provides teaching suggestions for speech and language-learning disorders. It includes a new section that addresses communication disorders, including stuttering,

and receptive and expressive language disorders and updates coverage of hearing impairments.

- Chapter 18 is retitled "Other Health Impairments" and now includes updated coverage of attention deficit disorder (ADD) for consistency with current laws.
- Maria Garcia is a real-life example of a child (whose name has been changed) given a comprehensive educational assessment at the Texas Woman's University Institute for Clinical Services and Applied Research. She is followed throughout the text to demonstrate the relationship between assessment and intervention, as well as to illustrate the critical connection between each of the instructional components. For example, her comprehensive adapted physical education assessment is used to develop her individual education program, strategies for working with her parents are considered, and her "matrix of friends" is developed, as are specific recommendations regarding the strategies that should be used to create an appropriate learning environment.
- Case studies provided in selected chapters encourage the reader to apply the content with a *real* learner in mind. Specific tasks to foster critical thinking are provided with each case study.
- Practical suggestions for teaching learners with disabilities in the general physical education program are integrated throughout the text.
- Helpful lists of websites, videos, and CDs conclude selected chapters to provide additional resources for readers.

Pedagogical Aids

- Objectives begin each chapter to identify and reinforce the goals to be accomplished.
- Case studies and accompanying "Application Tasks" and "Critical Thinking Tasks" in selected chapters help students gain an understanding of learners who are taught in the public schools and guide students to a real-world application of the content.

- Tasks in selected chapters encourage students to apply the chapter content for problem solving.
- Key terms are defined in the glossary at the back of the text.
- Chapter content is summarized to reinforce key concepts and aid students with test preparation.
- Review questions end each chapter to foster classroom discussion, review, and application of the concepts learned.
- Student activities help students apply the content learned and introduce topics for further exploration.
- References and suggested readings have been thoroughly revised to provide the most current documentation.
- Recommended websites, videos, and CDs in selected chapters encourage further exploration of topics.

Ancillaries

Instructor's Manual and Test Bank

Extensively revised to reflect the significant content revisions in the ninth edition, the *Instructor's Manual and Test Bank* provides instructors with lecture outlines, teaching suggestions, and new test questions. Entirely online, this resource is particularly helpful for first-time instructors and newer faculty for effectively teaching an introductory-level course. Visit our website at www.mhhe.com/hper/physed/humanperformance for more information.

Computerized Test Bank

The *Microtest Test Bank,* with over 300 matching, true/false, listing, and essay questions, is available in IBM Windows and Macintosh formats to qualified adopters.

Gross Motor Activities for Young Children with Special Needs

The new edition of the text includes this very useful resource tool, which is valuable to students and instructors alike. This revised handy pocket guide includes over 250 activities and games designed to promote equilibrium, sensory stimulation and discrimination, body image, motor planning, locomotor skills, cross-lateral integration, physical fitness, relaxation, "animal games," and cooperative play activities. This is an excellent resource for students and instructors looking for activities to use in the classroom. It is available with each new text purchase.

ACKNOWLEDGMENTS

The authors would like to gratefully acknowledge the many contributions of individuals who provided their wisdom, effort, and support in the preparation of the ninth edition of this text.

We would particularly like to thank Dr. Greg Reid, president of the International Federation of Adapted Physical Activity and Dr. Jan Seaman, executive director of AAALF, the American Association of Active Lifestyles and Fitness, of the American Alliance of Health, Physical Education, Recreation and Dance, for their vision statements, included in the text.

We would like to thank the following individuals for their exceptional commitment to quality play, leisure, recreation, sports, and physical fitness programs for individuals with disabilities and for their willingness to share photographs and program information with us:

- Ms. Barbara Brandis, president, Research Institute for Independent Living
- Dr. Ron Davis, professor, Adapted Physical Education, Ball State University, Muncie, Indiana
- Ms. Maureen Dowd, director, Manitoba, Canada, Special Olympics
- Dr. Ron French, professor, Adapted Physical Education, Texas Woman's University
- Dr. Lisa Silliman-French, director, Denton (TX) Independent School District Adapted Physical Education Program
- Dr. Luke Kelly, director, Adapted Physical Education National Standards (APENS) Project, and dean of the College of Human Performance, University of Virginia

- Dr. Jim Rimmer, director of the Center on Health Promotion Research for Persons with Disabilities, Department of Disability and Human Development, University of Illinois at Chicago
- Dr. George Smith, director of Unified Sports, Special Olympics International
- Dr. Tom Songster, sports director, Special Olympics International

We would also like to thank the following individuals, programs, and companies for sharing their invaluable photographs with us:

- Achilles Track Club
- Challenge Aspen
- Deming Designs
- Disability Options
- Endolite
- GPK Incorporated
- Handicapped Scuba Association
- Northwest Passage
- Orthomerica
- Orthotic and Prosthetic Athletic Fund
- Rudy Garcia, elite athlete, and his wonderful mother
- Texas Woman's University—parents, children, and students participating in the TWU Aquatics and Motor Development Program
- United States Association of Blind Athletes
- United States Electric Wheelchair Hockey Association
- Jason Wenning, elite athlete
- Wilderness Inquiry

In addition, we would like to acknowledge the efforts of

- Jimmie Lynn Harris, reference librarian, Texas Woman's University, with special thanks for her comprehensive, creative, computer-assisted library searches; she saved us hours in the library
- Andy Tucker, reference librarian, Texas Woman's University, with special thanks for his help in securing articles and documents needed for the text; he saved us hours in the library

• Dr. Trish Hughes, for developing the Bruininks-Oseretsky Test of Motor Proficiency summary data graph in Chapter 2

Comments and criticisms from users of the eighth edition were carefully considered and addressed in this edition. A panel of reviewers was selected to assist with the revision of the manuscript to meet the needs of the instructors and their students. To these colleagues, we would like to express our sincere appreciation:

Peter M. Aufsesser   *San Diego State University*
Elizabeth Bate   *University of Northern Colorado*
Jodi Johnson   *University of Missouri–Columbia*
Sandra L. Wilson   *Winthrop University (SC)*
Maeberta Bob   *Winthrop University (SC)*

Finally, we would like to thank our editors at McGraw-Hill. In particular, we would like to thank Vicki Malinee, executive editor, a friend and colleague, for her ongoing sensitivity and appreciation for our deeply felt passion and commitment to the field of adapted physical education. In addition, we would like to thank Michelle Turenne, our developmental editor, for her persistent (with a capital *P*) interest in the quality of the text. We would like to thank Sheryl Krato for her technical assistance in the developing and processing of the manuscript. And we would like to thank Marilyn Sulzer and her team for all their hard work and attention to the details during the production process.

David Auxter
Jean Pyfer
Carol Huettig

P A R T

I

The Scope

In this section we provide an overview of adapted physical education—what the term means, its historical development, the benefits strong programs have to offer persons with disabilities, and the barriers we must overcome if we are to provide meaningful services in the future. Distinguished individuals who have contributed significantly to our field have shared their visions of the directions we must continue to move if we are to fully realize the dream we all share—accessible, healthful, and fulfilling movement opportunities for everyone, throughout life, regardless of ability level.

CHAPTER

1

Adapted Physical Education

■ **OBJECTIVES**

Define adapted physical education.

Explain physical education as a mandated, direct educational service in special education.

List several of the benefits of physical education for learners with disabilities.

Briefly describe the many, varied roles of the adapted physical educator.

Briefly explain the major events in the history of physical education for individuals with disabilities.

Briefly explain the major indicators in the Healthy People 2010 initiative.

Share strategies for transforming physical education and physical education for individuals with disabilities in the twenty-first century.

Courtesy Endolite: North America, Centerville, OH.

Adapted physical education is the art and science of developing, implementing, and monitoring a carefully designed physical education *instructional* program for a learner with a disability, based on a comprehensive assessment, to give the learner the skills necessary for a lifetime of rich leisure, recreation, and sport experiences to enhance physical fitness and wellness.

The potential exists for the physical educator and the adapted physical educator to make an incredible difference in the life of a learner with a disability and the learner's family. As undergraduate or graduate students involved in the study of kinesiology or physical education, play, movement, leisure, recreation, fitness activities, or sport has been significant in your life. It is possible to share that experience with learners with disabilities. It is a truly rewarding experience to make a significant difference in the life of any learner, but somehow it may prove more rewarding to improve the quality of life of a learner with a disability.

Imagine the possibilities:

- Sharing with a mother her delight that her son, diagnosed with autism, learned the skills necessary to go swimming with his younger brother at the community pool
- Enjoying the success of an athlete who placed in the top ten in the Boston Marathon, Wheelchair Division
- Teaching a child with a visual impairment to play catch with a friend
- Helping a child with a severe/profound disability clap her hands to music
- Coaching a Special Olympian and helping her achieve a personal best in the 1,500-meter run
- Sharing with a father his joy that his son with Duchenne muscular dystrophy has learned functional swimming skills
- Hugging a grandmother to share her pleasure that her young grandson with pervasive developmental delays shared a toy with another child
- Coaching a teenager with a hearing impairment who wrestles on his high school wrestling team
- Developing an after-school "cooperative games" program in which children with and without disabilities can experience success
- Helping a student using a wheelchair learn to navigate an obstacle course and do a "wheelie"
- Working with a young parent to develop a home program to foster equilibrium in her toddler with Down syndrome
- Helping a student with severe dyslexia develop cross-lateral integration
- Teaching a young adult using an electric wheelchair to play hockey
- Developing strategies so a woman with multiple sclerosis can participate with her friends in an aqua aerobics program
- Helping a learner with a conduct disorder monitor and control his own behavior so he can participate in the general physical education program
- Taking a little boy with a passion for hockey to his first sledge hockey game
- Skiing downhill alongside a young woman using a sit-ski
- Watching an athlete you coached proudly accept a first-place medal at the Paralympics
- Enjoying a pizza party with your team after a victory in the United States Association of Blind Athletes regional track and field games
- Teaching yoga skills to a little girl with spastic cerebral palsy to help her maintain flexibility
- Helping a middle school student with asthma develop a personal conditioning program to prepare for the junior high school cross-country team
- Sharing with a grandfather his incredible pride that his grandson with fetal alcohol syndrome earned a spot on the school "play day" relay team
- Teaching a student using a walker the skills necessary to participate in an age-group soccer program with his buddies
- Helping a young child with intellectual delays ride a bicycle

- Assisting a young woman enroll in and use the weight-training equipment in a local fitness center
- Collaborating with a family making important decisions about the future of their child after graduation from high school

DEFINITION OF SPECIAL EDUCATION

The term *special education* means specially designed instruction, at no cost to parents, to meet the unique needs of an individual with a disability, including

1. Instruction conducted in the classroom, in the home, in hospitals and institutions, and in other settings
2. Instruction in *physical education*

DEFINITION OF PHYSICAL EDUCATION

Physical education for individuals with disabilities was specifically defined in P.L. 94-142, and that definition was retained in the Individuals with Disabilities Education Act (IDEA).[38,42]

1. The term means the development of
   a. Physical and motor fitness
   b. Fundamental motor skills and patterns
   c. Skills in aquatics, dance, and individual and group games and sports (including intramural and lifetime sports)
2. The term includes special physical education, adapted physical education, movement education, and motor development.

    The two essential components of physical education for persons with disabilities are developing and implementing an individual education program (IEP) and teaching the defined curricula of physical education. When specially designed physical education is prescribed on the child's IEP, educators will provide physical education to ensure children and youth with disabilities an equal opportunity to participate in those services and activities. Each child with a disability is to participate in physical education with children without disabilities to the maximum extent appropriate. [35, section b]

BENEFITS OF PHYSICAL EDUCATION FOR STUDENTS WITH DISABILITIES

The *good news* is that there are significant benefits of a quality physical education program for learners with disabilities:

- The development of equilibrium, sensory discrimination and integration, and sensory-motor function
- The development of locomotor and nonlocomotor skills
- The development of object-control skills
- The development of play, leisure, recreation, and sport skills
- The development of physical fitness for maintenance of daily living skills and health/wellness
- The development of a repertoire of movement skills necessary for independent living
- The development of physical and motor prerequisites to vocational skills required for independent living

    The benefits of a quality physical education program for learners with disabilities can not be minimized. The *bad news* is that, like general physical education programs, the benefits are not clearly understood by the administrators who make program decisions and allocate budgets.

THE ADAPTED PHYSICAL EDUCATOR

The adapted physical education (APE) teacher is the person responsible for developing an appropriate individual physical education program for individuals with disabilities. The APE teacher is a physical educator with highly specialized training in the assessment and evaluation of motor competency; physical fitness; play; and leisure, recreation, and sport skills. The APE teacher is a direct service provider, not a related service provider, because special physical education is a federally mandated component of special education services.[41]

Depending on the size of the school district, the numbers of students with disabilities who require adapted physical education, the case load, and the unique skills of physical education and special education professionals, the APE teacher may assume any or all of the following roles:

- Direct service provider (hands-on teaching)
- Assessment specialist, completing comprehensive motor assessments of individuals with disabilities and making specific program recommendations
- Consultant for physical education and special education professionals and paraprofessionals providing physical education instruction for individuals with disabilities
- IEP/multidisciplinary team committee member who helps develop and monitor the IEP
- In-service educator, providing training for those who will provide physical education instruction for individuals with disabilities
- Student and parent advocate
- Facilitator of a "circle of friends" for a learner with a disability
- Program coordinator who develops curricular materials, develops intra- and inter-agency collaborations to meet the needs of individuals with disabilities
- Transition facilitator who helps the IEP/multidisciplinary team develop an appropriate individual transition plan for those students preparing to leave school and move into the community[34]

PREVALENCE

The *good news* is that Child Find efforts to identify and serve children and youth with disabilities in the public schools has been successful. In the 1996-1997 academic year, over 5 million learners with disabilities received special education services.[35] Information regarding the number of children with specific disabilities served by special education is included in Figure 1-1.

Each year, the U.S. Department of Education, Office of Special Education and Rehabilitation Services (OSERS), reports to Congress pertinent facts about the education of learners with disabilities. Recent data indicate

- Children with disabilities in special education represent approximately 11 percent of the entire school-age population.
- Approximately twice as many males as females receive special education services.
- Approximately 85 percent of school-age children who receive special education have mild disabilities.[35]

In addition, almost three-quarters of a million (737,025) infants and toddlers with developmental delays and preschoolers with disabilities received early childhood intervention (ECI) services or preschool education for children with disabilities in 1996–1997. The *bad news* is that this represents a *60 percent increase* in the number of children needing service since 1990-1991.

The overwhelming number of infants, toddlers, and preschoolers requiring special education intervention is related to, but not limited to, the following:

- *Growing numbers of infants affected by drug and alcohol use in utero*
- *Inadequate prenatal care during pregnancy*
- *Drastically increased numbers of children being raised in poverty*
- *Increased numbers of children who are victims of abuse and neglect*
- *Parents with limited parenting skills*
- *Medical technology which allows more premature and medically fragile infants to survive*

There is also a reason for concern regarding the number of students who have been identified as needing special education services because of conduct, behavior, and emotional disorders. Less than 1 percent of school-age children in the United States are identified as having conduct, behavior, and emotional disorders for special education

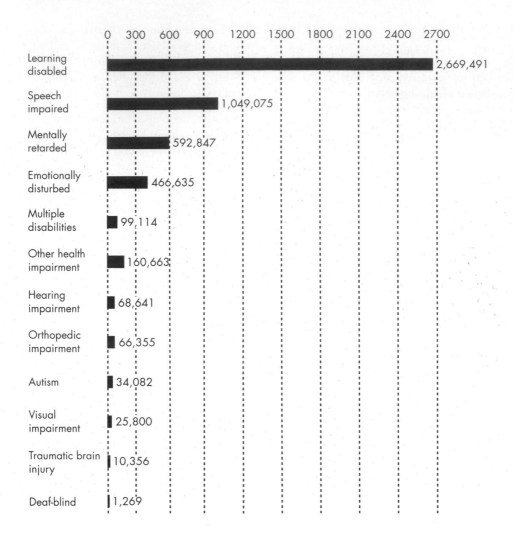

	0	300	600	900	1200	1500	1800	2100	2400	2700

- Learning disabled — 2,669,491
- Speech impaired — 1,049,075
- Mentally retarded — 592,847
- Emotionally disturbed — 466,635
- Multiple disabilities — 99,114
- Other health impairment — 160,663
- Hearing impairment — 68,641
- Orthopedic impairment — 66,355
- Autism — 34,082
- Visual impairment — 25,800
- Traumatic brain injury — 10,356
- Deaf-blind — 1,269

1996–1997 Total: 5,224,328

Figure 1-1   Number of School-Aged Children (Six to Twenty-One) with Disabilities Who Received Special Education Services in the 1996-1997 School Year[35]

From US Department of Education: Twentieth annual report to Congress on the Implementation of the Individuals with Disabilities Education Act, pps A 2-4.

purposes.[31] This figure appears to be a significant underestimation of the actual number of students who are in desperate need of quality intervention. Sachs wrote,

Due to federal law, schools cannot easily remove students who qualify for special education services. Consequently, the schools are

indirectly encouraged **not** to identify these students so they can remove them from their classrooms through in-school suspension, out-of-school suspension, a shortened school day, homebound instruction, alternative school placement, ignored truancy or expulsion. . . . While it is unrealistic to believe that special education services are going to "cure" a majority of these students, we do know that we can succeed with some of them. We can reduce the amount of pain and suffering that students with conduct disorders inflict on our environment and themselves.[31]

HISTORY OF ADAPTED PHYSICAL EDUCATION

The *good news* is that the history of adapted physical education is rich and reflects significant growth. The actual history of adapted physical education began with the implementation of P.L. 94-142 in

1975. The traditions associated with the profession, however, are tied to the advancements in the medical professions and in rehabilitation services.

Advancements in medicine, rehabilitation, and the education of individuals with disabilities have been tied, ironically, to war. World War I and World War II, in particular, found veterans returning to civilian life in need of significant medical and rehabilitation services. Many services previously considered hospital services became separate, recognized medical fields; these included physical therapy, occupational therapy, and corrective therapy.

Hand Propelled Bikes
Courtesy Northeast Passage, Chapter of Disabled Sports, USA, Durham, NH.

However, the main impetus for educating individuals with disabilities did not occur until early in the twentieth century, and as late as the early 1960s for persons with mental retardation or emotional disturbance. President Franklin D. Roosevelt made it infinitely clear, by his remarkable example, that a disability need not interfere with greatness. The incredible efforts of the Kennedy family, devoted to improving the lives of individuals with mental retardation, and the International Special Olympics program need to be acknowledged.

In 1952, the Committee on Adapted Physical Education of the American Association of Health, Physical Education, Recreation and Dance adopted a resolution to accommodate children with disabilities in physical education programs of diversified developmental activities designed specifically to meet their individual needs.[3] The commitment to individuals with disabilities was strengthened in the early 1970s when a group of adapted physical educators dedicated to providing appropriate programs for students with disabilities met in Washington, DC. The purposes of their meeting were to define what constituted appropriate physical education for persons with disabilities and to develop a strategy for ensuring that physical education was identified in P.L. 94-142. Some of the professionals who championed physical education as a mandated educational service at that important meeting included Dr. David Auxter, Dr. Lane Goodwin, Dr. Jean Pyfer, and Dr. Julian Stein. They were successful in their efforts, and that led to a national thrust to prepare physical educators with specialized training in providing programs for persons with disabilities. That definition appeared earlier in this chapter.

In the spring of 1991, the National Consortium for Physical Education and Recreation for Individuals with Disabilities (NCPERID) in conjunction with the National Association of State Directors of Special Education (NASDSE) and Special Olympics International conducted an "Action Seminar" on adapted physical education for state directors of special education and leaders of advocacy groups for individuals with disabilities. This conference had two goals:

- Identify the barriers that were preventing full provision of appropriate physical education services to individuals with disabilities
- Establish an action agenda for addressing and resolving these problems

To counter the trend of providing less than appropriate physical education experiences to students with disabilities, in 1994 the National Consortium for Physical Education and Recreation for Individuals with Disabilities published national standards for adapted physical education.[16] The purpose of the Adapted Physical Education National Standards (APENS) project was to ensure that physical education instruction for students with disabilities was provided by qualified physical education instructors.[1] To achieve this end, the project has developed national standards for the profession and a national certification examination to measure knowledge of these standards.

The definition of who was "qualified" to provide physical education services to individuals with disabilities was left to the individual states and their respective certification requirements. Unfortunately, unlike other special education areas ("mental retardation," "learning disabilities," "early childhood," etc.), most states did not have defined certifications or endorsements for teachers of adapted physical education. Please refer to Figure 1-2 for a list of the areas of information included in the APENS standards.

On May 10, 1997, the first national administration of the APENS certification exam was given at 46 sites around the country. A total of 219 teachers completed the exam, and 175 passed. As of July 16, 1997, the APENS project is managed by a standing committee within the NCPERID governance titled the APENS-NCPERID Committee. This committee is composed of seven members:

Ron French, C.A.P.E., Texas Woman's University, committee chair

Luke E. Kelly, University of Virginia

Figure 1-2   APENS Standard Categories

1. Human development
2. Motor behavior
3. Exercise science
4. Measurement and evaluation
5. History and philosophy
6. Unique attributes of learners
7. Curriculum theory and development
8. Assessment
9. Instructional design and planning
10. Teaching
11. Consultation and staff development
12. Student and program evaluation
13. Continuing education
14. Ethics
15. Communication

For more information regarding APENS standards please go to the APENS website at http://www.twu.edu/APENS.

Ron Davis, Ball State University

Nancy Megginson, San Jose State University

Christine Stopka, University of Florida

Stephen Butterfield, University of Maine

Georgia Frey, Texas A&M University

For more information about the many devoted professionals who made significant contributions to the development of the APENS project, please refer to the APENS website at http://www.twu.edu/APENS[1]

In the past several decades, the emerging discipline of Adapted Physical Education has witnessed amazing growth. The *Adapted Physical Activity Quarterly (APAQ)*, the official journal of the International Federation of Adapted Physical Activity, was first published in 1983. *APAQ* is the journal in which professionals share their research and opinions regarding the emerging discipline of adapted physical education. *Palaestra: The Forum of Sport, Physical Education, and Recreation for Those with Disabilities* is a quarterly publication released in cooperation with the United States Olympic Committee's Committee on Sports for the Disabled and the Adapted Physical Activity Council of the

American Alliance for Health, Physical Education, Recreation and Dance, dealing with adapted physical activity for individuals with disabilities, their families, and professionals in the field. *Sports 'n Spokes,* for the past two decades, has been a magazine dedicated to the *active* wheeler. *Sports 'n Spokes* covers competitive wheelchair sports and recreational opportunities for individuals who use wheelchairs.

The National Consortium for Physical Education and Recreation for Individuals with Disabilities (NCPERID) was formed in 1973 to promote, stimulate, and encourage significant service delivery, quality professional preparation, and meaningful research in physical education and recreation for individuals with disabilities. NCPERID has played a major role in shaping the direction of the adapted physical education profession. Its members—primarily adapted physical education and therapeutic recreation professionals—actively serve as advocates for favorable legislation and funding at the national, state, and local levels; disseminate information about new legislation; and stimulate and conduct research.[23]

The Adapted Physical Activity Council (APAC) is affiliated with the American Association of Active Lifestyles and Fitness of the American Alliance of Health, Physical Education, Recreation and Dance. APAC's mission is to promote quality movement experiences for individuals with disabilities through research, advocacy, publications, programs at conventions and workshops, position statements, standards of practice, and cooperation with other organizations committed to people with disabilities.[2]

In the spring of 1999, Dr. Jim Rimmer, director of the Center on Health Promotion Research for Persons with Disabilities, Department of Disability and Human Development, University of Illinois at Chicago, received a $7 million grant from the Centers for Disease Control and Prevention to establish the National Center on Physical Activity and Disability (NCPAD). The NCPAD is a clearinghouse for research and practice information to promote healthy lifestyles for persons with disabilities. This commitment to the health and wellness of individuals with disabilities is cause for celebration. In the new millennium, the field of adapted physical education has the potential to affect significant change in the health and wellness of individuals with disabilities.

The NCPAD was developed through a cooperative venture of the University of Illinois at Chicago and the Secondary Conditions Branch of the Centers for Disease Control and Prevention. The NCPAD is designed to gather, synthesize, and disseminate information related to fitness, physical activity, and disability. The goals of the new center are to help reduce the incidence of secondary conditions and to improve the overall quality of life for persons with disabilities through promotion of higher levels of fitness and healthy lifestyles.[28]

The NCPAD reflects a national priority to address the public health benefits of physical activity and physical fitness for individuals with disabilities. This is particularly critical because individuals with disabilities are more likely than the general population to be at risk of developing secondary health conditions—obesity, high blood pressure, diabetes—due to sedentary lifestyles.

The *bad news* is that many state education agency personnel, school board members, school district administrators, and parents have yet to understand the importance of physical education in the lives of students with disabilities. And, unfortunately, many fail to understand the significant impact of physical activity on the health and wellness of individuals with disabilities throughout the life span.

FEDERAL LEGISLATION AND THE RIGHTS OF PERSONS WITH DISABILITIES

The *good news* is that there is a long history of federal legislation that supports the education of learners with disabilities. Perhaps the most significant civil rights litigation tied to the education of learners with disabilities was *Brown v. Board of Education, Topeka, Kansas* in 1954.[7] Though the litigants, parents, sued in protest over "tracking" their

children who were African American into noncollege preparatory classes, the affirmation of the courts regarding the significance of education in the lives of ALL children was a landmark case. The court wrote:

> [Education] is required in the performance of our most basic responsibilities. . . . It is the very foundation of good citizenship. In these days, it is doubtful that any child may reasonably be expected to succeed in life if he [or she] is denied the opportunity of an education. Such an opportunity, where the state has undertaken to provide it, is a right which must be made available to **all** on equal terms.[7]

The rights of persons with disabilities became a central concern during the 1970s, when landmark court cases ruled that children with disabilities had a right to a free and appropriate education and training and that persons in institutions had a right to rehabilitation. These court decisions paralleled and created the initiative for federal legislation such as the Rehabilitation Act of 1973[37] and the Education of the Handicapped Act of 1975 (P.L. 94-142).[38]

At the beginning of the 1990s, the passage of the Americans with Disabilities Act (ADA) and the Individuals with Disabilities Education Act (IDEA) further addressed the rights of persons with disabilities. The ADA act had a significant impact on the civil rights of individuals with disabilities in the public and private sectors.

The rights of individuals with disabilities have been enhanced, primarily, through four major pieces of federal legislation. This legislation includes the Rehabilitation Act of 1973, the Education of the Handicapped Act of 1975, the Americans with Disabilities Act (ADA) of 1990,[39] and the Individuals with Disabilities Education Act (IDEA) of 1990.[40] These four pieces of legislation were created to provide equal opportunity for individuals with developmental disabilities. The similarities are

1. Equity of services for individuals with disabilities when compared with those without disabilities

A Javelin Thrower with an Above-the-Knee Amputation
Courtesy Orthotic & Prosthetic Athletic Assistance Fund, Inc., Alexandria, VA.

2. Accessibility to environments and programs so there is equal opportunity to derive benefits from services
3. Encouragement of integration of individuals with and without disabilities.

All of the acts apply these basic principles but focus on different contexts.

Table 1.1 is a brief summary of major legislation that has had an impact on the education of learners with disabilities. Each of the major laws will be considered in detail in the appropriate chapter. Court decisions that have had an impact on the education of individuals with disabilities are summarized, briefly, in Table 1.2. Each of the major court cases (litigation) that have had an impact on the education of individuals with disabilities will be considered in the appropriate chapter.

The *bad news* is that increasing litigation against the public schools has proved incredibly costly in terms of both financial cost human work hours. And, unfortunately, it has created a situation in which the parents with the most resources (money or power) can demand and receive for their children educational services that are not accessible or available to the children of the poor and disenfranchised.

EDUCATIONAL REFORM AND SPECIAL EDUCATION

There is a great deal of public criticism regarding the effectiveness of public education in the United States today. The findings of the thirtieth annual Phi Delta Kappa/Gallup Poll, 1998, of 1,151 adults, randomly selected to generalize to

TABLE 1.1	Federal Legislation That Has an Impact on Physical Education for Individuals with Disabilities

1966 P.L. 89-750 amendments to the Elementary and Secondary Education Act
Created the Bureau of Education for the Handicapped (now the Office of Special Education Programs) devoted to the professional preparation of personnel to serve individuals with disabilities

1973 P.L. 93-112 Section 504 of the Rehabilitation Act
Mandated that individuals with disabilities cannot be excluded from any program or activity receiving federal funds solely on the basis of the disability

1974 P.L. 93-247 Child Abuse and Protection Act
Created systems to protect children from abuse and mandated that a person who suspects child abuse must report it or commit a felony

1975 P.L. 94-142 Education for All Handicapped Children Act
- Mandated a free, appropriate public education for all children with disabilities between the ages of three and twenty-one years
- Mandated an individual education program (IEP) be developed for each student with a disability
- Mandated education in the least restrictive environment (LRE)
- Identified physical education as a direct instructional service required for students with disabilities
- Mandated that students with disabilities be included, where appropriate, in intramural and interscholastic opportunities.

1978 Amateur Sports Act
The United States Olympic Committee formed the Committee on Sports for the Disabled.

1986 P.L. 99-457 Education for All Handicapped Children Amendments of 1986
States were mandated to develop comprehensive early childhood intervention services for infants and toddlers with developmental delays and to expand services for preschoolers with disabilities.

1988 Technology-Related Assistance for Individuals with Disabilities Act
Ensured students with disabilities would have access to needed technology-related assistance

1990 P.L. 101-476 Individuals with Disabilities Education Act
Mandated the use of the term *disability* instead of *handicapped*

1990 P.L. 101-336 Americans with Disabilities Act
Expanded civil rights protections for individuals with disabilities with the public and private sectors

1994 School-to-Work Opportunities Act
Ensured all school-to-work programs are fully accessible to students with disabilities

1997 Individuals with Disabilities Education Act Amendment
- Emphasized education for students with disabilities in the general education program
- Increased the emphasis on parental participation in the assessment and IEP process

1998 Workforce Investment Act of 1998
One of the provisions is to develop research and demonstration projects to indicate how adapted physical education programs can develop health and related skills that improve work performance.

1998 Reauthorized Technology-Related Assistance for Individuals with Disabilities Act
Made technical amendments to the 1988 Technology-Related Act.

TABLE 1.2	Court Decisions (Litigation) That Have Had an Impact on the Education of Individuals with Disabilities

1970   *Diana v. State Board of Education* (California)
        Children cannot be placed in special education on the basis of culturally biased tests.

1972   *Mills v. Board of Education of the District of Columbia*
        Every child has a right to equal opportunity for education. Children with emotional disorders cannot be excluded from school; lack of funds is not an acceptable excuse for failure to provide services.

1972   *Larry B. v. Riles* (California)
        IQ tests cannot be used as the sole basis for placing children in special classes.

1979   *Armstrong v. Kline* (Pennsylvania)
        Children with disabilities who regress and cannot recoup their gains over extended layoffs from school are entitled to an extended school year through the summer.

1982   *Rowley v. Hendrik* (Hudson, New York School District)
        A child with a disability has a right to an IEP and the support services to ensure the child will benefit from it.

1984   *Irving Independent School District v. Tatro* (Texas)
        Services needed to enable a child to reach, enter, exit, or remain in school are required.

1988   *Polk v. Central Susquehanna Intermediate Unit* (Ohio)
        A school district cannot have a blanket policy that no child will get one-to-one physical therapy by a licensed physical therapist if that is what is needed.

1991   *Greer v. Rome City*
        A child with Down syndrome may enroll in a regular kindergarten program instead of a "substantially separate" special education class. It ruled that the child's IEP was inappropriate because (1) it failed to accommodate the child with supplementary aids and services in the regular class, (2) no attempts were made to modify the kindergarten curriculum, and (3) the school developed the IEP before the meeting and failed to inform the parents of the range of options available.[13]

1993   *Oberti v. Board of Education of Clementon School District*
        Ruled that a school district could not segregate a student who demonstrated disruptive behavior because the district failed to provide supplementary aids and services to reduce the child's disruptive behavior.

1994   *Sacramento City Unified School District v. Rachel*
        Developed a four-factor standard for educational placement in the least restrictive environment based on (1) the educational benefits of a full-time regular class, (2) the nonacademic benefits of a regular class, (3) the effects a student has on the teacher and children in the regular class, and (4) the cost of placement in a regular class.

1994   *Clyde K. and Sheila K. v. Puyallup School District*
        Ruled that, if children with emotional and behavioral disorders adversely affect the learning of other children and the educational environment, they may be removed and placed in a more restrictive educational environment.[9]

1999   *Cedar Rapids, Iowa, Community School District v. Garret*
        Ruled that school districts must provide necessary nursing services to ensure a student is educated in the least restrictive environment.[8]

the U.S. population as a whole, found that the general public had mixed feelings about the current performance and accomplishments of the public schools:

- Half of the parents felt the schools helped their children become eager learners.
- Thirty-four percent said their children simply tolerated learning.
- Fourteen percent said their children were "turned off" to learning.[30]

But, most of the problems the parents identified as significant problems in the public schools had little to do with education per se. The parents listed the following as the top five problems:

- Fighting and violence
- Lack of discipline
- Lack of financial support
- Use of drugs
- Overcrowded schools

Much of the criticism of the public school comes, however, from the business sector. Business leaders have expressed concerns that the public schools are not adequately preparing youth to assume their rightful place within the workplace. Dr. David Berliner has suggested that business leaders in this country have no right to criticize the public schools because the corporate contribution to the taxes that support the public schools has decreased dramatically in the past ten years from 50 percent to 30 percent. This is primarily a result of tax exemptions and tax reduction incentives to get "business and industry" to set up shop in a particular area.

The *good news* is that public education in this country is producing citizens ready to assume their roles. Berliner and Biddle have written an impassioned book that criticizes the public and government officials who created the "manufactured crisis" in public education (see Figure 1-3). They wrote,

> The Manufactured Crisis was not an accidental event. Rather, it appeared within a specific historical context and was led by identifiable critics whose political goals could be furthered

Figure 1-3   Myths Associated with the "Manufactured Crisis" in Public Education[6]

Berliner and Biddle note that there are *myths* about contemporary education that simply *are not true:*
- Student achievement in American schools—primary, secondary, and university-level—have declined.
- The problem-solving skills of America's young people have declined.
- American schools do not compare well with schools in other countries.
- America spends more money on its schools than other nations do.
- The amount of money spent is not related to student performance.
- The productivity of American workers is deficient; this is directly related to inadequate training in American schools.
- Public schools are not staffed by qualified teachers.

by scapegoating educators. It was also supported from its inception by an assortment of questionable techniques—including misleading methods for analyzing data, distorting reports of findings, and suppressing contradictory evidence. . . .

One of the worst effects of the Manufactured Crisis has been to divert attention away from the **real** problems faced by American education—problems that are serious and that are escalating in today's world. To illustrate, although many Americans do not realize it, family incomes and financial support for schools are much more poorly distributed in our country than in other industrialized nations. This means that in the United States, very privileged students attend some of the world's best private and public schools, but it also means that large numbers of students who are truly disadvantaged attend public schools whose support is far below that permitted in other Western democracies. Thus, opportunities are **not** equal in America's schools. As a result, the achievements of

Waterproofing a Blind Child
Photo by Carol Huettig.

students in schools that cater to the rich and the poor in our country are also far from equal.[6]

A number of educational reforms have been attempted to address the perceived problems in the public schools and in special education. These educational reform movements are discussed in Chapter 7.

The most significant educational initiative—the initiative that may actually make a difference in the education of an ethnically, culturally, linguistically, gender, gender preference, and ability/disability diverse student population—is an increased emphasis on the *family* as the critical unit in the education of students with and without disabilities. Dr. Dean Corrigan—speaking at the "Challenges for Personnel Preparation in Special Education"—sponsored by the Office of Special Education Programs, September 1999—suggested there is a need to switch from "child-centered" schools to "family-centered" schools.[11]

Dr. Corrigan also advocated for "full service schools." He advocated for a co-location of services in the schools, so *all* the services a family needs are easily and readily accessible. This would require significant inter-agency collaboration among education, social services, human services, and health services so the needs of families can be met. Dr. Corrigan used the term *inter-professional villages* to describe his vision for the schools of the future.[11]

The *bad news* is that few administrators in state and local education agencies share Dr. Corrigan's remarkable vision for the millennium. He is embracing, essentially, a return to the days when the school was the focus of the community and all community members worked together for the sake of the children. An African American proverb reminds that "it does, indeed, take a whole village to raise a child."

PHYSICAL FITNESS, HEALTH AND WELLNESS

The *good news* is that the critical relationship between a physically active life and health and wellness has been well established. Siedentop wrote,

> During this century we have witnessed what is now commonly referred to as the epidemiological transition, the shift in the main cause of death from infectious diseases to degenerative cardiovascular diseases and cancers. . . . To substantially increase the percentage of citizens who value physical activity enough to voluntarily make decisions to be regularly active despite attractive alternatives, we need to move from a traditional focus on remediation to a focus on prevention; and we need to view prevention not only as altering the risk-status of individuals but also as developing and sustaining attractive, inclusive, physical activity infrastructures for children, youth, and adults; that is, we need to focus on the social determinants of physical activity.[32]

Recommendations from the Centers for Disease Control and Prevention and the American College of Sports Medicine make it clear that every adult should accumulate 30 minutes or more of moderate intensity activity on most, preferably all, days of the week.[26] The Surgeon General of the United States released the following recommendations regarding physical activity and health.

• People of all ages can benefit from regular physical activity.
• Significant health benefits can be obtained by including a moderate amount of physical activity (e.g., 30 minutes of walking briskly or raking leaves, 15 minutes of running, or 45 minutes of playing volleyball) on most, if not all, days of the week.
• A modest increase in activity can improve the health and quality of life for most Americans.
• Longer and more vigorous activities can provide additional health benefits.
• Some of the prominent health benefits of appropriate activity include reduced risk for premature mortality, heart disease, colon cancer, hypertension, and diabetes mellitus.
• Other benefits include improved mental health and improved fitness of the muscles, bones, and joints.[36]

A coalition of major organizations committed to the health and wellness of individuals with and without disabilities has been formed in order to become a more vocal advocate. See Figure 1-4 for

Figure 1-4	The National Coalition for Promoting Physical Activity

American College of Sports Medicine
American Alliance for Health, Physical Education, Recreation and Dance
American Heart Association
Association for Worksite Health Promotion
International Health Racquet and Sportsclub Association
National Association of Governor's Councils on Physical Fitness

the names of the organizations that are involved in the coalition.

While there has been an increased focus on the physical activity needs of adults, there has also been an increased focus on the physical activity needs of children. The Council for Physical Education for Children (COPEC) of the National Association for Sport and Physical Education (NASPE) of the American Alliance for Health, Physical Education, Recreation and Dance developed the following guidelines for children:

• Elementary-school-age children should accumulate at least 30 to 60 minutes of age- and developmentally appropriate physical activity from a variety of physical activities on all, or most, days of the week.
• An accumulation of more than 60 minutes, and up to several hours, per day of age- and developmentally appropriate activity is encouraged for elementary-school-age children.
• Some of the child's activity each day should be in a period of time lasting 10 to 15 minutes or more and should include moderate to vigorous activity. This activity will typically be intermittent, involving alternating moderate to vigorous activity with brief periods of rest and recovery.
• Extended periods of inactivity are inappropriate for children.
• A variety of physical activities selected from the Physical Activity Pyramid is recommended for elementary school children.[27]

Clearly, the schools can and should meet the physical activity needs of children. McKenzie wrote,

> Schools have the potential to be the primary source of physical activity. . . . An established part of the community infrastructure, schools serve nearly all children and adolescents, have a staff of physical activity experts, require almost all children to take some form of physical education, and house facilities and equipment specifically designed to promote physical activity.[20]

However, it remains clear that many students do not have daily access to a quality physical education program that gives them the opportunity to engage in 30 minutes of moderately intense activity.[21] The *bad news* is that increasing demand for improved academic performance has caused administrators who do not understand the developmental needs of children and youth and who do not know the critical relationship between activity and brain function to reduce and/or eliminate physical education from the curriculum.

HEALTHY PEOPLE 2010

The *good news* is that there is an increasing interest in and understanding of the profound personal, community, and national impact of contemporary health practices in this country. Murray wrote,

> At the same time we are cutting back on physical education, our society is spending more than ever on health care. Last September, the U.S. Department of Health and Human Services (HHS) predicted that health care expenditures from 1997 to 2007 would increase from $1 trillion to more than $2.1 trillion. During that time, hospital growth is expected to lag behind growth in drug companies, number of physicians, and other professional health care services. Although the most optimistic projections suggest health care costs will double over the next decade, ironically, the public continues to treat the need for health-related education with benign neglect.[22]

The Committee on Leading Health Indicators for Healthy People 2010, Division of Health Promotion and Disease Prevention, Institute of Medicine, of the National Academy of Sciences released the "Leading Health Indicators for Healthy People 2010."[18] The complex report identified three proposed "sets" and their specific indicators:

1. Health determinants and health outcomes
2. Life course determinants
3. Prevention

It is interesting to note that three health indicators appear in each of the three sets, indicating the significance and comprehensive impact of each on personal, community, and national health:

1. Poverty
2. Tobacco use
3. Disability

Please refer to Table 1.3 for the summary of health indicators in Healthy People 2001.

There appears to be an almost linear correlation between poverty and poor health and disease. Americans with the lowest income have a significantly higher incidence of illness and disease. Tobacco abuse has been identified as a leading cause of death in the United States. Its use is causative in many forms of cancer and respiratory ailments and may create significant problems for a child exposed to its toxins in utero. In fact,

TABLE 1.3	Proposed Leading Health Indicator Sets, Healthy People 2010	
Health Determinants and Outcomes	**Life Course Determinants**	**Prevention**
Physical environment	Substance abuse	Poverty
Poverty	Poverty	Tobacco use
High school graduation	Physical activity	Childhood immunization
Tobacco use	Health care access	Cancer screening
Weight	Cognitive development	Hypertension screening
Physical activity	Violence	Diabetic eye exam
Health insurance	Disability	Health care access
Cancer detection	Tobacco use	Disability
Disability	Low birth weight	Preventable deaths

tobacco may be as toxic to the fetus in utero as alcohol or other drugs.

Disability is a major indicator because of its profound impact on the person, the family, and community. Individual and societal costs include significant medical expenses, loss or reduced productivity in the home and at work, increased education expenses, and perhaps a decreased quality of life. Of concern may be the secondary effects of the disability that are associated with sedentary lifestyles. Certainly, studying the impact of the secondary effects of a disability on health is one of the purposes of the National Center on Physical Activity and Disability (NCPAD).

As mentioned, poverty, tobacco, and disability are significant health indicators which are included in all three health indicator sets. Several variables are included in two of the three sets:

- Physical activity
- Health care access
- Preventable deaths

Increasingly, regular physical activity is understood to be significant in the maintenance of health and wellness. The Leading Health Indicators for Healthy People 2010 report stated,

> Regular and sustained physical activity has documented beneficial effects on cardiovascular functioning (e.g., reducing hypertension and hypercholesterolemia) but also on the prevention of osteoporosis and its sequelae (e.g., hip fractures), the effects of osteoporosis, and on such mental conditions as depression.[18]

Access to health care is a critical issue that is negatively related to poverty, homelessness, and migrancy. The *bad news* is that continued, regular care in the medical community is a critical factor in the maintenance of health that is not available to all in this society. *Preventable deaths* refers to intentional and unintentional injury. Intentional injury deaths include those from suicide and homicide and, thus, may be related to location of the individual's home or social environment. Preventable deaths are, for example, those caused by drunk driving.

ESCALATION OF HATE IN THE SCHOOLS

The *good news* is that concerned educators and parents have begun to address the reality that, reflecting the larger society, the public schools remain incredibly segregated and that hate and intolerance is a divisive force. Educators and parents have developed empathy programs, in-service education for professionals and paraprofessionals, and curricular materials to prevent and reduce or allow healing attitudes.

Parks suggests that there are three elements in an educational program that hopes to address racism.[25] These may be effective in addressing sexism, ageism, and homophobia in the schools, as well.

Prevention

Classroom instruction and professional development efforts that helps individuals identify racist influences and prevents them from growing include.

- Antiracism curricula
- Peace education
- Global education
- Moral reasoning
- Critical thinking
- Cooperative learning

The physical educator and adapted physical educator may be particularly effective and vital in the school community because of unique skills to foster cooperative play in and through cooperative games and challenges (low ropes course, etc.).

Abatement or Reduction

Abatement involves reducing tension between groups, using specific techniques to lessen distress:

- Conflict resolution
- Peer mediation
- Service learning
- Cooperative learning

Healing

The healing process may require a great deal of energy and certainly requires a willingness to engage in a critical self-examination regarding attitudes and feelings and to engage in dialogue with individuals representing different cultures, ethnic groups, religious groups, genders, and gender preferences. Certainly, it is critical that physical education teachers and adapted physical education teachers exhibit what Robinson and Rathbone call "cultural competence":

> Cultural competence may be best defined as a combination of sensitivity, attitudes, skills, and knowledge that allow an individual or system to establish or maintain productive relationships with members of a different ethnic group or culture.[29]

The *bad news* is that, after several decades of significant initiatives to desegregate the public schools, there is an incredible resurgence of racism, sexism, and homophobia in the schools. Increasingly violent actions of students in the schools give notice that many young people in this society are angry, have low self-esteem, and feel disenfranchised.

EDUCATIONAL STANDARDS

The *good news* is that school reform initiatives that focus on the improvement of educational standards increased dramatically after the passage of Goals 2000: Educate America Act in 1994. The lofty goals included in Goals 2000, while largely unmet, included the following:

By the Year 2000:—
- All children in America will start school ready to learn.
- The high school graduation rate will increase to at least 90 percent.
- All students will leave grades 4, 8, and 12 having demonstrated competency over challenging subject matter, including English, mathematics, science, foreign languages, civics and government, the arts, history, and geography.

- Every school in America will ensure that all students learn to use their minds well, so they may be prepared for responsible citizenship, further learning, and productive employment in our nation's modern economy.
- U.S. students will be first in the world in mathematics and science achievement.
- Every adult American will be literate and will possess the knowledge and skills necessary to compete in a global economy and exercise the rights and responsibilities of citizenship.
- Every school in the United States will be free of drugs, violence, and the unauthorized presence of firearms and alcohol and will offer a disciplined environment conducive to learning.
- The nation's teaching force will have access to programs for the continued improvement of their professional skills and the opportunity to acquire the knowledge and skills needed to instruct and prepare all American students for the next century.
- Every school will promote partnerships that will increase parental involvement and participation in promoting the social, emotional, and academic growth of children.

The Goals 2000 act provided federal funds to support the development and implementation of standards within the context of general school reform.[10] In his sixth annual State of American Education speech, delivered February 16, 1999, Richard Riley, the secretary of education, indicated that forty-eight of the fifty states had begun to address the critical issue of improved education standards. These include two types of standards:

- Content standards. These describe the knowledge and skills that students need to acquire in a given subject area.
- Performance standards. These describe, specifically, what a student needs to do to demonstrate he or she has indeed learned what is important within the content standards.[10]

Content and performance standards are particularly important for the physical educator serving students with disabilities. Certainly, the apparent intent of recent legislation and litigation is that students with disabilities receive their education within the general program using the general curriculum. The physical educator and adapted physical educator should play a critical role in the development of these standards to ensure that content and performance standards in physical education are high and consistent with best practice in the field.

The *bad news* is that few schools have actually implemented significant changes in order to help students meet higher standards. The physical educator can use his or her considerable energy to help his or her colleagues mobilize to implement changes to help students meet higher standards in motor performance, physical fitness, problem solving, and critical thinking.

THE TEACHER'S REALITY

The *good news* is that teachers continue to play a critical role in the lives of children and youth. Good physical education teachers continue to be the "pied pipers" of the professionals who work with children and youth. Children are drawn, of course, to teachers who love to do what children love to do—play and move. And those who truly love children and love to teach continue to be the backbone of this society. Certainly, the profession becomes even more important as children have more and more needs that must be met.

The *good news/bad news* is that there is a critical shortage of personnel with the training to meet the needs of children with disabilities. Teachers with training to meet the educational needs of students with disabilities in special education will be able to find jobs. In the 1995–1996 academic year, over 4,000 vacancies in special education were not filled, and 28,000 individuals teaching special education were not certified for their positions.[33]

The *bad news* is that physical education teachers are facing the following realities:

- More children enter the gymnasium with their basic needs unmet—food, shelter, safety,

warmth, and love. The teacher must address those needs in order for learning to occur.
- Teachers are increasingly asked to serve as quasi social workers, psychologists, counselors, nurses, and parents.[17]
- The children in the gymnasium may reflect significant ethnic, cultural, and linguistic diversity. It is not unusual for a physical education teacher to face a class in which most of his or her students don't speak the same language as the teacher.
- Teachers are tired of being grossly underpaid. This grows increasingly difficult because of the incredible amounts of money being paid others with gross motor and athletic skills— professional athletes. It is ironic and shameful that those who can "bounce the ball" are paid millions of dollars and those with the unique skills to teach children to bounce the ball struggle to make ends meet because they love children and have made a commitment to their society.
- Teachers are, unfortunately, not held in the same regard as they were at one time in our society. In fact, teachers and parents have moved into hostile relations.

O'Hanlon summarized,

> There are too many kids for too few classrooms and teacher's income are lower than plumbers' and private schools are skimming off the cream and aging taxpayers don't want to spend more money on education and more students are being home-schooled and a thousand other problems beset public education in the last days of the 20th century. But there's one problem that comes first and sets the tone for almost everything else: the discipline crisis.[24]

LEISURE AND RECREATION OPPORTUNITIES FOR INDIVIDUALS WITH DISABILITIES

The *good news* is that individuals with disabilities and their families now have the potential to participate, together, in a wide variety of quality

Competitive tennis provides opportunities for challenge and personal growth.
Courtesy National Foundation of Wheelchair Tennis.

Include all children in the least restrictive environment.
Photo by Carol Huettig.

leisure and recreation programs. Wonderful programs such as Wilderness Inquiry give individuals with disabilities and their families the opportunity to participate in quality outdoor recreation experiences together. Northeast Passage works to create an environment where individuals with disabilities can recreate with the same freedom of choice and independence as their able-bodied peers. The National Ability Center is dedicated to the development of lifetime skills for persons with disabilities and their families by providing affordable, quality sports and recreation experiences. The benefits of these experiences build self-esteem and confidence, enhancing active participation in the fabric of community life. Since 1976, the Breckenridge Outdoor Education Center has offered quality outdoor learning experiences for people of all abilities, including people with disabilities, those with serious illnesses and injuries, and "at-risk"

populations. As a nonprofit organization, the Breckenridge Outdoor Education Center is dedicated to helping people reach their full potential through custom programs for groups and opportunities for individuals. With adventure trips, internships, and volunteer positions, people of all abilities can get involved.

The *bad news* is that the schools, for the most part, have not seriously addressed transition issues in leisure, recreation, fitness, and sports programming for learners preparing to leave the public schools as adults. While many school districts have in place excellent school-to-work programs and provide job training, when appropriate, few are actually helping learners with disabilities and their families learn to access and enjoy leisure and recreation opportunities available in their communities.

SPORT FOR INDIVIDUALS WITH DISABILITIES

The *good news* is that sport opportunities continue to grow and improve for individuals with disabilities. Dr. Karen Depauw wrote,

> The U.S. Congress recently approved a change to the definition of elite athlete (as defined by the United States Olympic Committee) to include athletes with disabilities; a very positive end to a struggle that began more than a

decade ago. The significance of this action lies in the official recognition and acknowledgement that athletes with disabilities, both male and female, are indeed athletes.[12]

Dr. David Beaver wrote,

> On Wednesday, October 21, 1998, Senator Ted Stevens' (R-AK) much awaited amendments to the original Amateur Athletic Act, PL 95-606 (1978), were passed by Congress as part of the Omnibus Appropriations Bill. . . . Hailed by many as historic landmark legisla-

A young athlete competes in his chair.
Courtesy of Jefferson Parish Public Schools, Special Education Dept. Harvey, LA.

tion for athletes with disabilities, the new bill amends the original with provisions reflecting the growth of competition by athletes with disabilities within Olympic and amateur athletic programs, and ensures the continued development of sport opportunities for individuals with disabilities.

However, for those interested in the mission of *PALAESTRA,* the most important aspect of the amendments of 1998 lies in those sections recognizing sport for athletes with disabilities; on their parity with other athletes, and programs provided under the aegis of the USOC; in the recognition of the International Paralympic Committee, the Paralympic Games, as well as the acknowledgement of the USOC as the National Paralympic Committee for the United States.[5]

There are literally hundreds of organizations devoted to quality athletic competition for individuals with disabilities. You can gain easy access to information about many of those organizations at the Texas Woman's University Project INSPIRE website[34] or Dr. Gail Dummer's Disability Sport website at http://ed-web3.educ.msu.edu/Kin866/contents.htm

It is also very exciting to note that the business sector has started to realize there is definitely a market for carefully designed equipment necessary for the athlete with a disability to be more successful in his or her sport. Companies such as Radventure, Flex-Foot, Orthomerica, Endolite, Deming Designs, Disability Options, and Orthotic and Prosthetic Athletic Fund are deeply committed to providing quality sport equipment for individuals with disabilities. And major equipment and supplies companies, such as Sportime, have been innovative in the development of equipment for individuals with disabilities to use in leisure, recreation, fitness, and sports activities.

The *bad news* is that athletes with disabilities, particularly in the rural parts of the country, may find it difficult to access sports programs and competitions designed to meet their unique needs. It appears that virtual competition, using the Internet, may prove to be one avenue to allow individuals all over the world to compete in individual sports with athletes with similar disabilities. Although there are critical limitations to this type of competition—just as there are critical limitations in e-mail vs. personal communication—it may provide one vehicle for competition.

THE TRANSFORMATION OF PHYSICAL EDUCATION FOR ALL CHILDREN

The *good news* is that there are deeply passionate individuals who are striving to ensure that all children have a quality, daily physical education program that allows them to meet their basic physical needs. Certainly, the National Association for Sport and Physical Education of the American Alliance of Health, Physical Education, Recreation and Dance has taken the lead in establishing national standards for physical education. The NASPE National Standards for Physical Education suggest that a student should

- Demonstrate competency in many movement forms and proficiency in a few movement forms
- Apply movement concepts and principles to the learning and development of motor skills
- Exhibit a physically active lifestyle
- Achieve and maintain a health-enhancing level of physical fitness

Learning Colors Through Active Play
Photo by Carol Huettig.

- Demonstrate responsible personal and social behavior in physical activity settings
- Demonstrate understanding and respect for differences among people in physical activity settings
- Understand that physical activity provides opportunities for enjoyment, challenge, self-expression, and social interaction[27]

Vail wrote,

> Unfortunately, children who hate gym class grow into adults who associate physical activity with ridicule and humiliation. And dread of physical activity is taking its toll on our health. Report after report tells us that, as a nation, we are getting fatter and more sedentary than generations before us.[42]

Dr. Judith Young, executive director of NASPE said, "We've shifted focus from performance-related activities to reaching a level of fitness that supports good health."[42] Dr. Mary Marks, instructional coordinator of health and physical education of the Fairfax, Virginia, public schools has suggested that the schools must re-envision physical education in order to be sensitive to the needs of the students.[42] Physical education programs that are more sensitive to the developmental needs of children and youth and that focus on their fitness and health include activities in which they can participate actively as adults. These activities include, but are not limited to, aerobic dance, weight training, fitness walking, mountain biking, hiking, in-line skating, aqua aerobics, cross-country skiing, snow shoeing, swimming, yoga, rock climbing, kayaking, and canoeing.

Dr. Hal Lawson described an existing crisis in physical education and spoke passionately about the need to transform physical education if it is to serve all our children and maintain viability as a profession.[17] He suggested a number of action steps that would lead toward a transformation:

- Research the physical education needs of poor, vulnerable, and minority children and youth.
- Focus research on the child's family and community.

- Refocus the curriculum to ensure children are prepared for community-based leisure, recreation, fitness and sport activities.
- Refocus energies into supportive extra-school activities.
- Refocus the curriculum based on student interest.
- Re-establish physical education as a critical part of the neighborhood and community.

Dr. Rainer Martens has written eloquently of the need to transform physical education. Essentially, Martens noted that adults (teachers and parents) forget that children and youth like to play and move because it is *fun*. It is critical that physical educators and adapted physical educators avoid the following:

- Adult goals for organizing activities for children are often not the same goals the children have. Adults are often performance-oriented, and children often are seeking only to have fun. This discrepancy in goals often leads to conflict between teacher/coach and children.
- As part of adults' performance orientation, they routinize learning of physical activity skills into a routine to the point of making them exceptionally boring. It may be the best way to teach these skills on the short term, but it is not the best way to encourage children to participate in the activity for a lifetime.
- Adults may replace games and unstructured play with calisthenics, a pernicious way of exercising thought up surely by a sadistic military sergeant. Calisthenics are boding to most people, and people must be highly motivated to do them for extended periods of time. There are many more enjoyable ways than calisthenics to have children be physically active from which they will derive the health benefits we deem desirable.
- We squelch fun also by using physical activity as punishment for misbehaving. It's obvious to everyone (except all those who continue to prescribe to this practice) that doing so turns kids off to physical activity.[19]

Martens continues,

> It's far less important that young people master physical activity skills to a high level or win the game or championship when our long-term objective is to encourage children to be active for a lifetime. When this objective is foremost in the minds of adult leaders, then the emphasis shifts from the outcome of participation to the quality of the experience during participation. If that experience is positive, if that experience enhances children's perceptions of self-worth, or if that experience is fun, then children are far more likely to continue that activity, and to do so for a lifetime.[19]

Dr. James Kauffman wrote of special education,

> If we are going to survive as a viable professional field, then I think we are going to need to change the way we view our legitimacy in public education and develop a sense of self-worth and pride in what we do. I would like to see us become unapologetic about our function, our identity, our distinctiveness, our visibility.[15]

Kauffman's advice for special educators is equally appropriate for physical educators as well as adapted physical educators. Physical educators must not be apologetic about their significant place in the education of learners with and without disabilities. The Puritan dichotomy of mind and body continues to haunt educators committed to physical education. Physical educators must speak openly and without hesitation about the critical relationship between movement and brain function, movement and memory, and movement and learning.

Wilma Harrington, in the Thirty-Third Amy Morris Homans Commemorative Lecture, 1999, "Our Collective Future: A Triumph of Imagination," spoke of her inspiration after reading and contemplating the following poem by Brian Andreas

> *In my dream*
> *the angel shrugged*
> *& said, If we*
> *fail this time, it*
> *will be a failure of*
> *imagination*
> *& then she placed the world*
> *gently in the palm of my hand.*[4]

Certainly, as physical educators and adapted physical educators the very future of students with disabilities lies in the palms of our hands. And that future has not been placed in our hands gently; it has been thrust on us because of an incredible need for good teachers—physical education teachers who are committed to learners with disabilities—to step forward and make a difference. With imagination, we can transform our profession and refocus our energies[14] (see Figure 1-5). The *good news* is that we can make a difference. Imagine the possibilities:

- Helping a family get involved with a Wilderness Inquiry trip into the boundary waters in Minnesota
- Teaching a ten-month-old child with Down syndrome to swim
- Helping a streetwise adolescent use her remarkable basketball talent to score over 30 points in a Special Olympics game
- Clapping to acknowledge the remarkable dance of a troupe of boys with Duchenne muscular dystrophy
- Serving as a guide runner for a marathoner who just happens to be blind
- Taking a little boy with nemaline rod myopathy to see his first-ever sledge hockey tournament
- Encouraging older adults with secondary disabilities to participate in aqua aerobics
- Helping two little girls with spina bifida communicate via e-mail (modern-day pen pals), even though they live thousands of miles apart
- Sharing a pizza with a bocce team after a victory
- Helping an aerobic dance teacher modify the dance steps so an individual in a wheelchair can participate in her class
- Hugging a parent grieving the loss of her envisioned child
- Watching a father's joy as his little girl executes a perfect balance beam dismount
- Playing video golf with a young man with a traumatic brain injury

Figure 1-5   Thoughts Regarding the Future of Adapted Physical Education: The Visionaries in Our Field

Dr. David Auxter (in response to the request of his co-authors)
Senior scientist, Research Institute for Independent Living

The Centers for Disease Control and Prevention has identified insufficient leisure physical activity as a health risk for persons with disabilities. Physical activity is essential for the prevention and management of a host of chronic health conditions such as back pain, arthritis, diabetes, asthma, and other disorders that lead to disability or contribute to secondary disabling conditions. The economic consequences of poor health promotion programs that do not include physical activity are severe and have been recognized by the United States Congress. Health promotion through leisure physical activity was the rationale for the initiation of the recently introduced "Physical Education Progress Act." Worksite health promotion programs which include physical activity have proven to be effective; however, there are few persons with disabilities in worksite health promotion programs. Therefore, the twenty-first century requires a shift of emphasis from performance-based physical education programs in the schools for persons with disabilities to programs that generalize physical activity to leisure lifestyles in the community so they may derive health promotion and lifelong recreational benefits.

Dr. Greg Reid
President, International Federation of Adapted Physical Activity

While challenges always lie ahead, I am optimistic about the future of adapted physical activity. I believe we will see a modest shift of emphasis in outcome measures, from physical skill and fitness to physical activity, largely resulting from the philosophy of active living and the recent Surgeon General's report. We will increasingly be concerned with the needs of aging individuals with a disability. Also, our programs will place more emphasis on empowerment and self-determination, thus encouraging choice, decision making, self-observation, personal goal setting, problem solving, and self-evaluation. Finally, we will spend less time debating the pros, cons, and extent of inclusion and more time investigating and sharing means to improve the process.

Dr. Janet Seaman
Executive director, American Association for Active Lifestyles and Fitness

One day, educators will care as much as I do that children with disabilities have the same opportunities for physical activity as their able-bodied peers. Teaching education is changing from focusing on the elite performer to reflecting a more egalitarian philosophy—engaging ALL children in physical activity for the fun and lifelong values of activity for a healthy lifestyle. The new breed of pedagogists have helped the profession "turn the corner" from the physical training orientation to the new physical education—emphasizing lifelong skills, enjoyment of physical activity, and wellness.

Preservice physical educators are being prepared today to serve the diverse needs of ALL students in the new century. Their preparation will manifest in including multicultural and lifestyle variances as well as performance differences, providing sufficient depth and breadth to be challenging for all, and offering a comprehensive program rich in a variety of activities beneficial for enhancing the quality of life for ALL citizens. In my vision, society merely needs to reinforce and reward practice of that training.

- Losing a tennis game to your opponent who used a wheelchair
- Helping a teenager with spina bifida climb a rock wall
- Riding a tandem bicycle in a 25-mile road race with a partner with a vision impairment
- Walking three days a week for 30 minutes with a friend with an above-the-knee amputation and prosthesis
- Developing a play group for young mothers of children with Down syndrome who want their children to be active
- Sharing a sign language joke with a teammate
- Ocean kayaking to watch the whales with athletes with spina bifida
- Creating a web page designed to foster the growth of quality physical education for learners with disabilities

Practice makes perfect.
Courtesy Jefferson Parish Public Schools, Special Education Dept. Harvey, LA.

SUMMARY

The twentieth century saw drastic and remarkable growth in physical education for individuals with disabilities. Certainly, the law and litigation have provided the impetus for this growth.

There have been major changes in the public schools in the past several decades. These changes have at once challenged and frustrated the physical educator with a commitment to serving children and youth with and without disabilities. Certainly, the physical educator in the twenty-first century must demonstrate increased skills in facilitating cooperative play and in developing critical thinking skills and must demonstrate cultural competence.

There are increased opportunities for individuals with disabilities to lead full and healthy lives, enjoying leisure, recreation, fitness, and sport opportunities because of a quality physical education program. Certainly, this is possible only if physical educators re-envision the future of the discipline.

REVIEW QUESTIONS

1. What is adapted physical education? How does it differ, if it does, from general physical education?

2. What are the similarities among the major legislation affecting physical education for individuals with disabilities?

3. What are the benefits of a quality physical education program for indivdiuals with disabilities?

4. What is APENS? Briefly describe its impact on the field.

5. Briefly describe the basic physical activity guidelines for adults and children.

STUDENT ACTIVITIES

1. Join ADAPT-TALK at sportime.com/adapt-talk/subscribe

2. Join PE-TALK at sportime.com/pe-talk/subscribe

3. Join your state Association of Health, Physical Education, Recreation and Dance. Attend its state convention.

4. Visit the recommended websites and travel through their links into the world of cyberspace.

REFERENCES

1. Adapted Physical Education National Standards (APENS) http://www.twu.edu/APENS

2. American Association for Active Lifestyles and Fitness (AAALF) at http://www.aahperd.org/aaalf.html

3. American Association of Health, Physical Education, and Recreation: Guiding principles for adapted physical education, *J Health Phys Educ Rec,* p. 15, April 1952.

4. Andreas B: *Still mostly true,* Decorah, IA, 1994, Storey People.

5. Beaver D (Editor's Corner): A coming of age: Sports for athletes with disabilities and the Amateur Sports Act, *Palaestra,* 14(4):5, 1998.

6. Berliner DC, Biddle BJ: *The manufactured crisis: myths, fraud, and the attack on America's public schools,* New York, 1995, Pegasus Books.

7. *Brown v. The Board of Education,* 347 US, 483, 1954.

8. *Cedar Rapids, Iowa, Community School District v. Garrett,* U.S. Supreme Court, March 3, 1999, No. 96-1793.

9. *Clyde K, Sheila K v. Puyallup School District,* 21 IDELR 664 (9th Cir, 1994).

10. Cobb RB, Tochterman S, Lehmann J: *School reforms and students with disabilities: a review,* Ft. Collins, 1999, Colorado State University, School of Education.

11. Corrigan D: Keynote address. *Challenges for personnel preparation in special education conference,* Washington, DC, September 1999, Office of Special Education Programs.

12. DePauw KP: Girls and women with disabilities in sport, *JOPERD,* 70(4):50–52, 1999.

13. *Greer v. Rome City School District,* 950 F 2d 688 (11th Cir, 1991).

14. Harrington WM: Our collective future: a triumph of imagination. *Quest,* 51:272–284, 1999.

15. Kauffman JM: Commentary: today's special education and its messages for tomorrow, *J Spec Ed,* 32(4):244–254, 1999.

16. Kelly LE: *National standards for adapted physical education,* Washington, DC, 1994, U.S. Department of Education, Office of Special Education Programs.

17. Lawson HA: Rejuvenating, reconstituting, and transforming physical education to meet the needs of vulnerable children, youth, and families, *J Teaching in Phys Educ,* 18:2–25, 1998.

18. *Leading health indicators for healthy people 2010,* Final Report, Committee on leading health indicators for healthy people 2010, Chrvala CA, Bulger RJ, editors. Washington, DC, 1999, Division

of Health Promotion and Disease Prevention, Institute of Medicine, National Academy of Sciences.

19. Martens R: Turning kids on to physical activity for a lifetime, *Quest,* 48:303–310, 1996.

20. McKenzie TL: School health-related physical activity programs: what do the data say? *JOPERD,* 70(1):16–19, 1999.

21. McKenzie TL et al.: Student activity levels and lesson context during third grade physical education, *Research Q Exercise and Sport,* 66:184–193, 1995.

22. Murray BA, Murray KT: A nation out of shape, *Am School Bd J,* August:29–33, 1999.

23. National Consortium of Physical Education and Recreation for Individuals with Disabilities at http://ncperid.usf.edu

24. O'Hanlon, A: Time out for Alan, *The Washington Post Magazine,* June 21:3–15, 23–25, 1998.

25. Parks S: Reducing the effects of racism in schools, *Educational Leadership,* April:14–19, 1999.

26. Pate RR et al.: Physical activity and public health: a recommendation from the Centers for Disease Control and Prevention and the American College of Sports Medicine, *J Am Medical Assoc,* 273:402–407, 1995.

27. *Physical activity for children: a statement of guidelines,* Reston VA, 1998, Council for Physical Education for Children (COPEC) of the National Association for Sport and Physical Education an association of the American Alliance for Health, Physical Education, Recreation and Dance.

28. Rimmer J, Schiller WJ: New center announced, *International Fed Adapted Phys Act Newsletter,* 7(4):3, 1999.

29. Robinson EG, Rathbone GN: Impact of race, poverty, and ethnicity on services for persons with mental disabilities: call for cultural competence, *Mental Retardation,* August:333–338, 1999.

30. Rose L, Gallup A: The 30th annual Phi Delta Kappa/Gallup poll of the public's attitudes toward the public schools, *Phi Delta Kappan,* September:41–56, 1998.

31. Sachs J: The hidden conspiracy in our nation's schools, *Behavioral Disorders,* 25(1):80–82, 1999.

32. Siedentop D: Valuing the physically active life: contemporary and future directions, *Quest,* 48:266–274, 1996.

33. Study of personnel needs in special education (SPeNSE) at http://www.spense.org

34. Texas Woman's University, Project INSPIRE at http://venus.twu.edu/~f_huettig

35. U.S. Department of Education: Twentieth Annual Report to Congress on the Implementation of the Individuals with Disabilities Education Act, 1998, Washington, DC, pp. 2–4, 1998.

36. U.S. Department of Health and Human Services: Physical activity and health: a report of the surgeon general. Atlanta, 1996, U.S. Department of Health and Human Services, Centers for Disease Control and Prevention, National Center for Chronic Disease Prevention and Health Promotion.

37. U.S. Department of Health, Education, and Welfare: *504 regulations for the Rehabilitation Act of 1973, Rehabilitation Act amendments of 1974, and Education of the Handicapped Act,* Fed Reg 45:339–395, 1990.

38. U.S. 94th Congress: Public Law 94-142, November 29, 1975.

39. U.S. 101st Congress: Public law 101-336, August 9, 1990.

40. U.S. 101st Congress: Public law 101-476, October 30, 1990.

41. U.S. 103rd Congress: Individuals with Disabilities Education Act, 1995.

42. Vail K: Fit for life: trading in old-fashioned gym class for the "new PE," *Am School Bd J,* August:31–32, 1999.

SUGGESTED READINGS

Martens R: Turning kids on to physical activity for a lifetime, *Quest,* 48:303–310, 1996.

Siedentop D: Valuing the physically active life: contemporary and future directions, *Quest,* 48:266–274, 1996.

RECOMMENDED WEBSITES

Please keep in mind that these websites are being recommended in the winter of 1999. As such, the sites may have moved, been reconfigured, or disappeared from the Internet.

Centers for Disease Control and Prevention
http://www.cdc.gov

Surgeon General's Report
http://www.cdc.gov/nccdphp/sgr/ataglan.htm

National Coalition for Promoting Physical Activity
http://www.ncppaorg.ncppa

American College of Sports Medicine
http://www.acsm.org/sportsmed.

PE Central
http://www.chre.bt.edu/~/pe.central

Texas Woman's University Project INSPIRE
http://venus.twu.edu/~f huettig

Education Law
http://www.edlaw.net

Disability Sport
http://ed-web3.educ.msu.edu/Kin866/contents.htm

AAALF, American Alliance of Health, Physical Education, Recreation and Dance
http://www.aahperd.org/aaalf

RECOMMENDED VIDEOS

Aquarius Health Care Videos
5 Powderhouse Lane
PO Box 1159
Sherborn, MA 01770
www.aquariusproductions.com

> Beyond the Barriers
> 47 minutes, purchase price $90
> Item #DISBEYOND

> My Country
> 60 minutes, purchase $195
> Item #DISCOUNTRY

> No Barriers
> 48 minutes, purchase price $90
> Item #DISBARRIERS

> Without Pity
> 56 minutes, purchase price $129
> Item #DISWITHOUT

Fanlight Productions
Psychology, Social Work, and Disabilities
Video Collections, 1999-2000
4196 Washington Street
Boston, MA 02131

> Breathing Lessons: The Life and Work of Mark O'Brien
> By Jessica Yu
> Academic Award—Best Short Documentary
> 35 minutes, purchase price $195
> Order No. CV-180

> Challenge
> By Amy Kaplan
> Heartland Emmy Winner
> 28 minutes, purchase price $195
> Order No. CV-266

> Vital Signs: Crip Culture Talks Back
> By David Mitchell and Sharon Snyder
> Grand Prize, Rehabilitation International World Congress
> 48 minutes, purchase price $195
> Order No. CV-230
> Note: An excellent video, but it does contain strong language and nudity

Key Techniques

The types of services needed by learners are common; however, each individual has a unique profile that must be addressed in the most appropriate fashion. For learners to fully benefit from physical education, their specific needs must be identified, a program to address those needs must be designed, a teaching approach to facilitate each learner's needs should be provided in the most positive and inclusive environment, and school systems must provide the necessary resources to ensure programmatic success. We address each of these critical components in this part.

2

Determining Educational Needs Through Assessment

■ **OBJECTIVES**

List the different types of assessment.

Explain the purposes of assessment.

Identify four factors that must be considered when selecting an assessment instrument.

Explain what is meant by administrative feasibility.

Provide examples of techniques that can be used to organize test results.

Courtesy of Orthotic & Prosthetic Athlete Assistance Fund, Inc. Photo by Julie Gaydos.

As we enter the twenty-first century, it is becoming increasingly clear that traditional educational practices that have served our society well in the past must be modified to keep pace with changing societal demands, as well as the growing diversity of students being educated in our schools. It is becoming apparent that, for our society to survive and grow, all students, regardless of gender, ethnicity, and functional capacity, must be adequately prepared to participate successfully in a multicultural society that is increasingly dependent on advanced technology.[2] School curricula must be designed to provide students with information, skills, and problem-solving capabilities that will enable them to function fully in the career and community of their choice. A critical component of an effective curriculum is a means for determining at what levels students are functioning, the types of interventions needed to gain full benefits from their school experiences, their progress toward mastery of the school curriculum, and validation that what has been learned has application in the society.

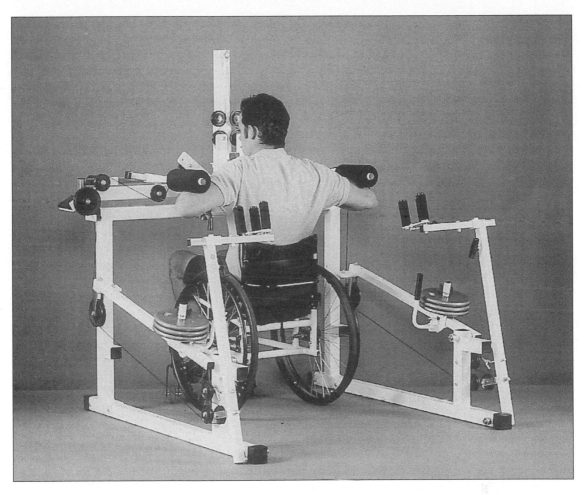

A person with tetraplegia strengthens his deltoids.
Courtesy of GPK, Inc. El Cajon, CA.

Appropriate assessment techniques can provide this information.

In this chapter a broad range of assessment information will be presented. The purposes of assessment, the types of instruments available to meet those purposes, ways to evaluate specific instruments to determine their appropriateness, and tips on administering tests have been included. Ways to arrange test results to facilitate interpretation will also be covered. Recommendations for instruments that can be used with students who have specific types of disabilities, and ways to modify the testing situation to meet their needs, will be included in each of the chapters that address those populations.

PURPOSES OF ASSESSMENT

Assessment is a problem-solving process that involves a variety of ways of gathering information. Testing is the administration of specific instruments that are used to gather assessment data.[4] Motor assessment instruments provide different types of information. It is important to match the selection of the instrument with the purpose of the assessment. Assessment instruments should provide the teacher information about what activities should be included in the curriculum. Too frequently, the teacher selects assessment instruments that reflect what is currently being taught. Assessment is an inseparable part of the student's ongoing educational program, and it is particularly critical for students with disabilities.

Assessment of students in educational settings has at least five purposes:

1. To identify those who might be experiencing developmental delays
2. To diagnose the nature of the student's problem or delay
3. To provide information to use to develop the IEP and determine appropriate placement
4. To develop instruction specific to the student's special needs
5. To evaluate student progress[4]

MATCHING TYPE OF ASSESSMENT TO PURPOSE

Both formal and informal tests serve important functions in the educational process. Formal tests are those that have been developed for a specific purpose and have been standardized. Informal tests are those that have been developed for a general purpose and have not been standardized. The purpose of the assessment should dictate the type of instrument selected and the standards the instrument must meet. The more critical the decisions that are made from the assessment, the more rigorous the requirements for the instrument the evaluator will use.

Informal techniques used for screening groups to determine whether any individuals are experiencing significant delays include checklists, activities used in the curriculum, an observation of students during their regular physical education class or during recess. Formal tests which are used to pinpoint specific areas of delays include physical fitness tests, gross motor development tests, and skill tests and/or motor proficiency tests that have

been standardized. Whatever the method used, it is recommended that the information be recorded so that documentation is available for the permanent record file. An example of an observational checklist that was developed for use in the Denton, Texas, Independent School District appears in Figure 2-1. Using an informal test, once a teacher observes a student not performing to the level of his or her classmates, it is understood that more rigorous testing is necessary to determine the extent and type delay. Parental approval is not required for informal testing; however, it is required for more in-depth testing.

Assessment information used for developing a student's IEP and for selecting appropriate activities can be gathered from a variety of sources, including parental reports, informal test procedures, and formal testing. Those areas found to be below expectations for the student's age become the present levels of performance that are required to be recorded on the IEP. The long-range goals selected for the student are directly related to the present level of performance areas found to be lacking. Frequently, the long-range goal selected for a person with a disability is the level of performance one would expect for a person without a disability. The short-term objectives lead from the present level of performance to the long-range goal. A well-designed IEP includes specific behavioral objectives and goals. The effectiveness of a physical education program can be continuously monitored by determining the extent to which the students are mastering short-term objectives and long-range goals that have been included on their IEPs.

LEGAL MANDATES FOR DETERMINING PRESENT LEVEL OF PERFORMANCE

The type of testing used for students with disabilities must conform to federal and state laws and district practices. Physical education appropriate for students with disabilities is broadly defined in the federal laws (see Chapter 1). Those laws do not dictate the type of testing that should be done but do set the conditions surrounding the testing

Denton Independent School District
Adapted Physical Education Prereferral/Referral Form

Dates Received: Sp. Ed. Sup.   Area Dir.   APE Teacher

Please Initial   ___ ___   ___ ___   ___ ___

Student _____ ID _____ DOB _____

School _____ Type of Class (Unit) _____

Evaluation Request by _____ Medical Concerns: _____

Educational Implications _____

Area of Difficulty in Physical Education _____

School Contact for APE Teacher _____

Method of Ambulation: _____ Form of Communication: _____

Dear Teacher,

    Below are some behaviors that indicate a student's ability to move efficiently and interact effectively with others. Please check the appropriate response.

Psychomotor Development	Yes		Sometimes		No	
	RE	APE	RE	APE	RE	APE
Moves without bumping into others						
Stands on one foot for 5 seconds						
Jumps in place for 5 consecutive times (two feet)						
Hops (one foot) for 5 consecutive times						
Skips 10 feet						
Kicks stationary ball						
Throws a softball 15 feet						
Bounces and catches a playground ball to self						
Turns own jump rope 5 consecutive times						
Uses free time for active play						
Awkward and clumsy when moving						
Performs tasks more slowly than others						
Falls excessively						
Body Mechanics/Postural Orientation						
❏ Posture						
❏ Muscular/Skeletal/Neuro Impairment						
❏ Underweight /Overweight						
Mobility Skills (Nonambulatory)						
❏ Transfer ❏ Reverse						
❏ Range of Motion ❏ Brake						
❏ Doorways ❏ Pivot						
❏ Ramps/Curbs ❏ Wheelie						
❏ Stairs ❏						
Cognitive Development						
Can remember visual or auditory information						
Exhibits appropriate on-task behavior						
Participates in team activities						
Communicates with others while participating in group activities						
Can follow directions						
Dependent on others to accomplish tasks						
Impulsive responses to difficult tasks						

Figure 2-1   **Denton Independent School District Adapted Physical Education Prereferral/Referral Form (*Continued*)**

Courtesy Denton, Texas, Independent School District.

Adapted Physical Education Prereferral/Referral Form—Page 2

Student _____

Affective Development	Yes		Sometimes		No	
	RE	APE	RE	APE	RE	APE
Has indicated a dislike for physical education						
Clinging/demanding attention from others						
Loneliness—Prefers solo play						
Self-destructive acts						
Low frustration tolerance, cries easily						
Tends to be impulsive, accident prone						
Verbal aggression toward others						
Physical aggression toward others						
Short attention span						
Distracts others						
Lying/cheating						
Temper tantrums						

Thank you for your time. Please return this completed form to the Special Education Diagnostician in your school.

- -

To be filled out by the APE teacher

Date of Classroom Visit(s): _____   _____   _____   _____   _____

Recommendations:

❏ The student is functioning within acceptable limits and does not need any further evaluation at this time.

❏ The student appears to be experiencing difficulty in the area(s) indicated above and will need further screening/evaluation.

❏ The student is able to be mainstreamed in regular Physical Education class with appropriate modifications as determined by the Adapted Physical Education Specialist.

❏ The student is experiencing difficulty in the area(s) indicated above and is recommended for evaluation by Adapted Physical Education teacher.

Comments: _____

_____

_____

_____

_____

_____

_____

_____	_____	_____
Signed	*Date*	*Area*

Figure 2-1   (*Continued*)
Denton Independent School District adapted physical education prereferral form.

Figure 2-2   1999 IDEA Evaluation Requirements

May not discriminate on a cultural or racial basis.

Are provided and administered in the child's native language.

A variety of assessment tools and strategies are used to gather functional and development information, including information provided by the parent, and information related to enabling the child to be involved in and progress in the general curriculum.

The standardized tests used in the process must have been validated for the specific purpose for which they are used and must be administered by trained and knowledgeable personnel in accordance with the provided instructions.

All variations from standard conditions must be described.

Child is assessed in all areas related to the suspected disability, including, if appropriate, health, vision . . . and motor abilities.

Assessment tools and strategies are used that provide relevant information that directly assists persons in determining the [physical] education needs of the child.

Assessment tools, required in the general [physical] education program must be administered to students with disabilities with modifications, if needed.

process. The basic requirements for testing conditions were included in P.L. 94-142. The 1999 amendments of IDEA expanded on the testing conditions and the types of information that can be used to determine a student's present level of performance. The latest IDEA revisions generally restate longstanding policy set out in the prior regulations.[3] Those requirements, including new revisions, are located in Figure 2-2.

In most school districts, the question of whether testing is done and the type utilized are left to the discretion of individual teachers. Because appropriate testing is basic to designing a physical education program that will meet the needs of the student with a disability, it is critical to the effectiveness of a teacher.

AUTHENTIC ASSESSMENT

Authentic assessment is testing that provides the teacher with information needed to develop a meaningful physical education program for each student. What is meaningful depends a great deal on the knowledge and skill of the teacher as well as the time available to him or her. Teachers who are committed to a predetermined curriculum will measure students' ability to demonstrate competence of the components of the curriculum (curriculum-based). The teacher who is preparing a transitional program for a student who is fourteen years or older will conduct task analyses of activities available in the community (ecological inventory) and then will design a program to teach the missing skills to the student. The teacher who believes all activity should primarily contribute to physical fitness will measure fitness levels. The teacher of the young student will focus on the basic locomotor, object-control, and perceptual motor skills needed to be successful later with sport-specific activities. The teacher with advanced training in basic neurological building blocks will probe down through physical fitness tasks and sport, functional, and perceptual motor skills to determine if all the

Figure 2-3   Types of Assessments for School-Age Students

Curriculum-based—Competency Testing for Adapted Physical Education (Louisiana), Motor Activities Training Program (National); Moving into the Future: National Standards for Physical Education (National), Skill Tests (Local)

Physical fitness—Brockport Physical Fitness Test: A Health-Related Test for Youths with Physical and Mental Disabilities; Physical Best and Individuals with Disabilities

Functional skills—Mobility Opportunities via Education (MOVE); Test of Gross Motor Development (TGMD); Ohio State University Scale of Intra Gross Motor Assessment (OSU-Sigma)

Sport skills—Methods of Assessing Motor Skills, 1999 (NASPE); Special Olympic Sport Skill Guides (Special Olympics)

Perceptual/motor skills—Purdue Perceptual Motor Skills

Sensorimotor skills—Southern California Tests of Sensory Motor Integration; DiGangi-Berk Test of Sensory Integration; Sensory Input Systems Screening Test

underlying sensorimotor components are functioning fully. The types of tests available to address each of these kinds of assessments are presented in Figure 2-3.

The scoring method used for any given test depends on what the test is designed to measure. Tests are designed to measure a person's performance against established criteria, components in the task, or components in a series of tasks (refer to Tables 2.1 and 2.2 and the content task analyses in Figures 2-4, 2-5, and 2-6). Tests that measure performance against established criteria are either normative-referenced or criterion-referenced. *Normative-referenced* means an individual's performance can be compared with that of others of the same age and gender. Most physical fitness test items are normative referenced. Criterion-referenced tests are designed to provide information about a person's mastery of a specific skill or behavior. An example of a criterion-referenced test item is the following: from a running start, kick a stationary $8\frac{1}{2}$-inch playground ball 30 feet.

Test items that are designed to measure components that make up a task are content-referenced. That is, the ability of an individual to demonstrate all of the content (task components) of a skill or pattern is what is observed. An example from the Test of Gross Motor Development is the content task analysis of the locomotor pattern of running is located in Figure 2-7.

Some tests include both criterion-referenced and content-referenced scoring techniques. For example, the task of kicking a playground ball 30 feet from a running start could also require the evaluator to indicate whether the student demonstrated the following components of the task: backswing of leg from knee, contact with foot, forward swing of the arm opposite the kicking leg, and follow-through by hopping on the non-kicking foot.

Checklists and ecological inventories are content-referenced because they are used to determine whether specific components of a task or a series of tasks are demonstrated. Checklists are frequently developed and used to delineate critical aspects of motor coordination and sport skills. The content task analysis of a softball throw is an example of such a checklist (see Figure 2-4). Checklists are useful for screening one student or a whole class of students before beginning a unit of

TABLE 2.1	Norms for the Standing Long Jump in the AAHPERD Physical Fitness Test			
	Test Scores (Meters)*			
Percentile Rank	**11 Years**	**12 Years**	**13 Years**	**Percentile Rank**
100th	2.56	2.26	2.59	100th
95th	1.87	1.98	2.15	95th
90th	1.82	1.90	2.08	90th
85th	1.77	1.85	2.03	85th
80th	1.75	1.82	1.95	80th
75th	1.70	1.80	1.90	75th
70th	1.67	1.75	1.87	70th
65th	1.67	1.72	1.82	65th
60th	1.65	1.70	1.82	60th
55th	1.62	1.67	1.77	55th
50th	1.57	1.65	1.75	50th
45th	1.57	1.62	1.70	45th
40th	1.52	1.60	1.67	40th
35th	1.49	1.57	1.65	35th
30th	1.47	1.54	1.60	30th
25th	1.42	1.52	1.57	25th
20th	1.39	1.47	1.52	20th
15th	1.34	1.44	1.47	15th
10th	1.29	1.37	1.39	10th
5th	1.21	1.26	1.32	5th
0	0.91	0.96	0.99	0

Source: From the American Alliance for Health, Physical Education, Recreation and Dance, Reston, VA.

*To convert to centimeters, move the decimal point two places to the right (1.95 m = 195 cm).

instruction. Through the use of the checklist, the teacher can determine which tasks need to be taught. Hyde[1] developed an instrument for screening kindergarten children for developmental delays (see Figure 2-5). Ecological inventories are developed to identify the behavioral contents (demands) of an environment. An example of an ecological inventory is located in Figure 2-6. That ecological inventory is a content analysis of a series of tasks that needs to be mastered to participate in the activity of bowling in the community. Ecological inventories are particularly helpful when designing a transition program for students fourteen years and older. A community-based ecological inventory completed by a teacher will identify what activities are available in the community and the series of tasks a student needs to master to participate in those activities.

TEST SELECTION CRITERIA

As indicated earlier in this chapter, depending on the purpose for the assessment, both standardized tests and less formal instruments are useful when working with students with disabilities. Once the purpose of the assessment has been decided, an appropriate assessment instrument is selected. Factors that must be considered to select the right test are (1) the need for utilizing a standardized test, (2) the adequacy of test standardization; (3) administrative

TABLE 2.2	Isometric Push-Up, Bench Press, Extended Arm Hang, Flexed Arm Hang, and Dominant Grip Strength: Specific Standards for Youngsters With Mental Retardation

Age	Isometric push-up[a] (s)	Bench press[a] (# completed)	Extended arm hang[b] (s)	Flexed arm hang[a] (s)	Dominant grip strength[c] (kg)
		Males			
10	20		23		12
11	20		23		14
12	20		23		16
13		10		6	19
14		16		8	22
15		20		8	24
16		23		8	28
17		25		8	32
		Females			
10	13		15		11
11	13		15		12
12	13		15		14
13		5		4	16
14		6		4	17
15		7		4	19
16		7		4	19
17		8		4	19

[a]Specific standards reflect a 50% adjustment to minimal general standards.
[b]Specific standards are 75% of minimal general standards.
[c]Specific standards are 65% of minimal general standards.

Source: Adapted with permission from The Cooper Institute for Aerobics and Research, 1992 and 1999, FITNESSGRAM, Dallas, Texas: Cooper Institute for Aerobics Research.

feasibility; and (4) the student's type of disability. Each of these factors will be discussed.

Need for Utilizing a Standardized Test

P.L. 94-142 and IDEA clearly specified that the use of standardized tests is necessary to determine a student's eligibility for special services—in this case, special (adapted) physical education. In the 1999 amendments of IDEA, the requirement of utilizing standardized tests is not clearly stated; however, individuals who monitored the public policy surrounding those amendments indicate the intent is implicit. That is, whereby many types of information may be used *in addition to* standardized tests, standardized tests indicating that a student's performance significantly lags behind his or her peers are still required.[3] What is clear in the most recent amendments is that, if a standardized test is used, the adequacy of the person administering the test and the fact that the test has been standardized must be demonstrated. That is, the person administering the test must be adequately trained in administration and interpretation and the test itself must be valid, reliable, and objective for the purposes it is being used.

Figure 2-4 Content Task Analysis of a Softball Throw

1. Demonstrate the correct grip 100 percent of the time.
   a. Select a softball.
   b. Hold the ball with the first and second fingers spread on top, thumb under the ball, and the third and fourth fingers on the side.
   c. Grasp the ball with the fingertips.
2. Demonstrate the proper step pattern for throwing the softball three out of five times.
   a. Identify the restraining line.
   b. Take a side step with the left foot.
   c. Follow with a shorter side step with the right foot.
3. Demonstrate the proper throwing technique and form three out of five times.
   a. Grip ball correctly.
   b. Bend rear knee.
   c. Rotate hips and pivot left foot, turning body to the right.
   d. Bring right arm back with the ball behind the right ear and bent right elbow leading (in front of) hand.
   e. Bend left elbow and point it at a 45-degree angle.
   f. Step straight ahead with the left foot.
   g. Keep the right hip back and low and the right arm bent with the ball behind the ear and the elbow leading.

   h. Start the throwing motion by pushing down hard with the right foot.
   i. Straighten the right knee and rotate the hips, shifting the weight to the left foot.
   j. Keep the upper body in line with the direction of throw and the eyes focused on the target.
   k. Whip the left arm to the rear, increasing the speed of the right arm.
   l. Extend the right arm fully forward, completing the release by snapping the wrist and releasing the ball at a 45 degree angle.
   m. Follow through by bringing the hand completely down and the right foot forward to the front restraining line.
4. Throw a softball on command three out of five times.
   a. Assume READY position between the front and back restraining lines with feet apart.
   b. Point the shoulder of the nonthrowing arm toward the restraining line.
   c. Focus eyes in the direction of the throw.
   d. Remain behind the front restraining line.
   e. Throw the softball on command.
   f. Execute smooth integration of skill sequence.

Permission for the Special Olympics Sports Skills Instructional Program provided by Special Olympics, created by The Joseph P. Kennedy, Jr., Foundation. Authorized and accredited by Special Olympics, Inc., for the Benefit of Mentally Retarded Citizens.

Standardization

To standardize a test means to give the test to a large group of persons under the same conditions to determine whether or not the test discriminates among ages and populations. When a test is going to be used for diagnostic purposes, adequacy of the standardized process must be verified. Questions that must be answered include (1) Were the appropriate procedures used to select the population used to standardize the instrument? (2) Did the author(s) demonstrate an appropriate type and level of validity? (3) Did the author(s) establish an appropriate type and level of reliability?

(4) Did the author(s) verify the objectivity of the instrument?

Selecting the Standardization Sample

Ideally, the sample that is used for the standardization of an instrument should include the same percentage of individuals in the socioeconomic groups, geographic locations (South, East, North, Northeast, etc.), ages, genders, and races represented in the general population according to the latest population census. Hence, if the year 2000 U.S. census reports that 52 percent of the population is female and 48 percent is male, those

| Name _____ | | Examiner _____ |
| Birthdate _____ Sex _____ | | Date _____ |

Category	Special Notes and Remarks		
Static balance	___does not attempt tasks	___heel-toe stand, 5 sec ___balance on preferred foot, arms hung relaxed at sides ___5 sec ___10 sec	___heel-toe stand, eyes closed, 5 sec ___balance on preferred foot, arms hung relaxed at sides, eyes closed ___5 sec ___10 sec
Hopping reflex	___no response ___no righting of head ___trunk no step in direction of push ___right___left ___forward___backward	___head and body right themselves ___step or hop in direction of push ___right___left ___forward___backward	
Running pattern	___loses balance___almost ___twists trunk ___leans excessively ___jerky, uneven rhythm	___elbows away from body in arm swing ___limited arm swing ___short strides	___full arm swing in opposition with legs ___elbows near body in swing ___even flow and rhythm
Jumping pattern	___loses balance on landing ___no use of arms ___twists or bends sideways	___arms at side for balance ___legs bent throughout jump	___arms back as legs bend ___arms swing up as legs extend ___lands softly with control
Throwing pattern	___pushing or shoving object ___loss of balance ___almost	___body shifts weight from back to front without stepping	___steps forward with same foot as throwing arm ___steps forward with foot opposite throwing arm
Catching pattern	___loses balance___almost ___shies away ___traps or scoops	___arms stiff in front of body	___arms bent at sides of body ___arms "give" as catch ___uses hands
Kicking pattern	___misses ___off center	___arms at sides or out to sides ___uses from knee down to kick	___kicks "through" ball ___arm opposition ___uses full leg to kick ___can kick with either foot

Figure 2-5   Motor Development Checklist
Courtesy Beverly Hyde.

Figure 2-6   Content Task Analysis of a Series of Tasks Needed to Bowl Independently

1. Can determine when bowling lanes are available.
   a. Finds the number of the bowling establishment in the phone book.
   b. Calls the bowling establishment to determine when open bowling is available.
2. Can get from home to the bowling establishment.
   a. Knows which bus to take to the bowling establishment.
   b. Walks to the nearest bus stop.
   c. Waits at the bus stop until the bus arrives.
   d. Checks the bus sign to make sure it is the correct bus.
   e. Gets on the bus.
   f. Checks with the bus driver to be sure the bus goes to the bowling establishment.
   g. Drops the fare into the box.
   h. Asks the driver to let him or her know where to get off.
   i. Moves to an empty seat and sits down.
   j. Listens for the driver's announcement of the correct stop.
   k. Pulls the cord to alert the driver that he or she wants to get off at the next stop.
   l. After the bus stops, departs from the bus.
   m. Checks to determine where the bus stop is for the return trip home.
3. Can reserve a lane, rent shoes, and select the appropriate ball.
   a. Goes to the counter and tells the clerk how many games he or she wants to bowl and asks for the correct-size bowling shoes.
   b. Pays for the games and shoes and receives the correct change.
   c. Takes a seat behind the lane that has been assigned and changes from street to bowling shoes.
   d. Searches for a ball that fits his or her hand span and is the correct weight.
   e. Selects a ball that fits and is not too heavy.
   f. Places the ball on the ball-return rack of the correct lane.
4. Can correctly deliver the ball.
   a. Picks up the ball with both hands.
   b. Cradles the ball in the nondominant arm while placing his or her fingers in the ball.
   c. Positions self in the center of the approach approximately 15 feet from the foul line.
   d. Holds the ball in both hands and aims.
   e. Walks to the line, coordinating the swing of the dominant arm and the walking pattern of the feet.
   f. Releases the ball from behind the foul line.
   g. Follows through with the dominant arm.
   h. Watches the ball move down the lane and strike pins.
5. Can retrieve the ball and continue bowling.
   a. Walks back to the ball-return rack.
   b. Awaits the ball's return.
   c. Continues to aim and deliver the ball, being careful not to throw the ball while the pins are being reset.
6. Stops bowling when the electronic scoring device indicates that three games have been completed.
   a. Returns the ball to the storage rack.
   b. Changes back into street shoes.
   c. Returns the rented shoes to the counter.
   d. Exits the bowling establishment.
7. Can return home from the bowling establishment.
   a. Goes to the bus stop and awaits the bus.
   b. Checks the bus sign to verify it is the correct bus.
   c. Gets on the bus.
   d. Asks the bus driver if the bus goes to the street he or she is seeking.
   e. Drops the fare into the box.
   f. Asks the driver to let him or her know where to get off.
   g. Moves to an empty seat and sits down.
   h. Listens for the driver's announcement of the correct stop.
   i. Pulls the cord to alert the driver that he or she wants to get off at the next stop.
   j. Waits for the bus to stop before rising from the seat and departing the bus.
   k. Walks home.

percentages should be duplicated in the test sample. If, in the same census, it is reported that the U.S. population is 40 percent African American, 34 percent Anglo, 18 percent Hispanic, 3 percent Native American, 2 percent Asian, and 3 percent other, then those percentages should be used to select the makeup of the sample to be tested. In addition, the test sample should include the ages of the persons with whom the test will be used selected at random from all areas of the country. Because few, if any, motor tests meet these stringent criteria, tests should

Figure 2-7 Content Task Analysis of a Locomotor Pattern—Run

1. Arms move in opposition to legs with the elbows bent
2. Brief period where both feet are off the ground
3. Narrow foot placement landing on heel or toe (i.e., not flat-footed)
4. Nonsupport leg is bent approximately 90 degrees (i.e., close to buttocks)

From Gallahue, D. L., and Ozmun, J. C.: *Understanding motor development,* Madison, WI: Brown & Benchmark, 1995. Reproduced with permission of the McGraw-Hill Companies.

be selected that come as close to the ideal as possible.

Establishing Validity

Test validity is a measure of how truthful an instrument is. A valid instrument measures what the authors claim it measures. There are three acceptable types of validity: (1) content-related, (2) criterion-related, and (3) construct (see Figure 2-8).

Content-related validity refers to the degree to which the contents of the test represent an identified domain (perceptual motor, physical fitness), body of knowledge, or curriculum. Content-related validity pertaining to a domain or a body of

TRANSITION: FROM WALKING TO STANDING	GRAD LEVEL	LEVEL I	LEVEL II	LEVEL III
I.1 Can stop walking and maintain a standing position without assistance.	☐ DATE			
I.2 Can stop walking and maintain a standing position when another person helps the participant maintain balance.		☐ DATE		
I.3 Can stop moving legs reciprocally and maintain hip and knee extension for standing while in a front leaning walker or while another person helps maintain balance.			☐ DATE	
Can tolerate fully prompted reciprocal leg movements while being supported in a front leaning walker or by another person. SEE: G.6.				☐ DATE
Can tolerate fully prompted extension of hips and knees. SEE: C.5.				☐ DATE
Can tolerate being placed in a vertical position. SEE: C.6.				☐ DATE

Excerpt from the M.O.V.E. (Mobility Opportunities Via Education)® Curriculum, copyright© 1990, 1999 Kern County Superintendent of Schools. All rights reserved. Reproduced here with permission of copyright holder. No part of this publication may be reproduced in any form or by any electronic, mechanical or other means (including the use of information storage and retrieval systems) without written permission from the copyright holder.

Figure 2-8   Move™ Top-Down Motor Milestone Test™
Used with permission from MOVE International, Bakersfield, CA.

knowledge is often determined by verifying that experts in the field agree about the components of the domain. To demonstrate content validity, first the author must provide a clear definition of what is being measured. Then, literature that supports the content is identified or the test is examined by a panel of judges selected according to a predetermined set of criteria (i.e., five or more publications in the field, recommended by three or more professionals as an authority in the field, etc.). The panel members independently review the items in the test to determine whether they are appropriate, complete, and representative. In the case of content-related validity pertaining to a curriculum, the test is usually constructed by a districtwide, statewide, or nationwide committee made up of professionals in the field. Those professionals select items to include in the tests that they believe are appropriate, complete, and representative of the physical education curriculum at each level (elementary, middle school, junior high, and senior high).

Appropriateness means that the most knowledgeable professionals would agree that items measure what it is claimed they measure. For example, if a test designer claims that the 50-yard dash measures cardiovascular function, few professionals would agree that the test content is appropriate.

Completeness is determined by whether there is a wide range of items or only a select few. To be complete, a test that is purported to measure physical fitness would be expected to sample cardiovascular endurance, upper body strength, abdominal strength, leg power, lower back and hip flexibility, and percent body fat. If only one measure of strength and one measure of cardiovascular endurance were included, the test would be deemed incomplete.

For a test to be declared representative of a given domain, several levels of performance would be sampled. This is accomplished by including a range of items from simple to complex or allowing a set amount of time to complete as many of the same tasks as is possible. In physical fitness tests, the representative requirement is frequently met by allowing the student to perform to the best of his or her ability within a given period of time. That is, the number of sit-ups executed in 30 seconds is counted. Students with well-developed abdominal muscles will perform more sit-ups than those who are less well developed. The content validity of a test is frequently as strong as the literature cited and/or the knowledge base of the professionals selected to evaluate and or develop the test. The broader the literature base and the more knowledgeable and critical the professionals, the stronger the content validity.

Criterion-related validity indicates the test has been compared with another acceptable standard such as a valid test that measures the same components. There are two types of criterion-related validity—concurrent and predictive. Concurrent criterion-related validity is achieved when the test scores on one test a accurately reflect a person's score on another test at point in time. For instance, if a student performs strongly on a 2-mile run, a strong performance on a bicycle ergometer test is expected. Predictive content-related validity means that the test scores can be used to predict accurately how well a student will perform in the future. Thus, if a student performs well on a motor ability test, the student should do well in a variety of sport activities.

Construct validity is the degree to which a test does what the author claims it will do. To establish this type of validity, an author sets out to develop a test that will discriminate between two or more populations. After identifying which populations the test should discriminate among, a series of studies is completed measuring each of the identified groups with the test. For example, an author might claim that students with learning disabilities will do significantly more poorly on the test than will students with no learning problems. After the test is designed, it is administered to two groups of students who have been matched on age and gender. One group has verified learning disabilities; the other does not. Each group's scores are compared to determine whether they are significantly different. If the group with learning disabilities scores significantly lower than the group with no learning disabilities, construct validity is claimed.

Different statistical techniques are used to evaluate validity. In the case of content validity relating to a domain or a body of knowledge, percentage of agreement among the judges on the panel is reported. Acceptable content validity can be declared when the judges agree on the appropriateness of items included in the test at least 90 percent of the time. Content validity relating to a curriculum is generally achieved by majority vote of the professionals developing the test. Criterion validity is usually reported as a coefficient that is derived from correlating the sets of scores from the two tests being compared. Ideally, a correlation coefficient of between +.80 and 1.00 is desirable. However, few motor tests reach this level of agreement. Construct validity is generally demonstrated by using a statistic that measures differences between the mean scores of each group. Thus, when construct validity is claimed at the .05 level of significance, it means that it is expected that the test will accurately classify an individual as belonging to one group rather than another 95 times out of 100.

Determining Reliability

Test reliability is a measure of an instrument's consistency. A reliable test can be depended on to produce the same scores at different times if no intervention, learning, or growth has occurred between test sessions. The two test reliability techniques used for most physical and motor tests are test-retest and alternate forms.

The test-retest technique is the most frequently used method for demonstrating reliability of physical and motor performance instruments. To establish test-retest reliability, the same test is administered to the same group of people twice in succession, and then the scores are correlated to determine the amount of agreement between them. The interval between administrations of the test should be carefully controlled. Never should a period of more than two weeks lapse between test administrations.

The alternate form reliability technique is also referred to as equivalent form reliability. When two tests are identified that are believed to measure the same trait or skill and have been standardized on the same population, they can be used to determine alternate form reliability. To estimate the degree to which both forms correlate, the tests are divided in half and administered to the same population. Half of the group will be tested by using Test A first and Test B second. The other half of the group will be tested with Test B first and then with Test A. The scores from Test A will be correlated with the scores from Test B to determine the amount of consistency (equivalency) between the tests.

Determining the extent to which sets of scores achieved during the testing sessions correlate is the most frequently used statistical method for estimating reliability. The stronger the correlation coefficient, the more reliable the test. A reliability coefficient between +.90 and +1.00 is most desirable because it means that 90 percent of the two test scores were the same; however, the larger the sample tested, the smaller the size of reliability coefficient that is acceptable.

Determining Objectivity

Objectivity means freedom from bias and subjectivity. The clearer and more concise the instructions, the more objective the instrument. Test objectivity is determined by having two or more scorers independently evaluate the performance of a subject being tested. The scorers' results are then correlated to determine amount of agreement. The greater the amount of agreement between the scores, the higher the correlation coefficient. An objectivity coefficient beyond +.90 would be considered an acceptable level of objectivity because it would indicate that all scorers agreed on the scores given 90 percent or more of the time.

Administrative Feasibility

Administrative feasibility means how practical and realistic is the test. Several factors must be considered when attempting to determine whether a given test is administratively feasible to use for a given purpose:

> Cost. Resources available to purchase test manuals and equipment must be carefully considered. Costs of tests continue to

increase; it is not uncommon for motor tests to range in cost from $250 to $1,000. To conserve resources, needed tests may be stored at a central source and made available for individuals to check out for brief periods of time.

Equipment. The amount and kind of equipment needed to administer tests vary widely. Frequently it is possible to build, rather than purchase, equipment; however, some items such as bicycle ergometers may be clearly out of the practitioner's price range.

Level of training to administer the test. Some tests require extensive training for accurate administration; indeed, some tests require evidence of professional training and certification of capability before the tests can be used. Other tests simply require practice and familiarity with the items. Professionals familiar with test administration, such as university professors who teach assessment courses, can be contacted to provide workshops for practitioners who are responsible for testing.

Level of training to interpret the test. Professional training in interpretation of test results is required for most tests. Educators should select tests they understand and can accurately interpret. Again, professionals can be retained to provide workshops in test interpretation.

Purpose of the test. How a test is to be used will determine which test to select. As indicated earlier, different types of tests are used for screening, diagnosing, and programming purposes. For a test to be useful, it must provide the needed information.

Length of time to administer. Limited time is available in school settings for test administration. However, too frequently a test selected because it can be administered in a short period of time yields little usable information. On the other hand, tests that require more than one-half hour administration time are unrealistic for school settings. Tests need to be selected that provide the needed information yet require a minimum of time to administer.

Personnel needs. Some tests can be used if adequate personnel are available to administer and score them. When paraprofessionals and/or volunteers are available, they must be carefully trained, particularly if they do not have a strong background in motor and physical development.

Standardization population. If the test information is going to be used to diagnose a student's movement problems to determine whether special services are required, the test must be standardized on a population the same age as the student being tested. Practitioners sometimes avoid using the appropriate standardized test because they are aware that their student cannot adequately perform the items in the test. One of the purposes of a standardized test is to establish that the student is performing significantly below same-age peers.

Type of Disability

The type of disability a student has greatly impacts the assessment process. There are some tests available that have been developed for use with individuals with specific types of disabilities. These tests obviously should be used for diagnostic purposes to determine whether a student qualifies for special services. Other tests, both formal and informal with minor modifications, can be used to provide the information needed for developing the IEP and determining intervention programs. An overview of tests appropriate for use with individuals with disabilities is presented in Table 2.3. More information about tests that are appropriate for use with specific types of disabilities, as well as suggestions about how they might best be used, will be presented in the chapters in which distinctive populations are discussed (see Figure 2-9).

TABLE 2.3 Selected Motor Tests Appropriate for Use with Individuals with Disabilities

Test	Source	Population	Components	Scoring Type
Brockport Physical Fitness Test for Youths with Physical and Mental Disabilities (1999)	Human Kinetics Publishers Box 5076 Champaign, IL 61820	Visually impaired, auditory impaired, orthopedically impaired, ages 10–17 yrs	Body composition, muscular strength and endurance, speed, power, flexibility, coordination, cardiorespiratory endurance	Criterion-referenced
Bruininks-Oseretsky Test of Motor Proficiency (1978)	American Guidance Services Publishers' Building Circle Pines, MN 55014	Normal, mentally retarded, learning disabled, ages 4 1/2–14 1/2 yrs	Speed and agility, balance, bilateral coordination, strength, fine motor, response speed, hand-eye coordination, upper limb speed and dexterity	Normative-referenced
A standardized test composed of subtests that can be administered individually to determine underlying sensory input and ability level delays:				
Competency Testing for Adapted Physical Education (1995)	Louisiana Department of Education Office of Spec Educ Ser PO Box 94064 Baton Rouge, LA 70804	Ambulatory individuals 6 yrs and older	Locomotor, manipulative, balance, sport, fitness, gymnastic, spatial relations	Content- and criterion-referenced
A task analyzed curriculum-imbedded program for all students with disabilities except for the most severely involved:				
I CAN (1978)	Hubbard Scientific Co. PO Box 104 Northbrook, IL 60062	Ambulatory individuals of any age	Preprimary motor and play skills; primary skills; sport, leisure, and recreation skills	Criterion- and content-referenced
A task analyzed curriculum-imbedded program for moderate-to low-functioning individuals:				
Mobility Opportunities Via Education (MOVE) (1990)	Kern County Superintendent of Schools 5801 Sundale Ave. Bakersfield, CA 93309-2924	Nonambulatory, severely and profoundly involved of any age	A sequence of motor skills that lead to independent self-management	Content- and criterion-referenced

A task analyzed curriculum-imbedded program to promote head, trunk, and limb control of severely and profoundly involved individuals:

| Motor Activities Training Program: Special Olympics Sports Skill Program (1997) | Special Olympics Intern 1325 G Street, NW Suite 500 Washington, DC 20005 | Severe handicaps of any age | Mobility, dexterity, striking, kicking, aquatics, manual and electric wheelchair | Content-referenced |

A task-analyzed program designed for persons with severe mental retardation who are not yet able to compete in a rigorous sports program:

| Movement Assessment Battery for Children (Movement ABC) (1992) | The Psychological Corp. Foots Cray High Street Sidcup, Kent DA14 5HP England | Motor development delays, ages 4–12 yrs | Balance, fine motor, object-control, locomotor | Normative- and content-referenced |

A standardized, updated version of the Stott-Henderson Test of Motor Impairment; designed to detect, quantify, and correct motor development delays:

| Moving into the Future: National Standards for Physical Education | National Assoc. for Sport and Physical Education AAHPERD 1900 Association Dr. Reston, VA 22091 | School-age individuals | Locomotor, balance, object-control, gymnastics, health-related, fitness, sport skills | Normative-referenced |

A national curriculum-based assessment developed by physical education professionals in the United States:

| Ohio State University Scale of Intra Gross Motor Assessment (OSU-SIGMA) (1979) | Mohican Publishing Co. PO Box 295 Loundonville, OH 44842 | Normal, ages 2½–14 yrs | Basic locomotor skills, ladder and stair climbing, throwing, catching | Content- and criterion-referenced |

A test to identify critical components of basic locomotor, climbing, and object-control skills:

| Oregon Data-Based Gymnasium (1985) | PRO-ED Publishing Co. 8700 Shoal Creek Blvd. Austin, TX 78758 | Severely disabled, any age | Movement concepts, elementary games, physical fitness, lifetime leisure skills | Criterion-referenced |

(Continued)

TABLE 2.3 *(Concluded)*

Test	Source	Population	Components	Scoring Type
A task analysis of discrete movement behaviors for individuals with severe and profound involvement:				
Physical Best and Individuals with Disabilities: A Handbook for Inclusion in Fitness Programs (1995)	AAHPERD 1900 Association Dr. Reston, VA 22091	Mild and moderate retardation, Down syndrome, nonambulatory, cerebral palsy, visual impairment, 5–17 yrs	Aerobic capacity, body composition, flexibility, upper and lower body strength and endurance	Criterion- and normative-referenced
A standardized test for measuring and developing the physical fitness levels of persons with disabilities:				
Physical Fitness and Motor Skill Levels of Individuals with Mental Retardation (1991)	Illinois State Printing Service Illinois State University Normal, IL 61761-6901	Mild and moderate mental retardation and Down syndrome, ages 6–21 yrs	Balance, body composition, muscular strength and endurance, power, flexibility, cardiorespiratory endurance, hand-eye coordination	Normative-referenced
A standardized physical fitness test with norms for persons with mental retardation:				
Project M.O.B.I.L.T.E.E. Curriculum Imbedded Assessment (1981)	Hopewell Special Education Regional Resource Center	Moderately and low functioning, ambulatory and nonambulatory, any age	Cardiovascular, speed, agility, power, strength and endurance	Content- and criterion-referenced

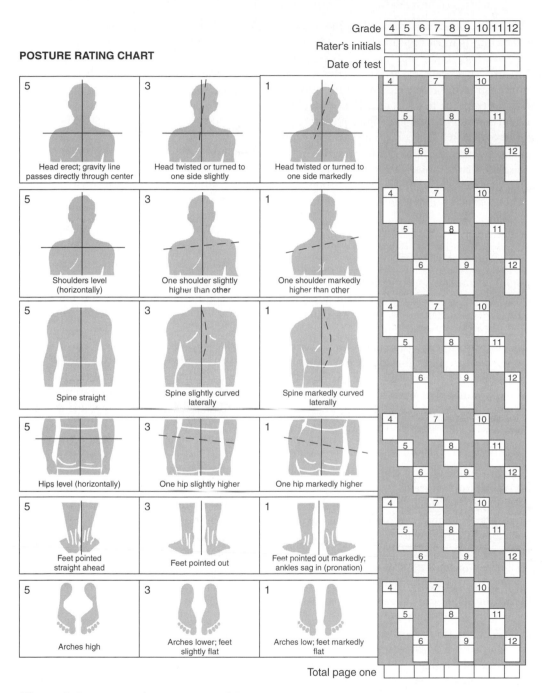

Figure 2-9 New York State Postural Survey
Courtesy New York State Education Department.

Care must be exercised to select the assessment tool that is most appropriate and administratively feasible. Once appropriate assessment instruments have been selected, it is critical that the administration, interpretation, and recommendations from the tests produce the type of information that can be used to design a physical education program that will contribute to the growth and independence of students, particularly those with disabling conditions. General guidelines for ensuring that the procedure results in appropriate educational programming are presented in the next section.

THE TESTING PROCESS

Although selecting an appropriate test is a critical step in gathering meaningful assessment information, the most important phase of the process is to ensure that the information gathered is truly representative of the student's capability. The effective evaluator fully prepares for the testing session, conducts the testing with care, and analyzes the information gathered as soon after the session as possible.

Preparations for Testing

After an appropriate instrument has been selected, it is important to give careful thought to the testing process. Not only should the evaluator become thoroughly familiar and comfortable with the test, but also should others who are assisting. Having practice sessions in advance with peers and/or children who do not have disabilities or observing a videotape of the correct procedure to use followed by discussion of the critical aspects of each item can be helpful. To avoid having to refer constantly to the test instructions during the actual testing session, evaluators may choose to prepare and use "crib" notes while testing. These notes can be used as reminders about what positions are required, time limitations, and unique cues that can be given during the testing session. When other personnel are going to assist with the testing session, they should be trained to the point where it is evident

that they are clear about how the test items are to be administered and scored. Once everyone is confident about the test procedures, decisions must be made about how, where, and when the test will be administered.

Administering the Test

Tests can be administered individually or in groups whenever possible in a natural rather than a contrived setting. Diagnostic tests are most frequently administered individually; however, screening and programming tests can be given to groups during the physical education period. When testing groups, the gymnasium can be divided into stations, with each station being designated for a particular test item, or the movements to be evaluated can be built into the lesson for the day.

Regardless of the procedure being used, it is important that a well-lighted, comfortably cooled, uncluttered area be selected. The more removed from noisy events and traffic zones, the better. Equipment that is required for the testing session should be arranged near the location where it will be needed and arranged so that it is accessible but not distracting to the students. The best time to administer tests is midmorning or midafternoon. Whenever possible, avoid administering tests early or late in the day, just before or after lunch, after a student has been ill, or prior to or just after an exciting event. Regardless of the time of day the tests are administered, the evaluators' attitude toward the students is a critical factor in obtaining optimum performance efforts.

Whenever possible, the test situation should be a positive experience for the students. Students who feel encouraged and valued will be motivated to try harder than will students who feel threatened and demoralized by the testing situation. Evaluators should be instructed to show interest in each child, offer words of encouragement, and reward every honest effort with praise. Unusual behaviors and ways of executing movements demonstrated during the session should be noted on the score sheet. Avoid rushing the students, verbally comparing their performance with those of others, and providing clues not permitted by the test. Some practical considerations to keep in mind include the following:

1. The test should be administered by an individual who can communicate in the child's preferred language and/or form of communication. If an adult is not available, use a bilingual peer to interpret the instructions.

2. How a child performs a task often can be more informative than whether the child is successful with the movement. Watch for extraneous arm, trunk, or leg movements and unusual head positioning as the child performs. Record these observations.

3. Keep the testing conditions as comfortable as possible. Children perform better when the surroundings are free from distractions and the evaluator is relaxed and unhurried. Spend a few minutes talking with the children to establish rapport, and convey your interest in them.

4. Keep the number of observers to a minimum. Children with disabilities are often hesitant about performing in front of peers or parents. When they are insecure about their ability to perform, they will try too hard or fail to give their best effort if people are watching them.

5. Repeat trials when you think the child might be able to perform adequately if given more time or is less tense. If a child is having difficulty with a given task, go on to easier tasks until he or she regains some confidence. Then go back to a task that was failed earlier and try again.

6. Observe the child on different days if possible. Children are just like adults—they have their good days and their bad days. If the testing can be spread over two or three days, the child will have the opportunity to show different performance levels.

7. Limit testing time to reasonable periods. Children will perform best for a period of 30 to 60 minutes. If the time is too brief, the child does not have time to get warmed up and into the procedure. If you go beyond an hour of testing time, fatigue and distractibility often interfere with performance.

A sensitive evaluator keeps the child's best interest in mind at all times. Focusing on the test rather than the child distorts test results and gives an inaccurate picture of the child's true capabilities. On completion of the testing session, observations and scores must be recorded, organized, and interpreted.

Organizing and Interpreting the Test Results

Once you have the test results in hand, it is important to analyze them as soon as possible. The shorter the time lapse between administering and interpreting the results, the easier it is to remember how the student performed individual tasks in the test. To facilitate reporting and interpreting the data, the test results should be organized. Actual test data for Maria Garcia are presented in Figures 2-10, 2-11, and 2-12. Examples of three ways to organize these test results appear after the actual score sheets.

There are several different ways to organize test results. Test performance can be charted, grouped according to strengths and weaknesses, or reported according to subset or subtest scores. Examples of each of these organizational techniques are presented in Figures 2-13, 2-14, 2-15, and 2-16. As will be seen by studying these examples, there are advantages and disadvantages to each.

Charted data provide a simple visual record of how the student performed in comparison with established normative standards. This form of reporting can be accomplished in a brief period of time; however, little information from which to establish goals and objectives and to develop an intervention program is available (see Figures 2-13 and 2-14). The reader is left to draw his or her own conclusions about the type of strength that is lacking and the extent to which Maria is at visual risk. This form of reporting test

					TGMD	TEST OF GROSS MOTOR DEVELOPMENT

Name *MARIA GARCIA*

School/Agency_____

Sex: Male _____   Female __X__   Grade __3__

TGMD

TEST OF
GROSS
MOTOR
DEVELOPMENT
Dale A. Ulrich

TESTING INFORMATION

1ST TESTING	Year	Month	Day	**2ND TESTING**	Year	Month	Day
Date Tested	99	2	3	Date Tested			
Date of Birth	89	1	21	Date of Birth			
Chronological Age	10	0	14	Chronological Age			

PYFER
Examiner's Name

ADAPTED PE SPECIALIST
Examiner's Title

TO DETERMINE GROSS MOTOR DEV
Purpose of Testing

Examiner's Name

Examiner's Title

Purpose of Testing

RECORD OF SCORES

1ST TESTING Subtests	Raw Scores	%iles	Std. Scores	**2ND TESTING** Subtests	Raw Scores	%iles	Std. Scores
Locomotor Skills	20	9	6	Locomotor Skills			
Object Control Skills	13	2	4	Object Control Skills			
Sum of Standard Scores =	10			Sum of Standard Scores =			
Gross Motor Development Quotient (GMDQ) =	70			Gross Motor Development Quotient (GMDQ) =			

COMMENTS/RECOMMENDATIONS

_____

_____

_____

_____

_____

_____

_____

_____

Additional copies of this form (#0552) may be purchased from PRO-ED, 8700 Shoal Creek Blvd., Austin, Texas 78757, 512/451-3246

Figure 2-10   (*Continued*)

LOCOMOTOR SKILLS

Skill	Equipment	Directions	Performance Criteria	1st	2nd
RUN	50 feet of clear space, colored tape, chalk or other marking device	Mark off two lines 50 feet apart	1. Brief period where both feet are off the ground	/	
		Instruct student to "run fast" from one line to the other	2. Arms in opposition to legs, elbows bent	/	
			3. Foot placement near or on a line (not flat footed)	/	
			4. Nonsupport leg bent approximately 90 degrees (close to buttocks)	/	
GALLOP	A minimum of 30 feet of clear space	Mark off two lines 30 feet apart	1. A step forward with the lead foot followed by a step with the trailing foot to a position adjacent to or behind the lead foot	/	
		Tell student to gallop from one line to the other three times	2. Brief period where both feet are off the ground	/	
		Tell student to gallop leading with one foot and then the other	3. Arms bent and lifted to waist level	/	
			4. Able to lead with the right and left foot	0	
HOP	A minimum of 15 feet of clear space	Ask student to hop 3 times, first on one foot and then on the other	1. Foot of nonsupport leg is bent and carried in back of the body	/	
			2. Nonsupport leg swings in pendular fashion to produce force	/	
			3. Arms bent at elbows and swing forward on take off	/	
			4. Able to hop on the right and left foot	/	
LEAP	A minimum of 30 feet of clear space	Ask student to leap	1. Take off on one foot and land on the opposite foot	/	
		Tell him/her to take large steps leaping from one foot to the other	2. A period where both feet are off the ground (longer than running)	/	
			3. Forward reach with arm opposite the lead foot	0	
HORIZONTAL JUMP	10 feet of clear space, tape or other marking devices	Mark off a starting line on the floor, mat, or carpet	1. Preparatory movement includes flexion of both knees with arms extended behind the body	/	
		Have the student start behind the line	2. Arms extend forcefully forward and upward, reaching full extension above head	/	
		Tell the student to "jump far"	3. Take off and land on both feet simultaneously	/	
			4. Arms are brought downward during landing	/	

Figure 2-10   (*Continued*)

LOCOMOTOR SKILLS

Skill	Equipment	Directions	Performance Criteria	1st	2nd
SKIP	A minimum of 30 feet of clear space, marking device	Mark off two lines 30 feet apart Tell the student to skip from one line to the other three times	1. A rhythmical repetition of the step-hop on alternate feet	0	
			2. Foot of nonsupport leg carried near surface during hop	0	
			3. Arms alternately moving in opposition to legs at about waist level	0	
SLIDE	A minimum of 30 feet of clear space, colored tape or other marking device	Mark off two lines 30 feet apart Tell the student to slide from one line to the other three times facing the same direction	1. Body turned sideways to desired direction of travel		1
			2. A step sideways followed by a slide of the trailing foot to a point next to the lead foot	1	
			3. A short period where both feet are off the floor	1	
			4. Able to slide to the right and to the left side	0	
LOCOMOTOR SKILLS SUBTEST SCORE					

2 0

OBJECT CONTROL SKILLS

Skill	Equipment	Directions	Performance Criteria	1st	2nd
TWO-HAND STRIKE	4-6 inch light-weight ball, plastic bat	Toss the ball softly to the student at about waist level Tell the student to hit the ball hard Only count those tosses that are between the student's waist and shoulders	1. Dominate hand grips bat above nondominant hand	1	
			2. Nondominant side of body faces the tosser (feet parallel)	1	
			3. Hip and spine rotation	1	
			4. Weight is transferred by stepping with front foot	0	
STATIONARY BOUNCE	8-10 inch playground ball, hard, flat surface (floor, pavement)	Tell the student to bounce the ball three times using one hand Make sure the ball is not underinflated Repeat 3 separate trials	1. Contact ball with one hand at about hip height	1	
			2. Pushes ball with fingers (not a slap)	1	
			3. Ball contacts floor in front of (or to the outside of) foot on the side of the hand being used	1	

Figure 2-10   (*Continued*)

OBJECT CONTROL SKILLS

Skill	Equipment	Directions	Performance Criteria	1st	2nd
CATCH	6-8 inch sponge ball, 15 feet of clear space, tape or other marking device	Mark off 2 lines 15 feet apart. Student stands on one line and the tosser on the other. Toss the ball underhand directly to student with a slight arc and tell him/her to "catch it with your hands." Only count those tosses that are between student's shoulders and waist.	1. Preparation phase where elbows are flexed and hands are in front of body 2. Arms extend in preparation for ball contact 3. Ball is caught and controlled by hands only 4. Elbows bend to absorb force	1 1 0 1	
KICK	8-10 inch plastic or slightly deflated playground ball, 30 feet of clear space, tape or other marking device	Mark off one line 30 feet away from a wall and one that is 20 feet from the wall. Place the ball on the line nearest the wall and tell the student to stand on the other line. Tell the student to kick the ball "hard" toward the wall.	1. Rapid continuous approach to the ball 2. The truck is inclined backward during ball contact 3. Forward swing of the arm opposite kicking leg 4. Following-through by hopping on nonkicking foot	1 1 0 0	
OVERHAND THROW	3 tennis balls, a wall, 25 feet of clear space	Tell student to throw the ball "hard" at the wall.	1. A downward arc of the throwing arm initiates the windup 2. Rotation of hip and shoulder to a point where the nondominant side faces an imaginary target 3. Weight is transferred by stepping with the foot opposite the throwing hand 4. Following-through beyond ball release diagonally across body toward side opposite throwing arm	1 1 0 0	
			OBJECT CONTROL SKILLS SUBTEST SCORE	13	

Figure 2-10   (*Concluded*)

Bruininks-Oseretsky Test
of Motor Proficiency

Robert H. Bruininks, Ph. D.

NAME _____ SEX: Boy ☐ Girl ☐ GRADE _____

SCHOOL/AGENCY _____ CITY _____ STATE _____

EXAMINER _____ REFERRED BY _____

PURPOSE OF TESTING _____

Arm Preference: *(circle one)*
　　RIGHT　　LEFT　　MIXED

Leg Preference: *(circle one)*
　　RIGHT　　LEFT　　MIXED

	Year	Month	Day
Date Tested	____	____	____
Date of Birth	____	____	____
Chronological Age	____	____	____

TEST SCORE SUMMARY

Complete Battery:

SUBTEST	POINT SCORE Maximum	Subject's	STANDARD SCORE Test (Table 23)	Composite (Table 24)	PERCENTILE RANK (Table 25)	STANINE (Table 25)	OTHER _____
GROSS MOTOR SUBTESTS:							
1. Running Speed and Agility	15	____	____				____
2. Balance	32	____	____				____
3. Bilateral Coordination	20	____	____				____
4. Strength	42	____	____				____
GROSS MOTOR COMPOSITE			*☐ SUM	☐	☐	☐	☐┆☐
5. Upper-Limb Coordination	21	____	*☐				____
FINE MOTOR SUBTESTS:							
6. Response Speed	17	____	____				
7. Visual-Motor Control	24	____	____				
8. Upper-Limb Speed and Dexterity	72	____	____				
FINE MOTOR COMPOSITE			*☐ SUM	☐	☐	☐	☐┆☐
BATTERY COMPOSITE			*☐ SUM	☐	☐	☐	☐┆☐

*To obtain Battery Composite: Add Gross Motor Composite, Subtest 5 Standard Score, and Fine Motor Composite.
Check result by adding Standard Scores on Subtests 1-8.

Short Form:

	POINT SCORE Maximum	Subject's	STANDARD SCORE (Table 27)	PERCENTILE RANK (Table 27)	STANINE (Table 27)
SHORT FORM	98	____	☐	☐	☐

DIRECTIONS

Complete Battery:

1. During test administration, record subject's response for each trial.
2. After test administration, convert performance on each item (item raw score) to a point score, using scale provided. For an item with more than one trial, choose best performance. Record item point score in *circle* to right of scale.
3. For each subtest, add item point scores; record total in circle provided

at end of each subtest and in Test Score Summary section. Consult *Examiner's Manual* for norms tables.

Short Form:

1. Follow Steps 1 and 2 for Complete Battery, except record each point score in *box* to right of scale.
2. Add point scores for all 14 Short Form items and record total in Test Score Summary section. Consult *Examiner's Manual* for norms tables.

Figure 2-11　Bruininks-Oseretsky Test of Motor Proficiency

Form T-1R

No. _____

Name   *MARIA GARCIA*   Date *2-4-99*

Address   _____   Age *10*

Sex: M ☐   F ☒

Occupation   *STUDENT*

Glasses Worn: No ☐   Always ☒   Near Only ☐   Far Only ☐   Multi-Focal ☐   Other _____

Difficulty with Vision: No ☐   Yes ☒   Last Exam by Doctor   *SUMMER 1998*

Comments:

	Test No.		Low Score					High Score	
FAR POINT TESTS 0	1	Vertical Phoria	R. Hyper ★	★	+			⊃⊂	⊖
			L. Hyper ■	■	▲				
	2	Lateral Phoria	Over CONVERGENCE	1 2 3 4 5				6 7	8
			Under	15 14 13 ⑫ 11				10 9	
	3	Central Fusion	Two	Four Far Apart	Four Close Together		Four Then Three	Three Boxes	
	Acuity		1	2	3	4	5	6	
	4	Left	(ECDBF)	(TPCDB)	CEZFL	EPCFZ	ZZOLF	TELDZ	
		Both	(LDZTC)	OETFL	DZEOP	LPTOB	ELTDC	OFLCT	
		Right	(TPEOB)	(BFZDL)	(TCPBO)	ELDTF	DCZOE	DZEOF	
	5	Stereo	L-R only	Forward runner		(A 2)	(B 5)	C 8	
	5a	Stereo	L-R only	(A 4)	(B 2)	(C 5)	(D 3) (E 4)	(F 2)	
	6	Color	(A 8)	(B 15)	(C 5)	(D 35)	4 out of 6	(All Correct)	
NEAR POINT 10	7	Lateral Phoria	Over CONVERGENCE	1 2 3 4 5				6 ⑦	8
			Under	15 14 13 12 11				10 9	
	8	Central Fusion	Two	Four Far Apart	Four Close Together		Four Then Three	(Three Boxes)	
	Acuity		1	2	3	4	5	6	
	9	Left	(DCF)	(FZDL)	DZEBO	LPCFZ	DCELT	YDZOF	
		Both	(BPE)	(PCDB)	FLTCP	DTFEP	LFZOE	VOTDZ	
		Right	(OTB)	(OETF)	(OPCEZ)	ELTOB	TZODC	EDFTC	

Test taken: With ☒   Without ☐   Glasses.

Referred: No ☐   Yes ☒

Tester   *PYFER*

Figure 2-12   Bioptor® Vision Tests

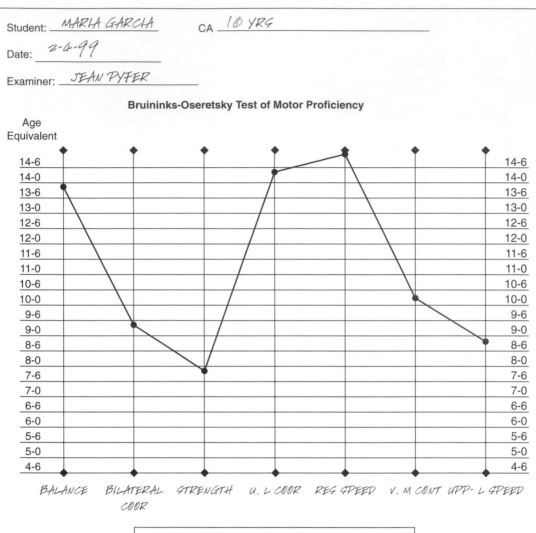

Student: _MARIA GARCIA_   CA _10 YRS_

Date: _2-4-99_

Examiner: _JEAN PYFER_

Bruininks-Oseretsky Test of Motor Proficiency

Age Equivalent

	BALANCE	BILATERAL COOR	STRENGTH	U. L COOR	RES SPEED	V. M CONT	UPP- L SPEED

| TEST OF GROSS MOTOR DEVELOPMENT |
| Raw Score Expectations for Ages 3 to 10 Years |
| (25th to 75th Percentile) |

Age	Locomotor 25th-75th	Object Control 25th-75th
10	23-26	17-18
9	22-25	15-18
8	22-25	14-17
7	18-23	11-16
6	16-21	8-13
5	14-17	5-11
4	(9-15)	4-6
3	6-10	(2-3)

Figure 2-13

Name: Maria Garcia

FAR POINT	OK	At risk
Vertical phoria	✓	
Lateral phoria		✓
Central fusion	✓	
Acuity Left		✓
Both		✓
Right		✓
Stereo vision	✓	
Color	✓	

NEAR POINT	OK	At risk
Lateral phoria	✓	
Central fusion	✓	
Acuity Left		✓
Both		✓
Right		✓

Comments _____

_____

COVER TEST---EACH EYE SWUNG IN LATERALLY TOWARD THE NOSE WHEN UNCOVERED; CONV-DIV---EYES MOVED EVENLY AND SMOOTHLY; TRACKING---EYES MOVED SMOOTHLY AND EVENLY.

Figure 2-14   Bioptor Visual Screening

results can be very helpful when large numbers of students are being tested with the same instrument more than once. The student's performance can be recorded in a different color each time, so that quick comparisons from one test period to the next can be made.

Highlighting Maria's strengths and weaknesses without providing subtest scores provides more information than simply charting the test results. Grouping test information according to strengths and weaknesses provides ready reference to areas of concern while acknowledging the student's stronger points (see Figure 2-15). However, the evaluator must be trusted to determine accurately what constitutes a strength and a weakness. With this form of reporting, it is possible to determine what Maria can and cannot do, but her performance cannot be compared with that of others her age.

Reporting test results according to subtest scores and including a narrative describing performance on tasks within the subtests give the reader the greatest amount of information (see Figure 2-16). Subtest scores reported in percentiles or age equivalency provide both the parent and teacher with a comparative picture of how the student is performing in relation to his or her age group. The narrative report gives the reader insight into what parts of the domain the student is having difficulty with, which will be very helpful in setting goals and objectives as well as designing the intervention program. Reporting of this sort facilitates communication between the evaluator and others who will read and use the information; however, it is very time consuming. If there are designated professionals whose major responsibility is testing students in a district, they may wish to use this form of reporting at least once every three years and just provide progress reports during the intermittent years.

When the test results are going to be used to determine whether a student's performance is significantly delayed to require special services, comparison with age-expected results is necessary and required by law. Usually any total or subtest score that falls beyond one standard deviation below the mean or below the 25th percentile or one year below the performance expected for the age of the child is considered a deficit area. But do not rely on those scores alone. Poor performance on individual tasks is a clue to deficit areas. If a child does well on sit-ups but poorly on push-ups, we cannot conclude that strength is adequate. Rather, we note that improvement of shoulder girdle strength is a very definite unique need.

ADAPTED PHYSICAL EDUCATION EVALUATION

NAME: Maria Garcia   DOB: 1-21-89   CA: 10 years

EXAMINER: Dr. Jean Pyfer, Adapted Physical Education Specialist   Date: February 3 and 4, 1999

Maria Garcia was referred to the TWU Institute of Clinical Services and Applied Research by her mother because the girl is experiencing difficulty in third grade. The Test of Gross Motor Development was administered to Maria in MCL 908 at Texas Woman's University on February 3 at 3:00 pm in the afternoon. The Bruininks-Oseretsky Test of Motor Proficiency and visual screening tests were administered at 4:15 pm on February 4. There were no observers present in the room.

STRENGTHS	WEAKNESSES
1. Running.	1. Follow through when leaping, kicking and throwing.
2. Hopping.	
3. Horizontal jump.	2. Leading with right foot during gallop and slide.
4. Stationary bounce.	
5. Leading with the left foot during gallop and slide.	3. Trapping ball against chest.
	4. Static balance with eyes closed.
6. Static and dynamic balance with eyes open.	5. Synchronizing limbs on opposite sides of the body.
7. Upper limb coordination.	6. Situps.
8. Response speed.	7. Pushups.
9. Visual convergence and divergence.	8. Leg power.
10. Visual tracking.	9. Tasks requiring visual attention.
11. Visual vertical phoria.	10. Lateral phoria of eyes at far point.
12. Central fusion of eyes at near and far.	11. Turning head to right and holding it close to the page when tracing mazes.
13. Stereo vision.	
14. Color vision.	12. Visual acuity at near and far point.

GENERAL OBSERVATIONS—Maria is a slightly built girl who willingly went with the examiner to the testing room. She answered all questions asked of her and volunteered additional information. She said she likes school and is best at math. Maria attempted every task requested of her and attended to all tasks throughout both days of testing. While tracing mazes, Maria turned her head to the right and held it 4 to 6 inches from the paper.

ANECDOTAL INFORMATION—Maria weighed 4 lbs. 7 oz. at birth and was kept in intensive care for observation for 10 days. Compared to the Garcia's other two older children, Maria was slow to develop; however, she looked forward to beginning kindergarten and interacted well with her teachers and other children until she reached second grade. At that time she was having difficulty grasping basic skills, could not read, and began acting out in class and with other children. At the mother's request Maria was tested by the school district and found to have a learning disability. Her Individual Education Program that was developed addressed her cognitive problems, but not her behavioral difficulties. She repeated second grade and began receiving pull-out services from a special education teacher. Maria is now in third grade and is still experiencing learning and behavior problems. Her classroom teacher reports that Maria is disruptive in class: the special education teacher reports that Maria is manipulative; Mrs. Garcia says that Maria complains a lot and tries to get out of her work. The teacher suggested that Maria get an eye examination because she was complaining of having headaches. Instead, the Garcia's brought her to the Institute for a full assessment.

Figure 2-15   Motor Test Results Arranged According to Strengths and Weaknesses (*Continued*)

CONCLUSIONS:
1. Maria's strong performance in running, hopping, horizontal jumping, stationary bounce, static and dynamic balance tasks with the eyes open, upper limb coordination tasks utilizing limbs on the same side of the body, and response speed indicate she comprehends instruction.
2. Maria's inability to balance for 10 seconds with eyes closed could indicate delayed vestibular (inner ear) development.
3. Her below average pushup, situp, and long jump scores indicate muscular weakness in the shoulder girdle and abdominal muscle groups as well as in explosive power in the legs.
4. Maria's inability to gallop and slide leading with either foot, inability to skip, lack of weight transfer during striking, kicking, and overhand throwing; as well as her failure to synchronize tapping of fingers and toes and arm and leg on opposite sides of the body indicate that cross lateral coordination has not yet developed.
5. Her tendency to trap when catching an 8" sponge ball, the under convergence at far point on the bioptor test, and the swinging in of the eyes after being uncovered indicate she may have some difficulty using both eyes in unison, and when given an option, prefers to use the left eye.
6. The below average scores on near and far point acuity (with glasses on), slow performance during upper limb and dexterity tasks requiring visual guidance and the tendency to hold her head close to the paper with tracing mazes suggest she may not be seeing clearly.

RECOMMENDATIONS:
1. Encouraging Maria to play games that she performs well should contribute to her sense of satisfaction and accomplishment.
2. Perform activities that promote vestibular development (turning, rolling, spinning).
3. Provide general strengthening program to improve shoulder girdle, abdominal, and hip flexor strength.
4. Perform activities that require her to reach across the center of the body and/or to coordinate limbs on opposite sides of the body (rope climbing, stepping with opposite foot when throwing, and swimming using the crawl stroke with breathing).
5. Have an eye examination done by a visual developmental specialist to determine both refractive and orthoptic visual status.

Figure 2-15 (*Concluded*)

ADAPTED PHYSICAL EDUCATION EVALUATION

NAME: Maria Garcia   DOB: 1-21-89   CA: 10 yrs

Dates tested: February 3, 4, 1999

EXAMINER: Dr. Jean Pyfer, Adapted Physical Education Specialist

---

Maria Garcia was referred to the TWU Institute of Clinical Services and Applied Research by her mother because the girl is experiencing difficulty in third grade. The Test of Gross Motor Development was administered to Maria in MCL 908 at Texas Woman's University on February 3 at 3:00 pm in the afternoon. The Bruininks-Oseretsky Test of Motor Proficiency and visual screening tests were administered at 4:15 pm on February 4. There were no observers present in the room.

Figure 2-16 **Motor Test Results Arranged According to Subtest Performance (*Continued*)**

GROSS MOTOR DEVELOPMENT

Locomotor Skills   Points

Demonstrated all components of the tasks run, hop, and horizontal jump.

Gallop—demonstrated all components of the task except the ability to lead with the right and the left foot (only led with the left foot); Leap—demonstrated all components of the task except reaching forward with the arm opposite the lead foot; Skip—did not demonstrate any components of the skip. She would step two or three times and then try to add a hop; Slide—demonstrated all components of the task except the ability to lead with the right and the left foot (only led with the left foot).

Locomotor skills subtest score   20

Object Control Skills

Stationary bounce—demonstrated all components of the task.

Two-hand strike—demonstrated all components of the task except she did not transfer her weight by stepping with the front foot; Catch—demonstrated all components of the task except catching the 8" ball and controlling it with the hands only. She trapped the ball against her chest on every catch; Kick—demonstrated all components of the task except forward swing of the arm opposite the kicking leg and follow through by hopping on the nonkicking foot; Overhead throw—demonstrated all components of the throw except she did not transfer her weight to the foot opposite the throwing hand, nor did she follow through diagonally across the body toward the side opposite the throwing arm.

Object control skills subtest score   13

MOTOR PROFICIENCY   Age
Equivalency   (years-months)

Gross Motor Subtests
1. Running Speed and Agility   Did not administer
2. Balance—Maria performed all tasks to maximum except standing on one   13-8
   foot with eyes closed (6 seconds).
3. Bilateral Coordination—She demonstrated the ability to tap feet alternately   9-5
   while making circles with fingers, synchronizing movement of the arm and leg on
   the same side, jumping up and touching her heels, and synchronizing tapping
   fingers and toes on the same side of the body. She jumped up and clapped her
   hands twice, and drew 7 lines and crosses simultaneously. She did not demonstrate
   the ability to synchronize tapping fingers and toes on the opposite side of the body
   nor did she synchronize movement of the art and leg on opposite side of the body.
4. Strength—Maria Completed 10 situps in 20 seconds and 9 knee pushups in   7-8
   20 seconds. She long jumped 30 inches.

Upper Limb Coordination Subtest
5. Upper-Limb Coordination—Maria performed all tasks to maximum except   14-5
   hitting a target with a thrown ball (she hit the target 4 out of 5 times).

Fine Motor Subtests
6. Response Speed—She stopped the dropped stick 7 out of 7 times with a   15-11
   median score of 14.
7. Visual-Motor Control—Maria executed all tasks to maximum except   10-2
   copying a horizontal diamond and overlapping pencils using her
   preferred hand.
8. Upper Limb Speed and Dexterity—Maria executed all tasks; however, those   8-8
   tasks requiring visual attention were done more slowly than those that did not.

Figure 2-16   (*Continued*)

VISUAL SCREENING

1. Cover Test—Each eye swung in laterally toward the nose when uncovered (exophoric).
2. Convergence-Divergence—Both eyes moved evenly and smoothly when tracking an object moved toward her nose from a distance of 16 inches to a distance of 4 inches and back.
3. Tracking—Both eyes moved smoothly and evenly when tracking an object moved laterally and diagonally about 16 inches from the bridge of the nose.

BIOPTOR TESTING

1. Far point
   a) Scored above average on vertical phoria
   b) Scored below average on lateral phoria (under converged)
   c) Scored above average on central fusion
   d) Scored below average on acuity when using each eye independently and when using both eyes together
   e) Scored average or above on both stereo tests
   f) Correctly identified all color test numbers
2. Near point
   a) Scored above average on lateral phoria and central fusion
   b) Scored below average on acuity when using each eye independently and when using both eyes together

GENERAL OBSERVATIONS—Maria is a slightly built girl who willingly went with the examiner to the testing room. She answered all questions asked of her and volunteered additional information. She said she likes school and is best at math. Maria attempted every task requested of her and attended to the tasks throughout the test session. While tracing mazes, Maria turned her head to the right and held it 4 to 6 inches from the paper.

ANECDOTAL INFORMATION—Marla weighed 4 lbs. 7 oz. at birth and was kept in intensive care for observation for 10 days. Compared to the Garcia's other two older children, Maria was slow to develop; however, she looked forward to beginning kindergarten and interacted well with her teachers and other children until she reached second grade. At that time she was having difficulty grasping basic skills, could not read, and began acting out in class and with other children. At the mother's request Maria was tested by the school district and found to have a learning disability. Her Individual Education Program that was developed addressed her cognitive problems, but not her behavioral difficulties. She repeated second grade and began receiving pull-out services from a special education teacher. Maria is now in third grade and is still experiencing learning and behavior problems. Her classroom teacher reports that Maria is disruptive in class: the special education teacher reports that Maria is manipulative; Mrs. Garcia says that Maria complains a lot and tries to get out of her work. The teacher suggested that Maria get an eye examination because she was complaining of having headaches. Instead, the Garcia's brought her to the Institute for a full assessment.

CONCLUSIONS:

1. Maria's strong performance in running, hopping, horizontal jumping, and static and dynamic balance tasks with eyes open, upper-limb coordination tasks utilizing limbs on the same side of the body, and response speed indicate she comprehends instructions.
2. Maria's inability to balance for 10 seconds with eyes closed could indicate delayed vestibular (inner ear) development.
3. Her below average pushup, situp and long jump scores indicate muscular weakness in the shoulder girdle and abdominal muscle groups as well as in explosive power in the legs.
4. Maria's inability to gallop and slide leading with either foot, inability to skip, lack of weight transfer during striking, kicking, and the overhand throwing, and failure to synchronize tapping of fingers and toes and arm and leg on opposite sides of the body, indicate that cross lateral coordination has not yet occurred.

Figure 2-16   (*Continued*)

5. Her tendency to turn her head to the right during tracking tasks, the under convergence at far point on the bioptor, her tendency to trap when catching an 8" sponge ball, and the swinging in of the eyes after being uncovered indicate she may have some difficulty using both eyes in unison, and when given an option, prefers to use the left eye.
6. The below-average scores on near and far point acuity (with glasses on), slow performance during upper limb and dexterity tasks requiring visual guidance, and the tendency to hold her head close to the paper when tracing mazes suggest she may not be seeing clearly.

RECOMMENDATIONS:

1. Encouraging Maria to play games that she performs well should contribute to her sense of satisfaction and accomplishment.
2. Perform activities that promote vestibular (inner ear) development (turning, rolling, spinning).
3. Provide a general strengthening program to improve shoulder girdle, abdominal, and hip flexor strength.
4. Perform activities that require her to reach across the center of the body and/or to coordinate limbs on opposite sides of the body (rope climbing, stepping with the opposite foot when throwing, and swimming using the crawl stroke with breathing).
5. Have an eye examination done by a visual developmental specialist to determine both refractive and orthoptic visual status.

Figure 2-16   (*Concluded*)

When the information is going to be used to develop an IEP, determine goals and objectives, and/or design educational programs, descriptive rather than comparative information is needed. Additionally, information about how a movement was performed will provide clues needed to determine what the underlying problem is and where to focus the intervention program. An IEP developed from Maria Garcia's test results is presented in Chapter 3, "Developing the Individual Education Program." A behavior modification program addressing Maria's needs is included in Chapter 6, "Behavior Management."

USING ASSESSMENT FOR CLASSIFICATION

Assessment is sometimes used to classify performers so that competition between individuals is as equal as possible. To classify competitors, performance in the skill is observed to determine what the athlete is capable of doing. Once the abilities of the performers are determined, those with similar capabilities compete against one another. A running classification for performers with physical disabilities follows:

1. Move a wheelchair forward continuously a distance of 10 yards
2. Move a wheelchair forward continuously a distance of 30 yards
3. Move a wheelchair continuously up a 10-degree incline that is a length of 10 yards
4. Move a walker continuously a distance of 10 yards
5. Move a walker continuously a distance of 30 yards
6. Move with crutches a distance of 10 yards
7. Move with crutches a distance of 25 yards
8. Move with a cane continuously a distance of 15 yards
9. Move with a cane continuously a distance of 30 yards
10. Move independently over a distance of 10 yards
11. Move independently a distance of 30 yards
12. Run a distance of 30 yards (flight phase)

SUMMARY

Assessment has become an integral part of the educational process. Students are evaluated for the purpose of (1) identifying those who have developmental delays, (2) diagnosing the nature of the student's problem or delay, (3) providing information to use to develop the student's IEP, (4) developing instruction specific to the student's specific needs, and (5) evaluating student progress. Evaluation instruments can be classified as informal or formal. Informal evaluation involves observing movements in a variety of settings, gathering information from parents, and/or using a checklist or clinical test. Formal evaluation involves using a standardized test instrument. Tests can be used to measure mastery of a general or specific curriculum, mastery of a functional or sport skill, level of physical fitness, perceptual motor development, or sensorimotor status. Performance is measured using a criterion or content reference. Criterion-referenced tests measure performance against a standard, whereas content-referenced tests are used to determine whether all components of a task or a series of tasks are demonstrated.

Which instrument is selected depends on established policy, whether standardization is required, administrative feasibility, and the student's type of disability. A variety of tests are available that are very useful for fitness and motor programming for students with disabilities. Evaluators should be trained in test administration and interpretation. Information gathered from assessment must be organized, interpreted, and reported in ways that facilitate communication and program development.

REVIEW QUESTIONS

1. What is the difference between a formal and an informal test?
2. What are the purposes of assessment?
3. When must a standardized test be used?
4. What is curriculum-based assessment?
5. What is administrative feasibility?
6. Describe, compare, and contrast three techniques for organizing test data.

STUDENT ACTIVITIES

1. Identify five assessment tools. Analyze and classify each according to whether the scoring method used is content- or criterion-referenced.
2. Using test results from a physical fitness test, identify present levels of performance.
3. Divide the class into small groups. Using made-up test results, have each group organize the test results by graphing, according to strengths and weaknesses, and according to subtest scores. Have the students discuss the advantages and disadvantages of each type of data presentation.
4. Observe teachers assessing learners. Indicate the types of assessment used.
5. Make a list of behaviors/skills a person with disabilities would need to successfully use a fitness center in your community.

REFERENCES

1. Hyde BJ: *A motor development checklist of selected categories for kindergarten children,* Unpublished thesis, Lawrence, 1980, University of Kansas.
2. Meisels SJ: Designing meaningful measurements for early childhood. In Mallory BL, New RS, editors: *Diversity and developmentally appropriate practices,* New York, 1994, Teachers College, Columbia University Press.
3. Silverstein R: *A user's guide to the 1999 regulations,* Washington, DC, 1999, ERIC.
4. Waterman BB: Assessing children for the presence of a disability, *National Information Center for Children and Youth with Disabilities (NICHCY) News Digest,* 4:1–24, 1994.

SUGGESTED READINGS

Horvat M, Kalakian LH: *Assessment in adapted physical education and therapeutic recreation,* Madison, WI, l996, Brown & Benchmark.

Kasser SL, Collier D, Solava DG: Sport skills for students with disabilities: a collaborative effort, JOPERD, 68(1): 50–53 1997.

National Association for Sport and Physical Education: *Methods of assessing motor skills,* Reston, VA, 1999, American Association for Health, Physical Education, Recreation and Dance.

National Association for Sport and Physical Education: *Moving into the future: national standards for physical education,* Dubuque, IA, 1995, McGraw-Hill.

Seaman JA, editor: *Physical best and individuals with disabilities: a handbook for inclusion in fitness programs,* Reston, VA, 1995, American Association for Active Lifestyles and Fitness.

Tannehill D, editor: *Physical education assessment series,* Reston, VA, 1999, National Association of Sport and Physical Education.

Veal ML, Russell M, Brown JL: Learning to use assessment, JOHPERD, 67(9): 21–25, 1996.

3

Developing the Individual Education Program

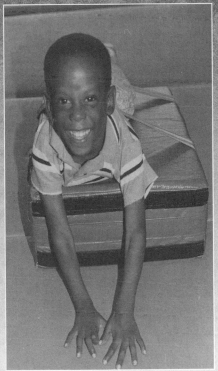

Photo by Carol Huettig.

Twenty-five years after the passage of the Education of the Handicapped Act (1975), the educational needs of children and young adults with disabilities are still not being met. Every child in the United States is entitled to a free, public education. This is true of every child with a disability as well. However, each child with a disability has unique abilities and unique needs. The very nature of a disability simply enhances that uniqueness and requires that the child be taught more carefully.

To ensure that every child with a disability receives an appropriate education, the Education of the Handicapped Act of 1975 (P.L. 94-142)

CASE STUDY

Maria Garcia

Please review the assessment of Maria Garcia in Chapter 2. Then, carefully review the individual physical education program (IPEP) included in Figure 3-1.

APPLICATION TASK

Would you have included any other objectives on the IPEP? Would you have added or eliminated any instructional modifications?

Figure 3-1 Individual Physical Education Program

Name: Maria Garcia
Date of birth: 1-21-89
Test dates: 2-4-99 and 2-5-99
Chronological age: 10 years
School: Wilson Elementary
Evaluator: Dr. Jean Pyfer, adapted physical education specialist

Tests administered:
   Bruininks-Oseretsky Test of Motor Proficiency
   Test of Gross Motor Development
   Bioptor Visual Test (acuity, color, and central fusion)

Present level of performance:
• Maria's inability to balance on either foot for 10 seconds with eyes closed could indicate delayed vestibular (inner ear) development.
• Her below-average push-up, sit-up and long jump scores indicate muscular weakness in the shoulder girdle and abdominal muscle groups as well as in explosive power in the legs.
• Maria's failure to synchronize tapping of fingers and toes and arm and leg on opposite sides of the body; her inability to gallop and slide leading with either foot; inability to skip; and lack of weight transfer during striking, kicking, and the overhand throw indicate that cross-lateral coordination has not yet occurred.

Annual physical education goals and short-term objectives

Annual goal
Maria will demonstrate vestibular function by balancing on her left foot for 10 seconds, with eyes closed.
   Short-term objectives:
   Maria will be able to do 5 consecutive log rolls to the right.
   Maria will be able to do 5 consecutive log rolls to the left.
   Maria will be able to do 3 consecutive log rolls to the right followed, immediately, by 3 consecutive log
      rolls left.

(Continued)

Figure 3-1   *(Continued)*

Annual goal
Maria will demonstrate improved abdominal strength by performing 20 abdominal curls in 1 minute.
> *Short-term objectives:*
> Maria will perform 12 abdominal curls in 1 minute.
> Maria will perform 15 abdominal curls in 1 minute.
> Maria will perform 18 abdominal curls in 1 minute.

Annual goal
To promote both cross-lateral integration and shoulder girdle strength, Maria will, while lying supine on a scooter board, pull herself, head first, the width of the gymnasium, hand-over-hand, on a rope suspended 2 feet above her head.
> *Short-term objectives:*
> Maria will, while lying supine on a scooter board, pull herself, head first, 10 feet, hand-over-hand, on a rope suspended 2 feet above her head.
> Maria will, while lying supine on a scooter board, pull herself, head first, 30 feet, hand-over-hand, on a rope suspended 2 feet above her head.
> Maria will, while lying supine on a scooter board, pull herself, head first, 50 feet, hand-over-hand, on a rope suspended 2 feet above her head.

Annual goal
To demonstrate development of cross-lateral integration, Maria will be able to throw, contralaterally, using her dominant hand, and demonstrate a follow-through, 5 out of 5 times.
> *Short-term objectives:*
> Maria will be able to throw, contralaterally, using her dominant hand, after assuming a stationary front-back stride.
> Maria will be able to throw, contralaterally, using her dominant hand, and demonstrate a follow-through, 3 out of 5 times.

Recommended physical education placement:
General fifth-grade physical education with support from an adapted physical education specialist to help her develop vestibular function, cross-lateral functioning capabilities, and physical fitness.

Modifications/adaptations

Please refer to the Modifications page of the IEP. (See Figure 3-5.)
Please refer to "Activities to Facilitate Movement Toward General Education Settings" (see Figure 3-6).

Duration of services: From March 15, 1999, to March 15, 2000

Date of annual review: March 15, 1999

mandated that an individual education program (IEP) be developed for each student with a disability. The IEP should be the cornerstone of the student's education. It should be a living, working document that the teacher and parents use as the basis for the instructional process.

The IEP is not a piece of paper; it is a process in which parents, educators, and the student work together to *ensure that the student is able to achieve his or her designated goals.*[50]

The IEP requires that educators and administrators be accountable for the education of the child with a disability. The IEP process, by and through which a child's education is planned and executed, requires a specific education program to be developed for each child with a disability. The federal mandates regarding the development of the IEP and the content of the IEP necessitate accountability.

Educators and administrators must be able to document the child's need, based on a comprehensive assessment and evaluation, and to outline specifically the methods, techniques, and procedures that will be used to educate the child, while keeping in mind the child's specific and unique needs.

Many educators are, however, deeply concerned that the intent of the law regarding the IEP has virtually been ignored. The IEP has too often become paperwork completed for the sake of doing paperwork. All too often, the IEP is neither individualized nor special. Espin et al. wrote,

> Although most special educators would agree that an individual focus is what makes special education special and that the IEP is the key to tailoring individual programs, questions have been raised recently regarding the extent to which individual programming remains central to special education. Most specifically, concerns have been raised regarding the extent to which the same degree of individual tailoring occurs in inclusive settings—general education classrooms where students with disabilities are educated with their peers—as in non-inclusive settings—where students receive special education outside the general education classroom.[15]

The emphasis on education within the general education program may have had a significant negative impact on the individualization long associated with quality special education programs. Teachers serving children with disabilities in "inclusive settings" are less likely than teachers in resource or self-contained classrooms to develop IEPs that meet the intent and specifications of the law.[15]

CONTENT OF THE IEP

The 1999 Reauthorization of the Individuals with Disabilities Education Act (IDEA) of 1990 explains the IEP and describes its required content.[48] There were several changes in the Reauthorization of the 1997 Amendments to IDEA:

1. The addition of "benchmarks" as an alternative way to measure education progress, instead of the short-term objectives
2. Increased emphasis on the education of the child in the general curriculum
3. The beginning of transition services at age fourteen years instead of sixteen years
4. The implementation of new requirements for reporting progress in the general education curriculum
5. Participation in state and local education agency mandated assessments

The individualized education program (IEP) is a written statement for a child with disabilities that is developed, reviewed, and created in a meeting with an IEP team or multidisciplinary team[48, section a] (see Figure 3-2). (S)

DESCRIPTION OF EACH COMPONENT OF THE IEP

Present Level of Educational Performance

For each child with a disability, the IEP must include a statement of the present level of educational performance. It is important that the statement of the child's present level of educational performance be based on *current, relevant* information about the child. Information should be obtained from a variety of sources, including

1. Information from the child's parents (There is an increased emphasis on parent involvement in every phase of the child's education)
2. The most recent evaluation of the child
3. Districtwide assessment results
4. Input from the child's general physical educator and/or adapted physical education teacher

The statement describing the present level of educational performance must include how the child's disability affects the child's involvement and progress in the general curricula or, in the case of preschoolers age three to five years, their participation in appropriate activities. Appropriate activities are age-relevant developmental abilities

Figure 3-2   Contents of the Individual Education Program

The IEP must include the following: (48, Section a)
- A statement of the child's present level of performance
- How the child's disability affects involvement and performance in the general physical education class
- How the disability affects the child's involvement and progress in the general curriculum
- A statement of annual, measurable goals
- A statement of how progress toward the annual goals will be measured
- Benchmarks or short-term objectives that relate to needs that result from the disability
- Indications of how the child can be involved and progress in the general curriculum
- A statement describing how each of the child's other needs that result from the child's disability will be met
- A statement describing special education and related services
- A statement describing supplementary aids and services
- A statement of program accommodations or modifications or supports for school personnel that will advance the child toward attaining educational goals
- A statement of services needed for the child to participate in extracurricular and other nonacademic activities
- A statement describing how the child is to be educated so he or she can participate with other children with and without disabilities
- An explanation of the extent, if any, to which the child will participate with children without disabilities in the general class
- The location of the services (Walsh)
- A statement describing how the child's parents will be regularly informed, at least as often as parents of children without disabilities, of their child's progress toward annual goals
- A statement that provides information of the extent to which progress is sufficient to enable the child to achieve his or her goals by the end of the year
- Beginning at age fourteen, a statement of transition service needs that focuses on the student's course of study
- Beginning at age sixteen, a statement of needed transition services of interagency responsibilities or any needed linkages
- A plan for positive behavioral management if the child is disruptive

or milestones that typically reflect the development of children of the same age.

One of the purposes of assessment is to determine the child's present level of educational performance and need for specially designed education and physical education arising from the child's disability. These assessments are needed to ensure the child's involvement and progress in the general education and physical education curriculum and any needed adaptation or modifications to the general curriculum.[48, section b]

The comprehensive determination of a student's present level of educational performance may include the following:

1. Intellectual assessment
2. Educational assessment
3. Developmental and sociological information
4. Emotional/behavioral assessment
5. Physical examination or health update
6. Speech and language assessment
7. Language dominance assessment
8. Motor and play assessment
9. Vocational assessment
10. Related services assessment(s)

The statement describing the learner's present level of performance in physical education must always be based on the results of more than one assessment instrument, one of which must be standardized. A comprehensive statement of the student's present level of performance in physical education may include a description of

1. Motor output that may cause one to suspect a sensory-input system dysfunction
   a. Inappropriate reflex behavior

b. Equilibrium dysfunction
c. Sensory integration deficit
d. Motor-planning deficit
2. The learner's locomotor and nonlocomotor competency
3. The learner's physical and motor fitness level
4. The learner's ability to participate in a variety of play, games, leisure, and recreation and sports activities
5. The learner's ability to participate in a variety of rhythms, dance, and aquatic activities
6. The learner's ability to use community-based resources to enable participation in play, games, leisure, and recreation and sports activities

The comprehensive assessment which determines the present level of performance is critical to the development of the IEP. A valid and extensive understanding of the student's present abilities and skills is the basis for the development of the annual goals and short-term objectives, or benchmarks.

Annual Goals

Measurable annual goals are critical to the strategic planning process used to develop and implement the IEP for each child with a disability. The annual goals and short-term objectives must be related to the child's ability to be involved and progress in the general curriculum.[9]

Once the IEP/multidisciplinary team has determined measurable annual goals, the team can develop specific strategies that will be most effective in achieving those goals. The annual goals should address the child's needs that result directly from the child's disability if the disability interferes with the child's ability to make progress in the general curriculum. The annual goals should also address the deficits or delays identified in the comprehensive assessment process. There should be a direct relationship among the present level of educational performance, the annual goals, and the short-term instructional objectives.

The criterion for mastery of a task, whether it is an annual goal or a short-term instructional objective, is the standard at which the task should be performed. Being able to perform the task to criterion level indicates mastery of the task and, hence, student progress. Reaching a criterion serves notice that one prerequisite in a series has been mastered and that the student is ready to begin working toward the next step. Measures for task mastery can take several forms:

- Number of repetitions (10 repetitions)
- Number of repetitions over time (20 repetitions in 15 seconds)
- Distance traveled (8 feet on a balance beam without stepping off)
- Distance traveled over time (200 yards in 25 seconds)
- Number of successive trials without a miss (4 times in a row)
- Specified number of successful responses in a block of trials (3 out of 5)
- Number of degrees of movement (flexibility in degrees of movement from starting to ending positions)
- Mastery of all the stated conditions of the task

Edelen-Smith[13] has suggested that only if the service provider (teacher or related service personnel) and parents believe a goal on an IEP is valid and meaningful will that individual make a concerted effort to help the student achieve that goal. Edelen-Smith suggests eight elements that are vital if the goals are to be perceived as being valid by professionals, parents, and the student (see Figure 3-3).

Short-Term Instructional Objectives

Short-term instructional objectives are measurable intermediate steps between present levels of educational performance and the annual goals. Because the present levels of performance are observable and measurable and all components of the IEP instructional process are related, the goals and objectives also should be observable and measurable. They are, literally, "the cornerstone of the individual education program."[49]

Data from Edelen-Smith P: *Intervent School Clin* 30(5):297–301, 1995.

Figure 3-3 Edelen-Smith's Criteria for Establishing Valid Goals

1. *Conceivable:* If all parties can conceive of the *outcome* that will result if these particular goals are met, the goals will have particular value for the student.
2. *Believable:* The student, parent, and professionals must believe the goal can be met. To be believable, the goal must also be consistent with family, cultural, and societal value systems.
3. *Achievable:* The comprehensive assessment, if done well, will provide data that make it possible to suggest goals that will be challenging but achievable.
4. *Controllable:* The student must feel as if he or she has had input in decisions regarding personal goals; if the student has had no control, the student will feel unempowered.
5. *Measurable:* The goal must be written so it can be measured.
6. *Desirable:* The goal must be something the student wants to achieve and the parent(s) and teacher(s) wants him or her to achieve.
7. *Stated with no alternative:* In order for a student, parent, or teacher to take a goal seriously, it must be perceived as a significant target, not one that will be adjusted without demonstrated effort.
8. *Growth facilitating:* The goals must seek desirable behaviors instead of seeking to eliminate undesirable behaviors.

The short-term objectives represent increasingly difficult steps leading from the present level of performance to the attainment of each annual goal. It is necessary to keep detailed records on each learner to monitor progress in the learning sequence. The mastery of one objective is a prerequisite to the next complex or more difficult objective.

In addition to the hierarchical linkage among the present level of performance, the annual goals, and each of the short-term objectives, the annual goals and short-term objectives must include four concepts:

- An action (what?)
- Conditions under which the action should occur (how?)
- A criterion for mastery of a specific task (at what level?)
- A performance better than the child's present level of educational performance

Action Concept

The action portion of the instructional objective indicates what the learner will do when performing the task. It is important that the action be stated in verb form, such as "throw," "strike," "kick," "do a sit-up," or "serve a volleyball."

Conditions

The conditions under which the action should occur describe how the learner is to perform at the task. It is important to be exact. Changing the conditions makes a task easy or more difficult, inefficient or efficient, simple or more complex. Examples of conditions are

- "With eyes closed and nonsupporting leg bent to 90 degrees, the student will be able to . . ."
- "From a prone position, the learner will . . ."
- "Keeping the back straight and arms at the side of the body, the student will . . ."
- "Floating on her back, the swimmer will . . ."

Statements of conditions are particularly necessary to ensure appropriate levels of difficulty in developmental sequences that lead to the attainment of long-range goals. If the conditions are not specified, it is impossible to determine the student's true capability and what activities are needed to make progress. If the conditions are not precise, it is unclear how the student is to perform the task, and once again the value of the objective is lost.

Well-written objectives include what, how, and at what level the behaviors are to be performed. Inappropriate objectives fail for several reasons:

- "Run as fast as you can."
  - Conditions: The condition, distance, or environmental arrangements, such as hurdles or nature of the course, are not specified.

- Criterion: Neither an objective, a measurable distance, nor a specified time has been included in the objective. "As fast as you can" is subjective. The students may believe they are running as fast as they can, but the teacher may have a different opinion.
- "Walk on a balance beam without falling off."
  - Conditions: The width of the balance beam, the position of the arms, and the position of the eyes make the task more or less difficult. None of these is specified.
  - Criterion: The distance to be traveled or distance over time is not specified.
- "Swim to the end of the pool."
  - Conditions: The type of stroke is not specified.
  - Criterion: Swimming pools are different lengths. It is unclear the exact distance the student is to swim.

Criterion of Mastery

It is critical that the level of performance the student is to demonstrate be included in the objective. There are three essential features to sound instructional objectives:

- Objectives must be relevant to the learner.
- Objectives should be so clear that another teacher or a related service professional knows exactly how the skill should be replicated.
- There must be agreement on what is to be taught and when it has been mastered by the student.

Please refer to Figure 3-4 for samples and descriptions of appropriate instructional objectives.

There is a provision in the 1997 Reauthorization of IDEA (P.L. 105-57) that relates to the previous measure of educational progress, the short-term instructional objective. Congress has given IEP/multidisciplinary teams the flexibility to use "benchmarks of progress" as opposed to short-term instructional objectives for reporting educational progress. Many state education agencies have adopted benchmarks, or standards for progress, in the general curriculum for students at all age levels. This provision allows the IEP team or multidisciplinary team to adopt, when

---

Figure 3-4   Appropriate Goals and Objectives and Evaluation of Criteria and Conditions

The student will be able to run 1 mile in 5 minutes 30 seconds.
> Action: Run
> Condition: 1 mile
> Criteria: 5 minutes 30 seconds

The student will be able to walk on a balance beam, 4 inches wide, heel to toe, with eyes closed and hands on hips, for 8 feet.
> Action: Walk
> Condition: A balance beam 4 inches wide
> Criteria: Heel to toe, eyes closed, and hands on hips for 8 feet

The student will be able to swim the breaststroke 50 meters in 1 minute 30 seconds.
> Action: Swim
> Condition: Breaststroke 50 meters
> Criteria: 1 minute 30 seconds

The learner will be able to roll his or her wheelchair through a 5 cone, figure 8 obstacle course in less than 2 minutes.
> Action: Roll wheelchair
> Condition: Through a 5 cone obstacle course
> Criteria: Less than 2 minutes

appropriate, benchmarks of progress in the general curriculum as measures of progress on a student's individual education program. Congress has allowed an IEP/multidisciplinary team to use either short-term instructional objectives or benchmarks, or a combination of the two, depending on the nature of the annual goals and the specific needs of the student.[48, section d] Those objectives should lead from the present level of performance to the annual goal.

Specific Educational Services

The dates of the initiation, the duration, the frequency, and the *location* (new mandate) of all services and supports must be made clear. In the broadest sense, the "specific educational services to be rendered" means what professional services (e.g., adapted physical education, remedial reading, speech and language therapy) will be made available to the student. Every activity selected should contribute toward reaching specific objectives or benchmarks.

The services to be provided must be clearly stated on the IEP so that the extent of the commitment of school district resources (personnel, equipment, and facilities) will be clear to parents and other IEP Team members.[48, section e] The specification of the extent of services should include

- Dates of initiation of services
- Duration of services
- Number of minutes a particular service will be delivered to the child per day, week, or month

  For example: Speech and language therapy, 30 minutes, two days per week

  The services may be specified by a range—for example, the student will participate in general physical education three times a week for 30–45 minutes.[48, section f]

- Specific service provider

  For example: Occupational therapy services will be supervised by a registered occupational therapist and implemented by an occupational therapy aide. For example, the student's direct service provider in physical education is the general physical educator who has access to a certified adapted physical educator who provides consultant services.

- Location at which the services will be provided

  For example, community-based instruction in bowling may be provided in a local bowling center.

Related Services

Related services help the student with disabilities benefit from the educational process. The goals and objectives of related service personnel may be a vital part of the child's IEP and should be consistent with those of direct service personnel. These services should focus on offsetting or reducing the problems resulting from the child's disability that interfere with learning and physical education performance in school.

The list of services in the 1997 Reauthorization of IDEA is not exhaustive. Depending on the unique needs of the child, other developmental, corrective, or supportive services may be required to help a child with a disability benefit from special education. Such services include nutrition services and service coordination between school-based physical education services and community-based agencies for health promotion purposes.[48, section g]

Extent to Which the Student Will *Not* Participate in Regular Education

The IEP for each child with a disability must include a statement of "the extent to which the child will NOT participate in general education, extracurricular and nonacademic activities."[9] The Reauthorization of IDEA and current litigation clearly place the burden of proof on the schools regarding participation in the general curriculum. It appears the intent of Congress was to encourage the schools to meet the needs of children with disabilities, whenever possible, in the general curriculum and within programs that exist to serve all children.

The 1997 Reauthorization of IDEA makes it clear that there should be high standards and clear performance goals (annual goals) for students with disabilities that are *consistent with the standards and expectations for all students.* For instance, in both the Senate and House of Representatives it was emphasized that, once a student has been identified as needing special education services, the connection among special education, related services, and the student's opportunity to experience and benefit from the general education curricula should be strengthened.[43] There must be provisions for appropriate and effective strategies and methods to ensure that students with disabilities have the opportunity to achieve the standards and goals of all children.[48, section h]

The IEP/multidisciplinary team's determination of how each child's disability affects the child's involvement and progress in the general curriculum is a primary consideration in the development of the child's IEP.

If the general physical educator has reason to believe that a child with a disability should *not* participate in the existing physical education program—for example, because the child is very disruptive—it is vital for the teacher to document aids and services, accommodations, and modifications attempted before suggesting an alternative placement at the IEP/multidisciplinary team meeting. It appears the intent of Congress is that educators try to help a student with a disability succeed in the general program and curriculum before suggesting alternative placements and programs.

Most states have forms designed specially to help members of the IEP/multidisciplinary team identify instructional modifications/supports which will help the student function effectively within the general education program. See Figure 3-5, which provides a sample of instructional modifications and supports recommended for Maria.

It is also vital that the instructional personnel make specific plans to help ensure student success in the general curriculum and program. Figure 3-6 is an example of an IEP supplement designed by the Texas Education Agency to help the IEP/multidisciplinary team develop specific strategies to facilitate movement toward general education

settings. In this case, the sample is designed to show strategies that could be used by Maria's adapted physical educator to help her succeed in the general physical education curriculum.

Modifications/Accommodations Needed for the Child to Participate in Statewide and Districtwide Achievement Tests

Consistent with congressional mandates regarding participation in the general curriculum is an increased emphasis on the participation of children with disabilities in state- and district-mandated achievement tests.[9] For example, if the local education agency requires a physical fitness assessment of every student, accommodations must be made to include students with disabilities in this assessment, as well. If the IEP/multidisciplinary team believes that the student cannot participate in this assessment, it is the responsibility of the team to explain why the test is inappropriate and to offer an alternative.

Statement of Needed Transition Services

A statement that describes the process by which a child with a disability will make the transition into community-based living must be included on the IEP of each child no later than age fourteen years. One of the primary purposes of the IDEA is to ensure that all children with disabilities have available to them appropriate physical education to prepare them for independent living, which includes physical activity. One of the major purposes of the 1997 Reauthorization of IDEA was to "promote improved educational [physical education] results for children with disabilities . . . through educational experiences that prepare them for later education challenges, i.e. healthful leisure activity."[27]

Beginning at the age of fourteen years, the IEP/multidisciplinary team, in determining appropriate measurable annual goals and services for a student, must determine the planned instructional and educational experiences that will prepare the student for transition from secondary education to

Figure 3-5 Instructional Modification/Supports

Page _____ of_____

*Instructional modifications/supports determined by ARD committee

Name of student __MARIA GARCIA__   Campus __WILSON ELEMENTARY__

The ARD committee has determined that the following modifications are necessary for the student to succeed:
Special language programs[1]

☐ Bilingual   ☐ ESL

Behavior management plan
☐ Yes
☑ No

Regular discipline plan
☑ Yes
☐ No

☐ Modifications not needed or not applicable

Goal & objective/subject

Alter assignments by providing:

	MATH	ENGLISH	P.E.	SOCIAL ST.	MUSIC			
Reduced assignments								
Taped assignments								
Extra time for completing assignments	✓	✓	✓					
Opportunity to respond orally								
Emphasis on major points	✓	✓	✓					
Task analysis of assignments								
Special projects in lieu of assignments								
Other:								
Other:								

Adapt instruction by providing:

	MATH	ENGLISH	P.E.	SOCIAL ST.	MUSIC			
Opportunity to leave class for resource assistance								
Short instructions (one or two steps)	✓	✓	✓					
Opportunity to repeat and explain instructions	✓	✓	✓					
Encouragement to verbalize steps needed to complete assignment/task								
Opportunity to write instructions								
Assignment notebooks	✓							
Visual aids (pictures, flash cards, etc.)			✓					
Auditory aids (cues, tapes, etc.)		✓						
Instructional aids								
Extra time for oral response								
Extra time for written response		✓						
Exams of reduced length	✓	✓	✓					
Oral exams								
Open book exams								
Study carrel for independent work								
Frequent feedback	✓	✓	✓					
Immediate feedback	✓	✓	✓					
Minimal auditory distractions								
Encouragement for classroom participation				✓				
Peer tutoring/paired working arrangement				✓				
Opportunity for student to dictate themes, information, answers on tape or to others								
Other:								
Other:								

[1]Special language programs are required for all students who are limited English proficient.
*Denotes required items.

Figure 3-5 (*Continued*)

Page _____ of _____

*Instructional modifications/supports determined by ARD committee, (continued)

Goal & objective/subject

	MATH	ENGLISH	P.E.	SOCIAL ST.	MUSIC				
Adapt materials by providing:									
Peer to read materials									
Tape recording of required readings				✓					
Highlighted materials for emphasis									
Altered format of materials									
Study aids/manipulatives									
ESL materials									
Large-print materials									
Braille materials									
Color transparencies									
Other:									
Other:									
Manage behavior by providing:									
Clearly defined limits	✓	✓	✓	✓	✓				
Frequent reminders of rules	✓	✓	✓	✓	✓				
Positive reinforcement	✓	✓	✓	✓	✓				
Frequent eye contact/proximity control									
Frequent breaks									
Private discussion about behavior									
In-class time-out									
Opportunity to help teacher									
Seat near the teacher									
Supervision during transition activities				✓					
Implementation of behavior contract									
Other:									
Other:									
Required equipment/assistive technology devices:									
Calculators									
Word processors									
Augmentative communication device									
Note taker/note-taking paper									
Interpreter									
Decoders for TV and films									
Access to equipment:									
Other:									

*Criterion referenced assessment (TAAS):[1]

✓ Will take reading   ____ Exempt in all areas
✓ Will take mathematics   ____ Will take science
✓ Will take writing   ____ Not offered for this
✓ Will take social studies   student's grade
                                  placement

Modifications as defined in test administration materials:
_____
_____

End-of-course examinations:[2]

____ Not enrolled in Algebra I or Biology I
____ Will take Algebra I
____ Will not take Algebra I
____ Will take Biology I
____ Will not take Biology I

Modifications as defined in test administration materials:
_____
_____

[1]Until Spanish TAAS tests are available, LEP students exempt from the English TAAS must be tested with the alternative measures of accountability.
[2]The only students not required to test are students receiving content modifications resulting in an "S" on the transcript, as stated in test administration materials. These materials also provide information about testing these students for local purposes.
*Denotes required items.

3/97
ARD-5

Figure 3-6

*DATE OF ARD:

3/15/99

┌─────────────────────────────┐
│   DISTRICT IDENTIFICATION   │
└─────────────────────────────┘

Page _____ of _____

ARD/IEP SUPPLEMENT
ACTIVITIES TO FACILITATE MOVEMENT TOWARD GENERAL EDUCATION SETTINGS

☑ Conference with general education teacher/other personnel: *PHYSICAL EDUCATOR*

☐ Conference with parent

☑ Training for general education teacher and/or other staff

Topic: *ADD & DYSLEXIA*

Provided by: *DR. JEAN PYFER*

☐ Training for special education staff

Topic: _____

Provided by: _____

☐ Special conference to allow parents and all services providers (e.g., counselors, therapists) to discuss the special needs of the student

☐ Discussion with students in the general class

Topic: _____

Provided by: _____

☐ Schedule for special education support

Length of time: _____

Purpose of support: _____

Person(s) responsible: _____

☐ Provide general education assignments to student while receiving services in a special education setting

☑ Assign peer mentor from general education class   *TRAINING BY DR. JEAN PYFER*

☐ Gradual transition into general class

Schedule for transition: _____

☐ Special education teacher and student visit the general education class

☐ Common planning time for general and special education teachers

☐ Other: _____

☐ Other: _____

☐ Other: _____

☐ Building level plan (for movement to general education settings) reviewed by campus administrator

*Denotes required items

3/97
ARDSUPGE

post-secondary life.[48, section j] The physical education component of the student's IEP, after the child is fourteen years of age, must focus on providing instruction and experiences that prepare the student for independent living, which includes participation in leisure, recreation, and physical fitness activities in community-based programs. More information about the Individual Transition Program (ITP) process is included later in this chapter.

Positive Behavior Management

One of the most contentious issues in the 1997 Reauthorization of the Amendments of IDEA is that of expulsion and suspension from school. Advocates of persons with disabilities viewed the rights of the public schools to expel or suspend a student with a disability as an attempt to deny the student his or her entitlement to a free appropriate public education (FAPE). Positive behavior-management strategies have proven to be successful in preventing and controlling disruptive behavior in the schools. Appropriate positive behavior-management strategies should be included in the contents of the IEP when the student's behavior interferes with his or her learning or disrupts the learning of others.[48, section k]

Special educators (including adapted physical educators), related service personnel, general educators, school administrators, school counselors, and parents need to work in concert to develop and implement a positive behavior-management plan. The focus, as in any good behavior-management plan, needs to be on prevention of disruptive or inappropriate behavior. Schoolwide implementation of a positive behavior-management plan which is consistent throughout the school building is the most effective, but difficult to implement.

There is some concern that students with disabilities are being inappropriately suspended or expelled from the public schools because of behavior that may be related to the student's disability. Individual states may require that public schools include in the child's record a statement of any current or previous disciplinary action. The statement may include

- A description of any behavior that required disciplinary action
- A specific description of the disciplinary action taken
- Any other relevant information

If the state education agency or department of public instruction finds that significant discrepancies occur in the rate of long-term suspensions or expulsions of children with disabilities, as compared with children without disabilities, the state must revise its policies, procedures, and practices. The state must re-evaluate policies, procedures, and practices related to the development and implementation of IEPs; the use of behavioral interventions, and the procedural safeguards to ensure that children with disabilities are not unfairly treated.[50]

Projected Dates for Initiation and Termination of Services

The projected dates for beginning and terminating educational and related services must be included on the IEP. This is just one more technique intended to ensure accountability. All IEPs must include a date when services should begin and an anticipated date when goals will be reached.

Appropriate Objective Criteria and Evaluation Procedures

Each IEP must also include a description of the techniques that were used to determine the child's present level of performance and to determine whether the child accomplishes each of the goals/objectives stipulated on the IEP. These must include specific evaluation/assessment instruments that allow each participant in the IEP staffing process to determine whether the student accomplished the goals/objectives in a clear and nonbiased way.

Figure 3-1 was Maria's Individual Physical Education Program (IPEP) that was developed from specific test results (see Chapter 2). The goals that were included were, in the adapted physical educator's opinion, the most critical areas needing immediate attention. All objectives lead directly from the present level of performance to the goals.

The physical educator and/or adapted physical educator is responsible for ensuring that all of the components of the IEP are included within the physical education component of the IEP.

Additional Components of Most School-Based IEP Documents

It is important for the physical educator to be aware that there are many other pieces of information that are included in most school-based documents. Because the IEP document has often become the basis of litigation by parents and/or advocacy groups and is highly scrutinized by review teams from the state department of public instruction and/or federal grant agencies, the actual document has become increasingly complex. It is not unusual for this document to be twenty to twenty-five pages long. In fact, many educators and parents find the documents to be prohibitively complex and, most certainly, anything but user-friendly.

This additional information, often kept as records within the principal's office, but often included on the IEP, includes

1. Information about the student
   a. Name
   b. Identification number
   c. Birthdate
   d. Native language/mode of communication
2. Information about the parent or guardian
   a. Address
   b. Phone numbers (work, home, emergency)
   c. Contact person/phone for parent without access
   d. Native language/mode of communication
3. Determination of eligibility statement (i.e., does the child have a disability as determined by federal mandates?)
4. Determination of placement or placement options along the service delivery continuum

5. Assurance of placement close to home and/or home school and a specific explanation if the child must receive services in a different setting
6. Waiver/nonwaiver status for state education agency–mandated examinations and specific techniques that will be used to ensure the student every opportunity to participate in state and local education agency assessments and, if that is not possible, modifications of assessments that will be provided
7. Specific modifications in instructional strategies to ensure learning throughout placement continuum
8. Goals/objectives for extended-year service (summer school) if it is feared that regression may occur without such service
9. Modified standards for participation in extracurricular activities, if necessary
10. Assurances that
    a. Placement in special education is not a function of national origin, minority status, or linguistic differences
    b. Placement in special education is not directly attributable to a different culture or lifestyle or to lack of educational opportunity
    c. Education will be provided in the student's least restrictive environment

PARENT/GUARDIAN RIGHTS

The often cumbersome IEP document is only one way in which school districts meet federal and state regulations regarding the rights of the child. In addition, there are specific mandated parent/guardian rights that must be made clear to the parent(s) or guardian(s) before a child is evaluated and either dismissed or admitted to a special education program.

Most school districts distribute a parent rights manual developed by their state education agency when the child is first referred by the parent or guardian, members of the extended family, classroom teachers, physical education teachers, social workers, day-care personnel, medical personnel, child protective services personnel, and/or workers in homeless shelters. Usually the parent rights manual is given to the parent by a case manager or transition specialist.

Because children need to be evaluated in their native language or mode of communication, parents and guardians need to be advised of their rights in their native language or mode of communication. While most state education agencies have parent rights manuals developed in at least two languages (English and Spanish), translators must be used to explain parent rights to those parents who use another language. It should be noted, though, that this process has become overwhelming, particularly for many large, urban school districts.[14] It is not unusual for children and parents within a given school zone to speak hundreds of different languages/dialects and represent that many different cultures.

In addition, the law is clear in its intent—it is not enough to simply hand parents a booklet explaining rights that they may or may not be able to read, much less understand; it is crucial that they really do understand, and a professional must use parent-friendly language to make these rights clear.

In the comprehensive assessment process, the parent or guardian has the right to
- Receive written notice (in native language) before the school assesses the child
- Receive information about the abilities, skills, and knowledge that are to be assessed
- Give or refuse consent for that assessment
- Inspect and review all assessment records before the IEP meeting
- Expect that the assessment information will be considered at the IEP meeting
- Expect that tests and other assessment materials will be in the child's native language or mode of communication
- Expect that no single procedure will be used as the sole basis for admission, placement, or IEP decisions
- Seek an external assessment, an independent educational evaluation, within reason, at the school district's expense, if the parent or guardian disagrees with the results of the evaluation

- Request mediation or a due process hearing if agreement on assessment procedures or results cannot be reached

In regard to the IEP meeting, the parent or guardian also has the right to

- Receive written notice of the IEP meeting before the meeting that explains the purpose, time, and location of the meeting and who will attend
- Receive written notice of what the school proposes for the child as a result of the meeting
- Have the IEP meeting scheduled at a time that is convenient for the parent or guardian and the school. It is considered best practice for the school administrator to make every effort to schedule at a time when both parents, or a parent and grandparent, can attend the meeting together. (If the parent or guardian is unable to attend, the school must contact the parent or guardian via a visiting teacher or personal conference.)
- Have an interpreter present if the parent or guardian is deaf and/or uses a language other than English
- Bring others to the meeting for support or advocacy
- Be an active and important participant in the IEP meeting and discuss any service the parent or guardian thinks the student needs
- Have the meeting reconvened at a later date if the parent or guardian disagrees with the recommendations of the committee
- Seek judicial intervention (due process) if the parent or guardian and school continue to disagree regarding the student's assessment, placement, or services
- Obtain an independent evaluation at public expense and to know where it may be obtained. For example, if the parent disagrees with the assessment report provided by the district's adapted physical educator, the parent may request an independent assessment.
- A written notice at a reasonable time before the school proposed and changes identification, evaluation, or educational placement

- An impartial hearing officer from the state education agency
- Be accompanied and advised by counsel and/or individuals with special knowledge or training with respect to children with disabilities
- Appeal if aggrieved by the findings and decisions made in the hearing

The IEP must be reviewed at least annually. It can and should be revised to address:

- Lack of progress toward annual goals
- Lack of progress in the general curriculum
- Information provided by the parent
- The student's anticipated needs[9]

PARTICIPANTS OF THE IEP/MULTIDISCIPLINARY TEAM MEETING

The IEP meeting must be attended by the following individuals:

1. The student, when appropriate
2. The parent(s) or guardian(s), or a designated representative
3. A representative of the school administration, other than the child's teacher, who is qualified to provide or supervise the provision of special education. This person must have the authority to allocate school district resources. In most school districts, the principal or principal's designee fills this role in the meeting.
4. The student's special educator
5. At least one general educator if the child will receive any services in the general education program. This may be the physical educator if the student is to participate in the general physical education program. Whether the student's general physical education teacher should be present at the IEP meeting should be determined on a case-by-case basis.[48, section 1]
6. A member of the evaluation team or a professional able to interpret assessment data (in many school districts, this is the educational diagnostician, but individual

state departments of education specify personnel who may fulfill this requirement)

In addition, the following personnel should be part of this IEP meeting:

1. Any direct or related service personnel who have assessed the student (adapted physical education specialist, occupational therapist, speech-language pathologist, etc.). The IDEA regulations do not expressly mandate that the IEP/multidisciplinary team include related services personnel. However, it is critical that those individuals attend the meeting if a particular related service is to be discussed at the meeting.
2. The school nurse, particularly if the student has a chronic and/or serious medical condition (e.g., asthma, AIDS, cancer) and/or requires special medical procedures (e.g., tube feeding, catheterization) in order to function in the school environment
3. An interpreter, as required
4. Representations of community agencies that will be responsible for implementing individual transition plans (after the student reaches age fourteen years)[9]

It is important to note that The American Academy of Pediatrics has taken an active interest in the role of the physician in the IEP process. The academy has particularly identified its role as a member of the IEP/multidisciplinary team for students who have been identified as other health impaired. The academy recommends that all pediatricians ensure that every child with a disability served by their practice have access to the following services:

- A medical home which provides care that is accessible, continuous, comprehensive, family-centered, coordinated, and compassionate.
- Comprehensive screening, surveillance, and diagnosis, particularly to check for the risk or existence of a disability or developmental delay
- Appropriate referral to early intervention and special education programs

- Active participation in the multidisciplinary assessment process
- Consultation with the IEP/multidisciplinary team regarding the development of the IEP
- Pediatrician's advocacy for improved community and educational services for children with disabilities[3]

The commitment of The American Academy of Pediatrics, the Committee on Children with Disabilities, is heartening. Certainly, a partnership among the pediatrician, school-based professionals, community agencies, and parents can only improve the quality of the IEP and the delivery of appropriate educational services.

Difficult and occasionally adversarial relationships between parents and school districts have created situations in which a parent may bring an advocate or a lawyer to an IEP meeting. If a student or parent advocate is present, the meeting should continue as scheduled; the advocate is representing the best interests of the student and/or parent and usually represents a nonprofit agency devoted to ensuring rights for children and adults with disabilities. The advocate may be helpful to the parent and other members of the IEP committee as strategies for developing and implementing the best possible IEP are discussed. If the parent brings a lawyer without providing appropriate prior notice to the school district so that the district's counsel may also attend, the meeting must be terminated and rescheduled so that both sides (the student and/or parent and the school district) are represented by counsel.

The intent of the IEP meeting is that every individual with important information about the child should meet with every other individual with important information about the child and share this information so that, in the end, the child receives the best possible education. Unfortunately, in the real world this is not always possible. For example, the adapted physical education specialist may be serving as a consultant for over 300 children. There may be only one physical therapist serving an entire district. As a result, not all the people who actually tested the

child or who may ultimately be serving the student can attend every meeting. The argument is made that it is neither expedient nor necessary for all evaluators and teachers to be present if those who do attend can interpret the test results and are qualified to develop an appropriate IEP. Adapted physical education teachers who find themselves in this situation should be certain that the person making the physical education report understands the evaluation results and why it is important to follow the physical education recommendations.

DISCIPLINE CONCERNS

The increase in violence and disruptive behavior in the schools has caused many school districts to adopt zero-tolerance statements, which indicate that a student will be expelled or removed to an alternative school for the following kinds of behavior:

- Hitting a teacher or another student
- Selling or otherwise distributing drugs
- Bringing a weapon into the school building or near school grounds
- Continuing verbal aggression toward a teacher or another student

A student served by special education is subject to the district or school's student code of conduct unless specific exceptions are noted on the student's IEP. The parent has a right to expect that his or her child's IEP will include, if necessary, a positive behavior-management plan that outlines disciplinary options to be used in addition to, or instead of, certain parts of the district code. This is to protect a student with a disability from being expelled, or seriously reprimanded, for behavior that is a direct result of his or her disability.

This is an increasingly serious issue in the schools. Escalating violence, murders, and assaults within the schools have caused many administrators and educators to endorse this zero-tolerance stance. Students with severe conduct, emotional, or behavioral disturbances may, for example, exhibit behaviors that are inconsistent with school conduct codes and may be unable to control that behavior.

Nevertheless, violent and aggressive behavior cannot be tolerated in a learning environment, much less in the larger society. The 1997 Amendments to IDEA addressed the issue of discipline without discriminating against students with severe conduct, behavioral, or emotional disorders.

THE IEP MEETING AGENDA

A productive IEP meeting proceeds as follows:

1. The principal or meeting leader welcomes all participants and thanks them for attending. This sets the tone for a cooperative effort.
2. Individuals attending the meeting either are introduced by the meeting leader or introduce themselves.
3. Meeting participants review the agenda for the meeting. Although an agenda is not required by federal mandates, it has proven very useful in keeping on task. In addition, it helps create the proper mind-set in the participants; the IEP meeting is a business meeting and should be treated as such.
4. At this point, the committee members should also agree on an individual who will take minutes of the meeting. These minutes are invaluable in the IEP process and in the maintenance of records. In IEP meetings that last three to four hours it is almost impossible to remember what was said and by whom, and, while the IEP document should reflect committee consensus, it often does not address important concerns regarding the student's education. In addition, in the event that a professional serving the student was unable to attend, the minutes will bring that person "up to speed" about the committee's decisions. These minutes should become a valuable part of the student's comprehensive educational record and an attachment to the IEP.
5. The principal or meeting leader should begin the meeting by expressing a personal interest in the student and commenting on at least one of the student's strengths.
6. The principal or meeting leader should explain the reason for the meeting. This may include
   a. Admission to special education: initial assessment/evaluation
   b. Review of assessment and/or the program
      1. Three-year comprehensive re-evaluation
      2. Annual review
      3. Parent's request to reconsider any component of the existing IEP for any reason
      4. Disciplinary review
   c. Dismissal from special education
7. If the IEP meeting has been called to discuss the three-year comprehensive re-evaluation or the annual review, each participant then addresses the student's present level of educational performance. It is vital that the parents be encouraged to begin that discussion and to provide their insight into their child's progress. This is also consistent with congressional mandates that the parents be much more involved in the total education of their child. Asking the parents to start the discussion validates the parents and increases the likelihood that they will be active participants in the meeting. Then each professional reports on the student's present level of performance within that person's area of expertise. This includes a concise report that includes the names of the tests administered, the results of the testing (including strengths and deficits demonstrated by the child), and the goals and objectives that should be set for the child. Whenever possible, the physical educator should relate findings to results found by other professionals (e.g., poor balance often can be tied to fine motor delays; visual problems can be tied to reading difficulties; poor self-concept can be associated with motivational problems in the classroom). If the meeting has been called at the parent's request or is a result of an ongoing disciplinary problem, the involved

participants should indicate specific behaviors that have necessitated the meeting.

8. An open discussion among the people present at the meeting usually is the next step. During this discussion, all the needs of the student and strategies for meeting these needs are explored. At this point, the true multidisciplinary nature of the meeting should surface. Each person must be willing to recognize the value of the services that other persons, particularly the parents, have to offer, as well as the value of his or her own expertise. The knowledgeable physical educator will understand and appreciate services that can be provided by the various therapies; however, he or she must also recognize that many activities in physical education can accomplish the physical and motor goals of the child in an interesting, novel fashion unique to the discipline.

9. The committee must then determine the annual goals and short-term objectives (or benchmarks) that are appropriate. Agreement must be reached among the participants about which of the child's needs are most pressing and which goals and objectives take precedence over others. Most states have determined specific expectations for their students at given age levels and within specific content areas. Whenever possible, the annual goals and objectives developed for the student with a disability should be similar to those expected by state department of education policies; the regulations regarding the use of benchmarks makes this possible.

10. After determining appropriate annual goals and objectives, the committee must consider the educational services that will be required for the student to meet goals and accomplish objectives. When contributing to these decisions, the physical educator should focus on the present level of educational performance evidenced by the child in the physical and motor areas. If, through testing,

the child is found to have significant deficits such as reflex abnormalities, vestibular delays, or range-of-motion limitations the physical educator does not believe can be included in the physical education program activities, referral to a related therapy may be the best recommendation. Such a recommendation does not mean the child should not or cannot participate in some type of physical education class. It simply means that the related therapies should focus on the immediate low-level deficits while the child continues to participate in a physical education program that is designed to reinforce the intervention programs provided by the other services. None of the related therapies should replace physical education; however, they could be used to help the student take a more active role in the physical education class.

11. The committee must then consider the extent to which the student will be educated in the regular education program. Given increased emphasis on inclusion, this is often one of the most difficult and potentially confrontational parts of the IEP meeting. Once again, the physical educator must remember that his or her services are valuable, regardless of the child's demonstrated functioning levels. Under no circumstances should the physical educator agree that the child should automatically be included in a regular physical education class or that motor services can better be implemented by an occupational or a physical therapist. Unfortunately, some parents and school personnel continue to perceive physical education as supervised "free play." Their perception that physical education is a nonacademic experience causes them to devalue physical education. Careful consideration should be given to the decision regarding placement.

12. Transition must be considered in three situations:

a.   If the child has just turned three years of age and is entering a public school preschool program

b.   If the child is turning six and will be leaving preschool for a school program

c.   If the student is approaching his or her fourteenth birthday and decisions need to be made to prepare the student for community transition when leaving school

13.   The committee must agree on dates for initiation and review of services.

14.   The members of the committee must discuss and agree on the criteria for evaluating the student's progress toward IEP goals and objectives.

15.   The minutes of the meeting should be read, carefully, so any participants can ask for clarification or can clarify.

16.   The meeting leader should briefly summarize the meeting and ask if any member of the committee has any additional questions or comments. All participants should sign the IEP document.

If the parents do not concur with the recommendations made by school personnel and refuse to sign the IEP, the IEP/multidisciplinary team must be reconvened, in most cases within 10 school days, to address the issues. If the parent, ultimately, continues to disagree, the parent then has the right to secure counsel.

IDEA 1997 establishes mediation as a primary process to be used in resolving conflicts between school and the parents of a child with a disability.[28] Each state is responsible for ensuring the following:

• Mediation is a voluntary process and is not used to deny a parent the right to due process.

• The mediation process is conducted by a qualified, impartial mediator who is well trained.

• A list of trained and qualified mediators is available to the school and parents.

• The schools are prepared to assume the cost of the mediation.

ENCOURAGING AND MAXIMIZING PARENT PARTICIPATION IN THE IEP PROCESS

The IDEA Amendments of 1997, P.L. 105-17, strengthen the role of parents and emphasize that one of the purposes of the amendments is to expand opportunities for parents and school personnel to work in new partnerships at the local education agency level.[27] The IDEA Amendments of 1997 require that parents have an opportunity to participate in meetings with respect to the identification, evaluation, and educational placement of the student. Parents must be a part of

• The team that determines what additional data are needed in an evaluation of their child

• The team that determines the child's eligibility

• The team that makes decisions on the educational placement of the child[48, section m]

In addition, the concerns of parents and the information they provide, with their unique perspective, must be considered in developing and reviewing IEPs. Parents must also be informed about the educational progress of their children, at least as often as are parents of children without disabilities, particularly as the information relates to progress in the general curriculum. This is particularly important for the general physical educator who is usually expected to provide a report card or progress report for all the children he or she teaches every six weeks. If the parents of children without disabilities get a physical education progress report every six weeks, the parents of children with disabilities must also receive a progress report every six weeks.

First, consider some of the advice that a parent of a student with a disability gives to other parents of students with disabilities. As a lawyer representing parents in "special education matters," Ebenstein[12] has provided strategies for parents of students with disabilities to use when dealing with a school district in order to guarantee the learner's rights and to maximize his or her educational opportunities (see Figure 3-7).

Figure 3-7   Strategies for Parents to Ensure the Educational Rights of Children with Disabilities

1. Maintain "business" records of your interaction with district personnel. Communicate only in writing and save a copy of *everything*. Do not rely on regular mail—hand deliver or send important materials certified mail.
2. Get support letters from your child's pediatrician, therapist, or other professional if you believe your child's needs are not being met.
3. Reevaluate your child's **educational classification.** Some services are available to a child with certain classifications that are not available to others.
4. Cooperate with the school district's *reasonable* evaluation system. If you disagree with an evaluation, review it carefully. Was your child sick that day? Was the child in transition from one medication to another? Was the evaluator trained to complete the evaluation? If you disagree with the district's evaluation, your child is entitled to an independent evaluation at district expense.
5. Demand IEP accountability. Make sure every professional who actually works with the student reads and understands the IEP. Make sure you know who is responsible for follow-up.
6. Try to settle major problems before the IEP meeting.
7. Don't hesitate to negotiate.
8. Be wary of proposals regarding inclusion. "Sometimes, a school district will include a child without providing needed services. Too often, this is a costcutting maneuver which sabotages the child's placement . . . ."
9. "Treat the annual review as your most important business meeting of the year." Insist the child's other parent be included.

Data from Ebenstein B: *Except parent* April: 62–63, 1995.

Figure 3-8 lists several things that parents have indicated they want at the IEP or ITP meeting. In addition, consider some of the reasons parents of a student may not attend or participate in the IEP meeting (see Figure 3-9). Understanding these reasons helps identify strategies for increasing the likelihood the parents will participate. Parents of a learner with a disability may miss the IEP meeting,

Figure 3-8   What Parents Want at the IEP Meeting[42]

- Meetings held in comfortable, homelike places
- Simple refreshments
- Furniture that allows all participants to sit in a circle
- Input into the time/date of the meeting
- An organized, well-planned meeting with an agenda
- An opportunity to prepare for the meeting
  - Information regarding the purpose of the meeting
  - Notice regarding invited participants
  - An opportunity to add agenda items
- Open, respectful, honest communication
- Clarity (avoidance of jargon)

Salembier GR, Furney KS: Speaking up for your child's future, *Except Parent,* July: 62–64, 1998.

or fail to participate actively if present, for a number of reasons.

To enhance parent participation in the IEP meeting, the climate of the meeting must be parent-friendly. The following are some specific strategies for ensuring this:

Duties of the Professionals

- Emphasize the positive. All parents want to hear good reports about their child; it is difficult for any parent to be bombarded by what the child cannot do.
- Use parent-friendly language. Explain assessment results and discuss goals and objectives without professional jargon or acronyms. The parents will be better able to make good judgments if they understand what is said.
- Use a parent's exact words, describing IEP goals and objectives. There is nothing more enabling for parents than having their thoughts and words embraced. The other bonus is that the parents will be much more likely to encourage the child to accomplish a goal they have understood and articulated.
- If possible, use audiovisual technology to share information with parents about their child. If it

Figure 3-9 Obstacles to Parental Attendance at or Participation in the IEP Meeting

- The parent may be in one of several stages of the grief cycle, which makes it difficult, if not impossible, to address his or her child's specific education needs.
- The parent is overwhelmed by the educational system and chooses to avoid interacting with professionals. This is common, particularly when the parent has not been treated, at previous IEP meetings, as a valuable member of the team of individuals seeking to educate the child.
- The parent, despite repeated attempts at notification, is unaware of the meeting. Difficulty notifying parents is typical in non-English-speaking families. It is also typical if parents are illiterate. Difficulty with notification is a particular issue with homeless families; as a rule, they are so transient it is difficult to maintain contact over the period of time required to complete the evaluation and/or paperwork.
- The parent is unable to attend the IEP meeting at the time it is scheduled. A constantly changing work schedule may be one reason for this problem. This is particularly true of migrant farm workers and other members of a temporary workforce.
- The parent cannot find transportation to the meeting site.
- The parent is unable to find a baby-sitter and is hesitant to bring other, younger children to the meeting.
- The parent's cultural background is such that he or she feels obligated to accept the decisions of the professionals involved; as such, the parent feels as if he or she has no input of value.
- The parent may have serious personal problems, developmental disabilities, or emotional disturbances, drug-related or otherwise, that preclude participation, without careful assistance, in the IEP process.

is true that a picture is worth a thousand words, a videotape of the child performing a movement activity may be worth a million words.

- Relate to common experiences whenever possible to enhance communication. The physical educator is in a particularly good position to develop rapport with the parent because most parents can identify with movement, play, leisure, and recreation experiences more readily than with a specific academic curriculum.
- Talk directly to the parent and not to the other professionals at the meeting. This is particularly important if there is an interpreter. Look at the parent and not at the interpreter.
- Listen to the parents. Body language and facial expressions must reflect an openness to their thoughts and feelings. This is often easier said than done. Sitting in an IEP meeting with parents you suspect of abusing their child and trying to validate them as human beings may be the most difficult experience an educator

experiences. Extending your work day for an evening IEP meeting that a parent attends intoxicated makes this very difficult. Enabling a parent who is being verbally abusive to you is almost impossible but is an indicator of professional maturity.

Duties of the Meeting Leader Before the Meeting

- Use every possible contact to ensure that a parent is informed of the IEP meeting, including visiting teachers, a parent who lives nearby to remind him or her, phone calls from a community service provider known to the parent, and a network of professionals serving the homeless.
- Schedule the meeting at a time that is convenient for the parent(s). This is seldom during regularly scheduled school hours.
- Help the parent with transportation difficulties by scheduling two meetings back-to-back and helping the parent carpool with a neighbor who does have transportation.

Duties of the Meeting Leader Immediately Before the Meeting

- Have a professional the parent already knows and likes greet the parent at the school office and escort the parent to the meeting room. There is nothing more intimidating for a parent than to enter a roomful of professionals, often strangers, alone.
- Ensure that the meeting table is round, so that all participants are given equal value; specifically, there is no head of the table.
- Ask if the parent cares for a cup of coffee or a soft drink.
- Have name tags and use first names. Titles are confusing and intimidating to most parents.

ENCOURAGING AND MAXIMIZING STUDENT PARTICIPATION IN THE IEP PROCESS

The IDEA Amendments of 1997 contain provisions that greatly strengthen the involvement of students with a disability regarding their own future, particularly to facilitate their movement from school to postsecondary activities. The amendments significantly expand the provisions by addition of an annual requirement to invite students, of any age, to attend the IEP meeting if the purpose of the meeting is for transition to "adult" life. Indeed, if more IEP/multidisciplinary team meetings were to emphasize outcome-based learning, every meeting would be about the student's eventual transition to "adult" life. If the student does not attend the IEP meeting, the school must take other steps to ensure that the student's preference and interests are carefully considered.[48, section m]

If at all possible, the student should be involved in the IEP meeting. In actuality, only students with the most severe and profound disabilities would have difficulty participating in some way. After all, it is the student's performance that is being reviewed and the student's plan that is being discussed and developed. Lovitt, Cushing, and Stump[34] interviewed twenty-nine students from two diverse high schools and found that "student opinions concerning IEPs reflected confusion, ambivalence, distance or a lack of interest." Few participated in the IEP process or saw a meaning to the process. One student they interviewed regarding the significance of annual goals said, "It really is pretty stupid because . . . I do my work and everything in school. I did everything that was on my list. . . . And each year the objectives are exactly the same. So, it's . . . just basically learning the same stuff over and over every year. And it's been like that since about eighth grade."

Many of the strategies for making the parent feel like a vital part of the IEP process can also make the student feel like a vital part of the IEP process. For example, professionals must make eye contact with the student while talking, instead of looking at other professionals in the room. In addition, the following are strategies for getting students' input concerning their goals and objectives. Before the IEP meeting,

1. Ask the middle or high school student to meet with his or her teachers and therapists to discuss and write goals/objectives that the student believes will be challenging but attainable. If writing is difficult, the student can record his or her goals and objectives on a tape recorder. Then the student will be prepared with input for the IEP meeting.
2. Ask the elementary school student to express his or her desires regarding goals or objectives in the following ways:
   a. Tell what he or she would like to learn to do.
   b. Draw a hero and describe the qualities he or she likes in that hero.
   c. Describe the things a friend does that he or she would like to be able to do. Use a tape recorder or allow the student to make a magazine collage representing his or her particular skills, abilities, and interests.
   d. Tell a story about his or her favorite character (e.g., Pocahontas, Snow White, Thomas the Truck, Barney) and describe the things the character does that he or she would like to do.

e. Make a list of the things he or she does best.

f. Describe the things he or she wants to do when he or she grows up.

Finally, and perhaps most important, professionals cannot hesitate to include goals and objectives in the child's language on the IEP. It will help create a situation in which the child is involved in the process.

CONCERNS REGARDING THE IEP PROCESS

In some school districts, the IEP has become a paper chase that is unrelated to the actual process of educating the child with a disability. Care and concern for the student ends up being buried underneath mounds of paperwork. Indeed, school personnel are asked, "Are you done with Juan's IEP?" or "Have you written the IEP for Demetric?" The IEP is seen as an end product rather than an ongoing process of evaluation, review, and adaptation of the program to meet the child's unique educational needs.

Smith has criticized the IEP process:

> Despite overwhelming evidence that IEPs have failed to accomplish their mission, little has been done to rectify the situation. . . . The IEP should be an essential component of instructional design and delivery that enhances and accounts for students' learning and teachers' teaching. Yet, data support the contention that IEPs are not functioning as designed, including being inept at structuring "specially designed instruction."[44]

Indeed, Gerardi et al.[20] have suggested that the IEP may be the "single most critical detriment to appropriate programming" for children in need of special education services. The researchers have suggested that the IEP process has created a huge, ineffective bureaucracy. It has been viewed as superfluous to the ongoing educational process and an educational burden from which many special educators would like to escape,[35] and it has been perceived as being troublesome and expensive to implement.[33]

While the potential for maximizing educational benefits for children with disabilities through the IEP process is great, there have been problems with IEP implementation. Specific problems and suggested solutions follow:

1. School district personnel write IEPs with goals and objectives that bear little relation to the teacher's instructional plans.[49] On the other hand, and perhaps more potentially devastating, teachers plan instruction (or, worse yet, don't plan instruction at all) that bears little relation to the learner's IEP. The good teacher embraces the notion that he or she can and must be able to document carefully the child's progress and, more important, be able to design an instructional environment so that the child can accomplish the specific goals and objectives.

2. Educators fear they will be held accountable if the child fails to achieve the goals of the IEP, so they suggest only goals and objectives that can be met easily. The IEP is not, however, a performance contract.[49]

3. The campus leader, the principal, fails to recognize his or her responsibility to ensure that the IEP is implemented. Perhaps this will happen only when a principal's performance (and subsequent promotion potential) is measured by student performance on state-mandated standardized tests and by student accomplishment of IEP objectives.

It appears that the IEP process can be used to hide ineffectual and inappropriate education for children with disabilities. The IEP process can, however, be used to carefully plan and monitor the education of children with special needs.

THE INDIVIDUAL TRANSITION PLAN

The individual transition plan (ITP) is an extraordinary idea with a promise and potential yet unfulfilled. The intent of the ITP is that those integrally involved in the life of a student with a disability will help plan and determine the "outcomes" of a lifetime of public education (see Figure 3-10).

Figure 3-10   Target Areas for Holistic Adult Lifestyle Transition Planning

1. Postsecondary education (choose one)

   _____   1.1 College
   _____   1.2 Junior college
   _____   1.3 Adult education
   _____   1.4 Vocational/technical training school
   _____   1.5 GED program
   _____   1.6 Other _____

2. Employment (choose one)

   _____   2.1 Competitive employment—no support
   _____   2.2 Competitive employment—transition support
   _____   2.3 Supported employment—at or above minimum wage, individual placement
   _____   2.4 Supported employment—subminimum wage, individual placement
   _____   2.5 Enclave—small group in business setting, ongoing support
   _____   2.6 Mobile crew—small group in a variety of businesses, ongoing support
   _____   2.7 Sheltered workshop
   _____   2.8 Day activity center
   _____   2.9 Other _____

3. Living arrangements (choose one)

   _____   3.1 Living on own—no support
   _____   3.2 Living on own—with support
   _____   3.3 With family or relative
   _____   3.4 Adult foster care
   _____   3.5 Group home—specialized training
   _____   3.6 ICF–MR—training, ongoing support
   _____   3.7 Adult nursing home
   _____   3.8 Other _____

4. Homemaking activities (choose all that apply)

   _____   4.1 Independent—needs no services
   _____   4.2 Needs personal care assistance
   _____   4.3 Needs housekeeping, laundry assistance
   _____   4.4 Needs meal preparation assistance
   _____   4.5 Needs menu planning, budgeting assistance
   _____   4.6 Other _____

5. Financial issues

   _____   5.1 Earned wages
   _____   5.2 SSI
   _____   5.3 SSDI
   _____   5.4 SSI/SSDI and earned wages
   _____   5.5 Unearned income—gifts, family support
   _____   5.6 Trust/will
   _____   5.7 Food stamps
   _____   5.8 Other _____

(Continued)

Figure 3-10   *(Concluded)*

6. Community resources (choose all that apply)

_____   6.1 Independent—needs no services
_____   6.2 Needs banking assistance
_____   6.3 Needs shopping assistance
_____   6.4 Needs assistance with identifying and using some resources (day care, voting, etc.)
_____   6.5 Needs assistance to use all or most community activities
_____   6.6 Other _____

7. Recreation and leisure (choose all that apply)

_____   7.1 Independent—needs no services
_____   7.2 Needs assistance—needs support to participate in all or almost all activities
_____   7.3 Participates in family activities
_____   7.4 Attends community recreation activities with disabled peers
_____   7.5 Attends community recreation activities with disabled and nondisabled peers
_____   7.6 Participates in church groups, clubs
_____   7.7 Other _____

8. Transportation (choose all that apply)

_____   8.1 Independent—needs no services
_____   8.2 Needs assistance—uses public transportation
_____   8.3 Needs assistance—uses specialized transportation
_____   8.4 Uses family transportation
_____   8.5 Uses car pool
_____   8.6 Uses group home or residential transportation
_____   8.7 Other _____

9. Medical services (choose all that apply)

_____   9.1 Covered by group insurance—Blue Cross, Medicaid, etc.—and needs no assistance
_____   9.2 Covered by group insurance but needs assistance—monitoring medical needs, appointments, etc.
_____   9.3 Needs extensive medical services and support—regular tests and/or daily monitoring of medicine and/or therapy
_____   9.4 Other _____

10. Relationships (choose all that apply)

_____   10.1 Independent—needs no services
_____   10.2 Desires family-planning assistance
_____   10.3 Desires support group
_____   10.4 Desires counseling assistance
_____   10.5 Desires family respite or family support services
_____   10.6 Desires peer or "buddy" friendship network
_____   10.7 Other _____

11. Advocacy/legal (choose all that apply)

_____   11.1 Independent—needs no services
_____   11.2 Desires some assistance—estate planning, will, etc.
_____   11.3 Desires extensive assistance—guardianship, etc.
_____   11.4 Other _____

Hasazi et al. wrote, "The Individuals with Disabilities Education Act emphasizes the importance of including students and parents as active participants in Individualized Education Program and transition planning, and using collaborative and interagency approaches to developing outcome-oriented plans based on students' needs, taking into account their preferences and interests."[22] Devlieger and Trach wrote, "The life transition process ultimately should be seen as comprised of intersecting and intertwining individual and social dimensions."[10]

The society hopes to prepare its young people for a productive and meaningful life after school. That is, indeed, one of the purposes of public education. Harold Hodgkinson, while he served as the director of the Center for Demographic Policy at the Institute for Educational Leadership, studied the ability of students to make a meaningful transition into an adult life; more specifically, he considered the students most in need of general education reform. He found that the top 20 percent of students graduating from high schools in the United States are "world class"; they would be successful with or without any educational reform. The next 40 percent are capable of completing a college-level education without educational reform. It is the bottom 40 percent about whom he is worried. He wrote,

> The lowest 40% of students are in very bad educational shape, a situation caused mostly by problems they brought with them to the kindergarten door, particularly poverty, physical and emotional handicaps, lack of health care, difficult family conditions and violent neighborhoods. . . . These are the children who are tracked into the "general" curriculum in high school, which prepares them neither for

Individuals with paraplegia enjoy snow skiing.
Courtesy of Challenge Aspen, Aspen, CO.

college nor for a job. . . . The best way to deal with this problem is to provide a seamless web of services, combining education, health care, housing, transportation and social welfare.[25]

Halpern[21] believes that this type of comprehensive re-evaluation and re-envisioning of general education, in toto, and of transition, in particular, must occur if students, with and without disabilities, leave the public schools in this country ready to assume a role as a productive member of the society.

Many of the children who are served in special education programs in the United States begin to receive early childhood intervention (ECI) services soon after their birth. They make a transition from ECI into public school programs at age three years, and many remain there until graduation at age twenty-two years. What is the point of nineteen years of programming? What is the goal? What are the desired educational outcomes?

Certainly, the physical educator and adapted physical educator can and must play a critical role in the individual transition plan process. Hawkins notes the vital role of leisure activities, "to promote health/wellness, life satisfaction, and rewarding personal relationships."[23] The physical educator is trained to teach the gross motor skills required for participation in many blue-collar vocations and has the expertise to help the student learn the skills necessary to participate in leisure, recreation, sport, and physical fitness activities. Piletic wrote, "Most physical educators are already preparing students to participate in activities offered through city recreation programs, YMCA's [and YWCA's], private gyms, racquet clubs, golf courses, bowling centers, and swimming pools. These are the community-based activities that should be included in transitional services for students with disabilities."[40] Dummer[11] suggested that, if individual transition plan goals and objectives are selected or modified from the core curriculum, the physical educator will be best prepared to use their experience and expertise to teach skills which will be critical in postschool years.

Educators and parents, working closely with the student, must have a preordained idea of what should be the specific "outcomes" of a lifetime of education.

Critical decisions must be made regarding the following:

- What specific social-emotional, cognitive-academic, and gross motor skills should be demonstrated as an adult?
- What vocational competencies does the individual need to guarantee independence and the least restrictive educational or work placement? Depending on the type of vocation planned, the skills can be varied:
  - Skills to lift, carry, push, pull
  - Skills to do research on the Internet
  - Skills to create or illustrate a children's book
  - Skills to plant, dig, prune, weed, and care for plants
  - Skills to write and edit a paper
  - Skills to join and participate in a discussion group in a community-based class
  - Skills to drive a car
- What survival skills does the individual need to guarantee his or her access to community-based programs, facilities, or activities?
  - Skills to manage and use public transit systems
  - Skills to navigate bus steps, move through revolving doors, step up and down from curbs, climb on and off a moving escalator
  - Skills to send and receive e-mail
  - Skills to use a phone for emergencies (dial 911) and for personal/social contact, simply to call and stay in touch with a friend
  - Skills to use and manage money, including buying and receiving goods
- What skills does the individual need to enjoy a life full of leisure, recreation, sport, and physical fitness activities?
  - Specific locomotor, object-control, and culturally determined patterns of movement to be successful in leisure, recreation, sport, and physical fitness activities
  - Specific skills to gain access to community-based programs, facilities, or activities—for example
    - Renting cross-country skis

- Going to a local sports club to watch the Green Bay Packers play the Minnesota Vikings
- Joining and using a local recreation department health center
- Packing a simple picnic dinner to attend a Ballet Folklorico performance in the park
- Buying and using shoes for an aerobic dance class
- Taking a bus to a mall to participate in an early bird walking program
- Buying a ticket to see a new movie and being able to carry popcorn and a drink into the theater
- What skills does the individual need to participate in a meaningful relationship with another adult?

Certainly, the process of planning for the future of a student, with or without a disability, after graduation from high school is a complex one that demands the efforts of all involved. The intent of the mandate regarding an individual transition plan, beginning at age fourteen, for students with a disability, is to focus the efforts of the student, parents, and professionals alike on the desired outcome—a full, rich, satisfying life. An individual transition plan must be developed for each student with a disability, no later than his or her fourteenth birthday. The transition plan must address, specifically, the instructional strategies that will be used to prepare the student for the transition from school to community and work environments.

Certainly, some adolescents with disabilities have a more difficult time making a meaningful transition into the community after completion of school-based programs. Only a small percentage of adolescents with emotional disorders enroll in postsecondary education programs.[7] Adolescents who have conduct, behavioral, or emotional disorders tend to have more difficulty securing a job, keeping a job, and developing or maintaining positive interpersonal relationships than do students with other disabilities.[7]

Like many other states, Minnesota mandates that the individual transition plan address

- Employment
- Community participation
- Home living
- Recreation and leisure
- Postsecondary education[36]

Preparing for a transition into the community and workplace after school requires systematic and careful planning.[19] The State of Minnesota has developed a comprehensive website, "A Guide to Plan Your Life After High School."[36] It includes specific suggestions for students four to five years before graduation to one to two years after graduation. This includes specific recommendations for students, "Planning Your Dreams," that have implications for adapted physical education and recreation:

Four to Five Years Before Graduation
- Take a community education class.
- Attend events to learn spectator or audience member skills.
- Learn how to plan recreation and leisure activities (where, when, cost, transportation).
- Establish exercise routines.
- Join a club or an organization in your community.

Three Years Before Graduation
- Explore new ways to use your free time.
- Identify supports needed to participate in activities of interest.

Two Years Before Graduation
- Try additional recreation and leisure activities.

One Year Before Graduation
- Continue to take part in activities of interest.

One to Two Years After Graduation
- Join and participate in adult recreation activities.

Stopka et al.[46] wrote that one of the significant concerns regarding the transition of students with disabilities into the vocational setting may be their lack of physical fitness for basic tasks, which include painting, stocking shelves, and doing basic laundry duties. Perhaps of more concern to the physical educator and/or adapted physical educator is the significant lack of attention paid to planning for a postsecondary life full of quality leisure, recreation, sport, and fitness activities. Although these goals, and physical education programs to attain these goals, are significant, leisure, recreation, sport, and fitness goals have been virtually ignored on individual transition plans.[16]

The Louisiana Department of Education has developed a visionary ITP that targets the following areas for holistic adult lifestyle transition planning:

- Postsecondary education
- Employment
- Living arrangements
- Homemaking activities
- Financial/income needs
- Community resources
- Recreation and leisure
- Transportation
- Medical services
- Relationships
- Advocacy/legal needs

The Louisiana plan addresses each of these issues and designates the desired adult outcome for each of the areas (see Figure 3-11). This plan then

---

INDIVIDUALIZED TRANSITION PLAN

LOUISIANA DEPARTMENT OF EDUCATION   Page___ of___

Comprehensive transition planning should consider each of the following areas.
Check each area that was addressed for this student in this year's plan.

1. ___ Postsecondary Education	4. ___ Homemaking Needs	7. ___ Recreation and Leisure	10. ____ Relationships
2. ___ Employment	5. ___ Financial/Income Needs	8. ___ Transportation Needs	11. ____ Advocacy/Legal Needs
3. ___ Living Arrangements	6. ___ Community Resources	9. ___ Medical Services	12. ____ Other _____

We, the undersigned, have participated in this transition plan and support its intent and recommendations.

STUDENT	STATE ID #	SCHOOL SYSTEM	DATE
PARENT/GUARDIAN		RELATED SERVICE PROVIDER(S)	
TEACHER			
ITP COORDINATOR		ADULT AGENCY SERVICE PROVIDER(S)	
ODR			

DATE	DESIRED ADULT OUTCOMES	SCHOOL ACTION STEPS	DATE	FAMILY ACTION STEPS	DATE	ADULT AGENCY ACTION STEPS	DATE

Figure 3-11   Individual Transition Plan Form
Courtesy Louisiana Department of Education.

defines the process required to ensure that the individual meets the goals or desired adult outcomes by stipulating the responsibilities of the school, the family, and adult agencies in meeting these outcomes. Included for each desired adult outcome are

- School action steps
- Family action steps
- Adult agency action steps

> An increasing number of leisure, recreation, and sport programs are designed to encourage individuals with disabilities to participate in an active lifestyle after school. For a comprehensive list of these agencies, please refer to the Texas Woman's University Project INSPIRE website at
>> http://venus.twu.edu/~f huettig
>> Click on the Recreation button.[47]

An increasing emphasis is being placed on effective transition from the school-based programs into the community. The physical educator and the adapted physical educator can and should play a vital role in this process. First and foremost, the physical education program must be outcome-based. The curriculum should prepare students to participate in leisure, recreation, and sports programs as adults. Second, the professional can and must be the liaison between the school and the community agencies. See Figure 3-12, Maria's projected ITP at age fourteen years.

The process of planning for the critical transition from school to employment, postsecondary school, community living and access, and participation in community activities is not something that can be managed in an IEP/multidisciplinary team meeting. It appears that the crucial decisions may best be made in the informal but trust-based communications between the learner, the parents, and the professionals who have earned the trust of the learner and parents.[10] The personal futures planning model may be a valid and appropriate process to ensure that the intentions of the federally mandated ITP are realized.

PERSONAL FUTURES PLANNING

Personal futures planning (PFP) is a process not unlike the IEP process. In fact, if the IEP and ITP process had evolved as its designers and creators had hoped, there would have been no need for PFP in the education of individuals with disabilities. The intent of the PFP process is to *really* examine the capabilities, strengths, and interests of the learner with a disability in interaction with family members, neighbors, and friends in the context of the community in which the learner lives. Given this matrix, the individuals involved in the planning process help the learner and his or her family dream about the future, immediate and long-term. Then, the individuals involved in the planning process advocate for the learner, so that the school's instructional program helps the learner and the family realize their dreams.

With the present educational system, this is a voluntary process, usually initiated at the request of a parent, and it involves dedicated individuals willing to make a long-term commitment to the well-being and growth of the learner who is the focus of the plan. This is an extended commitment to the learner and the learner's family and may require meetings several times a year.

Increasingly, community service agencies and residential facilities that serve individuals with disabilities are adopting this personal futures planning model. This process, however, is often met with resistance by agency personnel because it is time consuming. It may also cause serious conflicts with existing modes of service delivery.[45] For example, leisure and recreation service models in many community service agencies have typically been based on convenience and availability of services:[26] all program participants go bowling on Thursday afternoon from 2–4 P.M.; the bowling alley is empty, the bus is available, and the staff likes to bowl. This type of approach is in direct opposition to the philosophy of personal futures planning. How does the agency respond to the participant who would rather go fishing, go horseback riding, or go for a nature walk?

Figure 3-12 Recreation and Leisure Component of Maria's PROJECTED Individual Transition Plan (at age 14 years)

ADAPTED PHYSICAL EDUCATION INDIVIDUAL TRANSITION PLAN

Name: Maria Garcia

Date of birth: 1-21-89

Test dates: 2-4-2003 and 2-5-2003

Chronological age: 14 years

School: Martin Luther King Junior High School

Evaluator: Dr. Carol Huettig, CAPE

Tests administered:
>Louisiana Competency Test for Adapted Physical Education, Level V Family Interview re: Leisure, Recreation and Sport Preferences Community Inventory of Leisure, Recreation and Sport Programs

Present level of performance:
>On the CTAPE, Maria was unable to perform the locomotor skills combination because she is unable to skip. She was able to throw a softball and serve a volleyball but had difficulty in the performance of receipt skills such as catching and fielding a ball, striking a tossed softball. She was able to dribble a basketball and execute a 2-handed bounce pass. She was unable to complete the gymnastics skills. Her physical fitness skills were comparable to those demonstrated during her 3-year comprehensive evaluation in February 2002. She continues to lack abdominal and shoulder girdle strength. She was able to walk 1/2 mile in a time of 12 minutes 30 seconds, an indication of poor cardiovascular fitness.

>The family interview included the mother, Amelia Garcia; the father, Ernesto Garcia; and Maria's older sister, Christina, age 18 years. The mother reported the family, and the extended family, enjoys camping, biking, and horseback riding. The father said he was "into" dirt biking. Christina said she was "into" dancing and shopping but preferred to associate with her friends, not her family.

Annual transition goals and short-term objectives

Annual goal
To develop her cardiovascular fitness so she can participate in camping, biking, and horseback riding activities, Maria will be able to walk 1 mile in 20 minutes.
>*Short-term objectives*
>Maria will be able to walk 3/4 mile in 18 minutes.
>Maria will be able to walk 3/4 mile in 15 minutes.
>Maria will be able to walk 1 mile in 25 minutes.
>Maria will be able to walk 1 mile in 22 minutes.

Annual goal
Maria will be able to bicycle 3 miles, on a circuit around the school, with a partner, in 24 minutes.
>*Short-term objectives*
>Maria will be able to bicycle 1 mile, on a circuit around the school, with a partner, in 10 minutes.
>Maria will be able to bicycle 2 miles, on a circuit around the school, with a partner, in 18 minutes.

Annual goal
To develop abdominal strength so she can participate in horseback riding, Maria will be able to do 25 bent-knee crunches in 1 minute.
>*Short-term objectives*
>Maria will be able to do 15 bent-knee crunches in 1 minute.
>Maria will be able to do 20 bent-knee crunches in 1 minute.

Figure 3-12   (*Continued*)

Annual goal
Maria will participate, with a classmate, parent, or teacher, in a community bike-a-thon and complete a 3-mile ride.

Recommended physical education placement: General physical education with support from an adapted physical educator to enhance skills necessary for family/community participation.

Modifications/adaptations:

Please refer to the Modifications page of the IEP. (See Figure 3-5 for sample modifications; those presented were included as part of Maria's IEP at age 10 years.)

Duration of services: From March 15, 2003, to March 15, 2004

Date of annual review: March 15, 2004

Referral recommendations: Adapted physical educator will contact City Parks and Recreation Department and local bike riding club to assist with a smooth postschool transition.

Leatherby suggested that at least the following persons be included in the initial future planning meeting:

1. Learner
2. Parent(s) and at least one other family member, particularly a sibling
3. At least one friend of the learner
4. At least one community representative who is not a service provider
5. At least one human service agency representative or provider
6. At least one school representative who knows the learner well[32]

The first step of the process is to identify in a drawing the individuals who are part of the learner's circle. This maps the learner's relationships. Like a sociogram, it gives pictorial evidence of those relationships that the learner would like to emphasize and maintain and indicates problem areas if they exist. See Figure 3-13 for Maria's circle of friends.

The second step is to identify the learner's community interests. Critical in this process is the identification of family interests. Only if the family or extended family is interested in sharing and encouraging the activities can community-based par-

ticipation be a reality. Figure 3-14 is a diagram representing Maria's community interests.

The third step is to develop an action plan that identifies the steps that must be taken to maximize the learner's interaction within the context of his or her greater community. In addition, the action plan identifies a tentative time line for completion of these tasks.

The PFP process is an ongoing, lifelong commitment to the quality of life of the targeted learner, and it contributes to the quality of life of the learner's family and friends.[37] It is a proactive process in which, after the learner's abilities, interests, and skills are targeted, a specific plan is developed to maximize the learner's opportunities to use the skills within the community.

PROFESSIONAL PERSONNEL WHO MAY BE INVOLVED IN THE INDIVIDUAL EDUCATION PROGRAM AND/OR THE INDIVIDUAL TRANSITION PLAN

The variety of personnel who provide both direct and related services and who may be involved in the initial evaluation and in the child's subsequent

Mom

Dad

Classmates and friends

Sister

Mrs. Martinez,
Classroom teacher

Grandma

Maria

Dr. Simpson,
principal

Sister Maria
Margaretta

Father
Knowlon

APE teacher,
Jean Pyfer

Figure 3-13   Maria Garcia's Circle of Friends

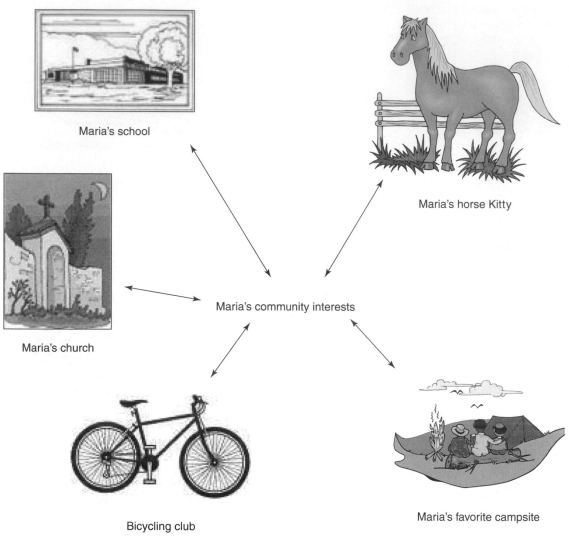

Figure 3-14   Maria Garcia's Community Matrix

individually designed education program are described in this section. IDEA stipulates those services that are to be "direct" and those that are to be "related." Direct services are those to be provided as part of the child's special education. These include (1) instruction conducted in the classroom, in the home, in hospitals and institutions, and in other settings and (2) *instruction in physical education.* The personnel involved in the provision of these services are described in the following paragraphs.

Direct Service Providers

Special Educators

Special educators are professional personnel who have received specific training in the techniques and methodology of educating children with disabilities. In the past, special educators were trained primarily to provide instruction to children with one particular disability. For example, special educators received training and subsequent certification in "mental retardation," "emotional disturbance," or "deaf education." Today, most professional preparation programs provide training that leads to a generic (general) special education certification. This general training and certification better prepares educators to serve children in the public schools who frequently have more than one disability. For example, one child may be diagnosed as having ADD (attention deficit disorder), dyslexia, and a conduct disorder. Each disability must be considered when the learning environment is being designed.

The level and type of instruction provided to children with disabilities depend on the child's present level of performance and expectations for future performance. For example, special educators working with children who have profound intellectual disorders and who are medically fragile require sensory stimulation experiences and health care (e.g., catheterization, tube feeding, medication). Special educators working with children who are autistic and developmentally delayed need to provide a very structured prevocational, self-care program. Special educators teaching children with a history of abuse and subsequent emotional disorders may use a pre-academic or academic curriculum within the framework of a structured, positive behavior-management program. The special educator, a classroom teacher, has primary responsibility for the child with disabilities.

Generally, as the child's primary teacher, the child's special educator is responsible for the implementation and monitoring of the IEP. The special educator should work closely with other professionals, including the physical educator and the adapted physical educator, to ensure that the child acquires developmentally appropriate motor skills. The physical educator should regularly communicate with the classroom teacher.

Hospital/Homebound Instructors

Hospital/homebound instructors are trained professionals who provide special education instruction to children who are hospitalized or who, because of severe medical disabilities, cannot be educated within the typical school setting. The education is the same; only the setting is different.

Increasingly, parents of children with disabilities are opting to provide home-based instruction; educators will need to make educational services available in the home.

Instructors in Institutions and Other Settings

For a variety of reasons, some children, particularly those with profound developmental delays and multiple disabilities, receive their education within an institutional setting. Within recent years, court mandates have significantly improved the quality of both instruction and care within these facilities.

Adapted Physical Educators

The art, the science, and the profession of adapted physical education are described throughout this entire text. The role of the adapted physical educator, as part of the IEP/multidisciplinary team, is summarized in this section.

Adapted physical educators are physical educators with specialized training. Specifically, these professionals have training in the assessment and evaluation of motor behavior and physical fitness, the development of the child's individual physical education program (IPEP), the implementation of the child's IPEP, and the processes of teaching and managing the behavior of children with disabilities in a venue which emphasizes play, leisure, recreation, sport, and physical fitness skills.

Due, specifically, to the incredible work of Dr. Luke Kelly, University of Virginia, a certification in adapted physical education is now available to trained professionals who meet rigorous standards of professional preparation and who complete/pass a comprehensive examination. Fulfilling the criteria mandated by The Adapted Physical Education National Standards (APENS) allows the adapted physical educator to use the title "certified adapted physical educator," or "CAPE." Many states, however (California, Louisiana, and Minnesota, for example), have extensive certifications which indicate a significant professional commitment and comprehensive training as well.

Physical education is mandated by law as a direct education service, not a related service. Adapted

Figure 3-15   Adapted Physical Education
Levels of Intervention

Adapted physical educators with specific training
and knowledge in the neurodevelopmental process
may intervene at a variety of levels that include
• Reflex integration
• Equilibrium development
• Sensory stimulation and sensory discrimination
• Sensorimotor development
• Body image and body cathexis
• Motor planning
• Locomotor and nonlocomotor skills
• Object-control skills
• Patterns for leisure, recreation, and sport skills
• Skills and knowledge related to physical fitness

physical educators with specific training and knowledge in the neurodevelopmental process may intervene at a variety of levels, depending on the extent of their training and commitment (see Figure 3-15).

The initial passage of P.L. 94-142, 1975, mandated that physical education is to be a vital part of each child's special education program. In fact, physical education was the only curricular area designated specifically as a required, direct service. The intent of the law was that specially trained adapted physical educators would provide quality, direct, hands-on, daily physical education instruction to children with disabilities. A lack of financial and personnel resources, as well as a lack of commitment to physical education in general, has made this scenario a dream, rather than a reality, in most school districts.

General Physical Educators

The intent of those who carefully crafted the wording of P.L. 94-142 was for physical educators with special training and certification to meet the unique motor needs of children with disabilities as part of their comprehensive education.[41] Increasingly, general physical educators are being asked to provide direct physical education instruction to learners with disabilities. General physical education professionals are, typically, professionals with

a state certification or license in physical education. In many states, the educator has an all-level certification that indicates the individual has the necessary education and skills to provide physical education instruction for learners from kindergarten through high school.

The general physical educator, typically, has specific training in the following:

• Motor development
• Motor learning
• Pedagogy, particularly as it relates to human movement
• Anatomy and physiology
• Exercise physiology
• Biomechanical analysis of movement
• Leisure, recreation, and sport instruction
• Coaching

More and more learners with disabilities are receiving their physical education instruction from general physical education teachers within the general curriculum. This is effective only if the general physical educator has access to the personnel (adapted physical education consultant), aids, and resources necessary to provide quality instruction.

Vision Specialists

Historically, a child with a severe visual impairment received educational services within a segregated environment. Typically, educational services were delivered in a separate residential school facility or within a self-contained room in a given school building. In that setting, the child's primary teacher was a vision specialist, a teacher specially trained to meet the educational needs of the child with a severe visual disability.

The increased emphasis on inclusion of learners with disabilities in the general curriculum has changed that scenario. Specifically, the learner with a visual impairment, whenever possible, is educated in his or her home school with support from vision specialists and orientation and mobility specialists. Children who are totally blind, legally blind, or partially sighted and those who have multiple disabilities (whose visual loss is only one of their impairments) may be educated with support within the regular education classroom in school districts embracing the concept of inclusion.

Vision specialists have the skills necessary to complete a visual evaluation and educational assessment to determine the extent of visual disability and the types of intervention that will make possible a successful educational experience. The vision therapist/teacher focuses on modification of instruction, which may include specific visual, tactile, and auditory learning techniques. Other modifications also may be required for the child to learn in the designated education setting. The therapist may suggest augmentative aids, such as a braille typewriter, a computer with auditory input/output capability, or a text enlarger, to meet the unique needs of the child.

Orientation and Mobility Specialists

Orientation and mobility was added to the Amendments to IDEA of 1997 as a direct educational service. Orientation and mobility means services provided to students who are blind or visually impaired to enable them to use skills systematically to orient them within their environments in the schools, home, and community.[48, section r]

Orientation and mobility services help students improve spatial and environmental concepts and use information received by the senses, such as sound and vibrations. Some children with disabilities other than visual impairments need travel training if they are to move safely and effectively within and out of the school environment. Travel training is often an integral part of the individual transition plan, the special education program that is designed to prepare students for postschool activities.

The orientation and mobility specialist works with the child and his or her general or special educators to help the child develop the skills necessary, for example, to use a cane or to successfully ascend and descend school bus stairs. The orientation and mobility specialist focuses on helping the learner develop the skills necessary to access his or her environment.

Related Service Providers

The law also specifies and defines related services. As indicated earlier in the chapter, these are services that must be provided to the child with disabilities so that the child can benefit from instruction. There are several related services that may assist the child to benefit from special education. The list of related services is not exhaustive and may include other corrective or supportive services, such as music or dance therapy, if they help the learner benefit from special education. The related service providers are described in the following paragraphs.

Audiologists

Audiologists are trained to complete a comprehensive evaluation of a child's hearing capabilities. This includes an evaluation of the child's response to the qualities of sound—intensity, pitch, frequency, and timbre. Based on the results of the evaluation, the audiologist makes recommendations to school personnel. The audiologist may suggest, for example, simple modifications in the educational environment of the child with a mild hearing impairment to facilitate learning; specifically, the child may be placed close to the teacher for instructional purposes. The audiologist may recommend that a hearing aid be provided for the child with a more severe hearing disability and may work closely with trained special educators who will help the child develop total communication skills, including sign language, speech reading, and oral language.

In addition, the audiologist may create and administer programs for prevention of hearing loss, as well as counsel parents and teachers regarding hearing loss. The audiologist may also determine children's needs when selecting and fitting an appropriate hearing aid and evaluating the effectiveness of amplification.[48, section o]

Counseling Services

Counseling services are services provided by a qualified social worker or other qualified personnel such as psychologists and guidance counselors.[48, section p]

Counseling services are becoming increasingly important in the total education process for all children, particularly children with disabilities. The school-based counselor may serve children with disabilities by implementing programs designed to enhance self-esteem, to teach children to identify and avoid sexual abuse, to share techniques for values identification and clarification, or to teach techniques and methods for dealing with grief.

Children with disabilities living within dysfunctional families may need a more comprehensive intervention. These children may need individual counseling services in order to benefit from educational services. Because the family unit must be addressed if counseling is to be of value and have long-lasting effects, the most effective programs involve each member of the family in the counseling process.

Medical Diagnostic Service Personnel

IDEA indicates that medical diagnostic services must be provided for a child who needs these services in order to benefit from his or her education. Many school districts have working partnerships with a hospital or rehabilitation facility, so that children who require medical diagnostic services can be referred to medical diagnostic service personnel at that hospital or center. It is important to note, however, that the law does not mandate medical services, just medical diagnostic services.

To be eligible for special education services, a child with an orthopedic impairment or other health impairment must be diagnosed as having a disability; this diagnosis must be made by a licensed physician. For a child to be identified as "emotionally disturbed," a licensed psychologist or psychiatrist must confirm the diagnosis.

Occupational Therapists

Occupational therapists improve, develop or restore functions impaired or lost through illness, injury, or deprivation, so that individuals can function independently.[48, section q] Occupational therapy must be made available to a child with a disability who requires this service in order to allow the child to be successful in the educational environment. Before passage of IDEA, the pediatric occupational therapist functioned primarily within hospitals, community-based agencies, home health care agencies, and rehabilitation facilities. Now pediatric occupational therapists are a vital part of the total educational process and can be an integral part of a motor development team.

The American Occupational Therapy Association has adopted occupational therapy performance areas[5] that are the focus of occupational therapists in all settings. See Figure 3-16 for a description of the services they provide.

Occupational therapists working within the educational setting have had to define their role and focus in relation to special education. As a

---

Figure 3-16 Occupational Therapy Performance Areas as Defined by the American Occupational Therapy Association[5]

1. Activities of daily living
   - Grooming
   - Oral hygiene
   - Bathing
   - Toilet hygiene
   - Dressing
   - Feeding and eating
   - Medication routine
   - Socialization
   - Functional communication
   - Functional mobility
   - Sexual expression
2. Work activities
   - Home management
   - Care of others
   - Educational activities
   - Vocational activities
3. Play or leisure activities
   - Play or leisure exploration
   - Play or leisure performance

American Occupational Therapy Association: Uniform terminology for occupational therapy, ed 2, Rockville, Md, 1989, The Association.

result, the school-based therapist has had to develop a strategy to function within the educational model rather than the medical model. The American Occupational Therapy Association has described the occupational therapist serving in the schools in the following way:

Registered occupational therapists in education systems are considered to be related service personnel. The occupational therapist is responsible for assessment, planning, and goal development and for providing appropriate intervention services designed to enhance the student's potential for learning. The occupational therapist assists the student in acquiring functional performance skills needed to participate in and benefit from the educational environment, and to help the student function independently.[4]

According to Orr, Gott, and Kainer[39] the occupational therapist in the school setting must focus on the student role. Within the schools, these professionals concentrate on activities of daily living that are part of the process of going to school. In addition, the school-based occupational therapist defines "school" as a child's "work." The occupational therapist is responsible for ensuring that the student with a disability can assume the role of student and benefit from instruction within the school setting. Orr, Gott, and Kainer define behaviors and activities that constitute the role of the student and then develop strategies to allow the child to be successful in the student role.

The school-based occupational therapist might contribute to the child's school success in a number of ways. The therapist may help wheelchair-enabled students move independently within the school by teaching them to carry a lunch tray on their lap, manage a ramp to and from the playground, and move through crowded halls without running into classmates. The therapist may assist a learning-disabled student by providing sensorimotor training to ready the child to receive instruction. The occupational therapist has usually had significant education and training in the skills necessary to promote sensory integration. The therapist may help the child with autism or conduct disorders develop basic play skills.

The occupational therapist will often work in cooperation with the physical educator, particularly to ensure student success in managing travel around the gymnasium or playground, in developing strategies to maximize the development of appropriate social skills and play behavior, and in contributing to the physical education individual exercise plan.

Parent Counselors and Trainers

Parents of children with disabilities are very important participants in the education of their children. This echoes the mandates of P.L. 105-17 that the parent is the child's first and primary teacher. Helping parents gain the skills that will enable them to help their children meet the goals and objectives of the IEP or the individual family service plan (IFSP) is critical.[48, section s] The services provided by parent counselors and trainers are vital to those facing the reality of raising a child with a disability. This counseling and training is even more crucial for a single parent raising a disabled child. The grief, financial struggles, loneliness, and fears are often overwhelming.

Parent counseling and training also focus on helping the parent(s) develop appropriate expectations regarding the child's growth and development. The parent must be helped to develop realistic, yet hopeful, goals for the child.

Physical Therapists

The physical therapist is trained to provide services that address range of motion, maintenance and development of muscle tone, gait therapy, and mobility assistance with and without physical aids or equipment. The physical therapist can be a vital and integral part of the motor development team. The therapist brings to the child with disabilities a vast wealth of information regarding human motion.

One of the major problems facing the public schools that are attempting to meet the mandates of the federal law is that it is increasingly difficult to hire a physical therapist to work within the schools. The services of physical therapists are sought by hospitals, rehabilitation facilities, and nursing homes. Generally, the public schools cannot compete financially to hire and retain physical therapists.

Psychologists

Psychological services for children with disabilities, and if necessary for their parent(s), have been designated as a related service. Their responsibilities include:

- Administer psychological and educational tests
- Interpret assessment results
- Interpret information about the child's behavior and condition related to learning
- Consult with other staff members in planning school programs to meet the special needs of children
- Conduct behavioral evaluations
- Plan and manage a program of psychological services
- Provide psychological counseling for parents and children
- Assist with developing positive behavior-intervention strategies[48, section t]

Many school districts provide these services by hiring a psychologist or psychiatrist as a consultant or on a per-child basis. Larger school districts may hire school-based psychologists as part of the assessment and intervention team.

These professionals are involved in the assessment of children with disabilities referred because of conduct, behavioral, or emotional disorders; aggressive behavior toward other children or their parent(s); severe depression; suicidal tendencies or attempted suicides; or reports of sexual or physical abuse or serious neglect.

Recreation Therapists

Recreation means assessment of leisure function, therapeutic recreation services, recreation programs in school and community agencies, and leisure education.[48, section u] The school-based recreation therapist provides instruction so that individuals with disabilities will be able to make wise choices in the use of leisure time. The intent is to provide instruction so students will be able to participate in community-based leisure activities. Because of the commitment of recreation therapists to community-based, lifetime activity development, these professionals play a vital role in the development of the child's ITP. The child's IEP in middle school and high school must include specific goals and objectives related to community-based leisure and recreation activities.

Rehabilitation Counselor

Rehabilitation counselors provide services in individual or group sessions that focus specifically on career development, employment preparation, and achievement of independence and integration in the workplace and community. These services include vocational rehabilitation services funded under the Vocational Rehabilitation Act of 1973 as amended.[48, section v]

The rehabilitation counselor focuses on helping the learner with a disability gain the confidence and learn the skills necessary to function as typically as possible. Most rehabilitation counseling and rehabilitation services address the needs of the learner with adventitious injuries or disabilities; these are injuries or disabilities that occur after the child has already experienced typical development.

Rehabilitation counseling addresses grief; specifically, the individual with a new injury or disability must grieve the loss of function or ability before he or she can get on with life. It also addresses strategies for the re-establishment of self-esteem. Techniques are taught so that the child can adapt or compensate for the injury or disability and live a full life. Play, games, leisure, recreation, and sports have been found to be effective tools in the rehabilitation process. Indeed, most major rehabilitation facilities encourage participation in these activities to facilitate recovery and development.

Assistive Technology Service Personnel

Legislative initiatives such as P.L. 100-407—The Technology-Related Assistance for Individuals with Disabilities Act of 1988 (Tech Act)—and IDEA illustrate the importance the federal government has placed on assistive technology service personnel. Congress defined assistive technology service as:

> Any service that directly assists an individual with a disability in the selection, acquisition, or use of an assistive technology device including
>
> (A) the evaluation of the needs of an individual with a disability, including a functional evaluation of the individual in the individual's customary environment;
> (B) purchasing, leasing, or otherwise providing for the acquisition of assistive technology devices by individuals with disabilities;
> (C) selecting, designing, fitting, customizing, adapting, applying, maintaining, repairing, or replacing of assistive technology devices;
> (D) coordinating and using other therapies, interventions, or services with assistive technology devices, such as those associated with existing education and rehabilitation plans and programs;
> (E) training or technical assistance for an individual with disabilities, or, where appropriate, the family of an individual with disabilities; and
> (F) training or technical assistance for professionals (including individuals providing education and rehabilitation services), employers, or other individuals who provide services to, employ, or are otherwise substantially involved in the major life functions of individuals with disabilities.[27]

The Tech Act and IDEA focused on the fact that an individual living in the twenty-first century must be comfortable with technology in order to thrive, in order to survive. Assistive technology services is a related service that must be provided to a child who needs such services in order to benefit from the educational experience. The technologies that must be made available to a child with disabilities include low-tech assistive technology, such as note-taking cassette recorders, simple switches, head pointers, and picture boards. High-tech assistance includes optical character recognition, speech synthesizers, augmentative communication devices, alternative keyboards, and word processors with spelling- and grammar-checking capabilities.[6]

A statement of the Instruction Systems Technology Division of the Dallas Independent School District included, "The population of students who stand to gain the most from microcomputer technology are those who have physical, sensory, emotional and/or cognitive limitations which have caused them to be isolated from their 'regular' peers."[18]

Cain[8] suggested six reasons why computer technology must be included within special education programs:

1. Computer technology is a vital component of "regular" education, so it should be a vital component of special education to ensure program equity.
2. These technologies prepare individuals with disabilities for the most productive life possible.
3. Computers can serve as a vital tool for compensatory, expressive, and receptive language.
4. Computers provide the opportunity for children with disabilities to experience the real world through simulation activities.
5. Computers serve as a prosthetic communication device for some learners with disabilities. For example, a learner who is deaf has an entire world of e-mail communication open in/through the use of computers.
6. Computers can provide a recreational alternative for children to enable them to "play" or "coach" soccer, golf, football, and ping-pong via computer.

School Health Service Personnel

School health services must be provided to students with disabilities. In most school districts, the school health service personnel are nurses. These health services include monitoring immunization records and monitoring and/or completing health procedures such as catheterization or tracheostomy tube suction. In *Irving Independent School District v. Tatro* (1984), the U.S. Supreme Court decided that health services needed to enable a child to reach, enter, exit, or remain in school during the day were required.[29] A careful consideration of *Garrett v. Cedar Rapids Community School District* will be considered in Chapter 7.

School health services for children with disabilities become more complex as more children who are medically fragile pursue their right to a free, appropriate public education as mandated by IDEA and Section 504 of the Rehabilitation Act.

Social Workers

Social work services were broadened in the 1997 Amendments to IDEA to include individual and group counseling and other mental health services.[48, section w] Some of the specific tasks done by social workers include

- Prepare social or developmental histories of children with disabilities
- Conduct group or individual counseling with parents and children
- Work in partnership with parents regarding aspects of the child's living situation that affect the child's adjustment to school
- Assist in developing positive behavior-intervention strategies

The licensed social worker intervenes within the family, seen as part of the total community, and helps the child with disabilities and his or her family deal with issues that directly relate to the disability—discrimination, fear, guilt, substance abuse, child abuse, medical expenses, and the intrusion of well-meaning professionals into their lives. The social worker is trained to assist the family in coping with the vast and often complex system designed to provide support for families in trouble. The social worker can, for example, help a parent apply for Aid for Dependent Children or, if necessary, unemployment compensation.

In some large school districts, community social service agencies have opened offices within the schools to improve access to needed social services.

This strategy has proved valuable in providing assistance to non-English-speaking children and their families.

Speech Therapists

Speech and language therapy has as its goal the improvement of communication behaviors of students whose speech and/or language deficits affect educational performance. Haynes[24] has identified four speech and language components that must be addressed by the speech therapist:

- Semantics (language content or meaning)
- Syntax (language structure or grammar)
- Pragmatics (language use or function)
- Phonology (the sound system of language)

If a student has a problem that the speech therapist cannot correct, the therapist will refer the student to medical personnel or rehabilitation specialists.[48 section x]

Service delivery in speech and language programs was historically based on a medical model in which the speech therapist provided therapy to children with speech and language deficits in a clinical, isolated setting. That is, the clinician provided speech and language programming in a setting removed from the child's regular education or special education classroom. That practice is changing.

Current, innovative practice in speech and language programs is based on the notion that speech and language are a basic and integral part of the child's total life experience. As Achilles, Yates, and Freese[1] have suggested, the child uses speech and language throughout the day, in a variety of environments, in response to a variety of stimuli, and in interaction with many different people; as such, speech and language use are ongoing processes. Therefore, speech and language therapy must be embedded within the total academic and nonacademic curriculum.

To allow classroom-based therapy to occur, the speech therapist functions collaboratively with the child's regular educator and/or special educator. A smart therapist is anxious to collaborate with the physical educator or the adapted physical educator because the advantages identified in classroom-based language instruction pertain to the physical education "classroom" or adapted physical education "classroom" as well. In fact, the nature of physical education makes it an exciting, language-rich opportunity. Children involved in dance, play, and games are functioning within their most natural environment; this environment demands communication in a variety of forms—gestures, signs, expressive facial behaviors, or expressive/receptive speech.

In addition, the therapist collaborates with the physical educator or adapted physical educator because of the obvious relationship between gross and fine motor development and the development of speech and language. Indeed, movement is speech; speech is movement.

Transportation Specialists

In *Alamo Heights v. State Board of Education* (1986), the court mandated that transportation, like other related services, must be included on the child's IEP.[2] The Office of Civil Rights has decreed that a child with a disability should not have to ride the school bus longer than other children. The Office of Civil Rights has also indicated it is a violation of civil rights if a child with a disability has a shorter instructional day than other children because of the school bus schedule. In addition, the child with a disability should have the same access to extracurricular, before-school or after-school, programs as any other child.[38] If the child needs an aide (transportation specialist) on the bus during transportation to and from school, litigation indicates it should be included on the IEP as well.

Transition Service Personnel

One of the major transition services offered by transition service personnel is vocational education. A quality vocational education program includes a comprehensive assessment of vocational potential and capabilities. The student with a disability is given the opportunity to demonstrate his or her unique skills and talents so that appropriate job training can be provided. As the student enters middle school and high school, the focus of the education provided is vocational, if appropriate. Special education instruction focuses on the skills necessary to function within a workplace. Actual work-related opportunities are provided in "work production" or "work simulation" classes. Some progressive school districts have job placement opportunities for children with disabilities in the last years of their special education career. In fact, some provide "job coaches" to work "shoulder to shoulder" with a student with a disability at the actual job site to assist the student with the technical aspects, as well as the social nuances, of the job. For example, if the student is being trained as a maid for a major hotel chain, the job coach accompanies the student to the hotel, both wearing the same uniform as every other employee, and helps the student learn the day-to-day routine and processes involved in being a successful employee.

Each of the professionals described above brings a special expertise to the child with a disability. Seldom does one child require the services of all these specialized professionals. However, the intent of the law is that these personnel must be made available, if necessary, for the child to benefit from the educational process.

Seldom are all these professionals on-staff personnel within a given district. Small school districts may rely on a special education center to provide such services. These centers are called by different names in different states. In Kansas, the term *cooperative special education center* is used. In Michigan, the title *intermediate school district* is given to centers that provide specialized services. In Texas, regional special education service centers work in close cooperation with local school districts. When this type of special education center is not available, school districts hire their own specialized personnel on a contractual basis or refer children to private practitioners and/or hospitals or rehabilitation centers for assessment/evaluation services and/or programming.

Summary

The process of designing individual education programs (IEPs) in physical education for the student with a disability is a basic component of effective programming. The role of the parents in this process has been heightened. In addition, there has been an increased emphasis on the provision of services in the general curriculum and program.

The type of physical education program developed for each student will depend on the student's identified needs. After the student has been assessed to determine specific levels of present performance and needs, annual goals and short-term objectives leading to each goal are determined by the IEP/multidisciplinary team. No later than age fourteen, an individual transition plan (ITP) must be developed that ensures the student's ability to function in a community when leaving the school setting.

Review Questions

1. Explain the importance of and difference among IEP, ITP, and PFP.
2. Explain the role of the adapted physical educator and physical educator in the development and implementation of the IEP, ITP, and PFP.
3. How can the physical educator or adapted physical educator make a parent or a student feel comfortable in the IEP/multidisciplinary team meeting?
4. Describe the role of the parent in the IEP, ITP, and PFP processes.

Student Activities

1. Visit the websites of the parent advocacy groups to get a sense of the feelings of parents regarding their rights and needs.
2. Review Maria's IEP, ITP, and the PFP process. Describe other ways the physical educator or adapted physical educator could help Maria and her family so they can enjoy community-based leisure, recreation, and sport experiences together.
3. Interview a parent of a student with a disability. Ask the parent to explain his or her frustrations with the proceedings of the IEP or ITP meeting. Discuss suggestions for making that a more parent-friendly process.
4. Interview a related service provider—an occupational therapist, physical therapist, speech and language therapist, etc.—to help clearly define his or her unique contributions to the education of a student with a disability.

References

1. Achilles J, Yates R, Freese J: Perspectives from the field: collaborative consultation in the speech and language program of the Dallas Independent School District, *Lang Speech Hearing Schools* 22:154–155, 1991.
2. *Alamo Heights v. State Board of Education*, 790 F 2d 1153 (5th Cir 1986).
3. American Academy of Pediatrics, Committee on Children with Disabilities: The pediatrician's role in development and implementation of an individual education plan (IEP) and/or an individual family service plan (IFSP), *Pediatrics* 104(1):124–127, 1999.

4. American Occupational Therapy Association: *Guidelines for occupational therapy services in school systems*, Rockville, MD, 1989, Author.

5. American Occupational Therapy Association: *Uniform terminology for occupational therapy*, ed 2, Rockville, MD, 1989, Author.

6. Behrmann M: Assistive technology for students with mild disabilities, intervention, *School Clin* 30(2):70–83, 1994.

7. Bullis M, Cheney D: Vocational and transition interventions for adolescents and young adults with emotional or behavioral disorders, *Focus Except Child* March:1–24, 1999.

8. Cain EJ: The role of the computer in special education: some philosophical considerations, *Pointer* 28:6–11, 1984.

9. California Department of Education: *Individualized education program fact sheet*, http://www.cde.ca.gov/spranch/sed/iep.htm

10. Devlieger PJ, Trach JS: Mediation as a transition process: the impact of postschool employment outcomes, *Except Child* 65(4):507–523, 1999.

11. Dummer G: Curriculum revision in adapted physical education, *Palaestra* 15(2):59, 1999.

12. Ebenstein B: IEP strategies: getting what your child needs from IEP meetings and annual reviews, *Except Parent* April:62–63, 1995.

13. Edelen-Smith P: Eight elements to guide goal determination for IEPs, *Intervent School Clin* 30(5):297–301, 1995.

14. Elmore RF, McLaughlin MS: *Steady work: policy, practice, and the reform of American education*, Santa Monica, CA, 1988, Rand Corporation.

15. Espin C et al.: Individualized education programs in resource and inclusive settings: how "individualized" are they? *J Special Ed* 33(3):164–174, 1998.

16. Felix M, Todd B: Transition plans in adapted physical education and recreation: An overlooked need. In D. Beaver, editor: *Proceedings of the 6th National Conference on Adapted Physical Activity*, 5–7, Macomb, IL, Western Illinois University Press.

17. Foss, PD: *Transition from school to community: what works for students with disabilities?* Unpublished master's thesis, 1991, University of Southern Florida.

18. A four-year plan to systematically integrate microcomputers, videodiscs, and other state-of-the-art technology into special education administration, management and classroom instruction. Dallas Independent School District, January 1987, Instruction Systems Technology Division, Department of Special Education.

19. Furney KS, Hasazi SB, DeStefano L: Transition policies, promises, and practices: lessons from three states, *Except Child* 63:343–356, 1997.

20. Gerardi RJ et al.: IEP—more paperwork and wasted time, *Contemp Educ* 56:39–42, 1984.

21. Halpern AS: *Transition: is it time for another rebottling?* Presented at the 1999 Annual OSEP Project Directors' Meeting, Washington, DC, June 14, 1999.

22. Hasazi SB, Furney KS, Destefano L: Implementing the IDEA transition mandates, *Except Child* 65(4):555–566, 1999.

23. Hawkins BA: Leisure and recreational programming. In Stainback W, Stainback S, editors: *Controversial issues confronting special education: divergent perspectives*, Boston, 1992, Allyn & Bacon.

24. Haynes C: Language development in the school years—what can go wrong? In Mogford K, Sadler J, editors: *Child language disability*, Clevedon, UK, 1989, Multilingual Matters.

25. Hodgkinson H: American education: the good, the bad, and the task. In Elam S, editor: *The state of the nation's public schools: a conference report*, Bloomington, IN, 1993, Phi Delta Kappa Foundation.

26. Holburn S, Vietze P: Acknowledging barriers in adopting person-centered planning, *Mental Retard* 37(2):117–124, 1999.

27. House of Representatives Report No. 105-95, p. 182, 1997): Senate Report No. 105-17, p. 4, 1997.

28. IDEA Amendments of 1997: News Digest, A Publication of the National Information Center for Children and Youth with Disabilities (NICHCY), 26 (revised edition), June 1998.

29. *Irving Independent School District v. Tatro*, 1984, 468 US 883.

30. Jankowitz W, Cort RH: Transition planning: will your child be ready for life after high school? *Except Parent* September: 83–84, 1999.

31. Kohler PD: Best practices in transition: substantiated or implied. *Career Develop Except Individuals* 16(2):107–121, 1993.

32. Leatherby J: *Reach for the stars—planning for the future: personal futures planning for young children.* Paper presented at the Ninth Annual Statewide Conference on Deaf-Blindness and Multiple Disabilities, Austin, TX, February 1994.

33. Lewis A: Churning up the waters in special education, *Phi Delta Kappan* 73:100–101, 1991.

34. Lovitt T, Cushing S, Stump C: High school students rate their IEPs: low opinions and lack of ownership, *Intervent School Clin* 30:34–37, 1994.

35. Lynch E, Beare P: The quality of IEP objectives and their relevance to instruction for students with mental retardation and behavioral disorders, *Remed Spec Educ* 11(2):48–55, 1990.

36. Minnesota Individual Transition Plans at http://www.disability.state.mn.us/pubs/trans/pyd.html

37. Mount B: *Dare to dream*, Manchester, CT, 1991, Communitas.

38. Office of Civil Rights, 1989, EHLR 326.

39. Orr C, Gott C, Kainer M: *Model of student role adaptation: merging the values of occupational therapy and special education*, Dallas, 1990, Dallas Independent School District.

40. Piletic C: Transition: are we doing it? *J Phys Ed Rec Dance* 69(9):46–50, 1998.

41. Pyfer J. Personal communication, Fall 1999.

42. Salembier GR, Furney KS: Speaking up for your child's future. *Except Parent* July: 62–64, 1998.

43. Senate Report No 105–17, p. 20: House of Representatives Report No. 105–95, p. 99, 1997.

44. Smith SW: Individualized education programs (IEPs) in special education—from intent to acquiescence, *Except Child* September: 6–13, 1990.

45. Stone DA: Policy paradox: the art of political decision making. Boston, 1997,W.W. Norton.

46. Stopka C et al.: Transition skills for wellness. *Teaching Except Child* January/February: 6–11, 1999.

47. Texas Woman's University Project INSPIRE at http://venus.twu.edu/~f huettig

48. U.S. Department of Education, 34 CFR Parts 300 and 303: Assistance to States for the Education for Children with Disabilities and the Early Intervention Program, *Federal Register*, March 12, 1999, Section a–x, Washington, DC.

49. U.S. Department of Education: Assistance to states for education of handicapped children: interpretation of the individual education program, *Federal Register,* January 19, 1981.

50. Walsh J: How to propose an IEP, run an ARD, develop a BIP, and comply with procedural safeguards. Walsh, Anderson, Brown, Schulze & Aldridge, P. C., 1998.

RECOMMENDED WEBSITES

Please note that the recommendations regarding websites are being made in the fall of 1999. These websites may have moved or been eliminated by the time you are reading this text.

State of Minnesota Individual Transition Plans
  http://www.disability.state.mn.us/pubs/trans/pyd.html

Draft IEP Checklist
  http://www.cde.ca.gov/spbranch/sed/iepcheck.htm

What Makes a Good Individual Education Plan for Your Child
      http://www.pacer.org/parent/iep.htm

Parent Advocacy Group—Mothers from Hell
  http:// www.apexcomm.net/~deviski/mfhmome.html

Parent Advocacy Group—Parent Panthers
  http://home.epix.net/~mcross/8panther.html

Recreation and Leisure Time as Part of the Transition Program for Individuals with Disabilities
  http://www.coe.ufl.edu/special/florida/leisure.htm

NTA Transition Practices Framework: Student-Focused Planning and Development
  http://www.dssc.org/nta/textonly/stusty t.htm

California Department of Education: IEP Fact Sheet
  http://www.cde.ca.gov/spranch/sed/iep.htm

SUGGESTED READINGS

Jankowitz W, Cort RH: Transition planning: will your child be ready for life after high school? *Except Parent,* September:83–84, 1999.

Piletic C: Transition: are we doing it? *Journal of Physical Education Recreation and Dance* 69(9):46–50, 1998.

RECOMMENDED VIDEOS

Aquarius Health Care Videos
5 Powderhouse Lane
PO Box 1159
Sherborn, MA 01770
    Raising Kids with Special Needs
    Item # LRNRAISING
    21 minutes, $89

My Country
Best of Show Superfest '98 Award
Item # DISCOUNTRY
60 minutes, $195

Teaching to Meet Learners' Needs

■ OBJECTIVES

Recognize the differences between the top-down and the bottom-up teaching approaches.

Discriminate between functional and sport skills.

Give an example of a content analysis.

Identify three functional adaptations a physical educator could make to accommodate students with disabilities.

Explain programmed physical education instruction.

The Camden, NJ, Courier-Post, Courtesy National Amputee Golf Association.

There is no question about the importance of motor development. In addition to its being a critical component of movement efficiency, it is also widely believed to underlie perceptual, cognitive, and affective function.[10] How infants' bodies grow and change has been widely studied in this country since 1920. From that time through the 1940s, Shirley, McGraw, and Gesell carefully observed and documented hundreds of motor milestones normally developing children demonstrate during their first few years of life. Those observations became the basis for the majority of motor development screening instruments available to us today (see Chapters 2 and 10 for specific screening instruments). Such instruments are frequently used to determine whether an infant is progressing neurologically at the expected rate because motor milestones are among the first visible indicators of central nervous system maturation. However, even though motor development screening instruments can be used to identify where a child is performing in comparison with normal expectations, such

CASE STUDY

CRITICAL THINKING TASK
Review Maria Garcia's individual education program (IEP) in Chapter 3 (see Figure 3-1). Note the areas of performance that were indicated as weaknesses. As you read this chapter, identify which type of intervention (top-down, bottom-up, or accommodation) that could be used to address each weakness.

instruments do not provide information indicating what is interfering with the slowly developing child's progress. That information must be predicted from formal sensory input, sensory integration or psychological tests developed specifically for those purposes, or informal clues provided by the child. More direct, absolute measures are, however, under development.

As we begin a new millennium, developmental psychologists, movement scientists, neuroscientists, and others are joining forces to try to build on the work of the early developmentalists to better understand the processes by which infants and children gain mastery over their bodies. Careful studies are being conducted to determine what aspects of nature and nurture are critical for maximal motor development. Advanced technology is being used to identify and monitor factors that impact favorably on a child's motor competence.[8]

Physical educators who teach individuals with disabilities agree that their primary goal is to facilitate development of purposeful skills for each student. There are, however, a variety of approaches to programming from which physical educators can select. They range from general physical education activities believed to benefit all children, regardless of degree of function, to developmentally sequenced activities that serve as building blocks of motor development, to activities that enhance very specific skills.

Which approach a physical educator selects depends on the amount of time available, the age and readiness level of the students, the capabilities of the teacher, and the number of individuals available to assist the teacher. In this chapter, the levels of function that contribute to sport and functional skills, ways to facilitate development at each of those levels, and adaptations that can be made to accommodate individuals with special needs will be addressed.

LEVELS OF MOTOR FUNCTION

The ultimate goal of physical education for individuals with disabilities is to equip them with motor skills that contribute to independent living. To plan these programs systematically, it is desirable to distinguish clearly the levels of function that contribute to the acquisition of the many specific sport skills.

Each of these levels makes a unique contribution to independent functioning: (1) basic neurological building blocks, (2) integration processes, (3) functional skills, and (4) sport and recreational skills (see Figure 4-1). The physical educator who understands the interrelatedness of these levels and can select intervention activities to facilitate functioning at any given level, depending on a student's needs, will realize success.

The functioning of the basic neurological building blocks depends on the integrity and operation of the sensory input systems. These systems include primitive reflexes, the vestibular system, refractive and orthoptic vision, audition, the tactile and kinesthetic systems, and equilibrium reflexes. Before information can reach the central nervous system for processing, these systems must be intact and functional. The physical educator who automatically assumes these systems are functioning and that adequate stimulation is reaching the central nervous system disregards an important component of purposeful movement.[9]

The second level of functioning is the integration processes. Like the basic neurological building blocks, these prerequisites enhance the acquisition of skill. If the basic neurological building blocks

Motor output

Sport skills

Dribbling, shooting, rebounding, spiking, volleying, serving, trapping, pitching, tumbling, punting, diving, skiing, batting

Functional skills

Locomotor	**Object control**
Rolling, crawling, walking, running, hopping, jumping, sliding, galloping, skipping, climbing stairs	Kicking, catching, throwing, striking, bouncing

---

Integration processes

Perceptual motor	**Physical fitness**	**Motor fitness**
Balance	Strength	Agility
Laterality	Flexibility	Power
Directionality	Muscular endurance	Speed
Body image	Cardiovascular endurance	Coordination
Spatial awareness		
Cross-lateral integer		

Basic neurological building blocks

Equilibrium reflexes
Vestibular, kinesthetic, refractive and orthoptic vision, tactile audition
Primitive reflexes

Figure 4-1   Motor Development Model

are functioning, integration processes develop concurrently with quality movement experiences. The integration processes include the perceptual-motor, physical fitness, and motor fitness categories. Examples of perceptual-motor abilities are balance, cross-lateral integration, laterality, directionality, body image, and spatial awareness. Physical fitness prerequisites are strength, flexibility, muscular endurance, and cardiovascular endurance. Motor fitness consists of power, agility, speed, and motor coordination.

The uppermost levels of motor development are functional and sport and recreation skills. Skills are motor behaviors that are specific to either functional living or to a sport or recreational activity. Examples of functional skills are the basic locomotor skills such as walking, running, hopping, and skipping and the object-control skills such as throwing, bouncing, and kicking. Sport and recreational skills include shooting a basketball, serving a tennis ball, skiing, and trapping a soccer ball. Functional skills, such as walking and running, usually emerge as the central nervous system prerequisite components mature. Proficiency at specific individual and team sport skills is usually developed through repetitious practice of the skill itself.

INCIDENTAL VERSUS PLANNED LEARNING

Most individuals learn from everyday interaction with the environment. This is particularly true if the environment is varied and the learner possesses all the prerequisites needed to convert environmental stimulation into motor patterns. This is known as *incidental learning*. The more ready an individual is (i.e., the more developed the neurological, cognitive, and motor functions are), the more that can be gained from interaction with the environment. Conversely, the fewer the number of developed prerequisites, the less a person gains from environmental exchanges.

The individual with a disability is often denied opportunities to interact with varied environments. This is a hindrance because, for the central nervous system to develop normally, a wide variety of stimulation is necessary.[7] Thus, attempts to protect these children from interaction with the environment often delay their development. Because of these delays, learners with disabilities do not always gain as much from incidental learning as do other learners.

Teachers of children with disabilities must be particularly sensitive to the needs of their students. Until a teacher determines the needs of students, appropriate intervention strategies cannot be selected. The physical education teacher must ensure that each student's motor learning improves. The general approach of providing a wide variety of activities to all students gives no assurance that motor learning will result. It is true that the children may have fun and could gain some physical fitness from their activities; however, the students will not make the same gains as would be possible if activities were selected specifically to meet the needs of the learners. There are many activities available that are enjoyable for all children in a class that also meet the needs of individual learners. The effective teacher will select those activities that benefit all of the children in his or her class.

FACILITATING SKILL DEVELOPMENT

Children and youth with disabilities frequently demonstrate physical and motor development lags. As a result, they often have difficulty learning chronologically age-appropriate skills. When developmental deficits become apparent, decisions about how to address the deficits have to be made. Questions that need to be answered include whether it is necessary to modify the teaching strategy used or will modifications/adaptations best accommodate the student's needs. In the following sections, three teaching techniques and several functional adaptations that are effective for accommodating the student with special needs will be presented.

Teach Specific Skills: Top-Down

Teaching the skill directly is known as the task-specific approach. Advocates of this approach stress what skills an individual will need for productive independence as an adult in the community where he or she lives. In the case of the physical educator, the targeted behaviors focus on the functional and recreational sports skills that an individual would have an opportunity to participate in as an adult in the community. The top-down approach places emphasis on the end of the skill sequence, the final motor countdown as an adult, rather than what is to be taught next. When using the top-down approach, it is necessary to monitor carefully the progress of learners with disabilities as they move from elementary to middle schools to high schools and then into adult life. To ensure that functional skills are being taught, it is necessary to gather information about the lesser restrictive environments the individual will function in as an adult. The focus of this approach emphasizes teaching skills and behaviors that are absolutely necessary for a person to function in a community environment.

To determine which skills an individual has in relation to skills that will be needed for ultimate functioning in the community requires the completion of an ecological inventory (community-based assessment). The ecological inventory provides critical information about current and future school and community environments (see Chapter 2, "Determining Educational Needs Through Assessment"). Selecting age-appropriate skills tends to maximize the normalization process during the life of a person with a disability. When using ecological assessment data, a major departure from traditional procedures is the need to take students into the community to do part of the instruction. This enables the student to practice the skills in a natural setting.

When using a task analysis approach to assess students' repertoires, the educator can determine which motor skills are present and which are yet to be learned. Once the deficient skills are determined, they are prioritized and analyzed to determine which portions have not yet been mastered, and the specific missing components are taught using a direct teaching method.

In general, there are two types of task analysis, content analysis of discrete tasks and content analysis of continuous skills. Examples of each appear in Figure 4-2. An example of a content analysis of a discrete task is given in Figure 4-3, and an example of a content analysis of continuous skills is presented in Figure 4-4. Once a task analysis is completed and the missing components are identified, a person using a task-specific top-down teaching approach would either teach each of the components found to be lacking or teach the entire movement from beginning to end.

Task analyses can be very formal or quite informal. Tests that are content-referenced are truly sets of analyzed tasks because they provide the components of each task in the test. However, frequently the physical educator relies

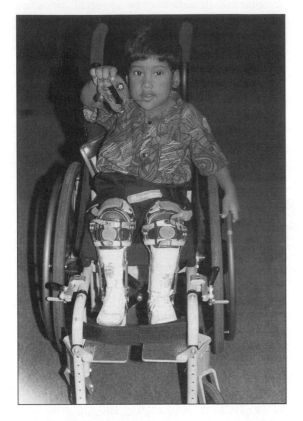

Every child can make music.
Courtesy Dallas Independent School District.

Figure 4-2   Task Analyses and Educational Performance

Type of task analysis	Type of task	Examples
Content analysis of discrete tasks	Discrete tasks broken down into parts that make up the entire task	Dressing, lay-up shot in basketball
Content analysis of continuous skills	Continuous task broken down into components that contribute to the skill	Running, jumping, throwing

Figure 4-3   Content Analysis of the Discrete Task of Executing a Lay-Up Shot in Basketball

1. Bounces a basketball with one hand
2. Bounces a basketball at waist height with one hand
3. Runs while bouncing a basketball at waist height
4. Takes a short step and jumps vertically off the foot opposite the shooting hand
5. Times the jump to occur just before the body reaches the area under the basket
6. Releases the ball at the top of the jump
7. Directs the ball to a point on the backboard that will permit the ball to rebound from the backboard into the basket
8. Controls the body when coming down from the jump

Figure 4-4   Content Analysis of the Continuous Task of Running

Mature stage of running

1. Stride length at maximum; stride speed fast
2. Definite flight phase
3. Complete extension of support leg
4. Recovery thigh parallel to ground
5. Arms swinging vertically in opposition to legs
6. Arms bent at approximate right angles
7. Minimal rotary action of recovery leg and foot

Courtesy of Gallahue, DL, Ozmun, JC (1995), *Understanding Motor Development,* Dubuque: McGraw-Hill Publishing.

on observation of performance to determine what parts of the task are inefficient. For example, if the physical educator observes that the student is performing all parts of the basketball lay-up task correctly except timing the jump to occur just before the body reaches the area under the basket and directing the ball to the correct point on the backboard, those are the two components that should be selected to be taught directly.

To correct the jump timing problem, it might be necessary to mark an area on the floor where the jump should be executed for a right-hand lay-up. The student practices approaching the mark and landing on it consistently with the left foot. When that movement becomes habitual, the student practices the approach and adds a jump off the left foot when reaching the mark on the floor. Then to direct the student's attention to the correct place to rebound the ball, an area could be marked on the backboard. The student then practices the correct approach, jump, and striking the outlined area on the backboard with the ball in one continuous motion. Minor adjustments may need to be added to modify the amount of force the student uses when releasing the ball.

Once a skill is learned, it should be practiced under a variety of conditions to assure the learner's ability to use the skill in different situations and environments. Conditions that can be modified include time (fast/slow, even/uneven), space (straight/circular/zig-zag, high/low, alone/with others, inside/outside), force (light/heavy, soft/hard), and flow (synchronized/unsynchronized, run/walk/hop, twist/turn). (See the "little red book," Gross Motor Activities for Children with Special Needs, that accompanies this text for additional examples.)

The task-specific top-down approach is probably the most realistic and expedient type to use with individuals with severe disabilities and higher-functioning individuals in middle school and beyond, but it may be inappropriate for younger children with disabilities. The essential question to ask when trying to decide whether to use this approach is "How much time is available?" Facilitating basic neurological building blocks and integration processes prior to teaching specific skills takes time, perhaps years. Also, there is evidence that children under the age of twelve years respond more readily than do older individuals. When the individual with a disability is older and severely involved and there is a limited amount of time available to develop functional skills needed to live in a natural environment, the task-specific approach is the most efficient intervention strategy.

Eliminate Deficiencies: Bottom-Up

Motor development is a progressive process. For each of us to learn to move efficiently, we must first be able to take environmental information into the central nervous system. Then it must be processed or integrated so that it can be used to direct movement patterns and skills. Only after the information is received and processed can the brain direct the muscles to work. If anything goes wrong before the information reaches the muscles, movement is inefficient or nonexistent. Advocates of the developmental approach agree that the ultimate goal of education is to produce productive adults who can function independently in their communities. To achieve this goal, the developmentalist would intervene in a child's life as early as possible to determine whether age-appropriate basic building blocks, integration processes, and skills were functional. If any age-appropriate developmental blocks were found to be deficient when the child was tested, then the developmentalist would select activities to promote development of the deficient areas. Thus, if a child were found to have a severe orthoptic (eye alignment) problem that would interfere with eye-hand coordination development, the child would be referred to a visual behavioral specialist for correction of the problem. If a child demonstrated failure to develop equilibrium reactions and/or adequate vestibular (inner ear) function, which are critical for balance development, activities to promote development in those areas would be prescribed.

The developmental approach can be considered a bottom-up teaching strategy because the evaluator tries to determine the lowest level of motor function and correct that problem before addressing specific skills (review Figure 4-1). Once the developmentalist determines which basic neurological building blocks and integration components appear to be poorly developed, activities that promote the functioning of each area found to be lacking are selected. The rationale is to ensure that the supporting building blocks and integration processes are fully functioning so that skill development will be facilitated.

In the following section, each of the basic neurological building blocks and perceptual motor integration processes will be described, clues that indicate that the systems are not fully developed will be given, and individual activities that promote development will be suggested. Group activities to use to facilitate development of these systems are included in the "little red activity manual" that accompanies this text.

Basic Neurological Building Blocks

The primitive reflexes and the vestibular, visual, kinesthetic, tactile, and auditory systems, as well as the equilibrium reflexes, are considered basic input systems because sensations arising from these systems' receptors provide the basic "stuff" from which integration processes and motor skills are built. These systems normally develop during the first five years of life. After they are functioning, perceptual-motor, physical fitness, motor fitness, and motor skill development occurs. Should any one or a combination of these systems fail to develop fully, all motor development is delayed and/or interfered with in some way.[5,7] For this reason, it is imperative to identify and remediate basic input system delays as early in life as possible. The point at which it becomes too late to attempt to facilitate development of any of these systems is not really known; however, some writers suggest that, if such delays are still present at age twelve years, the educator's time might better be spent teaching the child to accommodate to the delay. See Figure 4-5 for an informal screening test that can be used to identify sensory input delays.

Reflexes

Reflexes are innate responses that all normal children develop (see Table 4.1). Reflexes that affect movement are of interest to the physical educator because students whose reflex maturation is delayed have inefficient movement patterns. In

Figure 4-5   Sensory Input Systems Screening Test

	Pass	Fail
Reflex Test Items—Check Pass or Fail		
1. Tonic labyrinthine supine—(TLS) While lying on back, can bend knees to chest, wrap arms around knees, and touch head to knees. Child should be able to hold position for 10 seconds.		
2. Tonic labyrinthine prone—(TLP) While lying face down on mat with arms at side, child can lift head and upper body and hold off mat for 5 seconds.		
3. Positive support reaction—(PSR) Child is able to jump into air and, on landing, flex ankles, knees, and hips while maintaining balance for 5 seconds.		
4. Equilibrium reactions When placed on a tilt board, child will move hands out to side and maintain balance for 3 seconds when the board is suddenly tipped 15 degrees to one side and then to other side (check each side independently). Check child in each of these positions:		
a. Seated, start with hands in lap—move right		
b. Seated, start with hands in lap—move left		
c. On two knees, start with hands on hips—move right		
d. On two knees, start with hands on hips—move left Place child on all fours on tilt board and tip board 15 degrees to one side and then to the other. Child can maintain "all fours" position while holding head in a neutral position.		
e. When tipped to right		
f. When tipped to left		
Vestibular Test Items—Check Pass or Fail		
1. Seat child in a desk chair that can be rotated 360 degrees. Have child rest hands in lap or on arms of chair. Child should tip head down slightly (30 degrees). Turn chair 10 complete turns in 20 seconds (1 complete rotation every 2 seconds). Stop chair and watch child's eyes. Child's eye should flick back and forth for 7 to 13 seconds. After a 2-minute rest, repeat turning procedure in opposite direction. Check eye movement again.		
a. Turn to right		
b. Turn to left		
Fixation (Ocular Control)—Check Pass or Fail		
1. Child should sit in a chair facing a seated evaluator. Child can fixate with both eyes on an object held 18 inches in front of the nose at eye level for 10 seconds.		
2. Child should sit in a chair facing a seated evaluator. Cover child's left eye with your hand or a card. Child can fixate with right eye on an object held 18 inches in front of the nose at eye level for 10 seconds.		
3. Child should sit in a chair facing a seated evaluator. Cover child's right eye with your hand or a card. Child can fixate with left eye on an object held 18 inches in front of the nose at eye level for 10 seconds. NOTE: Any tendency to turn the head to one side, to blink excessively, or for the eyes to water could be an indication that the child needs to be referred to a visual development specialist for a refractive and orthoptic visual exam.		

Courtesy Jean L. Pyfer, Texas Woman's University, Denton, Tex., and Robert Strauss, Trinity University, San Antonio, Tex.

Figure 4-5   (*Continued*)

	Pass	Fail
Ocular Alignment (Depth Perception)—Check Pass or Fail		

Ocular Alignment (Depth Perception)—Check Pass or Fail

NOTE: On all of the following items start with the child looking at the object with both eyes. Then cover 1 eye and begin your observation.

1. Child is seated in a chair facing a seated evaluator. Child can fixate on an object held 18 inches in front of the nose at eye level without moving right eye as left eye is covered for 3 seconds. (Note whether the right eye moves and in what direction.)
2. Child is seated in a chair facing a seated evaluator. Child can fixate on an object held 18 inches in front of the nose at eye level without moving left eye as right eye is covered for 3 seconds. (Note whether the left eye moves and in what direction.)

Convergence-Divergence Ocular Control—Check Pass or Fail

1. Child is seated in a chair facing a seated evaluator. Child can visually follow with both eyes an object moved slowly from 18 inches directly in front of the nose (eye level), to 4 inches from the eyes (midpoint), and back to 18 inches. (Note whether the eyes move equally without jerking.)

Visual Tracking—Check Pass or Fail

1. Child is seated in a chair facing a seated evaluator. Child can visually pursue with both eyes without moving the head an object held 18 inches from the eyes as the object is moved in the following patterns:
   a. A square (12-inch sides)
   b. A circle (8- to 10-inch diameter)
   c. An *X* (10-inch lines)
   d. A horizontal line (12 inches)
2. Child is seated in a chair with left eye covered facing a seated evaluator. Child can visually pursue with the right eye without moving the head an object held 18 inches from the eyes as the object is moved in the following patterns:
   a. A square (12-inch sides)
   b. A circle (8- to 10-inch diameter)
   c. An *X* (10-inch lines)
   d. A horizontal line (12 inches)
3. Child is seated in a chair with right eye covered facing a seated evaluator. Child can visually pursue with the left eye without moving the head an object held 18 inches from the eyes as the object is moved in the following patterns:
   a. A square (12-inch sides)
   b. A circle (8- to 10-inch diameter)
   c. An *X* (10-inch lines)
   d. A horizontal line (12 inches)

   NOTE: During all tracking tasks, note any tendency for the eyes to (1) jump when the object moves across the midline of the body, (2) jump ahead of the object, (3) jerk while pursuing the object, (4) water, or (5) blink excessively. The watering and/or excessive blinking could be an indicator of visual stress, and such cases should be referred to a visual development specialist for a refractive and orthoptic visual exam.

Kinesthesis—Check Pass or Fail

1. Can touch finger to nose 3 times in alternating succession with index fingers while eyes are closed. (Failure if the child misses the tip of the nose by more than 1 inch.)

TABLE 4.1	Primitive and Equilibrium Reflex Development		
Reflex	**Age**	**Age Inhibited**	**Effect on Movement Patterns**
PRIMITIVE REFLEXES			
Flexor withdrawal	Birth	2 months	Uncontrolled flexion of leg when pressure is applied to sole of foot
Extensor thrust	Birth	2 months	Uncontrolled extension of leg when pressure is applied to sole of foot
Crossed extension 1	Birth	2 months	Uncontrolled extension of flexed leg when opposite leg is suddenly flexed
Crossed extension 2	Birth	2 months	Leg adducts and internally rotates, and foot plantar flexes when opposite leg is tapped medially at level of knee (scissor gait)
Asymmetrical tonic neck	Birth	4–6 months	Extension of arm and leg on face side or increase in extension tone; flexion of arm and leg on skull side or increase in flexor tone when head is turned
Symmetrical tonic neck 1	Birth	4–6 months	Arms flex or flexor tone dominates; legs extend or extensor tone dominates when head is ventroflexed while child is in quadruped position
Symmetrical tonic neck 2	Birth	4–6 months	Arms extend or extensor tone dominates; legs flex or flexor tone dominates when head is dorsiflexed while child is in quadruped position
Tonic labyrinthine, supine position	Birth	4 months	Extensor tone dominates when child is in supine position
Tonic labyrinthine, prone position	Birth	4 months	Flexor tone dominates in arms, hips, and legs when child is in prone position
Positive supporting reaction	Birth	4 months	Increase in extensor tone in legs when sudden pressure is applied to both feet simultaneously
Negative supporting reaction	Birth	4 months	Marked increase in flexor tone in legs when sudden pressure is applied to both feet simultaneously
Neck righting	Birth	6 months	Body rotated as a whole in same direction head is turned
Landau reflex	6 months	3 years	Spine, arms, and legs extend when head is dorsiflexed while child is held in supine position; spine, arms, and legs flex when head is ventroflexed while child is held in supine position
EQUILIBRIUM REFLEXES			
Body righting	6 months	Throughout life	When child is in supine position and initiates full body roll, there is segmented rotation of the body (i.e., head turns, then shoulders, then pelvis)

TABLE 4.1	(*Continued*)		
Reflex	**Age**	**Age Inhibited**	**Effect on Movement Patterns**
Labyrinthine righting 1	2 months	Throughout life	When child is blindfolded and held in prone position, head raises to a point where child's face is vertical
Labyrinthine righting 2	6 months	Throughout life	When child is blindfolded and held in supine position, head raises to a point where face is vertical
Labyrinthine righting 3	6–8 months	Throughout life	When child is blindfolded and held in an upright position and is suddenly tilted right, head does not right itself to an upright position
Labyrinthine righting 4	6–8 months	Throughout life	Same as labyrinthine righting 3, but child is tilted to left
Optical righting 1	2 months	Throughout life	Same as labyrinthine righting 1, but child is not blindfolded
Optical righting 2	6 months	Throughout life	Same as labyrinthine righting 2, but child is not blindfolded
Optical righting 3	6–9 months	Throughout life	Same as labyrinthine righting 3, but child is not blindfolded
Optical righting 4	6–8 months	Throughout life	Same as labyrinthine righting 4, but child is not blindfolded
Amphibian reaction	6 months	Throughout life	While child is in prone position with legs extended and arms extended overhead, flexion of arm, hip, and knee on same side can be elicited when pelvis on that side is lifted
Protective extensor	6 months	Throughout life	While child is held by pelvis and is extended in air, arms extend when child's head is moved suddenly toward floor
Equilibrium-supine position	6 months	Throughout life	While child is supine on a tiltboard with arms and legs suspended, if board is suddenly tilted to one side, there is righting of head and thorax and abduction and extension of arm and leg on raised side
Equilibrium-prone position	6 months	Throughout life	Same as equilibrium-supine, except child is prone on tiltboard
Equilibrium-quadruped position	8 months	Throughout life	While child balances on all fours, if suddenly tilted to one side, righting of head and thorax and abduction-extension of arm and leg occur on raised side
Equilibrium-sitting position	10–12 months	Throughout life	While child is seated on chair, if pulled or tilted to one side, righting of head and thorax and abduction-extension of arm and leg occur on raised side (side opposite pull)

(*Continued*)

TABLE 4.1	(*Concluded*)		
Reflex	**Age**	**Age Inhibited**	**Effect on Movement Patterns**
Equilibrium-kneeling position	15 months	Throughout life	While child kneels on both knees, if suddenly pulled to one side, righting of head and thorax and abduction-extension of arm and leg occur on raised side
Hopping 1	15–18 months	Throughout life	While child is standing upright, if moved to the left or right, head and thorax move right and child hops sideways to maintain balance
Hopping 2	15–18 months	Throughout life	While child is standing upright, if moved forward, head and thorax move right and child hops forward to maintain balance
Hopping 3	15–18 months	Throughout life	While child is standing upright, if moved backward, head and thorax move right and child hops backward to maintain balance
Dorsiflexion	15–18 months	Throughout life	While child is standing upright, if tilted backward, head and thorax move right and feet dorsiflex
See-saw	15 months	Throughout life	While child stands on one foot, another person holds arm and free foot on same side; when arm is pulled forward and laterally, head and thorax move right and held leg abducts and extends
Simian position	15–18 months	Throughout life	While child squats down, if tilted to one side, head and thorax move right and arm and leg on raised side abduct and extend

Data from Fiorentino MR: *Reflex testing methods for evaluating CNS development,* Springfield, IL, 1970, Charles C Thomas.

general, there is a series of reflexes that should appear and disappear during the first year of life. These early (primitive) reflexes are layered over by (integrated into) voluntary movement patterns. As a child begins to move voluntarily, a different set of reflexes appears. These later automatic patterns are equilibrium reflexes. They help maintain upright posture and should remain with us throughout life.

A child is considered developmentally delayed in reflex development if any of the following conditions exist:

1. The primitive reflexes do not appear during the first year of life.
2. The primitive reflexes appear at the normal time but do not disappear by the end of the first year.

3. The equilibrium reflexes do not appear by the end of the first year of life.
4. Equilibrium reflexes do not persist throughout life.

Primitive Reflexes

Tonic labyrinthine reflexes (supine and prone) help maintain trunk extension when the child is supine and help maintain trunk flexion when prone. If either of these reflexes does not become integrated, the following movement problems will be exhibited:

1. Supine
   a. Difficulty doing sit-ups
   b. A tendency to extend the trunk during the backward roll

c. Rolling over on one side when trying to rise from a back-lying position
2. Prone
   a. Difficulty doing a full push-up
   b. Inability to extend body fully when lying belly down on a scooter

These two reflexes are under the control of the labyrinthine portion of the inner ear. To facilitate integration of these reflexes, the physical educator should have the child perform activities that require lifting the head against the pull of gravity.

To promote integration of the tonic labyrinthine supine reflex, the child should do activities such as the following, which require flexing the head and body from a back-lying position:

1. Hold knees to chest and rock back-and-forth several times
2. Egg rolls
3. V-sits
4. Partial sit-ups

To promote integration of the tonic labyrinthine prone reflex, the physical educator should have the child do activities such as the following, which require extension of the head and body starting in a front-lying position:

1. Wing lifts
2. While lying prone on a scooter, roll down a ramp and toss a bean bag at a target hung overhead
3. Seal walk while looking at the ceiling
4. Rock back-and-forth on stomach while holding ankles with hands

The positive support reflex causes the legs to extend and the feet to plantar flex when the child is standing. Clues to its presence are apparent if there is an inability to bend the knees when attempting to jump or no "give" at the knees and hips on landing.

When the negative support reflex is present, there is flexion of the knees, hips, and ankles when pressure is removed from the feet. Inability to inhibit the expression of the reflex causes the following problems:

1. During vertical jumps, the legs will bend as soon as the weight is taken off the feet; hence, explosive power is lost.
2. Inability to maintain extension of the legs while bouncing on a trampoline

Both of these reflexes are caused from pressure to the soles of the feet. A child may have either the positive or negative support reflex, but not both at the same time. To facilitate integration of these reflexes, the physical educator should use activities that increase pressure on the soles of the feet, while the child controls the position of the legs.

To eliminate the positive support reaction, the child should flex the lower limbs while applying pressure to the soles of the feet. The following activities are suggested:

1. Bounce on an air mat and suddenly stop on landing by bending the knees
2. Play stoop tag
3. Bunny hop
4. Bounce on inner tubes and/or small trampolines (with the child's hands being held to reduce the chance of falling)

To eliminate the negative support reaction, the child should extend the lower limbs while applying pressure to the soles of the feet. The following activities are suggested:

1. While lying prone on a gym scooter, use the feet to push off from the wall; keep legs extended as long as the scooter is moving across the floor
2. Bounce while sitting on a "hippity-hop" ball
3. Practice jumping up vertically and putting a mark on the wall
4. Bounce on an air mat and try to keep legs straight

Presence of the asymmetrical tonic neck reflex enables extension of the arm on the face side and flexion of the arm on the skull side when the head is turned. Positioning the arms in this fashion when the head is turned is often referred to as the classic fencer's position. Early in life it directs the child's visual attention toward the extended hand. If it persists beyond the tenth month of life, it interferes with bringing the hands to the midline when the head is turned and thus prevents turning the head while creeping and throwing and catching a ball.

Activities that facilitate integration of this reflex include movements that require the child to turn the head toward his or her flexed limbs, such as the following:

1. Practice touching the chin to various parts of the body (e.g., shoulder, wrist, knee).
2. Balance on hands and knees while holding a bean bag between the chin and one shoulder. Then place the hand on the face side of the body on the hip.
3. Hold a bean bag between the chin and one shoulder. Crawl down the mat while keeping the object between the chin and shoulder.
4. Do a no-hands ball relay where the students have to hold a tennis ball between their chin and chest and pass it to one another without using their hands or feet.

When the symmetrical tonic neck reflex is present, the upper limbs tend to flex and the lower limbs extend during ventroflexion of the head. If the head is dorsiflexed, the upper limbs extend and the lower limbs flex. If this reflex does not become fully integrated within the first year of life, the child will demonstrate the following:

1. Instead of using a cross pattern creep, the child will bunny hop both knees up to the hands.
2. If, while creeping, the child lowers the head, the arms will tend to collapse.
3. If, while creeping, the child lifts the head to look around, movement of the limbs ceases.

Activities that require the child to keep the arms extended while the head is flexed, and the arms flexed while the head is extended, will promote integration of this reflex. Examples of such activities include the following:

1. While balancing on hands and knees, look down between the legs; then look up at the ceiling. Keep the arms extended and the legs flexed.
2. With extended arms, push against a cage ball while looking down at the floor.
3. Practice doing standing push-ups against a wall while looking at the ceiling.
4. Do pull-ups (look up when pulling up, and look down when letting oneself down).

Equilibrium Reflexes

The protective extensor thrust causes immediate extension of the arms when the head and upper body are suddenly tipped forward. The purpose of the reflex is to protect the head and body during a fall. The reflex is used during handsprings and vaulting. If the reflex does not emerge, the child will tend to hit the head when falling.

To develop this reflex, the child needs to practice extending the arms and taking the weight on the hands when the head and upper body are tipped toward the floor. The following activities represent ways to accomplish this:

1. While the child is lying prone on a cage ball, roll the ball slowly so that the head, shoulders, and arms are lowered toward the floor. Roll the ball far enough so that the child's weight gradually comes to rest on his or her hands.
2. Practice handstands while someone holds the child's feet in the air.
3. Practice mule kicks.
4. Wheelbarrow with a partner holding the child's knees.

Presence of the body righting reflex enables segmental rotation of the trunk and hips when the head is turned. As a result of this segmental turning, children can maintain good postural alignment and maintenance of body positions. Without it, for example, when doing a log roll, the child will tend to turn the knees, then the hips, and then the shoulders.

To promote development of the body, righting reflex, the child should practice turning the head first, then the shoulders, followed by the hips. The child should start slowly and then increase the speed both from a standing position and back-lying position.

Labyrinthine and optical righting reactions cause the head to move to an upright position when the body is suddenly tipped. Once the head rights itself, the body follows. Thus, these reflexes help us maintain an upright posture during a quick change of position. Without these reflexes, the child will fall down often during running and dodging games and even tend to avoid vigorous running games.

The labyrinthine reflexes are under control of the inner ear, whereas the optical righting reactions are primarily controlled by the eyes. Labyrinthine reflexes are facilitated when the head is moved in opposition to gravity. Any activity requiring the child to move the head in opposition to the pull of gravity will promote development of this reflex (see tonic labyrinthine prone and supine activities). Clinical observation indicates that poorly developed optical righting reactions most frequently accompany orthoptic visual problems (poor depth perception). Once the depth perception problem is corrected, the optical righting reactions begin to appear.

Like the labyrinthine and righting reactions, the other equilibrium reactions help us maintain an upright position when the center of gravity is suddenly moved beyond the base of support. If the equilibrium reactions are not fully developed, children fall down often, fall off chairs, and avoid vigorous running games.

Almost all of these types of equilibrium reactions are the result of the stimulation of muscle spindles and/or the golgi tendon apparatus. Both muscle spindle and golgi tendon apparatus reactions result from sudden stretch (or contraction) of the muscles and tendons. To promote these equilibrium reactions, the child should participate in activities such as the following, which place sudden stretch (or contracture) on the muscles and tendons:

1. Bouncing on an air mat while lying down, balancing on all fours, or balancing on the knees

2. Tug of war
3. Crack the whip
4. Wrestling
5. Scooter activities with a partner pulling or pushing the child who is seated on the scooter

Vestibular System

The vestibular receiving mechanism is located in the semicircular canals of the inner ear. As the body moves, sensory impulses from the vestibular system are sent to the cerebellum and to the brainstem. From these two areas, information about the position of the head is sent to the extraocular muscles of the eye, to the somatosensory strip in the cerebral cortex, to the stomach, to the cerebellum, and down the spinal cord. Accurate information from this mechanism is needed to help position the eyes and to maintain static and dynamic balance. When maturation of the system is delayed, students may demonstrate the following problems:

1. Inability to balance on one foot (particularly with the eyes closed)[10]
2. Inability to walk a balance beam without watching the feet
3. Inability to walk heel-to-toe
4. Inefficient walking and running patterns
5. Delays in ability to hop and to skip

Children who demonstrate these clues and who fail to demonstrate nystagmus after spinning are believed to have vestibular development delays and are in need of activities to facilitate development.[10] Concentrated activities to remediate balance problems that result from poor vestibular function should be administered by someone trained in observing the responses of such a child. However, some activities can be done in fun, nonthreatening ways in a physical education class or on a playground with the supervision of parents or teachers.

Anyone who uses vestibular stimulation activities with children should observe closely for signs of sweating, paleness, flushing of the face, nausea, and loss of consciousness. These are all indications that the activities should be stopped immediately. Also, spinning activities should not be used with seizure-prone children. Avoid rapid spinning activities.

The following vestibular stimulation activities should be nonthreatening to most children:

1. Log roll on a mat, changing directions frequently.
2. Spin self while prone on a gym scooter by crossing hand-over-hand; stop and change direction.
3. Lie on a blanket and roll self up and then unroll.
4. Let the child spin himself or herself on a scooter, play on spinning playground equipment, go down a ramp prone on a gym scooter, or other such nonthreatening activities that give the child an opportunity to respond to changes of his or her position in space (movement or spinning should not be so fast as to be disorienting or disorganizing).

Visual System

Both refractive and orthoptic vision are important for efficient motor performance. Refractive vision is the process by which the light rays are bent as they enter the eyes. When light rays are bent precisely, vision is sharpest and clearest. Individuals who have poor refractive vision are said to be nearsighted (myopic) or farsighted (hyperopic) or have astigmatism. The following problems are demonstrated by children with refractive visual problems:

1. Tendency to squint
2. Tendency to rub the eyes frequently
3. Redness of the eyes

Orthoptic vision refers to the ability to use the extraocular muscles of the eyes in unison. When the extraocular muscles are balanced, images entering each eye strike each retina at precisely the same point, so that the images transmitted to the visual center of the brain match. The closer the match of the images from the eye, the better the depth perception. The greater the discrepancy between the two images that reach the visual center, the poorer the depth perception. Clues to orthoptic problems (poor depth perception) follow:

1. Turning the head when catching a ball
2. Inability to catch a ball or a tendency to scoop the ball into the arms
3. Tendency to kick a ball off center or miss it entirely
4. Persisting to ascend and descend stairs one at a time
5. Avoidance of climbing apparatus

The physical educator is not trained to test for or correct refractive and orthoptic visual problems. However, a simple screening test that can be used to determine whether the possibility of a serious orthoptic (depth perception) problem exists is described in the screening test for developmental delays (see Sensory Input Screening Test). Individuals who fail the ocular alignment portion of the screening test should be professionally evaluated by a behavioral visual specialist (optometrist or ophthalmologist who has specialized training in orthoptics). Students suspected of having refractive vision problems should be evaluated by either an optometrist or ophthalmologist.

Kinesthetic System

The kinesthetic receptors are specialized proprioceptors located in the joints, muscles, and tendons throughout the body. Information from the kinesthetic receptors informs the central nervous system about the position of the limbs in space. As these joint receptors fire, sensory impulses are sent to the brain and are recorded as spatial maps. As the kinesthetic system becomes more developed, judgment about the rate, amount, and amplitude of motion needed to perform a task improves. Refined movement is not possible without kinesthetic awareness. Possible signs of developmental delays of the kinesthetic system are

1. Inability to move a body part on command without assistance
2. No awareness of the position of body parts in space

3. Messy handwriting
4. Poor skill in sports that require a "touch," such as golf ball putting, basketball shooting, and bowling

Activities to promote kinesthetic function include any activity that increases tension on the joints, muscles, and tendons. Some activities that have proven useful in promoting kinesthetic function are

1. Games involving pushing (or kicking) a large cage ball
2. Lying prone on a scooter, holding onto a rope, and being pulled by a partner
3. Using the hands and feet to propel oneself while seated on a gym scooter
4. Doing any type of activity while wearing wrist and/or ankle weights

Tactile System

The tactile receptors are located throughout the body and respond to stimulation of body surfaces. Some of the receptors lie close to the surface of the body; others are located more deeply. A well-functioning tactile system is needed for an individual to know where the body ends and space begins, and to be able to discriminate tactually among pressure, texture, and size. Children who are tactile defensive are believed to have difficulty processing sensory input from tactile receptors. Behaviors demonstrated by the tactile-defensive child include

1. Low tolerance for touch (unless the person doing the touching is in the visual field of the student)
2. Avoidance of activities requiring prolonged touch, such as wrestling or hugging
3. Avoidance of toweling down after a shower or bath unless it is done in a vigorous fashion
4. Tendency to curl fingers and toes when creeping

Activities believed to stimulate the tactile system and promote sensory input processing should begin with coarse textures and progress (over time) toward finer texture stimulation. A sequence of such activities follows:

1. Present the child with a variety of textured articles (nets, pot scrubbers, bath brushes). Have the child select an article and rub it on his or her face, arms, and legs. (Tactile-defensive children will usually select the coarsest textures to use for this activity.)
2. Using an old badminton net, play "capture me" while crawling around on a mat. The teacher should toss the net over the child as the child tries to crawl from one end of the mat to the other. When the child has been captured, rub the net over exposed parts of the body as the child struggles to escape. Repeat the activity with the child chasing and capturing the teacher.
3. Construct an obstacle course with several stations where the child must go through hanging textures (strips of inner tube, sections of rope) and/or squeeze through tight places.
4. Using a movement exploration teaching approach, have the students find various textures in the gym to rub a point or patch against (e.g., rough, smooth, wavy).

Perceptual Motor Processes

Integration processes, including perceptual motor, emerge after sensory input systems begin to stabilize, usually during the fifth through the seventh years of life. Development of these processes requires not only intact information from the sensory input systems but also the capacity to integrate those signals in the brain. When all sensory input systems are functioning and cortical reception and association areas are intact, integration processes and motor skills emerge and generalize with practice. Weakened, distorted, or absent signals from the sensory input systems will detract from the development of integration processes as well as all other motor performance. This is not to say that specific motor skills cannot be taught in the absence of intact sensory information. Specific motor skills can be taught, but only as splinter skills. A splinter skill is a particular perceptual or motor act that is performed in isolation and does not generalize to other areas of performance. If hard neurological damage or age of the learner prevents development of the sensory input systems, it becomes necessary to teach splinter skills. In such cases, the top-down approach (task analysis) is recommended. If, however, it is believed that sensory input systems are fully functioning and cortical integration is possible, practice in the following activities should promote development of a wide variety of perceptual-motor abilities.

Balance

Balance is the ability to maintain equilibrium in a held (static) position or moving (dynamic) position. Balance ability is critical to almost every motor function. Some literature suggests that, until balance becomes an automatic, involuntary act, the central nervous system must focus on maintaining balance to the detriment of all other motor and cognitive functions.[5,7] Balance, once believed to be a result of combining some sensory input system signals, is now seen as a skill that is learned from using many systems, including all available sensory systems, many muscles, and passive biomechanical elements, as well as many different parts of the brain.[4,12] Clues to poor balance development include

1. Inability to maintain held balance positions (e.g., stand on one foot, stand heel-to-toe) with eyes open
2. Inability to walk heel-to-toe on a line or on a balance beam
3. Tripping or falling easily
4. Wide gait while walking or running

Activities that can be used to promote static balance include

1. Freeze tag—play tag; the child who is caught is "frozen" until a classmate "unfreezes" by tagging the child; "it" tries to freeze everyone
2. Statues—each child spins around and then tries to make himself or herself into a "statue" without falling first

3. Tripod—child balances by placing forehead and both hands on the floor; knees balance on elbows to form tripod balance
4. Child balances bean bags on different parts of the body while performing balancing positions.

Activities that can be used to promote dynamic balance include

1. Hopscotch
2. Various types of locomotor movements following patterns on the floor
3. Races using different types of locomotor movements
4. Walk forward heel to toe between double lines, on a single line, and then on a balance beam; make this more demanding by having the child balance a bean bag on different body parts (e.g., head, shoulder, elbow, wrist) while walking the balance beam

Laterality

Laterality is an awareness of the difference between the two sides of the body. Children who have not developed laterality often demonstrate balance problems on one or both sides. Delays in the development of laterality may be indicated by the following types of behavior:

1. Avoiding the use of one side of the body
2. Sliding sideways in one direction better than the other
3. Using one extremity more often than the other
4. Lacking a fully established hand preference

Laterality is believed to develop from intact kinesthetic and vestibular sensory inputs. If these two input systems are believed to be functioning adequately, then a child will benefit from activities that require differentiation between the two sides of the body. Examples include the following:

1. Wear ankle and/or wrist weights on the weak (unused) side of the body while climbing on apparatus; moving through obstacle courses; and kicking, bouncing, throwing, or catching a ball.

2. Walk a balance beam while carrying objects that weigh different amounts in each hand (e.g., carry a small bucket in each hand, with different numbers of bean bags in each bucket).
3. Push a cage ball with one hand only.
4. Use only one hand in tug of war.

Spatial Relations   Spatial relations concerns the ability to perceive the position of objects in space, particularly as they relate to the position of the body (see Figure 4-6). Development of spatial relations is believed to depend on vestibular, kinesthetic, and visual development. Problems may be indicated by

1. Inability to move under objects without hitting them or ducking way below the object

2. Consistently swinging a bat too high or low when attempting to hit a pitched ball
3. Inability to maintain an appropriate body position in relation to moving objects
4. Inability to position the hands accurately to catch a ball

If it has been determined that none of the prerequisite input systems are delayed, spatial relations can be facilitated by practice in the following activities:

1. Set up an obstacle course with stations that require the child to crawl over, under, and through various obstacles.
2. Place a 10-foot taped line on the floor. Give the child a bean bag and ask him or her to place the bean bag halfway down the line. If the child makes an error, ask him or her to

Figure 4-6
A child must have spatial relationship abilities to fit the body through the circular tunnel.

walk from one end of the line to the other, counting the number of steps. Then have the child divide the number of steps in half, walk that far, and place the bean bag down at that point. The child should then stand to the side of the line and look from one end of the line to the bean bag. Continue practicing until the child is successful at estimating where, on several different lengths of line, the midpoint is.

3. Repeat Activity #2 with the child wearing ankle weights.

4. Place several chairs around the room with varying distances between them. Ask the child to point to the two chairs that are closest together, farthest apart, or a given distance from one another (e.g., 3 feet, 10 feet, 6 feet). If the child makes an error on any task, have him or her walk the distance between the chairs and/or measure the distance with a measuring tape.

Ocular-Motor Control   Ocular-motor control includes the ability to fixate on and to visually track moving objects as well as the ability to match visual input with appropriate motor response (see Figure 4-7). Observed deficiencies might include

1. Failure to locate visually an object in space
2. Failure to track visually a softball when attempting to hit it
3. Failure to track visually a fly ball or ground ball
4. Failure to keep a place when reading
5. Difficulty using scissors or tying shoelaces
6. Poor foot-eye coordination
7. Messy handwriting

Ocular control can be improved with practice if a child does not have serious orthoptic (depth perception) problems. If an individual does have depth perception problems, participation in ocular control activities can worsen the visual difficulties. Once it is ascertained that no depth perception problems exist, the following activities can be used to promote ocular control of the eyes:

Fixation
1. Child sits and rocks back-and-forth while keeping his or her eyes on a tape on the wall directly in front of him or her.
2. Child lies on back with eyes fixated on a point on the ceiling. Child then stands up (or does a series of stunts) while continuing to fixate on the spot.
3. Child is in a standing position fixating on a designated point on the wall. Child then jumps and turns 180 degrees and fixates on a designated point on the opposite wall.
4. Child is in a standing position fixating on a designated point on the wall. Child then jumps and turns completely around (360 degrees) and again fixates on the original point.

Convergence/Divergence
1. Draw two *X*s on the chalkboard (at shoulder height of child) approximately 36 inches apart. Have the child stand centered about 2 inches in front of the board and move his or her eyes back and forth between the two *X*s.
2. Have the child sit at a table and look from an object on the table to an object on the wall directly ahead; continue back-and-forth 10 times. The table should be about 15 inches from the wall.
3. The child sits with arms extended and thumbs up, looking back-and-forth from one thumb to the other.
4. The child sits with one arm extended and the other flexed so that the hand is about 6 inches from the nose with thumbs up. Have the child look back-and-forth from one thumb to the other 10 times.

Visual Tracking
1. The child lies on his or her back. Have the child visually track lines, pipes, or lights on the ceiling, without moving the head.
2. The child lies on his or her back. Attach a small ball to a string and swing the ball horizontally above the child's head. The child should track the swinging ball with his or her

Figure 4-7   Activities That Contribute to the Development of Visual Systems

Figure 4-7   (*Continued*)

eyes and then point to it as it swings. (The ball should be suspended approximately 16 inches above the child's head.)

3. The child throws a ball up in the air and follows the path of the ball with his or her eyes until it hits the floor. Repeat several times and encourage the child not to move his or her head while tracking the ball.

4. The child either sits or lies on his or her back, then hits a suspended ball with the hand and visually tracks the movement of the ball.

Cross-Lateral Integration   Cross-lateral integration is the ability to coordinate the use of both sides of the body. It normally follows the development of balance and laterality. A child who has not developed cross-lateral integration by age eight years is said to have a midline problem because there is difficulty using the hands efficiently at and across the center of the body. Teachers will note the following problems demonstrated by a child with a midline problem:

1. Difficulty using both hands to catch a ball
2. Tendency of eyes to jump when trying to track visually an object that is moving from one side of the body to the other
3. Inability to master a front crawl stroke with breathing while trying to swim
4. Inability to hop rhythmically from one foot to the other
5. Tendency to move the paper to one side of the body when doing paper-and-pencil tasks

Activities that will promote cross-lateral integration are as follows:

1. The child crawls down a rope or line on the floor, crossing hands back-and-forth over the line (rope) going forward, then crossing feet back-and-forth while crawling backward.
2. The child picks up objects (from right side of body) with the right hand and places them in a container on the left side of the body. This should be repeated using the left hand, picking up one object at a time.
3. The child plays pat-a-cake.
4. The child practices swimming the front crawl with breathing.

Body Awareness   Body awareness is a broad concept that includes how people picture their body, attitude toward their body, and knowledge of personal bodily capabilities and limitations. Body awareness develops from all sensory input system information as well as from experiences with the body. Indications of a poorly developed body awareness are

1. Lack of knowledge of where body parts are located
2. Distorted drawings of self
3. Lack of knowledge about what specific body parts are for
4. Poor motor planning

Activities that can be used to facilitate a child's body awareness include

1. Give verbal commands to the child (e.g., touch your knees, touch your ankles, touch your ears, touch your shoulders).
2. Have the child stand with eyes closed. The teacher touches various body parts, and the child identifies them. Then have the child touch the same part that the teacher touches and name the part.
3. Trace an outline of the child's body on a large piece of paper or with chalk on the floor. Then have the child get up and fill in the details (e.g., facial features, clothes, shoes). Perhaps make an "own self" body puzzle. After the child is finished drawing, laminate the body shape; cut it into pieces for the child to reassemble.
   a. Have the child name all the body parts.
   b. Leave out a part and see if the child notices.
   c. Have the child trace around the teacher and name all the body parts.
   d. Have the child trace certain body parts on the drawing with different colors (e.g., yellow for feet, blue for arms).
4. Draw an incomplete picture of a person on the chalkboard and have the child fill in the missing parts.

McLaughlin[8] documented the value of using the bottom-up approach when she followed up on children who were clumsy who had received this type of evaluation and intervention at the University of Kansas Perceptual-Motor Clinic. Before intervention, the children demonstrated varied sensory input and integration processing deficits. One to two years after the deficits had been eliminated and the children were released from the clinic program, every child was demonstrating age-appropriate motor skills.

When attempting to determine whether to use a bottom-up approach in the adapted physical education program, the teacher must again ask, "How much time is available?" The younger the child and the more time available to the teacher, the more appropriate it is to use this strategy. Examples of how each of these two teaching methods are applied to achieve the same principles are given in Tables 4.2 to 4.6.

TABLE 4.2	Teaching Approaches and Their Relation to Growth and Development Principles		
Principle	**Implication**	**Bottom-Up Teaching Approach**	**Top-Down Teaching Approach**
Each individual is unique.	Every child has a different motor profile.	Test for sensory input deficits and intervene to eliminate those before testing and programming for higher-level abilities and skills.	Test for specific functional motor skill deficits. If some are found, probe down into specific abilities that contribute to those skills. If deficits are found, probe down into sensory input areas.
	Every child learns at his or her own rate.	Select activities that appeal to the child and use those until the deficits are eliminated.	Program activities at the highest level of dysfunction. If the child does not learn quickly, probe down into contributing components for deficits.
Children advance from one stage of development to a higher, more complex stage of development.	Activities are selected appropriate to the level of development.	Select activities that are appropriate for the stage of development the child demonstrates.	Select activities specific to the skill deficits the child demonstrates. Begin an intervention program at the developmental level the child demonstrates.
	Progression to the next stage of development depends on physiological maturation and learning.	When a child appears to have mastered one stage of development, select activities appropriate for the next level of development.	When a child masters lower levels of a specific skill, select activities to promote learning of a more complex aspect of that skill.
Children learn when they are ready.	As neurological maturation takes place, we are capable of learning more.	Test from the bottom up and begin instruction with the lowest neurological deficit found.	Analyze a specific task from the top down until the present level of educational performance is found.
	There are critical periods of learning.	It is assumed the child will learn fastest if instruction is begun at the developmental stage at which the child is functioning.	The level of instruction determined by empirical testing verifies that the child is ready to learn.

TABLE 4.2 (*Continued*)			
Principle	**Implication**	**Bottom-Up Teaching Approach**	**Top-Down Teaching Approach**
Development proceeds from simple to complex.	Development begins with simple movements that eventually combine with other movements to form patterns.	Eliminate reflex and sensory input delays before teaching higher-level abilities and skills.	Functional skill deficits are identified. The pattern of the skill is analyzed to determine contributing components. Behavioral programs are constructed and implemented to develop pattern deficits.
	Development progresses from large to small movements (from gross to fine patterns).	Promote reflex and vestibular development to stabilize balance. Once balance becomes automatic, control of the limbs will follow.	Program to synthesize patterns that contribute to a specific skill.

Physical Fitness

Techniques for evaluating various aspects of physical fitness and teaching strategies to use are discussed in Chapter 8. As you read that material and observe individuals performing activities to evaluate or promote physical fitness, keep in mind the impact of the primitive reflexes as well as the kinesthetic system on performance. Recall that individuals who have difficulty demonstrating a sit-up may have a persisting trace of a tonic labyrinthine supine reflex which interferes with flexion of the head and trunk. Individuals having difficulty with a push-up may have a persisting trace of a tonic labyrinthine prone reflex which promotes flexion when a person is in a "belly down" position.

A well-functioning kinesthetic system is critical to muscle tone. If the muscle spindles are not continually firing and sending impulses to the central nervous system, definition (firm shape) of the muscle will be lacking.

Motor Fitness

Agility, power, speed, and coordination are the four components of motor fitness. Agility, the ability to

A young man learns to walk using prostheses.
Courtesy of Orthotic & Prosthetic Athletic Assistance Fund, Inc., Alexandria, VA.

TABLE 4.3	Teaching Approaches and Their Relation to the Generalization Process*		
Principle	**Implication**	**Bottom-Up Teaching Approach**	**Top-Down Teaching Approach**
Generalization procedures	Activities to promote generalization are selected in particular ways.	Activity is selected to develop sensory input systems, reflexes, and abilities that are believed to be prerequisite to many skills that could be used in a variety of environments.	Functional age-appropriate activities are selected to promote appropriate skills in a variety of natural environments.
Generalization process	There is a degree to which the learning environment matches the natural environment.	At the basic levels (reflexes, sensory inputs, and abilities), the environment is controlled only to ensure that the basics are learned. No attention is paid to the type of environment the eventual skills will be used in.	Skills are practiced in environments that correspond closely to the environment in which the skill will be used (e.g., practice shooting baskets in the gym).
Retention	The more meaningful the skill, the longer it is remembered.	It is believed that, once basic reflexes, sensory input systems, and abilities emerge, they remain stable (unless the child is traumatized in some way).	Activities are reviewed immediately after a lesson and then periodically to ensure retention.
Overlearning	Overlearning occurs when a skill or activity is practiced after it has been learned.	Overlearning occurs as the basic levels are interwoven into higher skill levels.	Ability levels prerequisite to skills should be substantially greater than minimum entry requirements needed to fulfill the needs of the task.

*A task is not considered learned until it can be demonstrated in a variety of environments.

change position in space quickly and accurately, is dependent on the visual, kinesthetic, and vestibular systems. Should any of these systems be delayed, agility is compromised.

Power, or explosive strength, requires the ability to rapidly contract and coordinate muscles to per-form to maximum effort.[4] Power is frequently evaluated by using a standing long jump. Thus, strength is a primary contributor to power. When the standing long jump is used to measure power, the physical educator is reminded that strength of the hip ad- and abductor muscles as well as the quadriceps

		TABLE 4.4 The Relation of Teaching Approaches to Attention of the Learner	

Principle	Implication	Bottom-Up Teaching Approach	Top-Down Teaching Approach
Get the attention of the learner.	Help the child attend to relevant rather than irrelevant cues.	Permit the child to participate in a free activity of his or her choice each day if the child enters the room and immediately focuses on the beginning task.	Keep bats, balls, and other play equipment out of sight until time of use.
	Give a signal (sometimes called a "ready signal") that indicates a task is to begin.	Structure each day's lesson the same way so the child knows that, when a given activity ends, the next activity will begin.	Teach the child precise signals that indicate a task should begin.
Provide the appropriate stimulation.	Stimulate the child to focus on the desired learning task.	Make the activities enjoyable so that the child will want to continue the task.	Use precise, detailed instruction that is designed around eliciting attention through the use of the following hierarchy: 1. Visual or verbal input only 2. Combined visual and verbal input 3. Combined visual, verbal, and kinesthetic instruction

greatly impact that movement. The stronger the hip stabilizers and flexors, the greater the distance jumped. In addition to muscular strength, good kinesthetic and vestibular information, as well as the absence of the negative support primitive reflex, is critical to jumping performance.

Speed is the ability to move quickly in a short period of time. Speed is dependent on reaction time and movement time. Thus, the time it takes to hear and respond to a signal, as well as how quickly a person moves after initiating the movement, is critical to speed. Speed is frequently measured using a 50-yard dash. Obviously, a person will be

able to demonstrate greater speed if the vestibular, kinesthetic, and auditory systems are fully functioning; the primitive reflexes are integrated; and the equilibrium reflexes are well developed. Speed is also dependent on the number of fast twitch muscle fibers that can be recruited during the movement. Fast twitch muscle fibers are believed to be genetically determined.

Coordination is "the ability to integrate separate motor systems with varying sensory modalities into efficient patterns of movement."[4] To demonstrate coordination, individuals are required to perform a series of moves accurately

TABLE 4.5	Managing the Instructional Environment Through Teaching Approaches		
Principle	**Implication**	**Bottom-Up Teaching Approach**	**Top-Down Teaching Approach**
Impose limits for use of equipment, facilities, and student conduct.	Children should learn to adhere to rules that are necessary in a social context.	Students are not permitted access to equipment and areas unless they have been given permission by the teacher.	The equipment and facilities a student has access to are specified in the behavioral program.
Control the social interaction among children.	Inappropriate social behavior among children may disrupt class instruction.	The teacher must consider the performance level and emotional stability of each child when grouping children for activities.	Tasks and environments are structured to reduce adverse interaction with peers.
Do not strive for control in all situations.	Children with disabilities must develop social skills that will promote social interaction in the natural environment. For this to occur, students must have an opportunity to adjust to situations independent from supervision or with minimum supervision.	Select activities that will meet the long-range goals of the students and promote social interaction. Pair children so that their interaction contributes to both students' objectives—for example, a child who needs kinesthetic stimulation might be given the task of pulling a child who needs to ride a scooter for tonic labyrinthine prone inhibition.	The students are permitted to interact with others as long as progress toward short-term objectives is occurring.

and quickly. Gross motor coordination involves the whole body; thus, balance, agility, and rhythm must be synchronized to enable a smooth, efficient movement pattern. Hand-eye and foot-eye coordination requires the ability to use visual information, muscular control, and kinesthetic information while maintaining balance. Should any one of the visual, kinesthetic, or vestibular systems or the primitive or equilibrium reflexes be compromised, the efficiency of the movement is impacted.

PROGRAMMED INSTRUCTION

Instructional strategies are the ways to arrange an educational environment so that maximum learning will take place. Instructional strategies discussed thus far are the task-specific, top-down approach and the developmental, bottom-up approach. A third approach, which will be discussed in this section, is programmed instruction. Factors that affect the type of instructional strategy selected include the amount of time available, the

		Bottom-Up Teaching	Top-Down Teaching
TABLE 4.6	**Nature of Activity and Quality of Experience as They Relate to Two Teaching Approaches**		
Principle	Implication	Bottom-Up Teaching Approach	Top-Down Teaching Approach
Learning occurs best when goals and objectives are clear.	Clear goals provide incentives for children to learn.	The desired outcome is clear to the teacher (e.g., 5 seconds of postrotatory nystagmus). The child may be advised of another goal (e.g., stay on the spinning scooter until it stops).	The goal and ongoing measurement of the attainment of the objectives that lead to the goal are shared by the teacher and the child.
Actively involve the student in the learning process.	The greater the amount of learning time and the lesser the amount of dead time, the more learning will occur.	The child stays active because activities that are enjoyable to the child are selected.	When and if the child learns to self-instruct and self-evaluate or do so with the help of peer tutors, the student will be active through-out the period. The well-managed class will have children work on nonspecific activities when not participating in behavioral programs.
Discourage stereotyped play activities that develop rigid behaviors.	Permitting children to participate in the same activity day after day deters learning.	The teacher must initiate new activities as soon as lack of progress is evidenced.	The ongoing collection of data makes lack of progress immediately apparent to the teacher and the child and serves notice that the activity should be changed.
Program more for success than failure.	Every satisfying experience decreases anxiety and increases confidence.	The teacher selects activities the child enjoys and from which the child gains a feeling of accomplishment.	The increment of the step sizes in the behavioral program is constantly modified to match the ability of the learner.

age and readiness level of the learner, the capabilities of the physical education teacher, and the number of persons available to assist in the educational process. An instructional strategy that meets the needs of a wide range of learners and that can be delivered by a limited number of personnel is more valuable for ensuring that individual needs are met than is a strategy that presumes homogeneous grouping. For learners with disabilities who have heterogeneous needs, an instructional

Gardening is an excellent leisure activity.
Courtesy of Orthomerica Products, Inc., New Port Beach, CA.

strategy that promotes individualized learning is not only desirable but absolutely necessary. See Figure 4-8 for an example of a standard teaching sequence.

Individualization of instruction can be realized through the use of programmed instruction. The major goals of programmed instruction are to promote students' abilities to direct their own learning and to develop a communication system between the student and teacher that enables them to become independent of each other. The teacher's primary goals are to guide and manage instruction according to the student's individual needs and learning characteristics. The programmed instruction approach enables a teacher to cope with heterogeneous groups of children and to accommodate large numbers of children in the same class without sacrificing instructional efficiency.

The most expeditious way to manage an average-size class in a public school, using the individualized approach, is by using a variety of stations arranged around the gymnasium, with a different activity performed at each station. Each activity is graduated from simpler moves to more demanding requirements. The needs of individual children are determined ahead of time, and each child performs only the level of the activity that is appropriate for that student. Self-instructional and self-evaluative materials composed of a prearranged series of objectives help students develop skills at their own rates.

Specific examples of techniques to provide appropriate inclusive environments for students with disabilities are included in Chapter 5, "Delivering Services in the Most Inclusive Environment."

FUNCTIONAL ADAPTATIONS

Functional adaptations are modifications such as using an assistive device, changing the demands of the task, or changing the rules to permit students with disabilities to participate. Making functional adaptations in accordance with a child's needs may enable immediate participation in age-appropriate activities selected to enhance specific skills. Following is a list of functional adaptations for children with physical, sensory, or motor deficits:

- Children who are blind can receive auditory or tactual clues to help them locate objects or position their bodies in the activity area.
- Individuals who are blind read through touch and can be instructed in appropriate movement patterns through manual kinesthetic guidance (i.e., the instructor manually moves the student through the correct pattern) or verbal instructions.
- Children who are deaf can learn to read lips or learn signing, so that they understand the instructions for an activity.
- Children with physical disabilities may have to use walkers, wheelchairs, or crutches during their physical education class.

STANDARD TEACHING SEQUENCE

The system requires only that the teacher note the child's progress using the following symbols: X = the steps (activities) in the standard teaching sequence that can be mastered by the student, in this case step nos. 1, 2, 3, and 4; / = immediate short-term instruction objective, in this case no. 5;* = goal, in this case no. 18. All behaviors between the present level (/) and the goal (*) are potential objectives (6 to 18).

Walks unsupported (step no.): X̶ X̶ X̶ X̶ 5̶ 6 7 8 9 10 11 12 13 14 15 16 17 18*19 20 21 22 23 24 25 26

Two-footed standing broad jump

Type of program: Shifting criterion
Conditions
1. Both feet remain behind restraining line before takeoff.
2. Take off from two feet.
3. Land on two feet.
4. Measure from the restraining line to the tip of the toe of the least advanced foot.
Measurement: Distance in inches.

Two-footed standing broad jump (inches)	60	62	64	6̶6̶	6̶8̶	7̶0̶	7̶2̶	74	76	78	80	82*	84
Date mastered				9/7	9/21	10/5							

The scoring procedure of the ongoing development of the person would be explained as follows. The program that the child is participating in is the two-footed standing broad jump. The child began the program at an initial performance level of 66 inches on September 7 and increased performance by 4 inches between September 7 and October 5. Thus, the present level of educational performance is 70 inches (note the last number with an X over it). The child will attempt to jump a distance of 72 inches (immediate short-term objective) until he or she masters that distance. The child will continue to progress toward the goal, which is 82 inches (note the asterisk). It is a mistake in the applications of learning principles to ask the child to jump the 82 inches when it is known that the goal far exceeds the present level of educational performance. Unreasonable instructional demands from the learner by the teacher violate the principle of learning in small steps, which guarantees success for the child.

The same procedure could be used when teaching a child to throw a ball for accuracy. In the following example, a shifting condition program is used. For instance, two hierarchies that are known in throwing for accuracy are the size of the target and the distance between the thrower and the target. Thus, a standard teaching sequence might be similar to the following sequence of potential objectives: demonstrate the ability to throw a 4-inch ball a distance of ___ feet and hit a target that is ___ feet square five out of five times.

Throwing for accuracy

Type of program: Shifting condition
Conditions
1. Remain behind the restraining line at all times.
2. Complete an overhand throw (ball released above the shoulder).
3. If the ball hits any part of the target, it is a successful throw.

Figure 4-8   Standard Teaching Sequence

STANDARD TEACHING SEQUENCE—cont'd

The previous information would be contained in a curriculum book. However, the specific standard teaching sequence would be placed on a bulletin board at the performance area in the gymnasium. This would enable the performer to read his or her own instructional objective. The measurement of the performer's placement in the standard teaching sequence would be indicated on the prescription sheet.

Criterion for mastery: Three successful hits out of three.

DISTANCE OF THROW	SIZE OF TARGET	DISTANCE OF THROW	SIZE OF TARGET
Step 1. 6 feet	3 feet square	Step 10. 18 feet	2 feet square
Step 2. 9 feet	3 feet square	Step 11. 21 feet	2 feet square
Step 3. 12 feet	3 feet square	Step 12. 24 feet	2 feet square
Step 4. 15 feet	3 feet square	Step 13. 27 feet	2 feet square
Step 5. 18 feet	3 feet square	Step 14. 30 feet	2 feet square
Step 6. 21 feet	3 feet square	Step 15. 21 feet	1 foot square
Step 7. 24 feet	3 feet square	Step 16. 24 feet	1 foot square
Step 8. 27 feet	3 feet square	Step 17. 27 feet	1 foot square
Step 9. 30 feet	3 feet square	Step 18. 30 feet	1 foot square

The steps of the standard teaching sequence can be reduced and tasks can be added that are more or less complex as the situation requires.

STUDENT RECORDING SHEET

Throwing for accuracy (step no.)	X	X	X	X	X	6	7	8	9	10	11	12	13	14*	15	16	17	18
Date mastered																		

Figure 4-8   (*Continued*)

- A child with asthma may be permitted to play goalie in a soccer game, which requires smaller cardiovascular demands than the running positions.
- Rules may be changed to accommodate the variety of ability levels demonstrated by children in the class (see Chapter 5, "Delivering Services in the Most Inclusive Environment").
- A buddy, peer tutor, or paraprofessional may be assigned to assist the student with special needs execute the required moves or stay on task.

In these examples, functional adaptations are necessary for the student with a disability to participate in chronologically age-appropriate physical education activities. The approach is most beneficial when the only motor prerequisites lacking are those that are a result of the student's disabling condition or when including the student to promote social interaction.

GENERALIZATION TO COMMUNITY ENVIRONMENTS

Time spent teaching skills in physical education training settings is wasted if the individual with disabilities cannot demonstrate competency in sport and recreation settings other than the schools and in the presence of persons other than the original teachers.[1] To ensure that generalization to community environments and activities does occur, simulated training conditions need to be developed. Although there are few studies in physical education that have examined the generalization of motor skill and sport performance from instructional to community environments, Budoff[2] indicates positive results of softball training of mentally retarded persons in integrated community environments. On the other hand, the literature on simulated settings versus training in the applied settings on nonphysical education tasks is mixed. It is critical that instruction not cease until the individual uses the new skills spontaneously and correctly in the community.

COMMERCIAL PROGRAMS

Since 1980, several physical and motor programs have been made available commercially. The achievement-based curriculum development in physical education (I CAN),[11] the Data-based Gymnasium,[3] and Mobility Opportunities Via Education (MOVE)[6] are excellent examples of commercial programs specifically developed to promote physical and motor capability.

Modified sports equipment opens the world to individuals with disabilities.
Courtesy of Challenge Aspen, Aspen, CO.

REPORTING THE RESULTS TO PARENTS

Parents should always be informed of their children's educational performance levels and the goals and objectives of the school curricula. IDEA requires that the parents be apprised of the educational status of their children and approve the IEP that has been designed for them. When the procedures described in this chapter are followed by the teacher and the information shared with the parents, there will be no question about the educational process. Parents may question whether appropriate goals have been selected for their children, but usually, when evaluation results and the importance of their child's achieving as normal a performance level as possible are explained, parents agree with the professional educator's opinion.

It is important to point out to the parents their child's specific deficiencies and how those deficiencies interfere with the child's functional ability. Wherever possible, basic level and integrative process deficiencies should be linked to skill performance. That is, the educator should explain not only what deficits exist but also how those deficits relate to the child's present and future levels of performance ability. Once parents understand these relationships, they usually endorse the school's efforts on behalf of their children. In addition to

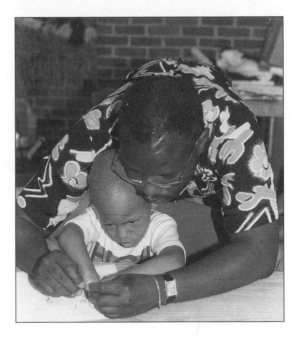

A creative teacher helps a child with no fingers enjoy arts and crafts.
Courtesy Dallas Independent School District.

pointing out a child's deficiencies, it is important to tell the parent about areas of strength their child has demonstrated. Parents of children with disabilities need to hear positive reports as frequently as possible. Do not overlook that need.

SUMMARY

Physical educators have traditionally included exercises, individual stunts and tumbling, games, sports, rhythmic activities, and gymnastics in their curricula. Often these activities are selected according to teacher bias. More recently, teachers have been sensitized to the need to provide appropriate learning environments for students who demonstrate a wide range of abilities. These teachers are exercising greater care in selecting meaningful activities to include in their programs. Even when following a set curriculum, more attention is being

paid to selecting activities that will meet a variety of learners' demonstrated needs.

The goal of a physical education program for students with disabilities is the development of motor behaviors that assist ultimate functional responses in the community environments. Maximizing performance of the many specific skills of the physical education curriculum is the unique role of the adapted physical educator. Individuals with disabilities often possess limited motor skills. Thus, the physical educator must determine which skills are needed and select appropriate intervention strategies to ensure that learning occurs. Teaching specific skills, fostering developmental sequences, and using programmed instruction are three acceptable intervention strategies. The amount of time available, the age and readiness of the learner, the capabilities of the physical education teacher, and the number of persons available to assist with the class dictate which intervention strategy to use. Regardless of the teaching approach used, functional adaptations may need to be made to enable the student to gain from the intervention strategy.

REVIEW QUESTIONS

1. What is the relationship between specific functional motor skills and the integrative process categories?

2. What are some examples of making functional adaptations for age-appropriate motor skills, and what are arguments for and against such functional adaptations?

3. Identify three perceptual-motor abilities.

4. What are the differences between bottom-up (developmental) and top-down (task-specific) approaches?

5. Name two sensory input systems, two categories of integration processes, and two specific skills.

6. What is incidental learning? Why are some children with disabilities unable to learn as much through incidental learning as children without disabilities?

STUDENT ACTIVITIES

1. Talk with adapted physical education teachers about how they determine what objectives and activities to use with their students with disabilities. Try to decide whether the teachers are using a top-down, bottom-up, or programmed instruction teaching approach.

2. Observe a physical education class that includes students with and without disabilities. Make a list of the functional adaptations used during the class. Select the two adaptations you believe aided the children most and tell why those adaptations were so helpful.

3. Conduct a content analysis of one functional skill and one sport skill. Identify each component required to successfully perform each of the skills.

4. Break the class into small discussion groups and have them share their bottom-up and top-down teaching approach suggestions for Maria's class with one another. Have each group agree on two suggestions for each teaching approach, and share them with the rest of the class.

5. Develop a task analysis of a specific sport skill.

REFERENCES

1. Billingsley F: Where are the generalized outcomes? An examination of instructional objectives, *J Assoc Persons Severe Handic* 9:186–192, 1984.

2. Budoff M: *The Massachusetts mixed softball league: a final report to Special Olympics International, Washington, DC,* Cambridge, MA, 1987, Research Institute for Educational Problems.

3. Dunn JM, Frederick H: *Physical education for the severely handicapped: a systematic approach to a data based gymnasium,* Austin, TX, 1985, PRO-ED.

4. Gallahue DL, Ozmun JC: *Understanding motor development,* Dubuque, IA, 1995, McGraw-Hill.

5. Horak FB, Henry SM, Shumway-Cook A: Postural perturbations: new insights for

treatment of balance disorders, *Physical Therapy* 77:517–533, 1997.

6. Kern County Superintendent of Schools: *Mobility opportunities via education,* Bakersfield, CA, 1990, Author.

7. Kohen-Raz R: *Learning disabilities and postural control,* London, 1986, Freund.

8. McLaughlin E: Follow-up study on children remediated for perceptual-motor dysfunction at the University of Kansas perceptual motor clinic, Unpublished master's thesis, 1980, University of Kansas.

9. Quiros JB, Schrager OL: *Neuropsychological fundamentals in learning disabilities,* San Rafael, CA, 1979, Academic Therapy.

10. Thelen, E: Motor development: a new synthesis, American Psychologist 50:79–95, 1995.

11. Wessel JA, Kelly L: *Achievement-based curriculum development in physical education,* Philadelphia, 1986, Lea & Febiger.

12. Westcott SL, Lowes, LP, Richardson, PK: Evaluation of postural stability in children: current theories and assessment tools, *Physical Therapy* 77:629–645, 1997.

Suggested Readings

Pyfer J: Teachers, don't let your students grow up to be clumsy adults, *J Phys Educ Rec Dance* 59:38–42, 1988.

Seaman JA, DePauw K: *The new adapted physical education,* Palo Alto, CA, 1989, Mayfield.

Wessel JA, Kelly L: *Achievement-based curriculum development in physical education,* Philadelphia, 1986, Lea & Febiger.

5

Delivering Services in the Most Inclusive Environment

All children can play together.
Courtesy of Sportime, Atlanta, GA.

■ OBJECTIVES

Define inclusion.

Suggest strategies for preparing the school and community for inclusion.

Describe the eight instructional variables that can be modified to accommodate a learner with a disability in the least restrictive environment.

Evaluate an existing physical education program to determine its appropriateness for students with disabilities.

Describe inclusive community-based leisure, recreation, and sports programs.

Explain strategies for embracing all learners within a school community.

The very good news is that physical education for students with disabilities was retained as a federally mandated, direct educational service, a vital component of special education in the Reauthorization of IDEA, 1997. Physical education remains the *only* educational service specifically listed in the definition of special education, a significant testimony to the efforts of devoted lobbyists committed to physical education, wellness, and a quality life full of meaningful leisure, recreation, and sport activities, professionals like Dr. David Auxter. [Thank you, Dave . . .]

CASE STUDY

Maria Garcia

Review Maria's IEP and the suggested modifications/ adaptations which the general physical educator might use to teach Maria and help her accomplish her IEP goals and objectives (see Chapter 3).

APPLICATION TASK

Describe the types of activities in which Maria is most likely to be successful in junior high and high school physical education. Describe the types of activities in which Maria is likely to struggle.

INCLUSION: THE CONTROVERSY CONTINUES

There are strong and passionate voices that support the inclusion of students with disabilities in the general education program and equally strong and passionate voices that believe the concept of least restrictive environment, if appropriately implemented, better addresses the unique needs of learners with disabilities. Judith Heumann, assistant secretary of the Office of Special Education and Rehabilitation Services (OSERS), an individual who has experienced firsthand discrimination because of her disability, spoke at the fifteenth National Institute on Legal Issues of Education for Individuals with Disabilities, May 1994. One of the most outspoken and articulate advocates of inclusion for individuals with disabilities at all levels, she paraphrased the famous words of Dr. Martin Luther King, Jr.

> Let us never succumb to the temptation of believing that legislation and judicial decree play only a minor role in solving problems. Morality cannot be legislated . . . but behavior can be regulated. Judicial decrees may not change the heart . . . but they can restrain the heartless. The law cannot make an employer love an employee or a teacher love a student . . . but it can prevent him/her from

refusing to hire me or teach me because of the color of my skin or my disabilities.[135]

Several of the major organizations that serve individuals with disabilities and their families have taken a stand in favor of inclusion. The delegate body of the ARC of the United States (formerly the Association for Retarded Citizens) adopted a position statement on "inclusion" in October 1995. It said,

> All people, with or without mental retardation, have the right to be fully included in their diverse communities. Children with mental retardation should:
> - live in a family;
> - grow up enjoying nurturing adult relationships both inside and outside a family;
> - learn in their neighborhood school in a regular classroom that contains children without disabilities;
> - play and participate with children, with and without disabilities, in community recreation and other leisure activities.[5]

TASH, the vocal and primary advocate for students with severe disabilities, formerly The Association for Individuals with Severe Handicaps, reaffirmed an earlier resolution in December 1993. In part, the TASH resolution stated:

> WHEREAS the democratic ideals of American society can be best served and protected when diversity is highly valued and seen as the norm in all schools; when ALL students are viewed as active, fully participating members of the school community; and when the reciprocal benefits of full inclusion for all students is understood and celebrated;
>
> BE IT RESOLVED that TASH reaffirms a definition of inclusion that begins with the educational and moral imperatives that students with disabilities belong in general education classrooms and that they receive the supports and services necessary to benefit from their education in the general education setting. Inclusion . . . is fully defined by a new way of thinking based upon current understandings about how ALL children and young people are educated—a new way of thinking that embraces a sociology of acceptance of ALL

children into the school community as active, fully participating members, that views diversity as the norm and maintains a high quality education for each student by assuring effective teaching, powerful pedagogies and necessary supports to each child in the general education setting.[116]

United Cerebral Palsy Associations, Inc., adopted a similar policy statement in 1993:

In the past two decades participation by individuals with disabilities in the activities of our nation has greatly enriched society as a whole. Yet, people with disabilities as a group still occupy an inferior status in our society; are severely disadvantaged socially, educationally, vocationally, and economically; and are segregated and relegated to lesser services, programs, activities, benefits and jobs. . . .

UCPA and its affiliate organizations support the goal of full inclusion of individuals with disabilities into every aspect of life and area of society, including the home, the school, the workforce and the community, regardless of severity of disability, as enumerated in the Americans with Disabilities Act.[125]

The organizations and individuals most ardent in support of inclusion as a philosophy and as an educational practice believe inclusion, educational equity, to be a fundamental right of children. McNulty et al. wrote,

Inclusive education requires a change in basic philosophy, from allowing "diverse" learners to enter a classroom to welcoming all students to share their gifts and learn with their peers. . . . However, if we can welcome and value all children, we can begin to address the real issue —excellence. How do we raise our expectations for all children? How do we hold ourselves accountable for elevating performance for all children? How do we ensure that all children have access to the "American dream"?[76]

Many professionals and advocates for learners with disabilities feel, with equal passion, that their unique educational needs cannot be met unless a continuum of service options are available, the

original intent of P.L. 94-142 and the continued intent of the Individuals with Disabilities Education Act. The major national organization which addresses the needs of children with disabilities, the Council for Exceptional Children, has adopted a stance in favor of the use/application of the least restrictive environment mandates of the federal law while acknowledging that inclusion is an ideal. The Council for Exceptional Children statement, in part, reads:

The Council for Exceptional Children believes all children, youth, and young adults with disabilities are entitled to a free and appropriate education and/or services that lead to an adult life characterized by satisfying relations with others, independent living, productive engagement in the community, and participation in society at large. To achieve such outcomes, there must exist for all children, youth, and young adults a rich variety of early intervention, educational, and vocational program options and experiences. Access to these programs and experiences should be based on individual educational need and desired outcomes. Furthermore, students and their families or guardians, as members of the planning team, may recommend the placement, curriculum option, and the exit document to be pursued.

CEC believes that a continuum of services must be available for all children, youth, and young adults. CEC also believes that the concept of inclusion is a meaningful goal to be pursued in our schools and communities. In addition, CEC believes children, youth, and young adults with disabilities should be served whenever possible in general education classrooms in inclusive neighborhood schools and community settings. Such settings should be strengthened and supported by an infusion of specially trained personnel and other appropriate supportive practices according to the individual needs of the child.[18]

While the Council for Exceptional Children retained a focus on the continuum of placements and services guaranteed by the least restrictive environment (LRE) mandates of the federal law, the Learning Disabilities Association, in a 1993 position paper, took a strong stand against inclusion for all students. The paper states,

> The Learning Disabilities Association of America does not support "full inclusion" or any policies that mandate the same placement, instruction, or treatment for ALL students with learning disabilities.[66]

The American Foundation for the Blind has also gone on record as affirming the necessity of implementing the least restrictive environment continuum of options. In its paper "Educating Students with Visual Impairments for Inclusion in Society," the committee wrote,

> There must be a full range of program options and support services so that the Individualized Education Program (IEP) Team can select the most appropriate placement in the least restrictive environment for each individual student with a visual impairment.[2]

The National Education Association (NEA), the nation's largest teacher organization, adopted a policy statement at its national convention in 1994 that supported and encouraged "appropriate inclusion." The statement, in part, reads as follows:

> The NEA is committed to equal educational opportunity, the highest quality education, and a safe learning environment for all students. The Association supports and encourages appropriate inclusion. Appropriate inclusion is characterized by practices and programs that provide for the following on a sustained basis:
> • A full continuum of placement options and services within each option. Placement and services must be determined for each student by a team that includes all stakeholders and must be specified in the IEP.
> • Appropriate professional development. . . .
> • Adequate time, as part of the normal school day, to engage in coordinated and collaborative planning on behalf of all students.
> • Class sizes that are responsive to student needs.
> • Staff and technical assistance that is specifically appropriate to student and teacher needs.

EMPHASIS ON EDUCATION WITHIN THE GENERAL EDUCATION PROGRAM

Like many social and educational movements, the trend toward including children with disabilities in the general education program has developed a momentum all its own. See Figure 5-1, which summarizes the relationship between inclusion and educational reform. The supporters of inclusion, particularly those committed to educational equity as an educational reform, have been very vocal. Indeed, it is the parents who believe their children should be included that continue to test the schools and, subsequently, the courts that interpret federal policy.

The basis of the trend toward inclusion is a widespread educational reform movement which challenges the public schools to meet the needs of its diverse students. Turner and Louis wrote,

> The common patterns of social responses to difference suggest that the goal of creating inclusive schools should not focus on the needs or concerns of students with disabilities. Instead, issues related to disability should be embedded in the broader context of difference and similarity. Only when we recognize the value of all differences that children bring to school will we be in a position to move toward the goal of cultural citizenship for a diverse society.[123]

However, those who fear that widespread inclusion may actually reverse the trend toward carefully designed, individual education programs for learners with disabilities are fearful of the movement.

Figure 5-1   Inclusion and Education Reform

Inclusion appears consistent with school restructuring and school reform movements:
• Detracking[70]
• Community schools
• Multicultural education
• Integrated curriculum[70]
• Emphasis on increased standards of excellence

Pugach wrote, "But inclusion poses a much greater challenge than conventional mainstreaming because it threatens the perceived safety net of traditional special education services within the public schools—although not everyone who supports inclusion, myself included, believes that all special education services should be dismantled."[92]

Federal Law

Congressional mandates regarding the education of children with disabilities has not changed appreciably since the passage of P.L. 94-142. The emphasis and interpretation of the law changed in the last twenty-five years of the twentieth century. These changes are a result of intense feelings of parents, professionals, and advocates who believe that children with and without disabilities should be educated together and learn and share together.

The inclusion movement has evolved because of the significant efforts of parents, professionals, and advocates devoted to the right to educational equity of children with disabilities.

The interpretation of the least restrictive environment mandates in the Reauthorization of the Individuals with Disabilities Education Act of 1997 appears to place the emphasis on the education of students with disabilities within the general education program using the general education curriculum.[122] The sections of the Reauthorization of IDEA that have a significant impact on the inclusion of children with disabilities in the general curriculum are underlined.

- The individual education program for each child with a disability must include a statement of the child's present level of educational performance, including how the child's disability affects the child's involvement and progress and involvement in the general curriculum.
- A statement of measurable annual goals related to meeting the child's needs that result from the child's disability to enable the child to be involved in and progress in the general curriculum.

- A statement of the special education and related services and supplementary aids and services.
- A statement of the program modifications or supports for school personnel that will be provided for the child to advance appropriately toward attaining the annual goals, to be involved and progress in the general curriculum, to participate in extracurricular and other nonacademic activities, and to be educated and participate with other children with disabilities and children without disabilities.
- States and local education agencies must provide for the participation of children with disabilities in general state and districtwide assessments—with appropriate accommodations and modifications in administration, if necessary.
- A general educator must be part of the IEP/multidisciplinary team if the child is to spend any of his or her time in the general education program.
- Each of the child's teachers, including the general education teacher(s) and provider(s), must be informed of his or her responsibilities related to implementing the child's IEP and the specific accommodations, modifications, and supports that must be provided for the child. This includes the physical education teacher.

See Figure 5-2, which outlines the potential benefits of inclusion.

Description of Placement Settings for Students with Disabilities

The Reports to Congress, Office of Special Education Programs, 1997, describe placement options as follows:

- General education class. Students who receive special education and related services outside of the general education classroom for less than 21 percent of the school day
- Resource room. Students who receive special education and related services outside the general education classroom for 21 percent to 60 percent of the school day

Figure 5-2   Benefits of Inclusion

- Improved social development for children without disabilities who are educated in inclusive classrooms[114]
- Improved social development for children with disabilities who are educated in inclusive classrooms, including[20,67,127]
  - Getting along with others
  - Interacting
  - Seeking assistance and lending assistance
  - Moving from one context to another
  - Asking questions
- KIIngner et al. wrote, "Students (LD) distinguished between the social benefits and the academic benefits of inclusion. The consensus was that pull-out was preferable for learning but inclusion was better for making friends."

Figure 5-3   Least Restrictive Environment Determination, as Mandated by the Courts[137]

School district determinations regarding the LRE should be based on the following:
- Has the school taken necessary steps to maintain the child in the general classroom?
  - What supplementary aids and services were used?
  - What interventions were attempted?
  - How many interventions were attempted?
- Benefits of placement in general education (with supplementary aids and services) vs. special education
  - Academic benefits
  - Nonacademic benefits (e.g., social, communication, peer-model)
- Effects on the education of other students
  - Is the education of other students adversely affected (e.g., if the student is disruptive)?
  - Does the student require a great deal of attention from the teacher, compromising the education of the other children?
- If the student is being educated in a setting other than the general classroom, is he or she interacting with peers without disabilities to the maximum extent appropriate?
  - In what academic settings is the student integrated with peers without disabilities?
  - In what nonacademic settings is the child integrated with peers without disabilities?
- Is the entire continuum of alternative services available?

- Separate class. Students who receive special education and related services outside of the general education classroom for more than 60 percent of the school day
- Separate school. Students who receive special education and related services in separate day schools (more than 50 percent of the school day), residential facilities (more than 50 percent of the school day), or homebound/hospital environments[4]

Essentially, placement practices differ widely across the nation, across states, and within local school districts. It appears that where a student lives is the major determining factor in his or her placement.[74] McClesky and Henry[75] developed a technique to evaluate the inclusion practices of states based on the placement of children with disabilities in the schools. Vermont had a Total Inclusion Index of 81, reflecting placements in the least restrictive environment. The District of Columbia had a Total Inclusion Index of −38, reflecting more placements in segregated learning environments.[74] They found that nine states rank among the top 25 percent in both educating students in general education classrooms and moving students out of restrictive, separate class, and separate school settings. These are

Vermont, North Dakota, Oregon, Colorado, Idaho, South Dakota, Minnesota, Alaska, and Iowa.

The Direction of the Courts

Since the early 1970s, the courts have led the country toward educational equity. See Figure 5-3, which includes the courts' interpretation regarding the least restrictive environment.

In *Pennsylvania Association of Retarded Citizens v. Commonwealth of Pennsylvania* (1972), the decision of the court was that

> . . . placement in a regular public school class is preferable to placement in a special public

school class and placement in a special public school class is preferable to placement in any other type of program.[76]

Many advocates of inclusion believe that inclusion is an educational reform which is a critical right assured by the Fourteenth Amendment of the Constitution of the United States. Wang and Reynolds wrote,

> We consider it a great moral victory for our society that wave after wave of legislative action has affirmed the right of all children—even those who are most difficult to teach—to an education that is inclusive and beneficial for each individual child. The universal right to education is now more than a rhetorical tradition; it is becoming a legal reality.[130]

Following are the summary decisions of major court cases which have had an impact on the education of learners with disabilities.

Daniel R.R. v. State Board of Education, 1989

Yell wrote, regarding *Daniel R.R. v. State Board of Education,* 1989,

> The Daniel R.R. court said it is then necessary to determine whether the child will receive educational benefit from regular class placement. The school must determine if the student will be able to understand the essential elements of the curriculum. This inquiry must extend beyond academics to the entire educational experience (e.g., social benefits).[137]

The 5th Circuit Court asked two main questions about mainstreaming with four subquestions:

1. Can education in the regular classroom, with the use of supplemental aids and services, be achieved satisfactorily for a given child?
   a. Has the state taken steps to accommodate children with disabilities in regular education, and, if so, are these efforts sufficient and within reason?
   b. Will the child receive an educational benefit from regular education? The Court says that "academic achievement is not the only purpose of mainstreaming. Integrating a handicapped child into a nonhandicapped environment may be beneficial in and of itself . . . even if the child cannot flourish academically."
   c. Is there any detriment to the child from the proposed mainstreaming?
   d. What effect will the presence of a child with a disability have on the regular classroom environment and on the education of the other students?
2. Has the child been mainstreamed to the maximum extent appropriate (this must occur if the decision is to remove the child from the regular education environment for a portion of the day).[65]

Greer v. Rome City School District, 1991

The Court found that the determination of LRE must be an individualized, fact-specific inquiry that includes a careful examination of the nature and severity of the child's particular disability and of his or her needs and abilities. This case further clarified the *Daniel R.R.* interpretation when Christy Greer's parents filed a law suit because they said school officials failed to consider the full range of supplemental aids and services. Instead, they said the school determined Christy's "severe impairment" justified placement in a self-contained special education classroom. The Court sided with the parents and said the school had made no effort to modify the kindergarten curriculum to accommodate Christy in the regular classroom. The Court also said school officials must share placement considerations with the child's parents at the IEP meeting before a placement is determined.[65]

Oberti v. Board of Education of the Clementon School District, 1993

In this case, the Court determined the school's responsibility for "burden of proof" in the event school personnel believe that a child cannot and should not be educated in the general program. It is not the parents' responsibility to prove the child should be educated within the "mainstream" but, rather, the school's responsibility to justify its decision to exclude a child from the regular classroom. The Court found that, clearly, school districts must make good-faith efforts to maintain students in regular class placement with appropriate aids and services.

Sacramento City Unified School District v. Rachel H., 1994

The Court addressed four issues:

1. The educational benefits available to the child within the general classroom, with supplementary aids and services, compared with the educational benefits of the special education classroom
2. The nonacademic (e.g., social, language, peer-model) benefits of each of the classrooms
3. The impact of the child's presence on others in the general classroom, particularly if the child's behavior is disruptive/distracting
4. The cost of educating the child within the general classroom

The 9th Circuit District Court defined LRE as a strong congressional preference. This opinion combines factors from several decisions to determine the least restrictive environment. Those factors, which have become known as the "Holland Test," include

- Educational benefits in a regular classroom
- Nonacademic benefits for the child with a disability in a regular classroom
- The child's effect on the teacher and other children in the regular class
- The cost of supplementary aids and services to mainstream the child with a disability; the court said cost is only a factor if it will significantly affect another child in the district

Yell wrote,

> Perhaps, the most important reason for school district losses in court cases involves the court's willingness to accept assertions of appropriateness of restrictive settings without proof by school districts as to the inappropriateness of the regular classroom.[137]
> *Clyde K. v. Puyallup School District* (9th Circuit, 1994)

Using the "Holland Test," the court ordered a self-contained placement for a fifteen-year-old student with Tourette syndrome and attention deficit disorder. The court found that the student did not benefit from regular education placement, even with supplementary aids and services, and was disruptive to the rest of the class. He was verbally and physically assaultive to other children. Clearly, while the courts appear to favor placement within the general education program, using the general curriculum, the courts, at least in this case, drew the line and would not mandate placement that was harmful and threatening to the rest of the class.[112]

Hartman v. Loudon County Board of Education (E.D.Va, 1996)

A school district was required to place an eleven-year-old student with autism in a regular education classroom with a one-to-one instructional aide and an appropriately adapted curriculum because the student had shown benefit from such placement in a previous school district.[112]

The significant impetus toward inclusion in the courts is based on widespread notions regarding equity within the broader social context. Educational equity not just for children with disabilities but for *all* children who represent a virtually endless myriad of cultures, races, languages, religions, socioeconomic classes, and family and community contexts is a critical part of the democratic process. Every child must be given the opportunity to receive an equitable education, an education designed to prepare him or her for a meaningful life within the society. According to Gallagher,

> Clearly, there is concern for equity in education. Are children of poor families or families from culturally different backgrounds getting a fair chance at a quality education? Fairness and equity are the key concepts, and the educational reactions to such concerns have been to return to an educational setting where children of all levels of ability, achievement, motivation, and family backgrounds would be together, more or less, ensuring that no group has been siphoned off and placed in an inferior setting with less opportunity.[37]

Kliewer wrote,

> Proponents of segregated special education maintain the myth of skill transmission. This suggests that we as special educators can delineate sets of skills necessary for community participation; transmit these to students in facilities separated from the complex community; and, when proficiency is achieved, allow the student to join that community where he or she will use those operant-induced skills to whatever degree possible.
>
> By contrast, proponents of inclusive ideas take seriously the fundamental meaning of education and recognize a severe flaw in the logic of segregation: One does not learn membership apart from being a member. An individual does not learn to be a citizen apart from being recognized as a citizen. Indeed, one cannot claim a culture without being a part of culture. Further, a person cannot be or do any of these things when he or she is contained apart from the community. [58]

The Impact of Inclusion

McLeskey and Henry wrote,

> If we are to truly understand the impact of inclusion not only on individual students but also on the social and academic fabric of the schools and communities where inclusion is either taking place or being resisted, it is necessary to have both objective and descriptive data to inform, argue, and do the hard work necessary to make school a better, more successful place for all students. [74]

Salend and Duhaney[103] completed a review of the literature with respect to inclusion. They summarized the literature as follows:

- The impact of inclusion programs on the academic performance and social development of students with disabilities has been mixed.
- The placement of students with disabilities in inclusion programs does not appear to interfere with their academic performance and may have social benefits.

- The responses of teachers to inclusion programs are complex and varied, and they change over time.

There is some evidence to suggest that there are potential social benefits for learners with disabilities who participate in the general education program.[36,55,126] However, data regarding the impact of placement in inclusive settings, particularly on academic performance, are varied. While some studies have indicated there are improved educational outcomes for learners with *mild* disabilities who participate in the general education program,[8,129] others indicate that academic performance is compromised in inclusive settings because students did not receive specially designed instruction to meet their educational needs.[7]

The impact of inclusion on students without disabilities is also complex. Several studies have found there is no negative impact on the academic performance of children without disabilities who are taught with children with disabilities.[48,105,111] In fact, there may be some academic benefit, from collaborative learning, for students without disabilities in the general education program.[102]

According to Giangreco et al.,

> Inclusive education provides opportunities for teachers to model acceptance of human diversity in its many forms (e.g., culture, race, gender, disability). If we are to encourage the next generation to accept and value diversity, what better opportunity than welcoming students with disabilities into the classroom as full, participating members? The expanding diversity of the student population reflects the corresponding expansion of diversity in our communities, which highlights the need for students to learn how to live, work, and play harmoniously with people who have an ever-widening range of personal characteristics. [40]

Inclusive education has been defined as education in which the following are true:

- All students are welcomed into the regular education classes in their home/neighborhood school.
- Students are educated in groups that represent the greater society (i.e., approximately

10 percent of the students in any class/school have identified disabilities).

- A zero-rejection philosophy is in place, so no student, regardless of the nature or severity of the disability, is excluded.
- Students with varying abilities share an educational experience, with specific modifications and accommodations to meet individual needs.
- Special education support is provided within the context of the general education program.[40,101]

All Children Belong (ACB)[1] is a joint project of the National Parent Network on Disabilities and the Statewide Parent Advocacy Network of New Jersey and is supported by the DeWitt Wallace Reader's Digest Fund. ACB's positions concerning inclusion are summarized in Figure 5-4.

Because of the growing national movement toward acceptance of the philosophy of inclusion and the implementation of educational practice to promote inclusion, this text includes a variety of strategies for meeting the needs of students with disabilities in an inclusive setting. Our decision to provide this information is not intended to imply an endorsement of the notion that all students' needs can best be met in the general physical education setting. We are deeply committed to the notion that the Least Restrictive Environment mandates better protect the individual rights and ensure a quality physical education experience. General guidelines, including types of activities that will meet the needs of all students in various school levels, are included in this chapter, and more specific strategies are addressed in each of the chapters dealing with specific disabilities.

NATIONAL STANDARDS FOR PHYSICAL EDUCATION

The National Association for Sport and Physical Education (NASPE) has developed a text titled *Moving into the Future: National Physical Education Standards: A Guide to Content and Assessment*.[82] This standards-based document seeks to define "what a student should know and be able to do." It seeks to bring physical education into the third millennium by defining the student outcomes of a quality physical education program and by focusing on the need for authentic assessment protocols and practices that address the desired outcomes. The NASPE task force examined content and performance standards for children in kindergarten, second grade, fourth grade, sixth grade, eighth grade, tenth grade, and twelfth grade. See Figure 5-5, which summarizes the NASPE standards.

Inclusion and Physical Education

Though there is a wide variety of definitions of inclusion, no particular definition of inclusion as it relates to physical education for learners with disabilities has been widely accepted by professionals in the field. Within the broad spectrum of physical education, the following definition of inclusion will be adopted for use in this text. Inclusion is a philosophy in which "all individuals can participate in physical activities that enable them to be

---

> **Figure 5-4**   All Children Belong Position Statement
>
> - Inclusion is a process, not a place, service, or setting.
> - Children and youth with disabilities have the right to participate in the same neighborhood schools, classrooms, extracurricular activities, and community programs they would attend if they did not have a disability.
> - Children and youth with disabilities should have all necessary supports to ensure successful experiences and achievement of potential.
> - Children and youth with disabilities bring their inherent gifts to their schools and communities.
> - Children and youth with disabilities must be afforded the dignity of risk.
> - Communities should have the capacity to support participation of children and youth with disabilities in all aspects of community life.
> - The value system of the school and community should be based on the belief that all children belong.

Modified from All children belong, *Except Parent*, July:43–46, 1994.

Figure 5-5   National Association of Sport and Physical Education Characteristics of a Physically Educated Person

The NASPE task force determined the characteristics of a physically educated person and suggests a physically educated person[26]
1. Demonstrates competency in many movement forms and proficiency in a few movement forms
2. Applies movement concepts and principles to the learning and development of motor skills
3. Exhibits a physically active lifestyle
4. Achieves and maintains a health-enhancing level of physical fitness
5. Demonstrates responsible personal and social behavior in physical activity settings
6. Demonstrates understanding and respect for differences among people in physical activity settings
7. Understands that physical activity provides opportunities for enjoyment, challenge, self-expression, and social interaction

Figure 5-6   Barriers to Inclusion of Students with Disabilities in General Physical Education

- Inadequate professional preparation at the college/university level
- Lack of infusion of information regarding learners with disabilities in kinesiology courses such as biomechanics, exercise physiology, and teaching and coaching methods courses
- Drastic shortages of well-trained and qualified adapted physical educators to provide support for the general physical educator
- Lack of support personnel
- Lack of or inappropriate staff development
- Inappropriate application of LRE principles in physical education
- Inappropriate assessment and evaluation
- Inappropriate and poorly written annual goals and objectives
- Huge class size
- Lack of equipment

motorically, cognitively, and affectively successful within a community that embraces diversity."[118]

It is clear that a carefully administered comprehensive assessment, a skillfully designed individual education program, systematic and qualified instruction, and continual monitoring of student progress are critical factors that positively impact motor performance and physical development.

Block and Krebs led the profession of physical education toward inclusion with their article "An Alternative to Least Restrictive Environments: A Continuum of Support to Regular Physical Education."[12] They outlined strategies for the provision of services in physical education for learners with disabilities. They wrote, "It is time to let go of the continuum of LRE options in physical education and adopt a continuum of support to regular physical education." However, Wang and Reynolds remind professionals that

Delivering special education as an integral component of one education system for all children requires a major restructuring of schools and of teacher education, revisions in funding and accountability systems, and changes in assessment and instructional grouping practices.[130]

Initially, assumptions were made that significant resources, including personnel, equipment, and assistive technology, would be available to the general physical educator to make inclusion a possibility. Unfortunately, however, that has not appeared to be the case. See Figure 5-6, which outlines the barriers to inclusion. In fact, even in relatively affluent school districts with ample resources and good reputations, few of these resources were made available to the general physical educator attempting to serve children with disabilities in the general program.[64] Apparently, even physical educators judged to be highly effective elementary school teachers, found the process of trying to include children with disabilities to be frustrating and guilt-producing, and it caused the children to feel inadequate.[64]

Research regarding academic learning time in physical education (ALT-PE)—quality, intensive time in which children are actively engaged in learning—has demonstrated that academic learning time is lower than in other academic disciplines.[63] This should be obvious, given the dynamics of physical education as opposed to those of the more traditional "academic" disciplines. Large class sizes; learners moving actively through a space which, traditionally, is not acoustically sound; and insufficient numbers of adults for instruction and supervision makes it difficult to keep all the children involved in learning.

It is critical to remember that the law remains clear. The IEP or multidisciplinary team is responsible for determining the appropriate education for the student. Block and Burke wrote, "The IEP team should decide what constitutes an appropriate physical education program, as determined by each child's age, unique needs, interests, parental interests, and what is available and popular in physical education and community recreation programs"[11] (see Figure 5-7).

Inclusion and Developmentally Appropriate Practice in Physical Education

The inclusion of learners with disabilities in the general physical education program can be best implemented in a classroom in which the physical educator uses *developmentally appropriate practices.* That is, the physical educator engages the learners in the class in activities that are age and interest appropriate for the learners. For example, learners with disabilities can most effectively be included in the general physical education curriculum for first and second graders if the emphasis in the program is the acquisition and refinement of basic locomotor and nonlocomotor patterns, movement exploration, cooperative play activities, and elementary rhythms and dance. If inappropriate practices are being used for example, team sports and competitive games—children with disabilities, like *all* young learners who are not "superstars," are doomed to failure and frustration.

The same is true of general physical education at the high school level. If the general physical educator concentrates on instruction in leisure and recreation skills for use as adults in postschool years and emphasizes the development of physical fitness, for example, most learners with disabilities can be successful in the general physical education environment. If inappropriate practices are being used—for example, team sports and competitive games—learners with disabilities, like *all* children who are not "superstars," are doomed to failure and frustration. See Figure 5-8, which reviews concepts regarding developmentally appropriate practice.

Figure 5-7   Problems Unique to Physical Education

There are problems unique to the physical education environment that make it difficult for the physical educator to ensure the student spends time actively engaged in learning physical education activities including
1. Large classes[26]
2. Teacher attrition[26]
3. Management problems unique to the physical education learning environment, including large, open spaces; active, moving bodies; and equipment that acts as "attractive nuisances"

Figure 5-8   Developmentally Appropriate Pedagogy and Inclusion

- Skills and activities must be age appropriate.[95]
- Skills and activities must be individually appropriate.[95]
- Skills must be broken down into small steps and introduced in sequence.[95]
- Activities must be chosen based on the interests and needs of the children.
- The curriculum must honor the play potential and level of the children.

PREPARING FOR INCLUSION— A PROACTIVE APPROACH

All too often, inclusion was something that "happened" within a given school community. Any change, particularly a dramatic change, in an educational environment must be preceded by careful and systematic preparation to ready all involved in the process.

For inclusion to be effective within a given community and school, significant preparation must occur. Unfortunately, all too often inclusion "happens" without forethought, consensus building, values modification, or comprehensive in-service education. In this section, suggestions are made for ensuring that inclusion is successful by preparing the community, administrators, parents, children, teachers, and paraprofessionals.

In many traditional Native American cultures, the purpose of the society is to produce courageous youth. That paradigm is of use in the development of appropriate inclusion programs. The desired outcomes for these carefully taught youth are identical to those critical in a community committed to inclusion (see Figure 5-9).

Figure 5-9 "Circle of Courage" Outcomes[120]

Belonging
Experiencing personal development, achieving social competence, making and keeping friends, and feeling part of the community

Mastery
Being able to communicate, developing competency in something, and reaching one's potential

Independence
Engaging in problem solving, assuming personal responsibility, being accountable for one's own actions, and being a life-long learner

Generosity
Exercising social responsibility, contributing to society, valuing diversity, and being empathetic

Preparing the Community

An increased emphasis on school-community partnerships necessitates a broad-based, public relations campaign to help focus community interest on issues tied to the quality of life of individuals with disabilities. Within a given community, visible, capable, and effective individuals with and without disabilities need to be part of a public relations campaign to educate and motivate its citizens to embrace appropriate inclusion in the schools. It is particularly critical that the school board—elected representatives of the public—has adopted a philosophy that emphasizes appropriate inclusion.[50] The school board—representatives of the taxpayers who continue to be overwhelmed with the financial responsibility of educating their children—must be able to communicate carefully and effectively to all its citizens the benefits of appropriate inclusion. This is particularly important if learners with disabilities are to have the opportunity to make a meaningful transition into the community.

The Building Principal: The Key to Effective Instructional Programs

Without a primary building administrator who is deeply committed to the philosophy and ideal of quality instruction for learners with special needs, schoolwide education programs for children with disabilities, particularly inclusion programs, can be badly applied and practiced. See Figure 5-10 for a summary of the practices of principals who encourage inclusion. Unfortunately, all too often children with disabilities are included in general physical education, art, music, library, and computer classes without careful regard to the unique needs and abilities of the child.

The IEP/multidisciplinary team may provide inclusion experiences—based solely on the social needs of the child—in the so-called special education program in order to meet parental demands for placement with typical children without jeopardizing student performance in the so-called academic components of the curriculum.

Figure 5-10 The Building Principal: The Key to Successful Inclusion in Physical Education

An administrator who values and supports the education of diverse learners is absolutely critical to successful inclusion.[120] The administrator committed to inclusion will do one of the following to ensure that quality physical education is received by all:

1. Decrease the class size by hiring additional professional personnel or arranging alternate scheduling patterns.
2. Decrease the student–teacher ratio by assigning trained paraprofessionals to assist the teacher and ensuring they do their job.
3. Decrease the student–teacher ratio by assigning school volunteers to assist the physical educator in the gymnasium.
4. Use creative alternative scheduling patterns for service delivery. Perhaps it is more prudent to have students attend a quality physical education class three times a week if the class size is limited to thirty students than to have them attend a large, ineffective baby-sitting service daily if class size is in excess of eighty students.
5. Arrange for university/community college interns to provide vital extra hands.

In addition to limiting the student–teacher ratio in physical education, the campus administrator must also provide support for the physical educator by addressing other concerns:

1. The physical educator must be encouraged to attend classes and in-service presentations that address the education of children with disabilities in the regular physical education program.
2. The physical educator must be given release time to participate actively as part of the motor development team or the multidisciplinary team in the assessment/evaluation of the child's gross motor skills and in the creation and implementation of the child's individual motor education plan (IMEP) or individual physical education plan (IPEP).

Administrative support for the appropriate inclusion of children with disabilities in general education, including general physical education, is vital if a nurturing educational environment is to be created. If the local campus administrator, principal, or dean of instruction supports the notion that some children with disabilities may be integrated effectively into the general physical education program, and that meets the child's social and/or physical/motor needs, then the administrator must support the physical educator in a number of ways.

The local campus administrator cannot expect a physical educator to create a nurturing, supportive environment for a child with a disability—for *any* child, for that matter—if saddled with huge class sizes. It is not uncommon in some school districts for a physical educator to have a class size in excess of eighty students. It is impossible to address the needs of each child in a class of this size, and it is ridiculous to assume that even the best teacher could accommodate even one more child, particularly a child with a disability. The safety of all children is jeopardized.

The IDEA's federally mandated participation of students with disabilities in state and district assessments may redirect school administrators to focus their efforts on the performance of students in special education. Unfortunately, many school administrators believe physical education and adapted physical education are simply peripheral or so-called special activities and focus their energies on test scores in the "general" education program (see Figure 5-11).

Preparing Parents

The perceptions of parents of children with and without disabilities toward inclusion are widely varied, depending on the focus of the parents in relation to their individual child. Parents' attitudes toward placement and instructional methodology are diverse, complex, and very emotionally charged. Palmer et al. wrote,

This lack of unity in opinion regarding the efficacy of inclusive practices may result from conflicting views regarding the primary

Figure 5-11   The Building Principal Committed to Educational Equity for Learners with Disabilities

The building principal committed to *real* educational equity will
- Actively recruit and hire teachers and staff members who represent diverse cultures, languages, races, religions, gender, gender preferences, and *abilities and disabilities.*
- Actively recruit persons for the school site–based committee who represent diverse cultures, languages, races, religions, gender, gender preferences, and *abilities and disabilities.*
- Provide significant proactive in-service training for teachers, paraprofessionals, and other building personnel (including the building secretary, custodian, school nurse, etc.) regarding a community of learners that includes individuals with disabilities.
- Reward and recognize teachers and staff whose actions give evidence of a commitment to the education of learners with disabilities.
- Encourage special educators and adapted physical educators to take an active leadership role in schoolwide planning and curriculum development that affects all learners.

Figure 5-12   Parents' Perceptions Regarding Essential Factors in Integrated Physical Education Programs[26]

- Small class size
- Instructional support—teacher and paraprofessional
- Parent support
- Administrative support
- Communication skills of the learner with a disability
- Student's health status
- Student's motivation
- Student's physical skills
- Student's language/communication skills
- Student's social/emotional skills
- Student's self-help skills
- Parent involvement in diagnostic/prescription process
- Parents were provided information regarding their child's language, cognitive, social, and motor skill progress.
- Student's age

mission of the schools. . . . It may then be that parents who share the inclusionist view of the relative importance of socialization are those who would tend to favor general class placements for their children. These parents are less likely to be concerned with any perceived negative effects regarding the impact of inclusion on their child's ability to receive special education services. Parents who place a higher value on the development of social skills may be willing to trade off "special education" benefits such as: (a) specialized curriculum, (b) easier access to ancillary services, and (c) more individualized instruction for the social benefits that they consider to be more attainable in a general education setting.[87]

Perhaps the most important phase of a successful inclusion program is the preparation of parents of children with and without disabilities.

Certainly, a broad-based public relations campaign within the community is a good start, but carefully designed parent education programs are vital. See Figure 5-12 to review parents' perceptions regarding the needs for the successful integration of children with disabilities into the general physical education program.

Parents of children with disabilities are often the primary advocates of inclusion programs. On occasion, however, parents of children with disabilities are fearful of the general education program. Particularly if their child has been educated in a self-contained special education program, they may like the safety and the security of that program. Parents fear their child may be teased or hurt, laughed at, and ridiculed by typically developing children. The best way to deal with these types of fears is to invite parents to visit the general physical education program before the IEP/multidisciplinary team considers the possibility of the child's attending the class. If the parents have the opportunity to see a caring, nurturing teacher and a well-organized, child-centered physical education program, particularly with sensible/safety-based numbers of children, their fears will be reduced.

Preparing the parents of children without disabilities for inclusion may be the most difficult part of the development of an inclusion education program. Most parents of children without disabilities are supportive of inclusion efforts if, and only if, they believe their children's education will not be compromised. Parents of children without disabilities are concerned that

- The teacher's time and energy will be exhausted dealing with a learner with disabilities.
- School resources and tax dollars will be allocated disproportionately for learners with disabilities.
- Their child's learning will be disrupted by a child with inappropriate learning behaviors— aggressive, acting out, and refusal behaviors, for example.
- Their child will begin to mimic inappropriate behaviors demonstrated by children with disabilities.
- Their child's safety will be compromised by a child with physically aggressive behavior.
- Their child's emotional well-being will be compromised by a child who is verbally aggressive or who uses inappropriate language.
- Their child's health will be compromised by a child who vomits, drools, spits, is not toilet trained, or has a communicable disease (e.g., AIDS, syphilis).

The single most important strategy for preparing parents of children without disabilities for inclusion is gradual and thoughtful inclusion of children with mild disabilities, at first. It appears that this is particularly effective if very young children with disabilities are included with their peers. If parents of children without disabilities can see that their children's education is not compromised, and, in fact, if they learn some important social skills about dealing with others, they will be more likely to support inclusion.

Another significant strategy is to give parents of children with and without disabilities the oppor-

Achilles Track Club sponsors a summer in Central Park for disabled children, which promotes family involvement.
Courtesy Achilles Track Club, New York, N.Y.

tunity to discuss their mutual and independent concerns in a carefully designed open forum. Often, if a parent becomes aware of the fears, needs, dreams, and hopes of another parent, an avenue of communication is opened that will transcend discriminatory practice.

Preparing Children

The single most effective strategy for preparing children with and without disabilities for inclusion is to begin inclusive education early. If infants, toddlers, and young children grow up learning together, as young adults there will be no question of "who belongs." In fact, if a school district is deeply committed to effective, inclusionary practice with a minimum of upheaval, the district would begin inclusionary practice in their birth-to-age-five program and then gradually, as the children who grew up learning together moved into the primary grades, would expand the program into the primary grades. Then, eventually, the program would be expanded into the middle and high schools. Although the total transformation would take up to eight years, at the end of that time the school district would be a place in which all children could learn together.

In fact, if inclusion is well done, there are innumerable benefits for all children. According to Rogers:

- The presence of an included classmate should provide opportunities for growth for the entire class.
- Classmates can develop a sense of responsibility and the enhanced self-esteem which results from such responsibility.
- Classmates' understanding of the range of human experience can be enhanced.
- Children can benefit from their classmates with disabilities as role models. As a result of advancements in medical science that allow most people to live ever longer lives, most of those children without disabilities will survive to become persons with disabilities themselves one day.
- Classmates are enriched by the opportunity to have had friends with disabilities who successfully managed their affairs and enjoyed full lives.[100]

Members of the community of persons with disabilities identify themselves as TABS (temporarily able-bodied) or CRABS (currently regarded as able-bodied).

Lockhart, French, and Gench reported that a number of factors have been identified as those that promote positive attitudes and improve social interaction in physical education:

- A conducive social climate
- An equal status contact
- An intimate, rather than casual, contact
- Pleasurable and satisfying contact
- Cooperative activity that engages all students in a common goal[68]

To ensure that this is a positive experience for all children, helping children without disabilities to understand what it is like to have a disability is an excellent first step. Children respond well to empathy experiences in which they have the opportunity to feel what it is like to have a disability. These empathy experiences help a child, in a concrete way, learn and accept. The child without a disability, or with a different disability, can be asked to do one or more of the following:

1. Spend a day in a wheelchair
2. Wear mittens when attempting to perform fine motor tasks
3. Endeavor to trace an object reflected in a mirror
4. Spend a day not speaking a word
5. Spend a day with cotton wads covered with vaseline or a headset covering the ears
6. Wear eye patches
7. Use crutches for a day
8. Spend a day with a yardstick splint on the dominant arm
9. Listen to teacher instructions given in a different language

In the physical education classroom, empathy experiences designed to help learners without disabilities understand the person with a disability might include instructions to

1. Navigate an obstacle course in a wheelchair
2. Wear mittens when trying to play catch with a friend
3. Play in the gymnasium and on the playground using only gestures for communication
4. Wearing a headset to cut out hearing, attempt to play in a game
5. Wearing eye patches, allow a classmate to walk the child around the playground and help him or her use each piece of equipment
6. Kick a ball while supporting self on crutches
7. With a yardstick splint on the dominant arm, catch, throw, and dribble with the nondominant hand and arm
8. Participate in class when the teacher uses only sign language to communicate

One of the most significant means of preparing an environment for a learner to be successfully included is to identify and encourage a circle of friends to be in place before the inclusion experience is attempted.[109] This helps provide a vital, caring, and humane transition into general education services. See Figure 5-13, which addresses peer

Figure 5-13   Improving Friendships Between Children with and Without Disabilities

The teacher must
- Model friend-first behavior
- Provide opportunities at the beginning of the school year and intermittently throughout the year for children to get to know one another[108]
- Use books, videos, and songs/dances that encourage friendship[108]
- Teach specific skills for being "friends." Increasingly, students come to school without the interpersonal skills necessary to create and maintain friendships.
- Ensure opportunity to practice the specific skills for being "friends." The skills are specific and "learned" and need to be practiced.
- Reinforce and reward "friendly" behaviors
- Teach children specific skills for handling a peer's rejection
- Provide structure, if needed, at lunch or recess to encourage appropriate social interactions[108]
- Stipulate annual goals and objectives directly tied to learning appropriate social skills (e.g., friendship skills) in the child's IEP[38]
- Identify and assign roles in a "cooperative learning" experience to foster friendship. For example, one child in the group could be specifically charged with being a "cheerleader" for the other group members.
- Help children create a "circle of friends" before moving into a new educational environment. For example, if a child is going to begin participating in general physical education, *before* the child starts, he or she should already have a "circle of friends" in place, ready to welcome the child into the learning environment.

friendships. A child with a disability is given the opportunity to make friends in a controlled, reverse mainstream setting before attempting to move into the general education/physical education setting. For example, if a six-year-old girl with Down syndrome is hoping to participate in the general education/physical education program, several six-year-old girls are asked to meet and play with the child in her classroom, preferably during a time in which interaction might occur (e.g., center time). Then, after the child has made friends, she is included in the general education/physical education program, more comfortable because of her friends.

Preparing older students, middle and high school age, for inclusion needs to be approached altogether differently. These students are more likely to be accepting of an individual with a disability if they are able to understand the disability on an intellectual level. Honest communication of information regarding the nature of a disability will reduce fear. They are also more likely to interact with a classmate with a disability if given a leadership role (e.g., as a tutor, personal assistant,

etc.). Only the truly mature adolescent is able to deal with peer pressure issues to only "hang with the in crowd." Selective assignment and recruitment of tutors and personal assistants must be used.

Preparing Professionals, Including the General Physical Educator

Clearly, undergraduate and graduate professional education programs need to be restructured to focus on real-world applications. An increased emphasis on the skills necessary to provide services to a variety of students is critical. The general educator must be prepared to meet the diverse needs of children representing a wide variety of cultures, races, languages, socioeconomic classes, abilities, and disabilities. And an increased emphasis needs to be placed on the professional skills necessary to work in collaboration with other professionals.

For a child with even a mild disability to be educated in the general physical education class, careful preparation must be made. There are three variables that must be considered before deciding to place a child in the general education/physical education program:

1. The professional preparation of the educator to teach a child with disabilities
2. The attitude of the educator toward learners with disabilities
3. The nature of the educator's previous experience working with learners with disabilities

See Figure 5-14, which describes the psychological preparation a teacher must do to ready him- or herself for inclusion, and Figure 5-15, which addresses the teacher's needs.

The first variable to be considered in the decision to include children with disabilities in general education/physical education programs is the professional preparation of the teacher. An introductory-level adapted physical education class at the undergraduate level that addresses the attitudes and feelings of preprofessionals is the basis of such preparation.[44] It is particularly critical

Figure 5-14   Psychological Preparation for Inclusion[89]

Teachers, paraprofessionals, and related service personnel must examine the following:
- Their "picture books"
  - Their expectations of each student
- Their lenses
  - Values
  - Beliefs
  - Prejudices
- Their "playbooks"
  - Actions: past, present, and future

Figure 5-15   Teachers' Perceptions of the Day-to-Day Support Required If Inclusion Programs Are to Be Successful

- Personalized, ongoing, specific training to meet the needs of a particular child[33,131]
  - Training designed to complement the teacher's learning style
  - Training components developed for use when the teacher has time
- Training and opportunity to develop a collegial staff[50]
- Goals and activities for the child that are tied to the general goals and activities of the classroom[48]
- Training that addresses the following:[56]
  - Cooperative teaching
  - Curriculum-based assessment
  - Behavior-management techniques
  - Multiple intelligences[88]
  - Trust building[134]
  - Conflict resolution[134]
- Opportunities to observe in other classrooms where inclusion programs are successful
- Opportunities for practice of specific techniques until a comfort level emerges[56]
- Support from a team of professionals
- In-class assistance[131]
- Administrative support
- Time to work with support team, parents, and the child
- Smaller class size[48,90]
- Additional money for class materials and supplies[33]
- The option/right to remove the child to another place (e.g., resource room of self-contained classroom) if significant misbehavior continues
- Reconfigured "roles" of personnel to allow flexibility in meeting children's needs[48]
- Schoolwide consensus on a set of values that affirms inclusion[48]
- Organizational and role flexibility[134]

that the preparation include hands-on experiences with children with disabilities in the physical education setting.[32,99] It appears that the nature of the practicum is critical in the quality of the experience as well. The controlled practicum, on a university campus, is characterized by the following:

- The faculty member is actively involved in ongoing supervision.
- Students are served in small teacher–student ratios.
- Students with disabilities are carefully selected for participation.

In one study, students who participated in the controlled, campus-based practicum had better attitudes toward working with students with disabilities than did those who participated in public school–based practicum experiences in which "control" of variables was more difficult.[44] These findings speak volumes about the critical nature of teacher preparation and the very fine line between creating comfortable learning environments and giving students real-world experience.

If the physical educator did not acquire knowledge of ways to accommodate learner with disabilities in the general curriculum during undergraduate or graduate professional preparation, the educator must be provided access to this information through in-service preparation before a child with disabilities is included in the general program. Subsequent, ongoing in-service training is vital in order to keep professional staff on the cutting edge in the provision of services to learners with disabilities in a general physical education setting. Teachers' perceived competence is significantly related to their attitudes toward students with disabilities.[99] See Figure 5-16 for a list of essential knowledge for the general physical educator if inclusion is to be successful.

The second variable that must be considered before placing a child with a disability in the general classroom is the teacher's attitude toward teaching those with disabilities. If the teacher has a negative attitude about including a learner with a disability in the class, the learner will know it instantly and be devastated by it; the learner with a

Figure 5-16 Essential Knowledge and Skills for General Education Teachers and Paraprofessionals Responsible for the Instruction of Children with Disabilities

1. Knowledgeable about the physical, mental, and emotional characteristics of children with disabilities
2. Knowledgeable about the learning styles of children with disabilities
3. Able to use teaching techniques and methodologies appropriate for children with and without disabilities
4. Proficient in using behavior-management strategies appropriate for children with and without disabilities
5. Able to modify play and games, and leisure, recreation, and sport activities to include children with disabilities
6. Capable of modifying curriculum objectives to meet the needs of children with disabilities
7. Able to modify evaluation and grading for children with disabilities

disability simply cannot be placed in a classroom or gymnasium in which he or she is not wanted.

Teachers may have negative attitudes toward students with disabilities for a variety of reasons, but attitudes are learned behaviors that, when necessary, can be changed.[91] According to Clark, French, and Henderson,[21] it is important to find ways to teach physical educators the knowledge and skills necessary to work effectively with students with disabilities in the general classroom and increase positive attitudes toward them. These are not mutually exclusive. Teachers may have negative attitudes toward students with disabilities because they do not know how to teach them.

Preprofessionals, those involved in preparation for careers as physical educators, express the intent to work with students with disabilities based on their role identity in society and their confidence in their ability to teach students with disabilities.[119] Downs and Williams[27] studied 371 preservice physical education students in four European countries to determine their attitudes toward serving learners with disabilities in their future careers. The researchers used the Physical Educators' Attitudes Toward Teaching the Handicapped (PEATH) developed by Rizzo.[97] They noted that learners with "some previous experience" with individuals with disabilities had a more negative attitude toward learners with disabilities than did those who did not have this experience. It is important to consider the nature of the experience; clearly, a well-planned, structured experience improves the attitudes of individuals toward those with disabilities. Contact, in and of itself, does not improve attitudes.

Downs and Williams noted that their European students expressed a more positive attitude toward teaching learners with physical disabilities than teaching those with learning disabilities. They suggest

> One could argue that people with physical disabilities are more suited to the physical activity setting since their "limitations" present only functional barriers whereas people with learning disabilities may be unable to grasp the fundamental, cognitive structures underlying the physical activity setting.[27]

In addition, Downs and Williams[27] reported that women were more likely to express a positive attitude toward teaching individuals with disabilities than were men. This is easily explained by societal expectations of women as nurturers and caregivers.

Clark, French, and Henderson[21] have recommended preservice or in-service training that would include empathy experiences, values clarification, volunteerism, experiences with learners with disabilities, group discussions, and lectures as vehicles for attitude change. See Figure 5-17 to consider staff development and attitudinal change. The following techniques are suggested for preservice or in-service presentations intended to alter the attitudes of physical educators toward the disabled.

Empathy Experiences

The general physical educator can be provided experiences that simulate the experience of being

Figure 5-17 Alternatives to Traditional Staff Development to Prepare Personnel for Inclusion

- Study groups[10]
- Directed web quests
- Action research[10]
- Independent study
- Visitations to classrooms where "inclusion" works[10]
- Collegial sharing
- E-mail problem solving
- Focus groups
- Invited program evaluation (internal and external)

disabled. For example, the individual can be asked to spend a day teaching in a wheelchair or to spend a night at home with his or her family while wearing a headset. Or the educator/physical educator can be asked to wear eye patches and a blindfold and allow a student to take him or her on a tour of the playground.

The same type of experience that might help a child understand the phenomenon associated with having a disability can help the professional, as well. A truly remarkable account of an empathy experience is the true story of an entire football team, players and coaches, who shaved their heads to commiserate with a teammate who lost his hair as a side effect of chemotherapy for cancer.

Illumination Experiences

The educator/physical educator can be exposed to information about the potential and the performance of individuals with disabilities. The physical educator might be asked, for example, to compare his or her running performance with the national marathon record of male and female racers who use wheelchairs. Better still, the physical educator can be given the opportunity to compete against an elite athlete with a disability. The teacher might have a chance to play tennis against a tennis player who uses a wheelchair. Or the teacher might have the opportunity to bowl against a member of the American Wheelchair Bowling Association or to play golf against a low-handicap player of the National Amputee Golf Association.

Observation Experiences

The physical educator can be invited to attend a local or regional sports competition for individuals with disabilities. These include events sponsored by, for example, the Special Olympics, the National Wheelchair Athletic Association, or the National Association of Sports for Cerebral Palsy. If this is not possible, the teacher can be given the opportunity to view tapes, for example, of a recent Special Olympics or Paralympics competition.

Volunteer Experiences

The physical educator can be given the opportunity to volunteer, in a carefully supervised experience, to work with learners with disabilities. The mere act of volunteering does not cause a change in attitude. But a positive experience, one in which the educator perceives his or her work to be of value—one that allows for important and honest communication between the educator and the individual with a disability—can alter an attitude for a lifetime.

Values Clarification

The physical educator can be led by a trained psychologist or school counselor through the process of identifying and clarifying prejudices, attitudes, and notions about individuals with disabilities. These values might best be clarified in and through conversations with disabled adults or with parents of children with disabilities. This type of conversation should be led by a psychologist or counselor, at first, to ensure that the individuals have a quality human interaction. Clark, French, and Henderson[21] have suggested that a "trigger story" may also help physical educators sort out feelings and attitudes toward teaching students with disabilities. For example, the physical educator can be asked to react to the following types of scenarios by identifying the emotions of the child, those of his or her classmates, and the fears or concerns the physical educator may have about the inclusion process:

> Atlantis is a moderately mentally retarded, emotionally disturbed child who cries for an

hour before being made to join the fifth-grade physical education class. No one in the class has befriended her; indeed, her classmates taunt and jeer at her throughout.

> Guadalupe is a five-year-old child with mild spina bifida. He is ambulatory and loves to play. He is not being allowed to go to the gym with his classmates and is depressed because of the decision.

Perhaps the most significant experience for a physical educator with hesitations about educating a student with a disability in his or her class is the opportunity to observe another professional physical educator teaching children with disabilities in the general program. This may have a positive effect on attitudes and may help the educator develop specific strategies for teaching learners with disabilities.

Preparing the Paraprofessional or Teacher Assistant

The paraprofessional or teacher assistant is often the key to the success of a learner with a disability in the general physical education program.

Paraprofessional personnel are often willing, but grossly underpaid, members of the teaching staff. Typically, these individuals are given the tasks the teacher does not want to do—changing diapers, feeding, supervising recess, and so on. These staff members can be the single most important force in the school life of a child with a disability. If a paraprofessional is given specific training, he or she can better meet the needs of the child. With success in intervention, the paraprofessional will be enabled and reinforced to continue (see Figure 5-18).

In-service training needs to be concrete and specific to the needs of the individual children the paraprofessional is expected to serve. The single most important part of the training is the management of the learner's behavior. If the paraprofessional can help the learner behave appropriately, the general educator/general physical educator will be more likely to embrace the learner in the classroom.

Figure 5-18   Paraprofessional Roles

A dedicated and well-trained paraprofessional may
serve in the following roles:
- Ensuring access to the general physical education
  setting
- Providing physical and emotional support for the
  learner with a disability
- Serving as an advocate for the learner
- Supplementing instruction by providing
  individualized instruction
- Being the child's "best friend"

DETERMINING ACCESSIBILITY OF THE PHYSICAL EDUCATION SETTING

Facilities for physical education at the elementary, middle, and high school level vary extensively from district to district and from state to state. Most schools have an indoor gymnasium/play area and an outdoor playground area available for class use. Some school districts have no gymnasium and rely entirely on outdoor facilities. Some inner-city schools, however, have no viable (safe, weapon-free, gang-free) playground area, and often the gymnasium is too small to allow appropriate activities.

Students with disabilities who receive physical education instruction within the general physical education program share these facilities with children in their class. It is, of course, necessary to evaluate the facilities with regard to the safety of all the learners. In addition, it is vital that the physical educator critically evaluate the facility with the unique needs of learners with disabilities in mind. The physical educator must ask the following questions regarding the learning environment:

- Is the indoor gymnasium/play area accessible for a student who uses a wheelchair, walker, or crutches?
- Can the student with a physical or neurological disability make an easy transition from the indoor gymnasium/play area to the outdoor playground area?

- If the gymnasium/play area is not easily accessible, what accommodations can be made to ensure that a student is not limited by a disability?
- If the student is unable to make an easy transition from the indoor to the outdoor play area—because of stairs, for example—what accommodations can be made to ensure that the child is not limited access to the program by the disability?
- Can the play areas be modified to provide a safe, secure, and nurturing learning environment for all learners?
- Are there accessible washrooms close to the indoor gymnasium/play area and the outside playground area?
- Can all learners, including those with disabilities, be safely evacuated from the indoor gymnasium/play area in the event of a fire?

It is important for the teacher to understand that Section 504 of the Rehabilitation Act of 1973 and subsequent legislation—specifically, the Americans with Disabilities Act of 1990[3]—mandate that all new public facilities be built to ensure access for individuals with disabilities. In the event, however, that the teacher is serving in an old building, the law mandates that a "reasonable accommodation" must be made to ensure that the student has access to programs offered to others. For example, if the primary pathway from the gymnasium to the playground is down a set of stairs, a student in a wheelchair may be unable to get to the playground using that route. A reasonable accommodation is for the physical education teacher to have the entire class use an accessible route—one with a ramp, for example—so that the learner using the wheelchair feels part of the group. The gymnasium and playground areas can be modified to make them more user-friendly for learners with disabilities:

- A constant sound source could be placed in the gymnasium or on the playground to allow the visually impaired student to orient self in both settings.
- A "safety strip" made of a material different from that of the major play area could surround

the gymnasium or playground area to warn the visually impaired or blind student of walls or fences.

- The playground area must be completely surrounded by fences if a learner with a conduct disorder, a student with autism, or a "wanderer" or "runner" is to be allowed to play and/or recreate outside. Actually, given the present climate in the society, it is critical that *all* school property is surrounded by a fence with gates that can be locked or supervised to control access to the school.
- The gymnasium should be well lighted to ensure use by a student with a visual disability.
- The gymnasium should have good acoustics to ensure that a learner with a hearing impairment can hear the teacher's instructions. Materials to absorb sound and prevent it from bouncing around the environment are critical for the learner with Asperger's syndrome and autism.
- The teacher should have access to a microphone to speak at levels that can be heard by a student with a hearing impairment.
- Major equipment should always be stored in the same place in the gymnasium to provide consistency for the visually impaired and autistic learner.

VARIABLES AFFECTING INSTRUCTION IN PHYSICAL EDUCATION IN THE LEAST RESTRICTIVE ENVIRONMENT

It is critical that *instruction, not placement,* be the deciding factor in the process of educating a learner with a disability. Unfortunately, all too often, learners with disabilities are "placed" in a particular educational setting and left there to learn or fail.

The most critical factor in the instruction of learners with disabilities is a comprehensive assessment. The assessment drives and is the basis for the development of the individual education program (see Figure 5-19). Then, and only then, should decisions be made regarding instruction and placement in the least restrictive environment.[47]

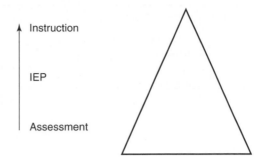

Figure 5-19

Decker and Jansma[24] have cautioned that federal mandates to provide education in the least restrictive environment have been largely ignored, and, indeed, many school districts have as few as two "service delivery options." Their research in 452 schools throughout the United States indicated that "the most widely used continuum (50.7%) was not a continuum at all, but rather a single placement option: full-time general class in a general school."[24] The frightening thing is that this study was conducted during the 1988–1989 school year, before the widespread national focus on inclusion programs. It seems logical to concur that this widespread abuse of the least restrictive environment alternatives has escalated. Careful consideration must be given the variables that affect instruction in physical education in the least restrictive environment:

- Curriculum
- Program participation
- Support personnel
- Teaching style
- Management of behavior
- Grading
- Assessment
- Equipment

It is impossible to determine what is the "least" or "most" restrictive when considering instruction. Generalizations regarding what is least or most restrictive are inappropriate when considering individual instruction for learners

Curriculum	Support personnel	Program participation	Equipment
Assessment	Management of behavior	Teaching style	Grading

Figure 5-20   Variables Affecting Instruction in Physical Education in the Least Restrictive Environment

with disabilities. The determination of least or most restrictive must be carefully considered by the IEP/multidisciplinary team. Each of the variables can be considered on a continuum (see Figure 5-20). However, the determination of least or most restrictive is an individual decision that must be made by the IEP/multidisciplinary team. For example, a teacher using a very autocratic, command-based teaching style may be the perfect answer for a student who requires a great deal of structure. The same teacher may make it impossible for a student with ADD/ADHD to be successful.

As the variables are considered, every effort should be made to maximize participation in the general physical education program. A student with mild to moderate dyslexia may participate under the following conditions:

- The physical education curriculum is based on the NASPE National Standards for Physical Education.
- The student is able to participate fully and independently in the general physical education program.
- The student's teacher is the general physical educator.
- The teacher develops individually designed programs for all learners in the program.

- The child's motor behavior is assessed using the same strategies/protocols used for all other learners.
- The same behavior expectations exist for all students in the class.
- There are modifications of expectations in some phases of the evaluation process. Specifically, knowledge tests are administered orally.
- The learner uses the same equipment as all other learners.

The consideration of variables affecting instruction provides maximum flexibility, with instruction designed to meet the unique needs of all learners. For example, a student with spina bifida who uses a wheelchair for ambulation may participate in the least restrictive physical education environment with these alternatives:

- The physical education curriculum is based on the NASPE National Standards for Physical Education.
- The student is able to participate fully and independently in some units (such as archery) but requires support in others (such as gymnastics) in the general physical education program.
- The student's teacher is a general physical educator who has consultative support from an adapted physical education specialist.
- The teacher develops individually designed programs for all learners in the program.
- The same behavior expectations exist for all students in the class.
- The student's gross motor behavior will be evaluated using the Brockport Test of Physical Fitness.
- There are modifications of expectations in some phases of the evaluation process for grading. For example, the student's cardiovascular fitness evaluation may be based on improvement in the number of minutes the student can wheel at a given rate without stopping.
- The child will take the same paper-and-pencil tests as other students.
- The learner uses the same equipment as all other learners and just happens to ambulate in a chair.

Curricular Variables Affecting Instruction in the LRE

The adoption of a given curriculum for use by some or all students within a given district is a critical variable affecting instruction in the creation of an inclusive learning environment. Increasing emphasis is being placed on the use of universally designed materials so teachers need to teach only one flexible curriculum in order to meet the needs of all of their students.

> In terms of learning, universal design means the design of instructional materials and activities that allows the learning goals to be achievable by individuals with wide differences in their abilities to see, hear, speak, move, read, write, understand English, attend, organize, engage, and remember. Universal design for learning is achieved by means of flexible curricular materials and activities that provide alternatives for students with disparities in abilities and backgrounds.[86]

The curriculum must be considered when determining instruction in the least restrictive environment (see Figure 5-21):

• NASPE National Standards for Physical Education as the basis of the school curriculum. The National Association for Sport and Physical Education has determined the standards of performance in physical education. If possible, learners with disabilities should participate in this curriculum.

• State education agency "essential elements" in physical education as the basis of the school curriculum. Most states have developed their own standards or "essential elements" for all curricular areas, including physical education. These essential elements may not be as global as those outlined by NASPE.

• Local education agency physical education curriculum. Many local districts have developed their own curriculum. Curricula developed at the local level tend to reflect the interests and attitudes of local school and community personnel.

• Modified physical education curriculum. According to Kelly,

> Physical educators must examine how they as professionals and their content area of physical education contribute to an inclusive school. This may involve issues such as revising the physical education curriculum so that it reflects the needs and interests of all the students and the community at the expense of what the physical education staff has traditionally taught or valued in the past.[20]

In some states, such as Wisconsin and Louisiana, the Department of Public Instruction/State Education Agency has actually spearheaded the development of a statewide adapted physical education

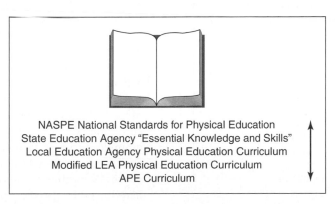

NASPE National Standards for Physical Education
State Education Agency "Essential Knowledge and Skills"
Local Education Agency Physical Education Curriculum
Modified LEA Physical Education Curriculum
APE Curriculum

Figure 5-21   Curricular Variables Affecting Instruction in LRE

curriculum, reflecting a "separate but equal" philosophy. Before the major impetus toward inclusive education, many educators within local school districts developed their own adapted physical education curriculum. The goals, objectives, and standards are typically modified to meet the needs of many students with disabilities served by the local education agency.

Program Participation Variables Affecting Instruction in the LRE

In determining the least restrictive environment, there are many alternatives that may be considered by the IEP committee (see Figure 5-22):

- Full, independent participation in general physical education. In actuality, the general physical educator has coped with the notion of

Full, independent participation in general PE
Full, independent participation in general PE with younger children
Independent participation in general PE in some units
Independent participation in some phases of the general PE class
Participation in general PE with specific APE instruction
Separate, but equal, APE with typical peers (reverse mainstreaming)
Separate, but equal, APE with peers with disabilities
APE in home, hospital, or institution

Figure 5-22   Program Participation Variables Affecting Instruction in the LRE

inclusion for years. It has been relatively standard, albeit inappropriate, practice to give students the opportunity for "socialization" in art, music, and physical education to pacify parents interested in having their child educated with typically developing peers.

- Full, independent participation in general physical education with younger students. Occasionally, it may be appropriate to integrate children with disabilities into physical education classes with younger children. This strategy, which is viable only at the elementary-school level, may be appropriate with children with delayed social and play skills. Under no circumstances, however, should a child with a disability be integrated into a physical education class serving children more than two years younger. To place a first-grader with a mild conduct disorder in a physical education class with kindergartners may prove to be a humane and creative way of allowing the child to develop social and play skills that the child lacks. It would, however, be inappropriate to place that child in a kindergarten class when the child has reached fourth-grade age. The child is not "included" in that environment; the child is set apart for ridicule by the very nature of size differences.

- Full, independent participation in some units in general physical education. On occasion, a decision about instruction in the least restrictive environment must be made on a unit-by-unit basis. For example, a learner with a behavior disorder may be able to participate independently in individual activities, such as bowling, bocci, or inline skating, but would be overwhelmed by a large-group game or sport activity.

- Full, independent participation in some phases of the daily lesson in general physical education. A mildly autistic learner, for example, may be able to participate in the structured warm-up/fitness phase of the physical education class but would be unable to handle a group game or sport.

- Participation in general physical education with specific APE instruction. A student with

Duchenne muscular dystrophy, for example, may be able to participate in the "relaxation" phase of the daily lesson. However, when the rest of the class is involved in a group game or competitive sport activity, the student should receive specific instruction in leisure and recreation activities, such as fishing or bird watching.

- Separate, but equal, adapted physical education in the school building with typically developing peers. In the event that a student requires a program participation limitation—separate, but equal, adapted physical education— a reverse mainstreaming model may be adopted. In that model, with parental permission, students without disabilities may be invited to participate in a physical education program specifically designed for students with disabilities. This is the basis of the Special Olympics Unified Sports concept. The intent of that instructional, recreation, and sports program is to allow individuals with mental retardation to be taught with, to recreate with, and to compete with individuals with disabilities.

- Separate, but equal, adapted physical education in the school building with peers with disabilities. Students with severe disabilities and/or delays may need to receive their physical education within a separate, adapted physical education class. This may, in fact, be the least restrictive environment for a student with severe behavior disorders, Rett syndrome, or severe/profound mental retardation.

- Adapted physical education in the home, hospital, or institutional setting. Students with profound disabilities and/or chronic, terminal illness may need to receive physical education, as well as the rest of their educational services, in an institutional setting, the hospital, or their home. Students with an illness or injury that requires hospitalization or causes them to be homebound for more than four weeks (this time line may vary from state to state) require educational services, including physical education, in the hospital or home.

Assessment Variables Affecting Instruction in the LRE

The Reauthorization of IDEA mandated that learners with disabilities be included, whenever possible, in state-mandated assessments. As an alternative to more traditional assessments, the State of Kentucky implemented the use of portfolio assessments for those students whose disabilities were so severe they could not participate in the state-mandated assessments.[53]

The challenge of including students with disabilities in state and districtwide assessments is great. Generally, students receiving special education services may participate in the education process in three ways: (a) in standard tests administered to all other students; (b) through the use of approved accommodations; and (c) through an alternative assessment designed to measure the progress of students who cannot participate, meaningfully, in the standard assessment process.[30] See Figure 5-23 for assessment variables affecting instruction in the LRE.

Udvari-Solner and Thousand wrote,

> Functional expressions of competence more readily allow teachers to identify skills that are discrepant or mastered, thus giving direction to instruction that is of the highest priority. Authentic assessment techniques also are less likely to be culturally biased relative to

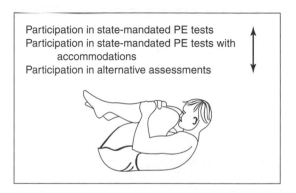

Participation in state-mandated PE tests
Participation in state-mandated PE tests with
  accommodations
Participation in alternative assessments

Figure 5-23   Assessment Variables Affecting Instruction in the LRE

students who are limited in English proficiency or in any other intellectual, physical, or emotional capacity.[124]

Support Personnel Variables Affecting Instruction in the LRE

Most physical educators demand personnel support in providing instruction for learners with disabilities in the least restrictive environment. Support personnel are critical if learners with disabilities are to be served in the LRE. Yasutake and Lerner reported that 41.9 percent of general educators believe that inclusion is not workable, regardless of the level of support provided; only 4.6 percent of the educators responded positively about the academic results of inclusion.[136]

The IEP/multidisciplinary team must carefully consider the learner's need for instructional support from a teacher, paraprofessional, volunteer, or peer buddy (see Figure 5-24).

- *No support required.* The least restrictive environment in terms of support is that in which the general physical education teacher requires no support in order to provide services. An IEP, however, is required if a student is to receive services in adapted physical education.
- *General physical educator with adapted physical education consultant support.* The general physical educator provides instruction and simply relies on an adapted physical education consultant for assessment/evaluation, IEP development, and the sharing of ideas and equipment.
- *Same-age peer buddy.* Often the only accommodation that must be made to allow a learner with a disability to function effectively within the general physical education class is to ask a given learner in the same class, a learner the same age, to be a special buddy. The buddy is asked to include the learner in play, games, or activities; often this is the only ice breaker necessary to allow the student to thrive in the general program. Trained peer tutors appear to be effective in improving the motor performance of learners with disabilities in integrated physical education classes[45,46,80] (see Figure 5-25).

King-Sears and Cummings found that the use of classwide peer tutoring facilitates the inclusion of

---

Student requires no support.
General PE teacher has APE consultant.
Same-age peer buddy
Older peer buddy
Older student as teacher assistant
Adult volunteer as teacher assistant
PE paraprofessional provides support.
Special education paraprofessional provides support.
APE teacher provides support in general PE program.
APE specialist as teacher

Figure 5-24   Support Personnel Variables Affecting Instruction in the LRE

Figure 5-25   Peer Tutor Instructions

Job description: peer buddy
Peer buddy: Molly Pyfer
Student: Cole Huettig
Physical education teacher: Dave Auxter

Physical education: Monday, Wednesday, and
Friday, 8:00 to 8:45

Every time your class goes to PE
1. Walk behind Cole in line. Take his hand if he starts to get out of line. Ask him, "Cole, walk with me, please." If he says, "No," drop his hand.
2. Sit next to Cole in the gymnasium.
3. Follow Mr. Auxter's directions so Cole can watch you and learn from you.
4. If Cole is not doing what the class is doing, tell Cole, "Watch me."
5. During free play, ask Cole, "Will you play with me?" If he says, "No," leave and go play with other friends.
6. If Cole does play with you, tell him, "I like playing with you, Cole."
7. If Cole hits, spits, or tries to wrestle with you, leave him and tell Mr. Auxter.

Figure 5-26   Classwide Peer Tutoring Model[46]

The beauty of the Classwide Peer Tutoring Model is that children with and without disabilities alike can serve interchangeably as peer tutors depending on the activity. The following steps are recommended to teach the classwide peer tutoring model:
1. Develop specific task sheets with criteria for successful performance for discrete skills.
2. Provide a model—teacher demonstration, demonstration by skilled student, or videotape.
3. Allow the students an opportunity to practice the skill.
4. Distribute the specific task sheets and criteria.
5. Provide a demonstration of the peer tutor process.
6. Review the process.

children with disabilities into the general classroom (see Figure 5-26). Specific student benefits include

- Increased opportunities to practice a skill
- Increased amount of engaged time
- Frequent feedback about their performance
- Reduction of off-task and acting-out behaviors[56]

Peers are powerful facilitators of learning. Once instruction becomes specific, it is not difficult for students to learn what it is they are to do and then communicate information to their peers. The peer instruction or modeling can be done by students with and without disabilities. Buddies must know what is to be done and have the ability to communicate with the learner.

The buddies should receive the same type of preservice and in-service training as does the professional, although the learning needs to be adapted, so that it is developmentally appropriate. Armstrong, Rosenbaum, and King[6] found that a controlled, direct-contact experience between children with and children without disabilities can significantly improve the attitudes of children without disabilities toward children with disabilities.

Empathy experiences are particularly valuable in the training of peer buddies. Also, just like paraprofessionals, the buddy should have a specific job description (review Figure 5-25). Working in close cooperation with the student's classroom teacher, this experience can be valuable for the peer buddy, as well as for the child with a disability.

- *Older peer buddy.* A student who is unable to function within the general physical education class with a same-age buddy may thrive if given the opportunity to work with an older buddy. This buddy should be carefully trained to help meet the special needs of the student without interfering with instruction and without setting the child apart from the others. This older, more mature student should receive training in the nature of the disability, in techniques for communicating effectively with the learner, and in methods of helping the learner (to move his or her wheelchair for example, or, if blind, to orient him- or herself in the gymnasium). Older students may serve as excellent models and, if carefully chosen, may serve as a magnet to draw other students toward the student with a disability (see Figure 5-27).
- *Older student as teacher's assistant.* Teacher's assistants in physical education can be indispensable in individualized learning environments. They can assume several responsibilities that contribute to class management and record progress in physical education, such as setting up and storing equipment before and after class, collecting data on themselves and others, and assisting with the instruction of younger students. These students are often honor students who are released from school or are scheduled with younger and slower-learning children. These students need to be thoroughly familiar with the programming if their assistance is to be valuable.
- *Adult volunteer as teacher's assistant.* The adult volunteer must be carefully trained to meet the needs of the student with a disability in the general physical education classroom. This may be a more effective instructional environment (the least restrictive one) for a learner with a behavior disorder that another child could not manage but a trained adult could manage.

Figure 5-27   Strategies for Developing Student Support Programs in General Physical Education

1. Discuss student support programs (peer buddy and older student assistant) in adapted physical education with the local campus administrator. At the request of the campus administrator, usually the principal, present program guidelines to the site-based management school committee.
2. Discuss the student support plan with the classroom teachers whose students will be affected. Suggest that the program be used as a reinforcer for good work in the classroom. For example, those students who had turned in homework assignments each day of a given week would be given the opportunity to serve as "peer buddies" or "student assistants" in the following week.
3. Secure permission of parents of students without disabilities in order for them to participate in the program. Outline potential benefits of participation in the program for students involved:
   a. Opportunity to learn responsibility
   b. Opportunity to assume a leadership role
   c. Chance to interact with children with different needs and abilities
4. Schedule a preservice orientation meeting for all teachers, students, and their parents. Include
   a. A description of the program
   b. Roles/responsibilities of all involved
   c. Characteristics of children with disabilities (use empathy experiences)
5. Provide in-service training for all teachers and students involved in the program. Invite parents to attend as well.
6. Develop a specific schedule for each classroom teacher whose children will be involved in the program.
7. Plan ongoing in-service education during each class period. Spend a few moments before each class reminding the student support personnel of their roles and responsibilities.
8. Informally evaluate the performance of the student support personnel; provide positive feedback whenever possible.
9. Honor the student support personnel at the end of the year in the student award assembly. *The greater the student perception of program importance, the greater the participation and personal investment.*

As funds become increasingly scarce, administrators and teachers are becoming more and more dependent on the use of volunteer resources to continue or improve programs. The effective recruitment and retention of volunteers is enhanced by effective communication. However, it is important for the general physical education teacher or adapted physical education teacher to understand the nature of the volunteer to effectively use the volunteer to meet program goals (see Figure 5-28).

Parents may take an active role as adult volunteers within the physical education program.[26] As with other volunteers, it is critical that parents receive training for their task. Downing and Rebollo wrote, "Parental roles as support personnel and/or adjunct educators of their children can only be as effective as their preparation to serve in these capacities."[26]

Schools and school districts have begun the process of actively recruiting volunteers to work with children within the schools. Schools may be "adopted" by a corporation or a civic organization. Corporate employees or members of a civic group may each serve the school in a unique way as a part of the "adopt a school" program. The general physical education teacher or adapted physical education teacher can increase the likelihood that a volunteer will choose to work in the gymnasium by following the suggestions in the box above.

The use of volunteers in the schools can greatly enhance the opportunities that can be given to children with disabilities. The physical educator can provide a chance for children to thrive and grow through the encouragement and help of program volunteers.

Physical Education Paraprofessional to Provide Support

General educators have indicated, overwhelmingly, that additional teaching support is critical if

Figure 5-28 Strategies for Increasing Volunteer Support in the Gymnasium

1. Develop a poster recruiting campaign that features the fact that it is "fun" and a great "change of pace" to work with children with disabilities in a play, leisure, recreation, or sport setting.
2. Actively recruit volunteers on the basis of their athletic skills; it is easier to recruit someone who has the perception of being needed because of particular skills.
3. Form a "dad's club" that allows fathers to contribute to their child's education in a format in which they may be comfortable.
4. Indicate the potential for learning new skills, particularly those that might be marketable. This is particularly valuable in recruiting individuals who are unemployed or seeking alternative employment opportunities.
5. Share program goals and objectives with the volunteer. Share specific goals and objectives for specific children the volunteer serves.
6. Write a specific job description for the volunteer. This is the key to successful volunteer recruitment and retention. The volunteer needs to understand his or her role within the program.
7. Ensure that the volunteer is recognized for his or her efforts. Help the children in the program express their thanks. This is perhaps the most valuable form of recognition for most volunteers. Develop a systematic strategy for recognizing the volunteer. This includes "volunteer highlights" in the adapted physical education newsletter, thank-you notes, plaques, and/or recognition dinners.

Figure 5-29 Perceptions of Paraprofessionals Regarding Their Role in Inclusion Programs

- Paraprofessionals assumed an advocate role for "their" students being included.[73]
- Paraprofessionals sought to make the experience positive for the general education teacher with whom they work.[73]
- They felt responsible for controlling all student behaviors to avoid disruption in the classroom.[73]
- They believed they are a critical liaison among parents, the general education teacher, and other school personnel involved with the child (school nurse, etc.).
- They believed themselves to be "experts" regarding the student to whom they are assigned.

students with disabilities are to be included, effectively, in the general program. Paraprofessionals and paraeducators are being used increasingly to meet that need.[28,35,80] The physical educator must, however, use the services of a paraprofessional with care (see Figure 5-29). It appears that the presence of an aide with a student with a disability may limit the potential for development of peer interactions.[38]

The student's least restrictive physical education environment may be the general physical education class with the support and assistance of a physical education paraprofessional. This paraprofessional literally serves as a second physical education teacher, who focuses interest and efforts on the children with special needs. In some instances, the general physical education teacher should insist that, if one or more learners with disabilities are to be included in the physical education class, a paraprofessional must be available (see Figure 5-30).

In many school districts, paraprofessionals or teacher's aides are assigned to assist a teacher in a given program without regard to their training or background. As such, it is possible that the physical education teacher will need to ensure that the paraprofessional attend preservice and in-service programs regarding physical education and, if students with disabilities are to be served, regarding physical education for children with disabilities.

At the very least, the paraprofessional must have the opportunity to share the same types of learning experiences recommended for teachers. Clark, French, and Henderson[21] have recommended preservice or in-service training for physical education teachers that includes empathy experiences, values clarification, volunteerism, experiences with children with disabilities, group discussions, and lectures as vehicles for attitude change. This same type of preservice or in-service

Figure 5-30 Example of Specific Responsibilities for a Special Education Paraprofessional

---

Class 1, 8:00–8:45

7: 55
Go to Room 109 to accompany Michelle to the gym. Insist she push her own chair.

8:00–8:15
Roam throughout the gymnasium while children are doing warm-up exercises, encouraging all the children to do well. If necessary, remind Michelle to do her modified warm-ups, which are posted on the wall.

8:15–8:40
Monitor Michelle's interactions with others in the class. Record and describe any inappropriate interactions on her behavior chart in the teacher's office. Refer to the description of appropriate and/or inappropriate behaviors on her chart.

8:40–8:45
Accompany Michelle to her room.

---

training must be included in the training regimen of the paraprofessional as well.

One of the most significant aspects of the supervision of a paraprofessional is the description of the paraprofessional's role and responsibilities. Most school districts have a job description for the paraprofessional. This description is, however, often vague regarding the specific role and responsibilities of the paraprofessional. In addition, the job description for the paraprofessional is usually prepared for the individual who will assist a classroom teacher. The duties and responsibilities of the paraprofessional working in the gymnasium are different from the duties and responsibilities of the paraprofessional in the classroom. As such, the general physical education teacher or adapted physical education teacher must work closely with the building principal to design a specific job description, particularly if the paraprofessional is to help teach children with disabilities.

A specific job description significantly alleviates potential problems. If respective roles and responsibilities are clear to both the physical education teacher and the paraprofessional, they can work together as a professional team, serving children in the best possible way. In addition, the wise physical educator should take every opportunity to reinforce the efforts of the paraprofessional. For example, the physical educator should write a letter to the principal praising the efforts of the paraprofessional. A copy should be shared with the paraprofessional. Or the physical educator should routinely orchestrate a class "thank-you" for the paraprofessional with cards, cake, and punch.

Special Education Paraprofessional to Provide Support

The presence of a special education paraprofessional in the gymnasium is more restrictive than if the student works with a physical education paraprofessional because of the stigma attached to having a "special ed" teacher accompany the learner to class. Every bit of information that applied to the physical education paraprofessional applies to the special education paraprofessional as well (review Figure 5-30).

The paraprofessional may play a particularly important role within the school as a liaison between the community and the school. The paraprofessional who lives within the school feeder system may be of critical value to the physical educator who seeks to provide a physical education program that is meaningful not only to the students but also to the community at large.[35]

Adapted Physical Educator to Provide Student Support

For a student to function within the general physical education program, it may be necessary for a specialist trained in adapted physical education to intervene with the student in the gymnasium. Unfortunately, by necessity, this would reduce the amount of time the student would spend in the general physical education program. In most districts, the adapted physical education specialist has too large a caseload to spend individual time with each student each day. When it is impossible for the APE to spend time daily with the student, the adapted physical education specialist may demonstrate strategies to the general physical educator that he or she may be able to use with this student and with other students with disabilities. In some situations, if the adapted physical educator provides a model while supporting a student with a disability in the general physical education setting, the general physical educator and/or paraprofessional can then adopt that behavior to facilitate inclusion.

Adapted Physical Educator as Teacher

Many school districts have not made a strong commitment to quality adapted physical education programming. In some schools, for example, the caseload of the adapted physical educator may be more than 200 students; there is no way that quality service can be delivered in that situation. A separate, but equal, service for students with disabilities has become a luxury, not a reality.

The adapted physical educator may provide direct service in some institutions or with a very specific type of student—those with traumatic brain injuries, for example—but, in general, staff priorities cause this form of direct service to students with disabilities and their parents to be rare.

Teaching Style as a Variable Affecting Instruction in the LRE

The teaching style of the general physical educator is a variable that must be considered carefully if a learner with a disability is to be taught in the general physical education class (see Figure 5-31). It is clear that most teachers have a set teaching style

```
Learner's individually designed program
      Guided discovery approach
         Self-check approach
           Reciprocal style
            Command style
```

Figure 5-31   Teaching Style as a Variable Affecting Instruction in the LRE

and are unwilling or unable to change that style; in fact, an adapted physical educator serving as a consultant is wise to make recommendations and suggestions that fit into the teacher's typical behavior and rhythm.[47] For example, there may be two physical educators in the same large high school. The IEP committee may need to evaluate the teaching style of both teachers to determine in which class the learner is likely to succeed. Certainly, a willingness to work with a student with a disability and a commitment to educating all are necessary and desirable traits in a teacher selected to work with a learner with a disability.

The selection of an instructional approach appears to be based heavily on the teacher's experience. Professional preparation training programs continue to produce teachers who are most likely to teach the way they have been taught. This cycle, unfortunately, continues to place teachers who remain teacher-directed and teacher-focused and who believe themselves to be the "givers of knowledge" in direct contact with students who would be more successful if given the opportunity to direct their own learning, to discover, and to take responsibility for their own learning. Following are different types of instructional strategies.

- *Learner's individually designed program.* The essence of this teaching style is that the focus is on each student and his or her needs. A teacher who is already focusing on individual students can easily accommodate and serve a student who just happens to have a disability. The learner is empowered to design and develop a series of tasks and activities that meet his or her needs, and the teacher serves essentially as a consultant—the teacher helps the student by asking important questions, reinforcing appropriate tasks and activities, and redirecting the student's efforts if the tasks or activities are not developmentally appropriate.
- *Guided discovery.* In this teaching style, the teacher asks questions, chooses and develops activities, and plans events to lead a student to a predetermined answer or solution.[79] The most common guided discovery teaching style in

physical education is movement exploration. For example, a student who uses a wheelchair may be guided through the following activities at the same time as his other-ambulatory peers:

1. Can you move in a large circle on the floor?
2. Can you move in a large circle on the floor in a different way?
3. What can you do to make the circle smaller?
4. What can you do to make the circle even smaller?

This type of approach empowers all movers and respects the individual's unique responses to movement problems and challenges. This teaching style is one in which learners with disabilities can be easily included.

- *Self-check.* In this teaching style, the teacher shares with the learner the skills needed to perform a task or activity individually.[79] The teacher has established criteria for successful accomplishment of a given task, so that the individual learner can evaluate his or her own success. If the teacher is serving a student with a disability, the teacher can help the student establish challenging, yet attainable, standards for success. Once again, the emphasis on meeting the needs of individual students facilitates the inclusion of students with disabilities.
- *Reciprocal style.* This teaching style is characterized by the establishment of learning partnerships.[79] While the teacher determines the activity or task and establishes the criteria for success, students work in partnership to provide each other feedback regarding performance. This teaching style easily accommodates learners with disabilities, even those who require the support of a same-age or older peer buddy to be successful. If every student has a learning buddy, it is easy for the learner with a disability to have a buddy as well.
- *Command style.* This teaching style has often been called the traditional teaching approach.[79] The teacher explains an activity, demonstrates it, and expects each learner to replicate it. The teacher-controlled atmosphere allows little individual variation in performance. Though

"When you adjust the height of the basket, I can be successful."
Picture by Carol Huettig.

this sounds restrictive, this teaching style may be exactly what a learner with a conduct disorder or autism needs in order to learn. The structure may prove very helpful.

The needs of learners in this new century demand that teachers of children, with and without disabilities, examine strategies to meet the needs of the children they serve. Most certainly, teachers have to focus on active rather than passive learning. Children, like adults, learn by doing, not by watching and certainly not by listening. And it is critical that teachers honor and respect the various ways that children learn.

Management of Behavior as a Variable Affecting Instruction in the LRE

The behavior of students with and without disabilities in a general education setting is often the major factor that determines the student's success or failure within that setting. Carpenter and McKee-Higgins wrote,

> A classroom climate characterized by learning and cooperative interactions with groups of students who are motivated, responsive to traditional authority figures and systems (e.g., teachers and schools), and compliant with established rules and routines may be jeopar-

Identical behavioral expectations
Slightly modified behavioral expectations
Individually designed reinforcement system
Individually designed behavior-management
    plan (BMP)

Figure 5-32   Management of Behavior as a Variable Affecting Instruction in the LRE

dized by the presence of students who have not learned or adopted behaviors that are compatible with performing within a community of learners.[17]

A proactive, positive behavior-management program is the key to the successful inclusion of students with disabilities in the general education program. The variables which must be addressed regarding the management of behavior are presented in Figure 5-32.

Identical Behavioral Expectations

Inappropriate behavior in the physical education classroom is the reason most often given that physical education teachers do not want a learner with a disability in the gymnasium. If a learner with a disability is to be readily accepted in the general physical education program, by the teacher and students alike, the learner must be able to meet the behavioral expectations and standards set for every other learner. Too often, a learner with a disability is excluded from the physical education environment, not because of a motor delay but because of the learner's inability to follow class rules (see Figure 5-33).

Figure 5-33   Skills Needed for Success in the General Program

One of the keys to the inclusion of children with disabilities in the general physical education program is, literally, teaching *all* the children the skills they need to be successful within the program. These specific behaviors include
• Following directions[19]
• Asking and answering questions[19]
• Beginning and completing tasks
• Getting, using, and returning equipment
• Sitting, standing, and walking in line

Slightly Modified Behavioral Expectations

General physical educators are often willing to include a learner with a disability in the general physical education program if it requires making only minor changes in behavioral expectations.[9] For example, if a student with an attention deficit disorder is unable to sit on a given spot while listening to directions, the teacher may accommodate the student by allowing the student to stay within a larger space (e.g., a free-throw circle).

Individually Designed Reinforcement System

As an example of this behavior-management system, a deeply committed physical educator teaching a high school student with Down syndrome was willing to abide by the recommendations of the IEP committee and completed a behavior checklist each week to be sent home to the student's parents. When the student willingly participated in class activities more than 50 percent of the time, she earned a coupon that she could use to rent a video on the weekend.

Individually Designed Behavior-Management Plan (BMP)

The most restrictive environment is one in which the student with a disability has an individual behavior-management plan (BMP) that is different from the plans of his or her classmates. The physical educator, often teaching large classes, will find it almost impossible to implement a specific behavior-management plan.

An individual behavior-management plan is almost impossible to implement in a physical education class without the support of an additional, trained adult in the gymnasium. Under no circumstances should a student, even an older student, be put in the position of implementing a behavior-management plan for another student. The ethical and legal implications of a student's being given the responsibility of managing the behavior of another student are frightening.

Grading as a Variable Affecting Instruction in the LRE

The Reauthorization of IDEA makes it infinitely clear that, if the school district has made a commitment to parents of children without disabilities to provide report cards every six weeks (six report cards per academic year), parents of children with disabilities have a right to have a report card explaining their students' progress every six weeks.

Grading is one of the most difficult issues facing the general physical educator (any educator, for that matter). All too often, children with disabilities are "placed" in the general physical education program, and the IEP/multidisciplinary team has made no recommendations regarding modifications/accommodations in grading. The continuum is described in Figure 5-34.

Same Expectations in Grading and Reporting Grade

In terms of instruction, the least restrictive environment in the physical education program is one in which learners with disabilities are able to meet the same expectations in all phases of the grading process. That includes the motor, physical fitness, knowledge, and behavioral components of grading. The teacher is able to use the same state or local assessments for the learner with a disability as he or she uses for other children and is able to report the results on the same instrument.

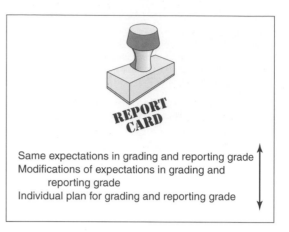

Same expectations in grading and reporting grade
Modifications of expectations in grading and reporting grade
Individual plan for grading and reporting grade

Figure 5-34   Grading as a Variable Affecting Instruction in the LRE

Modifications of Expectations in Grading and Reporting Grade

Occasionally a learner with a disability participates in the general physical education program successfully with basic modifications in expectations for grading and in the way that grade is reported to parents. For example, a student with severe dyslexia may need to have written tests administered verbally. A high school student with mild mental retardation may be required to answer only every third question on a written test. Or, a student with spina bifida who uses a wheelchair may be asked to "roll" instead of "run" in the cardiovascular-respiratory endurance phase of the physical fitness test. The modifications made must be reported on the standard school report card.

Individual Plan for Grading and Reporting Grade

A grade in any subject should promote educational goals and should reflect educational aims and objectives. For programs to be most effective, established objectives must indicate the desired goals of instruction so that they become the criteria on which grades are based. If the criteria are valid, successful measurement will result in valid evaluation. The grade, if one desires to translate behavioral performance, could reflect how well these criteria have been met.

The complexity of grading in physical education classes is magnified when an attempt is made to evaluate the performance of students with disabilities. The one common denominator among all students is the mastery of individual performance objectives. If students are graded on the basis of how well they meet their IEP objectives, a student with poor posture, a student with a cardiac disorder, an obese student, and a student who has just had surgery can all be properly evaluated for their grades in the class. In the case of a student with a disability, the student's IEP may be used as the tool for reporting progress (grade) to parents.

Equipment as a Variable Affecting Instruction in the LRE

Making instructional modifications for students with disabilities in physical education may be as simple as finding a different type of equipment for the student to use while learning. The continuum is outlined in the following paragraphs and in Figure 5-35.

- Same equipment. Every learner within the class shares and uses the same equipment.
- Similar, but different equipment. It is possible to improve instructional modifications simply by changing the type of equipment available for

student use. For example, a student with juvenile rheumatoid arthritis may not be able to participate in a volleyball game with a real volleyball but may be successful in a "volleyball" game that uses a beach ball instead. A child with a visual impairment may experience difficulty tracking a typical playground ball but would be able to participate in a game of catch if the ball were a bright, fluorescent color.

- Specially designed equipment. It is possible to enhance opportunities for inclusion by providing the learner with a disability with specially designed equipment to meet his or her needs. For example, a student with cerebral palsy may be able to bowl by using an "automatic grip release" or a ramp. A student with a below-the-knee amputation may be able to participate in downhill skiing with an "outrigger" ski pole.

Instruction within the least restrictive environment is a dynamic and evolving process. Unlike a determination of "placement," in which a student receives services without regard for acquisition of motor behaviors, social behaviors, or behavior, carefully designed instruction requires the physical educator to evaluate constantly the student's needs within each continuum.

WORKING DOCUMENT FOR THE IEP COMMITTEE: LEAST RESTRICTIVE ENVIRONMENT IN PHYSICAL EDUCATION

The Irving, Texas, Independent School District designed a special education program design matrix for the IEP/multidisciplinary committee in their consideration of the least restrictive environment within the general education program. The strength of this document is that it provides the members of the IEP committee with a working document that emphasizes a student's strengths and considers the realities of the general education experience. The committee members then try to match the student's strengths with the educational opportunity that will be provided.

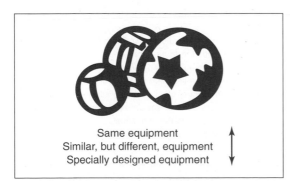

Same equipment
Similar, but different, equipment
Specially designed equipment

Figure 5-35   Equipment as a Variable Affecting Instruction in the LRE

This type of proactive effort in determining the least restrictive environment for learners with disabilities may be modified for use in physical education as well. Examples of matrixes for a unit and a daily plan are presented in Figures 5-36, 5-37, and 5-38. Figure 5-37 is an illustration of how the student's strengths are matched by unit(s) in which the student is likely to experience success. Focusing on the student's strengths is of particular value in the IEP/multidisciplinary team meeting. Parents are often much more receptive to the ideas of the committee members if the emphasis is on what the student *can do*, rather than what the student cannot do. In Figure 5-38, the student's strengths are matched with each phase of the daily lesson plan in the first-grade physical education program.

If an IEP/multidisciplinary team is truly focused on providing the best possible instruction for a student, within the federally mandated least restrictive learning environment, accommodations can/must be made to ensure success. Careful consideration of the student's abilities, the schedule and plan of the general physical educator, and the availability of support can all influence decisions involved in the construction of an appropriate learning environment.

Specific Strategies for Including Learners with Disabilities

In the following sections, specific instructional strategies for instructing learners with disabilities in the general physical education program are

A

Program Design Matrix

To facilitate positive and constructive admission, review, and dismissal meetings (ARDs) for all students, this program design matrix was developed at Irving Independent School District. It was during a difficult ARD that this matrix was scratched out for all participants to see a "picture" of the student. Because it focused on the strengths of the student, the ARD was able to maintain a proactive focus that generated an individual education program (IEP) for the student's needs. The successful and positive ARD supported the need for this matrix.

The following is a guide to implement the matrix.

1. The matrix is given to the teacher before the ARD to fill in the schedule of a regular school day. Copies are to be made to hand to all those attending the ARD.

2. After review of student's testing, progress, etc., you could begin the use of the matrix, explaining that this will help develop the IEP and programming for the student.

3. Next, identify strengths of the student. Everyone should participate and feel comfortable with the identified strengths before doing a cross-check with the classroom schedule.

4. As you do a cross-check, mark an X in the appropriate box and column to signify the student's specific strength(s) that could allow the student to be able to be successful in the classroom. It does not mean that the child could not get support if needed.

5. Empty boxes could indicate areas of concern that the ARD committee needs to address or that a box is not applicable. Circling an activity identified as an area of need will alert the committee to be sure to develop strategies to meet the student's needs in that area. Through ARD discussion, areas that could provide support through modification, consultation, pullout, collaboration, etc., could be identified. It is not to be assumed that support services are to be provided at the specific time scheduled for an activity identified as an area of need. The time assigned will allow the ARD committee to see how much time during the day is needed to program for special education support. The bottom boxes allow times to be totaled, which will help transfer information onto the time sheet.

6. Support suggestions can include equipment, peer tutor, buddy classmate, modifications to the lesson or activity, support personnel, etc.

Figure 5-36   Special Education Program Design Matrix to Facilitate Inclusion Based on Student's Strengths

A. Description of Matrix.

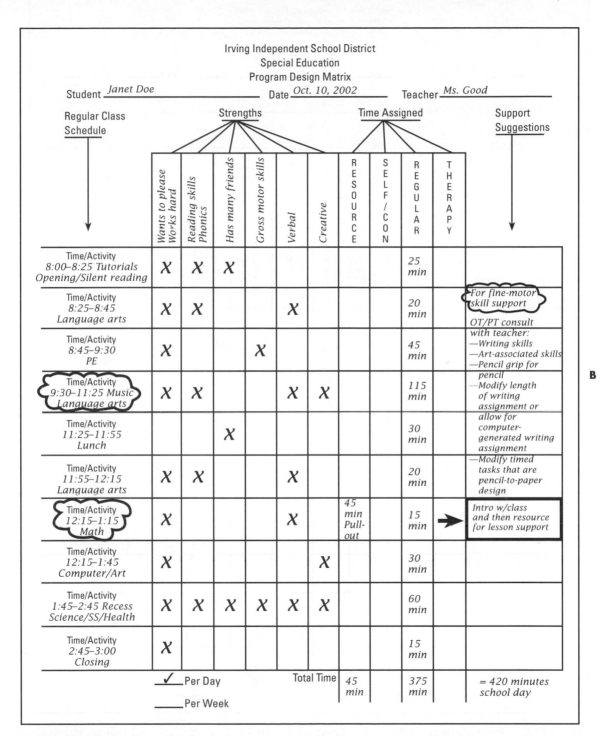

Figure 5-36 (*Continued*)

B. Example.

Courtesy Irving (Texas) Independent School District.

Least Restrictive Environment Design Matrix (Unit)
High School Physical Education
First Semester

Student _Julia Hernandez_   Date ___1/6/02___

Adapted Physical Education Teacher _Brett Favre_

Physical Education Teacher _Mr. Garcia_

Activity/ Unit	Student Strengths					Support Suggestions
	Good runner	Excellent flexibility	Works well independently	Responds well to music	Follows directions	
September, Weeks 1 & 2 Fitness Evaluations	✓	✓			✓	
September, Weeks 3 & 4, October, Weeks 1 & 2 Individual Fitness	✓	✓			✓	
October, Weeks 3 & 4 Archery			✓		✓	
November, Weeks 1 & 2 Flag Football						_Remove for separate, but equal program with low_
November, Weeks 3 & 4 Soccer						_pupil-staff ratio_
December, Weeks 1 & 2 Volleyball						
December, Week 3 Creative Dance			✓	✓		

Figure 5-37   Example of Least Restrictive Environment Design Matrix (Unit) to Facilitate Humane Inclusion in High School Physical Education Class

Least Restrictive Environment Design Matrix
First Grade Physical Education
Daily Lesson Plan

Student *Dione Haley*   Date *9/7/02*

Adapted Physical Education Teacher *Emmitt Smith*

Physical Education Teacher *Cassandra Williams*

Activity/ Unit	Basic locomotor skills	Balance	Rhythmic ability	Responds well to 1–1 instruction	Support Suggestions
	Student Strengths				
9:40–9:45 Roll				✓	*Pair with a buddy for roll/ directions*
9:45–9:55 Warm-Ups to Music			✓		
9:55–10:10 Movement Exploration	✓				
10:10–10:20 Large-Group Activity				✓	*Pair with a buddy for parallel activity*
10:20–10:25 Relaxation				✓	*Pair with a buddy for relaxation activity*

Figure 5-38   Example of Least Restrictive Environment Design Matrix (Daily Lesson Plan) to Facilitate Humane Inclusion in First-Grade Physical Education Class

considered at the elementary, middle, and high school level.

Elementary Physical Education

According to Ratliffe, Ratliffe, and Bie,[94] effective learning environments allow teachers to provide learning tasks, refine students' performance, and focus on students' skill and knowledge rather than on their behavior. Until such a learning envi-

ronment has been established, most of the teacher's time is spent attending to students' behavior and trying to keep students on task. Although the strategies outlined by these authors (see Figure 5-39) were designed for organizing instruction in the general elementary physical education class, they are appropriate for any physical education setting. The teacher approaches classroom organization proactively and creates a situation that enhances learning and prevents inappropriate behavior.

Williams[132] addressed the fact that many activities typically used in elementary physical education programs are inappropriate, not only for children with disabilities but for any child. He identified the "Physical Education Hall of Shame" to help physical educators take a close look at decisions regarding games that are inappropriate for any learner (see Figure 5-40). The intent of the 1996 Hall of Shame is to encourage educators to focus on developmentally appropriate activities to avoid the following:

- Embarrassing a child in front of his or her peers
  - One student performing while the others watch[133]
  - One line, one ball, one chance to participate[133]

Figure 5-39   Strategies for Reinforcing Appropriate Behavior

1. Reward appropriate behavior (e.g., smiley faces, stars, "happy-grams," stickers, hugs, smiles, or free time).
2. Remove distractions from the area before starting a lesson.
3. Provide equipment of the same type and color for all children to help prevent fights.
4. Strategically place students who are likely to exhibit inappropriate behavior in designated spots within the gymnasium (e.g., close to the teacher or near children who will be good models).
5. Have students practice "stopping" an activity by placing equipment on the floor in front of their feet. Have students practice returning equipment to the original storage place.
6. Develop a strategy for transition from the classroom to the gymnasium that allows maximum control. For example, have the students practice walking in a line with hands behind the back.
7. Consider an immediate individual activity when students sit on their designated spot, waiting for further instruction. For example, have the children join in singing a song while waiting for the entire class to be seated.
8. Reward students who listen and cooperate by letting them choose equipment first and take turns first.
9. Stand near a disruptive student. Make your immediate presence known by placing your hand firmly on the student's shoulder.
10. Provide a designated time-out area separate from the group, but easily monitored.

Data from Ratliffe T, Ratliffe L, Bie B: *J Phys Educ Rec Dance* 62:24–27, 1991.

Figure 5-40   Activities Included in the Physical Education Hall of Shame[132]

- Dodgeball
- Duck, Duck, Goose
- Giants, Elves, and Wizard
- Kickball
- Musical Chairs
- Relay races
- Steal the Bacon
- Line Soccer
- Red Rover
- Simon Says
- SPUD
- Tag

- Eliminating students from participation to allow only one "winner"
- Low participation time and low activity time
- Placing learners at serious risk for injury and harm
- "Rolling out the ball"[133]
- Inappropriately sized equipment, such as 10-foot basketball hoops in elementary schools
- Using exercise as punishment
- Allowing students to choose teams[133]

Young children who are still in the process of developing their basic sensory systems and their perceptual-motor integration processes are best served by using the bottom-up developmental model. Types of activities that have proved to be effective in resolving delays frequently demonstrated by young children whose development was compromised before, during, or after birth are discussed at length in Chapter 4.

As often as possible, activities that address specific areas of development should be incorporated into the activity of children demonstrating those delays. When programs for these youngsters are delivered in a general physical education program, it is possible to address their specific needs and still benefit other students within the class.

Games and activities that promote development in specific areas and are enjoyed by all children, regardless of ability level, are included in the supplement to this ninth edition of the text, *Gross Motor Activities for Young Children with Special Needs*. Over 200 group activities to promote reflex and equilibrium development; vestibular, tactile, proprioceptive, auditory, and visual sensory stimulation and discrimination; body image; motor planning; object-control skills; locomotor and nonlocomotor patterns; cross-lateral integration; fitness; and relaxation are included.

The Middle and High School Physical Education Program

One of the most successful techniques for designing physical education classes that appeal to and accommodate a wide range of ability levels is described in the book entitled *Changing Kids'* *Games* by Morris and Stiehl.[78] These authors suggest that an excellent way to pique students' interest and involvement in a physical education class is to engage them in a process that puts them in control of many aspects of the games included in the curriculum. They propose using a games' analysis technique in classes to enable students and teachers to identify and modify any aspect of a game or sport. Using a chalkboard or a flip chart, a teacher can lead the students through a process of systematically identifying the components that are included in the six categories that constitute a game.

The six categories included in every game are purposes, players, movements, objects, organization, and limits. Each category includes several components that have the potential to be changed, depending on the wishes of the group. The categories and their components are as follows:

1. Purposes. The purposes of a game include developing motor skills, enhancing self-worth, improving fitness, having enjoyment, gaining satisfaction, and developing cognitive skills. When deemed necessary, the components may be subdivided to identify specifics, such as which motor skills, what aspects of fitness, and which cognitive skills are included in the game.
2. Players. Analysis of the players category yields characteristics such as the number of players required, whether individual performance or group cooperation is needed, and the makeup of the groups. To create greater opportunities for students to be involved in a game, the number of team members could be increased, all teams could be made coeducational, efficient and inefficient movers could be placed on the same team, and students with disabilities and/or different cognitive levels could be included.
3. Movements. The components of the movements category include types (body awareness, locomotor versus nonlocomotor, reception versus propulsion, and physical

attributes); locations, including personal space (levels, directions, and pathways) and general space; quality (force, flow, and speed); relationships (objects, players, and group); quantity (number, unit of time, distance, and location); and sequences (task order within an episode). Students should be given the opportunity to alter the types of movement demands, so that everyone has a chance to participate fully. Individual games could be changed to partner or small-group efforts, and a variety of pathways from which players could choose could be built into the game. Players could be given the opportunity to play for a predetermined score rather than for time or vice versa.

4. Objects. The discussion of objects will center around the types and uses of the objects, the quantity needed, and their location. A game that requires everyone to use the same implements does not require much imagination. Why not give everyone the opportunity to use a batting tee, or to swing at a slow pitch rather than a fast pitch, or to catch with the mitt of choice rather than the one the rules call for?

5. Organization. Organizational patterns include patterns in the game (lines, circles, or scattered), number of players in the pattern, and locations of the players (close to one another or far apart, etc.). Differences among students can become less discouraging if the students are given opportunities to change things, so that they can be successful. Permitting the volleyball server to stand as close to the net as he or she chooses, designating specific players who have a difficult time keeping up to execute all of the throw-ins in soccer, working with peer partners who can help interpret written personal fitness program instructions, or allowing a hit after two bounces of the tennis ball can turn a dreaded class into a positive, uplifting experience.

6. Limits. Limits in games have to do with what is expected of players (the kind of

participation and the movements that are necessary) and the environmental conditions (boundaries, time limits, scoring, and rules). Wider boundaries, modified rules, shoulder instead of forward rolls, spotting instead of executing a cartwheel, smaller goals to defend, and more than one chance to execute a correct serve can include students who might never have had the opportunity to participate in a game with their classmates.

Students can be wonderfully creative when they are given an opportunity to analyze the components in a familiar game and are invited to invent ways to alter it by changing one or more components. In the beginning, the teacher may have to provide some examples—such as, if the game requires the use of one ball, what changes to the game would be necessary if two or more balls were used? How could the rules be changed if three rather than two teams were included in the game? What components would need to be modified to include the active participation of a student using a wheelchair? After the students catch on, they will have several ideas of their own to try. Once everyone agrees on the specific modifications, have them practice their newly designed game. An evaluation session should always follow. What did they like about their new game? What did they dislike? What other alterations would they like to try?

This approach has been used successfully with middle and high school students. It is a major focus of the physical education curriculum in use in the seventh and eighth grades at Cal Young Middle School in Eugene, Oregon.[117] In an attempt to increase student participation and involvement in physical education, it was decided to try the games analysis approach. After gaining the support and approval of the administration and parents, the physical education teachers implemented the program to foster the cooperation, creativity, and involvement of all the students. Students in the physical education classes were required to use a group approach to modify traditional games for the purposes of (1) maximizing the features of the game the students liked and minimizing those they did not like, (2) practicing the skills of the game, and (3) including students of all ability levels. For each of the traditional game units in the curriculum (e.g., softball, volleyball, soccer), teachers divided the class into equal teams, making a special effort to balance ability levels within each group. The groups, once formed, selected a team name that was positive and then analyzed the sport to determine the components of each of the six categories.

After identifying the components of the game, the students listed things each of them liked and disliked about the game and discussed and decided on ways to modify the game and the rules to better meet their needs and objectives. Modifications were expected to preserve the basic movements of the game (e.g., hitting, catching, throwing) yet accommodate the students' individual likes, dislikes, needs, and levels of ability. Every aspect of the game could be altered, and all students, regardless of ability level, were given the option of using any modification the team members had agreed on.

Before beginning to play the game, each student selected his or her own objectives to achieve in the sport. Afterward, the students determined the extent to which those objectives were met (see Figure 5-41). Student evaluations of their ability to

---

Self-Evaluation—Softball Unit

_____   _____
(First and last name)   (PE period)

Please rate yourself on the following questions. The rating scale is 1 (low) to 10 (high). Indicate which number best represents your contributions to your softball group. Your teachers hope that you will honestly evaluate yourself because this evaluation is not a part of your point total for the softball unit. The purposes are to have you see if you used your time constructively and in a positive manner for this 3-week instructional unit.

1. I gave some suggestions toward our team name. _____
2. I made a sincere effort to write down my own individual "likes and dislikes" about softball. _____
3. I contributed my ideas toward the game that we taught the class. _____
4. I understood most of the rules to the game that our group taught the class. _____
5. I thought I presented positive ideas and thoughts to my group. _____
6. I got along with the people in my group. _____
7. I became more acquainted with some people in my group that I did not know very well before we did the softball unit. _____
8. I tried to listen to other people's opinions in my group. _____
9. I was willing to try the new games that my classmates made up. _____
10. I became more aware of people's abilities and limitations. _____
11. I was willing to see adaptations made for people who needed some extra help when it came to practicing the skills of softball. _____
12. I learned to become more tolerant of my classmates' limitations. _____
13. I learned that if we can make modifications to the regular game of softball, we can have better participation by the entire class. _____
14. I have increased my awareness that everyone in my class has certain abilities and limitations when it comes to playing softball. _____
15. I would like to participate in another unit of instruction using some of the same ideas that were tried in the softball unit. _____

Please state the one thing you "liked the most" and "disliked the most" about the softball unit of instruction.

Figure 5-41   Self-Evaluation—Softball Unit
Courtesy L. Temple and J.D. Kelly, Eugene, Ore.

meet their own objectives were not part of the class grading system.

During any given unit, there were as many as five versions of the same sport being played in one class. When each team was satisfied with the game they had created, they presented it to the rest of the class.

Teachers reported that, after the initial period of uncertainty and confusion, the vast majority of students embraced and enjoyed the process. Teachers also reported that they personally grew in their ability to admit to not always having the "right" answers and to trust the students' abilities to make good decisions and evaluate their own progress.

Participation in Interscholastic Sports

The Americans with Disabilities Act makes it clear that students with disabilities have the right to participate in interscholastic sport activities sponsored by the school. Most coaches would agree that students with disabilities have a right to participate in interscholastic sport experiences. Most, however, also feel inadequately prepared to address the specific needs of individuals with disabilities in interscholastic sport settings.[60,98] Essentially, opportunities for learners with disabilities to participate in interscholastic sports at the middle and high school level are extremely limited.[60,61]

A variety of factors influence the lack of formalized opportunities for students with disabilities to participate in interscholastic sports in segregated programs, let alone a placement continuum:

- State interscholastic athletic agency policies
- Coach, administrator, and parent concerns regarding athlete safety
- Athletic program emphases on winning
- A lack of preparation, "infusion" of material, regarding coaching athletes with disabilities in the undergraduate professional preparation curriculum[25]

Rizzo et al.[98] has suggested that, if coaches had opportunities to coach young athletes with disabilities in integrated youth sport settings, the coaches would be better prepared to meet their unique needs at the middle and high school level.

Collaboration and Inclusion

The collaborative process, one in which two or more professionals share responsibilities, and subsequently thoughts and ideas, is often a difficult one for educators. It is particularly distressing to some professionals when the need for collaboration is thrust on them by programs or administrators (see Figures 5-42 and 5-43).

Always, the most successful collaborations are those that spring from grassroots, teacher-based efforts and that emerge naturally as professionals learn to trust each other and themselves. Sands wrote,

> Just as animals claim, enhance and protect their territories, so do disciplines assume ownership of particular bodies of knowledge, skills, or modes of intervention and, once established, promote and defend their turfs.[107]

Figure 5-42   Educators' Values and Beliefs That Support Collaboration

- Individual differences are valued.[59]
- Diversity is valued. Varied learning styles are honored.
- Active participation in the process is a key.
- Tolerant, reflective and flexible personalities are vital.[84]
- Team members work toward common goals.[42,59,110]
  - Co-teaching
  - Peer coaching
  - Assistance teaming
- Collaborative problem solving[42]
- Ethical behavior is expected.[121]
- Professionals can assume transdisciplinary roles and provide integrated related-therapy services or medical support.[42]
- Collaboration must be voluntary.[42]
- Collaboration necessitates equity between all participants in the process—teacher, aide, parent, and administrator.
- Participants are collectively responsible for the success/failure of the collaboration.[42,110]
- Specific purpose of the "team" is shared by team members and is an integral part of the larger school goals.

Figure 5-43 Strategies for Effective Collaborative Problem Solving

- Specifically defining the problem[42]
- Generating all possible solutions[104]
- Identifying the causes of the problem
- Screening solutions for feasibility[104]
- Setting specific, measurable objectives
- Identifying specific solution activities[42]
- Monitoring for success and evaluating the solution[104]

The process of working in collaboration is not typical within the professions and is certainly not easy. It requires a tremendous amount of work and involves professionals in activities that may cause them to feel vulnerable. Korinek et al. wrote,

> Most current models of collaboration stress the importance of well-developed relationships that are based on trust, parity, respect, and the value of each person's contributions. Other hallmarks of many collaborative models include voluntary participation, shared responsibility for problem solving and intervention implementation, intervention monitoring, scheduled follow-up, pooled resources, and professional accountability.[59]

According to Giangreco, Baumgart, and Doyle,

> The inclusion of students with disabilities in general education classrooms can serve as a catalyst to open classroom doors and change staffing patterns so that teachers can build collaborative alliances with other teachers and support personnel in order to have ongoing opportunities to engage in professional dialogue, problem solving, and various forms of co-teaching.[39]

The adapted physical educator must work in close cooperation with the general physical education personnel who are providing services to children with disabilities in the general physical education class. The physical educator may assume several roles in the capacity of delivering services to children with disabilities. Whatever the role, it is clear that an organizational system needs to be developed that coordinates the efforts of aides, volunteers, and special and general classroom teachers who deliver services, as well as itinerant and resource room teachers if they are involved in the program. Specific job descriptions, such as those provided in this chapter, are vital to the collaborative process (review Figure 5-25 and see Figures 5-44 and 5-45).

Shared responsibility necessitates significant communication and specific delineation of responsibilities. General, ongoing team meetings are necessary if this type of communication is to work. In addition, there must be a way for team members involved in the collaboration to communicate with others generally. Many teachers have found shared lunch periods and common planning periods to be

---

Job description: physical education volunteer

Volunteer: Beth Ann Huettig
Students: Alex, Talitha, Lashundra, and Jesus
Physical education teacher: Jean Pyfer
Physical education: Tuesday and Thursday, 10:10 to 10:50 A.M.

- Provide instructional support for Alex, Talitha, Lashundra, and Jesus.
- Please use the following strategies for encouraging appropriate behavior:
  1. Praise the child if "on task."
  2. Praise another child, in close proximity, who is "on task."
  3. Remind the child verbally regarding the task: for example, "Alex, we are all doing warm-ups now"; or "Alex, I'd like you to join the other children and do your sit-ups."
  4. Physically assist the child with the task. For example, sit down next to Talitha and help her hold onto the parachute handle.
- If the child demonstrates "off-task" or disruptive behaviors after using the four steps, request the teacher's assistance.
- Beth, remember you are responsible solely to me. If one of the children is abusive or aggressive, please let me intervene.

Figure 5-44   Job Description for an Adult Volunteer in an Elementary Physical Education Program

---

Job description: paraprofessional

To: Mr. Chen, special education assistant, self-
        contained classroom, Carthage Middle School
From: Jean Pyfer, adapted physical education consultant

Responsibilities for: Alejandro Moreno
Physical education: 11:00 to 11:50 A.M. every day

- Allow Alejandro to wheel himself to the gymnasium
  every day. Please leave 5 minutes before passing time
  so that Alejandro will not be late.

- Please watch quietly as Alejandro does his modified
  warm-ups with the class. Please note that his exercises are posted in the coach's office on the back of
  his door. He knows his exercises, but he may "pretend" he doesn't to avoid them.

- As the class begins their group activity, please use
  another student (one who hasn't dressed for activity)
  to work on skills with Alejandro. For example, if the
  class is playing basketball, demonstrate to the student
  how to bounce pass to Alejandro. Carefully monitor
  the activity to ensure that his peer is not too rough.

- When the class begins laps at the end of class (outside or inside), Alejandro should start his as well. At
  the beginning of the year, he was able to roll 2 times
  around the gymnasium in 10 minutes. Build, please,
  throughout the year by adding 1 lap per month. I
  would like him to be able to roll 6 times around the
  gymnasium in 10 minutes. Reward good effort with the
  football cards I gave you.

- You are responsible for Alejandro's safety and well-
  being in the gymnasium. If you have difficulty with his
  behavior, call me and we will develop a specific behavior-
  management plan. If he has a "bad" day (swearing,
  refusing, etc.), report it to his classroom teacher.

Figure 5-45   Job Description for a Paraprofessional for Middle School Physical Education

good times to discuss common problems and to create solutions.

Maguire[69] noted that there are four types of skills necessary for collaboration between educators in the school setting:

1. Exchanging information and skills
2. Group problem solving
3. Reaching decisions by consensus
4. Resolving conflicts

Exchanging Information and Skills

All professionals involved in collaboration must be able to share information and skills in a nonthreat-ening, nurturing way. As is true of all collaborative efforts, a teacher who is confident of his or her ability is delighted to share and receive informa-tion and skills from others. While this type of in-formation sharing can be accomplished in formal, in-service training experiences, often the most ef-fective information sharing occurs in small doses as professionals work together on an ongoing basis. This type of mutual learning occurs when teachers learn from watching another's behavior (modeling), observe another teacher's portfolio assessment, and share assessment/evaluation data.

Group Problem Solving

Historically, teachers have had their own, au-tonomous classroom or gymnasium. Decisions made within their rooms have been made inde-pendently. Collaborative teaching necessitates that teachers learn to make group decisions and solve problems together. The skills required for group problem solving include

- Identifying the problem
- Stating the problem
- Listing solutions
- Comparing solutions
- Deciding on the solution to the particular problem
- Reaching decisions by consensus

Reaching Decisions by Consensus

Although it is a more time-consuming process than making decisions by a vote, the collaborative process necessitates that all team members feel comfortable with group decisions. To reach con-sensus requires open and honest communication and, by necessity, a willingness to give and take for the sake of the program. For example, if a local campus received a small grant allocation and needed to determine how best to use the money to serve its students, the teachers (and, in the best educational environment, the students) would meet to discuss and prioritize needs. Together, all involved would come to a decision that all could accept.

Resolving Conflicts

As is true of any human community, conflicts may arise among members of that community. Teachers involved in a collaborative effort may find that there are times when disagreements occur and conflicts arise. One of the most important aspects of a collaborative effort is the willingness of those involved to address disagreements and conflicts openly and honestly. Left to fester, disagreements and conflicts will grow out of proportion. This type of open discussion requires professionals who are secure in their own skills and competencies. In the event that professionals cannot solve a dispute by themselves, a negotiator may be required to help find resolution.

The Consultant and Inclusion

The significant impetus toward including learners with disabilities in general physical education has drastically and dramatically changed the nature of adapted physical education in the schools and, at the same time, the nature of services provided by the adapted physical educator. Many adapted physical educators have been thrust into the role of consultant. Once placed in that role, concerns these individuals express include

- "The unique and specific needs of students with disabilities cannot be met in the general physical education program, particularly in large classes, regardless of the nature of support provided."
- "I have spent thousands of hours preparing to teach learners with disabilities and now I have to depend on others (who are usually not nearly as committed or well trained) to provide services."
- "I am responsible for assessment and implementation of an IEP, and if I'm lucky I see the student and am able to monitor progress once a month."
- "I fear that when I am not in the building, the program I designed is not being implemented

and my student has been relegated, once again, to watching, . . . collecting towels, . . . distributing equipment, . . . or timekeeping."
- "Some of the general physical education teachers that I need to help my students don't care about them and don't want them in their classes."
- "Because I am not an active presence in the lives of my students, I can't possibly make a difference in the quality of their lives."

For many physical educators specially trained to provide services to children and adults with disabilities, the process of changing roles from direct service provider to that of consultant has been difficult. Thrust into the often unwanted role, the adapted physical education consultant must create an educational environment that can be maintained without daily supervision.[47] The general physical educator can indeed provide an excellent program for students with disabilities if their adapted physical education consultant provides the following services:

- Assessment and evaluation of motor performance
- Evaluation of the learning environment
- Collaborative development of the IEP
- Monitoring of student progress toward annual goals and benchmarks
- Collaboration in the development of a portfolio assessment
- Help in solving student-related problems, particularly related to behavior
- Grading of modifications
- Curriculum modifications
- Activity modifications
- Demonstrations of teaching behavior[50]
- Work with parents to foster their participation in program development
- Communication skills
- Provision of specialized equipment

With this type of comprehensive support, a student with disabilities may be able to learn and thrive in the general physical education setting, and the general physical educator will be willing to serve children with special needs.

In the event that the student is unable to participate successfully without additional personnel support, the adapted physical education consultant may play a crucial role in the creation of a successful inclusion program. The adapted physical education consultant can

1. Create a personnel support program
2. Identify student needs
3. Determine the least intrusive personnel continuum that will meet the student's needs (e.g., a peer buddy is much less intrusive than a full-time paraprofessional)
4. Develop a training program
5. Write specific job descriptions for support personnel

It is vital that important communication be established with the principal, teachers, and parents of students with and without disabilities if a successful student support program is to be implemented. (Specific strategies to follow when initiating student support programs in physical education were presented in Figure 5-27.) In addition, communications with building personnel are a vital part of this process.

Creating concise job descriptions may be the single most important part of the process of serving as a consultant to the general physical educator. Specifically, a job description allows the adapted physical education consultant to ensure some quality control and takes a huge load off the shoulders of the general physical educator. The job description should include specific task requirements, dates/time involved, the extent of responsibility, the hierarchy of authority, and allowance for "storms." (Sample job descriptions used in a large, urban school district adapted physical education consultancy were presented in Figures 5-25, 5-44, and 5-45.)

Each job description is written in very different terms, using different language, depending on the sophistication of the service provider. It is vital that the information in the job description also be shared verbally for the support person who is unable to read. A translator may be required to communicate the components of the job description to a student, volunteer, or paraprofessional who uses a language not used by the consultant.

The job description can be used informally, as a simple method of communicating with support personnel. If it is determined that the job is not being done well—that is, the student with disabilities is not being served well—several options exist, including

1. Evaluate job performance in relation to the job description and provide supervisory support. Revise the job description if necessary.
2. Find another peer buddy, older student assistant, or volunteer.
3. Use the job description as a type of contract, and ask school personnel to sign the contract in the presence of the building principal.

The essence of the adapted physical education consultancy is communication. An example of a letter written to motivate, as well as inform, a general physical education teacher who is serving students with disabilities in the general class is presented in Figure 5-46. This type of letter is extremely effective for building cooperative teams with school personnel because it is personal and it compliments the physical education teacher. This is particularly important in school settings in which the teachers feel unempowered. An adapted physical educator consultant willing to take the time to thank and honor a general physical education teacher for his or her service to students with disabilities will have created a strong program supporter. The letter also provides a summary and review of communication that is important documentation of one's program and efforts. Copying the letter to the physical educator's principal and any other administrative "higher-ups" is reinforcing to the teacher. In addition, it provides the principal and the "higher-ups" with valuable information about the adapted physical education program.

Remembering to take the time to thank school personnel who serve students well is important. A simple handwritten or computer-generated thank-you note is a marvelous tool for reinforcing good efforts and developing a team of individuals willing

Dave Auxter
Physical education teacher
Lincoln Elementary School

September 1, 2002

Dear Dave,

Thank you for the *wonderful* work you do with our special children. I consult with hundreds of physical education teachers in the district, and I believe you to be among the very best. Your classroom management, organization, and commitment to *really teaching* movement skills is exemplary.

I so appreciate the special place you have in your heart, and the special place you have made in your classes so that our atypically developing children can be included with their peers. You provide a safe, nurturing, and consistent environment in which they can learn and enjoy movement and play. You have embraced the notion that all our children have a right to be educated . . . and you do it so well.

Dave, I wanted to provide a written review of our collaboration regarding some of the special children attending Lincoln Elementary School and what, if any, modifications are needed for them to continue to thrive in your physical education program.

Juan Garcia

Please continue to allow Juan to use the modified warm-up exercises he used last year. His weight gain over the summer prevents us from increasing the number of repetitions/resistance in his exercises. Juan knows you and knows what you expect, and I believe he will have another good year with you. His behavior seems much improved—in the gym and the classroom. As always, any encouragement is vital. [Note for readers: Juan has spina bifida and uses a wheelchair for ambulation.]

Chuck Nelson

As we discussed, Chuck has Duchenne muscular dystrophy, a disability associated with ever-increasing loss of muscle tone and strength. At present, Chuck has particular difficulty getting up from a sit and moving into a stand. In addition, he has problems with stop/start activities and those that require a rapid change in direction.

In addition, Chuck is beginning to have difficulty maintaining an erect sitting posture, and this may adversely affect his ability to assume the cross-legged/cross-armed sitting position you ask of your students during your introduction and between warm-up exercises. As you begin your heart healthy runs and other physical fitness components of your program, please be aware that Chuck will fatigue easily. He tries very hard to do what his peers do . . . and does not like to be singled out because of his disability.

Lucy Anderson

Lucy's classroom teacher, Ms. Joslyn, has very wisely chosen to gradually introduce Lucy into the physical education program. Actually, movement is one of her particular strengths—she does not have a gross motor delay at this point, typical of children with Down syndrome. She was successful in her kindergarten physical education program at Washington Elementary School and should experience more success here because of the gradual introduction to your program, smaller class size, and your wonderfully structured program.

The one time she is likely to experience difficulty is during free play . . . I'd be grateful for an extra eye on her.

Jason Washington

It's hard to believe Jason is really in the fifth grade. He should continue to participate in regular physical education during warm-up activities, skill-learning sessions, and free play. If, however, your class is going to engage in activities like dodgeball, team basketball, or team soccer, Jason must return to his class. Ms. Joslyn is aware of this and will welcome him back. [Note for readers: Jason is a learner whose movements are characterized as awkward and clumsy. He has a severe learning disability. His mother overfeeds to reward him and, subsequently, he also struggles with obesity.]

Dave, if I could clone you, I could retire. If only I had teachers like you all over the district to serve our children.

Please know I have nominated you as the Elementary Physical Education Teacher of the Year in the Texas Association of Physical Education, Recreation and Dance. If you are selected . . . and I expect that . . . I trust we will celebrate.

Yours,

Emily Unger
Adapted Physical Education Consultant
XXX Public Schools

cc: *Catherine Smith,* principal, Lincoln Elementary School

Figure 5-46 **Letter Written to Motivate and Inform a Regular Physical Education Teacher Serving Students with Disabilities**

to serve students with disabilities. Perhaps most effective is a note, voice tape, or work of art created by the student (with the help of the classroom teacher or art teacher) to thank his or her peer buddy, older student assistant, volunteer, or paraprofessional. This type of thank-you is also very important for the general physical educator. Samples of notes sent to paraprofessionals who served children very well are presented in Figures 5-47 and 5-48. Sending a copy to building principals, district physical education coordinators, and area special education coordinators enhances their impact.

One of the most difficult aspects of being an adapted physical education consultant is having a great deal of responsibility and very little, if any, authority. The consultant must be accountable for his or her actions and for the supervision provided to school personnel. Job descriptions, letters that outline responsibilities and summarize conversations, correspondence regarding support personnel programs, and copies of thank-you notes help document efforts. As important, the adapted physical education consultant must

1. Keep a copy of original assessment data, as well as the written report shared with the IEP committee

2. Attend as many IEP meetings as possible. There is simply no substitute for face-to-face communication with parents, general educators, building personnel, and related service personnel.

3. Keep a copy of the IEP and carefully document visits to campus sites to monitor achievement of goals/objectives

4. Maintain careful logs that document
   a. Direct student contact, including the date, length of time spent with the student, and the purpose on that date (e.g., assessment, team teaching, or modeling teaching behavior)
   b. Time spent in consultancy, including the date, length of time spent in collaboration, personnel with whom he or she consulted, and the purpose on that date (e.g., modifying grading, modifying activities, or developing a behavior-management program)
   c. The nature and extent of parent communication
   d. The nature and extent of any communication with the student's physician and/or related service personnel

5. Be visible on the local school campus. In addition to signing in at the office, make a point of speaking to the building principal, the office secretary, the child's general and/or special educator, and the physical educator.

6. Send a note home to the student's parent if the student has made progress or has accomplished a goal/objective and leave copies with the child's general and/or special educator and the physical educator

7. Keep transportation logs to verify campus visits

```
              Ms. Jones

  Thank you, Thank you, Thank you.

              We
  would not have been able to
       participate in the
  community-based swimming program
       without your help!

            Much love,

            Ernesto,
             Juan,
           Sharonda,
               &
             Glenn

  Dr. Carol says "you are an angel!"
```

cc.   Mr. Garcia, Principal, Caillet Elementary School

Figure 5-47   "Thank-You" Note Sent to a Paraprofessional Who Accompanied Four Wheelchair-Enabled Children to a Community-Based Swimming Program and Assisted in the Locker Room
The children signed the thank-you.

MEMO

To: Sharon Black
From: Carol Huettig, Adapted Physical Education Consultant
Subject: Deundrae Bowie, Dunbar Learning Center
Date: December 1, 1996

   I can't thank you enough for your efforts on Deundrae's behalf. He is so lucky to have you as a mentor and friend. Your willingness to provide him with special help has truly enhanced the quality of his life. His dribbling skills have really improved, as has his ability to maneuver his wheelchair.
   I thank you, once again, for your professionalism, dedication, and concern for your students.

cc: Mr. Moore, Principal, Dunbar Elementary School
      Dr. Pittman, Area Coordinator

Figure 5-48   "Thank-You" Memo Sent to a Paraprofessional

One of the unique difficulties associated with the consultancy is demonstrating, in a systematic way, the efficacy of the program and the effect it has on the lives of students with disabilities. As more and more school districts and school systems demand accountability of their staff members, the responsibilities of the consultant become more clear—the consultant must keep and maintain a paper trail to document service delivery.

Transition

The activities and skills learned in the physical education class should be applicable to community leisure and recreation activity. The intent of the physical education program from kindergarten through the senior year of high school must be to prepare all students, particularly those with disabilities, for a life enhanced and enriched by quality leisure and recreation experiences. According to Dattilo and Jekubovich-Fenton:

> The trend toward inclusive leisure services focuses attention on participants' strengths as opposed to weaknesses, thus providing all participants—including people with mental retardation—with choices of age-appropriate recreation activities in which they can participate with their peers.[23]

Active participation in leisure and recreation activities after leaving the school-based setting is only effective if the student has had the opportunity to learn, while in school, the skills needed to function with success in the community. Because few school districts hire therapeutic recreators to help in the transition process, the role of the adapted physical educator and general physical educator becomes ever more important. Krebs and Block[62] outlined eight responsibilities of the adapted physical educator in the transition process, which are summarized in Figure 5-49.

A model inclusive leisure, recreation, and sports program, Promoting Accessible Recreation Through Networking, Education, Resources and Service (PARTNERS), has demonstrated success in providing transition from rehabilitation services to a community-based leisure, recreation, and sports program. The multidimensional program includes the following components:

- AIM for Independence—activity instructional program. The quality instructional program is designed to give individuals with disabilities and their families and friends an opportunity to explore a variety of activities, including skiing, scuba diving, canoeing, kayaking, water skiing, stunt kite flying, sledge hockey, and weight training.
- Equipment rental program. The specially designed equipment necessary for an individual with a disability to participate in some leisure and recreation activities is often prohibitive

---

Figure 5-49 Transition Responsibilities of the Adapted Physical Educator

1. Identify accessible community-based resources and programs in which an individual with a disability would be made welcome.
2. Provide instructional and technical support to personnel within local leisure and recreation facilities.
3. Analyze the environments in which learners could participate in leisure and recreation programs and identify specific skills required for participation. These include gaining access to the facility, making choices regarding participation, skills required to prepare for the activity (changing into swimwear, for example, and using a locker), equipment necessary for participation, and motor skills and fitness levels required to participate.
4. Determine levels of support required (see Figure 5-3 for least restrictive environment continuum alternatives).
5. Identify personnel who may be available to provide support.
6. Participate actively in the individual transition plan (ITP) meeting.
7. Implement the program.
8. Conduct ongoing program evaluation.

Data from Krebs P, Block M: *Adapt Phys Act Q* 9:305–315, 1992.

---

financially. PARTNERS makes equipment such as sit-skis, bi-skis, and mono-skis available for rental.

- Sports development program. While providing a youth sports development program, PARTNERS is designed to be sensitive to groups of individuals with an interest in a particular activity. For example, if a number of individuals wish to explore winter camping, the staff mobilizes to provide needed instruction and to help find accessible facilities and necessary equipment.
- Education and advocacy. PARTNERS provides education and advocacy to enhance the likelihood that an individual with a disability who chooses to participate in a leisure, recreation, and sports program will be extended the hospitality and welcome that any individual has a right to expect.

The Denver Parks and Recreation Program provides a program titled Transition to Recreation Activities in the Community (TRAC), in which a certified therapeutic recreator provides direct services and support to individuals making a transition from a hospital or rehabilitation program into the community.

It is only through a comprehensive school-based adapted physical education program that emphasizes community-based programming based on individual and community needs and resources, paired with a dynamic leisure and recreation program, that a learner can make a successful transition into the community as an active participant, making independent choices regarding activities that meet his or her needs.

Inclusion in Leisure, Recreation, and Sports

Historically, society has tended to isolate and segregate individuals with disabilities, and, despite some improvements, such forms of discrimination against individuals with disabilities continue to be a serious and pervasive social problem. Discrimination against individuals with disabilities persists in such critical areas as employment, housing, public accommodations, education, transportation, communication, recreation, institutionalization, health services, voting, and access to public services. Individuals with disabilities continually encounter various forms of discrimination, including outright intentional exclusion; the discriminatory effects of architectural, transportation, and communication barriers; overprotective rules and policies; failures to make modifications to existing facilities and practices; exclusionary qualification standards and criteria; and segregation and relegation to lesser services, programs, activities, benefits, jobs, and other opportunities.

In essence, the Americans with Disabilities Act of 1990 expands the mandates of Section 504 of the Rehabilitation Act of 1973. That law indicated that no individual can, solely on the basis of a disability, be denied access to publicly supported facilities and programs. The Americans with Disabilities Act of 1990 expands that to include privately owned public facilities. The law states that

> No individual shall be discriminated against on the basis of disability in the full and equal enjoyment of the goods, services, facilities, privileges, advantages or accommodations of any place of public accommodation by any person who owns, leases (or leases to), or operates a place of public accommodation.[2]

In addition, the law mandates that individuals with disabilities be able to participate in the programs and activities of the public facility in the most integrated setting appropriate to the needs of the individual. A reasonable accommodation must be made to ensure access. A reasonable accommodation may include modifications of rules and policies, provision of assistive devices, or provision of support personnel.

However, despite federal and state mandates regarding access to community leisure, recreation, and sports programs, many adults with disabilities do not participate in recreation activities. Sands and Kozleski[106] asked 131 adults without disabilities and 86 adults with disabilities to complete a survey that addressed their perceived quality of life. Their findings regarding participation in recreation activities were frightening:

- Thirty-five percent of the adults with disabilities had not attended a movie in the past year (compared with 5 percent of the adults without disabilities).
- Eighty-three percent of the adults with disabilities had not participated in a community group in the past year.
- Eighty percent of the adults with disabilities had not gone to an athletic club in the past year.
- Sixty-four percent of the adults with disabilities had not attended a live theatre performance in the past year.
- Sixty-four percent of the adults with disabilities had not attended a music performance within the community in the past year.
- Fifty-eight percent of the adults with disabilities had not attended a sporting event within the community in the past year.

Inclusion in community-based activities, such as youth sports, is a concept and major guiding principle of the ADA, Americans with Disabilities Act. Burkour makes a compelling statement regarding the need for reasonable accommodations so children can participate in youth sports:

> A person with a disability is someone's child or parent, someone's neighbor and friend, an aunt or cousin, someone's co-worker or classmate. They live in houses on streets in neighborhoods, and they go to general schools, have real jobs, play sports, and have fun. . . . Anyone can become a person with a special need at any time.[15]

See Figure 5-50.

Four hundred thirty-four athletes participating in Wheelchair Sports USA, U.S. Association for Blind Athletes, and U.S. Cerebral Palsy Athletic Association national competitions completed a survey addressing disability-related problems that made it difficult for individuals with disabilities to participate in sports.[31] The athletes identified the following nonmedically oriented problems: lack of transportation, lack of equipment or equipment failure, lack of support personnel (guides), and difficulty with orthotics or prostheses. They identified the following medically oriented problems: general medical problems, pressure sores or skin breakdown, difficulties with medication, and seizures.

Figure 5-50   Coaching Strategies to Facilitate Inclusion

Youth sport coaches can use the following strategies to accommodate a child with a disability:
- Make simple changes in basic rules. For example, a batter who uses a wheelchair may need a "pusher" to help him or her get to base.[15]
- Make simple changes in basic equipment. Use a bright yellow soccer ball to help a child with a visual impairment follow the play.
- Carefully analyze the sport/play situation and identify all the physical, sensory, learning, communication, and social/play skills that are required.[15]
- Use a "team" approach to determine necessary accommodations. The parents, adapted physical educator, and other players can help develop these strategies.

One of the most serious obstacles for sports and recreation programs for individuals with disabilities is one of "critical mass." Simply, it is difficult for individuals with disabilities to find individuals with similar disabilities with whom to compete.[22]

Block and Malloy[13] found that children with disabilities who participated in a community-based fast-pitch softball league felt positively about including "hypothetical" children with disabilities in the program, as did their parents. They noted, however, that the coaches were undecided about the inclusion of this "hypothetical child" in the program.

While these data point dramatically to the obstacles to participation, widespread changes have occurred in leisure, recreation, and sports programs to increase the participation of individuals with disabilities. One of the most dramatic results of the emphasis on inclusion of individuals with disabilities in all public programs and facilities can be seen in the efforts of the National Park Service and the U.S. Forest Service to provide opportunities for individuals with disabilities to use and enjoy the programs and opportunities offered in the national parks.[29] The national parks listed in Figure 5-51 are accessible to individuals with disabilities.

Brasile[14] addressed the development of leisure and recreation skills of adventitiously injured individuals, within a social context. He suggested that an individual with a new physical disability moves through a series of developmental stages toward total social reintegration and participation in integrated leisure, recreation, and sport activities. He suggested that the individual participates before the injury in "typical life course participation." Immediately following the injury, the individual may participate in leisure, recreation, and sport activities for the primary purpose of postinjury rehabilitation. Then, the individual may participate in parallel activities, such as wheelchair basketball, amputee golf, or Paralympic track and field. In the last stages of recovery, the individual may be involved in total social reintegration, which includes participation in integrated or "inclusive" leisure, recreation, and sport activities.

The Amateur Sports Act of 1978 (P.L. 95-606) encourages the integration of persons with and

Figure 5-51 National Parks Accessible to Individuals with Disabilities[29]

Denali National Park and Preserve
Grand Canyon National Park
Death Valley National Monument
Sequoia National Park
Mesa Verde National Park
Rocky Mountain National Park
Everglades National Park
Gulf Islands National Seashore
Mammoth Cave National Park
Blue Ridge Parkway
Prince William Forest Park

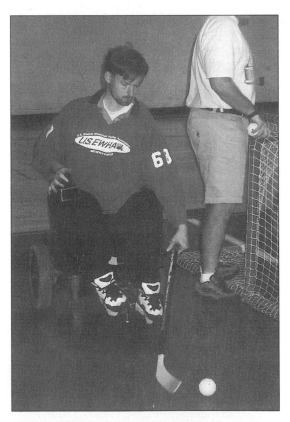

Floor hockey can be enjoyed by everyone.
Courtesy of United States Electric Wheelchair Association.

without disabilities into sports competition. The U.S. Olympic Committee provides assistance to amateur athletic programs for inclusion of individuals with disabilities in training and competition programs with individuals without disabilities.

In some cases, integration requires creative strategies. Special Olympics International has developed several creative programs designed specifically to enhance integration of individuals with and without disabilities into sports programs. The Partner's Club Program is designed to encourage high-school-age students to seek coaching certification and to be actively involved as coaches of athletes who are mentally retarded. The Unified Sports Program is designed to foster the integration of individuals with and without disabilities into training and competition programs by matching participants on the basis of age and ability. Then, children with and without disabilities can train and compete together, being mutually dependent on each other for the outcome of the event.

Part of the growth of leisure, recreation, and sports programs is due to an increased desire of individuals with disabilities to participate in leisure and recreation activities and to their willingness to serve as self-advocates in finding resources and programs that will address their needs. One of the major developments in leisure and recreation programs nationally is the trend toward participation by individuals with and without disabilities in programs with an emphasis on outdoor, environmental experiences. The Breckenridge Outdoor Recreation Center in Breckenridge, Colorado, is known for exceptional wilderness programming for challenged individuals. It is based on the following philosophy:

> There is therapeutic value in wilderness programming. Wilderness adventures can be strong tools for attitude changes and psychological growth providing experiences that bring out the best of the human spirit. . . . The real mission has to do with empowerment; instilling in participants the sense that who they are and who they can be is a product of their own hand, heart, and vision. Climbing, backcountry travel, and survival training are not

ends in themselves. Rather, such activities are methods to attain other goals.[77]

The innovative program includes the following winter activities: downhill and cross-country skiing, sit-skiing, mono-skiing, helicopter skiing, ice sledding, winter camping, backpacking, solo trips, and ropes courses. More and more community-based leisure and recreation programs are being made available to individuals with disabilities.

Many exciting and innovative programs encourage individuals with disabilities to participate with individuals without disabilities. Wilderness Inquiry of Minneapolis, Minnesota, has a model program that includes wilderness canoeing, backpacking and hiking, cross-country skiing, and dog sledding. Frei wrote, "The non-profit organization provides outdoor recreational programs all over the world for people of all abilities, making outdoor adventures fun and accessible."[34] Wilderness Inquiry has adopted a philosophy called "Universal Program Participation," which is the basis for all decision making regarding accessibility and programming. Wilderness Inquiry should particularly be recognized for its emphasis on family-based programming and services that meet the needs of the entire family (see Figure 5-52).

Challenge Aspen has a beautiful program that fosters an interest in and competency particularly in a variety of mountain snow-based activities such as skiing and snowboarding. The H.S.A. International

---

Figure 5-52   Universal Program Participation Skill

Wilderness Inquiry staff receive intensive training to prepare them for Universal Program Participation:
- Techniques for making the wilderness accessible without altering it
- Strategies for using adapted equipment
- Skills to communicate with individuals with and without disabilities
- Skills to ask a person regarding his or her specific needs
- Techniques for determining what each person can bring to the group

provides a variety of excellent programs to train scuba instructors to teach individuals with disabilities and provides an opportunity to develop dive buddy skills and open-water skills. Camp ASCCA-Easter Seals, Adaptive Aquatics, Inc., has a recognized program that focuses on water skiing and includes special instruction in slalom, barefoot, jumping, and trick skiing. Desert Breezes, Balloon Adventures, Inc., has developed a balloon basket customized and certified to fly passengers with disabilities. The Vinland Center has developed a comprehensive program for children and adults with disabilities. Vinland's programs are whole-person and focus on wellness, positive lifestyles, fitness, and productivity.

The Wisconsin Lion's Camp focuses on the development of individual competency through the use of a challenging "in the trees" ropes course, rock climbing, and aquatic activities. Other camping-based programs focus on the unique needs of the chronically ill child. Camp John Marc Myers, for example, in Bosque County, Texas, has been designed to give children with special health needs the chance to learn new skills, form peer relationships, and develop greater independence and self-esteem. Camp John Marc Myers is based on the following philosophy:

> Chronic disease and physical disability can rob children of the chance to just be kids, leaving them to spend the precious years of their youth watching from the sidelines. In lives that are filled with doctors, hospitals, and the painful awareness that they are not like other children, the chance to be a 'normal' kid is rare. Going away to camp gives children with special health needs that chance. The feeling of freedom experienced through camping provides an invaluable opportunity for these children to overcome preoccupation with illness and feelings of isolation.[16]

Other programs offer children with disabilities the opportunity to learn more community-based leisure and recreation skills. Kathy Corbin's "Never Say Never" program is a nonprofit organization that teaches golf to physically challenged individuals. The National Amputee Golf Association provides clinics in local schools and community centers to teach golf skills and golf-teaching skills

to those with amputations. The U.S. Tennis Association has a series of clinics that they offer in the public schools to teach beginning tennis to children with and without disabilities. The American Wheelchair Bowling Association works in close cooperation with the American Bowling Association to develop integrated bowling leagues.

Increasingly, more sophisticated sports and recreation equipment for individuals with disabilities is available to encourage participation and assure access. Deming Designs has created wheelchairs with supersize tires to allow individuals using wheelchairs access to beaches, woods, and other outdoor environments. Disability Options has created sophisticated "Kili-Kart" to allow athletes access to mountains and streams. Endolite has created sophisticated prostheses to allow individuals with amputations access to track and field, golf, and other leisure and sport experiences.

The Orthopedic and Prosthetic Athlete Assistance Fund, Inc., helps provide equipment for athletes that allow access to leisure, recreation, and sports activities. Orthomerica has designed prosthetics and braces to encourage and foster independent mobility and access to leisure and recreation activities.

Some colleges and universities offer sports camps for children with physical disabilities. Ball State University in Muncie, Indiana, the University of Texas at Arlington, and the University of Wisconsin-Whitewater are known for their children's sports training camps.

Embracing Multiculturalism

If the schools are to embrace the notion that all children have the right to educational equity and access to educational programs, it is critical that the movement toward inclusion embrace not just students with disabilities but also students who represent the diverse tapestry of contemporary society. Children who represent diverse cultures, religions, and ethnic groups; children who speak a variety of languages and dialects; children who represent a variety of economic backgrounds; children who have homes and those who are homeless;

children who have parents and those who are orphans; children who are being raising in traditional and those being raised in nontraditional families; those who are straight and those that are gay; and those with differing levels of ability and disability must be served *well* in our public schools if this society is to reverse its apparently self-destructive course.

According to Manning:

> Schools have long based expectations, perceptions of motivations and success, learning methodologies, and selection of curricular materials on middle-class, Anglo-American perceptions. This decision may have resulted from the belief that culturally diverse learners should acculturate toward middle-class Anglo-American perspectives, the belief that the schools should cater to the majority social class and culture, or the belief that culturally diverse learners did not deserve the advantages of the dominant culture. Regardless of the reason, the decision resulted in inequitable treatment of culturally different learners; and in the process, schools may have perpetuated racism, prejudice, and discrimination.[71]

The demographics within the United States and our schools have changed remarkably within the past decade. As Markowitz points out, "For the first time in U.S. history, the mainstream is about to become the minority, and the group that has held the power, made the laws, set the policies, controlled the money and dictated to everyone else is on the verge of being outnumbered."[72] Educators must seize every opportunity to embrace each child they serve—without regard to race, culture, socioeconomic status, religion (or lack thereof), gender, gender preference, and ability or disability. We have the responsibility to ensure that all public schools have equitable resources, all cultures are represented in the curriculum, and students representing all socioeconomic levels, as well as each gender and gender preference, are fairly treated.

To ensure educational equity, it has become increasingly obvious that the schools must be prepared to honor students representing diverse cultures. If students are to be empowered as learners

and as people, their families and their cultures must be respected. According to Markowitz,

> Multiculturalists argue that the price of cutting off a significant cultural legacy is internalized shame and diminished self-esteem. This is even more pronounced for those who come from cultures already in a one-down economic position, like refugees or people from developing nations, or those whose cultures include a history of colonization or persecution, like descendants of African slaves.[72]

This respect for the student's culture is particularly important because students who represent minority groups are much more likely to be in high-poverty schools and face discrimination and stereotypes; also, a much greater concentration of health, social, and neighborhood problems is found in high-poverty schools.[85]

Creating a school environment in which each child and the child's culture, in its broadest sense, are represented requires a serious commitment to understanding. It requires educators to examine seriously their values and their own cultural identity and to be willing to try new approaches in their classrooms in order to make their coursework relevant.[83]

The teacher must be able to engage in an honest, open dialogue with his or her learners, their parents, members of their extended families, and individuals within the communities in which the students live. Many dedicated educators choose to be involved in an experience known as a cultural plunge, in which they choose to live in or visit a setting that represents a culture very different from their own.[83] For example, a Hispanic teacher may choose to attend a church service attended primarily by African Americans. Or, an Anglo-American teacher may attend a Cinco de Mayo celebration. While this is only one step, it is the beginning of a process in which the teacher begins to develop empathy for and appreciation of the unique heritages and beliefs of his or her students.

According to Markowitz, "Ultimately, multiculturalism is a movement to make society a place in which people from all cultures have equal respect and equal voice and equal influence in shaping larger community values."[72] The physical educator or adapted physical educator can have an impact on the process of enabling all students to learn within the public schools and still retain dignity. The notion of culture is diverse and is not limited to one facet of the life of human beings. When educators consider culture, they must do so within a broad perspective because we all carry several cultures at once—our inherited cultures, the generation in which we were born, our gender, and our socioeconomic class. Each of these cultural facets impacts our perceptions and actions and may significantly affect our choices and options.

It is helpful to understand the impact culture has on behavior, because the teacher who is knowledgeable about and sensitive to cultural differences is capable of modifying instruction to fit the characteristics of the individual and group.[51] With a reminder that these cultural characteristics are basic and may not be true of all individuals representing a particular culture, in the same way that characteristics of individuals with disabilities may not adequately describe each individual, teaching strategies that can maximize the performance of students representing those cultures are presented in the following lists.

Hispanic Cultures

- Emphasize the importance of the extended family
- Celebrate cultural awareness by celebrating cultural holidays
- Emphasize respect for Hispanic cultural beliefs
- Expect moral and ethical behavior
- Encourage respect for Spanish as a living language
- Emphasize the primary role of family and family loyalty
- Acknowledge that students representing these cultures learn best in real-life situations and contexts
- Value quality interpersonal relationships
- May be awed by persons considered to be in a position of authority

Specific Teaching Strategies
1. Use demonstrations and rely on gestures and body language for communication.
2. Avoid competition and emphasize collaborative learning.
3. Use sequential learning.

African American Cultures

- Emphasize the importance of the extended family and kinship within the community
- Celebrate an awareness of African American history
- Emphasize the priority of the church as the central force within the community
- Emphasize a community responsibility for raising children
- Encourage respect for the elderly
- Acknowledge that the children learn best in real-life situations and simulations
- Recognize and embrace oral language and storytelling
- Value interpersonal relationships
- May distrust the public school system, and its teachers, as part of the larger "system" that has betrayed them

Specific Teaching Strategies
1. Emphasize collaborative learning and cooperative play.
2. Encourage individual expression.
3. Vary tasks frequently.
4. Help students develop personal goals and assist them by providing positive feedback.
5. Use active learning.
6. Embrace learning that recognizes bodily-kinesthetic, spatial, and musical intelligences.

Asian American Cultures

- Emphasize respect for individuals with authority
- Encourage respectful, quiet, cooperative behavior
- Establish and maintain very high academic and behavioral standards
- Emphasize the integrity of the family as a unit
- Teach children to avoid behavior that might embarrass the family
- Teach respect for the elderly
- Respect and value the complexity of language
- Emphasize the work ethic

Specific Teaching Strategies

1. Provide opportunities for individual and independent work.
2. Provide a hierarchy of challenges, so that each child can seek improvement.
3. Use overhead projectors and provide extra-credit reading assignments.

Native American Cultures

- Emphasize respect for all individuals
- Emphasize respect for nature and the environment
- Encourage the group welfare of the tribe and the family
- Put an emphasis on self-sufficiency and on providing children the skills needed to learn and grow early in life
- May distrust the public school system, and its teachers, as part of the larger "system" that has betrayed them
- Tend to learn best by participating in active learning
- Value personal and cultural dignity

Specific Teaching Strategies

1. Link the past to the present; emphasize the historical context of play, games, and sports.
2. Avoid competition and emphasize cooperative learning.
3. Analyze tasks to create a hierarchy of objectives.

Anglo-American Cultures

- Emphasize individual initiative
- View history from a limited, European perspective
- Emphasize respect for one's individual family
- Rely heavily on verbal rather than nonverbal communication
- Encourage increasing independence as children get older

Specific Teaching Strategies

1. Help students develop personal goals and develop skills to evaluate their own progress.
2. Provide a great deal of variety in the program.

See Figure 5-53 for a summary of all the strategies a general physical educator can use to demonstrate a commitment to multiculturalism and diversity.

Figure 5-53   Strategies the General Physical Educator Can Use to Demonstrate a Commitment to a Quality Education for All Children

- Know and use each child's name. This is a fundamental requirement if the teacher is to communicate the fact that the child is valued.
- Do not jump to conclusions regarding a child's behavior, particularly if the child represents a different culture. For example, children from many Asian cultures have been taught to lower their heads and their eyes to show respect to adults. A teacher insisting that the child, "Look at me when I'm talking to you" is literally asking the child to show disrespect.
- Ensure that there is someone available to translate if the teacher does not understand the language or dialect of the student. Often, another student can help communicate. While it would be wonderful for the teacher to be familiar with basic phrases in the native language or mode of communication of each child in his or her classes, it is not unusual in a large urban district for children to use more than ninety different languages and dialects.
- Minimize the use of verbal language and rely heavily on demonstrations.
- Use posters that reflect a diverse community.
- Recognize "heroes" that reflect a diverse community.
- Learn to read the student. Body language, gestures, and facial expressions can often communicate intent and feelings better than verbal language can.
- The teacher should select and use music that represents a variety of cultures.
- Invite parents and members of the community to teach dance, games, and other activities that represent the cultures of the children served.
- Honor diverse religious and cultural celebrations. Ask parents and other members of the community to share that diversity to celebrate, for example, Juneteenth, Cinco de Mayo, Rosh Hashanah, and the Chinese New Year.

SUMMARY

Adapted physical education has changed dramatically since inclusion was widely embraced as an educational philosophy and practice. Current legislation and litigation support the inclusion of students with disabilities. General physical educators are becoming increasingly responsible for providing instruction to students with disabilities. There are instructional strategies and procedures that can be used to ensure that appropriate services are provided.

Physical educators deeply committed to providing quality adapted physical education services have to cope with, adjust to, and create new collaborative and consultative procedures for providing services in inclusive settings. Careful preparation, communication, and documentation are needed for the process to work.

The physical educator can also use a variety of strategies to ensure that all students are embraced in the learning environment.

REVIEW QUESTIONS

1. Briefly describe the litigation that emphasizes the inclusion of students with disabilities.

2. What are the eight instructional variables that can be addressed to accommodate learners with disabilities in the least restrictive environment?

3. How can the least restrictive environment design matrices included in this chapter be used to evaluate appropriate physical education services for a student with disabilities?

4. What are the characteristics of an inclusive, community-based leisure, recreation, and sports program?

5. What factors can be considered when grading a person with a disability who is being served in an inclusive physical education setting?

6. What strategies can a teacher use to embrace multiculturalism and diversity in the general physical education program?

STUDENT ACTIVITIES

1. Consider each of the instructional variables that can be used to accommodate a learner with a disability in the general curriculum. Describe which accommodations would need to be made to include Maria in the general physical education program.

2. Write a job description for a peer buddy assigned to work with Maria in a general physical education class.

3. Interview a parent who is adamant about "full inclusion" and a parent who prefers his or her student to be educated in a safe and secure "special education" program. Compare.

4. Evaluate a physical education setting to determine if it is appropriate for a student with disabilities to be included in the general physical education program.

5. Develop a list of empathy experiences that a professional might experience in preparation for including a student with a disability in the general physical education program.

REFERENCES

1. All children belong, *Except Parent* July:43–46, 1994.

2. American Foundation for the Blind: http://www.afb.org/education/jtlipaper.html

3. Americans with Disabilities Act of 1990, P.L. 101-336, Alexandria, VA, 1991, National Mental Health Association.

4. Annual Reports to Congress on the Implementation of the Individuals with Disabilities Education Act by the Office of Special Education Programs, Washington, DC, 1997, U.S. Department of Education.

5. Arc of the United States: http://thearc.org/posits/integra.html

6. Armstrong RW, Rosenbaum PL, King SM: A randomized controlled trial of a "buddy" programme to improve children's attitudes toward the disabled, *Dev Med Child Neurol* 29:327–336, 1987.

7. Baker JM, Zigmond N: The meaning and practice of inclusion for students with learning disabilities: themes and implications from five cases, *J Special Ed* 29:163–180, 1995.

8. Banerji M, Dailey RA: A study of the effects of an inclusion model on students with specific learning disabilities, *J Learn Dis* 28:511–522, 1995.

9. Belka DE: Let's manage to have some order, *J Phys Educ Rec Dance* 62:21–23, 1991.

10. Beninghof A: Using a spectrum of staff development activities to support inclusion. *J of Staff Development* 17(3):12–15, 1996.

11. Block ME, Burke K: Are children with disabilities receiving appropriate physical education? *Teaching Except Child* 31(3):12–17, 1999.

12. Block ME, Krebs PL: An alternative to least restrictive environments: a continuum of support to regular physical education, *Adapt Phys Act Q* 9:97–113, 1992.

13. Block ME, Malloy M: Attitudes on inclusion of a player with disabilities in a regular softball league, *Mental Retardation* 36(2):137–144, 1998.

14. Brasile F: Inclusion: a developmental perspective. A rejoinder to "examining the concept of reverse integration," *Adapt Phys Act Q* 9:293–304, 1992.

15. Burkour CK: We want to play too! Including all children in youth sports and complying with the ADA, *Except Parent* June:72, 75, 1998.

16. Camp John Marc Myers, Special Camps for Special Kids, Dallas, TX.

17. Carpenter SL, McKee-Higgins E: Behavior management in inclusive classrooms. *Remedial Spec Educ* 17(4):195–203, 1996.

18. CEC (Council for Exceptional Children): http://www.cec.org

19. Chalmers L, Faliede T: Successful inclusion of students with mild/moderate disabilities in rural school settings, *Teaching Except Child* 29(1):22–25, 1996.

20. Chesley GM, Calaluce PD: The deception of inclusion. *Mental Retardation* 35:488–490, 1997.

21. Clark G, French R, Henderson H: Attitude development of physical educators working with the disabled, *Palaestra* 1:26–28, 1986.

22. Colon KM: Sports and recreation: many rewards, but barriers exist. *Except Parent* March:56–60, 1998.

23. Dattilo J, Jekubovich-Fenton Q: Trends: leisure services for people with mental retardation, *Parks and Recreation* May:46–52, 1995.

24. Decker J, Jansma P: Physical education least restrictive environment continua used in the United States, *Adapt Phys Act Q* 12:124–138, 1995.

25. DePauw KP, Goc Karp G: Integrating knowledge of disability throughout the physical education curriculum: an infusion approach. *Adapt Phys Act Q* 11:3–13, 1994.

26. Downing JH, Rebollo J: Parents' perceptions of the factors essential for integrated physical education programs. *Remedial Spec Ed* 20(3):152–159, 1999.

27. Downs P, Williams T: Student attitudes toward integration of people with disabilities in activity settings: a European comparison, *Adapt Phys Act Q* 11:32–43, 1994.

28. Doyle MB: *The paraprofessional's guide to the inclusive classroom.* Baltimore, MD, 1997, Paul H. Brookes.

29. Ellis W: Accessible camping in the national parks, *Sports 'n Spokes* 17:47–51, 1992.

30. Erickson R et al.: Inclusive assessments and accountability systems: tools of the trade in educational reform. *Teaching Except Child* November/December:4–9, 1998.

31. Ferrara M et al.: A cross-disability analysis of programming needs for athletes with disabilities, *Palaestra* Fall:32–42, 1994.

32. Folsom-Meek SL, Groteluschen W, Nearing RJ: Influence of academic major and hands-on experience on college students' attitudes toward learners with disabilities, *Brazilian Int J of Adapted Phys Ed Res* 3(1):47–66, 1996.

33. Fox NE, Ysseldyke JE: Implementing inclusion at the middle school level: lessons from a negative example, *Except Child* 64(1):81–85, 1997.

34. Frei CE: Sharing the adventure, *Except Parent* 29(5):50–55, 1999.

35. French NK, Pickett AL: Paraprofessionals in special education: issues for teacher educators, *Teacher Education and Special Education* 20(1):61–73, 1997.

36. Fryxell D, Kennedy C: Placement along the continuum of services and its impact on students' social relationships, *J Assn Persons with Severe Handicaps* 20:259–269, 1995.

37. Gallagher J: The pull of societal forces on special education, *J Spec Educ* 27:521–530, 1994.

38. Gelzheiser LM et al.: IEP-specified peer interaction needs: accurate but ignored, *Except Child* 65(1):51–65, 1998.

39. Giangreco M, Baumgart D, Doyle M: How inclusion can facilitate teaching and learning, *Intervent School Clin* 30(5):273–278, 1995.

40. Giangreco M et al.: Problem-solving methods to facilitate inclusive education. In Thousand J, Villa R, Nevin A, editors: *Creativity and collaborative learning: a practical guide to empowering students and teachers*, Baltimore, MD, 1994, Paul H. Brookes.

41. Heumann J, Hehir T: Questions and answers on the least restrictive environment requirements of the Individuals with Disabilities Education Act, U.S. Department of Education, Office of Special Education and Rehabilitative Services, November 23, 1994.

42. Hobbs T, Westling DL: Promoting successful inclusion through collaborative problem-solving, *Teaching Except Child* September/October:12–19, 1998.

43. Hodge SR: Prospective physical education teachers' attitudes toward teaching students with disabilities, *Physical Educator* 55(2):68–77, 1998.

44. Hodge SR, Jansma P: Effects of contact time and location of practicum experiences on attitudes of physical education majors, *Adapt Phys Act Q* 16:48–63, 1999.

45. Houston-Wilson C, Dunn JM, Van der mars H, McCubbin J: The effect of peer tutors on motor performance in integrated physical education classes, *Adapt Phys Act Q* 14:298–313, 1997.

46. Houston-Wilson C, Lieberman L, Horton M, Kasser S: Peer tutoring: a plan for instructing students of all abilities, *J Phys Ed Rec Dance* 68(6):39–44, 1997.

47. Huettig C: *But I didn't want to be a consultant.* Presentation at the 28th National Conference on Physical Education for Individuals with Disabilities, Costa Mesa, CA, October 1999.

48. Hunt P, Goetz L: Research on inclusive educational programs, practices, and outcomes for students with severe disabilities, *J of Special Education* 31(1):3–29, 1997.

49. Hunt P et al.: Achievement by all students within the context of cooperative learning groups, *J Assoc Persons with Severe Handicaps* 19:290–301, 1994.

50. Idol L: Key questions related to building collaborative and inclusive schools, *J Learning Disabilities* 30(4):384–394, 1997.

51. Jensen E: *Turning point for teachers*, Harrow Press Del Mar, CA, 1992.

52. Kauffman JM, Hallahan DP, editors: *The illusion of full inclusion*, Austin, TX, 1995, PRO-ED.

53. Kearns JF: Principal supports for inclusive assessment: a Kentucky story, *Teaching Except Child* November/December:16–23, 1998.

54. Kelly L: Preplanning for successful inclusive schooling, *J Phys Educ Rec Dance* 65(1):37–39, 1994.

55. Kennedy CH, Shuklas, Fryxell D: Comparing the effects of educational placement on the social relationships of intermediate school students with severe disabilities, *Except Child* 64:31–47, 1997.

56. King-Sears ME, Cummings CS: Inclusive practices of classroom teachers, *Remedial and Special Education* 17(4):217–225, 1996.

57. Klingner JK et al.: Inclusion or pull-out: which do students prefer? *J Learning Disabilities* 31(2):148–158, 1998.

58. Kliewer C: The meaning of inclusion. *Mental Retardation* August:317–321, 1998.

59. Korinek L et al.: Least restrictive environment and collaboration: a bridge over troubled water, *Preventing School Failure* 39(3):6–12, 1995.

60. Kozub FM, Poretta D: Interscholastic coaches' attitudes toward integration of adolescents with disabilities, *Adapt Phys Act Q* 15:328–344, 1998.

61. Kozub FM, Poretta D: Including athletes with disabilities: interscholastic athletic benefits for all, *J Phys Ed Rec Dance* 67(3):19–32, 1996.

62. Krebs P, Block M: Transition of students with disabilities into community recreation: the role of the adapted physical educator, *Adapt Phys Act Q* 9:305–315, 1992.

63. Lacy A, LaMaster K, Tommaney W: Teacher behaviors and student academic learning time in physical education, *Physical Educator* 53(1):44–50, 1996.

64. LaMaster K, Kinchin G, Gail K, Siedentop D: Inclusion practices of effective elementary specialists, *Adapt Phys Act Q* 15:64–81, 1998.

65. Law and Litigation: http://www.uni.edu/coe/inclusion/legal.html

66. Learning Disabilities Association of America: *Full inclusion of all students with learning disabilities in the regular education classroom*, Pittsburgh, 1993, Author.

67. Lipsky DK, Gartner A: *Inclusion and school reform: transforming America's classrooms*, Baltimore, MD, Paul H. Brookes, 1997.

68. Lockhart RC, French R, Gench B: Influence of empathy training to modify attitudes of normal children in physical education toward peers with physical disabilities, *Clinical Kines* 52(2):35–41, 1998.

69. Maguire P: Developing successful collaborative relationships, *J Phys Educ Rec Dance* 65(1):32–36, 1994.

70. Mamlin N: Despite best intentions: when inclusion fails, *J Special Education* 33(1):36–49, 1999.

71. Manning M: Understanding culturally diverse parents and families, *Equity Excel Educ* 28(1):52–57, 1995.

72. Markowitz L: The cross-currents of multiculturalism, *Networker*, June/August:20–28, 1994.

73. Marks SU, Scharder C, Levine M: Para-educator experiences in inclusive settings: helping, hovering, or holding their own? *Except Child* 65(3):315–328, 1999.

74. McClesky J, Henry D: Inclusion: what progress is being made across states? *Teaching Except Child* 31(5):56–62, 1999.

75. McClesky J, Henry D, Axelrod M: Inclusion of students with learning disabilities: an examination of data from reports to Congress, *Except Child* 66(1):55–66, 1999.

76. McNulty BA et al.: LRE policy: the leadership challenge, *Remedial and Special Education* 17(3):158–167, 1996.

77. Mobley M, Marlow P: Outdoor adventure: a powerful therapy, *Palaestra* 3:16–19, 1987.

78. Morris GS, Stiehl J: *Changing kids' games*, Champaign, IL, 1989, Human Kinetics.

79. Mosston M, Ashworth S: *Teaching physical education*, New York, 1994, Macmillan.

80. Murata NM, Jansma P: Influence of support personnel on students with and without disabilities in general physical education, *Clinical Kinesiology* 51(2):37–46, 1997.

81. Murphy DM: Implications of inclusion for general and special education, *Elementary School Journal* 96(5):470–493, 1996.

82. National Association for Sport and Physical Education: Moving into the future: national physical education standards: a guide to content and assessment, St. Louis, 1995, Mosby.

83. Nieto J et al.: Passionate commitment to a multicultural society, *Equity Excel Educ* 27(1):51–57, 1994.

84. Olson MR, Chalmers L, Hoover JH: Attitudes and attributes of general education teachers identified as effective inclusionists, *Remedial Spec Educ* 18(1):28–35, 1997.

85. Orfield G et al.: The growth of segregation in American schools: changing patterns of separation and poverty since 1968, *Equity Excel Educ* 27(1):5–8, 1994.

86. Orkwis R, McLane K: *A curriculum every student can use: design principles for student access.* ERIC/OSEP Special Project. The ERIC Clearinghouse on Disabilities and Gifted Education. Reston, VA, Fall 1998, The Council for Exceptional Children.

87. Palmer DS, Borthwick-Duffy SA, Widaman K: Parent perceptions of inclusive practices for their children with significant cognitive disabilities, *Except Child* 64(2):271–282, 1998.

88. Pankake AM, Palmer B: Making the connections: linking staff development interventions to

implementation of full inclusion, *J Staff Development* 17(3):26–30, 1996.

89. Parish TS, Boyd DA: The psychological ramifications of "full inclusion" within our nation's public schools, *Education* 116(2):238–240, 1996.

90. Pearman EL, Huang AM, Mellblom CI: The inclusion of all students: concerns and incentives of educators. *Education and Training in Mental Retardation and Developmental Disabilities* March:11–20, 1997.

91. Prom M: Measuring perceptions about inclusion. *Teaching Exceptional Children* 31(5):38–42, 1999.

92. Pugach MC: On the failure of imagination in inclusive schooling. *J Spec Ed* 29(2):212–223, 1995.

93. Rademaker B, Shirer W, Stocco D: *Project communicate: computer aided instruction for handicapped students*, Mosinee, WI, 1990, Mosinee School District.

94. Ratliffe T, Ratliffe L, Bie B: Creating a learning environment: class management strategies for elementary physical education teachers, *J Phys Educ Rec Dance* 62:24–27, 1991.

95. Reeves L, Stein J: Developmentally appropriate pedagogy and inclusion: "don't put the cart before the horse," *Physical Educator* Winter:2–7, 1999.

96. Reinhardt A: Personal communication, 1994, adapted physical education specialist, Stevens Point (WI) Area Public Schools.

97. Rizzo T: Attitudes of physical educators toward teaching handicapped pupils, *Adapt Phys Act Q* 1:267–274, 1984.

98. Rizzo T, Bishop P, Tobar D: Attitudes of soccer coaches toward youth players with mild mental retardation: a pilot study, *Adapt Phys Act Q* 14:238–251, 1997.

99. Rizzo T, Vispoel WP: Physical educators' attributes and attitudes toward teaching students with handicaps, *Adapt Phys Act Q* 8:4–11, 1991.

100. Rogers J: The inclusion revolution, *Research Bulletin* May:2–3, 1993, Phi Delta Kappa, Center for Evaluation, Development, and Research.

101. Sailor W: Special education in the restructured school, *Teacher Remed Spec Educ* 12(6):8–22, 1991.

102. Saint-Laurent et al.: Academic achievement effects of an in-class service model on students with and without disabilities, *Except Child* 49:192–202, 1998.

103. Salend SJ, Duhaney LM: The impact of inclusion on students with and without disabilities and their educators, *Remedial Spec Educ* 20(2):114–126, 1999.

104. Salisbury CL, Evans IM, Palombaro MM: Collaborative problem-solving to promote the inclusion of young children with significant disabilities in primary grades, *Except Child* 63(2):195–209, 1997.

105. Salisbury CL et al.: Strategies that promote social relations among elementary students with and without severe disabilities in inclusive schools, *Except Child* 62:125–137, 1995.

106. Sands D, Kozleski E: Quality of life differences between adults with and without disabilities, *Educ Train Ment Retard Dev Disabil* 29:90–101, 1994.

107. Sands RG: "Can you overlap here": a question for an interdisciplinary team, *Discourse Processes* 16:545–564, 1993.

108. Searcy S: Friendship interventions for the integrations of children and youth with learning and behavior problems, *Preventing School Failure* 40(3):131–134, 1996.

109. Shanker A: Inclusion and ideology, *Except Parent* September:43–46, 1994.

110. Sharpe MN, York JL, Knight J: Effects of inclusion on the academic performance of classmates without disabilities, *Remed Spec Educ* 15:281–287, 1994.

111. Sharpe T, Templin T: Implementing collaborative teams: a strategy for school-based professionals, *J Phys Ed Rec Dance* 68(6):50–55, 1997.

112. Sherman Consulting: http://www.sherm.com/inclusion/law/a5rulings.html

113. Skrtic TM, Sailor W, Gee K: Voice, collaboration and inclusion: democratic themes in educational and social reform initiatives, *Remedial and Spec Ed* 17(3):142–157, 1996.

114. Staub D et al.: Using nondisabled peers to support the inclusion of students with disabilities, *J of the Assn for Persons with Severe Handicaps* 21:194–205, 1996.

115. Stein J: Total inclusion or least restrictive environment? *J Phys Educ Rec Dance* 65(12):21–25, 1994.

116. TASH:http://tash.org/resolutions/R33INCED. html

117. Temple L, Kelly JD: *Break the rules: everyone plays.* Presentation at the American Alliance of Health, Physical Education, Recreation and Dance convention, Portland, OR, 1995.

118. Texas Woman's University Project INSPIRE website:http://venus.twu.edu/~f_huettig

119. Theodorakis Y, Bagiatis K, Goudas M: Attitudes toward teaching individuals with disabilities: application of planned behavior theory, *Adapt Phys Educ Q* 12:151–160, 1995.

120. Thousand J et al.: The evolution of secondary inclusion, *Remedial Spec Ed* 18(5):270–306, 1997.

121. Turnbull AP, Turnbull HR: Families, professionals, and exceptionality: a special partnership, ed. 2, Columbus, OH, 1990, Merrill.

122. Turnbull AP, Turnbull HR, Shank M, Leal D: *Exceptional lives: special education in today's schools* ed. 2, Upper Saddle River, NJ, 1999, Merrill.

123. Turner CS, Louis KS: Society's response to differences: a sociological perspective, *Remedial Spec Ed* 17(3):134–141, 1996.

124. Udvari-Solner A, Thousand JS: Creating a responsive curriculum for inclusive schools, *Remedial Spec Ed* 17(3):182–192, 1996.

125. United Cerebral Palsy: http://www.ucpa.org/text/advocacy/inclusion.html

126. Vaughn S, Elbaum BE, Schumm JS: The effects of inclusion on the social functioning of students with learning disabilities, *J Learn Dis* 29:598–608, 1996.

127. Vaughn S, Klingner JK: Students' perceptions of inclusion and resource room settings, *J Spec Ed* 32(2):79–88, 1998.

128. Voltz D et al.: Collaborative teacher roles: special and general educators, *J Learning Disabilities* 27:527–535, 1994.

129. Waldron NL, McLeskey J: The effects of an inclusive school program on students with mild and severe learning disabilities, *Except Child* 64:395–407, 1998.

130. Wang MC, Reynolds MC: Progressive inclusion: meeting new challenges in special education, *Theory into Practice* 35(1):20–25, 1996.

131. Werts et al.: Teachers' perceptions of the supports critical to the success of inclusion programs, *JASH* 21(1):9–21, 1996.

132. Williams N: The physical education hall of shame, part 2, *J Phys Educ Rec Dance* 65(2):17–20, 1994.

133. Williams N: The physical education hall of shame, part 3, *J Phys Educ Rec Dance* 67(8):45–48, 1996.

134. Wood M: Whose job is it anyway? Educational roles in inclusion, *Except Child* 64(2):181–196, 1998.

135. Wright PD: *Winds of change: major shifts in U.S. educational policies.* The Special Ed Advocate. http://www.wrightslaw.com/advoc/articles/Winds of change.html

136. Yasutake D, Lerner J: Teachers' perceptions of inclusion for students with disabilities: a survey of general and special educators, *Learning Disabilities: A Multidisciplinary Journal* 7(1):1–7, 1996.

137. Yell ML: Least restrictive environment, inclusion, and students with disabilities: a legal analysis, *J Spec Ed* 28(4):389–404, 1995.

SUGGESTED READINGS

Barbarash L: *Multicultural games,* Champaign, IL, 1997, Human Kinetics.

Houston-Wilson C, Lieberman L, Horton M, Kasser S: Peer tutoring: a plan for instructing students of all abilities, *J Phys Ed Rec Dance* 68(6):39–44, 1997.

Kasser SL: *Inclusive games: movement fun for everyone,* Champaign, IL, 1996, Human Kinetics.

Lieberman LJ, Houston-Wilson C, Butzler Y: *Practical inclusion strategies*, Champaign, IL, 2001, Human Kinetics.

Lipsky DK, Gartner A: *Inclusion and school reform: transforming America's classrooms*, Baltimore, MD, 1997, Paul H. Brookes.

RECOMMENDED WEBSITES

Please note: These websites are being recommended in the fall of 1999. Given the ever changing nature of the Internet, these sites may have moved or been replaced by the time you are reading this text.

Kids Together
        http://www.kidstogether.org/right-ed.html
Inclusion Education Website: The Renaissance Group—the What and How To of Inclusive Education
        http://www.uni.edu/coe/inclusion/

Inclusion: School as a Caring Community
        http://www.quasar.ualberta.ca/ddc/incl/intro.htm
Circle of Inclusion
                http://www.circleofinclusion.org
Family Village
        http://www.familyvillage.wisc.edu/recreat.htm

RECOMMENDED VIDEOS

Psychology, Social Work & Disabilities, Video Collections, 1999-2000.
Fanlight Productions
4196 Washington Street
Boston, MA 02131
As I Am
        Honorable Mention, Columbus International Film Festival, ***** Video Rating
        20 minutes, Purchase $99
        Order No. CV-058
A Passion for Justice
        Featured, Paralympic Disability Film Festival
        29 minutes, Purchase $99
        Order No. CV-164
One of Us: Four Stories of Inclusion
        27 minutes, Purchase $195
        Order No. CV-163

How We Play, by Curtis Graven, Texas Parks and Wildlife
        Featured, Council for Exceptional Children International Video Festival
        11 minutes, Purchase $99
        Order No. CV-092
Aquarius Health Care Videos
        5 Powderhouse Lane
        PO Box 1159
        Sherborn, MA 01770
They're Just Kids, 1998
        27 minutes, Purchase $99
        Item #DISTHEYRE

RECOMMENDED CDs

Willing and Able
Disability Education Program
Participation Division
Australian Sports Commission

PO Box 176, Belconnen, ACT 2616
E-mail: DEP@ausport.gov.au
http://www.ausport.gov.au/partic/dishome.html

CHAPTER

6

Behavior Management

■ **OBJECTIVES**

Give the four fundamental assumptions about behavior management.

Describe techniques that can be used to identify behaviors that need to be learned or changed.

Name and describe five techniques that can be used to facilitate performance of a skill or behavior.

Differentiate between behavior-management techniques for reducing disruptive behaviors in a group setting versus with individuals.

Give three examples of techniques to facilitate generalization.

Name and describe the components of a schoolwide behavior-management system.

Identify the circumstances that permit school personnel to suspend or expel a student with a disability.

Waterproof children at a young age.
Picture by Carol Huettig.

I n the past twenty-five years, discipline has become the number one concern in the schools in the United States.[34] Behavior problems, lack of discipline, student safety, and violence in schools are among the top concerns.[36] More and more children are going to school from homes where socially acceptable behavior is not taught. Children who are raised in homes where cultural, religious, and ethnic expectations differ vastly from the expectations of the schools cannot expect to thrive in school settings. Children from homes where patterns of abuse, verbal and physical, are the norm cannot be expected to demonstrate kindness and consideration for others, let alone wait quietly in line and take turns. Their everyday world has taught them to look out for themselves first and to mistrust adults.

CASE STUDY

CRITICAL THINKING TASK
In Chapter 2 one of the recommendations for Maria Garcia was that she be encouraged to play games that she performs well and contribute to her self-esteem. As you read this chapter, in addition to selecting games that favor Maria's skills, identify at least five ways that you, as the physical educator, could boost Maria's self-esteem while she is participating in your general physical education program.

How do teachers manage the behavior of children who are being raised in environments that, instead of meeting their basic needs, constantly threatens their safety and well-being?

In the past, teachers who became overwhelmed with a student's behavior would refer the "problem" to special education or to the school psychologist to be fixed. However, more recently, educators are coming to understand that the problem may not rest solely with the child. It is becoming clear that the structure of the learning environment, the types of behaviors that are taught directly, and the kinds of interactions that are allowed to routinely occur in that environment are critical factors that impact the behavior of students. Leading educators in this country have come to realize that they can maximize the amount of learning that occurs in a school setting if the entire school is engaged in a focused effort to create learning environments that address all of their students' needs. All teachers and support staffs must take responsibility for creating a learning environment that addresses the psychological as well as the cognitive and physical needs of the students. In this chapter, we will examine specific behavior-management strategies that have a positive impact on individuals' behavior and learning, and we will explore examples of school-wide behavior-management systems that are beginning to emerge across this country. Statutory regulations regarding procedures that may be implemented to discipline students with disabilities whose conduct is unacceptable will also be discussed.

The benefit of physical education programs can be maximized if acceptable principles of learning and development are applied to instruction. Teachers of children with disabilities bear the responsibility for ensuring that learning takes place. In the past, teachers often were assigned to children with disabilities on the basis of tolerance or because they enjoyed working with these children. The physical education programs that teachers designed often focused only on those activities that children enjoyed. If the children appeared to be having a good time, the teacher was judged to be effective. Since the advent of the Education of the Handicapped Act of 1975, the qualifications for teachers of learners with disabilities have changed dramatically. Now these teachers not only must enjoy their work but also must be masterful at determining what is to be taught and at designing educational environments that promote maximum learning. Maximizing learning involves the ability to generalize skills from the instructional settings to functional use in natural, integrated community environments.

Teachers of learners with disabilities must be able to test children; interpret test results; write appropriate long-range goals and short-term objectives that lead to those goals; and apply principles of learning, development, and behavioral strategies that contribute to classroom learning. In addition to these skills, the teacher provides patterns of behavior for the child to copy. From their teachers, immature children learn how the environment works and how persons cope with changing environments.

Teachers must be emotionally stable, flexible, and empathetic toward atypical behavior while encouraging learning. To best understand what the child with a disability is experiencing, teachers must be sensitive enough to perceive the importance of even the slightest change in the child's behavior. This degree of understanding provides a medium through which a child may better understand his or her own behavior and then modify it. This is no easy task. Being in contact with anxiety-provoking persons often stretches the teacher's emotional capacities. Some of the behaviors that teachers often tolerate are implied rejection from the child and conflicting demands, which range from demands that immediate needs be met to severe withdrawal, aggressive tactics, and immature behavior.

Teachers who work solely with normally developing children may be unaccustomed to the many behaviors demonstrated by students with disabilities. If inclusion is going to succeed, teachers must understand and accept the behavior patterns of atypical children while designing and implementing programs that ensure learning progress. The best defense a teacher has is knowledge of what is occurring coupled with teaching and behavioral strategies to move the child beyond present levels of educational performance.

SPECIFIC BEHAVIOR-MANAGEMENT STRATEGIES

Application and Use

Behavior-management strategies provide the teacher with information about how to structure the environment to produce changes in pupil behavior, thus allowing maximum learning to take place. The strategies can be used either to teach and maintain physical and motor skills or to lessen or eliminate disruptive behaviors. The general process is the same in both instances; however, certain techniques are beneficial in facilitating step-by-step learning of motor skills, whereas others are effective for managing disruptive behavior. The fundamental assumptions of behavior management are

- Most behaviors are learned.
- Most behaviors are specific to environments.
- Most behaviors can be changed or modified.
- Behavior-change goals should be planned and systematic.[40]

The physical education teacher has the responsibility of establishing learning environments that permit students to be productive. The environment must be arranged to facilitate skill learning and discourage disruptive behavior because disruptive behavior by one student interferes with that student's learning, as well as with the learning of the others in the class. There are several strategies physical education teachers can use to teach skills and manage classroom behavior; however, the most effective intervention programs are based on actual student performance data. Whether one is attempting to identify behaviors or skills that need to be learned or behaviors that need to be changed, the procedure is the same:

1. Identify the problem.
2. Identify the behavior that needs to be learned or changed.
3. Assess the frequency that the behavior occurs.
4. Select an intervention strategy.
5. Determine an appropriate reinforcer.
6. Begin the program.
7. Consistently reinforce the student's efforts to comply.
8. Observe the effects of the program.
9. Reevaluate to ensure that learning or change has occurred.
10. Fade out the program.

Identifying Behaviors That Need to Be Learned or Changed

The behavior to be observed and changed is the "target behavior." Target behaviors include the following:

- Behaviors that are dangerous to the child or others
- Behaviors interfering with the child's participation in activities
- Behaviors that interfere with the child's social integration
- Functional behaviors that the child will need in the real world
- Behaviors that make the child more socially acceptable
- Behaviors that enable the child to become more independent
- Negative behaviors that draw attention to the child[35]

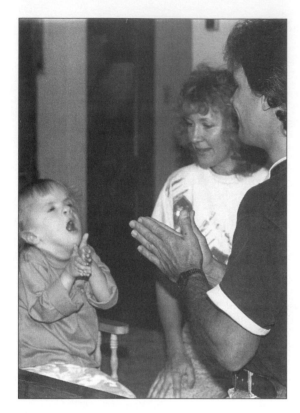

Parents model the behavior they want their child to demonstrate.

Student performance data can be gathered by using a formal instrument to assess motor, physical, or behavioral performance or by observing the students as they perform in educational settings. Formal physical and motor assessment instruments are presented in Chapter 2 of this text; formal observational instruments that can be used to identify teacher and student behaviors in educational settings are included in the Suggested Readings at the end of this chapter. Regardless of whether the behavior to be studied involves performance or the learning of tasks, or disruptive actions, the data collected must be accurate. If a formal instrument is not used, a measuring system must be developed that clearly identifies the behavior to be observed and enables the observer to systematically gather baseline data about the behavior.

Assess the Frequency of Behavior

When collecting baseline behavioral data, it is necessary first to select a measurement system and then decide who will observe and how often. Measuring systems available for collecting and recording behavior include the following components:

- Permanent product recording: a system that involves counting actual behaviors that are demonstrated
- Event recording: the number of times a specifically defined behavior occurs within a time interval (e.g., counting the number of times a student steps away from a line within one class period)
- Duration recording: the length of time a behavior occurs (e.g., how long a student can stay on a specific task)
- Interval recording: the occurrence or nonoccurrence of a behavior within a specific time interval (e.g., the teacher may observe that Jim was active during only two of the five 1-minute observation periods)

The method selected depends on the type of behavior, the kind of data to be gathered, and the ease of implementation by the observer. The most common behavior-measurement systems used in physical education are event, duration, and interval recordings (see Table 6.1).

Event recording produces frequency data that can be converted into percentages. Percentages and frequencies are appropriate measures for skill behaviors done in blocks of tasks. Percentages can be computed by counting the number of baskets made out of ten shots, or the number of successful kicks out of five at a goal in soccer. Frequency data are simply the number of occurrences of the behavior. To compare frequencies, the observation periods should be equal in length, and the student should have the same opportunity to demonstrate the behavior during each observation period. Frequency data can be converted into rate information. Rate is simply the number of times a behavior occurs

TABLE 6.1	Measures of Behavior		
Measure	**Derivation**	**Example**	**Application**
Percentage	Number of correct trials out of a block of trials	Seven basketball goals are made out of a block of 10 trials $\frac{7}{10} \times 100 = 70\%$ accuracy	A measure of accuracy without regard for time or proficiency
Frequency	$\frac{\text{Count of behavior}}{\text{Observation time}}$	Pupil tutor feeds back three times in 3 minutes $= \frac{3}{3}$	How often a distinct behavior occurs within a period of time
Duration	Direct measures of length of time	A child is off task for 45 seconds	The total length of time a continuous behavior occurs
Intervals	Number of fixed time units in which behavior did or did not occur	Children are observed for 20 seconds; then the observer records whether the behavior occurred during the interval; observers then repeat the process (usually data are expressed in terms of percentage of intervals during which the behavior occurred) $\frac{4 \text{ intervals}}{10 \text{ intervals total}} \times 100 = 40\%$ of intervals	When behavior occurs over a time frame

within a certain time limit, such as the number of times a student is able to set up a volleyball in 20 seconds.

Duration recordings are useful if the length of time a student engages in a behavior is of interest. For example, observers may note the amount of time a student requires to move from one activity to the next or how long a student is active or inactive. Duration can be recorded in actual time limits (e.g., Jack was on task for 5 minutes) or in percentages (e.g., Ralph was active for 40 percent of the time).

Interval recordings are particularly useful for the regular class teacher because they do not require that students be observed continuously. Behaviors can be counted throughout the time period (whole-interval time sampling), during the interval (partial-interval time sampling), or only at the end of the interval (momentary time sampling).

Selecting an Intervention Strategy to Facilitate Learning

The central purpose of the physical education program is to develop positive physical and motor behaviors that result in improved health and recreational activity. Intervention programs can be used to teach, maintain, or strengthen a new behavior or to weaken or eliminate undesirable behaviors.

The amount of productive behavior being demonstrated is the primary criterion for determining whether an intervention program is needed. To make this decision, the teacher must refer to the student's educational objectives and compare the behavior being demonstrated with those objectives.

If a behavior to be learned or maintained is not being demonstrated consistently, an intervention program is needed. If time off task and/or disruptive behavior is occurring to the extent that meaningful learning is not occurring, an intervention program is needed.

When a skill or behavior is being taught, maintained, or strengthened, several techniques can be selected to facilitate the performance. These include modeling, shaping, prompting and fading, use of task signals, chaining, peer tutoring, and repetition.

Modeling

Modeling is the demonstration of a task by the teacher or reinforcement of another student who performs a desirable behavior in the presence of the target student. When a teacher actually performs the desirable behavior, he or she is teaching the target student how the task is to be performed. When another student is used as the model and performs a task correctly, the teacher praises the behavior in the presence of the target student. For example, if a teacher wants all the children to maintain a curled back while doing sit-ups, those children who keep their backs curled are pointed out by the teacher and praised while they do their sit-ups. All other children who then perform the task correctly are also reinforced. Modeling can lead to a fairly close approximation of the desired response. Refinement of the response could be done at another time. The model, particularly in motor tasks that are continuous and cannot be broken into component parts, is a very efficient way of promoting learning. Still pictures, movies, and videotapes also may be used. The intent of the model is for the student to imitate the behavior that is demonstrated.

Shaping

Shaping involves the reinforcing of small, progressive steps that lead toward a desired behavior. It is the development of a new behavior through the use of an appropriate reinforcer. The technique of shaping is used to teach new behaviors and is particularly valuable in the performance phase of acquiring a skill. When shaping a new motor response, the physical education teacher has the choice of waiting for the learner to demonstrate the next small step toward the goal or helping the learner attain the

TABLE 6.2	Procedures for Shaping a Behavior
Procedure	**Example**
1. Define the behavior.	Balancing on one foot with eyes open for 10 seconds
2. Define a reinforcer.	Knowledge of task success
3. Determine the present level.	2 seconds on the task
4. Outline a series of small steps that lead to the desired behavior.	16 increments of 1/2 second each
5. Advance the learner on a predetermined criterion.	Each step three times in a row
6. Define the success level.	90 percent

objective through the use of a physical prompt. In either case, the specifically defined task (step) must be reinforced. The procedures for shaping a behavior are listed in Table 6.2.

Prompting and Fading

Prompting and Fading techniques can be included in any behavior-management system. Prompting means providing just enough assistance so that the student realizes some success at the task. Fading means gradually withdrawing the help. Usually prompting will enable a successful response or a close enough approximation so that shaping can be used to improve the performance level.

Physical priming,[1] or prompting, involves physically holding and moving the learner's body parts through the activity. Types of prompts include physical, auditory, and visual. An auditory prompt may involve clapping the hands or blowing a whistle to gain attention or terminate activity. Visual prompts involve hand signals that could be used to gain attention and terminate activity, footprints that indicate where one should stand or position the body for a skill, and visual targets.

Prompting should be used with the idea of eliminating the primers as quickly as possible so that the learner can begin to function independently. A general rule for prompts is to provide no more assistance than is necessary to elicit a successful outcome. Prompts should be faded as soon as possible to eliminate the learner's dependence on them. Students should be taught to reduce their dependence on the teacher and increase their ability to function independently. A way of structuring the environment from the most to the least assistance might involve (1) providing a great amount of physical help combined with verbal instruction, (2) providing a lesser amount of physical help combined with verbal instruction, (3) providing demonstration with verbal instruction, (4) providing verbal instruction only, (5) providing visual cues only, and finally (6) having the learner seek the auditory and/or visual cues needed to understand the task and be successful.[39]

Prompts can be combined with other behavior-management techniques to facilitate the learning of physical skills. One other technique that can be used in combination with prompting is positive reinforcement.[13] Combining positive reinforcement with auditory, visual, and/or physical prompts tends to reduce avoidance behaviors.[10]

Prompts are valuable if the tasks can be learned quickly. If the learner is not able to perform a task in a relatively short period of time, the teacher probes through prerequisite components to determine which ones are missing and need to be learned before the skill can be performed.

Task Signals

Signals that indicate the beginning and end of the activity and movement of the children from one part of the play area to another part increase the structure of the play environment (see Table 6.3). The characteristics of signals for providing structure to the instructional environment are as follows:

1. The command signals should be short and concise.
2. The signals should be no stronger than needed to elicit the response.

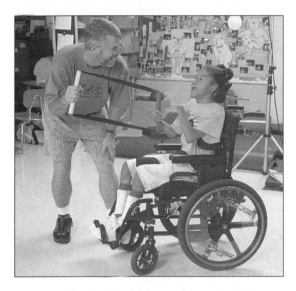

Equipment that enables participation reinforces a child's desire to participate.
Courtesy of Sportime, Atlanta, GA.

TABLE 6.3	Application of Task Signals to Specific Activities to Facilitate Effective Instruction	
Principles	**Instructional Conditions**	**Task Signals**
Secure a signal	Group or individualized instruction	Clap hands for attention, "ready go," "listen"
Short command	Guarding a nonmoving person in basketball	"Hand up"
	Preparation for catching a ball	"Watch the ball"
Signals no stronger than needed	Instruction on a task individualized to needs of the child	Tone of voice from a whisper to loud enthusiasm
Feedback signals	After successful catch of a ball	"Nice catch"
	Error correction in catching	"Watch the ball into your hands"

3. Signals may be needed to secure attention (such commands as "listen" and "look" may be needed to secure the attention of persons with more severe involvements).
4. Feedback signals about task mastery are needed to provide information to the learner; through the use of these signals, the teacher should indicate to the student the level of success he or she is experiencing.

Chaining

Chaining is the process of leading a person through a series of teachable components of a motor task. Each teachable component represents a discrete portion (link) in a task. When these links are tied together, the process is known as chaining. Some skills can be broken into components and taught by the chaining process more easily than others. Self-help skills are easily broken into parts. Clearly, grasping a spoon is an essential link in the process of eating; however, it is a behavior distinctly different from scooping the food with the spoon or placing the food in one's mouth. Each of these components is a necessary link that must be tied together (chained) to accomplish the skill of self-feeding. Continuous physical skills do not break into discrete teachable components and are difficult to chain. Other physical skills, such as the lay-up shot in basketball, can be broken into discrete components that lend themselves to chaining.

When forward chaining is being used, the first step is taught first, the second step is taught second, and so on until the entire task is learned. Most teachers use forward chaining when teaching motor and physical tasks.

When the last of the series of steps is taught first, the process is known as backward chaining. Self-help tasks, such as tying a shoe and dressing, are easily and effectively taught by backward chaining, as are skills used in team play. Teaching a basketball lay-up by means of backward chaining requires that the student (1) stand close to the basket, reach high with the arm, and shoot the basketball; (2) jump from the inside foot, reach high with the arm, and shoot the basketball; (3) run-jump from the inside foot, reach high with the arm, and shoot the basketball; and (4) dribble the basketball while running, jump from the inside foot, reach high with the arm, and shoot the basketball. The value of backward chaining is that the individual is reinforced during each step by completing the task successfully. Examples of the analysis of these tasks are given in Table 6.4.

Peer Tutoring

Peer tutoring has been shown to increase instructional effectiveness for persons with disabilities. Peer tutoring involves using same-age peers or cross-age (older) peers to interact with children with disabilities to keep them on task. Both the child with a disability and the peers benefit from the interaction.[20] The benefits to students with disabilities include (1) sustained positive interactions and friendships, (2) increased opportunities to practice needed skills, (3) age-appropriate role models, (4) development of social behaviors and communication skills, and (5) discovery of hidden strengths. Peer tutors gain from the experience by (1) increasing acceptance of individual differences, (2) developing a deeper sense of social justice and advocacy for others,[6] (3) increasing self-esteem,[9] and (4) developing a better understanding of how to communicate with and provide assistance to people with disabilities.[30]

Repetition

Repetition is the act of practicing the same physical movement over and over again. Repetition can be varied into massed or distributed schedules. Massed practice occurs all at once, whereas distributed practice sessions are spaced out over a period of several days or months. In general, distributed practice is considered the best technique for promoting learning and ensuring retention of a skill. Repetition can result in overlearning of a target skill, which in turn enhances the possibility of generalizing motor and physical skills from a class setting to a community recreational setting.

Reinforcement

Reinforcement is a strategy that follows and strengthens a behavior.[35] It is important to involve

TABLE 6.4	Examples of Skills Taught by Backward Chaining
Behavior	**Task Sequence**
Pass receiving in football	(1) Catch pass; (2) run and catch pass; (3) make cut, run, and catch pass; (4) release from line, run, cut, and catch pass.
Tackling in football	(1) Tackle ball carrier; (2) run pattern to intersect and tackle ball carrier; (3) release blocker, run pattern to ball carrier, and tackle ball carrier; (4) administer technique to neutralize blocker, release blocker, run pattern to ball carrier, tackle ball carrier.
Shooting a soccer goal	(1) Shoot soccer goal; (2) dribble and shoot soccer goal; (3) receive a pass, dribble, and shoot soccer goal.
Passing a soccer ball	(1) Pass soccer ball; (2) bring ball under control and pass soccer ball; (3) dribble, bring ball under control, and pass soccer ball.
Leg takedown in wrestling	(1) Take opponent to the mat; (2) secure legs and take opponent to the mat; (3) shoot move for legs, secure legs, and take opponent to the mat; (4) set up move, shoot move for legs, secure legs, and take opponent to the mat.
Fielding a ball and throwing a player out at first base in softball	(1) Throw to first base; (2) field the ball and throw to first base.

students in developing a list of potential reinforcers because it is critical that the reinforcer be something the student values. The discussion that follows focuses on positive reinforcers because they yield the most lasting results. Positive reinforcers include teacher or peer praise, stickers, a paper certificate, positive notes to parents, sports equipment, medals, first in line and squad leader privileges, selection of activities a student enjoys doing, and success on a task. Positive reinforcement is constructive because it helps individuals feel good about themselves.

Selection of Reinforcers

Reinforcers may be intrinsic (internal) or extrinsic (external). Intrinsic reinforcement comes from within the learner. Often knowledge of success on a task or the satisfaction of participating is sufficient reinforcement. Extrinsic reinforcement comes from outside the learner. Examples of extrinsic reinforcement are praise and other rewards from a person who acknowledges the learner's achievement. One objective of a reinforcement program is to move the learner from dependence on extrinsic

reinforcers to a search for intrinsic reinforcers. Once learners no longer have to rely on teachers for feedback, they can direct their own learning. It is important that both the learner and the teachers agree on what the reinforcer will be and how the system of reinforcement will work.

Reinforcement Procedures

Contingency management is a way of controlling the use of reinforcers. A contingency agreement is an agreement between the student and the teacher that indicates what the student must do to earn a specific reward. A token economy is a form of contingency management in which tokens (external reinforcers) are earned for desirable behavior. This type of system can be used with a single student, selected groups of students, or classes of students. Lewis and Doorlag[18] suggest the following procedure for setting up a token economy:

1. Specify the behaviors that earn tokens.
2. Use tokens that are appropriate for the student.
3. Pose a menu (list) of the types of available reinforcers.

4. Allow students to suggest reinforcers for the list.
5. Revise the menu regularly.
6. Use a clear recording system (of distributing the tokens) that is accurate.
7. Give students frequent opportunities to cash in their earned tokens.
8. The cash-in system should take a minimal amount of time.
9. Provide clear rules to staff and peer tutors for distribution of tokens.
10. Gradually reduce the value of the tokens to increase reliance on more natural reinforcers.

Token economy systems that have proved successful in the physical education program include those that allow students to cash in their tokens to buy the following:

A given number of minutes of supervised free play

The right to lead class warm-up exercises

The right to choose a class activity for 5 to 10 minutes on a given day

The privilege of being the "assistant" teacher for a given class

The privilege of 5 to 10 minutes of uninterrupted one-on-one play time with the physical education teacher

The right to eat lunch with the physical education teacher

A poster of a sports star

Recreation and sport equipment

Relatively inexpensive recreation and sport equipment can be purchased to support the token economy system. Children love having the privilege to earn jump ropes, balls, juggling scarves, and hackey-sacs. Parent-Teacher Associations often are willing to help with fund raising to help provide the physical education teacher with this type of equipment. There are corporations that have fund-raiser/promotional campaigns (e.g., Campbell Soup Company) that may help the physical education teacher secure this type of equipment without buying it out of an already small budget or an equally small personal salary.

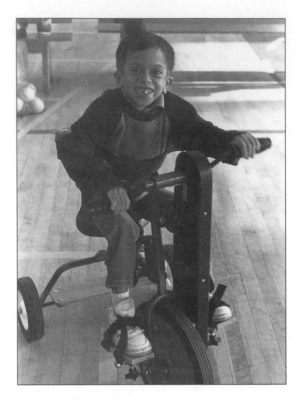

Equipment that enables participation motivates a child's desire to persist at a task.
Courtesy Dallas Independent School District.

Frequency of Reinforcement

The frequency of distributing reinforcers should be carefully controlled, so that the student continues to strive toward desirable goals. The frequency that reinforcers are given is called the reinforcement schedule (see Table 6.5). Schedules of reinforcement should move from continuous (a reinforcer every time the desirable behavior occurs) to a fixed ratio (e.g., one reinforcer for every three instances of desirable behavior). Interval reinforcement schedules provide reinforcement after an established period of time. The schedule should be changed eventually to a variable-interval ratio (e.g., one reinforcer for every three instances of desirable behavior followed by one reinforcer for every five instances of desirable behavior, or one reinforcer every minute followed by one reinforcer every 3 minutes). The variable-interval ratio is the most effective because, when

TABLE 6.5	Intermittent Schedules of Reinforcement		

| | | **Effects on Behavior** | |
Name of Schedule	Definition of Schedule	Schedule in Effect	Schedule Terminated (Extinction)*
Fixed ratio (FR)	Reinforcer is given after each X responses	High response rate	Irregular burst of responding; more responses than in continuous reinforcement, less than in variable ratio
Fixed interval (FI)	Reinforcer is given for first response to occur after each X minutes	Stops working after reinforcement; works hard just prior to time for next reinforcement	Slow gradual decrease in responding
Variable ratio (VR)	Reinforcer is given after X responses on the average	Very high response rates; the higher the ratio, the higher the rate	Very resistant to extinction; maximum number of responses before extinction
Variable interval (VI)	Reinforcer is given for first response after each X minutes on the average	Steady rate of responding	Very resistant to extinction; maximum time to extinction

From Walker HM: *The acting-out child: coping with classroom disruption,* New York, 1979, Allyn & Bacon.

*See pp. 236–41 for discussion on decreasing inappropriate behavior.

students are unable to predict when they will be reinforced, they tend to persist at a task.

Intervention Strategies to Control Disruptive Behaviors

Much of the previous discussion concerns the uses of reinforcement to increase efforts toward learning tasks. Very often, reinforcement procedures are used to decrease undesirable behaviors. The undesirable behaviors must be eliminated or substantially reduced so that the student can focus attention and effort on positive learning habits.

Because of self-concept and attention deficits, children with disabilities may disrupt classrooms and make it difficult for themselves and others to learn meaningful motor skills. When behavior-management strategies are applied to classroom management, it must be systematic, consistent, and concerned with both preventing disruptive behavior and promoting positive behavior. There are two

levels of classroom management: one for the group and another for individuals within the group.

Controlling Group Behavior

There are some techniques for managing behavior that are particularly effective for groups. These include positive teacher attitudes, prevention, establishment and enforcement of class rules, teacher intervention, flexibility in planning, appeals to values, control of the environment, and student leadership opportunities.

Positive teacher attitudes have a powerful impact on the learning of social behavior and physical skills. Some behaviors a teacher can demonstrate that will motivate a class to perform to their maximum include:

1. Be positive. Students work harder to gain rewards than they do to avoid punishment.
2. Teach enthusiastically. Use a comfortable verbal pace, varied inflection, and an encouraging tone of voice.

a. Set realistic expectations. Students will strive toward goals they believe they can accomplish.
b. Inform students about their progress. Students need to know they are on track and improving.
c. Reinforce every legitimate effort. Students are more motivated to persist when their efforts are noticed and reinforced.[29]

The single most effective method for controlling behavior is prevention. The most significant technique for controlling behavior is to "catch 'em being good." This proactive teaching response, in which the teacher consistently and enthusiastically embraces "good" behavior, allows the teacher and the students to focus on good behavior. It is crucial that, when addressing the behavior of a child or children, the focus is on behavior. When praising a child for good behavior, it is necessary that other children understand that it is the behavior that is being praised, so that those not being praised do not get the unintentioned message that they are somehow "bad." Examples of appropriate responses include the following:

- "Juan, thank-you for being such a good listener."
- "I really like the way that Thelma is following directions."
- "Carlos, I'm really proud of you for putting your ball away."
- "Way to be, Jason! I like the fact that you shared your toy with Julianna."

The good teaching technique of "catch 'em being good" is one of the basic elements of preventive planning, which consists of establishing class rules and enforcing them in the least intrusive ways possible. Rules for class conduct should communicate to students the behavior expected by the teacher. Effective class rules should (1) be few in number, (2) be a statement of behavior desired from the student, (3) be simple and clearly stated in a positive way, and (4) explain guidelines that the teacher can enforce. For example, a well-stated rule is "When lined up at the door waiting to pass

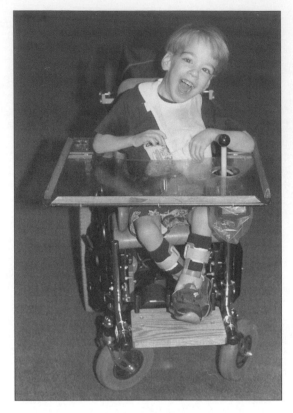

Children who enjoy activity are internally motivated to continue participation.
Courtesy Dallas Independent School District.

to the next class, keep your hands to yourself." Clearly stated expectations lead to appropriate classroom behavior. They provide learners with rules of conduct and identify behavior that will be rewarded. It is suggested that a list of rules be placed where students can observe it each day. The consequences for breaking rules should also be made clear to the students. These must be posted in the native languages of the children served. For example, if a school serves a large number of Hispanic students, rules and consequences should be posted in both English and Spanish. When serving young children or nonreaders, rules and consequences must be reviewed before each class period; in some situations, rules and consequences may need to be repeated periodically throughout the class.

Modifying equipment to enable everyone to play is a reinforcer to the child.
Courtesy Orthotic & Prosthetic Athlete Assistance Fund, Inc.

Rules cannot take care of every situation; often there is disruptive behavior not covered by the rules. The difficult decision each teacher must make is whether to intervene and stop the disruptive behavior. Teachers have a responsibility to interfere with behaviors that

> Present a physical danger to self or others
>
> Are psychologically harmful to the child and others
>
> Lead to excessive excitement, loss of control, or chaos
>
> Prohibit continuation of the program
>
> Lead to destruction of property
>
> Encourage the spread of negativism in the group
>
> Lead to conflict with others outside the group

Compromise the teacher's mental health and ability to function[28]

If the teacher does decide it is necessary to intervene to control disruptive behavior, several techniques are effective in controlling disturbances. Some specific techniques that have been identified by Redl to manage disruptive students in a physical education setting are as follows:

- Planned ignoring. Much of children's behavior is designed to antagonize the teacher. If this behavior is not contagious, it may be wise to ignore it and not gratify the child.
- Signal interference. The teacher can use nonverbal controls, such as hand clapping, eye contact, frowns, and body posture, to indicate to the child disapproval and control.
- Proximity control. The teacher can stand next to a child who is having difficulty. This is to let the child know of the teacher's concern regarding the behavior.
- Interest boosting. If a child's interest is waning, involve the child actively in class activities of the moment and let him or her demonstrate the skill that is being performed or discussed.
- Reduction of tension through humor. Humor is often able to penetrate a tense situation, with the result that everyone becomes more comfortable.
- Hurdle lesson. Sometimes a child is frustrated by the immediate task. Instead of asking for help, the child may involve his or her peers in disruptive activity. In this event, select and structure a task in which the child can be successful.
- Restructure of classroom program. If the teacher finds the class irritable, bored, or excited, a change in program might be needed.
- Support from routine. Some children need more structure than others. Without these guideposts they feel insecure. Structure programs for those who need it by clearly defining the rules, boundaries, and acceptable limits of behavior, as well as adhering to the same general routine each day.

- Direct appeal to value areas. Appeal to certain values that children have internalized, such as a relationship between the teacher and the child, behavioral consequences, awareness of peer reaction, and appeal to the teacher's power of authority.
- Removal of seductive objects. It is difficult for the teacher to compete against balls, bats, objects that can be manipulated, and equipment that may be in the vicinity of instruction. Either the objects have to be removed or the teacher has to accept the disorganized state of the group.[26]

In addition, whenever possible, students should be given opportunities to provide leadership within the class,[25] be given opportunities to select activities,[29] and engage in planning sessions on ways to modify games to include a wide range of student abilities (see Chapter 5).

Handling the Disruptive Student

The behavior problems of students with disabilities frequently contribute to their placement in special physical education programs. When students with special needs are placed in the physical education class, teachers are often concerned that their problem behaviors will interfere with the operation of the classroom.

Behaviors that interfere with classroom instruction, impede social interaction with the teacher and peers, or endanger others are considered classroom conduct problems. Examples of inappropriate classroom behaviors are talking out, fighting, arguing, being out of line, swearing, using equipment or facilities inappropriately, being noncompliant, and avoiding interactions with others. Breaking of the rules of the game, poor sportsmanship, and immature and withdrawn behaviors also fall under this category. Behaviors that interfere with the special student's motor skill development are considered skill problems. Typical skill problems result from poor attending behavior and failure to attempt tasks with a best effort.

Problem behaviors are exhibited in one of three ways: (1) there is a low rate of appropriate behaviors, (2) there is a high rate of inappropriate behaviors, or (3) the appropriate behavior is not part of the student's repertoire. Knowing the characteristics of the behavior is important, since different management strategies are linked to each.

One athlete reinforces another athlete's performance.
Courtesy Achilles Track Club, New York.

1. Low rate of appropriate behaviors. Students with low rates of appropriate behaviors do exhibit appropriate behaviors, but not as frequently as expected or required. For example, a student may be able to stay on task only 50 percent of the time. Also, students may behave appropriately in one setting but not in another. For instance, the special student may work well on individual tasks but find it difficult to function in group games. To alleviate these problems, the teacher sets up a systematic program to generalize on-task behaviors from one situation to another. An example of facilitating the generalization of on-task behavior toward functioning in a group setting is to gradually move a student from an individual task to a task that is paralleled by another student, to a task where two students assist each other in being successful (such as

taking turns spotting one another during free weight lifting).

2. High rate of inappropriate behaviors. Inappropriate behaviors that occur frequently or for long periods are troublesome to teachers. Examples are students who do not conform to class rules thirty to forty times a week, those who talk during 50 to 60 percent of class instruction, those who use profanity five to ten times in one class period, and those who are off task 70 to 75 percent of the class period. To overcome these high rates of inappropriate behavior, the physical education teacher attempts to decrease the frequency or duration of the undesired behavior by increasing appropriate behaviors that are incompatible. For instance, to decrease the incidence of hitting a peer while in class, the teacher can increase the rate of performing tasks or decrease the time between tasks.

3. Appropriate behavior not part of the student's repertoire. Students may not yet have learned appropriate behaviors for social interaction or classroom functioning. For instance, they may not know sportsmanship conduct in class games. Teachers must provide instruction to help students acquire new behaviors. Behavior problems do not occur in isolation. Events or actions of others can initiate or reinforce inappropriate behaviors. To understand and manage classroom problems, the teacher should examine the student in relation to the target behavior. For example, classmates who laugh at clowning or wisecracks tend to reinforce that type of disruptive behavior; as a result, the disruptive student continues to exhibit the undesirable behavior. Students show inappropriate behavior when they have not learned correct responses or have found that acting inappropriately is more rewarding than acting appropriately. These behavior problems do respond to instruction.

Several methods for decreasing inappropriate behavior are available. Walker and Shea have proposed the following continuum of behavior-modification interventions:

1. Reinforcement of behavior other than the target behavior. A reinforcer is given at the end of a specified period of time, provided that a prespecified misbehavior has not occurred during the specified time interval.
2. Reinforcement of an appropriate target behavior. A reinforcer is given following the performance of a prespecified appropriate target behavior.
3. Reinforcement of incompatible behaviors. A reinforcer is given following the performance of a prespecified behavior that is physically and functionally incompatible with the target behavior.
4. Extinction. The reinforcer that has been sustaining or increasing an undesirable behavior is withheld.
5. Stimulus change. The existing environmental conditions are drastically altered to ensure that the target behavior is temporarily suppressed.
6. Reprimand. A form of punishment that involves verbally chastising a student for inappropriately exhibiting a target behavior. The reprimand should
   - Be specific to the inappropriate behavior
   - Address the behavior, not the child
   - Be firm and administered immediately
   - Be accompanied by loss of privileges
   - Include a statement of appropriate behavior
   - Be done in a calm voice followed by observation of the child's reaction, so that the effect of the reprimand can be evaluated
7. Nonexclusionary time-out
   a. Head down on a desk or table in the work area in which the target behavior occurred
   b. Restriction to a chair in a separate area of the classroom but able to observe classroom activities
   c. Removal of materials (work, play)
   d. Reduction or elimination of room illumination

8. Physical restraint. It may be necessary to restrain a child physically if he or she loses control and becomes violent.

9. Negative practice or satiation. The target behavior is eliminated by the continued and increased reinforcement of that behavior.

10. Overcorrection. This punishment procedure requires the individual who misbehaves to improve the environmental effects of the misbehavior and/or repeatedly perform the appropriate form of the target behavior in the environment in which the misbehavior was exhibited.

11. Exclusionary time-out.
    a. Temporary distraction. When a student's behavior has reached the point at which he or she will not respond to verbal controls, the student may have to be asked to leave the room (to get a drink, wash up, or deliver a message—not as punishment, but to distract the student).
    b. Quiet room/think station. Some schools provide quiet spaces for students to use when it becomes necessary to remove oneself from a group setting to ponder about the misbehavior. The student should be continuously monitored, and the length of time should be limited to 2 to 10 minutes.
    c. In-school suspension.

12. Response cost lottery. Students are given a predetermined number of slips of paper. Each time the student violates a class rule, he or she must relinquish one slip of paper. The names of the students are written on the slips of paper the students still have at the end of a given time period and are placed in a hat for a lottery drawing. The winner of the drawing receives a prize.[35]

Consistent Management Techniques

There is consensus that successful schools use systems of firm, consistent management. Research confirms that clearly structured, secure environments permit students to master the objectives of

Encouragement by a teacher is critical to developing risk-taking behaviors.
Picture by Carol Huettig.

the program. Haring indicates that "teaching . . . necessitates finding a method of instruction which allows the child to learn."[8]

The preconditions for the application of learning principles are that there must be a precisely defined short-term instructional objective, and there must be incentives for the learner to master the objective. If either of these preconditions is not satisfied, the effect of the program is minimized. Effective learning is the result of mutual understanding between the student and the teacher. The student must understand what is expected and the consequences of not performing to expectations. Homme[11] provides nine rules to follow when using behavior-management techniques:

1. Praise the correct objective.
2. Praise the correct objective immediately after it occurs.
3. Praise the correct objective after it occurs and not before.
4. Objectives should be in small steps so that there can be frequent praise.
5. Praise improvement.

6. Be fair in setting up consequences for achieving objectives.
7. Be honest and provide the agreed-on consequences.
8. Be positive so that the child can achieve success.
9. Be systematic.

Praise the Correct Objective

To implement this principle effectively, persons involved with instruction (teachers, school administrators, parents, and related service personnel) must know precisely the objective or behavior that the learner is to carry out. That behavior must be praised only if it is achieved. The application of this principle must be consistent among all persons who work with the child.

There are two ways that this learning principle can be violated by a teacher, parent, or school administrator. First, he or she may provide praise even though the objective has not been achieved; second, he or she may neglect to provide praise even though the objective has been achieved. In the first case, the learner is being reinforced for doing less than his or her best and consequently will have a lessened desire to put forth maximum effort on subsequent trials. In the second case, if the teacher does not deliver the agreed-on consequence (explicit or implicit), the student's desire to perform the instructional task again will be reduced.

Praise Immediately After Completion of the Task

Learners need to receive feedback immediately after task performance. Homme[11] indicates that reinforcing feedback should be provided 0.05 second after the task for maximum effectiveness. Immediacy of feedback on task performance is particularly important with children functioning on a lower developmental level. If there is a delay between task performance and feedback, the child may be confused as to what the praise is for. For example, if a child walks a balance beam correctly but confirmation of task mastery is provided late (for instance, as the child steps off the beam), the behavior of stepping off the beam may be strength-ened to a greater degree than the desired objective of walking the beam. Thus, the timing of the feedback (immediately after the task has been completed) is important.

Praise at the Appropriate Time

If a child is praised for performing an objective before it is completed, there is a good chance that he or she will expend less effort to meet the objective.

Make Sure Objectives Are in Small Steps

If the step size is small, there will be a greater rate of success. As has been indicated, disruptive behavior may be triggered by lack of success. This principle may therefore be applied in attempts to control disruptive behavior in the classroom. Thus, if a child often exhibits many different types of disruptive behavior, objectives can be postulated to reduce the occurrence of these disruptive behaviors in small steps. For children with disabilities, learning by small steps permits much needed success.

Praise Improvement

The acquisition of skill toward an objective should be praised. Providing appropriate consequences for improvement may in some instances violate the principle of praising the correct objective. However, on tasks that cannot be broken into small steps, it is necessary to praise improvement. To do so, the instructor must know precisely the student's present level of educational performance. When the performance reflects an improvement on that level, the student must be reinforced with praise. Improvement means that the learner is functioning on a higher level than before. Therefore, it is unwise to praise or provide positive consequences to students who perform at less than their best effort, since to do so may encourage them to contradict their potential.

Be Fair in Setting Up Consequences

When there are specific objectives to be achieved to develop skill or appropriate classroom behavior, specific consequences can be arranged to support

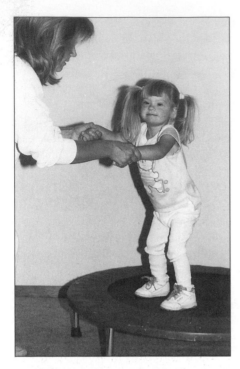

Equipment for the home provides play opportunity for child and parent.

the development of these objectives. However, if such arrangements are to be made between the learner and the teacher, there must be equity between the task and the incentives. If the learner does not have sufficient incentive to perform the tasks or to behave appropriately, he or she is unlikely to do so. This learning principle operates at very early ages.

In one clinical experience, a target objective was set up for an 18-month-old boy with Down syndrome to learn to walk. The task involved walking from one chair to another, which was placed 8 feet away. If the child walked the full distance, he was allowed to play for 15 seconds with the toys that were placed on top of the chairs. When this period elapsed, he would return to the task of walking a prescribed distance of 8 feet 1 inch, a short distance farther than the previous time. After a time, the child refused to participate in the activity. The child's mother suggested that he be permitted to play with the toys for 30 seconds rather than 15 seconds. This procedure was used, and the child again engaged in the instructional task. It was inferred that the child would participate in tasks if the opportunity to play was commensurate with the effort put forth to master the objective. This is an example of equity between incentive and performance.

Be Honest

Agreements between teachers and learners must be honored by both. If there is an implicit or explicit arrangement between the teacher and the learner and the teacher does not follow through with the arrangement when the learner has upheld his or her end of the bargain, then the learning conditions will be seriously weakened. It is not uncommon for teachers to inadvertently forget the arrangements that have been made. Therefore, it is important for teachers to have records of arrangements between themselves and learners. Forgetting the preconditions between learner and teacher may have a negative impact on the pupil's learning at a subsequent time.

If the teacher requests that a learner perform a specific task, the teacher must not provide the desirable consequences unless the learner achieves the proper objective. Honest delivery of the agreed-on consequences is similar to praise for the correct behavior. However, praise for the correct behavior usually connotes a specific short-term task, whereas an agreed-on consequence may involve a contractual arrangement between two parties. Principals and teachers who set policies may achieve positive results with the application of this principle.

Be Positive

The objective should be phrased positively, so that the learner can achieve the stated objective (e.g., "Walk to the end of the balance beam"). An example of a negative statement is "Don't fall off of the balance beam." In the negative instance, the child is avoiding failure, and there can be little value in mastering the desired behavior.

Be Systematic

To make the greatest positive impact on children with disabilities, it is necessary to apply all the learning principles all the time. Inconsistency confuses the learner with regard to the material to be learned and the type of behavior to maintain during class. The consistent use of behavior-management strategies enhances a child's ability to learn desirable behaviors. This learning principle is the most difficult one for teachers of children with emotional disturbances to master.

Contingency Contracting

A contract is an agreement, written or verbal, between two or more parties, that stipulates the responsibilities of the parties concerning specific items or activities.[35] Contingency contracting is a method used to individualize instruction to respond to the interests, needs, and abilities of children. When the students satisfactorily complete the conditions of their contracts, they receive something they have identified. Contingency contracts can be used to teach a new behavior, maintain existing behaviors, and decrease inappropriate behaviors. The values of this type of contracting include (1) the technique can be used with fairly large groups of students, (2) they allow for delay of reinforcement during busy period, (3) they allow one reinforcer for reinforcing many behaviors, and (4) reinforcers can be given without interruption of teaching the class.

Techniques to Ensure Persistence of Learning or Change

Maintenance is perpetuation of a trained behavior after all formal intervention has ceased. To determine whether a trained behavior is being maintained, it can be formally assessed, observational data can be gathered, and/or individuals who interact with the student can be interviewed. The most powerful indication that behavior has really been impacted and is being maintained is the extent to which the behavior has been generalized to other settings.

Figure 6-1 Methods for Promoting Maintenance

- Teach in a natural setting and avoid artificial training settings.
- Implement the program across settings and with different people.
- Identify common elements between the teaching environment and generalizing environments.
- Shift the artificial stimulus controls to natural stimulus controls.
- Shift from continuous to intermittent forms of reinforcement.
- Pair artificial reinforcers with natural reinforcers and consequences.
- Reinforce maintenance and generalization by telling your students when you notice gains.

Maintenance is the degree to which a behavior change is maintained over time. Methods for promoting maintenance are presented in Figure 6-1. Generalization is the ability to use a learned skill or way of behaving in places other than the instructional setting. The success of instruction can be measured by the extent to which a learned way of behaving can be used in a variety of practical settings. Such generalization assists with independence and adds to the quality of life for persons with disabilities.

In the past, generalization was an expected, yet unplanned, outcome of instructional programs;[31] however, during the past twenty-five years generalization has been more systematically planned and evaluated. Studies have documented that generalization of motor skills can be taught successfully. More recently, studies have been conducted to determine the process and variables that control the generalization of all types of behaviors to applied settings. LeBlanc and Matson[17] have developed a social training program that helps preschool children with disabilities to generalize behaviors to other social settings. The program uses protocols for modeling, feedback, and time-out from reinforcement. Other instructional packages directed at self-management, self-modeling, self-assessment, discrimination training, and co-operative efforts can be used for physical skill development.[2,21]

Although a number of considerations are a part of the development and application of generalization techniques, two are of paramount importance: (1) the techniques should support the generalization of functional motor skills to nontraining settings, such as recreational environments in the community and the home; and (2) the techniques should be reasonably efficient. Efficiency is the use of a skill in an applied setting with a minimum amount of training or assistance to produce the desired results. To ensure the transfer of learning to applied settings, it is critical that specific generalization goals be incorporated into the student with severe disability's educational program.[27]

Morris[22] describes three types of generalizations: (1) response maintenance, (2) situation or setting, and (3) response generalization:

1. Response maintenance generalization includes changes that are maintained even after the behavior modification has stopped.
2. Situation or setting generalization includes changes that occur from one environment to another and/or from one person to another.
3. Response generalization includes changes in behavior that was not targeted for intervention.

Generalization Variables

There are two basic forms of generalization in the curriculum content of physical education: (1) generalization of the acquired motor skills and (2) generalization of the cognitive and social dimensions that enable participation with others. Clearly, if the skills of a physical sport (e.g., basketball, soccer, or softball) are acquired but the social skill is inappropriate for participation in culturally acceptable environments in the community, then the person with a disability will not have the opportunity to express the attained skills.[38]

When using generalization procedures, the adapted physical educator should consider the cognitive and social ability levels of the student, the acquired level of proficiency of the target skill, and the features of the natural environment. The cognitive and motivational levels of the individual with disabilities and his or her attitude toward the skill are other dimensions of generalization. Also, it is important to understand the student's attitude toward competition. Some individuals do not enjoy participating in activities where there are winners and losers. If these individuals participate in competitive sports, they may be motivated by focusing on the importance of their contributions to the team effort rather than on bettering their opponents.[4,19]

Considerations for Generalization

There are at least two different types of environments associated with the process of generalization. One is the instructional environment, and the other is the natural environment. Instructional environments are settings where the education of students with disabilities is of explicit concern. Natural environments are those settings where the motor skills that are learned in school are actually used (e.g., community environments). Natural environments are those in which individuals without disabilities function and in which individuals with disabilities should be taught to function. To facilitate generalization from educational to community environments, it is recommended that the teacher (1) develop a management system to assess the generalized effect of the motor skill training program in nontraining environments, (2) determine the effects of training on the motor function of persons with disabilities, (3) analyze the ecological variables (i.e., community situations in which the motor skills will be used), and (4) manipulate environmental variables to facilitate the generalization of the use of the motor skills.[38]

Generalization is an important issue for students with severe disabilities because they typically do not learn motor skills sufficiently to enable participation in natural environments. Some persons with disabilities have difficulty generalizing newly learned motor behaviors to

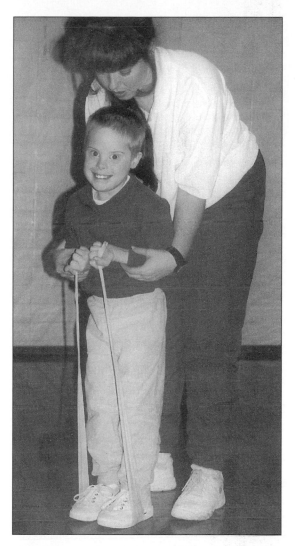

Prompting the student assures initial success.
Picture by Carol Huettig.

other settings, persons, and stimuli because of their limited motor capabilities. It is desirable to establish a comprehensive repertoire not only of motor behaviors that will permit sufficient immediate opportunities for participation in the community but also of motor skills that can be recombined to permit other opportunities to participate in an expanding number of recreational activities in the natural community. Fostering the ability to generalize across similar events in dissimilar settings is essential. A person can be aided in generalizing to new environments if he or she is taught the cues and correction procedures used in natural settings.

Cues and Correction Procedures

Cues and correction procedures are used to increase the probability that a skill learned in one setting will generalize to a second setting. The procedures range from those that provide maximum assistance to those that offer minimum guidance and those that occur exclusively in instructional environments to those that occur exclusively in natural environments.[5] There are three important considerations in the use of cues and correction procedures for generalization:

1. Know the cues and correction procedures that persons without disabilities typically use when performing a specific motor skill in the natural environment.
2. Know the specific motor response required to perform the particular skill.
3. Know how to use the environmental cues and correction procedures that shape and develop motor responses.

All three component parts of the instructional process must be fully comprehended, and detailed attention must be given to these three essential aspects of instruction.

Self-Management

Self-management of behavior should be taught to persons with disabilities.[24] The technique requires that the control over behavior be shifted from the teacher or parent to the student. Self-management has been used to teach individuals with disabilities play and social skills, as well as to lessen disruptive behavior.[15,16] The effectiveness of a variety of self-management procedures has been demonstrated in classroom settings. It has been shown that students can regulate their behavior by selecting appropriate goals; by self-instructing; and monitoring, reinforcing, and by evaluating responses.[3,12,23] Self-management procedures consist of one or more of the following strategies:

- Goal setting. Teaching students to select numerical targets to achieve leads to higher performance than not selecting goals or selecting vague goals.[14,32]
- Self-instruction. Teaching individuals to direct their own task performance is critical for independent functioning.
- Self-evaluation. Teaching individuals to observe, record, evaluate their performance according to a standard, and reward their own successes promotes ongoing growth and independence.[23]

Learning by Self-Correction

A mode of behaving that contributes to successful independent functioning in the community is learning by self-correction. Adults must learn to think about the effectiveness of their behaviors in order to identify aspects in need of change. Obviously, it is necessary that the individual have the cognitive ability needed to reflect on his or her performance and determine where or how errors occurred. The ability to learn by correction varies according to the learner's cognitive capabilities and the complexity of the task being attempted.

SCHOOLWIDE BEHAVIOR-MANAGEMENT SYSTEMS

Within the past decade, educators have come to understand that a lack of understanding of appropriate behavior, ineffective environments, and a lack of continuity between environments have directly resulted in escalating discipline difficulties in our schools. Because management by threat to punish was failing to motivate students to comply with school rules, more effective strategies were designed and tried. The earliest of these programs used schoolwide assertive discipline strategies that shifted the responsibility for appropriate behavior from the teacher to the student. As those programs

Figure 6-2 Elements of Effective Schoolwide Behavior-Management Systems

Schoolwide prevention

Unified discipline approach
Shared expectations for socially acceptable behaviors
Academic enrichment
Classroom prevention

Positive behavior-management strategies in use
Social skills instruction
Academic enrichment
School-family-community linkages

Parent partnerships
Community services

Modified from Warger, Eavy & Associates: *Prevention strategies that work,* Reston, VA, 1999, Author.

were implemented and evaluated, they were continually refined and expanded to involve more participants, including students, staff, family and the community. All of these model programs have been designed to address a specific school or district; however, the most effective share a number of elements, including the traditional principles of behavior management that have been covered in this chapter. Each uses a systematic, collaborative strategy to prevent and manage children's behavior in a positive fashion. The most common components incorporated in these programs are presented in Figure 6-2.

The schoolwide and class prevention programs require a total staff commitment to whatever behavior-management strategy is adopted. The program must include widely agreed-on attitudes, expectations, and consequences with clearly defined staff roles. The staff must define a clear, positive purpose for the program; define positively stated expectations for desirable social behaviors; select procedures for teaching the schoolwide expectations; identify a continuum of procedures to promote the expected behaviors; identify a continuum of procedures to discourage violations;

and select a method for monitoring implementation and effectiveness.[37]

The unified discipline approach uses a consistent management program throughout the building. Frequently a peer mediation program that is shared with everyone in the school is incorporated into the program. Students are taught directly how to be responsible, solve conflicts, and behave in socially acceptable ways. Selected students are taught how to mediate conflicts between their peers.

Academic enrichment at both the school and classroom levels involves remedial programs and uses both the classwide peer and cross-age peer tutoring discussed earlier in this chapter and in Chapter 5. These approaches have been shown to facilitate the development of basic literacy skills, active student engagement in instruction, and improved reading scores for students at risk for behavioral problems.[7]

Social skills instruction involves classroom survival skills such as listening, answering questions, and asking for help, as well as critical peer skills such as cooperating, showing empathy, and making friends (prevention strategies that work). In one program, the following behavior expectations were posted in every room:

> Be respectful.
> Be responsible.
> Follow directions.
> Keep hands and feet to oneself.
> Be there and be ready.[33]

Schoolwide prevention programs are most effective if parents are involved in the planning and implementation. Parents work closely with teachers to identify their child's emotional and behavioral issues. Whenever possible, contracts among the child, parent, and teacher are agreed on and implemented in both the school and the home (prevention strategies that work).

Whenever possible, particularly in large urban areas, it is critical that various human service agencies and services are offered within the schools. These services can include social service assistance, mental assessment and treatment for children and families, health and wellness services for students, and evening tutoring and recreational activities for students and parents.

VIOLATIONS OF SCHOOL CONDUCT RULES

The 1999 IDEA amendments clearly indicate to what extent students with disabilities may be disciplined. The new amendments re-emphasize the fact that, if a student's undesirable behavior is related to the child's disability, positive behavioral interventions, strategies, and supports that address that behavior should be included in the student's IEP. However, the student with a disability may be suspended or expelled from the school setting for infringement of rules to the same extent as students without disabilities if the misbehavior is not a direct result of the student's disability, with the following exceptions. If the student's behavior is likely to result in injury to the student or to others, or if the student brings a weapon to school or knowingly possesses or uses illegal drugs or sells or solicits the sale of a controlled substance while at school or a school function, removal is permissible. When a child with a disability has been disciplined by removal from school for more than ten days, the school must convene an IEP meeting and develop a functional behavioral assessment plan. After developing the plan and the assessment, the school must convene an IEP meeting to determine appropriate behavioral interventions to use with the student. When necessary, an interim alternative setting will be selected to enable the student to continue to participate in the general curriculum. In that setting, it is expected that "services will be provided to address the behavior relating to weapons and drugs, injury to the student or others, that are designed to prevent the behavior from recurring."[28]

Summary

Learning is facilitated and changes in behavior occur when a systematic process is used. New skills and behaviors can be learned and inappropriate behaviors can be diminished when appropriate procedures are followed. First, the behavior to be learned or changed must be identified. Second, intervention strategies and appropriate reinforcers must be selected. Finally, reinforcement must be consistently applied and change in behavior validated. The maintenance of a learned skill or behavior can be verified through re-evaluation in the educational or community setting. The true measure of learning is the extent to which the skill or behavior generalizes across several environments and contributes to independent functioning. Schoolwide behavior-management plans include schoolwide prevention and classroom prevention components, as well as school-family-community linkages. Students with disabilities who are expelled or suspended from school must be provided a functional assessment and intervention program that will be implemented in an alternative setting.

Review Questions

1. What techniques can be applied to maximize student achievement in motor skill development?

2. What are some positive teacher techniques that can be used to adapt instruction to the needs of the learner?

3. Describe some techniques for recording data that extend present levels of performance.

4. Describe the ways in which performance can be measured.

5. Name and describe some behavioral techniques for facilitating the development of positive behavior.

6. Indicate some principles for establishing class rules.

7. What are some techniques that can be used to manage disruptive classroom behavior?

8. List some types of reinforcers.

9. What are some of the characteristics of a teacher that can maximize the development of motor and social skills for individuals with disabilities?

10. What is generalization, and how does it apply to independent recreational sport and physical activity in the community?

11. What are some principles that may guide the physical educator to generalize the physical education activities learned in a class setting to activity outside of class?

12. What are the components of a schoolwide behavior-management plan?

13. Under what circumstances can a student with a disability be expelled or suspended from school?

14. What provisions must be made for students with disabilities who are expelled or suspended for more than ten days?

Student Activities

1. Working in small groups, identify ways the physical educator could boost Maria's self-esteem in the general physical education curriculum.

2. Make a list of class rules, other than those suggested in this chapter, that would minimize disruptive behavior in a physical education class.

3. Working in small groups, describe a scenario of a student who needs a behavioral intervention plan. Then exchange the scenarios, and assign each group the responsibility of developing an intervention plan that could be used to correct/improve the performance of the student described in the scenario.

4. Conduct an ecological assessment of the community to determine what activities should be included in physical education programs for individuals with disabilities in your community.

5. Use the Internet to find examples of schoolwide behavior-management plans. Report on their findings.

REFERENCES

1. Bellamy GT, Horner RH, Inman DP: *Habilitation of the severely and profoundly retarded,* Specialized Training Program Monograph No 2, Eugene, 1977, Center on Human Development, University of Oregon.

2. Berg WK et al.: A demonstration of generalization of performance across settings, materials, and motor responses with profound mental retardation, *Behav Modif* 19:119–143, 1995.

3. Ellis DN, Cress PJ, Spellman CR: Training students with mental retardation to self-pace while exercising, *Adapt Phys Educ Q* 10:104–124, 1993.

4. Ellis ES: The role of motivation and pedagogy on the generalization of cognitive training by the mildly handicapped, *J Learning Disabil* 19:66–70, 1986.

5. Falvey MA: *Community based curriculum: instructional strategies for students with severe handicaps,* Baltimore, MD, 1986, Paul H. Brookes.

6. Falvey M, Gage S, Eshilan L: Secondary curriculum and instruction. In Falvey M, editor: *Inclusive and heterogeneous schools: assessment, curriculum and instruction,* Baltimore, MD, 1995, Paul H. Brookes.

7. Greenwood C, Delquadri J, Carta J: *Together we can! Classwide peer tutoring to improve basic academic skills,* Longmont, CO, 1997, Sopris West.

8. Haring N, editor: *Developing effective individualized programs for severely handicapped children and youth,* Washington, DC, 1977, U.S. Office of Education, Bureau of Education for the Handicapped.

9. Helmsmetter E, Peck C, Giangreco M: Outcomes of interactions with peers with moderate or severe disabilities: a statewide survey of high school students, *J of Assoc for Persons with Severe Handicaps* 19:180–286, 1994.

10. Hoch TA et al.: Contingency contracting, *Behav Modif* 18:106–128, 1994.

11. Homme L: *How to use contingency contracting in the classroom,* Champaign, IL, 1970, Research Press.

12. Hughes CA, Korinck L, Gorman J: Self-management for students with mental retardation in public school settings: a research review, *Educ Train Ment Retard* 26:271–291, 1991.

13. Jayne D et al.: Reducing disruptive behaviors by training students to request assistance, *Behav Modif* 18:320–338, 1994.

14. Kahle AL, Kelley JL: Children's homework problems: a comparison of goal setting and parent training, *Behav Ther* 25:275–290, 1994.

15. Kohler FW et al.: Promoting positive supportive interactions between preschoolers: an analysis of group oriented contingencies, *J Early Intervention* 14:327–341, 1990.

16. Kohler FW et al.: Using group-oriented contingency to increase social interactions between children with autism and their peers, *Behav Modif* 19:10–32, 1995.

17. Leblanc LA, Matson JL: A social skills training program for preschoolers with developmental delays, *Behav Modif* 19:234–246, 1995.

18. Lewis RB, Doorlag DH: *Teaching special students in the mainstream,* Columbus, OH, 1983, Charles E. Merrill.

19. Licht BC, Kistner JA: Motivational problems of learning-disabled children: individual differences and their implications for treatment. In Torgesen JK, Wong BYL, editors: *Psychological and educational perspectives on learning disabilities,* New York, 1986, Academic Press.

20. Longwill AW, Kleinert HL: The unexpected benefits of high school peer tutoring, *Teach Exceptional Children* March/April:60–65, 1998.

21. Lonnecker C et al.: Video self monitoring and cooperative classroom behavior in children with learning and behavior problems: training and generalization effects, *Behav Disord* 20:24–34, 1994.

22. Morris RJ: *Behavior modification with exceptional children,* Glenview, IL, 1985, Scott, Foresman.

23. Nelson RJ, Smith DJ, Colvin G: The effects of a peer-mediated self-evaluation procedure on the recess behavior of students with behavior problems, *Remed Spec Educ* 16:117–126, 1995.

24. Nelson RJ et al.: A review of self-management outcome research conducted with students who exhibit behavioral disorders, *Behav Disord* 16:169–179, 1991.

25. Pierangelo RA: *A survival kit for the special education teacher,* West Nyack, NY, 1994, Center for Applied Research in Education.

26. Redl F: Managing surface behavior of children in school. In Long HJ, editor: *Conflict in the classroom,* Belmont, CA, 1965, Wadsworth.

27. Sailor W, Guess D: *Severely handicapped students: an instructional design,* Boston, 1983, Houghton Mifflin.

28. Silverstein R: *A user's guide to the 1999 IDEA regulations,* Center for the Study and Advancement of Disability Policy, Washington, DC, 1999, George Washington University School of Public Health and Health Services.

29. Spodek B, Saracho ON: *Dealing with individual differences in the early childhood classroom,* New York, 1994, Longman.

30. Staub D, Hunt P: The effects of social interaction training on high school peer tutors of school mates with severe disabilities, *Exceptional Children* 60:41–57, 1993.

31. Stokes TF, Baer DM: An implicit technology of generalization, *J Appl Behav Anal* 10:349–367, 1977.

32. Swain A, Jones G: Effects of goal-setting interventions on selected basketball skills: a single subject design, *Res Q Exerc Sport* 66:51–63, 1995.

33. Taylor-Greene S, Brown D, Nelson L, Longton J, Gassman T, Cohen J, Swartz J, Horner R, Sugai G, Hall S: Schoolwide behavioral support: starting the year off right, *J of Behavioral Education* 7:99–112, 1997.

34. U.S. Office of Special Education Programs: *Research connections in special education,* Washington, DC, 1997, Author.

35. Walker JE, Shea TM: *Behavior management: a practical approach for educators,* Columbus, OH, 1999, Charles E. Merrill.

36. Warger, Eavy & Associates: *Prevention strategies that work,* Reston, VA, 1999, Author.

37. Warger, Eavy & Associates: *Research connections in special education, a biannual review of research on topics in special education, focusing on research sponsored by the U.S. Office of Special Education Programs,* 4:3, Winter, 1999, Author.

38. Warren SF et al.: Assessment and facilitation of language generalization. In Sailor W, Wilcox B, Brown L, editors: *Methods of instruction for severely handicapped students,* Baltimore, MD, 1985, Paul H. Brookes.

39. Zhang J, Horvat M, Gast DL: Using the constant delay procedure to teach task-analyzed gross motor skills to individuals with severe intellectual disabilities, *Adapt Phys Educ Q* 11:347–358, 1994.

40. Zirpoli TJ, Melloy KL: *Behavior management,* Columbus, OH, 1995, Charles E. Merrill.

SUGGESTED READINGS

Darst PW, Zakrajsek DB, Mancini VH, editors: *Analyzing physical education and sport instruction,* Champaign, IL, 1989, Human Kinetics Books.

French RW, Henderson HL, Horvat M: *Creative approaches to managing student behavior in physical education,* Park City, UT, 1992, Family Development Resources.

Gardner R et al.: *A behavioral analysis in education,* Pacific Grove, CA, 1994, Brooks/Cole.

Metzler MW: *Instructional supervision for physical education,* Champaign, IL, 1990, Human Kinetics Books.

Walker JE, Shea TM: *Behavior management: a practical approach for educators,* Columbus, OH, 1999, Charles E. Merrill.

Wielkiewicz RM: *Behavior management in the schools: principles and procedures,* Boston, 1995, Allyn & Bacon.

RECOMMENDED WEBSITES

Please note: These websites are being recommended in the fall of 1999. Given the ever changing nature of the Internet, these sites may have moved or been replaced by the time you are reading this text.

Center for Effective Collaboration and Practice: *Addressing student problem behavior: An IEP team's introduction to functional behavioral assessment ad*

behavior intervention plans. Washington, DC, 1998, Chesapeake Institute.
http://www.air-dic.org/cecp/resources/problembehavior/main.htm

Fitzsimmons, M: *Functional behavioral assessment and behavior intervention plans,* ERIC/OSEP Digest E571. Reston, VA, 1998, Eric

Clearinghouse on Disabilities and Gifted Education.
http://ericec.org

National Information Center for Children and Youth with Disabilities: *Positive behavioral support: a*

bibliography for schools, Washington, DC, 1997, Author.
http://www.nichcy.org

PE Central. *Creating a positive learning environment.*
http://pe.central.vt.edu/climate/disciplinelis.html

RECOMMENDED VIDEOS

Classical and Operant Conditioning
56 minutes, color, purchase $129, rental $75
Films for the Humanities & Sciences
PO Box 2053,

Princeton, NJ 08543-2053
48 minutes, purchase price $150
Item # Berhome

7

Program Organization and Administration

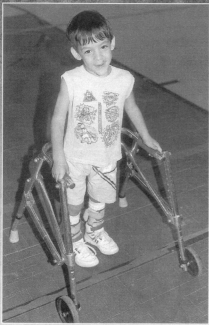

All children need to participate in physical activities.
Picture by Carol Huettig.

■ **O B J E C T I V E S**

Explain how the changing demographics of the student population in the United States affects the provision of educational services.

Describe the hierarchical structure within the U.S. educational system.

Describe the functions of the federal, state, and local education agencies in public education.

Describe the personnel involved and function of the members of a quality motor development team.

List and briefly explain school reform initiatives.

Explain how the "total quality" philosophy applies to adapted physical education.

Describe the six levels of involvement in a parent/school/community partnership and give examples of each.

Describe the factors that cause stress in families with children with disabilities.

List inexpensive equipment that can be used in the physical education program for children with and without disabilities.

CASE STUDY

APPLICATION TASK
Consider the personal and social forces that act upon Maria's parents. Discuss specific strategies that might be used by school personnel to better meet their needs.

The physical educator and/or adapted physical educator may play a critical role in serving not just Maria, but her parents, as well. Describe that role and specific intervention strategies.

CONTEMPORARY EDUCATION

Contemporary education in the new millennium is faced with real and critical issues. Tucker and Clark wrote,

> In the past, when educators have talked about accountability, they have asked, how can we produce public data on performance? But the public has been asking a different question: If students are not performing, who (among the professional educators) is responsible, and what should happen to them? The public is fed up with what it sees as excuses. It demands improved student performance at no increase in cost. Public educators do themselves no good by complaining. Whether we call it accountability to the public (as educators would have it) or better management (as business and government would have it), the challenge is to get much better results at no increase in cost.[64]

It is absolutely vital that educational leaders understand the public outcry of taxpayers and members of the business community who rely on the "products" of the public schools to maintain and encourage economic growth. Educational leaders must be grounded in reality and able to create and monitor an educational environment that meets the needs of all its students, parents, and community members.

Public outcry regarding schools' failing to meet students' needs is a reasonable response to the fact that more and more of our students who leave our high schools, with or without a diploma, have no more than an eighth-grade level of literacy.[64] In the article "Still a Nation at Risk," The Heritage Foundation asserted,

> In the midst of our flourishing economy, we are re-creating a dual school system, separate and unequal, almost half a century after government-sanctioned segregation was declared unconstitutional. We face a widening and unacceptable chasm between good schools and bad, between those youngsters who get an adequate education and those who emerge from school barely able to read and write. Poor and minority children, by and large, go to worse schools, have less expected of them, are taught by less knowledgeable teachers, and have the least power to alter bad situations.[31]

While the needs of some children are being met within the public schools, there remains an incredible disparity between educational opportunities in the public schools, particularly schools in the inner city and in poor rural areas, and public and private schools located in more affluent areas. Singham wrote,

> Educational achievement correlates more strongly (although not perfectly) with economic status than with any other single variable . . . since the black community lags badly behind the white in both income and wealth, the educational disparities are caused by the socioeconomic disparities.[59]

The relationship between effective general education and special education, given the numbers of children with special needs and circumstances in the schools, remains virtually inseparable. Fuchs suggested that there are three critical principles for contemporary education leaders:

1. There must be high expectation for all students.
2. There must be valid accountability systems in place.
3. "Best" instructional practices must be implemented.[24]

Federal and state policies to mandate educational opportunity have affected the quality of services in physical education provided to learners with and without disabilities.

THE LAW AND PUBLIC EDUCATION

Federal education policy typically reflects congressional priorities and interests. More and more often, policies regarding the education of children with and without disabilities have been mandated by the federal courts and challenged within the state and federal judicial system.

The U.S. Department of Education is challenged with the responsibility of interpreting federal legislation and helping the states implement such policies. Within the Department of Education there are several subagencies responsible for setting the agenda and providing direction for each state. The Office of Special Education and Rehabilitative Services (OSERS) has the primary responsibility for setting the agenda and providing direction regarding the delivery of educational services for students with disabilities.

The 1997 Reauthorization of the Individuals with Disabilities Education Act and litigation as it applies to physical education for children with disabilities is discussed, at length, in Chapters 2, 3, 5, and 10. Congressional priorities and interests, a reflection of the public's priorities and interests, have affected the language of the law included in the reauthorization.

It is important to remember that the law regarding the education of children with disabilities has not changed appreciably since the initial passage of P.L. 94-142, The Education of All Children Act, in 1975.

There are other U.S. laws that significantly affect the education of children with disabilities:

- P.L. 93-112, Section 504 of the Rehabilitation Act, 1973. This federal law was, in effect, the *civil rights* legislation that guaranteed that an individual with a disability could not be discriminated against solely on the basis of that disability. The basic statute said, "No otherwise qualified handicapped individual in the United States shall, solely by reason of his handicap be excluded from participation in, be denied the benefits of, or be subjected to discrimination under any program or activity conducted by an executive agency."[65] Increasingly, this law has taken on a significant meaning within the educational context; students with disabilities not covered under IDEA have rights guaranteed by Section 504. This is of particular significance to physical educators because Section 504 specifically requires that sport and athletic programs, offered in facilities that receive federal funds, must provide equal opportunities for comparable participation for individual with disabilities.[23]

- P.L. 93-247, Child Abuse and Prevention Act. This federal law created systems designed to protect children against abuse. The most significant part of the law—which remains in effect today—is that it is a *felony* to suspect child abuse and not report it. It is vital that the physical educator is aware of this law and knows the specific procedures in the school, school district, or educational cooperative for reporting suspected abuse.

- P.L. 99-457, Education for All Handicapped Children Amendments of 1986. This law mandated specific, family-based educational intervention for children with a developmental delay or disability, between birth and 3 years of age. The Individual Family Service Plan (IFSP) was a critical mandate of this law. This is considered more fully in Chapter 10.

- P.L. 101-407, The Technology Related Assistance Act of 1988. Assistive technology is defined as any item, piece of equipment, or product, whether acquired commercially, off the shelf, modified or customized, that is used to increase, maintain, or improve the functional capabilities of individuals with disabilities. It should be noted that the ability of a child to function effectively in leisure, recreation, and sport activities is significantly affected by the child's access, for example, to sport wheelchairs, prostheses designed to withstand the stresses involved in sport, and specially designed equipment such as bowling ramps, sit-skis, and beep balls that allow participation.

- P.L. 191-336, Americans with Disabilities Act of 1990 (ADA). The Americans with Disabilities Education Act (IDEA) prohibits discrimination in employment, public accommodations, transportation, state and local government services, and telecommunication relay services. The Americans with Disabilities Act broadened the scope of Section 504 and mandated nondiscrimination in the private sector as well. This legislation has a significant impact on adapted physical education because of its implications regarding access to leisure and travel services, and recreation and sport facilities such as bowling alleys, golf courses, curling centers, downhill and cross-country skiing centers, and boat and canoe rentals, for example.

Recent Litigation

Current trends in litigation have supported the inclusion of learners with disabilities in the general education program. More specific information can be found in Chapter 5.

The U.S. Courts of Appeals for the 4th Circuit may have shifted the momentum of the courts away from "inclusion" in *Hartmann v. Loudoun County,* 1997. The court listed the three situations in which a school district is not required to educate a student with a disability in the general education classroom:

1. Mainstreaming is not required if a student with disabilities will not receive educational benefits from a general classroom.
2. Mainstreaming is not required if any marginal benefit would be significantly outweighed by benefits obtained only in a separate instructional setting.
3. Mainstreaming is not required if the child is a disruptive force in the general education classroom.[30]

The *Hartmann v. Loudoun* decision may remind administrators, educators, and parents of the orig-

inal and existing intent of the law—that is, that students with disabilities are to be educated in the least restrictive environment. Yell notes that "to make a placement decision that all students will be in the general education classroom is just as illegal as placing all students with disabilities in special schools."[68]

Special education—that is, *specially designed education* for learners with disabilities—may have been seriously compromised by the thrust to educate learners with disabilities in the general education program, using the general education curriculum. Crockett and Kauffman noted,

> Inclusive but often inadequate instructional approaches for students with disabilities threaten to marginalize special education from the center of school reform, which emphasizes not downplays, the importance of curriculum, academic standards, and student and teacher accountability.[11]

The United States Supreme Court in its decision regarding *Cedar Rapids Community School District v. Garrett F.,* 1999, voted 7–2 in favor of Garrett, a young man with significant disabilities, some of which were health-related. In essence, the Cedar Rapids Community School District did not believe it to be its responsibility to provide catheterization and other procedures it deemed to be medical in order to allow Garrett to attend school all day. Administrators cited significant and burdensome costs. However, the Supreme Court decided that the school district was responsible for providing these "related services" in order to ensure that Garrett, like every other child, was guaranteed his right to an education with children who have disabilities whenever possible. The bottom line is that, if a child with a disability needs related services in order to have meaningful access to school, the school district must provide them, as long as they are not services that must be performed by a physician.[36] This decision of the Supreme Court of the United States is important for the physical educator and adapted physical educator because it virtually ensures that more and more children with significant disabilities, who are medically fragile, will receive their educational services within the public schools. The physical educator and the adapted physical educator must be prepared to meet the unique needs of these children.

The State and Local Education Agency

A state education agency is responsible for implementing federal policy at the state level and interpreting federal legislation to meet the needs of learners within the state. The state education agency or department of public instruction within each state has specific guidelines and policies that must be followed by each local education agency. Typically, the state education agency is responsible for decisions regarding the instructional standards and the strategies that will be used to evaluate whether students served within the local education agency are meeting those standards.

A local education agency or education cooperative, a cluster of small school districts without sufficient resources to provide education for their children independently, is responsible for implementing state policy and interpreting that policy to meet the needs of learners within the district or cooperative. It is the responsibility of the school to contribute to the fullest possible development of each student entrusted to its care. This is a basic tenet of our democratic structure. The notion of "home rule" is critical in the education of children within the United States. Since the founding of this country, citizens in individual communities have long held the belief that it is their responsibility and their right to educate their children.

In most school districts, the responsibility for educating the district's children is placed in the hands of the members of a school board. In most communities, individuals who serve on this school board are elected officials, responsible to the voters for their performance. The school board is responsible for implementing state policy and interpreting that policy to meet the needs of learners within the particular school district.

The primary administrator within the school district is usually called the "superintendent of schools." Recently there has been a trend toward naming this individual the "chief executive officer" of the district, in keeping with the trend in the private business sector to name the head of a company or corporation the "chief executive officer." The responsibilities of the superintendent or chief executive officer include the assurance of a quality education for all children. This individual, particularly in a large district, often has associate superintendents, who help with quality control and assist with decisions regarding student services, budget, personnel, and facilities and equipment.

Within that structure, historically, an individual has been designated as the director of special education or the operations executive. That person is responsible for implementing school board policy as it relates to students who are in need of special education services in order to be successful learners and, ultimately, productive and capable citizens.

ADAPTED PHYSICAL EDUCATION AND THE ADMINISTRATIVE HIERARCHY

Adapted physical education is usually, but not always, aligned administratively with the special education, rather than the physical education, department. See Figure 7-1 to consider the admin-

---

Figure 7-1 Administrative Hierarchy in the Local Education Agency and Adapted Physical Education

Local Education Agency School Board

Superintendent of Schools

Director of Special Instructional Services

Director of Special Education or Chief Executive Officer of Special Education

Coordinator of Instructional and Related Services

Department Chair or "Lead Teacher" in APE

Adapted Physical Educator

istrative hierarchy. This remains expedient because of the unique requirements of the law regarding specially designed physical education programs for children with disabilities and federal and state funding mandates and allocation of resources. It is critical, however, that the adapted physical educator is seen as part of the general physical education team.

In a small school district or small special education cooperative, the adapted physical educator or adapted physical education consultant may be directly responsible to the director of special education. Regardless of who has the responsibility for overseeing physical education services for students with disabilities, the adapted physical educator is accountable to the director of special education for the provision of quality adapted physical education services. See Figure 7-2 for the responsibilities of the adapted physical educator.

The responsibilities of the adapted physical educator in a large school district or large special cooperative are the same as those in a smaller district. In a large school district or large special service cooperative, one member of the adapted physical education staff may be designated as the lead teacher or department chair. This person is directly accountable for the activities of the staff and must report to his or her immediate supervisor. The responsibilities of the staff members are the same as those of educators in smaller districts. The layers of bureaucracy may simply be more complex.

One of the major responsibilities of the adapted physical educator is to communicate regularly and effectively with his or her direct supervisor. Frequently neither the director of special education nor the building principal understands the potential and importance of a quality adapted physical education program in the education of learners with disabilities. The adapted physical educator must be a vocal and tenacious advocate for the learner with a disability and for the field. The teacher should inform these persons about the requirements of the law and share legal updates and current articles describing state-of-the-art practices in adapted physical education.

The single most effective way to communicate the worth of the program is through demonstrated student results, based on assessment data, and through student and parent testimony regarding the effectiveness of the program.

Unfortunately, many administrators simply do not understand the nature or scope of the field of adapted physical education. Nor do they understand the critical role of general physical education in the lives of learners with disabilities.

Timely information that clarifies the goals and objectives of the program and describes the "before and after" status of students served in adapted physical education may help the administrator understand the value of the program. If possible, the administrator should be invited to attend a class or an activity that demonstrates quality programming to meet individual student needs and highlights the accomplishments of the students.

Figure 7-2   Responsibilities of the Adapted Physical Educator

- Assessment and comprehensive evaluation within the psychomotor domain
- Development of the individual physical education plan (IPEP)
- Implementation of the IPEP
- Representation of adapted physical education at individual education program (IEP) or multidisciplinary team meetings
- Provision of direct instructional services to children with disabilities, when appropriate
- Consultation with general physical education and general special education personnel
- Consultation with community-based leisure, recreation, and sport facilities managers regarding program and facility accessibility
- Curriculum development and/or revision
- Communication with parents
- Management of budget
- Purchase and maintenance of equipment

It is vital that the adapted physical educator secure the support of district administrators and building principals if the program is to receive its share of district and school resources and if the adapted physical educator is to be considered a vital and integral part of the instructional team within the district.[32]

The director of the adapted physical education program and its teachers are responsible for meeting federal, state, and local mandates regarding the provision of a quality physical education program for all children with disabilities who need a specially designed program in order to learn and grow. The components of a quality adapted physical education program include the following:

- Philosophy
- Definition of adapted physical education
- Goals and objectives
- Criteria for eligibility
- Referral process
- Assessment procedures
- IEP
- Continuum of services, placement, and personnel
- Accountability[16]

Philosophy

The philosophy of the program must reflect that of the school board and must be consistent with state and federal policy regarding the provision of services to children with disabilities. The Denton (Texas) Independent School District has developed a philosophy statement that indicates it will "provide all students, including those with disabilities, with an appropriate physical education program . . . and ensure that students with disabilities have access to a program that enables them to acquire the same essential elements of physical education as their nondisabled peers."[16]

Definition of Adapted Physical Education

An appropriate definition of adapted physical education may be adopted from IDEA:

1. The term means the development of
   a. Physical and motor fitness
   b. Fundamental motor skills and patterns
   c. Skills in aquatics, dance, and individual and group games and sports (including intramural and lifetime sports)
2. The term includes special physical education, adapted physical education, movement education, and motor development.

Goals and Objectives

The goals of the adapted physical education program should be consistent with those established by the state education agency for every learner who participates in physical education. This is critical, given the current emphasis on the inclusion of learners with disabilities in the general physical education program. The objectives or benchmarks of the program must also be consistent with the state mandates "essential elements" or "essential knowledge and skills." The Denton Independent School District included the following objectives in their program manual:

1. Psychomotor
   a. Develop sensory integration and perceptual motor function.
   b. Develop and maintain efficient fundamental motor skills and patterns.
   c. Develop and maintain an adequate level of physical and motor fitness.
   d. Develop the ability to relax.
   e. Develop skills in rhythmical movements.
   f. Develop skills in gymnastics and tumbling.
   g. Develop skills in individual and group games and sports.
2. Cognitive
   a. Develop knowledge and understanding for rhythmical movement.
   b. Develop knowledge and understanding required for gymnastics and tumbling skills.
   c. Develop knowledge and understanding of rules and strategies of individual and group games and sports.
   d. Develop knowledge of safety practices required for a variety of physical activities.
3. Affective
   a. Develop appropriate social interaction skills.

b. Develop respect for rules, authority figures, and others.

c. Develop a positive self-concept, body image, and confidence.

d. Develop and demonstrate cooperative and competitive skills through physical activity.

e. Accept limitations that cannot be changed and learn to adapt to the environment to make the most of strengths.[16]

Criteria for Eligibility

Specific criteria for eligibility for special education services are mandated by federal law. In addition, the individuals who may certify the eligibility statement are specified. For example, for a student to meet eligibility requirements for the category "other health impaired," a licensed physician must sign the statement.

The students who are eligible for special education services may also be eligible for adapted physical education. That is, if the learner cannot make adequate progress toward the successful acquisition of the "essential elements" of physical education in the regular physical education setting, he or she is eligible for adapted physical education services.

The specific criteria for eligibility for adapted physical education remain confusing and inconsistent from school district to school district. The local education agency must determine the eligibility criteria. Eligibility criteria may be established based on the extent of the learner's gross motor delay, age-related performance, or score on a given standardized instrument.

The failure of the state education agency and local school districts to identify specific criteria for eligibility makes it virtually impossible for itinerant adapted physical education consultants to serve learners with disabilities in the public schools. Individuals hired to conduct comprehensive adapted physical education consultants are asked to determine if the student assessed "qualifies" for adapted physical education; without specific criteria, this decision is based solely on the experience and judgment of the individual consultant.[32]

Referral Process

Referral, assessment, and placement procedures are the very foundation of the adapted physical education program and are vital to ensure that each eligible student receives the appropriate intervention, an individualized education program. The instructional model for adapted physical education follows these steps:

1. Accumulation of information about the student
2. Screening and, with parent consent, a comprehensive assessment
3. Development of a program to meet the student's individual needs as part of the IEP/multidisciplinary team
4. Determination of the instructional modifications necessary to meet the learner's educational needs
5. Consideration of placement
6. Implementation of the program
7. Monitoring of progress

See Chapter 2, Figure 2-1, for the Denton Independent School District prereferral and referral form.

Assessment Procedures

It is vital that the adapted physical education assessment be completed by a trained professional who has vast experience in assessment in the psychomotor domain (see Figure 7-3). Because it is unusual for a general physical educator to have

Figure 7-3 Assessment Skills of the Adapted Physical Educator

The carefully trained adapted physical educator has unique skills to assess and evaluate gross motor performance within the following areas:
- Reflex and equilibrium development
- Sensory stimulation and discrimination skills
- Sensorimotor integration
- Locomotor and nonlocomotor competency
- Play, game, leisure, recreation, and sport-specific motor patterns
- Physical and motor fitness

specific training in the comprehensive assessment that identifies gross motor delays and their causes, many school districts hire adapted physical education specialists specifically for assessing and recommending an appropriate instructional program. For more information regarding assessment procedures, refer to Chapter 2.

IEP

The IEP is the cornerstone of the educational process that ties together the parent and data from the comprehensive assessment and information from the child's classroom and physical education teacher, with a specific plan to intervene to meet goals and objectives specially designed for the student. For more information on the IEP process, refer to Chapter 3.

Continuum of Services, Placement, and Personnel

A continuum of instructional options is the basis of a district's ability to provide physical education services within the least restrictive environment. Information regarding the continuum of instructional and placement options is included in Chapter 5. The ways in which a multidisciplinary motor team can contribute to program development and delivery are discussed later in this chapter. Related service personnel roles are described in Chapter 3.

Accountability

The adapted physical educator must be accountable for the delivery of appropriate education services. In some states, federal and state funding of the local special education program is based on the number of documented contact hours between the professional and the student. Contact hours are usually documented with a service log. Service logs are used to record daily involvement in the adapted physical education program. Those logs are routinely checked by the adapted physical educator's supervisor. A sample of such a log is provided in Figure 7-4.

Figure 7-4   Sample Daily Service Log

Date	Service	Student(s) Served/School	Time
2/10	Direct service—teaching*	EC Class/Adams	8:00–9:00
	Direct service—teaching*	S/Ph Class/Adams	9:00–10:00
	Travel to Cabell		10:00–10:15
	Motor/fitness assessment	J. Flores/Cabell	10:15–12:00
	Lunch/travel to White		12:00–12:45
	Consultation—PE teacher	K. Black/White	12:45–1:30
	Travel to office		1:30–1:45
	Written report*	J. Flores/Cabell	1:45–3:15
	Prepare for IEP meeting		3:15–3:45
2/11	Direct service—teaching*	EC Class/Foster	8:00–8:45
	Direct service—teaching*	HI Class/Foster	9:00–9:45
	Travel to Cabell		9:50–10:00
	IEP meeting	J. Flores/Cabell	10:30–12:00
	Travel/lunch		12:00–12:45
	Direct service—teaching	S/Ph Class/Grant	1:00–1:45
	Travel to community pool		1:45–2:00
	Direct service	MD students/district	2:15–3:30
	Swimming instruction*		

* See attached lesson plans.

Figure 7-5 Daily Lesson Plan

Teacher:	Buddy Nelson
Class:	Preschool Program for Children with Disabilities
School:	Walnut Hill Elementary School
Date:	December 7, 2003
Warm-up: Rhythms:	"If You're Happy and You Know It" "What a Miracle," "Swing, Shake, Twist, Stretch," "Flick a Fly"
Equilibrium activities:	Magic Carpet Ride, Crazy Sidewalk, Freeze
Relaxation:	Pretend to be a rag doll and a sleepy kitten

In addition to a daily log that accounts for time and student contact, the adapted physical educator, like other teachers in the district, may be responsible for lesson plans that may have to be submitted to a building principal or to the lead teacher. Adapted physical education teachers with large caseloads (more than fifty students) will find it impossible to manage the paperwork, including daily lesson plans, without the use of computer technology. The teacher who can generate daily lesson plans using a basic word-processing system and a prepared template will save hours daily. The procedure greatly simplifies the process of writing plans because basic information required on every plan does not have to be written by hand. In addition, generating the plans on the computer allows the teacher to readily trace the progress of each student within each class. A sample lesson plan is included in Figure 7-5.

SERVICE DELIVERY IN ADAPTED PHYSICAL EDUCATION

The basic criteria for an adapted physical education program have been discussed previously. The strategies used to ensure that a student receives the instructional services she or he deserves varies greatly, depending on a number of variables:

- The number of students served by the school district

- The location and geographical size of the school district
- The administrative hierarchy
- The administrative commitment to adapted physical education
- Parent interest in and commitment to adapted physical education
- The number of trained/certified adapted physical educators hired to teach within the district
- The caseload

Few school districts have actually embraced the intent of P.L. 94-142 and the Individuals with Disabilities Education Act to address the physical education needs of learners with disabilities. One example, however, is the Jefferson County Parish outside New Orleans, Louisiana, led by a visionary adapted physical educator, Jennifer Wright, with significant support and assistance from the state director of physical education, Janice Fruge, boasts a staff of more than thirty-five adapted physical educators, five hired solely to do comprehensive adapted physical education assessments. These adapted physical educators are able to address the physical education needs of their students with disabilities to prepare them for quality leisure, recreation, physical fitness, and sport experiences throughout the lifetime. Unfortunately, this is the exception, not the norm. Because few school districts have actually made a commitment to adapted physical education within the curriculum, the strategy for delivering services varies dramatically. See Figure 7-6 for a continuum of service delivery strategies in adapted physical education.

Increasingly the well-trained adapted physical educator (CAPE or state-certified professional) finds himself or herself thrust into the role of consultant, even though his or her preservice training focused on the provision of instructional services to learners with disabilities.[3,32] See Figure 7-7 to consider the roles and responsibilities of the adapted physical education consultant.

It also becomes increasingly important that the general physical educator be able to take advantage of the services of the APE consultant. Few teachers have received adequate training to

---

Figure 7-6   Service Delivery Options

Required educational service by a CAPE or state-certified adapted physical educator

Assessment and IEP development by a CAPE or state-certified adapted physical educator who serves as a regular consultant to the general physical educator; instruction by general physical educator

Assessment and IEP development by a CAPE or state-certified adapted physical educator who serves as an occasional consultant to the general physical educator; instruction by general physical educator

Assessment and IEP development by a general physical educator or special educator with occasional review by a CAPE or state-certified adapted physical educator; instruction by general physical educator

---

Figure 7-7   Roles and Responsibilities of the APE Consultant[3,32]

- Complete a comprehensive adapted physical education assessment
- Make specific program recommendations
- Work with the IEP/multidisciplinary team to develop an individual physical education program
- Consider accommodations/modifications of the following instructional variables (refer to Chapter 5):
  - Curriculum
  - Assessment
  - Extent and nature of program participation
  - Instructional (personnel) support
  - Teaching style
  - Grading
  - Equipment
  - Management of behavior
- Work with the general physical educator
  - Identify needs
  - Develop a plan for addressing the needs
  - Develop a system for accountability for both the consultant and the general physical educator/special educator
  - Monitor progress

Figure 7-8   Strategies for the General Physical Educator to Maximize Use of the APE Consultant

---

- Make sure the APE consultant feels as if your gymnasium/school is his or her second home.
- Give the APE consultant a place to work (if possible, a phone) in your office or gymnasium.
- Put the APE consultant's scheduled visit on the bulletin board.
- Communicate with the APE consultant regularly via e-mail or campus mail.
- If the APE consultant deserves a "thanks," do so regularly with cards, notes, or letters with copies to the consultant's supervisor.
- Advise the APE consultant of upcoming IEP meetings (if the special education staff has advised you of the upcoming IEP meetings).
- Invite the APE consultant to PTA presentations, schoolwide play days, holiday celebrations, etc.
- Be sure to introduce the APE consultant to key building personnel.
- Be prepared for the consultant's visit with specific questions.
- When necessary, loan the APE consultant equipment needed for assessment/intervention.
- Regularly complete service logs or portfolio notes for the APE consultant.
- Videotape student performance or behavior so the consultant has all the information needed to intervene.

---

prepare them for their collaborative roles. See Figure 7-8 for specific suggestions for the general physical educator to maximize time spent with the adapted physical education consultant.

INTERACTION WITH OTHER SPECIAL EDUCATION PERSONNEL

Within the larger structure of the school district and local campus, the effective adapted physical educator works in close cooperation with other direct service providers and with related service personnel. The most crucial interactions are with the learner's general physical educator, special education teacher(s), and related service personnel.

The relationship between the adapted physical educator and the physical therapist, occupational therapist, and recreation therapist is particularly crucial, given the direct concern of each professional regarding the child's motor efficiency. Related service personnel play an important role in physical education programs for children with disabilities. In addition to providing services that will help the children benefit from the program, they may also enhance the program by

- Communicating directly with medical personnel
- Identifying students with special motor needs
- Making APE referrals of students with special motor problems
- Recommending specific exercises and activities
- Providing computer or assistive technology necessary for the student to learn auxiliary skills in physical education—for example, playing computer golf

Professionals involved in the education of a learner with a disability must share their knowledge, expertise, and technical skill not only with the learner but also with each other. The most efficient way to ensure cooperation among the adapted physical educator and related service personnel is to formalize the relationship by forming a multidisciplinary motor team.[61]

The use of a multidisciplinary team to provide services is an excellent way to ensure communication among service providers. The members of the interdisciplinary motor development team should include the adapted physical educator, the general physical educator, the physical therapist, the occupational therapist, and the recreation therapist. The speech therapist may also function as part of the motor development team. Common functions of members of motor development teams made up of adapted physical educators, physical therapists, occupational therapists, and recreation therapists can include the following:

1. To screen and evaluate students with functional and/or educational problems to determine needs for special services. See Figure 7-9, a motor team screening form developed in District 19, Oregon. This screening instrument gives direction to physical educators, special educators, and general educators who may need to refer children to the motor development team. Once the members of the motor development team receive the information, they decide which specialist should serve as the lead member of the evaluation process. That lead person initiates and organizes a subsequent full-scale gross motor evaluation, which reduces the amount of duplicated effort. For example, both the occupational therapist and the adapted physical educator routinely use the Bruininks-Oseretsky Test of Motor Proficiency. As a member of the motor development team, either the adapted physical educator or the occupational therapist may administer the test and share results with other professionals on the team.

2. To develop an IEP or ITP, as part of the total multidisciplinary team, to specifically address the child's motor needs. Members of the motor development team develop an IEP or ITP that addresses the needs of the child.

3. To implement an intervention program that facilitates learning. Once the IEP or ITP is approved by the entire IEP/multidisciplinary team, the members of the motor development team implement the intervention program. Like the assessment, the intervention program is cooperative. Each member of the team addresses the child's motor needs. Instead of limiting focus to one component of motor development, all professionals on the team share responsibility for implementing the program or designate one service provider to represent the team.

4. To manage and supervise motor programs. Each member of the motor development team assumes a specific responsibility for the management and supervision of the program. If a team leader has been designated, each member of the motor development team will communicate directly

Figure 7-9   District 19 Motor Team Screening Form

Name: _____   DOB _____

Date of referral: _____   Grade: _____   Teacher: _____

School: _____

Specialist: _____   Physician _____

Was student retained? _____ Yes _____ No

PE time: _____   Recess time: _____

Current disabling conditions: _____

_____

Does the student use adaptive equipment (braces, crutches, etc.)? _____

_____

Please check those items that have been observed.

Gross Motor

____Lacks age-appropriate strength and endurance

____Difficulty with run, jump, hop, or skip compared with others his or her age

____Stiff and awkward in his or her movements

____Clumsy, seems not to know how to move body, bumps into things, falls out of chair

____Demonstrates mixed dominance

____Reluctant to participate in playground activities

____ Play pattern is inappropriate for age group (does not play, plays by self, plays beside but not with, stereotypical) (Circle one)

____ Has postural deviations

____ Complains of pain during physical activities

____ Demonstrates unusual wear patterns on shoes and/or clothing

Fine Motor

____Poor desk posture (slumps, leans on arm, head too close to work) (Circle)

____Difficulty drawing, coloring, copying, cutting

____Poor pencil grasp and/or drops pencil frequently

____Lines drawn are light, wobbly, too faint, or too dark

____ Breaks pencil often

____ Lack of well-established dominance after six years of age

____ Student has difficulty using both hands together (stabilization of paper during cutting and paper activities)

Self-Care Skills

____Difficulty with fasteners (buttons, zippers, snaps, shoe tying, lacing) (Circle)

____Wears clothes backward or inside out; appears messy

____Has difficulty putting clothes on or taking them off

____ Difficulty with the eating process (opening packages, feeding self, spilling, using utensils) (Circle)

____ Oral-motor problems (drools, difficulty chewing, swallowing, difficulty drinking from straws) (Circle)

____ Needs assistance with toileting (wiping, flushing, replacing underwear/clothes) (Circle)

Academic (Check Those Areas Presenting Problems)

____Distractibility

____Following directions

____Hyperactivity

____Memory deficit

____Difficulty naming body parts

____ Slow work

____ Restlessness

____ Organizing work

____ Finishing tasks

____ Attention deficit

Figure 7-9 *(Continued)*

Tactile Sensation

___ Seems to withdraw from touch
___ Craves touch
___ Tends to wear coat when not needed; will not allow shirtsleeves pulled up
___ Has trouble keeping hands to self, will poke or push other children
___ Apt to touch everything he or she sees ("learns through fingers")

___ Dislikes being hugged or cuddled
___ Avoids certain textures of foods
___ Dislikes arts-and-crafts activities involving different textures (clay, finger paints)
___ Complains of numbness, tingling, and other abnormal sensations

Auditory Perception

___ Appears overly sensitive to sounds
___ Talks excessively
___ Likes to make loud noises
___ Has difficulty making self understood

___ Appears to have difficulty understanding teacher/paraprofessional/peers
___ Tends to repeat directions to self

Visual Perception

___ Difficulty discriminating colors and shapes doing puzzles
___ Letter and/or number reversals after first grade
___ Difficulty with eye-tracking (following objects with eyes, eyes and head move together)
___ Difficulty copying designs, numbers, or letters

___ Has and wears/doesn't wear glasses
___ Difficulty transcribing from blackboard or book to paper
___ Difficulty with eye-hand or eye-foot coordination (catching, striking, kicking)

Emotional

___ Does not accept changes in routine easily
___ Becomes easily frustrated
___ Acts out behaviorally; difficulty getting along with others
___ Tends to be impulsive, heedless, accident prone
___ Easier to handle in large group, small group, or individually (Circle)

___ Marked mood variations, outbursts or tantrums
___ Marked out-of-seat behavior
___ Noncompliant
___ Unstable home situation
___ Notable self-stimulatory behaviors

Additional Concerns

Assigned to: _____

Date received: _____   Evaluation date: _____

with that person regarding the student's progress.

5. To document service delivery. Careful documentation of services delivered is a vital part of the process. Each member of the team must be accountable not only to the child served but also to each other. The motor development team, if it is to function effectively, demands professional accountability. This is often done by using a service provider log. See Figure 7-10, a sample of a motor development team service provider log. If the IEP/multidisciplinary team agrees to collaboratively address one or more objectives on the learner's IEP or ITP, this type of log is vital for communication

Figure 7-10   Motor Team Service Log for Maria Garcia

To address one of Maria Garcia's annual goals in adapted physical education

To promote both cross-lateral integration and shoulder girdle strength, Maria will, while lying supine on a scooter board, pull herself, head first, the width of the gymnasium, hand-over-hand, on a rope suspended 2 feet above her head.

Date	Service provider	IEP goal	Child's performance
11/12	C. Orr, OTR	See above	Supported body weight 20×, for 1 second when rolled over a therapy ball, prone
11/14	H. Unger, PT	See above	Use medium theraband in biceps curl 10×
11/15	C. Huettig, CAPE	See above	Played "scooter board" tag, prone, with peers in the gymnasium, 10 minutes
11/19	C. Orr, OTR	See above	Supported body weight 20×, for 2 seconds when rolled over a therapy ball, prone
11/20	C. Huettig, CAPE	See above	Played "bridge over the river," pulled self head first 20 feet

among professional members of the motor development team. The log may also serve as crucial documentation of the services provided during the annual review of the child's progress.

6. To cooperatively provide or create resources that help other professionals meet the motor needs of students with disabilities. Members of the motor development team have specialized knowledge that should be shared with educators who are in daily contact with the learners. In some school districts or special service cooperatives, the members of the motor development team have created motor development handbooks for use by teachers in early childhood classrooms, self-contained special education classrooms, or the general physical education. In others, the members of the motor development team have developed curricula for use by special educators in prevocational preparation programs.

7. To conduct cooperative in-service motor development training for other school personnel, parents, and volunteers. Professionals on the motor development team share common functions yet retain professional integrity and responsibility for the motor development and motor proficiency of the child served.[61] Each has a unique contribution to students and professionals who provide direct or related instructional services to students with disabilities. The traditional emphasis by each professional who may function as a member of a motor development team is illustrated in Figure 7-11.

It is important to note that this model is not restrictive. The intent of the motor development team is to share professional competency, judgment, and expertise. For example, members of the adapted physical education staff of the Jefferson Parish, Louisiana, Project Creole are actively involved in the in-service and preservice education of physical and occupational therapists to train those professionals to teach children to use their wheelchairs in sport, leisure, and recreation. An occupational therapist on a multidisciplinary team may provide sensory integration in-service to physical educators to ensure that the students receive ongoing, appropriate intervention services.

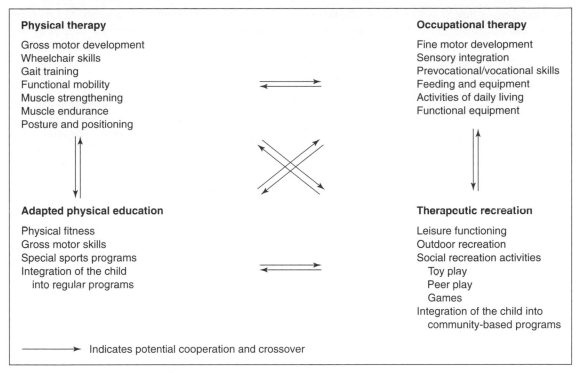

Figure 7-11   Motor Development Team
From Sugars A: *The adapted physical educator as a member of the motor development team.* TAHPERD State Convention, Lubbock, Tex, 1990.

This type of model for the delivery of services to children with motor deficits is particularly important in school districts and cooperatives unable to locate sufficient numbers of certified, trained professional staff. For example, if a school district is unable to hire and retain a licensed physical therapist as part of the staff, it may be necessary for other professionals to implement the program designed by a contracted therapist. In school districts with limited adapted physical education teachers, it is vital that the general physical educator who provides direct service be provided information necessary to deliver appropriate educational services.

Physical education services must be provided to students with disabilities enrolled in public education. Though the law makes it infinitely clear that "lack of money" or "lack of personnel" is not

an adequate reason for failure to provide the services, in reality the quality of those services will depend on the availability, training, and knowledge of the service providers. In best-case scenarios, all direct service providers will be equipped to determine and provide the needed services. However, in the vast majority of schools, personnel knowledgeable about the physical and motor development needs of students with disabilities are limited. It appears the "Puritan" dichotomy of mind and body continues to negatively affect the priority of educational services within the public schools.

Those who are designated to provide instruction related to gross motor performance frequently work under the supervision of the director of special education and have responsibility for assessing, defining goals and objectives, recommending instructional modifications, determining placement, and providing or directing direct instructional services to the student. Those individuals must be accountable to their supervisors through record keeping and the filing of daily lesson plans with their supervisors. Because of the limited number of professionals trained in the physical and motor development of individuals with disabilities, motor development teams that share responsibilities are formed. These teams, through direct teaching, consulting, and resource development, allow greater continuity of services to learners with special needs.

Once the adapted physical education program has been established, its success will depend on the quality of services provided, the ability of personnel to communicate effectively, and the flexibility of the program. Flexibility to function within a school district is crucial because of the number of changes public education is undergoing in this country. In the following section, a number of initiatives that surfaced during the 1990s are presented. The adapted physical educator is challenged to explore ways to participate and contribute to these new frontiers.

School Reform Initiatives

The public schools in this country, and the students they serve, are in the midst of a crisis that is undermining the very fabric of the nation. The schools are failing to prepare students for informed participation in our democracy, for full and vital participation in careers and vocations, for effective parenting, for active volunteerism and social service, and for creative use of leisure and recreation time.[5] This is occurring at a time in which the vast inequality between the "haves" and "have nots" continues to escalate and entitlement programs are being slashed.

As a result, the structures of schools in the United States are changing, as is the nature of the students and parents who are being served. These changes, known collectively as school reform initiatives, impact the role and the responsibility of the physical educator and the adapted physical educator. The initiatives have great potential for improving the quality of education for every student. As professionals who take their responsibility seriously, physical educators should be on the cutting edge of these changes. Darling-Hammond wrote,

> Rather than seek to make the current system of schooling reform more efficient by standardizing practice, school reform efforts must focus on building the capacity of schools and teachers to undertake tasks they have never before been called upon to accomplish. . . . Reforms that rely on the transformative power of individuals to rethink their practice and to redesign their institutions can be accomplished only by investing in individual and organizational learning, in the human capital of the educational enterprise—the knowledge, skills, and dispositions of teachers and administrators, as well as those of parents and community members.[14]

Clearly, the process of reforming public education is not a matter of adopting the most current "fix." Rather, it must be a process of developing and maintaining high-achieving learning environments. Maria Patterson, principal of Hollinger Elementary School in Tuscon, said,

> High-achieving learning environments involve students in a variety of learning activities that are challenging and aligned with learning goals, promote engaged learning, and draw on the culture, life experiences, and knowledge of all students. They allow students to discuss, argue, and analyze issues and concepts. Students explore, solve problems and construct knowledge rather than just memorizing it. Their work is authentic, engaging, and important, and it builds understanding from in-depth investigation.[10]

The Changing Nature of the Schools

According to the U.S. Department of Education, the National Center for Educational Statistics, 46.4 million children were enrolled in public elementary and secondary schools in the fall of 1997. As early as 1995, the General Accounting Office of the United States reported that $112 billion would be needed just to repair or upgrade existing schools.[27] This amount does not begin to cover estimated costs of building new schools to meet the escalating number of children who will need to receive an education, especially when inflationary prices are considered.

The students and parents served by the public schools have changed dramatically in the past century. Children served by the public schools are increasingly at risk because of poverty, homelessness, abuse and neglect, and inadequate or ineffective parenting. Providing a quality education for all of America's children becomes more complex because of the changing nature of the children/families served.

Increasingly, administrators and teachers in the public schools are faced with the reality and promise of teaching children with diverse economic, ethnic, cultural, linguistic, and religious backgrounds. At the same time, they are faced with the responsibility of teaching children who represent both genders, differences in gender preference, and children with a wide variety of abilities. These children, more often than not, come from single-parent families and are often raised by their mother or grandmother. Approximately one-quarter of the children in the schools are neglected or abused. And one of ten of the students in public schools today is served by special education.

Increased Segregation in the Schools

Of increasing concern to many educators and parents alike is the trend toward sanctioned segregation in the public schools. It is clear to any educator, parent, or student who has visited the schools in any of major urban area—New York City, Los Angeles, Chicago, Dallas, Houston, East St. Louis, and so on—that the segregation of students, based on race and poverty, is a reality.

Decades of Court-mandated desegregation efforts began with the 1954 Supreme Court Decision in *Brown v. Board of Education*. In that remarkable civil rights case, the Court decision to eliminate "tracking" of children into particular

academic and nonacademic programs based on race, was extended and had a remarkable impact on the education of children with disabilities. However, after almost fifty years of Court-mandated desegregation efforts, it is clear there is a widespread return to segregation in the public schools. Orfield et al. wrote,

> Segregation is increasing for blacks, particularly in the states that once mandated racial separation. For Latinos, an even more severe level of segregation is intensifying across the nation. . . . Racial and ethnic segregation of African American and Latino students has produced a deepening isolation from middle-class students and from successful schools.[52]

Issues surrounding the education of immigrants to the country have been contentious, at best. The appropriate education of immigrants to this country has been a cornerstone of education within this country. Certainly, without regard to other issues regarding immigrant status, the children who live in this country are the future of this country. They must receive a good education, or our society is doomed to significant failure.

Over the past decade, more than 2 million immigrant children and youth enrolled in the U.S. public schools.[45] While this number is staggering and has certainly complicated the process of teaching children and youth in our schools, McDonnell and Hill report,

> With very few exceptions, the teachers and administrators who serve immigrant children do so with care and enthusiasm. Nevertheless, the school districts serving the largest numbers of immigrant students are deeply troubled and frequently fail to provide high-quality educational services to students of all sorts, including native-born, low-and middle-income children, as well as immigrants. . . . Few schools have routine, easy access to the educational, health and social support services desperately needed by students who must cope with the effects of poverty and the traumas associated with leaving one culture and adjusting to another.[45]

Many of the problems associated with the education of children who are immigrants are absolutely inseparable from the problems associated with contemporary education, particularly problems associated with education in large, urban school districts. A large proportion of immigrants to the country settle in large, urban areas. McDonnell and Hill noted,

> Despite the unique needs of immigrant students, however, many of the service gaps they experience also adversely affect U.S. born students. These stem from the current condition of big-city school districts—their inability to cope with growing fiscal deficits, facility overcrowding, shortages of qualified teachers, and weak links to other community institutions.[45]

It is important to note, however, that many of the immigrant children in this country are part of migrant families who move from place to place within the country to find work.[15] See Figure 7-12 for information about providing educational services to children who are migrants.

Figure 7-12   Suggestions for Working with the Parents of a Migrant Child[39]

- Emphasize personal contact. Migrant parents respond better to a person contact than to vague contact with a "school."
- Establish one person as the liaison, go-between, or contact person.
- Allow the liaison to establish trust with the parent.
- Ask the liaison to share school documents with the parent and help the parent return important paperwork to school authorities.
- Take the parents to the classrooms in which their child will receive primary services to allow the parents to become familiar and at ease with the school.
- Ask questions to probe for understanding. Parents may appear to agree without really understanding.
- Help the parents develop a file or an envelope in which to share all school papers to ease transition when moving from work to work settings.

It is important to note, however, that the proportion of foreign-born citizens in this country has actually decreased since the turn of the previous century. In 1910, 16 percent of individuals in America were foreign-born; in 1990, 7.9 percent of the population were foreign-born.[38] The influx of foreign-born students into the public schools is, most certainly, not the cause of existing problems within the education system. It may simply complicate existing problems.

School reform and school restructuring initiatives are occurring in many districts in response to heightened public concern regarding the quality of public education. Figure 7-13 includes a description of the major school reform initiatives.

Site-Based Management

Site-based management is a strategy to increase school effectiveness by allowing the major players (e.g., the principal, teachers, parents, students, and community members) more control over policies and procedures that affect their school. David wrote,

> For all its guises, site-based management is basically an attempt to transform schools into

---

Figure 7-13   School Reform Initiatives

These reform initiatives include the following:
- Site-based management[12,26]
- Re-envisioning of the nature of leadership[60]
- Restructuring of curriculum and instruction[26]
- Restructuring of school calendars/time[26]
- School choice options[26]
- School vouchers[56]
- Magnet schools[40,55]
- Charter schools[8]
- Home schooling[57]
- Integration of technology into the standard curriculum[33]
- Implementation of total quality management in the schools[6]
- Community-school-parent partnerships[22,63]
- Embracing of multiculturalism[42,49,53]
- Inclusion (see Chapter 5)
- Privatization of schools[48]

communities where the appropriate people participate constructively in major decisions that affect them. . . .

Finally, the goal of transforming schools into communities where everyone has a voice goes beyond issues of school reform to the heart of our democratic society. The creation of models of collaboration and participatory decision making for students to witness and become involved in—not only in classrooms but also in their community—ultimately benefits not just the school community but our entire society.[12]

When 170 principals from 12 suburban school districts in the Indianapolis and Minneapolis/St. Paul areas were surveyed, they found that

- Meaningful change is most likely to occur at the school level rather than the school district level (87.9 percent agreement).
- For change to occur, individual schools need flexibility with regard to regulations (83.2 percent agreement).
- Broad representation of the school community in the decision-making process produces a level of commitment necessary to bring about change (86.6 percent agreement).[25]

The actual implementation of site-based management differs significantly, based on the following variables:

- Is site-based management mandated by the state education agency?
- If the state requires site-based management, has the state actually transferred legal authority from the state to the local education agency to the school itself for the education of its students?
- Is the school still accountable for state-mandated "essential knowledge or skills" or a given performance standard on state-mandated assessment tests?
- Is the intent to balance authority among the state, local education agency, and school?
- Is the intent to empower the people directly responsible for the education of the students— the parents, teachers, staff members,

community members—or to shift blame for some school failure away from district administrators?[12]

The potential beauty of site-based management is that the very people responsible for the quality of learning are held directly accountable for that learning and are given greater decision-making authority in that process. However, the site-based management process is only as good as the building leader(s).

If the school has a visionary principal, virtually any management style will be effective in bringing about significant learning outcomes for children with and without disabilities.

If the principal is empowered to mobilize school and community resources to identify student needs, develop a comprehensive plan to meet those needs, and reward school and community personnel who are critical in the process, school reform will be a reality. However, if the building leader is abusive, authoritarian, or ineffectual for other reasons, no management strategy will allow significant change to occur.

At present, in many districts, it is virtually impossible for the instructional leader on the local campus to get rid of low-performing and, sometimes, abusive teachers. That will change when the school principal is given more authority to hire and fire. In addition, the school principal is often controlled by district policies that limit the authority of teachers and parents. Site-based management gives teachers more responsibility for decision making in and through campus-based committees. It gives parents and students the opportunity to provide input and to serve on campus-based decision-making committees. In addition, it gives members of the community the opportunity to serve its constituents and to help train the students who will eventually be part of the workforce.

The physical educator and the adapted physical educator can and must be a part of the school-based team. When the physical educator is involved in decision making, the program can be recognized as an integral part of the total educational process. See Figure 7-14 for the administrative hierarchy in a site-based management school, Figure 7-15 for information regarding site-based management teams, and Figure 7-16 for the role of the physical educator/adapted physical educator in a site-based management school.

Re-envisioning the Nature of Leadership

The nature of leaders in contemporary education must evolve to meet their rapidly changing constituency, increased societal demands and expectations, and renewed public demands for accountability. Smith suggests that leaders committed to a renewal of educational reform must learn to

- Establish and honor a shared mission
- Work as change agents
- Collaborate with colleagues
- Think inclusively about all constituents
- Make clear the vital connections between educational theory and practice[60]

The notion that a leader in educational reform must value the shared mission of all of the constituents served is critical. It is vitally important that all educators, parents, volunteers, taxpayers, and students share the mission and strive for accountability. Educational leaders must seek purposeful change in and through collaboration. Most important, the leader must be able to recognize and honor the team members who are struggling with the change.

For example, some general physical educators are resistant to the inclusion of learners with disabilities in their classroom. An effective leader—whether the superintendent of schools, president of the school board, building principal, director of physical education, or adapted physical education lead teacher—honors the feelings of concern, fear, denial, anger, and despair that may characterize the

Figure 7-14   Site-Based Management Hierarchy

Site-Based School Committee

Instruction and Curriculum Sub-Committee

School Principal

Assistant Principal or Dean of Instruction

School ◄┈┈┈► Adapted Physical Educator
Special Education
Committee

Figure 7-15   Characteristics of Effective Site-Based Management Teams

- Carefully designed committee structure[12]
- Leadership which enables the council to function[12]
- Clear mission, developed by consensus
- Commitment to community-based decisions regarding the education of its students
- Specific focus on student outcomes
- Focus on the learning potential for all professionals, paraprofessionals, parents, and community members and the resources to provide access to such learning
- A commitment to long-term existence of the site-based team
- Specific designated authority and designated responsibility

Figure 7-16   Unique Contributions of the Physical Educator in a Site-Based System

The physical educator, adapted or general physical educator, is uniquely trained to do the following:

- Lead site-based committees or teams in cooperative learning activities based on the "New Games" philosophy
- Develop campus-based wellness programs for teachers, staff, students, and their parents
- Help develop a before- or after-school program to keep children in a safe and nurturing environment while parents work
- Assume leadership of a committee designed to develop positive relationships between community members and the school

emotions of the hesitant teacher. Indeed, the truly effective leader understands that each of the emotions is part of the continuum of grief that is typical when an individual faces a real or imaginary loss.[60] After the feelings are honored, only then are efforts made to redirect the emotions into positive action.

Restructuring the Curriculum and Instruction

Gaul, Underwood, and Fortune[26] reported that the restructuring of curriculum and instruction occurring in the following areas is making a difference in the quality of education:

Computer instruction programs

Programs for at-risk students

Foreign language instruction

Adoption of a common core curriculum

Dropout prevention programs

Whole-language instruction

Restructuring of school calendars and time

Most reform initiatives have included lengthening the school year and expansion of extended-year services (summer school). Additional initiatives include before- and after-school programs, such as tutorials, and block scheduling.

School Choice Options

In some states and local school districts, parents will be given the option of which school in the district their children may attend, including magnet or charter schools. Increasingly, school districts with low-performing schools have given parents the option to send their children to other schools within the given school district at no cost. Unfortunately, many parents are unable to take advantage of this option because of an inability to assume the financial responsibility for transportation of their student to the new school.

School Vouchers

School choice options may be enhanced by school vouchers. Ramirez wrote,

> The magic of the marketplace is not sufficient to guarantee the success of a school voucher program. Educators and policymakers must first address the down-to-earth issues of capacity and accountability.[56]

Individuals who support voucher systems believe that the approach will allow market forces to have a positive impact on public school education. This economic rationale for vouchers has little objective supporting data.[56] Opponents of the voucher system suggest that there is little potential for improving the system in any substantial way and, actually, temporarily takes pressure off low-performing public schools. Ramirez wrote,

> Ultimately, vouchers are about politics, not about improving education. Vouchers will be an educational life preserver for a small percentage of poor students who are stuck on sinking educational ships. However, the current voucher strategy does nothing to address the needs of those youngsters who must stay behind. The economic theory of open-market competition as a justification for vouchers and as the solution to an ailing education system is voodoo economics.[56]

Magnet Schools

U.S. Department of Education statistics indicate that the number of students enrolled in magnet schools has tripled in the past decade.[55] Magnet schools were originally developed to increase integration in school districts where school attendance zones tended to be racially segregated. A magnet school is a school or an education center that offers a special curriculum capable of attracting substantial numbers of students of different racial backgrounds.[40] To encourage desegregation, a local education agency may reassign children or faculty to reduce, eliminate, or prevent the isolation of a given minority group. The schools are able to entice parents to send their children to magnet schools because of a specially designed curriculum or focus that is not a part of the typical curriculum or program offered for students of a particular age or grade level. For example, a magnet school may be a science-technology center or a center for the performing arts. Funds for magnet schools are provided by the U.S. Department of Education's Magnet Schools Assistance Program (MSAP).[40]

Charter Schools

Many states have adopted legislation that allows individuals to enter into a contract—a charter—to provide educational services to students. The attraction is the potential to change the way schools provide services without the significant restraints tied to state-mandated public education. Many of the charter schools have been awarded funding which was made available under the 1994 Improving America's Schools Act. Charter schools are as different as the people who dream them. "Some charters look a lot like magnet schools or traditional public schools that have strong site-based decision-making and parent involvement. Others are run by homeschoolers, are 'housed' on-line, or serve teen mothers. No two are alike."[8]

Home Schooling

An increasing number of parents are choosing to educate their children at home. There are over 1 million children being home schooled in this country. Rudner[57] defines homeschooling as educating children at home rather then in public or private school. There are several strategies which parents may use to homeschool their children:

- "Unschooling" or child-led education. The parents follow the children's natural interests and curiosities.
- "School at home." Parents purchase the textbooks for all subjects and follow much the same curriculum in place in the public schools.
- Classical approach or trivium. This approach concentrates on the basics, classic languages, and higher-order thinking skills.
- Unit studies. Using unit studies, a parent can integrate content from a variety of disciplines while concentrating on a given theme.

Rudner summarized the demographics and major findings regarding home schooling.[57]

Demographics

- Home school parents have more formal education than parents in the general population; 88 percent continued their education beyond high school, compared with 50 percent for the nation as a whole.
- The median income for home school families ($52,000) is significantly higher than that of all families with children ($36,000) in the United States.
- Almost all home school students (98 percent) are in married-couple families.
- Home school students watch much less television than typical students nationwide; 65 percent of home school students watch one hour or less per day.

Achievement

- Almost 25 percent of home school students are enrolled one or more grades above their age-level peers in public and private schools.
- Student achievement test scores are exceptionally high (70th–80th percentile in every subtest).
- Students who have been home schooled their entire academic lives have higher scholastic achievement test scores than do students who have also attended other educational programs.
- There are no meaningful differences in achievement by gender, whether the student is enrolled in a full-service curriculum or a parent holds a state-issued teaching certificate.

Integrating Technology into the General Curriculum

The 1997 Reauthorization of the Individuals with Disabilities Education Act emphasizes the use of technology, not for rehabilitation purposes but as an integral component of instructional technology.[33] Davidson, McNamara, and McGillivray wrote that, with careful and thoughtful implementation of a technology program, the following can happen:

> Four years later, teachers communicate regularly by e-mail, classroom computers are

networked, teachers are infusing a myriad of technologies into their daily lessons and using web pages to share ideas, and students are becoming adept at using the Internet and multimedia presentation tools such as Powerpoint.[13]

They continued,

The changes have extended beyond hardware and software. Classroom observations document changes in teaching practices, classroom management, and relationships between teachers and students. Clearly, technology has been the impetus for teachers to try new instructional approaches.[13]

Implementing Total Quality Management in the Schools

As Glasser[29] pointed out, the recommendations in *A Nation at Risk* focused on lengthening the school day and year and implementing stiffer graduation requirements; however, no suggestions were made as to how teachers might better teach and manage student behavior. Simply increasing the time spent in an ineffective educational environment will not improve learning.

A philosophy for enabling teachers to provide more effective instruction, manage behavior better, and inspire excellence is called total quality management. This movement is based on the work of Dr. W. Edwards Deming, a philosopher, Rennaissance man, visionary, and world leader who provided the impetus for radical change in the way that Americans do business. This change agent helped transform many American businesses from top-down, authoritarian, unempowering organizations into vital, energy-based, enabling organizations in which the contributions of individuals are respected, honored, and valued. The emphasis in Dr. Deming's philosophy of life and business is that individuals must be given the opportunity to do quality work.

Dr. Deming summarized his philosophy in fourteen tenets[4], discussed in this section as they apply to the total quality management movement that is impacting education. Their potential impact on physical education for individuals with disabilities is also addressed.

1. Create constancy of purpose for improvement of product and service. The emphasis in education would be on the learning process, not on the product. A lifelong excitement and interest in learning would be encouraged. In the adapted physical education program, the emphasis would be on a deep and abiding commitment to individual wellness and to the continuous exploration of individual potential in play; games; and leisure, recreation, and sport activities so the individual can enjoy an active life.

2. Adopt the new philosophy. The primary tenet of Deming's philosophy is that every individual and every organization must seek continued improvement. The physical educator must be committed to the continuous improvement of his or her program. This requires an ongoing evaluation (plan-do-review) process. Unfortunately, all too often the adapted physical educator is so overwhelmed with the stresses of day-to-day instruction that it is almost impossible to be proactive in program review and development. In the adapted physical education program, every student would be recognized for his or her abilities and encouraged in every possible way to seek continual improvement.

3. Cease dependence on mass inspection. If education is to evolve to really meet the learning needs of the students it serves, the emphasis must shift from often invalid mass state- and district-mandated testing of students to individual consideration of student needs. In this, special education and adapted physical education have the potential to be on the cutting edge with the implementation of the IEP. If Deming's principles were truly embraced, every student (with or without disabilities) would have an IEP. Also as important, every student would

be given the opportunity to learn to evaluate his or her own progress using portfolio assessments or other nontraditional strategies.

4. End the practice of doing business on the basis of price tag alone. In the development of a quality school, the emphasis would be on the student and the student's family as customers. School district administrators would stop concentrating on the "cost" of educating learners with disabilities and admit the society can simply not afford the "costs" if learners with disabilities are not educated. To that end, the school's program and curricula would be specially designed to meet the needs of the student and the family. To ensure that this happened, the school would be involved in an effort to be a vital part of the community. The physical education program would be designed to be sensitive to the needs of the student and the student's family within the community. For example, in Wisconsin, part of the program would address activities such as show-shoeing, cross-country skiing, ice skating, and sledding—activities that would hardly be appropriate for students growing up in the South. If the students served in the school represent a largely Hispanic community, rhythms and dance activities that represent their culture would be infinitely more significant to them than the "Hokey Pokey."

5. Improve constantly and forever the system of production and service. School administrators committed to the notion of quality would empower their faculty and staff to grow and learn and experiment with teaching techniques and strategies in order to constantly improve the existing system. Faculty and staff would be encouraged to engage in the constant cycle of plan-do-review to keep program evaluation ongoing. The physical educator would be involved in the constant process of evaluating the quality of services given to students with disabilities. The teacher would conduct ongoing needs

assessments of students with disabilities and their parents. The building administrator would constantly assess student progress toward the attainment of IEP and ITP goals and objectives.

6. Institute programs of training. In-service education programs would be designed by the faculty and staff to meet their needs—not the needs of an administrator. Training programs would be made available to parents who want to address their child's motor needs in the home and on the local playground.

7. Institute leadership. In a system of true quality, only the leaders capable of managing in a system of trust, in which the faculty/staff and students were empowered to grow and change, would be allowed to remain in a position of leadership. Those with a top-down and autocratic management style would be encouraged to seek employment elsewhere. Only the physical educators able to encourage students to learn, grow, and change in an environment sensitive to their needs would be allowed to remain in a position of leadership. Those whose classes resembled a quasi-military setting would be asked to seek employment elsewhere. Students would be taught to learn to set and measure personal goals in relation to play; games; and leisure, recreation, and sport activities. In addition, students would be given the skills necessary to evaluate personal fitness levels.

8. Drive out fear. According to Bonstingl, "Fear is counterproductive. . . . Fear is destructive of the school culture and everything good that is intended to take place within it."[4] The verbally or physically abusive teacher has no place in our schools.

9. Break down barriers between staff areas. Multidisciplinary school teams, multiage groupings of students, community-parent-faculty collaborative efforts, and cooperative learning would be the focus of the quality school. The motor team would be one

excellent example of this process of breaking down barriers between individuals representing differing professions.

10. Eliminate slogans, exhortations, and targets for the workplace. Catchy phrases and slogans may be fun, but they should not replace a fundamental and basic commitment to quality within the school.

11. Eliminate numerical quotas. In the school setting, this means that the focus of learning would be on learning as a process, not on arbitrarily determined state standards. Teachers would not teach for "test success" but would help students learn how to learn. The physical educator would eliminate mass physical fitness tests, for example, in favor of individual self-testing of health-related fitness. Children would be given the opportunity to receive instruction, as needed, without the formal "eligibility" requirements for special education.

12. Remove barriers to pride and joy of workmanship. The instructional leader would develop an environment where his or her teachers would feel pride in their work. The teachers would create a learning environment in which the students could take pride in their performance, learning, and accomplishments. The joy in learning would return to the schools. Schools would cease being empty shells in which children were treated disrespectfully and would become joyous places in which children were revered and held in a place of honor.

13. Institute a vigorous program of education and retraining. Everyone in the school would be excited about learning and would be given every opportunity to seek new learning and new joy in the process. Teacher- and parent-driven in-services would be planned. Teachers would be reinforced for participation in graduate-level education and/or participation in other specific training.

14. Take action to accomplish the transformation. The responsibility for change lies with the professional educator who cares about students. Individuals who favor protecting the status quo should leave. Dr. Deming would shake his head in disgust at educators who claim that such a transformation could not occur. He would simply tell them to "make it happen . . . now."

School/Family/Community Partnerships

A vital part of any school reform movement involves the child, the child's family, and the community and school as partners in educating and embracing the child. A wonderful African saying that should be the watchword for education in the twenty-first century is "It takes a whole village to raise a child." Epstein wrote,

> The way schools care about children is reflected in the way schools care about the children's families. If educators view children simply as students, they are likely to see the family as separate from the school. That is, the family is expected to do its job and leave the education of children to the schools. If educators view students as children, they are likely to see both the family and the community as partners with the school in children's education and development. Partners recognize their shared interests in and responsibilities for children, and they work together to create better programs and opportunities for students.[22]

Epstein[22] has developed a model for the development of school/family/community partnerships to best serve the children within any given community. She has identified the following six types of involvement of families and community members within the schools:

- *Type 1:* Parenting. Help all families establish home environments to support children as students.
- *Type 2:* Communicating. Design effective forms of school-to-home communications about school programs and children's progress.
- *Type 3:* Volunteering. Recruit and organize parent help and support.

- *Type 4:* Learning at home. Provide information and ideas to families about how to help students at home with homework and other curriculum-related activities, decisions, and planning.
- *Type 5:* Decision making. Include parents in school decisions, developing parent leaders and representatives.
- *Type 6:* Collaborating with the community. Identify and integrate resources and services from the community to strengthen school programs, family practices, and student learning and development.

The following are suggestions for the regular physical educator and adapted physical educator for increasing involvement in each of the six types of involvement:

Type 1: Parenting

- Provide parents and members of the learner's extended family with information that will help them develop reasonable expectations regarding the motor development of a student with a developmental delay or disability.
- Provide parents and members of the learner's extended family with information regarding developmentally appropriate play (e.g., the child needs to learn to engage in cooperative play before he or she can engage in competitive experiences with success).
- Model appropriate play and motor intervention strategies for parents (e.g., toss the ball in a horizontal path when a student is learning to catch, so that the child is not overwhelmed by trying to track an object moving through horizontal and vertical planes).
- Share information with parents about strategies for making inexpensive equipment for the student to play with in the home (e.g., an old mattress or an old tire covered with a secured piece of carpeting makes a wonderful trampoline).
- Share information about community resources and opportunities for students with disabilities to participate in play; games; and leisure, recreation, and sport activities.

- Provide family support and information regarding securing health services for the student.
- Serve as an advocate for the parent and family.

Type 2: Communicating

- Use your computer to generate a physical education and/or adapted physical education newsletter or ask for a column or space in the school newspaper.
- Develop an adapted physical education website for the school and/or district to communicate with parents and community members.
- Send home brief notes to communicate with the student's family, such as the computer-generated certificate shown in Figure 7-17.
- Videotape a class activity and make the video available for parent checkout.
- Call a parent to discuss student progress. This is particularly effective if the physical educator or adapted physical educator calls to praise a child. Much too often, teachers communicate with parents only when there is a problem.
- Be an active participant in regularly scheduled parent-teacher conferences. Communicate with parents a willingness to meet at other times as well.
- Write positive comments on student report cards.

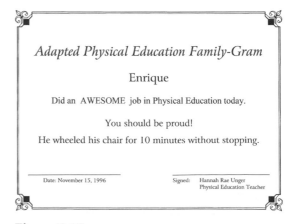

Figure 7-17

A customized certificate is an excellent way to communicate with a student's family.

Type 3: Volunteering

- Encourage parents to serve as the following:
  - An assistant in classes
  - A director or an assistant in before- and after-school recreation, intramural, or sports programs
  - An assistant coach
  - A director or assistant in school play day
  - The editor or publisher of the newsletter
  - A parent-to-parent trainer
  - A raffle organizer to raise money for equipment
  - An assistant playground supervisor
  - A clerical assistant to generate certificates, progress charts, and so on

Type 4: Learning at Home

- Provide information to parents regarding curriculum and activities required at each grade level.
- Provide information to parents with strategies for helping the learner develop the motor skills necessary to participate in play; games; and leisure, recreation, and sport activities; include information regarding the development and maintenance of physical fitness.
- Demonstrate age-appropriate activities that parents can use with groups of children—at a park or in an open area within their apartment or project complex, for example.
- Provide a calendar for parents that helps them follow unit themes and special activities.
- When appropriate, recommend websites or listserves in which parents might be interested.
- Recommend television shows or videotapes that reflect the philosophy of your program. For example, suggest that the family share the following:
  - Television coverage of the Olympics
  - Television coverage of the Paralympics
  - Television coverage of the Special Olympics
  - A videotape of *The Jim Thorpe Story*
  - A videotape of *The Babe Didrickson Story*

Type 5: Decision Making

- Invite parent participation as a member of the site-based school committee.
- Invite parent participation in a subcommittee of the Parent-Teacher Association/Organization (PTA/PTO) that addresses the physical education/adapted physical education program.
- In districts where there is a special education advisory committee, ensure that a parent with a commitment to physical education/adapted physical education is on that committee.
- Encourage parents to serve as advocates for adapted physical education programs and services.

Type 6: Collaborating with the Community

- As the physical educator or adapted physical educator, ask to serve on boards or committees of community recreation and/or sports organizations.
- Develop a collaborative physical education or recreation program to meet the needs of learners within the community, using shared facilities, shared equipment, and, if possible, shared personnel.
- Recruit community personnel to help develop and build playgrounds for the schools. Particularly in large, urban districts, playgrounds are often nonexistent or antiquated.
- Encourage older learners to provide service within the community as coaches and recreation leaders.
- In a very diverse community, invite the parents and other relatives of children into the school to teach games, sports, and dances of their country of origin. McGehee and Reekie wrote, "In school districts with diverse ethnicities and nations of origin, it is exciting to encourage children's relatives to visit the class and teach an activity of their homeland. This helps families feel involved in their children's education, and also makes the child proud that an activity of his or her heritage is important enough to be included in the school."[46]

Increasingly, leading educators have suggested that the public school appears to be the most viable place to serve as a "hub" for the community it serves. In the 1800s and early 1900s in this country, the school served as the cultural, civic, and social hub of the community.

At a fall 1999 conference sponsored by the Office for Special Education Programs,[9] Dr. Dean Corrigan, Texas A&M University, in his keynote speech, advocated for a co-location of services in the schools, so that *all* the services a family needs to access are easily and readily accessible.[9] That is, he suggested the school should once again serve as a hub in the respective community. He recommended that the school be the one point of contact for families who need education, social services, human services, and health services.

The U.S. Department of Education and the U.S. Department of Health and Human Services joined efforts and developed a document titled "Together We Can: A Guide for Crafting a Profamily System of Education and Human Services." It said, in part,

> A pro-family system will eventually benefit the entire community and the many neighborhoods where children and families live. Creating such a system will require the united efforts of many partners—key leaders from different sectors who come together to find solutions to shared problems . . . a collaborative is a group of community leaders who have agreed to be partners in addressing shared problems.[63]

Embracing Multiculturalism

It is vital that the public schools, as reflections of the community, embrace multiculturalism and help teach children and their families learn to value others who are different. According to Manning,

> Schools have long based expectations, perceptions of motivations and success, learning methodologies, and selection of curricular materials on middle-class, Anglo-American perceptions. This decision may have resulted from the belief that culturally diverse learners

should acculturate toward middle-class Anglo-American perspectives, the belief that the schools should cater to the majority social class and culture, or the belief that culturally diverse learners did not deserve the advantages of the dominant culture. Regardless of the reason, the decision resulted in inequitable treatment of culturally different learners; and in the process, schools may have perpetuated racism, prejudice, and discrimination.[41]

The demographics within the United States and our schools have changed remarkably in the past decade. As Markowitz points out, "For the first time in U.S. history, the mainstream is about to become the minority, and the group that has held the power, made the laws, set the policies, controlled the money and dictated to everyone else is on the verge of being outnumbered."[42] Educators must seize every opportunity to embrace each child they serve—without regard to race, culture, socioeconomic status, religion (or lack thereof), gender, gender preference, and ability or disability. We have the responsibility to ensure that all public schools have equitable resources; that all cultures are represented in the curriculum; and that students representing all socioeconomic levels, as well as each gender and gender preference, are fairly treated.

To ensure educational equity, it has become increasingly obvious that the schools must be prepared to honor students representing diverse cultures. If students are to be empowered as learners and as people, their families and their cultures must be respected. According to Markowitz,

> Multiculturalists argue that the price of cutting off a significant cultural legacy is internalized shame and diminished self-esteem. This is even more pronounced for those who come from cultures already in a one-down economic position, like refugees or people from developing nations, or those whose cultures include a history of colonization or persecution, like descendants of African slaves.[42]

This respect for the student's culture is particularly important because minority students are much more likely to be in high-poverty schools and face discrimination and stereotyping. Also, a much greater concentration of health, social, and neighborhood problems is found in schools located in high-poverty areas.[53]

Creating a school environment in which each child and the child's "culture," in its broadest sense, are represented requires a serious commitment to understanding. It requires educators to seriously examine their values and their own cultural identity and to be willing to try new approaches in their classrooms in order to make their coursework relevant.[49] McGehee and Reekie wrote,

> In response to the need to recognize and appreciate diversity, K–12 schools should strive to internationalize their curricula. As international cultural and economic interactions continue to increase, an appreciation of other cultures, political and social systems, religions, and languages can help promote international and peace and improve the business and social relationships between people of different nations [and within our nation].[46]

The teacher must be able to engage in an honest and open dialogue with his or her learners, their parents, members of their extended families, and individuals within the communities in which the students live. Many dedicated educators choose to be involved in an experience known as a "cultural plunge," in which they choose to live in or visit a setting that represents a culture very different from their own.[49] For example, a Hispanic teacher may choose to attend a church service attended primarily by African Americans. An Anglo-American educator may opt to live with a family in a South American country in order to learn the language and culture. Or an African American teacher may attend a Cinco de Mayo celebration. While this is only one step, it is the beginning of a process in which the teacher begins to develop empathy for and appreciation of the unique heritages and beliefs of his or her students.

According to Markowitz, "Ultimately, multiculturalism is a movement to make society a place in which people from all cultures have equal respect and equal voice and equal influence in shaping larger community values."[42] The physical educator or adapted physical educator can have an impact on the process of enabling all students to learn within the public schools and still retain dignity.

The notion of culture is diverse and is not limited to one facet of the life of human beings. When educators consider culture, it must be understood within a broad perspective because we all carry several cultures at once—our inherited cultures, the generation in which we were born, our gender, and our socioeconomic class.[42] Each of these cultural facets impacts our perceptions and actions and may significantly affect our choices and options. It is helpful to understand the impact culture has on behavior, because the teacher who is knowledgeable about and sensitive to cultural differences is capable of modifying instruction to fit the characteristics of the individual and group.[34]

Privatization of the Schools

In direct response to the concerns of parents and taxpayers regarding the effectiveness of the public school system, private, for-profit organizations are seeking to attract business and are offering, for a significant profit, to take on the responsibility of educating our children. The National Education Association has, for example, criticized one of the major for-profit educational corporations:

> Of course there is no silver bullet, no outsider who can solve the problems of schools and children. In the end, school improvement is accomplished through the hard work of school staff, with administrative and parent support. Everything the for-profit companies say they'll do has already been done in publicly run public schools. Every curriculum and program they use is available for every school in America to implement on its own—without adding corporate managers and without subtracting corporate profit.[48]

The investment community uses the acronym EMO, educational management organizations, to describe for-profit, private companies that manage schools. In fact, EMOs are a $300 billion–a–year industry in the United States.

Like any other business, the for-profit school is self-promoting. Unlike the public schools, which must remain accountable for their performance in a public way, the for-profit school can emphasize success and minimize, or ignore, failure. There are two major educational management organizations. The TesseracT Group is focusing its efforts on charter schools after a history, which was less than successful, as the Educational Alternatives, Inc. The Edison Project, the leading for-profit public school management corporation has a history of limited success but is proactive in seeking new business. Furtwenger wrote,

> It is too early to determine the success or failure of the privatization venture in public education. What do available evaluation reports tell about the success or failure of EMOs? An obvious finding is that EMOs, particularly the most viable Companies, do not seek an outside evaluation of their programs.[25]

Communication with Parents

Increasingly, the parent(s) and members of the learner's extended family are being encouraged to be active participants in the learner's education and are increasingly part of the education system at all levels—as members of the state board of education, as members of a local school board, as members of site-based management committees, as active participants in the day-to-day operation of the school, and as tutors, for example.[28] See Figure 7-18 for strategies the physical educator can use to help the school become part of the "extended family."

In many situations, the parents may be effective participants in the total assessment/evaluation process, providing evaluators with information about the learner's behavior in the home and on the neighborhood playground.[58] The reauthorization of IDEA makes it clear that the parents play a vital role in the assessment/evaluation process and are a critical part of the IEP/multidisciplinary team.

One of the most challenging aspects of the role of the adapted physical educator is effective

Figure 7-18   The School as Part of the Extended Family

Strategies for enhancing the family-school partnership:
- Find out what the parents really want from the school. What "outcomes" do they expect after their children receive educational services?
- Encourage many different types of parental involvement in the school, based on the comfort level of the parents.[22]
- Make communications with parents positive. Unfortunately, all too often, parents are only contacted by the school when their child is in trouble.
- Create parent-involvement opportunities that are sensitive to parents' work schedule, time constraints, needs for child care, etc.[22]
- Find and develop a small room designated for the parents, which has child development information, computer/Internet access, access to a printer, etc.

communication with the parents. This vital communication, which can and should lead to an effective partnership between the teacher and the parent and between the school and the home, is often challenging because of cultural, ethnic, and socioeconomic differences. According to Olson, "As the two major forces entrusted with educating and socializing children in society, parents and teachers should be natural allies. But far too often, they find themselves on opposite sides of an exceedingly high fence."[51]

To communicate effectively with the parents and families of learners with disabilities, the physical educator or adapted physical educator must be aware of the comprehensive effects of a child's disability on the total ecology of the family. There are three major theories regarding the impact of a child's disability on the child's parents, siblings, and extended family: chronic sorrow syndrome, dominant stage theory, and nonsequential stage theory.

Chronic sorrow syndrome describes the reactions of parents or siblings when faced with the constant reminder of "loss" associated with disability.

The parent or sibling with chronic sorrow syndrome may cope relatively well with the day-to-day requirements of providing support for the child with a disability, but the individual's underlying emotions include sadness, fear, anger, and guilt.[50]

The dominant stage theory suggests that the parent or sibling of a child with a disability experiences emotions and reactions that are identical to those that are experienced by an individual facing the death of a loved one or facing a terminal illness. These stages of grief—denial, bargaining, anger, depression, and acceptance—were first described in the teachings of Dr. Elisabeth Kübler-Ross.[51] It is important to note that these emotional stages also parallel those experienced by a child or an adult with an adventitious disability (a condition acquired after a history of "normal" development).

The nonsequential stage theory suggests that the parents, siblings, or extended family members may experience some or all of the stages of grief described by Kübler-Ross, but not necessarily in predictable stages. The nonsequential stage theory suggests that a response to the child's disability may be the result of facing particular milestones.[6] The initial diagnosis of disability may cause denial, anger, and depression. These emotions may resurface when the parents are faced with the fact that their child needs to receive special education services; again as the child reaches adolescence and the parents must deal with the realities of sexuality; and/or as the parents deal with their own aging and the inevitability of providing alternate care for their offspring.

Parent support groups have acknowledged the serious need for parents of learners with disabilities to deal, proactively, with their grief in order to continue to function not only as parents but also as human beings. Blanchard[2] suggests that a parent needs to actively release the "dream" that accompanies the loss of the child imagined during pregnancy—a child with the physical skills of Michael Jordan, the cognitive/language skills of Barbara Jordan, the artistic ability of Picasso, the musical ability of Joan Baez, the looks of Robert Redford or Whitney Houston, and the altruism of Mother Teresa. A grieving ritual allows parents to identify all the characteristics they hoped their child would have and gives them permission to release that. Blanchard describes that extremely painful process:

> I began by leafing through magazines to find pictures of my "dream child"—the child I didn't get. I cut out any picture that moved me. I especially looked for pictures of the ideal birth where everyone is smiling and the wet, shining baby is laid on the mother's chest. I found pictures of babies sitting up and crawling, of young girls running and playing. I cut out a paper doll from a large piece of blank paper and was amazed that holding this piece of paper to my chest caused me to cry. I glued my dream child pictures all over the paper doll. I decorated her with glitter, paint and colorful markers. I cut out a back for her, and stuffed her with more of my "dreams". . . . I had decided to burn this dream child to transform her energy and let her float away. So after discussing my dreams with my friends, I put the paper doll in the fireplace, lit a match and let her go.[2]

Understanding the response to a child with a disability is further complicated by the fact that there appear to be sociocultural differences in parent reactions. Mary[43] studied the reactions of African American, Hispanic, and white mothers toward their child with a disability and found that Hispanic mothers reported an attitude of self-sacrifice more often than the other mothers. In addition, Hispanic mothers noted greater spousal denial of the disability than other mothers.

Willoughby and Glidden[67] studied forty-eight married, middle-class, predominantly Anglo-European parents and found that, when fathers participated actively in the care of the child with a disability, both parents expressed greater satisfaction in the marriage. Sharing time and stress demands appeared to lessen the stresses associated with coping in both spouses.

The adapted physical educator hoping to work successfully in the home must not only recognize the emotional responses of family members to a child with a disability but also be sensitive to the forces that affect the family. The family is often over-whelmed by the need to interact with the huge, often impersonal medical bureaucracy. The sense of despair is often heightened by the sense of feeling helpless and unempowered when facing the barrage of medical personnel, hostile medical insurance representatives, and incomprehensible medical bills. New HMO and other insurance reforms have heightened the sense of helplessness experienced by the family of a learner with a disability. The family may experience a sense of isolation as friends and others in the community respond in fear. The family may be frustrated by huge time constraints involved in the care of a child with a disability. According to Bratlinger, "Parenting is always demanding, but having a child with a handicapping condition usually adds to the complexity of the task."[6] Parents of children with disabilities are more likely than others to experience significant stress, and Blacher[1] reported that these parents are more likely to develop emotional and personality disorders. Dyson[19] found that such stress is persistent even in the absence of other socioeconomic disadvantages.

Weiss[66] and McConachie[44] reported that parents of children with significant developmental delays experience a great deal of stress, including

- The experience of dealing with professional and other support services
- Family strains
- Stigmatization
- The child's aberrant behavior
- Sleepless nights
- Concerns regarding their own future mental/emotional health

Fears regarding the child's future, including financial planning, residential versus community living, and vocational and social integration. It is interesting to note that, in a study of fifty-seven adult caregivers and their adult children with mental retardation, over half had not made any long-term plans for their children.[35]

These stressors are not uncommon to the parents of any child with a disability. The nature of the disability and its severity have a direct bearing on the extent and type of stress. In addition, the nature of the support resources offered to parents and siblings has a direct impact on the stress and coping ability of the family members.[44]

CONTEMPORARY ADAPTED PHYSICAL EDUCATION USING COMPUTER TECHNOLOGY

Computer technology has literally created a "worldwide classroom" for learners, their teachers, their parents, and members of communities all over the world to share.[20,47] In addition, it has virtually changed the way that educators manage their day-to-day responsibilities as well. There are a number of ways physical educators and adapted physical educators can use the computer and the Internet to enhance the performance of learners with and without disabilities in their classes:

- Promote physical education classes and activities via a Web page.[47]
  - Post student achievements, accomplishments, and awards on the Web.
- Conduct sporting events with learners from all over the world.[20]
  - Have a track and field competition, with specified metric events, between physical education classes in Rosholt, Wisconsin, USA, and Perth, Australia.
  - Compare sports and games with a group of students in a school in another country.
- Promote professional development through e-mail, listservs, and discussion groups with other physical education professionals.[20,47]
  - NASPE (National Association for Sport and Physical Education) e-mail discussion group
  - PE-Talk at sporttime.com/pe-talk/subscribe
  - Adapt-Talk at sportime.com/adapt-talk/subscribe
- Promote personal and professional development through participation in listservs and discussion groups designed to serve parents of learners with disabilities.
- Gain access to information from physical education, adapted physical education, and disability sport websites.

- PE Central at http://pe.central/vt.edu[54]
- TWU Project INSPIRE at http://venus.twu.edu/~f_huettig[62]
- Dr. Gail Dummer's Disability Sport site[18] at http://ed-web3.educ.msu.edu/kin866/contents.htm
- Assign students to gain information via the Web rather than using more traditional learning strategies. For example, they can gain information regarding the history of sport (Negro Baseball Leagues—http://www.blackbaseball.com), rules, equipment, sport organizations, techniques, etc.
- Use computer technology to generate and maintain IEPs, IFSPs, or ITPs. Computer software has been designed to help physical educators generate individual education programs. Most school districts have IEP templates available so the physical educator or adapted physical educator can simply "fill in the blanks." If the school district does not have such a template, the IEP form can be easily created by scanning an existing paper form.
- Use computer technology to facilitate the assessing and monitoring of student performance. The process of completing an assessment report in adapted physical education has been simplified by Dan Cariaga, an accomplished adapted physical educator with the San Luis Obispo County, CA, Student Services Division. He has developed a computer-based system that converts raw data on a given assessment tool, provided by the physical educator or adapted physical educator, into standardized scores and assessment reports appropriate for presentation to the IEP/multidisciplinary committee.[7]
- Organize, monitor, and analyze fitness test data using computer technology. Specific software, such as Fit-N-Dex, is designed to organize, monitor, and analyze fitness test results quickly and efficiently. It allows the physical educator to enter the data and get results on individual student performance, class performance, or grade performance and compare the data year

to year, and so on. It allows the physical educator to create reports for students, parents, and administrators that are professional and easy to read. This is available from Cramer Software Group (http://www.cramersportsmed.com). It is, of course, possible to use a database to develop an individually designed system.
- Participate in programs such as the President's Physical Fitness Challenge by accessing its home page at preschal@indiana.edu
- Use interactive computer programs available on the World Wide Web to study subjects such as human anatomy (www.innerbody.com).
- Use computer software to enhance instruction. Dr. Peter Ellery, University of South Florida, has developed an interactive video titled "Physical Education Sign Language Program" that allows physical educators to learn the sign language skills necessary to communicate with learners who are deaf or who use sign language for other reasons.[21]
- Use computer software to facilitate inclusion. Dr. Peter Downs and Active Australia[17] have created an interactive software program called "Willing and Able: Count Me In," designed to foster inclusion in physical education and sport.
- Embrace innovative physical education programs such as SPARK and/or share that information with general classroom educators and/or special educators, available at www.foundation.sdsu.edu/projects/spark/index.html
- Use inexpensive software and free Web-based materials to get graphics, fonts, templates, and so on to create newsletters, banners, posters, certificates, and thank-you notes that can be used to motivate, generate interest, and inform students, parents, and members of the greater school community regarding the physical education and adapted physical education program.
- Use CD-ROM computer technology to maintain and preserve portfolio assessment data. See Chapter 10 for more information about the portfolio assessment process.

- Encourage learners and their parents to use interactive CD-ROM computer technology to participate in games that encourage the learning of rules, strategy, and technique. These computer games—golf, tennis, football, baseball, and so on—allow even a child with limited movement potential to play with a peer. Programs such as Maniac Sports allow a student who is confined to bed the opportunity to experience hang gliding, mountain climbing, and downhill skiing vicariously. For example, a learner in the last stages of Duchenne muscular dystrophy may have only limited control of one hand. With that hand, the learner can manipulate the joystick. This type of software also exists for high school students studying the human body and the way it works.

EQUIPMENT

The physical educator or adapted physical educator is responsible for a great deal within the school community. One of the responsibilities is securing and maintaining equipment for learners with disabilities to use in a variety of instructional arrangements in the schools.

Equipment for Elementary School Physical Education for Children with Disabilities

As mentioned earlier, if children with disabilities are able to receive physical education instruction in the regular physical education program, they generally share equipment with the other children. The physical education teacher who serves children with disabilities in the regular elementary physical education program may wish to supplement basic equipment needed for quality elementary physical education instruction with additional equipment. The following is a list of the basic equipment needed for such a program. This list also represents the basic requirements for an adapted physical education program in a more restricted environment.

1. Locomotor skills
   a. Wide balance beams or balance boards (6, 8, 10, and 12 inches wide)
   b. Oversize scooter boards
   c. Shoe polish/washable paint for marking floors
   d. Plastic hoops
   e. Jump ropes
2. Manipulative skills
   a. Balloons
   b. Punch balls and beach balls
   c. Balls (assorted sizes, types, textures)
   d. Velcro paddles and Velcro balls for catching
   e. Wands with ribbons attached
   f. Small balls with ribbons attached
   g. Beanbags (including large and heavy beanbags)
3. Low-organized group games
   a. Huge group parachutes
   b. Cage balls
   c. Tug of war rope
4. Lead-up games for individual and team sports
   a. Oversize tennis and badminton racquets
   b. Oversize, soft and short, bats
   c. Nerf-type soccer balls, footballs, and volleyballs
   d. Junior-size balls
   e. Height-adjustable equipment
5. Tumbling and developmental gymnastics
   a. Floor mats
   b. Incline mats
   c. Carpeted barrels
   d. Inner tubes (covered with 1- to 2-inch mats for jumping)
6. Rhythms and dance
   a. Portable "boombox"
   b. Assorted tapes and CDs
   c. Music-making equipment (bells, drums, maracas, etc.)

With some ingenuity, the teacher can provide an excellent adapted physical education program for students at the elementary school level with minimum equipment. Play equipment can be made inexpensively. Following are suggestions for inexpensive equipment for use in the physical education program:

- Rope for skipping, making shapes, jumping over, and climbing under
- Cardboard boxes to climb in and through, to catch with, and to use as targets (particularly empty refrigerator, television, and washer/dryer boxes)
- Tape to make shapes on the floor for moving on, around, and in
- Chalk for making "own body" shapes and puzzles
- Half-gallon or gallon plastic jugs for catching, throwing, knocking over, and so on
- Scrap lumber for balance beams
- Yarn for yarn balls
- Carpet squares to skate on, slide on, sit on, and use as targets
- Cardboard barrels to roll in and throw objects into
- Old garden hoses to make hula hoops
- Old ladders to walk on and through
- Traffic cones for obstacle courses
- Balloons (for children at least four years old)
- Wire clothes hangers and old nylons (nylons suspended around the clothes hangers make inexpensive racquets)
- Butcher paper for body tracings and targets
- Paper bags filled with sand for "barbells"
- Dowel rods cut into sections for lumni sticks

Equipment for Middle and Secondary School Physical Education for Children with Disabilities

Equipment for a fitness program, as well as leisure, recreation, and sports, at the middle and secondary school levels should allow the participation of all students, with different levels of ability.

Fitness Equipment

1. Mirrors
2. Wide, padded benches
3. Multistation, heavy resistance machines on which students can exercise a number of different areas of the body; Cybex, Nautilus; or other isokinetic machines should be used

4. Stationary bicycle
5. Stationary rowing machine
6. Stationary cross-country skiing simulator
7. Stair stepper
8. Treadmill

Equipment for Leisure, Recreation, and Sports

1. Archery
   a. Lightweight bows
   b. Large, fluorescent target faces
   c. Beepers to attach to target
2. Badminton
   a. Oversize racquets
   b. Oversize shuttlecocks
3. Basketball
   a. Adjustable-height basketball standards
   b. Basketball standards with return nets
   c. Junior-size basketballs
4. Bowling
   a. Bowling ball with retractable handle
   b. Portable bowling ramp
   c. Wooden shuffleboard sticks for pushing the ball down the floor
   d. Lightweight balls with an assortment of appropriate holes (4- to 6-inch balls)
   e. Beepers for target at end of lane
   f. Bumpers
5. Goal ball
   a. Goal ball with beeper
   b. Goal ball nets
6. Golf
   a. Clubs with enlarged heads
   b. Fluorescent golf balls
   c. Fluorescent golf-size wiffle balls
7. Rhythms and dance
   a. "Boombox" with excellent bass adjustment
   b. Percussion instruments
8. Snow skiing
   a. Sit-skis
   b. Pulk skis
9. Softball
   a. Adjustable T-ball stands
   b. Beeper softballs
   c. Large, soft softballs

d. Oversize bats

e. Fluorescent bases

10. Tennis

a. Oversize racquets

b Fluorescent balls

11. Track and field

a. Beep cones

b. Guide ropes with movable plastic holder

c. Lighter shot-puts

12. Volleyball

a. Beach balls, brightly colored

b. Adjustable net standards

13. Skiing

a. Sit-skis

Modification of Equipment

The modification of equipment frequently enables individuals with disabilities to participate in leisure, recreation, sport, and physical fitness activities from which they would otherwise be excluded. Entrepreneurs have come to understand that individuals with disabilities are as serious about quality leisure, recreation, sport, and physical fitness activities as individuals without disabilities. Within the past few years, there has been a remarkable growth in the manufacturing of equipment that enhances athletic performance for individuals with and without disabilities. There are hundreds of types of shoes that can be selected specifically to improve performance in a given activity. There is also a wide variety of sport wheelchairs and modified equipment designed to improve performance in a given activity. There are, for example, specific wheelchairs designed for sprint racing, distance road racing, basketball, tennis, rugby, football, and wilderness trekking.   ❧

SUMMARY

The nature of the educational system—both the structure and the nature of the students and parents served—is changing rapidly. The physical educator must respond to these changes in order to ensure a valid place within the educational community.

The physical educator is one of the many professionals who has a vested interest in students' growth, development, and maturation. The adapted physical educator has the responsibility for ensuring that each student with a disability is provided an appropriate physical education experience. The physical education teacher and adapted physical education teacher must work together as advocates of a quality program for children with and without disabilities.

The quality adapted physical education program requires excellent communication among all involved. Adapted physical educators and regular physical educators serving learners with disabilities may serve a vital role as a member of a motor development team made up of professionals with a particular commitment to motor performance.

A number of educational reform initiatives are in place in many schools/districts as educators, administrators, parents, and members of the community seek excellence in the public schools. The most important initiative is the increased involvement of parents in the lives of their children; the focus of education in the new millennium must be the family.

REVIEW QUESTIONS

1. What is the role of the physical educator and adapted physical educator in school reform initiatives?

2. Describe the motor development team and the roles of the professionals involved.

3. Describe the grief reactions of parents of students with disabilities. Explain strategies the professional may use to be sensitive to these feelings.

STUDENT ACTIVITIES

1. Attend a celebration or an event that represents a culture different from your own. Ask a participant, honestly, what he or she expects of his or her child's teacher.

2. Talk with a physical therapist, occupational therapist, or recreation therapist regarding his or her perceptions of the adapted physical educator as part of the motor development team.

3. Talk with parents regarding the process they went through to cope with the disability of their child.

4. Join a listserve or discussion group of parents of children with a particular disability. These can be found at the home page of the major national and international organizations that serve individuals with a particular disability.

5. Join NASPE, PE-Talk, or Adapt-Talk listservs to communicate with professionals in the field.

6. Interview a principal who has gone through the process of converting to site-based management.

REFERENCES

1. Blacher J: Sequential stages of parental adjustment to the birth of a child with handicaps: fact or artifact? *Ment Retard* 22:55–68, 1984.

2. Blanchard S: Grieving a dream, *Except Parent* October:26–30, 1994.

3. Block ME, Conatser P: Consulting in adapted physical education, *Ad Phys Act Q* 16:9–26, 1999.

4. Bonstingl J: *Schools of quality: an introduction to total quality management in education,* Alexandria, VA, 1992, Association for Supervision and Curriculum Development.

5. Bracey GW: The eighth Bracey report on the condition of public education, *Phi Delta Kappan* October:112–131, 1998.

6. Bratlinger E: Home-school partnerships that benefit children with special needs, *Elementary School J* 91:249–259, 1991.

7. Cariaga, D: *Adapted physical education,* San Luis Obispo County, CA, Student Services Division. (dcariaga@tcsn.net)

8. *Charter schools: education reform's quiet revolution.* Communicator. The National Association of Elementary School Principals, October 1996. http://www.naesp.org/comm/c1096.htm

9. Corrigan, D: *Keynote presentation at the Office of Special Education Programs National Conference,* Washington, DC, September 1999.

10. *Creating high-achieving learning environments,* http://www.ncrel.org/sdrs/areas/issues/educatrs/leadrshp/le400.htm

11. Crockett JB, Kauffman JM: Taking inclusion back to its roots, *Educ Leadership* October:74–77, 1998.

12. David JL: *Site-based management: making it work,* http://www.ascd.org/pubs/el/decjan/david.html

13. Davidson J, McNamara E, McGillivray K: *Achieving whole-school change with technology,* http://www.electronic-school.com/199909/0999f5.html

14. Darling-Hammond L: Reframing the school reform agenda, *Phi Delta Kappan* June:754, 1993.

15. Delgado-Gaitan C: School matters in the Mexican-American home: socializing children to education, *Am Educ Res J* 29(3):495–513, 1992.

16. Denton Independent School District: *Adapted physical education program guide,* February 1995, Author.

17. Downs P, Active Australia: *Willing and able: Count me in,* Disability Education Program, Participation Division, Australian Sports Commission, PO Box 176, Belconnen, ACT 2616, http://www.ausport.gov.au/partic/dishome.html

18. Dummer G: Disability sport web site, http://ed-web3.educ.msu.edu/kin866/contents.htm

19. Dyson L: Families of young children with handicaps: parental stress and functioning, *Am J Mental Retard* 95:623–629, 1991.

20. Ellery PJ: Embracing computer technology in physical education instruction, *Chronicle Physical Education in Higher Education,* 7(3):3, 18, 1996.

21. Ellery P. School of Physical Education, Wellness and Sport Studies, University of South Florida, 4202 East Fowler Avenue, PED 214, Tampa, FL.

22. Epstein J: Theory to practice: school and family partnerships lead to school improvement and student success. In Fagnano C, Werber B, editors: *School, family, and community interactions: a view from the firing lines,* Boulder, CO; 1994, Westview Press.

23. French et al.: Revising Section 504, physical education and sport, *J Phys Educ Rec Dance,* 69(7):57–63, 1998.

24. Crockett JB, Kauffman JM: *The least restrictive environment: its origins and interpretations in special education.* Mahway, NJ, in Associates press, Lawrence Erlbaum.

25. Furtwenger CB: Heads up! The EMOs are coming, *Educ Leadership,* October:44–47, 1998.

26. Gaul T, Underwood K, Fortune J: Reform at the grass roots, *Am School Board J* January: 1994.

27. General Accounting Office: *School facilities: condition of America's schools,* Washington, DC, 1995, Author.

28. Giroux H: Educational leadership and the crisis of democratic government, *Educ Res* 21(4):4–11, 1992.

29. Glasser W: *The quality school: managing students without coercion,* New York, 1992, HarperCollins.

30. *Hartmann v. Loudon County Board of Education,* 26 IDELR 167 (4th Circuit, 1997).

31. Heritage Foundation: Still a nation at risk, *Policy Review* July/August:23–29, 1998.

32. Huettig C: *But I didn't want to be a consultant,* presentation at the 28th Annual Physical Activity for Exceptional Individuals Conference, Costa Mesa, CA, October 1999.

33. Integrating technology into the standard curriculum: Extending learning opportunities for students with disabilities. *Research Connections Spec Ed* Fall (3):2–3, 1998.

34. Jensen E: *Turning point for teachers,* Del Mar, CA, 1992.

35. Kaufman A et al.: Permanency planning by older parents who care for adult children with mental retardation, *Ment Retard* 29:293–300, 1991.

36. Kerr SD: *Analysis of the U.S. Supreme Court decision in* Cedar Rapids Community School District v. Garret F, http://www.kerrlaw.com/legal/garretanal.html

37. Kübler-Ross E: *On death and dying,* New York, 1969, Macmillan.

38. Labovitz P: *Immigration—just the facts,* http://www.math.harvard.edu/~pak/25labo.html

39. Lozano JR, Castellano JA: *Assessing LEP migrant students for special education services,* http://www.ael.org/eric/digests/edor9810.htm

40. Magnet Schools, http://www.maec.org/mag-schl.html

41. Manning M: Understanding culturally diverse parents and families, *Equity Excel Educ* 28(1):52–57, 1995.

42. Markowitz L: The cross-currents of multiculturalism, *Networker* June/August:20–28, 1994.

43. Mary N: Reactions of black, Hispanic, and white mothers to having a child with handicaps, *Ment Retard* 28:1–5, 1990.

44. McConachie H: Implications of a model of stress and coping for services to families of young disabled children, *Child Care Health Dev* 20:37–46, 1994.

45. McDonnell LR, Hill PT: *Newcomers in American schools,* http://www.rand.org/publications/MR/MR103/MR103.html

46. McGehee RV, Reekie SH: Using sport studies and physical activities to internationalize the K–12 curriculum, *JOPERD* 70(6):38–46, 1999.

47. Mills B: Opening the gymnasium to the World Wide Web, *JOPERD* 68(8):17–19, 1997.

48. National Education Association: *Student achievement in Edison project schools: separating fact from fiction,* http://helpfrom.nea.org/issues/corpmngt/respond.html

49. Nieto J et al.: Passionate commitment to a multicultural society, *Equity Excel Educ* 27(1):51–57, 1994.

50. Olshansky S: Chronic sorrow: a response to having a mentally retarded child, *Soc Casework* 43:190–193, 1962.

51. Olson L: Parents as partners: redefining the social contract between families and schools, *Educ Week* April: 17–24, 1990.

52. Orfield G et al.: Deepening segregation in American public schools: a special report from the

Harvard Project on school desegregation, *Equity Excel Edu* 30(2):5–23, 1997.

53. Orfield G et al.: The growth of segregation in American schools: changing patterns of separation and poverty since 1968, *Equity Excel Educ* 27(1):5–8, 1994.

54. PE Central, http://pe.central/vt.edu/

55. Proceedings of the Magnet School/Title IV Desegregation Programs 1993 Conference, *Equity, excellence and school reform: a new Paradigm for desegregation,* Ann Arbor, MI, April 1995, Programs for Educational Opportunity, in cooperation with the U.S. Department of Education.

56. Ramirez A: Vouchers and voodoo economics, *Educ Leadership* 56(2): 1998, http://www.ascd.org/pubs/el/oct98/externalramirez.html

57. Rudner LM: *Scholastic achievement and demographic characteristics of home school students in 1998.* ERIC Clearinghouse on Assessment and Evaluation, College of Library and Information Services, University of Maryland, College Park, 1998, http://olam.ed.asu.edu/epaa/v7n8/

58. Simeonsson R: Family involvement in multidisciplinary team evaluations: professional and parent perspectives, *Child Care Health Dev* 21(3):199–213, 1995.

59. Singham M: The canary in the mine: the achievement gap between black and

white students, *Phi Delta Kappan* September:9–15, 1998.

60. Smith WF: Leadership for educational renewal, *Phi Delta Kappan* April:602–605.

61. Sugars A: *The adapted physical educator as a member of the motor development team,* TAHPERD State Convention, Lubbock, TX, 1990.

62. Texas Woman's University Project INSPIRE, http://venus.twu.edu/~f_huettig

63. *Together we can: a guide for crafting a profamily system of education and human services,* 1993, U.S. Department of Education and U.S. Department of Health and Human Services, http://www.nwrel.org/cnorse/booklets/educate/8.html

64. Tucker MS, Clark CC: The new accountability, *Am School Bd J* January:26–29, 1999.

65. United States Congress, P.L. 93-112, Rehabilitation Act, 1973.

66. Weiss S: Stressors experienced by family caregivers of children with pervasive developmental disorders, *Child Psychiatry Hum Dev* 21:203–215, 1991.

67. Willoughby J, Glidden L: Fathers helping out: shared child care and marital satisfaction of parents of children with disabilities, *Am J Ment Retard* 99(4):399–406, 1995.

68. Yell ML: The legal basis of inclusion, *Ed Leadership* October:70–73, 1998.

SUGGESTED READINGS

Block ME, Conatser P: Consulting in adapted physical education, *Ad Phys Act Q* 16:9–26, 1999.

Bracey GW: The eighth Bracey report on the condition of public education, *Phi Delta Kappan* October:112–131, 1998.

RECOMMENDED WEBSITES

Please note: These websites are being recommended in the fall of 1999. Given the ever changing nature of the Internet, these sites may have moved or been replaced by the time you are reading this text.

Charter Schools
  http://www.edweek.com/context/topics/charter.htm
  http://www.ncee.org/ac/intro.html

Educational Reform
  http://www.edreform.com/forum/
  http://familyeducation.com
  http://eric-web.tc.columbia.edu/

Home Schooling for Children with Special Needs
  http://www.geocities.com/Athens/8259/special.html

Magnet Schools
>http://www.maec.org/mag-schl.html
>http://www.magnet.edu/
>http://www.ascd.org/pubs/eu/mar197.html
>http://isis.ebrps.subr.edu/~rculpepp/elem.html

Multicultural Education
>http://curry.edschool.Virginia.EDU/go/
>multicultural/teachers.html
>http://www.cgcs.org/services/onissues/

Privatization of Education
>http://www.ncpa.org/pi/edu/

School Choice
>http://edreform.com

Site-Based Management
>http://www.mcrel.org/standards/
>articles/8-questions.asp

RECOMMENDED VIDEOS

Fanlight Productions
4196 Washington Street
Boston, MA 02131
>Surviving Death: Stories of Grief
>1998 Wilbur Award, Best TV Documentary
>47 minutes, purchase price $245
>Order # CV-270
Aquarius Health Care Videos
5 Powderhouse Lane

PO Box 1159
Sherborn, MA 01770
>We're Almost Home Now
>Elizabeth Kübler-Ross
>48 minutes, purchase price $150
>Item # Berhome

Children and Youth at Risk

Today, more than any other time in our history, an increasing number of children are entering our schools with significant physical, social, and psychological disadvantages. Many arrive in this world addicted to drugs and/or malnourished; spend their first few years without having their basic physical, safety and affection needs addressed; and have little exposure to activities beyond their home and culture. Their at-risk status continues to escalate when they enter school because they lack adequate skills, knowledge, and resources to benefit fully from what education has to offer. Fortunately, a quality physical education program has the potential to address and ameliorate the majority of these delays using powerful experiential strategies not available to the classroom teacher. In the gymnasium setting, fun activities are used to promote physical, motor, social, and intellectual development; physical educators provide opportunities for children to build self-esteem by mastering their bodies in their own time at their own speed; physical educators help them learn to take responsibility for their own actions by allowing them to establish and honor rules that apply equally to everyone; and physical educators give them the opportunity to experience the deep satisfaction that comes from working with others by using cooperative learning initiatives. The challenges these children represent to themselves and society will be addressed in this part, as will the programmatic strategies the physical educator can use to help all children grow and reach their full potential.

Physical Fitness and Sport Conditioning

■ **OBJECTIVES**

Identify five of the national standards for physical education.

Cite at least five values to persons with disabilities of participating in a regular physical activity program.

Identify the potential dangers of a sedentary lifestyle.

Identify the unique problems persons who are undernourished or overweight present for the physical educator.

Identify at least three types of physical fitness tests.

Construct a circuit training program that addresses a wide range of physical fitness levels.

Identify three ways to involve students' families in an active lifestyle.

Compare and contrast a general and a specific sports conditioning program.

Proper training yields successful performance.
Courtesy of Jason Wening. Gold Medal winner 400M Free (World Record) IPC World Swimming Championships, New Zealand, 1998.

One of the objectives of physical educators is to assist students in developing an activity repertoire that will promote life-long physical activity. Individuals who are physically fit are healthier, are able to perform motor skills competently, and are able to perform daily living activities without undue fatigue. During a child's early years, activity is an intregral part of living—most young children love to move. However, the biological drive for physical activity declines as we grow, and extrinsic factors affecting activity levels become more important motivators. This reliance on extrinsic motivation peaks in adolescence, when the need for peer acceptance, sexual attractiveness,

CASE STUDY

APPLICATION TASK
Review Maria Garcia's test results (see Chapter 2) to determine what physical fitness deficiencies she demonstrated. As you read this chapter, identify potential activities other than calisthenics that you could build into your physical education program that Maria and her classmates would enjoy while in school and after school. What are some ways you could involve Maria's parents in her physical activity program?

self-concept, and physical capabilities become prominent influences on whether or not an individual participates in regular physical activity.[42] Obviously, the individual who is physically gifted will use sports as a primary source for attention getting. Those individuals less gifted will turn to other activities. It is those less gifted movers that present the greatest challange to the physical educator. Without assistance, these are the persons who are at risk for becoming sedentary adults.

The surgeon general's 1996 report on physical activity and health addresses the many benefits of regular physical activity, as well as the failure of many Americans to participate on a regular basis. The report indicates that the benefits of regular physical activity include positive effects on the musculoskeletal, respiratory, cardiovascular, and endocrine systems. In addition to improved health, regular participation in physical activity reduces the risk of developing many debilitating conditions. However, even though we are aware of the many benefits that are derived from regular activity, more than 60 percent of American adults and 50 percent of teenagers do not regularly participate in vigorous exercise.[57] Until more Americans adopt an active lifestyle, we truly are a nation at risk.

Participation in a regular physical activity program is as important, if not more important, for persons with disabilities. The lack of physical de-

velopment and low vitality of persons with disabilities constitute a major concern of physical education. Chronically ill persons with debilitating conditions are particularly prone to poor physical vitality and development. Persons with cardiorespiratory conditions such as chronic bronchitis and various heart defects also show a tendency toward poor physical fitness. Increasing numbers of children who are medically fragile are now being educated in the public schools. Children with disabilities and children without disabilities often lack the physical and motor abilities that are prerequisite to successful participation in sports and the activities of daily living. It is of primary importance that the physical educator take responsibility for identifying the physical fitness needs of all students and for designing interesting, fun, and challenging programs that will motivate students to adopt a healthy, active lifestyle. This chapter includes a discussion of physical fitness and special problems demonstrated by persons who are undernourished, obese, visually impaired, and/or mentally and physically impaired. To assist the coach who becomes involved with sport programs, the chapter also discusses sport conditioning.

DEFINITION OF PHYSICAL FITNESS

The American Alliance for Health, Physical Education, Recreation and Dance (AAHPERD) describes physical fitness "as a physical state of well-being that allows people to perform daily activities with vigor, reduce their risk of health problems related to lack of exercise, and establish a fitness base for participation in a variety of activities."[48] In 1995 the National Association for Sport and Physical Education (NASPE), a member of AAHPERD, developed national standards for physical education. Those standards are presented in Figure 8-1.

Developing and maintaining an appropriate level of physical fitness is critical for persons with disabilities because, frequently, the disabling condition itself interferes with the ability to move efficiently. The problem is compounded when physical fitness levels are not adequate, because appropriate levels of muscular strength, joint flexibility,

A physically educated person

1. Demonstrates competency in many movement forms and proficiency in a few movement forms
2. Applies movement concepts and principles to the learning and development of motor skills
3. Exhibits a physically active lifestyle
4. Achieves and maintains a health-enhancing level of physical fitness
5. Demonstrates responsible personal and social behavior in physical activity settings
6. Demonstrates understanding and respect for differences among people in physical activity settings
7. Understands that physical activity provides opportunities for enjoyment, challenge, self-expression, and social interaction (AAHPERD, NASPE)

muscular endurance, and cardiovascular endurance are requisite for movement efficiency. A sedentary lifestyle that results from inadequate levels of physical fitness and lack of movement efficiency can contribute to a number of health problems, including obesity, hypertension, low back pain, osteoporosis, coronary heart disease, diabetes, colon cancer, anxiety and depression, and premature mortality.[27]

The primary value of physical activity for persons with disabilities is that it increases the number of years of quality living.[27,41] However, there are additional values for persons with disabilities to participating in systematic physical activity programs, including (1) prevention of secondary disabling conditions, (2) enhancement of independent living, (3) improved physical fitness for quality recreational experiences and sport, (4) physiological benefits related to health, and (5) enhancement of the quality of life. The following are examples of specific benefits of physical activity that have been proven through research:

Prevention of Disabling Conditions

- Decreases the risk of diabetes[43]
- Decreases the risk of depression and anxiety[11,43]
- Prevents hypertension[52]
- Reduces the risk of colon cancer[29]
- Lessens backaches[8]
- Enhances insulin production in persons who have diabetes[8]
- Prevents or delays the onset of osteoporosis[8]

Independent Living

- Improves functional independence[21,47]
- Increases pain-free weight-bearing capacity[50]
- Reduces medical expenditures[49]
- Reduces potential falls of persons with balance and ambulatory problems[33]
- Contributes to mobility[18]

Physical Fitness

- Allows maximal muscle power[9]
- Improves aerobic fitness[32,56]
- Prevents physical reconditioning[44]
- Increases and maintains muscular strength and endurance and contributes to mobility[27,41]
- Improves hand function, reaction time, tapping speed, and coordination[25]
- Enables a person with severe disabilities to lift the head, roll over, and maintain a sitting position[34]

Biological Measures

- Improves efficiency in ventilatory capacity[36]
- Improves stroke volume[45]
- Diminishes fluid retention in varicose veins[8]

General Health and Quality of Life

- Improves psychosocial health[37]
- Reduces depression[11]
- Improves sleep patterns[8]
- Facilitates weight reduction[8]
- Enhances postural stability[18]
- Enables a person with moderate to mild disabilities to engage in leisure-time activities in the community

Thus, participating in activities to improve physical fitness enhances a person's attitude about life, enhances ability to perform the activities of daily living, enhances sport and leisure skills, improves and maintains health, and reduces the chances of developing additional disabling conditions.

Once minimum levels of physical fitness are achieved, development and use of motor fitness can contribute to additional physical fitness development. That is, once an individual begins to use agility, balance, and coordination in daily living activities, as well as in games and sports, physical fitness levels continue to rise, and health continues to improve.

PHYSICAL ACTIVITY IN THE UNITED STATES

Although the United States appears to be involved in a fitness boom, there is evidence that the general population is not as active as one would believe.

Only 15 percent of the adult population engages in vigorous physical activity three or more days a week for 20 or more minutes.[57] Only slightly more than 20 percent of the adult population is mildly to moderately active for at least 30 minutes five or more times per week.[57] Furthermore, there is evidence that women and persons of minorities and of lesser education are at considerable health risk because they are less likely than Caucasion males to participate in leisure-time physical activity.[43] Major cardiovascular diseases account for almost 40 percent of the leading causes of death in this country.[40] Because conditions that contribute to cardiovascular disease have their beginning in childhood, there is renewed concern about the

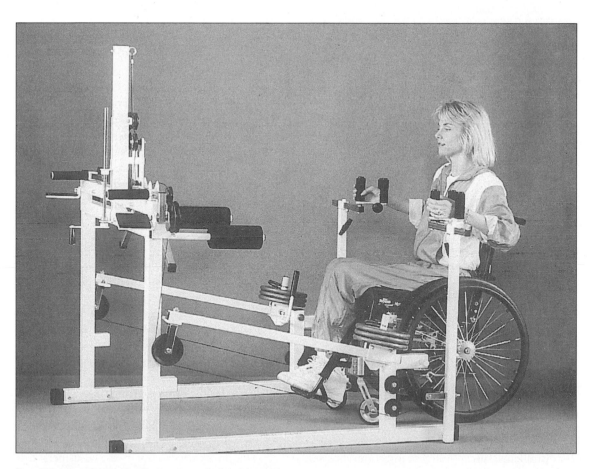

Specialized equipment facilitates strength development.
Courtesy of GPK, Inc. El Cajon, CA.

activity level of children. This concern is justified because (1) the nation's schoolchildren have become less active and fatter during the past decade; (2) if this trend continues, it is predicted that these children will be at greater risk for illness when they become adults; and (3) less than one half (46 percent) of physical education teachers have as their major goal the improvement of the physical fitness of students.[22] It is apparent that children in the United States are not as physically fit as experts believe they should be, and it is evident that youth with disabilities are less fit than their peers without disabilities.

All physical fitness test results that have been normed using children and youth with disabilities have shown lower physical fitness levels than results normed using children who lack disabilities.[14,48,54] Individuals with moderate mental retardation do poorer on cardiorespiratory function tests than do those with mild retardation.[14] Males and females between the ages of six and eighteen years who are mentally retarded are heavier than individuals the same age who are not retarded.[14] Individuals between the ages of ten and seventeen years who have visual impairments and those with spinal neuromuscular conditions have higher percentages of body fat than those the same age with no disabilities.[54] Males and females between the ages of ten and seventeen who have visual impairments,[54] moderate mental retardation, or Down syndrome[14] have less flexibility (sit-and-reach test) than youth without those disabilities. It is evident that physical educators who serve children and youth with disabilities must address the physical fitness deficiencies these youngsters demonstrate.

CAUSES OF POOR PHYSICAL FITNESS

Several factors contribute to poor physical fitness, including health status, developmental delays, lack of opportunity, lack of confidence by the child or the caregiver, and poorly designed physical education programs. Examples of health status problems include obesity; asthma and other chronic respiratory problems; susceptibility to infectious diseases, including the common cold; poor nutrition; inad-

equate sleep; motor limitations such as paralysis, muscular dystrophy, and cerebral palsy;[5] cardiopulmonary or metabolic limitations, including advanced cyanotic heart disease, cystic fibrosis, scoliosis, and undernutrition;[5] minority status; low income;[43] sensory and motor impairment in the lower limbs;[30] use of psychoactive medications; risk-taking behavior;[33] mobility impairments;[30] and balance or gait abnormalities.[31]

Developmental delays that can impact physical fitness levels include abnormal reflex development, delayed vestibular function, poor vision, delayed cross-lateral integration, inadequate spatial awareness, poor body image, and any other factor that limits the ability to move efficiently. Lack of opportunities to participate in physical fitness activities results from environmental barriers, such as limited access to community, group, or private exercise facilities;[11] insufficient programs as a result of inadequate testing procedures; lack of instructor knowledge; and limited curriculum offerings in the school system.[55]

Caregivers, including parents, medical personnel, and educators, sometimes encourage children to "take it easy" because they fear the children will overdo or hurt themselves during activity participation.[5] Also, some individuals with disabilities may be exceptionally self-conscious, and they may lack self-confidence. Their fear of failure may result in avoidance of both instructional and extracurricular physical activity.[38] It is important to determine why a person's fitness is low (i.e., why they are avoiding physical activity), so that the physical fitness program that is developed will focus on cause, as well as effect.

The quality of the physical education program being offered in the school setting is critical to students with and without disabilities. Poorly managed physical education programs result in 60 percent of the class time being spent standing or sitting, and only 8 percent of the time devoted to vigorous physical activity.[19] Well-designed physical education programs offer a variety of activities and keep the students moving and motivated to participate.

The physical educator is the ideal person to address the deterrents to exercise; however, before

Courtesy Dallas Independent School District.

joint could seriously affect the attainment of specific daily living or sport skills. Thus, a full evaluation of physical education needs would involve assessing the strength of major muscle groups, range of motion of many joints, and factors that affect cardiovascular efficiency.

It should be obvious that there is seldom enough time or personnel in a school system to assess every child comprehensively. Therefore, the physical educator usually only samples some physical and motor fitness components. Which components are measured is usually determined in one of two ways. Either a specific test (e.g., Physical Best and Individuals with Disabilities) is administered or test items that measure specific aspects of a given daily living skill or motor skill are selected and administered.

The ultimate purpose of preevaluation in the areas of physical fitness is to determine which activities will meet the unique needs of the child with disabilities. The procedures to be used for determining the needs in the areas of physical fitness are as follows:

1. Identify motor skills to be taught in the physical education program that contribute to physical fitness and can be expressed as recreational skills and activities of daily living for independence in the community.
2. Select physical fitness areas associated with the skills needed for independent living in the community.
3. Identify levels of physical fitness necessary for independent recreation and activities of daily living in the community.
4. Test for present levels of educational performance in the physical fitness domain.
5. Compare the child's performance with normative community standards to determine whether there is sufficient discrepancy to indicate an educational need.
6. If it is determined that there are physical fitness needs, establish long-range goals and short-term objectives that lead to those goals.

There are at least four orientations to physical fitness testing. One type is "health-related fitness,"

a program can be implemented, the student's present level of performance must be ascertained. With those results in hand, a physical activity program can be established to benefit the student.

EVALUATING PHYSICAL FITNESS

The full evaluation of the physical fitness of a child with a disability requires comprehensive assessment of ability areas identified through research (see Chapter 2). One does not just measure strength as a single entity. Rather, one measures the strength of specific muscle groups, such as the knee extensors, elbow flexors, or abdominal muscles. In the same manner, when flexibility is evaluated, it is necessary to determine range of motion at specific joints in the body. A severe loss of strength in any muscle group or limited range of motion in any

which refers to the components of physiological functioning that are believed to offer protection against such degenerative diseases as obesity, disk degeneration, and coronary heart disease.[24] A second type includes tests designed to develop aspects of physical fitness such as optimal strength, endurance, and flexibility to be used in sport activities. A third orientation, which is preferred by Evans and Meyer[15] for individuals with disabilities, is a function-specific type of physical fitness that relates to independent functioning in the community. The American College of Sports Medicine recommends a fourth type of testing, which is termed problem-oriented exercise management.[35] Problem-oriented exercise management involves five steps, including (1) collection of subjective data, (2) collection of objective data, (3) assessment and generation of a problem list, (4) formulation of a diagnostic or therapeutic plan, and (5) periodic reassessment.[35]

Health-related tests include measures of cardiovascular/cardiorespiratory endurance, abdominal strength, percentage of body fat, and flexibility. The performance of children and youth with disabilities has been measured using items included in the Health-Related Physical Fitness Test and the Prudential FITNESSGRAM. These types of tests are meaningful when individuals with mild or moderate cognitive and physical disabilities are being evaluated. AAHPERD has incorporated those test items in its Physical Best and Individuals with Disabilities evaluation (see Chapter 2). Winnick and Short's[54] Brockport Physical Fitness Test is an excellent criterion-referenced health-related test that can be used with children and youth with different types of disabilities. Nonambulatory severely and profoundly involved students would benefit from the test items and curriculum presented in Mobility Opportunities Via Education (MOVE) (see Chapter 2).

Individuals with severe disabilities who are ambulatory require functional physical fitness tests that relate specifically to what an individual needs to meet the daily demands of the environment. Examples of such test items are walking to develop endurance to walk to and from one's home from designated areas in the neighborhood, developing sufficient balance to remedy a wide shuffling gait, and performing specific heel-cord stretching exercises to lengthen tight heel cords, so that the entire foot will strike the ground when walking. The type of fitness test selected depends on the goals and objectives of the physical education program. Inactive persons frequently cannot sustain exercise for more than 5 minutes. Therefore, the physical educator must use good judgment when selecting test items. For the sedentary person, heart rate after a 6-minute or 12-minute walk may be the best indicator of cardiovascular endurance.

PROGRAMMING FOR PHYSICAL FITNESS

Physical fitness encompasses muscular strength and endurance, flexibility, body composition, and cardiovascular endurance. Each of these factors must be addressed in the training program.

Muscular Strength

Muscular strength is the ability to contract a muscle against resistance. Types of contraction include

- Concentric. Muscle tension is greater than the amount of applied resistance, so that the muscle shortens and movement occurs.
- Isometric (static). Muscle tension equals the amount of applied resistance, so that no movement occurs.
- Eccentric. Resistance is greater than the muscle tension, so that the muscle lengthens without relaxing.

Muscular strength can be improved by using the overload principle. The overload principle is applied by gradually increasing the resistance (load or weight) used over time (days or months). Isotonic exercises use progressive resistance with free weights or Nautilus or Universal weight machines. When isotonic exercises are being performed, the greatest resistance is during the start or finish of the movement. Isokinetic exercises provide resistance throughout the entire range of motion. Isokinetic exercise machines include the Cybex and Orthotron. When isometric exercises are being performed, the resistance is so great that the contracting muscles do not move.[40] The physical educator is cautioned to be sure to include instruction about proper breathing during both isotonic and isometric exercises. The person involved in exercise should be instructed to breathe out while executing an exercise such as a sit-up or a bar press and to breathe in when returning to the starting position.

Muscular Endurance

Muscular endurance is the ability to continue to contract a muscle against resistance. Muscular endurance is developed by gradually increasing the number of repetitions completed during an exercise period.

Flexibility

Flexibility is the range of motion possible at any given joint. Flexibility can be improved through the use of static stretching, which is accomplished by slowly lengthening a muscle group that surrounds a joint and then holding the extended position for 30 to 60 seconds.

Body Composition

Body composition refers to the muscle, bone, fat, and other elements in the body.[40] Usually in a discussion of physical fitness, the term is used to express the percentage of body fat in comparison with lean tissue. Overweight and obese individuals have high percentages of body fat. There is controversy as to what percentage of body fat is most desirable; however, most fitness experts agree that levels less than 30 percent are healthiest.

Cardiovascular Endurance

Cardiovascular endurance is the ability of the heart and vessels to process and transport oxygen from

Warming up with stretching exercises helps prevent injury.
Courtesy of Orthotic & Prosthetic Athletic Association Fund, Alexandria, VA.

the lungs to muscle cells for use. The greater the cardiovascular endurance, the longer the period of time that a person is able to continue exercising. Cardiovascular endurance can be improved by persisting at activities that increase the heart rate to between 60 and 90 percent of maximum.

PRINCIPLES OF TRAINING

In 1990 the American College of Sports Medicine (ACSM) made recommendations in the following five areas for achieving and maintaining physical fitness:

1. Mode of activity. It is recommended that any continuous physical activity that uses

large-muscle groups and that can be rhythmic and aerobic be used.[40] Activities such as walking, running, inline skating, hiking, rowing, stair climbing, swimming, dancing, and cycling are suggested.

2. Frequency of training. Frequency of training is the number of times per week a person should exercise. Rest periods are interspersed between training sessions to permit the body to recover.[16] The surgeon general's report on physical activity and health includes a recommendation that people of all ages include a minimum of 30 minutes of physical activity of moderate intensity most, if not all, days of the week.[57]

3. Intensity of training. Intensity is the magnitude (percentage of one's capacity) of exercise during one exercise session. Usually the higher the intensity, the greater the benefit from the activity. In aerobic activity, the faster the pace, the greater the intensity. In resistance training, the heavier the weight, the greater the intensity.[26] Individuals with disabilities who have been sedentary should begin their exercise program with a short duration of moderate intensity and gradually increase the duration or intensity until the preset goal is reached.[57] Low to moderate intensity will provide these advantages: (1) less chance of cardiovascular problems, (2) possibly fewer injuries, and (3) a greater probability that the individuals will continue their exercise programs after formal instruction.

4. Duration of training. Duration is the length of time a person exercises at a given time. Duration of exercise applies primarily to cardiorespiratory endurance development. The surgeon general recommends setting a goal of 30 minutes of sustained activity.[57] High-intensity activities (80 to 90 percent of maximum heart rate) require shorter periods of time; activities that generate a lower level of intensity (less than 70 percent

of maximum heart rate) require longer periods of time. The duration time should include at least a 10-minute warm-up period and a 5- to 10-minute cool-down period that includes stretching and reduced exertion exercise (e.g., walking slower). When one is working with students who have disabilities, it is better to begin with a shorter duration of less intense activity and gradually work toward lengthening the time and intensity of the activity. There is some evidence that cardiorespiratory fitness gains are similar when persons engage in several short sessions of activity (e.g., 10 minutes) as when they participate in a 30-minute session.[57]

5. Resistance training. The goal of resistance training is to improve overall muscular strength and endurance. The intensity of exercise will vary, depending on the condition of the individual; however, in general, to develop and maintain a healthy body composition, it is recommended that moderate intensity strength training be used. The workout should begin with two to three repetitions initially and eventually build to three sets of eight to twelve repetitions three times weekly. Isotonic or isokinetic exercises of major muscle groups should be included. To develop strength, it is recommended that at least 60 percent of the maximum resistance a person can move be used. The number of times the weight is moved depends on the repetition continuum selected. The training effect is increased in proportion to the number of times an exercise is repeated, up to a point.[4] Once a student can repeat the exercise eight times in a row with ease, the number of sets should be increased by one. As the amount of resistance is increased, the number of repetitions is decreased and then gradually increased. Rest ranging from 30 seconds to 5 minutes should always occur between the sets.

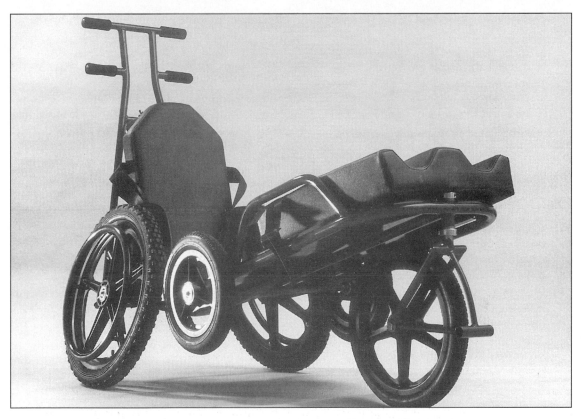

The Kili-Kart is an off-road all-terrain cart to enable persons with physical disabilities access to outdoor activities.
Courtesy of Clark James Mishler Photography for Disability Options, Inc. Palmer, AR.

DEVELOPING TRAINING PROGRAMS

Resistance training is well established as an effective method for developing musculoskeletal strength. Major health organizations including the American College of Sports Medicine,[3] the American Heart Association,[2] and the surgeon general[57] recommend strength training to improve strength, endurance, and health and have developed resistance exercise guidelines for health promotion. Their recommendations are one set of eight to twelve repetitions of eight to ten exercises two to three times per week for persons under fifty years of age.

Fitness instruction for students with disabilities should be conducted in conformance with the individual education program (IEP). This means that there should be measurable, observable objectives and that present levels of educational performance should be determined for each student when the activity program is begun. To accommodate the changing demands of the ability level of each learner, the following principles are suggested:

1. Individual differences. Every student's IEP should be based on specific assessment data that indicate the unique needs for alleviating deficits in prerequisites for self-sufficient living.
2. Overload/shaping principle. Increases in strength and endurance result from small increments of workload greater than the

present ability. Overload can be achieved in the following ways:

   a. Increase the number of repetitions or sets.

   b. Increase the distance covered.

   c. Increase the speed with which the exercise is executed.

   d. Increase the number of minutes of continuous effort.

   e. Decrease the rest interval between active sessions.

   f. Any combination of the above

3. Maintenance or development of physical fitness. Training sessions can be used to maintain or develop physical fitness. The data on the frequency of the training will indicate whether the training results maintain or develop physical fitness levels.

4. Physical fitness for a purpose. Values gained from exercises should be relevant to the development of functional skills and/or health components. Exercises are highly specific; they need to be done at intensity levels commensurate with the ability of the student.

5. Active/voluntary movement. Benefits are greatest when the exercise is active (done by the student) rather than passive (done by the therapist or teacher). When the student performs the activity, it is possible to provide behavioral measurement and apply learning principles from research and demonstration.

6. Recovery/cool-down. Students should not lie or sit down immediately after high-intensity exercise. This tends to subvert return of blood to the heart and cause dizziness. Cool-down should entail continued slow walking or mild activity.

7. Warm-up. At least 10 minutes of warm-up exercises using movements specific to training should precede high-intensity exercise sessions or competitive games. The warm-up is particularly important for persons with chronic respiratory problems or cardiovascular conditions. Warm-ups should emphasize stretching exercises that facilitate range of motion (flexibility) rather than ballistic (bouncing) exercises.

Examples of ways to write behavioral physical fitness goals are provided in Figure 8-2.

Contraindications

Physical educators should know what exercises and activities are contraindicated for each individual. Lasko-McCarthey and Knopf[28] recommend avoiding the following movements during exercises:

- Head circles that involve circumduction/hyperextension of the cervical spine
- Trunk circling that involves flexing the spine from a standing position with the legs straight
- Shoulder stands
- Hyperextension of the spine from a prone (face-down) position
- Standing toe touches with straight legs
- Bilateral straight-leg raises
- Sit-ups with feet held and hands behind head
- Sit-ups with straight legs
- Trunk twists from a standing position
- Deep knee bends (squats)
- Bench press performed with the feet on the floor
- Hip flexor stretches from a prone or kneeling position
- Hurdle stretches
- Prone flies from a standing position
- Military presses with head extended (dorsiflexed)
- Isometric exercises for individuals over age forty or those with a history of cardiovascular disease
- Immediate rest after intense exercise

In addition, the medical records of individuals with disabilities should always be reviewed to determine whether specific exercises and activities have been identified as contraindicated by medical personnel.

Static Stretching Exercises

Adapted physical education requires that tasks be adapted to the ability level of each learner. When this occurs, each student with a disability can be

Figure 8-2 Behavioral Statements for Development of Physical Fitness

Many physical fitness tasks are measurable. Usually, if measure can be incorporated into a task, performance difficulty can be prescribed for the individual learner. Below are statements that involve physical and motor tasks requiring specifications of measurement to be ascribed to the tasks. Many children with disabilities will be able to participate in these tasks at their ability level if objectives are sequenced.

1. Walk a specified distance at a heart rate of 120 beats per minute.
2. Jog and walk alternately 50 steps for a specified distance.
3. Run in place lifting the foot a specified distance from the floor a specified number of times for a specified period of time.
4. Run in place 100 steps in a specified amount of time.
5. Run a specified distance in a specified period of time.
6. Perform a modified push-up a specified number of times.
7. Perform a modified chin-up a specified number of times.
8. Climb a rope a specified distance in a specified amount of time.
9. Perform toe raises with a specified amount of weight a specified number of repetitions.
10. Perform a sit-up (modified if necessary) a specified number of repetitions; sit-up difficulty can be modified by performance on an incline, where gravity assists with the sit-up.
11. Perform a specified number of dips on the parallel bars (lower and raise the body by straightening and bending the arms) with a specified amount of weight attached to a belt; if one dip cannot be done, reduce the range of motion of the dip.
12. Perform arm curls with a specified weight and a specified number of repetitions.
13. Curl the toes and pick up a specified number of pencils or sticks of the same size; move them a specified distance to a target of a specified size over a specified time frame.
14. Perform a wrist roll in which a rope of specified length has a weight of specified pounds attached to it a specified number of repetitions over a specified time frame.
15. Perform toe curls with a towel with the heels flat on the floor; bunch up the towel under the feet and put a weight of a specified number of pounds on the towel a specified distance from the toes.
16. Perform a wrist curl in which the wrist is over the edge of a table or a chair; then bend and straighten the wrist, holding a weight of a specified amount a specified number of repetitions.
17. Jump and reach a specified height.
18. Throw a medicine ball of specified weight from a sitting position a specified distance.
19. Run a specified distance over a specified period of time.
20. Run around a hoop 4 feet in diameter a specified number of times over a specified time frame.
21. Leap over a rope placed at a specified height.
22. Leap over 2 lines on the floor that are a specified distance apart.
23. Step up and then down on a bench of a specified height a specified number of repetitions over a specified time frame.
24. Run in a figure-eight fashion around a specified number of cones set a specified distance apart a specified number of times during a specified time frame.
25. Perform a shuttle run in which the parallel lines are a specified distance apart a specified number of trips in a specified amount of time.

accommodated. Usually, individuals with disabilities have tight muscles and connective tissue, which limits joint range of motion. Stretching is an important activity for increasing movement of desired joints. Lasko-McCarthey and Knopf[28] recommend the following practices for achieving a permanent increase in flexibility: (1) engage in a 5- to 10-minute warm-up before stretching; (2) do not apply too much force to the stretch; (3) hold the stretch for a duration of 30 to 60 seconds; (4) do not perform stretching if pain, infection, or edema is present; and (5) incorporate stretches at the end of the cooldown to prevent adaptive shortening and promote relaxation of muscles.

Walk-Run Program for Cardiovascular Endurance

A walk-run program has at least two variables that can be manipulated to make it more or less difficult: (1) the distance that the individual should run and (2) the length of time permitted to travel the prescribed distance. Suggested distance intervals are 1/4 mile, 1/2 mile, 3/4 mile, and 1 mile. Suggested target criterion times for each distance could be 5 minutes for 1/4 mile, 8 minutes for 1/2 mile, 12 minutes for 3/4 mile, and 15 minutes for 1 mile.

Jumping Rope for Cardiovascular Endurance

When a cardiovascular fitness program is being conducted for individuals with disabilities, each individualized program should have specific objectives tailored to the student's present level of ability. A continuum of exercise activities can be used to accommodate individual differences. A procedure for constructing an individualized physical fitness program of rope jumping may be as follows:

1. Make a 4-minute musical tape recording that uses a cadence of seventy jumps per minute.
2. Test the students to determine how long they can jump without a rest interval.
3. Prescribe each individual to continue for 2 seconds longer each day.
4. When an individual can jump continuously for 4 minutes, substitute another tape that uses a cadence of eighty jumps per minute.

Under these conditions, there would be two stations of different frequencies, but each person at each of those stations would be performing for specific lengths of time commensurate with their present levels of ability. Increasing cadences could be added to the program as individuals increase in cardiovascular endurance. Another factor that could be introduced into the program to make it more or less difficult is to vary the length of the rest intervals between repeated bouts of exercise.

Exercise in Water

Exercise in water is an excellent activity mode for persons with disabilities.[12] Walking, running, and swimming contribute to cardiovascular endurance and strength.

Accommodation of Individual Differences

Physical fitness activities for students with disabilities must be individually tailored to abilities and to the severity of the condition. The goals of the exercise program for persons with disabilities will vary, depending on the type of impairment, and will differ from those of individuals with no disabilities.[35]

Exercises can be modified in several ways to accommodate the ability level of each student with a disability:

1. The number of repetitions can be modified to make the task easier or more difficult. The fewer the number of repetitions, the less difficult the activity.
2. The position of the body in relation to gravity during the activity can be modified. Strength exercises done using gravity for assistance are the least demanding (e.g., executing a sit-up on a slant board with the head higher than the feet). Strength exercises done in a side-lying position will eliminate the effect of gravity (e.g., going from a full body extension to a crunch position while in a side-lying position). Exercises done against gravity are the third most demanding (e.g., executing a sit-up from a supine position or on a slant board with the head lower than the feet). The most demanding strength exercises are those done with resistance and against gravity (e.g., individual leg extensions from a sitting position while wearing ankle weights).
3. The time that it takes to complete a set of repetitions can be shortened or lengthened. The shorter the time interval for completing the work, the more difficult the exercise task.

4. The number of sets of repetitions can be modified. Greater numbers of sets are associated with more intense and difficult training regimens. The number of sets can be decreased to accommodate the individual's present level of ability.

5. Theraband, surgical tubing, and sections of inner tubes can be used for strengthening specific muscle groups. These types of exercises are particularly valuable for individuals with physical disabilities who do not have access to weight-training equipment.

6. The use of floatation devices in the pool for the nonswimmer will enable that person to realize the benefits of moving in the water.

7. Stationary bikes, recline cycles, and arm cranking devices can be used by individuals with balance difficulties or those who are nonambulatory.

8. Large therapy balls can be used to develop trunk and abdominal strength.

9. For the sedentary person, the distance to be traveled and the time to engage in the activity can be shortened.

10. Self-selected rest periods can be allowed during the class time.

11. Relaxation practice can be built into each class period.

12. Low-impact exercises can be used.

Circuit Training

Accommodation for individual differences for most students with disabilities can be easily accomplished if a circuit training program is used. Circuit training involves using a series of stations with different types of activities at each station. Individual differences can be accommodated by altering the intensity and workload required of each student. To meet the individual physical needs of each student in circuit training, the following modifications can be made:

1. Develop a wide variety of activity levels, the lower of which can accommodate most individuals with disabilities.

2. Assign students with disabilities to only those stations in the circuit that meet their assessed needs.

3. Modify the nature of the activity at each station, so that each student can participate at the appropriate ability level.

4. Provide peer assistance, if available, and special instructions for the use of specific apparatus or equipment.

5. Provide verbal encouragement.[46]

6. Pair higher-functioning individuals with lower-functioning persons who need assistance at each station.[46]

Accommodating for Specific Types of Disabilities

Students with varying types of disabilities may need specific accommodation in circuit training exercises. Visually impaired and deaf students need assistance with communication systems that provide them with instructional information, whereas students with physical disabilities need accommodation for impaired motor functioning. Students who are mentally retarded or who have a specific learning disability, on the other hand, may need assistance in comprehending the task. Youngsters with autism need a structured environment with as few distractions as possible. The following are suggestions for accommodating students with a variety of disabilities.

Visual Disabilities

Students with visual impairments need confidence to cope with training programs. They may need for the exercise environment to be modified, or they may need help from others to participate in training activities. Some environmental aids and supplemental assistance that may enable the student with a visual disability to benefit from circuit training can be found in Figure 8-3.

Physical Disabilities

Students with physical disabilities may need accommodations to move physically through the environment and to manipulate exercise equipment.

Figure 8-3 Circuit Training: Environmental Aids and Supplemental Assistance for Students with Visual Disabilities

1. Provide boundaries that define the general exercise area to facilitate mobility of the student within the exercise area.
2. Use boundaries to define the location of each specific exercise station.
3. Use sighted peers, if available, to help the student with visual disabilities move from station to station and to comprehend each task.
4. Provide a complete explanation of the way to use specific apparatus or equipment.
5. Arrange the exercise area the same way every time so that the student with visual disabilities will be able to move through a familiar environment.
6. Arrange for enlarged type or braille descriptions of the activity at each session.
7. Physically move the student through the exercise several times.
8. Plan the circuit so that movement to different areas for exercise is minimized.
9. Provide initial reference points that indicate where the student starts in the circuit.
10. Use brightly colored objects as boundaries to assist students with residual vision.

Some accommodations to enable these individuals to participate in circuit training follow:

1. Select activities that involve functional body parts (e.g., if the legs are impaired, prescribe activities for the arms).
2. If an individual has limited function of the wrists and fingers, place pads on the forearms and select activities that will enable the individual to move the weights with the padded forearms.
3. If necessary, attach weights to the body or attach a body part to a piece of equipment with Velcro straps (e.g., if the student has difficulty keeping the feet in bicycle stirrups, attach the feet to the pedals with Velcro straps).
4. Establish an exercise environment that is accessible for students in wheelchairs.

Cognitive Disabilities

Students who are learning disabled or who are mentally retarded can benefit from pictures of exercises that are to be practiced at each station on the circuit. Rimmer[46] suggests that a variety of cardiovascular endurance activites be used when working with individuals with short attention spans. Specifically, the following 2-minute stations would be included in a training circuit: walk briskly around the track, jump on a mini trampoline, step up and down the bleachers, pedal a stationary cycle, perform jumping jacks, and use the rowing machine. A 30- to 60-second rest should occur between each station. Families of individuals with mental retardation should be encouraged to join their youngsters in a walk after dinner, use community-based fitness centers as often as possible, and perform light calisthenics between commercials while watching TV.[46]

SELECTED FITNESS PROBLEMS

As mentioned earlier in this chapter, the problems of underdevelopment and low physical vitality are closely associated to a great number of organic, mental, physiological, and emotional problems, which are discussed throughout this book. However, three major problem areas transcend the others: malnutrition, overweight, and obesity.

Malnutrition

The term *malnutrition* means poor nutrition, whether there is an excess or a lack of nutrients to the body. In either instance, the malnourished individual has relatively poor physical fitness and other serious disadvantages.

It is important that the cause of physical underdevelopment be identified. One cause of physical underdevelopment may be a lack of physical activity, which, consequently, does not provide an opportunity for the body to develop its potential. However, some children are physically underdeveloped partially because of undernutrition. When a person's body weight is more than 10 percent below the ideal weight indicated by standard age and weight tables, undernutrition may be a cause. Tension, anxiety, depression, and other emotional factors may restrict a person's appetite, causing insufficient caloric intake and weight loss. The most severe emotional disturbances causing insufficient caloric intake and weight loss are anorexia nervosa and/or bulimia. Impairment in physical development may also ensue. In culturally deprived areas, common in the urban inner city, children may lack proper nutrition as a result of insufficient food resulting from poverty or the use of money for other priorities (e.g., drugs), idiosyncrasy, or loss of appetite caused by an organic problem. Proper nutrition and exercise go hand in hand in growing children. One without the other may cause lack of optimum physical development. The role of the physical educator in dealing with the underweight person is to help establish sound liv-

ing habits with particular emphasis on proper diet, rest, and relaxation.

Students from affluent families should be encouraged to keep a three-day food intake diary, after which, with the help of the teacher, a daily average of calories consumed is computed. After determining the average number of calories taken in, the student is encouraged to increase the daily intake by eating extra meals that are both nutritious and high in calories.

The physical educator must be sensitive to the unique problems of the child who is homeless, the child living in poverty, and the child who is nutritionally abused. A change in caloric intake is not a simple matter of the child's understanding the relationship between caloric intake and health. Often the child is a victim, unable to control the powerful forces around him or her. The physical educator

The successful athlete devotes many hours to general and specific training.
Courtesy of College Park, For Disability Options, Inc., Palmer, AR.

may take the lead in arranging for the child to have a federally or state-subsidized free breakfast or lunch. This may be the only meal the child eats during the day. In addition, the physical educator may use fresh fruit as a reward, always seeking an opportunity to allow the hungry child to earn the reward.

Overweight and Obesity

Many persons in the United States are overweight. Obesity, particularly in adults, is considered one of the great current medical problems because of its relationship to cardiovascular problems and other diseases. The frequency of overweight among patients with angina pectoris, coronary insufficiency, hypertension, and coronary occlusions is considerable.

Overweight can be defined as any excess of 10 percent or more above the ideal weight for a person, and obesity is any excess of 20 percent or more above the ideal weight. Obesity constitutes pathological overweight that requires correction. Several factors must be considered in determining whether a person is overweight. Among these are gender, weight, height, age, general body build, bone size, muscular development, and accumulations of subcutaneous fat.

In the past, sufficient attention has not been given to the diagnosis of overweight among many children in our society. The incidence of overweight among children in our schools has been estimated at 10 percent or more—a rate of such significance that attention to prevention and remediation should be provided by public school doctors, nurses, and health and physical educators.

Overweight persons have a greater tendency to contract diseases of the heart, circulatory system, kidneys, and pancreas. They also have a predisposition to structural foot and joint conditions because of their excess weight and lack of motor skill to accommodate the weight.

The basic reason for overweight is that the body's caloric consumption is greater than the energy expended to use the calories. Consequently, the excess energy food is stored in the body as fat,

leading to overweight. In many instances, overeating is a matter of habit. Thus, the body is continually in the process of acquiring more calories than are needed to maintain a normal weight.

Overweight and obesity have many causes. Among them are (1) caloric imbalance from eating incorrectly in relation to energy expended in the form of activity; (2) dysfunction of the endocrine glands, particularly the pituitary and the thyroid, which regulate fat distribution in the body; and (3) emotional disturbance.

There is impressive evidence that obesity in adults has its origin in childhood habits. There seems to be a substantial number of overweight adults whose difficulty in controlling their appetite stems from childhood. Social environment definitely influences obesity. The time youngsters spend in front of the TV or computer has greatly increased in the past decade. In inner cities where gangs, crimes, and violence are prevalent, it is simply not safe for children to play outside. In the past thirty years, the percentage of young people who are overweight has more than doubled.[58] Unless appropriate intervention is provided, these youngsters will grow up to be obese, sedentary adults.

Adverse Effects of Obesity

Many obese children exhibit immature social and emotional characteristics. It is not uncommon for obese children to dislike the games played by their peers, since obesity handicaps them in being adept at the games in which their peers are adequate. These children are often clumsy and slow, are objects of many stereotyped jokes, and are incapable of holding a secure social position among other children. Consequently, they may become oversensitive and unable to defend themselves and thus may withdraw from healthy play and exercise. This withdrawal from activity decreases the energy expenditure needed to maintain the balance that combats obesity. Therefore, in many instances, obesity leads to sedentary habits. It is often difficult to encourage these children to participate in forms of exercise that permit great expenditures of energy.

Obesity may be an important factor as children form ideas about themselves as persons and about how they think they appear to others. The ideas that they have about themselves will be influenced by their own discoveries, by what others say about them, and by the attitudes shown toward them. If the children find that their appearance elicits hostility, disrespect, or negative attention from parents and peers, these feelings may affect their self-concept. Traits described by their parents and peers may affect their inner feelings and may be manifested in their behavior, since children often assess their worth in terms of their relationships with peers, parents, and other authority figures.

When children pass from the child-centered atmosphere of the home into the competitive activities of the early school years, social stresses are encountered. They must demonstrate physical abilities, courage, manipulative skill, and social adeptness in direct comparison with other children of their age. The penalties for failure are humiliation, ridicule, and rejection from the group. Obesity places a tremendous social and emotional handicap on children. Therefore, educators should give these children all possible assistance and guidance in alleviating or adjusting to obesity.

Programming for the Obese Child

Since children who are overweight often cannot efficiently perform the activities of the physical education program, it is not uncommon for them to dislike many of these activities. As a result of their inability to participate in the program, they are often the objects of practical jokes and disparaging remarks made by other children. In such an environment, boys and girls who are obese become unhappy and ashamed and often withdraw from the activity to circumvent emotional involvement with the group. The physical educator should attempt to create an environment that will enable the obese child to have successful experiences in the class, thus minimizing situations that could threaten the child's position as a person of worth. The physical educator is also challenged in regard to developing the attitudes of other students in the classes. Consequently, proposing to the class the acceptance of children who are different is an important and worthwhile goal of the physical educator.

Conducting a Weight-Control Program

The conduction of a weight-control program should follow the basic procedures according to the instructional process of the Education of the Handicapped Act. First, there must be a goal—a desirable body weight that the individual is to achieve. Next, the present level should portray the weight of the person at the present. Third, short-term instructional objectives that lead from the present weight to the eventual goal must be developed. For instance, if the present body weight is 100 pounds and the desirable body weight is 90 pounds, then the series of short-term objectives could be in 1- or 2-pound increments. The weight-loss goal will be reached most quickly if diet control is practiced while the exercise program is conducted. Appropriate goal setting will contribute not only to immediate weight loss but also to changes in lifelong diet and exercise habits.

The use of behavior-management techniques contributes to success in weight-control programs by controlling the positive influences and minimizing the negative variables of the program. Some of the positive aspects of behavior management that will strengthen weight control behaviors are (1) encouragement by the instructor, (2) a safe environment that keeps the student free from injury, (3) a variety of activities to reduce boredom, (4) a regularly scheduled routine, (5) a compatible, supportive social group, (6) feedback about progress toward short-term objectives, and (7) social reinforcement when weight losses occur. Punishing features that should be minimized are (1) poor program advice, (2) inconvenient time and place, (3) muscle soreness and/or injury, (4) lack of progress, and (5) disapproval about participation in the program by peers and family.

There can be no one program for the remediation of children who are obese. It is necessary that the true cause of the problem be found. When the cause of obesity is known, several avenues are available for treatment. Some rules to be applied for successful weight control are provided in Figure 8-4.

Obese students should be guided into activities that can be safely performed and successfully

Figure 8-4   Guidelines for a Safe and Effective Weight-Control Program

1. Know your desirable weight.
2. Count calories.
3. Try to calculate the energy expenditure through controlled workouts.
4. Do not cut out the food you like; cut down on the amounts you eat.
5. Seek medical treatment in the case of a glandular dysfunction.
6. Seek counseling when emotional causes are at the root of the problem.
7. Seek counseling on the consequences of obesity to the total personality.
8. Disrupt sedentary ways of living.

Courtesy Canadian Association of Athletes with a Mental Handicap.

achieved. This will tend to encourage them to participate in more vigorous activities. Some of the activities that can be used to combat obesity are general conditioning exercises, jogging, dancing, rhythmical activities, swimming, and sports and games. Much can be done for these children through individual guidance, encouragement, and selection of the proper developmental experiences. Loss of weight results in a decrease in the amount of stored adipose tissue; however, which stores of adipose tissue will decrease cannot be predicted. Therefore, it is impossible to spot reduce.

FAMILY INVOLVEMENT IN ACTIVE LIFESTYLES

Lifestyles of physical activity are shaped in part within the school setting and in part within the home. The family unit provides the primary social learning environment for the child. Parents serve as role models for children's attitudes and practices, and the extent to which the parents participate in physical activity does impact their child's attitude and behavior.[23] When family members support and cooperate with teachers, participation in physical activity is reinforced. For this reason,

teachers should routinely reach out to the home to communicate their program goals and seek support.[10]

Effective collaboration of schools and families to facilitate physically active leisure lifestyles for persons with disabilities involves a blend of convenience, acceptability of information sent to the home, home-based curricula, and family learning opportunities. When these factors are controlled, the vast majority of families participate with the school to enhance their child's well-being.[20] Some successful components of a parent training program follow:

- Home packets that list the values of exercise, suggest types of activities, identify community resources, and highlight upcoming special physical activity events can be distributed to students on a regular basis by the physical education teacher.
- Family fun nights can be used to generate interest in the physical program, raise awareness of the value of exercise, and inform all members of the family about the joy and benefits of regular participation in physical activity. The evening should be a mini-health fair aimed at improving health habits. Events can be structured that demonstrate games and activities that individuals and families should participate in to enhance their health.
- Family scorecards should be distributed to families to allow them to record the amount and frequency of physical activity in which the child with a disability and the family participate. The scorecard should include specific activities for which points can be earned, the activities and points earned by the student, and the activities and points earned by the family as a whole.[23]

IMPLICATIONS FOR PHYSICAL EDUCATION

Physical education has emerged with new importance as awareness of the deleterious effect of inactivity on the sedentary adult population has increased. Through the efforts of many disciplines, the public is beginning to realize that proper exercise can be a deterrent to many characteristics of premature physiological aging, as well as to their concomitant diseases.

Research and studies have resulted in new concepts about the type of physical fitness activities best suited for adults. Acquisition of motor skills in physical education could encourage participation in ongoing physical activity, which in itself assists in maintaining physical fitness and controlling weight. Continuity of well-planned activities can serve as a preventive conditioner.

A multidisciplinary approach has resulted from medicine's concern for premature cardiovascular disease and the positive effects of proper exercise. The physician, physical educator, exercise physiologist, sports nutritionist, and many other professionals are lending their skills to help solve the problem of lack of physical fitness among adults. With the implementation of many medically oriented adult physical education programs, there is an increased need for trained teachers of adapted physical education who understand the problems and needs of the adult population. Establishing individual physical education programs for adults is one of the greatest challenges of our time.

SPORT CONDITIONING

Opportunities for top-level competitive sports for persons with disabilities are increasing,[7] particularly in the area of physical disability.[39] Competition is designed to bring out the best qualities of performance of individuals with and without disabilities. Many competitions have been arranged for persons with disabilities at the local, state, national, and international levels. Athletes who are serious about competition strive to participate at the highest level. To qualify for participation at the upper levels of competition requires effective training and conditioning programs. The value of intensive conditioning has been demonstrated by the Manitoba Special Olympics Medallian Program, which will be described in Chapter 11, and

by the Paralympic performances of dedicated elite athletes with disabilities. In this section, we will examine sports conditioning components and procedures that maximize physical performance.

Match Program to Abilities, Needs, and Interests

Sports conditioning programs for persons with disabilities should be designed to match their abilities, needs, and interests. The challenge for designing effective sports conditioning programs is to select activities that promote general conditioning, as well as activities that maximize transfer to improved performance in competition. *General conditioning* refers to developing the prerequisite physical, motor, and perceptual factors that generalize across many sporting activities for many persons. *Specific conditioning* refers to developing the muscular strength and endurance and movements that are critical for success in the event of choice. Stopka reminds us that effective training involves attention to duration, intensity, and frequency.[51] She goes on to say, "We must train within, not beyond" our limitations.[51] The goal of conditioning is improvement in both overall and sport-specific strength, endurance, flexibility, power, and relaxation.

Year-Round Training Regime

Whereas the recreational athlete focuses on training in the weeks just prior to competition, the training regime followed by elite athletes is year-round. Typically, the first two or three months of the training year are dominated by laying a base for what is ahead. Early season goals include improved strength, endurance, flexibility, power, and aerobic capacity. The strength goals are aimed at muscle groups specific to the sport. Weight lifting and theraband or surgical tubing exercises are used that target the muscle groups used in the sport. For swimmers, exercises may emphasize development of the biceps, triceps, and latissimus dorsi muscle groups, as well as simulate the arm-pulling patterns in the types of strokes used in competition.[13] Runners

Figure 8-5   Variations in Resistance Exercise Programs

Result	Resistance	Frequency	Rest
Muscular endurance	Light loads (less than 70 percent of 1 maximum repetition)	12–20 reps × 3 sets	20–30 secs
Muscle definition	Moderate loads (70 to 80 percent of 1 maximum repetition)	8–12 reps × 3–6 sets	30–90 secs
Strength	Heavy loads (80 to 100 percent of 1 maximum repetition)	1–8 reps × 3–5 sets	3–5 mins

would focus on developing their quadriceps, hamstrings, gastrocs, and hip ab- and adductors, as well as abdominal strength. Sprinters would add explosive strength to give them an advantage when coming out of the blocks. Muscular and cardiovascular endurance activities should take place from five to seven times per week, with a focus on movements specific to the sport performance (e.g., stroke and turning techniques, lay-ups, wheelchair mobility). The types of activities that can be used to promote muscular endurance, muscle definition, and strength are presented in Figure 8-5.

The mid-year training regime usually lasts four months and involves more frequent and intense practices, with a focus on building a strong aerobic base as well as improving range of motion and upper body, limb, and abdominal strength. Interval training which involves mixing slow with faster exercises is built into each workout. For sports requiring explosive moves, plyometric training is freqently used. Plyometric exercises involve rapid stretching of a muscle, which is undergoing stress while lengthening, followed by a rapid contraction of that muscle. The rapid stretching of the muscle results in the storing of energy in the muscle, which will be used immediately when the muscle is contracted.[17] An example of a plyometric exercise appropriate for gymnasts, divers, and high jumpers is pike jumping. In pike jumping, the person starts in a standing position with the feet shoulder width apart. The action involves swinging the arms backward, then forward, and bending the knees while jumping vertically. Straighten the legs while in the air until they are parallel to the floor. Then move the legs to under the body for landing. The activity is immediately repeated. To reduce the potential for injury, coaches frequently have the athletes practice plyometric exercises in the water. For the plyometric training program to be effective, it should be specific to the activity the athlete competes in. Resistance training combined with plyometric training has shown to increase sports performance more than either resistance or plyometric training alone.[53]

The next few months prior to one month before competition is generally known as the in-season training program Focus is on maintaining fitness and refining performance skill. A constant effort should be made to improve the efficiency and accuracy of the movements involved in the competition. Overpracticing skills is recommended to reinforce the efficiency of the motor units involved in specific skills.

Workouts during the last few weeks prior to competition differ according to the sport. All sports require continual work on timing, concentration, and mental imagery. However, endurance sports require ongoing endurance training. Specific training regimes used by world-class elite athletes with disabilities appear in each article of *Palaestra*. Refer to those issues for more specific information about sports conditioning.   ❧

SUMMARY

Americans are underexercised. As a result, we are at high risk for developing a number of health problems, including obesity, hypertension, low back pain, osteoporosis, coronary heart disease, diabetes, colon cancer, anxiety and depression, and premature mortality. AAHPERD defines physical fitness as a physical state of well-being that allows people to perform daily activities with vigor, to reduce their risk of health problems related to lack of exercise, and to establish a fitness base for participation in a variety of activities. Physical educators have a unique and important role in encouraging active lifestyles for all individuals.

Because each person possesses a unique composition of physical and motor abilities, individual assessments should be used to determine the needs of each person. Activity programs should be constructed so that the physical and motor fitness tasks can be adapted to the ability level of each learner. Circuit training can be used to develop a wide range of performance levels. Fitness training should include both resistance training and aerobic activities. Programs of activity should include mode of activity, frequency of training, intensity of training,

duration of training, and resistance training. Although collectively persons with the same disability may be similar, each student with a disability needs to be in a program that benefits his or her unique needs.

Undernourished and obese students present a challenge to the physical educator. The physical educator must be sensitive to the environmental conditions that contribute to these students' eating problems. A carefully designed exercise program guided by an appropriate behavior-modification plan should be developed and implemented for each child with a weight problem.

Family interest and involvement in physical activity enhances the probability that a child will have a positive attitude toward and will participate in an active lifestyle. Teachers should reach out to the home to encourage the understanding of and participation in healthful activities.

Sports conditioning regimes can be used to improve the performance of athletes with disabilities. The serious elite competitor participates in year-round general and sport-specific conditioning programs designed to enhance strength, agility, endurance, flexibility, relaxation, and specific sport skills.

REVIEW QUESTIONS

1. What is a physically educated person?
2. What are the values of exercise for persons with disabilities?
3. How would one determine a unique physical fitness need for a specific functional skill?
4. Why do some people choose not to participate in regular physical activity?
5. What special challenges do students with eating problems present to the physical educator?
6. What are the critical components of general and sport-specific conditioning programs?

STUDENT ACTIVITIES

1. In small groups or individually, identify selected group activities that could be used in a regular physical education class that would be fun for the class and would address Maria Garcia's physical fitness deficiencies (see Chapter 2).
2. Working in small groups, with each group assigned a particular muscle group (e.g.,

abdominals, quadriceps, biceps), develop four levels of strengthening exercises (with, without, and against gravity and against gravity with resistance) for your assigned muscle group.
3. Construct a circuit training program that includes three levels of activities to promote shoulder girdle

strength, abdominal strength, quadricep endurance, and cardiovascular endurance.

4. Design and implement a weight-reduction program of exercise and diet that incorporates behavior-management principles.

5. Develop a general and specific sports conditioning program for a specific sport. Reference the activities included in the conditioning program from the literature.

REFERENCES

1. American Alliance for Health, Physical Education, Recreation and Dance, National Association for Sport and Physical Education, http://www.aahperd.org

2. American Association of Cardiovascular and Pulmonary Rehabilitation: *Guidelines for cardiac rehabilitation programs,* ed. 2, Champaign, IL, 1995, Human Kinetics.

3. American College of Sports Medicine: *Resource manual for guidelines for exercise testing and prescription,* ed. 3, Baltimore, MD, 1998, Williams and Wilkins.

4. Bar-Or O: Trainability of physical fitness measures, *Physician Sportsmed* 17:70–82, 1989.

5. Bar-Or O: Importance of differences between children and adults for exercise testing and exercise prescription. In Skinner JS, editor: *Exercise testing and exercise prescription for special cases,* Philadelphia, 1993, Lea & Febiger.

6. Bove AA, Sherman C: Active control of hypertension, *Physician and Sportsmed* 26:45–53, 1998.

7. Campbell E, Jones G: Precompetition anxiety and self-confidence in wheelchair sport participants, *Adapted Physical Education Quarterly* 14:95–107, 1997.

8. Carlucci D et al.: Exercise: not just for the healthy, *Physician Sportsmed* 19(7):47–54, 1991.

9. Coelho CW, Velloso CL, Brasil LO, Conceicao FL, Vaisman M, Arajo GS: Six-week home-based resistance training improves muscle power in adult patients with GH-deficiency, *Medicine and Science in Sports and Exercise,* Supplement 31:S268, 1998.

10. Cooper P: *Update on comprehensive school health programs in West Felciana Parish.* Paper presented at the Louisiana Association for Health, Physical Education, Recreation and Dance, New Orleans, LA, 1992.

11. Coyle CP, Santiago MC: Anaerobic exercise training and depressive symptomatology in adults with physical disabilities, *Arch Phys Med Rehabil* 76:647–652, 1995.

12. Dowzer CN, Reilly T, Cable NT: Maximal physiological responses to deep and shallow water running, *J of Sports Science* 16:514–515, 1998.

13. Dummer GM, Anderson NE: Focus on training, *Palaestra* 8:50–53, 1992.

14. Eichstaedt C et al.: Physical fitness and motor skill levels of individuals with mental retardation, Normal, IL, 1991, Illinois State University Printing Service.

15. Evans IM, Meyer L: *An educative approach to behavior problems,* Baltimore, MD, 1985, Paul H. Brookes.

16. Fleck SJ, Kraemer WJ: Resistance training: basic principles, *Physician Sportsmed* 16:160–171, 1988.

17. Haff GG: Explode with plyometrics, *Muscular Development* 36:92–98, 1999.

18. Hamdorf PA et al.: Physical training effects on the fitness and habitual activity patterns of elderly women, *Arch Phys Med Rehabil* 73:603–607, 1992.

19. Heath EM, Coleman KJ, Pope RP, Hernandez D, Alcala I, Jewell SL: Characterization of elementary physical education in a predominantly Mexican-American culture, *Medicine and Science in Sports and Exercise,* Supplement 31:S175, 1998.

20. Hearn MD et al.: Involving families in cardiovascular health promotion: the CATCH feasibility study, *J Sch Health* 23:22–31, 1992.

21. Huany Y, Macera CA, Blair SN, Rill NB, Kohl HW, Kroenenfeld JJ: Physical fitness, physical activity, and functional limitations in adults aged 40 and older, *Medicine and Science in Sports and Exercise* 31:1430–1435, 1998.

22. Humphrey JH: An overview of childhood fitness, Springfield, IL, 1991, Charles C Thomas.

23. Johnson CC et al.: CATCH: family process evaluation in a multicenter trial, *Health Educ Q* 2:S91–S106, 1994.

24. Katch FI, McArdle WS: *Nutrition, weight control and exercise,* ed 2, Philadelphia, 1983, Lea & Febiger.

25. Kauranen KJ, Siira PT, Vanharanta HV: A 10-week strength training program; effects on the motor performance of an unimpaired upper extremity, *Archives of Physical Medicine and Rehabilitation* 79:925–930, 1998.

26. Kraemer WJ, Fleck SJ: Resistance training: exercise prescription, *Physician Sportsmed* 16:69–81, 1988.

27. Kujala UM, Kaprio J, Sarna S, Koskenvuo M: Baseline leisure physical activity and future mortality in twins, *J of Sports Science* 16:508–509, 1998.

28. Lasko-McCarthey P, Knopf KG: Adapted physical education for adults with disabilities, ed. 3, Dubuque, IA, 1992, Eddie Bower.

29. Lee IM, Paffenbarger J, Hsieh E: Physical activity and the risk of developing colorectal cancer among college alumni, *J of the National Cancer Institute* 83:1324–1329, 1991.

30. Luukinen H, Koski K, Kavella SL: Predictors for recurrent falls among the home-dwelling elderly, *Scandinavian J of Primary Health Care* 13:294–299, 1995.

31. Maki BE, Holliday PJ, Topper AK: A prospective study of postural balance and risk of falling in an ambulatory independent elderly population, *J of Gerontology* 49:M42–M49, 1994.

32. McMurray RG, Ainsworth BE, Harrell JS, Griggs TR, Williams OD: Is physical activity or aerobic power more influential on reducing cardiovascular disease risk factors? *Medicine and Science in Sports and Exercise* 31:1521–1529, 1998.

33. Means KM, Rodell DE, Sullivan PS: Obstacle course performance and risk of falling in community-dwelling elderly persons, *Archives of Physical Medicine and Rehabilitation* 79:1570–1576, 1998.

34. Modell SJ, Cox TA: Fitness activities for children with severe profound disabilities, *Teaching Exceptional Children* January/February:24–29, 1999.

35. Moore GE, Durstine JL: Framework. In Durstine JL, editor: *Exercise management for persons with chronic diseases and disabilities,* Champaign, IL, 1997, Human Kinetics.

36. Myers J, Dziekan G, Goebbels U, Dubach P: Influence of high-intensity exercise training on the ventilatory response to exercise in patients with reduced ventricular function, *Medicine and Science in Sports and Exercise* 32:929–937, 1999.

37. Nacher S, Valenzuela J, Nogues J, Rodriguez FA: The effects of self-administered swimming and walking programmes on health and fitness in previously inactive adults, *J of Sports Science* 16:508–509, 1998.

38. Pagenoff SA: The use of aquatics with cerebral palsied adolescents, *Am J Occup Ther* 38:469–473, 1984.

39. Pensgaard AM, Roberts GC, Ursin H: Motivational factors and coping strategies of Norwegian Paralympic and Olympic winter athletes, *Adapted Physical Activity Quarterly* (APAQ) 16:238–250, 1999.

40. Payne WA, Hahn DB: *Understanding your health,* ed. 4, St. Louis, 1995, Mosby.

41. Pommering TL et al.: Effects of an aerobic program on community-based adults with mental retardation, *Ment Retard* 32:218–226, 1994.

42. President's Council on Physical Fitness and Sports: Adolescence: a "risk factor" for physical inactivity, *Research Digest* 3:1–8, 1999.

43. Ransdell LB, Wells C: Physical activity in urban white, African-American, and Mexican-American women, *Medicine and Science in Sports and Exercise* 31:1608–1617, 1998.

44. Raven PB, Welch-O'Conner RM, Shi X: Cardiovascular function following reduced aerobic activity, *Medicine and Science in Sports and Exercise* 31:1041–1052, 1998.

45. Raymond J, Davis GM, Climstein M, Sutton JR: Cardiorespiratory responses to arm cranking and electrical stimulation leg cycling in people with paraplegia, *Medicine and Science in Sport and Exercise* 32:822–828, 1999.

46. Rimmer JH: *Fitness and rehabilitation programs for special populations,* Madison, WI, 1994, Brown & Benchmark.

47. Sandstrom RM, Mokler PJ, Hoppe KM: Discharge destination and motor function outcome in severe

stroke as measured by the functional independence measure function-related group classification system, *Archives of Physical Medicine* 79:762–765, 1998.

48. Seaman JA, editor: Physical best and individuals with disabilities: a handbook for inclusion in fitness programs, Reston, VA, 1995, American Association for Active Lifestyles and Fitness.

49. Shepard RJ, Emter M, Finne M, Stalenheim G: A 3-year follow-up of asthmatic patients participating in a 10-week rehabilitation program with emphasis on physical training, *Archives of Physical Medicine and Rehabilitation* 79:539–544, 1998.

50. Shepard RJ: Do work-site exercise and health programs work? *The Physician and Sportsmedicine* 27:48–72, 1999.

51. Stopka C: Managing common injuries in individuals with disabilities; prevention comes first, *Palaestra* 12:28–31, 1996.

52. Trudeau F, Laurencelle L, Tremblay J, Rajic M, Shepard RJ: Daily primary school physical education: effects on physical activity during adult live, *Medicine and Science in Sports and Exercise* 32:111–117, 1999.

53. Waller MA, Piper TJ: Plyometric training for the personal trainer, *J of Strength and Conditioning* 21:9–14, 1999.

54. Winnick JP, Short FX: *The Brockport physical fitness test manual,* Champaign, IL, 1999, Human Kinetics.

55. Wiseman DC: *Physical education for exceptional students: theory to practice,* Albany, NY, 1994, Delmar.

56. Woolf-May K, Kearney EM, Jones DW, Davison RC, Coleman S, Bird SR: The effects of two different 18-week walking programmes on aerobic fitness, selected blood lipids and factor XIIa, *J of Sport Science* 16:701–719, 1998.

57. U.S. Department of Health and Human Services: *Physical activity and health: a report of the surgeon general,* Atlanta, GA, 1996, National Centers for Chronic Disease Control and Prevention.

58. U.S. Department of Health and Human Services: *Promoting lifelong physical activity,* Atlanta, GA, March 1997, National Centers for Chronic Disease Control and Prevention.

SUGGESTED READINGS

Dummer G: Sports Disabilities website from Michigan State University, http://ed.web3.educ.msu.edu/kin866/contents.htm

Durstine JL, editor: *Exercise management for persons with chronic diseases and disabilities,* Champaign, IL, 1997, Human Kinetics.

Rimmer JH: *Fitness and rehabilitation programs for special populations,* Dubuque, IA, 1994, William C. Brown.

RECOMMENDED WEBSITES

Please note: These websites are being recommended in the fall of 1999. Given the ever changing nature of the Internet, these sites may have moved or been replaced by the time you are reading this text.

ADA and Disability Information
http://www.public.iastate.edu/~sbilling/ada.html

Canadian Wheelchair Basketball Federation
http://www.cwba.ca

International Wheelchair Basketball Association
http://www.iwbf.org

Sports Disabilities
http://ed.web3.educ.msu.edu/kin866/contents.htm

United States Handcycling Federation
http://www.ushf.org/

United States Quad Rugby Association
http://www.quadrugby.com

Wilderness Inquiry Outdoor Adventures
http://www.wildernessinquiry.org/

RECOMMENDED VIDEOS

Insight Media
2162 Broadway
New York, NY 10024-0621
    Abilities taken for granted: the disabled
    16 minutes, purchase price $159
    color 1997
    Wheelchair athletes
    27 minutes, purchase price $225
    color, 1996

The Chariot Races: A Journey from Disabled to Enabled
27 minutes, purchase price $139
color, 1997
A Dream Comes True
13 minutes, purchase price $189
color, 1992

9

A Child Engaging in Solitary Play
Courtesy Callier Center for Communications
Disorders, Dallas, TX.

Children in Crisis: Psychosocial Delays

■ OBJECTIVES

Describe the nature of infant mortality in the United States.

Explain the impact of prenatal exposure to drugs on children with and without disabilities.

Describe the nature of abuse and neglect of children with and without disabilities.

Explain the relation of poverty and homelessness to inadequate psychosocial development in children with and without disabilities.

Describe some of the causes of violence in our society, and chronicle the significant growth of school violence.

List some of the signs/symptoms that a child or an adolescent may be a gang member or a gang member "wannabe."

Describe cooperative learning and the "New Games" approach to physical education.

Describe Don Hellison's physical education programs, and explain why they are effective.

Educators must respond to the increased psychosocial needs of the infants, children, and adolescents they serve. Children are living in a society that is plagued by hatred, violence, racism, ageism, classism, and homophobia. Children with and without disabilities are entering the public school system unprepared, understimulated, abused, abandoned, homeless, unloved, frightened, distrustful, tired, hungry, unkempt, angry, as members of gangs, as gang member "wannabe's," and distrustful of the public schools. The school, as a microcosm of the society, reflects and mirrors the larger society.

Children are exposed daily to inordinate and unnecessary violence on television. They spend more time watching television and playing video games than reading or interacting with family members.

Essentially, a child lucky enough to be born without an identifiable disability is entering a society in which the deck is literally "stacked" against the child. The society is taking children with the potential for normalcy and, perhaps, giftedness and destroying the potential (see Figure 9-1).

Any of the myriad of societal factors which will be addressed in this chapter, individually, may have a serious detrimental impact on the psychosocial development of children and may cause them to be at risk for failure in school and in the society in general. In combination, however, children with all these strikes against them struggle to function within the school and in society in general. Essentially, children who do not already have diagnosed disabilities are becoming virtually "disabled" by the tremendous forces that act on them and their families.

Children with disabilities may also demonstrate delayed psychosocial development. Factors that contribute to this delay will be discussed in this chapter. In addition, strategies for enhancing psychosocial development in and through participation in developmentally appropriate play, games, leisure/recreation, and sport in a well-designed physical education program will be considered.

Marian Wright Edelman, president of the Children's Defense Fund, wrote,

> Can our children save our nation's soul again? Can this nation—flush in wealth—confront itself and its hypocrisy between professed and practiced values, and make a commitment to *Leave no Child Behind?* How can we expect our children to believe us and in our ideals if we do not value them enough to provide them the healthy, fair, and safe start, and quality education in our public schools *every* child in any rich, compassionate, democratic society should be assured? ... Investing in and educating all American children is an urgent moral and practical imperative.
>
> Is it fair that poor children in the poorest neighborhoods have the poorest schools, the poorest prepared teachers, the poorest equipment, the poorest school buildings, libraries and laboratories, the fewest computers, counselors, school nurses and enrichment programs, and the lowest expectations by teachers and a public that blame them for achieving poorly on the tests for which we have not prepared them?[80]

Many special educators are exceptional, talented, and dedicated teachers. However, it is particularly frightening to note that children with disabilities, receiving special education services, may be the most likely to be taught by emergency-licensed teachers with no background in any type of education. Zahn and Schultze wrote, "A severe shortage in fully trained special education teachers has resulted in an increasing number of emergency-licensed teachers—who have the least amount of training—assigned to the most challenging students."[102]

The children who most need support and nourishment are the very children most in jeopardy. According to Karen Thomas,

> On playgrounds, in school hallways, on street corners, and in their homes, children in New York City and Washington, D.C. are fantasizing

Figure 9-1   How America Stands[80]

Among industrialized countries, the United States ranks	
1st	In military technology
1st	In defense expenditures
1st	In military exports
1st	In health technology
1st	In gross domestic product
1st	In the number of millionaires and billionaires
16th	In living standards among our poorest children
17th	In efforts to lift children out of poverty
17th	In low birth-weight rates
18th	In infant mortality
18th	In the gap between rich and poor children
21st	In eighth-grade math scores

Modified from Children's Defense Fund, 1999, Author.

about the day that their lives will abruptly end. They are picking colors for the satin of their coffins, instructing their parents what they would like to be buried in and describing details to make their funerals different from the others they have already witnessed. Kids are "playing" funeral.[86]

The physical educator, standing before a gymnasium full of sixty children, can assume that at least twenty of those children are at significant risk for school failure because of overwhelming poverty, homelessness, abuse, and inappropriate or nonexistent parenting. This is an overwhelming, humbling experience. It is even more overwhelming and more humbling when the physical educator knows and loves the children reflected in those statistics.

It is critical that physical educators be aware of the nature and extent of the problems that affect our children in society and in the schools. Figure 9-2

summarizes the perceptions of school principals regarding problems within the schools. The social malaise which appears to perpetuate hate, violence, and an ever growing difference between societal access of the "haves" and the "have-nots" creates an increasingly challenging venue for teachers who would like to make a difference in the lives of children, with and without disabilities, and their families. According to Cowley,

> Children have never had it easy. A fair proportion have always been beaten, starved, raped or abandoned, and until quite recently even the loved ones faced daunting obstacles. . . . Nearly one in four is born into poverty, a formidable predictor of lifelong ill health, and a growing number lack such basic advantages as a home, two parents, and regular access to a doctor. Every year thousands die violently from abuse or preventable accidents. Millions go unvaccinated against common childhood diseases. . . . American children remain the most neglected in the developed world.[13]

INFANT MORTALITY

The most obvious indication of the neglect that Cowley[9] describes is the fact that the United States ranks behind nineteen developed nations in its infant mortality rate. There is encouraging news, however:

Infant Mortality Rates
- 7.2 deaths per 1,000 live births in 1997
- 20 deaths per 1,000 live births in 1970[66]

Other data that give reason for hope include the fact that increasing numbers of pregnant women, 81.8 percent, are seeking prenatal care during the critical first trimester of pregnancy.[57] However, infant mortality continues to be a reflection of racial prejudice and issues tied directly to poverty. The gap remains frightening among infant mortality figures for Caucasian infants, African American infants, and Native American/Alaska Native infants. U.S. Surgeon General Dr. David Satcher noted that African American babies are more than twice as likely as white babies to die before their

Figure 9-2	Principals' Perceptions of Discipline Issues in Their Schools[67]

Most pressing issue
- Student tardiness
- Student absenteeism
- Physical conflicts among students
- Robbery or theft of items worth over $10
- Vandalism of school property
- Student alcohol use
- Student drug use
- Sale of drugs on school grounds
- Student tobacco use
- Student possession of weapons
- Trespassing
- Verbal abuse of teachers
- Physical abuse of teachers
- Teacher absenteeism
- Teacher alcohol or drug use
- Racial tensions
- Gangs

Modified from Principals' Perceptions of Discipline Issues in Their Schools, Violence & Discipline Problems in US Public Schools: 1996–97 http://nces.ed.gov/pubs98/violence/98030007.html

first birthday and that the stresses of racism—including environmental toxins, violence, discrimination, and other stress—may be to blame.[56] The Native American/Alaska Native infant mortality rate is 70 percent higher than the white infant mortality rate.

While infant mortality figures have improved, there has been a significant increase in the number of low-birth-weight and very low-birth-weight infants born in the United States. Farel and colleagues noted that "although most children with disabilities are born at term, children born prematurely contribute disproportionately to disabilities in childhood."[23] More and more preterm and low-birth-weight babies survive, in part, because of the increasingly sophisticated technology that allows for intensive prenatal and perinatal intervention. In fact, in neonatal centers characterized by aggressive neonatal and perinatal management, death rates as low as 21 percent have been seen in very premature or very low-birth-weight infants.[60] But the immature and incomplete in utero development of these children causes them to be at serious risk for developmental disabilities throughout their lives. These low-birth-weight infants who survive have high risks of deafness, blindness, mental retardation, and other disabilities. In addition, these infants will be at a serious disadvantage in every skill required for adequate, much less successful, performance in school.[23,63,83]

Also of concern is the number of infants who die each year as a result of injury. The major categories include drowning, fires/burns, intentional injury, and suffocation. Scholer et al.[71] have identified the characteristics of the mother which cause the infant to be ten times as likely to suffer from an injury-related death:

- The mother is less than twenty years old.
- The mother has less than a high school education, compared with a college education.
- The mother has more than two other children, compared with no other children.
- The mother is unmarried.
- The infant birth weight is less than 1,500 grams, compared with 2,500 grams.

CASE STUDY

Mark

Mark entered a public school at age five years. His aunt, his legal guardian, was very open with school personnel regarding his background. The aunt indicated her sister, Mark's mother, had used and abused just about every drug known during pregnancy. Mark was born addicted to crack/cocaine and, presumably to the other drugs that had affected his system in utero. He went to school with a violent, uncontrollable temper, no sense of cause-effect, and no apparent social conscience.

CRITICAL THINKING TASK

The prekindergarten- and kindergarten-age students all go to the gymnasium for physical education at the same time. Develop a list of specific tasks you want Mark's one-on-one aide to perform while he is in the gymnasium, so you are free to teach and the other children are safe.

ALCOHOL AND OTHER DRUG ABUSE

According to Greer,

> We are facing the emerging of what some are now calling a bio-underclass; a frightening proportion of the next generation of school children will have impairments which, in the words of Dr. Harold Nickens of the American Society of Addiction Medicine, may require the medical community to define an entirely new, organic brain syndrome based on the physical and chemical damage done to fetal brains by drug-abusing mothers.[29]

The escalation of the use and abuse of alcohol and other drugs has had a profound impact on the quality of life of millions of infants, children, and adolescents with and without disabilities. Between 11 and 15 percent of babies born in the United States today are exposed, in utero, to alcohol and illicit drugs. Over 1 million women in the United

Figure 9-3   Effects of in Utero Exposure to Alcohol (Fetal Alcohol Syndrome)[16,18,82,99]

Infancy	Early school years	Adolescence
Low birth weight	Gross motor deficit	Significant social deficit
Short stature	Fine motor deficit	Social withdrawal
Craniofacial defect	Attention deficit disorder	Difficulty with friendships
Cleft palate	Hyperactivity	Dependency
Lip palate	Delay in spoken language	Difficulty in group settings:
Small eye openings	Difficulty with verbal comprehension	School and work
Extra skin fold at eyes	Poor impulse control	Difficulty with attention
Low-set ears	Poor visual motor memory	
Receding chin	Difficulty with social skills	
CNS dysfunction	Aggressive behavior	
Abnormal reflexes		
Sleep disorder		
Tremors		
Hypertonia		
Hypotonia		
Heart defects		
Spinal defects		
Difficulty ignoring sensory stimuli		

States who use and abuse alcohol, nicotine, marijuana, cocaine, or other drugs and continue to abuse the drugs during pregnancy, give birth to babies with significant developmental delays.[18] Fetal alcohol exposure is now the nation's leading known cause of mental retardation, surpassing Down syndrome. The figures are staggering. Between 5,000 and 10,000 children are born with severe fetal alcohol syndrome each year. Figure 9-3 summarizes the effects of in utero exposure to alcohol on infants.

Tarr and Pyfer[84] did a comprehensive meta-analysis of fifty-six studies in the research literature that examined the impact of alcohol and other drugs on infants and young children. They found that the use and abuse of illicit substances, alcohol, or both by the mother does significantly affect the physical and motor development of neonates/infants exposed in utero (see Figure 9-4). The process of analyzing the data, however, was difficult because of difficulty differentiating between the effects of the drugs and the effects of other environmental factors, including poverty, hunger, a lack of or late prenatal medical intervention,

Figure 9-4   Motor and Physical Consequences for Infants Exposed to Drugs in Utero[84]

- Decreased birth weight
- Decreased birth length
- Decreased head circumference
- Decreased Apgar scores (measures of the neurological integrity of the infant) at 1 and at 5 minutes after birth
- Decreased gestational age (preterm birth)
- Increased irritability
- Increased tremors and convulsions
- Increased hypertonicity or hypotonicity
- Decreased Bayley Motor Development Index Scores on the Psychomotor Development Index at 6 months, 12 months, 18 months, and 24 months

inappropriate or absent parenting skills, homelessness, child abuse and neglect, community violence, and genetic variables. The researchers reported it was also difficult to separate the drug effects in the

Figure 9-5   Characteristics of Infants and Children Exposed Prenatally to Crack/Cocaine[28,69,92,96]

Infants	Young children	Adolescents
Poor body state regulation	Passivity	Continued difficulty with:
Tremors	Passivity in learning	Learning
Chronic irritability	Difficulty learning	Social skills
Poor visual orientation	Hyperactivity	
Small heads	Desperate need for structure	Pathological conscience
Missing bowels		Tendency toward
Malformed genitals	Inappropriate social behavior	aggression
	Tendency toward aggression	
Prone to strokes		
Prone to seizures	Lack of social conscience	Lack of social conscience
	Lying and stealing	
Difficult and serious		
withdrawal behavior	Speech and language delays	

research. Many of the mothers involved used or abused a combination of drugs, including alcohol, marijuana, heroin, methadone, cocaine, poly drugs, nicotine, and caffeine.

It is almost impossible to imagine the impact of this prenatal child abuse—women literally abusing their babies with alcohol, crack, heroin, PCP, and poly drugs when the infants are in utero. Figure 9-5 briefly describes the effects of the drugs on infants and children. The child protective service agencies, child welfare agencies, and foster care systems are being bombarded because of this abuse. Not only have these infants been abused during the prenatal experience, but often these infants are subsequently abandoned on the streets, in dumpsters and bathrooms, and in the hospitals. The women who give birth to these infants commonly continue to be drug abusers and often are unable to care for themselves, much less an infant.

Abandoned infants and children, without extended family willing to assume responsibility, generally are placed in the protective custody of the state. The first placement is generally in a foster care home. A study of the foster care system in New York revealed an escalated need and increased demand on the child protective service system. In 1980, 19 percent of the children placed in foster homes were under the age of five; in 1990, over 50 percent of the children placed in foster homes

An adolescent with mental retardation experiences the challenge of an "in-the-trees" ropes course.
Courtesy Wisconsin Lions Camp, Rosholt, Wis.

were under the age of five. This dramatic increase is directly attributable to crack abuse.[1]

It is frightening to note that the foster care system, meant to provide a web of protection for infants and children at risk, may actually compound and escalate the very abuse which caused the referral into the system. Over 500,000 children are currently placed within the foster care system in this country every year.[24] While the vast majority of foster parents and their families are attempting to provide a valuable and important service for infants and children in need, a critical number perpetuate the abuse the infants, toddlers, and children are trying to escape. And, unfortunately, the foster care system is a huge bureaucracy that devotes a vast amount of money to removing children from their homes to place them in alternative settings. A fraction of the money used to support foster care may be better used to support and nurture family health dynamics.

Abuse, disenfranchisement, and a lack of stability may be typical of the lives of children placed in the foster care system. The significant educational needs of children with disabilities may be more than a foster parent can manage. The care required to ensure that a foster child with a disability receives appropriate special education services is overwhelming (see Figure 9-6).

CASE STUDY

Anthony

Anthony is a four-year-old boy who lives with his mother in a shelter for women who are victims of domestic abuse. Lisa, Anthony's mother, finally left her husband after her husband physically abused Anthony as well. Anthony's mother, twenty-two years old, is seeking employment but struggling to secure care for Anthony while at work.

Anthony's mother is trying to get him admitted to a school near the shelter, but school officials have not been particularly helpful. Since the shelter is not a permanent address, school officials hesitate to invest a great deal of time in Anthony's enrollment. His enrollment status is further compromised by the fact that Anthony has been diagnosed by a physician as having ADD/ADHD. When Anthony takes his medication, he functions well within the shelter and in community settings. However, his mother finds it impossible to get to the community-based medical center, where she can receive free medication. As a result, his behavior is unpredictable, and, more often than not, he is in trouble at the shelter and difficult to manage in community settings.

Anthony needs an educational diagnostician's evaluation and perhaps a social worker's intake evaluation prior to admission to the public schools. He may be eligible for placement within a preschool program for children with disabilities classroom or a prekindergarten classroom.

CRITICAL THINKING TASK
As you read this chapter, consider the multiple factors which affect Anthony's potential for success in school. Describe a kindergarten physical education program that would meet Anthony's needs.

Figure 9-6 Inappropriate Special Education Services for Children with Disabilities Living in Foster Care[97]

- Failure to identify a child's disability in a particular area
- Failure to identify a child as eligible for special education services when a need exists
- Significant time line violations
- IEP violations, including inappropriate persons at IEP meeting, failure to implement services guaranteed on the IEP, and failure to have required info on the IEP
- Inappropriate programming
- Inadequate resources to address the child's needs
- Inappropriate job performance by teachers/aides because of lack of training
- Parent/foster parent advocacy problems
- Lack of coordination of services
- Lack of services because of dependent status within the court system
- Lack of services because of difficulties with transportation

POVERTY AND HOMELESSNESS

Dr. Lillian Parks, superintendent of the East St. Louis schools, said, "Gifted children are everywhere in East St. Louis, but their gifts are lost to poverty and turmoil and the damage done by knowing they are written off by their society."[49] A young child's risk for living in poverty appears to depend on three major factors:

1. Single parenthood. Single-parent families, headed by women, represent 34 percent of the homeless population.[5]
2. Low educational attainment of the parent
3. Part-time or no employment of the parent[101]

See Figure 9-7 for more information regarding children living in poverty.

In fact, 85 percent of children under the age of six are living in poverty if neither parent is employed and if neither has a high school diploma.[101] However, the demographics regarding poverty are changing. It is important to note that nearly two-thirds of all young children in poverty live in a family in which at least one parent is employed. Parents, struggling and working to make a life for their children, remain in poverty because of the nature of the employment available to them—minimum-wage and below-minimum-wage jobs. The significant gap between the rich and the poor continues to grow, and it appears that the gap between the extremely rich and the "middle class" is growing as well.

Victor Sidel, M.D., noted, "Hunger, even if there are no direct signs of malnutrition, can affect children's health, can affect their ability to learn."[44] Clearly, a child whose basic needs are not being met—and one of those needs is adequate and nutritious food—cannot be free to learn, to grow, and to move toward self-actualization. The primary concern of a child who is hungry is food, and this dominates thought.

Poverty may also be tied to substandard housing, if the family has housing. Significant dangers to children inherent in substandard housing include:

- Faulty wiring, which can lead to fires
- Overcrowding, which helps spread infectious disease
- Cockroach infestations, which can exacerbate allergies and asthma
- Rat infestations
- Chipped or flaking lead paint, which can cause lead poisoning[15]

Figure 9-7   Facts: Children Living in Poverty[68,101]

- The poverty rate for young children remains far higher than for any other age group in the society.
- In 1997, 5.2 million children were living in poverty.
- In 1997, 42 percent of American children under the age of 6 years were living in poverty or near poverty.
- Approximately 1 in 10 young children was extremely poor (10.4 percent in 1997).
- Almost 2.5 million young children lived in extreme poverty, a family of 4 living on less than $8,000 per year.
- In 1997, 40 percent of young children in poverty were African American.
- In 1997, 38 percent of young children in poverty were Hispanic. This rate is approximately 3 times as high as for young white children, at 13 percent.
- The single greatest increase in child poverty, in the past several years, occurred in the suburban areas. There was a 49.6 percent increase in young child poverty in the suburban areas, a 43.2 percent increase in the rural areas, and a 31.2 percent increase in urban areas.

Poverty and Access to Technology

Certainly not as critical, in terms of life and death, as many of the other issues tied to poverty and race, but nevertheless a very real problem associated with poverty, is the ever escalating gap between those who have the means to access the Internet and other technology-based information and those who do not. A 1997 U.S. Commerce Department study showed that whites are more than twice as likely to own computers as African

Americans or Hispanics and that whites are roughly three times as likely to have Internet access as African Americans and Hispanics. Larry Irving, an administrator of the National Telecommunications and Information Administration said, "There is a gap, it is widening and what should be done is not only a civil rights issue but a matter of public policy."[31] While it is difficult to determine if it is an issue related to poverty, race, or education, the result is the same. Individuals without access to Internet technology are being put at a significant disadvantage for acquiring information critical to living in a contemporary society that requires access to information.

Homelessness

The number of people who are homeless in this country is escalating dramatically:

The Increase and Changing Nature of Homelessness

> 1988   Five to six hundred thousand people were homeless in the United States.
>
> 1999   Over 2 million people were homeless in the United States.
>
> Seven hundred thousand people were homeless on any given night.[39]
>
> Forty percent of the homeless were families with children.[75]
>
> Twenty-five percent of the homeless were children under age eighteen.[87]

Several major factors appear to be related to the overwhelming increase in homelessness:

- An overwhelming increase in poverty[39]
- A growing shortage of safe, available, affordable housing
- A significant increase in alcohol and other drug abuse

See Figure 9-8 for more information regarding homeless children in the United States.

According to Bassuk,

> During critical, formative years, homeless children lack the basic resources needed for normal development. They undergo experi-

Figure 9-8   Homeless Children: America's New Outcasts[30,90]

Within a single year,

- Ninety-seven percent of homeless children move, many up to three times.
- Forty percent of homeless children change schools.
- Twenty percent of homeless school-age children don't attend school.
- Homeless children are twelve times more likely to end up in foster care.
- Homeless children have twice as many ear infections.
- Homeless children have six times as many speech/language problems.
- Homeless children are more likely to have chronic illnesses such as asthma, headaches, and eczema.
- Almost half of homeless children suffer from anxiety or depression.

ences resulting in medical, emotional, behavioral, and educational problems that may plague them forever.... Homeless shelter workers report that homeless children often suffer from depression and rage, and their aspirations/expectations are low. Homeless teenagers are particularly susceptible to the ravages of the streets—drug abuse, alcohol abuse, violence, gangs, pregnancy and juvenile crime. It is startling to note that the response of homeless children and adolescents to their situation has been compared to that of post-traumatic stress syndrome most typically associated with the effects of war.[5]

And Griffin writes, "Tonight, like any other, more than a million children will sleep in shelters, abandoned buildings, cars or public parks."[30] Homeless children experience more acute and chronic medical problems than do poor children who have homes. Health care workers find high incidences of diarrhea and malnourishment, as well as asthma and elevated blood levels of lead, in children who live in shelters.

Lack of consistent health care, inadequate nutrition, and inadequate rest cause significant health risks for the child who is homeless. The Children's Defense Fund, an active child advocate agency, has reported that children who are homeless are three times more likely to have missed immunizations than are poor children with apartments, trailers, or houses.[80]

Children who are homeless are at high risk not only for health problems but also for problems in psychosocial development. In addition to a chaotic family life, homeless children frequently also experience a loss of friends, a loss of familiar neighborhood surroundings, school disruptions, exposure to many strangers, and threatening situations on the streets and in the shelters.

These children's lives are in jeopardy. Of significant concern is the fact that, in the past, homeless children had difficulty gaining access to one of their fundamental rights—a free, public education. Those that make it to school are frightened, exhausted, hungry, and disenfranchised. The children feel unempowered and overwhelmed by the uncertainty of their lives. They are often embarrassed because they have difficulty getting access to showers and baths, as well as to washers/dryers, to keep them and their clothes clean. They are also embarrassed because they lack

the basic materials required for school—school supplies, etc. Children who are homeless are among those most at risk for delays in psychosocial development because they are denied the most basic of human rights—to be warm, protected, and safe. See Figure 9-9 for information about how the physical educator can help children who are homeless and poor within the school setting.

A federal law, the Stewart B. McKinney Homeless Assistance Act, enacted by Congress July 1987, and its amendments of 1990, mandates that all children, including homeless children, have a right to access a free, appropriate public education and that school residency laws may not be used to prevent homeless children from attending school[81] (see Figure 9-10). In the past, homeless children were often denied access to school because of a lack of address as a "legal and permanent resident" of a district, and/or because parents were unable to locate or provide health records. In addition, parents of homeless children may fail to register their child for school because of the seemingly impossible obstacles of providing transportation from shelters, abandoned cars, or empty buildings to school; of sending the child to school clean and

---

Figure 9-9   Strategies the Physical Educator Can Use to Help Homeless Students and Those Living in Poverty

- Provide healthy snacks as rewards and create situations where hungry students get the "rewards" often:
  - Fresh fruit
  - Fresh vegetables (Most supermarkets will gladly donate fruit and vegetables to teachers for use in the schools.)
  - Peanut butter crackers
  - Crackers and cheese
- If you bring your lunch to school, bring two and share it with a student who needs it. If you buy your lunch, buy an extra sandwich, piece of fruit, etc., and share it.
- Allow *supervised* locker room use by students needing to shower, shave, brush teeth, etc. Ask other faculty and PTA members
  - To save the "stuff" they find in their hotel/motel rooms—shampoo, soap, hand and body lotion.
  - To donate toothbrushes given them by their dentists and ask their dentists to donate toothpaste samples.
  - To donate the travel kits given them on international and long domestic flights.
- Be one of the faculty who volunteers to help wash and dry clothes.
- Keep a box of clean clothes, socks, and shoes that have been left in the gym for use by students who need them.
- Use school supplies as "rewards," and create situations in which the learners win and get the rewards.

Figure 9-10   The Stewart B. McKinney Homeless Assistance Act[81]

Teachers must help parents understand their rights:
- Parents do not need a permanent address to enroll a child in school.
- Parents have a choice of school placement. A child may remain at the same school he or she attended before becoming homeless or may enroll at the school serving the attendance area where he or she is receiving temporary shelter.
- A homeless child cannot be denied school enrollment just because school records or other enrollment documentation are not immediately available.
- The homeless child has the right to participate in all extracurricular activities and all federal, state, and local programs for which the child is eligible, including food programs, before- and after-school programs, vocational education, and Title I and other programs for gifted, talented, and disadvantaged learners.
- The child cannot be isolated or separated from the mainstream school environment solely due to homelessness.

Working with peer tutors often leads to forming friendships that extend beyond the class.
Photo by Carol Huettig.

in clean clothes; and of securing needed school supplies. In addition, the parents may be fearful that children will be reported by school authorities and taken away from them by social service agencies.

CASE STUDY

Tasha

Tasha gave birth to her baby during her senior year in high school. Tasha attended a special education center which served, primarily, students with severe and profound mental retardation. Tasha was reported to Child Protective Services for failing to care for her child, and her child was placed in a foster home at age two years. Tasha cries daily because she can't find her doll.

CRITICAL THINKING TASK

What role, if any, should a physical educator play in health and sex education in the school for students with severe and profound mental retardation?

PARENTAL INSTABILITY

One of the major issues in the psychosocial development of infants, young children, and adolescents, with and without disabilities, is the presence of a stable, caring, nurturing primary adult (parent) in their lives. Without the security of a stable, caring, and nurturing adult, children are not free to explore the world around them and, subsequently, are at significant risk for developmental delays.

While a slight majority of children still live in nuclear families, a rising number live with single parents, with other relatives, in foster homes, in institutions, in homeless shelters, or on the streets. A Census Bureau study found that 4,125,000 children are living in homes headed by grandparents. Of particular concern is the fact that single grandmothers who head households are at significant risk of being poor.[58] But those children would be even more in crisis had not these grandparents stepped up and assumed roles as caregivers for the children of their children.

One in every four children in this country lives in a single-parent household, and most of these single parents are women living in poverty. While single parents can be very effective parents, when the process is complicated by lack of money and a lack of education, parenting becomes a very difficult process.

Literally, babies are having babies. Often in hopes that they will now "have someone who loves me." These young teenagers, often incapable of caring for themselves, certainly lack the parenting skills necessary to raise a child, particularly if that process is made more difficult because of a lack of support from the father, poverty, insufficient education to seek and keep a good job, and lack of access to appropriate, affordable child care.

SCHOOL VIOLENCE AND THE GANG CULTURE

The schools are simply a microcosm of the greater society that is characterized by escalating violence and rage. Hatred, intolerance, bullying, racism, homophobia, and the real and noxious presence of gangs haunt this society. Increasingly, the schools are becoming places in which violence is common; in which hatred is evident; and in which gangs meet, conduct their "business," and recruit new members.

Children and adolescents are faced with violence on a daily basis. A bulletin board, made by a prekindergarten class in a core, inner-city

elementary school in Dallas, celebrated Martin Luther King's birthday. Each four-year-old child in the class was asked to complete the statement "I have a dream. . . ." Eighteen of the twenty-two children in the class responded with statements such as: "I have a dream . . . the shooting will stop"; "I have a dream . . . my momma won't get dead"; and "I have a dream . . . the guns will stop so I can sleep." These four-year-old children, and other victims like them, experience symptoms like those in posttraumatic stress disorder:

- Anxiety
- Heightened sense of hearing, smell, and sight
- Hypervigilance or "tuning out" the environment[95]

While these symptoms prepare the child for "fight or flight" reactions in stressful situations in the streets or in their homes, these reactions interfere significantly with learning in school. Unable to tune out the background, or tuning it out completely, makes it difficult for these children to learn.

School Violence

For the first time in its history, the American Academy of Pediatrics is advocating that violence prevention and the promotion of nonviolence be part of the education, clinical practice, and community activities of pediatricians. Pediatricians have acknowledged the fact that violence is a health issue

CASE STUDY

Clifford

Clifford is a five-year-old with severe asthma and significant learning disabilities. Clifford lives in a housing project in which violence is a routine part of his days, and particularly his nights. The Preschool Program for Children with Disabilities teacher who serves Clifford has simply made a safe haven for him to sleep during the day, because he can't sleep at night because of gun fire and sirens.

CRITICAL THINKING TASK
What could the physical educator do to help Clifford deal with his incredible stress?

CASE STUDY

Alicia

Alicia, a thirteen-year-old junior high student, was wounded by her former boyfriend in a school shooting. The bullet did so much damage that Alicia will probably walk with a walker the rest of her life.

CRITICAL THINKING TASK
Describe the role of the physical educator in assisting Alicia to recover from this school violence.

that may cause children who have been exposed to violence struggle with adult health problems, including substance abuse, depression, suicide attempts, high-risk sexual behaviors, obesity, and smoking.[3]

Warren Skaug, a pediatrician in Jonesboro, Arkansas, wrote regarding the school massacre on the afternoon of March 24, 1998:

Lesson 1: The Jonesboro school shooting and other individual acts of school violence are not random events. They are part of an epidemic of homicide, suicide, and firearm-related deaths that has grown to become the second greatest cause of death for youth in our country. It is not merely an urban, rural, or regional problem. All communities are at unacceptable risk.

Lesson 2: Although anger and frustration are universal, a wealth of research has shown that violence is a learned behavior—learned from witnessing or experiencing violence in the home, learned from television and other media.[77]

(See Figure 9-11.)

Rene Girard, a French scholar, has developed a theory regarding human violence. His theory of "scapegoating" suggests that humans lash out when they feel threatened or harmed. They exhibit a powerful, often unconscious, need to maintain order and unity among the groups with which they identify. This is consistent with the work of Dawn Perlmutter, who suggests that schoolyards are "sacred grounds" where popular students—notably, athletes and cheerleaders—are idolized.[76]

Increasingly, school violence appears to be tied to young, white men who feel disenfranchised and feel as if they are outcasts within the school society (see Figures 9-12 and 9-13). It appears that school

Figure 9-11 Cycle of Family Violence

The cycle of violence for children who grow up in abusive homes escalates. The Texas Council on Family Violence[20] has indicated that children who grow up in violent homes, as opposed to children who grow up in homes where violent behavior is not tolerated, are
- Six times more likely to commit suicide
- Twenty-four times more likely to commit sexual assault
- Fifty times more likely to abuse alcohol or drugs
- Seventy-four times more likely to commit crimes against other people
- Fifty-three percent more likely to be arrested as a juvenile
- Thirty-eight percent more likely to be arrested as an adult

Figure 9-12 Early Warning Signs That a Student Is at Risk for Committing School Violence[19]

The signs listed below are indications that there is reason for concern. However, viewed individually none of these is an indication the student will actually commit a violent act.
- Social withdrawal
- Excessive feelings of isolation and aloneness
- Excessive feelings of rejection
- Being a victim of violence
- Feelings of being teased, bullied, and picked-on
- Poor academic performance
- Little interest in school
- Expression of violence in writing, drawing, websites, or music
- Uncontrolled anger
- Constant hitting, intimidating, and bullying
- History of discipline problems
- History of violent/aggressive behavior
- Intolerance for difference and prejudices
- Drug and alcohol use
- Affiliation with gangs
- Inappropriate access to, possession of, and use of firearms
- Serious threats of violence

Signs that violent behavior is imminent
- Serious physical fighting with peers/family
- Severe destruction of property
- Severe rage for seemingly minor reasons
- Detailed threats of lethal violence
- Possession and/or use of firearms/weapons
- Self-injurious behavior/threats of suicide

Modified from Early Warning, http://www.air.org/cecp/guide/files/3.htm

Figure 9-13   Checklist of Characteristics of Youth Who Have Caused School-Associated Violent Deaths[72]

The following characteristics should alert school administrators, teachers, counselors, and parents that a student is troubled and may engage in violent behavior:

1. ___Has a history of tantrums and uncontrollable angry outbursts
2. ___Characteristically resorts to name calling, cursing, and abusive language
3. ___Habitually makes violent threats when angry
4. ___Has previously brought a weapon to school
5. ___Has a background of serious disciplinary problems at school and in the community
6. ___Has a background of drug, alcohol, or other substance abuse or dependency
7. ___Is on the fringe of his or her peer group with few or no close friends
8. ___Is preoccupied with weapons, explosives, or other incendiary devices
9. ___Has previously been truant, suspended, or expelled from school
10. ___Displays cruelty to animals
11. ___ Has little or no supervision and support from parents or a caring adult
12. ___Has witnessed or been a victim of abuse or neglect in the home
13. ___Has been bullied and/or bullies or intimidates peers or younger children
14. ___ Tends to blame others for difficulties and problems he or she causes him- or herself
15. ___Consistently prefers TV shows, movies, or music expressing violent themes, rituals, and abuse
16. ___Prefers reading materials dealing with violent themes, rituals, and abuse
17. ___Reflects anger, frustration, and the dark side of life in school essays or writing projects
18. ___Is involved with a gang or an antisocial group on the fringes of peer acceptance
19. ___Is often depressed and/or has significant mood swings
20. ___Has threatened or attempted suicide

Printed with permission from The National School Safety Center.

violence may be escalated, even caused, by situations that cause students to feel there is no justice and no fairness. Adams and Russakoff, writing for the *Washington Post* immediately following the slaughter at Columbine High School, Littleton, Colorado, said,

> Columbine may be no different from thousands of high schools in glorifying athletes.... Increasingly, as parents and students replay images of life at Columbine, they are freeze-framing on injustices suffered at the hands of athletes, wondering aloud why almost no one—not teachers, not administrators, not most students, not parents—took the problem seriously. No one thinks the high tolerance for athletic mischief explains away or excuses the two boys' horrific actions. But some parents and students believe a schoolwide indulgence of certain jocks—their criminal convictions, physical abuse, sexual and racial bullying—intensified the killers' feelings of powerlessness and galvanized their fantasies of revenge.

(See Figures 9-14 through 9-17.)

Gang Culture

Many children and adolescents in this society do not feel secure, loved, wanted, needed, or respected. The gang, as a sociological phenomenon, has always been present in cultures in which individual members of that culture feel unempowered and disenfranchised (see Figure 9-18).

In many ways, the gang replaces the family as the primary source of security. In addition, participation in a gang may provide the gang member with a sense of power and recognition that is missing in other relationships. *Gang* has been defined as a formal or an informal association of three or more persons who have a common name or identifying signs, color, or symbols and who individually or collectively engage in a pattern of criminal activity involving felony crimes and violent misdemeanor offenses.[26]

Figure 9-14   Violence in U.S. Schools, 1997–1999[89]

May 20, 1999
> A student opened fire at Heritage High School, near Conyers, Georgia, and injured six schoolmates.

April 20, 1999
> Two young men, students, wearing long black trench coats opened fire in a suburban high school in Littleton, Colorado. They injured twenty people. Fifteen people died, one teacher and fourteen students, including the two gunmen.

June 15, 1998
> A male teacher and a female guidance counselor were shot in a hallway in a Richmond, Virginia, high school.

May 21, 1998
> A fifteen-year-old student in Springfield, Oregon, opened fire in the school cafeteria and killed two students. The student's parents were later found dead in their home.

May 21, 1998
> A fifteen-year-old girl was shot and wounded in a suburban Houston high school when a gun in the backpack of a classmate went off in a biology class.

May 19, 1998
> An eighteen-year-old honor student killed a classmate who was dating his ex-girlfriend in the parking lot of a high school in Fayetteville, Tennessee.

April 24, 1998
> A forty-eight-year-old science teacher was shot to death in front of students at a graduation dance at James Parker Middle School in Edinboro, Pennsylvania.

March 24, 1998
> Four girls and a teacher were shot to death and ten others wounded during a false fire alarm at Westside Middle School in Jonesboro, Arkansas, when two boys, ages eleven and thirteen, opened fire from the woods.

December 1, 1997
> Three students were killed and five others wounded while participating in a prayer circle at Heath High School in West Paducah, Kentucky.

October 1, 1997
> A sixteen-year-old student in Pearl, Mississippi, shot nine students; two died.

February 19, 1997
> A sixteen-year-old student killed the principal and another student in Bethel, Alaska.

Modified from Violence in U.S. Schools, http://abcnews.go.com/sections/us/DailyNews/school shootings

The gang culture has a profound influence within the schools. Though only 10 percent of young people join gangs,[8] their presence in schools significantly increase the likelihood that students and teachers will be affected negatively by fear and violence (see Figure 9-19).

The very nature of the gang culture leads the children and adolescents in gangs into direct confrontation with law enforcement personnel. Graffiti is used to claim territory and to mark an area as that of the gang. Violence is typical. Gang members feel that any disrespect (being "dissed") is just cause for retaliation. Intimidation techniques include, but are not limited to, extorting lunch money, forcing others to pay "protection" money, beating others, raping others, participating in drive-by shootings, and committing murder. While gang presence has long been thought to be a vestige of the urban core of huge metropolitan areas, nothing could be further from the truth. In fact, gangs and gang activity are now common phenomenan in small, rural communities as well. Part of the reason

Figure 9-15   Centers for Disease Control and Prevention Facts About Violence in Schools[22]

- Of school-associated violent deaths, 65 percent were those of students.
- Of school-associated violent deaths, 11 percent were those of teachers or other staff members.
- Of school homicide or suicide victims, 83 percent were males.
- During the thirty days preceding the survey, 8.3 percent of high school students carried a weapon (e.g., gun or knife).
- During the thirty days preceding the survey, 5.9 percent of high school students carried a gun.
- During the twelve months preceding the survey, 7.4 percent of high school students were threatened or injured with a weapon on school property.
- During the twelve months preceding the survey, 14.8 percent of students had been in a physical fight on school property one or more times.
- Approximately one-third (32.9 percent) of students nationwide had property (car, clothing, or books) stolen or deliberately damaged on school property.

Modified from the Center for Disease Control's Youth Risk Behavior Survey, 1997.

Figure 9-16   School Violence: Methods of Death, 1992–1999[72]

Methods	Number
Beating/kicking	11
Hanging	1
Heart attack (from fright)	1
Jumping	1
Shooting	195
Stabbing/slashing	35
Strangling/asphyxiation	4
Unknown	3
Number of deaths as a result of school violence, 1992–1999	**251**

Figure 9-17   Locations of School Deaths, 1992–1999[72]

Location	Number
Athletic field	18
Restroom	10
School bus	15
Cafeteria	5
Classroom/office	22
Hallway	35
Library	7
Playground	2
Parking lot	29
	143
Near school	47
On campus	61
	108

CASE STUDY

Robert

Robert's grades have started to fall, and increasingly he is in trouble with his teachers. Though he has struggled for years with ADHD, he had been a good student. His parents are concerned that he no longer spends time with his family or his old friends. He quit the part-time job he had after school as a pizza deliverer but he seems to have money to spend. He has started to wear only black.

CRITICAL THINKING TASK
Robert used to be a member of the boys high school cross country team and ran the 3 mile event in track and field. How could the physical educator help get Robert re-aligned with a school team?

"wannabes." These children and adolescents who want to be part of a gang may actually be more dangerous than gang members themselves; the "wannabe" may be willing to participate in a violent ritual in order to prove worthy of gang membership. And the bottom line is that many children and adolescents in small, rural areas also do not feel

for this phenomenon is that gang members from large cities literally recruit members in smaller, rural areas, in order to expand membership.[25] In addition, there is a growing number of gang

Figure 9-18 Signs and Signals of Gang Involvement

- The child decreases the amount of communication he or she has with family members.[38]
- The child's personality changes abruptly.[38]
- The child has a new circle of friends and "hangs" with them; he or she doesn't bring these friends home.
- The child doesn't communicate any longer with old friends.
- The child begins wearing a particular color or style of clothing, excluding other clothes he or she used to wear.
- The child uses a walking gait that he or she didn't use before (e.g., the child struts).
- The child begins to use a language that includes slang the parent/teacher does not understand.
- The child's school work begins to suffer and grades fall.
- The child is truant more often.
- Clothing, posters, notebooks, diaries, etc., have graffiti-like symbols on them.[38]
- The child becomes confrontational with teachers and parents and may exhibit violent behavior.[38]
- The child ignores hobbies or other activities that used to be important in order to "hang" with his or her friends.
- The child has a tattoo or other distinctive mark on his or her skin, including self-inflicted scars from knives or rubbing erasers on the skin until it bleeds, picking the scab, and repeating the process until a scar exists.
- The child begins to carry weapons—pocket knives, sharpened screwdrivers, switchblades, and guns.

Figure 9-19 Nonfatal Teacher Victimization[62]

- In a 5-year period from 1992 to 1996, teachers were the victims of 1,581,000 nonfatal crimes at school.
- Teachers were the victims of serious violent crimes (rape or sexual assault, robbery, and aggravated assault) 18,000 times per year.
- Middle and junior high school teachers (59 crimes per 1,000 teachers) were more likely to be victimized than high school teachers (32 crimes per 1,000 teachers), who were more likely to be victims than elementary school teachers (17 crimes per 1,000).

Figure 9-20 Clearinghouse on Urban Education Intervention to Prevent Gang Presence in the Schools[8]

- Target students who are vulnerable to gang recruitment for mentoring, counseling, and conflict-resolution programs.
- Include moral and ethical education, values clarification, and conflict resolution within the curriculum.
- Create a learning environment in which each student feels valued.
- Provide in-service education for all faculty and staff regarding gangs.
- Offer parent education programs regarding gangs that is culturally sensitive and in a variety of languages to meet community needs.
- Carefully monitor youths who "hang out" near school property who are not enrolled.
- Provide opportunities for students to discuss gangs, their concerns, their fears, etc.

secure, loved, wanted, needed, or respected. A gang becomes a natural and viable place, in their minds, to find what they need (see Figure 9-20).

CHILD ABUSE AND NEGLECT

Child abuse and neglect are defined as physical or mental injury, sexual abuse, negligent treatment, or maltreatment of a child under eighteen years of age.[6] In 1997, over 3 million (3,195,000) children were reported for child abuse and neglect to Child Protective Service agencies in the United States.[93] The United States Department of Health and Human Services, Administration for Children and Families, reported almost 1 million (963,870) cases of substantiated child abuse and neglect in 1997.[88] It is frightening to note that these are the substantiated cases; child abuse and neglect are often unreported and may be very difficult to prove.

The U.S. Advisory Board on Child Abuse and Neglect,[1] completing a nationwide research project, found that fatal abuse and neglect is much more widespread than previously believed; at least 2,000 children are killed each year, and over 140,000 children are seriously injured due to neglect and abuse.

Over 700 children were killed, as a result of abuse and neglect, in Texas alone. But the data reflect the fact that most child abuse is an abuse of power. The most helpless—the youngest children—are the victims.

Between 1995 and 1997, 78 percent of the children who lost their lives as a result of abuse were younger than five years of age. Thirty-eight percent were under one year of age.[93]

Shaken baby syndrome has become epidemic in this country. Shaken baby syndrome accounts for 10 to 12 percent of deaths due to abuse and neglect in the United States.[73] A baby's brain, along with the blood vessels and other support tissues connecting the skull to the brain, are fragile and underdeveloped. If a baby is shaken, the brain rebounds around the skull, causing brain damage, which may result in mental retardation, speech and learning disabilities, paralysis, seizures, hearing loss, and even death. The diagnosis of shaken baby syndrome is based on the triad of subdural hematoma (bruising), cerebral edema (swelling), and retinal hemorrhage.[74] Theodore and Runyon wrote, "The problem of child abuse and neglect is different from most medical conditions because it is an entirely socially constructed problem. There is as yet no biological basis for the abuse and neglect that children suffer, and the social and environmental context of their upbringing are greater determinants of the outcome 'abused' or 'not abused.'"[85]

Violence does, indeed, breed violence. The student who is exposed to violence in the home cannot leave that violence, clearly a learned behavior, at home. The student who threatens other children and/or the teacher, the student who verbally or physically abuses other children and/or the teacher, or the child who abuses the class pet is one who has learned these behaviors. This child, often the student most difficult to teach, is the very student who most needs a constancy of support, love, and nurturing in the classroom.

Wang and Daro[93] noted the following types of abuse:

1. Physical abuse (22 percent). Physical abuse involves the physical battery of a child[6] (see Figure 9-21).

Figure 9-21   Indicators of Possible Physical Abuse the Physical Educator Should Know[4,10,40,43,46,54,100]

Affective disturbances
Low self-esteem
Hopelessness
Depression
Nonresponsiveness
Flat affect
Anxiety
Aggressive behavior
Posttraumatic stress disorder
Increased suicide risk
Substance abuse

Soft-tissue damage (most common site—buttocks, hips) Soft-tissue bruises, particularly multiple bruises
Bruise colors in different stages of healing
  • Days 1–2   Red/blue
  • Days 3–5   Blue/purple
  • Days 6–7   Green
  • Days 8–10   Yellow/brown

Burns
Burns in areas child could not reach
Burns shaped in patterns of objects used to inflict burn (curling item, steam iron, light bulb, immersion)

Head trauma
Cephalohematoma
Skull fracture
Intercranial soft-tissue damage

Joint dislocations, abdominal trauma, spiral fractures

---

2. Sexual abuse (5 percent). Sexual abuse includes oral-genital, genital-genital, genital-rectal, hand-genital, hand-rectal, or hand-breast contact. It includes showing pornography to a child or using a child in the production of pornography. Sexual intercourse includes vaginal, oral, or rectal penetration[10] (see Figure 9-22).

3. Neglect (54 percent). Neglect includes failure to meet a child's basic physical needs (e.g., food, clothing, shelter) and health needs (e.g., adequate medical intervention, regular physical

Figure 9-22   Indicators of Sexual Abuse the Physical Educator Should Know[10,21,40,43]

Clinical manifestations of sexual abuse

Pregnancy
Sexually transmitted disease
Vaginal, penile, or rectal injuries, lesions, or pain; redness of area or a discharge with or without bleeding
Soft-tissue injuries on/around the mouth and breasts
Pain and irritation during urination or defecation

Behaviors associated with sexual abuse

Seductive behavior
Activity of a sexual nature with peers, animals, or objects
Preoccupation with age-inappropriate sexuality
Prostitution

Affective disorders associated with sexual abuse

Deficit with age-appropriate play behaviors
Deficit in age-appropriate social skills
Fearfulness of adults
Sleep disorders
Regression
Aggression
Feelings of hopelessness and despair, suicide attempts
Self-mutilation
Poor school performance (especially if it had been good)
Eating disorders

Figure 9-23   Indicators of Neglect the Physical Educator Should Know

Failure to thrive
Below-average height for age
Underweight for age

Malnutrition
Poor physical fitness levels
Low energy levels
Complaints of hunger

Inappropriate clothing for weather (e.g., no socks in winter)

Figure 9-24   Indicators of Psychological Abuse the Physical Educator Should Know

Long-term psychological deprivation, the absence of appropriate nurturing, can have long-term effects on the mental, social, and emotional health of the child. The indicators of psychological abuse include[11,26,27,33]

Affective disturbances
Flat affect
Volatility, or "acting out" behaviors
Inability to maintain significant relationships
Inability to participate in age-appropriate play

Physical indicators
Failure to thrive
Malnutrition
Frequent illness

examinations, and needed inoculations against childhood disease)[26,27] (see Figure 9-23).

4. Emotional maltreatment (4 percent). Emotional abuse includes intentional verbal or behavioral acts that result in adverse emotional consequences. Emotional neglect occurs when a caregiver intentionally does not provide the nurturing verbal and behavioral actions that are needed for health development[10] (see Figure 9-24).

5. Other (12 percent). Behaviors included in this category are abandonment, medical and educational neglect, substance and alcohol abuse, and lack of supervision or bizarre discipline.

Wang and Daro[93] also identified the causes of child abuse and neglect. The three primary causes include (1) substance abuse; (2) poverty and economic strains, including inadequate housing and unemployment; and (3) lack of parenting skills. Other significant factors include a history of abuse, homelessness, and inadequate parental education.

Unfortunately, society perpetuates and allows the abuse of children. Child abuse and neglect must be considered within the context of the society. Child abuse is not usually "something" done to a child by a stranger. Child abusers are most often parents, siblings, other relatives, or people entrusted with the care of the child—babysitters, child-care workers, and youth group leaders, for example. One of the most tragic issues surrounding child abuse and neglect is that the abuser is almost always someone the child trusts and/or someone on whom the child is dependent.

Child abuse must be considered within the context of a society that endorses the notion that children are the property of the parent. The courts typically have supported the notion that the best possible place for a child to be raised is with the natural parents. The efforts of professionals involved in child protection are often thwarted by the interpretation of laws that continue to support the notion that the parents "own" their child and, subsequently, have the right to treat the child, the "property," as they see fit. Teachers who report suspected child abuse are often dismayed to learn that an abused child is returned to the home, the place where abuse occurs, after investigation.

The issue of child abuse must also be addressed in a society that endorses corporal punishment and assumes that parents have the right to spank, slap, and in other ways physically punish their children. If a woman hits another person's child on the street, that woman would be prosecuted for assault and battery. If that woman strikes her own child on the street, passersby are fearful to intervene. Corporal punishment as a technique for childrearing is still endorsed in some states and allowed by some school districts. It is based on the notion that suggests that to "spare the rod" is to "spoil the child." There are other, much better, strategies for dealing with children. The physical educator should, under no circumstance, participate in corporal punishment within the school setting.

Children with disabilities were 1.7 times as likely as other children to experience some form of abuse or maltreatment.[14]

Children with disabilities may be at greater risk of abuse and neglect than children who do not have disabilities.[17,45,51,98] Sobsey[78] found that more boys are physically abused and neglected, but more girls are sexually abused and that boys with disabilities are overrepresented in all categories of abuse. In fact, the very characteristics of some children with disabilities puts them in jeopardy. Children particularly at risk are those with mental retardation, behavior disorders, attention problems, difficulty maintaining reciprocal relationships, premature infants (particularly colicky and crying babies), and children with behavioral problems (see Figures 9-25, 9-26, and 9-27).

Children who are abused or neglected are at greater risk of becoming emotionally disturbed, language-impaired, mentally retarded, and/or physically disabled than are children who are not abused. In fact, adolescents who have been physically abused are much more likely to have difficulty with internalizing issues (depression, suicide, withdrawal, attentional problems) and externalizing issues (aggression, delinquent behavior, and aggressive behavior) than are adolescents who have not been abused.[47]

Children who are abused or neglected are also more likely to end up in trouble with the law; more than a third of the women in state prisons and jails say they were physically or sexually abused as children.[42] Having suffered from abusive behavior as a child not only tends to create a scenario in which abusive behavior continues, but, clearly, the abused individual seeks alcohol, marijuana, and other drugs to escape the feelings associated with the abuse.[32] Women who were sexually and physically abused as children suffer from stigmatization, feelings of betrayal and powerlessness, traumatic sexualization, and posttraumatic stress disorder.[7,12]

The impact of the cycle of abuse of our most precious resource, our children, has yet to be fully understood. It is infinitely clear, however, that our children must be protected.

Figure 9-25 Ways Children with Disabilities May Differ Psychosocially from Children Without Disabilities

- They may have difficulty with basic communication skills and, as such, lack ability to relate to others and respond appropriately.
- They may lack impulse control.
- They may have significant difficulty following directions and rules.
- They may have difficulty in age-appropriate social interactions with peers and teachers, particularly in a structured school environment.
- They may be verbally or physically aggressive toward self, peers, teachers, and parents.
- They may be totally passive in the social environment, avoiding interaction with others and exhibiting completely subservient behavior in any interaction with another.
- They may demonstrate no interest in play or the play environment.
- They may have difficulty taking turns and sharing equipment, particularly toys, balls, etc.
- They may have difficulty understanding social cues and, subsequently, respond inappropriately to others.
- They may exhibit difficulty processing and understanding gestures, facial expressions, and vocal inflections that are crucial to understanding the context of an interaction with another.
- They may exhibit "out-of-control" behaviors or temper tantrums, particularly in response to overstimulation or change in routine.
- They may exhibit developmental delays in play behaviors, basic to the social development of children.

Figure 9-26 Children with Disabilities and Their Susceptibility to Abuse

Children with disabilities may have one or more of the following characteristics, which make them more susceptible to child abuse and neglect than children without disabilities:[98]
- Need for expensive medical intervention/ therapy and the pressure that puts on the caregiver
- Inability to follow expected developmental patterns in motor, speech, social, and play skills
- Dependency on others to take care of basic daily living needs
- Dependency on others to take care of social/friendship needs
- Inability to take control of own life, which causes long-term need for caregiver
- Inability to effectively communicate needs and wants
- Inability to participate in reciprocal relationships
- Lack of knowledge about sex and misunderstanding of sexual advances
- Inability to differentiate between acceptable and nonacceptable touch
- Inability to defend self

TEACHING STRATEGIES FOR PHYSICAL EDUCATORS WORKING WITH CHILDREN WHO HAVE BEEN ABUSED

The physical educator is in a unique position to see the indications of child abuse. In addition, the physical educator is more likely than other school personnel to see children and adolescents who are not fully clothed. A child with legs badly bruised from being kicked may be able to hide them in the regular classroom but may have difficulty hiding the bruises if the required dress is shorts, for example. A child whose back has been beaten may be able to sit in a chair in the classroom by adjusting his or her posture; that child may find it impossible to lie on a mat to do a sit-up.

If a physical educator suspects abuse, he or she must report it. It is a felony to suspect child abuse or neglect and not report it.

Most school districts have policies that outline the steps the teacher should take to report it. Referrals are usually made to Child Protective Service agencies or the police through the school principal. However, if those responsible for reporting the suspected abuse do not do so, the teacher must take the responsibility to ensure that the child's rights are protected.

Figure 9-27   Characteristics of the Parents of Children with Disabilities That May Make The Parents More Prone to Abuse Their Children

The parents of children with developmental disabilities may be more prone to abuse their children because of the following:

- The parent's obligation to provide constant care
- Significant financial and time obligations and restraints
- The parent's guilt, denial, and frustration[98]
- The parent's lack of understanding regarding the developmental sequence of the learner with a developmental delay
- The tendency to compare the child's development with that of nondelayed children
- Failure to develop appropriate expectations regarding the child's behavior
- Frustration because of intervention, and perceived intrusion, by care providers, e.g., teachers, therapists, social workers, etc.
- Frustration because of the child's lack of reciprocal relationship capability
- Frustration due to the child's lack of ability to express needs and wants
- Feelings of helplessness
- Disputes between parents regarding care of the child with a disability
- Alcohol and drug abuse[98]
- The parents' own developmental delay
- The parents' own history of abuse

The physical education program should be adjusted to accommodate the abused child's physical, social, and motor needs. Children who can't keep up with their classmates because of underdevelopment, malnourishment, or behavioral problems must be able to learn in an environment in which it is possible for them to succeed. The preschool and elementary school programs should focus on the development of age-appropriate play behavior. The middle school and secondary physical education programs should be used to help these students develop self-responsibility.

Because the young child who has been abused may be delayed socially as well as physi-cally, placement in a physical education setting with younger children might allow the child to function best. That placement should never deviate more than two grades from the child's age-appropriate placement.

PSYCHOSOCIAL DEFICITS OF CHILDREN AND YOUTH WITH DISABILITIES

At-Risk Children and Youth with Disabilities

Students receiving special education services in the United States are disproportionately at-risk minority children. Kozol wrote:

> Nationwide, black children are three times as likely as white children to be placed in classes for the mentally retarded but only half as likely to be placed in classes for the gifted: a well-known statistic that should long since have aroused a sense of utter shame in our society.[49] (emphasis ours)

The U.S. Department of Education, in IDEA, noted,

> Greater efforts are needed to prevent the intensification of problems connected with mislabeling and high dropout rates among minority children with disabilities. More minority children continue to be served in special education than would be expected from the percentage of minority students in the general school population. Poor African American children are 2.3 times more likely to be identified by their teacher as mentally retarded than their white counterparts. Although African Americans represent 16 percent of elementary and secondary enrollments, they constitute 21 percent of total enrollments in special education. The drop out rate is 68 percent higher for minorities than for whites. More than 50% of minority students in large cities drop out of school.[41]

African American students were 2.4 times more likely to be identified as mildly mentally retarded and about 1.5 times as likely to be identified as seriously emotionally disturbed than their non-African American peers.[65] Oswald and associates wrote, "Minority children with disabilities who live in urban and high poverty environments are believed to be at particularly high risk for educational failure and poor outcomes because of inappropriate identification, placement and services."[65]

Children with disabilities face even more problems in society and in the schools than children without disabilities; this is particularly true of at-risk children, poor or homeless children, and abused children who happen to have disabilities. Their lives are more complex and more frightening because of an even more overwhelming sense of lack of power than that experienced by children facing only the disabilities.

Children and Youth with Disabilities

Children with disabilities may find it difficult to experience typical psychosocial development for a number of reasons. They may face rejection, overt or covert, by their parents, siblings, teachers, or peers. These rejections are generally borne of fear, guilt, pity, or the process of equating disability with illness.

The psychosocial development of children with disabilities may be seriously affected by the prejudice of others. In fact, the prejudice of others may predispose the child to have low self-esteem. Children with disabilities may be overprotected and, subsequently, prevented from developing age-appropriate play and interaction skills. Well-meaning parents and teachers may keep children with disabilities from participating in activities with their siblings and peers.

Individuals with disabilities generally experience more problems in individual and social development and adjustment than do their peers without disabilities. Some of the problems with psychosocial development are a function of the prejudice and expectations of others. Some of the problems may be a function of the behaviors of children without disabilities. Some disabilities cause, by their very nature, serious difficulties in social interaction skills. The autistic child or the child with childhood schizophrenia, for example, is deemed to be disabled primarily because of the difficulties the child experiences in interacting with other people.

PHYSICAL EDUCATION FOR AT-RISK CHILDREN AND YOUTH, INCLUDING THOSE WITH DISABILITIES

James Garbarino, the director of the Family Life Development Center at Cornell University, has noted that children are growing up in a world so "socially toxic" that all are at risk simply by being in the environment.[70] Garbarino has suggested that in a physically toxic environment the most affected are the most vulnerable. In a socially toxic environment, it's the same. The effects are seen first among children with disabilities, homeless children, and poor children.[70] The social toxins which affect children—violence, poverty, hunger, homelessness, inadequate parenting, abuse and neglect, drug abuse, racism, classism, ageism, and homophobia—seriously compromise quality of life. These multivaried psychosocial "pollutants" precipitate a delay in the psychosocial development of children. They are particularly devastating to infants and children in the critical early years of development. Indeed, the very foundation of all psychosocial development lies in the early years between birth and three years. In the first year of life, infants who are raised in a caring, nurturing environment in which their needs are met will learn to be trusting, loving, and caring children, adolescents, and adults.

In contrast, infants who are raised in an environment characterized by chaos, violence, abandonment, poverty, and parental inconsistency learn to be fearful, mistrustful, wary, anxious, impulsive, and stressed. Without effective parenting, particularly in the critical time from birth to three years, young children are unable to develop the basis for social behaviors—the conscience or an internal sense of right and wrong.[50] Wallach, one of the founders of the Erikson Institute, wrote,

> Development in the first five or six years should prepare children for successful school experiences. When they enter elementary school, they

are expected to have the social and cognitive skills that will make them good group members who are reasonably cooperative with adults. However, many children have not been prepared for this step. They do not come to school eager to learn and to put aside their immediate wants in order to be part of the group and win the teacher's approval. Rather, they arrive at school with all the internal stress and external fears that result from living with violence. Managing this stress takes all their energies, which are then not available for tasks such as learning to read and write or learning mathematics, history, or science[91] (as physical educators—this addition is critical).

Garbarino identified eight elements that children need in order to overcome the social toxicity in their environment.[70] It is crucial that physical educators honor these needs and ensure that their actions and programs meet these needs:

Children Need These to Overcome Social Toxicity

1. Stability
2. Security
3. Affirmation of worth
4. Time with teacher
5. Belief in ideology
6. Access to basic resources
7. Community
8. Justice[70]

These crucial needs of children can be met within the physical education setting. Each will be discussed in the following sections with specific strategies for meeting the child's psychosocial needs in the physical education environment.

Stability

The single most important variable in maintaining stability in the physical education environment is a professional educator able to exhibit consistent, calm, and nurturing behavior; there is no room for volatility when teaching children whose lives are in chaos.

- Class rules need to be posted, in clear view, and must remain consistent. They should be posted in the primary languages of the children whenever possible.
- Rules need to be written in specific, behavioral terms. For example, "Be good!" has little or no meaning to young children who have been raised in chaos, but "Listen when the teacher talks" gives the child the specific information he or she needs to follow directions.
- Class rules need to be written in positive terms, rather than in negative terms. For example, "Keep your hands and feet to yourself" conveys a much more positive message than "No hitting or kicking."
- There should be rewards for following the rules, as well as consequences for breaking the rules. Consequences for breaking the rules need to be provided as choices to help the children learn cause-effect and must be the same for every child, every time.

Sparks wrote, "All students, but especially at-risk students, must accept responsibility for the decisions they make. This is a learned process. At-risk students often refuse to acknowledge this responsibility by accepting very little ownership in a decision. They often look for excuses, blame someone else, or even society in general for a situation they do not like or cannot control."[79]

Security

The single most important variable in maintaining security in the physical education environment is a professional educator able to exhibit consistent, calm, and nurturing behavior; there is no room for volatility when teaching children whose lives are in chaos.

- The routine should be consistent from class to class.
- It must be clear to all children that verbal and physical abuse of others will not be tolerated (as made clear by the rules).
- Verbal or physical abuse of children is *never* a consequence of misbehavior. Even in districts and states in which corporal punishment is allowed, the physical educator must *never* allow

that to be part of the program. By its nature, it perpetuates the violence and chaos which has caused the children to be at risk in the first place.

Affirmation of Worth

- Know and use each child's name.
- Expect excellence from all your students.[64] O'Neil has suggested that having high standards for at-risk students is vital if they are to be successful and is crucial to their self-esteem.
- Always "catch 'em being good" and acknowledge that behavior.
- Praise often and well.
- The emphasis in the physical education setting, at all levels (elementary, middle school, junior high school, and high school) must be on cooperative, not competitive, experiences. At-risk children have difficulty experiencing success even in cooperative experiences. Competition causes some children to lose; these children simply don't need to lose any more than they already have.

Time with Teacher

- While it may be difficult for the physical educator to find time every day for each child, warm-up time, station time, and relaxation time offer excellent opportunities for interpersonal communication—a compliment, a question, or a pat-on-the-back (ask for permission to touch a child until you know he or she will be receptive to your touch) will be significant for the student.
- Use time with the teacher as a reward for good behavior. A student or a small group of students can be rewarded if you do something as simple as have lunch with them in the cafeteria, buy them a soft drink and talk for 5 minutes after school, or shoot baskets with them for 5 minutes during your lunch break.

Belief in Ideology

- The student must be given the opportunity to feel that his or her life matters and that there is

some sense in the "big picture." This is desperately hard for many children who have come to believe that their only option is prison or death. You can help with this process in a small but significant way.

- Give students specific responsibilities as part of the class experience. For example, most young children would almost kill, literally, to be line leader. Develop a system so that all children have the opportunity to assume responsibility and be rewarded for performing the given task.
- Load your gymnasium with pictures and posters that represent ethnic, cultural, gender, and ability diversity. Invite role models such as area athletes and professional or college or university athletes, including those with disabilities, to participate in your program as a guest speaker or mentor.

Access to Basic Resources

- Playground areas are often disregarded in school planning, particularly in urban, poor school districts. Organize a community/parent campaign to design and build a playground area.
- Use inexpensive and homemade equipment so that, when appropriate, each child has access to his or her own piece of equipment. (Many children have never had even a balloon to play with.)

Community

The focus in play, games, leisure/recreation, and sport must be based on the adoption of the philosophy espoused in the "New Games" movement.[59,61] In this philosophy, individuals have an opportunity to learn to move while learning cooperative, rather than competitive, behaviors. There is no winner and, subsequently, no loser in the New Games, or Cooperative Play, movement. For example, instead of trying to score a "kill" in a competitive volleyball game with only six people per side, a New Games volleyball game would include as

Children need to experience success when participating in age-appropriate activities.
Photo by Carol Huettig.

many people as want to play who work together to see how long they can keep the volleyball from hitting the ground.

- Use ethnic and culturally diverse music for warm-ups and rhythm/dance activities.
- Expand the curriculum to include ethnic and culturally diverse play, games, leisure/recreation, and sports.

Justice

Every child must be treated the same way as every other child, all the time, if children are to believe the physical educator to be just.

MODEL PHYSICAL EDUCATION AND RECREATION PROGRAMS FOR AT-RISK CHILDREN AND YOUTH

The physical educator is in a unique position to address some of the issues that plague at-risk children and youth, with and without disabilities. In fact, the physical educator can help children who have psychosocial delays by providing the opportunity to develop the social skills necessary to function within play, games, leisure/recreation, and sport. Many of the skills necessary to participate successfully in the physical education program are those necessary to participate successfully within the schools and within society at large. Sometimes, however, it is difficult to address the social skills of at-risk students because the skills necessary for their street survival are not the skills necessary to survive in "middle-class" society.

Hellison and his associates at the University of Illinois–Chicago Circle have developed a beautiful, innovative, model physical education and sports program for at-risk children and youth that honors their street skills and builds on those skills.[35] Hellison and his associates have based their program on the notion that the physical education class, or a team within a class, is a microcosm of the greater society and that children can learn to develop values and behaviors necessary to participate in play, games, leisure/recreation, and sport; those social skills are at the very foundation of an individual's ability to function within the society at large.[37] The intent of the program is to develop the child's self-responsibility and social responsibility:

> Self-responsibility is conceptualized as empowering at-risk youth to take more control of their own lives, to learn how to engage in self-development in the face of a variety of external forces, including socialization patterns, peer pressure, self-doubt, lack of concepts and skills, and limited vision of their own options. Social responsibility is conceptualized as the development of sensitivity to the rights, feelings, and needs of others. Indicators include movement beyond egocentrism and ethnocentrism,

The development of trust is often difficult for children.
Courtesy Wisconsin Lions Camp, Rosholt, Wis.

Figure 9-28   Hellison's Four-Level Model of Behavior/Value Development

Level 1: Sufficient self-control to respect the rights and feelings of others
Level 2: Participation and effort in program activities
Level 3: Self-direction with emphasis on independence and goal setting
Level 4: Caring about and helping others

Data from Hellison D: *J Phys Educ Rec Dance* 61:38–39, 1990.

tion. Indeed, many children and youth simply have not been taught the necessary skills for communicating basic needs, for negotiating, and for expressing emotions that are socially appropriate. The children's models have used verbal and physical aggression to communicate; young people simply mirror what they have learned and what they have seen. Specific strategies for modifying games to better meet students' needs are presented in Chapter 5.

Hellison and his associates have used student logs and diaries in which the student explains behavior and indicates his or her progress on skills at each of the four levels of social development.[34,36] The culmination of the acquisition of socially desirable behaviors includes the student's efforts to provide help, care, and support for others. Hellison and his colleagues provide the opportunity for children to learn the skills that are expected within the larger society, in a structured environment, which allow the children to self-test and grow.

Martinek and Hellison[52] have suggested that an effective way to foster resiliency, the ability to survive and thrive despite the circumstances, is an extended day program. They suggest that before-school, after-school, and evening programs provide an opportunity for at-risk children and youth to develop the social competence, autonomy, optimism, and hope required to succeed. Martinek and Hellison suggest that the extended

recognition of the rights and feelings of others, caring and compassion, service to others, and concern for the entire group's welfare.[35]

Hellison's programs have been based on the notion that children, even those who are most seriously at risk, can learn the social and emotional skills necessary to function in play, games, leisure/recreation, and sport and, perhaps more important, can generalize those skills to participation in the larger society. Hellison suggests a four-level model of behavior/value development for the physical education program (see Figure 9-28).[36]

At-risk children and youth are given the opportunity in Hellison's program to develop the fundamental skills necessary for human interac-

day program, if it is to be successful, must follow these guidelines:

1. Treat the children and youth as resources with potential, not as problems.
2. Focus on the whole child or youth—addressing emotional, social, educational, and economic needs.
3. Respect the individuality of the child or youth, including his or her cultural, developmental, and behavioral characteristics.
4. Encourage participation in the program by fostering active participation and allowing a decision-making voice in the program.
5. Ensure there are clear expectations and values associated with the program.
6. Help the child or youth envision and plan a future (other than death or prison).
7. Ensure a physically and psychologically *safe* environment.
8. Foster and nurture links with community leaders—ministers, business leaders, parents, and teachers.
9. Conquer the system obstacles.
10. Help ensure that the child or youth has regular contact with an adult who is a mentor.

Physical activity programs provide the most logical opportunity for the development of the skills required for resiliency: social competence, autonomy, and optimism. Martinek and Hellison have found that goal-setting skills, particularly significant in physical activity programs, are critical in the development of resiliency and autonomy. They note, however,

> Certain barriers must be negotiated before any kind of goal-setting can take place. These barriers are: (1) the school culture, (2) combative values, (3) dysfunctional home life, and (4) fear of making choices.[53]

Essentially, Martinek and Hellison, both with extensive experience working with at-risk youth, have found in their "club" system and extended school day programs that many at-risk youth are not able or willing to participate in traditional, school-based goal-setting experiences because they perceive the school culture as that of the "enemy"; they prefer fighting to problem solving; their models may have been abusive; and they may avoid making choices because it requires a commitment and accountability. Martinek and Hellison, writing to physical education professionals, said,

> You have to value this work, to have a passion for it. Without sufficient internal drive, we would have given up long ago. When we do workshops for teachers and youth workers, we always make the point: "You have to outlast them!" We refer not only to the children, who reflect the influences in the community, but also to all attempts to derail your efforts. We often say that our most important goal is to hang in there (white-knuckled) through thick and thin—all the rest "is details."[53]

Children participating in cooperative play.
Photo by Carol Huettig.

Children participating in parallel play.
Photo by Carol Huettig.

They suggest that, in club and extended day programs, it is vital that deeply committed professionals help create an alternative culture. Martinek and Hellison suggest it is vital "to respect the children—their culture, their struggles, their individuality, their voices (they 'know things' we don't but should), and their capacity for decision making."[53]

Miller, Bredemeier, and Shields have suggested that physical education may be the perfect discipline in which to provide socio-moral education. They wrote,

> Physical educators have equal opportunity to create competitive or cooperative environments in their physical education classes. In our program, we have changed the goal structure of many "traditional" competitive activities, such as basketball, baseball, ultimate Frisbee . . . through employing superordinate goals. Instead of head-to-head competition in ultimate Frisbee, for example, we challenged the entire group to make more successful passes in three minutes than they did the previous week. On another day, we implemented a team juggling exercise in which a group of 10 students tried to "juggle" 10 tennis balls at the same time by tossing the balls to each other in a pre-arranged pattern.[55]

These types of cooperative activities provide a perfect venue for the development of a moral community, in which learners empathize with one another.

HIERARCHY OF INCENTIVES FOR DEMONSTRATING SOCIALLY APPROPRIATE BEHAVIOR

There may be a hierarchy of incentives for demonstrating developmentally appropriate behavior in social situations. Children learn appropriate behavior, as their social conscience evolves, from models who are capable of demonstrating appropriate behavior in social situations. Children and adults without a strong social conscience, and without a perception of right and wrong, exhibit behavior in social situations based on incentives that may not be related to an inherent, gut-level sense of what behavior is appropriate. Kohlberg[48] suggests the sequence of psychosocial development shown in Figure 9-29. Social behavior in the child or adult without a well-defined morality may be based solely on avoidance of punishment; the more evolved child or adult may exhibit developmentally appropriate social behavior simply to maintain self-respect and self-esteem.

Figure 9-29   Kohlberg's Hierarchy of Psychosocial Development

1. Obey rules to avoid punishment.
   If there is no punishment, the rules will not be obeyed.
2. Conform to obtain rewards.
   If there are no rewards, there may be inappropriate social behavior.
3. Conform to obtain approval from others.
   If there is little recognition from the group, there is little incentive to maximize participation.
4. Conform to avoid censure by authority figures.
   If there is no authority censure, there is insufficient incentive to participate.
5. Conform to maintain the respect of the social community.
   If the social community cannot express respect, there is insufficient incentive to participate.
6. Conform to maintain self-respect and integrity.
   If there is little desire to be a person of integrity, there is less incentive to participate.

Data from Kohlberg L: The cognitive-development approach to moral education. In *Values, concepts, and techniques,* Washington, DC, 1971, National Education Association.

An understanding of Kohlberg's hierarchy is crucial for the physical educator. A child who is unloved, unwanted, uncared for, and in other ways neglected may not respond to the promise of a reward or punishment. If the child comes from a situation in which cause-effect has not been addressed fairly—specifically if the child is treated differently for exhibiting the same behaviors on two different occasions (e.g., "If Mom is sober, I can say 'hello,'" or "If Mom is drunk and I say 'hello,' she'll hit me")—the child comes to school either being unwilling to act or acting out. If the child is socially immature, and exhibits appropriate social behavior only to avoid punishment, the physical educator committed to the notion that corporal punishment is unethical, immoral, and counterproductive may be hard-pressed to develop a plan which provides a punishment which will be fair and consistent but still a deterrent. If the child demonstrates socially appropriate behavior only when that behavior is rewarded, the physical educator must give serious consideration to the nature of the reward. For example, if the child is hungry, earning a "smiley face" sticker may have little or no meaning; earning an apple may reward behavior and meet the child's basic need—food. The child who exhibits some social behaviors to obtain approval from peers can provide a challenge for the physical educator. Specifically, the child more interested in demonstrating social behaviors endorsed and supported by his or her gang—defiance, violence, and aggression—may create significant problems for the teacher.

One of the major problems in school settings today is that many children simply have little or no regard for authority figures—particularly if an authority figure represents a different culture or is perceived by the child to be part of the system that is abusive to the child. The physical educator must earn the respect, and subsequently authority, from his or her students by consistently attempting to create a learning environment that is caring and nurturing and meets the needs of the students. Obviously, it is hoped that children and adolescents will demonstrate appropriate social behavior in order to maintain the respect of the social community and to maintain self-respect and integrity. This is a difficult and long-term process that requires careful planning and thought.

Horseback riding develops Spencer's balance and confidence.
Courtesy of Roxanne and Randy Roberson, Spencer's Mom and Dad.

With just a little help and encouragement, a child realizes success.
Photo by Carol Huettig.

Figure 9-30   In the Two Hours It Took You to Read This Chapter. . .[80]

7,200	Public school students have been suspended.
800	High school students have dropped out of school.
800	Public school students have been corporally punished.
450	Children have been arrested.
288	Babies have been born to an unmarried mother.
194	Babies have been born to a mother who is not a high school graduate.
180	Babies have been born into poverty.
120	Babies have been born without health insurance.
120	Babies have been born to a teenage mother.
60	Babies have been born at low birth weight (less than 5 lbs 8 oz).
40	Babies have been born to a mother who had late or no prenatal care.
40	Children have been arrested for drug abuse.
20	Children have been arrested for a violent crime.
12	Babies have been born at very low birth weight (less than 3 lbs 4 oz).
7	Babies have died.
3	Children or youths under 20 have died from an accident.
1	Child or youth under 20 has been killed by a firearm.
1	Child or youth under 20 has been a homicide victim.

Every 4 hours a child or youth under 20 commits suicide.
Every 11 hours a young person under 25 dies from HIV infection.

Modifed from The Children's Defense Fund: Moments in America, for all children, Washington, DC. 1990.

PSYCHOLOGICAL GOALS AND OBJECTIVES ON THE IEP

Psychosocial goals and objectives are a crucial part of the IEP. The nature of a carefully developed physical education program that includes developmentally appropriate play, games, leisure/recreation, and sport gives the physical educator the opportunity to focus on the attainment of psychosocial goals and objectives. (See Chapter 3 for more information on IEP goals and objectives.)

John Hope Franklin, an African American scholar who wrote *From Slavery to Freedom: A History of African Americans,* speaking before the North Carolina Assembly, July 22, 1997, said,

It surely is not enough for the most powerful nation in the world to have an educational system that is impoverished not only in terms of its dilapidated physical facilities but also in terms of inequities along racial and class lines among schools and school districts. I hope that you will agree that it is not enough for us to move at a snail's pace in wiping out the remnants of racial and ethnic strife. In doing so, we merely add to the burdens we must bear in leading the world toward a lasting peace, devoid of the sentiments and enmities that have already brought on huge wars time and time again. We can do better than that, and I hope that you agree.[94]

(See Figure 9-30.)

SUMMARY

Children with and without disabilities in this society are at serious risk. Children are among the most ignored and neglected of our people. Children with and without disabilities are entering the public school system

unprepared, understimulated, abused, homeless, unloved, fearful, tired, hungry, and unkempt. All of these factors have an impact on the psychosocial development of children. In combination, the effect is devastating. At-risk individuals and individuals with disabilities sometimes demonstrate delayed psychosocial development. Factors that contribute to this delay include differences in appearance and behavior, overprotective environments, lack of opportunity to interact with others in play, and rejection by others. Psychosocial development can be promoted through participation in developmentally appropriate play, games, leisure/recreation, and sport in a well-designed physical education program. The physical education program must carefully address the student's needs, the student's play skills, and motivations for social interaction and must create a nourishing, nontoxic learning environment.

REVIEW QUESTIONS

1. Explain the relationship between maternal prenatal neglect and low-birth weight infants.

2. List some of the reasons that children with disabilities are more at risk for child abuse and neglect than other children.

3. Describe the impact of poverty and homelessness on infants, children, and their families.

4. Describe the turbulent nature of the schools in contemporary society.

5. Describe Hellison and Martinek's model physical education programs for at-risk children and youth.

6. Describe the nature of a New Game.

STUDENT ACTIVITIES

1. Work in groups of three to five students. Create New Games for use with children with psychosocial deficits.

2. Divide into six groups and develop an appropriate physical education program for each of the children/learners described in the case studies—Mark, Anthony, Tasha, Clifford, Alicia, and Robert.

3. Interview a physical education teacher working in the inner city. Interview a physical education teacher working in an affluent suburb. Compare and contrast their experiences. Ask specific questions regarding the out-of-school lives of their children.

4. Volunteer at a shelter for the homeless or at a shelter for abused women and children.

REFERENCES

1. *A nation's shame: fatal child abuse and neglect in the United States,* Washington, DC, 1995, Author. U.S. Advisory Board on Child Abuse and Neglect.

2. Adams L, Russakoff D: Game plan for disaster: Culture that permitted athletes to run amok may have contributed to tragedy at Columbine, *Dallas Morning News,* June 20, 1999.

3. *Advocating for children: the pediatrician's role in violence prevention,* Atlanta, GA, 1999, Author. American Academy of Pediatrics.

4. Allen DM, Tarnowski KJ: Depressive characteristics of physically abused children, *J Abnorm Child Psychol* 17:1–11, 1989.

5. Bassuk EL: Homeless families, *Sci Am* 265:66–72, 1991.

6. Beers MH, Berkow R, editors: *The Merck manual of diagnosis and therapy,* Whitehouse Station, NJ, 1999, Merck Research Laboratories.

7. Briggs L, Joyce P: What determines post-traumatic stress disorder symptomatology for survivors of childhood sexual abuse, *Child Abuse Negl* 21(6):575–582, 1997.

8. Burnett G, Walz G: *Gangs in schools,* Clearinghouse on Urban Education Digest, http://eric-web.tc.columbia.edu/digests/dig99.html

9. Checklist of Characteristics of Youth Who Have Caused School-Associated Violent Deaths. National School Safety Center, http://www.NSSC.org/reporter/checklist.htm

10. Child Abuse, http://www.childabuse.com

11. Claussen AH, Drittenden PM: Physical and psychological maltreatment: relations among types of maltreatment, *Child Abuse Neg* 14(5):5–18, 1991.

12. Coffey P, Leitenberg H, Henning K, Turner T, Bennet RT: Mediators of the long-term impact of child sexual abuse: perceived stigma, betrayal, powerlessness, and self-blame, *Child Abuse and Negl* 20(5):447–455, 1996.

13. Cowley G: Children in peril, *Newsweek Spec Issue* Summer 1991.

14. Cross SC, Kaye E, Ratnofsky AC: *A report on the maltreatment of children with disabilities,* Washington, DC, 1993, National Center on Child Abuse and Neglect.

15. Dangerous homes: substandard housing is a health risk for kids, *Dallas Morning News,* April 13, 1999.

16. D'Entremont D: *Intervention strategies for school age children,* report # (CG023529). University of Southern Maine. (ERIC Document Reproduction Service # ED 334514).

17. Diamond LJ, Jaudes PK: Child abuse in a cerebral-palsied population, *Dev Med Child Neurol* 1:12–18, 1987.

18. Dodge NN: *Effect of legal and illegal substances used by women during pregnancy.* Paper presented at "Understanding the Impact of Alcohol and Other Drugs on Young Children and Their Families," April 16–17, 1999, Region 20 Education Service Center, Richardson, TX.

19. Early Warning, Timely Response: A Guide to Safe Schools, http://www.air.org/cecp/guide/files/3.htm

20. Easley J: We are failing to protect our children, *Dallas Morning News,* March 16, 1995.

21. Elliott DJ, Tarnowski KJ: Depressive characteristics of sexually abused children, *Child Psychiatry Hum Dev* 21:37–47, 1989.

22. *Facts about violence among youth and violence,* Atlanta, GA. April 21, 1999, Author. Centers for Disease Control and Prevention.

23. Farel AM et al.: Very-low-birthweight infants at seven years: an assessment of the health and neurodevelopmental risk conveyed by chronic lung disease, *J Learn Dis* 31(2):118–126, 1998.

24. Foster Care. http://home.rica.net/rthoma/foster03.htm

25. *Gangs/recruiters find fertile turf beyond big city, Milwaukee Journal Sentinel,* June 18, 1995.

26. Garbarino J, Garbarino AC: *Emotional maltreatment of children,* Chicago, 1986, National Committee for Prevention of Child Abuse.

27. Garbarino J, Guttman E, Seely JW: *The psychologically battered child,* San Francisco, 1986, Jossey-Bass.

28. Green C: Infant mortality rate may rise: poverty, drug use, AIDS among factors cited in panel's report, *Dallas Morning News,* February 27, 1990.

29. Greer JV: The drug babies, *Except Child* February: 382–384, 1990.

30. Griffin L: Welfare cuts leaving more families homeless, study finds, *Dallas Morning News,* July 1, 1999.

31. Hadnot I: Digital divide: experts wonder how to close gap between whites and minorities in computer use, *Dallas Morning News,* June 27, 1999.

32. Harrison PA, Fulkerson JA, Beebe TJ: Multiple substance abuse among adolescent physical and sexual abuse victims, *Child Abuse Neg* 21(6):529–539, 1997.

33. Hart SN, Grassard MR: A major threat to children's mental health: psychosocial maltreatment, *Am Psychol* 42:160–165, 1987.

34. Hellison D: Making a difference—reflections on teaching urban at-risk youth, *J Phys Educ Rec Dance* 61:33–45, 1990.

35. Hellison D: Physical education for disadvantaged youth, *J Phys Educ Rec Dance* 61:37, 1990.

36. Hellison D: Teaching PE to at-risk youth in Chicago—a model, *J Phys Educ Rec Dance* 61:38–39, 1990.

37. Hellison D, Templin T: *A reflective approach to teaching physical education,* Champaign, IL, 1991, Human Kinetics.

38. Hillsborough County Street Gang Awareness, Hillsborough County Anti-Drug Alliance Multi Agency Gang Related Committee, Hillsborough County, Florida.

39. *How many people experience homelessness?* Fact Sheet #2. The National Coalition for the Homeless, February 1999, http://nch.ari.net/numbers.html

40. Huettig C, DiBrezzo R: *Factors in abuse and neglect of handicapped children.* Paper presented at American Alliance of Health, Physical Education, Recreation and Dance National Convention, Las Vegas, April 1987.

41. IDEA, P.L. 195-17; Section 601; U.S. Department of Education, 1995b.

42. Jailed women often abused as kids: study finds rate twice as high as in the general female population, *Dallas Morning News,* April 12, 1999.

43. Jason J: Child abuse or maltreatment. In Conn RB, editor: *Current diagnosis,* ed. 7, Philadelphia, 1985, WB Saunders.

44. Jasperse P: Four million U.S. kids "hungry," *Milwaukee Journal Sentinel,* July 20, 1995.

45. Jaudes PK, Diamond LJ: The handicapped child and child abuse, *Child Abuse Negl* 9:341–347, 1985.

46. Johnson CF: Inflicted injury versus accidental injury, *Pediatr Clin North Am* 37:791–814, 1990.

47. Kaplan S et al.: Physically abused adolescents: behavior problems, functional impairment, and comparison of informants' reports, *Pediatrics* 104(1):43–50, 1999.

48. Kohlberg L: The cognitive-development approach to moral education. In *Values, concepts, and techniques,* Washington, DC, 1971, National Education Association.

49. Kozol J: Savage inequalities: children in America's schools, New York, 1991, Crown.

50. Leroux C, Schreuder C: Crucial beginnings: a child's first few months can determine its future, *Dallas Morning News,* November 29, 1994.

51. Lifka BJ: Hiding beneath the stairwell—a dropout prevention program for Hispanic youth, *J Phys Educ Rec Dance* 61:40–41, 1990.

52. Martinek TJ, Hellison D: Fostering resiliency in underserved youth through physical activity, *Quest* 49:34–49, 1997.

53. Martinek T, Hellison D: Values and goal-setting with underserved youth, *J Phys Educ Rec Dance* 69(7):47–52, 1998.

54. McClelland CQ, Kingsbury GH: Fractures in the first year of life: a diagnostic dilemma, *Am J Dis Child* 136:26–29, 1982.

55. Miller SC, Bredemeier BJ, Sheilds DL: Sociomoral education through physical education with at-risk children, *Quest* 49(1):114–129, 1997.

56. *Minority health: racism linked to high infant mortality rate,* Kaiser Family Foundation Reproductive Health Report, March 22, 1999, http://report.kff.org/repro/db2/1999/03/kr990322.4.html

57. *Morbidity and mortality, weekly report,* Centers for Disease Control, 49(9):185–189, Atlanta, GA, March 12, 1999.

58. More children being raised by grandparents, Census Bureau finds, *Dallas Morning News,* July 1, 1999.

59. *More new games and playful ideas from the New Games Foundation,* Garden City, NY, 1981, Headlands Press.

60. Msall M et al.: Multivariate risks among extremely premature infants, *J Perinatology* 14(1):41–47, 1994.

61. *New games,* Garden City, NY, 1976, Headlands Press.

62. Nonfatal Teacher Victimization at School Teacher Reports. Indicators of School Crime and Safety, 1998, http://nces.ed.gov/pubs98/safety/teacher/html#attacked

63. Olsen P et al.: Psychological findings in preterm children related to neurologic status and magnetic resonance imaging, *Pediatrics* 102(2):329–336, 1998.

64. O'Neil J: Transforming the curriculum for students "at-risk," *Curr Update* pp. 1–3, 6, 1991.

65. Oswald DP et al.: Ethnic representation in special education: the influence of school-related economic and demographic variables, *J Spec Educ* 32(4):194–206, 1999.

66. Preventing Infant Mortality, Health and Human Services. http://www.keepinformed.com/HHS/PR/1997/09/970911e.html

67. Principals' Perceptions of Discipline Issues in Their Schools, Violence and Discipline Problems in U.S. Public Schools: 1996–97. http://nces.ed.gov/pubs98/violence/98030007.html

68. Rise in urban needy reported, *Dallas Morning News,* December 21, 1989.

69. Rotholz D et al.: A behavioral comparison of preschool children at high and low risk from prenatal cocaine exposure, *Ed and Treatment of Children* 18(1):1–18, 1995.

70. Rummler G: Children's world may be "socially toxic," *Dallas Morning News,* August 15, 1994.

71. Scholer SJ, Hickson GB, Ray WA: Sociodemographic factors identify U.S. infants at high risk of injury mortality, *Pediatrics* 103(6):1183–1188, 1999.

72. *School associated violent deaths,* The National School Safety Center's Report. www.nssc1.org

73. Shaken Baby Syndrome Fact Sheet. http://www.dphhs.mt.gov/quickfacs.shaken.htm

74. *Shaken baby syndrome,* The National Conference on Shaken Baby Syndrome. Keynote Addresses. Salt Lake City, UT, December 1996.

75. Shinn M, Weitzman B: Homeless families are different. Homeless in America, 1996. Washington, DC, 1996, National Coalition for the Homeless.

76. Sieder JJ: Scholars take look at anatomy of violent acts, *Dallas Morning News,* June 12, 1999.

77. Skaug WA: The Jonesboro school shootings: lessons for us all, *Am Acad Pediatrics* 1999.

78. Sobsey D, Randall W, Parrila RK: Gender differences in abused children with and without disabilities, *Child Abuse Negl* 21(8):707–720, 1997.

79. Sparks W: Promoting self-responsibility and decision making with at-risk students, *J Health Phys Educ Rec Dance* 64(2):74–78, 1993.

80. *State of America's children yearbook, 1999,* Washington, DC, 1999, Author. Children's Defense Fund.

81. Stewart B: McKinney Homeless Assistance Amendment Act, P.L. 100–645, 1990 U.S. Code Cong. & Ad. News (104 Stat.) 4673. (1990).

82. Streissguth A et al.: Fetal alcohol syndrome in adolescents and adults, *J Amer Med Assoc* 265:1961–1967, 1991.

83. Sykes DH: Behavioral adjustment in school of very low birthweight children, *J Child Psychol Psych* 38(3):315–322, 1997.

84. Tarr S, Pyfer J: Physical and psychomotor development of neonates/infants prenatally exposed to drugs: a meta-analysis, *Adapt Phys Act Q* 13(3):269–287, 1997.

85. Theodore AD, Runyon DK: A medical research agenda for child maltreatment: negotiating the next steps, *Pediatrics* 104(1):168–178, 1999.

86. Thomas K: This is sick: kids planning their funerals, *Dallas Morning News,* March 23, 1995.

87. U.S. Conference of Mayors: *A status report on hunger and homelessness in America's cities,* Washington, DC, 1998, Author.

88. U.S. Department of Health and Human Services, Administration for Children and Families. http://www.acf.dhhs.gov/news/stats/caperps.htm

89. Violence in U.S. Schools. http://abcnews.go.com/sections/us/DailyNews/schoolshootings

90. Vissing Y: *Out of sight, out of mind: homeless children and families in small town America,* Lexington, KY, 1996, University Press of Kentucky.

91. Wallach L: Children coping with violence: the role of the school, *Contemp Educ* 65(4):182–184, 1994.

92. Waller M: Crack babies grow up: what happens when drug-exposed children get older? *Am School Board J* 1994.

93. Wang CT, Daro D: *Current trends in child abuse reporting and fatalities: the results of the 1997 annual fifty state survey,* Chicago, IL, 1998, Prevent Child Abuse America.

94. Washington V, Andrews JD, editors: *Children of 2010,* Washington, DC, 1999, Author.

95. Wasserman J: Surviving the mean streets, *Dallas Morning News,* January 12, 1995.

96. Wehling D: The crack kids are coming, *Principal* May: 12–13, 1991.

97. Weinberg LA: Problems in educating abused and neglected children with disabilities, *Child Abuse Negl* 21(9):889–905, 1997.

98. Westcott H: The abuse of disabled children: a review of the literature, *Child Care Health Dev* 17:243–258, 1991.

99. Williams B, Howard V, McLaughlin T: Fetal alcohol syndrome: developmental characteristics and directions for future research, *Educ Treat Children* 17(1):86–97, 1994.

100. Wilson EF: Estimation of the age of cutaneous contusions in child abuse, *Pediatrics* 60:750–752, 1977.

101. *Young children in poverty: a statistical update: June 1999 edition.* National Center for Children in Poverty, The Joseph L. Mailman School of Public Health of Columbia University. New York.

102. Zahn M, Schultze S: Children with special needs often get teachers with little training, *Milwaukee Journal Sentinel*, May 24, 1998.

SUGGESTED READINGS

Fluegelman A, editor: *New Games book,* Garden City, NY, 1976, Headlands Press.

Hellison D, Templin T: *A reflective approach to teaching physical education,* Champaign, IL, 1991, Human Kinetics.

Kozol J: Amazing grace: *the lives of children and the conscience of a nation,* New York, 1996, Harper Perennial.

Kozol J: *Savage inequalities: children in America's schools,* New York, 1991, Crown.

Martinek T, Hellison D: Values and goal-setting with underserved youth, *J Phys Educ Rec Dance,* 69(7):47–52, 1998.

Project Effort: *Getting kids to try: manual for goal-setting with underserved populations,* Greensboro, NC, 1997, University of North Carolina at Greensboro.

The Children's Defense Fund: *The state of America's children yearbook,* Washington, DC, 1999, Author.

RECOMMENDED WEBSITES

Please be advised that these websites are being recommended in the summer and early fall of 1999. Though they are websites of organizations with consistent histories of information and service, the sites may not exist by the time you read this text.

National Center for Children in Poverty
http://cpmcnet.columbia.edu/dept/nccp/

National Coalition for the Homeless
http://nch.ari.net/numbers.html

Clearinghouse on Urban Education
http://eric-web.tc.columbia.edu/digests/dig99.html

Infant Mortality
http://www.keepinformed.com/HHS/PR/1997/09/970911e.html

Shaken Baby Syndrome
http://www.capcenter.org

The One Stop Internet Resource for Child Abuse Information
http://www.childabuse.com

RECOMMENDED VIDEOS

National School Safety Center
http://www.NSSC1.org/
School Crisis Under Control
Narrated by Edward James Olmos
25 minutes, purchase price $75.00

High Risk Youth at the Crossroads
Hosted by Lavar Burton
22 minutes, purchase price $50.00

Set Straight the Bullies
A "trigger film"
18 minutes, purchase price $75.00

What's Wrong With This Picture
Award—National Association of Government
Communications
18 minutes, purchase price $50.00

Total Marketing
http://www.totalmarketing.com
Kids in the Crossfire: Violence in America
Narrated by Peter Jennings

70 minutes, purchase price $24.98
Order No. 11242

T. Berry Brazelton: The Changing Family and
Its Implications
Hosted by T. Berry Brazelton
50 minutes, purchase price $34.98
Order No. 11687

Needs of Specific Populations

I n this part, specific types of disabilities and suggestions for intervention strategies are described. While we recognize that each person has unique qualities and needs, for ease of communication we have grouped similar conditions together. Each condition is defined, characteristics are given, means of testing are suggested, and specific programming and teaching techniques are detailed. The conditions addressed in each chapter have been reorganized to be consistent with the 1999 Amendments to IDEA. Expanded coverage has been given to categories of conditions that are increasing in incidence. These include pervasive developmental disorders, conduct disorders, speech impairments, traumatic brain injuries, and spinal cord injuries.

CHAPTER

10

Courtesy Dallas Independent School District.

Infants, Toddlers, and Preschoolers

■ OBJECTIVES

Explain the difference between IDEA mandates for early childhood intervention (ECI) birth to three years and preschool programs for children three to five years.

List and describe each of Howard Gardner's eight forms of intelligence and explain the implications for assessment and intervention.

Describe the infant-family interaction process.

Explain effective modeling techniques for parents who are trying to improve motor and play skills in their infant or toddler.

Describe developmentally appropriate practice in assessment and intervention in preschool learning environments, including preschool movement programs.

Discuss strategies for identifying a child's anger and helping the child deal with the anger.

Design an active learning center for indoor and outdoor play.

Describe strategies to develop an antibias active learning center.

Jacob

Hospital personnel advised Jacob's parents to contact an early childhood intervention agency before Jacob was scheduled to be released from the hospital several months after his birth. Jacob has been receiving significant medical intervention in neonatal intensive care. Jacob was born prematurely and has been struggling with the "failure to thrive" syndrome.

TASK

Explain the responsibilities of the early childhood intervention agency and then, eventually, the preschool program for children with disabilities in order to prepare Jacob for school success.

E arly and developmentally appropriate intervention during the crucial years in which central nervous system development is "plastic," marked, and pronounced has a profound impact on cognitive, language, social-emotional, and motor performance. Attention to these factors is important for all children; however, it is critical for children who are born at risk for failure to thrive and failure to develop along expected lines.

In this chapter we introduce the most recent theories of intellectual development, as well as the gross motor, cognitive, receptive and expressive language, symbolic play, drawing, fine motor, constructive play, self-help, and emotional characteristics of the typically developing child from birth through five years. Techniques for identifying the developmental level of young children and intervention strategies to facilitate their developmental processes are explained. In addition, federal mandates that address required services for at-risk infants, toddlers, and young children are discussed. The central role of the parents and other family members, including the extended family, in this process is emphasized. The characteristics and importance of developmentally appropriate learn-

ing environments designed to facilitate the primary learning tool of the young child—play—are highlighted.

THE POTENTIAL OF QUALITY EARLY INTERVENTION

The Zero-to-Three Organization advocates for early intervention for infants and toddlers at risk for developmental delays or who already have an identified disability. The organization reminds parents and early childhood educators that the first three years are characterized by amazing development:

> The first three years of life are a period of unparalleled growth in all areas of your baby's development. Recent research about how rapidly babies' brains grow and develop underscores the importance of the first three years for getting your baby off to a good start. While we know that the development of a young child's brain is a "work in progress" that takes years to complete, we also know that development in the early years is quite dramatic and can establish patterns for life-long learning.
>
> We now understand that . . . the human brain is not fully developed at birth. In fact, a newborn's brain is about 25% of its approximate adult weight. By age 3, it has grown dramatically by producing billions of cells (neurons and other brain cells) and hundreds of trillions of connections between these cells (synapses). Taken together, they form a complex control center for sensing the world and enabling the baby not only to see, hear, move, taste and touch but also to think, feel, and behave in particular ways. In other words, the baby's and young child's brain is vastly more active and complex than previously known. Neuroscientists are not only trying to learn more about the physical structure and functioning of the brain but are also beginning to focus their attention on the ways in which early nurturing experiences such as holding, feeding, and comforting impact the way a baby's brain develops.[76]

It is obvious that there is a significant window of opportunity in which a quality, family-based early intervention program can make a significant difference in the lives of a young child and, subsequently, his or her family and the greater community. The National Association for the Education of Young Children[54] describes the incredible results of the Abecedarian Study, released in October 1999 by researchers at the Frank Porter Graham Child Development Center. Specifically, the report demonstrates the long-lasting benefits for children enrolled in an experimental early education program. Of the 111 children studied, 57 children were continuously enrolled from infancy through age five years in a high-quality early childhood program. The program specifically addressed the variables that have been identified as critical in quality early childhood education. Specifically, the program components included

- Good adult–child ratios
- Ongoing professional development
- Staff salaries commensurate with that of teachers in the public schools
- An individualized curriculum that focused on learning games

The other 54 children constituted the control group and did not receive services.

Researchers conducted a longitudinal study that followed children who participated in the program and those in the control group until age twenty-one years. Their findings go beyond demonstrating school readiness and success to identifying positive educational and social outcomes during young adulthood; there were significant differences in individual abilities and achievements. At age twenty-one, those who received quality early intervention were more likely to

- Score higher on tests of intelligence (intelligence quotient)
- Score higher on reading and math tests
- Be enrolled in or graduate from a four-year college
- Delay parenthood
- Be gainfully employed

Researchers suggest the project is a model for early childhood education that could be replicated for approximately $11,000 per year per child. While the investment is significant, communities that commit to high-quality education beginning from infancy can expect lower costs associated with:

- Low academic achievement[54]
- Special education[54]
- Teen pregnancy[54]
- Unemployment
- Juvenile detention and adult incarceration

THE EIGHT TYPES OF INTELLIGENCE—THE PHILOSOPHICAL FOUNDATION OF EFFECTIVE AND APPROPRIATE EARLY INTERVENTION

Huettig, Zittel, and Goodway[34] discussed issues related to social validity and the education of preschoolers, particularly the physical education of at-risk preschoolers and those with developmental delays or disabilities. They identified the issues that must be addressed if, indeed, physical education for preschoolers with disabilities is to be socially valid. The questions that must be asked include, but are not limited to

- Do the annual goals and specific objectives (benchmarks) established for preschoolers make sense? Will it make a real difference in the child's life if the child acquires/achieves the goals/benchmarks?
- Are the goals and objectives consistent with family priorities?
- Does the program make sense to the parent?
- Is the parent satisfied with the program?
- Does the parent share common goals with the teacher?
- Do the goals and objective reflect society's (school and community) goals for preschoolers?
- Is the child happy when engaged in the performance of activities tied to the goals and objectives?
- Would the child choose the activities if offered as a choice?
- Does the child ask to "do it again"?[34]

A socially valid physical education program for preschoolers at risk, with developmental delays or disabilities is based on the premise that professionals, parents, and other family members acknowledge, recognize, accept, and embrace the notion that there are eight types of intelligence.

Howard Gardner,[22] in his classic work *Frames of Mind: The Theory of Multiple Intelligences,* suggests that, if educators are to conceptualize cognition, it must be considered in a far broader realm than that typically used to identify or quantify an individual's ability to think and learn. Specifically, Gardner suggests that those instruments used typically to assess and evaluate intelligence tend to ignore many types of human intelligence in lieu of measuring those that are easiest to measure—namely, linguistic and mathematical abilities.

Gardner's theory of multiple intelligence has been widely embraced by enlightened educational communities. His theory continues to be ignored by those satisfied with the status quo.

Gardner defines intelligence as the ability to solve problems or create products valued within one or more cultural settings. His emphasis on multicultural settings is of particular value in consideration of the philosophy. His work has gained recognition as educators seek to explore and define strategies to evaluate the intelligence of children representing a wide variety of cultures and as they seek educational intervention strategies that meet their diverse needs.

Widely used norm-referenced linguistic and mathematically based "intelligence tests" have widespread cultural, racial, socioeconomic, and gender biases. Historically, these tests have been used to include and exclude children from learning environments and experiences. The tracking of black and poor children, which provided the impetus for *Brown v. Board of Education* (Kansas), 1954, is a practice that, unfortunately, still exists. If Gardner's theory of multiple intelligences were widely embraced and practiced, educational assessment would more appropriately and equitably evaluate the performance and potential performance of all children. And, as important, educational intervention would be more appropriate and equitable,

and more children would love school and want to stay in school to learn. Movement and play programs would be embraced as a vital and integral part of the total education process. Movement and play would be recognized for its significant potential in the lives of young children.

Each of Gardner's theorized intelligences is considered here with examples of the behaviors of infants, toddlers, and young children that reflect these intelligences.[22]

Linguistic Intelligence

Linguistic intelligence is expressed in and through the use of oral language (receptive and expressive) and the use of written language (reading and writing). It represents a sensitivity to and interest in the use of words, the sound and rhythm of words, and the functions of language—to express wants and needs, to convince, to share, and to explain. The young child demonstrates this intelligence by

    Cooing and babbling
    Scribbling and drawing
    Asking questions
    Repeating nonsense rhymes
    Telling stories
    Listening to stories
    Identifying simple words or signs
    Rote counting

Logical-Mathematical Intelligence

Logical-mathematical intelligence reflects an individual's ability to group and sequence objects, to order and reorder them, to describe their quality and quantity, and to see and understand patterns. The young child demonstrates this intelligence by

    Separating dinosaurs from zoo animals
    Stacking rings, diminishing in size, on a base
    Collecting sticks and separating the long ones from the short ones
    Sequencing blocks in patterns, such as three blue, two red, three blue
    Arranging balls from the largest to the smallest

Musical Intelligence

Musical intelligence reflects an individual's ability to recognize sounds and distinguish one from another, identify and see patterns in music, be sensitive to rhythm and time variables, know and appreciate timbre and tone, and express feelings and emotions through music. The young child demonstrates this intelligence by

> Seeking one "favorite" musical instrument
>
> Moving the body to a beat
>
> Using pots and pans as drums
>
> Turning off the tape recorder if he or she does not like the music
>
> Asking to sing a favorite song, over and over
>
> Clapping or toe tapping to a particular rhythm or beat
>
> Singing or humming
>
> "Rapping" a favorite song

Spatial Intelligence

Spatial intelligence includes the ability to identify shapes and differentiate between objects in terms of size, to see commonalities in shape or size, to perceive the visual world accurately, to perform simple transformations of visual images, and to recreate a graphic image of a visual representation, such as maps or graphs. The young child demonstrates this intelligence by

> Putting puzzles together
>
> Building a block structure
>
> Building a "Lego" bridge
>
> Drawing self
>
> Sorting objects by shape and size
>
> Copying a given figure
>
> Drawing a particular shape in a variety of positions[20]
>
> Identifying a child who is larger or smaller than self
>
> Identifying a child who is taller or shorter than self

Bodily-Kinesthetic Intelligence

Bodily-kinesthetic intelligence is characterized by the ability to use the body in highly differentiated and skilled ways, for expressive and goal-directed purposes. The young child demonstrates this intelligence by

> Crawling, creeping, and walking in, around, and between objects
>
> Using gestures to express needs and wants
>
> Using facial expressions to convey emotions
>
> Reaching to get a favorite toy
>
> Rolling over
>
> Hurling a ball
>
> Catching a rolled ball
>
> Jumping over a set of blocks, arranged in an ever taller sequence
>
> Kicking a ball
>
> Using the body to pretend to be "mad," "sad," or "glad"
>
> Carrying a toy from the toy box to the play area

Interpersonal Intelligence

Interpersonal intelligence is one in which an individual can identify and empathize with the feelings and emotions of others. The young child demonstrates this intelligence by

> Crying if another child cries
>
> Telling a parent or other caregiver if a friend is hurt or sad
>
> Comforting a friend who is upset
>
> Noticing that the parent or caregiver is having a "bad day"
>
> Engaging in cooperative play

Intrapersonal Intelligence

Intrapersonal intelligence is one in which the individual is able to identify his or her own feelings, emotions, and motives and is basically inner-directed (i.e., internally driven). The young child demonstrates this intelligence by

Seeking solitary play experiences

Judging his or her own art project

Keeping a journal of pictures, drawings, or symbols that reflect feelings

Expressing emotion in housekeeping play experiences

Preferring an independent plan-do-review process to a group process

Naturalistic Intelligence

In later works, Gardner identified yet another form of intelligence. At first, he suggested that it might be a "spiritual" intelligence. In more recent works he has called it "naturalist" intelligence. In fact, it appears that the eighth intelligence is probably a combination of "spirituality" and a profound sense of "nature." Gardner suggested that:

> The intelligence of the naturalist involves the ability to recognize important distinctions in the natural world (among flora, fauna). It can also be applied to man-made objects in our consumer society (cars, sneakers, etc.). Obviously, this skill is crucial in hunting or farming cultures, and it is at a premium among biologists and others who work with nature in our own society.[30]

The young child demonstrates this intelligence by

Identifying flowers with similar petals

Collecting leaves and sorting them

Preferring to be outside to being inside

Taking loving care of the class pet

Perhaps only when educators, lawmakers, voters, school board members, and state education agency personnel acknowledge that there are at least eight different types of intelligence; that, in order to thrive and grow, our society needs individuals with each of these types of intelligence; and that the educational system must nurture each child representing every culture, race, socioeconomic status, and gender will the educational system truly meet the needs of all its constituents—all its constituents.

DEVELOPMENTALLY APPROPRIATE ASSESSMENT OF INFANTS, TODDLERS, AND PRESCHOOLERS

While the move toward assessment that acknowledges multiple forms of intelligence has been embraced by some educators, there is a desperate need for assessment that is sensitive to the unique needs of infants, toddlers, and young children (i.e., developmentally appropriate practice). This is critical because assessment drives eligibility. Eligibility drives decisions regarding goals and objectives on the IEP and individual family service plan. Goals and objectives drive placement and programming decisions.

In this section, we address developmentally appropriate assessment of movement and play for infants, toddlers, and young children, with an emphasis on play-based, transdisciplinary assessment practices and the development of a movement/play portfolio assessment process to follow the child from infancy through adulthood.

Shepard[65] has suggested three basic principles to guide assessment of young children:

1. Only testing that can be shown to lead to beneficial results should take place.
2. Assessment methods, particularly the language used, must be appropriate to the development and experiences of the children being tested.
3. Assessment features, including content, form, evidence of validity, and standards for interpretation, must be tailored to the specific purpose of the assessment.

Before the passage of P.L. 99-457, The Education of the Handicapped Amendments of 1986, assessment and intervention efforts directed toward children under five years of age focused on those children with obvious disabilities, such as Down syndrome, cerebral palsy, or visual impairment. P.L. 99-457 represents a major step toward meeting the needs of individuals with disabilities because, in addition to serving children with recognized disabilities, infants and toddlers with less-well-defined problems, who are at-risk or who experience developmental delays, now qualify for services. The inclusion of at-risk children and those with developmental delays has far-reaching implications for screening, assessment, and intervention activities. Tasks and opportunities relevant to screening and assessment outlined in P.L. 99-457 include

1. Using a multidisciplinary approach to screen and assess children from birth through five years of age
2. Identifying infants and young children with known disabilities and developmental delays and, at states' discretion, identifying children from birth through two years of age who are at risk for developmental delays (including physical delays)
3. Planning comprehensive services for young children with special needs, including a model of periodic rescreening and reassessment
4. Involving the family in all levels of assessment, identification, and intervention

Levels of services included in the law are

1. Child Find activities
2. Developmental and health screening, including administration of screening instruments, questioning of parents, and administration of medical, vision, and hearing examinations
3. Diagnostic testing, including formal testing, parent interviews, and home observation
4. Individual program planning[48]

Traditionally, adapted physical educators serving young children with disabilities have been involved with Child Find searches and developmental screening. However, the expansion of services mandated by P.L. 99-457 has enabled the physical educator to become more fully involved in identifying and remediating delays evidenced by a wider range of young children. This provides a significant opportunity to have a positive impact on the lives of growing numbers of at-risk children in those critical early periods of life to help ready them for school.

GUIDELINES FOR SCREENING AND ASSESSMENT OF INFANTS, TODDLERS, AND PRESCHOOLERS

The following guidelines for screening and assessing young children are recommended by Meisels and Provence:

1. Screening and assessment are services—as part of the intervention process—and not only a means of identification and measurement.
2. Processes, procedures, and instruments intended for screening and assessment should be used only for their specified purposes.
3. Multiple sources of information should be included in screening and assessment.
4. Developmental screening should take place on a recurrent or periodic basis. It is inappropriate to screen young children only once during their early years. Reassessment should continue after services have been initiated.
5. Developmental screening should be viewed as only one path to more in-depth assessment. Failure to qualify for services based on a single source of screening information should not become a barrier to further evaluation for intervention services if other risk factors (e.g., environmental, medical, familial) are present.
6. Screening and assessment procedures should be reliable and valid.
7. Family members should be an integral part of the screening and assessment process. Information provided by family members is critical for determining whether to initiate more in-depth assessment and for designing appropriate intervention strategies. Parents must give complete, informed consent at all stages of the screening process. Suen et al.[69] write eloquently of the need of significant parent input in the screening and assessment process,

> Parents, on the other hand, have more longitudinal evidence of their child's development. While their ideas of child

development may not be as rich in formal theory, the sheer amount of time spent with their own child over multiple situations lends a great deal of credence to their observations. Indeed, some newer approaches emphasize ecological/authentic information collection and rely on periodic parent appraisals of their children, especially when professional in-site assessment is not feasible. . . .[69]

8. During screening or assessment of developmental strengths and problems, the more relevant and familiar the tasks and setting are to the child and the child's family, the more likely it is that the results will be valid.
9. All tests, procedures, and processes intended for screening and assessment must be culturally sensitive.
10. Extensive and comprehensive training is needed by those who screen and assess very young children.[49]

Selected motor assessment instruments that are appropriate for use with preschool children are included in Table 10.1.

TRANSDISCIPLINARY, PLAY-BASED ASSESSMENT

The Individual with Disabilities Education Act (IDEA) mandates a comprehensive assessment, for children from birth to three, and three to five, to determine eligibility and to serve as the basis for the development of the individual family service plan or the IEP. The standard within the profession is transdisciplinary, play-based assessment (TPBA), described by Linder as follows:

> Transdisciplinary play-based assessment involves the child in structured and unstructured play situations with, at varying times, a facilitating adult, the parent(s), and another child or children. Designed for children functioning between infancy and 6 years of age, TPBA provides an opportunity for developmental observations of cognitive, social-emotional, communication and language, and sensorimotor domains.[42]

The assessment process must be transdisciplinary; that is, it should be done by a team of individuals with a commitment to infants, toddlers, and young children representing various disciplines. The child's parents are the most important members of the team—the parents are the best source of information about the child.

Professionals with unique abilities and skills in one or more of the domains are a vital part of the team as well. These professionals may include, but are not limited to, (1) an educational psychologist, (2) a speech and language therapist, (3) an occupational therapist, (4) a physical therapist, (5) an adapted physical educator with specific training and experience working with little ones, and (6) a play therapist. A transdisciplinary approach to assessment with infants, toddlers, and young children allows the team members to gain vital information regarding the child's development and to share that information with other professionals.

It is vital that the professionals and parents understand their feelings during the evaluation process. Simeonsson[66] found a significant disparity between the feelings that parents acknowledged they felt during the evaluation process and those that the professionals attributed to them. Professionals, clearly, attributed many more negative feelings to the parents than the parents reported actually feeling:

Feelings Experienced During Transdisciplinary Evaluation

Parental Feelings (%)		Feelings Professionals Attributed to Parents (%)
Afraid	17%	70%
Angry	8	24
Confused	13	61
Worried	42	89

In order for the parents and professionals to function effectively as part of the transdisciplinary team, honest and open communication between them is vital, so that this type of misperception does not persist.

TABLE 10.1	Selected Motor Assessment Instruments for Infants, Toddlers, and Preschoolers			
Test/Description	**Source**	**Age**	**Components**	**Reference**
Alberta Infant Motor Scale (AIMS) (1994) A tool for assessing the early postures of the developing infant	Piper & Darrar: Motor Assessment of the Developing Infant W.B. Saunders Company 6277 Sea Harbor Drive Orlando, FL 32821	0–19 mos	Prone, supine, sit, stand postures	Content-referenced
Bayley Scales of Infant Development II (1992) This revised scale is sensitive to differences between children who are at risk for developmental delay and those who are not.	The Psychological Corp. 555 Academic Court San Antonio, TX 78204	1–42 mos	Posture, locomotor, fine motor	Norm-referenced
Brigance Diagnostic Inventory—Revised (1991) A widely used, teacher-friendly scale that also includes speech and language, general knowledge and comprehension, social and emotional development, reading readiness, basic reading skills, manuscript writing, and basic math assessment techniques	Curriculum Assoc., Inc. 5 Esquire Road North Billerica, MA 10862	Birth–7 yrs	Preambulatory, motor skills, fine motor, gross motor, self-help skills	Content-referenced
Callier-Azusa Scale (1978) A developmental scale designed to aid in the assessment of deaf-blind and profoundly disabled children. It also includes daily living skills, cognition, communication and language, and social-developmental milestones.	The University of Texas at Dallas The Callier Center for Communication Disorders 1966 Inwood Road Dallas, TX 75235	Birth–7 yrs	Postural control, locomotion, fine motor, visual-motor and visual, auditory, and tactile development	Content-referenced

TABLE 10.1 (*Continued*)

Test/Description	Source	Age	Components	Reference
DeGangi-Berk Test of Sensory Integration (1983) An excellent instrument for use by individuals familiar with sensory integration theory and development	Western Psychological 12031 Wilshire Blvd. Los Angeles, CA 90025	3–5 yrs	Postural control, bilateral motor integration, reflex integration	Content- and norm-referenced
Denver Development Scale II (1988) This easy-to-use screening tool also includes screening for language and personal-social skills (self-help).	Ladoca Publishing Found. 5100 Lincoln Street Denver, CO 80216	Birth–6 yrs	Gross motor skills, fine motor–adaptive skills	Content-referenced
Hawaii Early Learning Profile (HELP) (1988) A curriculum-embedded developmental checklist that also includes cognitive, language, social, and self-help skills	VORT Corp. PO Box 601321 Palo Alto, CA 94306	0–36 mos	Gross motor, fine motor, self-help	Content-referenced
Miller Assessment for Preschoolers (1988 Rev.) An instrument that also includes evaluation of a child's speech and language and cognitive abilities and provides guidance in determining whether a child's behavior during testing ranges from severely dysfunctional to normal	The Psychological Corp. 555 Academic Court San Antonio, TX 78204-2498	2.9–5.9 yrs	Sense of position and movement, touch, basic movement patterns, gross motor, fine motor	Content-referenced

(*Continued*)

TABLE 10.1	(Continued)			
Test/Description	**Source**	**Age**	**Components**	**Reference**
Movement Assessment of Infants (1980) An instrument that enables the evaluator to determine whether a child is developing normally during the first year of life	Movement Assessment of Infants PO Box 4631 Rolling Bay, WA 98061	Birth–12 mos	Muscle tone, primitive reflexes, equilibrium reflexes, volitional movement	Content-referenced
Peabody Developmental Motor Scales (1983) A curriculum-embedded assessment tool that is widely used by preschool teachers	DLM Teaching Resources One DLM Park Allen, TX 75002	Birth–83 mos	Fine motor, gross motor	Norm-referenced
Test of Sensory Functions in Infants (1989)	Western Psychological 12031 Wilshire Blvd. Los Angeles, CA 90025	4–18 mos	Reaction to tactile deep pressure adaptive motor functions, visual-tactile, integration, ocular-motor	Content-referenced

The adapted physical educator may add a unique perspective to the transdisciplinary team because of specific competencies. Cowden and Torrey[9] suggest the "adapted motor developmentalist" should have the following competencies:

- Knowledge of normal and abnormal motor development
- Curriculum- and judgment-based assessment techniques
- Appropriate response-contingent toys and materials for sensory stimulation and physical and motor development
- Strategies for relaxation, socialization, and play

The assessment process is sensitive to the unique needs of the child and allows flexibility in order to see the child's very best. In and through play—the most natural phenomenon of early childhood—the assessment team has the opportunity for developmentally appropriate observations within the cognitive, social-emotional, communication and language, and sensorimotor domains.

The more traditional assessment/evaluation model is inappropriate for infants, toddlers, and preschoolers for a number of reasons:

- Infants, toddlers, and preschoolers are not comfortable with strangers. It is frightening to meet a stranger, much less be asked to leave a parent or "more comfortable" adult to go with a stranger into a room to "play."
- Young children are uncomfortable outside of their natural setting—their home, their neighborhood, their child-care setting. Little children will not behave naturally when asked to perform outside of their natural setting.
- Young children may be asked to play with an evaluator, but the child does not control the situation—the unfamiliar adult does. The

child is asked to play without favorite toys, and, to facilitate evaluation, the child may find a toy he or she enjoys playing with and then be asked to return the toy to move on to another task.

- Assessment protocols often discriminate against a child with a disability. For example, most "intelligence tests" rely heavily on language and prelogical/mathematical skills; the performance of a child may be significantly negatively affected by a dialect unfamiliar to the examiner.
- Many developmental assessment scales assume that there is a typical developmental sequence; many children with disabilities simply do not acquire developmental milestones in a typical way.
- Many of the tasks that infants, toddlers, and young children are asked to perform have little or no meaning for the child or the child's parents. This has, unfortunately, been part of the clinical "mystique," which has presumed that the professionals have the answers and the parents are dependent on the professionals for information.

The TPBA process must be used in the motor assessment process as well. The motor assessment instrument presented in Figure 10-1 was designed to identify motor development delays in preschoolers three years of age and older. Data are collected through observation of play in structured and unstructured situations. It provides wonderful information for the parent and preschool adapted physical education specialist developing the individual education program (IEP) and the individual family service plan (IFSP).

COMPREHENSIVE MOTOR ASSESSMENT

The assessment of movement and play behaviors in infants, toddlers, and young children requires a special sensitivity to the fact that major developmental changes occur during the crucial years from birth to five years. Federal mandates require a child's assessment to include results of standardized and validated tests, particularly when decisions are being made about eligibility (review Table 10.1). These instruments are developmental scales that allow the adapted physical education specialist to evaluate the progress of the infant, toddler, and young child in relation to "typical" child development. Typical child development is considered later in this chapter.

While federal mandates require that a child's assessment include results of standardized and validated tests, information can be gathered for a comprehensive and formal assessment using the TPBA approach and while honoring the unique needs of the child. Formal assessment and the TPBA process are compatible. For example, the adapted physical education specialist may observe most of the motor and play components of the Brigance Diagnostic Inventory of Early Development–Revised while simply observing the infant, toddler, or child engaged in play in the home, child-care center, or preschool classroom. To maintain an emphasis on child-appropriate assessment, strategies sensitive to the needs of the child can be used to gain information regarding the skills the child does not demonstrate during natural or structured play. For example, to see the child perform particular skills, the evaluator may use hand puppets and tell a story about animals that "do" the skills that the evaluator needs to see. A pony puppet may be used to tell a brief story in which the pony gallops, for example. Or a puppy puppet may be used to tell a story in which the puppy catches a bounced ball.

ECOLOGICAL ASSESSMENT

Whenever possible, the assessment and evaluation of an infant, a toddler, or a young child should be completed in the child's most natural environment—the home, child-care setting, or neighborhood play area. In addition to being sensitive to the child's natural environment, the assessment must be culturally, linguistically, socioeconomically, and gender sensitive.

Figure 10-1   Motor Development Delay Indicators: Three Years and Older*

I. Muscle tone status (check all that apply):
  a. Low tone (proprioceptive problems):
    Difficulty holding up head _____
    Slumped posture _____
    Tendency to put legs in a W position when sitting _____
  b. High tone (overflow/tension):
    Stiff body movements _____
    Fisting of one or both hands _____
    Grimacing of mouth or face when concentrating _____
II. Strength and endurance—demonstrates any of the following:
    Tires during play before other children _____
    Gets out of breath before other children _____
    Has breathing difficulties sometimes _____
III. Equilibrium/extensor muscle control (check all that apply):
  a. Does not raise and control head when:
    Lying face down _____
    Balancing on hands and knees _____
    Sitting _____
  b. Does not roll from front to back _____
  c. Does not prop on forearms _____
  d. Does not reach for a toy when:
    Lying face down _____
    Balancing on hands and knees _____
    Sitting _____
  e. Cannot remain standing without support _____
IV. Equilibrium/flexor muscle control (check all that apply):
  a. Has difficulty with the following moves from a back-lying position:
    Rolling from back to front _____
    Sitting up _____
    Standing up _____
    Reaching for toy _____
V. Equilibrium when moving (check all that apply):
    Does not use sequential movement when rolling (head, shoulders, hips, followed by legs) _____
    Stands/walks/runs on balls of feet _____
    Uses a wide base of support during walk/run _____
    Loses balance when suddenly changing directions _____
    Does not put arms and hands out to break fall _____
    Avoids walking on narrow supports (balance beam, curb) _____
VI. Visual status (indicators of depth perception problems)—demonstrates any of the following:
    Both feet are not off ground momentarily when running _____
    Does not jump down from bottom step _____
    Watches feet when moving on different surfaces _____
    Marks time when ascending and descending stairs _____
    Avoids climbing apparatus _____
    Turns head when catching ball _____
    Cannot bounce and catch playground ball with both hands _____
    Misses ball when kicking _____

*Activities that can be used in preschool and elementary grades to promote motor development can be located in the handbook *Gross Motor Activities for Young Children with Special Needs,* which accompanies this text.

Figure 10-1 (*Continued*)

(NOTE: Children demonstrating three or more of the preceding eight behaviors should be referred to a visual development specialist for an orthoptic visual examination.)

VII. Coordination (check all that apply):
   a. Does not bring the hands together at midline when:
   Lying down _____
   Sitting up _____
   b. Does not demonstrate the following:
   Uses arms in opposition to legs when crawling _____
   Uses arms in opposition to legs when walking _____
   Uses arms in opposition to legs when running _____
   Arms are bent at waist height when running _____
   Use of both arms to assist during jump _____
   Slides leading with one side of body _____
   Gallops _____
   c. Does not demonstrate the following when kicking:
   Swings kicking leg behind body when preparing to kick _____
   Follows through with kicking leg after contact _____

VIII. Additional information:
   a. What are the primary means of moving during play?_____
   _____
   b. What motor skills does the child avoid?_____
   _____
   c. Can the child imitate a movement pattern that is demonstrated?_____
   d. Can the child demonstrate a sequence of movements when requested to do so?
   _____
   e. Check the stages of play the child demonstrates:
   Solitary (onlooker or ignores others) _____
   Parallel (plays alongside or with similar toys) _____
   Associative (follow the leader) _____
   Cooperative (social interaction) _____

IX. Comments/observations/concerns _____
   _____
   _____

THE PORTFOLIO ASSESSMENT PROCESS

Sensitivity to the fact that assessment is not, and should never be, a six-month, annual, or three-year comprehensive event but, rather, a day-to-day, ongoing process has led educators to the portfolio assessment. Just as caring parents have historically saved documentation of their child's progress—pictures, drawings, height/weight information, "new" words, etc.—caring educators must begin to save, carefully, documentation of the progress of the children they teach.

Danielson and Abrutyn[14] have identified three types of portfolios:

1. Display or showcase portfolios. The display portfolio captures, usually with photos, the many activities children actually engage in in a classroom. It is a visual picture of what goes on in the classroom but does not document an individual child's performance or development. A showcase portfolio shows only a child's best work and, subsequently, does not accurately reflect actual consistent performance.

2. Working portfolios. One way to get more accurate documentation about how a child is growing and developing is in a working portfolio. A working portfolio shows the process of learning new concepts and applying new understanding to tasks. The work samples document the child's strengths and weaknesses in meeting certain goals or learning objectives. Gronlund suggests that a collection of "work samples" that pertain to a child's goals and objectives are key in the assessment of educational progress:

> The work samples document the child's strengths and weaknesses in meeting certain goals or learning objectives. The work is not representative of the child's best work, but rather is evidence of her typical, everyday performance. In this way a teacher can really look at the child's work samples and decide on teaching strategies to help that child grow and develop in her skills and knowledge. And, on a practical level, if the teacher collects only work samples that pertain to goals and objectives, s/he significantly limits the number of things that will be collected and stored . . . .[25]

3. Assessment portfolios. Danielson and Abrutyn wrote, "Documentation for assessment purposes must be more than photos and work samples. Teacher commentary becomes an essential source of information for evaluating the work. . . . Identifying what makes a quality piece of work or an informative work sample for portfolio collection is critical."[14]

The portfolio assessment process allows educators to address each of the eight types of intelligence to carefully document and monitor the progress of the infants, toddlers, and preschoolers they serve.[32] If the parent and teacher are sensitive to the fact that their role should not be intrusive but, rather, supportive, not as the director of learning but as the facilitator of learning, the portfolio is a natural and obvious conclusion. If the educator is actively watching and learning from the children, the teacher will become adept at documenting each child's progress.

The adapted physical educator has a great deal to contribute to the child's total portfolio. In fact, this specialist may contribute information and data for the portfolio in all eight types of intelligence. Sharing these type of data with the early childhood educator helps validate the active play and learning process and encourages teachers and parents to perceive the adapted physical educator as a professional who can and does make a significant contribution. Examples of movement and play data that might be collected to reflect each of the eight types of intelligence are included here.

Linguistic Intelligence
- A child tells a story about a favorite movement, and the story is recorded on audiotape.
- A toddler says, "Ball" when he or she wants the teacher to roll the ball to the child; the teacher records the utterance on the child's daily log.
- The child sings a simple "rap" song while jumping; the teacher videotapes the child.

Logical-Mathematical Intelligence
- A child builds a tower with giant soft blocks, and the teacher takes a picture of the structure.
- A group of children line up to form a "train," and the teacher videotapes the group performing to the song "Chug-a-Long Choo Choo."

Musical Intelligence
- Several children dance to Hap Palmer's "What a Miracle"; the teacher videotapes the child being assessed.
- A child walks to the beat of a drum; the teacher notes the progress.
- An infant looks about to find the source of a sound; the teacher notes the milestone.

Spatial Intelligence
- A toddler can trap a 13-, 10-, 8-, or 6-inch ball rolled to the child sitting in a V-sit position; the parent notes the ability and shares the information with other team members.
- An infant crawls toward and reaches a toy; the preschool movement/play specialist records that on the ongoing motor development assessment instrument.

Bodily-Kinesthetic Intelligence

- A nine-month-old child creeps on all fours. The teacher takes a picture of the child moving in this position.
- A two-year-old toddler hurls a ball; the teacher records the progress on the child's portfolio.
- A five-year-old with Down syndrome climbs up and down a set of five stairs, holding the railing; the teacher records the milestone.
- A child slides down a playground slide for the first time; the teacher catches the "first" on film.

Interpersonal Intelligence

- A child engages in parallel play in a sandbox. The teacher videotapes the play.
- A child identifies the children he or she likes to play with and those he or she does not like to play with; the teacher records this on a sociogram.

Intrapersonal Intelligence

- A child describes the way he or she feels when playing a simple game with a friend. The teacher catches this on audiotape.

Naturalistic Intelligence

- A child names a flower on a nature walk; the teacher notes it.
- A child describes how she feels chasing her shadow; it is recorded on audiotape.

Contemporary communication, technology, and computer capabilities now make it possible for parents and teachers to save vast amounts of information about the development of young children. Baby-boomers have sepia photographs of their parents as children and their grandparents as adults. The children of the 2000s have audio and visual memories stored on CD-ROM or on personal websites.

The technology exists to begin a portfolio for every infant that can follow the child throughout his or her development. The beauty lies in the capability to save and store information that could increase the likelihood that infants, toddlers, and young children grow and learn in the best possible way. When the infant makes the transition into a toddler program, when the toddler makes the tran-sition into a preschool program, and when the preschooler makes the transition into first grade, his or her teachers will have a comprehensive and complete record of the child's progress.

The most significant questions related to the assessment process with infants, toddlers, and preschoolers include, but are not limited to

1. Does the assessment process yield important information that relates to eligibility, placement, and programming?
2. Does it do no harm? That is, can the infant, toddler, or preschooler be hurt in any way by the process? If so, it should not be done under any circumstance.
3. Does the assessment discriminate against children on the basis of culture, socio-economic base, or gender? It must not.
4. Does the process provide information that the parents and other practitioners can use?

Assessment can be intrusive. A transdisciplinary, play-based approach to assessment completed in the child's natural ecosystem reduces the potential that the assessment may be frightening to the child or parent.

Assessment can also be discriminatory. Recognizing eight different types of intelligence and monitoring progress using a portfolio assessment minimizes that possibility as well. Most important, the unique sensitivities of an infant, a toddler, or a young child must be respected and acknowledged.

AGES AND STAGES— UNDERSTANDING TYPICAL AND ATYPICAL DEVELOPMENT

It is vital that the adapted physical education specialist be aware of the development of the whole child. It is also necessary for the educator to embrace the notion that there is no such thing as a "typical" child. Each child is a unique being who develops in a unique way.

The description of the approximate ages at which a child usually acquires a new skill is charted in Table 10.2. Certainly, the educator must know what is typical in order to deal with a child with

TABLE 10.2	Ages and Stages of Typical Child Development			
Months	**Typical Gross Motor Development**	**Typical Play Development**	**Typical Fine Motor/ Constructive Play**	**Typical Cognitive Development**
0–3	Optical righting (2 mos)—child uses vision to align head when body is tilted; labyrinthine righting prone (2 mos)—when body is tilted, head orients to normal position	Gets excited when a toy is presented; shakes rattle if placed in hand	Puts fist in mouth; brings hands to chest and plays with hands and fingers; refines movements that satisfy needs (e.g., thumb sucking)	Follows object with eyes; continues actions to produce interesting reactions (e.g., kicks, coos, babbles)
3–6	Labyrinthine righting supine (6 mos)—when body is tilted, head orients to normal position; body righting (6 mos)—when body is tilted, body orients to normal position	Smiles, laughs in response to parent's speech, smile, or touch; enjoys simple songs, tickling, vocal games	Early grasping patterns emerge; plays with hands and feet; rubs, strikes, and shakes things to make noise; reaching patterns develop; uses both hands together; reaches and grasps objects	Uncovers partially hidden object; imitates simple familiar actions
6–12	Supine and prone equilibrium reactions (6 mos); crawling (6–7 mos); hands and knees equilibrium reactions (8 mos); Creeping (7–9 mos); sitting equilibrium reaction (10–12 mos); cruises holding onto furniture	Likes to bang things together; begins to imitate social games; prefers play with a parent to play with a toy; bites/chews toys; explores environment with adult help	Imitates simple actions (e.g., clapping, lying down; thumb begins to help with grasp; loves to shake and bang toys; begins to move intentionally; real pincer emerges at 12 months; begins to release objects)	Uncovers hidden object; imitates somewhat different actions; puts familiar actions together in new combinations; moves to get toy
12–18	Standing equilibrium (15 mos); walks up stairs, marking time; stands alone; walks alone with wide base of support; starts and stops walking; pushes a playground ball back and forth with a partner; makes a whole-body response to music; pulls or pushes a toy while walking	Enjoys piling objects and knocking them down; engages in solitary play; swings on a swing; plays alone contentedly if near an adult; likes action toys but plays with a variety of toys; uses realistic toys on self (e.g., pretends to brush hair with brush)	Stacks hand-sized blocks; combines objects; puts on/takes off pan and jar lids; takes objects out of a container; begins to scribble; holds crayon in hand with thumb up	Modifies familiar actions to solve new problems; imitates completely new actions; activates toy after adult demonstration

TABLE 10.2	*(Continued)*

Typical Social-Emotional Development	Typical Development of Receptive Language	Typical Development of Expressive Language	Typical Development of Self-Help
Begins to find ways to calm and soothe self (e.g., sucking); draws attention to self when distressed; learns adults will answer (if, indeed, an adult answers); likes face-to-face contact; responds to voices	Notices faces of others; coos in response to pleasant voice; may stop crying when someone enters room	Cries and makes vowel-like sounds; uses "different" kinds of cries; makes pleasure sounds	Depends on parent for everything
Cries differently in response to adults; shows excitement when adult approaches to lift, feed, or play; regards adult momentarily in response to speech or movement; smiles when parent smiles; laughs and giggles; smiles at mirror image	Turns eyes and head toward sound; responds to sound of own name	Varies tone to express feelings; new sounds emerge; stops making sounds when adult talks; begins vocal play; squeals; babbles; coos; "talks" to toy or pet	Depends on parent for everything
Asserts self; demonstrates curiosity; infant tests relationship with caregiver; exhibits anxiousness over separation; shows awareness of difference between parent and "stranger"; gives hugs and kisses; likes to play simple adult-child games; exhibits sensitivity to other children (e.g., cries if another child cries); demonstrates emotions—joy, fear, anger	Shows interest in sounds of objects; understands and recognizes own name; understands "no" and "stop"; imitates simple sounds; gives objects on request	Makes same sounds over and over; uses gestures; imitates adults' sounds; enjoys simple games such as "peek-a-boo"; appears to sing along with familiar music; asks for toys/food by pointing and making sounds; says "da-da" and "ma-ma"	Pulls off own socks; feeds self finger foods; holds bottle independently to drink
Demonstrates initiative; imitates; "me do it" attitude; explores (if feels safe); exploration inhibited if child feels insecure; begins to comply with simple requests; resists change; demonstrates affection with parent; follows simple one-step directions; initiates interactions with other children	Recognizes names of people and some objects; points to some objects; responds to a simple command; points to one to three body parts when asked; acknowledges others' speech by eye contact, speech, or repetition of word said	Jabbers; understands simple turn-taking rules in simple play; tries to communicate with "real words"; uses one to three spoken words; calls at least one person by name	Spoon-feeds and drinks from cup with many spills; sits on toilet supervised for 1 minute

(Continued)

TABLE 10.2 (*Continued*)

Months	Typical Gross Motor Development	Typical Play Development	Typical Fine Motor/ Constructive Play	Typical Cognitive Development
18–24	Walks down stairs, marked time, one hand held; walks backward; hurls a tennis ball while standing	Engages in parallel play; likes play that mimics parent's behavior; adds sounds to action (e.g., talks to a teddy bear); play themes reflect very familiar things (e.g., sleeping, eating); engages in play beyond self (e.g., child holds doll and rocks it)	Builds tower of 4 blocks; turns a key or crank to make a toy work; fits simple shapes into form boards; pours/ dumps objects out of a container; scribbles vigorously; begins to place scribbles in specific place on paper	Points to pictures of animals or objects; chooses pictures to look at; points to mouth, eyes, nose; looks for familiar person who has left room; uses stick to get out-of-reach toy
24–30	Runs; jumps over a small object; stands on tiptoes momentarily	Likes rough and tumble play; pretends with similar objects (e.g., a stick becomes a sword); uses a doll to act out a scene; imitates adult activity in play (e.g., pretends to cook or iron)	Stacks 5-6 objects by size; nests cups by size; puts together simple puzzles; dresses/undresses dolls; strings objects; turns doorknob; scribbles begin to take on forms and become shapes; imitates circular, vertical, and horizontal strokes; rolls, pounds, and squeezes clay	Points to and names pictures; likes "read-to-me" books; loves stories that include him or her; points to arms, legs, hands, fingers; matches primary colors
30–36	Walks to and kicks a stationary playground ball; climbs on/off child-sized play equipment	Shares toys with encouragement; plays with other children for up to 30 minutes; pretend play reflects child's experience; pretends with dissimilar objects (e.g., a block becomes a car)	Draws a face; makes pancakes with clay; moves fingers independently; snips on line using scissors	Understands "front"/"back" and "in"/"out"; matches objects that have the same function (e.g., comb, brush)
36–48	Stands on one foot for 5 seconds; walks up stairs, alternating feet; runs contralaterally; hops on "best" foot three times; catches a bounced playground ball; throws a ball homolaterally; does a simple forward roll	Plays with an imaginary friend; prefers playing with other children to playing alone; pretends without any prop (e.g., pretends to comb hair with nothing in the hand); pretends after seeing, but not experiencing, an event; assumes "roles" in play and engages others in theme; acts out simple stories	Builds 3-D enclosures (e.g., zoos); makes specific marks (e.g., circles, crosses); draws a simple face; drawings represent child's perceptions (adult should not try to name/label); makes balls and snakes out of clay; cuts circles with scissors	Fills in words and phrases in favorite books when an adult reads; corrects adult if adult makes an error in reading (or tries to skip part of the story); points to thumbs, knees, chin; matches brown, black, gray, white; names red and blue when pointed to; matches simple shapes; understands "over"/"under"; classifies animals, toys, and modes of transportation

TABLE 10.2 (*Continued*)

Typical Social-Emotional Development	Typical Development of Receptive Language	Typical Development of Expressive Language	Typical Development of Self-Help
Expresses emotions by acting them out; likes cuddling; follows simple rules most of the time; begins to balance dependence and independence; "no" becomes a favorite word; remains unable to share	Recognizes common objects and pictures; follows many simple directions; responds to "yes" or "no" questions related to needs/wants; listens as pictures are named; points to 5 body parts when asked; understands approximately 300 words	Uses simple two-word phrases (e.g., "Bye-bye, Daddy" or "Cookie, more"); uses simple words to request toys, reject foods, or answer simple questions; favorite word may be "no"; names familiar objects; has an expressive vocabulary of at least twenty-five words; refers to self by name	Chews food; begins using fork
Separates easily from mother in familiar situations; exhibits shyness with strangers; tantrums when frustrated; imitates others' actions; may be bossy and possessive; identifies self with children of same age and sex	Understands simple questions; understands pronouns ("I," "me," "mine"); follows a related 2-part direction; answers "what" questions; understands approximately 500 words	Begins to put together three- and four-word phrases; says first and last name; uses "I" and "me"; asks simple questions; uses "my" and "me" to indicate possession	Uses spoon, spills little; takes off coat; puts on coat with help; washes and dries hands with help; gets drink from fountain; helps when being dressed; tells adult regarding need to use toilet in time to get to toilet
Comforts others; relates best to one familiar adult at a time; begins to play with others with adult supervision; is conscious of and curious about sex differences	Listens to simple stories; follows a 2-part direction; responds to simple "yes" or "no" questions related to visual information; points to pictures of common objects by use (e.g., "Show me what you eat with"); understands approximately 900 words	Begins to tell stories; plays with words/sounds; has 300-word vocabulary; asks "why" and "where" questions; adds "ing" to words	Stabs food with fork and brings to mouth; puts on socks and shirt
Begins to say "please" and "thank-you"; shows affection for younger siblings; enjoys accomplishments and seeks affirmation; begins to form friendships	Answers "who," "why," and "where" questions; responds to 2 unrelated commands; understands approximately 1,500 words	Begins to use tenses, helping verbs; uses simple adjectives—"big," "little"; uses language imaginatively when playing; uses 3–4 word sentence; repeats simple songs; asks lots of questions; uses speech to get/keep attention of others; has 900- to 1,000 word vocabulary; repeats simple rhymes	Eats independently, with little help; brushes hair; spreads with knife; buttons/unbuttons large buttons; washes hands independently; uses tissue, with verbal reminder; uses toilet independently, with assistance to clean and dress self; puts on/takes off shoes and socks (Velcro closures); hangs up coat (child-sized cubbies)

(*Continued*)

TABLE 10.2	(Continued)			
Months	Typical Gross Motor Development	Typical Play Development	Typical Fine Motor/ Constructive Play	Typical Cognitive Development
48–60	Walks down stairs, alternating feet; walks to an even beat in music; jumps forward ten times consecutively; hops on nonpreferred foot; catches using hands only; gallops with one foot leading; slides in one direction; throws contralaterally; swings on a swing and self-propels	Plays a table game with supervision; acts out more complex stories; creates stories that reflect that which child has not experienced; plays cooperatively with two or three children for 15 minutes	Prints first name; repeats patterns in structure (e.g., three red blocks, three blue, three red); draws self with primary and secondary parts; creases paper with fingers; begins to distribute shapes/objects evenly on paper; begins to draw bodies with faces; completes eight-piece puzzle; threads small beads on string	Follows along in a book being read; tries to read book from memory; names green, yellow, orange, purple; names circle and square when pointed to; understands "forward"/ "backward," "above"/ "below"; classifies food/people
60–72	Gallops with either foot leading; may skip; bounces and catches tennis ball	Plays several table games; engages in complex sociodramatic play	Combines drawings of things the child knows (e.g., people, houses, trees); draws pictures that tell stories; folds paper diagonally and creases it; colors within the lines; pastes and glues appropriately	Retells story from a picture book; reads some words by sight; names triangle, diamond, rectangle when pointed to; understands "right"/"left"; classifies fruits and vegetables; matches letters

delays or disabilities. But it must be understood that each child develops uniquely. For example, it is not uncommon for an abused or neglected child to demonstrate typical gross and fine motor development but demonstrate marked delays in social-emotional, cognitive, receptive, and expressive language development. It is not uncommon for a child struggling to learn English as a second language to demonstrate typical gross and fine motor development but demonstrate delays in play behavior and receptive and expressive language development.

Not only does the adapted physical educator need to understand and identify delays, but the knowledge of typical development makes it possible for the educator to sensitively teach the whole child. With that information, the educator can bet-

ter plan and design an appropriate learning environment for the whole child. An understanding of typical development allows the educator to better meet the needs of the child in early childhood intervention and preschool programs for children with disabilities.

EARLY CHILDHOOD INTERVENTION PROGRAMS—BIRTH TO THREE YEARS

Infants, Toddlers, Young Children, and Their Families

Federal mandates (IDEA Reauthorization, 1999) to provide educational services to infants, tod-

TABLE 10.2 (Continued)			
Typical Social-Emotional Development	Typical Development of Receptive Language	Typical Development of Expressive Language	Typical Development of Self-Help
Begins to describe feelings about self; acknowledges needs of others and may offer assistance; starts to initiate sharing; tends to exaggerate; shows good imagination	Understands approximately 2,500 words; knows words associated with direction (e.g., "above," "bottom")	Uses adjectives; uses past tense; can retell a story; defines simple words; can describe differences in objects; can describe similarities in objects; uses five to six word sentence	Cuts easy food with knife; does laces; buttons smaller buttons; uses toilet independently; uses zipper
Asks for help from adults; cares for younger children; waits for turn for adult attention; has "best friend"; seeks autonomy	Participates in conversation without dominating it; understands words related to time and sequence; understands approximately 10,000 words; understands opposites	Participates in give-take conversation; uses words related to sequence; uses "tomorrow" and "yesterday"	Dresses self completely; makes simple sandwiches; brushes teeth alone; likes to make simple purchases; can assist in setting table, making beds; complete independence in bathing

dlers, and preschoolers have opened a window of opportunity for adapted physical education professionals. However, the strategies for intervention with infants, toddlers, and preschoolers are significantly different from those used in traditional educational programs. Consistent with the direction of the Office of Special Education Programs (OSEP), the most recent legislation has emphasized the importance of the family unit in providing early services to infants and children. Steps were taken to ensure that the family takes a central role in providing for children, particularly those children with high probability for lagging in their developmental process. Kay Hopper, the director of the Richardson (TX) Development Center, spoke eloquently of the parent and family role in the education of infants, toddlers, and young children:

> In over 30 years of work with families of children with disabilities, first as a speech therapist and later as the Director of the agency, I have found 98% of the parents deeply committed to their child. Some parents lack the specific skills to meet the needs of the child but almost ALL want to be GOOD PARENTS.[29]

The Families of Children with Disabilities Support Act of 1994 was reauthorized and enacted as P.L. 103-382, and included as Part I in IDEA. This legislation provides financial assistance to states to support system changes that put an emphasis on the family unit in the provision of services. The mandates support the following initiatives:

- To develop and implement, or expand and enhance, a statewide system of family support for families of children with disabilities
- To ensure the full participation, choice, and control by families of children with disabilities
- To enhance the ability of the federal government to identify those programs that help or hinder family support in families of children with disabilities
- To provide technical assistance and information and to evaluate programs

The shift toward embracing the family in the early intervention process represents an entire philosophical and pedagogical shift from past practices. The growing societal awareness of the importance of early intervention for positively impacting the quality of children's lives and the current national emphasis on parental involvement in programs for at-risk children have the potential for dramatically modifying educational experiences of all children.

Lip service has been paid, in the past, to the critical role of the family in the development of the infant, toddler, and young child. However, best practices in early childhood programming have seldom, if ever, really addressed the needs of the family members. Strategies for fostering the participation of parents in ECI programs are summarized in Figure 10-2.

Central to early childhood intervention is a respect for the family unit—in whatever form that takes. The child must be seen as part of that dynamic unit with the parent (or parent substitute) as the infant's primary and most significant teacher. Dawkins et al.[13] acknowledged that there has been a wonderful transformation in the provision of services to infants, toddlers, and young children:

The "family-centered approach" has become the foundation of early intervention. Families are seen as having enormous strengths and making the critical difference that enables a child to reach his or her potential. In the family-centered approach, families are allowed to choose their role at each

Figure 10-2 Fostering Parents' Participation in Early Childhood Intervention Programs[47, 58]

- The emphasis should be on families, not children alone.[58]
- Program practices should be directly tied to the characteristics and circumstances of families served.[58]
- The emphasis should be on expanding on the parents' strengths.
- Frequent, personal, and enabling conversation appears to be the key to parent-faculty relations.[58]
- Parent must be honored in/for life/roles separate from that of "parent."

stage and professionals are there not to direct, but to support the family and provide services.[13]

To consider movement and play intervention with an infant or young child, it is vital that the adapted physical educator be sensitive to the unique needs of the child within the family unit and to the needs of the parent(s) in response to the child. The interactions of the child and parent may be seriously compromised if the infant has a disability or if the parent is ill prepared for the role.

Klemm and Schimanski wrote in "Parent to Parent,"

Parents have to adjust emotionally to the fact that our experiences with our child are different than we thought they would be, and that we have been thrust into a whole new world. This world contains professionals we never knew existed, words and acronyms that are unfamiliar, reactions from friends and family that we never would have anticipated. We must learn about the disability itself and what this will mean for our child and our family. We often feel scared, alone, lost.[39]

Stern has described a representational model that helps explain the complexities of the infant-parent interaction.[15] It is vital that the educator who hopes to intervene successfully understand the nature of the interaction. Every attempt must

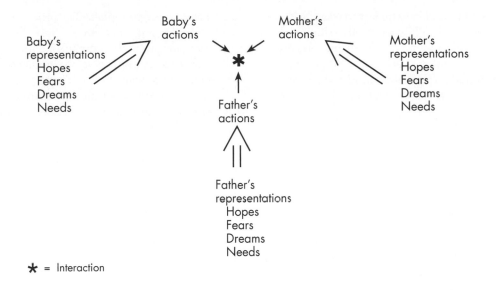

Figure 10-3   Stern's Model for Infant-Parent Interaction Analysis Before Caregiving

be made to see every parent as an individual of value—as one who wants the best for the child (see Figure 10-3).

The interaction between the infant and the parent is complex because the actions of the infant and the parent may represent hopes, fears, and dreams that the parent finds difficult, if not impossible, to articulate and may be a result of learned behavior. Subsequently, the infant's and parent's actions may be grounded in representations that are often difficult to understand. The relationship between the infant and parent, and their unique representations, are considered here.

The initial actions of the infant are reflex behaviors (rooting, for example) and responses to basic physiological needs (crying when hungry, for example). Subsequent actions are a result, at least in part, of the primary caregiver's responses to the initial actions. The infant's life is driven by the need to create a "global pattern perception," in which there is constancy and a predictable routine. Indeed, if the parent is able to make a natural response to the baby's natural needs, the baby will have a regular, schedule-based, and predictable

routine, which, as with older children, is the critical basis for the infant's development.

Stern described the "motherhood constellation,"[15] a complex of hopes, fears, dreams, and needs that have an impact on the mother and the way the mother acts and reacts to her child:

Survival and growth. The mother believes her primary responsibility is to keep the baby alive and growing. The mother's major fear is that something may happen to the baby. This shared instinct is one of the reasons members of this society react so violently to mothers who abandon their infants in trash bins or kill their children.

Fear regarding competence. The mother fears that she will be unable to fill her role as a mother, that she lacks the basic skills required for meeting the needs of the infant. Unfortunately, all too often this fear is well grounded. Consider the example of one child who was born naturally, full-term, and healthy. The very young mother took the child home but did not understand she needed to feed her child, who was hospitalized with severe malnutrition and dehydration four days after being released into the mother's care. The child now has profound mental retardation and severe quadriplegic spastic cerebral palsy as a result of the profound deprivation. And, as one would expect, the mother is guilt-ridden.

Primary relatedness. The mother fears she will be unable to love the baby or that the baby will be unable to love her. The mother knows that society expects that the infant and mother will have a natural bond and that the mother will be the primary and most important person in the infant's life. The significant bond between the infant and the mother is relatively set by twelve to eighteen months. These bonds tend to take one of three forms: (1) secure attachment pattern; (2) insecure attachment pattern; or (3) disorganized attachment pattern. Insecure and/or disorganized attachment patterns are typical in very young mothers and in mothers who are abusing drugs. Insecure and/or disorganized attachment patterns are also typical in the mothers of children with infantile autism or those born addicted to drugs. The infant may be unable to make the responses expected by the mother. Thus begins a vicious cycle in which the infant-mother connection evolves into one that is confusing and frightening for both.

Validation as caregiver. The mother, particularly if the child is her first, is in desperate need of validation. That is, the mother needs to have other women perceive her to be a good mother. The new mother is, in particular, in need of validation from her own mother. If her relationship with her own mother has been secure, she is more likely to be able to form a secure attachment with her new baby. If her relationship with her own mother has been insecure or disorganized, she is more likely to form an insecure or disorganized attachment pattern with her new baby.[15]

Identify reorganization. The process of becoming a mother causes a vast reorganization of a woman's identity. The woman goes from being her mother's daughter to being her child's mother and, usually at the same time, moves from being a wife to being a parent. This causes significant adjustments in her perception of herself. The same type of identity reorganization occurs in professional women who have a first child; the woman may have been validated as a professional in the workplace and now seeks validation in the role of parent. This process may be complicated by the fact that job requirements are often relatively basic—do this, and you will be perceived to be a good employee. Being a parent is simply not that easily defined, and this may result in confusion.

The mother's perception of the baby is complex and is formed, at least in part, by seeing the baby in diverse roles:

- Baby as individual being
- Baby as my son or daughter
- Baby as my husband's son or daughter
- Baby as a grandchild
- Baby as a sibling
- Baby as a niece or nephew

The mother's perception of the baby begins while the fetus is still in utero, and these perceptions are heightened by seeing a sonogram and/or feeling the baby move and kick. The mother's expectations of the infant are heightened, as well, when the infant achieves basic milestones related to growth and development. For example, when the child first sits up independently and manipulates an object (at approximately seven to eight months), the mother's expectations may change, and the child may be envisioned as a pianist or author. When the child first walks independently (at eleven to thirteen months), the mother's expectations may change, and the child may be envisioned as an architect or a firefighter.

Not as much research has been done on the role of the father in this process. But the father, who is critical in this process, shares many of the same questions and fears regarding validation as a parent and, most certainly, shares expectations regarding the child and the child's future. And there is a great deal of evidence that the father suffers from a significant period of confusion when the infant replaces the father as the predominant interest in the wife's existence. The father may experience the following:

- Concern regarding ability to care for and support the infant and mother—financial and emotional concerns
- Fear regarding ability to assume the role of father
- Concern with loss of primary importance in his wife's (or girlfriend's) life
- Expectations regarding his child's future

Being sensitive to the families of infants, toddlers, and young children with disabilities is much more complex, given the vast diversity in the families served in early childhood intervention programs and their ethnic, cultural, linguistic, and economic characteristics. Skinner, Rodriguez, and Bailey wrote,

> People draw upon a variety of cultural models to make sense of different situations and act in them, set goals, make plans, manipulate the environment, evaluate and anticipate the behavior of others, understand oneself, and describe experiences. . . .
>
> When we communicate with members of our same group (whether it be a religious, ethnic, gender, generational, ability, work, or some other kind of group), we assume much shared knowledge that we do not explicitly state. The exegesis of this shared knowledge is seldom necessary when we are speaking to people from our same cultural and linguistic background, and, in many cases, we may be only vaguely aware of the cultural models that guide our thoughts and actions.[67]

Religion may play a significant role in the family relationships that exist in a family in which a child has a disability.[62,67] Religion may provide a significant support to families of children with disabilities or chronic illness. Rogers-Dulan indicated that

religious support within the African American community has provided a framework in which the family can understand disability.[62] Within the Latino community, five religious themes have emerged in qualitative research examining the role of religion in the families of children with disabilities:

- God sent the child as a means for parents to become better people.
- God recognized the parents as special individuals capable of raising such a child.
- The child is a test that God sends to see how parents will respond.
- The child with a disability is a punishment for previous acts.
- A child with a disability is not a sign from God.[67]

Obviously, the role of religion within the family of a child with a disability is profoundly personal and individual. The role of religion, however, needs to be considered and honored when a professional interacts with a family member. It is, once again, a matter of cultural competence—honoring the family's culture. Suggestions for providing culturally competent services are outlined in Figure 10-4.

Infant-Parent Relationships in Families with an Infant with a Disability

The myriad of actions and representations of the infant, mother, and father, especially when complicated by actions and representations of members of the extended family, is difficult enough in the growth and development of an infant or child who develops typically. The process is much more complex when the infant or child has a developmental delay or disability.

There are early indicators that an infant may be at risk for delay and/or disability. Typically, these infants present one of two profiles: the "model" baby or the "irritable" baby. The model baby is lethargic, prefers to be left alone, and places few demands on parents. These behaviors, which cause these babies to be perceived to be "good" babies, may be due to neurological or neuromuscular pathology. A typically developing infant

Figure 10-4   Cultural Competence[11]

- The family, in whatever form, must be the focus of treatment and services.
- Americans with diverse racial/ethnic backgrounds are often bicultural or multicultural. As a result, they may have a unique set of needs.
- Families make choices based on their cultural backgrounds. Service providers must respect and build on their own cultural knowledge as well as the families' strengths.
- Cross-cultural relationships between providers and consumers may include major differences in world views. These differences must be acknowledged and addressed.
- Cultural knowledge and sensitivity must be incorporated into program policymaking, administration, and services.
- Natural helping networks such as neighborhood organizations, community leaders, and natural healers can be a vital source of support to consumers. These support systems should be respected and, when appropriate, included in the treatment plan.
- In culturally competent systems of care, the community, as well as the family, determines direction and goals.
- Programs must tailor services to their consumers—the family.
- When programs include staff who share the cultural background of their consumers, the programs tend to be more effective.

Parents are the child's most important teachers.

seeks contact with the parents, particularly the mother, engages in social interaction (at seven weeks the infant seeks to make eye contact), and makes his or her needs known.

The irritable baby cries excessively, sleeps fitfully, is difficult to console (does not respond to rocking, caress), and has difficulty nursing or eating. Mothers of infants later diagnosed as having attention deficit disorder or attention deficit hyperactivity disorder have suggested that the fetus is irritable within the uterus and that the kicking and other movements of the fetus are not like those of other children. Again, these behaviors may have a neurological or neuromuscular basis.

Other behaviors associated with atypical infant development (potential indicators of developmental delay or disability) include the following:

- Lack of response to sound (parent's cooing or singing)
- Lack of response to parent's presence (face or smile)
- Limited imitation of parent's expressions, gestures, or vocalizations
- Difficulty with gaze behavior (avoiding eye contact or staring)
- Limited response to parent's play attempts
- Unnatural attachment to objects

Comprehensive and early medical evaluation of infants makes it possible for a child with a potential for developmental delay or disability to be identified early in many cases. In fact, many potential delays or disabilities may be identified when the fetus is in utero.

Early identification of an at-risk fetus or infant provides the parents with early warning and may give them the opportunity to begin the grief process. However, this grief process is as complex and multidimensional as the actions and representations of the infant, parents, and members of the extended family. Typically, the grief process is similar to that described by Kübler-Ross in her classic works regarding death and dying. The grief of parents and others when confronting the delay or disability of an infant is often much more profound than that of an individual dealing with the death of an individual who has lived a long and purposeful life.

The contrast between the expectations and dreams for the infant and the reality is often vast. The parent who dreams of his or her child's being the first female president of the United States grieves unbelievably when the parent learns that that is most probably not an option for her daughter with Down syndrome. The father who dreams of his son as a professional hockey player grieves terribly when he learns his son has Duchenne muscular dystrophy and that, unless there is a cure soon, playing professional hockey is probably not an option.

The stages of grief that a parent may experience in response to an infant with a delay or disability are detailed in Table 10.3. Also presented is a range of appropriate responses from the professional educator. The parent moves through these phases of grief in a fluctuating way—simple events may cause the parent to experience all these feelings all over again. For example, if the infant is still unable to walk at age three years, the parent may begin the grieving process all over again. If the child requires placement in a preschool program for children with disabilities at age three, the parent may need to envision the dream all over again. If the child can't make a transition into kindergarten on entering school, the parent may face denial and anger all over again. The professional working with the parent must consistently focus on honest, open communication and redirect the parent to focus on the child's abilities rather than disabilities.

Early Childhood Intervention in Natural Settings

Best practices in early childhood intervention (ECI) acknowledge that infants and toddlers between birth and three years of age must be educated in their most natural environments. In fact, an amazing number of infants and toddlers spend time outside the home in regulated and unregulated child-care centers.[40] Specifically, increasing numbers of children receive care outside the home because of the following:

- Increased numbers of parents/families unable to provide care within the home
- Increased numbers of parents/families unwilling to provide care within the home
- Increased numbers of parents/families living in poverty and the subsequent need for both parents (if there are two parents) to work
- Increased requirements for job training and work for parents receiving social support services
- Increased numbers of single parents, particularly young women, trying to support their children
- Increased numbers of children with significant developmental delays and disabilities with special needs because of improved medical technology that allows infants to survive who would have died in the natural selection process in earlier civilizations

The ECI natural settings initiative is in direct response to programs that in the past served typically developing infants and toddlers as well as infants and toddlers with developmental delays or disabilities, in training/school centers or provided programs in hospital-based or university-based clinical settings. Advocacy groups such as Advocacy Incorporated and the Association for Retarded Citizens have lobbied actively for service provision in the most inclusive and natural setting. According to Crais:

> The suggested changes involve moving from client-centered to family-centered services, from professionally-driven to family-driven

TABLE 10.3 **Stages of Parental Grief and the Educator's Role in Response to Infants with Development Delays or Disabilities**

Stage	Parent's Behavior	Role of the Educational Professional
Denial	The parent does not acknowledge that the infant has a delay or may have a disability. In the initial stages of grief, this is a self-protective mechanism that keeps the parent from being totally destroyed by this information.	During this time, the professional working with the parent may help in the following ways: • Share information about the infant and the infant's progress; far too often, the parent is exposed only to what the infant cannot do rather than what the infant can do • Deal with the present rather than projecting the future • Express a willingness to listen. Use open-ended questions to allow the parent to discuss feelings and thoughts • Share information in writing (simple, direct writing) so the parent can review the information in private and on the parent's terms
Negotiation	During this stage, parents may try to negotiate or "make a deal" with their God or a force in the universe. The parents may promise to "do good works" in order to have their infant cured.	The professional working with the infant and the parent should continue to work with the parent as if in denial.
Guilt/grief	During this stage, the parent may experience tremendous guilt and grief. This is particularly true if the cause of the delay or disability is genetic or a result of parental alcohol or other drug abuse. This is often a time in which parents may blame each other for the child's disability. This is difficult if there is no blame to be had; it is devastating if one of the parent's behavior did, indeed, have a cause-effect relationship in the disability.	The professional working with the infant and the parents should • Encourage parents to express guilt and "get it in the open" • Encourage parents to examine their belief system • Help parents meet other parents who have experienced the same thing—contact existing support groups or help parents make contact with parents of other infants • Share realistic expectations regarding their infant's development • Reinforce any parent attempt to play or interact with the infant
Depression	The parent may become overwhelmed with the contrast between the expectation and the reality. Stern described a mother's reaction to having a severely disabled infant as a narcissistic wound.[15] The depression, ultimately, allows parents to abandon their dream and may help the parent move to self-acceptance.	The professional dealing with the parent who is depressed must do so with great care, since the parent is very fragile at this time. The professional must keep an open line of communication that is nonjudgmental and caring.
Anger	Though this may be the most difficult stage for the professional to deal with, when the parent finally gets angry, the parent is on the way to healing (a process that may take a lifetime).	During this time, the professional must • Acknowledge that anger directed toward him or her may be displaced (or the parent may simply be angry with the motor specialist) • Encourage the parent to express anger • Encourage the parent's effort to play with the child and help the parent develop skills to avoid directing the anger toward the child

decision making, and from focusing on problems to identifying and developing family and child strengths.[10]

Specifically, the focus is on a family-centered approach, in which the family and its culture are honored. Winston[75] and Crais[10] have suggested that the following underlying principles must be the crux of the family-centered, natural setting initiative:

1. Families are the constants in their children's lives, whereas service systems and professionals may only be sporadic.
2. Services should be ecologically based and therefore focus on the mutual influence of the contexts surrounding the child and family.
3. Families should be equal partners in the assessment and intervention process.
4. Services should foster families' decision-making skills and their existing and developing skills while protecting their rights and wishes.
5. Professionals need to recognize the individuality of children and their families and to modify their own services to meet those needs.
6. Services must be delivered using a coordinated, "normalized" approach.

This has resulted in ECI mandates, at the federal and state level (in most states), that expect the family-centered individual family service plan (IFSP) process—including assessment, IFSP development, and service delivery (see Chapter 3)—to relate to the family's ability to choose services that reflect and support the child in the family's natural settings. Basic to this process is the fact that a natural environment is a setting that is natural or "normal" for the child's age peer who has no disabilities and includes home and community settings in which children without disabilities participate. These natural settings include

- Home
- Family and for-profit or nonprofit agency child-care settings
- Church and synagogue programs and activities
- Community playground
- Park and recreation department programs and activities
- Library "reading times"
- Grocery stores

The assessment and the IFSP must provide information regarding the infant's or child's eligibility and the level of functioning in the following areas:

- Cognitive development
- Physical development, including vision and hearing, gross and fine motor skills, and nutrition status
- Communication development
- Social-emotional development
- Adaptive development or self-help skills[55]

In addition, the assessment must include the child's unique strengths and needs "in relation to the child's ability to function in settings that are natural or normal for the child's peers who do not have disabilities, including home and community settings in which children without disabilities participate."[55]

Recent mandates also require parent input regarding their child's functional abilities and the extent of their participation in settings that are natural or normal for their child's age peers without disabilities. The focus is on the family's perception of their needs if they are to provide quality parenting in natural environments.

Mandates exist that ensure that each child and family has a plan of services that meets the unique needs of the child and family and reflects and supports the collaborative partnership between parents and professionals. The program must provide service coordination and an IFSP for all eligible children (see Table 10.4).

The IFSP must:

- Be written within forty-five days of referral
- Be jointly developed through a face-to-face meeting of a team of professionals that includes the parents
- Be based on information from a comprehensive evaluation and assessment performed by an interdisciplinary team

TABLE 10.4	Comparison of the Individual Education Program and the Individual Family Service Plan	
	Individual Family Service Plan	**Individual Education Program**
Focus	Family-centered and needs-based	Child-centered
Children served	Children from birth to age three years with developmental delays	Children from age three to twenty-two years with disabilities
Emphasis	Education in natural environment	Education in least restrictive environment
Eligibility	Based on developmental delay, atypical development, or medical diagnosis	Based on educational need
Response to referral	Requires development of an IFSP with forty-five days of referral	Requires development of an IEP within ninety days of referral
Provision of services	Services continually provided twelve months of year	Services provided during nine-month school year, unless identified concern regarding regression necessitates extended year services
Progress review	Six-month and annual reviews (arranged by ECI service coordinator)	Annual reviews and three-year comprehensive evaluations
Team participants	Parent(s) of child	Parent(s) of child
	Other family members or child-care persons, as requested by parent	Other family members, as requested by parent
	Advocate(s) or person(s) outside family, as requested by parent	Advocate(s) or person(s) outside family, as requested by parent
	A minimum of two professionals from different disciplines	Child's special educator
		Representative from regular education
		Related service personnel
		Building principal (or representative)
	Service coordinator	Case manager
	Person directly involved in evaluation/assessment	Professional able to interpret assessment data
Contents	Summary of child's health/medical history	Statement of present level of educational performance
	Statement describing present level of	
	• Cognitive development	
	• Physical development, including vision and hearing, gross/fine motor skills, and nutrition skills	
	• Communication development	
	• Social-emotional development	
	• Adaptive development or self-help skills	
	Description of child's unique strengths and needs in relation to ability to function in natural settings: home, child care, neighborhood, community playground, church, restaurants, grocery stores, etc.	
	Review of need for assistive technology: assessment, services, and devices	
	Statement of major outcomes and strategies for achieving outcomes	Annual goals and short-term objectives

TABLE 10.4	(*Continued*)	
	Individual Family Service Plan	**Individual Education Program**
	FILM (frequency, intensity, location, and method of delivering services)	Statement of specific educational services to be provided
	Summary of opportunities for inclusion in family and community life and with peers	Statement regarding extent to which student will participate in regular education program
	Starting dates and expected length of services	Projected dates for initiation/duration of services
	Transition plan for child leaving program (beginning at two years)	Transition plan for student leaving program (beginning at fourteen years)
	Medical and other services required and method of payment	Appropriate objective criteria and evaluation procedures
Procedural safeguards	Families protected by procedural safeguards outlined in Part H of IDEA	Families protected by procedural safeguards outlined in Part B of IDEA
Additional features	With agreement of family, the IFSP may include	
	• Integrated summary of procedures for identifying family's concerns, priorities, and resources	
	• Statement regarding family's ability to enhance the child's development, as identified by family	
	• Description of intervention required to meet needs of family and payment plans	

- Be developed to include the services to be provided, the child's ability to function in natural environments, and the family's ability to meet the child's needs
- Coordinate services with all other providers, including child-care providers
- Address the need for assistive technology assessment, services, and devices
- Include a statement that describes the child's health and medical history
- Include a statement that describes the present level of development
- Contain major outcomes and strategies for achieving outcomes
- Include frequency, intensity, location, and method of delivering services (FILM)
- Contain a summary of opportunities for inclusion in family and community life and life with peers

- Address starting dates and expected length of services
- Include medical and other services required and the method of payment
- Include a transition plan, beginning at two years, into preschool programs[55]

With the permission of the family, the IFSP may also include a summary of procedures for identifying the family's concerns, priorities, and resources. In addition, it will include information regarding the family's ability to enhance the child's development. If required, it may stipulate plans for intervention required to meet the needs of the family.

It is exciting to note that the Reauthorization of IDEA makes it possible for educators in preschool programs for children with disabilities to extend the IFSP into the child's preschool years and, potentially, into the school years, as well. This is, certainly, a direct reflection of Congress's commitment to the provision of services to the family.

The Movement Program and the ECI Natural Settings Initiative

The ECI natural settings initiative has a broad and comprehensive impact on the adapted physical education specialist. It is no longer appropriate to pull infants, toddlers, and young children out of their natural settings to provide intervention, including intervention with parents, in a clinic based in a service agency, on a public school campus, or on a university campus. Far too often in the past, an infant or a toddler was removed from the familiar home and neighborhood environment and taken into an enhanced learning environment (e.g., a clinical setting with all the necessary materials and equipment [toys, for example]).

The opportunity for learning and development is great during the time the child receives services within the clinical setting. Cowden, Sayers, and Torrey,[8,64] reported significant success in motor intervention for infants, and toddlers with disabilities in a university-based clinical setting that focused on the following:

- Increase or decrease of muscle tone to facilitate effective movement
- Inhibition of primitive reflexes
- Reciprocal innervation
- Neurodevelopmental repetitive facilitation of movements
- Stimulation of automatic equilibrium reactions
- Tactile stimulation for warm-up, flexibility, range of motion, and relaxation
- Positioning for increasing muscle tone, strength, and balance of specific muscles
- Coordination of stability and mobility
- Resistance training

However, university-based clinical experiences provide little or no opportunity for transfer of the learning experience into the home or neighborhood. Cheatum and Hammond[6] address that in their text, a recommended reading. Also, parents are often overwhelmed by the clinical setting and become observers rather than leaders in the learning process.

The adapted physical educator must be prepared to provide services in settings described as "natural" for children from birth to age three years:

- Home
- Child-care or family day-care
- Neighborhood recreation center
- Community playground

Intervention within a child's natural setting provides many advantages. The first, and most important, is that an infant or a toddler will be most at ease in the familiar environment. The specialist will have the opportunity to see the child moving in his or her most natural play environment and will be able to develop a movement/play program designed to work within that context. The second advantage is that the specialist will have an opportunity—in the home, in the child-care setting, in the neighborhood recreation center, and on the community playground—to provide meaningful intervention with the parent in a context familiar to the parent or other caregiver. Strategies can be developed to help the parent develop skills for facilitating the child's development in the environment most familiar to both the parent and the child. The likelihood that the parent will become an active participant in the child's learning is enhanced.

There are, however, some disadvantages and problems associated with the provision of services in the natural setting. These disadvantages and problems, which are increased in inner-city and other poverty-stricken areas, including Native American reservations and camps for transient migrant workers, include

- The safety of the professional may be compromised within a given community, particularly in the late afternoons and evenings. Unfortunately, there are simply some homes and some neighborhoods in which the lives of professionals (even when traveling in pairs) are in jeopardy.
- The health of the professional may be compromised in homes in which basic health

care standards are not met (lack of cleanliness or appropriate immunizations).

- The provision of services in a clinical setting provides professionals the opportunity, if only for a brief time, to meet an infant's or toddler's basic health and safety needs. For example, infants and toddlers are often bathed and fed nutritious meals while attending the clinic. That type of opportunity is not readily available in some homes and neighborhoods.
- The professional feels as if he or she has no base and only limited connection with other early childhood professionals.

Movement and Play in the Individual Family Service Plan

The trend toward intervention within the natural context can be effective only if the goals and objectives (and the specific strategy for accomplishing these objectives) are functional, can be generalized, can be integrated within the natural setting, are measurable, and reflect a hierarchical relationship between long-range goals and short-term objectives. It is critical to put real-life skills into the IFSP.[56] This is true of movement and play, as well. The following are examples of real-life goals and objectives:

- *Functionality.* Will the movement or play skill increase the child's ability to interact with people and objects in the environment? For example, facilitating the development of sitting equilibrium increases the likelihood that a child will be able to sit and play with a toy. An appropriate annual goal may be "The child is able to retain sitting equilibrium while being bounced on a mattress with hands held."
- *Generality.* Can the movement or play skill be used in several different settings? For example, if a child is able to grasp and release small objects, the child can (1) at home—help pick up toys and put them in a bucket, (2) at child care—build with large Duplo blocks, (3) on the playground—collect and stack twigs. An appropriate annual goal may be "The child is

able to grasp and release a variety of small objects."

- *Integrated into natural setting.* Can the movement or play skill be used within the child's daily environment? For example, if a child is able to participate in parallel play, he or she can (1) at home—sit and look at a book while the parent looks at a newspaper, (2) at child care—share a water table with another child, (3) on the playground—share a sandbox and engage in filling and pouring like another child. An appropriate annual goal may be "The child is able to engage in parallel play with adults and peers."
- *Measurable.* Can the movement or play skill be measured? A goal or objective is of no use if the educator or parent cannot determine if the objective has been met. For example, "The child will be able to run better" is not an appropriate goal or objective. An appropriate annual goal may be "The child will be able to run, using arms in opposition to the legs."
- *Hierarchical annual goals and objectives.* Can the movement/play goals and objectives be expressed in hierarchical fashion? The only appropriate annual goals and objectives are those in which the objectives can build on one another, leading to an annual goal.[56]

Role of the Adapted Physical Education Specialist with Infants and Toddlers in Natural Settings

The role of the adapted physical educator is the same in each of the natural settings—home, child-care setting, neighborhood recreation center, and community playground. The first responsibility is the completion of a comprehensive, developmentally appropriate, ecological assessment and the initiation of the portfolio assessment process.

After the completion of the initial assessment and the initiation of the ongoing portfolio assessment process, the adapted physical education specialist working with infants and toddlers is responsible for working closely with the parents or caregivers to help them understand the importance of play to the infants and toddlers and to help them acquire the skills necessary to facilitate play. It is clear that infants and toddlers are more responsive to parents who are playful than to those who are not and that infants and toddlers develop stronger bonds with parents who play with them.[35] There are several techniques for introducing parents to the play process:

1. Informal discussions regarding developmental milestones in typically and atypically developing children
2. Films and videotapes that illustrate child development
3. Films and videotapes that demonstrate parent-child interaction[35]

The most effective strategies, however, are those in which the adapted physical educator actually demonstrates the techniques for the parent with the infant or toddler and then encourages and re-inforces the parent while practicing under a watch-ful eye. These strategies and techniques are de-scribed in the following sections.

Modeling Strategies and Techniques for Enhancing Sensory Stimulation

Vestibular Stimulation

1. Hold and rock the infant or toddler in your arms or rock in a rocking chair.
2. Bounce the infant or toddler on your lap with the child lying on his or her stomach, sitting, and standing.
3. Gently pat the bed or couch cushion next to the infant or toddler while the child lies prone.
4. Dance, holding the infant or toddler in your arms.
5. Carry the child in a baby backpack.

Tactile/Proprioceptive Stimulation

1. Do infant massage. Hold (or lie down next to) the infant or toddler and gently stroke the child with the fingertips and fingers. Apply slightly more pressure as the massaging hand moves down the long bones in the arms and legs, and down the spine.
2. Play with the child's fingers and toes.
3. Introduce Koosh balls and squishy animals for the child to hold and feel.

4. Grasp the child's feet and gently pump up and down while chanting or singing a simple song: "Molly is kicking, kicking, kicking, Molly is kicking all day long" (sung to "London Bridge").
5. Lift and move the child's arms and legs, stretch and bend.
6. Use different types of materials to gently rub on the child's body—flannel, silk, cotton, fake fur, terry cloth, feathers, sponge, etc.
7. Wiggle the child's fingers and toes in water, sand, cereal, whipped cream, etc.
8. Help the child do finger play in a scoop of pudding on the child's high chair tray.
9. Plan simple games such as "This Little Piggy" while touching and pulling gently on the baby's toes and fingers.
10. Let the child pound on chunks of refrigerated cookie dough.
11. Put pillows on the floor for the child to crawl and creep on or over.
12. Let the toddler push and pull objects such as laundry baskets.

Auditory Stimulation

1. Talk, coo, and sing to the baby.
2. Read. If the parent cannot read, help the parent select auditory tapes of simple books or, better still, urge the parent to participate in a parent/child literacy program.
3. Tell the child simple stories that include the child. Use the child's name often in the story.
4. Expose the infant or toddler to different types of music—classical, jazz, rock, and country-western.
5. Allow the infant or toddler to stimulate his or her own auditory system using rattles.
6. Attach a large jingle bell to the child's arm or foot using a ponytail holder; help the child kick the foot.

Visual Stimulation

1. Expose the newborn to black/white contrasts.
2. As the infant matures, expose the baby to vibrant, primary colors.
3. Imitate the baby's gestures and expressions.
4. Encourage the child to look at self in a mirror.

5. Jiggle a brightly colored toy or noisemaker in front of the child's face. When the child's eyes locate the object, jiggle it again.

Olfactory Stimulation

1. Hold the child very close to the body, allowing the child to pick up the body's unique odor.
2. Expose the child to the varying odors of perfumes and spices.

Modeling Strategies and Techniques for Enhancing the Development of Equilibrium Behaviors

Supine Equilibrium

1. With the infant or toddler supine, jiggle a bright toy or noisemaker above the child's face (no closer than 12 inches to the child's face).
2. With the child supine on your lap, with the head supported by a hand under the head, gently bounce the infant or toddler on your lap.
3. Put a brightly decorated sock on the baby's foot to encourage the child to reach for his or her toes.
4. Lie on your back with the child supine on your chest. Supporting the child's head and body, roll from side to side.

Prone Equilibrium

1. With the infant or toddler in the prone position, place a bright toy or noisemaker in front of the child's head to encourage the child to lift the head.
2. With the infant or toddler in the prone position, walk your fingertips up the child's back, with fingers on either side of the spine.
3. Use textures to stimulate the muscles in the baby's back and neck. Try using a paintbrush, washcloth, and sponge.
4. Lie on your back with the child prone on your chest. Supporting the child's head and body, roll from side to side.
5. Put a rolled-up towel under the child's shoulders, allowing the hands and arms to move freely in front of child. Blow bubbles for the child to track or use a music box or rhythm instrument to encourage the child to hold the prone position, bearing weight on the forearms.

Sitting Equilibrium

1. Hold the child on your lap, supporting the child's head on your chest, and gently rock from side to side.
2. Hold the child on your lap, supporting the child's head on your chest, and gently bounce the child up and down.
3. Prop the child up in a sitting position using pillows. Put toys or musical wind-ups above eye level to encourage the child to hold the head up.
4. Place the baby in a high chair, an infant seat, or a walker. Hold a toy in front of the child and encourage the child to reach for it.
5. Prop the baby in the corner in a sitting position with pillows for support. Encourage the child to reach for a toy and play with it while sitting.
6. When the child can sit independently, place a number of toys within the child's reach and a number just beyond easy reach, so that the child has to adjust equilibrium to get the toys.
7. Play games such as "Pat-a-Cake."
8. With the child seated on a mattress or pillow, gently pull or push the child to force the child to regain equilibrium.
9. Let the older child sit on a rocking-horse, etc.
10. With the child in a sitting position, put a bucket in front of the child and objects to be placed in the bucket at the sides and near the back of the child.
11. Put a wheeled toy in front of the child and let the child roll it back and forth, causing the child to need to readjust equilibrium.

Standing Equilibrium

1. With the child supine, put the palms of your hands against the bottom of the child's feet and push gently.
2. After the child has head-righting capabilities, hold the child in a standing position with the child's feet on your lap. Bounce the child and gently move the child from side to side, keeping the feet in contact with the lap.

3. Play "Soooooo Big"—lift the child above your head while keeping the child in a vertical position.
4. While supporting the child in standing position, "dance" back and forth, and forward and back, keeping the child's feet in contact with the floor.
5. Let the child stand on your shoes as you dance around the room.

Modeling Strategies and Techniques for Developing Simple Locomotor Competency

Rolling

1. Gently lift the infant's right hip from the supine toward the side-lying position; alternate and lift the left hip from the supine toward the side-lying position. Let the return happen naturally.
2. If the infant is supine, place a favorite toy on either side of the child's head to encourage the child to roll the head to look for the toy.
3. Place the child on a blanket or towel on the stomach or back. Gently raise one side of the blanket to assist the child in rolling to the side. (Do not use this activity if the infant arches his or her back during the roll.)
4. Jiggle a favorite toy or noisemaker in front of the child's eyes (never closer than 12 inches) while the child lies supine; when the child focuses on the toy, slowly move it to a position at the side of the child's head on the crib mattress.
5. Place the child on a small incline so that the child has a small hill to roll down.
6. With the child supine, gently bend one leg and bring the leg across the midline of the body. Go slowly so that the child's body follows the movement.

Pull to Sitting

1. Sit with your back against a support and with your knees bent to make an incline for the child to lie on. The baby lies with the head near the knees and the hips cradled by your chest, so that the child faces you. Carefully, and with head support, round the baby's shoulders toward you and lift the baby into a sitting position. As the baby develops strength and sitting equilibrium, gradually reduce the amount of support.

Crawling

1. Sitting on the floor with your legs stretched out, place the child over your leg and shift the child so that the child's hands are in contact with the floor, and gently roll the child toward his or her hands so that the child gradually takes more weight on the hands.
2. Repeat 1, but this time shift the weight so that the child gradually takes more weight on his or her knees.
3. Place the child on a carpet or mat and remove shoes and socks. Place a favorite toy in front of the child to encourage the child to move toward the toy. If needed, help the child move by placing a palm against the child's foot, so that the child has something to push off from.

Creeping

1. Place a bolster or rolled-up towel in front of the child and encourage the child to creep over it to get to a favorite toy.
2. Make a simple obstacle course with sofa cushions, pillows, rolled-up towels, and rolled-up newspapers and encourage the child to move through the obstacle course toward a favorite toy.

Pull to Standing

1. Place a favorite toy on the edge of the seat of a sturdy, cushioned chair or sofa; when the child expresses interest in the toy, move it back just a little from the edge.
2. When the child is in a sitting or kneeling position, periodically throughout the day grasp the child's hands and pull gently to standing.

Cruising

1. Put a small, child-sized chair with metal feet on a tile or wooden floor. Help the child pull to stand near the chair and "cruise," holding weight on the chair.

2. Put several well-cushioned chairs close together and increase interest in cruising by placing toys on the chair seats.

Modeling Strategies and Techniques for Facilitating/Scaffolding Symbolic Play Behavior

1. Imitate the infant or toddler's facial expressions and gestures.
2. Demonstrate simple strategies for the child to communicate the following and model parent response:
   a. Behavioral regulation
      1. Requesting objects
      2. Requesting actions
      3. Protesting
   b. Social interaction
      1. Greeting
      2. Calling
      3. Requesting social routine
      4. Requesting permission
      5. Showing off
   c. Joint attention
      1. Commenting
      2. Requesting information
      3. Providing information[59]

Strategies and Techniques for Scaffolding Learning

The adapted physical educator may help the parent develop the scaffolding skills necessary to gently nudge the child toward more sophisticated symbolic play as he or she moves through the sequence of development of symbolic play skills.[2,24,59,74] Lyon noted that symbolic play develops in a specific progression:

- Increasing decentration movement from pretend directed toward the self to pretend directed toward others
- Increasing integration of single pretend actions into sequences
- Increasing decontextualization pretend play behavior that is decreasingly dependent on realistic objects or contexts and increasingly depending on imagination and symbolism[45]

Understanding this sequence can make it possible for the teacher and parent to more readily facilitate and scaffold symbolic, "pretend play," behavior.

Pre-Pretense or Accidental Pretense The child puts a comb in his or her hair or a telephone to his or her ear. The adult can help scaffold learning by responding, "Emily, you're combing your hair," or the adult can pretend to put a telephone to his or her own ear and say, "Hello, Hannah. This is. . . ."

Self-Pretend The child actually pretends to do familiar things. The most typical are eating and sleeping. The adult can help scaffold learning by saying, "Is it good? Can I have some, too?" or the adult can cover the child and say out loud, "Ssshhhh, Molly is sleeping."

Other-Pretend The child pretends to do things that he or she has seen significant others do. For example, the child may pretend to feed a baby or drive a car. The adult can help scaffold learning by saying, "Lashundra, what a good mommy you are being, feeding your baby." Or the adult may sit down next to the child and make "vvvvvvroooom" sounds. The adult may facilitate other-pretend play by providing appropriate props after a trip—for example, to the grocery store: garbage bags, boxes of food, an old wallet.

Imaginary Objects and Beings The child not only uses a variety of real or child-sized replicas of real objects in play but also uses imaginary objects to engage in pretend behavior. For example, the child might ride an imaginary horse or pretend a block is an ice cream cone. The adult may provide support for play by joining in—riding an imaginary horse while twirling a rope or giving the child another "scoop" of ice cream. This type of play is best facilitated when the child has access to props that can be anything—blocks, for example.

Animated Play The child uses toy people and toy animals, for example, and assigns them words or actions. The toy horse may gallop across the range while "neeeeiiiiighing." The adult can facilitate play by galloping and then jumping over "fences."

Sequential Play (Thirty Months or Older)   The child is moving into sophisticated play scenarios, and the play represents a sequence of events. For example, the child may "go to the store, buy groceries, bring them home, and fix dinner." The adult can scaffold learning by asking simple questions about the sequence but should not intrude on or change the child's plan.

Modeling Strategies and Techniques for Facilitating Constructive Play Behavior

1. Put four blocks on the floor. Pick one up and put it into a small box. Pick up a second block and put it into the box. Pick up a third block and put it into the box. Wait for the toddler to pick up the last block and put it into the box.
2. Sit near the child and stack two blocks. Stack three, etc.
3. Sit near the child and roll play dough in your hands. Offer some to the child.

Demonstrating How Simple Materials Found in the Home or Other Settings Can Be Used to Facilitate Play and the Development of Gross Motor and Fine Motor Skills

1. Use mattresses as "trampolines."
2. Provide pillows as "mountains" for climbing over and rolling down.
3. Provide wooden spoons, strainers, funnels, and old pans to make music or pretend to "cook."
4. With the child lying on a quilt, pick up an edge of the quilt to help the child roll from the stomach to the back.
5. Put a favorite toy just out of reach of the child to encourage crawling, creeping, cruising, or walking to the toy.

Demonstrating the Use of Simple Toys

1. Securely attach objects (large hair curlers, clean jar lids, plastic rings) to a dowel and tie it across the crib.

2. Put dry oatmeal, cereal, or macaroni in film canisters.
3. Make building blocks out of 2 × 4s (saw and sand the blocks).
4. Recycle empty cereal boxes as building blocks.
5. Use cardboard rolls from paper towels and toilet paper for building and rolling.
6. Make available things to crumple and crinkle—waxed paper, aluminum foil, tissue, used wrapping paper, newspaper, etc.
7. Clean a 1-liter soda bottle and fill it with water. To enhance the effect, add food coloring. Close the lid tightly and seal with duct tape. To help the child with discrimination of weight, etc., put varying amounts of water in a number of bottles.

Helping the Parent (or Other Caregiver) Select Toys That Facilitate Communication Between the Caregiver and the Child

1. Toys that draw attention to the parent's actions
   a. Push toys that make noise
   b. Musical instruments
   c. Rattles
2. Toys that draw attention to the parent's face
   a. Bubbles
   b. Pinwheels
   c. Scarves
3. Toys that facilitate reciprocal interaction
   a. Puppets
   b. Push toys (cars, trains, trucks)
   c. Balls

Helping the Parent Select Toys that Empower the Child

1. Toys that allow the child to see cause and effect (bang pan with spoon and make noise)
2. Toys the child can push and pull
3. Toys with which the child can follow the action (ball is dropped into the top and rolls down the series of chutes)

THE PRESCHOOL PROGRAM FOR CHILDREN AGES THREE TO FIVE YEARS

A comprehensive, family-focused, early childhood intervention program based in natural settings has the potential to prepare a three-year-old child for participation in "regular day care" or for continued home/community involvement. If a child deemed at risk for developmental delays exhibits a disability at age three years, the child will usually make the transition into a preschool program for children with disabilities within a community agency or public school program.

A natural and logical extension of a quality early childhood intervention program is a quality preschool program for children ages three to five years to help prepare the children for school. Washington, Johnson, and McCracken wrote:

> When former President George Bush and the nation's governors hammered out their six most important national education goals in 1989, this goal emerged as the first—Goal One: "By the year 2000, all children will start school ready to learn."[72]

Three objectives were specified to achieve Goal One:

1. All children with disabilities and from less advantaged families would have access to good-quality, appropriate preschool experiences.
2. All parents would devote time every day to help their preschoolers learn, and they would have access to training and support needed to do that.
3. Children would receive the nutrition and health care needed to arrive at school healthy.

The critical components necessary for children to achieve their potential are

- Health
- Nutrition
- Family and community stability
- Cultural competence
- Self-esteem
- Quality of early learning experience

Improvements in even one component increase children's opportunities to succeed in school and life. Given blatant poverty, the abuse and neglect of young children, homelessness, and cultural deprivation, the quality of the early learning experience becomes even more important. The importance of a quality preschool learning experience has been well documented in the research literature. The most noteworthy of the studies is the Perry Preschool Project,[4] which is a comprehensive, longitudinal study of 123 African American children from families with low incomes—children who were believed to be at risk for school failure. The study examined the long-term effects of participation versus nonparticipation in a high-quality early education program.

Children ages three and four years were selected at random from a single school attendance area and were randomly assigned to an experimental group, which received high-quality preschool education, or to a control group, which did not. Information was collected annually on these children from ages three to eleven years, and then at ages fourteen, fifteen, and nineteen. The following variables were considered: family demographics; child abilities, attitudes, and scholastic performance; involvement in delinquent and criminal behavior; use of welfare assistance; and employment.

The results were astonishing and demonstrated lasting benefits of quality preschool education. This is consistent with the findings of the Abecedarian Study of the effectiveness of birth-to-five intervention. When compared with the control group, the individuals in the experimental group demonstrated the following:

- Improved cognitive performance during early childhood
- Improved scholastic performance during school years
- Decreased delinquency and crime
- Decreased use of welfare assistance
- Decreased incidence of teenage pregnancy
- Increased graduation rates
- Increased frequency of enrollment in postsecondary education and vocational training programs
- Increased employment

Not only is this evidence impressive from a human success standpoint, but it is also incredible because the return on the dollar is so significant. "Over the lifetimes of the participants, preschool is estimated to yield economic benefits with an estimated present value that is over seven times the cost of one year of the program."[4] Unfortunately, current legislative thrusts ignore the simple findings. If society spends $1 to educate a three-year-old child, it will save $7 later on costs associated with special education, social services, unemployment, and prisons.

Preschoolers are, unfortunately, being bombarded by a host of forces over which they have little or no control. In order for preschool education to be effective, teachers must address the children's anger and fears. Certainly this is most effective if done in concert with the family. The typical causes of anger in toddlers and preschoolers is addressed in Figure 10-5. Strategies the teacher can use to help the young children deal with their anger constructively are outlined in Figure 10-6.

It is also critical that preschool educators help young children deal with the realities of violence in their lives. Strategies a teacher can use to help a preschooler deal with violence in his/her life are outlined in Figure 10-7.

The preschool educator is also faced with the reality of teaching many children whose language he or she does not share. It is not uncommon for a

---

Figure 10-6   Helping Toddlers and Preschoolers Develop Skills to Deal with Anger

- Create a safe environment for expression of emotion.[46]
- Model responsible anger management[46] and discuss it with the children.
- Help children develop self-regulatory anger-management skills.
- Help the children give a name to their anger. Teachers typically encourage children to "use your words . . . ."
- Encourage children to talk about situations that cause anger.
- Read books and talk about books that help children talk about anger.

Figure 10-5   Typical Causes of Anger in Toddlers and Preschoolers

- Conflict over possessions or space[46]
  Children get angry if another child takes a toy with which they are playing or moves into a space, such as a spot at the sand table, that the child had "claimed."
- Physical assault
  Toddlers and preschoolers get angry if jostled, pushed, or hit.
- Verbal aggression
  Toddlers and preschoolers, like other individuals, get angry if teased, taunted, or ridiculed.
- Lack of recognition or acceptance
  Children get angry, particularly, if not allowed to participate, if they want to play and peers say "no."
- Compliance issues[46]
  Children may get angry when asked to do something they believe interferes with their plans, such as washing their hands, putting away toys, or stopping to go to the bathroom.

Figure 10-7   Helping Young Children Deal with Violence[68]

Early childhood educators can help young children deal with violence by
- Helping children identify violence, find a name for it, and talk about its consequences
- Talking *with* children about real-world violence
- Recognizing and responding to children's traumatic reactions to violence
- Training young children in basic violence-related safety and self-protection
- Eliminating "disciplinary" violence against children
- Supporting families trying to help children cope with violence
- Providing a safe haven for young children and their families

teacher in a preschool program for children with disabilities to be working with children who represent four or five different linguistic backgrounds. In a typical prekindergarten or kindergarten class in an urban, core area, the children may speak as their first languages as many as fifteen languages. When combined with other factors affecting so many children—poverty, abuse, parents with limited parenting skills—the language issue becomes overwhelming. When it is difficult to communicate with a child, it is difficult to teach and to provide support, love, and care. The developmental sequence of second language acquisition is illustrated in Figure 10-8. Strategies for the teacher of preschoolers who use English as a second language are outlined in Figure 10-9.

Children, more than ever, have a critical need for early and effective intervention. A quality preschool learning experience is vital. Perhaps a quality preschool experience is so effective because it drastically affects the perceptions of the children, the parents, and the teachers. Expectations are high—and children rise to meet those expectations.

> Preschool, then, enables children to better carry out their first scholastic tasks. This better performance is visible to everyone involved— the child, the teacher, the parents, and other children. Children realize they have this capacity for better scholastic performance and believe and act accordingly, developing a stronger commitment to schooling. Teachers recognize better scholastic performance and react to it with higher expectations and eventually with scholastic placements that reflect these higher expectations.[4]

A quality preschool learning environment is one in which expectations for children's performance are high and the learning environment encourages active exploration. A quality learning environment for three- to five-year-old children is play-based.[43] A child's natural drive to play is encouraged, fostered, and respected. Play is a vehicle through which a child's motor, language, social-emotional, and cognitive skills are scaffolded in and through interaction with another child or a gentle,

---

Figure 10-8 Developmental Sequence of Second-Language Acquisition (Tabors) in Young Children[70]

Home language use
  Children continue to use their home language, even in settings in which it is not used by others, and seem not to understand that their language is not the one being used by others.

Nonverbal period in the new language
  Children realize their home language is not that being used and, in frustration, they stop using the home language. Instead, the child uses crying, whimpering, whining, pointing, and other forms of gesturing to communicate wants and needs.

Telegraphic and formulaic language
  Children use language that helps them get along—"OK," "yea," "mine," "bye-bye," "I don't know," etc.

Productive use of the language
  At first, it may appear that the child has regressed in the use of language; in actuality, the child is just struggling with the nuances of the English language.

Figure 10-9 Basic Strategies for the Teacher of Preschoolers with English as a Second Language

- Rely heavily on nonverbal communication.
- Rely heavily on demonstrations.
- Use visual images—pictures, graphics, photographs—to help communicate.
- Combine gestures with the important words in a sentence.
- Use a buddy system to pair an outgoing English-speaking child with a second language learner.[70]
- Establish and keep a predictable routine in the class.
- Use graphics to help the students anticipate activities.
- Use music and simple dances in which the sequence of movements is very predictable.
- Use favorite music, dances, and movements often.

caring adult. Play by any name—symbolic play, fantasy play, make-believe, pretend play, dramatic play, imaginative play—is the foundation or focus of the development of cognition, social-emotional skills, and language.[2] According to Gowen:

> It is during this second developmental period (preoperational) that children begin to develop their symbolic function, or representational competence. This is the function that allows children to go beyond the limitations of immediate experience by using symbols to represent (re-present) past experiences and to imagine future possibilities.[24]

Rubin, Fein, and Vandenberg,[63] in their significant review of the research regarding symbolic play, indicate that it is at the core of the development of a diverse set of abilities, including creativity, sequential memory, group cooperation, receptive vocabulary, conceptions of kinship relationships, impulse control, spatial perspective-taking skills, affective perspective-taking skills, and cognitive perceptive-taking skills. One of the major features of all symbolic play is that the children playing make rules regarding the play. Although it may not appear to be rule-governed behavior, even the most basic pretend play has rules that the child takes very seriously. A sensitive adult will hear the protests of a child to another child or to the adult (e.g., "Not that way"; "That isn't a puppy"; "You can't cook with that"; or "That goes in the blocks center"). In and through rules over which the child has some control, the child learns to function in a rule-governed society. According to Berk and Winsler:

> Adults and peers scaffold young children's play, nurturing the transition to make-believe and its elaboration throughout the preschool years. Representational play serves as a unique, broadly influential zone of proximal development within which children advance themselves to ever higher levels of psychological functioning.[3]

Vygotsky emphasized the role of representational play, or fantasy play, as a leading factor in child development:

> Play creates a zone of proximal development in the child. In play, the child always behaves beyond his average age, above his daily behavior; in play it is as though he were a head taller than himself. As in the focus of a magnifying glass, play contains all developmental tendencies in a condensed form and is itself a major source of development.[71]

In most child-care and preschool settings, this play-based, quality educational environment is one that is centers-based. That is, there are unique, separate, and distinct areas within the classroom that are specifically designed and equipped for active exploration. Dodge and Colker[18] recommend the following centers for the preschool classroom:

Blocks

House corner

Table toys

Art

Sand and water

Library

Music and movement

Cooking

Computers

Outdoors

A center provides children the opportunity to explore and interact with a wide variety of materials that engage a whole spectrum of senses, encourages sensory integration, and allows the children to be involved in an extended process of "pretend" and real play. For example, a housekeeping center may include the following:

- Child-sized furniture, including a stove, refrigerator, sink, comfortable chair, sofa, kitchen table and chairs, doll bed, stroller
- Play props, including pots and pans, cooking and eating utensils, a coffee pot, glasses and cups, a broom, a mop
- Baby dolls reflecting diversity—cultures, genders, abilities
- Doll clothes
- Dress-up clothes, including hats, scarves, costume jewelry
- A full-length mirror

A puppet theatre and puppets reflecting a variety of people, animals, and so on may also encourage "pretend" and real play. An area that can be used to simulate a post office, grocery store, or restaurant and the necessary props to stimulate play may also encourage pretend play.

Given this type of play support, the young child who is just developing pretend play skills will be "nudged" toward more sophisticated play. Eventually, the child will not need actual objects to stimulate play but will be able to substitute any object for another in play.

Quality Movement/Play Experiences in Preschool Programs

The process of preparing every child for a successful school experience includes providing quality movement/play experiences. A position statement of The National Association for Sport and Physical Education (NASPE), developed by the Council on Physical Education for Children (COPEC), describes appropriate and inappropriate practice in movement programs for young children in a twenty-one-page pamphlet titled "Developmentally Appropriate Practice in Movement Programs for Young Children Ages 3–5."[11] The major premises outlined by NASPE and COPEC follow.

NASPE/COPEC—Three-, Four-, and Five-Year-Old Children Are Different from Elementary School-Age Children[17]

Widespread condemnation of the American public school system in the 1980s and early 1990s caused an academic "trickle down" that has had a devastating impact on the education of young children. Specifically, a knee-jerk response to the criticism caused academicians and administrators to allow curricula to trickle down to younger grades. For example, material that was once considered appropriate for the sixth grade is now being introduced in the fourth and fifth grades. What was once considered appropriate for first-graders is now being introduced in prekindergarten and kindergarten classes. According to Shepard,

Because what once were first grade expectations were shoved down to kindergarten, these shifts in practice were referred to as the "escalation of curriculum" or "academic trickledown." The result of these changes was an aversive learning environment inconsistent with the learning needs of children. Developmentally inappropriate instructional practices, characterized by long periods of seatwork, high levels of stress, and a plethora of fill-in-the-blank worksheets, placed many children at risk by setting standards for attention span, social maturity, and academic productivity that could not be met by many normal 5-year-olds[41] [much less children with disabilities and developmental delays—comment ours].

This has been true not only in "academic" content areas but in movement and physical education programs as well. This trickle down effect has seriously compromised the movement and play experience of young children, as children have been expected to

- Sit and wait "forever" for a turn
- Sit and listen "forever" to directions given by an adult
- Participate in an activity predetermined by an adult and be given no choice regarding participation
- Participate in large-group activities when the child is not yet able to play with another one-to-one
- Share equipment before the child is ready to share equipment
- Use modified equipment—mini-basketballs, shortened baskets, large plastic bats—with a stereotypical *adult* expectation regarding the use of the equipment
- Perform skills for which they are not ready, because the teacher or parent does not understand developmental sequence (e.g., a five-year-old trying to bat an arched, pitched ball)
- Play cooperatively or compete with other children when the child is developmentally at onlooker, solitary play, or parallel play stage

Preschoolers are ready for movement and play activities that prepare them for school. But they are, by nature and design, not prepared for activities that would be part of the school curricula for six-year-olds. There is a vast difference between the capability and interests of three-year-olds and those of six-year-olds.

NASPE/COPEC—Young Children Learn Through Interaction with Their Environment[17]

Preschoolers learn only through active play and active involvement with their environment. They do not learn by watching someone else perform or by listening to directions—they learn by doing, experimenting, and experiencing.[26] Active, experiential play is the very foundation for the active learning center and the outdoor play center.

NASPE/COPEC—Teachers of Young Children Are Guides or Facilitators[17]

Vygotsky has theorized that all children learn best when their learning is scaffolded, or supported by an adult or another child.[3] Traditional practice in education, including physical education, embraces the teacher as the "giver of wisdom" and the child as the "learner." Vygotsky, a philosopher and social theorist,[71] and early childhood educators have reminded us that that simply is not the way young children learn.

The adapted physical education specialist must, by necessity, rethink and re-evaluate traditional teaching models and strategies and embrace a model in which the teacher is simply an unobtrusive facilitator of children's learning. Preschool children hate whistles, unless they happen to be blowing them. They hate lines, unless they happen to be drawing them. And they hate speeches, unless they happen to be giving them.

The adapted physical educator best serves preschoolers by becoming a facilitator of learning. The role of the facilitator includes the following:

- Carefully observing children in play
- Carefully observing children moving—their locomotor and nonlocomotor patterns, their object-control skills, and the way they use equipment and materials
- Recreating the learning environment by including materials that encourage further

exploration of the environment or enhance self-testing. For example, if the child is successfully running and jumping off an incline ramp that is 6 inches at the tallest point into a large landing mat, ask the child if he or she would like to try running and jumping off an incline ramp that has been raised so that it is 12 inches at the tallest point.
- Redirecting the child's learning and activity, with permission. For example, if the child is bobbling a balloon in the air with ease, ask the child if he or she would like to try bobbling two balloons at the same time.
- Honoring and respecting the play of children:
  - Ask to join their play and respect their decision if they choose *not* to play with you.
  - Engage in parallel play so that a child can observe you without being told what it is he or she should do. For example, if a child is having difficulty pushing a wheelbarrow because the load is not distributed equally, position yourself near the child and redistribute materials in your wheelbarrow as a model.
  - Support the child's play by providing adequate time and appropriate equipment and materials to challenge the child.

NASPE/COPEC—Young Children Learn and Develop in an Integrated Fashion[17]

Physical education must not be a separate, 30-minute period of time. Or, worse yet, "physical education" cannot be relegated to the "outside time" or teachers' break time. Movement must be, inherently, an integral part of all learning, in all centers, and an important part of every special activity. For example, in the blocks center, children will engage in gross motor activity when given the opportunity to build using large foam or wooden blocks. In the best scenario, children in the blocks center will be freed to use their body as building blocks. In the music center, children will engage in gross motor activity when given the opportunity to perform locomotor and nonlocomotor actions to music. In the language and literacy center, children will have the opportunity to use their large muscles and engage in gross motor activity when given the opportunity to pretend to be the turtle, snake, or rabbit in the story. At lunch, the children will have the opportunity to use their gross motor skills to carry a pitcher of milk to the table. Movement must be an integral part of all learning all day.

NASPE/COPEC—Planned Movement Experiences Enhance Play Experiences[17]

The adapted physical education specialist may plan movement experiences for children—but under no circumstances should children be required to participate in those experiences. Young children have such widely diverse motor capabilities, play skills, and needs that it is developmentally inappropriate to force a child into any activity. A developmentally appropriate movement experience allows individual, solitary activity and a choice to participate in small and/or large-group activities. For example, the adapted physical education specialist may have a plan to involve children in a "snowball fight" with rolled-up socks or white yarn balls. If a child is ready—physically, motorically, neurologically, and socially—he or she will choose to participate. If the child is not ready, the teacher must have some other option—independent play on a scooter, play with covered balloons, play with large playground balls—readily accessible and available for the children. The movement program for young children with disabilities—indeed, for any young children—must be designed to meet their needs and be responsive to their interests.

Developmentally Appropriate Practice

The focus of this chapter continues to be the need for movement and play programs for young children with and without disabilities to focus on the needs and interests of the children, not the needs and interests of the adults. The activity suggestions that follow must be used within the broader framework of developmentally appropriate practice. Dr. Denise Jenks, consultant and authority on best practices in early childhood education, reminds professionals, however, that the term *developmentally appropriate practice* has been vastly overused

and is misunderstood.[37] And, unfortunately, though many educators claim to use developmentally appropriate practice, a small percentage of teachers (20 to 33 percent) actually use teaching practices that are appropriate for young children in their classrooms.

Specifically, when one is working with young children, the movement activities must always be presented as a choice—not an expectation. If the movement activities are appropriate, most children will be drawn to them and will want to participate. If the movement activities are inappropriate, children will choose not to participate, will act out if made to participate, or will lose interest quickly.

The intent of a quality movement/play program for preschoolers with and without disabilities is to provide young children access to neurodevelopmentally appropriate activities that enhance the development of

- Equilibrium
- Sensory discrimination
- Sensory-motor function (body image and motor planning)
- Basic locomotor and nonlocomotor competency
- Cross-lateral integration
- Object-control skills
- Fitness

Examples of activities that enhance the development of each of these follow. Additional activity suggestions can be found in *Gross Motor Activities for Young Children with Special Needs,* which accompanies this text.

Equilibrium

A young child develops equilibrium in static positions and movements, at first, in which the center of gravity is very close to a large base of support (e.g., in the supine and then the prone position). As the child develops, he or she begins to be "in balance" in static and dynamic situations in which the center of gravity is farther away from a smaller base of support (e.g., walking on tiptoes on a balance beam).

The intent of these activities is to develop tone and strength in the muscle groups that provide shoulder and hip stability and to enhance postural adjustments.

Supine Equilibrium
Bubble Out Ask the child to lie on his or her back and try to break bubbles with a finger as you blow them over his or her face and chest.

Prone Equilibrium
Trampoline Fun Ask the child to lie on his or her stomach on a mini-trampoline. Sit next to the child and push the mini-trampoline at various spots near the child's body. Vary the pressure and the area of focus. A nap mat or 1-inch-thick play mat placed over an inner tube makes a great, inexpensive mini-trampoline.

Sitting Equilibrium
Little Red Wagon Ask the child, or a group of children, to sit on a crash-type mat or clean mattress. To the song "Little Red Wagon," the children can act out the experience of "joltin' up and down in the little red wagon." The song can be found on the cassette *Hello Everybody* by Rachel Buchman.

Hands and Knees Equilibrium
Pet Parade Ask a number of children to get into a hands/knees position on a long scooter board and "parade by" by moving their scooter board

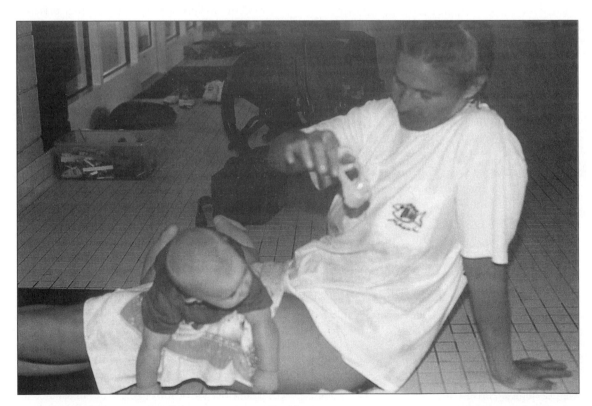

An Activity to Promote Equilibrium in Prone Position
Photo by Carol Huettig.

with their hands. To make it a great deal of fun, the pets can wear special costumes for the parade.

Kneeling Equilibrium
Rodeo Rider Ask the child to straddle a bolster, with the knees on a mat on both sides. Let the child pretend to be a "rodeo rider" while the teacher lifts either end of the bolster and tries to roll it back and forth while the child sits on it. This is even more fun if the children sing "Rodeo Rider" from the cassette *What I Want to Be* from Kids Songs.

Standing Equilibrium
Body Boogie Ask the children to stand and join you in the dance "Swing, Shake, Twist and Stretch," on the record/cassette *Walter the Waltzing Worm* by Hap Palmer. Certainly, children using a wheelchair can perform the same activities while remaining seated.

Sensory Discrimination

Movement and play programs for three- to five-year-old children with and without disabilities should focus on the development of sensory discrimination, although children with severe and profound disabilities may require ongoing sensory stimulation. The intent is to provide children with the opportunity to integrate sensory stimuli, so that they can make an appropriate motor output. Examples of activities to stimulate the development of sensory discrimination follow.

Tactile Discrimination
Line-Em-Up Ask the child to sit in a long V-sit position with his or her eyes closed. Roll a variety of balls (different textures and different shapes) to the child (yarn ball, whiffle golf ball, tennis ball, 6-inch playground ball, volleyball, nerf football, 20-inch beach ball, beep ball, etc.) and ask the child to arrange the balls from "smallest" to the "biggest." If the child peeks, the child *needs* to peek.

Obstacle Course On a mat, establish an obstacle course with mats, rolled-up towels, bolsters, incline mats, beanbag chairs, etc. Ask the children, one at a time, to move through the obstacle course with their eyes closed. If the child peeks, the child *needs* to peek.

Vestibular Discrimination
Spin-A-Way Ask the child to sit and spin on a scooter board. Once the child has demonstrated, for example, a 360-degree spin, the teacher can ask the child permission to spin the child 360 degrees, as well.

Proprioceptive Discrimination
Pull-A-Thon Ask the child to close his or her eyes. Tie jump ropes to a variety of objects that can be pulled (scooters with other kids sitting on them, a tire, a wagon with a mat in it, etc.). Let the child pull one "object" and replace it. Then let the child pull all "objects" until the child finds the one he or she pulled first. At first, make the contrast very obvious so the child experiences success; as the child gets more sophisticated, the differences can be made more subtle.

Auditory Discrimination
You Can't Find Me Ask two or more children (depending on their auditory discrimination capability) to hide, each using one rhythm instrument. Ask a child to close his or her eyes and try to locate the child shaking the tambourine, for example, as opposed to the child beating on the drum.

You Can't Catch Me; I'm the Ginger-Bread Man Ask the children to crawl or creep while trying to catch the child who is reciting, "Run, run, as fast as you can . . . You can't catch me; I'm the gingerbread man." This is even more fun if the class has already heard the story "The Gingerbread Man."

Visual Discrimination
Texas Round-Up Blow up several dozen balloons (several different colors) and put them on a parachute in the corner of a room. The children play cowgirl or cowboy and try to "round up" the balloons after they have escaped. (The teacher and several children lift the parachute up into the air to send the balloons flying.) Children are asked to

round up the "little doggies." Children may be encouraged, for example, to use only their feet for the round up. If the children need to use their hands, however, they should be allowed to do so.

Body Image

Having a good body image indicates that a child has an internal understanding of how the body works, how the parts of the body relate to one another, how much space the body occupies, and what the body looks like. The development of body image can be enhanced by activities as simple as participating in the dance, "What a Miracle" on Hap Palmer's *Walter the Waltzing Worm* record/cassette. Or the activities can be more complex, as in the following example.

My Own Special Movement A group of children sit in a circle. Each child is asked to show a "special" movement. The teacher can help prompt. For example, if the child is asked to show a special movement and the child simply shrugs the shoulders, the teacher can thank the child for sharing the "shoulder shrug." Then the activity starts. The group chants the child's name while doing the child's shoulder shrug three times. For example, the group chants "Tommy, Tommy, Tommy" while shrugging the shoulders three times, once for each time the name is repeated.

If the next child, Maria, chooses a hand clap as her movement, the group practices saying, "Maria, Maria, Maria" while clapping three times. Once the group has practiced, the activity starts over. The group chants, "Tommy, Tommy, Tommy" while shrugging and then "Maria, Maria, Maria" while clapping.

The number of children in the circle is determined by the children's interest and attention span. This is an empowering activity—having your own movement and having others chant your name—so most tend to stay involved. This is a particularly wonderful activity if a child in the group has limited movement potential. For example, if Roshard's athetoid cerebral palsy limits his voli-

tional movement to a head roll, the group can chant, "Roshard, Roshard, Roshard" while rolling their heads.

This dance or game can be enhanced by adding music to the chants so the children are working on rhythm skills at the same time as they are doing motor planning and auditory and kinesthetic sequencing and using motor memory.

Basic Locomotor and Nonlocomotor Competency

Locomotor and nonlocomotor skills can be enhanced as young children are given every opportunity to explore movements and their variables: time, space, force, and flow. Examples of how basic movements can be modified by manipulating those four variables follow.

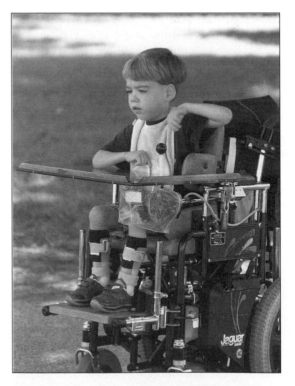

A motorized chair gives a child the opportunity to control his or her destiny.

Time   The child swings his or her arms to

1. A 4-4 beat
2. The song "Freeze" on the cassette *We All Live Together II* by Greg and Steve
3. The beat of a drum
4. Follow the arm-swinging motion of a partner

Space   The child creeps

1. Forward and backward
2. Up and down an incline mat
3. In, around, and between a series of obstacles
4. Through a tunnel
5. On a "crazy sidewalk": A series of mats is placed on varying surfaces, such as beanbag chairs, so that the surface "gives" when the student moves, causing postural adjustments.

Force   The child runs

1. While pushing a wheelbarrow
2. While pulling a partner sitting on a scooter, each holding one end of the rope
3. While pumping arms and legs vigorously
4. While trying to get as high off the ground as possible

Flow   The child pushes his or her wheelchair

1. Three times and then stops
2. Forward three times, stops; backward three times, stops
3. In an alternating pattern, right hand, left hand, right hand, left hand
4. In "wheelies" (wheels on ground) right three times, and "wheelies" left three times

Cross-Lateral Integration

Cross-lateral integration is the ability to coordinate the use of both sides of the body, particularly in activities that require movement about the midline of the body. Examples of activities that may facilitate the *beginning* of the neurological development required for cross-lateral integration follow.

Ribbon Activities   The child holds a wand with a ribbon of Mylar or crepe paper and makes the following movements, alternating hands:

1. Figure eight, which crosses the midline of the body
2. Huge *X*s, which cross the midline of the body

Ball Activities

1. The child, while sitting, rolls a ball all the way around the body.
2. The child performs alternate-hand dribbling in front of the body.

Object-Control Skills

Object-control skills are simply those that involve the process of using an object. Examples of activities that facilitate the development of object control follow:

1. Ask the child to sit in a long V-sit, and roll a series of balls to the child, asking the child to roll them back. The intensity (quickness) should be adjusted so that the child is successful.
2. Ask the child to lie supine and bobble a balloon above the body using knees and feet.
3. Ask the child to sit and "trap" as many balloons as possible with the arms and legs.
4. Ask the child to wad newspaper into balls as quickly as possible and then throw them as far as possible.
5. Scatter balls and beanbags of as many different sizes, weights, and textures as possible in a given space. Ask the child to throw them all to another space—over a net, for example.
6. Scatter balls and beanbags of as many different sizes, weights, and textures as possible in a given space. Ask the child to kick them all to another space—over a net, for example.

Fitness

Fitness activities for young children, ages three to five, should be redundant. If a young child is involved in a quality, developmentally appropriate movement program, the child will develop and maintain fitness. The natural inclination of a young child to move—to play—if honored, should provide the child ample opportunity to develop strength, flexibility, and cardiovascular endurance. Any attempt to structure that fitness experience may encourage fitness in the preschooler but will ultimately discourage the child from a lifetime of fitness commitment.

Activities designed particularly for the young child who uses a wheelchair for ambulation or who has limited movement potential can be found in the book that accompanies this textbook, *Gross Motor Activities for Young Children with Special Needs.*

THE INDOOR ACTIVE LEARNING CENTER

The active learning center for preschoolers with and without disabilities, like other centers designed in the developmentally appropriate learning environment, should provide children with the opportunity to move, self-test, explore, interact, and play. Ideally, the adapted physical education specialist should create the active learning center *with* the children. And the specialist should be sensitive to the needs of the children and create and recreate the environment on the basis of the materials and equipment to which the children are drawn. The following materials and equipment enhance the learning environment and encourage active exploration and active experiences in movement and play:

- Mats of different types and densities, including "crash-type" mats
- Large foam-filled forms of different shape (pyramids, cubes, donut holes, etc.) for kids to roll on, jump on, and climb in, around, over, and through
- Large empty boxes for children to climb in, around, over, and through
- Giant tumble balls (17-, 23-, and 30-inch)
- Hippity hops
- Large balls for catching (10- to 13-inch)

- A wide variety of small balls and beanbags to throw
- Tricycles and child-sized safety helmets
- Scooters and child-sized safety helmets
- Wagons and wheelbarrows
- A variety of scooter boards, with and without handles (Sportime has some excellent "huge" scooter boards that two children can share)
- Sheets and blankets to make forts and tunnels
- Steps for climbing and a slide for sliding
- An incline ramp
- Nets and ropes for climbing
- Big trucks, cars, etc.
- Hula hoops
- Parachutes (6-, 12-, and 20-foot)
- Tug of war rope and shorter ropes for pulling and jumping over
- Cones
- Paper and markers to identify a play area (e.g., Pooh's house)

This indoor active learning center provides a wealth of opportunity for children to explore and move. It provides a myriad of experiences that enhance learning in other centers as well. For example, the active learning center is a vital part of a centers-based, developmentally appropriate program. The children should have the opportunity to participate in independent, adult-supported play experiences. In addition, the active learning center can provide a wonderful opportunity for the enhancement of a given theme or unit. For example, if the preschoolers are learning about winter, activities in each of the centers may enhance this learning and make it more real. The following are examples of the types of activities that may occur in each center.

Science or Discovery Center   To examine ice and its properties, the teacher can freeze water on cookie sheets and let the children feel how slippery and cold the ice really is. Then they can watch it melt and, if possible, refreeze.

House Center   The children may pretend to make hot chocolate or warm cider on the stove. The children may get all dressed up to go out in the cold weather.

Art Center   The children can use cottonballs ("snowballs") in their art. The children can cut or tear white paper and make snowflakes, or the children may decide to use black or brown paper and make "rainflakes."

Music Center   The children can sing and dance to "Frosty the Snowman."

Language Center   The children can read the story of "Frosty the Snowman" and then act out the story. The children can make up stories about "Hannah [the child's name] the Snowman." It should be noted that Connor-Kuntz and Dummer[7] have acknowledged the potential for language intervention and instruction within physical activity. They found

> First, language enrichment can be added to physical education activities without lengthening the activities and without compromising improvement in motor skill performance. Second, previously documented gains in motor skill performance as a result of intervention have been extended to a broader range of skills. Third, preschool children with cognitive and/or language impairments, preschoolers of low socioeconomic status, and preschoolers who might be considered privileged all benefited from language enriched physical education activities.[7]

Cooking Center   The children can make "snowball" cookies by cutting prepackaged rolls of refrigerated sugar cookie dough into small quarters, sprinkling the cookies with shaved coconut, and baking the cookies (with the teacher's help).

Blocks and Center   The children can use blocks and Duplos/Legos to build snowpeople and snow forts, or the children may decide to make a "Teletubby."

Active Play Center

1. The children may pretend to be people cutting and stacking firewood and shoveling snow.
2. The children may pretend to be ice skaters, skating on pieces of waxed paper on the wood or tile floor.
3. The children can use large building blocks to make snow forts and have a "snowball" fight using yarn balls or rolled-up white socks.
4. The children can ride tricycles and pretend to be snowmobilers.
5. The teacher can fold a large rope between panels of a mat. Several children can ride on the "sleigh" while the teacher and other children are the horses. To make it even more fun, the children can jingle "sleigh bells" and sing "Jingle Bells."
6. The teacher can push children lying prone on scooter boards, and the children can pretend to be sledding.

Movement is an end in itself. Children need to move, and they must be given every opportunity to do so. It may be easier, however, for the adapted physical education specialist to convince other preschool educators to involve children in gross motor activity if the teachers believe the activity will reinforce learning that occurs in other centers or supports a given "theme". The opportunities for learning that are inherent in the active learning center are endless and meet the needs of young children to use their bodies and to participate in play, all the while reinforcing other learning.

As mentioned earlier, the equipment, materials and other props simply help the adapted physical educator establish the learning environment. The learning opportunities are endless. They are endless, however, only if each child has adequate play opportunities. There is nothing so sad as seeing a group of young children in a huge open play space with only two or three balls to share.

Careful preparation of the play environment will maximize learning opportunities and minimize the potential for arguments. The key to the preparation of any learning environment for young children is the creation of at least 2.5 play units per child. Sharing is one of the things that preschoolers really struggle with—to force them to do something for which they are developmentally unprepared is to create conflict between children. Fewer play units (play materials, equipment, and spaces) increase the likelihood that children will argue about materials, equipment, and space.

Wetherby[73] describes the different types of play units:

- Simple play unit: A play area that occupies one child and is not conducive to cooperative interaction
- Complex play unit: A play area that occupies up to four children, such as a sand table with pouring utensils for each child or a puppet stage with puppets for each child
- Super play unit: A play area that occupies up to eight children, such as a dramatic play area with eight costumes or a block area with at least twenty-five interlocking or fifty unit blocks per child

With young children, the leap from independent, solitary play in a simple play unit to play in a complex play unit may be overwhelming. A "partner" play unit is developmentally appropriate as children learn first to deal with one other child and then with small groups of children. Teachers must create opportunities for play with only one other child as well. A play unit analysis for indoor active play centers is presented in Figure 10-10.

The consideration of play units must also address the nature of the toys selected for inclusion in the learning center. Some toys tend to foster the development of cooperative play; some tend to "isolate" children in a play setting.[36] Cooperative play is much more likely when social toys are available. Social toys support a more equal balance between parallel and cooperative play.[36] Careful selection and use of toys is an important tool.[38] In fact, it may be the most significant instructional strategy available for an early childhood educator and/or an adapted physical education specialist working with preschoolers with and without disabilities. Ivory identified the following as social toys:

- Blocks
- Dress-up clothes
- Dolls and dollhouse
- Housekeeping materials such as spoons, ice cube trays, bowls
- Puppets
- Toy trucks and cars[36]

Figure 10-10 Active Learning Center, Indoors: Play Unit Analysis

Following is a sample evaluation of an indoor active learning center that a preschool adapted physical education specialist would complete before involving young children in its use. Required: 2.5 play units per child.

Materials, Equipment, Spaces	Number of Play Units
Simple play units (1 point each)	
5 tricycles	5
3 wheelbarrows	3
2 small slides (height = 6 feet)	2
2 small balance beams (6 inches wide, 6 inches long)	2
6 scooter boards (2 feet × 3 feet)	6
3 wooden trucks	3
3 plastic fire trucks	3
2 "jumpin jiminy"	2/26 play units
Partner play units (2 points each)	
3 small pull wagons (1 child pulls, 1 rides)	6
2 two-seat rockers	4
6 huge (refrigerator/stove) empty boxes	12/38 play units
Complex play units (4 points each)	
1 cassette player with songs for dancing	4/42 play units
Super units (8 points each)	
1 large parachute with handles for 16	16/58
	68 play units

Play area is adequate to support quality play of 27 children!

THE OUTDOOR ACTIVE LEARNING CENTER

The outdoor play experience for young children with developmental delays or disabilities should be an extension of learning that occurs within the home, day-care center, recreation center, neighborhood playground, and active learning center. As in every other setting, the outdoor play of young children needs to be respected and valued, and it may serve as a scaffold for the development of

- More complex and sophisticated play
- Gross and fine motor skills
- Interpersonal skills
- Communication and language

The outdoor active learning center must also focus on the provision of adequate play units if the environment is to enhance learning. An example of an outdoor active play center play unit analysis is found in Figure 10-11.

The opportunity to play and learn outdoors is as vital to a child as the air he or she breathes. Children, as resilient people, will find a way to play—in almost any outdoor setting. Being able to use "outside voices" and to do the things that come naturally to many children—running, jumping, climbing, swinging, hanging—creates the opportunity for a joyful learning experience. However, as Rivkin reminds us,

> Although no person or government planned it, habitats for children, especially in industrialized countries, have been greatly altered—often destroyed—in this century, especially in recent decades. . . . Children's access to outdoor play has evaporated like water in sunshine.[61]

Unfortunately, this alteration and destruction of play environments for children—the ruination of their habitats—has significantly compromised the quality of young children's lives. In many urban environments, children simply cannot "go out to play," for fear of drive-by shootings or kidnapping, contact with drug paraphernalia, and contact with toxic substances. In fact, many children have the opportunity to play outdoors only under the supervision of teachers and assistants in a day-care or preschool program. A vital and integral part of a total early childhood education program, the outdoor play experience should be a part of the daily schedule.[50] Children must have the opportunity to play outside every day. The only exception, of course, is during inclement or dangerous weather, including weather "warnings," storms with lightning, severe heat or severe

Figure 10-11   Active Play Center, Outdoors: Play Unit Analysis

Following is a sample evaluation of an outdoor play area that a preschool adapted physical education specialist would complete before involving young children in its use. Required: 2.5 play units per child.

Materials, Equipment, Spaces	Number of Play Units
Simple play units (1 point each)	
5 tricycles	5
3 wheelbarrows	3
2 small slides (height = 6 feet)	2
2 small balance beams (6 inches wide, 6 inches long)	2
6 scooter boards (2 feet × 3 feet)	6
3 wooden trucks	3
3 plastic fire trucks	3
2 "jumpin jiminy"	2/26 play units
Partner play units (2 points each)	
3 small pull wagons (1 child pulls, 1 rides)	6
2 two-seat rockers	4/10 play units
Complex play units (4 points each)	
1 water table (with a spoonful of dishwashing detergent) 2 buckets 2 measuring cups 2 watering cans 4 bubble makers	4/4 play units
Super units (8 points each)	
1 large sandbox 5 buckets 5 shovels 4 rakes 4 pancake turners 2 sieves	8
1 small parachute with handles for 8	8
1 large play structure	8/24 play units
	64 play units

Play area is adequate to support quality play of 25 children!

cold, and, particularly for children with asthma and other respiratory problems, ozone and other pollution alerts.

Most preschool educators would agree that the ideal outdoor play setting is one in which the child has the opportunity to interact with and learn from nature. This gives the child with a "naturalistic" intelligence the opportunity to learn and grow and use that intelligence. It is vital not only for their physical and social development but may inherently be vital for the development of their souls. The ideal preschool outdoor play area is nature-based (Figure 10-12) and includes the following:

- Flowers, bushes, and trees native to the area

- Natural play surfaces: grass (short and tall grasses), dirt, sand, hills, and valleys
- Apparatus for climbing, swinging, and hanging: trees, rocks, vines
- Apparatus for balancing, self-testing: tree stumps, fallen logs
- Play areas for digging and pouring: dirt/mud, sand, stream/pond
- Play materials for building and stacking: rocks, twigs
- Play materials for sorting and classifying: flowers and weeds, leaves, seeds (acorns)

In the event that the outdoor play area is not in a natural setting, there are still ways for the creative adapted physical educator to help design an

Figure 10-12   Natural Outdoor Play Area

outdoor play area that meets the fundamental needs of young children (see Figure 10-13). The "asphalt" play area could include the following:

- Flowers, bushes, and trees native to the area (flower boxes, potted trees, potted bushes)
- Play surfaces: wood chips, sand, dirt, pea gravel, incline ramps
- Apparatus for climbing, swinging, hanging, and sliding: net climbers, tire climbers, swings, slides, steps/ladders, horizontal poles, vertical poles
- Apparatus for balancing, self-testing: railroad ties, 4 × 4's
- Play areas for digging and pouring: sandbox, dirt/mud, sand table, sand, water table, plastic swimming pool, sprinkler, garden plots
- Play materials for building and stacking: plastic blocks, rocks, wooden blocks, twigs

In some inner-city areas it is virtually impossible to maintain a developmentally appropriate outdoor play area because of theft and vandalism. Large play structures that can be cemented into the ground may be the only option to provide any play spaces for children. And educators have to be concerned that parts of those play structures that can be disconnected to be sold to gain recycling dollars. There are some creative play structures that provide access for all children that are difficult to disassemble and difficult to hurt.

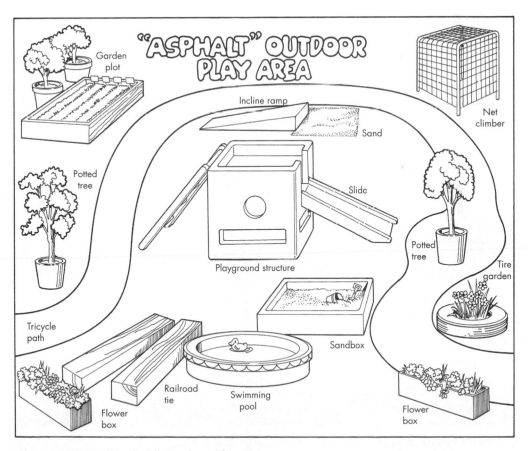

Figure 10-13   "Asphalt" Outdoor Play Area

Basic Standards for the Preschool Outdoor Play Area

The adapted physical education specialist must determine the safety and developmental appropriateness of the outdoor play area. The following must be considered:

1. Is the outdoor play area large enough to allow children to move freely (75 to 100 square feet per child)? If the play area is not that large, can scheduling patterns be devised to limit the number of children using the outdoor play area at any given time?
2. Can the teachers and assistants see all children in the outdoor play area without obstruction?
3. Is the area accessible to all children?
4. Is the area adjacent to bathrooms and water fountains? Are those accessible to all children?
5. Is there a phone available in the event of an emergency?
6. Does the outdoor play area provide areas that are sunny and areas that are shaded?[18]
7. Is the area fenced in to provide protection? Is there an area that serves as a buffer between the street and the play area?
8. Are there child-sized places to rest and relax (e.g., child-sized picnic tables or benches)?
9. Is the area free of debris, litter, and broken glass?[18]
10. Are playground structures no taller than twice the height of the tallest preschooler using the play area? Actually, some playground safety experts believe that climbing structures should be significantly limited. A cautious rule of thumb is 1 foot of height for every year of age. A three-year-old can climb a ladder/mound to 3 feet. A five-year-old can climb a ladder/mound to 5 feet.[60]

It is easy for a child with a developmental delay to catch a slowly moving scarf.
Photo by Kerrie Berends.

11. Does any of the equipment have rust, cracks, or splinters?[18]
12. Are there any hazards, such as sharp edges or places where a child can be pinched?

Careful attention should be paid to the safety of the outdoor play area. Careful review of safety standards, on a daily basis, is a vital part of the role of the adapted physical educator.

Extending Learning Center Activities Outdoors

Far too often, outdoor play time is considered a "recess" time or a time for teachers to relax and regroup. The outdoor play time is one of the most vital and significant parts of the day and can, if carefully planned, not only prove crucial in the development of more complex and sophisticated play skills, gross and fine motor skills, interpersonal skills, and communication/language skills but may also enhance learning opportunities initiated in indoor learning centers. The following are examples of how activities that are part of the centers experience can be expanded and enhanced in learning activities out-of-doors.

Sociodramatic Play   Children wearing dress-up hats and "pretending to be" wear the hats outside and

1. Put out the fire in the house (playground structure)
2. Use the wagons as ambulances when playing doctor
3. Climb on buildings (climbers) as construction workers
4. Chase robbers in squad cars (tricycles)

Art
1. Children use large brushes and water and "paint" the outside of the building.
2. Children make sand sculptures in the sandbox.
3. Children make texture rubbings on trees, with leaves and flowers.
4. Children make shadow drawings.

Discovery (Science)
1. Children fly kites to experiment with the wind.
2. Children slide down slides to experience gravity.
3. Children collect acorns, seeds, leaves, weeds, flowers, etc., for a collage.

Blocks
1. Children collect and arrange rocks in sequence from large to small.
2. Children see how many "laps" they can drive on their tricycle in a given amount of time.
3. Children take large foam and large wooden blocks outside to create structures that augment those that already exist.

Language and Literacy   Children act out stories learned in the classroom. They become large muscle/gross motor activities when acted out outside:

1. "Billy Goat Gruff" (incline ramps/play structure as bridge)
2. "Pocahontas" (outdoor play area is the wilderness)

Music   Children move to music while climbing, hanging, swinging, bending, stretching, and twisting on apparatus, trees, rocks, etc.

This approach allows the "inside" and "outside" learning experiences to augment and enhance each other. Outdoor play does not require any justification and certainly is not designed to supplement anything. It is, inherently, a vital and integral part of the child's total educational experience.

PRESCHOOL INCLUSION PROGRAMS

If this society is, indeed, committed to the notion that all individuals should have the opportunity to learn together—a commitment not based on administrative feasibility or perception of cost reduction—the best possible place to begin inclusionary practices is with infants, toddlers, and young children, yet Lamorey and Bricker[41] estimated that less than one-third of young children eligible for early intervention services are

Physical educators must appraise play facilities with the needs of students with disabilities in mind.
Courtesy Collier Center for Communicative Disorders, Dallas, TX.

receiving those service in integrated or inclusive settings. The decision regarding the extent to which a child should be included, if the child should be included, must be based solely on the child's individual needs.[51]

Young children are, inherently, very accepting of other children. Their curiosity is natural and, if their questions are answered honestly, they accept their playmates naturally and without hesitation. A child-sensitive inclusion program would begin with inclusive infant, toddler, and preschool programs. As children who have played together enter school together, they are able to learn together and, eventually, be citizens together in peace.[44]

Including and using children's books that are designed to foster acceptance, empathy, and understanding regarding a fellow child's disability is a vital part of the preschool learning experience. Figure 10-14 lists excellent books for preschoolers that address the issue of disability in an enlightened and humane way. In fact, it appears that children make play choices, to include or not to include another child, based on behaviors, not disability. Preschoolers do not want to play with children who are aggressive or destructive.[31,53] Millspaugh and Segelman[52] suggested

Figure 10-14   Books for Preschoolers that Encourage Understanding Regarding Disabilities[5]

Rabe B: Where's Chimpy? Morton Grove, IL, 1988, Albert Whitman.
Emmert M: I'm the Big Sister Now, Morton Grove, IL, 1989, Albert Whitman.
Wright C: Just Like Emma: How She Has Fun in God's World, Minneapolis, MN, 1993, Augsburg Fortress.
Bunnett R: Friends in the Park, Bellingham, WA, 1992, Our Kids Press.
Hesse K: Lester's Dog, New York, 1993, Crown.
Cowen-Fletcher J: Mama Zooms, New York, 1993, Scholastic.
Karim R: Mandy Sue's Day, New York, 1994, Clarion Books.
Kastner J: Naomi Knows It's Springtime, Honesville, PA, 1993, Boyds Mills.
Damrell L: With the Wind, New York, 1991, Orchid Books.

that preschoolers are so willing to accept other children with disabilities because each preschooler is virtually disabled in the so-called adult-designed world. According to them,

Figure 10-15   Preschool Movement/Play Inclusion Checklist for Children with Severe Disabilities

Student:_____ Age:_____ Date:_____	Y/N

1. Is the child in a position to participate in all phases of the movement/play activity? If the child uses a wheelchair or crutches, is the activity taking place on a surface that is accessible?   _____

2. Does the child participate in the same movement/play activities as the other children? If not, are the modifications kept to a minimum?   _____

3. Does the child engage in movement/play activities at the same time as the other children?   _____

4. Is the child actively involved, or does the child spend a great deal of time watching others move/play?   _____

5. Does the child receive physical assistance from an adult only when absolutely necessary?   _____

6. Is the adult careful not to interrupt the play of the child?   _____

7. Does the child receive only the most unobtrusive prompts from adults to help the child participate in the activity?   _____

8. Do other children seek out the child for play (e.g., ask the child to play)?   _____

9. Does the child seek out other children for play?   _____

10. Does the child have gestures, signs, or pictures to help him or her communicate if the child is unable to communicate verbally?   _____

11. Do teachers interact with the child the same way as they do with the other children—the same type of praise, stickers, hugs, etc.?   _____

12. Does the child have the same opportunities as other children for responsible roles in the active learning center (e.g., selecting music, distributing equipment)?   _____

"Society systematically handicaps all small children by making drinking fountains too high to manage, stairs too deep to climb, and toilet paper dispensers too far (away) to reach."[52] A checklist that can be used to evaluate the extent to which a child with a severe disability is actually included in a preschool activity program is presented in Figure 10-15.

A publication written for the W.K. Kellogg Readiness Initiatives, supported by the W.K. Kellogg Foundation in cooperation with the National Association for the Education of Young Children, *Grassroots Success: Preparing Schools and Families for Each Other,*[72] suggested that schools that are ready for children

- Welcome all children and families in the community
- Design curriculum content and daily routines that promote children's self-motivated learning: social, emotional, cognitive, and physical
- Offer challenging, hands-on, relevant learning activities that build on what children already

know and prepare them to contribute to a democratic society

- Ensure that staff are well prepared to work with the ages and abilities of the children
- Use appropriate methods to assess children's progress and evaluate possible special needs
- Prepare environments that enable children to construct knowledge and understanding through inquiry, play, social interaction, and skill development

As is true of school-based inclusive adapted physical education programs (see Chapter 5), a great deal of preparation must occur to address attitudes and biases, abilities and skills, and, most important when addressing inclusive learning with preschoolers, the developmental appropriateness of the learning environment. Children with diverse abilities and disabilities can learn and thrive together in developmentally appropriate learning environments with few, if any, modifications in curriculum or pedagogy.[33]

RESPONSIBILITIES OF THE ADAPTED PHYSICAL EDUCATION SPECIALIST

Goodway and Rudisell[23] have provided an incredible challenge to adapted physical educators and other early childhood educators to provide quality motor programming for children with disabilities and those at risk. They found that African American preschoolers who are at risk for school failure or developmental delays start school feeling competent and good about themselves. However, data have shown that by the third grade these feelings of competence and acceptance have declined.[57] Clearly, the adapted physical educator, like every other educator, needs to take heed and to address the issue.

The responsibilities of the adapted physical educator who works with preschoolers include the following:

1. Address the gross motor and play goals/objectives on the IEPs of each of the children with disabilities.
2. Collect data for each child's portfolio assessment, those children with and without disabilities.
3. Create a learning environment in which all the children, those with and without disabilities, have the opportunity to work on gross motor and play skills. The key to a successful, developmentally appropriate motor/play learning environment is the work done before the children are present to prepare the learning environment.
4. Coordinate and plan the learning experience to support the theme or focus of the child-care or preschool program.
5. Model appropriate motor and play behavior for all students.
6. Encourage and support age-appropriate interaction among all students.
7. Provide support for the children with disabilities who are having difficulty with a gross motor or play skill, not by separating the children for individual instruction but by encouraging a small group of children to work together.

PARENT NOTE

It is very important that you know . . .

You can be very proud of _____ . Your child did some great things this week:

       Played in a small group

       Caught a bounced 6-inch playground ball

You could help at home by

       Complimenting play at home that doesn't include fighting

       Playing catch with your child

Thank you for sharing your great kid with me.

       Emily Unger, Preschool Motor Specialist

Figure 10-16 **Parent Note**

---

8. Model and provide consultative support for the early childhood educators and assistants and other preschool regular and special educators and their paraprofessionals.
9. Communicate with parents through notes and newsletters (see Figures 10-16 and 10-17).

An example of including all children in a learning center that reflects a child-care or preschool theme is provided in Figure 10-18. In this example, the theme for the week was "transportation," and the adapted physical educator created an active learning center to support that theme. The active learning center, indoor or outdoor, for preschoolers with and without disabilities, designed to support a transportation theme would include the following:

- A marked roadway for automobiles, buses, and trucks with tricycles, scooter boards, and wagons, including stop signs, etc.
- An incline ramp with crash mat to simulate an airplane take-off
- Different-sized boxes for the children to decorate as race cars, police cars, firetrucks, etc.

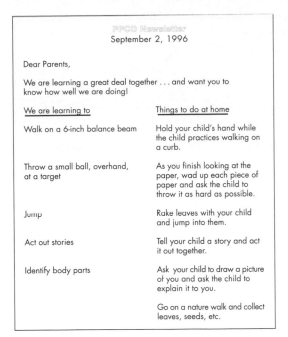

PPCD Newsletter
September 2, 1996

Dear Parents,

We are learning a great deal together . . . and want you to know how well we are doing!

We are learning to	Things to do at home
Walk on a 6-inch balance beam	Hold your child's hand while the child practices walking on a curb.
Throw a small ball, overhand, at a target	As you finish looking at the paper, wad up each piece of paper and ask the child to throw it as hard as possible.
Jump	Rake leaves with your child and jump into them.
Act out stories	Tell your child a story and act it out together.
Identify body parts	Ask your child to draw a picture of you and ask the child to explain it to you.
	Go on a nature walk and collect leaves, seeds, etc.

Figure 10-17   PPCD Newsletter

- A roadway created with a series of mats to provide varied surfaces for the cars to move on
- An obstacle course for the automobiles, buses, and trucks to move on, over, between, and through
- A cassette player with a tape including the following songs: "The Freeze" (We All Live Together, Volume 2); "Yellow Submarine" (Mod Marches); "Chug A Long Choo Choo" (Preschool Aerobic Fun, Georgiana Stewart)

Once the active learning center is designed to expand on the theme, the role of the adapted physical educator is that of *facilitator.* Following are examples of techniques that can be used to address IEP goals/objectives and still serve all the children in the program:

- If a four-year-old with Down syndrome is having difficulty with jumping skills and performing a vertical jump[6] using a definite flexion-extension pattern with hips, knees, and ankles is one of her short-term objectives, the teacher may position himself or herself near the "airplane take-off area" and offer to spot for all the children as they run and jump into the crash pad. All children gravitate to a teacher who is actively supporting and encouraging children. In this way, the teacher can work on the child's IEP goals without singling the child out from the others.
- If a three-year-old child with low muscle tone is having difficulty lifting his head and shoulders when in a prone position, the teacher may sit on the floor and play "supergirl" or "superboy" by letting children get on scooter boards on their stomachs and then push them so they race until they run out of gas.
- If a five-year-old with spina bifida is using a manual wheelchair to ambulate and one of her annual goals is "Elaine will be able to stop and start her wheelchair to avoid bumping into other children in the hallway," the teacher can help her decorate her wheelchair as a police car and then work with all the children on starting/stopping activities in the figure-eight raceway.
- If a four-year-old child with ADHD (who has difficulty playing with other children) has an annual goal that reads "Jeremiah will be able to participate in a small-group cooperative play activity," the teacher may invite three or four children to play "Freeze," an active parallel play experience.

If preschoolers with disabilities are receiving services from an adapted physical education teacher, it is usually as a consultant rather than as a direct service provider. The general physical educator may work with preschoolers who are three, four, or five years old but in many school districts the early childhood educator is responsible for addressing the child's gross motor and play needs. Thus, the major task of the adapted physical education specialist is to help local campus staff follow through and continue the activity and actions throughout the week when the teacher is not present.

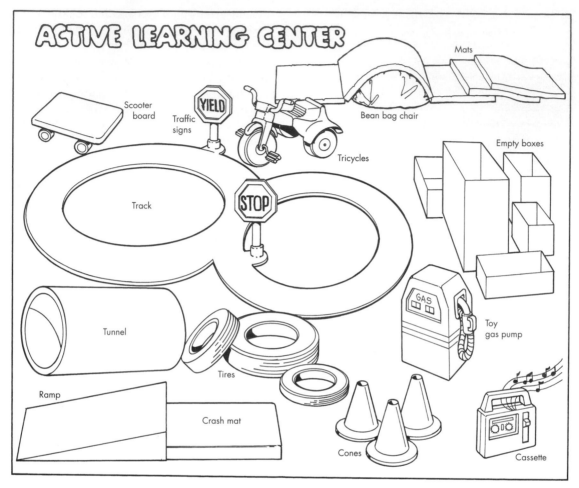

Figure 10-18 **Active Learning Center to Support a Transportation Theme**

Atypical Play Behavior

Curry and Arnaud wrote,

> For young children, play is the most natural and spontaneous of activities, on a par with eating, sleeping, talking, moving, and elimination. Accordingly . . .
>
> Play is a lawful, predictable phenomenon that shows clear developmental regularities, although the degree to which these regularities are expressed is much influenced by the child's environment.
>
> Play serves to integrate complex cognitive, emotional, and social elements in the child's thinking and behavior.

> Disturbances in play often reflect disturbances in the child's personality and social functioning.[12]

The adapted physical education specialist, as an acute and trained observer of children's behavior, may note disturbances in a child's play that should alert the specialist to a potential problem.[12] The play behavior of young children with disabilities may reflect their developmental delays. Bergen stated:

> Most at-risk young children engage in the first stage of play development (sensorimotor/practice play) although the quantity and quality of the play is influenced by the nature and

severity of their handicaps, biological risk, or environmental risk conditions. For example, visually impaired, autistic, and motorically-impaired children have narrower ranges of sensorimotor play behaviors, severely multiply-handicapped children initiate less sensorimotor play, and abused/neglected children may be hypervigilant and less exploratory. Down syndrome and hearing impaired children, however, seem to show sensorimotor play behaviors that are very similar to those of children who are not at risk.[1] [Author's note: No attempt was made to change this quotation to reflect person-first language.]

The preschool movement/play specialist, always a careful observer of young children at play, must be sensitive to the following types of idiosyncrasies in play:

1. Significant preoccupation with a single play theme may be an indicator of a behavior disorder or an autistic-like behavior. Most young children seek repetition as a means of gaining and keeping control of their environment. Any parent who has been urged to read a story "one more time" or any teacher who has grown weary of a particular song or dance understands this phenomenon.
2. Unchanging repetition of a play theme
   a. May indicate an emotional disturbance or a cognitive delay
   b. May indicate a need for control of part of the child's life, as is typical of children living with abuse and neglect or parental drug abuse
3. Unusual or morbid play themes (drive-by shooting, funeral) may indicate a child has had the experience and is trying to put it into perspective.
4. Imitation of sexual acts and practices may indicate the child is being or has been sexually abused or molested.
5. Lack of awareness of other children
   a. May indicate a developmental delay (in children age three or older)
   b. May indicate an emotional disorder
   c. May indicate autism or pervasive developmental disorder

6. Fragmentary play—an inability to sustain play
   a. In children older than three years may indicate a developmental delay or attention deficit disorder
   b. May indicate that a child is unable to cope with a significant, acute, or chronic trauma
7. Difficulty separating self from a play role (e.g., the child is a Power Ranger, not Sally playing "Power Ranger") may be typical of a child who has been treated aggressively.
8. Difficulty joining groups at play without disrupting others may be typical of a child with a developmental delay.
9. Tendency to lash out and spoil play (knock down the block structure) of other children may indicate the child has a disability that makes it difficult to participate, so the child acts out in frustration.

Management of Behavior in the Preschool Learning Environment

Zittel and McCubbin wrote,

> Best practice in early childhood education, for children with and without developmental delays, calls for the design of environments that are more child- versus teacher-directed.[77]

If educators design a learning environment that is more child-directed, management of behavior is simplified. The beauty of the developmentally appropriate, play-based, learning environment is that behavior problems are minimized.[19] The following environmental variables encourage appropriate behavior and minimize behavior problems:

- A small student–teacher ratio (young children demand and require the attention and care of adults; a ratio of no more than 8:1 is vital)
- Age-appropriate, child-driven activity
- A routine that the child can count on during the day, every day
- Child choices regarding activity
- A daily schedule sensitive to a child's basic needs—nutritious snack and lunch time, quiet or nap time

- A daily schedule that provides an opportunity for solitary, partner, small-group, and large-group activities
- A daily schedule that allows for a mix of indoor and outdoor play
- A quiet place where a child can retreat at any time during the day
- An adequate number of play units (there must be a sufficient number of materials so children are not expected to share)

If these basic variables are controlled, most children's behavior will be controlled as well. To encourage consistency, just as in any other setting, rules must be clear and concise, brief and understandable.

The most basic strategy for establishing a positive learning environment in which a preschooler will be successful is to be proactive and to "catch 'em being good" whenever possible. There are some important constraints, here, however, for the adapted physical educator to consider.

The preschool adapted physical educator is aware that there are effective and ineffective ways to acknowledge the play (work) of the young child. Programs such as High Scope acknowledge that, if an adult praises a young child, the child gets two messages. First, the child learns that the adult can praise or withhold the praise; inherent here is a power that may be frightening to the child. If an adult says, "Good boy" or "Good girl," the child may be concerned or frightened that if he makes a mistake or disappoints the adult he or she may no longer be "good."

Professionals need to consider the difference between encouragement and praise.[27] Encouragement acknowledges the adult's interest in the play/work of the child and reinforces that play/work. The use of praise inherently causes a value judgment—"good" and "bad," "appropriate" and "inappropriate," "right" and "wrong." The young child, still inherently dependent on the adult, quickly understands that "if my actions can be 'good,' they can also be 'bad'; if my behavior is 'appropriate,' it can also be 'inappropriate'; and, if my work can be 'right,' it can also be 'wrong.'" This may be very frightening to a young child.

Encouragement, however, acknowledges interest in and respect for a child's efforts and is specific enough that there is no judgment of "goodness," "badness," "rightness," and "wrongness." Examples of encouragement are

- "You jumped 2 feet!"
- "You threw that ball and hit the target!"
- "You bobbled the balloon eight times before it hit the floor!"
- "You hopped on your other foot! All right!"
- "You wheeled your chair up the ramp! Way to be!"
- "You climbed over that huge cube mat!"

Teachers who care about children and their feelings struggle with a way to communicate caring and love without communicating "power." Adults who use negativity, sarcasm, and brutal comparisons simply need to find another job. Inappropriate language for use with preschoolers include

- "No—not like that!"
- "No way."
- "You're being stupid."
- "You can't be serious."
- "Your brother was such a great kid; what happened to you?"
- "Why can't you be like . . ."

Young children (and older children and adults, for that matter) do not need to be treated with that type of disrespect. There is nothing to be gained, and young souls to be lost.

Cultural Diversity in the Active Learning Centers

The adapted physical education specialist needs to be particularly sensitive to the diverse cultures, languages, socioeconomic backgrounds, genders, and abilities/disabilities of the children served. Even very young children begin to develop stereotypical notions regarding performance and potential. The wisest response from educators is to openly address issues related to culture, socioeconomic forces, gender, gender preference, age, and ability/disability and, specifically, to be willing to address the many questions that young children will raise.

According to Derman-Sparks and the Anti-Bias Curriculum (A.B.C.) Task Force, research data reveal that

- Children begin to notice differences and construct classificatory and evaluative categories very early.
- There are overlapping but distinguishable developmental tasks and steps in the construction of identity and attitudes.
- Societal stereotyping and bias influence children's self-concept and attitudes toward others.[16]

Even the young child is engaged in the process of sorting and categorizing. By age three many children have begun to notice gender, racial, and cultural differences and may have begun to notice children with physical disabilities, in particular. This process begins earlier. According to Derman-Sparks and the A.B.C. Task Force,

> By 2 years of age, children are learning the appropriate use of gender labels (girl, boy) and learning color names, which they begin to apply to skin color. By 3 years of age (and sometimes even earlier), children show signs of being influenced by societal norms and biases and may exhibit "pre-prejudice" toward others on the basis of gender or race or being differently-abled. Between 3 and 5 years of age, children try to figure out what are the essential attributes of their selfhood, what aspects of self remain constant. By 4 or 5 years of age, children not only engage in gender-expected behavior defined by socially prevailing norms, they also reinforce it among themselves without adult intervention. They use racial reasons for refusing to interact with children different from themselves and exhibit discomfort and rejection of differently abled people. The degree to which 4-year-olds have already internalized stereotypic gender roles, racial bias, and fear of the differently abled forcefully points out the need for antibias education with young children.[16]

Antibias education is particularly crucial if young children with disabilities are to be included in preschool programs.[44] Froschl and Sprung[21] observed 158 preschoolers between the ages of 2 1/2 and 5 years. They noted that girls and children with disabilities were likely to be overhelped and overpraised:

> If a 3-year-old boy and girl are getting ready to go out to play and are attempting to put on jackets, the girl is more likely to receive help. If both receive help, the girl will probably have her jacket put on for her, the boy will be shown a technique for putting it on himself. If the same situation arises and one child is disabled, it is the disabled child who will have the jacket put on, whether a girl or a boy. This is the beginning of the syndrome of "learned helplessness."[21]

The adapted physical education specialist must be part of the cadre of professionals willing to create a learning environment in which each child is embraced, nurtured, and challenged. There are vast opportunities to explore cultural, socioeconomic, gender, age, and ability/disability issues within the learning environment. Henninger wrote:

> To insure that multicultural play experiences happen, learning centers must be arranged in such a way that diversity issues encountered elsewhere and those inherent in the materials themselves can be understood as children select materials and engage in playful interactions with them and their peers. Rather than "visiting" these multicultural experiences for brief, disconnected learning opportunities children can more naturally experience diverse cultures when multicultural materials and activities are integrated into the art, manipulative, housekeeping, dramatic play, and outdoor learning centers.[28]

To create an antibias learning environment within the active learning center, the adapted physical educator must do the following:

1. Display posters and photographs of people that reflect a broad variety of cultures, socioeconomic status, gender, age, and ability/disability.
   a. Posters and photographs should empower all children.
   b. Posters and photographs should correctly reflect daily life with an emphasis on movement, sport, recreation, and leisure activities.

2. Use CDs/cassettes of various types of music common to the cultures of children in the program.

    a. Use a broad assortment of music that features males and females as lead performer.

    b. Choose a broad assortment of music that features young and old performers.

    c. Use CDs/cassettes that reflect diversity: "You Are Super the Way You Are" (Joining Hands with Other Lands), "Mi Casa, My House" (Joining Hands with Other Lands), "Somos El Barco" (Head First and Belly Down), "Sister Rosa" (The Neville Brothers), "Native American Names" (Joining Hands with Other Lands), "La Bamba" (Dancin' Magic), "Shake It to the One You Love the Best" (Shake It to the One You Love the Best, Cheryl Mattox)

    d. Use records/cassettes that honor young children as they are: "Ugly Duckling" (We All Live Together, Volume IV, Greg and Steve), "What a Miracle" (Walter the Waltzing Worm, Hap Palmer), "Free to Be You and Me" (Free to Be You and Me, Marlo Thomas), "Self Esteem" (B.E.S.T. Friends)

3. Use music that includes culturally distinctive instruments.

4. Provide a variety of cultural musical instruments:

    a. Kenyan double stick drum

    b. Zulu marimba

    c. Indian sarangi

    d. Mexican guiro

    e. West African balaphon

    f. Japanese den den

    g. Native American dance bells

    h. Chilean rainstick

5. Teach dances that reflect a variety of cultures and experiences.

    a. Ask parents and grandparents of the children to teach the songs and dances of their childhood.

    b. Provide materials of color that have cultural connotations to enhance celebrations and studies of different cultures (e.g., red and gold to celebrate Chinese festivals; red, white, and green to represent the Mexican flag for Cinco de Mayo celebrations).

6. Introduce simple games that reflect a variety of cultures and experiences. Ask parents and grandparents of the children to teach simple games.

7. Use language that is gender-free when referring to the activities and play of children. If the child, for example, is zooming around the room "pretending to be," be certain the words you use reflect no bias. The child is a "firefighter," a "police officer," or a "postal worker."

8. Read and act out stories of children involved in diverse play, sport, leisure, and recreation experiences.

The creation of an antibias active learning center provides young children with yet one more learning experience that honors young children. The adapted physical education specialist can also help embrace diversity by encouraging the preschool educators to provide dolls, puppets, and puzzles for the classroom that reflect children with disabilities.

SUMMARY

New federal and state initiatives have had a dramatic impact on early childhood intervention and preschool education programs. A heightened respect for the integrity of the family unit, in whatever form, and a sense that infants, toddlers, and young children should be educated in the most natural, least restrictive environment has placed a new emphasis on providing services to infants and toddlers within the home and the child's community and on providing educational services to preschoolers in private and public child care and other natural settings.

The adapted physical education specialist has a unique role to play in the child development process. The professional must be a consultant, or a teacher of teachers—including the parent.

A developmentally appropriate learning environment for infants, toddlers, and young children is one in which adults are sensitive to the unique needs of the children and are responsive to those needs. The learning environment allows active exploration with others and with materials. A developmentally appropriate learning environment for movement reflects the same needs.

REVIEW QUESTIONS

1. Compare and contrast the behavior of a typically developing infant, toddler, or preschooler with that of an infant, a toddler, or a preschooler who has a delay or disability.

2. Explain the differences between the individual family service plan and the individual education program.

3. List each of Howard Gardner's eight forms of intelligence and give examples of behaviors tied to each.

4. Describe modeling techniques that parents or teachers could use to improve an infant's or a toddler's motor and play skills.

5. Describe developmentally appropriate assessment practices for preschool-age children.

6. Describe developmentally appropriate intervention programs for preschool-age children.

7. Describe a developmentally appropriate preschool learning environment.

8. Describe the essential elements of an antibias active learning center.

STUDENT ACTIVITIES

1. Visit a child-care center and evaluate the play units in its outdoor play area.

2. Volunteer in a child-care center/preschool for children at risk.

3. Working in small groups, design an active learning center for indoor play and one for outdoor play.

Present your group's center to the rest of the class and explain the purpose of each component and why it was included in the plan.

REFERENCES

1. Bergen D: *Play as the vehicle for early intervention with at-risk infants and toddlers.* Paper presented at the annual conference of the American Educational Research Association, Chicago, April 1991.

2. Berk L: Vygotsky's theory: the importance of make-believe play, *Young Children* November:30–39, 1994.

3. Berk L, Winsler A: *Scaffolding children's learning: Vygotsky and early childhood education,* Washington, DC, 1995, National Association for the Education of Young Children.

4. Berrueta-Clement J et al.: *Changed lives: the effects of the Perry Preschool Program on youths through age 19,* Monographs of the High/Scope Educational Research Foundation, No 8, Ypsilanti, MI, 1985, High/Scope Press.

5. Blaska JK, Lynch EC: Is everyone included? Using children's literature to facilitate the understanding of disabilities, *Young Children* March:36–38, 1998.

6. Cheatum BA, Hammond AA: *Physical activities for improving learning and behavior: a guide to sensory*

motor development, Champaign, IL, 1999, Human Kinetics.

7. Connor-Kuntz FJ, Dummer GM: Teaching across the curriculum: language-enriched physical education for preschool children, *Adap Phys Act Q* 13:302–315, 1996.

8. Cowden JE, Sayers LK, Torrey CC: *Pediatric adapted motor development and exercise: an innovative, multisystem approach for professionals and families,* Springfield, IL, 1998, Charles C Thomas.

9. Cowden J, Torrey C: A ROADMAP for assessing infants, toddlers, and preschoolers: the role of the adapted motor developmentalist, *Adapt Phys Act Q* 12:1–11, 1995.

10. Crais E: *"Best practices" with preschoolers: assessing within the context of a family-centered approach,* Chapel Hill, NC, 1991, Carolina Institute for Research on Infant Personnel Preparation, Frank Porter Grahman Child Development Center.

11. *Cultural competence in serving children and adolescents with mental health problems,* U.S. Department of Health and Human Services, Substance Abuse and Mental Health Services Administration, Center for Mental Health Services, Rockville, MD, 1999, Author.

12. Curry N, Arnaud S: Personality difficulties in preschool children as revealed through play themes and styles, *Young Children* May:4–9, 1995.

13. Dawkins C et al.: Perspectives on early intervention, *Except Parent* February:23–27, 1994.

14. Danielson CL, Abrutyn L: *An introduction to using portfolios in the classroom,* Alexandria, VA, 1997, Association for Supervision and Curriculum Development.

15. *A day with Daniel N. Stern, M.D.* Presentation sponsored by the Texas Association for Infant Mental Health, February 20, 1995, Dallas.

16. Derman-Sparks C, A.B.C. Task Force: *Anti-bias curriculum: tools for empowering young children,* Washington, DC, 1989, National Association for the Education of Young Children.

17. *Developmentally appropriate practice in movement programs for young children ages 3–5,* Reston, VA, 1994, National Association for Sport and Physical Education.

18. Dodge D, Colker L: *The creative curriculum for early childhood,* Washington, DC, 1992, Teaching Strategies.

19. Dunn L, Kontos S: What have we learned about developmentally appropriate practice? *Young Children* July:4–13, 1997.

20. Eddowes EA: Drawing in early childhood: predictable stages, *Dimens Early Child* Fall:16–18, 1995.

21. Froschl M, Sprung B: Providing an anti-handicappist early childhood environment, *Interracial Books Child Bull* 14:7–8, 1983.

22. Gardner H: *Frames of mind: the theory of multiple intelligences,* New York, 1983, Basic Books.

23. Goodway JD, Rudisell ME: Influence of a motor skill intervention program on perceived competence of at-risk African American preschoolers, *Adapt Phys Act Q* 13:288–301, 1996.

24. Gowen J: The early development of symbolic play, *Young Children* March:75–84, 1995.

25. Gronlund G: Portfolios as an assessment tool: is collection of work enough? *Young Children* May:4–10, 1998.

26. Hayes T, Shaffer K, Wiens A: *Promising practices: active learning lab.* Presentation at the Texas Education Agency "Promising Practices" conference, Austin, TX, Fall 1994.

27. Hendrickson-Pfeill S: *Encouragement,* 1990, San Antonio, Communication Skill Builders.

28. Henninger M: Supporting multicultural awareness at learning centers, *Dimens Early Child* Summer:20–23, 1995.

29. Hopper K: *Early childhood intervention: working with parents.* A presentation to the Project INSPIRE staff at Texas Woman's University, November 1999.

30. *Howard Gardner on the eighth intelligence: seeing the natural world—an interview, Dimens Early Child* Summer:5–6, 1995.

31. Huettig C, Hughes J, Clemons M: *Play preferences of preschoolers with and without disabilities.* Report to the Meadows Foundation, 1996, Dallas, TX.

32. Huettig C, Pyfer J: *The motor portfolio assessment process with young at-risk children.* Presentation at the First Annual National Conference on At-Risk Children and Youth, Denton, TX, June 1995.

33. Huettig C, Tomlinson D: *The Macon project: a developmentally appropriate school-based inclusion project for at-risk children.* Presentation at the First Annual National Conference on At-Risk Children and Youth, Denton, TX, June 1995.

34. Huettig C, Zittel L, Goodway J: *Social validity: the value of subjective measurement in early childhood,* Minneapolis, MN, October 1998, North American Federation of Adapted Physical Activity.

35. Hughes F, Elicker J, Veen L: A program of play for infants and their caregivers, *Young Children* January: 52–88, 1995.

36. Ivory JJ, McCollum JA: Effects of social and isolate toys on social play in an inclusive setting, *J Spec Ed* 32(4):238–243, 1999.

37. Jenks D: *Developmentally appropriate practice.* Presentation to the Project INSPIRE Staff at Texas Woman's University, December 4, 1999.

38. Jones HA, Rapport MJ: Research-to-practice in inclusive early childhood education, *TEACHING Except Child* November/December:57–61, 1997.

39. Klemm D, Schimanski C: Parent to parent: the crucial connection. *Except Parent* September:109–112, 1999.

40. Lally J: The impact on child care policies and practices on infant/toddler identity formation, *Young Children* November 34–36, 1995.

41. Lamorey S, Bricker D: Integrated programs: effects on young children and their parents. In Peck C, Odom S, Bricker D, editors: *Integrating young children with disabilities into community programs,* Baltimore, MD, 1993, Paul H. Brookes.

42. Linder T: *Transdisciplinary play-based assessment: a functional approach to working with young children,* Baltimore, MD, 1993, Paul H. Brookes.

43. Linder T: *Transdisciplinary play-based intervention: guidelines for developing a meaningful curriculum for young children,* Baltimore, MD, 1993, Paul H. Brookes.

44. Lubeck S: The politics of developmentally appropriate practice: exploring issues of culture, class, and curriculum. In Mallory B, New R, editors: *Diversity and developmentally appropriate practices: challenges for early childhood education,* New York, 1994, Teachers College Press.

45. Lyon ME: Symbolic play and language development in young deaf children, *Deafness and Education* 21(2):10–19, 1997.

46. Marion M: Guiding young children's understanding and management of anger, *Young Children* 52(7):62–67, 1997.

47. McBride SL: Family-centered practices, *Young Children* 54(3):62–68, 1999.

48. Meisels SJ: Developmental screening in early childhood: the interaction of research and social policy. In Breslow L, Fielding JE, Love LB, editors: *Annual review of public health,* vol. 9, Palo Alto, CA, 1988, Annual Reviews.

49. Meisels S, Provence S: *Screening and assessment: guidelines for identifying young disabled and developmentally vulnerable children and their families,* Washington, DC, 1989, National Center for Clinical Infant Programs.

50. Miller K: *The outside play and learning book: activities for young children,* Mt. Ranier, MD, 1989, Gryphon House.

51. Mills PE, Cole KN, Jenkins JR, Dale PS: Effects of different levels of inclusion on preschoolers with disabilities, *Except Child,* 65(1):79–90, 1998.

52. Millspaugh F, Segelman M: Neither fear nor pity: public-service announcements about differences. In Harmonay M, editor: *Promise and performance: children with special needs,* Cambridge, MA, 1977, Ballinger.

53. Nabors L: Playmate preferences of children who are typically developing for their classmates with special needs, *Mental Retardation* 35(2):107–113, 1997.

54. National Association for the Education of Young Children. www.naeyc.org/naeyc

55. "Natural Environment" draft policy recommendations, Texas Interagency Council on Early Childhood Intervention, March 31, 1995.

56. Notari-Syverson A, Shuster S: Putting real-life skills into IEP/IFSP's for infants and young children, *TEACHING Except Child* Winter:29–32, 1995.

57. Overby LY, Branta C, Goodway J, Smith Y: *The relationship of parental attitudes to perceived competence, motor development and physical fitness of at-risk youth.* Paper presented at the National Convention of the American Alliance for Health, Physical Education, Recreation and Dance, Denver, CO, April 1994.

58. Powell DR: Reweaving parents into the fabric of early childhood programs, *Young Children* September:60–67, 1998.

59. Prizant B, Meyer E: Socioemotional aspects of communication disorders in young children and their families, *Am J Speech-Lang Pathol* 2:56–71, 1993.

60. Readdick CH, Park JJ: Achieving great heights: the climbing child, *Young Children* 53(6):14–19, 1998.

61. Rivkin M: *The great outdoors: restoring children's right to play outside,* Washington, DC, 1995, National Association for the Education of Young Children.

62. Rogers-Dulan J: Religious connectedness among urban African American families who have a child with disabilities, *Mental Retardation* 36:91–103, 1998.

63. Rubin K, Fein G, Vandenberg B: Play. In Hetherington E, editor: *Handbook of child psychology, vol. 4, Socialization, personality, and social development,* New York, 1983, John Wiley & Sons.

64. Sayers LK et al.: Qualitative analysis of a pediatric strength intervention on the developmental stepping movements of infants with Down syndrome. *Adapt Phys Act Q* 13:247–268, 1996.

65. Shepard L: The challenges of assessing young children appropriately, *Phi Delta Kappan* November: 206–212, 1994.

66. Simeonsson R: Family involvement in multidisciplinary team evaluation: professional and parent perspectives, *Child Care Health Dev* 21:109–215, 1995.

67. Skinner D, Rodriguez P, Bailey DB: Qualitative analysis of Latino parents' religious interpretations of their child's disability, *J Early Intervention* 22(4):271–285, 1999.

68. Slaby RG, Roedell WC, Arezzo D, Hendrix K: *Early violence prevention: tools for teachers of young children,* Washington, DC, 1995, National Association for the Education of Young Children.

69. Suen HK, Logan CR, Neisworth JT, Bagnato S: Parent-professional congruence: is it necessary? *J Early Intervention* 19(3):243–252, 1995.

70. Tabors PA: What early childhood educators need to know: developing effective programs for linguistically and culturally diverse children and families, *Young Children* 53(6):20–26, 1998.

71. Vygotsky L: The role of play in development. In Cole R et al., editors: *Mind in society,* Cambridge, MA, 1978, Harvard University Press.

72. Washington V, Johnson V, McCracken J: *Grassroots success: preparing schools and families for each other,* W.K. Kellogg Readiness Initiatives, Washington, DC, 1995, National Association for the Education of Young Children.

73. Wetherby A: Communication and language intervention for preschool children, Buffalo, NY, 1992, Educom.

74. Wetherby A: *Best practices for enhancing communication and education for children with autism or pervasive developmental disorder.* Presentation at the Region X Education Service Center, Richardson, TX, August 20, 1994.

75. Winston P: *Working with families in early intervention: Interdisciplinary perspectives,* Chapel Hill, NC, 1990, Carolina Institute for Research on Infant Personnel Preparation.

76. Zero-To-Three. www.zerotothree.org

77. Zittel LJ, McCubbin JA: Effect of an integrated physical education setting on motor performance of preschool children with developmental delays, *Adapt Phys Act Q* 13:316–333, 1996.

Suggested Readings

Cheatum BA, Hammond AA: *Physical activities for improving learning and behavior: a guide to sensory motor development,* Champaign, IL, 1999, Human Kinetics.

Dodge D, Colker L: *The creative curriculum for early childhood,* Washington, DC, 1992, Teaching Strategies.

Slaby RG, Roedell WC, Arezzo D, Hendrix K: *Early violence prevention: tools for teachers of young children,* Washington, DC, 1995, National Association for the Education of Young Children.

RECOMMENDED WEBSITES

Please note: These websites are being recommended in the fall of 1999. Given the ever changing nature of the Internet, these sites may have moved or been replaced by the time you are reading this text.

Zero to Three
    http://www.zerotothree.org

National Association for the Education of Young Children
    http://www.naeyc.org

IDEAS That Work
    http://www.ideapractices.org

Family Voices
    http://www.familyvoices.org

RECOMMENDED VIDEOS

Psychology, Social Work, & Disabilities
Video Collections, 1999–2000
Fanlight Productions
4196 Washington Street
Boston, MA 02131
   When Parents Can't Fix It: Living with a Child's
   Disability
   By Sharon Thompson and Dr. Virginia Cruz
   First Place, National Council on Family Relations
   Media Awards

58 minutes, purchase price $245
Order No. CV-255

They Don't Come with Manuals
By Paul Uzee
Featured, National Council on Family Relations
Film Festival
29 minutes, purchase price $145
Order No. CV-038

11

Mental Retardation

■ OBJECTIVES

Define mental retardation as it appears in IDEA.

Explain how the IDEA and ARC definitions of mental retardation differ.

Identify three causes of mental retardation.

Identify typical motor development delays demonstrated by persons with Down syndrome.

Describe how physical education needs might differ for persons with mild retardation and persons with severe retardation.

Describe modifications the physical educator should make when programming exercise for students with mental retardation.

I t is now recognized that mental retardation is not a fixed, unalterable condition that condemns an individual to a static, deprived lifetime of failure to achieve. Rather, today we understand that cognitive, psychomotor, and affective behaviors are dynamic processes that, if properly stimulated, can be developed further than ever before imagined. Early concepts of mental retardation viewed the condition as an inherited disorder that was essentially incurable. This notion resulted in hopelessness on the part of professionals and social and physical separation of persons who were mentally retarded. After years of research and innovative programming, it is now recognized that intelligence and other functions depend on the readiness and experience of the child, the degree and quality of environmental stimulation, and many other variables.

In the late 1960s and early 1970s, institutions that served persons with mental retardation began designing and implementing educational programs intended to develop independent living skills to enable them to function in community settings. As institutionalized

CASE STUDY

Luther

Luther is a six-year-old boy with Down syndrome. His gross motor skills are significant strengths. He is able to perform the following:

- Run contralaterally, stopping and starting with ease
- Broad jump a distance of 3 feet
- Hop on his left foot five times in a row and two times on his right foot
- Gallop with ease with a left-foot lead
- Throw a tennis ball, with his right hand, using a contralateral pattern, a distance of 50 feet
- Kick a stationary ball with his left foot, with a good plant and follow through
- Dribble a basketball ten times using his right hand

At present, he is receiving his instruction in physical education in the general kindergarten class. Luther is having difficulty with behavior problems. Specifically, he hugs and wrestles with other children. Because he is strong, the children are becoming frightened of him.

APPLICATION TASK

Describe the types of low-organized games and activities in which Luther is likely to be successful. Consider the strategies the physical educator might use to help eliminate his inappropriate behaviors.

individuals rose to the challenge of these educational programs, a movement began to promote their placement in communities. During the 1970s, thousands of persons with mental retardation were removed from institutions and allowed to take their rightful place as contributing members of communities. As institutions began to develop viable educational programs, public schools took up their responsibility toward young children with mental retardation who lived in the communities. Professionals trained in appropriate teaching techniques were hired by the school systems to provide educational opportunities for these children. As a result of efforts by both institutions and public school systems, all except those individuals who are the most severely mentally retarded are living, going to school, and working in the community. Today these individuals have more opportunities for optimum social interaction than ever before. However, the social awareness and commitment required to maximize the physical and social community opportunities for individuals with mental retardation are still in their infancy.

DEFINITION OF MENTAL RETARDATION

The labels assigned to different groups of individuals with mental retardation vary depending on who is doing the labeling.[45] Traditionally, levels of retardation were determined by IQ scores. The 1994 edition of the *Diagnostic and Statistical Manual of Mental Disorders*,[3] while recognizing the importance of adaptive functioning, bases severity of intellectual impairment on the following IQ scores: mild = 50–55 to approximately 70; moderate = 35–40 to 50–55; severe = 20–25 to 35–40; and profound = below 20 or 25. The definition of mental retardation that was adapted by the American Association on Mental Retardation (now the Association for Retarded Citizens—ARC) in May 1992 reads as follows:

> Mental retardation refers to substantial limitations in present functioning. It is manifested by significantly subaverage intellectual functioning, existing concurrently with related limitations in two or more of the following applicable adaptive skill areas: communication, self-care, home living, social skills, community use, self-direction, health and safety, functional academics, leisure, and work. Mental retardation begins before age 18.[1]

The ARC definition differs from past definitions in three ways:

1. Mental retardation refers to substantial limitations in certain, but not all, personal capabilities. The personal capabilities

identified include cognitive, functional, and social abilities.

2. Mental retardation is manifested as significantly subaverage intellectual functioning plus related disabilities in two or more specific adaptive skill areas. The inclusion of at least two specific adaptive skill areas assures the inclusion of individuals who are limited in fully accessing independent functioning in our society.

3. The fact that mental retardation must be evident before age eighteen is clearly stated; however, the condition may not always be of lifelong duration. The recognition that mental retardation is not necessarily permanent speaks directly to a point many of us have argued for years. That is, with appropriate and timely intervention services, individuals who are born mentally retarded can be taught to perform to acceptable (normal) personal and social standards. Clearly, we must increase our efforts to use the most up-to-date information and technology to help individuals who are mentally retarded advance to the point where they can become fully functioning, independent citizens in society.

The ARC classification system includes only two levels—mild and severe retardation. The diagnostic system is divided into six parts: (1) intellectual functioning and adaptive skills; (2) psychological and emotional considerations; (3) health and physical considerations; (4) etiological considerations; (5) environmental considerations; and (6) appropriate supports. Use of this diagnostic system yields an overall profile of each mentally retarded individual that should greatly facilitate programming for these students.

In applying the definition, the following four assumptions are essential:

1. Specific adaptive disabilities often coexist with strengths in other adaptive skills or other personal capabilities.

2. The existence of disabilities in adaptive skills occurs within the context of community

environments typical of the individual's age peers and is indexed to the person's individualized needs for support.

3. With appropriate supports over a sustained period, the life functioning of the person with mental retardation will generally improve.

4. Valid assessment considers cultural and language diversity as well as differences in communication and behavioral factors.

According to ARC's definition, mental retardation is environmentally determined; therefore, IQ score is not used to determine the severity of retardation. Instead, individuals are assessed in ten adaptive skill areas—communication, home living, community use, health and safety, leisure, self-care, social skills, self-direction, functional academics, and work. Level of retardation (mild or severe) is based on functioning in the adaptive skill areas and on the amount of support the individual needs. The four levels of support are presented in Figure 11-1.

Figure 11-1 Levels of Support Required by Individuals with Mental Retardation

Intermittent	Supports are on an as-needed basis. Supports may be high- or low-intensity when needed.
Limited	Supports are needed consistently over time (e.g., employment training, transitional support when moving from school to an adult).
Extensive	Supports characterized by regular involvement (e.g., daily) in at least some environments (at work or at home).
Pervasive	Supports are constant, high-intensity, and across environments. The person needs constant care on a 24-hour basis and may include the maintenance of life support function/systems.[69]

Figure 11-2   Characteristics of Mild and Severe Levels of Mental Retardation

Mild retardation	Severe retardation
IQ of 70 to 35	IQ of 35 or below
Insufficient school progress in regular class	Needs training focusing on self-help skills
Minimum educability in reading, writing, spelling, math	Likely to be dependent on others for care
Capacity for school adjustment to a point	Noticeable motor deficits
	Physical and motor problems
Needs special adaptation for appropriate education	Restricted movement
Can manage independently in the community	Skeletal deformities
Can make productive adjustments at an unskilled or semiskilled level	Sensory disorders
	Seizure disorders

The public schools have not adopted the ARC definition. Rather, they are adhering to the definition that appears in the rules for implementing the Individuals with Disabilities Education Act (IDEA):

> Mental retardation means significantly subaverage general intellectual functioning existing concurrently with deficits in adaptive behavior and manifested during the developmental period that adversely affects a child's educational performance.[68]

Most schools consider an IQ score lower than 70 as significant subaverage general intellectual functioning. Thus, IQ scores lower than 70 accompanied by deficits in adaptive behavior qualify a student for the mental retardation classification and services. If the public schools in this country were to adopt ARC's two suggested levels of mental retardation, IQ scores and adaptive behaviors that might be used to assist in identifying types of needed services at each of the two levels of retardation could be defined in a manner similar to that presented in Figure 11-2.

INCIDENCE OF MENTAL RETARDATION

Approximately 3 percent of the total population is retarded. The individuals with less severe forms of mental retardation (those needing intermittent and limited support) are often associated with lower socioeconomic groups. Those individuals with the more severe forms which require extensive or pervasive support occur in all levels of socioeconomic groups.[9] During the 1996-1997 school year, the number of children and youth reported to be served under federal requirements was 592,847.[88]

CAUSES OF MENTAL RETARDATION

Although frequently there is no clear cause of mental retardation,[39] some causes that have been identified include

- Chromosomal abnormalities (e.g., Down syndrome, fragile X syndrome)
- Genetic metabolic and neurologic disorders (e.g., phenylketonuria, Tay-Sachs disease, neurofibromatosis, tuberous sclerosis)
- Congenital infections (e.g., rubella, herpes simplex)
- Prenatal drug exposure (e.g., alcohol, cocaine, medications)
- Perinatal factors (e.g., CNS bleeding, high forceps delivery, prematurity, low birth weight)
- Postnatal factors (e.g., severe malnutrition, asphyxia, lead or mercury poisoning, viral infection)[9]

CHARACTERISTICS OF MENTAL RETARDATION

Although research tends to generalize the characteristics of people who are mentally retarded, these individuals are diverse in cognitive, social, and physical functions. The performance of mentally retarded athletes in the 1999 Special Olympics World Games in Raleigh, North Carolina, where performance exceeded expectations, is testimony to their competence. On the other hand, some persons with mental retardation are unable to participate in regular sports events and need modification of the activities to be successful in their efforts to play. Other persons with severe mental retardation may not be ambulatory or have the physical capability needed to participate in play of any sort.

Because of the diversity within the group, it is difficult to generalize a set of characteristics to the total population. However, there are general characteristics that are representative of the group. The cognitive and physical characteristics of this population provide basic guidelines and alert the physical educator to the potential nature of the physical education programs they need.

Cognitive Characteristics Related to Skill

In addition to the considerable variability in intelligence as measured by standardized tests, individuals demonstrate variance in processing information, comprehension, and memory. Cognitive limitations associated with mental retardation are difficulty in organizing thoughts, persistence in using incorrect methods even when they have repeatedly resulted in failure to learn through imitation, and difficulty in evaluating self.[49] However, there are aspects of intelligence that may be superior to many with so-called "normal" intelligence. For instance, some persons with mental retardation have phenomenal memories.

As a group, persons who are mentally retarded are not as adept in perceptual attributes that relate to motor skills as are comparable nonretarded individuals. They may be clumsy and awkward and lack balance, which affects their ability to perform motor tasks efficiently. A review of the literature reveals that there are many perceptual and cognitive characteristics that may inhibit the learning of motor skills. Early studies reported that individuals with mental retardation demonstrated less preparation and slower actual movement times.[84] Also, when compared with other persons, they are less able to spontaneously predict changing conditions of a motor task. They are slower than others to estimate the amount of time needed to plan activities[40] and to intercept moving objects.[21] Even youngsters with mild mental retardation often inaccurately perceive their competence to perform motor skills. Perceived motor competence relates directly to motivation, self-esteem and, social development.[95] Individuals with negative perceptions regarding their motor competence do not persist at participating in physical activities.[76]

The good news is that, studies show that, when intervention occurs, even individuals with severe mental retardation improve their planning and movement times.[14] Others report that, as subjects with IQs of 40 and above increased in chronological age, their reaction times and individual variability decreased.[93] Thus, it is reasonable to expect individuals who are mentally retarded to benefit from appropriate intervention programs. Well-designed physical education programs can promote physical and motor gains.

Persons with severe mental retardation most likely have adverse performance in social, cognitive, language, and motor development. Many students who are severely mentally retarded have difficulty interacting with others. This may stem from abnormal behavior, which may include self-abusive acts as well as behavior that is injurious to others. Furthermore, stereotyped behaviors and bizarre acts, such as rocking back-and-forth, waving the hands in front of the eyes, and making strange noises, may also adversely affect social interaction with others. In addition, those who are severely mentally retarded may have problems with self-help skills, such as dressing, feeding, and basic motor functioning.

Attention, Memory, and Decision Making

Attention, regardless of how it is defined, is generally considered to be a critical aspect of information processing. As a result, attention plays a prominent role in a wide range of cognitive and behavioral activities.[12] Two important aspects of learning motor skills are the attention that one gives to the instructional task and the ability to remember and respond to movement cues. DePauw and Ferrari[26] indicate that individuals who are not mentally retarded have a more difficult time performing tasks when some interference occurs than do persons with mental retardation. Thus, once individuals who are mentally retarded are on task, they are not distracted by extraneous cues and information. Furthermore, Newell[64] found no difference between subjects who were mentally retarded and those who weren't on adopting memory strategies for the recall of movement cues on a motor task. Thus, it seems that persons with mental retardation can make improvements in their movement accuracy if they are helped to understand and remember essential movement information.

Decision-making capability varies widely among persons with mental retardation. Some persons with mental retardation may be able to make decisions that enable independent functioning in the community, while others may be totally dependent on others for cognitive decisions. One unique study, which focused on the impact of exercise on problem-solving skills, reported that moderate-intensity exercise (55 to 60 percent VO_2 max) for 20 minutes resulted in an increase in speed of problem solving in teenagers with average IQ scores of 60.[22] It has also been shown that persons with mental retardation can be made aware of exertion levels during physical exercise[6] and can successfully engage in self-management practices.[31]

Persons who are severely mentally retarded frequently have impaired cognitive and language

Trust in others is difficult for individuals who are emotionally disturbed.
Courtesy Wisconsin Lions Camp, Rosholt, Wis.

development. Many are unable to respond to simple commands. Thus, it is difficult for them to grasp instruction. Furthermore, they may lack the ability to generalize skills learned in one setting to another setting. They often have problems with language. This further makes communication during instruction difficult.

Motor Development Delays

Motor delays are very common among persons who are severely mentally retarded. Delays in developing postural reflexes[93] impact the ability to perform such basic tasks as grasping objects, holding the head up, sitting, standing, and walking. In addition, these delays, to varying degrees, negatively impact their motor and physical capabilities.

They may be less capable in strength, flexibility, agility, coordination, and balance.

Physical Health

There is an increasing frequency of chronic health conditions among persons with mental retardation. These individuals have a higher incidence of infections and cancers, poorer dental health, and a greater incidence of motor vehicle accidents than persons with normal intelligence.[44]

Health promotion which involves physical activities directed at persons with mental retardation can significantly improve this group's health status. Individuals who are helped to develop lifestyles that maintain and enhance the state of well-being will frequent community-based programs.[82]

In the past there has been a lack of overall policies regarding health promotion for people with mental retardation. Despite the research that has demonstrated significant health and physical fitness benefits for persons with mental retardation, their individual transition plans have consisted mainly of vocational skills and activities of daily living.[77]

The 1999 Amendments to IDEA retain both physical education as a direct service and recreation as a related service for persons with disabilities. To enable individuals with mental retardation improve their health status and ability to function well in their job settings, physical educators must make a significant effort to include and promote strength and endurance activities in each person's ITP.

Postural Development

Many individuals who are mentally retarded have postural abnormalities that include malalignment of the trunk or the legs. One of the most obvious postural deficiencies is that of the protruding abdomen, which may be associated with obesity[72] and/or lack of abdominal strength. In addition, because of depth perception problems and/or delayed vestibular and equilibrium reflex development, there may be a tendency to hold the head flexed, externally rotate the legs, and use a wide base of support when walking and running. Delays in reflex development always result in delays in the appearance of motor milestones.[43]

Physical Fitness Development

In general, individuals with mental retardation are in need of intervention programs to improve their physical fitness levels.[23] In many individuals, regardless of retardation level, poor respiration and susceptibility to respiratory infections may accompany the underdeveloped cardiovascular system.[19,37,52] There is, however, strong evidence that physical fitness, including cardiovascular endurance, can be developed through training regimens. Canadian Special Olympic athletes who were given opportunity to participate in the Manitoba Special Olympics Medallion program demonstrated outstanding improvement in physical fitness and skill performance levels. The six-month-long, intensive, three-times-a-week training program for selected Special Olympic athletes in Manitoba combines both fitness and skill-specific training akin to generic sport training, as well as nutritional counseling.[5] Frey et al.[37] studied physical fitness levels of trained runners with mild mental retardation and those without retardation and found no difference in percentage of body fat, peak oxygen consumption, and lower back/hamstring flexibility. Merriman et al.,[60] using a twelve-week, three-times-a-week training program, reported significant improvements in the muscular endurance, cardiorespiratory endurance, and flexibility of twenty-two adults whose retardation ranged from severe to mild. The Canadian program and studies in the United States verify that, when individuals with mental retardation are given appropriate practice opportunities and guidance, they demonstrate high levels of fitness and motor performance.

Individuals with mental retardation who have not been given opportunities to exercise and build work capacity demonstrate low levels of function,[20] as well as low muscle mass and strength.[34] When provided instruction in physical fitness and given opportunities to practice, they demonstrate improvement, but at a slower rate than their peers who are not retarded.[19,67] Fernhall[32] indicates that individuals with mental retardation may take between sixteen and thirty-five weeks to show improved VO_2 max; however, functional capacity gains frequently occur sooner. Investigations using subjects who are mentally retarded indicate that it is possible to strengthen all muscle groups when using appropriate training regimes.[5,13,73,96]

Social Development

The social characteristics of individuals who are mentally retarded also vary greatly. Some persons with mental retardation are dependable, are cooperative, and can delay their gratification, while others are self-centered and impulsive.[75]

Competition

Competition is an important motivator to bring out the best efforts of athletes. While evidence exists that persons who are mentally retarded can benefit through competition such as Special Olympics, some youngsters who are retarded may not understand the concept of competition. The central goal in most sport competition is to win; however, Special Olympics places the challenge on participation rather than winning. Bringing the participants to the starting line is more important than the sport skills that carry the athletes across the finish line.[29] Everyone deserves a chance to do his or her best.[71] The athlete who is severely mentally retarded may not comprehend "Run as fast as you can," "Jump as high as you can," and "Score more points than your opponent." Also, studies show that besting an opponent is not important to some persons with mental retardation;[97] as a result, their competitive performance is not adversely affected by anxiety.[70] In addition, individuals with mental retardation frequently demonstrate lower levels of self-determination than others in the same situations;[89] thus, their workouts must be supervised by individuals willing to motivate them to persist.

TESTING TO DETERMINE FUNCTIONING LEVELS

Development of the individual education program (IEP) requires that present functioning levels be determined. Several formal tests that can be used with mentally retarded students were listed in Table 2.1 of this text. Although there are tests to assess the areas of physical fitness of individuals who are mentally retarded, there has been increased interest in the validity of using general physical fitness tests with individuals who are mentally retarded. Some of the studies to validate physical fitness tests have examined VO_2 max as a predictor of aerobic capacity[33] the walk-run tests of different lengths,[37] and the Eurofit physical fitness test.[57] Preference should be given to measuring physical fitness, locomotor skills, object-handling skills, and balance. Reliable strength measures can be obtained from individuals who are mentally retarded.[83] When measuring strength, it is suggested that the mean of three trials be used to best represent the individual's capability.[47,48] For individuals who appear to demonstrate poor posture, postural alignment should be assessed and followed by specific programming to correct any abnormalities. Lavay et al.[55] reviewed three physical fitness tests to determine their validity for use with individuals with mental retardation and concluded that all three tests were appropriate. The items included in the tests were sit and reach for flexibility; strength measures, including grip strength, sit-ups, isometric push-ups, bench press (for age thirteen years and older); and run, jog, march, walk, exercise bicycle, or propel oneself in a wheelchair or on a scooter board for 12 minutes while maintaining a heart rate between 140 and 180 beats per minute for cardiovascular endurance. Winnick and Short's Brockport Physical Fitness health-related test for youth is an excellent test for use with youngsters between the ages of ten and seventeen years.[92] Other acceptable ways to evaluate the functioning levels of this population are task analysis and observation of the students as they perform a hierarchical sequence of activities. These techniques are described in Chapters 4 and 6.

Figure 11-3 Practices to Ensure Valid Test Results[32]

During all testing

- Provide ample time for individuals to become familiar with the test procedures, environment, and staff.
- Tailor the test procedures to the individual. (Allow staff members to adjust the testing procedures, to ensure validity of test results and safety of the person being tested.)
- Provide an environment in which the individual feels like a participating member.

When using a treadmill for testing

- Permit the person being tested to walk at a speed that is comfortable.
- Increase grade, but not speed.
- Use work stages of 1 to 2 minutes.

Figure 11-4 Techniques for Improving Response to Requests to Perform Test Items

1. If after the student has been told what to do the response is incorrect, demonstrate the position or movement.
2. If demonstration does not elicit the correct performance, manually place the student in or through the desired position or pattern.
3. Use positive reinforcement (praise, tokens, free play) to encourage the student.

Fernhall[32] cautions about the importance of determining whether any potential congenital cardiovascular problems exist prior to beginning testing, particularly for individuals with Down syndrome. To help ensure valid testing results, the recommendations presented in Figure 11-3 should be followed.

One of the most difficult problems of testing individuals with mental retardation is determining whether poor comprehension or poor motor development is the reason for their inability to perform a specific task. Because it is difficult to determine whether a student who is mentally retarded understands directions given during test situations, the suggestions presented in Figure 11-4 may help the evaluator elicit the best performance possible.

Because persons with mental retardation who participate in competitive sports such as Special Olympics are more likely than most athletes to experience sport-specific injuries,[85] it is strongly recommended that physical examinations tailored to each athlete be administered prior to participation. Athletes with Down syndrome should always be assessed for atlantoaxial instability prior to participation.

FETAL ALCOHOL SYNDROME, DOWN SYNDROME, AND FRAGILE X SYNDROME

The three most common causes of mental retardation are fetal alcohol syndrome (FAS), Down syndrome, and fragile X syndrome.

Fetal Alcohol Syndrome

Fetal alcohol syndrome (FAS) is the leading known cause of mental retardation. Estimates of the number of individuals born with fetal alchol syndrome range from 5 per 10,000 to 1 per 100 live births.[28] It is caused by maternal alcohol use during pregnancy, and it usually results in lifelong consequences, including mental retardation, learning disabilities, and serious behavioral problems.[28] The most severe form of FAS results from the mother's heavy drinking during pregnancy; lesser degrees of alcohol abuse result in milder forms of FAS.[9]

Both anatomical and cognitive modifications can accompany the condition. More than 80 percent of all children with FAS have pre- and postnatal growth deficiencies, microcephaly, and characteristic facial features (saddle-shaped nose and gap between the front teeth). Adults with fetal alcohol syndrome who have a normal IQ demonstrate difficulty with tasks requiring higher levels of attention, organizational skills, and judgment.[51] Poor motor coordination, hypotonia, and attention deficit hyperactivity disorders are characteristic of half of the children.[16] Behavioral problems demonstrated by these students may be the biggest challenge to the physical educator.

Down Syndrome

Down syndrome is the most common chromosomal disorder leading to mental retardation. In about 95 percent of the cases, there is an extra chromosome #21.[9] The incidence rates are about 1 in 800, of whom 80 percent score between 25 and 50 on IQ tests.[8] Some physical characteristics of individuals with Down syndrome are

- Small skull
- Slanting, almond-shaped eyes
- Ears slightly smaller than average
- Flat-bridged nose
- Protruding tongue
- Palmar crease
- Short stature
- Short fingers
- Short limbs
- Short neck
- Overweight
- Substantial delays in reflex integration
- Varied levels of mental retardation
- Looseness of joints
- Lack of muscle tone during infancy

There has been considerable interest by researchers concerning the specific physical and motor characteristics of individuals with Down syndrome. When compared with the general population, people with Down syndrome may differ in the following ways:

- Demonstrate less power and strength[74]
- Function lower than average on cardiovascular measures[52]
- Have deficient leg strength associated with lower cardiovascular measures[52]
- Begin the aging process earlier than expected[63]
- Have less capability for decision making that relates to motor control[54]
- Have difficulty in planning goal-directed movements[46]

- Have a greater incidence of obesity
- Have atlantoaxial instability

It is believed that effective programs of physical activity can significantly impact physical and psychomotor deficiencies. Clinical intervention programs that begin early in life can promote reflex integration, vestibular function, and kinesthetic impulses that impact muscle tonacity. Development of these input systems is critical to gaining locomotor and object-control patterns and skills. Other intervention programs have also shown to be effective. Ulrich et al.[87] demonstrated facilitation of stable walking patterns through the use of treadmill programming. Once locomotor and object-control skills are developed, the control child with Down syndrome will be more likely to participate actively with peers and may be less likely to develop obesity.

The atlantoaxial segments of the cervical spine of children with Down syndrome may have a tendency to develop localized anomalies that are in danger of atlantoaxial dislocation. As a result of this potential danger, in 1983 a group of physicians, including experts in sports medicine and the surgeon general of the United States, met at the Joseph P. Kennedy, Jr., Foundation to discuss the perceived dangers of atlantoaxial instability among individuals with Down syndrome. Of particular concern were the thousands of athletes in Special Olympics with Down syndrome.

The incidence of atlantoaxial instability is in question. The range of incidents is reported from 10 to 30 percent of the Down syndrome population. However, the American Academy of Pediatrics' Committee on Sports Medicine reports 15 percent.[56]

Atlantoaxial instability is a greater than normal mobility of the two upper cervical vertebrae—C1 and C2—at the top of the neck. The condition exposes the victims to possible serious injury if they forcibly flex the neck, because the vertebrae may shift and thereby squeeze or sever the spinal cord. A dislocation involves an actual displacement of the bone from the normal position in the joint. Awareness of the significance of atlantoaxial instability can aid in the prevention of injuries at the upper cervical spine level. The instability is due to (1) the laxity of the transverse ligament that holds the odontoid process of the axis (C2) in place against the inner aspect of the inner arch of atlas (C1) and (2) abnormalities of the odontoid. These conditions allow some leeway between the odontoid and the atlas, especially during flexion and extension of the neck. This results in an unstable joint. The atlantoaxial instability can be gradual and progressive.

The two types of symptoms of atlantoaxial dislocation are observable physical symptoms and neurological signs. Some of the behavior symptoms are

- Fatiguability
- Difficulty in walking, abnormal gait
- Neck pain, limited neck mobility, torticollis (head tilt)
- Weakness of any of the extremities
- Incoordination and clumsiness[17]

Some of the neurological signs associated with atlantoaxial dislocation are

- Spasticity
- Sensory deficits
- Hyperreflexiveness[56]

Special Olympics has taken the lead in the formulation of policies for the participation of athletes with Down syndrome who may have atlantoaxial instability. Tens of thousands of mentally retarded individuals with Down syndrome have participated in Special Olympics over the past twenty-five years. However, officials of Special Olympics International believe that none have suffered injury related to atlantoaxial instability while participating in Special Olympics training or competition. However, as a precaution, Special Olympics has developed a policy requiring that all athletes with Down syndrome receive neck X rays before they participate in its nationwide competitive program.

Professionals in physical education need to be aware of the potential injury-inducing activities and situations for persons with atlantoaxial instability. The adapted physical educator should be aware of each student's medical status, including the condition of the atlantoaxial joint. Results of medical examinations should be kept in the student's permanent health file at the school. The American Academy of Pediatrics' Committee on Sports Medicine reported in 1995 that only three of the forty-one recorded pediatric cases had worsening of atlantoaxial instability during organized sport participation; however, the committee urges pediatricians to follow the Special Olympics policy to conduct lateral neck X rays on all athletes with Down syndrome.[2] The Special Olympics policy and the Committee on Sports Medicine[15] guidelines are presented in Figure 11-5.

Fragile X Syndrome

Fragile X syndrome is the most common inherited cause of mental retardation, and it is recognized as

---

Figure 11-5   Guidelines to Follow When Individuals with Down Syndrome Participate in Physical Education and/or Special Olympics

1. Check the medical files to determine which individuals have the atlantoaxial instability condition.
2. If there is no record of neck X-ray results, with the principal's permission, contact the parents and explain the importance of screening.
3. Discuss the medical options and the situation with the student's parents or guardians.
4. Have the parents sign a consent form allowing the child to participate in the physical education program.
5. Restrict participation in gymnastics, diving, the butterfly stroke in swimming, the diving start in swimming competition, the high jump, soccer, and any warm-up exercises that place pressure on the neck muscles.
6. Design a physical education program with activities that are not contraindicated for those with atlantoaxial instability.
7. Watch for the development of the symptoms indicating a possible dislocation.
8. Adhere to the physician's recommendations.

second only to Down syndrome as a specific chromosomal cause of developmental disability.[9] Prevalence rates are estimated to be 1 in 1,000 births, with males being affected more often than females.[9]

Cause

The condition is a result of an abnormally long X chromosome, which appears to have "fragile" ends, hence its name.[81] The fragile site on the X chromosome results in a folic acid deficiency.[27] Fragile X syndrome usually expresses itself less fully in females because they have two X chromosomes, with one being normal and the other abnormal. Because males have only one X chromosome, the condition manifests itself more fully. In addition, two distinct categories of variation at the fragile X locus have been identified. A mosaic premutation results in milder deleterious features than the fuller, nonmosiac, mutation.[9] The fuller mutation is the one associated with the developmental delays that affect development.[9]

Characteristics

Approximately 95 percent of the males with the full mutation are mentally retarded (moderate to severe range), whereas only about 50 percent of the females with the full mutation are mentally retarded; however, those who are not retarded usually demonstrate learning disabilities.

There are several differences in the physical features between the genders, with males being more affected than females. When full expression of the condition prevails, there are several distinct physical features in the newborn male. The baby may be large and have a high forehead; a heavy lower jaw; large, low-set ears; and large head, nose, hands, and feet. These features become more prominent with age, with the face narrowing and lengthening.[66] Other distinguishing characteristics in males are large testicles (70 percent of the time), strabismus (56 percent), mitral valve prolapse (50 percent), hypotonia, and joint laxity (50 percent).[41] Behaviors demonstrated by males include autistic-like behaviors such as hand flapping, perseveration, hand biting, and poor eye contact. Frequently, these children are hyperactive, have attention deficits, and engage in aggressive outbursts.[90]

Females have an increased prominence of the ears but few of the other physical characteristics that the males demonstrate.[90] They tend to be shy, depressed, anxious, hypersensitive, and somewhat hyperactive as children and socially impaired as adults.[9]

Whereas most young fragile X syndrome boys demonstrate moderate mental retardation, some (estimates vary between 25 and 75 percent) tend to deteriorate cognitively with age. The greatest change in cognitive ability is seen between the ages of eight and thirteen years.[91] By adulthood, most males test in the moderate to severe range of mental retardation.[9] Interestingly, these males frequently have good verbal expressive skills and are socially engaging; however, they tend to avoid direct eye contact during conversation, they have a short attention span, they are hyperactive, and they demonstrate motor delays.[42]

Approximately 50 percent of the females are mildly mentally retarded; those who are not retarded usually have learning disabilities, particularly in mathematics.[78] Most of the fragile X syndrome females, regardless of degree of affect, demonstrate deficits in short-term memory for nonverbal information, deficits in mental flexibility, and visual-motor performance deficits.[9]

Both genders frequently have sensory-motor integration deficits, which result in delayed balance (probably related to recurring middle ear infections), poor coordination, motor planning deficits, and tactile defensiveness.[41]

The physical limitations of the males require careful motor programming. Hypotonia and joint laxity could predispose students to a tendency to hyperextend joints during contact sports; strabismus could create depth perception difficulties that would limit success in games and sports requiring object control; and a prolapsed mitral valve might limit cardiovascular endurance. Activities such as weight training could contribute muscle tone and greater joint stability, as well as enhanced self-esteem.

Students of both genders should receive sensory integration activities, particularly vestibular, kinesthetic, and tactile stimulation, as early in life as possible. Later in life, when motor skills are being learned, short-term memory lapse and difficulty mastering sequential information will require that attempts be made to teach the whole task in the context where it will be used.[58] The greater the teacher's success at presenting the "whole picture," the easier it will be for the student to learn.

TEACHING STRATEGIES

The mentally retarded are a very heterogeneous group. Many techniques of instruction are necessary to elicit a desired response. Therefore, it is difficult to make generalizations that may be helpful in the instruction of physical education activities for mentally retarded persons. However, as a guide, some strategies for teaching physical education to individuals with mental retardation appear in Figure 11-6.

Every student, regardless of disability, can learn. The teaching methodology selected to use with the individual who is severely retarded depends on age. All children who are mentally retarded should engage in a bottom-up developmental program in the early ages of life because they need to develop their sensory-motor and perceptual motor systems, as well as learn the basic elements of fundamental movement skills. A bottom-up approach is critical for persons who are severely or profoundly involved because of the extent to which they are motorically delayed. The Special Olympics Motor Activities Training Program (MATP) is designed for this population.

Older individuals who are severely retarded learn specific skills best with a defined instructional

Every child should be waterproofed at a young age.
Photo by Carol Huettig.

Figure 11-6   Strategies for Teaching Physical Education to Persons with Mental Retardation

1. Employ methods that are compatible with individualized instruction

Use strong visual, tactile, and auditory stimuli for the children who are more severely involved, because these often bring the best results.

Have many activities available, because the attention span is short.

Use a systematic style of instruction where the behaviors are defined, measured, modeled, and monitored for acquisition.

Keep verbal directions to a minimum. They are often ineffective when teaching children who are more severely retarded.

Use demonstration as an effective instructional tool. It is particularly effective to use a peer demonstrator.

Use **manual guidance** as a method of instruction. The proprioceptors are great teachers of movement. The less ability the child has to communicate verbally, the more manual guidance should be considered as a tool for instruction.

Help students develop sound self-management procedures so that they can learn to plan and complete tasks independently, evaluate their own performance, compare their performance with a standard, and make adjustments.[61]

Provide opportunities for choice of activities to foster self-motivation and decision making;[11] these practices decrease social avoidance and reduce problem behavior[36] and noncompliance.[18]

2. Involve students actively in activities they can do successfully

Structure the environment in which the activity takes place so that it challenges the students yet frees them from the fear of physical harm and gives them some degree of success.

Analyze tasks involved in activities to be sure you are clear about all the components of the skill you are about to teach.

Work for active participation on the part of all the students. Active involvement contributes more to neurological development than does passive movement.

Modify the activity so that each child can participate up to his or her ability level.

3. Facilitate participation in group activities

Use markers to indicate where students are to participate.

Have students hold hands as they organize for instruction (e.g., in a circle).

Use peer partners during group exercises.[53]

Use a token or point system to reward compliant behavior.[20]

4. Interact appropriately with students

Be patient with smaller and slower gains of students who are more severely involved. Often gains that seem small when compared with their peers are tremendous for students who are retarded.

Do not underestimate the ability of students who are mentally retarded to perform skilled movements. There is a tendency to set goals too low for these children.

Convey to all students that they are persons of worth by reinforcing their strengths and minimizing their weaknesses.

5. Teach for generalization to community environments

Remember that children with lower levels of cognition must be taught to play. This means that physical education programs are responsible for creating the play environment, developing basic motor skills that are the tools of play, identifying at what play level (self-directed, onlooker, solitary, parallel, associative, or cooperative) the child is functioning, and promoting development from that point.

Use effective maintenance and generalization programs to ensure that the skills attained in physical education are used in community settings.[24] If possible, teach the skills within the community-based setting that will be used for leisure, recreation, or sports participation.

Create a safe play environment but do not necessarily provide security to the extent that the students are unduly dependent on you for physical safety.

procedure that uses a top-down teaching approach. That procedure includes (1) assessing the present level of the student in defined target skills, (2) arranging the skills in an appropriate sequence so that objectives can be identified, (3) providing clear cues during the instructional process, (4) providing precise feedback immediately after the task is completed, (5) including strategies to promote generalization of skills to meaningful community environments, and (6) measuring and evaluating the performance gains to enable appropriate subsequent instructional decisions.

Behavior modification coupled with task analysis is usually recommended when teaching students who are mentally retarded.[7] This system involves selecting a signal or a request to cause the desired behavior. After selecting the skill to be taught, divide it into its component parts. Teach the parts using backward or forward chaining. If the task is a continuous one (such as running or jumping), shaping, rather than task analysis, is more appropriate. Once the physical skill has been performed, reinforce the student (see Chapter 6).

THE PHYSICAL EDUCATION PROGRAM

Knowledge of the characteristics of persons who are mentally retarded provides information about the types of programs that need to be implemented to serve them. However, designing whole physical education programs around these characteristics for the purpose of teaching groups of these persons may not meet the needs of individuals within the group. Clearly, the assessed needs of each individual must be taken into consideration when designing the individual physical education program.

It is true that individuals who are mentally retarded have developmental lags in intellectual quotients and usually have parallel lags in motor and social development. Figure 11-7 shows the mental and chronological ages of individuals who are mentally retarded with a conversion of motor behaviors one would expect from individuals with delayed mental ages. Children with a chronological age of two to five years who are mildly retarded

would be expected to attempt locomotor patterns. Those between six and nine years would be attempting to learn to jump and balance on one foot briefly, as well as learning to throw. This information provides a good basis for constructing curricula for group activity because it is simple and straightforward. However, full assessments of the physical education needs of mentally retarded persons will reveal deviations from behaviors indicated in Figure 11-7.

Every effort must be made to provide each student who is mentally retarded with an appropriate physical education program that will promote the motor growth and development of that child. Children under the age of nine years will benefit from a physical education program that focuses on promoting sensory input and perceptual-motor integration. Older students should be taught to perform culturally relevant community-based recreational skills that can be used throughout their lives to promote and maintain a healthy lifestyle in social settings.

Numerous studies have demonstrated that individuals who are mentally retarded benefit from physical fitness training coupled with reinforcement.[73,86,96] Treadmill exercise regimes which are individualized have been proven safe and beneficial for improving and maintaining cardiovascular fitness.[4] In addition, training in a modified form of judo is a valuable therapeutic, educational, and recreational tool for persons with mental retardation. A biweekly, six-month-long program resulted in gains in physical fitness as well as developmental skills such as walking, stair climbing, running, jumping, and hopping.[38] Appropriate motivation, high teacher expectations, and carefully designed learning sequences appear to be the keys to promoting learning among individuals who are mentally retarded.

Stopka et al.[82] report significant results for secondary students with mental retardation when using a twice-weekly program consisting of 5 to 10 minutes of warm-up and stretching, 20 to 25 mintues of resistance training or weight training, and 20 to 30 minutes of sports and recreation skills and games. When determining repetitions, they recommend weight be increased for seventeen- to

Figure 11-7	Conversion of Behavior in Physical Education Activity Adjusted for Mental Age of Persons with Moderate Mental Retardation

Chronological age	Activities for normal children by chronological age	Activities for those with mild mental retardation adjusted for mental age	Mental age
4 to 8 years	Generalization of running, jumping as subroutines into play activity; low organized games (i.e., Follow the Leader, Tag).	Learning to run; balance on one foot; manipulate objects; engage in activity that requires simple directions.	2 to 4 years
8 to 12 years	Can play lead-up games to sport skills that involve throwing and catching. Can play games of competition where there is team organization. Can learn rules and play by them.	May be able to generalize running and locomotor skills into play activity. May be able to play games of low organization and follow simple direction. May socially interact in play; may play by self, or may play in parallel.	4 to 6 years
12 to 17 years	Can play games of high organization. Can further develop skills that involve racquet sports and balls and require high levels of skill. Can participate in team games and employ strategies in competitive activity.	Can participate in modified sport activity. Is better in individual sports (e.g., swimming, bowling, and track), where there is a minimum of social responsibility. Can throw and catch balls, but it is difficult to participate in meaningful competitive activity.	6 to 8 years
Over 17 years	Can participate independently in recreational activities in their chosen community.	Can participate in community recreational sport and physical activity in special programs and with assistance from others.	Over 10 years

twenty-two-year-olds when eight to twelve repetitions can be easily performed and for thirteen- to seventeen-year-olds when fifteen to twenty repetitions can be easily performed.

Fernhall[32] recommends that the following modifications be made when working with individuals with mental retardation:

1. Exercise intensity shoud be between 60 and 80 percent of maximal functional capacity.
2. Exercise should be supervised.
3. Provide a longer training duration to achieve the desired effects.
4. Motivational techniques, such as token rewards, may be necessary to maintain adherence to the program.
5. Strength training using machines rather than free-weights should be incorporated

whenever possible because this may have important ramifications for vocational productivity and independence.

Physical education programs should be based on the nature and needs of the learner. As mentioned previously, there is great variability among the populations of individuals who are mentally retarded. This is attributable to inherent differences between mild and more severe retardation, the causes of mental retardation, and the many other disorders that accompany the condition.

Disorders associated with mental retardation may be sensory impairments such as blindness, hard-of-hearing, or deafness; emotional disturbances; and neurological disorders such as cerebral palsy, muscular dystrophy, and problems in perception. It is apparent that physical education programs for persons who are mentally retarded must meet a multitude of needs at all age levels and all levels of intellectual and physical development. Programming principles to use for persons with mental retardation appear in Figure 11-8.

Figure 11-8 Programming Principles for the Physical Education Program for Persons with Mental Retardation

1. Select activities that meet the needs of the students in the class.

Select activities to meet the students' interest levels. However, precaution should be taken against participation in one particular activity to the exclusion of others. Be aware of students' tendency to favor the single activity with which they are most familiar.

Consider individual differences when selecting the activities. There are many games that allow for differences in abilities among class members.

Select activities according to the needs of the students who are mentally retarded.

2. Include appropriate physical and social opportunities.

Select sensory-perceptual-motor activities to promote specific and general development of the young child who is retarded and to develop recreational skills of older students to make it possible for these individuals to integrate socially with peers and members of their families now and in later life in community activity.

Select activities primarily on the basis of the development of motor skills; however, chronological ages should bias your selection of activities. Whenever possible, the activities should be age appropriate as well.

Provide a broad spectrum of activities that have recreational and social significance for later life.

Teach specific social skills that are meaningful within a specific social environment so that the behavioral change results in functional social performance.[59]

Work for progression toward skill development. For young children, use sensorimotor activities that contribute to sensory input system development; for older children, use task analysis with sequential progression methodology.

Whenever possible, students who are mentally retarded should be integrated with their peers into regular physical education classes. If they cannot participate successfully in regular classes, they should be given special developmental physical education commensurate with their capacity and needs. The regular physical education class may not provide adequate placement for all students who are mentally retarded. These children have social and motor deficits that make it difficult for them to participate equally with members of the regular class. Consequently, they often are found on the periphery of activity and do not involve themselves in the games and activities of the physical education class. An effort must be made to integrate mentally retarded persons into regular class activities; however, if this is not possible, special physical education programs should be adapted to the particular needs of the children.

The physical educator is cautioned against generalizing about the motor functioning level and learning capability of the student who is mentally retarded. As in all cases of students with disabilities, the children and youth should be thoroughly tested for motor skill functioning level and physical fitness before decisions are made as to what type of physical education program is needed. If testing shows a student to be deficient in areas of motor behavior performance, a thorough task analysis should be completed before the student's program is determined. Program adjustments may be required to ensure maximum benefit for students with mental retardation. In this section ways to meet the needs of students with mild and those with severe mental retardation in a segregated or inclusive setting are addressed.

Adaptations for Students Who Are Mildly Retarded

The most apparent difficulty for persons with the mildest forms of mental retardation is comprehension of complex playing rules and strategies. Often the student who is mildly retarded who is included in the regular physical education class is inappropriately accused of trying to cheat, when, in reality, he or she honestly does not understand what the rule or proper move is. Such accusations by peers or teachers often lead to momentary or prolonged rejection of the student. Rejection leads to feelings of low self-esteem, which contribute directly to withdrawal or retaliation by the student. Acting out then becomes an everyday occurrence, and before long such students perceived by peers or teachers as trouble makers. The vicious cycle can be avoided if the teacher anticipates comprehension difficulties and acts to counter them before they occur. Some suggestions for dealing with lack of understanding of rules or playing strategies are as follows:

1. Place the student in a less demanding position.
2. Overteach and constantly reinforce cognitive aspects of each game.
3. Help the other students in the class develop an understanding of and sensitivity toward the student's learning difficulties.

If the student who is retarded has a propensity toward excessive body fat, this problem will be detected when the AAHPERD Health Related Fitness Test or a similar test is given early in the school year to all students. Every student identified as having excessive body fat should be provided with appropriate aerobic activities and, possibly, nutritional counseling to reduce body fat stores. There is a need for routine health-related testing of all students in all schools, at every level. The sooner children learn the importance of controlling body fat levels through diet control and exercise, the higher the chance that these good habits will carry over to adulthood.

To enhance the probability that children with mental retardation will interact with their families and peers in healthful leisure-time pursuits, care must be taken to teach students to play games and sports that are typically pursued in community settings. The child who finds success and enjoyment in vigorous activity at a young age will continue participation as an adult.

Modifications for the Student Who Is Severely Retarded

With the development of instructional technology in the late 1970s, it was possible to demonstrate the competence of individuals who are severely mentally retarded. Project MOVE and the Data Based Gymnasium are examples of programs that use instructional technology for improving the movement capability of persons who are severely involved.[30,62] Through implementation of the available information from research and demonstration (i.e., best practice), it has been demonstrated that it is possible to maximize the potential of this group of individuals for meaningful participation in society. Physical education, which develops the motor capabilities of this group, is an integral part of their education.

It is true that these children who are severely mentally retarded often demonstrate delayed motor development milestones early in life and learn slower than children who are not retarded. However, the early childhood intervention programs that are gaining in popularity may help offset the marked motor delays more involved children demonstrate when they reach school age.

When designing the adapted physical education program, the physical educator should work closely with both physical and occupational therapists, who often test students who are severely involved to determine range of motion and level of reflex development. Consultation with the therapists and creative modification of traditional physical education activities will benefit students who are severely delayed. Some common activities used by physical and occupational therapists with this population are presented in Figure 11-9.

Special considerations must be made for the student with profound mental retardation and developmental delays. Many of these students spend a great deal of the instructional day, or day at home, in wheelchairs, in recliners, or on pillows or bolsters. The aquatic environment can afford a student with profound mental retardation a singular opportunity for freedom. There are remarkable flotation devices that can help the student maintain a relatively upright position in the water and

Figure 11-9 Activities for Persons with Severe Mental Retardation

- To stretch hip and knee flexors, remove the student who is nonambulatory and severely mentally retarded from a sitting position and allow him or her to stretch out on a mat.
- To improve range of motion, encourage the individual to reach for an object held just a few degrees beyond the range of capability. To hold interest, permit the person to reach the object occasionally.
- Place the student face down on the mat and place a pillow or bolster under the upper chest. Encourage the student to look up (lift head) from this position as often as possible.
- Place the student who is severely mentally retarded face down on a long scooter. Pull the scooter and encourage the individual to try using hands and feet to propel him- or herself.
- Place the student in a supine position on an air mat or a trampoline. Gently bounce the surface around the student.
- Praise every attempt the student makes to initiate movement.
- Hook a lightweight Theraband strip or an elastic loop around each of the student's limbs (one at a time) and encourage him or her to pull against the loop.

allow any action a cause-effect reaction. *Abilitations*, published by Sporttime, has a catalog specifically devoted to aquatics for individuals with disabilities.

Most aquatic educators do not recommend the widespread use of flotation devices when teaching students with disabilities to swim. However, as it is unlikely that the student who is profoundly mentally retarded will learn to swim independently or is independently mobile enough to put himself or herself in jeopardy of falling into a pool, the flotation devices simply increase freedom from restraint. Large flotation mats may be helpful for the student with severe contractures. Massage in a warm-water environment may be very helpful in maintaining circulation and preventing further contractures.

Because many students with profound mental retardation have significant difficulty maintaining thermal equilibrium, care must be taken to watch for signs of overheating—flushed face and rapid respiration—or of significant cooling—blue lips, shivering, chattering teeth, goose pimples, etc. The student must be removed from the pool if these signs exist.

Students with an educational/medical diagnosis of profound mental retardation may retain significant primitive reflexes which interfere with movement in the water in the same way the reflexes interfere with movement on dry land. The aquatic environment is great for these learners, however, because the viscosity of the water reduces gravity's impact on movement.

Attention must also be given to apparatus attached to the body, as well as the toileting habits of the students. Stomas used for providing oxygen or other nutrients to the body or for removing body water must be covered securely with waterproof tape. Depending on the child's toileting schedule, if necessary, a catheter must wear "Huggies Swimwear" or the like. Adults must wear a "Depend" undergarment specifically designed to prevent disintegration when in contact with water, or secure plastic undergarments must cover the diapers.

Many students with profound delays respond particularly well to music. Music may be calming and encourage relaxation. (For more information about appropriate accommodations, refer to Project INSPIRE Aquatics Pages: http://venus.twu.edu/~f_huettig)

Special Olympics International has developed training materials for use with individuals who are severely mentally retarded.[79] Activites in the Special Olympics Training Program (MATP) are broken down into the following components: dexterity, reaching, grasping, releasing, posture, head control in prone and supine positions, sitting in a chair, rolling, crawling, use of an electric wheelchair, sensory awareness, visual-motor, auditory-motor, and tactile awareness. Each of these activities is sequenced to maximize the potential for learning. The motor development curriculum promotes improvement in coordination and control of the body when performing a variety of motor activities. It is designed to develop age-appropriate sport and recreation skills as well as physical fitness, sensory awareness, and the sense of being part of a group. Included in the curriculum is a motor activities assessment instrument that should be used to evaluate mobility, dexterity, striking, kicking, and aquatic activity, as well as manual and electric wheelchair mobility skills. Also included are Special Olympics activities specifically adapted for severely mentally retarded athletes. These include aquatics, track and field, basketball, bowling, gymnastics, softball, volleyball, and weight lifting. Each sport is task analyzed for inclusion of the motor activities in the guide. Criteria and standards are identified to inform the teacher as to when the skill or task has been mastered. Furthermore, data sheets on which to record the types of instruction used (physical assistance, physical prompts, demonstration, verbal cues, and visual cues) are included. Spaces are also provided for recording the type of reinforcement used (e.g., edible, social, token), as well as the schedule of reinforcement (continuous, fixed, or intermittent).

Integration

The ultimate goal of sports and physical activity for persons who are mentally retarded is participation in integrated physical activity in natural community environments. For the most part, integration models for acquiring physical skills for persons with mental retardation in the public schools offer a choice of participation in regular or special physical education programs. When including the student with mental retardation in the regular class, careful selection of activities, frequent positive feedback, and opportunities to interact successfully with other students are critical.

Individuals with disabilities have a basic right to be provided opportunities that will lead to their full integration into community recreational settings. (Special Olympics has initiated several such integration programs, which will be detailed later in this chapter.) To achieve this integration, the process should include the following opportunities:

1. There should be a continuum of lesser restrictive environments in both instructional settings in the schools and in community recreational environments, and they should be coordinated for the benefit of each individual.
2. Persons with mental retardation should be placed in the most appropriate environment that is commensurate with their social and physical abilities.
3. Persons with mental retardation should be provided with a support system commensurate with their needs to adapt to present restrictive environments and advance to lesser restrictive environments.

When this procedure to achieve integration is used, individuals with disabilities will have a much greater opportunity to interact successfully in community recreational settings than they now have. Just placing students who are mentally retarded in a regular physical education class and hoping they gain all that is needed has not been successful. The current mainstreaming practice of chance placement must be replaced by a carefully planned integration process.

To enable individuals with disabilities to progress toward integration into community recreation programs, a continuum of lesser and lesser restrictive environments is needed. Three major environments that would promote the participation of individuals with disabilities into a sport activity are (1) a training environment restricted to individuals with disabilities, (2) a mixed or integrated athletic competition, and (3) a normal community environment (see Figure 11-10).

A persons-with-disabilities-only training/playing environment, where athletes receive special training from teachers and trained peer tutors, is a critical starting place for many individuals who are mentally retarded (see Figure 11-11). They need opportunities to learn basic fundamental movement skills before being placed with persons who do not have a disability. The next most appropriate

Figure 11-10 **Continuum of Lesser Restrictive Environments That Enable Progression Toward Independent Recreational Participation in a Specific Sport Activity**

environment is mixed or integrated athletic competition, where the composition of the team is at least 50 percent athletes without disabilities. This step is important because, to facilitate functioning in natural settings, athletes who are mentally retarded need exposure to peers who are not retarded and who have specific training in the principles of integration. The next step would be participation in integrated settings with nontrained peers without disabilities who are willing to assist with the integration process. In the fourth step, individuals who are mentally retarded would participate in integrated leisure, recreational, and sport activities with the assistance of nonparticipants. The ultimate goal is to participate without assistance in natural community, school, and recreation environments such as church, YMCA, and community recreation programs. Modifications of the major integration environments may be made to serve the unique needs of each athlete. It is most important that the thrust of integration be a process to move the students through the continuum of restrictive environments in specific sports to lesser restrictive environments to independent recreational functioning in sport activities that occur in communities.

Physical skill is one variable to consider for placement of persons with mental retardation in integrated settings with persons who are not mentally retarded. The ability to adapt to others when participating in activity is critical for the successful integration of individuals into leisure, recreation, and sport activity. The ability to cooperate and work harmoniously with others, to compete, to display sportsmanship, to respond to coaching and instruction, and to control one's emotions are necessary social behaviors if a person is to participate successfully in an integrated leisure, recreation, or sport activity. In addition to considering the physical and social abilities of individuals who are mentally retarded, the social complexity and the entry level of skill required to participate need to be considered. Individual sports such as track and field, bowling, and swimming require less social ability than team sports with complex rules, such as basketball or soccer. Specific examples of integration techniques follow.

Marathon Running Integration

A project was designed to integrate Special Olympics' athletes into 5- and 10-kilometer marathons. This project was conducted by a committed volunteer who was a marathon runner and coach of Special Olympics' track athletes. The athletes participated in a series of training and

Figure 11-11   Aquatics for Learners with Mental Retardation

- In an aquatic environment, a small teacher–student ratio is necessary. Students with mild mental retardation can be served safely in/through small-group instruction (one teacher to four to seven children). Students with profound mental retardation require careful, well-trained one-to-one instruction.
- A whole-part-whole approach to instruction appears to be most effective particularly when dealing with stroke skills. The use of David Armbruster's (famous coach of the University of Iowa Swimming Team and extraordinary swimming teacher) technique in which the student is introduced to all swimming strokes via the human stroke or dog paddle is particularly viable. Once the student can human stroke (dog paddle) on his or her stomach, each side, and back, the foundation is laid for the development of each of the basic swimming strokes. Then refinement of stroke mechanics and technique can be introduced.
- When possible, use the least invasive/directive strategy to provide instruction. Keep verbal instruction simple. Use one-word and two-word directions. If possible, keep verbal instructions simple but age appropriate. For example, don't ask a teenager to lie on his or her "tummy"; it is much more appropriate to ask the student to lie on his or her stomach. Pair the verbal instruction with a simple physical demonstration to clarify instruction.
- It is vital that the demonstration be done in the same place as the activity should be performed. For example, it is very confusing for a student with mental retardation to watch an instructor demonstrate the arm pattern for the back crawl with the instructor standing. Preferably, the instructor demonstrates in the water in the proper position; if that is not possible, the instructor should lie on the pool deck to demonstrate.
- If necessary, pair strong tactile and proprioceptive cues using patterning with a simple verbal (or sign) associative cue. For example, hold the student's hand and move it through a pulling motion, pairing that with the word (or sign) "pull." The student with mental retardation will find it easier to manage his or her own behavior if given the opportunity to choose a particular activity or activity sequence. For example, the teacher can give the student the opportunity to decide if he or she wants to practice flutter kicking first or practice back float first.
- Using "if then" strategies may be particularly effective in dealing with stubborn students—for example, "If and only if you bob five times will you be allowed to play with the beach ball."
- Repetition is key to learning in the student with mental retardation and developmental delays. The instructor can ensure this will happen without boredom by modifying the activity to involve other students and different types of equipment. For example, the student can practice the flutter kick while doing the following:
Flutter kick while being towed by teacher
Flutter kick while kicking at a beach ball
Flutter kick with fins
Flutter kick "fast" and "slow"
Flutter kick as part of a song, "If you're happy and you know it "kick your feet"

For more information refer to Project INSPIRE Aquatics Pages:
http://venus.twu.edu/~f_huettig

competitive environments. The first environment was made up of all Special Olympic athletes who were trained for distance running. However, to advance to a lesser restrictive environment, it was necessary for the athletes to acquire greater skill. To achieve this, Special Olympic runners were given additional training with marathon runners who were also mentally retarded. After additional skill and higher performance levels were achieved, the prime athletes were integrated in training with adult marathon runners who were not retarded. The final step of the integration process was competition with runners in a regular marathon. Thus athletes progressed through three training environments—Special Olympics training, extended Special Olympics training conducted by a parent, and integrated training with competitors who were not mentally retarded in 5- and 10-kilometer races.

Softball Integration

There is a concept in the integration process that is known as reverse mainstreaming. In this procedure, persons who are not mentally retarded are integrated into activities designed for persons who are retarded. Modification of this technique was initiated in the development of the Massachusetts Special Olympics softball integration project.[10] Special Olympics International subsequently funded the Research Center for Education Achievement to study the effects of Special Olympics' softball integration on coaches and players who were mentally retarded and those who weren't retarded. (The integrated softball game is composed of teams on which at least 50 percent of the players are not mentally retarded.) Reverse mainstreaming can be used with individuals with any type of disability.

Integrated softball is a lesser restrictive environment than traditional Special Olympics where a different social support system is provided to produce positive results. Through the construction of social networks of lesser restrictive environments in which individuals who are retarded and those who aren't participate on the same team, impressive social and physical gains can be made.

Budoff[10] has conducted research on integrated (Special Olympics) softball. In this activity, the individuals who are not retarded participate on the same team as an equal number of players who are retarded. Budoff, in comparing the play of the players who are retarded in integrated softball with all other softball games made up entirely of players who are retarded, makes the following comments: "The contrast between the mixed (integrated) and all-mentally retarded teams is so stark as to make the same slow-pitch softball game look like a dramatically different game."[10] As a result of a three-month season of integrated softball, the athletes who were mentally retarded demonstrated lateral movement and intelligent positioning for the ball as it was coming toward them. There were few "dead spots," where players were immobile and did not move when a ball was directed to them. The team members worked well together. To explain this phenomenon, Budoff comments that "it seems

Recreation and leisure activities provide opportunities for joy throughout the life span.
Courtesy Recreation Services, Division Care and Treatment Facilities, Department of Health and Social Services, Northern Wisconsin Center for the Developmentally Delayed.

that playing alongside of non-handicapped players helped to steady their [mentally retarded players] game, even when there were no overt signs of instruction."

An integrated team promotes the playing and understanding of the players who are mentally retarded because (1) the coach and the nonmentally retarded players are commited to teaching and supporting the players who are retarded and (2) the players who are not retarded serve as models on the field. According to Budoff, "There seems to be no doubt of the individual development observed in the play and sense of the game among players who are mentally retarded during this past season on the integrated (mixed) teams."[10] Thus, there are strong indications that an integrated environment in sport activity is a critical factor that benefits individuals who are mentally retarded.

Integrated Basketball with Adolescent Who Are Severely Mentally Retarded

The previous descriptions of integrated activity with participants who were not retarded were based on modeling procedures and intuitive coaching techniques. Many of the athletes in both the marathon running and integrated softball projects had the potential for integrated activity without a highly technical support system. However, there are persons with mental retardation who may always need support systems for integrated play in sports.

Pilot research has been done in integrated basketball play with individuals who were severely retarded.[7] In this activity, an equal number of college students preparing for professional roles in human service served as player-coaches. The rules of the basketball game were modified so that the athletes who were mentally retarded were required to perform the basic skill aspects of the game. The modified rules were (1) a player who was mentally retarded could travel and double dribble; (2) players who were not retarded could not dribble, shoot the ball, or pass to a teammate who was not retarded; and (3) only players who were mentally retarded could shoot. To increase scoring, another modification to the game was to award one point when the ball hit the rim. This modification provided more reinforcement to the conditions of play.

Each player who was not retarded was paired with a specific athlete with mental retardation. This athlete-coach then provided direct instruction as to when and to whom the ball was to be passed, when to dribble, and when to pass. These specific behaviors were reinforced. Thus, play and technical instruction were combined. When using this procedure, the stimulus cues and reinforcing properties by peer player-coaches are withdrawn as the athlete who is mentally retarded improves social and physical skills and can perform tasks without the cues. The limitations to this type of integrated play are that the desirable ratio of player-coach volunteers is one to one and prerequisite training is needed for direct instruction by player-coaches.

Roles of Player-Coaches

The roles assumed by the player-coaches in the complex social interactive game (e.g., basketball and softball), which may require direct coaching of

social and cognitive strategies, appear to be critical to the integration process. The complexities of the social and cognitive judgment of the athletes in marathon running were not as great as basketball and softball. Therefore the demand on the coaches was not as great. Nevertheless, attention by the coach was necessary to adapt integrated environments and training regimens commensurate with the ability of the athletes who were mentally retarded.

In all three integration environments, there was commitment by those who conducted the coaching. The attitudes of the coaches involved in all three projects supported the notion that, in an educational setting with teachers who favor integrating individual with disabilities, mainstreaming has a reasonable chance of success. On the other hand, the evidence also suggests that, where teachers oppose integration, the prognosis for success is not good. Thus, because Special Olympics is a volunteer activity for coaches, it is logical to assume that volunteers bring with them good attitudes toward the integration process.

Competition and Integration

The evidence from these integration programs is that they were beneficial to the performance of athletes with mental retardation. Inasmuch as there is some debate on the values of competition for persons who are mentally retarded as compared with play, the preliminary findings from these studies would indicate support for the findings of Karper, Martinek, and Wilkerson.[50] Their study investigated the effects of competitive and noncompetitive learning environments on motor performance in mainstreamed physical education classes. They found that the performance of the students who were mentally retarded dropped during noncompetitive treatment following a competitive one. Although there is no way of knowing whether competition was the cause for behavioral changes, the effects of competition on the performance of athletes who are mentally retarded may be a significant and fruitful avenue for future research.

COMMUNITY-BASED OPPORTUNITIES

Opportunities to learn motor skills and participate in leisure and recreation using learned skills should be available to all persons beyond the normal years of public-sponsored education. After leaving school, individuals must be able to find recreation using the skills and activities taught during the formal years of schooling. Opportunities for such recreation should be available to persons of all ages and capability levels. Those who have not had opportunities to participate and to learn motor skills should be provided with instruction in skills and ways of using leisure time for physical activity. Programs using direct instruction in appropriate warm-up and weight-training techniques report that their "graduates" continue participation in community-operated and commercial health and fitness programs.[82]

Children who are mentally retarded need to be taught to play regardless of their level of retardation. Fine, Welch-Burke, and Fondario[35] propose a three-dimensional model designed to enhance the leisure functioning of individuals with mental retardation. Levels of social play are autistic, solitary, parallel, cooperative, and competitive. Levels of cognitive play are functional, constructive, dramatic, and games with rules. Areas of skill development range from acquisition of prerequisite fine and gross motor skills and functional play to toy-play, art, simplified table games, exposure to the community, self-initiated play, and leisure education. Following is the five-step model designed to promote the achievement of higher levels of play:

1. Assessing current levels of skill and play
2. Setting goals consistent with individual needs
3. Teaching goal behaviors
4. Generalizing newly learned skills to higher levels of skill and to other environments
5. Teaching individuals to apply skills in natural environments

Recreational opportunities for children who are mentally retarded should be provided after school, during school vacations, and after formal educational training. There should be adequate provision in the recreation program for vigorous activity such as sports, dancing, active games, swimming, and hiking. Intramural and community sports leagues should be provided to reinforce skills developed in the instructional program. In addition, winter snow games should be made available. Camping and outdoor education programs are other ways of affording expression of skills and interests.

Recreation

Though at least one study has shown that mildly retarded adolescents can generalize motor skills from one setting to another,[84] whenever possible, recreational activities for persons with mental retardation should take place in a community-based integrated setting. Recreational activities should be designed to stimulate interaction between individuals who are mentally retarded and those who aren't.[25] Adults who are mentally retarded are more apt to socially integrate when they are given the opportunity to select leisure activities of interest to them.[11]

In conjunction with the recreation program, special events scheduled throughout the school year stimulate interests, motivate the children, and inform the community about the progress of the physical education program and about the abilities of youngsters who are mentally retarded. Examples of such events are demonstrations for PTA meetings, track and field meets, swimming meets, play days, sports days, "hoop-it-up," pass-punt-kick contests, hikes, and bicycle races.

Overcoming Barriers to Full Recreational Inclusion

Some of the barriers to full inclusion in recreational programs that adults with mental retardation face are

- Restrictive attitudes of parents and family
- Opposition from some members of the community
- Lack of widely available guidelines for planning and implementation of integrated programs
- Lack of skill[49]

Part of the solution to overcoming these barriers is fostering and improving social relationships.[65] What is needed is a community commitment to provide programs for all the citizens. Some ways a community can meet the needs of its citizens with mental retardation are

1. Develop guidelines for planning and implementing integrated recreational programs.
2. Provide opportunities for individuals who are retarded to socialize with persons who are not retarded.
3. Use existing materials to train personnel to work with individuals who are mentally retarded.
4. Change attitudes toward persons with mental retardation by "showcasing" their capabilities during local fairs and festivities.

Volunteer Assistants

Individuals who are severely mentally retarded often require individual attention. Volunteers trained in specific duties can be of assistance to the instructional program as well as to after-school and vacation recreation programs. Parents of children who are retarded, members of high school and college service clubs, and scouting groups are becoming increasingly active as volunteers. Instructors can seek out these people and ask them to become involved with the programs for individuals who are mentally retarded. A 1- or 2-hour training session can be planned to teach these volunteers what needs to be done, how to do it, what to expect from individuals who are retarded, and how to deal with behavior problems.

The Home Program

The amount of time that the physical educator will be involved personally with students who are mentally retarded is relatively small. If maximum benefits are to be derived from programs, it is necessary to have a follow-up of activities taught in the form of a home program. An educational program for parents describing the children's program and its purpose should be provided for implementation in the home. Parents should receive direction and assistance in methods for involving their children in physical activity taking place in the neighborhood and the home.

Special Olympics

Probably no single program has done as much to foster the participation of individuals who are retarded in physical activities as has the Special Olympics program. This program, which is now international in scope, was begun in 1968 by the Joseph P. Kennedy, Jr., Foundation. The program includes training in physical fitness and sports and provides competition at the local, district, state, national, and international levels for children and adults who are retarded. Special Olympics also has been instrumental in developing integration programs for athletes who are mentally retarded.

The Special Olympics philosophy is expressed by its motto, which is "Let me win, but if I cannot win, let me be brave in the attempt." The stated mission of Special Olympics is

> To provide year-round sports training and athletic competition in a variety of Olympic-type sports for all children and adults with mental retardation, giving them continuing opportunities to develop physical fitness, demonstrate courage, experience joy, and participate in a sharing of gifts, skills, and friendship with their families, other Special Olympic athletes, and the community.[80]

The philosophy and mission are supported by four basic programs:

1. *Special Olympic Sports Skill Program.* This program is based on illustrated guides for each sport, which include the rules under which the athletes must compete, task-analyzed skills, goals and objectives, and pre- and posttraining assessments.
2. *Unified Sports Program.* This program uses an equal number of players with and without mental retardation to participate in the sponsored events. Principles that guide this

program are age and ability groups. Usually unified teams compete with other unified teams.

3. *Special Olympics Motor Activities Training Program (MATP).* This program serves persons with severe mental retardation.[79] The program provides a wide range of activities and stresses the following points:
   a. Training should be fun.
   b. Ultimately, athletes should be able to choose their own activities.
   c. Activities should be age-appropriate.
   d. Participants should demonstrate their newly developed skills to significant others.
   e. Functioning level guides activity selection.
   f. Even partial participation has value.
   g. Creativity should be used when providing community-based sports and recreational activities.
4. *Demonstration Sports Program.* This program explores and researches the appropriateness of incorporating new sports into the Special Olympics program.

Twenty-three official sports are offered in the Special Olympics national and international programs—alpine and Nordic skiing, basketball, badminton, bowling, diving, Frisbee throwing, floor hockey, gymnastics, figure skating, field hockey, physical fitness and weight training, rhythmic movements, softball, speed skating, walking, poly hockey, soccer, swimming, track and field events, volleyball, and wheelchair events.

Some of the rules of the Special Olympic sports program are

1. Athletes can participate beginning at age eight years.
2. Competition is conducted according to age and ability.
3. Competition must be preceded by at least eight weeks of training.
4. Records of performance levels during practice must be submitted prior to competition to establish competition divisions.
5. Head coaches must be formally trained.
6. Event managers must complete formal training.

SUMMARY

Mental retardation refers to substantial limitations in certain personal capabilities. It is manifested as significantly subaverage intellectual functioning, existing concurrently with related disabilities in two or more of the following adaptive skill areas: communication, self-care, home living, social skills, community use, self-direction, health and safety, leisure, functional academics, and work. Mental retardation begins before age eighteen but may not always be of lifelong duration. The prevalence of mental retardation in the population is approximately 3 percent. Two levels are recognized—mildly retarded and severely retarded. Persons with mental retardation can be expected to learn and develop.

Physical educators can expect to have students with mental retardation in the classes they teach. Those students' motor skills and physical fitness levels may be lower than those of students who are not mentally retarded. These students can be taught and can improve. Carefully selected teaching strategies and program adaptations will yield positive motor development results. Students should be tested to determine their specific motor strengths and weaknesses, as is true for most performance abilities. Physical education programs should be designed around these test results.

Physical education programs in the public schools should provide assistance for transition of the recreational skills acquired in physical education classes to independent, integrated recreational activity in the community. Participation in recreation, home programs, and Special Olympics should be encouraged. Special Olympics has taken the lead in developing programs to include individuals who are mentally retarded in integrated sports activity.

REVIEW QUESTIONS

1. How does the IDEA definition of mental retardation differ from the Association for Retarded Citizens (ARC) definition?

2. What types of physical education program modifications need to be made for individuals with Down syndrome who have atlantoaxial instability?

3. What causes fetal alcohol syndrome? How prevalent is it in the United States?

4. What types of modifications are recommended for use when programming exercises for persons with mental retardation?

5. What are five specific teaching strategies that can be used with persons with mental retardation?

6. How are adaptations of physical activity different for persons with mild and severe mental retardation?

7. What accommodations are needed outside of school to enable persons with mental retardation to participate in community recreation programs?

8. What Special Olympic programs are available for persons with mental retardation?

9. What is necessary to conduct successful integration of persons with and without retardation into community sports activities?

STUDENT ACTIVITIES

1. With the class divided into small groups have them select appropriate games for Luther's class. When each group reports its selection of games, have each group give its rationale for each selection.

2. Students select three behavior management techniques for all of Luther's teachers to use to control his behavior, and describe how they would use those techniques in an inclusive physical education class.

3. Locate one of the journals that deals with mental retardation. (Some of these journals are *Adapted Physical Education Quarterly; Palaestra: The Forum of Sport, Physical Education and Recreation for the Disabled; Exceptional Children; Retardation; Education and Training of the Mentally Retarded;* and *Journal of Intellectual Disability.*) Look through recent issues for articles that might be applied to

conducting physical education programs for students who are mentally retarded.

4. Visit classes in which youngsters with mental retardation are included. Compare the performance of these students with that of the other students in the class. List the ways their performance and/or behavior differs.

5. Talk with a physical education teacher who has worked with students who are mentally retarded and ask which teaching strategies have proven successful with specific types of learners on specific tasks.

6. Observe a Special Olympics meet. Describe how the meet was conducted to accommodate the different abilities of the participants so all could engage in meaningful competition.

REFERENCES

1. American Association on Mental Retardation: *Classification in mental retardation,* Washington, DC, 1992, Author.

2. American Academy of Pediatrics Committee on Sports Medicine: Atlantoaxial instability in children with Down syndrome, *Pediatrics* 96:151–154, 1995.

3. American Psychiatric Association: *Diagnostic and statistical manual of mental disorders,* vol. 4, Washington, DC, 1994, Author.

4. Anchuthengil JD, Neilsen DH, Schulenburg J, Hurst R, Davis MJ: Effects of an individualized treadmill exercise training program on cardiovascular fitness

of adults with mental retardation, *J of Ortho, Sports, and PT* 16:229–237, 1992.

5. ARA Consulting Group: *The Winter Medallion Program of Manitoba Special Olympics: an evaluation.* Winnipeg, Canada, 1994, Author.

6. Arnold R, Ng N, Pechar G: Relationship of rated perceived exertion to heart rate and workload in mentally retarded young adults, *Adapt Phys Act Q* 9:47–53, 1992.

7. Auxter DM et al.: *Prediction of playing basketball and basketball skills among persons with severe mental retardation.* Unpublished paper, Special Olympics International, Washington, DC, 1987.

8. Baumgardner TL, Green KE, Reiss AL: A behavioral neurogenetics approach to developmental disabilities: gene-brain-behavior associations, *Current Opinion in Neurology* 7:172–178, 1994.

9. Beers MH, Berkow R, editors: *The Merck manual of diagnosis and therapy,* Whitehouse Station, NJ, 1999, Merck Research Laboratories.

10. Budoff M: *The evaluation of the mixed teams softball in Massachusetts Special Olympics—coaches' views,* Cambridge, MA, 1987, Research Institute for Educational Problems.

11. Bullock CC, Mahon MJ: Decision making in leisure: empowerment for people with mental retardation, *JOPERD* 63:36–39, 1992.

12. Burack JT, Enns JA: *Attention, development and psychopathology,* New York, 1997, Guilford Press.

13. Chanias AK, Reid G, Hoover ML: Exercise effects on health-related physical fitness of individuals with an intellectual disability: a meta-analysis, *Adapt Phys Act Q* 15:119–140, 1998.

14. Choi S, Meeuwsen HJ, French R, Stenwall J: Learning and control of simple aiming movements by adults with profound mental retardation, *Adapt Phys Act Q* 16:167–177, 1999.

15. Committee on Sports Medicine: Atlantoaxial instability in Down syndrome, *Pediatrics* 74:152–154, 1984.

16. Committee on Substance Abuse, Committee on Children with Disabilities: Fetal alcohol syndrome and fetal alcohol effects, *Pediatrics* 91:1004–1006, 1993.

17. Cooke RE: Atlantoaxial instability in individuals with Down's syndrome, *Adapt Phys Act Q* 1:194–196, 1984.

18. Cooper LJ, Wacker DP, Thursby D, Plagmann L, Harding J, Millard T, Derby M: Analysis of the effects of task preferences, task demands, and adult attention on child behavior in outpatient and classroom settings, *J of Applied Behav Analysis* 25:823–840, 1992.

19. Croce R: Effects of exercise and diet on body composition and cardiovascular fitness, *Educ and Train in Mental Retard* 25:176–187, 1990.

20. Croce R, Horvat M: Effects of reinforcement-based exercise on fitness and work productivity in adults with mental retardation, *Adapt Phys Act Q* 9:148–178, 1992.

21. Croce R, Horvat M: Coincident timing by nondisabled mentally retarded, and traumatic brain-injured individuals under varying target-exposure conditions, *Perc Motor Skills* 80:487–496, 1995.

22. Croce R, Horvat H, Roswal G: A preliminary investigation into the effects of exercise duration and fitness level on problem solving ability in individuals with mild mental retardation, *Clinical Kinesiology* 48(3):48–54, 1994.

23. Croce RV, Pitetti KH, Horvat M, Miller J: Peak torque, average power, and hamstrings/quadriceps ratios in nondisabled adults and adults with mental retardation, *Arch Phys Med Rehabil* 77:369–372, 1996.

24. Danforth DS, Drabman RS: Community living skills. In Matson JL, editor: *Handbook of behavior modification with the mentally retarded,* New York, 1990, Plenum Press.

25. Dattilo J, Schlein SJ: Understanding leisure services for individuals with mental retardation, *Mental Retard* 32:53–59, 1994.

26. DePauw K, Ferrari N: The effect of interference on the performance on a card sorting task of mentally retarded adolescents, *The Phys Educ* 43:32–38, 1986.

27. De Vries LB, Halley DJ, Oostra BA, Niermeijer MF: The fragile X syndrome: a growing gene causing familial intellectual disability, *J of Intellectual Disability* 38:1–8, 1994.

28. Division of Child Development, Disability, and Health: Fetal Alcohol Syndrome, *Centers for Disease Control and Prevention webpage,* http://www.cdc.gov/nceh/programs/cddh/fasfact.htm, Atlanta, GA, 1999.

29. Downs SB, Wood TM: Validating a Special Olympics volleyball skills assessment test, *Adapt Phys Act Q* 13:166–179, 1996.

30. Dunn JM, Morehouse JW, Fredericks HD: *Physical education for the severely handicapped: a systematic approach to a data based gymnasium,* Austin, TX, 1986, PRO-ED.

31. Ellis DN, Cress PJ, Spellman CR: Using self management to promote independent exercise in adolescents with moderate mental retardation in a school setting, *Educ and Train of Ment Retard* 27:51–59, 1992.

32. Fernhall B: Mental retardation. In Durstine JL, editor: *Exercise management for persons with chronic diseases and disabilities,* Champaign, IL, 1997, Human Kinetics.

33. Fernhall B, Pittetti KH, Vukovich DS, Hensen T, Winnick JP, Short FX: Validation of cardiovascular fitness field tests in children with mental retardation, *Amer J of Ment Retard* 102:602–612, 1998.

34. Felix M, McCubbin J, Shaw, J: Bone mineral density, body composition, and muscle strength in premenopausal women with mental retardation, *Adapt Phys Act Q* 15:345–356, 1998.

35. Fine A, Welch-Burke C, Fondario L: A developmental model for the integration of leisure programming in the education of individuals with mental retardation, *Ment Retard* 23:289–296, 1985.

36. Foster-Johnson L, Ferro J, Dunlap G: Preferred curricular activities and reduced problem behaviors in students with intellectual disabilities, *J of Appl Behav Analysis* 27:493–504, 1994.

37. Frey GC, McCubbin JA, Hannigan-Downs S, Kasser SL, Skaggs SO: Physical fitness of trained runners with and without mild mental retardation, *Adapt Phys Act Q* 16:126–137, 1999.

38. Gleser JM, Margules JY, Mier Nyska SP, Mendelberg H: Physical and psychological benefits of modified judo practice for blind mentally retarded children: a pilot study, *Perc Motor Skills* 74:915–925, 1992.

39. Gillberg C: Practitioner review: physical investigations in mental retardation, *J Child Psychol Psyc* 38:889–897, 1997.

40. Grskovic JA, Zentail SS, Stormont-Spurgin M: Time estimation and planning abilities: students with and without mild disabilities, *Behavior Disorders* 20:197–203, 1995.

41. Hagerman, R: Behaviour and treatment of the fragile X syndrome. In Davies KE, editor: *The fragile X syndrome.* Oxford, England, 1989, Oxford University Press.

42. Hagerman R: The ARC's Q&A on Fragile X. http://thearc.org/faqs/fragqa.html

43. Haley S: Postural reactions in infants with Down syndrome: relationship to motor milestone development and age, *J Am Phys Therapy* 66:17–22, 1986.

44. Hallahan DP, Kauffman JM: *Exceptional learners: introduction to special education,* Boston, 1997, Allyn & Bacon.

45. Hickson L, Blackman LS, Reis EM: *Mental retardation: foundations of educational programming,* Boston, 1995, Allyn & Bacon.

46. Hodges NJ, Cunningham SJ, Lyons J, Kerr TL, Digby E: Visual feedback processing and goal directed movement in adults with Down syndrome, *Adap Phy Act Q* 12:52–59, 1995.

47. Horvat M, Croce R, Roswell G: Magnitude and reliability for measurements of muscle strength across trials for individuals with mental retardation, *Perc Motor Skills* 77:643–649, 1993.

48. Horvat M, Croce R, Roswal G, Scagraves F: Single trial versus maximal or mean values for evaluating strengths in individuals with mental retardation, *Adapt Phys Act Q* 12:176–186, 1995.

49. Ittenbach RF, Abery BH, Larson SA, Speigel AN, Prouty RW: Community adjustment of young adults with mental retardation: overcoming barriers to inclusion, *Palaestra* 11(2):32–42, 1994.

50. Karper WB, Martinek TJ, Wilkerson JD: Effects of competitive/non-competitive learning on motor performance of children in mainstream physical education, *Am Correct Ther J* 39:10–15, 1985.

51. Kerns KA, Audrey D, Mateer CA, Streissguth AP: Cognitive deficits in nonretarded adults with fetal alcohol syndrome, *J of Learning Disabilities* 30:685–693, 1997.

52. Kim S, Kwang HK: Cardiorespiratory function of educable mentally retarded boys. In Yabe K, Kusano K, Nakata H, editors: *Adapted physical activity: health and fitness,* New York, 1994, Springer-Verlag.

53. King D, Mace FC: Acquisition and maintenance of exercise skills under normalized conditions by adults with moderate and severe mental

retardation, *Educ and Train in Ment Retard* 28:311–317, 1990.

54. Latash ML, Almeida GL, Corcos DM: Preprogrammed reactions in individuals with Down syndrome: the effects of instruction and predictability of the person, *Archives of Physical Med and Rehab* 74:391–398, 1993.

55. Lavay B, McCubbin J, Eichstaedt C: Field-based physical fitness tests for individuals with mental retardation. In Vermeer A, Davis WE, editors: Physical and motor development in mental retardation, *Medicine and Sport Science* 40, 168–180, Basil, Karger, 1995.

56. Leshin L: Atlantoaxial Instability: Controversy and Commentary. http://www.ds-health.com/aai.htm

57. MacDonncha A, Watson A, McSweeney T, O'Donovan DJ: Reliability of Eurofit physical fitness items for adolescent males with and without mental retardation, *Adapt Phys Act Q* 16:86–95, 1999.

58. Maes et al.: Cognitive functioning and information processing of adult mentally retarded men with fragile-X syndrome, *American J of Medical Genetics* 50:190–200, 1994.

59. Martin JE et al.: Consumer-centered transition and supported employment. In Matson JL, editor: *Handbook of behavior modification with the mentally retarded,* New York, 1990, Plenum Press.

60. Merriman WJ, Barnett BE, Jarry ES: Improving fitness of dually diagnosed adults, *Percept Motor Skills* 83:99–104, 1996.

61. Monroe H, Howe C: The effects of integration and social class on the acceptance of retarded adolescents, *Educ Train Ment Retard* 6:21–24, 1971.

62. M.O.V.E, MOVE International, Bakersfield, CA, website. http://www.MOVE-International.org

63. Nakaya T, Kusano K, Yare K: Decreasing motor ability in adults with Downs syndrome. In Yabe K, Kusano K, Nakata H, editors: *Adapted physical activity: health and fitness,* New York, 1994, Springer-Verlag.

64. Newell R: Motor skill orientation in mental retardation: overview of traditional and current orientation. In Clark JH, Humphrey J, editors: *Motor development: current selected research, vol. I,* Princeton, NJ, 1985, Princeton Book Co.

65. Newton SJ, Horner RH, Ard WR, LeBaron N, Sappington G: A conceptual model for improving the social life of individuals with mental retardation, *Mental Retard* 32:393–402, 1994.

66. Patel, BD: The fragile X syndrome, *British J of Clinical Practice* 48(1):42–44, 1994.

67. Pitetti KH, Rimmer JH, Fernhall B: Physical fitness and adults with mental retardation: an overview of current research and future directions, *Sports Medicine* 16:23–56, 1993.

68. P.L. 101-476 Rules. *Federal Register,* September 29, 1992.

69. Polloway EA, Patton, JR, Smith TE, Buck GH: Mental retardation and learning disabilities: conceptual and applied issues, *J of Learn Disabilities* 30:297–308, 345, 1997.

70. Porretta DL, Moore W, Sappenfield C: Situational anxiety in Special Olympics athletes, *Palaestra* 9(3):48–50, 1993.

71. Privett C: The Special Olympics: a tradition of excellence, *Exceptional Parent* May:28–36, 1999.

72. Rimmer JH, Braddock D, Fujiura G: Prevalence of obesity in adults with mental retardation: implications for health promotion and disease prevention, *Mental Retardation* 31:105–110, 1993.

73. Rimmer J, Kelly L: Effects of a resistance training program on adults with mental retardation, *Adapt Phys Act Q* 8:146–153, 1991.

74. Schantz OJ: Adaptation in students with Downs syndrome: an experimental study on the trainability of strength and power. In Yabe K, Kusano K, Nakata H, editors: *Adapted physical activity: health and fitness,* New York, 1994, Springer-Verlag.

75. Schroeder SR et al.: Self-injurious behavior. In Matson JL, editor: *Handbook of behavior modification with the mentally retarded,* New York, 1990, Plenum Press.

76. Shapiro DR, Drummer GM: Perceived and actual basketball competence of adolescent males with mild mental retardation, *Adapt Phy Act Q* 15:179–190, 1998.

77. Smith D: *Introduction to special education: teaching in an age of challenge,* Needham Heights, MA, 1998, Allyn & Bacon.

78. Smith S: Cognitive deficits associated with fragile X syndrome, *Mental Retardation* 31(5):279–283, 1993.

79. Special Olympics International: *Adapted physical education sports skill assessment resource manual, Special Olympics Bulletin,* Washington, DC, 1991, Author.

80. Special Olympics International: *Special Olympics motor activities training guide,* Washington, DC, 1989, Author.

81. Steinbach P et al.: Molecular analysis of mutations in the gene FMR-1 segregating in fragile X families, *Hum Genet* 92:491–498, 1993.

82. Stopka C, Pomeranz J, Siders R, Dykes MK, Goodman A: Transitional skills for wellness, *Teach Ex Child* 7:6–11, 1999.

83. Suomi R, Surburh PR, Lecius P: Reliability of isokinetic and isometric measurement of leg strength on men with mental retardation, *Archives of Phys Med and Rehab* 74:848–853, 1993.

84. Surburg PR: The influence of task incompletion of motor skill performance of mildly retarded adolescents, *Am correct Ther J* 40:39–42, 1986.

85. Tanji JL: The preparticipation exam, *The Physician and Sportsmed* 19:61–69, 1994.

86. Taylor J, French R, Kinnison L, O'Brien T: Primary and secondary reinforcers in performance of a 1.0 mile walk/jog by adolescents with moderate mental retardation, *Percept Motor Skills* 87:1265–1266, 1998.

87. Ulrich BD, Ulrich DA, Collier DH, Cole EL: Developmental shifts in the ability of infants with Down syndrome to produce treadmill steps, *Phys Ther* 75:17–23, 1995.

88. U.S. Department of Education: *Twentieth annual report to congress on the implementation of the Individuals with Disabilities Education Act,* Washington, DC, 1998, U.S. Government Printing Office.

89. Wehmeyer ML, Metzler CA: How self-determined are people with mental retardation? The national consumer survey, *Mental Retard* 33:111–119, 1995.

90. Wiebe E, Wiebe A: Fragil X syndrome, *Can Fam Physician* 40:290–295, 1994.

91. Wiegers AM, Curfs LMG, Fryns J-P: A longitudinal study of intelligence in Dutch fragile X boys, *Birth Defects: Original Article Series* 28(1):93–97, 1992.

92. Winnick JP, Short FX: The Brockport Physical Fitness Test, Champaign, IL, 1999, Human Kinetics.

93. Yabe K et al.: Developmental trends of jumping reaction time by means of EMG in mentally retarded children, *J Ment Defic Res* 29:137–145, 1985.

94. Yang JJ, Porretta DL: Sport/leisure skill learning by adolescents with mild mental retardation: a four-step strategy, *Adapt Phys Act Q* 16:300–315, 1999.

95. Yun J, Ulrich DA: Perceived and actual physical competence in children with mild mental retardation, *Amer J on Ment Retard,* 102:147–160, 1997.

96. Zetts RA, Horvat MA, Langone J: Effects of a community-based progressive resistance training program on the work productivity of adolescents with moderate to severe intellectual disabilities, *Educ Train Ment Retard Dev Disab* June:66–178, 1995.

97. Zoerink DA, Wilson J: The competitive disposition: views of athletes with mental retardation, *Adapt Phys Act Q* 12:34–42, 1995.

SUGGESTED READINGS

American College of Sports Medicine: *Exercise management for persons with chronic diseases and disabilities,* Champaign, IL, 1997, Human Kinetics.

Eichstaedt C, Lavay B: *Physical activity for individuals with mental retardation: infant to adult,* Champaign, IL, 1992, Human Kinetics.

Hickson L, Blackman LS, Reis EM: *Mental retardation: foundations of educational programming,* Boston, 1995, Allyn & Bacon.

Rimmer JH: *Fitness and rehabilitation programs for special populations,* Dubuque, IA, 1994, Wm. C. Brown.

Taylor RL: *Assessment of individuals with mental retardation,* San Diego, 1998, Singular.

RECOMMENDED WEBSITES

Please note: These websites are being recommended in the fall of 1999. Given the ever changing nature of the Internet, these sites may have moved or been replaced by the time you are reading this text.

Association for Children with Down's Syndrome
http://www.mrpc.com/acds/acdshome.html

Canadian Centre on Substance Abuse—Fetal Alcohol Syndrome
http://www.ccsa.ca/fasgen.htm

Down's Syndrome Empowerment Home Page
http://wvlink.mpl.com/users/casten_t/downsyn.html

Fragile X Syndrome
http://www.worx.net/fraxa

Project INSPIRE Aquatics
http://venus.twu.edu/~f_huettig

The Association of Retarded Citizens (ARC)
http://TheARC.org/welcome.html

RECOMMENDED VIDEOS

Special Needs Students in Regular Classrooms?
Sean's Story
45 minutes, color, $149 purchase price, $75 rental
Films for the Humanities & Sciences
PO Box 2053
Princeton, NJ 08543

Raymond's Portrait
27 minutes, color, $175 purchase price
Fanlight Productions

4196 Washington Street
Boston, MA 02131

Down Syndrome: A Parent's Perspective
19 minutes, color, $150 purchase price
Aquarius Health Care Videos
5 Powderhouse Lane
PO Box 1159
Sherborn, MA 01770

The child who is autistic requires cardiovascular activities.
Photo by Carol Huettig.

Pervasive Developmental Disorders

■ OBJECTIVES

Briefly explain pervasive developmental disorders.

Briefly describe autism, Asperger's disorder, Rett syndrome, childhood disintegrative disorder (CDD), and pervasive developmental disorder–not otherwise specified (PDD-NOS).

Explain specific strategies for providing instructional services for students with all five pervasive developmental delays in the most inclusive environment.

Give examples of each of the physical education activities appropriate for learners with all five of the pervasive developmental delays at various stages of development.

Explain simple strategies to encourage appropriate behavior in learners with pervasive developmental disorders.

Describe the leisure/recreation and fitness activities that may be appropriate in a community-based program for learners with each of the pervasive developmental disorders making a transition from school into the community.

Compare and contrast the five types of PDD, based on the *DSM-IV-Revised*.

Briefly explain the causes of each pervasive developmental disorder.

For learners with PDD, give specific examples of activities to develop physical and motor fitness; fundamental motor skills and patterns; and skills in aquatics, dance, and individual and group games and sports (including intramural and lifetime sports).

Explain the critical role of parents in assessment of and IEP development for individuals with PDD.

Briefly explain instructional and behavioral methodologies used for individuals with PDD, including Daily Life Therapy (Higashi), TEACCH and Applied Behavioral Analysis.

Write individual transition plans for learners with each of the types of PDD to demonstrate your ability to differentiate among each.

461

PERVASIVE DEVELOPMENTAL DISORDERS

Definition

Individuals with pervasive developmental disorders (PDD) present an exciting, wonderful, and ever challenging opportunity for physical educators. Their unique approach to life, their reaction to sensory stimulation within the environment, and their fascinating human interaction and communication/language skills provide the opportunity for physical educators, adapted and general physical education teachers alike, to test and teach skills.

Tsai[79] in a National Information Center for Children and Youth with Disabilities (NICHCY) briefing paper, reported ever increasing interest in the nature of individuals with pervasive developmental disorders and significant confusion for both parents and professionals regarding the various diagnostic categories included under the large umbrella of PDD. Tsai suggested that all types of PDD are neurological disorders that are usually evident by age three years. In general, children who have a type of PDD have difficulty in talking, playing with other children, and relating to others, including their families. This is consistent with the *DSM-IV-R* definition:

> Pervasive Developmental Disorders are characterized by severe and pervasive impairment in several areas of development:
> - social interaction skills;
> - communication skills; or
> - the presence of stereotyped behavior, interests, and activities.[2]

For the sake of clarity, pervasive developmental disorders can be considered the large category under which there are five types: autistic disorder, Asperger's disorder, Rett's disorder, childhood disintegrative disorder, and PDD-NOS (see Figure 12-1).

Autistic disorder is one of the five disorders included under the large umbrella of pervasive developmental disorder (PDD). Classic autism, originally known as Kanner's syndrome, was first described by Dr. Leo Kanner in 1943.[47] The major characteristics of autism are significant developmental delays, global and comprehensive language disorders, abnormal and stereotypical behavior patterns, social isolation, and often, but not always, mental retardation.

In 1944, Hans Asperger introduced an autistic disorder that is now widely known as Asperger's disorder.[73] Individuals with this condition, known originally as high-level autism, share many of the same symptoms as individuals with autism. However, there are some significant differences. One of the major differences between Asperger's disorder and others within the PDD category is that an individual with Asperger's disorder has average to above average intelligence.[5]

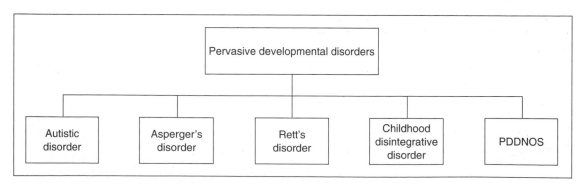

Figure 12-1   Pervasive Developmental Disorders
Modified from Tsai L: *Pervasive developmental disorders,* NICHCY Briefing Paper, FS20, 1–15, 1998.

The individual with Asperger's disorder usually does not have a significant delay in basic communication and language skills but may struggle with the subtleties of conversation, including humor, sarcasm, and irony, and may have some difficulty "reading" subtle facial expressions or gestures.[81] One of the other distinguishing characteristics of Asperger's disorder is that some students with the disorder demonstrate motor clumsiness and awkwardness.

Rett's disorder is a neurological disorder first described in 1966 in Germany by A. Rett.[68] The condition is characterized by normal development during the first six to eighteen months of life followed by loss of acquired gross and fine motor skills, impaired language skills, gait apraxia (unusual or atypical gait), and the appearance of stereotypic hand-wringing, hand-washing movements.[69] Rett's disorder is distinguished from the others under the PDD umbrella because of the significant nature of the loss. Children with Rett's disorder typically are classified as having severe or profound mental retardation.

Childhood disintegrative disorder (CDD) is an extremely rare disorder in which a significant loss or regression exists in many areas, including movement, bladder and bowel control, and social and language skills. One of the critical features of this condition is that the diagnosis of CDD is made only if the symptoms occur after there have been at least two years of apparently normal development and if the regression begins prior to the age of ten years.[7] The critical factor is that in childhood disintegrative disorder the learner must have been developing "typically" for at least two years prior to the beginning of the regression.

Pervasive developmental disorders–not otherwise specified (PDD-NOS) is a term used to describe learners who do not meet the specific criteria for diagnosis in any of the other four forms of pervasive developmental disorder, as specified in *DSM-IV*. They share, however, significant, severe and pervasive delays in the development of social interaction and communication skills.

Incidence

The United States Department of Education, Office of Special Education and Rehabilitation Services, in its annual report to Congress on the Implementation of the Individuals with Disabilities Education Act, February 1998, reported that 45,000 children, from birth to age twenty-one, received educational services in the broad category of "autism and other." These children were served in a variety of educational settings:

Regular class	10.8%
Resource room	9.4
Separate class	54.7
Public separate school facility	15.2
Public residential facility	0.7
Private residential facility	2.2
Homebound/hospital environment	0.5[80]

Causes

The causes of pervasive developmental disorders have been widely studied. But, as is often true in the educational diagnostic process, contemporary research has not yet significantly distinguished among each of the five types of PDD. Too often, researchers lump together "autism" and "PDD–NOS," or "Asperger's disorder" and "high-functioning autism." It is safe to say, however, that each of the five types of PDD is characterized by significant neurological impairment. Autism and the other PDDs appear to share common genetic mechanisms.[7,30,74,77] However, MacLean et al.[59] have suggested that higher- and lower-functioning learners with pervasive developmental disorders may result from separate genetic mechanisms. In this section, the specific etiology of each of the five types of PDD will be considered separately.

The causes of autism have been widely studied. It is believed that autism has a neurological basis. This may include chromosomal defects; disorders of neuron cell migration; congenital brain malformation, including megancephaly (large brain); electrophysiological abnormalities; and defects in neurotransmitter and receptor structure.[6,18,26,77,83]

There are also significant concerns that the environmental ecosystem has become so toxic that children are being significantly affected by the toxins, and this may be related to an increase in the incidence of autism.[19] The toxins may also have a negative impact on the genetic endowment of individuals.

It has been difficult for researchers to identify specific causative factors associated with Asperger's disorder because of the presumed strong relationship between the "high-functioning" autistic individual and an individual with Asperger's disorder. Asperger's disorder and autism are, however, two different conditions, even though they share the same PDD umbrella.[13]

Like the other forms of PDD, there appears to be a strong genetic component in Asperger's disorder. Pauls[64] has provided data based on family self-reports as one part of a series of studies at Yale University in the Social Learning Disabilities Project. Family members surveyed indicated that 32 percent of their fathers had social difficulties, as did 33 percent of their uncles and 22 percent of their grandfathers. The same family members said that 12 percent of their fathers had attentional problems, as did 16 percent of their uncles and 6 percent of their grandfathers. The reported incidences were much lower for their mothers, aunts, and grandmothers.

The cause of Rett's disorder is unknown; however, because only females are affected, it is assumed that it is a result of a dominant mutation of an X-linked gene, which would be lethal in a male fetus.[51] Possible causative factors include immune system abnormalities; atrophy in the frontal lobe of the cortex, abnormal neurotransmitter function, deterioration of the corpus callosum (the part of the brain that connects the right and left parts of the brain) and brainstem-vestibular dysfunction.[31,32,66]

The cause of childhood disintegrative disorder is unknown, but it appears to be a result of central nervous system pathology. Unlike Rett's disorder, more boys than girls appear to be affected.[65]

The causes of PDD-NOS are difficult to identify, specifically, because of the failure to distinguish between PDD-NOS and other types of PDD.

COGNITIVE, MOTOR, PHYSICAL, BEHAVIORAL, AND PSYCHOSOCIAL CHARACTERISTICS

It must be understood that every individual with a pervasive developmental disorder is unique. It is, however, helpful for the physical educator to have an understanding of "typical" characteristics associated with each of the five types of pervasive developmental disorders.

Autism

The primary classification system used to identify pervasive developmental disorders is the *DSM-IV-Revised* system developed by the American Psychiatric Association (1994).[2] Autism is one of the primary forms of pervasive developmental disorders (see Figures 12-2 and 12-3).

Current research has identified other cognitive, motor/physical, language, behavioral, and psychosocial factors as well. Many children with autism have difficulty completing academic tasks within the school setting, though this may have no relationship to their intelligence. Learners with autism may simply find it difficult to function within the school environment.

Learners with autism may exhibit gross and fine motor delays. Manjiviona and Prior found that 66.7 percent of high-functioning children with autism had definite motor problems, as measured on the Test of Motor Impairment-Henderson revised, and performed at a level significantly lower than their same-age peers.[60] Learners with autism may also display unusual gross and fine motor behaviors. Rapin noted,

> Motor sterotypies are often striking and, besides hand flapping, may include pacing, spinning, running in circles, twirling a string, tearing paper, drumming, and flipping light switches. . . .[67]

Most learners with autism struggle with expressive and receptive language. To communicate an intention, the learner with autism may use atypical means such as having temper tantrums,

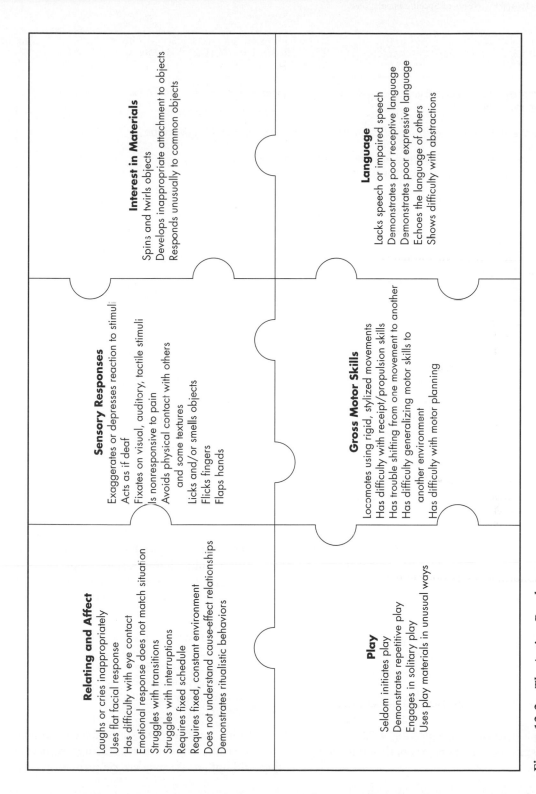

Relating and Affect

Laughs or cries inappropriately
Uses flat facial response
Has difficulty with eye contact
Emotional response does not match situation
Struggles with transitions
Struggles with interruptions
Requires fixed schedule
Requires fixed, constant environment
Does not understand cause-effect relationships
Demonstrates ritualistic behaviors

Sensory Responses

Exaggerates or depresses reaction to stimuli
Acts as if deaf
Fixates on visual, auditory, tactile stimuli
Is nonresponsive to pain
Avoids physical contact with others
and some textures
Licks and/or smells objects
Flicks fingers
Flaps hands

Interest in Materials

Spins and twirls objects
Develops inappropriate attachment to objects
Responds unusually to common objects

Play

Seldom initiates play
Demonstrates repetitive play
Engages in solitary play
Uses play materials in unusual ways

Gross Motor Skills

Locomotes using rigid, stylized movements
Has difficulty with receipt/propulsion skills
Has trouble shifting from one movement to another
Has difficulty generalizing motor skills to
another environment
Has difficulty with motor planning

Language

Lacks speech or impaired speech
Demonstrates poor receptive language
Demonstrates poor expressive language
Echoes the language of others
Shows difficulty with abstractions

Figure 12-2   The Autism Puzzle
Developed by Virginia Nelson, Autism Specialist, Dallas Independent School District, together with Carol Huettig and Jean Pyfer.

465

Figure 12-3   Summary of Characteristics of Individuals with Autistic Disorder

For a formal diagnosis of autism, the *DSM-IV-R* system requires that at least eight of the following behaviors be demonstrated:

Qualitative impairment in reciprocal social interaction as manifested by at least two of the following
A. Marked lack of awareness of the existence of feelings of others
B. No or abnormal seeking of comfort at times of distress
C. No or impaired imitation
D. No or abnormal social play
E. Gross impairment in ability to make peer friendships

Qualitative impairment in verbal and nonverbal communication, and in imaginative activity, as manifested by at least one of the following
A. No mode of communication, such as communicative babbling, facial expression, gesture, mime, or spoken language
B. Markedly abnormal nonverbal communication, as in the use of eye-to-eye gaze, facial expression, body posture, or gestures to initiate or modulate social interaction
C. Absence of imaginative activity, such as play acting of adult roles, fantasy characters, or animals, lack of interest in stories about imaginary events
D. Marked abnormalities in the production of speech, including volume, pitch, stress, rate, rhythm, and intonation
E. Marked abnormalities in the production of speech, including stereotyped and repetitive use of speech

Markedly restricted repertoire of activities and interests, as manifested by at least one of the following
A. Stereotyped body movements (e.g., hand flicking or twisting, spinning, head banging, complex whole body movements)
B. Persistent preoccupation with parts of objects
C. Marked distress over changes in trivial aspects of environments (e.g., insisting that exactly the same route always be followed when shopping)
D. Markedly restricted range of interests and a preoccupation with one narrow interest (e.g., interested only in lining up objects, in amassing facts about meteorology, or in pretending to be a fantasy character)
Onset during infancy or childhood

Modified from *DSM-IV-R.*

grabbing a teacher's hand to take the teacher where the learner wants the teacher to be, and performing self- and other-aggression.[70] To communicate verbally, the learner may use language patterns that include

- Echolalia, echoing the language of another
- Neologisms, made up words or sounds
- Singing or sing-songing particular words or phrases or humming
- Poorly articulated and agrammatical speech
- Jargon
- "Overlearned scripts," repeating words
- High-pitched, sing-song or poorly modulated speech[67]

Many have difficulty with behavior, and most experience difficulties in psychosocial experiences—play, cooperative behaviors, and attention to another person.[53,58] When describing younger children, Rapin wrote,

> Young children with autism do not know how to play. They may manipulate or line up toys without apparent awareness of what the toys represent, and they do not engage in pretend play, which, in normal children, starts before the age of two.[67]

During unstructured, unplanned free play, children with autism, when compared with children without autism matched on mental age, play

CASE STUDY

Mike

Mike is a twelve-year-old with an educational diagnosis of autism. He has in-home therapy in the mornings to address behavior and academic skills; he attends the public school in the afternoon for socialization in a third-grade class. He is basically nonverbal, but his receptive language skills appear to be quite good. He follows simple directions. He is able to imitate gross motor skills with ease.

Mike is able to swim, using a stylized human stroke (dog paddle) pattern, 200 yards without assistance. He has a good repertoire of locomotor skills—walking, running, and jumping—but has difficulty with object-control skills. He appears to enjoy walking on a treadmill and stationary cycling.

APPLICATION TASK
Suggest the physical activities in which Mike is likely to be most successful in the middle school physical education curriculum. Describe the physical activities in which Mike may be successful interacting with a peer without autism.

with fewer toys, are less focused on play, and seldom initiate interaction or communication with their play partners.[9,48] They play better, however, in more structured play experiences.

Many students with autism have difficulty in social situations. They may have difficulty responding to typical social stimuli, such as having their names called; difficulty with spontaneous verbal or nonverbal greeting or "good-bye"; and difficulty establishing eye contact.[18,39,40] But they do appear to be sensitive to another human in distress.[10]

Temple Grandin, a high-functioning individual with autism who has earned a Ph.D. in animal science described her particular difficulty with social skills. She and other individuals with autism tend to identify with *Star Trek* heroes Data and Mr. Spock. She believes most human beings have some innate and implicit knowledge of social conventions and

codes; however, she and other individuals with autism lack that knowledge.[34] She said, "I couldn't figure out what I was doing wrong. I had an odd lack of awareness that I was different. I thought the other kids were different. I could never figure out why I didn't fit in."[71]

There are particular characteristics of individuals with autism that have a dramatic impact on their ability to learn:

- Learners with autism may be unable to impose meaning on their experiences. Their reality is of apparently unrelated experiences and events.
- Learners with autism may focus on minute details but have difficulty seeing the "big picture."
- They may be distractible and focus on stimuli that compete with the information a teacher is trying to share.
- They may have difficulty with abstract concepts and symbols.
- Learners with autism may find it easy to understand and remember individual facts or concepts but have difficulty combining or integrating ideas.
- They may have difficulty organizing acts or thoughts in a logical sequence.
- They may learn a fact or concept in one situation but be unable to generalize to another, similar situation.
- Learners with autism are often very persistent in seeking out and getting what they want—whether it is a particular smell, object, or toy.
- They may be anxious. This is often a combination of biological and psychological factors.
- Learners with autism may process sensory stimuli in atypical ways.[15]

Howard Gardner, in his classic work *Frames of Mind*, suggested that individuals with autism demonstrated a variety of intelligences, including logical-mathematical and musical but had particular difficulty with intelligences associated with social-emotional skills, the interpersonal and intrapersonal types of intelligence.[29] In the broadest sense, if educators and other professionals were to

This autistic child became so confident in the water that he now dives off his parents' boat into the lake.
Photo by Carol Huettig.

embrace the notion that there are different types of intelligence and, as such, different ways to assess and teach EVERY learner, the needs of ALL LEARNERS could be met.

Asperger's Disorder

Perhaps the major difference between an individual with autism and one with Asperger's disorder is this: "People with Asperger's disorder can tell us of their experiences, their inner feelings and states, whereas those with autism cannot. With Asperger's disorder there is self-consciousness and at least some power to introspect and report."[71] The individual with Asperger's disorder is typically bright, with average or above-average intelligence. The individual with Asperger's disorder is often highly verbal but verbalizes about unusual things[78] (see Figure 12-4).

Rett's Disorder

Rett's disorder is devastating for the family and learner. A girl with Rett's disorder appears to be perfectly normal during eighteen months of life and exhibits typical social, emotional, language, cognitive, and motor development (see Figure 12-5). At some point between her first and second birthday, a relentless regression begins. Iyama describes the process as follows:

> She stops playing with toys. She stops responding to the spoken word and stops using the few single words she has learned. She becomes withdrawn and loses interest in social interaction. She may stop walking. Purposeful hand use is replaced by stereotypic hand movements. The lost developmental skills are never recovered, and she moves through childhood at a level of profound mental retardation.[46]

Figure 12-4 Summary of Characteristics of Individuals with Asperger's Disorder

Diagnostic criteria for Asperger's disorder, while similar to those described in autism, include the following:[2]

Qualitative impairment in some types of social interaction
- Restricted repetitive and stereotyped patterns of behavior, interests, and activities
- All-absorbing, circumscribed interest
- Imposition of routine or interest
- Clinically significant impairment in social, occupational, or other important areas of functioning
- No significant general delay in language
- Difficulty with nuances in communication in spite of superficially excellent expressive language skills
- Limited understanding of nonverbal expressive language skills
- No significant delay in cognitive development or in the development of age-appropriate self-help skills; adaptive behavior, except in social interaction; and curiosity about the environment in childhood
- Motor clumsiness[33]

Modified from *DSM-IV-R.*

Figure 12-5 Summary of Characteristics of Individuals with Rett's Disorder

Necessary diagnostic criteria for Rett disorder are as follows:[2]

A. Apparently normal prenatal and perinatal periods
B. Apparently normal psychomotor development through the first six months
C. Normal head circumference at birth
D. Deceleration of head growth between ages five months and four years
E. Loss of acquired purposeful hand skills between ages six and thirty months, temporally associated with communication dysfunction and social withdrawal
F. Development of severely impaired expressive and receptive language, and presence of apparent severe psychomotor retardation
G. Stereotypic hand movements such as hand wringing, hand washing, squeezing, clapping/tapping, and mouthing that appear after purposeful hands skills are lost
H. Appearance of gait apraxia and truncal apraxia/ataxia between ages one and four years
I. Diagnosis tentative until two to five years of age

Modified from *DSM-IV-R.*

In the girl's early preschool years, motor performance is severely compromised by ataxia and difficulty with motor planning; this causes the girl to fix her joints into positions of stability, reducing her ability to change positions.[11] The regression appears to reach a plateau during the early school years. While no further loss occurs (there is, unfortunately, little left to lose), few functional skills are acquired after this time. In adolescence and early adulthood, motor deterioration is pronounced, and typically the young woman experiences muscle wasting, spasticity, and scoliosis, and she becomes dependent on a wheelchair for ambulation. In addition, a diminished ability to use and store calcium results in low bone density, and the incidence of fractures is higher than in the general population.[11,37,56]

Childhood Disintegrative Disorder

Childhood disintegrative disorder, a rare condition, was described by Theodore Heller in 1908 and, as such, is also known as Heller's syndrome.[53] One of the characteristics identified in research being done at the Developmental Disabilities Clinic at Yale University is an apparent lack of interest in the social environment.[65] Children with CDD have significant delays in all phases of development (see Figure 12-6).

Pervasive Developmental Disorder–Not Otherwise Specified

Pervasive developmental disorder–not otherwise specified is a "subthreshold" condition identified

CASE STUDY

Charles

Charles is an eighteen-year-old with Asperger's disorder. Charles is preparing to graduate from high school. He has been quite successful academically in high school because of his excellent memory, mathematical, and computer skills. However, he has had and continues to have difficulty with social skills and doesn't have any friends.

His functional locomotor skills are quite good. He throws well but has difficulty catching, kicking, and striking. He walks, runs, and jumps with ease. He runs 2 miles every evening with his father in about 20 minutes. He struggles, however, in his high school physical education program because the emphasis throughout is on team sports.

APPLICATION TASK

Describe the steps you would go through before writing a draft of an individual transition plan for Charles to help him prepare for a community-based leisure and recreation program. What information would you need? Whom would you ask?

CASE STUDY

Ramona

Ramona is a five-year-old girl with Rett's disorder. She has lost previously acquired gross motor skills; she no longer hops, jumps, slides, catches, or kicks. She does hurl a bean bag, however. In fact, her gross motor skills resemble those of an eighteen-month-old child. She has started hand wringing. She is no longer speaking in full sentences. She uses one-word utterances to communicate her needs. Though toilet trained at age three years, she has lost bowel and bladder control and is, once again, wearing diapers. She has begun head banging and is now required to wear a helmet to prevent injury from the head banging and frequent falls. It is difficult to assess her receptive skills and understanding. She does, however, appear to enjoy music and likes animal crackers.

APPLICATION TASKS

You are responsible for presenting information regarding her present level of gross motor competency at the M-Team or IEP meeting. Try to put yourself in the parents' position. Their once apparently "typical" child is now regressing. Write an outline of your report, thinking carefully about what you would say and how you would say it.

Figure 12-6   Summary of Characteristics of Individuals with Childhood Disintegrative Disorder

- Apparently normal development for the first two years of life
- Significant loss or regression of previously acquired skills (before age ten years)
  - Expressive or receptive language skills
  - Social skills or adaptive behavior
  - Bowel or bladder control
  - Play
  - Motor skills
- Abnormalities in functioning
  - Social interaction skills
  - Communication skills
  - Restricted, repetitive, and stereotyped behaviors, interests, and activities

Modified from *DSM-IV-R*.

by the American Psychiatric Association in *DSM-IV-R*. PDD-NOS, also referred to as "atypical personality development," "atypical PDD," or "atypical autism" is a condition in which the learner exhibits some of the traits commonly associated with autism and PDD:

- Marked impairment of social interaction
- Marked impairment of communication
- Stereotypical behavior patterns or interest patterns

However, in PDD-NOS, other diagnostic criteria are not met.[65]

CASE STUDY

Hee Jung

Hee Jung is a six-year-old with CDD. She had been developing typically until age five years, when she began to regress. The regression occurred rapidly, and she now has the gross motor, fine motor, language, and social skills of a twelve-month-old child.

APPLICATION TASK

What kind of behaviors is she likely to demonstrate? (Chapter 9 has a summary of early childhood development.)

TESTING FOR PDD

A powerful case can be made for the use of transdisciplinary and portfolio assessment strategies for the learner with pervasive developmental delays. (See Chapter 10 for more information about transdisciplinary assessment and a more comprehensive explanation of the portfolio assessment process.) A comprehensive eco-behavioral, portfolio assessment, completed by parents together with professionals representing a variety of fields and interests, is crucial if the educational progress of the learner with pervasive developmental delays is to be measured. This is vital if the student's individual education program is to be appropriate and maximize progress. This type of assessment is particularly important for the learner with pervasive developmental disorders because most traditional assessment strategies require performance-on-request behavior that is typically impossible for learners with PDD.

Ongoing observational data regarding the learner in a variety of settings are vital to the entire process. The student's behavior must be evaluated in the home; in natural settings such as the grocery store; in a variety of school settings, including the classroom, and particularly the playground, lunchroom, and library; in small- and large-group activities; in structured and free play; in academic/

CASE STUDY

Steven

Steven is a four-year-old boy, diagnosed with pervasive developmental disorder-not otherwise specified. Steven was adopted by his parents when he was a week old. Both of his parents are deeply committed to him and very actively involved in all aspects of his life. At present, Steven participates in a university-based aquatics program. When he began the program a year ago, he was unable to swim. He is now able to jump off the diving board in the deep end of the pool. He is also able to swim, using a human stroke, 25 feet independently. Steven is also participating in a hippotherapy (equine therapy) program and a developmental gymnastics program.

His gross motor skills reflect his significant gross motor strengths. His Test of Gross Motor Development (2nd edition) scores for each item and subtests are as follows:

INDIVIDUAL SKILL SCORES

Run-8; Striking-10; Gallop-6; Stationary Dribble-8; Hop-8; Catch-6; Leap-4; Kick-6; Horizontal Jump-6; Overhand Throw-8; Slide-4; Underhand Roll-2; Locomotor Subtest-36; Object-Control Subtest-40

APPLICATION TASK

Consider Steven's physical education needs as he enrolls in the public school for kindergarten level education services at age five years. Identify which specific motor and fitness competencies Steven needs to develop, from kindergarten through high school graduation, in order to enjoy a life full of rich and varied leisure, recreation, and sport experiences.

prevocational work experiences; and in community-based leisure, recreation, and sport venues. Motor competency must also be evaluated in each of these settings.

Information regarding the motor performance of the learner with pervasive developmental delays may include (1) videotapes of the learner moving in a variety of settings (e.g., navigating stairs in the home, pushing a grocery cart in the grocery store, using a piece of playground equipment, using a broom in a work setting, swimming, or engaging in simple dance with peers); (2) photographs which represent the learner's play behavior (e.g., building block structures); (3) narratives describing the learner's social interaction/play behaviors; and (4) teacher and parent anecdotal records. This information may be supplemented by medical data, behavior frequency counts, behavioral checklists, developmental rating scales, and formal assessment/evaluation instruments.

Formal assessment/evaluation is a critical part of a comprehensive portfolio assessment process. However, whether the intent is to assess social behavior, cognitive and intellectual skills, and/or motor behavior, standardized instruments are often very difficult to use with individuals under the PDD umbrella.

Carter et al., 1998, developed supplementary normative scores on the Vineland Adaptive Behavior Composite for individuals with autism under the age of thirty-five years. Specifically, they developed special population norms for four groups of individuals with autism:

1. Mute children under age ten years
2. Children with at least some verbal skills, under age ten years
3. Nonspeaking (mute) individuals who are age ten or older
4. Verbal individuals who are age ten or older[12]

These norms will make it possible for educational diagnosticians and social workers doing "intake" evaluations for special education to more effectively and appropriately assess the daily living skills, socialization, and communication performances of children and young adults with autism.

The Test of Non-Verbal Intelligence–2nd Edition (TONI) has been demonstrated to be a powerful alternative to more traditional intelligence testing for individuals with autism. Edelson and associates, 1998, found the TONI to be a valuable alternative for predicting intelligence in individuals with autism because it is a nonverbal test, it is not timed, and it is an abstract measure of intelligence that does not measure "traditional" class-

based knowledge to which an individual with autism may not have been exposed.[20]

The Childhood Autism Rating Scale (CARS) is a very useful instrument which allows the educational diagnostician or specially trained assessor to evaluate the learner's abilities in the following areas: (1) relating to people; (2) imitation; (3) emotional response; (4) body use; (5) object use; (6) adaptation to change; (7) visual response; (8) listening response; (9) taste, smell, and touch response and use; (10) fear or nervousness, (11) verbal communication; (12) nonverbal communication; (13) activity level; (14) level and consistency of intellectual response; and (15) general impressions. The evaluator is able to share with parents and teachers a total score indicating that the learner is in the nonautistic, mildly-moderately autistic, or severely autistic range.[72] Increasingly, parents are being asked to evaluate their own learner with autism using the CARS so parents, educational diagnosticians and teachers can compare perceptions regarding performance. These data often allow a heightened understanding for parents and professionals, alike (see Figure 12-7).

In addition, there are several instruments which teachers use for identifying autistic behaviors and referring students for diagnostic testing. These instruments vary in length and sophistication. For example, the Autism Behavior Checklist (ABC)[54] is a fifty-seven-item questionnaire that requires yes/no answers. The Autism Prescreening Checklist, which was developed by the Dallas Independent School District Autism Task Force, in cooperation with the Dallas Society for Autistic Children, includes fourteen behavioral signs and symptoms of autism.[16] Preschool and elementary teachers are taught to use this instrument so that children with autistic-like behaviors can be identified early and more extensive testing can be initiated.

One of the best instruments for evaluating the learning of the adolescent, young adult, or adult with autism has been developed by the North Carolina TEACCH (Treatment and Education of Autistic and Related Communication-Handicapped Children) program. This instrument identifies and evaluates functional skills, including (1) vocational skills, (2) independent functioning, (3) leisure

society as an adult. An excerpt from the TEACCH web page follows:

> While strongly urging and promoting "normalizing" experiences for autistic students, TEACCH has also adhered to other equally important principles. These include individualization, reliance on empirically-based approaches rather than ideologically-based philosophies, and treatment and education that begins with and emphasizes an understanding of the problems of autism. The elaboration and operationalizing of these principles has led to a network of educational programs in North Carolina. Among the options developed, one can find highly structured, intensive specialized classrooms for autistic students, cross-categorical classrooms that serve one or more students with autism, and regular education classrooms that serve one or more learners with autism. Oftentimes, placement for learners with autism involves a combination of educational settings. Individualization, when properly carried out, leads to optimal, unique solutions for each student, based on his/her needs rather than ideology. The heterogeneity one sees in autism requires many options and possibilities, not one solution for all.[45]

One of the unique teaching strategies recommended for learners with autism is to use the individual's daily routines to facilitate learning, particularly communication skills. Most learners with autism seek and demand a consistent, predictable routine. TEACCH recommends the use of a joint activity routine, "a powerful teaching tool for learners with communication disorders. This term describes a routine in which the learner and the adult engage in a meaningful activity together and communicative behaviors are taught within the routine of the activity."[45]

TEACCH professionals suggest that the following are key characteristics of joint activity routines:

- They occur in a meaningful and functional context, such as meal or naptime routines.
- They focus on the learner's interests and strengths.

- They are social, requiring two people, and emerge at the learner's level of understanding and within the broad context of the learner's ability to play (observational, parallel, associative, cooperative, etc.).

The adult has specific responsibilities in this process. The adult is responsible for identifying the routine, for creating the learning environment, for adding visual or other sensory supports (such as pictures or objects) to encourage the routine and add meaning, and for continuing the routine.

The TEACCH program has trained and used parents as co-teachers. This unique program is based on three crucial principles that acknowledge the dynamics of family interaction and the impact of that interaction on the professional attempting to intervene. Schopler et al. describe those three concepts:

> First, it serves as a reminder that professional-family relations are defined not only by the expertise communicated from the professional to the parent but also by the parent's resources, aspirations and questions directed at the professional. . . . Second, and equally important, is the recognition that handicapped (sic) children and even infants have an impact on their parents every bit as real as the effect parents have on their children. Third, the interaction concept is probably most important for the TEACCH model in evaluating the outcome of educational and other intervention efforts. That is, the outcome is the product of two kinds of change. Either the learner acquires better skills or reduces dysfunctional behavior, on the one hand, or the environment (home, school, community) develops greater acceptance of the learner's deficits, on the other hand.[73]

Acknowledging the vital interactive process, and empowering the parents as teachers, may have a vast impact on the physical education of the learner with autism. A home-based program to supplement the school-based program may have exciting results. Armed with information about facilitating play, supporting movement attempts, and interacting in and through movement activities, the parent may become more effective.

Ozonoff and Cathcart, 1998, found a home-training program for preschoolers with autism to be effective.[63] The preschoolers with autism performed significantly higher than their matched typically developing peers overall on the Psycho-educational Profile-Revised (PEP-R) and on subtests which included gross motor, fine motor, imitation, and nonverbal conceptual skills. The home-training program was effective for three primary reasons:

- Home training is cost-effective.
- Parents can and will be involved as their learner's primary advocate and liaison. As such, parent education and empowerment is critical to effective intervention throughout the learner's lifetime.
- Parents may feel empowered, feel more competent, and exhibit less depression when participating in an effective home program.

The TEACCH program has been implemented well in programs throughout the world. It is a comprehensive, broad-based program designed with one outcome in mind—to prepare learners with autism for a life within the greater society.

Applied Behavioral Analysis

The third of the major intervention strategies is Applied Behavior Analysis. Applied Behavior Analysis (ABA) is usually labeled the Ivar Lovaas approach, even though Dr. Lovaas and his associates at UCLA are only one group of clinicians and researchers using this approach to dealing with behavior disorders in learners with autism and other disabilities.

Applied Behavioral Analysis is a style of teaching that uses a series of trials to shape a desired behavior or response. The desired responses tend to be communication-based, although other parts of the learner's development are addressed, as well. It demands ongoing and precise performance evaluation. A thorough individual analysis of a learner's functioning is undertaken. The intent is to identify the skills needed for improved performance and functioning. Then, the behavior

manager or educator completes a detailed task analysis to break down the skills into the simplest parts that can be learned. Discrete trial training is used in a very specific and systematic methodology to address performance and functional needs.

In discrete trial training, each skill is taught in very small and brief units called "trials." Each trial consists of an instruction, a prompt, an opportunity/response, and immediate feedback. The instruction, prompt, and feedback are given in very clear language the individual learner can understand.

Specific behavioral treatment is data-based and requires documentation of the learner's performance on a daily basis. The treatment is very directive and instructionally based, and it requires, optimally, at least 40 hours per week. Most parents who wish to implement an ABA program with their learner use a combination of clinical intervention and a home-based program. The nature of the ABA program, and its rigors, typically makes it difficult to implement such a program within the public schools.[3]

The specific, behavioral strategies used to teach very precise skills has been shown to be effective for approximately 50 percent of the higher-functioning individuals with autism. However, the exaggerated claims regarding the usefulness of ABA has caused many educators to view the program with suspicion. Of particular concern is the fact that devotees of Applied Behavior Analysis have suggested that, if a parent/family embraces the training, their learner or young adult with autism can be "cured." Gresham and MacMillan suggested, "ABA and discrete trial intervention programs are useful tools; however, there are serious doubts about whether these strategies can be used to cure autism."[36]

Other teaching and intervention strategies have been espoused and supported for learners with autism. The often devastating impact of autism on the learner and the learner's family creates a situation in which the parents, in particular, are often extremely vulnerable to claims for quick fixes for a condition for which there is, at least at present, no cure.

Several specific teaching and intervention strategies will be considered in general; in the next section, those that are applicable within the physical education program will be considered more fully.

Other Intervention Strategies

There are many effective intervention strategies being used for learners with autism.[38] They include Holding Therapy, Gentle Teaching, Options Approach, Choice Making, and Floor Time as interventions based on relationships. Holding Therapy is based on the notion that autism results from a broken symbiotic bond between the mother (or father) and the learner.[76] Hefflin and Simpson suggest, "Holding Therapy seeks to restore the bond between the learner with autism and his or her caregiver. Even when not 'holding' the learner, the caregiver must remain in close physical proximity with breaks of no longer than 2 hours."[38] While this therapy is being used in Europe, American educators and parents appear to believe that the therapy is invasive and not respectful of the learner's need for privacy.[38]

Gentle Teaching emphasizes success. The learning environment is created so the learner with autism is accepted unconditionally. The adult seeks to create a bond, characterized by warmth and caring with the learner with autism. The learning environment is designed so there is "errorless learning"; the learner is redirected to appropriate responses through prompting and careful task analysis. The strategy has not been proven effective consistently.

The Options Approach is designed to foster the development of an intense bond between the learner and adult to develop and maintain a mutually beneficial relationship.[49] The Options Approach is, in actuality, a comprehensive program to enhance human performance and human potential. The particular Option program of interest to physical educators who teach children with autism is The Son-Rise Program. The Son-Rise Program, at the Option Institute, is devoted to the unique and pivotal relationship between the parent and the learner. Describing that relationship to parents, Son-Rise personnel write,

> Here at the Option Institute, we not only acknowledge parents as the learner's most important resource, but seek to empower them to the learner's advantage. Your knowledge, your lifelong interest and caring can never be matched by anyone else. Professionals do the best they can and, certainly, can provide meaningful assistance. But you can do much, much more because of your unique position in your learner's world.[75]

The Son-Rise Program describes its approach to education of children with autism:

> We believe that the most effective way to "teach" children, young people and adults is to draw information, understanding and insight from them, and to help them develop and build on their talents, skills and interests. . . . The parent, the instructor, the therapist or facilitator becomes the student of the learner's world. . . . observing, learning, assisting and supporting the learner's flowering in a loving and nonjudgmental environment.[75]

There are, most certainly, wonderful reports of the success of this intensive, learner-centered philosophy and program. However, there is little empirical evidence of its effectiveness. Implementation of the program requires total devotion to the learner, almost to the exclusion of anyone else in the parent's life.

Choice Making strategies were described by Moes.[61] The findings support the use of learner choice as a teaching strategy to improve the academic and behavioral performance of learners with autism. It appears that providing learners with autism opportunities to make choices improves their productivity, improves their emotional affect, and reduces their disruptive behaviors. Like providing Choice Making opportunities, Baker et al.[8] found that capitalizing and building on the learner's obsessions and interests had a positive effect:

> The results of this investigation showed that the obsession themes of children with autism, which are typically viewed as problematic, can

be transformed successfully into common games to increase positive play interactions between children with autism and their typically developing peers in inclusive school environments. These increases in appropriate social play interactions maintained in the absence of the adult who initially prompted the game. Further the appropriate social play generalized to other nonobsession theme games following intervention. Additionally, both the children with autism and their nondisabled peers' affect increased positively, showing improved interest and happiness following intervention.[8]

Floor Time, developed by renowned child development authority Stanley Greenspan, is a systematic approach to intervention based on an understanding of and sensitivity to the learner's unique developmental sequence. Floor Time is designed to develop human interaction skills that begin with gesture and, later, verbal interactions. This approach has had success because at its core is developmentally appropriate teaching. Literally, the adult honors the learner enough to get down on the floor and teach where the learner is comfortable, using only activities that are developmentally appropriate.

Skill-based treatment programs include Picture Exchange Communication Systems, Joint Action Routines, Visual Schedules, and Facilitated Communication. The first Picture Exchange Communication Systems, developed by Frost and Bondy[27] at the Delaware Autistic Program was originally designed for preschoolers with autism but has been widely used with individuals with autism throughout the life span. Simply, a learner with autism is taught to exchange a picture of a desired item or experience for the actual item or experience. Like many other augmentative communication systems, this has been used successfully by teachers and clinicians alike.

The use of Joint Action Routines was briefly described in the section describing the TEACCH program. Simply, the teacher uses established routines or events associated with daily experiences to teach needed skills.

Visual Schedules help the learner with autism anticipate and predict what will occur during the regular school day or at home. It capitalizes on the visual skills of learners with autism and their need for routine. Horizontal visual schedules that allow the learner with autism to work on the immediate past, present, and immediate future is the basis for the development of more complex notions regarding time.

One of the most controversial practices in the education of individuals with autism is Facilitated Communication. This practice involves using a helper to support the hand, wrist, or shoulder of a learner while the learner makes selections on a communication device such as a keyboard. Claims have been made that, given this simple assistance, the learner with autism can be freed to express thoughts, feelings, and emotions. Hostler, 1996, suggested that Facilitated Communication is rapidly fading from the educational scene because of lack of objective evidence.[41] Claims that children "locked" in autism were being freed to express their true intellect were made as parents flocked to yet another quick fix. The American Academy of Pediatrics noted that families spent considerable and unnecessary resources, time and money, on Facilitated Communication when the time and money could be better invested in behavioral and/or educational programs.[1]

Cognitive behavioral methods include cognitive behavioral modification, behavioral contracts, social scripts, and social autopsies. These intervention strategies acknowledge the fact that individuals with autism, particularly high-functioning individuals with autism, can monitor and manage their own behavior. Cognitive behavioral modification is a strategy designed to teach learners with autism to monitor their own behavior, including delivering self-reinforcement. This has shown to be effective particularly with high-functioning individuals with autism with specific, discrete tasks. Some learners, particularly high-functioning individuals with autism, may experience success with a simple behavior contract. They may also prepare for success using social scripts. If the learner is going to be faced with a new experience, the learner can prepare for the event by "practicing" what will happen. The script, like that written for a play, can help the learner face the situation. Social autopsies allow the learner to examine social incidents and identify, where possible, cause-effect relationships that promoted the behaviors. They allow the student to rethink what happened, particularly if the learner experienced discomfort or undue anxiety or had an "acting out" or "out of control" experience.

Like specific strategies for teaching individuals with autism, there are specific strategies for teaching learners with Asperger's disorder. Those are presented in Figure 12-8.

In the early stages of the onset of Rett's disorder, many of the teaching strategies outlined for

---

Figure 12-8   Specific Teaching Strategies for Teaching Learners with Asperger's Disorder

Insistence on sameness
- Provide a predictable environment.
- Maintain a consistent routine and minimize transitions.

Impairment in social interaction
- Place the learner in situations in which his or her reading, vocabulary, and memory skills can be viewed as an asset by peers.
- Create a bully-free learning environment for the sake of all.
- Older students with Asperger's disorder may be paired well with a sensitive buddy to help the student learn appropriate social skills and to reduce the tendency to be reclusive.

Limited range of interests
- If possible, designate a particular time during the day in which the learner with AS may discuss his or her preoccupation or interest.
- Initially individualize learning opportunities and experiences to build on the specific interest of the learner.

Poor concentration
- Use frequent teacher interaction, feedback, and redirection.
- Time work sessions; start short and build to longer sessions.
- Establish a signal to alert the student to "refocus."

Poor motor coordination
- Involve the learner in a health/fitness curriculum, rather than a competitive sports program.

Academic difficulties
- Provide an individualized program to ensure consistent success.
- Capitalize on the learner's typically excellent memory skills.
- Use activity-based learning, which should be at the core of all physical education experiences, whenever possible.
- Use graphics, pictures, and/or demonstrations.

Emotional vulnerability
- Help the learner develop a three-step routine to cope with stress.
- Especially when working with adolescents with Asperger's disorder, be very sensitive to the student's depression.
- A learner who is included, in particular, must have an identified staff member to provide emotional support.

Difficulties with language
- Teach specific skills regarding turn taking.
- Teach specific skills for seeking help/assistance.
- Pause after instruction and probe, with questions, to determine if the student has understood the information or directions.

Sensory sensitivities
- Minimize background noise and fluorescent lighting.
- Watch carefully for signs that the student is becoming overwhelmed by stimuli—self-abusive behaviors, crying, flushing, or hyperventilation.

Modified from Williams, http://www.sasked.gov.sk.ca/curr_inst/speced/asper.html

learners with autism may prove very useful in teaching. Effective teaching strategies for individuals with advanced Rett's disorder probably more closely resemble those that are effective when intervening with learners who are severely mentally retarded. (See Chapter 11 for more specific suggestions.)

In the early stages of the onset of childhood disintegrative disorder, many of the teaching strategies outlined for learners with autism may prove very useful in teaching. Effective teaching strategies for individuals with advanced childhood disintegrative disorder probably more closely resemble those that are effective when intervening with learners that are severely mentally retarded. (See Chapter 11 for more specific suggestions.)

Strategies for teaching individuals with PDD-NOS should be consistent with those suggested for autistic disorder and Asperger's disorder. The principles should remain the same.

GENERAL TEACHING STRATEGIES FOR PHYSICAL EDUCATION TO MAXIMIZE OPPORTUNITIES FOR INCLUSION

Teaching strategies for learners who fall under the broad umbrella of pervasive developmental disorders in the general physical education program are, essentially, consistent with good teaching. In this section, teaching strategies that have been found effective for individuals under the large umbrella of pervasive developmental disorders will be considered for the general physical education class and/or a more separate learning environment, if required, to ensure success. Figure 12-9 shows teaching strategies for learners with PDD in physical education.

As is true for all individuals, a quality physical education experience is a critical component in the lives of individuals with pervasive developmental disorders. An individually designed, comprehensive physical education program which addresses both the deficits and strengths identified in a comprehensive assessment is critical to the health, wellness, and long-term ability of the individual to

enjoy a life full of quality leisure, recreation, and sport experiences (see Figure 12-10).

At the crux of a quality physical education program for individuals with PDD is a comprehensive assessment. As mentioned earlier in this chapter, a portfolio assessment appears to be the most viable strategy for gaining valid and appropriate information. Based on the information gained in and through the portfolio assessment process, the individual education program must be developed to meet the unique needs of the learner, as mandated by federal law. Only then should consideration be given the appropriate placement in which the IEP goals and objectives can be met.

As discussed in Chapter 1, the Reauthorization of IDEA, 1999, and recent litigation support the intent of Congress to allow individuals with disabilities to participate, whenever possible, within the general program, using the general curriculum. The decision about the physical education placement of the learner with PDD remains, however, one that must be made by the multidisciplinary, individual education program team or committee.

The IEP team must consider the following variables when determining placement:

- Curriculum
- Support personnel
- Equipment
- Program participation
- Management of behavior
- Teaching style
- Grading

(See Chapter 5 for a complete discussion of these variables.)

Activity suggestions for learners with PDD are appropriate for the general physical education program and a less restrictive program. The types of activities included in the physical education program for the learner with PDD depends to a great degree on the type of PDD, the severity of the disorder, and the age of the learner (see Table 12.1). However, regardless of the type of PDD, the severity of the disorder, and the age of the learner, vigorous, aerobic exercise is critical daily because it

Figure 12-9   General Teaching Strategies for Physical Education to Maximize Opportunities for Inclusion

Adopt a "gentle teaching" philosophy.
- Ensure that the learner has every possible opportunity to succeed in the physical education learning environment. Start slowly, with simple skills, and build on them gradually.

Establish and maintain a consistent class routine.
- Each learner should have a separate and carefully marked "home base." The learner with PDD may be most comfortable if the home base is on the periphery of the gymnasium or other learning environment, rather than in the center.
- The physical educator should ensure each class has the same routine.
- If warm-ups are to be done to music, the physical education teacher should use the same songs over and over; a new song may be introduced after others have been mastered.
- If a given motor skill is to be practiced, the same class organization and equipment should be used. If the class is working on catching, for example, the teacher should use the same size and color ball.
- When using terms to describe a given activity or motion, the teacher should use the same term every time. For example, if each learner is assigned a plastic dot to serve as his or her home base, the teacher should refer to the plastic dot by calling it "dot" and not "circle."

Use joint activity routines.
- Use natural, teachable moments to help the learner acquire skills. For example, when the student enters/exits the gymnasium, he or she should be expected to greet the teacher, verbally or using a gesture.

Use a visual schedule.
- Place a horizontal visual schedule in a central place on the gymnasium wall to allow the learner with a PDD to predict and expect the next event.

Use picture exchanges.
- If the learner with PDD has difficulty understanding the simple visual symbol schedule, the physical educator can use a picture exchange system to help the students more effectively predict the sequence of events. The individual learner with PDD may have his or her own visual schedule, with each component on an individual card. As each event is about to begin, the learner pulls the card from his or her schedule and puts it in a pile, face down, until the entire class is completed.

Provide opportunities for social interaction.
- Carefully trained and sensitive peer buddies may encourage appropriate social interaction.
- Create and maintain a bully-free learning environment.

Allow choice making to encourage participation.
- Give the learner two options or choices from which he or she can choose. This is enabling and gives the learner some critical control over his or her environment. For example, while holding each ball in his or her hands, the teacher asks, "Ricardo, would you like to throw the red or the yellow ball?" and waits for the learner to grasp one ball, or "Dominique, do you want to start at the 'push-up' station or the 'sit-up' station?"

Spend quality "floor time" with the learner.
- Literally, get down on the floor with young learners with PDD to interact at their eye level.
- Ensure the activities are developmentally appropriate. A learner with a PDD is much more likely to be successful, for example, in a first-grade general physical education class if the teacher is concentrating on the foundations of locomotor and nonlocomotor patterns, object-control skills, and basic rhythmic activities than if the teacher is inappropriately focusing on team sports.

Address the interests of the learner with a PDD.
- Part of the lesson should focus specifically on the strengths of the individuals with a PDD. If the elementary school learner with a PDD has a particular interest in animals, for example, then the student should be given the opportunity to describe an animal before members of the class act like the animal. If the high school learner with Asperger's disorder, for example, has a particular interest in aerodynamics, the learner with a PDD should have an opportunity to explain the principles of aerodynamics before his or her classmates throw a Frisbee.

(Continued)

Figure 12-9 (*Continued*)

Acknowledge and honor the learner's difficulty attending to task.
- Provide frequent feedback.
- Use simple redirection strategies to return the learner's attention to task. For example, the physical educator could remind the student, "John, which station is next on your list?" or "Ramon, how many push-ups have you already done?"

Be consistent with behavior-management system.
- Adopt the behavior-management system used by the learner's classroom teacher and the learner's parents.
- Develop a behavior contract for learners with Asperger's disorder and high-functioning autism. This also needs to be consistent with that used in other parts of the curriculum.
- Redirect inappropriate behaviors. Since the learner with PDD often does not understand cause-effect relationships, it is ineffective to scold the learner for misbehavior or to say, "No." It is much more effective to redirect existing behavior. For example, if the learner is kicking furniture, replace the furniture with a ball.
- Simplify the task if the learner is misbehaving while attempting a task. Often, a learner with a pervasive developmental delay "acts out" as a result of frustration. Simplifying the task at hand may allow the learner to succeed at the task while reducing inappropriate behaviors.
- If the learner is acting out or is out of control, moving the learner to a less stimulating area may allow the learner to regain control of his or her behavior. An ideal place in the gymnasium is a bean bag chair or soft chair just inside the teacher's office.

---

effectively reduces self-stimulatory and off-task behaviors, increases time on academic and vocational tasks, and, as important, improves gross motor performance.[11,22,28,32,43,50,57] Physical education programs for individuals with pervasive developmental delays, at all levels of development, should include exercise that promotes the development of cardiovascular-respiratory endurance.

Infants and toddlers with pervasive developmental disorders need to be exposed to a wide variety of activities designed to enhance and develop equilibrium, to stimulate sensory-motor systems, and to develop basic locomotor and nonlocomotor skills *to prepare* the child for an active lifestyle.[60] Preschoolers should be given the opportunity to continue to develop equilibrium, perceptual-motor function, sensory-motor function including the development of body image and motor planning, as well as locomotor and nonlocomotor skills. The preschooler must also have the opportunity to develop object-control skills, basic movement patterns, and play skills. The preschooler must have the opportunity, daily, to participate in developmentally appropriate active play—walking, running, tricycling, climbing on playground equipment, or swimming.[42]

Kindergarten Through Third Grade Physical Education

The physical education program for young learners with pervasive developmental delays, kindergarten through third grade, should emphasize cardiovascular-respiratory endurance activities, whole body movement, dance and rhythm activities, activities to foster primary body part identification, and the development of onlooker and parallel play skills.

The National Association for Sport and Physical Education has developed guidelines about appropriate physical activity for preadolescent children including the following:

- An accumulation of more than 60 minutes, and up to several hours, per day of age- and developmentally appropriate activities is encouraged for elementary school children.
- Some of the child's activity each day should be in periods lasting 10 to 15 minutes or more and include moderate to vigorous activity. This activity will typically be intermittent involving alternating moderate to vigorous activity with brief periods of rest and recovery.[62]

Figure 12-10
A carefully designed visual schedule can help the learner with PDD anticipate the sequence of events in the PE class. This simple visual schedule reminds the student that the class will begin with announcements, followed by calisthenics, jogging or running, and dance, and will culminate with a given leisure activity.

Developmentally appropriate cardiovascular-respiratory endurance activities should be the basis of the program. The program should allow the child the opportunity to run, swim, tricycle/bicycle, climb on playground equipment, dance, do aerobic walking, do stationary cycling, and engage in structured aerobic dance that emphasizes the use of large muscle groups.

The development of equilibrium responses is a fundamental component of the physical education program of young learners with all five types of PDD. As is true in Daily Life Therapy, the emphasis should be on broad and varied activities that stimulate the vestibular system. These equilibrium activities include the following:

Scooter Board Activities Depending on the learner's level of development, the learner should assume a supine, prone, sitting, or kneeling position on a scooter board. Initially, the activity will be teacher-initiated and teacher-controlled. Gradually, the teacher should fade out involvement so that the scooter-spinning activity is learner-initiated and learner-controlled.

TABLE 12.1 Physical Education Activities Which Allow Age-Appropriate Inclusion for Learners with Pervasive Developmental Disorders

Individuals with PDD	Physical and Motor Fitness	Fundamental Motor Skills and Patterns	Aquatics	Dance	Individual and Group Games	Intramurals
K–3rd	"Animal Actions" "Chug Along Choo Choo" "Bend, Twist, Shake" "Warm-Up Time" Circuit Training	Locomotor Nonlocomotor Object control	Water orientation Water games Safety skills	"What a Miracle" "Sally . . . Swinging Snake" "Hokey Pokey" Locomotion to music	Parachute	NA
4th–6th	Jogging Stationary cycling Stationary rowing Circuit training	Locomotor Nonlocomotor Object control	Stroke development Entry and exit skills Safety skills	Basic line dance Circle dance	Parachute	Cooperative games New Games
7th–9th	Jogging Stationary cycling Stationary rowing Circuit training Inline skating	Object control	Stroke development Entry and exit skills Safety skills	Basic line dance Circle dance	Bocci Horseshoes Bowling Croquet Lead-up games	Cross-country running Cross-country skiing Swimming
10th–12th	Jogging Stationary cycling Stationary rowing Circuit training Inline skating Aerobic dance	Prevocational skills Vocational skills	Swimming for fitness AquaRobics	Basic line dance Aerobic dance	Bocci Horseshoes Bowling Inline skating Croquet Golf	Cross-country running Cross-country skiing Swimming
Adult	Walking Stationary cycling Stationary rowing Aerobic dance	Prevocational skills Vocational skills	Swimming for fitness AquaRobics	Basic line dance Aerobic dance	Bocci Horseshoes Bowling Inline skating Croquet Golf	NA

Crazy Sidewalk   Place a mat, or series of mats, over the top of other, pliable objects such as bean bag chairs, throw pillows, and rolled up mats. Then, depending on the learner's developmental level, ask the learner to crawl, creep, walk, or run over the top of the ever shifting surface.

Magic Carpet Ride   Have the learner assume a supine lying, prone lying, sitting, all-fours, or kneeling position on a mat or blanket. The teacher and other children, together, hold the edge of the mat or blanket and pull the learner around the room.[44]

Whole body movement which stimulates the vestibular and kinesthetic systems is also a curricular priority for the young learner with autism. This includes "wrap-em-ups" (roll the learner in a sheet or blanket, grasp the edge and lift, rolling the learner out of the sheet/blanket), log rolls, egg rolls, shoulder rolls, and forward/backward rolls.

In addition, simple songs and dances may be used to encourage the development of primary body part identification skills and rhythmic responses, as well as to provide an ideal opportunity for the learner to be engaged in parallel play with peers. The rhythmic experiences are particularly critical for the learner with Rett's disorder.[11] Songs and dances for young learners with PDD should have the following characteristics: (1) simple, clear, and often repeated directions; (2) repetitive phrasing; (3) an even beat; (4) a dominant rhythm instrument; and (5) nonintrusive "background" accompaniment. Hap Palmer and Greg and Steve songs and dances are particularly effective.

Young children with PDD are usually very fond of parachute play. Parachutes, particularly those with handles, help the learners function with a secure base for activity.

A crucial focus of the physical education program for young learners with autism is the development of age-appropriate playground skills. Sacks wrote,

> At one such school, as I approached, I had seen some learners in the playground, swinging and playing ball. How normal, I thought—but when I got closer I saw one learner swinging obsessively in terrifying semi-circles, as high as the swing would go; another throwing a small ball monotonously from hand to hand; another spinning on a roundabout, around and around; another not building with bricks but lining them up endlessly, in neat, monotonous rows.[71]

The adapted physical educator, working with the general physical educator, the classroom teacher, and the learner's parent need to develop a systematic plan for developing skills necessary for successful participation in playground activities. A learner with PDD who is able to "pump" a swing and swing independently has a wonderful opportunity to participate in parallel play with other learners' also swinging. Playground skills that many learners take for granted may often need to be task-analyzed for learners with PDD. The physical educator may need to break down the process of approaching and climbing the stairs and then sitting and sliding down a slide into several discrete components, for example.

Technology exists to provide wonderful interactive toy experiences for more severely disabled young children, such as those with Rett's disorder and childhood disintegrative disorder. Specifically, there are toys that combine bright colors and sounds and allow children to experience cause-effect relationships as they use adaptive switches on computers. In addition to providing interactive toys, the physical educator will need to focus on the basic skills required for ambulation and functional movement for learners with severe delays/regressions typical of those with Rett's or childhood disintegrative disorders.

Fourth Through Sixth Grades Physical Education

The physical education curriculum for learners with pervasive developmental disorders in the fourth through sixth grades must continue to emphasize cardiovascular-respiratory endurance activities. These activities may include aerobic walking, stationary cycling, aerobic dance, jogging/running, and stationary rowing.

The development of "functional" locomotor skills is a vital part of the physical education curriculum for learners in these grades. The learner should be given the opportunity to develop "ownership" of basic locomotor skills such as walking, running, and jumping in the following situations:

1. Ask the learner to move over different surfaces:
   a. Sidewalk-grass-sidewalk
   b. Grass-sand-grass
   c. Dry sidewalk–icy sidewalk–dry sidewalk
2. Ask the learner to move over, around, and through objects/obstacles:
   a. Step in and out of holes.
   b. Walk around and jump over puddles.
   c. Step over an object or a series of objects.
   d. Walk up and down inclines.
   e. Walk up and down stairs, varying the number, height, and surface of stairs.
   f. Walk through a revolving door.
3. Ask the learner to move, carrying an object or objects: groceries, umbrella, backpack, ball tucked under the arm.
4. Ask the learner to push or pull an object: a wagon or wheelchair.

More sophisticated equilibrium activities, which continue to stimulate the vestibular and proprioceptive systems, are also an important part of this program. These include self-testing balance activities. The learner moves, for example, on a tapered balance beam. Or the learner steps from one stone to another as the stones get smaller. Or the learner performs a series of increasingly complex tasks on a balance beam: walking and stepping over an object on the beam; walking and stopping to pick up an object on the beam; sliding in both directions; galloping on the beam; and performing such stationary balances on the beam as stork stands and airplane balances. Bouncing activities are also emphasized. Using a minitrampoline, an air mattress, or a gym mat placed on top of a tire, help the learner "bounce" while sitting, kneeling, or standing.

Rhythm activities and low-organization games are important to learners with PDD in this age range. Rhythm activities are critical to the development of an even and purposeful gait. Performing locomotor or nonlocomotor skills to the beat of a drum and starting and stopping to the music in songs such as the "Freeze" or cooperative "Musical Chairs" are particularly helpful.

Games with simple rules may be used particularly well to teach skills such as taking turns and sharing equipment. The development of these skills is crucial to individuals under the broad umbrella of PDD. A more sophisticated use of playground equipment is also critical and must be a part of the physical education curriculum if the young learner with PDD is to have the opportunity to share recess and playground time with other learners.

The development of more sophisticated object-control skills is also critical. Typically, the young learner with PDD will be more effective in closed propulsion skills, that is, a skill in which the learner propels a stationary object, than in others. Giving the learner the opportunity to throw and kick using a variety of balls with different textures, sizes, and shapes will be the key to developing truly effective skills.

Middle and Junior High School Physical Education

Learners with PDD in the middle and junior high school program should have the opportunity to develop basic leisure, recreation, sport, and fitness skills. The learner with PDD will usually be more successful in closed individual activities. For example, the middle and junior high school learner with PDD may be very successful in activities such as bowling, darts, frisbee golf, croquet, horseshoes, and golf.

This is often a critical and difficult time for learners with PDD. Children who are particularly sensitive to others but who struggle with their social behaviors, such as those with Asperger's, may find themselves teased and secluded from others. Difficulty dealing with their social-emotional issues makes it even more critical for learners this age to participate in vigorous, aerobic activities at least an hour per day. The vigorous activity allows the learners to better control impulses and other behavior. Learners with PDD tend to have the most success in walking, jogging, running, stationary cycling, stationary rowing, basic aerobic dancing, swimming, and inline skating.

High School

In high school the primary curricular emphasis needs to continue to be on cardiovascular-respiratory endurance. In addition, there is an emphasis on the development of leisure and recreation skills. These include bowling, fishing, horseshoes, golf, bocci, horseback riding, roller skating or inline skating, skateboarding, and basket shooting.

High school students should be preparing for the important transition from school-based programming into community-based experiences. In addition to the leisure, recreation, sport, and fitness skills discussed earlier, the learner should have the opportunity to develop skills required for prevocational programs and work. The adapted and general physical educator must work closely with the learner's parents and vocational education coordinator to ensure the learner has the necessary motor skills to do a job. Specific job tasks need to be identified and a task analysis done in order to determine which motor skills need to be taught. For example, if the learner is preparing for work at a nursery or as a gardener, then the prerequisite gross motor behavior would include (1) raking leaves; (2) digging with a shovel; (3) moving a wheelbarrow; (4) picking up and hauling large bags of peat moss; (5) using a trowel; etc. If the individual is planning on a life as a university professor, like Temple Grandin, other skills are particularly critical: (1) climbing stairs carrying a briefcase and (2) maintaining an erect sitting posture while working on the computer. The individual may need to work on skills such as lifting and carrying objects; climbing the steps of a bus; standing on a bus, train, or metro and holding a strap; walking up and down a flight of stairs, carrying a bag of groceries; pushing a shopping cart through a crowd; etc.

Decisions regarding the transition curriculum in physical education should be based on the learner's need to function within the community, the accessibility of programs and facilities, family and extended family interests, and community interests. For example, it is unfair to foster a love of horseback riding in a learner from a poor family if the learner's only access to a horse involves expensive rental. It would seem much more humane to help the learner develop the skills needed to participate in activities with other learners in the neighborhood, such as bocci, shooting baskets, inline skating, and skateboarding. If no one in the learner's family likes to bowl, it is ridiculous to teach bowling unless family members are willing to make a commitment to transporting the learner to a community-based bowling program.

A critical part of the process of preparing for the transition from school-based programming to community-based experiences is the development of self-determination. Field et al. defined self-determination:

> Self-determination is a combination of skills, knowledge, and beliefs that enable a person to engage in goal-directed, self-regulated, autonomous behavior. An understanding of one's strengths and limitations together with a belief in oneself as capable and effective are essential to self-determination. When acting on the basis of these skills and attitudes, individuals have greater ability to take control of their lives and assume the role of successful adults in our society.[24]

Parents and physical educators, general and adapted, play a critical role in helping learners with PDD develop self-determination.[24,25] One of the strategies used to begin the process of planning a future is the development of a "life map," using words and pictures to depict one's present life and what one wants one's life to look like in five years, for example. Fullerton and Coyne suggest that the intention of the life map is to serve as a self-created visual organizer that helps students see how the parts of their lives fit together and communicate their views of their lives to others.[28] This process is similar to that described in Chapter 3.

Aquatics

Aquatics may be one of the best venues to teach physical education for individuals with pervasive developmental disorders. Attwood wrote, "It is interesting that the ability to swim appears least affected, and this activity can be encouraged to enable the child to experience genuine competence and admiration for proficiency with movement,"[4] and Kitahara wrote,

> Swimming is an exercise that exercises the whole body and is one of the physical exercises most suited to diffusing bodily energies. It is a particularly good exercise for autistic children because it especially requires coordination of hand and leg movements. Swimming has been generally accepted as being effective with autism. Murashina Higashi Gakuen has a heated pool and a special physical education instructor gives special guidance in swimming all through the year to autistic children.[52]

See Figures 12-11 and 12-12 for more information about aquatics for learners with pervasive developmental disorders.

Figure 12-11   Teaching Strategies for Learners with PDD in the Aquatic Environment

- To meet the unique needs of a swimmer with a PDD in an aquatic environment, very small teacher–student ratios are required; typically, a one-to-one ratio will be necessary.
- Be aware of the swimmer's response to the change of sensory stimuli in the aquatic setting. The environment may heighten sensory overload because of the number of swimmers, toys, and objects in the pool setting. The environment may change sensory stimulation and perception as the swimmer is exposed to a different medium, different temperatures, waves, light reflection on the water, and different pressure sensations. If the swimmer moves while under the surface of the water, the stimulation may actually be reduced and be more manageable—noise may be muted, kinesthetic and proprioceptive sensations are negated because of constant hydrostatic pressure, and visual images may be blurred.
- During the swimming instruction period, a visual schedule will help the swimmer move, for example, from a warm-up activity to stroke work or from kicking drills to a water game. A similar plan needs to be in place to assure a transition to the activity in which the student will engage after swimming. For example, the swimmer may have a symbol card that shows a person taking a shower, then dressing, and leaving the pool.
- Typically, the best strategy for intervention includes the following:
  Use the swimmer's name.
  Pair the demonstration with a one-word or two-word cue.
  Always pair the same demonstration with the same cue.
- The swimmer should have a "home base" in every setting, a place designated specifically for him or her. For example, in the pool, the swimmer should have a particular spot on the side to which he or she returns after a given activity.
- The teacher should use equipment of the same type, color, and texture to work on the same skills. For example, if the swimmer with autism started working on the flutter kick using the yellow, nubby-textured, frog kickboard, then the teacher should always use the yellow, nubby-textured, frog kickboard when working on the flutter kick.
- If at all possible, the aquatics instructor should use the behavior-management plan being used by the child's classroom teacher or that used in the home (they should be the same).
- Swimmers with a PDD often choose to swim, almost dolphinlike, primarily underwater, because it reduces and mutes sensory stimuli. The instructor can best facilitate acquisition of swimming skill by spotting to ensure the swimmer learns to get breaths regularly, instead of waiting until he or she is out of breath; this facilitates aerobic activity. This can best be accomplished by observing the student and noting when paddling movements begin to be randomized and less effective. Then, the teacher can help by pushing the swimmer toward the surface; this is easier if the teacher is also swimming underwater.

Figure 12-12   Reducing Inappropriate Behavior in Aquatics for Learners with PDD

There are several strategies that are effective in eliminating or reducing inappropriate behavior:

1. Redirect the swimmer. If the swimmer is spitting, lower the face close to the water to allow him or her to blow bubbles. If the swimmer with PDD is kicking at the teacher, put him or her in a prone or supine position to allow him or her to kick at the surface of the water.
2. Simplify the task. If the swimmer with PDD experiences frustration, he or she may act inappropriately. Make the task simpler. For example, if the swimmer is having difficulty pulling his or her arms contralaterally, demonstrate the most basic pull—a homologous pull (both arms move together).
3. Reduce the stimulation. If the swimmer is having difficulty dealing with the stimuli in the aquatic environment, the teacher might move the swimmer to a smaller pool, a corner of the deck to do land drills, etc.

Modifications/Adaptations/ Inclusion Techniques

High-functioning learners with pervasive developmental disorders are capable of successful placement within the general physical education setting if the general physical education teacher is a GOOD teacher. Many learners with PDD can function successfully within the general physical program if the teacher is well organized, teaches developmentally appropriate activities, uses age-appropriate behavior-management strategies, and uses the teaching strategies outlined earlier in the chapter. For many learners with PDD, however, the general physical education class is restrictive because the nature of the physical education experience often includes large numbers of learners moving, with a great deal of noise, in a relatively unstructured environment.

Many variables need to be considered before deciding to place a learner with PDD in the regular

Figure 12-13   Characteristics of a Regular Physical Education Setting Appropriate for Children Who Are Mildly Autistic

Class dynamics

The teacher–student ratio must be less than 1:20. The class must be highly structured. The class routine must be consistent.

Instructional staff

The physical education teacher must be willing to create an environment that will facilitate learning for the learner with and without autism. A physical education aide or special education aide must be present. The physical education staff must be willing to work closely with special education personnel to learn strategies for managing the instructional environment.

Instructional program

The focus of the instructional program must be individual skills rather than group games and team sports.

Gymnasium and/or playground

The gymnasium must be relatively free of distractions—fans, standing equipment, etc. The playground must be surrounded by a fence.

physical education setting. Figure 12-13 describes the general physical education class that may be appropriate for a learner with mild PDD.

More severely involved learners with PDD respond favorably to a top-down task-analytic instructional model that includes physical, visual, and verbal prompts to guide learning.[14] These students need to receive physical education instruction within a small-group, self-contained setting. In order to give the learner with more severe pervasive disorders the opportunity to interact with typically developing peers, other learners may be included in the small-group physical education experience. These learners need, however, to be aware of the nature and needs of the learner with PDD. The role of peers and other support personnel is discussed in detail in Chapter 5.

The Adult with PDD

Like other adults, adults with PDD require consistent, moderate daily activity to maintain health and fitness. Their need for vigorous activity, such as fitness walking, jogging, swimming, stationary cycling, stair stepping, or inline skating, may continue to be tied to their need for exercise to help them monitor and control behavior and impulses.

Usually, adults with PDD are most successful in leisure and recreation activities that are closed, such as bowling, croquet, bocci, Frisbee golf, golf, and horseshoes. Other activities that may enhance the quality of life of adults with PDD include gardening, taking nature walks, and raising animal companions.   ⬠

Summary

Pervasive developmental disorders delays is the large umbrella under which fall five types of distinct delays: autism, Asperger's disorder, Rett's disorder, childhood disintegrative disorder, and PDD-NOS. Characteristics common to all forms of PDD are communication difficulties, abnormal behaviors, and poor social skills.

Physical education programs require set routines and careful transitions between each part of the instructional day. The key component in a quality physical education program for individuals with PDD is daily, vigorous, aerobic activity.

Review Questions

1. Name and briefly explain the five types of pervasive developmental disorders.
2. Briefly describe the primary emphasis on cardiovascular respiratory/aerobic activity with individuals with PDD.
3. Give some examples of equilibrium activities that could be included in a physical education program for learners with PDD in elementary school.
4. Explain some strategies the general physical education teacher could use to help learners with PDD experience success in the program.
5. Compare and contrast Daily Life Therapy, TEACCH, and Applied Behavior Analysis as the primary methodologies used with individuals with PDD.
6. Describe the physical education curriculum for learners from infancy through high school graduation. Describe the desired outcomes of a quality physical education program. What skills and competencies should a high school graduate with PDD possess?
7. Explain teaching strategies that have been demonstrated to be effective with learners with autism and Asperger's disorder and explain how those strategies might be adapted in the physical education program.

Student Activities

1. Arrange to observe a physical education class in the public schools that serves a learner with PDD. Describe the learner's behavior.
2. Interview a parent of a learner with PDD. Ask the parent to describe the impact of the diagnosis on the family.
3. Complete a web search to identify sources of information about PDD.
4. Arrange to observe a physical education class in the public schools that serves a learner with PDD. Compare the learner with the children described in the case studies.

5. Ask a parent of a learner with PDD for permission to attend an IEP multidisciplinary team meeting. Carefully consider the roles of each person attending the meeting.

6. Read the following book, a remarkable autobiography of Temple Grandin, a woman with autism who has earned a Ph.D. and has a successful consulting business devoted to the humane treatment of farm animals: Grandin T, Scarino M: *Emergence labeled autistic,* Navato, CA, 1986, Arena Press. Develop an individual physical education plan for a young "Temple" that would prepare her for adult community-based leisure/recreation activities.

7. Read a remarkable book: Attwood T: *Asperger's syndrome: a guide for parents and professionals,* Philadelphia, 1998, Jessica Kingsley.

8. Develop a "Web Quest" for high school students regarding PDD.

9. Refer to the Project INSPIRE web site at http://venus.twu.edu/~inspire and consider material regarding PDD.

10. Compare and contrast the physical education curriculum that would be appropriate for each of the learners described in the case studies.

REFERENCES

1. American Academy of Pediatrics Committee on Children with Disabilities: Auditory integration training and facilitated communication for autism, *Pediatrics* 102(2):431–433, 1998.

2. American Psychiatric Association: *DSM-IV-R diagnostic and statistical manual of mental disorders (revised),* Washington, DC, 1994, Author.

3. Applied Behavior Analysis. http://home.vicnet. qu/~abia/McEachin2.htm60

4. Attwood T: *Asperger's syndrome: a guide for parents and professionals,* Philadelphia, 1998, Jessica Kingsley.

5. Autism Society of America: *Asperger's syndrome information package,* Bethesda, MD, 1995, Author.

6. Bailey A et al.: A clinicopathological study of autism, *Brain,* 121:889–905, 1998.

7. Bailey A et al.: Autism: the phenotype in relatives, *J Autism Dev Disord* 28(5):369–392, 1998.

8. Baker MJ et al.: Increasing the social behavior of young children with autism using their obsessive behaviors, *JASH* 23(4):300–308, 1998.

9. Bieberich AA, Morgan SB: Brief report: affective expression in children with autism or Down syndrome, *J Autism Dev Disord* 28(4):333–338, 1998.

10. Blair RJ: Psychophysiological responsiveness to the distress of others in children with autism, *Personality Ind Diff* 26:477–485, 1999.

11. Braddock S et al.: Rett syndrome: an update and review for the primary pediatrician, *Clin Pediatrics* October:613–626, 1993.

12. Carter FR et al.: The Vineland Adaptive Behavior Scales: supplementary norms for individuals with autism, *J Autism Dev Disord* 28(4):287–302, 1998.

13. Cheng EM: Asperger syndrome and autism: a literature review and meta-analysis, *Focus Autism Other Dev Dis* 13:234–245, 1998.

14. Collier D, Reid G: A comparison of two models designed to teach autistic children a motor task, *Adapt Phys Act Q* 4:226–236, 1987.

15. Culture of Autism: From Theoretical Understanding to Educational Practice. http://www.mplc.co.uk/eduweb/sites/autism/culture.html#cult

16. Dallas Independent School District Autism Task Force: *Autism prescreening checklist,* 1988. Adapted with permission of Randal-Short, University of Queensland, Brisbane Children's Hospital, Australia.

17. Dawson G et al.: Neuropsychological correlates of early symptoms of autism, *Learner Dev* 69(5):1276–1285, 1998.

18. Dawson G et al.: Children with autism fail to orient to naturally occurring social stimuli, *J Autism Dev Disord* 28:479–485, 1998.

19. Edelson SB, Cantor DS: Autism: xenobiotic influences, *J Advance Med* 12(1):35–46, 1999.

20. Edelson MG et al.: Factors predicting intelligence scores on the TONI in individuals with autism, *Focus Autism Other Dev Dis* 13:17–26, 1998.

21. Ehlers S et al.: A screening questionnaire for Asperger syndrome and other high-functioning

autism spectrum disorders in school age children, *J Autism Dev Disord* 29(2):129–141,1999.

22. Elliott R et al.: Vigorous, aerobic exercise versus general motor training activities: effects on maladaptive and stereotypic behaviors of adults with both autism and mental retardation, *J Aut Dev Disord* 24:565–575, 1994.

23. Fantasia, Robert A., Executive Director and Principal, Boston Higashi School, Presentation at the 27th Annual California Activity Conference, Santa Rosa, CA, October 1998.

24. Field S, Hoffman A: The importance of family involvement for promoting self-determination in adolescents with autism and other developmental disabilities, *Focus Autism Other Dev Dis* 14(1):36–41, 1998.

25. Field S et al.: *A practical guide to teaching self-determination,* Reston, VA, 1998, Council for Exceptional Children.

26. Fisher E: Recent research on the etiologies of autism, *Infants Young Child* 11(3):1–8, 1999.

27. Frost LA, Bondy A: *The picture exchange communication system training manual,* Cherry Hill, NJ, 1994, Pyramid Educational Consultants.

28. Fullerton A, Coyne P: Developing skills and concepts for self-determination in young adults with autism, *Focus Autism Other Dev Dis* 14(1):42–52, 1999.

29. Gardner H: *Frames of mind: the theory of multiple intelligences,* New York, 1983, Basic Books.

30. Gillbert C: Chromosomal disorders and autism, *J Autism Dev Disord* 28(5):415–425, 1998.

31. Gillberg C: Autism and pervasive developmental disorders, *J Learner Psychol Psychiatry* 31:99–119, 1990.

32. Gillberg C: The borderland of autism and Rett syndrome: five case histories to highlight diagnostic difficulties, *J Autism Dev Disord* 19:545–559, 1989.

33. Gillberg I, Gillberg C: Asperger syndrome—some epidemiological considerations: a research note, *J Learner Psychol Psychiatry* 30:631–638, 1989.

34. Grandin T: An inside view of autism. In Schopler E, Mesibov G, editors: *High-functioning individuals with autism,* New York, 1992, Plenum Press.

35. Greenspan S: *Infancy and early childhood: the practice of clinical assessment and intervention with emotional and developmental challenges,* Madison, CT, 1992, International Universities Press.

36. Gresham FM, MacMillan DL: Autistic recovery? an analysis and critique of the empirical evidence on the Early Intervention Project, *Beh Disord* 22:185–201, 1997.

37. Haas RH et al.: Osteopenia in Rett syndrome, *J Pediatrics* 131:771–774, 1997.

38. Hefflin LJ, Simpson RL: Interventions for children and youth with autism: prudent choices in a world of exaggerated claims and empty promises. Part I: Intervention and treatment option review, *Focus Autism Other Dev Dis* 13:194–211, 1998.

39. Hobson RP, Lee A: Hello and goodbye: a study of social engagement in autism, *J Autism Dev Disord* 28(2):117–127, 1998.

40. Hobson RP, Lee A: Imitation and identification in autism, *J Child Psychol Psychiat* 40(4):649–659, 1999.

41. Hostler SL: Facilitated communication, *Pediatrics* 97(4):583–584, 1996.

42. Huettig C, O'Connor J: Wellness programming for preschoolers with disabilities, *Teach Except Child* 31(3):12–17, 1999.

43. Huettig C, O'Connor J, Shapland C, Goff D: *A case study of the benefits of an aquatic and gross motor program on a four year old with pervasive developmental delays.* Paper presented at the International Federation of Adapted Physical Activity, Barcelona, May 1999.

44. Huettig C, Pyfer J, Auxter D: *Gross motor activities for preschoolers with special needs,* St. Louis, 1993, Mosby.

45. Inclusion for Children with Autism: The TEACCH Position. http://www.unc.edu/depts/teacch/inclus.htm

46. Iyama C: Rett syndrome, *Advances in Pediatrics.* St. Louis, 1993, Mosby-Year Book.

47. Kanner L: Autistic disturbances of affective contact, *Nervous Learner* 2:217–250, 1943.

48. Kasari C: Focused and social attention of autistic children in interactions with familiar and unfamiliar adults: a comparison of autistic, mentally retarded, and normal children, *Develop Psychopath* 5:403–414, 1993.

49. Kaufman B, Kaufman S: The Option Institute. http://www.option.org/guidedintro/intro4html

50. Kern L et al.: The effects of physical exercise on self-stimulation and appropriate responding in

autistic children, *J Autism Dev Disord* 12:399–419, 1982.

51. Killian W: On the genetics of Rett syndrome: analysis of family and pedigree data, *Am J Med Genet* 24:369–376, 1986.

52. Kitahara K: *Daily life therapy, volume III,* Boston, 1984, Nimrod Press.

53. Klin A, Volkmar F: Autism and the pervasive developmental disorders. In Nospitz JD, editor: *Basic handbook of learner psychiatry,* New York, 1993, Basic Books.

54. Krug D, Arick J, Almond P: Autism behavior check-list for identifying severely handicapped individuals with high levels of autistic behavior, *J Learner Psychol Psychiatry* 21:221–229, 1980.

55. Landrus R, Mesibov G: *Preparing autistic students for community living: a functional and sequential approach to training,* Division TEACCH, Department of Psychiatry, University of North Carolina, 1985, Chapel Hill.

56. Leonard H: A population-based approach to the investigation of osteopenia in Rett syndrome, *Dev Med Child Neurol* 41:323–328, 1999.

57. Levinson L, Reid G: The effects of exercise intensity on the stereotypic behaviors of individuals with autism, *Adapted Phys Activity Quart* 10:255–268, 1993.

58. Libby S: Spontaneous play in children with autism: a reappraisal, *J Autism Dev Disord* 28:487–497, 1998.

59. MacLean JE: Familial factors influence level of functioning in pervasive developmental disorder, *J Amer Acad Learner Adolescent Psychiat* 38(6):746–753, 1999.

60. Manjiviona J, Prior M: Comparison of Asperger syndrome and high-functioning autistic children on a test of motor impairment, *J Autism Dev Disord* 25:23–39, 1995.

61. Moes DR: Integrating choice-making opportunities within teacher-assigned academic tasks to facilitate the performance of children with autism, *JASH* 23(4):319–328, 1998.

62. NASPE releases first ever physical activity guidelines for children, *NASPE News* 51:1, 4, 1998.

63. Ozonoff S, Cathcart K: Effectiveness of a home program intervention for young children with autism, *J Autism Dev Disord* 29(1): 25–32, 1998.

64. Pauls D: *Family genetics of Asperger's syndrome: preliminary results of the Yale Social Learning Disabilities Project.* Paper presented at the American Academy of Learner and Adolescent Psychiatry, Toronto, CA, 1997.

65. PDD-NOS: Yale University web site. http://info.med.yale.edu/chldstdy/autism/

66. Quill K, Gurry S, Larkin A: Daily life therapy: a Japanese model for educating children with autism, *J Autism Dev Disord* 19:625–635, 1989.

67. Rapin I: Autism, *New Eng J Med* 337(2):97–104, 1997.

68. Rett A: Uber ein eigenartiges hirnatrophisches syndrom bei hyperammonamie im kindersalter, *Weiner Med Wochenschrift* 116:723–726, 1966.

69. The Rett Syndrome Diagnostic Criteria Work Group: Diagnostic criteria for Rett syndrome, *Ann Neurol* 23:425–428, 1988.

70. Rollins PR: Early pragmatic accomplishments and vocabulary development in preschool children with autism, *Am J Speech-Language Path* 8:181–190, 1999.

71. Sacks O: A neurologist's notebook: an anthropologist on Mars, *The New Yorker,* 106–125, January 3, 1994.

72. Schopler E et al.: *The childhood autism rating scale (CARS),* Los Angeles, 1988, Western Psychological Services.

73. Schopler E: Convergence of learning disability, higher level autism, and Asperger's syndrome, *J Autism Dev Disord* 15:359, 1985.

74. Simonoff E: Genetic counseling in autism and pervasive developmental disorders, *J Autism Dev Disord* 28(5):447–456, 1998.

75. Son-Rise Program. http://www.Son-Rise.org/heart.html

76. Stades-Veth J: Autism broken symbiosis: persistent avoidance of eye contact with the mother. Causes, consequences, prevention and cure of autistiform behavior in babies through "mother learner holding." (ERIC Document Reproduction Service No. ED 294 344), 1998.

77. Szatmari P: Genetics of autism: overview and new directions, *J Autism Dev Disord* 28(5):351–368, 1998.

78. Thompson R et al.: *Pervasive developmental disorder: new subtests, new criteria.* Presentation at

Texas Speech-Language-Hearing Association, Houston, TX, April 22, 1995.

79. Tsai L: *Pervasive developmental disorders*, NICHY Briefing Paper, FS20, 1–15, 1998.

80. U.S. Department of Education, Office of Special Education and Rehabilitation Services: *Annual report to Congress on implementation of IDEA,* February 1998, Author.

81. Volkmar FR, Klin A, Pauls D: Nosological and genetic aspects of Asperger syndrome, *J Autism Dev Disord* 28(5):457–463, 1998.

82. Williams K: Understanding the student with Asperger syndrome: guidelines for teachers. Focus on Autistic Behavior, 10, 2. Modified with permission from Barb Kirby, Web Master, O.A.S.I.S. web page. http://www.udel.edu/bkirby/asperger/karen_williams_guidelines.html

83. Woodhouse W: Head circumference in autism and other pervasive developmental disorders, *J Child Psych Psychiat* 37(6): 665–671, 1996.

RECOMMENDED WEBSITES

Please note: These websites are being recommended in the fall of 1999. Given the ever changing nature of the Internet, these sites may have moved or been replaced by the time you are reading this text.

Educating the Student with Asperger Syndrome
http://www.sasked.gov.sk.ca/curr_inst/speced/asper.html

Inclusion for Children with Autism: The Teacch Position
http://www.unc.edu/depts/teacch/inclus.htm

Understanding the Student with Asperger's Syndrome: Guidelines for Teachers
http://www.udel.edu/bkirby/asperger/karen_williams_guidelines.html

RECOMMENDED VIDEOS

Fanlight Productions
4196 Washington Street
Boston, MA 02131
Psychology, Social Work, & Disabilities
Video Collections, 1999-2000
    Breakthroughs: How to Reach Students with Autism
    Chris Award and Silver Apple Award
    25 minutes, purchase price $195, Order # CV-252

    Autism
    28 minutes, purchase price $149, Order # CV-215
    Understanding Autism, by NewsCart Productions Inc.
    Council for Exceptional Children Video Festival
    19 minutes, purchase price $195, Order # CV-100

    Autism: A World Apart, by Karen Cunningham
    Blue Ribbon, American Film and Video Festival
    29 minutes, purchase price $195, Order CV-039
Films for the Humanities & Sciences
PO Box 2053
Princeton, NJ 08543-2053
Phone: 609-275-1400
    Autism: The Child Who Couldn't Play
    $149 purchase price, $75 rental
Amazon.Com
    Visual Thinking of a Person with Autism, by Temple Grandin.
    $29.95, ASIN:1885477503.
    Asperger's Syndrome. $89.95. ASIN:1885477465.

13

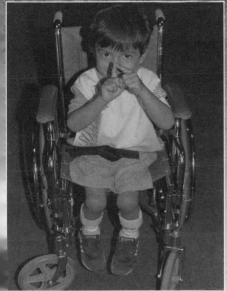

A child participates in creative storytelling at camp.
Courtesy Dallas Independent School District.

Specific Learning Disability

■ OBJECTIVES

Define specific learning disability.

Identify the types of behavior problems youngsters with a learning disability frequently demonstrate.

List five motor/physical development delays youngsters with a learning disability might demonstrate.

List at least three teaching strategies a physical educator could use to promote learning for students with specific learning disabilities.

Identify three techniques that might be effective in keeping a student with a specific learning disability on task during a physical education class.

Probably no disability has proven to be more controversial or has undergone more name changes than what we now call *specific learning disabilities.* Confusion about the condition is reflected in the number of terms associated with disability. Over the past thirty years individuals with these disabilities have been classified as perceptually handicapped, brain injured, brain damaged, minimal brain dysfunctionate, dyslexic, and/or developmentally aphasic. In every case, each term was selected in an attempt to convey the fact that persons with a specific learning disability have normal intelligence but fail to demonstrate the same academic competencies that most individuals do whose IQs fall within the normal range.

495

Shawn

Shawn is an eight-year-old who is having problems with his coordination, handwriting, and concentration, he also has trouble getting along with his second-grade classmates, following instructions, and remaining quiet in class when the teacher is giving instruction.

Shawn has a verbal IQ of 107 and a performance IQ of 91. Even though he has a normal overall IQ (99), he is reluctant to engage in any tasks requiring sustained mental effort, and he does not follow through on chores and assignments. He is performing to age level in math but struggles with comprehending material he reads.

He does not like to participate in competitive games. When he does, he frequently loses his temper and strikes out at other players. He prefers to play alone and particularly enjoys riding his bike; however, he still uses training wheels, which other kids in the neighborhood make fun of.

CRITICAL THINKING TASK

As you read this chapter, think about the problems Shawn is experiencing. Identify the self-esteem behaviors and motor proficiency problems he demonstrates that are often typical of individuals with learning disabilities. Determine how you, the physical educator, could create a positive learning environment for Shawn.

DEFINITION OF SPECIFIC LEARNING DISABILITY

Specific learning disability was defined in the Individuals with Disabilities Education Act (IDEA) of 1990. It is a disorder in one or more of the basic psychological processes involved in understanding or using language, spoken or written, which may manifest itself in the imperfect ability to listen, think, speak, write, spell, or perform mathematical calculations. Such disorders include such conditions as perceptual disabilities, brain injury, minimal brain dysfunction, dyslexia, and developmental aphasia. The term does not include children who have learning problems that are primarily the result of visual, hearing, or motor disabilities; mental retardation; emotional disturbance; or environmental, cultural, or economic disadvantage.[15]

Specific types of learning disabilities include a problem with arithmetic (discalculia), reading (dyslexia), handwriting (dysgraphia), spelling, and understanding and/or using verbal and nonverbal abilities (developmental aphasia, dysnomia, expressive language).[4] Many children and adolescents who have been identified as having a learning disability also have concurrent emotional and behavioral problems.[30] And, as would be expected of individuals who despite their best efforts continue to fail, self-concept is reduced.

INCIDENCE OF SPECIFIC LEARNING DISABILITY

Estimates of the prevalence of the condition range from 3 to 15 percent of the population,[4] depending on the number of characteristics included in the definition. Regardless of which characteristics are included, it is widely accepted that 70 to 90 percent of the children identified as having a specific learning disability are male; however, there is growing speculation that both genders are equally affected but males are identified more frequently because they tend to act out more and be more disruptive than females.[1] In 1977 there were approximately 800,000 learning disabled individuals; however, by 1990, the incidence of learning disability had more than doubled (i.e., more than 2 million). In the year 2000, the reported incidence has grown to 10 percent of the population. As would be expected, research on this disability has greatly increased in recent years. Specific learning disability is the most prevalent disabling condition of individuals in the United States.

CAUSES OF SPECIFIC LEARNING DISABILITY

What is known is that children who were once believed to be prone to daydreaming, inattentive, mischievous, or just plain "dumb" in school do indeed have an organic basis for their behaviors.[24] Technologically sophisticated equipment has been used to document neurological differences in the brains of persons with specific learning disabilities as compared with normal individuals,[13,19,21,25] yet the specific impact of neurological differences, the subcategories of the disability, and the causes have not been identified. The best we can do at this point in time is describe the behaviors demonstrated by this varied group of learners, and share whatever has been found to work successfully with them.

For more than forty years theorists postulated that sensory-perceptual-motor functioning delays underlie specific learning disabilities. Technology developed in the past decade has enabled researchers to demonstrate neurological differences in individuals with learning disability; however, the extent to which these deficits are tied to academic performance is still unknown. During the 1960s, when the perceptual-motor theories of Getman, Kephart,[23] and Frostig and Maslow[18] were emerging, great hope was placed in using physical activity to "cure" learning disabilities. The perceptual-motor pioneers proposed that the basic "stuff" from which cognitive information is constructed includes perceptual and motor components. Educational researchers speculated that if they could identify that perceptual-motor delays exist and intervene with a movement program to overcome the delays, cognitive function would be facilitated. Special educators with little or no background in motor development seized on these theories as the possible answer to resolving the academic learning problems manifested by individuals with learning disabilities. Kephart's and Frostig and Maslow's programs of activities were tried on groups of learning disabled students. Almost without exception, the wholesale application of these theories proved disappointing to the academic community. In most cases the learning disabled student improved in perceptual-motor function but demonstrated no immediate change in reading or mathematical ability. As a result, many special educators abandoned the notion that there could be a causative relationship between motor and cognitive functioning.

As the perceptual-motor theories faded in popularity, other neuropsychological theories emerged that advanced the belief that cognitive function could be facilitated by controlling types and qualities of sensory and motor experiences. These theories differed from earlier ones in that they advanced the notion that, prior to efficient perceptual motor and cognitive functioning, sensory input stimuli must be organized so that it can be used by the central nervous system.

Prominent advocates of a definitive relationship between the sensory, motor, and cognitive domains were Ayres,[2,3] deQuiros and Schrager,[12] and Dennison.[11] Ayres, a well-known researcher in the area of sensory integration therapy, advocated that "learning and behavior are the visible aspects of sensory integration"[2] and that sensory integration results from sensory stimulation and motor activity. Schrager and deQuiros believed that primary learning disabilities have their bases in vestibular, perceptual modalities, and cerebral dysfunctions. They advocated the use of sensory-perceptual-motor activities to assuage vestibular and perceptual problems. Dennison built on Sperry and Ornstein's model of brain function and developmental optometry's theories and developed a program of specific movements to use to enable individuals to access different parts of the brain. He called his approach Educational Kinesiology.

Research studies have validated that both sensory integration and Educational Kinesiology have a positive impact on perceptual-motor function; however, their value for enhancing cognitive functioning has been less apparent.[8,20] Studies that have reported academic gains from sensory integration therapy programs suffer from sampling, group assignment, treatment, and analysis inadequacies.[20] One study that looked at the efficacy of Educational Kinesiology concluded that the treatment is not effective in improving academic skills as measured by the Comprehensive Test of Basic Skills for Language, Arithmetic, and Reading.[8]

The development of functional independent leisure skills can enhance the quality of life.
Courtesy Wisconsin Lions Camp, Rosholt, Wis.

Interest in the relationship between motor and cognitive function continues. A carefully designed study carried out in England reported that over 95 percent of a sample of children with learning disabilities in the areas of reading, arithmetic, and spelling demonstrated depressed balance (with eyes closed) and low muscle tone.[17] It will take well-designed research studies such as this to tease out the existence of the specific types of sensory and motor components that exist concomitantly with cognitive problems. Once the underlying delays are identified, intervention programs will need to be developed and used with youngsters who have learning disabilities. After that, longitudinal studies that follow individuals who have been exposed to contemporary sensory-perceptual-motor intervention programs will need to be carried out. To understand the problem and potential solutions, dialogues among educators, neurologists, visual and hearing specialists, and researchers will need to be initiated and fostered. The questions to be answered must be approached with open minds, honest and critical analysis, and persistence.

CHARACTERISTICS OF SPECIFIC LEARNING DISABILITY

All children differ in their psychomotor, cognitive, and behavioral characteristics. Likewise, children with learning disabilities differ from one another, and there is considerable overlap in abilities between the child with learning disabilities and other children. However, there are some similar group characteristics that differentiate individuals with specific learning disabilities from individuals who lack disabilities.

Evidence that the central nervous system is involved includes problems of arousal, attention, activity level, temperament, alertness, and tone during the first two years of life. Delays in motor milestones, neuromuscular integrity, and fine and gross motor function, as well as speech delays, articulation problems, and dysfluency, are evident from two to four years of age. Between the ages of four to six years, these children have difficulty with printing, cutting, and drawing. After entering school, problems specific to school subjects are affected, and gradually the self-concept suffers.[6]

Figure 13-1 Characteristics That Affect Motor Performance

Neurophysiological differences

Neurological building blocks

Information processing

Language differences

Memory

Attention span

Children can differ in motor performance for many reasons, including (1) neurophysiological differences, (2) sensory input processing differences, (3) problems processing information, (4) language differences, (5) memory deficits, and (6) short attention span. (See Figure 13-1.)

Neurophysiological Differences

Most of the research and theory on learning disability has been done by cognitive theorists. However, in the past fifteen years there has been increased emphasis on neurophysiological functioning of the brain as it relates to learning disability. Studies of the brains of individuals with specific learning disabilities have been done using electroencephalography (EEG), auditory brainstem-evoked response (ABER), regional cerebral blood flow (rCBF), and magnetic resonance imaging (MRI). The purpose of this research is to determine whether any significant differences exist between the brain structure and function of normal and learning disabled individuals. Some differences have been reported.

Using EEG, Johns[21] demonstrated that the evoked potentials of groups of students with learning disabilities were significantly different from students with no learning problems. Other investigators have reported significant differences in re-

gions of blood flow,[25] brainstem-evoked responses during speech processing tasks,[19] and the width of the structure connecting the two hemispheres of the brain.[13] Neurophysiological tools such as these show great promise for the early identification of children with specific learning disabilities. Once unique brain structure and function profiles are identified and correlated directly to specific learning difficulties, it will be possible to develop educational intervention strategies specific to each child's needs.

Sensory Input Processing Differences

An analysis of neurological building blocks important to skilled motor performances indicates that exteroceptors (e.g., eyes, ears, and tactile receptors) and proprioceptors (e.g., vestibular and kinesthetic receptors) are important avenues for receiving information from the environment. Deficits in receiving and processing information from these senses may result in deficits in the performance of physical activities.

There is strong evidence that persons with learning disabilities may be impaired in their ability to balance. Good balance depends on accurate information from the vestibular system as well as normal reflex and depth perception development. When vestibular information is not received or processed efficiently, impaired balance results. In addition, persisting primitive reflexes and/or a delay in the development of postural (equilibrium) reflexes also inhibit a person's ability to achieve and maintain balance. Depth perception deficiencies interfere with an individual's ability to use visual cues in the environment to assist in balancing. Impaired balance interferes with postural and locomotor efficiency as well as foot-eye and hand-eye coordination.

Children with learning disabilities also may possess deficits in kinesthetic perception. Recent literature that points out the low muscle tone demonstrated early on by children with learning disabilities supports deficits in kinesthetic perception. When the kinesthetic receptors are not fully functioning, information about precise position

Aquatic skills can open a new world.
Photo by Carol Huettig.

and rate of movement of body parts in space does not reach the central nervous system. Kinesthesis is an essential prerequisite for sophisticated, refined sport skills that require precise movements, such as putting a golf ball, shooting a basketball, setting a volleyball, and performing any other movements that require qualitative forces for success. Most physical education activities require an awareness and control of body parts in space (i.e., kinesthetic perception). Thus, kinesthesis is considered an important prerequisite for movement control, which generalizes to many other physical and sport activities. Cermak and Henderson[9] estimate that 60 to 95 percent of these children have poor static and dynamic balance, coordination problems, low muscle tone, poor spatial orientation, and delayed acquisition of equilibrium reactions. Morrison, Hinshaw, and Corte[26] also report that this population demonstrates significantly more primitive reflexes and vestibular and equilibrium delays than do children without disabilities. Fawcett and Nicolson[17] validate the reports of poor static balance and low muscle tone.

Many children who have learning disabilities are uncoordinated and lack control of motor responses. Individuals with poorly developed balance and kinesthetic systems tend to have problems in changing direction or body position. As a result, these individuals commonly have difficulty learning to perform efficient specific sport and motor skills. Girls with learning disabilities perform motor tasks significantly poorer than do boys with learning disabilities.[31]

Problems Processing Information

There is evidence that many persons with learning disabilities differ from their unaffected peers as a result of their inability to process information efficiently.[7,17] Information processing relates to how one retains and manipulates information—how information is acquired, stored, selected, and then recalled. Although there appears to be agreement that as a group the population with learning disabilities has problems in information processing, the specific locus of the problem is disputed.

Cermak[9] indicates that processing deficits appear in the speed of rehearsal strategies. On the other hand, Karr and Hughes[22] indicate that the problem may not be a processing deficit. They demonstrated that this population is able to handle information associated with increased task difficulty in the same manner as nondisabled persons; however, a problem may exist in the very early input stages of the processing mechanism (i.e., getting information into the processing system).

Individuals with impaired depth perception misjudge where objects are in space. As a result, they are unable to catch and kick balls, descend stairs one at a time, and avoid climbing apparatus. Figure-ground perception involves the ability to distinguish an object from its background. It requires selecting and attending to the appropriate visual cue among a number of other cues that are irrelevant to that task at a particular moment. If the visual object to which the individual is to respond is not well defined, then chances are the motor task will be less proficient than desired. Individuals with poor depth perception almost always demonstrate deficits in visual figure-ground perception.

Another visual characteristic that may be impaired in this population is ocular saccadical abilities, which permit the learner to refix the eye on differing targets accurately and quickly. The ocular saccadical ability is required in sports in which an individual must concentrate on a moving ball as well as a moving target (e.g., in football, when a quarterback throws a ball to a second receiver after seeing that the first potential receiver is covered; in basketball, when focusing on a rebounding ball and then refocusing vision to find an outlet player to pass to). Any visual deficiency that interferes with visual discrimination needed for the proficient performance of a given sport will impair the performance of that sport.

The auditory mechanism may not be as critical in the performance of sport activity as is the eye; however, impaired ability of the individual to use auditory information may result in performance that is below normative expectations. Some of the sport activities requiring auditory discrimination and perception are dancing and floor routines in gymnastics. Auditory figure-ground discrimination is important to skill proficiency. Anytime there are extraneous auditory sounds, auditory figure-ground perception is needed (e.g., when players participating in a noisy gym must attend closely to hear the coaches' instructions and officials' calls).

Ayres[2] suggests that learning disabled individuals may have deficits in motor planning. Eichstaedt and Kalakian[16] describe motor planning as the ability to execute behaviors in a proper sequential order. Sport skill tasks require the integration of discrete component parts in sequence for task success. When learning a motor task, each component part of the skill must be planned and carried out in sequence before the skill can be executed correctly. With practice, the skill becomes a subroutine that is stored in long-term memory, and motor planning requirements are lessened. However, when learning new skills that are composed of component parts that must be sequenced, each component part must be present for the skill to be learned. Individuals with learning disabilities who demonstrate difficulty with motor planning may not have the necessary components (e.g., vestibular, kinesthetic, or visual information) available to them.

Language Differences

The physical education teacher should recognize individual language usage differences among students with learning disabilities.[14] Such knowledge can be used to modify teaching strategies that involve comunication through language. There are at least three language categories: (1) receptive language, (2) expressive language, and (3) inner language.

Receptive language involves the ability to comprehend the meaning associated with language. Deficits in receptive language may be either visual or auditory. Visual deficits are reflected by the inability to organize and interpret visual information appropriately. For example, a child may be unable to interpret facial gestures appropriately. Auditory receptive language deficits may be reflected in a failure to follow directions or an inability to discriminate between sounds.

Expressive language involves the ability to communicate through either audition or the visual mechanism. Auditory deficits are expressed through impaired speech, whereas visual expressive language deficits are writing problems. Problems in visual expressive language are the inability to reproduce simple geometric forms, the persistent reversal of letters, the rotation or inversion of letters, and the reversed sequence of letters.

Inner language processes refers to the ability to transform experience into symbols. This, of course, is dependent on experiences. Inasmuch as young children gain much of their experience with the world through play and motor activity, environmental exploration with the body is an important aspect of the development of inner language.

Memory Deficits

Many individuals with learning disabilities also have deficits in long-term and short-term memory. Four steps are necessary for learning to occur: (1) a stimulus must be registered in the brain, (2) that stimulus must be maintained while its relevance is determined, (3) the stimulus must be processed in light of material present in long-term storage, and (4) the stimulus must be placed in long-term storage. Thus, deficits in either short-term or long-term memory limit the benefits of prior experiences and practice.

Memory is also a prerequisite for closure, the ability to recognize a visual or an auditory experience when only part is presented. The partial image is compared with complete images that are stored in the memory for identification. An example of visual closure occurs when a baseball player is batting. The batter must make inferences as to where the ball will be when it crosses the plate. If a batter is not able to estimate where the ball will cross the plate, it is impossible to determine where the bat should be swung. More experienced batters have more comparative images stored in their memory banks; thus, they are better able to estimate the flight of an incoming ball than are less experienced batters.

Individuals with learning disabilities also may be deficient in cue selection. *Cue selection* is the ability to attend to relevant cues and block out irrelevant stimuli. Individuals with memory, visual, or auditory deficits will not make efficient cue selections.

Short Attention Span

Approximately 80 percent of all individuals with specific learning disabilities are estimated to also have some form of attention deficit disorder.[5] Attention deficit conditions are discussed in Chapter 18 of this text.

Motor Performance Profile

Any one or all of these factors will affect the success level of a child in physical education. Children with cognitive processing problems may not understand or remember instructions. Perceptual difficulties lead to spatial awareness or body image problems. Clumsy motor performance caused by delayed reflex and/or vestibular development, as well as depth perception problems, directly influence a student's ability to master basic movement tasks and to combine those tasks into the complicated patterns necessary to succeed in sports or leisure-time activities.

It is, however, difficult to group together all children with specific learning disabilities when trying to determine precisely what movement difficulties they will demonstrate. In an attempt to determine whether there is a clear-cut motor profile demonstrated by this population, over an eleven-year period Pyfer[28] administered a wide variety of tests to approximately 400 children with learning disabilities. Analysis of those data revealed that approximately 12 percent demonstrated no motor delays, 75 percent scored average on some tests but below average on other tests, and the remaining 13 percent were severely delayed in all areas tested. The youngsters who demonstrated motor delays were deficient in balance, spatial awareness, body image, visual-motor control, and/or fine motor development. Additionally, those youngsters had a performance IQ score that ranged from 12 to 20 points lower than their verbal

IQ scores. These findings agree with those of the studies cited earlier in this chapter. That is, no one performance profile characterizes all individuals with learning disabilities. These children constitute a heterogeneous group and, as such, they need to be treated as individuals. What is critical is to identify their motor delays as early in life as possible and to intervene to correct those problems. The fact that preschool children with learning disabilities can make significant motor gains when placed in a structured program has been validated.[29]

TESTING TO DETERMINE MOTOR FUNCTIONING LEVELS

Appropriate tests to use with this population include any instruments that will provide information about the functioning of neurological building blocks (vestibular, kinesthetic, visual efficiency, and reflex development), balance, fine motor control, and visual motor control. An instrument that can provide several clues about the motor functioning level of this population is the Bruininks-Oseretsky Test of Motor Proficiency. Subtests that are helpful for pinpointing possible vestibular, kinesthetic, visual efficiency, bilateral coordination, and physical fitness delays are Gross Motor, Upper-Limb Coordination, and the Visual-Motor Control section of the Fine Motor Subtest. Rather than using the subtest scores to determine whether delays exist, it is recommended that the evaluator examine the performance of specific components of the subtests. Specific clues to developmental delays were presented in Chapter 4. When Shawn was tested using the Bruininks-Oseretsky test, his performance was as follows:

- He scored at the six-year, eleven-month level on the balance subtest. He balanced for 10 seconds with his eyes open and only 5 seconds with his eyes closed.
- He scored at the seven-year, eleven-month level on the bilateral coordination subtest; however, he could not demonstrate any of the tasks requiring him to coordinate movements on the opposite side of the body.
- He scored at the seven-year, eight-month level on the strength subtest. He

demonstrated six bent-knee push-ups and six sit-ups.
- His upper-limb coordination subtest score was at the ten-year, five-month level, with no areas of concern.
- He scored at the six-year, eleven-month level on the visual-motor control subtest and at the six-year, eight-month level on the upper-limb speed and dexterity subtest. He erred on all of the tracing mazes tasks and when trying to draw geometric figures.

TEACHING STRATEGIES

Regardless of what type of program a physical educator favors, tests should be administered to determine the motor functioning level of the child with a specific learning disability. After areas of deficiency have been identified, activities can be selected to promote development in these problem areas. If appropriate activities are selected and carefully taught, the prognosis for the motor development of these students is quite good.

Specific activities to use with students with specific learning disabilities can be found in Chapters 4 and 5. General points to keep in mind when working with these students follow:

- Whenever possible, use a New Games approach that accommodates a wide range of motor competency, so that your students' self-concepts are enhanced rather than demoralized by failure to contribute.
- Use a positive behavior-management program to get students to finish tasks (e.g., use tokens or let them select their favorite activity once each day if they stay on task).
- Give brief instructions and ask the children to repeat those instructions before starting an activity. Doing this prevents problems that arise from the limited memory some of the children demonstrate.
- To enhance the children's opportunities for success and willingness to persist at tasks, break tasks into small learning steps and praise every legitimate effort they make.

See Figure 13-2.

A parent is a child's first teacher.

Figure 13-2	Teaching Strategies

Use a new games approach.

Use positive behavior management.

Give brief instructions.

Break tasks into small steps.

The Physical Education Program

It is critical that these students' participation be limited in group activities that are beyond their capabilities. Such practices only reinforce their feelings of inferiority. When including these students with the regular physical education class, the more activities that use an individualized approach that enable each student to work at his or her level without being compared with peers, the better will be this student's opportunity to realize some success. At the elementary school level, activities should promote development of the neurological building blocks before concentrating on perceptual-motor integration or motor output behaviors. The greatest amount of carryover will occur if educators "fill in the blanks" of missing building blocks and perceptual components before teaching motor output behaviors. Several activities that can be used with elementary children of all ability levels are included in Gross Motor Activities for Children with Special Needs, that accompanies this text. At the middle and high school levels, programs should encourage and reward individual effort. Examples are changing the way games are played to accommodate a variety of performance capabilities and having personal fitness programs that are specifically patterned to affect an individual's present level of performance.

When providing small-group or whole class programs for students with specific learning disabilities, it is easier to focus on their particular needs. However, there is controversy among physical educators as to whether a bottom-up developmental approach or a task-specific, top-down approach should be used in the instruction of motor skills for the learning disabled. A bottom-up approach to facilitate movement efficiency would begin with sensory stimulation activities to provide prerequisite components for meaningful, culturally relevant skills. With such an approach, there would be extended periods during which students are engaging in specific activities to facilitate basic sensory and reflex systems. Once the basic sensory and reflex systems are functioning, and those stimuli are integrated, perceptual-motor development as well as learning of specific motor skills will occur. Admittedly, the number of components of sensory input systems as well as perceptual-motor functions is considerable. All of the senses, the integration of each of the senses, the perceptual-motor characteristics of the individual, the way in which information is processed, and associative and organizational structures of perceptual skills that can be linked with each of the sensory modes are taken into consideration. Effective use of this approach requires extensive knowledge on the part of the teacher and the willingness to delay instruction in what many consider culturally relevant skills.

The top-down approach to facilitating movement efficiency would start with the culturally

A paraprofessional leads a class in rhythm activity to develop body part identification skills.
Courtesy Dallas Independent School District.

relevant skills and work down toward prerequisite components when it becomes apparent a learner is not benefiting from direct instruction of a specific task. Which approach to use can be determined through thorough evaluation and interpretation of results. When evaluation results clearly indicate no sensory or reflex deficits, the most economical method would be the top-down approach. Also, the older the learner, the less appealing the bottom-up approach is.

Modifications

Teaching and program modifications that are helpful for students with specific learning disabilities include the following:

- *Control attention.* One of the methods for controlling attention is to establish routines that are repeated day after day. This enables the child to develop a pattern of activities. The teaching techniques, behavior-modification program, and organizational patterns should be kept as structured and consistent as possible.
- *Control extraneous stimuli in the environment.* In addition to stable routines, the environment should appear relatively the same from one day to the next. Positioning of equipment and systematic procedures to store equipment should be established and maintained.

- *Control of desired behaviors.* There should be instructionally relevant stimuli to focus the attention of the students (e.g., designate specific spots on the floor where students are to begin class each day). Visual cues can be used that indicate where the hands are to be placed for a push-up or a forward roll. Specific visual or auditory information can be introduced that indicates to the individual specifically what to do with body parts to enhance motor control.
- *Control methodology.* If the learner has a tendency to disassociate visually or auditorially, use the whole-part-whole method of teaching. Later, attention to details of performance can be emphasized.
- *Use more than one sensory modality.* In addition to verbally describing the task to be performed, use visual stimuli (e.g., a picture, drawing, or demonstration). In this way, if the learning disabled student has either visual or verbal deficits, another sensory avenue can be used to comprehend the instruction. Kinesthetic aids, such as manually moving a child through sequences, also can be used.

Community-Based Opportunities

Individuals who grow into adulthood with specific learning disabilities must be taught compensation skills to enable them to recreate in the community. Too frequently, middle and high school students with specific learning disabilities who have not had their conditions properly identified and attended to develop all types of anxiety, guilt, and feelings of inadequacy.[27] Because they have IQs within the normal range, they are bright enough to realize that, no matter how much effort they exert, as the school material becomes increasingly complex and demanding their peers are going to outperform them academically. It is no wonder that these youngsters balk at continuing in school, demonstrate significant conduct problems, and frequently become alcohol-dependent. Professionals must make every effort to ensure that students who are not performing to adequate academic standards are properly assessed, so that intervention that will match their needs can be implemented. Their transition program should match their needs to the opportunities available in the community.

It is critical that every curriculum for individuals with learning disabilities address day-to-day tasks that will contribute to their overall levels of independence as adults. The needs identified for persons with learning disabilities are presented in Figure 13-3.

Probably the most significant knowledge these young adults require is that they are not to blame for their learning difficulties. The next most important piece of information they need is an understanding about their specific information-processing deficits. With those understandings the maturing individual can make informed decisions that will enable them to participate successfully in work and social activities.

Figure 13-3 Transition Needs of Persons with Learning Disabilities

Occupational/vocational training

Social skills development

Leisure-time activities

Life skills taught in natural settings[10]

Knowing there is a reason for the academic and social struggles they have experienced reduces the guilt, acting out and avoidance behaviors, and feelings of alienation from society. As a result, their self-confidence increases, and they become more motivated to attempt and persist at difficult tasks. With knowledge about the nature of their limitations, they can then either determine the types of assistance needed to realize success or select activities that circumvent their problem areas. Frequently, selecting an activity partner to assist with decision making is sufficient. For example, if determining distances is a problem, a golfer should select a partner or caddy who is willing and able to read the layout of the course and make club recommendations. When canoeing or kayaking for any distance or on an unfamiliar body of water, a partner versed in orienteering is essential. Adults with learning disabilities should be discouraged from attempting to participate in activities requiring skills for which they are unable to compensate. ❧

SUMMARY

Specific learning disability is a condition that is manifested through disabilities in listening, thinking, writing, speaking, spelling, and mathematical calculations. The majority of children with this disability also demonstrate soft neurological signs early. Frequently, these soft neurological signs are later expressed in delayed motor development. In addition to addressing the specific types of academic subject delays these students demonstrate, it is crucial that physical and motor delays also be determined and corrected. To determine what types of delays these students are experiencing, testing must be done. Selected parts of the long form of the Bruininks-Oseretsky Test of Motor Proficiency can be used to identify areas of concern. When including this type of student in the regular physical education class, either select activities that will be of benefit to them and to their classmates or allow for individualized programs for all students. When dealing with students with specific learning disabilities there are two types of programs that will benefit them: (1) a bottom-up approach that focuses on facilitating deficit sensory input and reflex systems is appropriate for younger children, and (2) top-down, skill-development approach that focuses on instruction in specific performance tasks that are available in the community is critical for the middle and high school student. During the school years, every effort should be made to address the academic, motor, and life skills these individuals require to attain independence and cope in the community.

REVIEW QUESTIONS

1. What are the cognitive, affective, and motor characteristics of individuals with specific learning disabilities?

2. What teaching strategies could a physical educator use to promote attending behavior of the student with specific learning disabilities?

3. What activities could a physical educator include in an elementary physical education class that would benefit both the students with learning disabilities and those without?

4. What types of information are helpful to the young adult with specific learning disabilities who is trying to cope in the community?

5. What is meant by the term *specific learning disability?*

STUDENT ACTIVITIES

1. Identify two behaviors Shawn in the case study demonstrates that must be extinguished to improve his chances of benefiting from his physical education experience. Develop one long-range behavioral goal and three short-term objectives leading to each goal that address these problem areas.

2. Divide the class into several small groups. Have each group review Shawn's test results and identify at least five activities he would have difficulty performing in physical education.

3. Divide the class into some small groups. Assign each group one of Shawn's physical/motor problem performance areas. Develop one long-range goal and three short-term objectives that progress from the present level of performance in that area. Then identify three activities that could be incorporated into a second-grade physical education class that would be of interest to the class and would lead Shawn toward his long-range goal.

REFERENCES

1. American Psychiatric Association: *Diagnostic and statistical manual of mental disorders DSM-IV,* Washington, DC, 1994, Author.

2. Ayres AJ: *Sensory integration and the child,* Los Angeles, 1980, Western Psychological Services.

3. Ayres AJ: *Sensory integration and learning disorders,* Los Angeles, 1972, Western Psychological Services.

4. Beers MH, Berkow R, editors: *Merck manual of diagnosis and therapy,* Whitehouse Station, NJ, 1999, Merck Research Laboratories.

5. Blau M: A.D.D: the scarlet letters in the alphabet, *New York Magazine,* December: 44–51, 1993.

6. Blumsack J, Lewandowski L, Waterman, J: Neurodevelopmental precursors to learning

disabilities: a preliminary report from a parent survey, *J of Learning Disabil* 30:228–237, 1997.

7. Brunt D, Magill R, Eason R: Distinctions in variability of motor output between learning disabled and normal children, *Percept Mot Skills* 57:731–734, 1983.

8. Cammisa K: Educational kinesiology with learning disabled children: an efficacy study, *Percept Mot Skills* 78:105–106, 1994.

9. Cermak LS: Information processing deficits in children with learning disabilities, *J Learning Disab* 16:599–605, 1983.

10. Cronin ME: Life skills curricula for students with learning disabilities: a review of the literature, *J of Learning Disab* 29:53–68, 1996.

11. Dennison P, Hargrove G: *Personalized whole brain integration*, Glendale, CA, 1985, Edu-Kinesthetics.

12. deQuiros JB, Schrager OL: *Neuropsychological fundamentals in learning disabilities*, Novato, CA, 1979, Academic Therapy.

13. Duane D, Gray B, editors: *The reading brain: the biological basis of dyslexia*, Parkton, MD, 1991, York Press.

14. Dunn JM, Fait H: *Special physical education*, Dubuque, IA, 1989, Wm. C. Brown.

15. EDLAW, Inc.: *Individuals with disabilities education act*, Potomac, MD, 1991, Author.

16. Eichstaedt CB, Kalakian LH: *Developmental/adapted physical education*, New York, 1987, Macmillan.

17. Fawcett AJ, Nicolson RI: Performance of dyslexic children on cerebellar and cognitive tests, *J of Motor Behavior* 31:68–78, 1999.

18. Frostig M, Maslow P: *Movement education: theory and practice*, Chicago, 1970, Follett.

19. Grant D: *Brainstem level auditory function in specific dyslexics and normal readers*, Ann Arbor, 1980, University of Michigan Press, DAI 3376-B.

20. Hoehn T, Baumeister A: A critique of the application of sensory integration theory to children with learning disabilities, *J of LD* 27:338–350, 1994.

21. Johns ER: *Neurometric evaluation of brain function in normal and learning disabled children*, Ann Arbor, 1991, University of Michigan Press.

22. Karr R, Hughes K: Movement difficulty and learning disabled children, *Adapt Phys Act Q* 5:72–79, 1987.

23. Kephart N: *The slow learner in the classroom*, Columbus, OH, 1971, Charles E. Merrill.

24. Leary PM, Batho K: The role of the EEG in the investigation of the child with learning disability, *S Afr Med J* June: 867–868, 1981.

25. Millay K, Grant D, Pyfer J: *Structural and functional differences in brain organization in developmental dyslexics*. Unpublished paper, Denton, TX, 1991, Texas Woman's University.

26. Morrison D, Hinshaw S, Corte E: Signs of neurobehavioral dysfunction in a sample of learning disabled children: stability and concurrent validity, *Percept Mot Skills* 61:863–872, 1985.

27. Naylor MW, Staskowski M, Kenney MC, King CA: Language disorders and learning disabilities in school-refusing adolescents, *J Am Acad Child Adolesc Psychiatry* 33:1331–1337, 1994.

28. Pyfer JL: *Sensory-perceptual-motor characteristics of learning disabled children: a validation study*. Unpublished paper, Denton, TX, 1983, Texas Woman's University.

29. Rimmer JH, Kelly LE: Gross motor development in preschool children with learning disabilities, *APAQ* 6:268–279, 1989.

30. Rock EE, Fessler MA, Church RP: The concomitance of learning disabilities and emotional/behavioral disorders: a conceptual model, *J of Learning Disab* 30:245–263, 1997.

31. Woodard RJ, Surburg PR: Fundamental gross motor skill performance by girls and boys with learning disabilities, *Percept Mot Skills* 84: 867–870, 1997.

SUGGESTED READINGS

Ayres AJ: *Sensory integration and the child*, Los Angeles, 1980, Western Psychological Services.

Morris GS, Stiehl J: *Changing kids' games*, Champaign, IL, 1998, Human Kinetics.

Rich, J: *Gym Dandy series*, Durham, NC, 1994, Great Activities.

RECOMMENDED WEBSITES

Please note: These websites are being recommended in the fall of 1999. Given the ever changing nature of the Internet, these sites may have moved or been replaced by the time you are reading this text.

Dyslexia, the Gift
  http://www.parentsplace.com/readroom/dyslexia/
            index.cgi

Special Education Resources on the Internet (SERI)
  http://www.hood.edu

RECOMMENDED VIDEOS

Dyslexia: A Different Kind of Mind
color, $129 purchase price
Films for the Humanities & Sciences
PO Box 2053
Princeton, NJ 08543

Dyslexia in the Primary Classroom
color, $149 purchase price
Films for the Humanities & Sciences
PO Box 2053
Princeton, NJ 08543

Learning Disabled
color, $129 purchase price
Films for the Humanities & Sciences
PO Box 2053
Princeton, NJ 08543

Understanding Learning Disabilities
16 minutes, color, $125 purchase price

Aquarius Health Care Videos
5 Powderhouse Lane
PO Box 1159
Sherborn, MA 01770

We're Not Stupid: Living with a Learning Difference
15 minutes, color, $125 purchase price
Aquarius Health Care Videos
5 Powderhouse Lane
PO Box 1159
Sherborn, MA 01770

Video of National Center for Learning Disabilities 1999 Summit to Reveal Keys to Learning success for all Children (available online) http://www.ncld.org/summit99keys99-top.htm

CHAPTER

14

Courtesy Dallas Independent School District.

Conduct, Behavior, and Emotional Disorders

■ OBJECTIVES

Briefly explain the varied types of conduct, behavior, and emotional disorders.

Explain the causes of conduct, behavior, and emotional disorders.

Briefly describe the effect of urbanization on mental health.

Describe behavior-management strategies that the physical educator can use in the gymnasium.

Explain the physical education teacher's role in the IEP process.

Briefly explain the activities that should be emphasized in the physical education program for learners with conduct, behavior, and emotional disorders.

Over one-third of all "new" teachers will leave the profession in the first three years of their career. Most of these teachers leave because of the frustrations of dealing with inappropriate student behavior.

This chapter will deal with the continuum of student conduct, behavior, and emotional disorders. In its least serious form, a student may choose to ignore a teacher's directions the morning after his mother "grounded him" for being late for curfew. In its most serious, and sociopathological form, the student may commit suicide or shoot his or her classmates and teachers. The physical educator must be prepared to deal with any and all of these possibilities.

CASE STUDY

Logan

Logan is a sixteen-year-old boy. Until his parents divorced when Logan was thirteen, he had been an excellent student-athlete, a member of the junior high school track and cross-country teams. Logan now spends one-half of his year with his mother and one-half of his year with his father; he also splits his time between two high schools.

During the past several months, Logan has become increasingly disruptive and argumentative in class. In the gym, Logan attempted to hit a classmate with a baseball bat; the teacher and several other students had to break up the fight. Logan was placed in in-school suspension for a week. He attended an alternative school for one month after he had been found using alcohol on the school campus.

He has just returned to his general high school campus. The physical educator has reported the following behavior to the Assistant Principal responsible for discipline:

- Verbally aggressive behavior, particularly swearing, directed at his classmates and the teacher
- Physically aggressive behavior, including, pushing, shoving, and tripping his classmates; throwing and kicking balls at others; and swinging bats and racquets at other children
- Destroying equipment
- Exhibiting violent mood swings with no apparent trigger
- Refusing to obey teacher requests and rules

APPLICATION TASK
Can the physical educator help Logan? How?

A critical part of teaching all children in this society is the process of creating an emotionally safe physical education program. John Helion wrote,

> What constitutes safe physical education? A physically and emotionally safe program is developmentally appropriate. It allows students

to succeed because the lessons are planned around their needs and abilities. A safe educational setting is one in which there is no fear of trying because there is no fear of ridicule, where students will attempt something new because there is no penalty for failure, and where students are free to grow as individuals because they are not being constantly compared with or pitted against their classmates.[23]

DEFINITION OF CONDUCT, BEHAVIOR, AND EMOTIONAL DISORDERS

A conduct disorder is typically associated with specific actions, or failure to act, which causes a student to be in trouble within the home, school, or community. Behavior and emotional disorders are conditions in which the behavior or emotional responses of a student are so different from generally accepted, age-appropriate, ethnic, or cultural norms as to result in significant impairment in self-care, social relationships, educational progress, classroom behavior, work adjustment[39] or personal happiness.[27]

However, in a very diverse society, behavior that is acceptable in some groups is unacceptable in others.[27] Thus, some of the elements defining a specific behavior disorder may be (1) a description of the problem behavior, (2) the setting in which the problem behavior occurs, and (3) the person who regards the behavior as a problem.

The physical educator and other school professionals are faced, increasingly, with a larger society in which the understanding of appropriate behavior is not clear. For example, seemingly responsible adults engage in road-rage behaviors they would never demonstrate at work. These same, seemingly responsible adults use language in the locker room they would never use in front of a spouse or their own children. Television and radio programs, videos, and video games are increasingly violent and pornographic and include offensive language. There is widespread confusion regarding what is and what is not acceptable behavior.

The school is, very simply, a microcosm of the larger society. Though expectations regarding student behavior were very clear for the teachers on *Little House on the Prairie,* and parents supported teacher decisions regarding behavior, that is simply no longer true within the contemporary public education system. The challenges are overwhelming but must be addressed.

The reauthorization of the Individuals with Disabilities Education Act, 1999, eliminated the word "serious" from the description of students eligible to receive special education services. Previously the term describing students eligible to receive educational services was "serious emotional disturbance."

Emotional disturbance is defined in IDEA Sec 300.7 as follows:

(i) The term means a condition exhibiting one or more of the following characteristics over a long period of time and to a marked degree that adversely affects a child's educational performance:
  (A) An inability to learn that cannot be explained by intellectual, sensory, or health factors.
  (B) An inability to build or maintain satisfactory interpersonal relationships with peers and teachers.
  (C) Inappropriate types of behavior or feelings under normal circumstances.
  (D) A general pervasive mood of unhappiness or depression.
  (E) A tendency to develop physical symptoms or fears associated with personal or school problems.
(ii) The term includes schizophrenia. The term does not apply to children who are socially maladjusted, unless it is determined that they have an emotional disturbance.[4]

It must be understood that federally mandated *special education* services are available only to students who have been assessed and determined to have a serious emotional disturbance. Students with other disorders may be able to receive support as a result of other federal initiatives—for example, programs designed to prevent truancy—and/or support from school-based counseling, music therapy, and gang reduction programs.

CONTINUUM OF CONDUCT, BEHAVIOR, AND EMOTIONAL DISORDERS

Conduct, behavior, and emotional disorders must be considered within the realm of a continuum of behaviors from those that are deemed "appropriate" to those that are deemed "inappropriate," or from those that are considered "socially acceptable" to those that are considered "socially unacceptable." It must be understood that within the broad continuum of conduct, behavior, and emotional disorders there exists a continuum within each separate type of disorder. For example, a student may experience significant anxiety when faced with state-mandated achievement tests; this anxiety is transient and usually ceases after the tests have been completed. Within the category of "anxiety disorders," a student may have school phobia so traumatic that the student must be home schooled.

Conduct, Behavior, and Emotional Disorders of School-Age Children

- Conduct disorders
  - Oppositional-defiant disorder
- Anxiety disorders
  - Phobia
  - Posttraumatic stress disorder
  - Panic disorder
- Dissociative disorders
  - Amnesia
  - Dissociative identity disorder
- Personality disorders
  - Odd/eccentric
  - Dramatic/erratic
  - Anxious/inhibited
- Mood disorders
  - Childhood Bipolar disorder
  - Childhood depression
- Emotional disorders
  - Childhood schizophrenia
- Suicidal behaviors

Students who find themselves in situations in which there is a significant conflict between the expectations of the professionals in the school system

Establishing a friendship with an animal may be the first step in trusting.
Courtesy Recreation Services, Division of Care and Treatment Facilities, Department of Health and Social Services, Northern Wisconsin Center for the Developmentally Delayed.

and the expectations of the parents and immediate community struggle to make sense of their reality. One of the problems associated with the classification and identification of conduct, behavior, and emotional disorders is that the determination of "appropriate" and "acceptable" behavior is situational. A student who is praised in his or her home for being an active, inquisitive, curious learner who readily questions adults while seeking information may be perceived as "insolent" by an insecure teacher who expects students to accept the teacher's opinions as gospel. Students whose parents, and immediate community, share a distrust of the "system" may, for example, refuse to give their child Ritalin for fear it is a tool of the "system" to depress and subjugate their children.

Of significant concern is the fact that African American students are more highly represented in special education classes that serve students with conduct, behavior, and emotional disorders.[36] This overrepresentation is caused by a significant failure to embrace active/interactive learning styles. Essentially, there appears to be a "mismatch" between the cognitive (learning) styles of children from minority cultural groups and the cognitive styles emphasized in the schools. As a result, children may be inappropriately identified as

having a conduct, behavior, or emotional disorder and may be inappropriately taught, increasing the disorder.[34]

The situation is a significant component of the determination of a conduct, behavior, or emotional disorder. The severity of the behavior is another important variable. Almost everyone occasionally reacts to stress, fatigue, grief, or uncertainty in ways that might be considered "abnormal" or "inappropriate." For example, faced with the death of her beloved dog, a professional may crawl into bed for several days, watching endless, mindless television before returning to work. If that behavior were to continue for weeks or months, the individual could be determined to be clinically depressed. For example, faced with the imminent break-up of her parents, a teenage girl may engage in binge drinking for a period of time. If that behavior were to persist, the girl may be considered clinically depressed and may be referred for an alcoholism evaluation.

Although, typically, a conduct, behavior, or emotional disorder is one in which a specific behavior, or a cluster of behaviors, persists over a period of time, one significant, atypical, antisocial behavior may be an indicator of a significant emotional disorder that may have been unnoticed or undiagnosed. For example, a second-grader who stabs a classmate with a knife in order to join his older brother's gang may never have exhibited this type of antisocial behavior before, yet the significance and nature of the behavior make it vital for serious consideration to be given the child's emotional disorder.

TYPES OF CONDUCT, BEHAVIOR, AND EMOTIONAL DISORDERS

It is important for the physical educator to distinguish carefully between the student who may, occasionally, misbehave and the student who has been diagnosed as having a conduct, behavior, or emotional disorder. As teachers struggle to teach more and more students who will not follow rules, reject discipline, and despise authority, the lines between students who exhibit problematic behavior and those who actually have a psychoeducational diagnosis become distorted.

Conduct Disorders

Bailey described a conduct disorder as follows:

> Conduct disorder in childhood includes excessive levels of fighting or bullying; cruelty to animals or other people; severe destructiveness to property; fire setting, stealing, repeated lying; frequent and severe temper tantrums; defiant provocative behavior and persistent severe disobedience; truancy from school; and running away from home. One of the most prevalent types of conduct disorders is oppositional-defiant disorder.[3]
>
> **"Oppositional-Defiant Disorder"**
> Oppositional-Defiant Disorder is antisocial behavior characterized by extreme disobedience, aggression, loss of temper, arguing with adults and others in authority. Literally, these children "sit" when asked to "stand" and "run" when asked to "walk."[17]

See Figure 14-1 for behaviors of children with conduct disorder and Figure 14-2 for the diagnostic criteria of conduct disorder.

Figure 14-1 Behaviors of Children with Conduct Disorder[6]

- Lack sensitivity to the feelings of other children
- Act aggressively with little remorse
- Tend to be suspicious
- Believe other children are threatening
- Have difficulty tolerating frustration
- Are impulsive
- Are reckless

Boys tend to
- Fight
- Steal
- Vandalize

Girls tend to
- Lie
- Bully
- Run away

Anxiety Disorders

Anxiety disorders cause intense feelings of anxiety and tension when there is no real danger. The symptoms cause significant distress and interfere with daily activities. Sufferers of anxiety disorders usually take extreme measures to avoid situations that provoke anxiety. The physical signs of anxiety are restlessness, irritability, disturbed sleep, muscle aches and pains, gastrointestinal distress, and difficulty concentrating. Anxiety disorders are often accompanied by the symptoms of depression and can lead to chronic anxiety such as phobia, posttraumatic stress disorder, or panic disorder.

Phobia

A phobia is a significant, persistent, yet unrealistic and often debilitating fear of an event, a person, an activity, or an animal/insect. For example, school phobia is a significant, and often debilitating, fear of going to school. Hydrophobia is a fear of water. Agoraphobia ("fear of the marketplace" in Greek) is an anxiety disorder characterized by intense fear of being caught or trapped in situations where no help is available should some incapacitating (e.g., losing control) or embarrassing (e.g., fainting) event occur in the presence of others. Agoraphobia can be brought on by repeated panic attacks and over time, if untreated, can lead to the fear of leaving one's house.

Posttraumatic Stress Disorder

A posttraumatic stress disorder is characterized by an overwhelming traumatic event that is re-experienced; this causes intense fear, helplessness, horror, and avoidance of stimuli associated with the trauma.[6] Posttraumatic stress disorder used to be a term associated with combat veterans and victims of criminal violence. Increasingly, children living in abusive homes and children who are living in homes within violent communities are demonstrating the symptoms associated with posttraumatic stress disorder.

Panic Disorder

Many children experience occasional panic attacks. Few suffer from panic disorder, which

Figure 14-2   Diagnostic Criteria of Conduct Disorders

A. A repetitive and persistent pattern of behavior in which the basic rights of others or major age-appropriate societal norms or rules are violated, as manifested by the presence of three (or more) of the following criteria in the past twelve months, with at least one criterion present in the past six months:

Aggression to people and animals
1. Often bullies, threatens, or intimidates others
2. Often initiates physical fights
3. Has used a weapon that can cause serious physical harm to others
4. Has been physically cruel to people
5. Has been physically cruel to animals
6. Has stolen while confronting a victim (e.g., mugging)
7. Has forced someone into sexual activity

Destruction of property
8. Has deliberately engaged in fire setting with the intention of causing serious damage
9. Has deliberately destroyed others' property

Deceitfulness or theft
10. Has broken into another's house, building, or car
11. Often lies to obtain goods or favors
12. Has stolen items without confronting a victim (e.g., shoplifting)

Serious violations of rules
13. Stays out at night despite parental rules, beginning before age thirteen years
14. Has run away from home overnight at least twice while living in parent or surrogate home (or once for a lengthy stay)
15. Is often truant from school, beginning before age thirteen years

B. The disturbance in behavior causes clinically significant impairment in social, academic, or occupational functioning.

C. If the individual is age eighteen years or older, criteria are not met for antisocial personality disorder.

Modified from: http://www.mentalhealth.com/dis1/

usually originates in adolescence and is more common among women than men.[6] See Figure 14-3 for the symptoms associated with a panic attack.

Dissociative Disorder

A dissociative disorder is one in which the individual is unable to integrate his or her memories, perceptions, identity, or consciousness normally.[6] The dissociative disorders include amnesia and dissociative identity disorder.

Amnesia

Amnesia is partial or complete loss of memory, which can be caused by head injury or severe psychological trauma.

Figure 14-3   Symptoms of a Panic Attack[6]

Nausea or abdominal distress
Numbness
Tingling sensations
Sweating
Trembling or shaking
Shortness of breath
Choking
Dizziness
Crying
Chest pain or discomfort

Dissociative Identity Disorder or Multiple Personality Disorder

This is characterized by two or more identities or personalities that alternately take over the person's behavior.[6] Although this has been overdramatized and misrepresented on television and in movies, this is a serious, although uncommon, disorder.

Personality Disorder

The *DSM-IV* divides personality disorders into three clusters, the odd/eccentric, dramatic/erratic, and anxious/inhibited.[2]

Odd/Eccentric

Odd/eccentric personality disorders include paranoid personality and schizoid personality. A person with a paranoid personality tend to be cold and controlling in interpersonal relationships and act with suspicion in interactions. A schizoid personality is one in which the person is introverted, withdrawn, solitary, cold emotionally, and distant.[6]

Dramatic/Erratic

This cluster of disorders includes borderline personality, in which the person is unstable in self-image, mood, behavior, and interpersonal relationships. An antisocial personality is one in which an individual exploits others, suffers from an inability to tolerate frustration, and acts out in compulsive and hostile ways. A narcissistic personality is one in which the person believes himself or herself to be superior and expects and demands that others acknowledge the superiority. An individual with a histrionic personality seeks attention, sympathy, or sexual activity in a dramatic and theatrical way.[6]

Anxious/Inhibited

The cluster of personality disorders described as anxious/inhibited includes a dependent personality, in which the person completely surrenders responsibility for his or her own life to others. Another personality disorder within this cluster is an avoidant personality; the person avoids fear and rejection by withdrawing from human interaction. An obsessive-compulsive disorder is characterized by recurrent, unwanted, intrusive ideas, images, or impulses that seem silly, weird, nasty, or horrible (obsessions) and by urges to do something that will lessen the discomfort due to the obsessions (compulsions).[6] Students with obsessive-compulsive disorders feel compelled to perform repetitive, purposeful behaviors to control their obsessions.[6] For example, the student may need to wash his or her hands hundreds of times a day in order to prevent contamination. Or the child may endlessly pick lint from a sweater to keep the sweater clean.

Mood Disorders

Mood disorders are characterized by significant and prolonged moods over which the learner has little or no control. Two of the most serious of these mood disorders are childhood bipolar disorder and childhood depression.

Childhood Bipolar Disorder or Manic/Depression

Bipolar disorder is a serious, debilitating disorder that involves extreme mood swings or highs (mania) and lows (depression). During the manic phase, the individual may be elated, irritable, or hostile. The child may experience inflated self-esteem and may be boastful. The child may be overactive, experience weight loss because of increased activity, and may not require sleep. In the depressive phase, the individual may be depressed, irritable, or anxious. The child may lack self-confidence and have low self-esteem. The child may focus on the negative and appear hopeless and helpless. The child will experience significant fatigue.[6]

Childhood Depression

Childhood depression is a mood disorder among children that resembles depression in adults but shows up in very different ways in children. Children with depression may appear persistently sad, may no longer enjoy activities they normally enjoyed, or may frequently appear agitated, or irritable. Depressed children may frequently complain

Figure 14-4 Characteristics of Childhood Schizophrenia[8]

- Most children with childhood schizophrenia have subtle, soft neurological signs of brain abnormalities.
- The largest risk factor for childhood schizophrenia is having an affected relative.
- Prenatal and perinatal exposure to viral infections and fetal hypoxia appear to be risk factors which may be preventable.
- Most children with childhood schizophrenia show developmental delays in speech, cognition, play, and motor development.
- Most children with childhood schizophrenia have significant educational delays.

Figure 14-5 High-Risk Factors and Behaviors Associated with Suicide[6]

- Male sex
- Talking about suicide
- Previous suicide attempt
- Making detailed suicide plans
- Family history of suicide or affective disorder
- Social isolation
- Depression
- Anxiety, restlessness, and motor agitation
- Significant feelings of guilt, inadequacy, and hopelessness
- Impulsive, hostile personality
- Alcohol or drug abuse
- Preoccupation with death and dying
- Loss of interest in things in which the person was previously interested
- Calling relatives and friends with whom the person rarely has contact
- Giving away possessions
- Getting one's affairs in order

of physical problems such as headaches and stomachaches and often have frequent absences from school or poor performance in school. They may appear bored or low in energy and frequently have problems concentrating. A major change in eating or sleeping patterns is frequently a sign of depression in children and adolescents.

Emotional Disorder

An emotional disorder is one of the most significant in the continuum of conduct, behavior, and emotional disorders. One of the more devastating, to the child and family alike, is childhood schizophrenia. Childhood schizophrenia is part of a continuum with the adult form of schizophrenia.[6] The behavior of children with schizophrenia is characterized by withdrawal, apathy, flat affect, thought disorder, hallucinations (perceiving stimuli which do not exist), and delusions (a tendency to take on the personality of another). See Figure 14-4 for more characteristics of childhood schizophrenia.

Suicidal Behavior

In the United States, about seventy-five people commit suicide every day. Suicide is epidemic, particularly among adolescents; it is the second leading cause of death, second only to accidents.[6]

Suicidal behavior includes suicide gestures, attempted suicide, and completed suicide. Suicidal behavior also includes plans and actions that appear to be unlikely to be successful; it is believed that these plans and actions are, indeed, a plea for help. An attempted suicide is an act that is not fatal; this may also be a significant plea for help. See Figure 14-5 for the high-risk factors and behaviors associated with suicide.

INCIDENCE OF CONDUCT, BEHAVIOR, AND EMOTIONAL DISORDERS

Conduct, behavior, and emotional disorders exist on a continuum. Because of the significant stigma attached to conduct, behavior, and emotional disorders, the reported incidence is probably significantly lower than the actual number of individuals who struggle with these disorders. It is also important to acknowledge the fact that special education services provided for students with conduct, behavior, and emotional disturbances are limited to those students who have been identified as having a "serious emotional disturbance."

There has been an ever increasing incidence of "serious emotional disturbance" in children from birth to twenty-one years of age served in federally supported programs for individuals with disabilities. In 1976-1977, just after the initial implementation of P.L. 94-142, there were 283,000 students identified as having a serious emotional disturbance. That number has increased steadily and dramatically in the past twenty years. In the 1996-1997 academic year, 446,000 students with serious emotional disturbance were served in special education programs. That number represented 7.5 percent of the students served in special education.

The percentages of students with "serious emotional disturbance" who were served in particular education settings follow:

General education class	22.1%
Resource room	24.0%
Separate class	35.2%
Public school separate facility	8.3%
Private school separate facility (only students who have "multiple disabilities" are more likely to receive educational services in a private school facility)	5.4%
Public residential facility	1.7%
Private residential facility	1.6%
Hospital/homebound environment	1.8%[45]

CAUSES OF CONDUCT, BEHAVIOR, AND EMOTIONAL DISORDERS

The causes of conduct, behavior, and emotional disorders can only be understood within the broad context of the total ecosystem of the individual. The disorders are a function of the interaction of a number of variables:

- Heredity and genetic predisposition
- Biochemical and neurotransmitter imbalance, which may be congenital, appearing in utero and at birth; this may occur as a result of glandular dysfunction and may be adventitious, caused by the use or abuse of alcohol or other drugs

- Neuroendocrine imbalance[10]
- Low birth weight and decreased head circumference[8]
- Significant failure of the parent to regulate homeostatic and physiological status of the infant[10]
- Breakdown in the family unit
- Parental mood disorders, particularly in the mother, characterized by withdrawal, depression, or hostility[10]
- Parental conflict[44]
- Parenting difficulties; conduct, behavior, and emotional disorders are particularly linked to abusive families
- Sexual and physical abuse and emotional neglect[1, 50]
- Lack of support by the extended family
- Poverty[3]
- Peer pressure, particularly gang involvement
- Community expectations regarding behavior
- Environmental toxins
- Inappropriate, inflexible teaching strategies
- Discrimination

Grossman[22] indicates that teachers may contribute to conduct, behavior, and emotional disorders in the schools by discriminating against the students and criticizing them in a harsh manner.

The causes of conduct, behavior, and emotional disorders may actually be systemic and profound. There is considerable evidence that the very process by which urbanization has occurred is causative in psychoses, depression, sociopathy, substance abuse, alcoholism, crime, delinquency, vandalism, family disintegration, and alienation.[32] See Figure 14-6 for more information about urbanization and mental illness.

CHARACTERISTICS OF CONDUCT, BEHAVIOR, AND EMOTIONAL DISORDERS

Learners with conduct, behavior, or emotional disorders constitute a very heterogeneous group. The physical educator seeking to teach learners with conduct, behavior, and emotional disorders must

Figure 14-6   Urbanization and the Causes of Mental Health and Social Deviancy[32]

Environmental
- Air pollution and toxins (lead, carbon monoxide)
- Noise pollution
- Traffic congestion, accidents, road rage
- Excessive stimulation

Sociological and economic
- Poverty
- Unemployment and underemployment
- Crime, violence, and gangs
- Crowded and substandard housing/ homelessness
- Marginalization

Psychosocial
- Family disintegration
- Cultural disintegration and confusion
- Racism and secularization

Psychological
- Powerlessness
- Isolation and loneliness
- Fear and anxiety
- Lack of quality of life

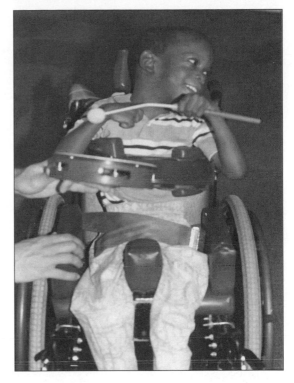

Make a joyous noise.

work closely with the learners' parents, the school counselor, and the learners' primary educators within the school building. This is critical in order to learn each student's specific conduct, behavior, and emotional characteristics.

Learners with conduct, behavior, or emotional disorders struggle within the school setting. Disruptive and antisocial learners, in particular, are excluded from school groups and find it difficult to maintain friendships. They tend to seek out each other and form separatist groups.[30]

There is considerable evidence that children and youth with conduct, behavior, or emotional disorders have educational difficulties:

- Many children and youth with conduct, behavior, and emotional disorders receive inappropriate educational, social, and medical services; as a result, families make tremendous financial sacrifices to secure needed services for their children.[11,28]

- Most students who have been diagnosed with an emotional disorder have lower grade point averages than their classmates.[49]

- Almost 40 percent have learning disabilities,[27] not to be confused with problems learning.

- Almost 50 percent fail at least one high school course.[49]

- One-fifth are arrested once before they drop out of school.[49]

- More than half leave school without graduating (most by the tenth grade).[46]

When children and youth are struggling with conduct, behavior, and emotional issues, the physical education teacher may be one of the first to notice the signs that a student is in trouble and needs help. The very nature of a physical education class—a great deal of movement, excitement, and noise and the necessity to work as part of a team—make some conduct, behavior, and emotional disorders more evident than they would be if a learner were just sitting at a desk. The signs that a learner may need help include

1. Learning
   a. Poor work habits in practicing and developing motor skills
   b. Lack of motivation in achieving goals not of an immediate nature
   c. Disruptive class behavior
   d. Lack of involvement in class activities
   e. Inability to follow directions
   f. Unwillingness to seek help
   g. Demands for constant attention by the teacher and other students
   h. Short attention span
   i. Poor coordination
   j. Development of physical symptoms (stomachache, headache, etc.) when confronted with physical activities with which the person is not secure
   k. Overactivity
   l. Restlessness
   m. Distractibility
   n. Forgetfulness
   o. Memory impairment[10]
   p. Daydreaming
   q. Fear of teacher and other adults
   r. Fear of other children
   s. Resistance to authority
   t. Fear of criticism
2. Interpersonal relationships
   a. Lack of conscience
   b. Loss of emotional control
   c. Formation of superficial relationships, if relationships are formed
   d. Shyness
   e. Hypersensitivity
   f. Detachment
   g. Unsocialized aggressiveness
   h. Hostility
   i. Quarrelsomeness
   j. Destructiveness
   k. Temper tantrums
   l. Hostile disobedience
   m. Physical and verbal aggressiveness
   n. Group values of delinquency
   o. Fear
   p. Flight reaction
   q. Apprehension
   r. Anxiety
   s. Feelings of inadequacy
   t. Disrespect of others
3. Inappropriate behavior under normal conditions
   a. Unhappiness or depression
   b. Inconsistencies in responses
   c. Rigid expectations of everyday life
   d. Carelessness, irresponsibility, and apathy
   e. Immaturity
   f. Timidity
   g. Feelings of rejection
   h. Tendency to seek retribution
   i. Aggressive behavior
   j. Withdrawal and self-isolation
   k. Negativism
   l. Noncooperation and contrariness
   m. Unreasonable expectations regarding own behavior (Cicchetti)[10]
   n. Incorrigibility
   o. Impulsiveness
   p. Repetitious behavior
   q. Aimless behavior
   r. Disorderliness
   s. Tendency to giggle or cry for no apparent reason
   t. Change of modes
   u. Physical and verbal abusiveness
   v. Tendency to attribute hostile intentions to the conduct of others (Bailey)[3]
4. Physical and motor characteristics
   a. Poor physical condition caused by withdrawal from activity
   b. Retardation of motor skill development caused by withdrawal from activity
   c. Disorientation in space and time
   d. Poor body image

TESTING

The student with a conduct, behavior, or emotional disorder is typically able to participate in any state- or local education agency-mandated physical fitness, motor, sport skill, or knowledge assessments regarding rules, techniques, and/or health/wellness concepts. Decisions regarding who will administer such tests is often left to the IEP or multidisciplinary team and may be a function of the placement of the student in general or adapted physical education.

If the student has been identified as having a motor deficit, the choice of assessment instruments is determined primarily by the student's age. The Test of Gross Motor Development may be very appropriate for an elementary-school-age student with a conduct, behavior, or emotional disorder. The Louisiana Competency Test in Adapted Physical Education may be very useful for a student in middle school or high school.

When testing students who have conduct, behavior, or emotional disorders, the teacher must be sensitive to the fact that these students may feel extremely threatened by test situations. When placed in threatening situations, more acting-out behavior can be expected. Aggressive or withdrawing behaviors can be avoided if the student does not have to perform in the presence of peers and if the teacher is supportive of the student's efforts. It is usually advisable, if testing a student with a serious disorder, to include the student's favorite teacher or a significant peer in the testing situation. The physical educator should be aware of the fact that the most appropriate assessment of a learner with conduct, behavior, or emotional disturbance includes not only an assessment of the learner but of the learner's parents as well.[3]

SPECIAL CONSIDERATIONS

One of the major problems associated with the education of students with conduct, behavior, and emotional disorders is the stigma attached to the label of disorder. A stigma means a mark or sign of shame, disgrace or disapproval, of being shunned or rejected by others. Individuals who struggle with emotional disorders and their families may feel stigmatized and rejected and, in fact, may be stigmatized and rejected. Unfortunately, this stigma often causes families to avoid seeking pro-

fessional help so that identification of a problem is delayed.

Cicchetti and Toth wrote,

Evidence . . . suggests that the failure of the school environment to facilitate development as children progress into middle schools may contribute to motivational and mental health problems. Inappropriate school environments during early adolescence can place many young children at risk for the negative trajectories that some lives take, including alienation from prosocial activities and peers, depression, and involvement in antisocial pursuits.[10]

The education of learners with disabilities cannot be seen in a framework outside of the family unit. Family management practices are key to the collaboration between the school and the home:

- Parents learn how to identify problematic behavior and track occurrences of the behavior at home.
- Parents learn to use reinforcement techniques such as praise, point systems, and rewards.
- Parents learn to use a "mild" consequence for inappropriate behavior, such as a one-hour loss of computer or video-game use.
- Parents are taught specific strategies to monitor their child's behavior.
- Parents are taught strategies to communicate clearly with their child. They learn to use "alpha" commands or instructions instead of "beta" commands. An alpha command is clear, specific, and direct and allows the child a limited time to respond. A "beta" command or instruction is one that is vague and conveys only frustration and anger. For example, if a parent wants the child to put toys away, an alpha command is "William, put your toys in the closet." A beta command, however, is "William, I've had a really long day. And I need some cooperation around the house. I can't be expected to work all day and worry about dinner and then come home and find the house is a mess. The least you could do is put away your toys." The physical educator also needs to learn to use alpha commands.[3,21]

It is important for physical educators, and other educators, to be aware of one emotional disorder of parents of children with disabilities that is receiving increasing attention. Munchausen by proxy is a fascinating and frightening disorder in which the parent, almost always the mother, harms her own child. The child abuse is pervasive and destructive. The psychological illness and substantial need of the mother is the major clinical symptom. The mother appears to medical and educational personnel to be very caring and concerned and, apparently, feeds off the emotions shared by these personnel. Typically, the harm is done in one of three ways:

1. The mother lies about symptoms or signs associated with an illness or a disability, including heating a thermometer to demonstrate elevated fever.
2. The mother actually alters medical records or laboratory specimens, including tampering with urine, blood, or fecal samples.
3. The mother causes the illness or disability. Some of the common reported abuses include
   a. Drug poisoning, using over-the-counter, illegal, and prescription medication (prescribed for someone else)
   b. Salt poisoning, including adding salt to breastmilk
   c. False allegations regarding sexual or physical abuse
   d. Inducing asthma, diabetic coma, etc. by withholding medications[24,41]

DISCIPLINE FOR CHILDREN WITH DISABILITIES

The 1999 Reauthorization of IDEA included some key changes regarding discipline for children with disabilities. These changes reflect serious consideration of the concerns of school administrators and teachers regarding

- Ensuring school safety
- Helping schools respond appropriately to a child's behavior
- Promoting the use of appropriate behavioral interventions
- Increasing the likelihood of success in school and school completion for at-risk students.

School personnel have the ability to remove a child for short periods of time as long as the removal does not constitute a change of placement. In this regulation, a disciplinary "change of placement" occurs when a child is removed for more than ten consecutive school days or when the child is subjected to *a series of removals that constitute a pattern* because they cumulate to more than 10 school days in a school year, and because of factors such as the length of the removal, the total amount of time the child is removed, and the proximity of the removals to one another (Sec. 300.519).

If the removal is pursuant to school personnel's authority to remove for not more than ten consecutive days (Sec. 300.520(a)(1)) or for behavior that is not a manifestation of the child's disability, consistent with Sec. 300.524 services must be provided to the extent necessary to enable the child to continue to appropriately progress in the general curriculum and appropriately advance toward the goals in his or her IEP (Sec. 300.121(d)).

Changes in the IDEA emphasize the need of state and local educational agencies to work to ensure that superintendents, principals, teachers, and other school personnel are equipped with the knowledge and skills that will enable them to appropriately address behavior problems when they occur.

The early identification of children who are at risk for conduct, behavior, and emotional disorders is critical. It is recognized that the earlier educators and mental health specialists can address the problem, the greater the prospect for preventing, ameliorating, or remedying the disorder. It is important to note, however that, in the absence of obvious external behaviors (a preschooler setting his apartment on fire or sexually molesting another child, for example), it is difficult to predict future conduct, behavior, and emotional disorders in young children.[7] Certainly, prevention is the key.

Teachers who work with toddlers and preschoolers have the unique privilege and responsibility to

- Help toddlers and preschoolers identify violence and its consequences[40]
- Talk openly with young children about real-world violence[40]
- Respond to young children's reactions to violence[40]
- Help them develop basic safety skills for self-protection[40]
- Never use corporal punishment; clearly, the last thing they need in their lives is more violence
- Work closely with families to help parents help their children deal with violence[40]

See Chapter 10 for specific suggestions regarding facilitating play in infants, toddlers, and preschoolers and strategies for helping young children deal with violence.

The physical educator should be aware that many children with conduct, behavior, and emotional disorders take medication that affects their performance during the school day. It is critical that the physical educator be aware of the medications a student is taking, particularly because some may inhibit motor control and have a negative impact on balance, for example. No attempt will be made in this chapter to list the types of medications and the potential impact on the child. Pharmacology is a rapidly evolving discipline; the drugs that are prescribed at the end of the 20th century will, most certainly, have changed by the beginning of the 21st century.

Most parents are thrilled if the physical educator takes enough interest in the student to ask for specific information regarding a medication. A physician will not release information about medication—or anything else, for that matter—to a teacher without signed parent permission. Most state education agencies have a standard form to request a release of information from a physician. The physical educator can ask the school nurse to complete such a request.

Psychological tests are required to establish the presence of conduct, behavior, and emotional disorders. However, the psychological data and the labels associated with the data often do not provide specific information to assist the physical education teacher in planning instruction. The physical educator should work closely with the child's special education teachers and counselors to plan and modify instruction. If at all possible, the physical educator should adopt the instructional strategies and behavior-management strategies used during the rest of the child's instructional day. This type of consistency is critical to the success of a student with a conduct, behavior, or emotional disorder. This will be considered more completely later in this chapter.

Specific ways the physical educator can collaborate with other professionals who work with the student as well as the student's IEP team are as follows:

- Share information about the student's physical and motor needs
- Listen and act on relevant suggestions made by parents and other professionals
- Share materials and ideas with individuals working with the student
- Solicit support from parents and colleagues that contributes to the physical education program effectiveness
- Use resource personnel effectively[16]

TEACHING STRATEGIES

The children who need great teachers the most may be the very children who are the most difficult to teach. The teacher of a child who has behavior, conduct, or emotional disorders must be grounded, self-assured, confident, patient, and competent. The teacher must be able to see the student's behavior within the broader context of a conduct, behavior, or emotional disorder and not respond to inappropriate behavior as if it were directed toward the teacher. The ability to separate self from inappropriate student behavior is critical to the effective teacher of students who have conduct, emotional, or behavior disorders. See Figures 14-7 and 14-8 for specific strategies of behavior management for the physical educator.

Figure 14-7   Behavior Management: Learners with Conduct, Behavior or Emotional Disorders[43]

- Effective intervention must duplicate the strategies used in other phases of the learner's life—school, home, recreation center, and/or work environment. This is crucial so the individual has consistent feedback and reinforcement.
- Teachers need to be well grounded and self-assured. Learners with conduct, behavior, and emotional disorders often "push the buttons" of perceived authority figures. The teacher must be secure enough to understand that inappropriate emotions/behaviors are not directed at him or her. These behaviors include but are not limited to
  - Absolute rejection of the authority figure
  - Conflicting demands. One minute the learner may be clingy, demand constant attention, and seek affection; the next moment, he or she may be shouting, "I hate you."
  - Temper tantrums, rages, and outbursts
  - Unpredictable changes in emotions and moods
  - Physical and/or verbal aggression
  - Significant withdrawal
  - Negativism, noncompliance, and refusal behaviors
  - Impulsiveness
  - Destruction of equipment and materials
- The limits and expectations regarding behavior must be clearly defined.
- Rules need to be posted in simple language or symbols or pictures. The learners need to be reminded *daily* of the rules and consequences if that behavior is not followed.
- Positive behavior and its positive consequences must be made clear. Always "catch 'em being good" and reward the appropriate behavior.
- The minimum amount of reinforcement should be used to encourage appropriate behavior:
  Smiles
  Verbal praise
  Verbal praise with a sign—"thumbs up"
  Verbal praise paired with a physical reinforcer: high, medium, low, or behind the back "5"
  Tangible reinforcers: stickers or praise notes for young learners
  Primary reinforcers: goldfish or graham crackers
- With older learners, more appropriate reinforcers may be
  Choice of activity
  "Free time"
  Choice of music to listen to in the background (careful screening is important)
  Baseball or football cards
  Sports posters
  Slice of pizza
  "Alone with me" time—teacher commits to time spent with the learner, shooting baskets or swimming laps together.
- Inappropriate behavior and its negative consequences must be clear. The learner must be reminded that the behavior and consequence is a choice. Always the consequence must occur and it must be explained to link cause-effect—e.g., "I'm sorry, Timmy, but you chose to [cite misbehavior]. You know this is the consequence."

The teacher of a child with a conduct, behavior, or emotional disorder has a tremendous responsibility. The most critical responsibility is for consistent, effective classroom management designed to prevent problems and minimize behaviors that disrupt learning. In fact, many school-based discipline strategies, such as in- and out-of-school suspensions, may actually be dumping grounds for students whose teachers simply are unprepared to manage their classroom. Nichols et al. wrote, "While classroom management and student discipline is a clear concern of teachers, parents and local communities, the effectiveness and impact of strategies

Figure 14-8   Behavior-Management Self-Check for Physical Educators

1. Are the majority of statements you make during the school day to your students in physical education *positive?*[25]
2. Are class expectations stated *positively?*[25]
3. Are class expectations and consequences reviewed regularly?
4. Do you remind students that *behavior is always a choice?*
5. Do you *always* follow through with consequences?
6. In a given day, are most of the consequences *positive?*
7. Do you know and use the names of your students? (Knowing and using their names is a basic sign of respect.)
8. Do you reinforce a student's appropriate behavior specifically, rather than making general comments that are meaningless, such as "Good job"?[25]
9. Are the activities you choose age and developmentally appropriate?
10. Are you careful *not* to use sarcasm?
11. Do you avoid verbal and physical confrontations when a student is angry?[25]
12. Do you model/teach your students the skills they need to deal with their anger?[25]
13. Do you praise in public and correct in private?
14. Do you act calm and controlled, even if you feel different?

A teenager prepares for the challenge of an above-the-ground (30 feet) ropes course.
Courtesy Wisconsin Lions Camp, Rosholt, Wis.

- Carefully model caring, sensitive, adult behavior.
- A gentle, calm, but structured teaching style will promote learning for any/all students, but particularly students with conduct, behavior, or emotional disorders.
- Teach so children with each of Gardner's eight types of intelligence can learn.
- Establish and use a set class routine.
- Set, define, and post positively worded rules and expectations that are age appropriate. Make clear not only the behaviors that are appropriate but those that are inappropriate. (See Figure 14-9 for a brief example of positive gymnasium expectations.)
- Consistently acknowledge and reward appropriate behavior.
- Consistently assure fair and humane consequences for inappropriate behavior.

such as in-school suspension, out-of-school suspension, and expulsion of students continue to be topics of great debate."[36] In fact, it appears that the practices of suspension and expulsion are associated with negative outcomes, which include poor student attitudes toward school, academic failure, retention in grades, and increased dropout rates.[36] Nichols et al. wrote, "The unfortunate circumstance of being young, male, economically deprived, and of minority status serves as a four-fold precipitator of possible disciplinary inequity in the public school system."[36]

The principles which guide the teacher of children who have conduct, behavior, or emotional disorders in physical education are, very simply, the BASIC PRINCIPLES OF GOOD TEACHING:

Figure 14-9   Gymnasium Expectations
Stated in a Positive Way

1. Raise your hand before speaking.
2. Remain on your spot until advised to leave it.
3. Keep your hands and feet to yourself.
4. Use school-appropriate language.
5. Use equipment as demonstrated.

Corporate punishment is not a fair and humane consequence in the public schools.[14]

- Remind the student of the consequences of inappropriate behavior.
- Emphasize cooperative activities. Competitive activities are appropriate only for older students who have been taught the specific skills required to deal with losing.
- Assure that each student has a designated spot with enough personal space to avoid physical contact with other students.
- Assure there is a safe space to which a student can retreat for a self-imposed "time-out."
- Have enough equipment so young children, in particular, will not have to share equipment.
- Remove distracting objects. Bats, balls, and other play equipment should be kept out of sight until the time of use, if possible.
- Maintain class control but do not use "power" for the sake of showing "power."
- Pair children for learning tasks carefully.
- Avoid activities that promote aggressive behavior—wrestling, for example.
- Ask for and use the behavior-management plan developed by the student's IEP/multidisciplinary team.
- Select activities which allow *all* students to experience success.

THE PHYSICAL EDUCATION PROGRAM

A developmentally appropriate, well-taught physical education program is critical for individuals with conduct, behavior, and emotional disorders. The potential benefits are the same as for any individual. It appears particularly important to provide students with conduct, behavior, and emotional disorders the opportunity to participate regularly in sustained, vigorous, aerobic activities. For preschoolers and young elementary learners, this includes dance activities such as "Chug Along Choo Choo" and "Bendable Stretchable," tricycling and bicycling, and vigorous, sustained playground activity. For older elementary-age students, these activities include walking, jogging/running, cross-country skiing, or swimming. Middle school and high school students can get the appropriate level of activity using walking, jogging/running, cross-country skiing, swimming, stationary cycling, stationary rowing, and aerobic dance or aquaRobics. See Figure 14-10 for more information about aquatics. There is significant evidence that participation in these activities may release endorphins, which improve a person's mood and reduce stress. Exercise programs have been effective in reducing the stereotypic, self-injurious, and disruptive behavior of individuals with severe behavior disorders.[4,33] There is also evidence that participation in systematic exercise may enhance self-esteem and body image.[48]

MODIFICATIONS/ADAPTATIONS/INCLUSION TECHNIQUES

Although there has been considerable emphasis in the past on identifying causes before alleviating disruptive behavior, Kauffman states that "the first or ultimate cause of behavior disorders almost always remains unknown. . . . The focus of the educator should be on those contributing factors that can be altered by the teacher."[26] Under most conditions, the physical education teacher cannot control the cause of inappropriate behavior, even if it is known. Thus, it is essential that the adapted physical education teacher plan for developing skills included on the individual education program (IEP) through the use of appropriate behavioral strategies.

A typical strategy for including students with disabilities into the general physical education program is to assign "peer tutors." This is, at best, a questionable practice when working with students with conduct, behavior, and emotional disorders.

Figure 14-10   Aquatics for Learners with Conduct, Behavior, or Emotional Disorders[43]

- The aquatic program must be such that the student's success is guaranteed. A careful initial assessment will ensure success. Please refer to Texas Woman's University Project INSPIRE Aquatics Web Page: http://venus.twu.edu/~f_huettig
- Start with "familiar" skills (walking, running, jumping in the water, for example) and move, slowly, to unfamiliar skills.
- Create small learning stations or areas for students so there is a "safe space." This can be done with lane lines, for example, or a tethered floating mat.
- From the minute they enter the locker room, absolutely every minute needs to be planned and monitored carefully. The locker room is the most potentially volatile situation for these learners. Issues tied to abuse, in its many forms, are more evident in this vulnerable setting. Supervision is crucial.
- With a particularly confrontational student, the best environment may be one in which the learner is, literally, over his or her head. It may be easier for the teacher to control behavior if the learner is dependent on the teacher.
- Touch, even for spotting, needs to be carefully explained and done with care. A learner with a history of abuse may misinterpret well-intentioned touch.
- There must be a "fail safe" plan for an emergency—a student "out of control." The lifeguard on deck must be able to contact another teacher/administrator instantly.

Simply, a young student has neither the training nor the emotional set to deal with a peer whose behavior is unpredictable.

It is critical that a physical educator serving a student with a conduct, behavior, or emotional disorder adopt the behavior-management plan developed by the IEP/multidisciplinary team. The most critical need of the student with a conduct, behavior, or emotional disorder is *consistency*. It is vital that the same behavior-management plan is used by all teachers and other school personnel working with the student. For example, the Boys Town curriculum has been adopted by many public schools that serve students with conduct, behavior, and emotional disorders. Indeed, the best possible scenario is one in which school personnel and the parents use the same strategies; this provides the student with the best possible opportunity to succeed.

In many school-based programs for students with conduct, behavior, and emotional disorders, the student literally "earns" the right, by demonstrating appropriate behavior, to participate in school programs such as physical education. The unique characteristics of the physical education program must be discussed with the IEP/ multidisciplinary team before any decision is made to include a student with a severe disorder in the physical education environment. Perhaps the major issue in many physical education programs, unfortunately, is large class size. Typically, the student with a conduct, behavior, or emotional disorder requires a great deal of attention. This is difficult, if not impossible, for the physical educator teaching three or more classes simultaneously.

COMMUNITY-BASED OPPORTUNITIES

The development of the individual transition plan for students who have reached the age of fourteen years takes on a special meaning for students with conduct, behavior, or emotional disorders. The IEP/multidisciplinary team must work closely with the physical educator who can assist the team with the process of identifying community-based resources in which the adult would be well received. Unfortunately, the stigma attached to mental illness often creates a situation in which individuals with these disorders do not have a venue for participation at the community level. It appears that the emphasis, for adults, as well as school-age children, with conduct, behavior, and emotional disorders needs to be on vigorous aerobic activity. Participation in this type of activity appears to enhance self-esteem, that may, in addition to increasing physical fitness, positively influences the adult's behavior and makes community-based participation a reality.

SUMMARY

Increasingly, physical education teachers and other school professionals a struggle to teach learners with conduct, behavior, and emotional disorders. It is critical that the physical educator be able to identify the signs of disorder; the physical education class may be the situation in which the signs are most easily identified. The physical educator must create a carefully designed classroom learning environment in which behavior management is used constructively to enhance learning and promote learners' self-esteem.

REVIEW QUESTIONS

1. What are some signs or symptoms of conduct, behavior, and emotional disorders?

2. What is the impact of urbanization on mental health? What are other causes of conduct, behavior, and emotional disorders?

3. What is a stigma?

4. What are some of the basic techniques the physical educator should use to teach learners with conduct, behavior, or emotional disorders?

5. What should be the emphasis in the physical education curriculum for students with these disorders?

6. How can the physical education teacher facilitate a student's transition from the school to the community setting?

STUDENT ACTIVITIES

1. Break the class into small groups to discuss how or if the physical educator could help Logan in the case study.

2. Observe a physical education class in a public school nearby. List the behaviors you see that are associated with conduct, behavior, or emotional disorders.

3. Conduct a web search for information regarding support services available for learners with conduct, behavior, or emotional disorders. Conduct a community-based assessment to determine which of these support services are available near your university.

4. Articles about physical education for students with emotional disturbances can be found in the *Adapted Physical Activity Quarterly* and *Palaestra: The Forum of Sport, Physical Education and Recreation for the Disabled*. Read two articles that discuss techniques for working with students with emotional disturbances, and write a report summarizing one of the articles.

5. Interview a person from psychological services or a school counselor. Determine whether a schoolwide or districtwide behavior-management system is used and why. If a system is used, describe the system.

6. Read the material about Don Hellison's programs for students at-risk (Chapter 9). Compare the strategies recommended by Hellison with those suggested in this chapter.

REFERENCES

1. Ackerman PT et al.: Prevalence of post traumatic stress disorder and other psychiatric diagnoses in three groups of abused children (sexual, physical and both), *Child Abuse Negl* 22(8):759–774, 1998.

2. American Psychiatric Association: *Diagnostic and statistical manual DSM-IV*, Washington, DC, 1994, Author.

3. Bailey VFA: Intensive interventions in conduct disorders, *Arch Disease in Childhood* 74:352–356, 1996.

4. Baumeister AA, MacLean WE: Deceleration of self-injurious behavior and stereotypic responding by exercise, *Applied Research Mental Retard* 5:385–393, 1982.

5. Bay-Hinitz J, Peterson RF, Quiltch RH: Cooperative games: a way to modify aggressive and cooperative behaviors in young children, *J Applied Behavioral Analysis* 27:435–446, 1994.

6. Beers MH, Berkow R: *The Merck manual of diagnosis and therapy,* Whitehouse Station, NJ, 1999, Merck Research Laboratories.

7. Bennett KJ et al.: Predicting conduct problems: can high-risk children be identified in kindergarten and grade 1? *J Consulting Clin Psychol* 67(4):470–480, 1999.

8. Cannon M, Murray RM: Neonatal origins of schizophrenia, *Arch Disease Childhood* 78(1):1–3, 1998.

9. Cartlege G, Milburn JF: *Teaching social skills to children and youth: innovative approaches,* ed. 3, Needham Heights, MA, 1995, Allyn & Bacon.

10. Cicchetti D, Toth SL: The development of depression in children and adolescents, *Amer Psychologist* 53(2):221–241, 1998.

11. Cohen R, Harris R, Gottlieb S, Best AM: States, use of transfer of custody as a requirement for providing services to emotionally disturbed children, *Hospital Community Psychiatry* 42:526–530, 1991.

12. Coie JD: Toward a theory of peer rejection. In SR Asher and JD Coie, editors: *Peer rejection in childhood,* Cambridge, England, 1990, Cambridge University Press.

13. Colbert RS: Team approach: involving parents in the treatment and education of youths with severe emotional disturbance, *J of Special Education* 18:54–61, 1994.

14. Corrigan D: Office of Special Education, Challenges for Personnel Preparation Conference, Washington, DC, September 8–10, 1999.

15. Depression. http://www.health.gov.au/hsdd/mentalhe/nmhs

16. Dettmer P, Thruston LP, Dyck N: *Consultation, collaboration and teamwork for students with special needs,* Boston, 1993, Allyn & Bacon.

17. Donovan SJ: A new approach to disruptive behavior disorders and the antisocial spectrum. Medscape Mental Health.

http://www.medscape.com/Medscape/psychiatry/journal/1998

18. Ervin CE: Parents forced to surrender custody of children with neurological disorders, *New Directions of Mental Health Services* 54:111–116, 1992.

19. Evans IM, Meyer PL: *An educative approach to behavioral problems—a practical decision model for intervention with severely handicapped learners,* Baltimore, MD, 1985, Paul H. Brookes.

20. Farmer TW, Hollowell JH: Social networks in mainstream classrooms: social affiliations and behavioral characteristics of students with emotional and behavioral disorders, *J Emotional Behav Disord* 1:223–234, 1994.

21. Forehand RL, McMahon RJ: Helping the non-compliant child: a clinician's guide to parent training, New York, 1981, Guilford Press.

22. Grossman H: *Special education in a diverse society,* Boston, 1995, Allyn & Bacon.

23. Helion JG: If we build it, they will come: creating an emotionally safe physical education environment, *J Health Phys Ed Rec Dance* 67(6):40–44, 1996.

24. Herold BC: Polymicrobial bacteremia: a commentary, *Clin Pediatrics* 36(7):419–422, 1997.

25. Johns BH, Carr VG: Techniques for managing verbally and physically aggressive students, Denver, 1995, Love.

26. Kauffman JN: *Characteristics of behavior disorders of children and youth,* ed. 4, Columbus, OH, 1989, Charles E. Merrill.

27. Kirk S, Gallagher J, Anastasio NJ: *Educating exceptional children,* ed., Boston, 1993, Houghton Mifflin.

28. Knitzer J, Steinberg Z, Fleisch B: Schools, mental health and the advocacy challenge, *J of Clinical Child Psychology* 20:102–111, 1990.

29. Koyangi C, Gaines S: *All systems failure: an examination of the results of neglecting the needs of children with serious emotional disturbance,* Washington, DC, 1993, National Mental Health Association.

30. Kupersmidt JG, Core JD, Dodge KA: The role of peer relationships in the development of disorders. In Asher R, Core JD, editors: *Peer rejections in childhood.* Cambridge, England, 1990, Cambridge University Press, pp. 274–308.

31. LaGreca AM: Social skills training with children: where do we go from here? *J of Clinical Child Psychology* 22:288–298, 1993.

32. Marcella AJ: Urbanization, mental health, and social deviancy: a review of issues and research, *Amer Psychologist* 53(6):624–634, 1998.

33. McGimsey JF, Favell JE: The effects of increased physical exercise on disruptive behavior in retarded persons, *J of Autism and Dev Disorders* 18:167–179, 1988.

34. McIntyre T: Does the way we teach create behavior disorders in culturally different students? *Ed Treatment Child* 19(3):354–370, 1996.

35. Mental Health. http://www.mentalhealth.com/dis1/

36. Nichols JD, Ludwin WG, Iadicola P: a darker shade of gray: a year-end analysis of discipline and suspension data, *Equity and Excellence in Ed* 32(1):43–55, 1999.

37. Oppenheimer J, Ziegler S: *Suspension, alternatives to suspension and other approaches to discipline,* #189. Toronto, CA, 1988, Toronto Board of Education.

38. Rainsworth B, York J, MacDonald C: *Collaborating teams for students with severe disabilities: integrating therapy and educational services,* Baltimore, MD, 1992, Paul H. Brooks.

39. Shea TM, Bauer AM: *Learners with disabilities: a social system perspective in special education,* Boston, 1994, Allyn & Bacon.

40. Slaby RG, Roedell WC, Arezzo D, Hendrix K: *Early violence prevention: tools for teachers of young children,* Washington, DC, 1995, National Association for the Education of Young Children.

41. Souid A, Keith DV, Cunningham AS: Munchausen syndrome by proxy, *Clin Pediatrics* 38(8):497–503, 1998.

42. Stigma. http://www.health.gov.au/hsdd/mentalhe/nmhs/what/stigma/index.htm

43. Texas Woman's University Project INSPIRE web page. http://www.twu.edu/inspire

44. Tripp JH, Cockett M: Parents, parenting and family breakdown, *Arch Disease Childhood* 78(2):104–107, 1998.

45. U.S. Department of Education, Office of Special Education and Rehabilitative Services: *Annual report to Congress on the implementation of the Individuals with Disabilities Education Act,* February 1998.

46. U.S. Department of Education: *To assure the free appropriate public education of all children with disabilities: sixteenth annual report to Congress on the implementation of the Individuals with Disabilities Education Act,* Washington, DC, 1994, Author.

47. U.S. Department of Health, Education, and Welfare: *Regulations for the Education for All Handicapped Children Act of 1975,* Fed Reg, vol 4, August 23, 1977.

48. Van de Vliet P, Coppenolle HV: Physical measures, perceived physical ability, and body acceptance of adult psychiatric patients, *Adapted Phys Act Q* 16:113–125, 1999.

49. Wagner M, Blackorby J, Hebbeler K: *Beyond the report card: the multiple dimensions of secondary school performance for students with disabilities,* Menlo Park, CA, 1993, SRI International.

50. Whitbeck LB, Hoyt DR, Ackley KA: Families of homeless and runaway adolescents: a comparison of parent/caretaker and adolescent perspectives on parenting, family violence, and adolescent conduct, *Child Abuse Negl* 21(6):517–528, 1997.

SUGGESTED READINGS

Helion JG: If we build it, they will come: creating an emotionally safe physical education environment, *JOHPERD* 67(6):40–44, 1996.

Johns BH, Carr VG: *Techniques for managing verbally and physically aggressive students,* Denver, 1995, Love.

RECOMMENDED WEBSITES

Please note that these recommendations are being made in the fall of 1999. It is possible the websites have moved or do not exist at the time you read this.

Virtual Resource Center in Behavioral Disorders
http://www.coe.missouri.edu/~vrcbd

Medscape Mental Health
http://www.medscape.com/Medscape/psychiatry/
journal/1998

Teenage Suicide
http://www.save.org

School Psychological Resources Online
http://www.bcpl.lib.md.us/~sandyste/
school_psych.html

Internet Mental Health Resources
http://www.mentalhealth.com

TrackStar
http://scrtec.org/track/tracks

SERI (Special Education Resources on the Internet)
Behavior Disorders
http://www.hood.edu/seri/behavior.htm

RECOMMENDED VIDEOS

Fanlight Productions
4196 Washington Street
Boston, MA 02131
Psychology, Social Work and Disabilities
Video Collections, 1999-2000

Step on a Crack: Obsessive Compulsive Disorder, by Arlene Lorre
29 minutes, purchase price $195
Order # CV-222

When the Brain Goes Wrong, by Jonathon David and Roberta Cooks

45 minutes, purchase price $195
Order # CV-131

First Break, by Silva Basmafian and Adrienne Amato
51 minutes, purchase price $195
Order # CV-254

Depression and Manic Depression
28 minutes, purchase price $149
Order # CV-193

Rudy Garcia-Tolson, Ten Years Old, Youngest Bilateral Amputee to Ever Complete an Entire Solo Triathlon
Courtesy of the Total Technology Company and Rudy Garcia-Tolson.

Physically Disabling Conditions

■ OBJECTIVES

Describe at least one physically disabling condition that is representative of each of the three categories in this chapter.

Identify the stages of the concussion grading system.

Describe the types of spina bifida and the types of physical education program modifications required of each.

Describe how to modify three physical education activities to include a student in a wheelchair.

Give three examples of principles for adapting physical activity to accommodate persons with physical disabilities.

There are many different types of physically disabling conditions. Afflictions can occur at more than 500 anatomical sites. Each person who has a disabling condition has different physical and motor capabilities. Thus, each person must be treated in such a manner that his or her unique educational needs are met.

In this chapter we suggest a procedure to accomplish this task. The processes involved in this procedure are to (1) identify the specific clinical condition, (2) identify which activities are contraindicated on the basis of medical recommendations, (3) determine needed functional physical fitness and motor skills, (4) determine the activities that will assist the development of the desired fitness and motor skills, and (5) determine aids and devices that will enable the individual to function in the most normal environment.

More than twenty disabilities are presented in this chapter. Many of these conditions, though differing in cause, result in similar movement limitations. To aid you in focusing on the commonalities across physically disabling conditions, the format of this chapter is slightly different from that of some of the other chapters dealing with specific populations. Under the headings of "Neurological Disorders," "Orthopedic Disabilities," and "Traumatic Injuries," specific conditions are identified and defined, the incidence and cause of each condition are given, the characteristics are delineated, special considerations are discussed, and suggestions for programming and teaching are presented. Following the unique aspects of all of the specific conditions, common testing suggestions; modifications, adaptations, and inclusion techniques; and community-based opportunities are presented.

DEFINITION AND SCOPE OF PHYSICALLY DISABLING CONDITIONS

Physical disabilities affect the use of the body as a result of deficiencies of the nerves, muscles, bones, and/or joints. The three main sources of disabilities are neurological impairments, orthopedic (musculoskeletal) disabilities, and traumatic injuries. Neurological disabilities are chronic debilitating conditions that result from impairments of the central nervous system. The neurological conditions discussed in this chapter include amyotrophic lateral sclerosis, cerebral palsy, epilepsy, multiple sclerosis, muscular dystrophy, Parkinson's disease, poliomyelitis and post-polio syndrome, and spina bifida.

Orthopedic conditions are deformities, diseases, and injuries of the bones and joints. The orthopedic conditions discussed in this chapter include arthritis, arthrogryposis, congenital hip dislocation, coxa plana, Osgood-Schlatter condition, osteogenesis imperfecta, osteomyelitis, and spondylolysis and spondylolisthesis.

Traumatic conditions are the result of damage to muscles, ligaments, tendons, or the nervous system as a result of a blow to the body. Traumatic head injuries, spinal cord injuries, and amputations are discussed in this chapter.

Because of the number of conditions included in this chapter, case studies have only

been developed to be representative of each of the three groups of disabilities. Spina bifida has been selected in the neurological disorder category, juvenile rheumatoid arthritis in the orthopedic disabilities category, and traumatic brain injury in the traumatic injuries section.

Neurological Disorders
Amyotrophic Lateral Sclerosis

Amyotrophic lateral sclerosis (ALS) is a progressive neurological disorder of an unknown cause that results in degeneration of the nerve tracts to the voluntary muscular system.[89] The reported incidence in the United States is 5,000 persons diagnosed each year.[5] The disease is infrequent in school-age populations and is more common in adulthood, with the median age of onset being fifty-five years.[6] It affects men two to three times as often as women. Lou Gehrig, the hall-of-fame first baseman of the New York Yankees, who finally missed a game after more than 2,000 successive starts, was forced to retire as a result of the disease. It has since been named Lou Gehrig disease.

Characteristics and Testing The central feature of the disease is atrophy and muscle wasting, resulting in marked weakness in the hands, arms, shoulders, and legs and in generalized weakness. The site of onset is random, and it progresses asymmetrically.[6] Cramps are common, and muscular weakness may cause problems with swallowing, talking, and respiration. Concomitant spinal conditions may include ruptured intervertebral disks, spinal cord tumors, and spinal malformations. Manual muscle testing is used to determine the amount of functional strength.

Special Considerations There is no specific medical treatment for ALS. The rate of decline of muscular strength varies, with some losing strength quickly, and others more slowly.[67] Seventy percent of those afflicted with ALS die within five years of the onset of the disease.[6]

The Physical Maintenance Program The major goals of the ALS physical education program are to maintain physical capability as long as possible. There is some anecdotal evidence that exercise that strengthens the healthy muscle fibers permits an individual with ALS to maintain strength and a higher level of function over time.[67] Walking and recumbent cycling daily is recommended for maintaining endurance. Range of motion exercises with light weights and use of weight machines are recommended for maintaining strength.[67] It might also be desirable to focus attention on activities that maintain efficient movement of the body for the activities of daily living. Leisure skills should be taught that have functional use at present or in the near future. The nature of the physical activities will depend on the physical capabilities of the individual at each point in time. The caregiver should be supportive and understanding. Consultation with an occupational therapist should be sought for advice about assistive devices to enable the activities of daily living.

Cerebral Palsy

Cerebral palsy is a condition rather than a disease. The term *cerebral palsy* is defined as a nonprogressive lesion of the brain before, during, or soon after birth (before age five years). The condition impairs voluntary movement and is a lifelong condition. It is the most frequent cause of severe disabilities in children.[56]

The incidence of cerebral palsy is 1 to 2 per 1,000 live births.[6] Although earlier studies indicated that the vast majority of cerebral palsy cases were caused by external factors such as prolonged labor, instrumental deliveries, and breech births, it is now believed that only 15 percent of cases result from these causes.[6] The most recent studies indicate that central nervous system abnormalities, such as enlarged ventricles in the brain, decreased brain hemisphere size, and viral infections, are probably critical factors that impair function.[52]

Certain groups of infants, including those with prolonged birth anoxia, very low birth weight, and abnormal neurological symptoms, are possible candidates for cerebral palsy.[13] Many children with cerebral palsy possess poor postural adjustment.

As a result, simple gross motor movements (e.g., kicking, throwing, and jumping) are difficult to perform effectively.[80]

Characteristics and Types The degree of motor impairment of children with cerebral palsy ranges from serious physical disability to little physical disability. The limbs affected are identified with specific titles:

- Monoplegia involves a single limb.
- Hemiplegia indicates involvement of both limbs on one side, with the arm being more affected than the leg.
- Paraplegia indicates involvement of both legs with little or no involvement of the arms.
- Quadriplegia or tetraplegia denotes involvement of all the limbs to a similar degree.
- Diplegia is an intermediate form between paraplegia and quadriplegia, with most involvement being in the legs.

Since the extent of the brain damage that results in neuromotor dysfunction varies greatly, diagnosis is related to the amount of dysfunction and associated motor involvement. Severe brain injury may be evident shortly after birth. However, cases of children with cerebral palsy who have slight brain damage and little motor impairment may be difficult to diagnose. In the milder cases, developmental lag in the motor and intellectual tasks required to meet environmental demands may not be detected until the children are three or four years old. As a rule, the clinical signs and symptoms of cerebral palsy reach maximum severity when children reach the age of two to four years.

Individuals with cerebral palsy usually demonstrate persistence of primitive reflexes and frequently are slow to develop equilibrium (postural) reflexes. It is difficult for most performers to execute simple gross motor movements effectively unless appropriate postural adjustments occur to support such movements[87] and individuals are given additional time to plan and execute the movements.

Some of the secondary impairments that accompany cerebral palsy are mental retardation, hearing and vision loss, emotional disturbance, hyperactivity, learning disabilities, loss of perceptual ability, and inability to make psychological adjustments.[83] Ferrara and Laskin[32] report that 60 percent of all children with cerebral palsy have seizures. Seizures are sudden involuntary changes in behavior that range from a short period of loss of consciousness to jerks of one or two limbs or the whole body.[6]

Various authors agree that more than 50 percent of children with cerebral palsy have oculomotor defects. In other words, children with brain injury often have difficulty in coordinating their eye movements. For this reason, these children may lack depth perception and have difficulty accurately determining the path of moving objects.

The different clinical types of cerebral dysfunction involve various obvious motor patterns, commonly known as hard signs. There are four clinical classifications: spasticity, athetosis, ataxia, and mixed. Of persons with cerebral palsy, 70 percent are clinically classified as spastic, 20 percent as athetoid, and 10 percent as ataxic; the remaining are mixed conditions (usually spasticity and athetosis).[6]

Muscular spasticity is the most prevalent type of hard sign among persons with cerebral palsy. It results from damage to an area of the cortical brain.[26] One characteristic of spasticity is that muscle contractures that restrict muscular movement and hypertonicity give the appearance of stiffness to affected limbs. This makes muscle movement jerky and uncertain. Children with spasticity have exaggerated stretch reflexes, which cause them to respond to rapid passive stimulation with vigorous muscle contractions. Tendon reflexes are also hyperactive in the involved part. When the upper extremities are involved, the characteristic forms of physical deviation in persons with spastic cerebral palsy include flexion at the elbows, forearm pronation, and wrist and finger flexion. When the spastic condition involves the lower extremities, the legs may be rotated inward and flexed at the hips, the knees may be flexed, and a contracted gastrocnemius muscle holds the heel off the ground. A scissors gait is common among persons with this type of cerebral palsy. Spasticity is most common in the antigravity muscles of the body. Contractures are more common in children with spastic cerebral palsy than in children with any of the other types of cerebral palsy. In the event that contractures are not remedied or addressed, permanent contractures may result. Consequently, good posture is extremely difficult to maintain. Because of poor balance among reciprocal muscle groups, the innervation of muscles for functional motor patterns is often difficult, which frequently results in a decreased physical work capacity.[31] Individuals with spastic hemiplegia or paraplegia usually have normal intelligence; however, they may demonstrate some learning disabilities. Mental retardation is more frequently seen in individuals with spastic quadriplegia and mixed forms of cerebral palsy.[6]

Athetosis, which results from basal ganglia involvement, is the second most prevalent clinical type of cerebral palsy. The distinguishing characteristic of the individual with athetosis is recognizable incoordinate movements of voluntary muscles. These movements take the form of wormlike motions that involve the trunk, arms, legs, and tongue or muscle twitches of the face. The unrhythmical, uncontrollable, involuntary movements increase with voluntary motion and emotional or environmental stimuli and disappear during sleep. Because of the presence of primitive reflexes and the inability to control muscles the individual with athetosis has postural control difficulties that threaten balance. Impairment in the muscular control of hands, speech, and swallowing often accompanies athetosis.

Ataxia, a primary characteristic of the ataxic type of cerebral palsy, is a disturbance of equilibrium that results from involvement of the cerebellum or its pathways.[6] The resulting impairment in balance is evident in the walking gait. The gait of the person with ataxic cerebral palsy is wide and unstable, which causes weaving during locomotion. Standing is often a problem. Kinesthetic awareness seems to be lacking in the individual with ataxia. Weakness, incoordination, and intention tremor create difficulties with rapid or fine movements.[6]

Mixed forms are the least common of all types of cerebral palsy. Spasticity and athetosis are the most frequent characteristics, with ataxia and athetosis demonstrated less frequently.[6]

Special Considerations   Increasingly, the medical community and society at large have come to understand that the focus of medical intervention should be on the prevention of disabilities through appropriate prenatal care and early intervention with at-risk children. The five procedures prevalent in the medical treatment of individuals with cerebral palsy are early intervention to promote a more normal neuromotor developmental sequence (physical therapy), casting, orthotics (bracing), medication, and neurosurgical management.[26] Physical therapy focuses on reducing the effect of persisting primitive reflexes and promoting range of motion at the joints. Casting involves placing a cast on an extremity to hold it in line with the limb to which it

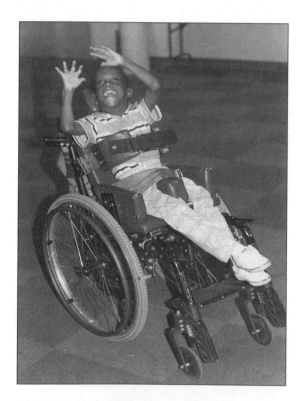

A five-year-old boy participates in creative dance.
Courtesy Dallas Independent School District.

is attached. Orthotics help delay the development of contractures, limit the amount of spasticity that can occur, and decrease consumption of energy.[26] Medication usually serves two functions: aiding in relaxation of muscle groups when neuromuscular exercise therapy is attempted and controlling epileptic seizures through the use of anticonvulsant drugs. Neurosurgical management involves surgery to release tight muscles and tendons.

There are various opinions as to the value of orthopedic surgery for persons with cerebral palsy. Certain types of operative procedures have met with considerable success, especially with particular types of cerebral palsy. The physical growth of children affects the efficiency of muscle and tendon surgery; however, surgical operation, for the most part, is not curative but, rather, assists the functional activities of daily living. Tenotomy (tendon cutting) of the hip adductor and hamstring muscles seems to be the most valuable surgical procedure for adults with cerebral palsy.

The use of electrical stimulation on the anterial tibial muscles of children with spastic hemiplegia proved to be useful in increasing the range of passive dorsiflexion of the ankle; however, the gait pattern was not significantly improved.[40] This type of intervention does hold promise as an alternative to surgery for reducing contractures.

Individuals with cerebral palsy have lower maximal oxygen consumption and distinctly subnormal values for peak anaerobic power and muscular endurance than do their able-bodied peers. Frequently, during aerobic testing, these individuals do not demonstrate a plateau in oxygen consumption; thus, a peak aerobic power test is considered reliable for this population. Also, anaerobic power is considered a better measure of functional capacity than is maximal aerobic power.[84]

The Physical Education Program and Teaching Strategies   There is no treatment for the repair of a damaged brain. However, the portion of the nervous system that remains intact can be made functional through a well-managed training program. Intervention by the physical educator and other personnel is needed to build functional developmental motor patterns with the operative parts of the body. Each child should be evaluated closely, and programs that foster those functional abilities should be formulated. Developmental programs should be constructed to correct deficiencies that respond to treatment. The specific child should be considered when the exercise regimen is being determined. Because of their numerous involuntary muscular activities, children with athetosis are much more active than children with spasticity and ataxia.

There is growing evidence that some of the sensory and perceptual delays can be improved through training. Sensory-motor and perceptual-motor training programs are designed to reduce primitive reflex involvement and develop locomotor patterns, balance, rhythm, and ocular control. These areas are the focus of physical therapists early in the life of the child. All of these activities are inherent in most elementary physical education programs; however, the quality of physical education programs could be improved by consciously selecting activities of this nature for classes that include students with spastic cerebral palsy. The handbook *Gross Motor Activities for Young Children with Special Needs,* which accompanies this text, includes several games that would be appropriate for the elementary-school-age child.

The individual education program (IEP) of the student with cerebral palsy should include activities to address the individual's unique needs. Some of the therapeutic activities and techniques that could be recommended follow:

1. Muscle stretching to relieve muscle contractures, prevent deformities, and permit fuller range of purposeful motion (consult with physical therapists about this procedure)
2. Gravity exercises that involve lifting the weight of the body or body part against gravity
3. Muscle awareness exercises to control specific muscles or muscle groups
4. Neuromuscular re-education exercises that are performed through the muscles' current range to stimulate the proprioceptors and return the muscles to greater functional use (consult with physical therapists about this procedure)
5. Reciprocal exercises to stimulate and strengthen the action of the protagonist
6. Tonic exercises to prevent atrophy or maintain organic efficiency
7. Relaxation training to assist in reducing muscle contractures, rigidity, and spasms
8. Postural alignments to maintain proper alignment of musculature
9. Gait training to teach or reteach walking patterns (consult with physical therapists about this procedure)
10. Body mechanics and lifting techniques to obtain maximum use of the large muscle groups of the body
11. Proprioceptive facilitation exercises to bring about maximum excitation of the motor units of a muscle with each voluntary effort to overcome motor-functioning paralysis (consult with physical therapists about this procedure)
12. Ramp climbing to improve ambulation and balance
13. Progressive, resistive exercise to develop muscle strength

Failure to provide children with cerebral palsy the opportunity to participate in progressive exercise may leave them short of their potential development. The opportunities for physical education to maximize the physical development of these children are great. Furthermore, children with cerebral palsy frequently do not develop adequate basic motor skills because of their limited play experiences.

When a child with cerebral palsy participates in a group activity, it may be necessary to adapt the activity to the child's abilities or to modify the rules or environment. A child with quadriplegic spastic cerebral palsy may be given the opportunity to play the bells during a rhythm activity, instead of being asked to dance with his or her feet. A wheelchair-enabled child with rigid cerebral palsy may "hold" one handle on the parachute with the edge of his or her chair. A child with ataxia may play a sitting circle game with classmates while propped in the teacher's lap or propped against a wall.

In addition to adaptation of activity, the capabilities of each individual must be considered. Children with spasticity, those with athetosis, and those with ataxia differ greatly in function. For instance, the child with spasticity finds it easier to engage in activities in which motion is continuous. However, in the case of the child with athetosis, relaxation between movements is extremely important to prevent involuntary muscular contractions that may thwart the development of skills.

Children with ataxia have different motor problems—they are usually severely limited in all activities that require balance. The motor characteristics of the basic types of cerebral palsy, as well as of each child, are important variables in the selection of activities. Rest periods should be frequent for children with cerebral palsy. The length and frequency of the rest periods should vary with the nature of the activity and the severity of the disability. The development of a sequence of activities varying in degree of difficulty is important. This sequencing provides an opportunity to place each child in an activity that is commensurate with his or her ability and proposes a subsequent goal to work toward.

Physical activities described under the definition of physical education in IDEA are appropriate for children with cerebral palsy. At the early elementary level, the focus should be on the development of sensory-motor function, body image, and rhythmicity. Appropriate motor activities might include fundamental motor patterns, such as walking, running, and jumping, and fundamental motor skills, such as throwing, kicking, and catching. Aquatics is a vital part of the curriculum for children with cerebral palsy. The buoyancy of the water frees the child from the pull of gravity, which activates many primitive reflexes and allows for greater range of motion. Rhythm activities are also a vital part of the quality physical education program for children with cerebral palsy; expressive dance may prove to be vital in the development of language and communication, as well as motor

skills. If possible, the physical education program for children with cerebral palsy at the elementary school level should include age-appropriate, geographically appropriate leisure and recreation skills. Horseback riding is a particularly effective intervention activity for even the most severely involved child. Other leisure and recreation skills are also an important part of the total program. The child should be introduced, for example, to the skills needed to participate in bowling, including the use of automatic grip release balls and ramps, if necessary. If geographically appropriate, the child should learn the skills necessary to sled with family and friends.

The middle school curriculum should focus on the development of physical fitness, body mechanics, and relaxation techniques. Once again, aquatics is a vital component of the curriculum. Increased focus should be placed on exposing the student to community-based leisure and recreation activities and, where appropriate, competitive sports programs.

In the high school program, it is important that students with cerebral palsy maintain adequate levels of physical fitness, practice body mechanics, and develop more sophisticated relaxation tech-

A lower leg prosthesis enables this runner to compete.
Courtesy of Orthotic and Prosthetic Athlete Assistance Fund, Inc., Alexandria, VA.

niques. There is impressive evidence that motor skills, muscular endurance, and strength can be developed in individuals with cerebral palsy through progressive exercise. Fernandez and Pitetti[31] reported that individuals with cerebral palsy who exercised regularly demonstrated improvement in functional capacity. Holland and Steadward[44] have identified Nautilus weight-lifting exercises that develop the neck, chest, and arms. These authors conclude that persons with cerebral palsy can participate in intense strength-training programs without sacrificing flexibility or increasing spasticity.

The secondary student's IEP must address techniques that will allow the student to make the transition from school-based to community-based leisure and recreation programs. For example, the IEP may address the skills necessary for the student to register for and participate in an adult bowling or archery league. These skills may include independent management of a ramp, for example. In addition, these students should be made familiar with the activities and programs of the U.S. Cerebral Palsy Athletic Association (see Appendix C for address).

Because of the many health and social benefits of staying active, individuals with cerebral palsy should be encouraged to participate in ongoing physical activities. Sport and recreation opportunities for individuals with cerebral palsy and other nonprogressive brain lesions (e.g., traumatic brain injury, stroke) are growing.[32] A functional classification system developed by Cerebral Palsy–International Sport and Recreation Association (CP-ISRA) is presented in Figure 15-1.

Figure 15-1 CP-ISRA Functional Classification System

CP1 Severe spastic or athetoid quadriplegia	Unable to propel a manual wheelchair independently; has nonfunctional lower extremities, very poor or no trunk stability, severely decreased function in upper extremity
CP2 Moderate to severe spastic or athetoid quadriplegia	Is able to propel a manual wheelchair slowly and inefficiently; has differential function abilities between upper and lower extremities, fair static trunk stability
CP3 Moderate spastic quadriplegia or severe spastic hemiplegia	Is able to propel a manual wheelchair independently; may be able to ambulate with assistance; has moderate spasticity on the lower extremities, fair dynamic trunk stability, moderate limitations to function in the dominant arm
CP4 Moderate to severe spastic diplegia	Ambulates with aids over short distances; has moderate to severe involvement of the lower extremities, good dynamic trunk stability, minimal to near-normal function of the upper extremities at rest
CP5 Moderate spastic diplegia	Ambulates well with assistive devices; has minimal to moderate spasticity in one or both lower extremities; is able to run
CP6 Moderate athetosis or ataxia	Ambulates without assistive devices; lower-extremity function improves from walking to running or cycling; has poor static and good dynamic trunk stability, good upper-extremity range and strength, poor throwing and grasp and release
CP7 True ambulatory hemiplegia	Has mild to moderately affected upper extremity, minimal to mildly affected lower extremity
CP8 Minimally affected diplegia, hemiplegia, athetosis or monoplegia	

Modified from Ferrara M, Laskin J: Cerebral Palsy. In Durstine, JL, editor: *Exercise management for persons with chronic diseases and disabilities,* Champaign, IL, 1997, Human Kinetics.

Epilepsy

Epilepsy is a disturbance resulting from abnormal electrical activity of the brain. It is not a specific disease but a group of symptoms that may be associated with several conditions. It is defined as a "recurrent disorder of cerebral function characterized by sudden, brief attacks of altered consciousness, motor activity, sensory phenomena, or inappropriate behavior caused by abnormal excessive discharge of cerebral neurons."[6] The estimated incidence of epilepsy is 2 percent of the population. Many persons with epilepsy experience their first attack during childhood. No cause can be found in 75 percent of the young adults who have epilepsy. Common causes are brain damage at birth, alcohol or other drug abuse, severe head injury, brain infection, and/or brain tumor.[30]

Characteristics and Types   There are several types of epilepsy, and each type has a particular set of characteristics. Although there are several methods of classifying various types of epilepsy, the one most commonly used includes four categories of seizure: grand mal, petit mal, focal, and psychomotor.

The grand mal, French for "big illness," is the most severe type of seizure. The individual often has an "aura" that immediately precedes the seizure, and the aura may give the individual some warning of the imminence of the seizure. The aura is usually a somatosensory flash—a particular smell, a blur of colors, or an itching sensation, for example. The seizure itself usually begins with bilateral jerks of the extremities, followed by convulsions and loss of consciousness. The student may be incontinent during the seizure, losing control of the bowels and bladder. After the seizure, the individual is usually confused, often embarrassed, and exhausted. Approximately 90 percent of individuals with epilepsy experience grand mal seizures.[6]

The onset of the petit ("little") mal seizure is sudden and may last for only a few seconds or for several minutes. Usually the individual appears to simply stare into space and have a lapse in attention. It is often characterized by twitching around the eyes or mouth. There is a loss of consciousness but no collapse. The individual remains sitting or standing. Seizures of this type usually affect children between the ages of five and twelve years and may disappear during puberty. The student with petit mal seizures may experience serious learning difficulties. It is not uncommon for a child to have hundreds of petit mal seizures a day. If a child has 100 seizures and each lasts only 30 seconds, the child will have lost a full 50 minutes of learning time. Approximately 25 percent of individuals who have epilepsy experience petit mal attacks.[6]

The focal seizure is similar to the grand mal seizure. It is characterized by a loss of body tone and collapse. The student usually remains conscious during the attack, but speech may be impaired. In jacksonian focal seizures, there is a localized twitching of muscles in the extremities, which move up the arm or leg. If the seizure spreads to other parts of the brain, generalized convulsions and loss of consciousness result.

A psychomotor seizure is characterized by atypical social-motor behavior for 1 or 2 minutes. The behaviors may include uncontrollable temper tantrums, hand clapping, spitting, swearing, or shouting. The individual is unaware of the activity during and after the seizure. Psychomotor seizures can occur at any age.

Several factors can cause seizures. Some of these factors are (1) emotional stress such as fear, anger, or frustration; (2) excessive amounts of alcohol; and (3) menstruation.

Special Considerations   Teachers should be cognizant of which students have epilepsy and whether they are taking drugs to control their seizures. Anticonvulsant drugs are the preferred medical treatment for approximately 95 percent of individuals with epilepsy. Drug therapy can completely control grand mal seizures in 50 percent of the cases and greatly reduce seizures in another 35 percent. In the case of petit mal seizures, drug therapy will completely control the condition in 40 percent of the cases and reduce the number of seizures in 35 percent of the cases.[6] The type of drug that should be given and the optimum dosage are difficult to determine and highly individualized. Teachers should be sensitive to the side effects of these drugs, which may impair motor performance. Dilantin, for example, can produce lethargy, dizziness, and mental confusion. Phenobarbital sometimes contributes to drowsiness and learning difficulties.[6] Drugs taken to control petit mal seizures lead to drowsiness and nausea.[6] These side effects may be detrimental to the student's performance and safety in certain activities. Information about the student's drug treatment program should be discussed during the IEP meeting.

Physical education teachers should be familiar with procedures for handling seizures. Perhaps the most significant procedure for handling a seizure is to educate the student's class members about epilepsy. If the child's classmates are knowledgeable about seizures, the child will not have to suffer from postseizure embarrassment.

In the event a child has a grand mal seizure, the physical educator should do the following:

1. Help the student to the floor or ground and place the student in a back-lying position.
2. Clear the area of dangerous objects.
3. Loosen all restraining clothing, such as a belt or shirt collar.
4. If the student is experiencing breathing difficulty, tilt the student's head back to open the airway.
5. Do not try to insert an object into the person's mouth or attempt to restrain the individual who is having a seizure.
6. Once the convulsion has stopped, place a blanket or towel over the student to eliminate embarrassment if the student has lost bowel or bladder control.
7. Allow the student to rest.
8. Report the seizure to the appropriate school official.[78]

A grand mal seizure is not a life-threatening event and should be treated as a routine event. The seizure process is dangerous only if the student moves into status epilepticus—has a series of grand mal seizures without a break. If this happens, emergency medical personnel must be contacted immediately.

If the student experiences a focal or psychomotor seizure, the child should be removed to an isolated part of the gymnasium, if possible. If the student experiences a petit mal seizure and the teacher is aware of it, the teacher should repeat any instructions given previously.

The Physical Education Program and Teaching Strategies If medication is effective and the child's seizures are under control, the student should be able to participate in a physical education program. However, activities that involve direct blows to the head should be avoided, including boxing, soccer, and full-contact karate. Activities that are performed while a considerable height from the floor, swimming in cold water, and unsupervised scuba diving should also be avoided. Swimming should be carefully supervised. Individuals who have uncontrolled seizures should avoid gymnastics, ice hockey and ice skating, sailing and waterskiing, and horseback riding.[78]

Multiple Sclerosis

Multiple sclerosis is a chronic and degenerative neurological disease affecting primarily older adolescents and adults. It is a slowly progressive disease of the central nervous system, leading to the disintegration of the myelin coverings of nerve fibers in the brain and spinal cord, which results in hardening or scarring of the tissue that replaces the disintegrated protective myelin sheath.[6] The cause of multiple sclerosis is unknown, but immunologic abnormality is suspected.[6] Multiple sclerosis occurs in 1 of 2,000 births in temperate climates and in 1 of 10,000 births in tropical climates.[6]

Characteristics The symptoms of multiple sclerosis include sensory problems, such as visual disturbances, tremors, muscle weakness, spasticity, speech difficulties, dizziness, mild emotional disturbances, partial paralysis, fatigue, and motor difficulties. Multiple sclerosis generally appears when the person is between the ages of twenty and forty years and results in several periods of remissions and recurring exacerbations. Some persons have frequent attacks, whereas others have remissions that last as long as ten years.[6]

The Physical Activity Program There is no treatment that can repair the damage to the nervous system caused by degeneration. However, each person should be evaluated individually, and programs of resistive exercise should be administered to maintain maximum functioning. In addition, Jacobson relaxation techniques and active and passive range-of-motion exercises should be used to counter contractures in the lower extremities. The goal of these programs is to maintain functional skills, muscle strength, and range of motion. It is particularly important to teach the skills necessary for the functional use of walkers, crutches, and/or wheelchairs. In addition, the individual should be given the opportunity to develop compensatory skills—skills needed to function because of changes in central nervous system function. For example, these include skills to compensate for disequilibrium. Braces may be introduced at the later stages of the disorder to assist with locomotion.

Inactivity may contribute to the progressive weakening of the muscles needed for daily activity. Instructors should constantly encourage as active a lifestyle as possible. Individuals should be urged to participate in an exercise program that maintains cardiovascular respiratory functioning and sufficient muscle strength to allow participation in the activities of daily living. Because involvement of the lower extremities interferes with balance, stationary cycles using the arms or legs are recommended for testing and exercise. Begin with an unloaded warm-up and progress to exercising in 3- to 5-minute increments.[64] Swimming[54] and aquatic aerobic exercises are recommended because they require less effort than activities on land. Individuals who enjoy competition should be encouraged to participate in wheelchair sports when their condition is in remission.

Muscular Dystrophy

Muscular dystrophy is a group of inherited, progressive muscle disorders that differ according to which muscles are affected.[6] All types result in the deterioration of muscle strength, power, and endurance.[5] The rate of progressive degeneration is different for each set of muscles.[59] Although the exact incidence of muscular dystrophy is unknown, estimates place the number of persons with the disorder in excess of 200,000 in the United States. It is estimated that in more than half of the known cases, the age of onset falls within the range of three to thirteen years.

Characteristics and Types The physical characteristics of persons with muscular dystrophy are relevant to the degenerative stage as well as to the type of muscular dystrophy. In the late stages of the disease, connective tissue replaces most of the muscle tissue. In some cases, deposits of fat give the appearance of well-developed muscles. Despite the muscle atrophy, there is no apparent central nervous system impairment.

The age of onset of muscular dystrophy is of importance to the total development of the children. Persons who contract the disease after having had an opportunity to secure an education, or part of an education, and develop social and psychological strengths are better able to cope with their environment than are those who are afflicted with the disease before the acquisition of basic skills.

Although the characteristics of patients with muscular dystrophy vary according to the stage of the disease, some general characteristics are as follows:

1. There is a tendency to tire quickly.
2. There may be a tendency to lose fine manual dexterity.
3. There is sometimes a lack of motivation to learn because of isolation from social contacts and limited educational opportunities.
4. Progressive weakness tends to produce adverse postural changes.
5. Emotional disturbance may exist because of the progressive nature of the illness and the resulting restrictions placed on opportunities for socialization.

There are numerous classifications of muscular dystrophy based on the muscle groups affected and the age of onset. However, three main clinical types of muscular dystrophy have been identified:

Duchenne (pseudohypertrophic), Becker, and facioscapulohumeral (Landouzy-Dejerine).[6]

The Duchenne (pseudohypertrophic) type is an X-linked recessive disorder that usually presents itself during the ages of three to seven years. It occurs in 1 in every 3,000 live male births. It affects the pelvic girdle first, followed by the shoulder girdle.[6] Symptoms that give an indication of the disease are the following:

1. Waddling gait
2. Toe walking
3. Lordosis
4. Frequent falls
5. Difficulty getting up after falling
6. Difficulty climbing stairs[6]

As the disease progresses, imbalance of muscle strength in various parts of the body occurs. Deformities develop in flexion at the hips and knees. The spine, pelvis, and shoulder girdle also eventually become atrophied. Contractures and involvement of the heart may develop with the progressive degeneration of the disease. The motorized wheelchair has increased the independence of children in the advanced stages of muscular dystrophy. Though unable to perform activities of daily living, the child using a motorized wheelchair retains a measure of mobility that promotes independence and allows integration into many school-based and community-based programs.

Becker muscular dystrophy is also an X-linked disorder; however, it is less severe than the Duchenne type. The advancement of this type of dystrophy mimics the Duchenne type, but the Becker type progresses more slowly. As a result, few individuals are required to use wheelchairs until they approach their twentieth year, and most survive into their thirties or forties.[6]

The facioscapulohumeral (Landouzy-Dejerine) type of muscular dystrophy, which is the third most common type, is characterized by weakness of the facial muscles and shoulder girdles. The onset of symptoms or signs of the facioscapulohumeral type is usually recognized when the person is between the ages of seven and twenty years. Both genders are equally subject to the condition. Persons with this form of muscular dystrophy have trouble raising the arms above the head, whistling, drinking through a straw, and closing their eyes. A child with this type of disease often appears to have a masklike face, which lacks expression. Later, involvement of the muscles that move the humerus and scapula will be noticed. Weakness usually appears later in the abdominal, pelvic, and hip musculature. The progressive weakness and muscle deterioration often lead to scoliosis and lordosis. This type of muscular dystrophy is often milder than the Duchenne type, and life expectancy is normal.[6] Facioscapulohumeral muscular dystrophy usually progresses slowly, and ambulation is seldom lost.

Special Considerations Duchenne muscular dystrophy is one of the most serious disabling conditions that can occur in childhood. Although not fatal in itself, the disease contributes to premature death in most known cases because of its progressive nature. The progress of the condition is cruel and relentless as the child loses function and moves toward inevitable death. However, it is worth noting that scientific research may be close to solving unanswered questions regarding the disease, and eventually the progressive deterioration may be halted.

The Physical Education Program and Teaching Strategies An individually designed activity program may significantly contribute to the quality of life of the individual affected by muscular dystrophy. Inactivity seems to contribute to the progressive weakening of the muscles of persons with muscular dystrophy. Exercise of muscles involved in the activities of daily living to increase strength may permit greater functional use of the body. Furthermore, exercise may assist in reducing excessive weight, which is a burden to those who have muscular dystrophy. Movement in warm water—aquatic therapy—may be particularly beneficial for the child with muscular dystrophy. It aids in the maintenance of muscle tonus and flexibility, and it encourages circulation.

The child's diet should be closely monitored. Prevention of excess weight is essential to the success of the rehabilitation program of persons with progressive muscular dystrophy. For individuals whose strength is marginal, any extra weight is an added burden on ambulation and on activities of daily living.

A great deal can be done to prevent deformities and loss of muscle strength from inactivity. If a specific strengthening and stretching program is outlined during each stage of the disease, the child may extend the ability to care for most of his or her daily needs for many additional years. In addition to the administration of specific developmental exercises for the involved muscles, exercises should include the development of walking patterns, posture control, muscle coordination, and the stretching of contractures involved in disuse atrophy. However, all exercises should be selected after the study of contraindications specified by a physician. It is desirable to select activities that use the remaining strengths so that enjoyment and success can be achieved.

All the types of muscular dystrophy cannot be considered to be the same; therefore, the physical and social benefits that children can derive from physical education and recreation programs are different. However, all children with muscular dystrophy can profit from a well-designed program to enhance quality of life. The focus of the program, particularly for children with Duchenne muscular dystrophy, is on the development of leisure and recreation skills that will be appropriate as the child progressively loses function. For example, a child with Duchenne dystrophy should be taught to fish and to play bocci because those are skills that can be enjoyed throughout the life span. Also, the child should be given the opportunity to learn board and video games that will provide entertainment and joy.

One focus of the program should be the development of relaxation techniques. The progressive loss of functional skills causes a great deal of stress, as does facing the inevitability of an early death; the quality of the child's life can be enhanced if the child has learned conscious relaxation skills.

Perhaps more important, a significant dance, music, and art therapy program should be a part of the child's total program. Movement and dance, even dance done in a motorized wheelchair, can help the child or adolescent express emotions—grief, rage, frustration love, joy. Music and art therapy provide vital avenues of expression as the child loses motor capabilities. In addition, a trained therapist can be of value as the child moves through the stages of grief. The intent of the program is to enhance the quality of the child's life and, with professional support, allow the process of dying to be as humane, caring, and ennobling as possible. Specific programs are suggested in Figure 15-2.

Parkinson's Disease

Parkinson's disease is a slow, progressive disorder that results in physical debilitation. The disease usually appears gradually and progresses slowly. It may progress to a stage where there is difficulty with the routine activities of daily living. There is no known cause; however, it is believed to result from a combination of genetics and environment (e.g., exposure to toxins).[75] The condition may be aggravated by emotional tension or fatigue. It affects about 1 percent of the population over

---

Figure 15-2 Recommended Programming Ideas for Persons with Muscular Dystrophy

Provide realistic short-term goals to the individuals and parents.

Use submaximal resistance exercises while focusing on maintaining muscle endurance, peak power, and strength.

Reduce the intensity of the activity if the person complains of exercise-induced cramps or excessive fatigue.

Include as many gamelike, fun situations as possible.

Provide nutritional counseling in conjunction with physical training to help avoid becoming overweight.

Modified from Bar-Or O: Muscular dystrophy. In Durstine DL, editor: *Exercise management for persons with chronic diseases and disabilities,* Champaign, IL, 1997, Human Kinetics.

sixty-five years of age, with an onset between forty and sixty years.[6] A juvenile form of parkinsonism, which has its onset prior to age forty years, has also been identified.

Characteristics The observable characteristics of Parkinson's disease are infrequent blinking and lack of facial expression, tremor of the resting muscles, a slowing of voluntary movements, muscular weakness, abnormal gait, and postural instability.[6] These motor characteristics become more pronounced as the disease progresses. For instance, a minor feeling of sluggishness may progress until the individual is unable to get up from a chair. The walking gait becomes less efficient and can be characterized by shuffling of the feet for the purpose of postural stability. In addition, voluntary movements, particularly those performed by the small muscles, become slow, and spontaneous movements diminish.

In general, most persons require lifelong management consisting of physical therapy and drug therapy. Physical therapy consists of heat and massage to alleviate the muscle cramps and relieve tension headaches that often accompany rigidity of the muscles of the neck.

The Physical Activity Program Because of the degenerative nature of the disease, the goals of physical activity programs are to preserve muscular functioning for purposive movement involved in the activities of daily living and required for the performance of leisure and recreation skills. The general types of physical activities that may be of value are general coordination exercises to retard the slow deterioration of movement and relaxation exercises that may reduce muscular incoordination and tremors. In addition, balance activities and those that teach compensation for lack of balance should be included. Exercises directed at maintaining postural strength and flexibility should be a part of the program plan. Care must be taken when the individual is on antiparkinsonian medications because of the varied side effects.[75] A physician's and or a physical therapist's guidance should be sought as the disease progresses.

Poliomyelitis and Post-Polio Syndrome

Poliomyelitis (polio) is an acute viral infection with a wide range of manifestations.[6] In the serious cases (nonparalytic and paralytic), an inflammation affects the anterior motor cells in the spinal cord, which in turn affects the muscles. Extensive vaccination has virtually eradicated polio; however, an increasing number of individuals who had polio as children are developing a post-polio syndrome (PPS). Almost one-fourth of the individuals who contracted polio during peak epidemics are now developing symptoms similar to that experienced during the initial onset of the disease. The most common complaints are fatigue, weakness, and muscle and joint pain.[7]

Characteristics and Types There are two basic patterns—minor illness (abortive) and major illness (paralytic or nonparalytic). Minor poliomyelitis accounts for 80 to 90 percent of the clinical infections and occurs chiefly in children.[6] This form does not involve the central nervous system. The symptoms are headache, sore throat, mild fever, and nausea.

Major poliomyelitis involves the central nervous system. In addition to the symptoms of minor poliomyelitis, the victim might experience a fever, severe headache, stiff neck, and general and specific pain in and acute contractions of one or more muscle groups located in the upper and lower extremities or the back. Individuals with the nonparalytic form recover completely. Individuals with the paralytic form develop paralysis of muscle groups throughout the body. Twenty-five percent of these individuals have a severe permanent disability, 25 percent have a mild permanent disability, and 50 percent recover completely.[6]

A post-polio syndrome has been identified that occurs many years after a paralytic poliomyelitis attack. The characteristics include muscle fatigue and decreased endurance, accompanied by weakness, and atrophy in selected muscles.[6]

The Physical Activity Program Exercise programs should focus on motor tasks that develop strength, endurance, flexibility, and coordination.

Orthopedic deformities resulting from the residual effects of polio do not totally restrict movement. Children learn quickly to compensate for the inconvenience of an impaired foot or arm. At the elementary school level, many children with polio can achieve considerable athletic success. However, as they progress through school life, accumulated developmental lags, as a rule, influence skill development. Wheelchair sports are popular for polio victims who cannot walk.

For adults who experience post-polio syndrome, it appears that the muscle units that were not originally impaired become fatigued from overwork. These individuals appear to benefit from moderate-intensity aerobic exercise and resistive training. To conserve energy, it is recommended that exercising should take place in the morning of relatively unstressful days, and overextending effort should be avoided.[7]

Spina Bifida

Spina bifida is the most common congenital spinal defect. The condition is a result of defective closure of the vertebral column. The severity ranges from spina bifida occulta, with no findings, to a completely open spine (spina bifida cystica).[6] The incidence of spina bifida is estimated at 2 per 100 live births, making it one of the most common birth defects that can lead to physical disability.

Characteristics In spina bifida occulta, the vertebral arches fail to fuse; however, there is no distension of the spinal cord lining or of the cord itself. In spina bifida cystica, the protruding sac can contain just the lining (meninges) of the spinal column (meningocele) or both the meninges and the spinal cord (myelomeningocele).[65] See Figures 15-3 and 15-4. Meningocele usually can be repaired with little or no damage to the neural pathways. Myelomeningocele, the more common of the two types, produces varying degrees of neurological impairment ranging from mild muscle imbalance and sensory loss in the lower limbs to paralysis of one or both legs. Paralysis usually affects bladder and bowel function,[6] and bladder and kidney infections are frequent. Over 70 percent of children born with

CASE STUDY

Josue

Josue is a first-grader with spina bifida myelomeningocele. His parents divorced in the first year after Josue's birth. His mother is having serious difficulty dealing with Josue's disability. She is in denial to the extent that she believes and tells Josue every day that he will not have spina bifida as an adult. She admitted in an individual education program (IEP) meeting that she is severely depressed and suicidal. As a result, Josue is developing behavior problems at home and at school. Though a bright little boy, he often engages in refusal behavior when asked to work.

Josue is very mobile in his chair. He is able to wheel in a straight line and in a circle, can stop and start with ease, can move backward, and is learning to do a "wheelie." He is able to get in and out of his wheelchair independently. At a recent IEP meeting, it was recommended that Josue participate in the regular physical education class and in community-based sports programs; however, his mother was very reluctant to agree.

APPLICATION TASK
Identify strategies for convincing Josue's mother to permit him to participate in the regular physical education class and in community-based sports programs for young children with disabilities. Modify the warm-up regimen the regular class uses, and develop a cardiovascular program so Josue can participate in the warm-up and heart-healthy portion of the curriculum. Identify the types of wheelchair maneuvers and skills he should practice in class in order to be successful in a sports program. Identify types of physical education activities where the use of a wheelchair may endanger the other children, and suggest alternative activities Josue could do with a peer on the sidelines. Develop a behavior-management plan that should be implemented when he refuses to participate in classroom activities.

myelomeningocele also have hydrocephalus. In these cases, usually a shunt is inserted to drain off cerebrospinal fluid that is not being reabsorbed properly. Removing the excess cerebrospinal fluid

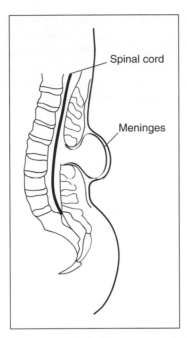

Figure 15-3   Meningocele

In this form, the sac contains tissues which cover the spinal cord (meninges) and cerebrospinal fluid. This fluid bathes and protects the brain and spinal cord. The nerves are not usually badly damaged and are able to function; therefore, there is often little disability present. This is the least common form.

Courtesy of Association for Spina Bifida and Hydrocephalus.

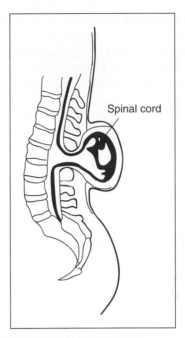

Figure 15-4   Myelomeningocele (Meningomyelocele)

This is the more common of the two meningoceles and the most serious. Here the sac or cyst not only contains tissue and cerebrospinal fluid but also nerves and part of the spinal cord. The spinal cord is damaged or not properly developed. As a result, there is always some degree of paralysis and loss of sensation below the damaged vertebrae. The amount of disability depends very much on where the spina bifida is and the amount of nerve damage involved. Many children and adults with this condition experience problems with bowel and bladder control.

Courtesy of Association for Spina Bifida and Hydrocephalus.

protects the child against brain damage resulting from pressure on the brain. Children who are paraplegic from spina bifida are often able to move about with the aid of braces and crutches. It is also interesting to note that many children who have spina bifida are allergic to latex.

Special Considerations   Activities that could distress the placement of any shunts or put pressure on sensitive areas of the spine must be avoided. Of considerable concern is the prevention of contractures and associated foot deformities (e.g., equinovarus) through daily passive flexibility exercises.

Many social problems result from spina bifida. In addition to the physical disability, there are often problems associated with bowel and bladder

control, which draw further attention to the children as they function in a social environment. In many cases, this has a negative social impact on the children. Often, children with spina bifida need catheterization. If someone must do it for them, the attention of others is drawn to these circumstances. However, in many cases older children may be taught to catheterize themselves. The physical disability and the associated physiological problems result in stressful social situations because groups must adapt to the child with spina bifida's physical disabilities and associated physiological problems. Social circumstances can be made more favorable if these children are integrated into regular classes in the early grades and if social integration strategies are used (see Chapter 9).

The Physical Education Program and Teaching Strategies   No particular program of physical education or therapy can be directly assigned to the student with spina bifida. Some students have no physical reaction and discover the condition only by chance through X-ray examination for another problem. On the other hand, a person may have extensive neuromuscular involvement requiring constant medical care. A program of physical education or therapeutic exercise based on the individual needs of the person should be planned.

The child with spina bifida myelomeningocele is often able to participate in a regular physical education program more effectively in a wheelchair than with the use of a walker or crutches and braces. While the child with spina bifida should be encouraged to walk whenever possible, it may be difficult for the child to participate in activities safely in a crowded gymnasium.

Simple modifications can be made to allow the child using a wheelchair to participate actively in regular physical education. Specific suggestions for including young children in wheelchairs in a regular physical education program are presented later in this chapter in the section on spinal cord injuries.

Orthopedic Disabilities
Arthritis

The term *arthritis* is derived from two Greek roots: arthro-, meaning joint, and -itis, meaning

A swimmer with an above-the-knee amputation participates in world-class competition.
Courtesy of Orthotic and Prosthetic Athlete Assistance Fund, Inc., Alexandria, VA.

CASE STUDY

Roberto

Roberto was diagnosed with severe juvenile rheumatoid arthritis (JRA) at age three years. At age five years, Roberto is unable to move without severe pain. Roberto uses a wheelchair for ambulation but needs someone to push him. He has severe flexion contractures at most of his joints. His hands and fingers are so affected that he is unable to grasp an object.

Roberto lives in a small, rural community. His parents, migrant workers, struggle to provide care. His pain and anti-inflammatory medication are both very expensive. Their transient life style and the cost of medication make it difficult for them to keep him on a regular medication schedule.

APPLICATION TASK
Identify types of things the adapted physical educator can do to help improve the quality of Roberto's life. What role, if any, might the general physical educator play?

inflammation. It has been estimated that more than 12 million people in the United States are afflicted with some form of arthritic disease. Since arthritis inflicts a low mortality and high morbidity, the potential for increasing numbers of those afflicted and disabled is great. It is assumed that a great many factors may predispose one to arthritis. Major contributors could be infection, hereditary factors, environmental stress, dietary deficiencies, trauma, and organic or emotional disturbances.

Types, Causes, Incidence, and Characteristics
In most cases, arthritis is progressive, gradually resulting in general fatigue, weight loss, and muscular stiffness. Joint impairment is symmetrical, and characteristically the small joints of the hands and feet are affected in the earliest stages. Tenderness and pain may occur in tendons and muscular tissue near inflamed joints. As the inflammation in the joints becomes progressively chronic, degenerative and proliferative changes occur to the synovial tendons, ligaments, and articular cartilages. If the inflammation is not arrested in its early stages, joints become ankylosed and muscles atrophy and contract, eventually causing a twisted and deformed limb. Three common forms of arthritis are rheumatoid, osteoarthritis, and anklyosing spondylitis.

Rheumatoid arthritis is the nation's number one crippling disease, afflicting more than 3 million persons. It is a systemic disease of unknown cause. Seventy-five percent of the cases occur between the ages of twenty-five and fifty years and in a ratio of 3 to 1, women to men. A type of rheumatoid arthritis called Still's disease, or juvenile arthritis, attacks children before the age of seven years. Approximately 285,000 children in the United States are afflicted with rheumatoid arthritis, making it a major crippler among young children.[2] The most significant physical sign is the thickening of the synovial tissue in joints that are actively involved (inflamed). Inflamed joints are sensitive to the touch. Individuals with rheumatoid arthritis are stiff for an hour or so after rising in the morning or after a period of inactivity.[6]

Osteoarthritis, the second most frequent type of arthritis, is a disorder of the hyaline cartilage primarily in the weight-bearing joints. It is a result of mechanical destruction of the coverings of the bone at the joints because of trauma or repeated use. Although evidence of the breakdown can be documented during the twenties, discomfort usually does not occur until individuals are in their forties. Initially the condition is noninflammatory, and it impacts only one or a few joints. Pain is the earliest symptom, and it increases initially with exercise. The condition affects men and women equally.[6]

Ankylosing spondylitis affects the axial skeleton and large peripheral joints of the body and is most prevalent in males.[6] It usually begins between the ages of twenty and forty years, and it is the most common type experienced by persons under thirty-five years of age.[54] Common symptoms are recurrent back pain, particularly at night, and early morning stiffness that is relieved by activity.

Special Considerations   Interventions for these types of arthritis include proper diet, rest, drug therapy, reduction of stress, and exercise. Because of its debilitating effect, prolonged bed rest is discouraged, although daily rest sessions are required to avoid undue fatigue. A number of drugs may be given to the patient, depending on individual needs; for example, salicylates such as aspirin relieve pain, gold compounds may be used for arresting the acute inflammatory stage, and adrenocortical steroids may be used for control of the degenerative process. Drugless techniques of controlling arthritis pain, such as biofeedback, self-hypnosis, behavior modification, and transcutaneous nerve stimulation, are often used as adjuncts to more traditional types of treatment.

The Physical Activity Program and Teaching Strategies   Physical exercise is critical to reduce pain and increase function. The exercises required by patients with arthritis fall into three major categories: exercises to improve and maintain range of motion, exercises that strengthen muscles that surround and support affected joints, and aerobic exercises to improve cardiovascular endurance.[54] The physical educator should encourage gradual or

Ankle-foot orthotics are custom-built to fit individuals' needs.
Courtesy of Orthomerica Products, Inc., Newport Beach, CA.

static stretching, isometric muscle contraction, and low-impact aerobic exercise daily. Exercising in a pool, biking, and rowing are highly recommended.[62]

Maintenance of normal joint range of movement is of prime importance for establishing a functional joint. Stretching may first be passive; however, active stretching is of greater benefit because muscle tone is maintained in the process. Joints should be moved through pain-free range of motion several times daily.[54]

Isometric exercises that strengthen muscles that support affected joints should be practiced during the day when the pain and stiffness are at a minimum. Weight-bearing isotonic exercises that cause compression of joints should be avoided.

Aerobic exercises that require a minimum of weight bearing should be used. Bicycling, swim-

ming, and aquatic aerobics are highly recommended. Whenever possible, water activities should take place in a heated pool because the warmth enhances circulation and reduces muscle tightness. One recreational activity that has been shown to improve cardiovascular endurance and to counteract depression, anxiety, and tension is dancing.[68]

An individual with arthritis may need rest periods during the day. These should be combined with a well-planned exercise program. Activity should never increase pain or so tire an individual that normal recovery is not obtained by the next day.

Arthrogryposis (Curved Joints)

Arthrogryposis is a condition of flexure or contracture of joints (joints of the lower limbs more often than joints of the upper limbs) that is present at birth. The incidence is estimated to be 1 in 3,000 births.[4]

Characteristics   The limbs may be fixed in any position. However, the usual forms are with the shoulders turned in, the elbows straightened and extended, the forearms turned with the palms outward (pronated), and the wrists flexed and deviated upward with the fingers curled into the palms. The hips may be bent in a flexed position and turned outward (externally rotated), and the feet are usually turned inward and downward. The spine often evidences scoliosis, the limbs are small in circumference, and the joints appear large and have lost their range of motion. Deformities are at their worst at birth, and a regular exercise program improves function; active physical therapy early in life can produce reduced contracture and improved range of motion.

Several physical conditions are associated with arthrogryposis, including congenital heart disease, urinary tract abnormalities, respiratory problems, abdominal hernias, and cleft palate. Intelligence is usually normal. Children with arthrogryposis may walk independently but with an abnormal gait, or they may depend on a wheelchair.

Special Considerations   Surgery often is used to correct hip conditions, as well as knee and foot deformities. Surgery is sometimes used to permit limited flexion of the elbow joint, as well as greater wrist mobility.

The Physical Education Program and Teaching Strategies The awkwardness of joint positions and mechanics causes no pain; therefore, children with arthrogryposis are free to engage in most types of activity. Muscle strengthening and range-of-motion exercises prove to be very beneficial.[4]

Congenital Hip Dislocation

Congenital hip dislocation, which is also known as developmental hip dislocation, is a disorder in which the head of the thigh bone (femur) doesn't fit properly into, or is outside of, the hip socket (acetabulum) (see Figure 15-5). It is estimated that it occurs more often in females than in males; it may be bilateral or unilateral, occurring most often in the left hip. One of every sixty births has a hip dislocation.[15]

The cause of congenital hip dislocation is unknown, with various causes proposed. Heredity seems to be a primary causative factor in faulty hip development and subsequent dysplasia. Actually, only about 2 percent of developmental hip dislocations are congenital.

Characteristics Generally, the acetabulum is shallower on the affected side than on the nonaffected side, and the femoral head is displaced upward and backward in relation to the ilium. Ligaments and muscles become deranged, resulting in a shortening of the rectus femoris, hamstring, and adductor thigh muscles and affecting the small intrinsic muscles of the hip. Prolonged malpositioning of the femoral head produces a chronic weakness of the gluteus medius and minimus muscles. A primary factor in stabilizing one hip in the upright posture is the iliopsoas muscle. In developmental hip dislocation, the iliopsoas muscle displaces the femoral head upward; this will eventually cause the lumbar vertebrae to become lordotic and scoliotic.

Detection of the hip dislocation may not occur until the child begins to bear weight or walk. Early recognition of this condition may be accomplished by observing asymmetrical fat folds on the infant's legs and restricted hip adduction on the affected side. The Trendelenburg test (see Figure 15-6) will reveal that the child is unable to maintain the pelvic level while standing on the affected leg. In such cases, weak abductor muscles of the affected leg

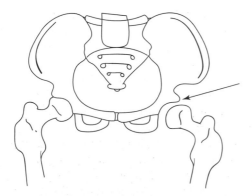

Figure 15-5 Developmental Hip Dislocation

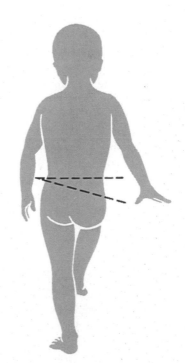

Figure 15-6 Trendelenburg Test

allow the pelvis to tilt downward on the nonaffected side. The child walks with a decided limp in unilateral cases and with a waddle in bilateral cases. No discomfort or pain is normally experienced by the child, but fatigue tolerance to physical activity is very low. Pain and discomfort become more apparent as the individual becomes older and as postural deformities become more structural.

Special Considerations   Medical treatment depends on the age of the child and the extent of displacement. Young babies with a mild involvement may have the condition remedied through gradual adduction of the femur by a pillow splint, whereas more complicated cases may require traction, casting, or surgery to restore proper hip continuity. The thigh is slowly returned to a normal position.

The Physical Education Program and Teaching Strategies   Active exercise is suggested, along with passive stretching to contracted tissue. Primary concern is paid to reconditioning the movement of hip extension and abduction. When adequate muscle strength has been gained in the hip region, a program of ambulation is conducted, with particular attention paid to walking without a lateral pelvic tilt. A child in the physical education or recreation program with a history of developmental hip dislocation will, in most instances, require specific postural training, conditioning of the hip region, continual gait training, and general body mechanics training. Swimming is an excellent activity for general conditioning of the hip, and it is highly recommended. Activities should not be engaged in to the point of discomfort or fatigue.

Coxa Plana (Legg-Calvé-Perthes Disease)

Coxa plana is the result of abnormal softening of the femoral head. It is a condition identified early in the twentieth century independently by Legg of Boston, Calvé of France, and Perthes of Germany. Its gross signs reflect a flattening of the head of the femur (see Figure 15-7), and it is found predominantly in boys between the ages of five and ten years.[6] It has been variously termed osteochondritis deformans juvenilis, pseudocoxalgia, and Legg-

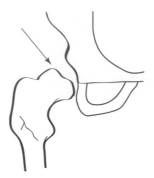

Figure 15-7   Coxa Plana

Calvé-Perthes disease. The exact cause of coxa plana is not known; trauma, infection, and endocrine imbalance have been suggested as possible causes.

Characteristics   Coxa plana is characterized by degeneration of the capital epiphysis of the femoral head. Osteoporosis, or bone rarefaction, results in a flattened and deformed femoral head. Later developments may also include widening of the femoral head and thickening of the femoral neck. The last stage of coxa plana may be reflected by a self-limiting course in which there is a regeneration and an almost complete return of the normal epiphysis within two to three years.[6] However, recovery is not always complete, and there is often some residual deformity. The younger child with coxa plana has the best prognosis for complete recovery.

The first outward sign of this condition is often a limp favoring the affected leg, with pain in the hip or referred to the knee region. The individual with coxa plana experiences progressive fatigue and pain on weight bearing, progressive stiffness, and a limited range of movement.

Treatment of coxa plana primarily entails the removal of stress placed on the femoral head by weight bearing. Bed rest is often used in the acute stages, with ambulation and nonweight-bearing devices used for the remaining period of incapacitation. The sling and crutch method for nonweight bearing is widely used for this condition (see Figure 15-8).

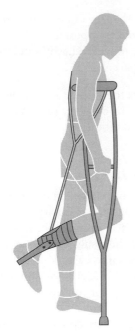

Figure 15-8   Sling and Crutch for Hip Conditions

Weight-bearing exercise is contraindicated until the physician discounts the possibility of a pathological joint condition.

The Physical Education Program And Teaching Strategies The individual with an epiphyseal affection of the hip presents a problem of muscular and skeletal stability and joint range of movement. Stability of the hip region requires skeletal continuity and a balance of muscle strength, primarily in the muscles of hip extension and abduction. Prolonged limited motion and nonweight bearing may result in contractures of tissues surrounding the hip joint and an inability to walk or run with ease. Abnormal weakness of the hip extensors and abductors may cause shortening of the hip flexors and adductors and lead the individual to display the Trendelenburg sign (review Figure 15-6).

A program of exercise must be carried out to prevent muscle atrophy and general deconditioning. When movement is prohibited, muscle-tensing exercises for muscles of the hip region are

conducted, together with isotonic exercises for the upper extremities, trunk, ankles, and feet.

When the hip becomes free of symptoms, a progressive, isotonic, nonweight-bearing program is initiated for the hip region. Active movement emphasizing hip extension and abduction is recommended. Swimming is an excellent adjunct to the regular exercise program.

The program of exercise should never exceed the point of pain or fatigue until full recovery is accomplished. A general physical fitness program emphasizing weight control and body mechanics will aid the student in preparing for a return to a full program of physical education and recreation activities.

Osgood-Schlatter Condition

Osgood-Schlatter condition is not considered a disease entity but, rather, the result of trauma to the patellar tendon where it inserts on the tibia. Major features are pain, swelling, and tenderness over the insertion point.[6]

The Osgood-Schlatter condition usually occurs in active boys between the ages of ten and fifteen years and girls between the ages of eight and thirteen, and it is more common in males.[6] Furthermore, the condition occurs twice as frequently in the left knee than in the right knee.

Characteristics Disruption of the blood supply to the epiphysis results in enlargement of the tibial tubercle, joint tenderness, and pain on contraction of the quadriceps muscle. The physical educator may be the person who detects this condition based on complaints of the student. When this happens, the student should be immediately referred to a physician.

Special Considerations If the Osgood-Schlatter condition is not properly cared for, deformity and a defective extensor mechanism may result; however, it may not necessarily be associated with pain or discomfort. In most cases, the Osgood-Schlatter condition is acute, is self-limiting, and does not exceed a few months' duration. However, even after the arrest of symptoms, the Osgood-Schlatter condition tends to recur after irritation.

Local inflammation occurs when the legs are used and eases with rest. The individual may be unable to kneel or engage in flexion and extension movements without pain. The knee joint must be kept completely immobilized when the inflammatory state persists. Forced inactivity, provided by a plaster cast, may be the only answer to keeping the overactive adolescent from using the affected leg.

The Physical Education Program and Teaching Strategies   Early detection may reveal a slight condition in which the individual can continue a normal activity routine, excluding sport participation, excessive exercise, strenuous running, jumping, deep knee bending, and falling on the affected leg. All physical education activities must be modified to avoid quadriceps muscle strain while preparing for general physical fitness.

While the limb is immobilized in a cast, the individual is greatly restricted; weight bearing may be held to a minimum, with signs of pain at the affected part closely watched by the physician. Although the Osgood-Schlatter condition is self-limiting and temporary, exercise is an important factor in full recovery. Physical education activities should emphasize the capabilities of the upper body and nonaffected leg to prevent their deconditioning.

After arrest of the condition and removal of the cast (or relief from immobilization), the patient is given a graduated reconditioning program. The major objectives at this time are re-education in proper walking patterns and the restoration of normal strength and flexibility of the knee joint. Strenuous knee movement is avoided for at least five weeks, and the demanding requirements of regular physical education classes may be postponed for extended periods, depending on the physician's recommendations. Although emphasis is placed on the affected leg during the period of rehabilitation, a program also must be provided for the entire body.

The following are criteria for the individual to return to a regular physical education program:

1. Normal range of movement of the knee
2. Quadriceps muscle strength equal to that of the unaffected leg
3. Evidence that the Osgood-Schlatter condition has become asymptomatic
4. Ability to move freely without favoring the affected part

After recovery, the student should avoid all activities that tend to contuse, or in any way irritate again, the tibial tuberosity.

Osteogenesis Imperfecta (Brittle Bone Disease)

Osteogenesis imperfecta is a condition marked by both weak bones and elasticity of the joints, ligaments, and skin. It occurs once in 20,000 births.[29] Most cases are the result of a dominant genetic defect, although some cases result from a spontaneous mutation.[69] There are four types, ranging from mild to severe involvement.

Characteristics   The bones of children with this condition are abnormally frail and may have multiple fractures at the time of birth. The underlying layer of the eyeball (choroid) shows through as a blue discoloration. Individuals who live are shorter than average and have a triangular-shaped face.

As growth occurs in individuals with the disease, the limbs tend to become bowed. The bones are not dense, and the spine is rounded and often evidences scoliosis. The teeth are in poor condition, easily broken, discolored, and prone to cavities. The joints are excessively mobile, and the positions that the children may take show great flexibility.

Special Considerations   No known chemical or nutrient has been shown to correct osteogenesis imperfecta, and the most satisfactory treatment is the surgical insertion of a steel rod between the ends of the long bones. This treatment, plus bracing, permits some youth to walk. Many persons with brittle bone disease need a wheelchair at least part of the time, and those with severe cases require a wheelchair exclusively.

The Physical Education Program and Teaching Strategies   Some authorities have suggested that physical activities are to be ruled out for this population, whereas others encourage exercise to promote muscle and bone strength. Swimming and water therapy are strongly recommended. These individuals are also encouraged to maintain a healthy weight and avoid activities that deplete bone (smoking, steroid use).[69]

Physical education teachers should be sensitive to the presence of children in their classes whose bones are highly susceptible to injury, trauma, or breakage because of this and related conditions. These children, who approach normalcy in other areas, continue to require a highly adapted physical education program that is limited to range-of-motion exercises. Although the diagnosis of osteogenesis imperfecta is assigned only to severe cases, many children seem to have a propensity for broken bones. Physical educators should take softness of bones into consideration when developing physical education programs for children.

Osteomyelitis

Osteomyelitis is an inflammation of a bone and its medullary (marrow) cavity. Occasionally referred to as myelitis, this condition is caused by bacteria, mycrobacteria, and fungi.[6] In its early stages osteomyelitis is described as acute. If the infection persists or recurs periodically, it is called chronic. Since chronic osteomyelitis may linger on for years, the physical educator should confer with the physician about the nature of an adapted program.

Characteristics   The bones most often affected in osteomyelitis are the tibia, femur, and humerus. Pain, tenderness, and soft tissue swelling are present, and heat is felt through the overlying skin. There are limited effects on range of joint movement. The child may limp because of the acute pain.

Special Considerations   If medical treatment is delayed, abscesses work outward, causing a sinus (hole) in the skin over the affected bone from which pus is discharged. This sinus is covered with a dressing that must be changed several times daily. The medical treatment is rest and intensive antibiotic therapy. Through surgery, the infected bone can be scraped to evacuate the pus.

The Physical Education Program and Teaching Strategies   Rehabilitation activity under the direction of a physician can restore motor functions so that normal activity can be resumed. Exercise is always contraindicated when infection is active in the body.

Spondylolysis and Spondylolisthesis

Spondylolysis and spondylolisthesis result from a congenital malformation of one or both of the neural arches of the fifth lumbar vertebra or, less frequently, the fourth lumbar vertebra. Spondylolisthesis is distinguished from spondylolysis by anterior displacement of the fifth lumbar vertebra on the sacrum. Both conditions may be accompanied by pain in the lower back.

Forward displacement may occur as a result of sudden trauma to the lumbar region. The vertebrae are moved anteriorly because of an absence of bony continuity of the neural arch, and the main support is derived from ligaments that surround the area. In such cases, individuals often appear to have severe lordosis.

Characteristics   Many individuals have spondylolysis, or even spondylolisthesis, without symptoms of any kind, but a mild twist or blow may set off a whole series of low back complaints and localized discomfort or pain radiating down one or both sides.

Special Considerations   The pathological condition eventually may become so extensive as to require surgical intervention.

The Physical Education Program and Teaching Strategies   Proper therapy may involve a graduated exercise program to help prevent further aggravation and, in some cases, remove many symptoms characteristic of the condition. A program should be initiated that includes stretching the lower back, strengthening abdominal muscles, walking to stimulate blood flow, and engaging in a general conditioning program. Games and sports that overextend, fatigue, or severely twist and bend the lower back should be avoided. In most cases, the physician will advise against contact sports and heavy weight lifting.

Traumatic Injuries

Traumatic Brain Injuries

Definition   A traumatic brain injury is an injury to the head that results in minor to serious brain damage. It is the most common cause of acquired disability in childhood and adolescence.[49] The effects of head injuries on school behavior depend on the extent of the insult to the brain tissue.

Incidence   Approximately 1.5 million traumatic brain injuries (TBI) occur in the United States each year, with 20 percent resulting from recreational sports.[82] Of those who seek medical intervention, 1 million are treated and released from hospital emergency rooms, 230,000 are hospitalized and survive, and 50,000 die.[14]

Causes   The causes of TBI include motor vehicle accidents (most common in adolescence), falls, bicycle accidents, child abuse, assaults, and sport injuries. In 1996, thirty-four percent of sports or recreation-related injuries were mild and did not require a physician's attendance, 55 percent received outpatient care, and 12 percent were hospitalized.[82]

Characteristics   The location and severity of brain damage greatly affect the characteristic behaviors of the child and the speed of recovery. Generally, attention/concentration; memory; executive functions; cognition; and motor and language functions are impaired to some extent. These posttrauma reactions frequently lead to a misdiagnosis of learning disabled, mentally retarded, or emotionally disturbed.[60] Although rapid recovery of most functions occurs during the first two or three years after injury, problems frequently persist for longer periods. When the frontal lobe is involved, cognitive impairments include impairments in attention, executive functioning, and problem solving. Damage to the temporal regions of the brain result in problems with learning new information.[49] Gross motor impairments are more frequent than fine motor impairments.[77] Static and

CASE STUDY

Bubba

Bubba is the nickname of a seven-year-old boy who was hit by a drunk driver while riding his bicycle near his home in West Texas. Bubba was described by his parents before the accident as "all boy," "outgoing," "athletic," "rough and tumble," and "friendly."

An adapted physical education assessment six months after his traumatic brain injury described the following behaviors and characteristics:

- He is able to walk, with a cane, independently on flat and known surfaces without falling.
- He is able to recover from a fall to a stand.
- He is unable to run, gallop, jump, hop, or skip.
- Bubba cannot ascend or descend stairs without support from a teacher's aide.
- He is able to throw a yarn ball, with excellent directionality, a distance of 10 feet without falling.
- He is able to "kick" an 8-inch ball by pushing at it with his left foot.
- He is unable to stand on one foot and maintain a balance with eyes open.

Complicating his re-entry into the elementary school in his neighborhood is the fact that the speech centers of the brain were also apparently affected. He is demonstrating speech and language behaviors similar to that of a person with Tourette syndrome. The teachers and staff have worked very hard to teach him to use alternatives to swear words that appear to "pop" out of his mouth without reason.

APPLICATION TASK

Bubba has a one-on-one paraprofessional who spends the entire day with him. She adores Bubba and is willing to do anything to help him. Describe the activities she could do to help him regain functional skills.

dynamic balance as well as activities requiring coordination of the two sides of the body are usually impacted the most.[33] Difficulty processing and integrating information, as well as abnormal brain activity, contributes to negative behaviors, including low tolerance for frustration, aggression, impulsiveness, and noncompliance. In addition, seizures are three times more likely among individuals with TBI, with the risk doubling as late as five years after the injury. The extent and frequency of these problems should be addressed in the student's IEP.

Testing   The type of test administered will depend on the extent and severity of the student's brain damage. If an individual is having difficulty organizing sensory input, decision and movement time will be compromised, as well as movement efficiency. The type of teaching approach (bottom-up or top-down) a teacher uses will dictate the assessment instrument used. The teacher who wants to address functional performance will measure physical fitness and specific sporting skills.[77] The teacher who uses the bottom-up approach will elect to sample sensory input function. To determine what types of sensory input problems exist, the physical educator may wish to administer a sensory input screening instrument similar to the one presented in Chapter 4.

If the evaluator is more interested in simply pinpointing the areas of motor functioning that have been affected, a motor development or motor proficiency test such as the Test of Gross Motor Development or the Bruininks-Oseretsky Test of Motor Proficiency (balance, strength, and bilateral coordination subtests) should be administered.

Special Considerations   The extent of the brain damage will determine the number of special considerations that must be made. The person who suffers from TBI will have good days and bad days. On a good day, it is relatively easy to attend, follow directions, and tolerate minor frustrations. On a bad day, everything is blown out of proportion—it is hard to sit still, listen to instructions, overlook minor problems, and comply with rules. The sensitive teacher will attend carefully to clues that indicate the type of day the student with brain damage is experiencing and adjust expectations for the student accordingly. Allowance must always be made

for basic organizational problems and learning difficulties that have resulted from the insult to the brain tissue. The more positive and user-friendly the educational environment, the better.

D'Amato and Rothlisberg[24] recommend using a structure, organization, and strategy (S.O.S.) approach to assist the student with TBI who is struggling to function in a school setting. Structuring involves keeping the learning environment as structured and stable as possible. Organization involves providing the student with TBI the necessary environmental cues and aids to foster new learning. That is, provide advance organizers, key words, and clear guidelines when teaching these students. Instruction in strategies to use to problem solve include multimodal teaching styles that provide visual, auditory, and kinesthetic cues. Croce, Horvat, and Roswal[18] have demonstrated that individuals with TBI will acquire motor skills more rapidly when provided practice schedules with summary and/or average knowledge of results, rather than every trial or no feedback.

It is critical that students who have suffered a traumatic head injury, no matter how mild, be carefully monitored before returning to participation in sports. The reason for this is that the effects of repeated concussions are cumulative. A concussion grading scale recommended for physical educators, athletic trainers, and coaches is presented in Figure 15-9.[50]

Teaching Strategies   Physical education personnel should be particularly attentive to the posttrauma student's ongoing psychomotor, cognitive, and behavior problems. Care must be exercised in sequencing motor tasks, providing instructions, and simplifying motor demands. Tasks should be reduced to their simplest components without making the student feel babied; instructions should be brief and to the point; and game strategies should be simple rather than complex. The student should be given the option of timing himself or herself out when the demands of the class prove to be too frustrating to handle on a given day. Any adjustments that will reduce the student's frustration to a minimum and increase his or her

Figure 15-9　Concussion Grading Scale and Playing Status[50]

Grade	Symptoms	Playing status
1	Transient confusion; no loss of consciousness; concussion symptoms or mental status abnormalities resolve in less than 15 minutes	Remove and examine every 5 minutes; return after 15 minutes
2	Transient confusion; no loss of consciousness; concussion symptoms or mental status abnormalities last more than 15 minutes	Remove from play and disallow return that day; examine next day allow return after one full week without symptoms
3	Loss of consciousness, which may be a few seconds or minutes	Transport player to a hospital if still unconscious for a thorough neurologic evaluation; allow return after two to four full weeks without symptoms

capability of cooperating in a group setting will contribute to the possibility of the student's success in physical education.

The Physical Education Program　Physical exercise has been shown to improve motor function, elevate mood, and contribute to perceptions of better health in individuals with TBI.[37] The type of physical education provided for the student with TBI will depend on the test results and the teacher's judgment of the student's capability. The more individualized the program, the less frustration the student will experience. Being required to contribute to a competitive team effort where winning is highly valued will create significant problems for the individual who is slow to make critical playing decisions and moves. If the student is given opportunities to pursue his or her own exercise program, a buddy system should prove to be effective in keeping the student with TBI on task and following appropriate safety procedures.

Depending on the extent and severity of brain damage, educational modifications that may need to be included in the IEP are

- Reduced course load
- Scheduling of the most demanding courses in the morning when the student is fresh
- Resource room with the assistance of an aide
- Rest breaks as needed

- Adapted physical education or a modified regular physical education program
- Peer tutoring
- Counseling
- Provisions for taping lectures and extra time for completing written work and examinations[63]

The individual with a strong support system made up of friends and family will have greater opportunities to be active in community settings than will the individual who has little or no outside support. Persons with TBI who understand the components of a healthy lifestyle and who have been taught to select activities that will promote that lifestyle will seek out opportunities to stay active on their good days. On their bad days, their support group will provide them with the encouragement and motivation they need to expend the extra effort to stay active. Caution should be exercised when selecting activities. Highly competitive sports, particularly those that involve contact, can easily provoke a sensitive individual and result in undesirable impulsive, aggressive behaviors. Less competitive games and exercise routines will provide the same level of benefit without the potential negative emotional and physical outcomes.

Spinal Cord Injuries

Spinal cord injuries usually result in paralysis or partial paralysis of the arms, trunk, legs, or any

An individual with a spinal cord injury hand pedals his bike.
Courtesy of Challenge Aspen, Aspen, CO.

combination thereof and loss of sensation, depending on the locus of the damage. The spinal cord is housed in the spinal or vertebral column. Nerves from the spinal cord pass down into the segments of the spinal column. Injury to the spinal cord affects innervation of muscle. The higher up the vertebral column the level of injury, the greater the restriction of body movement. Persons with spinal cord injuries are usually referred to as paraplegics or tetraplegics (quadriplegics). In paraplegia, the legs are paralyzed. In tetraplegia, both the arms and legs are affected. There are 8,000 to 10,000 new cases of spinal cord injury in the United States every year.[51] Fifty-six percent of spinal cord injuries occur among individuals in the sixteen- to thirty-year age range; males outnumber females 4 to 1.[66]

Characteristics   Spinal cord injuries are classified according to the region of the vertebrae affected. The regions affected are cervical, thoracic, lumbar, and sacral. Half of all spinal cord injuries occur at the cervical level and result in tetraplegia. Paraplegics make up the other half of spinal cord injuries; their lesions occur in the thoracic, lumbar, and sacral segments of the spine.[66] A description of the movement capability at each level of the lesion follows:

• Fourth cervical level. There is use of only the neck muscles and the diaphragm. Upper limb function is possible only with electrically powered assistive devices. The individual needs complete assistance moving to and from the wheelchair.

- Fifth cervical level. There is use of the deltoid muscles of the shoulder and the biceps muscles of the arm. The arms can be raised; however, it is difficult to engage in manipulative tasks. Persons with this level of involvement can perform many activities with their arms. However, they need assistance with transfer to and from the wheelchair.

- Sixth cervical level. There is use of the wrist extensors, and the student can push the wheelchair and make use of an overhead trapeze (a bar hung overhead to be grasped). Some persons afflicted at this level can transfer the body to and from the wheelchair.

- Seventh cervical level. There is use of the elbow and wrist extensors. Movement of the hand is impaired. However, the person afflicted at this level may be able to perform pull-ups and push-ups and participate in activities that involve the grasp release mechanism.

- Upper thoracic levels. There is total movement capability in the arms but none in the legs. There is some control in the muscles of the upper back. The individual can control a wheelchair and may be able to stand with the use of long leg braces.

- Lower thoracic levels. There is control of the abdominal musculature that rights the trunk. The use of the abdominal muscles makes it possible to walk with the support of long leg braces.

- Lumbar levels. There is control of the hip joint, and there is a good possibility of walking with controlled movement.

- Sacral level. There is muscular functioning for efficient ambulation. The functional level of the bladder, anal sphincters, and external genitals may be impaired.

In general, spinal cord injury results in motor and sensory loss below the level of injury, autonomic nervous system dysfunction if the injury is at T3 or lower (e.g., bowel/bladder, cardiovascular, and temperature regulation), spasticity, and contractures.[22] Specific physical characteristics are as follows:

1. Inappropriate control of the bladder and digestive organs
2. Contractures (abnormal shortening of muscles)
3. Heterotopic bone formation, or laying down of new bone in soft tissue around joints (during this process, the area may become inflamed and swollen)
4. Urinary infections
5. Difficulty in defecation
6. Decubitus ulcers on the back and buttocks (caused by pressure of the body weight on specific areas)
7. Spasms of the muscles
8. Spasticity of muscles that prevent effective movement
9. Overweight because of low energy expenditures
10. Scoliosis
11. Respiratory disorders

Persons with spinal cord injury have muscle atrophy and impaired aerobic work capacity because of fewer remaining functional muscles and impaired blood flow.[61] If the injury is above T3, the heart rate may be impacted (120 beats per minute is high). Athletes with spinal cord injuries between C6 and T7 have maximal heart rates of 110 to 130

Seth Ritchey, who is paralyzed from the waist down, skis using a sit-ski.
Courtesy of Challenge Aspen, Aspen, CO.

beats per minute.[21] Thermal regulation may also be impaired because of a loss of normal blood flow regulation and the inability to sweat below the level of injury.[21] For this reason, individuals with tetraplegia should not be left in the sun or cold for any length of time. Individuals with tetraplegia who exercise are encouraged to wear support hose and use abdominal strapping to promote venous blood flow to the heart.[22]

Special Considerations Athletes with disabilities frequently experience injuries. The most frequent types of injuries suffered by wheelchair athletes, some prevention techniques, and treatments are summarized in Table 15.1. For activities that require trunk stabilization, strapping is necessary.[33]

The Physical Education Program and Teaching Strategies The physical education program for persons with spinal cord injury should be based on a well-rounded program of exercises for all the usable body parts, including activities to develop strength, flexibility, muscular endurance, cardiovascular endurance, and coordination. Young chil-

dren need to be taught ways to use their wheelchairs in a variety of environments and should be encouraged to interact with their ambulatory peers. The middle school and high school student should develop the physical fitness necessary to participate in the sports of their choice.

Movement and dance therapies have been used successfully in rehabilitation programs for persons who have spinal cord injuries. Figure 15-10 includes an example of modifications that can be made in a typical warm-up session for a kindergarten or first-grade class.

The emphasis in the physical education program should be on functional movement skills. The child, if wheelchair enabled, should be given every opportunity to move in the chair. Individuals with upper body function can perform most physical education activities from a wheelchair. The physical education program should include wheelchair mobility training. Project C.R.E.O.L.E. is an excellent curriculum that promotes functional training in wheelchair use.[90] The child should practice moving in the chair with activities that modify the movement variables of time, space,

TABLE 15.1 Most Common Injuries Suffered by Wheelchair Athletes

Injury	Prevention	Treatment
Soft tissue damage (overuse syndromes: tendonitis, bursitis)	Taping, splinting, protective padding; proper wheelchair positioning	Rest; selective strengthening, muscle balancing
Blisters	Taping, gloves, padding, cushioning, and callous formation	Be aware of areas that lack sensation; treat blister
Lacerations/abrasions	Check equipment for sharp surfaces, wear padding, use cushions and towels for transfers; camber wheels	Treat injury; be aware of areas that lack sensation
Decubitus/pressure areas	Adequate cushioning; proper weight shifting; dry clothing, skin inspection; good nutrition and hygiene	Bed rest to remove all pressure from weight-bearing surface; treat open wounds
Sprains/contusions	Equipment safety; appropriate padding; sport-specific spotting	Treat injury; check for signs of fracture in athletes without movement or sensation

Data from Curtis KA: *Injuries and disability-specific medical conditions of athletes with disabilities.* Unpublished paper, Coral Gables, FL, 1993, University of Miami.

Figure 15-10   Warm-Up Session with Modifications for Children in Wheelchairs

Class Activity (Song/Dance)	Modifications
"Warm-up Time"	
Clap hands	None
Swing arms	None
Bend knees	Child lifts knees with hands
Stamp feet	Child slaps feet with hands
"What a Miracle"	
Clap hands	None
Stamp feet	Child slaps feet with hands
Swing arms	None
Bend and stretch legs	Child lifts knees with hands
Twist and bend spine	None
One foot balance	Child pushes into push-up position
"Swing, Shake, Twist, Stretch"	
Swing	Child swings arms or head
Shake	Child shakes hands, elbows, or head
Twist	Child twists trunk
Stretch	Child stretches arms
"Bendable, Stretchable"	
Stretch to sky, touch floor	Child stretches to sky, touches toes
"Run, Run, Run in Place"	
Run in place	Child spins chair in circle
"Simon Says Jog Along"	
Jog	Child rolls chair in time to music
Walk	Child rolls chair in time to music

force, and flow. For example, the child should be able to do the following:

1. Time
   a. Wheel fast, then slow.
   b. Wheel to a 4/4 beat.
2. Space
   a. Wheel up and down inclines.
   b. Wheel on cement, linoleum, grass, a gymnasium floor, etc.
   c. Wheel around obstacles.
   d. Wheel over sticks.
   e. Wheel, holding a glass of water.
   f. Wheel, holding a ball on lap.
3. Force
   a. Wheel with a buddy sitting on lap.
   b. Wheel while pulling a partner on a scooter board.
   c. Push hard and see how far the chair will roll.
4. Flow
   a. Roll forward, spin in a circle, roll forward.
   b. Roll forward, stop, roll backward, stop.

The same type of movement activities should be made available to the child using crutches and braces.

In addition to wheelchair mobility, younger children should be taught fundamental motor skills such as throwing, hitting, and catching. Once these skills are mastered, games that incorporate these skills may be played. Modifications of games that have been described previously are appropriate for children in wheelchairs. Children in wheelchairs can participate in parachute games and target games without accommodation. They can maintain fitness of the upper body through the same type of regimens that the nondisabled engage in. Strengthening of the arms and shoulder girdle is important for propulsion of the wheelchair and for changing body positions when moving in and out of the wheelchair. Swimming is a particularly good activity for the development of total physical fitness. The emphasis should be on the development of functional movement skills.

It is possible to increase the heart rate response, blood pressure response, stroke volume and cardiac output, and respiration rate and depth through the use of arm exercises.[22] Development may be attained through arm pedaling of a bicycle ergometer, pushing of a wheelchair over considerable distances, and agility maneuvers with the wheelchair. DiCarlo[27] reported that males with tetraplegia with lesions at the fifth to seventh

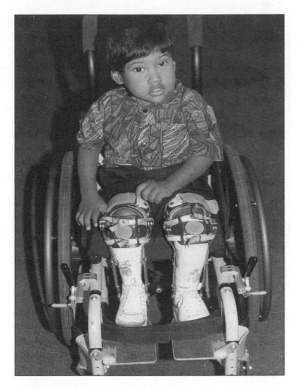

A Three-Year-Old Child with Long Leg Braces
Courtesy Dallas Independent School District.

cervical level were able to increase their wheelchair propulsion endurance and cardiopulmonary function by engaging in arm cycle ergometry exercises three times a week for eight weeks. Hardison, Isreal, and Somes[38] demonstrated the same types of gains with paraplegic males with lesion levels ranging from T4 to T12. They demonstrated improved oxygen utilization with a training program consisting of a 70 rpm ergometer cranking rate at 60 percent of the subject's maximum VO2. Physical activity also has been shown to counter some of the increase in body fat that is typical of individuals with spinal cord injury.[53] Curtis[21] cautions that there are several physiological response differences between upper and lower extremity exercise. During upper body exercise, (1) maximum value of oxygen utilization is 70 percent of that of lower body exercise; (2) heart rate is approximately

20 percent higher; (3) stroke volume is 10 to 18 percent less; and (4) lactic acid concentrations are higher.

Stretching exercises should always be used to improve flexibility and enable an individual to achieve full joint range of motion. They are also critical for reducing the chance of stress injuries to muscles, tendons, and ligaments. Curtis[19] recommends that stretching be done both before exercise and following cooldown. The following stretches should be executed for 15 to 30 seconds each, while sitting in a wheelchair:

Trunk Stretching

1. Exhale and lean forward to touch the ground; hold and return to sitting position.
2. Inhale. Bend over at waist and reach out, keeping arms and head parallel to the ground; hold and return to sitting position.
3. Arch left arm over the head and lean to the right; repeat to other side.

Shoulder Stretching

1. Intertwine fingers from both hands, inhale, and lift hands overhead, pushing palms upward.
2. Intertwine fingers from both hands behind back, exhale, lean forward, and lift hands high behind back.
3. Clasp hands behind head and push elbows backward.

Shoulder-Elbow Stretching

1. Raise arms to shoulder height with palms facing forward; push arms backward while keeping elbows straight.
2. Bend arm across chest, reaching for opposite shoulder blade; push on elbow. Repeat with other arm.
3. Raise arm up next to head; reach down the back with the hand; push against elbow with other hand. Repeat with other arm.

Elbow-Wrist Stretching

1. Raise left arm out in front of body, keeping elbow straight; with right hand, pull left hand and fingers into extension (fingers toward the sky). Repeat with other hand.

2. Raise left arm out in front of body, keeping elbow straight; with right hand, pull left hand and fingers into flexion (fingers toward the ground).

When developing strength exercise regimens to enhance sport performance, specificity of training is critical. Manually propelling a wheelchair tends to develop the flexor muscles in front of the body; thus, attention must be paid to developing unused muscle groups located in the back of the body. As a general rule, for all exercises executed in front of the body, do twice as many in the opposite direction.[22] Include backward wheelchair pushing to develop the muscles that work in opposition to the pectorals.[22] Because of the need to lift the arms to propel the wheelchair, arm abductors tend to be stronger than the adductors; thus, exercises to strengthen the adductors are indicated.[22] Coordination training should also be sport-specific. General power and endurance training is recommended for rounding out the exercise program.

Power training could include throwing and catching a medicine ball thrown against a small trampoline and wind sprints in the wheelchair. Endurance training should involve wheelchair pushing for 20 minutes and longer three times a week at the target heart rate (220 minus age if the injury is below T3).

Routine exercise programs are critical for the individual who uses a wheelchair for ambulation, because the act of manually wheeling the chair produces imbalances in muscle strength. Imbalances in muscle strength lead to postural deviations that, if left unaddressed, will eventually become structural and further impair the individual's health. The physical educator who helps the individual in a wheelchair develop a realistic exercise program that can be continued throughout life will contribute to the quality of that person's life.

Amputations

Amputation is missing part or all of a limb. Amputation is sometimes performed to arrest a malignant condition caused by trauma, tumors, infection, vascular impairment, diabetes, or arteriosclerosis.

The number of amputees in the United States exceeds 500,000.[48]

Characteristics and Types   Amputations can be classified into two categories: acquired amputation and congenital amputation. The amputation is acquired if one has a limb removed by operation; it is congenital if the child is born without a limb. Congenital amputations are classified according to the site and level of limb absence. When an amputation is performed through a joint, it is referred to as a disarticulation.

Special Considerations   Frequently, individuals with an amputation elect to use a prosthetic appliance to replace the missing limb. The purpose of the prosthetic device is to enable the individual to function as normally as possible. The application of a prosthetic device may be preceded by surgery to produce a stump. After the operation the stump is dressed and bandaged to aid shrinkage of the stump. After the fitting of the prosthesis, the stump must be continually cared for. It should be checked periodically and cleaned to prevent infection, abrasion, and skin disorder. The attachment of a false limb early in a child's development will encourage the incorporation of the appendage into natural body activity more than if the prosthesis is introduced later in life.

It is not practical to fit a prosthesis on some forms of amputations. Consider the case of Mark Pietranski (see Figure 15-11), who was born with two small appendages where the legs should have been. One appendage had to be removed early in life; the other is not strong enough for functional use. Mark does not let his lack of legs interfere with his activities. In Figure 15-11 Mark is a member of his middle school football team—despite the fact that he uses only his hands and arms to propel himself. He also swims regularly.

The Physical Education Program and Teaching Strategies   The ultimate goal of a person with an amputation is to perform physical activity safely. Amputees must develop skills to use prostheses; effective use demands much effort. The remaining

Figure 15-11
Mark Pietranski, a double amputee, participates in football with his classmates.
Courtesy *Denton Record Chronicle*.

Adrienne Slaughter doesn't let the loss of a leg interfere with her love for rock climbing.
Courtesy Challenge Aspen, Aspen, CO.

muscles needed for prosthetic use must be strengthened, and standing and walking must be practiced until they become automatic. To regain adequate postural equilibrium, individuals with lower limb amputations have to learn to link altered sensory input to movement patterns.[35] Practice in walking, turning, sitting, and standing is needed.

Amputees are often exposed to beneficial exercise through the use of the prosthesis. Exercises should be initiated to strengthen muscles after a stump heals. Training also enhances ambulation, inhibits atrophy and contractures, improves or maintains mechanical alignment of body parts, and develops general physical fitness.

There are several adaptations of physical activity that can be made for children with impaired ambulation. For these children, the major disadvantages are speed of locomotion and fatigue to sustained activity. Some accommodations that can be made are shortening the distance the child must travel and decreasing the speed needed to move from one place to another.

Persons with amputations below the knee can learn ambulation skills well with a prosthesis

and training. Persons with amputation above the knee but below the hip may have difficulty in developing efficient walking gaits. Amputations at this level require alteration of the gait pattern. Steps are usually shortened to circumvent lack of knee function.

Authorities agree that children with properly fitted prostheses should engage in regular physical education activities. Amputees have considerable potential for participation in adapted sports and games. The National Amputee Golf Association, for example, provides clinics nationwide to introduce children and adults with disabilities to the sport of golf and to train teachers and coaches to adapt methods and instruction to meet the needs of amputees. There are opportunities for persons with prostheses to participate in official sports competition. Persons with above-the-knee amputations can walk well and engage in swimming, skiing, and other activities with the proper aids. Persons with arm amputations who have use of their feet can participate in activities that require foot action, such as soccer and running events, as well as other activities that involve the feet exclusively.

Physical fitness of amputees should be an important part of a physical education program.

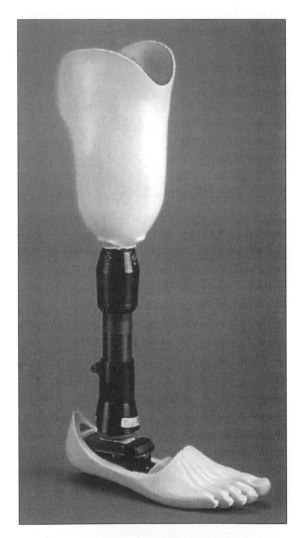

Newly designed prosthetic devices normalize walking patterns.
Courtesy Endolite: North America, Centerville, OH.

Strength and flexibility and power of the unafflicted limbs are important. Furthermore, Lasko-McCarthey and Knopf[54] stress the importance of developing and maintaining the amputee's level of cardiovascular efficiency.

TESTING

The type of test used depends on the functioning level of the individual, as well as the purpose for the assessment. Several types of tests and the populations they can be used with are presented in Chapter 2. Persons who are ambulatory, including those with cerebral palsy who have spastic hemiplegia, can usually be tested using standard equipment. Fernandez and Pitetti[31] used a bicycle ergometer, a Schwinn Air Dyne ergometer, a treadmill, and an arm-crank ergometer to determine the physical work capacity of individuals with cerebral palsy. They recommended using an ergometer rather than a treadmill to avoid discriminating against persons with gait anomalies or those who are nonambulatory for whatever reason. Ponichtera-Mulcare et al.[74] recommend that a combination leg and arm ergometer be used to assess maximal power output and peak aerobic power, as well as for training. The Brockport Physical Fitness Test, Project M.O.B.I.L.T.E.E., and the *Physical Best and Individuals with Disabilities Handbook* by the American Alliance for Health, Physical Education, Recreation and Dance (AAHPERD) all suggest accommodations for ambulatory and nonambulatory individuals.

In addition to formal testing, it is frequently just as important to appraise individuals' functional movement capabilities. Motor programs can then be developed to meet their unique needs. The assessment should provide information about the potential for movement of each action of the body. This would involve knowledge of the strength, power, flexibility, and endurance of specific muscle groups. In addition, there should be information about which movement actions can be coordinated to attain specific motor outcomes. For instance, several throwing patterns that children with severe impairments use when participating in the Special Olympics can help circumvent movement problems of the arms and hands. The desired throwing pattern is one of extension of the arm and elbow and flexion of the wrist. If either of these actions is impaired, alternate throwing patterns need to be found. Some throwing patterns developed to circumvent extreme disability of the arm, elbow, and wrist are underhand movement, horizontal abduction of the arm and shoulder, flexion of the arm and elbow (over the shoulder), horizontal abduction of the arm (side arm), and overhand movement with most of the force generated from a rocking motion of the trunk. To maximize the potential of each of these types of throwing patterns, it is necessary to conduct training programs that will consider each child's assets and develop them fully. However, another option is to provide therapeutic exercise for each of the desired actions and then teach it as a functional, normalized movement pattern.

The ability prerequisites of strength, flexibility, endurance, power, and coordination can be applied to many wheelchair activities. Some of these activities involve (1) basic mobility skills, (2) transfer skills from and to the wheelchair, (3) performance on mats, (4) performance on gymnastics apparatus, (5) ability to maneuver vehicles, (6) motor capabilities in a swimming pool, (7) ability to walk with aids, and (8) ability to push and pull objects. The ability prerequisites for each fundamental movement pattern should be studied to identify specific problems, so that appropriate intervention can be undertaken. Examples of the categories of activities or abilities follow:

1. Basic mobility skills[90]
   a. Moving up and down ramps
   b. Moving from a wheelchair to another chair
   c. Transporting objects
2. Transfer skills
   a. Standing from a wheelchair
   b. Moving from a wheelchair to another chair
   c. Moving from a wheelchair to mats
   d. Moving from a wheelchair to different pieces of equipment
3. Performance on mats
   a. Forward and backward rolls
   b. Partner activity
   c. Climbing on low obstacles and elevated mats
4. Performance on gymnastics apparatus
   a. Rings
   b. High bar
   c. Parallel bars
5. Ability to maneuver vehicles
   a. Floor scooters
   b. Hand-propelled carts
   c. Tricycles
   d. Upright scooters with three wheels
6. Swimming pool activity
   a. Getting into and out of the pool
   b. Using the railing for resting
   c. Swimming
7. Walking with aids
   a. Different types of canes
   b. Crutches
   c. Walkers
8. Ability to push and pull objects
   a. Throwing a ball or pushing a ball
   b. Propelling scooters with the hands
   c. Pushing a cage ball

Each of these should be analyzed to see if the student's strength, flexibility, endurance, power, and coordination are sufficient for acquisition and proficiency of the activity. In the case of Duchenne dystrophy, manual muscle testing (determining how much resistance is left in a muscle group by having the student flex or extend each limb) can give the evaluator some indication of the remaining strength. Students with other types of muscular dystrophy can be tested with standard tests.

Another group of persons in wheelchairs have severe impairment of the upper appendages. They may have spasticity or contractures. It is not uncommon for these children to adopt unique throwing patterns to maximize performance. Their physical structure rules out the use of standard testing techniques and the teaching of mechanically sound sport skill patterns. Specific techniques must be determined for each child.

MODIFICATIONS, ADAPTATIONS, AND INCLUSION TECHNIQUES

Many physically challenged children who participate in physical education programs use a wheelchair for locomotion, wear braces, and/or use some other assistive device. Assistive devices are used to enable fuller use of the upper limbs or aid locomotion when the legs are debilitated. Some assistive devices are hooks, canes, walkers, and crutches. There are a number of orthoses available to enable persons with paraplegia to move about with the aid of canes or walkers.[39]

Although it is difficult to substitute for the human hand and fingers, it is possible to achieve dexterity with the use of a utility arm and split hook. These aids enable the use of racquets for paddle games if both arms are amputated. Persons who have lost a single arm can play most basic skill games and participate in more advanced sport activity without modifications. Special devices can be built by an orthotist to fit into the arm prosthesis to hold sports equipment such as gloves.

A major problem for students who use canes, walkers, and crutches is the need to learn balance to free one hand for participation in activity. Use of the Lofstrand crutches, which are anchored to the forearms, enables balance to be maintained by one crutch. This frees one arm and enables participation in throwing and striking activities.

The physical educator should have a working knowledge of the care and maintenance of wheelchairs. In conjunction with related services, the child's classroom teacher, family, and physical educator should develop a program to maximize the use of ambulation devices in the physical education setting and beyond the school boundaries. In addition, any problems that arise with the ambulation devices should be communicated to the special or regular class teacher or the parents.

Wheelchairs

The purpose of wheelchairs is to provide a means of locomotion for persons who lack strength, endurance, or flexibility of muscles prerequisite for ambulation. Persons who can walk but cannot rise from a seated position to a standing position or those who need to transport objects but cannot do so may also need a wheelchair.

The technology is available to provide almost every person who has a severe physical disability with mobility.[46] The primary goals when designing wheelchairs are to maximize the function, comfort, and independence of those who use the technology. More specifically, the goals and objectives of wheelchair seating are to (1) maximize safety and functional independence, (2) maximize independent mobility through the ability to control the direction and speed of the chair, and (3) maximize functional communication with others in all life environments, including leisure physical activity.[86]

There are many types of wheelchairs. Some of the types identified by Wilson follow:

- Standard: Wheelchairs that have a folding frame with large driving wheels in the rear and small caster wheels in the front
- Manual: Wheelchairs propelled by the occupant
- Attendant: Manual wheelchairs that are propelled by another person because the occupant cannot or should not use either a manual or powered chair
- Powered: Wheelchairs driven by electric motors that run on batteries
- Lightweight: Standard wheelchairs refined to reduce overall weight
- Sport: Light standard wheelchairs that are easily disassembled
- Racing: Wheelchairs designed solely for competitive racing[88]

Nonstandard vehicles that have been developed specifically for children with orthopedic disabilities include the following:

- Hand-driven tricycle that includes a lever system that transmits arm power into the rear wheel axles
- Tricycle foot attachments that strap a child's feet to the pedals and allow the child with muscle weakness or spasticity to ride a tricycle

- Modified tricycle that includes a back support and a seat belt to stabilize the child's body
- Castor carts (large scooter boards) that enable a child to participate in activity at the floor level[52]

There have been many advances in recent years in upgrading wheelchairs to facilitate the mobility of youth and adults.[58] Platform motorized wheelchairs that can be driven at moderately high speeds are popular. Options for controlling powered wheelchairs include joysticks, single switches, and voice controls.[55]

Wheelchair design is a continuous process, the goal of which is to make the wheelchair more functional. Many special features can be added to make a wheelchair more functional or comfortable, including armrests, footrests, legrests, and headrests, all of which can be removed. Leg spreaders have also been incorporated into some wheelchairs to prevent the scissoring of legs. Analog devices for aligning the rear wheels have been developed to maximize efficiency in propelling the wheelchair.[16] Many wheelchairs can be folded for easy storage. Some other features of a wheelchair are unique folding mechanisms that allow it to double as a stroller or car seat, adjustable Velcro fasteners, pads, and attachable trays. Wheelchairs have also been designed for off-road recreation. Figure 15-12 contains a checklist that will enable physical education teachers to assess wheelchairs as they relate to optimum functioning and comfort of the individual.[85]

Specialized Adapted Seating

Adapted seating for individuals who are severely disabled has been a subject of increasing concern. Inappropriate seating of severely afflicted individuals can result in severe scoliosis with vertebral rotation. Severe contractures may result from fixed postures in a wheelchair. To avoid this, extensive adaptations of the chair may be necessary. Hundertmark[47] indicates that the anterior and posterior tilt of the pelvis and the vertical angle of the backrest are important considerations in achieving therapeutic seating for the person who has a severe multihandicap.

Adaptations for Wheelchair Sports Competition

Wheelchair competitive sports are becoming more and more popular. Competitive wheelchair users are faced with an array of decisions when

Figure 15-12 Checklist for Wheelchairs

Wheelchair

A. Arms
 1. Are the armrests and side panels secure and free of sharp edges and cracks?
 2. Do the arm locks function properly?

B. Back
 1. Is the upholstery free of rips and tears?
 2. Is the back taut from top to bottom?
 3. Is the safety belt attached tightly and not frayed?

C. Seat and frame
 1. Is the upholstery free of rips and tears?
 2. Does the chair fold easily without sticking?
 3. When the chair is folded fully, are the front post slides straight and round?

D. Wheel locks
 1. Do the wheel locks securely engage the tire surfaces and prevent the wheel from turning?

E. Large wheels
 1. Are the wheels free from wobble or sideplay when spun?
 2. Are the spokes equally right and without any missing spokes?
 3. Are the tires free from excessive wear and gaps at the joined section?

F. Casters
 1. Is the stem firmly attached to the fork?
 2. Are the forks straight on sides and stem so that the caster swivels easily?
 3. Is the caster assembly free of excessive play both upward and downward, as well as backward and forward?
 4. Are the wheels free of excessive play and wobble?
 5. Are the tires in good condition?

G. Footrest/legrest
 1. Does the lock mechanism fit securely?
 2. Are the heel loops secure and correctly installed?
 3. Do the foot plates fold easily and hold in any position?
 4. Are the largest panels free of cracks and sharp edges?

(Continued)

Figure 15-12 *(Continued)*

With student sitting in wheelchair

A. Seat width
1. When your palms are placed between the patient's hip and the side of the chair (skirtguard), do the hands contact the hip and the skirtguard at the same time without pressure?
2. Or is the clearance between the patient's widest point of either hips or thigh and the skirtguard approximately 1 inch on either side?

B. Seat depth
1. Can you place your hand, with fingers extended, between the front edge of the seat upholstery and to the rear of the knee with a clearance of three or four fingers?
2. Or is the seat upholstery approximately 2 to 3 inches less than the student's thigh measurement?

C. Seat height and footrest
1. Is the lowest part of the stepplates no closer than 2 inches from the floor?
2. Or is the student's thigh elevated slightly above the front edge of the seat upholstery?

D. Arm height
1. Does the arm height not force the shoulders up or allow them to drop significantly when the student is in a normal sitting position?
2. Is the elbow positioned slightly forward of the trunk midline when the student is in a normal sitting position?

E. Back height
1. Can you insert four or five fingers between the patient's armpit area and the top of the back upholstery touching both at the same time?
2. Is the top of the back upholstery approximately 4 inches below the armpit for the student who needs only minimum trunk support?

With student pushing or riding in wheelchair

A. Is the wheelchair free from squeaks or rattles?
B. Does the chair roll easily without pulling to either side?
C. Are the large wheels and casters free of play and wobble?

designing, building, buying, and racing wheelchairs. The ability to propel the wheelchair safely and quickly is an important factor for effective wheelchair sports competition. That capability is dependent on the user's ability, the design of the chair, and the suitability of the chair to the user. Interest in improving performance has spurred researchers to study ways to increase the efficiency of wheelchairs. Modifications in seat position,[46] the number of wheels, and the positioning of the body during propulsion all impact the speed at which the chair can be propelled.

The seat of a wheelchair should be adjusted to fit the width of the athlete's hips; the seat height should be altered to maximize the use of forces generated at the shoulder; and lowering the height of the back of the chair will increase mobility. The number of wheels is also an important competitive factor.

Three- and four-wheeled chairs are available for competition. Higgs[42] studied the comparative advantages of both of these chairs and reported that the advantages of three-wheeled chairs are that they have less rolling resistance, are lighter, and have less aerodynamic drag. The disadvantages of the three-wheeled chairs are that they have less stability and more skill is required to safely handle the chair. The position of the body in the chair, the use of hand pads, and strapping also impact speed and efficiency.

Gehlsen, Davis, and Bahamonde[34] indicate that a forward lean of the trunk may allow the individual to increase the range of hand-handrim contact. Hedrick et al.[41] indicate that a wheelchair racer's speed can be increased when he or she rotates the upper torso sideways or maintain a flexed position while coasting. Alexander[1] describes a technique to increase propulsion of the wheelchair in which the backs of the hands propel the wheelchair by drawing the hands up and over the wheel and finishing the power stroke with the lower arms in supination. Pads are used to increase friction between the hands and the wheelchair and allow the student a longer power phase. In addition, Burd and Grass[12] describe procedures for strapping students in wheelchairs to correct posture deviations

Ross Davis, a Silver Medal Winner in the Barcelona Paralympics
Courtesy Disabled Sports Association of North Texas, Dallas.

that diminish the full propulsive stroke on the handrim of the wheelchair.

In addition to improved techniques for wheelchair propulsion, research has been conducted on motivational variables that may facilitate competition in wheelchairs. Dummer et al.[28] suggest that teaching students the right strategies that are compatible with their abilities and helping them enjoy the activity and competition enhance their desire to compete. Brasile and Hedrick[11] suggest that intrinsic, task-related reasons for participation are important motivators for success in physical activity for students with orthopedic and neurological disabilities.

Assistive Technology

Every effort should be made to involve individuals with physical disabilities in play and games. To facilitate that participation, it may be necessary to adapt equipment to bridge an individual's functional limitations with the demands of the activity. Some devices that may improve functional movement include

- Chest straps that improve functional reach [23]
- Elasticized abdominal binders[23]
- Seat inserts or molded cushions that improve trunk stability[23]
- Chair anchors that stabilize the wheelchair and facilitate throwing activity[70]
- Wheelchair designs that enable propulsion with the legs rather than arms for athletes with functional leg strength[70]
- Wheelchair seats that can be rotated 180 degrees to allow participants to sit backward, which enables a strong push-off for propelling the chair[70]
- Padded workout gloves[81]
- Push rim padding[81]
- Lighter steering mechanisms[81]
- Increase the camber of the wheels[81]
- Spoke and finger protectors [81]
- Carbon spoke wheels that offer less resistance and facilitate faster acceleration than traditional chairs[70]

However, individuals who use specialized devices must anticipate and guard against the following problems: failure of the device, incorrect fit with

A Footless Climber Being Transported to Where He Will Begin His Ascent
Courtesy of City of Phoenix, AZ.

the individual's need, lack of appropriate instruction in use of the device, awkwardness of the device, and denial of the disability.[36]

There are several commercially available pieces of equipment that enable persons with physical disabilities to participate in bowling. Some of the adaptations are a bowling ball with handles, a fork that allows the person to push the bowling ball as in shuffleboard, and a ramp that enables gravity to act on the ball in place of the force provided by movement. Each of these adaptations in equipment accommodates for a specific physical problem related to bowling. The adapted equipment for bowling is paired with the nature of the physical problem.

Equipment	Accommodation of Disability
Handles	Needs assistance with the grip but has use of the arm and wrist
Fork	Has use of the arm but has limited ability to control the wrist and an underhand throwing pattern
Ramp	Has limited use of the arm, wrist, and fingers as they apply to an underhand movement pattern

Computer-Controlled Movement of Paralyzed Muscles

In the past, it was thought that paralyzed muscles could not contract to produce purposeful movement. Computer-controlled electrical stimulation for controlling movement is called functional neuromuscular stimulation (FNS), which involves placing electrodes made of conductive rubber over the motor point of a muscle. Small electrical currents are then conducted through the electrodes and the skin. The currents cause underlying motor nerves to discharge, which results in precise movement of muscle groups. Movement of whole limbs can be facilitated in this manner.[72] Recent studies involving FNS with individuals with paraplegia or tetraplegia report decreased venous pooling, increases in oxygen uptake, and significant increases in blood pressure during exercise.[73,76,91]

Modifications

Many games and sports in which students regularly participate in physical education classes can, with minor modification, be made safe and interesting for persons with physical disabilities. In general, the rules, techniques, and equipment of a game or activity should be changed as little as possible when they are modified for students with disabilities. Following is a suggested procedure for adapting a sport or game for a student with a disability:

1. Select and analyze the play, game, or sport.
2. Identify the problems the individual will have in participating in the play, game, or sport.
3. Make the adaptations.
4. Select principles of adaptation that may apply to the specific situation. Specific ways that regular physical education and sport activities can be modified are the following:
   a. The size of the playing area can be made smaller, with proportionate reduction of the amount of activity.
   b. Larger balls or larger pieces of equipment can be introduced to make the game easier or to slow down the tempo so physical accommodations can be made.
   c. Smaller, lighter balls or striking implements (plastic or styrofoam balls and plastic bats) or objects that are easier to handle (a bean bag) can be substituted.
   d. More players can be added to a team, which reduces the amount of activity and the responsibility of individuals.
   e. Minor rule changes can be made in the contest or game while as many of the basic rules as possible are retained.
   f. The amount of time allowed for play can be reduced via shorter quarters, or the total time for a game can be reduced to allow for the onset of fatigue.
   g. The number of points required to win a contest can be reduced.
   h. Free substitutions can be made, which allows the students to alternately participate and then rest while the contest continues.

These modifications can be made in a game or contest whether the student participates in a segregated or integrated physical education class. If the child with a disability participates in a segregated class, it is possible to provide activities similar to those of regular physical education classes by practicing many of the culturally accepted sport skills in drill types of activities. An example is playing basketball games such as "twenty-one" and "around the world" or taking free throws as lead-up activities to the sport. Pitching, batting, throwing, catching, and games such as "over the line" can be played as lead-up activities for softball. Serving, stroking, and volleying can be practiced as lead-up activities for tennis. Such activities can be designed to accommodate physical limitations (see Table 15.2). Students with temporary injuries may become more skillful in various activities so that, when they return to an unrestricted class, they may participate in the whole game or sport with a reasonable degree of success.

Students with disabilities do not always need to be involved in competitive activities. Individuals in wheelchairs should be taught to dance and to participate in water activities. The ability to move to music can be very satisfying; water activities frequently enable a freedom of movement not possible in a chair.[57]

The physical educator who is attempting to accommodate a student with a disability for participation in physical activity should work closely with school nurses and physicians. Some children with orthopedic and neurological conditions will be taking medication that may affect their attention span or level of alertness. Peck and McKeag[71] recommend that youngsters be carefully observed during activity, noting any side effects. Also, students with bladder problems (e.g., infections, ruptures, incontinence) need to be given special attention to help them avoid the embarrassment of wetting themselves.[71]

Inclusion Techniques

There are several ways to accommodate students with limited movement in the regular class setting with their peers. First, activities and games may be selected that circumvent the inability to move. However, it is obvious that such activity will constitute only a small part of the activity, games, and sports of the total physical education program. Second, in team sports it is not uncommon for specific positions of a sport to require different degrees of movement; thus, students who have limited movement capability may be assigned to positions that require less movement. Third, the rules of the game can be modified, enabling equitable competition between persons with and without disabilities. Fourth, aids can be introduced that accommodate inability, so that adjustments can be made to the game. Any one or a combination of these principles of adaptation may be used to enable children with disabilities to participate in regular classes.

COMMUNITY-BASED OPPORTUNITIES

Persons with physical disabilities should develop skills that can be expressed in leisure and recreational activity in the community. One of the desired outcomes of the acquisition of sport skills is participation in competitive sports. Therefore, the instruction in the physical education program should match opportunities for sports participation in the community.

The generalization of the sport skills acquired by the student who is physically challenged in the instructional phase of the physical education program requires close study of several variables. Some considerations are the nature of the specific disability, the equipment required for participation (wheelchairs and ancillary equipment), and ways of structuring competition to maximize fulfillment for the individual.

In addition to opportunities for community and home-based individual and team sport activities, there are an increasing number of recreational and camping opportunities for persons with physical disabilities. There are mountain resorts that offer adaptive recreation activities.[66] These programs include horseback riding, swimming, water skiing, tennis, and outdoor education programs.

TABLE 15.2	Principles for Adapting Physical Activity	
Activity	**Modification**	**Consequence**
REDUCE SIZE OF PLAYING AREA		
Soccer	Reduce size of field	Less distance to cover; ball moves from one end of field to other faster
Soccer	Reduce size of goal commensurate with student's movement ability	Less distance to cover
Badminton	Reduce size of court	Less distance to cover; accommodation can be made to equate movement capability of disabled student with that of nondisabled student
Softball	Shorten distance between bases when disabled person bats	Disabled student has equitable amount of time to reach base.
INTRODUCE LARGER PIECES OF EQUIPMENT		
Softball	Use balloon or beach ball	Speed of the object and tempo of game are reduced.
Softball	Use larger ball	Chance of success is enhanced and tempo of game is reduced.
Soccer	Use larger ball	Area where ball can be propelled successfully is increased.
Volleyball	Use beach ball	Area of contact is increased, enhancing success and requiring less finger strength to control ball.
INTRODUCE LIGHTER EQUIPMENT		
Softball	Use lighter bat	Bat can be moved more quickly so there is greater opportunity to strike ball.
Soccer	Use lighter ball	Speed is reduced and successful contact is more likely.
Bowling	Use lighter ball	Weaker person has greater control of ball.
Archery	Use lighter bow	Weaker person can draw bow.
Tennis	Use aluminum racquet	Weaker person can control racquet.
MODIFY SIZE OF TEAM		
Volleyball	Add more players	Less area for each person to cover
Soccer	Add more players	Less distance each person must cover in team play
Softball	Add more players	Less area for each person to cover
Handball/tennis	Play triples	Less area for each person to cover

(Continued)

TABLE 15.2 (*Continued*)		
Activity	**Modification**	**Consequence**
MAKE MINOR RULE CHANGES		
Wrestling	Use physical contact on take-down for blind persons	Blind person will always be in physical contact with opponent, enables him or her to know where opponent is at all times.
Volleyball	Allow person with affliction in arms/hands to carry on a volleyball hit	Opportunity for success is greater.
Soccer	Reduce size of goal	Opportunity for success is greater.
Gymnastics	Strap legs of paraplegic together	Strap controls legs when body moves.
REDUCE PLAYING TIME		
Basketball/soccer	Substitute every 3 or 4 minutes	Accommodation is made for fatigue.
Swimming	Swim beside pool edge and rest at prescribed distances of travel or time intervals	Accommodation is made for fatigue.
REDUCE NUMBER OF POINTS REQUIRED TO WIN CONTEST		
Handball/paddleball/tennis	Lessen number to fatigue level of individual	Physical endurance will not be factor in outcome of game.
Basketball	Play until specified number of points are made	

Camping opportunities are also available, with a wide variety of accommodations. When considering camping programs, it is suggested that each camp be evaluated to determine the staff's knowledge and experience with persons with physical disabilities.[8]

OPPORTUNITIES FOR PARTICIPATION IN COMPETITION

Persons with physical disabilities need opportunities to express attained sport skills in competition. Many public schools have limited numbers of students of similar ages and ability who are physically challenged. This makes organized competition among those with specific disabilities difficult. Therefore, cooperative efforts need to be made among schools to provide opportunities for competition among the athletes. Wheelchair sports events are sponsored by sports associations for persons with disabilities and are staged for competition in most states in the country. Several colleges and universities also have intercollegiate wheelchair sports programs. The University of Illinois has developed one of the best intercollegiate wheelchair sports programs. Several other universities also have well-developed intercollegiate athletic programs.

The missions of sports organizations for individuals with disabilities are to provide training opportunities and promote competition. These organizations provide a forum and an incentive to maximize proficiency in sports for competition. Wheelchair sports competitions are held at the local, national, and international levels. There is a movement for the organization of games for individuals with generic disabilities at the state level. Project GUMBO in Louisiana is a good example of games organized for the physically challenged at the state level.[17] More sophisticated competition is held by the International Sports Organization for the Disabled. Over 5,000 athletes with a variety of physical disabilities competed in the Paralympics in Atlanta in 1996. Competitions are intense. As a result, training camps have been developed to improve performance at international games.[25] International games have developed not only in the intensity of competition, but also in the magnitude of participation. Thus, opportunities exist for many individuals with physical disabilities to participate in competitive sports at their ability level with incentive to increase skills to a world-class level. A current list of sports organizations for individuals with physical disabilities is included in Appendix C.

Nature and Scope of the Program

Sport activity programs involve sports that can be performed while wearing prostheses or while seated in a wheelchair. Some of the available sport activities include archery, basketball, billiards, bowling, flying, golf, hockey, tennis, racquetball, rugby, road racing, shooting, skiing, softball, table tennis, track and field, water sports, and weight lifting. There is also a movement to enable persons with disabilities to participate with nondisabled athletes in major sporting events. For example, wheelchair athletes participate at the classic running event, the Boston Marathon.[45]

Differences in Abilities

Clearly, individuals in wheelchairs do not have equal abilities. Therefore, to provide equitable competition in school-based activities for persons with physical disabilities, it may be necessary to test skill performances and group the participants according to ability in the individual sports.

Official wheelchair sports competition is based on a medically designed neurological functioning classification system (see Table 15.3). As will be noted when reviewing Table 15.3, sports organizations for athletes with disabilities use slightly different systems for classifying athletes for competitive purposes. In Table 15.3, three classification systems are described in relation to muscular involvement and spinal level of impairment.

The National Wheelchair Basketball Association (NWBA) uses three categories for competition purposes: I, which encompasses impairments of the cervical and thoracic spine through T7 (seventh thoracic vertebra); II, which includes impairments from T8 (eighth thoracic vertebra) through L2 (second lumbar vertebra); and III, which includes all impairments to vertebrae below the second lumbar area.[79] Wheelchair Sports, U.S.A., and the International Stoke-Mandeville Games Federation (ISMGF) use similar classification systems. These two organizations categorize athletes with cervical level impairments as IA, IB, or IC, depending on the level of impairment: category II includes T1 through T6 impairments; category III encompasses T7 through T10 vertebral impairments; category IV includes T11 through L2 impairments; and category V includes all impairments from the third lumbar vertebra down.

The purpose of the classification system is to allow for fair competition. Tests are administered to determine the level of muscular function. Such tests do not take into account the proficiency of the athletes in competition. Several writers have questioned the validity of the existing medically designed classification systems because proficiency is not taken into account.[9,10,43] Those concerns have led to the development of several functional, sport-specific classification systems.

Functional classification systems allow for the observation and rating of the actual movement patterns used during sport performance. According to Curtis,[20] an ideal functional classification system should reflect the differences in

TABLE 15.3	Comparison of Wheelchair Classification Systems Based on Medical Model			

	NWBA		Wheelchair Sports U.S.A.	ISMGF (Except Basketball)
C5		IA	Triceps 0–3	IA
C6		IB	Triceps 4–5	IB
C7			Wrist flexion/extension present	
		IC	Finger flexion/extension 4–5	IC
C8			No useful hand intrinsics	
			No useful abdominals	
T1	I	II	No lower intercostals	II
T2	Motor loss at T7 or above			
T3				
T4	Sitting balance poor			
T5				
T6			Upper abdominals good, no	
T7		III	useful lower abdominals, no	III
			useful lower trunk extensors	
T8	II			
T9	Abdominal and spinal		Poor to fair sitting balance	
	extensor			
T10	muscle strength 3–5			
T11	Sitting balance fair to good	IV	Good abdominals and spinal	IV
T12			extensors, some hip flexors/ adductors	
L1	Hip flexors ≤4		Fair to good balance	Good balance
	Hip adductors ≤3		Quad strength <3	1–20 points traumatic
	Quadriceps ≤2		Includes bilateral hip disarticulation amputees	1–15 points post-polio
L2	Includes bilateral hip disarticulations			Amputees not included
L3	III	V		
	Trunk control, pelvic control		Normal balance Quad strength ≥3	
L4	Sitting balance good to normal		<40 points Most amputees AK and BK	V Normal balance
L5	Quads 3–5		In V/VI	21–40 points traumatic
S1	All other amputees		VI (swimming only) ≥40 points	16–35 points polio Amputees not included VI (swimming only) 41–60 points traumatic 36–50 points polio Not eligible >61 points traumatic >51 points polio

Modified from Weiss M, Curtis KA: Controversies in medical classification of wheelchair athletes. In Sherrill C: *Sport and disabled athletes—the 1984 Olympic Scientific Congress proceedings,* vol. 9, Champaign, IL, 1986, Human Kinetics.

Jason Wening, who is footless, prepares to start a race during the 1996 Atlanta Paralympics.
Courtesy of Jason Wening, World Record Holder.

Figure 15-13
Volleyball players with amputations compete in sitting volleyball at the 1992 Paralympics.
Courtesy Ron Davis, Ball State University, Muncie, Ind.

movement seen during performance of the sport by athletes who either have or lack the function of key muscle groups. Typical functional classification systems include evaluation of the following areas:

- Arm function (e.g., triceps strength for wheelchair push)
- Hand function (e.g., finger flexion adequate for grasp of a field implement such as a discus)
- Trunk function for rotation (e.g., rotating the trunk during the release of the discus)
- Trunk stability to maintain balance in an upright position (e.g., in table tennis, ability to leave the back of the wheelchair while serving without losing balance)
- Trunk function for forward-and-backward movement or upward-and-downward movement (e.g., recovery for the next wheelchair stroke by lifting the upper back and shoulders)
- Pelvic stability from side to side (e.g., increasing the reach to the side for a two-handed rebound in basketball)[20]

It is predicted that functional classification systems that are based on the movements inherent in the sport will replace the neurologically based systems within the next few years. Information about classification systems used in competition for specific sports can be obtained directly from the sport associations listed in Appendix C.

Amputees are considered to possess a lesser disability when compared with other athletes confined to wheelchairs. Sometimes they play volleyball standing up, and there are occasions when they play volleyball sitting down (see Figure 15-13). In efforts to equalize competition, they are classified according to the number of amputations and the location and length of the stumps. Amputations may occur on one or both sides of the body, above or below the knee.

SUMMARY

The three types of physical disabilities discussed in this chapter are neurological conditions, orthopedic disabilities, and conditions caused by trauma. Afflictions can occur at more than 500 anatomical sites. Each student with a disability has different physical and motor capabilities and is to be provided with accommodations that enable participation in modified games and sport activity. Contraindicated activity as identified by medical personnel must be avoided.

Physical educators should address two types of program considerations to meet the physical education needs of persons with physical disabilities. One is to implement developmental programs that enhance prerequisite motor patterns, sport skills, and physical and motor fitness. The other is to structure the environment so that students with disabilities can derive physical benefits through participation in competitive sporting activities (this may be facilitated by the use of aids for specific types of activities and disabilities).

The physical educator should be ready to accommodate the individual program needs of physically disabled persons by identifying unique needs through formal and functional assessment, using adaptive devices to permit active involvement, and modifying activities to enable the student to participate in a variety of settings.

Many national organizations have been developed to enable persons with disabilities to participate in sports competition. Functional classification systems are being developed to replace the older medical models to equalize competition among individuals with varying levels of function.

Modified sports equipment opens the world to individuals with disabilities.
Courtesy RADVENTURES, Inc.

Ocean Escapes, a pioneer in aqua therapy for wheelchair-enabled individuals, offers weightlessness through scuba diving to individuals who, on land, are trapped by gravity.
Courtesy Ocean Escapes.

REVIEW QUESTIONS

1. What are some principles for adapting physical activity for students with physical disabilities?

2. Provide illustrations how principles for adapting physical activity can be applied to a specific disability in a specific activity.

3. What are some motor and nonmotor characteristics of individuals with cerebral palsy?

4. What are the grades of concussion?

5. What are some specific examples of ways physical education activities can be modified to accommodate a student in a wheelchair?

6. What types of spina bifida are there and what accommodations must be made for each?

STUDENT ACTIVITIES

1. Working in small groups, share the applications you developed for Josue, Bubba, and Roberto and come to an agreement about how best to accommodate for each of these three students.

2. Working in small groups, determine what sports programs would be appropriate for Josue, Bubba, and Roberto and develop a list of skills/abilities each will need to participate in those sports.

3. Write a letter to convince Josue's mother that participation in the regular physical education class and a community sports program will improve the quality of his life.

4. Discuss with the rest of the class the type of behavior-management program that might be successful with Josue.

5. Select one or two major journals in the field of physical or special education. Some of these journals are *Journal of Health, Physical Education, and Recreation; Exceptional Children; Adapted*

Physical Activity Quarterly; Palaestra: The Forum of Sport, Physical Education and *Recreation for the Disabled; and Sports n' Spokes.* Look through the issues from the past few years for articles that present useful suggestions for adapting instruction for students with physical disabilities. Make a file of these suggestions.

6. Visit a school, shopping center, or municipal building and identify architectural barriers that would deny access/use to individuals with disabilities. Evaluate the accessibility of drinking fountains, phones, different floors, eating facilities, playing areas, and emergency exits. What types of activities might enable persons with physical disabilities to gain access to these facilities?

7. Discuss the pros and cons of conducting separate sports programs for individuals with physical disabilities. When are separate sports programs appropriate and under what conditions?

REFERENCES

1. Alexander MJ: New techniques in quadriplegic wheelchair marathon racing, *Palaestra* 3:13–16, 1987.

2. American Juvenile Arthritis Organization. http://www.arthritis.org/ajao/

3. Amyotrophic Lateral Sclerosis Association. http://www.alsa.nationalorg/

4. AVENUES. http://www.sonnet.com/avenues/pamphlet.html

5. Bar-Or O: Muscular dystrophy. In Durstine JL, editor: *Exercise management for persons with chronic diseases and disabilities,* Champaign, IL, 1997, Human Kinetics.

6. Beers MH, Berkow R: *The Merck manual of diagnosis and therapy,* Rahway, NJ, 1999, Merck Sharpe Dohme Research Laboratories.

7. Birk TJ: Polio and post-polio syndrome. In Durstine JL, editor: *Exercise management for persons with chronic diseases and disabilities,* Champaign, IL, 1997, Human Kinetics.

8. Burkhour CK: Let's go to camp, *Exceptional Parent,* May: 66–67, 1998.

9. Brasile F: Wheelchair basketball proficiencies versus disability classification, *Adapt Phys Act Q* 3:6–13, 1986.

10. Brasile F: Performance evaluation of wheelchair athletes more than a disability classification level issue, *Adapt Phys Act Q* 7:289–297, 1990.

11. Brasile F, Hedrick BN: A comparison of participation incentives between adult and youth wheelchair basketball players, *Palaestra* 7:40–46, 1991.

12. Burd R, Grass K: Strapping to enhance athletic performance of wheelchair competitors with cerebral palsy, *Palaestra* 3:28–32, 1987.

13. Cambell SK, Wilhelm IJ: Development from birth to three years of age of 15 children at high risk for central nervous system dysfunction, *Phys Ther* 65:463–469, 1985.

14. Centers for Disease Control and Prevention. http://www.cdc.gov/ncipc/dacrrdp/tbi.htm

15. Child Health. http://www.delphi.com/child/hip.html

16. Cooper RA: A new racing wheelchair rear wheel alignment device, *Palaestra* 4:8–11, 1988.

17. Cowden JE: Project GUMBO . . . games uniting mind and body, *Palaestra* 4:13–27, 1988.

18. Croce R, Horvat M, Roswal G: Augmented feedback for enhanced skill acquisition in indviduals with traumatic brain injury, *Perceptual and Motor Skills* 82:507–514, 1996.

19. Curtis KA: Stretching routines, *Sports 'n Spokes* 7(5):1–3, 1981.

20. Curtis KA: Sport-specific functional classification for wheelchair athletes, *Sports 'n Spokes* 17:45–48, 1991.

21. Curtis KA, editor: *Guide to sports medicine needs of athletes with disabilities*, Coral Gables, FL, 1993, University of Miami School of Medicine.

22. Curtis KA: *Injuries and disability-specific medical conditions of athletes with disabilities.* Unpublished paper, Coral Gables, FL, 1993, University of Miami.

23. Curtis KA et al: Functional reach in wheelchair users: the effects of trunk and lower extremity stabilization, *Arch Phys Med Rehabil* 76:360–372, 1995.

24. D'Amato RC, Rothlisberg BA: How education should respond to students with traumatic brain injury, *J of Learn Dis* 29:670–683, 1996.

25. Davis RW: Elite wheelchair training camp, *Palaestra* 4:48–52, 1988.

26. DeLuca PA: The musculoskeletal management of children with cerebral palsy, *Pediatric Clinics of North America* 43:1135–1151, 1996.

27. DiCarlo S: Effect of arm ergometry training on wheelchair propulsion endurance of individuals with quadriplegia, *Phys Ther* 68:40–44, 1988.

28. Dummer GM et al.: Attributions of athletes with cerebral palsy, *Adapt Phys Act Q* 4:278–292, 1987.

29. Engelbert RH, Pruijs EH, Beener FA, Helders PJ: Osteogenesis imperfecta in childhood: treatment strategies, *Archives of Phys Med and Rehab* 79:1590–1593, 1998.

30. Epilepsy. http://disabilities.miningco.com/health/disabilities/

31. Fernandez JE, Pitetti KH: Training of ambulatory individuals with cerebral palsy, *Arch Phys Med Rehabil* 74:468–472, 1993.

32. Ferrara M, Laskin J: Cerebral palsy. In Durstine JL, editor: *Exercise management for persons with chronic diseases and disabilities*, Champaign, IL, 1997, Human Kinetics.

33. Figoni SF: Spinal cord injury. In Durstine JL, editor: *Exercise management for persons with chronic diseases and disabilities*, Champaign, IL, 1997, Human Kinetics.

34. Gehlsen GM, Davis RW, Bahamonde R: Intermittent velocity and wheelchair performance characteristics, *Adapt Phys Act Q* 7:219–230, 1990.

35. Geurts ACH et al.: Dual-tasks assessment of reorganization of postural control in persons with lower limb amputation, *Arch Phys Med Rehabil* 72:1059–1064, 1995.

36. Gitlin LN, Levine R, Geiger C: Adaptive device use by older adults with mixed disabilities, *Arch Phys Med Rehabil* 74:149–152, 1993.

37. Gordon WA, Sliwinski M, Echo J, McLoughlin M, Sheere M, Meili TE: The benefits of exercise in individuals with traumatic brain injury: a retrospective study, *J Heal Trauma Rehabil* 13:58–67, 1998.

38. Hardison GT, Isreal RG, Somes G: Physiological responses to different cranking rates during submaximal arm ergometry in paraplegic males, *Adapt Phys Act Q* 4:94–105, 1987.

39. Harvey LA, Davis GM, Smith MB, Engel S: Energy expenditure during gait using the walkabout and isometric reciprocal gait orthosis in persons with paraplegia, *Arch of Physic Med and Rehab* 79:946–951, 1998.

40. Hazelwood ME et al.: The use of therapeutic electrical stimulation in the treatment of hemiplegic cerebral palsy, *Dev Med Child Neurol* 36:661–673, 1994.

41. Hedrick B et al.: Aerodynamic positioning and performance in wheelchair racing, *Adapt Phys Act Q* 7:41–51, 1990.

42. Higgs C: A comparison of three- and four-wheeled designs, *Palaestra* 8:29–35, 1992.

43. Higgs C et al.: Wheelchair classification for track and field events: a performance approach, *Adapt Phys Act Q* 7:22–40, 1990.

44. Holland LJ, Steadward RD: Effects of resistance and flexibility training on strength, spasticity/muscle tone and range of motion of elite athletes with cerebral palsy, *Palaestra* 6:27–31, 1990.

45. Huber JH: Wheelchair division of the 93rd Boston Marathon: new world records, issues, trends, *Palaestra* 5:44–46, 1989.

46. Hughes CJ et al.: Biomechanics of wheelchair propulsion as a function of seat position and user-to-chair interface, *Arch Phys Med Rehabil* 73:263–269, 1992.

47. Hundertmark LH: Evaluating the adult with cerebral palsy for specialized adapted seating, *Phys Ther* 65:209–212, 1985.

48. Hunter D et al.: Energy expenditure of below-knee amputees during harness-supported treadmill ambulation, *J Orthop Sport Phys Ther* 21:268–276, 1995.

49. Kehle TJ, Clark E, Jenson WR: Interventions for students with traumatic brain injury: managing behavioral disturbances, *J of Learning Dis* 29:633–642, 1996.

50. Kelly JP, Rosenberg JH: the development of guidelines for the management of concussion in sports, *J Head Trauma Rehabil*, 13:53–65, 1998.

51. Kirshblum SC, O'Connor KC: Predicting neurologic recovery in traumatic cervical spinal cord injury, *Arch Phys Med Rehab* 79:1456–1466, 1998.

52. Khaw CWH, Tidemann AJ, Stern LM: Study of hemiplegic cerebral palsy with a review of the literature, *J Paediatr Child Health* 30:224–229, 1994.

53. Kocina P: Body composition of spinal cord injured adults, *Sports Med* 23:48–60, 1998.

54. Lasko-McCarthey P, Knopf KG: *Adapted physical education for adults with disabilities,* ed. 3, Dubuque, IA, 1992, Eddie Bowers.

55. Lee K, Thomas D: Control of computer-based technology for people with physical disabilities: an assessment manual, Toronto, 1990, University of Toronto Press.

56. Lepage C, Noreau L, Bernard PM: Association between characteristics of locomotion and accomplishment of life habits in children with cerebral palsy, *Physical Therapy* 78:458–469, 1998.

57. Levin S: Aquatic therapy, *Physician Sportsmed* 19:119–126, 1995.

58. Letts RM: *Principles of seating the disabled,* Boston, 1991, CRC Press.

59. Liu M, Chino N, Ishihara T: Muscle damage in Duchenne muscular dystrophy evaluated by a new quantitative computed tomography method, *Arch Phys Med Rehabil* 74:507–514, 1991.

60. McLean KP, Skinner JS: Effect of body training position on outcomes of an aerobic training study on individuals with quadriplegia, *Arch Phys Med Rehabil* 76:139–150, 1995.

61. Midha M, Schmitt JK, Sclater M: Exercise effect with the wheelchair aerobic fitness trainer on conditioning with metabolic function in disabled persons: a pilot study, *Arch Phys Med Rehabil* 80:258–261, 1999.

62. Minor MA, Kay DR: Arthritis. In Durstine JL, editor: *Exercise management for persons with chronic diseases and disabilities,* Champaign, IL, 1997, Human Kinetics.

63. Mira M, Tyler J: Students with traumatic brain injury: making the transition from hospital to school, *Focus Except Child* 23:1–12, 1991.

64. Mulcare JA: Multiple sclerosis. In Durstine JL, editor: *Exercise management for persons with chronic diseases and disabilities,* Champaign, IL, 1997, Human Kinetics.

65. National Information Center for Children and Youth with Disabilities. http://www.nichcy.org

66. National Spinal Cord Injury Statistical Center. http://www.spinalcord.uab.edu/cgi-bin/noframes/driver/faq.data.html

67. Nau JL: Amyotrophic lateral sclerosis. In Durstine JL, editor: *Exercise management for persons with chronic diseases and disabilities,* Champaign, IL, 1997, Human Kinetics.

68. Noreau L, Moffet H, Drolet B, Parent E: Dance-based exercise program in rheumatoid arthritis, *Amer J of Physi Med and Rehab* 76:109–113, 1997.

69. Osteogenesis Imperfecta Foundation. http://www.oif.org/tier2/fastfact.htm

70. Paciorek MJ: Technology only a part of the story as world records fall, *Palaestra* 10:14, 42, 1993.

71. Peck DM, McKeag DB: Athletes with disabilities: removing medical barriers, *Physician Sportsmed* 22:59–63, 1994.

72. Petrofsky JS, Brown SW, Cerrel B: Active physical therapy and its benefits in rehabilitation, *Palaestra* 9:23–27, 61, 1992.

73. Phillips W, Burkett LN: Arm crank exercise with static leg FNS in persons with spinal cord injury, *Medicine and Science in Sports and Exercise* 27:530–535, l995.

74. Ponichtera-Mulcare JA et al.: Maximal aerobic exercise of individuals with multiple sclerosis using three modes of ergometry, *Clin Kines* 49:4–13, 1995.

75. Protas EJ, Stanley RK, Jankovic J: Parkinson's disease. In Durstine JL, editor: *Exercise management for persons with chronic diseases and disabilities,* Champaign, IL, 1997, Human Kinetics.

76. Raymond J, Davis GM, Climstein M, Sutton JR: Cardiorespiratory responses to arm cranking and electrical stimulation leg cycling in people with paraplegia, *Medicine & Science in Sports & Exercise* 31:822–828, 1999.

77. Rossi C, Sullivan SJ: Motor fitness in children and adolescents with traumatic brain injury, *Arch Phys Med Rehabil* 77:1062–1065, 1996.

78. Sirven JI, Varrato J: Physical activity and epilepsy: what are the rules? *The Physician and Sportsmedicine* 27:63–70, 1999.

79. Strohkendl H: The new classification system for wheelchair basketball. In Sherrill C, editor: *Sports and disabled athletes,* Champaign, IL, 1986, Human Kinetics.

80. Stolting JC: The National Ability Center; enhancing mind, body and soul, *Exceptional Parent* March: 32–35, 1999.

81. Stopka C: Managing common injuries in individuals with disabilities: prevention comes first, *Palaestra* 12(2):28–31, 1996.

82. Thurman DJ, Branche CM, Sniezek JE: The epidemiology of sports-related traumatic brain injuries in the United States: recent developments, *J Head Trauma Rehabil* 13:1–8, 1998.

83. United Cerebral Palsy of Central California. http://www.iccc/prg/whatis.htm

84. Unnithan VB, Clifford C, Bar-Or O: Evaluation by exercise testing of the child with cerebral palsy, *Sports Medicine* 26:239–251, 1998.

85. Venn J, Morganstern L, Dykes MK: Checklist for evaluating the fit and function of orthoses, prostheses, and wheelchairs in the classroom, *Teach Except Child,* Winter: 51–56, # 1979.

86. Ward E: *Prescriptive seating for wheelchair mobility,* Kansas City, MO, 1994, Health Wealth International.

87. Williams HG, McClenaghan B, Ward DS: Duration of muscle activity during standing in normally and slowly developing children, *Am J Phys Med* 64:171–189, 1985.

88. Wilson AB: *How to select and use manual wheelchairs,* Topping, VA, 1992, Rehabilitation Press.

89. World Federation of Neurology ALS. http://www.wfnals.org/

90. Wright J: *Project C.R.E.O.L.E.: wheelchair sports and mobility curriculum,* Harvey, LA, 1989, Jefferson Parish Public School System.

91. Yamamoto M, Tajima F, Okawa H, Mizushima T, Umezu Y, Ogata H: Static exercise-induced increase in blood pressure in individuals with cervical spinal cord injury, *Arch Phys Med Rehabil* 80:288–293, 1999.

SUGGESTED READINGS

Durstine JL, editor: *Exercise management for persons with chronic diseases and disabilities,* Champaign, IL, 1997, Human Kinetics.

Rimmer JH: *Fitness and rehabilitation programs for special populations,* Madison, WI, 1994, Brown & Benchmark.

RECOMMENDED WEBSITES

Please note: These websites are being recommended in the fall of 1999. Given the ever changing nature of the Internet, these sites may have moved or been replaced by the time you are reading this text.

American Juvenile Arthritis Organization
  http://www.arthritis.org/ajao/

Amyotrophic Lateral Sclerosis Association
  http://www.alsa.nationalorg/

AVENUES
  http://www.sonnet.com/avenues/pamphlet.html

Centers for Disease Control and Prevention
  http://www.cdc.gov/ncipc/dacrrdp/tbi.htm

Child Health
  http://www.delphi.com/child/hip.html

Duchenne Muscular Dystrophy
  http://www.softconn.co.za/~mpeters/dmd.html

Epilepsy
  http://disabilities.miningco.com/health/disabilities/

Muscular Dystrophy Association
  http://www.webnet.com.au/mda/

National Information Center for Children and Youth with Disabilities
  http://www.nichcy.org

National Spinal Cord Injury Statistical Center
  http://www.spinalcord.uab.edu/cgi-bin/noframes/driver/faq.data.html

Osteogenesis Imperfecta Foundation
  http://www.oif.org/tier2/fastfact.htm

World Federation of Neurology ALS
  http://www.wfnals.org/

RECOMMENDED VIDEOS

A Dream Comes True for a Swimmer with an Amputation
color, 13 minutes, 1992, $189 purchase price
Insight Media
2162 Broadway
New York, NY 10024-0621

Adaptive Skiing Teaching Methods: A Practical Guide to Teaching Disabled Skiers
color, 75 minutes, 1994, $279 purchase price
Insight Media
2162 Broadway
New York, NY 10024-0621

Cerebral Palsy: What Every Parent Should Know
color, 19 minutes, $89.95 purchase price
Films for the Humanities & Sciences
PO Box 2053
Princeton, NJ 08543-2053

Epilepsy: The Storm Within
color, 27 minutes, $149 purchase price,
$75 rental
Films for the Humanities & Sciences
PO Box 2053
Princeton, NJ 08543-2053

Mentally Handicapped and Epileptic: They Don't Make a Fuss
color, 30 minutes, $149 purchase price,
$75 rental
Films for the Humanities & Sciences
PO Box 2053
Princeton, NJ 08543-2053

Muscular Dystrophy
color, 26 minutes, $149 purchase price,
$75 rental
Films for the Humanities & Sciences
PO Box 2053
Princeton, NJ 08543-2053

Polio and Post-Polio Syndrome
color, 28 minutes, $149 purchase price,
$75 rental
Films for the Humanities & Sciences
PO Box 2053
Princeton, NJ 08543-2053

The Chariot Races: A Journey from Disabled to Enabled
color, 27 minutes, 1997, $139 purchase price
Insight Media

2162 Broadway
New York, NY 10024-0621

Understanding the Disabled: Dances with the
Minotaur
color, 45 minutes, 1998, $119 purchase price
Insight Media
2162 Broadway
New York, NY 10024-0621

Without Pity: A Film About Abilities
color, 56 minutes, $129 purchase price

$75 rental
Films for the Humanities & Sciences
PO Box 2053
Princeton, NJ 08543-2053

Wheelchair Athletes
color, 27 minutes, 1996, $225 purchase price
Insight Media
2162 Broadway
New York, NY 10024-0621

Communicative Disorders

16

■ OBJECTIVES

List three motor characteristics of individuals who are deaf.

Briefly describe cultural issues within the Deaf community that have an impact on the education of learners who are deaf and hearing impaired.

Demonstrate five specific signs that can be used in physical education to communicate with students who are deaf or hard of hearing.

List five techniques a teacher can use for enhancing communication with students who are deaf or hard of hearing.

Describe the two most widely accepted communication systems used by persons who are deaf or hearing impaired in this country.

Briefly describe one speech disorder, one language disorder, and one voice disorder.

Describe strategies the teacher can use to make a child who stutters more comfortable speaking in the physical education program.

Describe several strategies to create a "bully-free" environment in the physical education program so children with speech and language delays or disorders are not the victims of teasing.

A child develops play skills.
Courtesy Callier Center for Communicative Disorders, Dallas.

Fundamental to the human experience is communication with other human beings. Children who have difficulty expressing their thoughts, feelings, ideas, and dreams and children who have difficulty understanding the thoughts, feelings, ideas, and dreams of others struggle to make sense of their existence. It is difficult to make sense of their world and all the stimuli and experiences to which they are exposed without the capacity to describe, evaluate, and share these experiences.

Children with communicative delays and disorders may have a difficult time being successful in the educational environment. While they may have excellent physical and motor skills, they also may struggle with the psychosocial component of the physical education experience.

DEAFNESS AND HEARING IMPAIRMENTS

The challenges for the physical educator seeking to provide a quality education experience for learners who are deaf or hearing impaired are immense. Part of the challenge is associated with the growing educational trend to consider students who are deaf or hearing impaired as bilingual members of a bicultural minority,[52] rather than simply as children with a disability. This trend is emerging, in part, to honor the unique culture, language, history, and legacy of the Deaf community. In order to do this, educators must honor diversity among all minority groups.

It is particularly vital that the unique needs of the student who is deaf or hearing impaired and who represents another cultural/racial minority be acknowledged. For example, a young child who is African American and deaf must deal with the realities of learning and existing within three separate and distinct cultures. The responsibilities of "membership" and "belonging" within each of these cultures vary greatly. This can be very confusing, particularly to a young child or adolescent. This is especially critical because children who are deaf or hearing impaired and who represent another minority group, as well, do not do well,

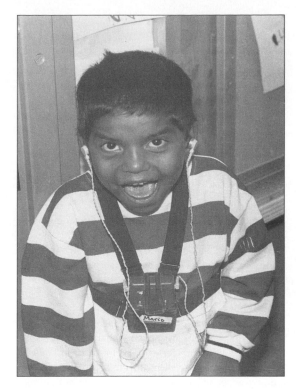

Courtesy Callier Center for Communicative Disorders, Dallas.

historically, in existing education programs.[52] Parasnis wrote,

> Shifting the focus from disability to diversity when considering deaf learners might bring about a change in perspective that would enhance the educational experiences of all deaf learners and would not be inconsistent with the general goal of the sociopolitical movement to consider deaf people as a bilingual, bicultural minority group in America.[52]

In addition to broader cultural issues, children who have permanent hearing losses usually have delays in expressive and receptive language, play and other social skills, and motor development. The purpose of this chapter is to provide a background into the nature of hearing loss and the needs of persons who are deaf and hard of hearing and to discuss the role of physical education in meeting these needs as part of the total educational

CASE STUDY

Juana

Juana is a eighteen-year-old student who is profoundly deaf. She is presently receiving educational services in a self-contained class for hard of hearing/deaf students in a school-based vocational preparation program in a large southern city. Although her recent three-year assessment indicated an IQ score of 70, her teachers believe she is much brighter and that her deafness compromised her performance during the assessment. She is able to do some lipreading and uses American Sign Language functionally. She is able to speak, but, until one gets to know her and becomes accustomed to her speech, she is very difficult to understand. Her gross and fine motor skills are excellent, and she performs at age level on physical fitness tests.

She is the youngest of five daughters and spends the majority of her time away from school baby-sitting for her sisters' children. Her work performance at Wolfe's Nursery has been excellent during her junior and senior years in high school. Her mother, who is hearing, has indicated that, when Juana graduates, Juana will assume the role of full-time baby-sitter for the family.

APPLICATION TASK

Juana's last transitional physical education plan is due. As you read through this chapter, think about the types of community activities in which she might be successful. What additional strategies could the physical educator use to help Juana, and her family, prepare her for participation outside her home?

process. Classifications of hearing loss, characteristics of individuals who are deaf and hearing impaired, types of communication systems, teaching techniques, and ways to serve these students in the most inclusive environment are discussed.

Definition

In the Education for All Handicapped Children Act, retained within the Individuals with Disabilities Education Act (IDEA),[66] *deaf* means a hearing impairment which is so severe that the child is impaired in processing linguistic information through hearing, with or without amplification, which adversely affects educational performance (Section a.5.b.3). *Hard of hearing* means a hearing impairment, whether permanent or fluctuating, which adversely affects a child's educational performance but which is not included under deaf in this section (Section 121a.5.b.3).[66] This definition is useful to physical educators because it requires focus on the child as he or she participates in tasks in physical education. If there is performance deficiency, the question can be asked, "Is the deficiency the result of hearing loss?" If the answer is yes, accommodation for the child should be made.

The continuum of degree of hearing loss and ability to understand speech ranges from that of little significance to that of extreme disability (see Figure 16-1). The degree of an individual's deafness is determined by the amount of decibel loss and the individual's ability to perceive conversation[49] (see Figure 16-2).

Incidence

Approximately 68,000 learners, from birth to age twenty-one years, received educational services in the 1996-1997 academic year because of a diagnosis of deafness or hearing impairment. This represents 1.1 percent of all the students served in early intervention and school-based programs. The school-age learners were served in the following educational placements:

- General education class: 35.4 percent
- Resource room: 19.1 percent
- Separate class: 28.5 percent
- Separate public school facility: 3.8 percent
- Separate private school facility: 2.7 percent
- Public residential facility: 9.3 percent
- Private residential facility: 1.0 percent
- Homebound/hospital: 0.2 percent[65]

Many individuals who are deaf or hard of hearing have concomitant disabilities. Specific conditions associated with deafness are included in Figure 16-3.

Figure 16-1 Characteristics of Children with Hearing Loss[4,23,33]

Mild hearing loss (15–30 decibel hearing loss)
- Children develop speech and language spontaneously.
- They may have difficulty hearing faint speech.

Moderate hearing loss (31–60 decibel hearing loss)
- Children will benefit from hearing aids as soon as possible after diagnosis.
- Children will rely on visual information to supplement auditory information.
- They may have difficulty with delayed language and speech skills, particularly in the pronunciation of consonants.
- They will do better in a classroom setting with preferential seating.

Severe hearing loss (61–90 decibel hearing loss)
- Children will have difficulty hearing conversational speech.
- They will be able to respond to sounds that are high in intensity, at close range, with amplification.
- They will require amplification and significant speech and language therapy to function in the educational setting.

Profound hearing loss (91–120 decibel hearing loss)
- Children with a profound hearing loss are unlikely to benefit from auditory input and will rely on tactile and visual cues.
- They will usually need to use total communication or manual communication.
- With little residual hearing, they may still have intelligible speech.

Total hearing loss (121 + decibel hearing loss)
- Children with total hearing loss do not hear even with an auditory amplification device.
- They will depend on vision as their primary modality.

Figure 16-2 Continuum of Educationally Significant Hearing Loss[44]

Most severe
- No residual hearing
- Severe to profound bilateral SNHL
- Mild to moderate bilateral SNHL
- Unilateral SNHL
- Minimal hearing loss
  Conductive/recurrent otitis media
  Speech or language delay
- Normal hearing

SNHL = sensorineural hearing loss

Figure 16-3 Specific Conditions Associated with Deafness[33]

Speech and learning disability	8.5 percent
Mental retardation	7.8 percent
Attention deficit disorder	4.6 percent
Cerebral palsy	3.0 percent
Legal blindness	1.6 percent
Other	3.8 percent

Causes

The acquisition of speech and language skills, like the acquisition of motor skills, is basic to the subsequent development of the individual. Therefore, the time of onset of deafness is a critical factor in determining the effects that it may have on the learning situation. Essentially, individuals are divided into two basic categories, those who are prelingually deaf and those who are postlingually deaf. If a child becomes deaf before the acquisition of any linguistic or speech skills, the child has little, if any, chance of acquiring typical speech and language skills. If an individual suffers a hearing loss after having acquired speech and language skills, postlingually, the individual may have already acquired and be able to retain typical speech and language skills.

In the past several years, an aggressive program has been established in many states to ensure early identification of deafness/hearing impairments and subsequent early intervention for affected infants and toddlers. This early identification, specifically with newborns, has been endorsed by the Joint Committee on Infant Hearing and the National Institutes of Health. The intent is the universal detection of hearing loss in newborns and involves three phases: (1) birth hearing screening; (2) follow-up and specific diagnosis; and (3) intervention services.[25] Each of these phases is critical in identifying and then providing early intervention services for newborns with a hearing loss. Clearly, the earlier the diagnosis can be made, the earlier the infant or child and his or her parents can receive the health and educational services which are vital to the development of the infant or child.

The proper diagnosis of hearing disabilities may provide assistance for the development of physical education programs. The uniqueness of each deaf child requires individualized assessment and intervention by teachers. Categories of hearing loss that should be considered in the educational planning for the student are the following.

Conductive Hearing Impairments

A conductive hearing loss, while interfering with a child's detection and recognition of speech, also causes fluctuating hearing levels. A conductive hearing impairment is, typically, a condition in which the intensity of sound is reduced before reaching the inner ear, where the auditory nerve begins. A conductive hearing loss can also result when the membranes in the inner ear undergo physical changes that reduce the transfer of energy to the hair cells.

The most prevalent cause of conductive hearing loss is otitis media, an infection of the middle ear. Hearing impairments and deafness from otitis media are particularly critical if a young child has suffered a series of infections at a young age. Intermittent or persistent conductive hearing loss, as a result of otitis media, may have a significant impact on the subsequent learning and behavior of school-age children. A history of middle ear disease is associated with articulation disorders in children in the "lower" social classes, hyperactive behavior in the "middle" social classes, and language problems in the "upper" social class.[37]

Another infection that may cause conductive hearing loss is mastoiditis. Mastoiditis occurs when there is chronic inflammation of the middle ear that spreads into the air cells of the mastoid process within the temporal bone. Other causes of conductive hearing loss include perforation of the eardrum from a blow to the head, allergies that make the eustachian tube swell, tumors of the external auditory canal, the presence of foreign objects in the external ear, insect bites, and an excessive build-up of ear wax.

Sensorineural Hearing Impairments

A sensorineural hearing loss (SNHL), while interfering with a child's detection and recognition of speech, may also filter and distort sound. A sensorineural hearing loss is a condition caused by an absence or a malfunction of a sensory unit. The damage may be present in the cochlea (sensory) or the eighth cranial nerve (neural). If the dysfunction is in the inner ear, the individual has difficulty discriminating among speech sounds. Sound can be heard, but often meaning cannot be derived from high-frequency sounds. Causes include recessive genetic sources, maternal Rubella (German measles) or venereal disease during the pregnancy, lesions or tumors in the inner ear or on the eighth cranial nerve, and infections of childhood such as mumps, inner ear infection, meningitis, and encephalitis.

One of the most threatening causes of significant hearing loss in the new millennium is the epidemic of noise-induced hearing loss, which results from exposure to any source of intense noise and/or to constant noise, an environmental toxin, at best, over an extended period of time.

Central Auditory Processing Problems

Deafness may result from damage at the brain stem level or in the cortex itself. This type of deafness can occur concurrently with sensorineural impairments.[53]

Unilateral Hearing Loss

A child who is affected by a unilateral hearing loss may struggle more than others within the school environment. He or she is frequently misunderstood as being able to hear "what he or she wants to hear." In fact, the child with a unilateral hearing loss has difficulty hearing the teacher, especially if the acoustics are bad and he or she is at any distance from the child. In order to track sound, the child may move his or her head and body toward the sound; unfortunately, a teacher without specific training may assume the child is simply fidgeting and not attending.[23]

Clues That Indicate Hearing Loss

Early identification of deafness and hearing loss is critical.[24] Parents and teachers should be alert to signs of hearing loss:[8,24]

1. Hearing and comprehension of speech
   a. General indifference to sound
   b. Lack of response to the spoken word
   c. Response to noises as opposed to words
   d. Head and body leans toward the source of sound
   e. Requests for repeated statements
   f. Tinnitus—buzzing, ringing, roaring, whistling, or hissing sounds
2. Vocalization and sound production
   a. Monotonal quality
   b. Indistinct speech
   c. Lessened laughter
   d. Vocal play for vibratory sensation
   e. Head banging, foot stamping for vibratory sensation
   f. Yelling, screeching to express pleasure or need
3. Visual attention
   a. Augmental visual vigilance and attentiveness
   b. Alertness to gesture and movement
   c. Vehement gestures
4. Social rapport and adaptation
   a. Subnormal rapport in vocal games
   b. Intensified preoccupation with things rather than persons
   c. Puzzling and unhappy episodes in social situations

d. Suspiciousness and alertness, alternating with cooperation
   e. Marked reaction to praise and affection
5. Emotional behavior
   a. Tantrums to call attention to self or need
   b. Tensions, tantrums, resistance due to lack of comprehension
   c. Frequent stubborn behavior
   d. Irritability at not making self understood
6. Motor behavior
   a. Vertigo, an abnormal sensation of rotary movement associated with difficulty in balance, gait, and navigation of the environment[8]
7. Physical and health
   a. Earaches, particularly chronic
   b. Jaw pain
   c. Chronic sinus infections[8]

The percentage of students who are deaf or hard of hearing who have specific functional limitations in cognitive/behavioral, communication, and physical domains is included in Figure 16-4.

Psychological, Behavioral, and Cognitive Characteristics

Hearing loss can have a profound effect on an individual's behavior. The very self-concept and identity (self-theory) of the developing child may be negatively affected. Parents are the major influence on the development of self-theory. The young child is dependent on the parent for significant feedback, which is the foundation of the child's understanding of self. Communication between the parent and the child who is deaf or hard of hearing is often confusing. This creates a stressful situation for the child struggling to understand his or her parents' responses and the meaning of the parents' reactions.[31] Misunderstandings can create awkward and hurtful situations in which the child is inadvertently given incorrect impressions about his or her behavior and the parents' perceptions regarding the behavior.

Deafness and hearing loss, in addition to the profound affect on self-concept and identity, also affect language and speech development, learning

Figure 16-4   Percentage of Students Who Are Deaf and or Hard of Hearing Reported to Have Functional Limitations[33]

	Mild/moderate (percent)	Severe/profound (percent)
Cognitive/behavioral social		
Thinking/reasoning (32.9 percent)	24.4	8.5
Maintaining attention to classroom tasks (35.1 percent)	27.1	8.0
Social interaction/classroom behavior (27.5 percent)	20.8	6.7
Communicative		
Expressive communication (45.6 percent)	31.7	13.9
Receptive communication (46.9 percent)	34.8	12.1
Physical		
Vision (12.5 percent)	10.4	2.1
Use of hands, arms, and legs (10.4 percent)	7.8	2.6
Balance (8.6 percent)	6.6	2.0
Overall physical health (9.5 percent)	7.6	1.9

and cognitive function, play, and social adjustment. Comprehension and production of language are significantly affected by hearing loss.

The degree of hearing loss has a great impact on language development. In both conductive and sensorineural hearing losses, the development of auditory skills that are critical prerequisites to the development of receptive and expressive language skills, as well as speech intelligibility, is delayed. The auditory skills that are compromised include detection, discrimination, recognition, comprehension, and attention.

If an infant or a developing child is unable to hear the oral language produced within his or her environment, it is impossible for the child to reproduce the language. If the child is unable to hear the rhythm and rhyme, the form (syntax), the use of language (pragmatics), the tone, the timbre and flow of the language, and the content (semantics), the child will be unable to produce sounds that replicate what was heard. It is generally understood that, the more severe the hearing loss, the less intelligible a child's speech will be.[69]

The young child who is deaf or hearing impaired is particularly apt to struggle within the traditional school setting. Until the child is able to read, the child is, typically, almost completely dependent on the auditory modality to learn.[44] This places the child who is deaf or hearing impaired at a significant disadvantage.

However, if a young child who is deaf or hearing impaired is given every opportunity to develop the intelligences (Howard Gardner's eight intelligences) not specifically associated with language—the musical, logical-mathematical, or bodily-kinesthetic, for example—there is no reason the child cannot succeed and, indeed, thrive in the educational community. Hearing loss may also have a significant impact on the child's ability to function within the classroom environment. The hearing loss may affect the child's ability to (1) comprehend class material, (2) follow directions, (3) follow class rules, (4) exhibit age-appropriate classroom behaviors, and (5) follow and participate in class discussions.[57]

In the past, unfortunately, psychoeducational assessment relied heavily on tests which discriminated against children who were deaf and hearing impaired and inappropriately portrayed them as lacking intelligence. In fact, all that the students lacked were the specific skills necessary to take the specific language-based test.

While many students who are deaf or hearing impaired are very successful in the educational community, many deaf students do not graduate from high school until they are about twenty years of age. This appears to be related to several factors. First, federal law mandates that a student with a disability has a right to a free, appropriate education from three to twenty-two years; many parents and students choose to take advantage of the educational and related services available during that time. Second, the amount of instructional time devoted to curricular content required by the state education agencies is often compromised because of the amount of time required to teach American Sign Language, speech reading, or other skills required to function effectively within the society.

There is reason for concern that at the time most students who are deaf or hearing impaired leave school at age twenty, their average reading skills are at grade 4.5, and their overall academic skills are behind those of their hearing peers.[69] It must be remembered, however, that most students who graduate from public high schools in the United States have functional reading skills typical of a fourth- or fifth-grader, and that is also a reason for concern.

The most significant issue tied to deafness and hearing ability, particularly in young children, is their difficulty with play. Play is the foundation of the development of young children. Difficulty with communication makes it difficult for a young child who is deaf or hearing impaired to interact with ease with other children. Lyon wrote,

> Play is one of the most important contexts in which children learn how to talk about objects and their own actions with them and how to interact with other people. Play also affords children the opportunity to work through and learn to deal with their feelings and emotions in situations which are non-threatening and under their control. . . . Play is thus related to developments in all major areas of development, physical, linguistic, cognitive, social and emotional. . . .

Research has found that children who are deaf and hearing impaired may, indeed, develop symbolic play even in the absence of spoken language. However, in that study, language did not develop in the absence of play.[41] It appears that young children who are deaf or hearing impaired develop the skills to engage in "pretend play" without oral/verbal communication. Apparently, it is much like the play typical of young children who have not yet developed spoken language—the play of young toddlers, for example.

Each child's psychosocial development is based on how well or poorly others in the environment accept her or him (see Figure 16-5). Unfortunately, the psychosocial development of some children

Figure 16-5 Holcomb's Categories of Identity of Individuals Who Are Deaf[31]

Balanced bicultural
The person who is deaf feels equally comfortable in deaf and hearing cultures.

Deaf-dominant bicultural
The person is primarily involved in the deaf community but can relate well to hearing people.

Hearing-dominant bicultural
The person feels comfortable within the hearing community and has limited involvement in the deaf community, perhaps because of lack of access.

Culturally separate
The person identifies with and prefers to associate exclusively with others who are deaf.

Culturally isolated
The person rejects involvement with other individuals who are deaf. The person is comfortable in and prefers the hearing community and perceives sign language to be a "crutch" for those unable to learn oral skills.

Culturally marginal
The person is uncomfortable in the deaf community and the hearing community.

Culturally captive
The person who is deaf and has had no opportunity to meet others who are deaf and learn about deaf culture.

who are deaf or hearing impaired is delayed because it reflects the negative stereotypes attributed to them.[43] Stereotypes associated with individuals who are deaf or hearing impaired include nonsocial behavior, reservedness, lack of communicativeness, and preference for solitary behavior.[17]

Children who are deaf and raised by parents who are deaf, about 10 percent of the children who are deaf, are generally better adjusted than deaf children reared by hearing parents because of the shared nature of the experience. This should be no surprise. If the child's parent has experienced the confusion, frustration, and pain associated with difficulty communicating with others and has also experienced discrimination within the community and larger society, the parent will be much more likely to understand the feelings of his or her child. In addition, the infant born to deaf parents has a definite advantage in communication skills because the child is exposed to sign language from infancy, in the same way that a hearing child of hearing parents is exposed to the oral language of the parents from infancy.

In addition, if the parent's natural language is sign, the child and parent will find it much easier to communicate than will a child and parent learning the language together. It is easy to compare this to the process a child goes through learning a verbal-based language. If the parent's native language, for example, is Spanish, it will be easy for the child to learn Spanish; the language is used in the home, and the inferences, nuances, and intricacies of the language are shared daily. If both the parents and the child are struggling to learn English as a second language, the process is much more difficult.

Motor Characteristics of Hearing-Impaired Individuals

Impairment of the semicircular canals, vestibule of the inner ear, and/or vestibular portion of the eighth cranial nerve has a negative effect on balance. Siegel, Marchetti, and Tecclin[60] reported significantly depressed balance performance by children with sensorineural hearing loss of below 65 decibels. Another study that did not examine etiological factors evaluated motor performance and vestibular function of a group of hearing impaired children. The vast majority (65 percent) of the studied group demonstrated abnormal vestibular function but normal motor proficiency except for balance, whereas 24 percent had normal vestibular function and motor proficiency, including balance. Eleven percent had normal vestibular function but poor motor proficiency and balance.[20]

Butterfield et al.[16] found that nine of eighteen deaf boys and girls, receiving their educational services in a residential school for the deaf, had significant balance deficits as characterized by extraneous movement when performing the Bruininks-Oseretsky Test of Motor Proficiency Subtest 2, Item 8. Each child was asked to walk on a balance beam and step over a stick, held at knee level, without falling off the balance beam. The students who fell appeared dependent on the visual system for their information about their performance; they watched their feet while walking on the beam. Each student who fell appeared dependent on the visual mechanism for information about their balance. This would be typical of children with a vestibular deficit, though no specific test was used to determine if such a deficit was present.

Friends at Play
Courtesy Callier Center for Communicative Disorders, Dallas.

Butterfield and Ersing[15] found that the cause of hearing impairment may have an impact on balance proficiency. In their study, a group of hearing-impaired persons with acquired deafness performed significantly better than a group with congenital deafness, deafness present at birth. Thus, it is important to point out that the balancing deficit associated with some hearing-impaired children cannot be generalized. The individual education program must be based on the needs of each child.

Another characteristic that may be negatively affected by a hearing impairment is motor speed (i.e., the time it takes the child to process information and complete a motor act).[14]

Children Who Are Deaf-Blind

Children who are deaf-blind have loss of both vision and hearing. They have less than 20/20 vision for a field of 20 degrees or less. In addition, they have a loss of hearing of 25 decibels or more. Thus, they are often unable to be educated in a class for the deaf or the blind. Children who are deaf-blind have problems that are similar to those of the blind child and the deaf child; however, their problems are exponential rather than additive. There is practically no foundation for communicative skills. Residual sight, hearing, or both can be the basis of communication. If there is no residual sight or hearing, communication is then made kinesthetically through the hands.

Wheeler and Griffin[67] have suggested a motor-based approach to teaching communication and language skills to young children who are deaf-blind. The critical role of the physical educator, as the motor expert, in each of these phases must be emphasized:

- Resonance. In this phase, the physical educator mirrors and expands on movements the student initiates. For example, if the student is holding a ball, the teacher may grasp the ball as well and begin to move it in a circular path.
- Coactive movement. In this phase, the emphasis is on the physical relationship between the teacher and the student, including frequent touch and physical contact between the two. It also includes movements done together—for example, sitting, singing, rocking, and playing "row, row, row your boat."
- Nonrepresentation reference. In this phase, the teacher helps the student develop the basis of body image by encouraging the student to replicate the position of a three-dimensional object—the teacher, a doll, a teddy bear, or a "gumby."
- Deferred imitation. The teacher, in this phase, asks the student to imitate a series of body positions, which become increasingly complex. An example of this activity is playing "angels in the snow."

In and through the development of the most basic body image, the physical educator can help the learner who is deaf and blind develop the foundation which is critical to the development of future movement, communication, and language skills.

Testing

Infants and toddlers who have been identified, early in life, as deaf or hearing impaired can and should be evaluated by a diagnostician or an educator using the same developmentally appropriate instruments used with any other child at risk for a delay. Chapter 10 contains more information about the assessment of infants, toddlers, and preschoolers.

Any evaluation instrument that allows the evaluator, or a peer, to *demonstrate* the skills involved can be used with students who are deaf or hearing impaired. Most elementary and middle school students who are deaf or hearing impaired can participate in the physical fitness and motor competency tests which are part of the general physical education program.

The Test of Gross Motor Development (TGMD) would be appropriate for the elementary- and middle-school-age child who is deaf or hearing impaired and has a motor delay. In addition, the balance subtest from the Bruininks-Oseretsky Test of Motor Proficiency could be used to determine whether there is a possibility of vestibular delay. Comparison of static balance ability with eyes open and eyes closed will provide clues to vestibular delay or damage. Keep in mind that should the physical educator or adapted physical educator suspect that poor vestibular functioning is interfering with the student's ability to balance with eyes closed it may not be possible to correct the condition. If the deafness is caused from damage to the portion of the eighth cranial nerve which also carries the vestibular impulse, activities to stimulate the vestibular system will not help the balance problem. In these cases, it is best to simply teach the child to execute the balance moves needed to be successful in motor activities.

High school students who are deaf, and have a motor delay or disorder, may best be assessed using the McCarron-Dial system designed to help identify strengths and deficits for the performance of tasks in the workforce. This type of assessment may be useful, in particular, in the development of the individual transition plan.

Special Considerations

For optimum learning to occur, a teacher must be able to communicate effectively with the students (see Figure 16-6). Students with hearing losses have the greatest opportunity to learn when they have maximum hearing correction and a teacher who has mastery of the communication system the student has elected to use. New technological advances continue to improve methodology for maximizing hearing capability (see Figure 16-7). And

Figure 16-6   Communication Strategies for Teachers Working with Students Who Are Deaf or Hearing Impaired[4]

- If a student is using an interpreter, the students in the class must be taught to communicate directly with the student who is deaf or hearing impaired, not the interpreter.
- If the student is working with a sign interpreter, the interpreter should be positioned, at the request of the student, directly in front of the student, near the teacher on the platform or in front of the gymnasium, or following the teacher about the room.
- If the student is working with an oral interpreter, the interpreter should be posited close to the student for presenting information via mouth movement, facial expression, gestures, and appropriate rephrasing.
- If the student is using an assistive learning device, the teacher can wear a lapel microphone attached to an amplifier in his or her pocket.
- Group discussions that include students who are deaf or hearing impaired must be carefully controlled.
  - Only one student can speak at a time.
  - A student who relies on speech reading should be given the time to refocus on the new speaker.
- The teacher should use the following strategies to enhance oral communication:
  - The teacher should enunciate clearly and speak at a moderate pace.
  - The teacher should face the class.
  - During question-and-answer periods, the teacher should repeat the questions carefully.
  - If the teacher needs to write on the board, he or she should write, then stop, and give the students time to process what has been written before going on. The use of overhead projectors allows the teacher to continue to face the class.
  - The teacher should not wear facial hair and should not use chewing gum.
  - Visual materials and handouts are particularly helpful.
- The teacher should use the following strategies to enhance the student's written communication:
  - Meet with the student regularly to review and correct written work.
  - Help the student learn to use spelling/grammar checks available as part of most computer software and to understand the changes the software makes.
- The teacher may encourage best performance on a test by allowing the student to take a written exam and then giving the student the opportunity to explain answers orally.

Figure 16-7 Auxiliary Learning Aids (Media, Materials, and Technology) for Individuals with Hearing Impairments[3,23]

Qualified interpreters
Note takers
Transcription services
Printed materials
Microcomputers and computer systems
Videotapes and interactive video disks
Instructional CDs and software
Telephone handset amplifiers
Assistive listening devices and systems
Telephones compatible with hearing aids
Closed caption decoders
Open and closed captioning systems
Telecommunication devices for the deaf (TDD)
Videotext displays
Soundfield amplification systems

Figure 16-8 Cyberspace: Learning Laboratory for Students Who Are Deaf or Hearing Impaired

- The Internet provides the opportunity for learners who are deaf or hearing impaired to learn at their own rate, independently.
- The Internet allows the students to capitalize on the visual learning mode.
- The Internet gives students who are deaf or hearing impaired the opportunity to interact with other individuals who are deaf or hearing impaired all over the world.
- DEAF-L, a listserve that provides an electronic forum for the discussion of questions, topics, and concerns of interest to the deaf community, is a well-established computer-mediated communication vs. "other human"–mediated communication.
- Cyberspace makes it possible for critical mentorships to be established.
- E-mail allows students to communicate without the need for an interpreter or a mediator of any kind (such as TTD).
- Cyberspace provides an opportunity for a learner who is deaf or hearing impaired to learn and interact on a "level playing field."

computer-mediated instruction has opened up a whole new world of communication and information exchange for individuals who are deaf or hearing impaired (see Figure 16-8).

Technological Hearing Assistance

Hearing aids amplify sound and are effective for conductive and sensorineural hearing losses that are greater than 30 decibels. They can also be helpful for individuals whose sensorineural hearing losses are in the high-frequency range. There are two primary types of hearing aids—air conduction and bone conduction. Air conduction hearing aids are worn on the body, behind the ear, on the temple bars of eyeglasses, or in the ear and are hooked to the receiver located in the ear canal by an open tube or airtight seal. For profound hearing losses, the most powerful hearing aid is the body type, which is worn in a shirt pocket or in front of the body in a harness and is connected to a receiver located in the ear canal. For moderate to severe hearing losses, an ear-level aid is fitted behind the pinna, or outer ear. Eyeglass aids which are built into the temple bar of a person's eyeglasses and in-the-ear aids are appropriate for mild and moderate

hearing losses.[8] Bone conduction aids are used when a person can't wear an ear mold. The generator is placed in contact with the mastoid bone (behind the ear) and held in place with a spring. The sound is conducted through the bone to the cochlea.[8] The Contralateral Routing of Signals (CROS) aid is used by an individual with a severe unilateral hearing loss. A hearing aid microphone is placed in the nonfunctioning ear, and sound is routed to the "hearing ear."[8] Cochlear implants are available for surgical implantation in persons who are profoundly deaf who can't be helped with hearing aids. These implants may enable the individual who is profoundly deaf to distinguish when a word begins and ends, the rhythm of the speech, and intonations.[8] While some cochlear implants have enabled spectacular successes in the person fitted with the implant, the failure rate is relatively high (47 percent)[56] (see Figure 16-9).

Figure 16-9   Cochlear Implants for the Individual with a Profound Hearing Loss[30]

Individuals who are profoundly deaf who cannot be helped by a hearing aid to read lips or hear environmental sounds may be helped by a cochlear implant.

- A "cochlear implant or implantation" is a surgical procedure that implants a device into an individual's inner ear. It takes the place of part or all of the function of the damaged inner ear structures.
- The goal of the implant process is to improve recognition of speech and acoustical information by converting sounds into electrical impulses that are projected over nerve endings of the eighth cranial nerve (auditory nerve) to the central nervous system.
- Each implant is "mapped" at the time of fitting; an audiologist individually calibrates the device.
- Static electricity will "demap" the implant and needs to be avoided. Children who have cochlear implants should avoid running on carpeting, sliding down slides, and performing any other activity likely to foster the development of static electricity.

Though hearing aids, particularly with new and advanced technology, are particularly helpful to the person who is deaf or hearing impaired, a "hearing aid effect" has been noted in research; individuals tend to associate negative connotations with the wearer of the hearing aid. Caucasian females asked to judge preteenage Caucasian males rated the wearer of the hearing aid with negatives in appearance, personality, assertiveness, and achievement. However, African American females, asked to judge preteenage African American males, found males without hearing aids to be more attractive than those wearing hearing aids but made no negative assumptions regarding personality, assertiveness, and intelligence based solely on wearing a hearing aid.[21]

Communication Systems

The two prevalent philosophies in the education of persons who are deaf or hard of hearing are the oral method and the total communication method. With the oral method, children are provided amplification of their residual hearing and are taught through speech reading (lipreading). They express themselves through speech. The use of signs and fingerspelling is prohibited. The total communication method combines the oral method with the use of signs and fingerspelling. Children are provided amplification of sound and are taught through speech reading, fingerspelling, and signs. They express themselves through speech, fingerspelling, and signs.

The term *total communication* refers to both a method of instruction and a philosophy of education. As a philosophy, it refers to the right of every person who is deaf or hard of hearing to select whatever form of communication is preferred. That is, depending on the circumstances, the person should have the right to choose to communicate through speech, signs, gesture, or writing. If taught through a total communication system, a person has the option to communicate in a way that best suits his or her need.[59] Classroom instruction of individuals who are deaf is predominantly through the total communication method. A variety of forms of manual communication systems may be incorporated into the total communication method.

The manual communication systems range from simple homemade gestures to fingerspelling. Signing systems between these two extremes include Pidgin Sign Language, American Sign Language, Manually Coded English, and fingerspelling. A description of each follows:

- Homemade gestures. A primitive gestural system is developed to communicate between individuals or among small groups.
- Pidgin Sign Language. It is mixture of English and American Sign Language. Key words and phrases are signed in correct order; prepositions and articles are usually omitted.[59]
- American Sign Language. ASL is a visual-gestural language that is governed by rules. The visual-gestural language involves executing systematic manual and nonmanual body

movements simultaneously. Manual movements involve shapes, positions, and movements of the hands; nonmanual gestures involve the shoulders, cheeks, lips, tongue, eyes, and eyebrows. The rules that govern this language relate to how the language works (e.g., functions of the language, meaning, structure, and organization of sentences and the sound, or phonetic, system).[20,50]

- Manually Coded English. Signs are produced in English order, and fingerspelling is used for words and concepts that do not have a sign equivalent. Forms of Manually Coded English include Seeing Essential English, Signing Exact English, and Signed English. All are variations of American Sign Language that attempt to model the vocabulary and syntax of the English language.[53]
- Fingerspelling. Each word is spelled letter-by-letter using a manual alphabet that consists of twenty-six letters. The hand is held in front of the chest, and letters are formed by using different single-hand configurations. Fingerspelling is also known as the Rochester method because it originated at the Rochester School for the Deaf in the late nineteenth century.[53]

Although many educators of students who are deaf or hard of hearing argue that it is in their best interest to be educated using some form of Manually Coded English,[53] the most widely used signing system used by adults who are deaf in this country is American Sign Language.

Effective and efficient communication with students who are deaf is a great challenge to teachers. Physical education teachers can and should improve their instructional ability by learning to communicate in a variety of ways to accommodate a wide range of pupils. Communication through hand signals will assist in communication with students who are deaf and those who are hard of hearing. Some of the basic survival signs needed by physical education teachers to communicate with hearing-impaired persons are presented in Figures 16-10 and 16-11. Most signs are for concepts and ideas rather than for words. Pointing, motioning, demonstrating, and signaling are perfectly acceptable.[24]

Parent Involvement

Parents are the critical forces in the lives of their children. They must be viewed by the physical educator and other educators as key to their child's success. Certainly, federal educational mandates have made it clear that parents must be included in all decisions regarding their child's education. In a broader sense, educators must embrace, in a real way, parents as partners in the education process.

Parents are particularly dependent on medical and educational personnel for early identification of their child's deafness or hearing impairment. Meadow-Orlans et al., 1997, reporting on data garnered in a national survey, found that the average age at which parents suspected a hearing loss was seventeen months. The average age at which the diagnosis was confirmed or denied was twenty-two months, with a lag time of five months. The average delay before their child received free, appropriate educational services was reported by the parents in the survey:

- A delay of 7.9 months to receive a hearing aid
- A delay of 9.6 months prior to receiving speech services
- A delay of 10.2 months prior to receiving auditory services
- A delay of 11.2 months prior to receiving instruction in sign language[45]

The delays were more significant for children identified as deaf as opposed to hard of hearing. One dismaying fact was that white children were exposed to sign language sooner (8.5 months after diagnosis) than either Hispanic children (15.4 months after diagnosis) or African American children (19.1 months after diagnosis). Though, in general, early identification and early intervention with children who are deaf or hearing impaired appears to be working, it is critical that the needs of children are met in a timely manner. A delay of one year in the life of a young child, during the most important time for the development of central nervous system function, is a year that is lost forever.

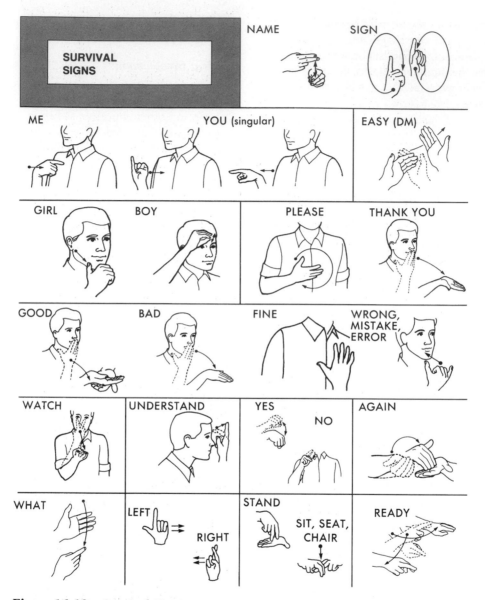

Figure 16-10   Survival Signs
Reprinted with permission from the *Journal of Physical Education, Recreation, and Dance.*

Parents who participated in the Meadow-Orlans et al. survey[45] reported that they were particularly appreciative of deaf education teachers. They found the information they provided very helpful, as was training in sign language. One-half of the fathers and three-quarters of the mothers participated in sign language classes offered by the early childhood intervention program. Although individual counseling was offered as a service to the parents of children identified as deaf/hearing

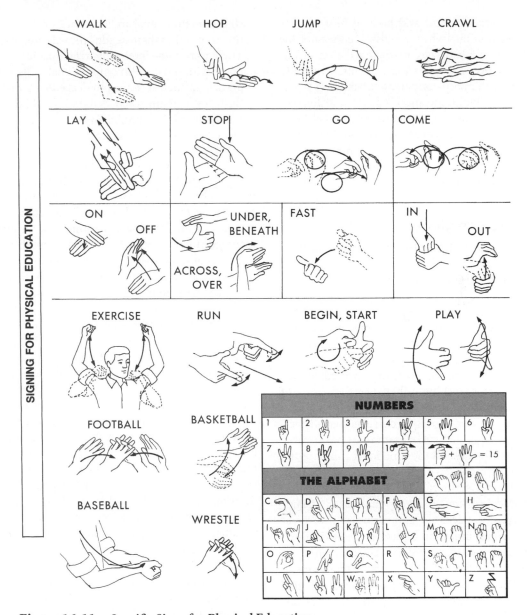

Figure 16-11 Specific Signs for Physical Education
Reprinted with permission from the *Journal of Physical Education, Recreation, and Dance.*

impaired, only 25 percent of the fathers used the counseling; however, 70 percent of the mothers took advantage of the offered service.

There have been significant changes in the demographics of the general populations; these are reflected in the demographics of children enrolled in special education as well. There has been a significant, disproportionate, increase in the numbers of non-native children in deafness-specific programs.[58] Easterbrooks, 1999, wrote, "About 40 percent of students who are deaf and hard of hearing may come from homes where English is either not the primary home language or where a dialect of English may prevail."[23] Increasing attention needs to be paid to the needs of parents of children struggling with communication issues as trilingual-tricultural parents of children who are deaf or hearing impaired. The parents speak and write their native language and struggle to communicate in English and in American Sign Language or another form of communication.

Teaching Strategies

In the past several decades, the emphasis in most special education programs has been on the process of teaching, actual teaching strategies and techniques, rather than the content of what is taught. This appears to be particularly true within deaf education[10] and most certainly, the adapted physical educator and the general physical educator who seek to communicate with students who are deaf or hearing impaired, have focused, too, on the process of teaching rather than the nature of the curriculum.[42] There must be a greater emphasis on the physical education curriculum, and decisions regarding that curriculum must be outcome based and focused on the functional ability of the student. An emphasis on hands-on demonstration, technological support, peer-to-peer instruction, self-paced learning, high expectations, independent learning packages, and exposure to a great deal of communication and interaction heighten the effectiveness of the learning environment.[11]

Karchmer and Allen,[33] reporting the results of the Gallaudet University comprehensive 1997-1998 Annual Survey of Deaf and Hard and Hearing Children and Youth, found

- Classroom limitations were much greater for the children who were deaf or hard of hearing than that predicted solely based on the traditional categorical approach.
- It appears that educational and related services for children who are deaf or hard of hearing need to be based on the children's functional ability or lack of function rather than an educational category.
- There were some interesting relationships noted within the realm of functional skills. Of particular interest to the physical educator is the fact that many teachers found the child's arm and limb functioning to be critically related to effective communication.

The ability to communicate effectively is important in instructional settings and while participating in play, games, leisure, and recreation and sporting events. When there is effective communication and the learning environment is properly managed, there may be little need to modify the demands of the physical activity.[15] However, when communication impairments are present, the student may perform motor and social skills less well, solely because of the communication problem. The physical educator who works with deaf or hard-of-hearing students must do everything possible to ensure effective communication.

Students who wear hearing aids are easily identifiable and should be given special consideration. One adjustment that can be made easily is to place the child close to the instructor, so that greater amplification of speech is received. A second adjustment that may help is for the instructor to keep the face in view of the child who is hard of hearing. Visual aids can also be used to communicate. Visual demonstrations, chalkboard work, films, and slides are important instructional aids for the deaf. To get the attention of the hearing-impaired child, waving the hands or turning off and on lights has proven effective in some instances.

Persons who are deaf, because of an inability to comprehend information through auditory means, must rely mainly on visual and kinesthetic information during physical education instruction. Therefore, when residual hearing is insufficient for communication, these sensory media should be used. According to Ling,[38] no single method can meet the individual needs of all children with hearing disorders, and whenever possible a total communication system should be used. Verbal instructions that describe movements are ineffective for deaf individuals who cannot read lips. It is critical that precise visual models be presented to deaf individuals. To promote kinesthetic feedback, it is also helpful to move a child through the desired movement pattern. Moving the child in this fashion helps the student feel the temporal-spatial relationship of movements associated with a skill. Using both visual and kinesthetic instruction provides opportunities for two avenues of sensory information. A quick visual model followed by physical prompting of the behavior may facilitate learning.

Some older children who are deaf can read lips and thus receive directions through verbal means. If the child has residual hearing or is skilled at lipreading, the physical educator should make the environment conducive to reception of the spoken word. Instruction must be given close enough to the child so that precise movement of the lips and tongue can be deciphered. The instructor should be in front and in clear view of the deaf student. When movement in a game requires the child to perform an activity at a distance at which lips cannot be read, it is then necessary to use a combination of signing to communicate. Eichstaedt and Seiler[24] have suggested forty-five signs specific to physical education to communicate with the deaf. Use of these signs will assist the physical education teacher in communicating with the student who is deaf. Another source of communication with these students may come from trained hearing paraprofessionals (teacher aides) or peers who can facilitate instruction by gaining the attention of the child who is hearing impaired and then relaying instructions through visual models, signs, or tactual inputs that guide the hearing-impaired child into class activities (see Figure 16-12).

The Physical Education Program

Considerable differences about the ways individuals respond to stimuli exist among persons who are deaf or hard of hearing. These differences must be taken into consideration when programming; of course, programming for each child who is deaf or hearing impaired is dependent on the child's IEP.

One of the major problems associated with physical education programs for learners who are deaf or hearing impaired are the poor acoustical conditions that exist in many classrooms.[44,51] The poor acoustical and reverberation effects in the typical classroom is nothing like those that exist in the gymnasium. Most gymnasiums are essentially large, empty rooms with a great deal of space, wood floors, high ceilings, and few materials or surfaces to absorb sound. As a result, any child may be bombarded by the noise and find it difficult to listen to and hear directions. The child who is deaf or hearing impaired may find it impossible to function in this type of environment. Adding sound-absorbing materials such as carpet, acoustic ceiling tiles, curtains, and corkboard may help reduce the reverberations.[11]

More effective acoustics are critical to the physical educator trying to teach *all* children, and particularly children with hearing impairments. Teachers need to talk approximately 15 decibels louder than the background noise in the classroom in order to be heard;[2] in the gymnasium, maintaining this level of volume is almost impossible throughout the teaching day.

Children who are deaf who have impaired semicircular canals, which affect balance, should not climb to high places. Also, some children with hearing loss should not participate in activity where there is excessive dampness, dust, or change in temperature because of increased likelihood of acquiring a middle or inner ear infection.

Instruction should be directed toward play, motor, and social skills that will enable the student to participate in leisure, recreation, and sport activity in the community.[54] To encourage maximum participation, the skills and attitudes of the instructor are important.

The objectives of a physical education program for children who are hard of hearing are the same as those for children who are not hearing impaired. At the preschool and early elementary school levels, the focus should be on developing basic locomotor and nonlocomotor skills through play, games, rhythm, and parachute activities. Percussion instruments such as cymbals, triangles,

Figure 16-12 Techniques for the Physical Educator to Enhance Communication

Techniques for the physical educator to enhance communication with these students follows:

1. Position yourself where the child who is deaf can see your lips and maintain eye contact; do not turn your back on the child and talk (e.g., writing on the blackboard).
2. When out of doors, position yourself so that you, rather than the child who is deaf, face the sun.
3. Use only essential words or actions to transmit messages.
4. Use visual attention-getters.
5. Make sure that the teaching environment has adequate lighting.
6. Allow the child to move freely in the gymnasium in order to be within hearing and sight range.
7. Encourage the use of residual hearing.
8. Use the communication method (oral, total communication) that the child uses.
9. Present games with straightforward rules and strategies.
10. Familiarize the student with the rules and strategies of a game before introducing the activity.
11. Learn some basic signs and use them during instruction (e.g., good, bad, okay, better, worse, line up, start, go, finish, stop, help, thank you, please, stand, sit, walk, run).
12. Use visual materials to communicate body movements (e.g., lay out footprints to indicate the foot placements required in a skill).
13. Refrain from having long lines and circle formations when presenting information to the class.
14. Keep objects out of your mouth when speaking.[46]
15. Use body language, facial expression, and gestures to get an idea across.[46]
16. Avoid verbal cues during the game or activity. It is important that the student who is deaf fully understands his or her role prior to the beginning of the game or activity and that the role does not change.[46]
17. Inside facilities should be equipped with special lighting systems easily turned on and off by the instructor to get the students' attention.[46]
18. Flags or bright objects can be useful in getting the attention of students out-of-doors. However, it must be made clear to the student that it is his or her responsibility to be aware of the teacher's presence throughout the lesson. Under no circumstances should the student be allowed to manipulate the teacher by ignoring attempts to gain attention.
19. Captioned videotapes and other visual aids can be helpful in explaining strategies.
20. Demonstrate or have another student demonstrate often. It may help the student form a mental picture of how to perform a particular skill correctly.
21. Keep instructions simple and direct.
22. Emphasize action rather than verbal instruction.
23. Stand still while giving directions.
24. Correct motor errors immediately.[46]
25. Select activities that allow all the children to be actively involved throughout; avoid activities that require children to spend a great deal of time sitting and waiting to participate.
26. Make use of the "buddy system" to help the student understand instructions and to help the student know when a phase of the activity is completed.
27. Assign a home base to every student in the class. The home base of the student who is deaf/hearing impaired should be close to the space from which the teacher usually communicates.
28. Delimit the area in which members of the class may move.
29. Children who are deaf or hearing impaired require a great deal of structure in order to feel comfortable.
30. The teacher should use the same sequence of activities for each class—for example, warm-up, dance, calisthenics, jogging/running, etc.
31. A visual schedule will be helpful for the student who is deaf; it will help the student predict what is coming and to prepare for it.

drums, and tambourines are valuable for rhythm activities, because they are capable of producing vibrations to which the child can respond.

An important area of concern is balance. If vestibular functioning appears to be delayed and damage to the eighth cranial nerve can be ruled out, activities in gross motor activities for young children with special needs would be appropriate. Should eighth cranial nerve damage be suspected, balance should be taught directly. Balance activities that may be included in a program are (1) standing on one foot so that the other foot can be used for kicking and trapping, (2) walking a balance beam to develop leg, hip, and trunk strength, and (3) performing drills that build balance skills for chasing, stopping, starting, and dodging. The physical education program at the elementary level should focus primarily on prerequisites for competent motor performance such as vestibular, kinesthetic, and visual stimulation.

At the middle and secondary school levels, these students can participate in the same activities as their hearing peers. Care should be taken to assure they develop skills that will enable them to participate in physical fitness and leisure-time activities available in their community. Activities that enhance kinesthetic development and that are popular with middle and secondary school students who are deaf or hearing impaired include handball and racquetball, wrestling, tae-kwon-do, cross-country running or skiing, swimming, weight lifting, golf, aquatics, and bowling (see Figure 16-13).

Integrating the Student Who Is Deaf or Hearing Impaired

It should no longer be assumed that all persons who are deaf or hearing impaired should or want to fit into and function in the hearing world. In some large cities, there are whole communities of individuals who are deaf, similar to communities of immigrants who choose to live together to share their unique culture, lifestyle, language, foods, and religion.

Requiring individuals who are deaf or hard of hearing to meet the demands of the hearing popu-

Figure 16-13 Aquatics for Individuals Who Are Deaf or Hearing Impaired

- Hearing aids will need to be removed before individuals who are deaf or hearing impaired enter the pool area. In fact, they should probably be removed in the locker room and stored carefully in a locked locker.
- The individual who is deaf or hearing impaired should wear ear plugs and waterproof headbands to prevent water from entering the ear canal.
- A visual emergency signal must be in place.
  - Flicking on and off the lights, above and below water level
  - Warning flags waved by lifeguard or teacher
- In an open-water swimming area, the designated safe swimming area must be carefully delineated and marked by colorful buoys. The individual who is deaf or hearing impaired must always swim with a buddy; in fact, it is the best practice in aquatics for all individuals always to swim with a buddy.
- In a pool, the deep-water areas must be carefully identified and separated from the shallow end.
- Demonstrations, particularly by classmates, are effective in presenting information.
- The individual who is deaf or hearing impaired should not dive to enter the pool area and certainly should not snorkel or scuba dive without his or her physician's specific permission because of the risk associated by increased hydrostatic pressure.
- The individual who is deaf or hearing impaired may experience difficulty with the maintenance of equilibrium. The individual must be given the opportunity to explore the aquatic environment and a variety of positions within that environment and to practice vital safety skills such as recovering to a stand from a float or glide.

lation's culture may not always be in their best interest. For example, Grimes and Prickett[29] argued that insisting that children who are deaf use only what hearing people consider "proper" English (or Spanish, Vietnamese, or Czech) may lead to feelings of inferiority and inadequacy. For this and other reasons, the issue of the placement of children who are deaf in an inclusive environment is a highly emotional and controversial issue with the deaf community. Physical educators can make a major contribution to the education of a child who is deaf by being sensitive to his or her individual needs and providing an appropriate and acceptable physical education program (see Figure 16-14). It is important to note that simply "sharing" the same physical space does not mean that students with and without hearing impairments will automatically develop empathy and mutual understanding.[47] The physical educator must help create an environment in which there is the opportunity for quality interaction and quality time; the students must participate in specific educational experiences designed to foster empathy and understanding.

The most inviting school for students who are deaf or hearing impaired is that in which the administration, faculty, staff, and students are prepared to welcome the students within the community. Stonewall Jackson Elementary School, a Regional Day School for the Deaf, in Dallas, Texas, received a United States Blue Ribbon School Award in 1999 for its unique and exceptional efforts in educating all children within the school. Beginning in kindergarten, all students who attend Stonewall Jackson receive instruction in American Sign Language so they can communicate with their peers who are deaf or hearing impaired. The principal and all members of the faculty, and most staff members, are able to communicate in sign as well.

Parents of some students prefer to enroll them in residential or day schools that provide segregated programs. These schools are preferred by many parents because they have a higher percentage of teachers who are deaf educators, and the students have the opportunity to participate in an extensive array of academic and vocational courses as well as a wide range of athletic and social programs.[62]

Gallaudet University provides evidence of the success of segregated school programs. This well-known university for individuals who are deaf routinely competes successfully against hearing competitors in baseball and soccer.[41] The Wisconsin School for the Deaf in Janesville, Wisconsin, for example, is nationally known for not only academic excellence but athletic excellence as well. Athletes from the Wisconsin School for the Deaf make regular appearances in the Wisconsin Interscholastic Athletic Association postseason tournament play in football, wrestling, and track and field.

For students who are deaf or hard of hearing who choose to interact with a hearing population in leisure, recreation, sport, and physical education activities, communication, whether verbal or nonverbal, promotes unity and stability. It is in these settings that children with hearing loss interact naturally with hearing children. This is an important step in fostering social interaction skills.

Physical educators are challenged to assist all students to develop effective social skills through participation in integrated settings. There are certain physical education activities that enable the integration process to be accomplished with minimum support systems. Activities that require less social interaction and communication skills are

---

Figure 16-14   Teaching Strategies for Including the Student Who Is Deaf or Hearing Impaired[4,32]

- Group discussions must be carefully controlled for students who rely on speech reading (lipreading).
  - The speech reader must be given enough time to refocus on the next speaker.
  - Only one student may speak at a time.
- The teacher of a student who relies on speech reading should not wear facial hair, particularly mustaches and beards which obstruct sight of the lips and mouth.
- The classroom or gymnasium must be well lighted; the speakers must avoid being in shadows.
- Group discussions must be carefully controlled for students who rely on an interpreter.
  - The interpreter must be seated within easy view of the student yet in a position that does not interfere with contact with other students.
  - Participants in the group discussion (and any discussion) must be taught to talk directly to the student and not the interpreter.
- The teacher may wear a lapel microphone, attached to an amplifier, for the student who is wearing an assistive listening device.

movement exploration programs in the elementary school and individual sports such as bowling, archery, and weight lifting at the advanced levels. More complex team sports such as basketball, which requires frequent response to whistles and verbal communication involved in strategic situations among teammates, are more difficult to integrate, but a highly motivated athlete may be very successful.

Organized football is perhaps the most difficult because of the need for ongoing information exchange between coaches and players while the game is in progress. The task is not, however, impossible. Kenny Walker, a football player who is deaf, was outstanding at the University of Nebraska and later played in the National Football League with the Denver Broncos. Through his interpreters, he was integrated into the game at the highest levels of competition. He is an excellent example of how a person who is deaf can be successfully integrated into a complex sport with the use of supplemental aids and services.

The introduction of a child who is deaf or hearing impaired into a general physical education class without prearranged support systems may be devastating. Assistance with what is expected and required to be successful in the regular setting must be provided. A peer support system is an excellent way to ease a student into the inclusive setting. As is the case with all support systems, only the amount of assistance necessary for the individual to experience success should be provided. The teacher has the major responsibility for assisting students who are deaf or hard of hearing adjust to the learning environment. See Figure 16-15 for some techniques that are beneficial to these students.

Community-Based Activities

The individual transition plan is a critical part of the process of preparing a student who is deaf or hearing impaired for transition from a school-based program into the community. Leisure, recreation, fitness, and sports available in the community are important outlets for persons with a hearing impairment. Community recreational

Figure 16-15   Creating a Learning Environment to Promote Acceptance to a Student Who Is Deaf or Hearing Impaired

1. Provide immediate acceptance of the child who is deaf or hearing impaired because this relationship can be observed by other students.[2]
2. Plan activities that constantly challenge the students but allow success.
3. Adjust the movement expectations for students with equilibrium impairments.
4. Provide the student who is hearing impaired with opportunities to participate in out-of-school activities, particularly on weekends and in the summer.
5. Facilitate peer interaction by planning activities that encourage turn taking and allow the students to work together in pairs and in small groups.
6. Plan activities that require group cooperation to achieve a goal.
7. Praise all students when it is deserved.
8. The program should meet the needs and interests of the participants and should reflect the needs interests of the community in which they will participate in leisure, recreation, and sport activities.

facilities and opportunities should be reviewed with high school students, their parents, and other members of the IEP/multidisciplinary team, so that they can make an informed decision about what activities are available after the school years. Those activities should be included in the transitional programs and instruction provided to the students.

One avenue for participation for children and adults who are deaf or hearing impaired is the United States of America Deaf Sports Federation (USADSF). This organization provides comprehensive opportunities for individuals who have a hearing loss of greater than 55 decibels. The USADSF describes its philosophy: the USA Deaf Sports Federation embraces universal values of self-respect, sportsmanship, and competition, which transcend all boundaries of geography, nationality, political philosophy, gender, age, race, and religion.[64] Its mission is to "provide year-round training and athletic competition in a variety of sports at the state, regional, national, and international level for developing and elite athletes."[64] The USADSF has programs in hockey, softball, soccer, table tennis, tennis, swimming, water polo, badminton, bowling, cycling, golf, team handball, wrestling, basketball, track and field, skiing, snowboarding, baseball, and flag football. In addition, it has "mini-games" for children who are deaf or hearing impaired just beginning their athletic careers.

SPEECH AND LANGUAGE-LEARNING DISORDERS

Though most children with speech and language disorders, as their only disability, do not have any gross motor delays, the physical educator teaches children with speech and language-learning disorders every day. In fact, approximately 10 percent of the population have identifiable speech and language-learning disorders. It is important that the teacher have a basic understanding of the types of disorders and their potential impact on the student. Gallegher wrote,

> Limited language facility can also negatively affect children's interpersonal functioning by constraining their social-interactional encoding and decoding options and contributing to interpersonal miscommunication and misperception.[28]

Certainly, the physical educator who teaches children with disabilities works closely with children who have speech and language disorders associated with other disabilities (e.g., cerebral palsy or Down syndrome). More than 20 percent of students receiving special education services have speech and language disorders.

For the purpose of this text, however, only a brief introduction to speech and language disorders will be included. Most students with speech and hearing disorders have typical gross motor skills, and the physical education can provide a quality educational experience with simple modifications to honor the students' individual needs.

CASE STUDY

Joshua

Joshua is a nine-year-old boy with a fluency disorder. Specifically, Joshua stutters. His motor skills are excellent. In fact, he is one of the more talented students in the physical education class.

He struggles, however, with interaction with other students. A number of boys tease him when the teacher is not watching. As a result, Joshua is rapidly becoming a loner and an angry child.

APPLICATION TASK
Describe some of the strategies the physical educator can use to create a "bully-free" learning environment. Describe some of the specific techniques he or she can use to heighten Joshua's social status.

Definition

Speech and language disorders are problems in communication and related areas such as oral-motor function. These delays and disorders range from simple sound substitutions to the inability to understand or use language or use the oral-motor mechanism for functional speech and feeding.[48] A speech and language disorder is usually only one aspect of a "complex set of correlates that may also include, for example, motor impairment, cognitive deficits, or academic difficulties."[39] Language-learning disorders are "most often associated with or are secondary to a host of other conditions, each of which has a complex epidemiology [cause]. . . . Comorbidity is clearly evident in the consistent use of the term language-learning disabilities adopted by professionals in recent years."[39]

Incidence

In the 1996-1997 academic year, 1,045,000 children between birth and twenty-one years with speech and language-learning disabilities were served in federally supported programs for individuals with disabilities. The school-age children within this population were served in the following educational settings:

- General education class: 87.6 percent
- Resource room: 7.5 percent
- Separate class: 4.5 percent
- Public school separate facility: 0.2 percent
- Private separate school facility: 0.1 percent
- Public residential facility
- Private residential facility
- Hospital/homebound: 0.1 percent[65]

Causes

One of the major causes of speech and language-learning disorders is hearing loss. Even a minor or fluctuating hearing loss (e.g., as a result of otitis media) may significantly influence speech and language skills. In addition, neurological disorders, traumatic brain injury, alcohol or other drug abuse, physical impairments such as cleft lip or palate, and vocal abuse (use of cigarettes or caffeine) or misuse may cause speech and language-learning disorders.[48]

There are many forms of communicative disorders. Under the broad umbrella of communicative disorders fall the following:

- Speech disorders
- Voice disorders
- Language disorders

Speech Disorders

The global term *speech disorders* refers to difficulties producing speech sounds or problems with voice quality that interfere with an individual's ability to communicate effectively. A speech disorder may be characterized by an interruption in the flow or rhythm of speech, called dysfluency or a fluency disorder. Stuttering is an example of this type of dysfluency. Speech disorders may also be problems with the way sounds are formed, called articulation or phonological disorders, or they may be difficulties with the pitch, volume, or quality of the voice.[48]

Fluency Disorders: Stuttering   Children and adults who stutter experience disruptions in the smooth flow of their speech more often than the average speaker of their age. Interruptions in the flow of speech commonly referred to as dysfluencies are the most obvious feature of stuttering. The interruptions may differ from person to person. Common dysfluencies include part or whole-word repetitions, phrase repetitions ("m-m-m-m-mummy"), prolonged sounds at the beginning of words ("C-a-a-a-an I have that," hesitations, and silent blocks when the person silently struggles to begin a word). "Typical" early stuttering is characterized by an appreciable range of individual variability.[1] Although virtually ALL children exhibit some disfluencies, very early stuttering is distinct from normal dysfluency. See Figure 16-16 for specific tips for the physical educator who is teaching a child who stutters.

Early in the disorder's course, there are about twice as many males as females who stutter. But, in older children and adults, there are four or five males who stutter to every female.[1]

Fluency Disorders: Cluttering   Cluttering is characterized by often rapid, slurred, or imprecise speech, which can also have some periods where the person seems to get "stuck," almost as if his or her mind is racing faster than the mouth can keep up.

Delayed Speech   If a child has delays in speech, this is an indicator of a problem. Like many developmental skills, the acquisition of speech is predictable in typical children. See Chapter 10 for information about typical speech development.

Articulation Disorders   People with speech disorders have trouble using some speech sounds, which can also be a symptom of a delay. They may say "see" when they mean "ski," or they may have trouble using other sounds such as "l" or "r." Listeners may have trouble understanding what someone with a speech disorder is trying to say (see Figure 16-17).

Motor-Speech Disorders: Developmental or Acquired Apraxia   Apraxia occurs when the part of the brain that controls the ability to voluntarily sequence muscle movements, particularly those

Figure 16-16 Tips for the Physical Educator Teaching a Child Who Stutters[63]

- Listen to and answer the child in a patient, calm, and unemotional way.
- Talk privately with the child who stutters. Explain to the child that when we learn to talk—just like learning new things in physical education—we make mistakes. We bobble sounds, just as we bobble a ball, or repeat or get tangled up on words, just as our feet get tangled in a jump rope.
- Assure the child that stuttering does not bother you. You want him or her to talk so you can learn the way he or she feels, what he or she thinks about, what he or she has learned and wants to learn.
- Initially, until he or she adjusts to the physical education class, ask the child questions that can be answered with one or two words.
- If every child is going to be asked a question, call fairly early on the child who stutters. The stuttering will be worse if the child has to wait and worry.
- Listen to what the child is saying. Respond to that, rather than the stuttering.
- Give appropriate responses to what the child is saying, such as head nods and smiles. Don't interrupt the child with "uh-huh" or "yes." The verbalization will cause the child to hesitate.
- Maintain natural eye contact when the child is talking.
- Don't rush the child by interrupting or finishing words for him or her.
- With the child and his or her parents' permission, spend a brief period of time early in the semester sharing specific information about stuttering or do "empathy" experiences to help the child's classmates understand the problem.

Figure 16-17 Signs and Symptoms of Articulation Disorders[35]

- The child has difficulty with frontal and lateral lisps.
- The child has difficulty articulating the <r> sound.
- The child substitutes the <j> (the "y" sound) for the <l> sound.
- The child has difficulty with the pronunciation of blends <r, l, and s> (i.e., *brake, clown, slow*).
- The child demonstrates speech sound errors which occur in a variety of syllables and words.

Note: These articulation errors are typical of preschoolers and are usually not cause for concern.
If the errors persist past age five, an evaluation is necessary.

speech deficit.[35] They are often poor readers who have difficulty with content area material (science, math, history) because of vocabulary[7] (see Figure 16-18).

Motor-Speech Disorders: Dysarthria Dysarthria occurs when there has been an injury to the nerves that control the muscles used to breathe and talk. The muscles may be weak and/or uncoordinated. The person's speech will be unclear as a result. Dysarthria can occur after a stroke or traumatic brain injury, as one symptom of cerebral palsy, or as a symptom of a neurological disease such as Parkinson's disease.

Speech Difficulties Due to Cleft Lip or Palate Children and adults with cleft lip and/or palate may experience speech difficulties due to structural problems in or around the mouth caused by their cleft lip or palate. The oral structures needed to speak include the lips, the teeth, the tongue, and the palate. Some speech sounds are more affected by a cleft lip or palate than others. The severity of the original clefting, and how effective the repairs were, will determine how clearly a child or an adult will be able to say these sounds. Children with cleft lip typically have the lip surgically repaired at two to three months of age, while children with cleft

involved in the production of speech (oral-motor), does not work as it should. Pronouncing even a single short word requires this ability because spoken words are sequences of speech sounds voluntarily produced by sequential muscle movement. Long words and sentences are even harder.

The student with apraxia may have difficulty with unintelligible speech, a significant motor-

Figure 16-18   Early Signs and Symptoms of Developmental Apraxia[35]

- The infant fails to coo or babble.
- Typical first words, such as *Mama*, may not appear at all; instead, the infant/toddler may point and "grunt."
- First words are delayed with many phonemes deleted or replaced with other (easier) phonemes.
- The child may not use many consonants. The child may only be able to use / b, m, p, t, d, h /.
- The child may simplify words by deleting consonants or vowels and/or replacing difficult phonemes with easier ones.
- The child may favor a particular syllable and emphasize it in all words.
- A word—a real word or a nonsensical utterance—may be used to convey other words.
- The child may articulate one word well, but his or her speech becomes unintelligible if the child attempts a sentence.
- The child may have verbal perseveration; the child gets stuck on a word or phrase and repeats it continuously.
- The child may have other fine motor deficits as well.

palate typically have the palate repaired about twelve months of age.[68]

Phonological Delays or Disorders   NICHCY described children with phonological delays or disorders as having trouble learning the sound system of their native language. The speech of these children can be very difficult to understand. While all toddlers and young preschoolers simplify their speech to make the words easier to say, children with a phonological delay use these simplified word forms much longer.[48]

Voice Disorders

People with voice disorders may have difficulty with the way their voices sound.

Vocal Hyperfunction   The voice of an individual with vocal hyperfunction may sound hoarse or breathy. Voice disorders may be caused by a history

of exposure to chemicals, smoke, low humidity, allergies, dust, smoking, alcohol abuse, or excessive caffeine and/or overuse.[34] It is particularly crucial that the physical education teacher be sensitive to the incredible overuse of the voice that is required in the gymnasium and on the playground.

Resonance Disorder   An individual with a resonance disorder has a voice that sounds very "nasal" or lacks "nasal quality." Resonance is the quality of voice that results from sound vibrations in the pharynx, oral cavity, and nasal cavity. Hypernasality is caused by velopharyngeal inadequacy; hyponasality is caused by a blockage in the nasopharynx or nasal cavity.[36]

Language Disorders

NICHCY defines a language disorder as "an impairment in the ability to understand and/or use words in context, both verbally and nonverbally."[48] Individuals with language disorders may have difficulty using inappropriate words and confuse their meanings, may struggle to express their ideas, may use inappropriate grammatical patterns, may have a small vocabulary, or may have difficulty following directions. One or a combination of these characteristics may occur in children who are affected by language-learning disabilities or a developmental language delay.[48]

Language Delay   A language delay is characterized by a delay "across the board" in the ability to understand language. See Chapter 10 for specific information about the approximate age at which a typical child acquires and demonstrates language skills.

Language Dysfunction: Receptive Language Dysfunction   A receptive language dysfunction is a central auditory processing deficit. A receptive language dysfunction is a difficulty in the decoding and storing of auditory information, typically incoming verbal messages (see Figure 16-19).

Language Dysfunction: Expressive Language Dysfunction   An expressive language disorder is one in which the individual has difficulty with verbal

Figure 16-19   Signs and Symptoms of Receptive Language Disorder[35]

- The child demonstrates echolalia. He or she repeats back words or phrases either immediately or at a later time without understanding the meaning.
- The child is unable to follow directions, though he or she may follow routine, repetitive directions.
- The child shows inappropriate, off-target responses to "wh" questions, "who," "what," "when," "where," and "why."
- The child demonstrates re-auditorization; he or she repeats back a question first and then responds to it.
- The child has difficulty responding appropriately to "yes/no" and "either/or" questions.
- The child does not attend to spoken language.
- The child uses a lot of jargon.

Figure 16-20   Signs and Symptoms of Expressive Language Disorder[35]

- The child has word retrieval difficulties. The child has difficulty naming objects or "talks in circles" around subjects with lack of appropriate vocabulary.
- The child demonstrates dysnomia, misnaming items.
- The child has difficulty acquiring syntax, the rules of grammar.
- The child has difficulty with morphology, changes in verb tense.
- The child has difficulty with semantics, word meaning.

expression. The individual struggles to put words together to formulate thoughts and to share those thoughts with others (see Figure 16-20).

Aphasia   Aphasia is an impairment of language that affects the production or comprehension of speech and the ability to read or write. It may affect a single aspect of language use, such as the ability to retrieve the names of objects, the ability to put words together into sentences, or the ability to read. It is more common, however, that many aspects of communication are impaired while some communication channels remain accessible for a limited exchange of information.

Aphasia is always due to injury to the brain—most commonly from a stroke, particularly in older individuals. But brain injuries resulting in aphasia may also arise from head trauma, from brain tumors, or from infections.[5]

Psychological and Behavioral Characteristics

Typically developing children use their speech, language, and voice skills to share information, express their feelings and emotions, initiate and terminate play, and negotiate with others. Children with impaired language skills interact differently than their typically developing peers in a classroom setting, are less preferred playmates than their typically developing peers, and experience problems with basic social interactions and tasks.[26] These children are often lonely within the school setting; their feeling of loneliness is influenced by their lack of acceptance by peers, lack of participation in friendship, nonsustainable or poor quality of friendships, and the perception they are victimized by their peers.[6] Children with a severe language impairment are less socially skilled than their typical peers and demonstrate more behavior problems. The social skills that appear to be affected include introducing oneself, joining in play and other activities, initiating and sustaining interactions, making friends, and compromising.[26] Children with severe language impairments are also more reticent,[27] are likely to prefer solitary play, and tend not to join a group for lunch, snack time, or recess.

It appears that early delays or difficulties with speech and language skill development, a critical component of communication, may limit subsequent growth in cognition, metacognition, and other language skills.[40] This may be a function of parent and teacher reactions to the delays.[4] They may be more likely to concentrate on remediating the problem than addressing academic content that is critical in their development.

Students with specific language disabilities may also have difficulties with "executive functions"—that is, "inhibiting actions, restraining and delaying responses, attending selectively, setting goals, planning, organizing, as well as maintaining and shifting set or focus of attention."[61] These executive function skills are critical for success in the school environment. For example, the student must be able to stay seated, an inhibiting action, even if the student really wants to get up, wander to the window, and watch the bird on the sill.

There appears to be a significant relationship between language problems and emotional/behavioral problems. A majority of children being treated for emotional/behavioral problems (62 to 95 percent) have been reported to have moderate to severe language problems.[18] In fact, many educators believe that children with severe language problems should be screened for emotional/behavioral problems and children with emotional/behavioral problems should be screened for language problems.

The communication needs of adolescents when interacting with peers and with teachers was examined. Skills required for communication with peers, such as skills associated with empathy, perspective taking, and use of voice/tone in interaction were more important than skills required for communicating with adults.[55]

Motor Characteristics

Children and adults with speech and language disorders do not exhibit any significant gross motor delays or disorders. The physical educator should be concerned with and concentrate, instead, on the individual's functional play and social skills.

Testing

The student with a speech and/or language disorder should be able to participate in any school, district, or state-mandated physical fitness, motor, or sport-skills assessment. Occasionally, the physical educator may be asked to help with the motor component on a broad-based developmental assessment instrument, such as the Brigance Diagnostic Inventory of Early Development.

Special Considerations

Speech and language pathologists who serve children with communication disorders are, increasingly, serving children within the general classroom environment.[9] Excellent speech and language pathologists, aware of the critical relationship between movement and language, may ask to provide services in conjunction with the physical educator or the adapted physical educator in the movement experience. The professionals serving the student will find that more language occurs in the context of play, leisure, recreation, and sport activities than in any other.

The speech and language pathologist will enhance and expand on language opportunities that occur naturally in the general education setting. Fujiki et al. wrote,

> The most effective school treatment contexts will most likely include those places where social interaction is the most intense: classrooms, playgrounds, and lunchrooms.[27]

Like children who are deaf or hearing impaired, children with speech and language disorders have difficulty in play interactions.[6,19] The physical educator has a unique opportunity to help the child with a speech and language impairment develop critical, developmental play skills. See Chapter 10 for more information about facilitating play.

Teaching Considerations

The primary focus of the physical educator is teaching the student with a speech-language disorder functional and developmentally appropriate play skills. The secondary focus is to increase the effectiveness of gross motor, physical fitness, and leisure, recreation/sport skills in the same way the teacher develops those skills in typical students (see Figure 16-21).

Figure 16-21   Physical Education Teachers' Strategies for Enhancing Interpersonal and Relationship Skills for Children Who Have Speech-Language Disorders

- Eliminate competitive activities from the physical education curriculum at the preschool, elementary school, and middle school levels.
- Emphasize cooperative activities, such as "New Games."
- Teach specific skills:
  - Initiating play
  - Taking turns
  - Negotiating rules
  - Resolving conflict
  - Coping with success and failure
- Include socially appropriate behavioral expectations within gymnasium rules. Talk about the rules. Post the rules. Enforce the rules.
- Under no circumstances allow bullying behavior. The gymnasium must be considered a "bully-free zone."

Figure 16-22   Facts About Bullying in the Schools[13]

- Over 160,000 children purposely miss school daily because they're afraid to go.
- One of every four children is bullied.
- Bullying occurs in *every* school and in *every* grade in this country. There are no exceptions. Anyone who thinks otherwise is being extremely unrealistic.
- Girls bully other girls and even boys as much, if not more, than boys bully boys.
- Kids get bullied on the bus, in the bathroom and the halls, at recess, in the locker room, and in physical education.
- Kids have said that the following kids get bullied: new kids, fat kids, skinny kids, boys that don't do well in sports, boys that act gay, lesbians, kids who are smart, kids who are dumb, geeks, nerds, computer-freaks, kids who wear out-of-style clothes, kids who smell, teachers' pets, kids with dirty hair, "retarded" kids, kids who talk funny, kids who walk funny, kids in wheel-chairs, kids who get good grades, kids who get bad grades, girls with blonde hair, kids who have freckles, kids who have funny-looking ears or noses, and kids with diseases—in other words, most kids.

In addition, however, the role of the physical educator is to create a learning environment in the gymnasium and on the playground that is "bully-free." Unfortunately, children with speech and language disorders are often the targets of bullies; this makes their educational experience a threatening and frightening experience (see Figure 16-22).

Bullying is a series of repeated, intentionally cruel incidents, involving the same children in the same bully/victim roles. Bullying can also consist of a single interaction. The intention of bullying is to put the victim in distress in some way. Bullies seek power.[12]

Unfortunately, teasing and bullying occur frequently in the locker room, in the gymnasium, and on the playground. As such, the physical educator is a vital component of a schoolwide effort to address and eliminate bullying.

Schools that have been successful in eliminating bullying have used the following strategies:

- All students have a "safe haven" where they may escape.

- At the "safe haven," students who have received particular experience as good listeners do just that for the student in trouble.
- The faculty and specially selected students have been trained to identify a student in crisis.
- The emphasis is on the 85 percent of the students who are neither the bully nor the victim in any given situation but who are uncomfortable and confused about what they see happening around them. Bully proofing attempts to shift the balance of power to the silent majority and away from the bullies.[22]
- The physical educator can help teach specific skills to the students who are neither the bully nor the victim. Students can take action in many different ways to help reduce bullying in their school. Refusing to watch bullying, reporting bullying incidents, and/or using

distraction with either the bully or the victim are all effective ways of making a difference.

- Acts of kindness and a sense of shared responsibility toward others are encouraged and rewarded.
- First and foremost, teachers must make it safe for students to report bullying. It is crucial that teachers, administrators, and other school personnel respect the anonymity of the victim and/or reporting students. Until students trust this will happen, bullying will go unreported, and bullies will continue to thrive.[22]

- The physical educator can help teach the bullies how to behave in a socially acceptable manner; sometimes, the child simply doesn't know another way to interact.
- The physical educator can help teach the victims develop friendship skills and learn to interact with assertiveness and confidence. Cooperative games are particularly effective in teaching these skills.
- The physical educator can help identify the "loner" in the class and make a special effort to befriend the child; usually bullies pick on a child without a support group.

SUMMARY

Children with communicative delays and disorders may have a difficult time being successful in the educational environment. Though they may have excellent physical and motor skills, they may struggle with the psychosocial component of the physical education experience.

When working with students who are deaf or hard of hearing, physical educators are concerned primarily with the extent to which the hearing loss affects ability to participate in play, leisure, recreation, and sport activity. The classification of hearing loss is often based on the location of the problem within the hearing mechanism. Conductive losses interfere with the transfer of sound. Sensorineural problems result from damage to the inner ear and/or the eighth cranial nerve. Central hearing impairments occur at the brain stem or the auditory cortex. Hearing aids and cochlear implants are used to amplify sound and enhance the communication capability of individuals who are deaf or hard of hearing. Types of communication systems used to communicate with deaf or hard of hearing individuals are the oral method and the total communication method. Considerations for effective communication by teachers of the individuals who are deaf or hearing impaired during instruction are teacher-learner position, visual feedback, intensity of the commands, and special attention to the environment. Few changes are required in the physical education program. Athletic opportunities should be provided for students who are deaf or hard of hearing so that they have the opportunity to participate in activities that will provide enjoyment and help maintain a healthy lifestyle after their school years.

The physical educator, teaching children with speech and language disorders, should focus on the development of functional and developmentally appropriate play skills. In addition, the physical educator should concentrate on the creation and maintenance of a bully-free gymnasium and playground.

REVIEW QUESTIONS

1. What are the different categories of deafness?
2. What are the indicators of hearing loss that can be observed by the physical education teacher while teaching a class?
3. Discuss two different methods of communicating with persons who are deaf.
4. What are some teaching strategies that can be used with students who are deaf?
5. What are the three major types of speech and language disorders?
6. What are some of the strategies that can be used to create a bully-free learning environment in the gymnasium and on the playground?

STUDENT ACTIVITIES

1. Prepare a list of points you could share with Juana's mother to convince her of the need and value of encouraging her daughter to participate in community-based activities instead of being confined to her home as a baby-sitter.

2. Observe students who are deaf or hearing impaired participating in a physical education class. What teaching strategies were used by the teacher? What adaptations were made to accommodate the children in activity? What were the behavioral characteristics of the children?

3. Complete a community survey. What leisure, recreation, and sport opportunities are available in your community for adults who are hard of hearing or deaf?

4. Ask for permission to observe a middle school or high school physical education class. Watch for signs of bullying. Identify any students who appear to be frightened. Describe the strategies the physical educator can use to help Joshua deal with his role as a victim.

5. Request permission to subscribe to DEAF-L, the listserv of the Deaf community to learn more about the culture.

6. Practice using basic survival signs for the physical educator with a peer.

7. Access the Project INSPIRE website at http://venus.twu.edu/INSPIRE http://www.twu.edu/~f_huettig and refer to the information provided about adapted physical education for students who are deaf or hearing impaired.

REFERENCES

1. Ambrose NG, Yairi E: Normative disfluency data for early childhood stuttering. *J Speech Lang Hear Res,* 42:895–909, 1999.

2. American Speech-Language-Hearing-Association. Position statement and guidelines for acoustics in educational settings, *ASHA,* 37(suppl.14):15–19, 1995.

3. Americans with Disabilities Act of 1990, 42 U.S.C. 12101, 1990.

4. Apel K: An introduction to assessment and intervention with older students with language-learning impairments: Bridges from research to clinical practice. *Lang Speech Hear Serv Schools,* 30:228–230, 1999.

5. Aphasia. http://www.aphasia.org/ NAAfactsheet.html

6. Asher SR, Gazelle A: Loneliness, peer relations, and language disorder in childhood. *Top Lang Disord,* 19(2):16–33, 1999.

7. Bahr RH, Velleman SL, Ziegler MA: Meeting the challenge of suspected developmental apraxia of speech through inclusion. *Top Land Disord,* 19(3):19–35, 1999.

8. Beers MH, Berkow R (Eds): The Merck Manual of Diagnosis and Therapy, Whitehouse Station, NJ, 1999, Merck Research Laboratories.

9. Blosser JL, Kratcoski A: PACs: A framework for determining appropriate service delivery options. *Lang Speech Hear Serv Schools,* 28:99–107, 1996.

10. Bowe F: Approaching equality: Education of the deaf. Silver Spring, MD: TJ Publishers, 1991.

11. Brackett D: Intervention for children with hearing impairment in general education settings. *Lang Speech Hear Serv Schools,* 28:355–361, 1997.

12. Bully Beware. http://www.bullybeward.com/ story4.html

13. Bully. http://www.members.tripod.com/ ~Ghoul2x/Bully3A.html

14. Butterfield SA: Deaf children in physical education, *Palaestra* 4:28–30, 1988.

15. Butterfield SA, Ersing WF: Influence of age, sex, etiology and hearing loss on balance performance by deaf children, *Percept Mot Skills* 62:659–663, 1986.

16. Butterfield SA et al: Kinematic analysis of a dynamic balance task by children who are deaf. *Clin Kines* 52(4):72–78, 1998.

17. Cambra C: A comparative study of personality descriptors attributed to the deaf, the blind, and individuals with no sensory disability. *Am Ann Deaf,* 141(1):24–28, 1996.

18. Cohen N et al: Unsuspected language impairment in psychiatrically disturbed children: Prevalence and language and behavioral characteristics. *J Am Acad Child Adol Psychiat,* 32:595–603, 1993.

19. Craig HK, Washington JA: Access behaviors of children with specific language impairment. *J Speech Hear Res,* 36:322–337, 1993.

20. Crowe T, Horak F: Motor proficiency associated with vestibular deficits in children with hearing impairments, *Phys Ther* 68:1493–1499, 1988.

21. Davis M et al: The hearing aid effect in African American and Caucasian males as perceived by female judges of the same race. *Lang Speech Hear Serv Schools,* 30:165–172, 1999.

22. Devine School. http://www.lcbe.edu.on.ca/sites/Devine/bully.html

23. Easterbrooks S: Improving practices for students with hearing impairments. *Except Child,* 65 (4):537–554, 1999.

24. Eichstaedt CB, Seiler P: Communicating with hearing impaired individuals in a physical education setting, *J Health Phys Educ Rec Dance,* May 1978, pp 19–21.

25. Finitzo T, Albright K, O'Neal J: The newborn with hearing loss: Detection in the nursery. *Pediatrics,* 102(6):1452–1460, 1998.

26. Fujiki M, Brinton B, Todd C: Social skills of children with specific language impairment. *Lang Speech Hear Serv Schools,* 27:195–201, 1996.

27. Fujiki M et al.: Withdrawn and sociable behavior of children with language impairment. *Lang Speech Hear Serv Schools,* 30:183–195, 1999.

28. Gallegher TM: Interrelationships among children's language, behavior, and emotional problems. *Top Lang Disord,* 19(2):1–15, 1999.

29. Grimes UK, Prickett HT: Developing and enhancing a positive self-concept in deaf children, *Am Ann Deaf* 133:4, 1988.

30. Hilgenbrinck L: Disability Fact Sheet on Cochlear Implants, Project INSPIRE at http://venus.twu.edu/~f_huettig

31. Holcomb TK: Development of deaf bicultural identity. *Am Ann Deaf,* 142(2):89–93, 1997.

32. Kalivoda K, Higbee JL, Brenner DC: Teaching students with hearing impairments, *J Dev Educ,* 20(3):10–16, 1997.

33. Karchmer MA, Allen TA: The functional assessment of deaf and hard of hearing students. *Am Ann Deaf,* 144(2):68–77, 1999.

34. Kereiakes TJ: Clinical evaluation and treatment of vocal disorders. *Lang Speech Hearing Serv in Schools,* 27:240–243, 1996.

35. Kid Speech   http://www.kidspeech.com/signs.html

36. Kummer AW, Lee L: Evaluation and treatment of resonance disorders, *Lang Speech Hear Serv Schools,* 27:271–280, 1996.

37. Lindsay RL et al: Early ear problems and developmental problems at school age. *Clin Pediatrics,* 38:123–132, 1999.

38. Ling D: Early total communication intervention: an introduction in early intervention for hearing-impaired children: total communication options, San Diego, 1984, College Hill Press.

39. Lubker BB, Tomblin JB: Epidemiology: Informing clinical practice and research on language disorders of children. *Top Lang Disord,* 19(1):1–26, 1998.

40. Lyon GR: Overview of reading and literacy initiates. Paper presented to the Committee on Labor and Human Resources, Washington, DC, April, 1998.

41. Lyon MF: Symbolic play and language development in young deaf children. *Deafness and Ed,* 21(2):10–20, 1997.

42. Lytle RR, Rovins MR: Reforming deaf education: A paradigm shift from how to teach to what to teach. *Am Ann Deaf,* 142(1):7–15, 1997.

43. Martinez C, Silvestre N: Self-concept in profoundly deaf adolescent pupils. *Inter J Psychol,* 30(3):309–316, 1995.

44. Matkin ND, Wilcox AM: Considerations in the education of children with hearing loss. *Ped Clin North Am,* 46(1):143–152, 1999.

45. Meadow-Orlans KP et al.: Support services for parents and their children who are deaf or hard of hearing. *Am Ann Deaf,* 142(4):278–288, 1997.

46. Minter MG: Factors which may prevent full self-expression of deaf athletes in sports, *Palaestra* 5:36–38, 1989.

47. Most T, Weisel A, Tur-Kaspa H: Contact with students with hearing impairments and the

evaluation of speech intelligibility and personal qualities. *J Sped Ed*, 33(2):1-3–111, 1999.

48. NICHCY, http://www.kidsource.com/NICHCY/speech.htm

49. Nowell R, Marshak, L: An orientation for professionals working with deaf clients. In Nowell R, Marshak L, editors: Understanding deafness and the rehabilitation process, Boston, 1994, Allyn and Bacon.

50. O'Rourke IJ: ABC's of signing, Silver Springs, Md, 1987, National Association of the Deaf.

51. Palmer CV: Hearing and listening in a typical classroom. *Lang Speech Hear Serv Schools*, 28:213–217, 1997.

52. Parasnis I: Cultural identity and diversity in deaf education, *Am Ann Deaf*, 142(2):72–79, 1997.

53. Paul P, Quigley S: Education and deafness, New York, 1990, Longman.

54. Reagan T: Cultural considerations in the education of deaf children. In Moores DF, Meadow-Orlans KP, editors: Education and development of aspects of deafness, Washington, DC, 1990, Gallaudet University Press.

55. Reed VA, McLeod K, McAllister L: Importance of selected communication skills for talking with peers and teachers: Adolescents' opinions. *Lang Speech Hear Serv Schools*, 30:32–49, 1999.

56. Rose DE, Vernon M, Pool AF: Cochlear implants in prelingually deaf children. *Am Ann Deaf*, 141(3):258–261, 1996.

57. Ross M, Brackett D, Maxon AB (eds): Assessment and management of mainstreamed hearing-impaired children. Austin, TX: PRO-ED, 1991.

58. Schildroth AN, Hotto SA: Annual survey of hearing impaired children and youth: 1991–92 school year, *Am Ann Deaf* 138:163–171, 1993.

59. Scott P: Certified Educator of the Deaf, Texas Woman's University, Denton, Tex, Personal communication, October, 1991.

60. Siegel J, Marchetti M, Tecclin J: Age-related balance changes in hearing-impaired children, *Phys Ther* 71:183–189, 1991.

61. Singer BD, Bashir AS: What are executive functions and self-regulation and what do they have to do with language-learning disorders? *Lang Speech Hear Serv Schools*, 30:265–273, 1999.

62. Stinson M: Affective and social development, In Nowell R, Marshak L, editors: Understanding deafness and the rehabilitation process, Boston, 1994, Allyn and Bacon.

63. Stuttering. http://www.mankato.msus.edu/dept/comdis/kuster/stutter.html

64. USA Deaf Sport Foundation. http://www.usadsf.org

65. United States Department of Education, Office of Special Education and Rehabilitative Services, Annual Report to Congress on the Implementation of the Individuals with Disabilities Education Act, February, 1998.

66. US Department of Health, Education, and Welfare: Regulations for the Education for All Handicapped Children Act of 1975, *Fed Reg* 44:42476, Aug 23, 1977.

67. Wheeler L, Griffin HC: A movement-based approach to language development in children who are deaf-blind. *Am Ann Deaf*, 142(5):387–390, 1997.

68. Widesmiles. http://Widesmiles.org

69. Wolk S, Schildroth A: Deaf children and speech intelligibility: A national study, In Schildroth A, Karchner M: Deaf children in America, San Diego, CA, 1986, College Hill.

SUGGESTED READING

Lieberman, L., & Cowart, F. (1996) Games for People with Sensory Impairments: Strategies for Including Individuals of All Ages, Champaign, IL: Human Kinetics.

RECOMMENDED WEBSITES

Please note that these websites are being recommended in the summer and early fall of 1999. By the time you read this text, the websites may no longer exist or may be at a different URL.

USA Deaf Sports Federation
http://www.usadsf.org

World Recreation Association of the Deaf
http://www.wrad.org/wradint.html

Deaf Nation News
http://www.deafnation.com/news/index.html

Kid Speech
http://www.kidspeech.com/signs.html

Kid Source (NICHCY)
http://www.kidsource.com/NICHCY/speech.htm

Bullying
http://www.members.tripod.com/~Ghoul2x/
Bully3A.html
http://www.bullybeware.com/tips.html

Cleft Lip and Cleft Palate
http://Widesmiles.org

National Institute on Deafness and Other Communicative Disorders
http://www.nih.gov/nidcd

RECOMMENDED VIDEOS

Fanlight Productions
4196 Washington Street
Boston, MA 02131
Psychology, Social Work, and Disabilities
Video Collections, 1999-2000
A Sign of the Times by James Shasky and Bonnie MacBird
23 minutes, purchase price $145, order # CV-236
Voices in a Deaf Theater by Margo Meisel
24 minutes, purchase price $195, order # CV-229
See What I'm Saying by Thomas Kaufman
CINE Golden Eagle 5 Star Award
31 minutes, purchase price $195, order # CV-090
Stuttering
28 minutes, purchase price $149,
order # CV-239

Available from Sporttime at http://www.Sportime.com
Cooperative Games, $29.95
New Games, $39.95
New Games from Around the World, $25.95
Bully Beware Products
1421 King Albert Avenue
Coquitlam, British Columbia, CA V3J1Y3
Bully Beware: Take Action Against Bullying. $19.95
These videos are available for purchase through Bigstar.com. Many are also available at a local video rental store.
Children of a Lesser God
For a Deaf Son
The Heart is a Lonely Hunter
In the Land of the Deaf
Mr. Holland's Opus
The Miracle Worker

Visual Impairments

Identify and describe three types of visual impairments.

List the general characteristics of children who are congenitally blind.

List five ways to modify the play environment to make it safe for students who are blind.

List eight ways to modify activities to accommodate a sightless learner.

Describe devices specially designed to enable sport participation by individuals with limited or no sight.

Describe a process for integrating individuals with and without sight into a sporting activity.

Jennifer Armbruster competes in goal ball during the 1996 Atlanta Paralympic Games.
Courtesy United States Association of Blind Athletes, Colorado Springs, CO.

V isual impairments include both permanent and functional conditions. Children with visual disorders represent a unique challenge to the physical educator, because in addition to their visual impairments they usually demonstrate developmental lags. Many of these children have not had opportunities to physically explore the environment during their early years. As a result, intact sensori-motor systems are not stimulated adequately, and motor development suffers. Low vitality and perceptual-motor development lags can prevent the children from participating in activities not contra-indicated by the primary visual disorder.

CASE STUDY

Hosea

Hosea is a twelve-year-old Hispanic boy who lives in a small town in a southwestern state. He was diagnosed as blind as a result of retinopathy of prematurity (born prematurely and placed on high concentrations of oxygen during the first few months of life). He is an only child who has an identified learning disability and a mild seizure disorder that is controlled with medication. He received educational intervention by a vision specialist from the age of six months to two years. Currently he is in fifth grade, two years behind his peers of the same age.

Although it is reported that Hosea did not walk until age two years and he exhibits poor self-help and social skills, his motor skills are quite good. Even though he is totally blind, his balance and most loco-motor skills are excellent; however, he has not yet developed cross-lateral integration (e.g., he has a midline problem). His cardiovascular endurance, body composition, and abdominal and upper body strength are all within the average range; however, his flexibility as measured by the sit-and-reach test is below the 25th percentile for his age group.

CRITICAL THINKING TASK

As you read the chapter, think about ways to include Hosea in an inclusive physical education class and eventually in community recreation settings with sighted participants.

DEFINITION OF VISUAL IMPAIRMENTS

There are varying degrees of visual impairments. Individuals at one end of the continuum have little residual vision and are unable to perceive motion and discriminate light. If a person is not totally blind, it is still possible to make functional use of whatever vision remains. Some persons who are considered blind are capable of perceiving distance and motion but do not have enough residual vision to travel; others, although classified as legally blind, can perceive distance and motion and have enough usable residual vision to move about with a minimal amount of assistance.

Children with loss of vision are, for educational purposes, classified as blind (those who are educated through channels other than visual) or partially sighted (those who are able to be educated, with special aids, through the medium of vision, with consideration given to the useful vision they retain). Visual impairment is determined by visual acuity and is expressed in a ratio with normal vision in the numerator and actual measured vision in the denominator; for example, 20/30 vision means that the eye can see at the distance of 20 feet what a normal eye can see at 30 feet.

The term *partially sighted* describes persons who have less than 20/70 visual acuity in the better eye after correction, have a progressive eye disorder that will probably reduce vision below 20/70, or have peripheral vision that subtends an angle less than 20 degrees. Legally blind are those who have visual acuity of 20/200 or less in the better eye after maximum correction or who have a visual field that subtends an angle of 20 degress or less in the widest diameter.

The term *low vision* refers to a severe visual impairment, not necessarily limited to distance vision.[17] Individuals with low vision may have reduced central vision with normal side vision, or vice versa, or have severely reduced vision at either close or far distances; or they may see only a blur or haze or suffer from extreme sensitivity to light. Others may not perceive colors or have blind areas in their field of vision, or they may be unable to see at night or under low lighting conditions.[5]

For a child to qualify under the law for special services in physical education, the visual disability must adversely affect the child's physical education performance. Children with visual disorders who qualify for adapted/developmental physical education programs demonstrate one or both of the following:

1. A visual disability that, even with correction, adversely affects the child's educational performance; the term *visual disability*

includes partially sighted, low vision, and legally blind children.

2. When hearing and visual impairments occur together, the combination of which causes such severe communication and other developmental and educational problems that the child cannot be accommodated in special education programs solely for deaf or blind children.

Functional conditions not covered under the law that have an impact on motor performance efficiency are depth perception, eye-hand coordination, visual form perception, visual memory, visual-spatial development, and visual-spatial integration. Children who have any of these conditions may experience movement problems, even though they are not classified as visually impaired.

INCIDENCE OF VISUAL IMPAIRMENTS

Visual impairments occur in individuals under the age of eighteen at the rate of 12.2 per 1,000. Severe visual impairments (legally or totally blind) occur at a rate of .06 per 1,000.[17]

CAUSES OF VISUAL IMPAIRMENTS

The underlying causes of visual loss are existing visual conditions, structural anomalies, and inefficient extraocular muscle control. Existing conditions impact the integrity of the visual impulse in the eye, on the optic nerve, or in the visual cortex. These conditions include diabetes, accidents and injuries, poisoning, tumors, excessive oxygen at birth, and prenatal influences such as rubella and syphilis. Structural anomalies include deviations of the eye structure. Functional causes that compromise visual efficiency are extraocular muscle imbalances caused by postural deviations, poor reading habits, and visual acuity problems.

Visual Conditions

Visual conditions that affect visual acuity include congenital causes, diseases, insult or injury to the eye, and aging. Two congenital causes are albinism and retinitis pigmentosa. With albinism, there is a lack of pigment in the eyes. Extreme light sensitivity may require the use of dark glasses. Retinitis pigmentosa is a hereditary condition in which the retinal rods become defective, which initially reduces night vision. Retinopathy of prematurity is an example of injury to the retina caused by excess oxygen during incubation of premature babies. Cataracts can be caused by aging, exposure to X rays, disease, or exposure to heat from infrared or ultraviolet light.[3] Cataracts cause an opacity of the normally transparent lens. Glaucoma is generally considered a disorder resulting from aging; however, it can occur in any age group.[3] Glaucoma creates increased pressure inside of the eye, which results in visual loss and decreased peripheral vision. As deterioration continues, central vision is reduced.

Structural Anomalies

Structural abnormalities of the eye alter the way light waves are bent (refracted) as they move into or through the eye. The resulting visual problems are called refractive errors. They include hyperopia, myopia, and astigmatism. Hyperopia, or far-sightedness, is a condition in which the light rays focus behind the retina, causing an unclear image of objects closer than 20 feet from the eye. The term implies that distant objects can be seen with less strain than near objects. Myopia, or nearsightedness, is a refractive error in which the rays of light focus in front of the retina when a person views an object 20 feet or more away. Astigmatism is a refractive error caused by an irregularity in the curvature of the cornea, so that portions of the light rays from a given object fall behind or in front of the retina. As a result, vision may be blurry.

Inefficient Extraocular Muscle Control

Singular binocular vision involves coordinating the separate images that enter each eye into a single image in the visual cortex of the brain. When the two eyes function in unison and are coordinated, the images entering each eye are matched in the visual cortex, and binocular fusion results. If, however, the supply of energy to one or more of the six extraocular muscles attached to the outside of each eyeball is out of balance, the eyes do not function in unison. When this occurs, the images from one eye deviate from those of the other eye, and the images do not match in the visual cortex. The amount of visual distress experienced because of mismatched images (strabismus) depends on the degree of deviation of the eyes and the ability of the central nervous system to correct the imbalance. Amblyopia results when the image from an eye has been suppressed by the brain for a long time because a conflict exists between the two eyes. The eye with amblyopia does not function because the brain will not accept the deviant image. Individuals who use each eye independently from the other, suppressing first one eye and then the other, are known as alternators. When a person has visual suppression problems with one or both eyes, depth perception is always compromised.

The two most prevalent dysfunctions resulting from lack of extraocular muscle balance are heterotropias and heterophorias. Heterotropias are manifest malalignments of the eyes during which one or both eyes consistently deviate from the central axis. As a consequence, the eyes do not fixate at the same point on the object of visual attention. Tropias always create depth perception difficulties.

Heterophorias are tendencies toward visual malalignments. They usually do not cause serious visual distress because, when slight variations in binocular fusion occur in the visual cortex, the central nervous system tends to correct the imbalance between the pull of the extraocular muscles. However, after prolonged use of the eyes, such as after reading for several hours, the stronger set of muscles overcomes the correction and the eyes swing out of alignment. An individual becomes aware of the malalignment when the vision of the printed page begins to blur. Phorias create depth perception difficulties only after the correction is lost.

Nystagmus involves rapid movement of the eyes from side to side, up and down, in a rotatory motion, or a combination of these. See Table 17.1 for descriptions of visual impairment conditions and specialists.

CHARACTERISTICS OF VISUAL IMPAIRMENTS

Vision loss has serious implications for the general development of motor, academic, intellectual, psychological, and social characteristics. There are widespread individual differences among persons with limited vision. However, certain characteristics appear more often than in sighted persons. Some of the characteristics that have implications for physical education are motor development, physical fitness, and psychological and social adjustment.

Motor Development

Limited vision restricts physical motor activity, which in turn limits the range and variety of experiences the children may encounter. Infants who are blind have little motivation to hold the head up because of lack of visual stimulation; as a result, all postural development, including trunk control, sitting, and standing, is delayed. Because postural control precedes gross and fine motor development, these children are slow to walk, run, skip, reach, grasp, and develop other gross and fine motor skills.

The child with normal sight makes judgments as to where objects are in space by pairing sensory information from vision with movement information received when moving to and from objects. Because persons with severe visual impairments cannot visually compare objects at varying distances in the environment, they are unable to formulate visual judgments.

The child with a severe visual impairment is often unaware of the movement potential of body parts. This lack of awareness of potential may restrict movements, which in turn retards the development of the muscles and balancing mechanisms needed for the development of complex motor skills.

TABLE 17.1	Visual Impairment Conditions and Specialists
Term	**Description**
Alternator	Uses each eye independently of the other (e.g., one eye may be used for near-point activities and the other for distance activities)
Amblyopia	A type of strabismus that causes the affected eye to be nonfunctional
Astigmatism	A refractive error caused by an irregularity in the curvature of the cornea of the lens; vision may be blurred
Esophoria	A tendency for an eye to deviate medially toward the nose
Esotropia	A condition in which the eye(s) turn(s) inward (cross-eyed)
Exophoria	A tendency for an eye to deviate laterally away from the nose
Exotropia	A condition in which the eye(s) turn(s) outward
Hyperopia	A condition in which the light rays focus behind the retina, causing an unclear image of objects closer than 20 feet from the eye (farsighted)
Hyperphoria	A tendency for an eye to deviate in an upward direction
Hypertropia	A condition in which one or both eyes swing upward
Hypophoria	A tendency for an eye to deviate in a downward direction
Hypotropia	A condition in which one or both eyes swing downward
Myopia	A condition in which the light rays focus in front of the retina when a person views an object 20 feet or more away from the eye (nearsighted)
Nystagmus	Rapid movement of the eyes from side to side, up and down, in a rotatory motion, or in a combination of these motions
Ophthalmologist	A licensed physician specializing in the treatment of eye diseases and optical defects
Optician	A technician who grinds lenses and makes glasses
Optometrist	A specialist in examining the eyes for optical defects and fitting glasses to correct those defects
Orthoptic vision	The ability to use the extraocular muscles of the eyes in unison
Orthoptician	A person who provides eye exercises to refine control of the eye (e.g., visual developmental specialist)
Refractive vision	The process by which light rays bend as they enter or pass through the eyes
Tunnel vision	A loss of side vision while retaining clear central vision; also called peripheral vision
Visual development specialist	An optometrist or ophthalmologist with specialized training in evaluating and correcting orthoptic visual problems

Studies have confirmed these delays. Ribadi, Rider, and Toole[18] indicate that congenitally blind individuals are less capable on static and dynamic balance tasks than are their sighted peers. The ways that delayed balance impact movement patterns were described by Gordon and Gavron.[9] They studied twenty-eight running parameters of sighted and blind runners and found that, as a group, the blind runners did not have sufficient forward lean while running. They demonstrated insufficient hip, knee, and ankle extension at takeoff, which limited their power, and range of motion of the hip and the ankle was limited. The play of preschool children with visual impairments lags behind children with sight. Children with low vision demonstrate play behavior more advanced than that of children who are functionally blind.[10]

Physical Fitness

Individuals with visual impairments demonstrate a wide range of physical fitness. Individuals who adopt a passive lifestyle can be expected to demonstrate poor physical fitness; however, when appro-

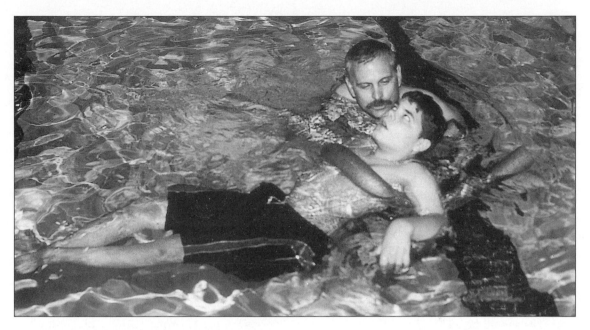

A totally blind child learns to relax and enjoy the water.
Photo by Carol Huettig.

priate activity programs are available, individuals who are blind can develop excellent levels of physical fitness.[16] Children with visual impairments have less muscular and cardiovascular endurance, less muscular strength, and more body fat than children who are sighted.[12] Kleeman and Rimmer[11] tested thirty adults with visual impairments and reported that over 70 percent scored in the average range on cardiovascular endurance, body mass index, and flexibility. Their scores for sit-ups were slightly below average, and 23 percent were categorized as overweight.

Psychological and Social Adjustment

The emotional and social characteristics of persons who are visually limited vary. Depending on early life experiences, students who are blind may have personality problems as well as physical incapacities. Research available regarding the social maturity of children who are blind reveals that, in general, they receive significantly lower social maturity scores than do sighted children.[6]

The psychological and social adjustment of individuals with severe visual impairments depends a great deal on the extent and success of their interactions with others.[14] Sighted persons acquire social habits by observing and imitating people they esteem. Individuals with severe visual impairments do not have the same opportunity to develop those skills because they are unable to observe social interactions. Any limitation in observing and interpreting gestures of individuals as they talk results in less information about what a person is attempting to communicate. Lack of opportunity to read body language and assess the social surroundings in terms of what is appropriate may limit the social development of individuals who are blind.

Some individuals who are blind may exhibit self-stimulatory behavior, or blindisms, such as rocking the body or head, placing fingers or fists into the eyes, flicking the fingers in front of the face, and spinning the body around repetitiously. The cause of these self-stimulatory behaviors is unknown; however, it is suspected that the individuals are attempting to access vestibular, kinesthetic, and tactile stimuli to substitute for loss of visual stimulation. Efforts to eliminate these behaviors seldom are successful for any length of time.[16]

TESTING

Children with visual disabilities must be approached in accordance with their own unique educational needs. A child who has a loss of vision also may be impaired in the function of mobility and may be less able than sighted children in motor abilities. There is a great need for children with visual impairments to be provided with opportunities, through physical education, that will compensate for their movement deficiencies. All children who are blind or partially sighted should have a full evaluation as to the degree of visual loss.

Physical fitness and motor proficiency and skill tests should be administered to all students, regardless of visual status. Physical fitness tests that might be used include the Brockport Physical Fitness Test, M.O.B.I.L.T.E.E., and Physical Best. To determine motor proficiency, the balance and bilateral coordination portions of the Bruininks-Oseretsky Motor Proficiency Test are recommended. Motor skills can be assessed using the Test of Gross Motor Development. Regardless of what tests are used, modifications must be made to accommodate the lack of vision. Recommendations for exercise testing are presented in Table 17.2.

TABLE 17.2	**Recommendations for Exercise Testing**

Have all instructions described verbally or on audiotape.
Allow the person to describe or demonstrate the test protocol before the test begins.
Give tactile and verbal reinforcement to motivate the participant.
Allow the person to lightly touch handrails or the tester when necessary.[4]

When testing sport skills, a hitting tee or cone should be used, rather than throwing the ball; and a ball to be kicked should be placed in front of the person's foot.

Vision tests are extremely important in order to identify and remedy vision disorders and to facilitate the education of visually disabled persons. A widely used test of vision is the Snellen test, which is a measure of visual acuity. This test can be administered with expediency to a child by nonprofessional personnel and is applicable to young children. The Snellen chart primarily is used to detect myopia (nearsightedness). It does not give indications of near-point vision, peripheral vision, convergence ability, binocular fusion ability, or oculomotor dysfunctions. A thorough vision screening program must include tests supplementary to the Snellen test. Other visual screening tests that may provide additional information are the Keystone Telebinocular test, which measures depth perception, and the Orthoptor test, which measures acuity, phoria, central fusion, and colorblindness.

Limitations in peripheral vision constitute a visual disability, particularly in some activities involving motor skills. Consequently, knowledge of this aspect of vision may assist the physical educator in determining methods of teaching and types of activities for the visually impaired child. Peripheral vision is usually assessed in terms of degrees of visual arc and is measured by the extent to which a standard visual stimulus can be seen on a black background viewed from a distance of about 39 inches when the eye is fixed on a central point.[13]

It is difficult to evaluate the results found on a given test of vision because two persons with similar visual characteristics on a screening test may display different physical, social, and psychological behaviors. Although objective screening tests of vision are important, it is suggested that daily observations be made to supplement the screening tests. Daily observation for the symptoms of eye trouble has particular importance in the early primary years. The detection of visual disabilities early in development enables early intervention, which maximizes skill development. Symptoms that might indicate eye disorders and might be observed by educators appear in Figure 17-1.

New techniques for evaluating vision and assisting individuals with visual disorders are available through low-vision clinics. This training assists the person with visual impairment to use what vision they have to maximum. Low-vision aids include "magnifying lenses, field enlargement lens systems, telescopic lenses mounted on eyewear frames, non optical aids such as special illumination, filters and large print materials, and electronic TV monitor magnification systems."[5]

Functional visual problems related to misalignment of the eyes are frequently treated using vision training, or vision therapy, defined as "the teaching and training process for the improvement of visual perception and/or the coordination of the two eyes for efficient and comfortable binocular vision."[20] The purpose of vision therapy is to treat functional deficiencies in order for the person to achieve optimum efficiency and comfort.[1] Although the value of this type of therapy has long been debated, when carried out by well-trained visual behavioral specialists, there is strong scientific support for its efficacy in modifying and improving oculomotor, accommodative, and binocular system disorders.[2]

SPECIAL CONSIDERATIONS

Differences Between Acquired and Congenital Visual Disorders

There are two basic types of visual disorders: (1) congenital, those present at birth, and (2) adventitious, those acquired after birth. The onset of blindness has an impact on the development of the child.

The child with congenital blindness lacks visual information on which motor responses may be built. Also, overprotection may hamper the development of the individual who is congenitally blind. Frequently, parents and teachers tend to restrict the activity of children who are blind.[12] The overprotection complicates development because the child is not permitted to explore the environments necessary for the development of motor responses. It is obvious that, depending on when blindness occurred, the child who is blinded after birth will have some opportunities to explore environments and receive environmental information through the visual senses for development. Previous sight experience impacts favorably on the physical and motor development of adventitiously blind persons. However, they are usually despondent over their loss of sight and need assistance in adjusting and coping. The sooner intervention counseling can begin, the better.

Figure 17-1   Symptoms Indicative of Common Disorders of the Eye

1. Confuses right/left directions
2. Complaints of dizziness or frequent headaches
3. Poor balance
4. Frequent rubbing of the eyes
5. Difficulty concentrating; short attention span; easily distracted
6. Difficulty following a moving target
7. Squinting
8. Eyes turn in or out
9. Walking overcautiously
10. Faltering or stumbling
11. Running into objects not directly in the line of vision
12. Failure to see objects readily visible to others
13. Sensitivity to normal light levels
14. Difficulty in estimating distances
15. Complaints of double vision
16. Going down steps one at a time
17. Poor hand-eye and/or foot-eye coordination
18. Avoidance of climbing apparatus
19. Holding the head close to the desk during paper and pencil tasks
20. Turning the head and using only one eye while moving

Modified from The Visual Fitness Institute Symptoms of Visual Skill Disorders website (http://visualfitness.com/symptoms.html).[23]

Mobility Training

Mobility is the ability to move from one point to a second point. Orientation is the ability to relate body position to other objects in space. Obviously, these abilities are related and required for efficient movement in a variety of environments.

Mobility training is an adaptive technique that applies to children with visual impairments. It enables them to learn about their physical play areas. Mobility training increases their confidence in moving with greater authority and provides greater safety while they are participating. It is a valuable way to enhance participation in the physical education program.

There are several prerequisites to efficient mobility training. Some of these are (1) sound discrimination, (2) sound location, (3) concentration, (4) memorization, (5) retention of information, and (6) physical skill. These prerequisite skills provide the environmental awareness needed for travel. Deficits in these prerequisites may be a deterrent to proficient performance.

Although specific techniques are used by professionals for mobility training, physical educators may reinforce many of the concepts that are a part of sophisticated mobility training programs. Goodman[8] suggests that routes be learned for both indoors and outdoors. Routes are organized in units and are purposely chosen courses from a starting to finishing point for which a strategy is developed. Routes are selected according to the blind student's skills, interests, and needs. Usually routes progress in difficulty from simple, straightforward routes to more complicated ones. Activities in the physical education class that would reinforce professional mobility training programs are (1) practice walking straight lines while maintaining good posture, (2) locate sounds in the environment, (3) follow instructions where movements have to be made that conform to instruction (memory), (4) practice the reproduction of specific walking distances with respect to time, (5) find one's way back to starting points on different surfaces, and (6) practice changing body positions.

Orientation and training programs should help visually impaired persons cope effectively with physical surroundings.[8] Training programs should also assist in the successful interaction with peers, as well as with the physical facilities and equipment. The teacher should remember that some persons with visual impairments have travel vision. The individual capabilities of each child should be assessed to determine the extent of the appropriate mobility training program.

TEACHING STRATEGIES

The Teacher

The effective physical education teacher is one who respects all students, regardless of their ability level; who is a skilled observer of motor performance; who recognizes and accommodates individual differences; and who uses teaching methods and curricula appropriate for the students. Such professionals establish educational environments conducive to optimum growth. They assess the needs, abilities, and limitations of all of their students and design a program to meet those needs. These are challenging tasks for all teachers; however, those who instruct students with visual impairments have an added dimension to their work. Rather than using the old standby, demonstration, as their main form of communicating a desired movement, they must be prepared to substitute a variety of other forms of sensory experiences that are meaningful to the student with a visual impairment. Adults with visual impairments who attended public school during the 1980s reported that their experience could have been improved if their physical educators had had more knowledge about visual impairments and had provided more information about health, wellness, and the benefits of exercise.[11]

Teaching Modifications

The child who has visual limitations must depend on receiving information through sensory media other than vision. Audition is a very important sensory medium of instruction. Another sensory medium that can be used is kinesthesis. The correct feel of the movement can be communicated through manual guidance administered by an instructor or another student. Also, because the child with visual limitations has little or no understanding of spatial concepts such as location, position, direction, and distance, skin and muscular sensations that arise when the student is moved through the activity area provide the information needed to participate. The manual guidance method accompanied by verbal corrections is often effective in the correction of faulty motor skills because two senses are used for instruction. A technique that has met with some success in the integrated class is for the teacher to use the child who has a visual impairment in presenting a demonstration to the rest of the class by manually manipulating the child through the desired movements. This enables the child who is being used to demonstrate to get the tactual feel of movement, and instruction to the sighted class members is not deterred. Providing information, rules, and tests in braille for advance study of a class presentation may enable the visually limited child to better understand the presentation.

Persons with visual limitations need concrete experiences with objects and events for learning to occur. To promote participation with sighted players, Richardson and Mastro[19] suggest that audible balls be used for relay and in such games as "Steal the Bacon." With the audible ball, blind players can know where the ball is most of the time. For bowling, Stanley and Kindig[22] suggest that improvised rope guide rails in conjunction with a carefully placed carpet can be used to identify foot positions and distance traveled during the instruction of a four-step approach. The carpet may replace the permanence of a guide rail and enable lesser restricted participation in bowling alleys; also, the carpet can be rolled and transported conveniently. Individuals with visual impairments can participate in alpine skiing with the help of a guide who stays within 5 to 8 feet of the skier with low vision. The guide and the skier

ski independently; however, the guide keeps an eye on both the course and the skier who is visually impaired.

Both guide wires and guide runners have been shown to be effective for runners. Guide wires are ropes or heavy string stretched 36 inches above the lane markers; they help runners feel the perimeters of the lane. A guide runner is a person who runs alongside the visually impaired runner and verbally describes the distance to the finish. In competition, the guide runner is also permitted to touch the elbow of a runner who has a visual impairment to indicate any lateral off-step.[15]

Because of the great visual content included in the components of certain games, some skill activities are more difficult than others to adapt for persons with visual limitations. In the case of total blindness, participation in the more complex activities may be extremely difficult to modify. However, the skills constituting a game can be taught, and lead-up games with appropriate modifications are usually within the child's grasp.

There are several considerations that physical educators must make to effectively accommodate children with low vision in the diverse activities and environments where instruction takes place. The application of principles of accommodation may help the physical educator teach a wide variety of activities. A number of practical guidelines are presented in Figure 17-2.

Cognitive Instruction

The communication of information and the testing of knowledge are part of physical education instruction. Accommodations must be made for students with visual impairments during the communication of the physical education program:

1. Use large-print letters and numbers (which can be perceived by many persons who are partially sighted).
2. Use braille, a shorthand for tactile reading. Dots in a cell are raised on paper to indicate letters, numbers, punctuation, and other signs.

This blind skier can enjoy downhill skiing by using a sighted guide and two poles.
Courtesy Aspen Challenge, Aspen, CO.

3. Make better use of listening skills and position students with visual impairments where they can best hear instructional information. This may be directly in front of the instructor.

4. Substitute kinesthetic (manual) guidance for vision when the components of skills are to be integrated in space and time.

5. Encourage the use of residual vision during the cognitive communication process between the instructor and a student with low vision.

6. Arrange seats to accommodate range of vision.

7. Design appropriate light contrasts between figure and ground when presenting instructional materials.

8. Be alert to behavioral signs and physical symptoms of visual difficulty in all children.

A blind runner and her guide compete together.
Courtesy United States Association of Blind Athletes, Colorado Springs, CO.

Figure 17-2 Physical Education Principles for Working with the Visually Impaired

1. Design the instructional environment to accommodate the individual.
2. Introduce special devices, aids, and equipment to assist the individual.
3. Use special instructional techniques to accommodate the individual.
4. Introduce precautionary safety measures to meet the individual's needs.
5. Provide special feedback for tasks to facilitate learning.
6. Use sighted peers to provide individual attention and maximize participation.
7. Train the individual for mobility and understanding of the environment.
8. Allow the person with the visual impairment to decide if assistance is needed or wanted.[9]
9. Keep equipment and objects in the same place. Moving objects without telling the person with a visual impairment can be frustrating to that person.
10. Assist with the initiation of social interactions with peers.

Control of the Environment—Safety First

The instructional environment for individuals who have visual impairments should be safe and familiar and possess distinguishing landmarks. As a safety precaution, play areas should be uncluttered and free from unnecessary obstructions. Children with visual impairments should be thoroughly introduced to unfamiliar areas by walking them around the play environment before they are allowed to play.

Environmental characteristics can be amplified. For instance, gymnasiums can be well lighted to assist those who possess residual vision. Bound-aries for games can have various compositions, such as a base or path of dirt and concrete or grass for other areas. Brightly colored objects are easier to identify. Also, equipment may be designed and appropriately placed to prevent possible injuries. For instance, two swings on a stand are safer than three. A third swing in the center is difficult to reach without danger when the other two swings are occupied. Attention to the safety and familiarity of the environment specifically designed for persons with visual impairments represents some degree of accommodation.

There are two parts to the management of safe environments. One is the structure of the environment, and the other is the teacher's control of the children as they participate in the environment. Suggestions to ensure safe play are presented in Figure 17-3.

Figure 17-3   Safety Measures to Prevent Injury

1. Alter the playing surface texture (sand, dirt, asphalt); increase or decrease the grade to indicate play area boundaries.
2. Use padded walls, bushes, or other soft, safe restrainers around play areas.
3. Use brightly colored objects as boundaries to assist those with residual vision.
4. Limit the play area.
5. Limit the number of participants in the play area.
6. Play in slow motion when introducing a new game.
7. Protect the eyes.
8. Structure activities commensurate with the ability of the student with a visual impairment.
9. Protect visual aids, such as eyeglasses.
10. Select safe equipment.
11. Structure a safe environment.
12. Instruct children to use the environment safely.

The following are applications of safety principles:

Principle	Safety Measure
Protection of aids	Protect all body parts; use spotting in gymnastics.
Protection of eyeglasses	Use a restraining strap to hold glasses in place.
Safe equipment	Use sponge ball for softball, volleyball, or any other projectile activities.
Safe environment	Check play areas for obstacles and holes in ground.
Activity according to ability	Avoid activities that require children to pass each other at high speeds.
Close supervision of all potentially dangerous activity	The teacher positions self close to the student with a visual impairment during activity, anticipates dangerous situations, and helps the student avoid them.

Special Instructional Methods

The application of special methods requires astute observation of the characteristics of each blind student. A list of special methods follows:

1. Give clear auditory signals with a whistle or megaphone.
2. Instruct through manual guidance.
3. Use braille to teach cognitive materials before class.
4. Encourage tactual exploration of objects to determine texture, size, and shape.
5. Address the child by name.
6. Individualize instruction and build on existing capabilities. Do not let the child exploit visual limitations to the extent of withdrawing from activity or underachieving in motor performance.
7. Use the sensory mode that is most effective for specific learners (tactile, kinesthetic, haptic, auditory).
8. Manage the instructional environment to minimize the need for vision. Use chains where children touch one another. Participate from stationary positions. Establish reference points to which all persons return for instruction.

Special Task Feedback

Children who are blind need to know the effects of their performance on physical tasks because they receive little or no visual feedback. Task feedback must come through other sensory modes. For example, buzzers or bells can be inserted inside a basketball hoop to inform the person when a basket has been made. Gravel can be placed around the stake in horseshoes to indicate accuracy of the toss. Peers can also give specific verbal feedback on tasks that involve projectiles. Effective feedback is an important reinforcing property to be incorporated into physical activity for persons with visual impairments.[7]

Peer Assistance

Peers without disabilities can assist children with disabilities in integrated settings. The nature of the assistance depends on the nature of the task. Peer assistance in providing feedback of task success is one example. Students with low vision may choose to have sighted guides. For safety in travel skills, a blind person should grasp the guide's upper arm, above the elbow, with the thumb on the outside and the fingers on the inside of the guide's arm. Both student and guide hold upper arms close to the body. When approaching doorways or objects, the guide moves the entire arm behind the back, so students with low vision understand to walk directly behind the guide. Verbal cues inform the student when there are stairways and curbs. When children without disabilities provide such assistance, it is necessary to manage their time so as not to impede their own education.

Physical education teachers working with children who are visually impaired should attempt to minimize the stereotyped manner in which the child with visual limitations receives an education and should encourage seeing children to accept their peers on a personal basis.

THE PHYSICAL EDUCATION PROGRAM

Physical Education Needs

Loss of vision, by itself, is not a limiting condition for physical exercise. A considerable amount of developmental exercises to promote muscular strength and endurance can be administered to such children. Through developmental exercise, the child with visual limitations develops qualities such as good posture, graceful body movement, and good walking and sitting positions. Furthermore, physical education programs develop and maintain a healthy, vigorous body with physical vitality and good neuromuscular coordination. In addition to physical benefits, the physical education program contributes to social-emotional outcomes such as security and confidence and sighted peers' acceptance of children who are blind.

The ultimate goal of the class atmosphere for children with vision losses is to provide experiences that will help them adjust to the seeing society in which they live. The selection and method of experiences in the physical education program are critical. These experiences should not be overprotective to the extent that growth is inhibited; rather, the experiences should provide challenge yet remain within the range of the children's capabilities for achieving skill objectives.

Children with limited vision are capable of participating in numerous activities; however, the degree of participation possible depends on each child's particular abilities. Broad curriculum areas should be available at appropriate levels of development to accommodate each child. Children with visual impairments may represent a cross section of any school population with regard to motor abilities, physical fitness characteristics, and social and emotional traits. The purpose of adapting methods and activities for the student with visual limitations is to provide many experiences that children with sight learn primarily through visual observation. A goal of group activity in which a child with limited vision participates is to assign a role to the child that can be carried out successfully. It is undesirable for the child to be placed in the position of a bystander.

The adaptation of the physical education program for individuals with visual limitations should promote their confidence to cope with their environment by increasing their physical and motor abilities. It should also produce in them a feeling of acceptance as individuals in their own right. To achieve these goals, the program should include the adaptation of the general program of activities, when needed; additional or specialized activities, depending on the needs of the child; and special equipment, if needed.

Perceptual Development

Children with limited vision use other sensory abilities better as a result of increased attention to them in attempts to learn about and cope with the environment. A sighted person might be unaware of particular auditory stimuli, whereas a person who is blind might attach great significance to them.

These children need to use full kinesthetic, auditory, tactile, and space perception. Each form of perception contributes to the blind child's ability to adapt to the environment. The kinesthetic and vestibular systems can enable a person with limited vision to maintain balance. Balance experience is acquired through participation in activities that require quick changes of direction. The kinesthetic receptors are stimulated if the tasks increase the amount of pressure applied to the joints such as weight lifting or pushing and pulling movements.

Interrelationship of Sensory Systems in Movement

The role of vision as it relates to movement has been the focus of much research. Visual information that assists with performing specific motor skills is integrated with information from the vestibular apparatus and kinesthetic signals resulting from reflex and voluntary movements. Organization of these sensory inputs plays a central role in successfully maintaining posture and executing movement. Sensory organization is responsible for determining the timing, direction, and amplitude of movement based on information from vision, kinesthesis, and the vestibular sense. The execution of static and dynamic balance requires a combination of several senses, one of which is vision. When vision is compromised, other senses must be used more fully.

Space Perception

Early visual experience of spatial relations establishes a method for processing information that affects cognitive and motor learning. Persons who have low vision often cannot perceive the relationship of objects to each other in space. They also have an impaired ability to relate themselves to objects in space. Therefore, the auditory, vestibular, kinesthetic, and tactile senses are used to establish spatial relationships.

Physical Education Activities

A sound physical education curriculum is one that includes a wide variety of activities selected to meet the needs of the students. Obviously, student needs vary depending on their developmental levels, ages, and interests. Fundamental motor skills and patterns are essential prerequisites for successful, enjoyable participation in recreational sport activities. Some of these activities are running, jumping, throwing, and striking. They involve coordinated movements.

Games of low organization are an important part of elementary school physical education programs. The games that require the least modification for persons with visual impairments are those in which there is continuous contact with the participants, such as tug of war, parachute activity, end man tag, ring around the rosy, hot potato, over and under relay, and wheelbarrow races.

Activities that require mimimum amounts of vision for participation are (1) wrestling (the only modification is contact with an opponent at a takedown), (2) individual fitness exercises, (3) gymnastics or tumbling, and (4) swimming. Suggestions for including learners with visual impairments in aquatic activities are presented in Figure 17-4. Team sports that are highly loaded with visual information require considerable accommodation. Such games include basketball, soccer, and football because the ball as well as the offensive and defensive players move continually.

Variable Adaptation

Physical activities need various amounts of adaptation for participants who are blind. Considerations for the selection of activities for players who have visual impairments are as follows:

1. Activities that require a considerable amount of vision are most difficult.
2. Activities that require great amounts of movement in the environment are usually the most difficult to adapt.

Figure 17-4   Aquatics for Learners with
Visual Impairments

- The swimmer should wear goggles to prevent any possible damage from chlorine and other chemicals in the water.
- Bright, colorful toys should be used: beach balls, kickboards, pails and shovels, water-use stuffed animals, water squirters (not squirt guns), etc.
- The swimmer must be given the opportunity to explore the learning environment to orient him- or herself. This careful exploration can be enhanced if there is a constant sound source: a soft radio or the like for the swimmer to use for orientation.
- The swimmer must be given a chance to learn self-protective skills that include sensing the end of the lane because of the reaction of the waves in response to the incoming body, sensing the presence of another swimmer because of splashing and waves, and announcing intentions if planning to jump into the water.
- A swimmer who is totally blind may learn best if given the opportunity to "feel" the movement of another; this is particularly effective if paired with patterning the movement of the swimmer.
- Open turns, rather than flip turns, give the swimmer a little leeway when lap swimming to find the wall rather than being surprised by it.
- Lane lines help the swimmer stay oriented in the pool. The swimmer may want to wear tight-fitting gloves to avoid being cut by the lane lines if off course.

For more information refer to Project INSPIRE Aquatics pages: http://venus.twu.edu/~f_huettig

Scott Moore, a blind athlete competes in Judo.
Courtesy United States Association of Blind Athletes, Colorado Springs, CO.

6. The more equipment that needs to be modified, the more complex the accommodation of the motor task for the learner.

Safety Precautions

The physical educator who administers activities to children with limited vision should take special safety precautions. Some considerations that may enhance the safety factor in physical education programs for the students with visual limitations are

1. Secure knowledge, through medical records and observation, of the children's limitations and capabilities.
2. Orient the children to facilities and equipment.

3. The greater the number of visual cues required for participation, the more difficult the accommodation.
4. Environments in which there is continual change of visual cues rather than stable visual cues (e.g., team games such as basketball, football, and soccer) are most difficult.
5. The more modifications that have to be made in the environment, the more difficult the accommodation for the player with a visual impairment.

3. Provide special equipment indicating direction, such as guide lines in swimming and running events, as well as deflated softballs.

Educational Settings

The physical education teacher may be requested to instruct a class in which children with visual limitations are integrated into the regular class, to instruct a class composed solely of visually limited children, or to instruct classes of multidisabled children. There is a growing awareness that similarities are greater than differences when children with visual limitations are compared with sighted children. Therefore, the inclusion of children with visual limitation into classes with their seeing peers should take place whenever possible. Such placement emphasizes the positive aspects of the children and minimizes differences.

In the past, it was not uncommon for children with limited vision to be referred to and placed in residential schools. However, with the implementation of The Education of the Handicapped Act, a countertrend has grown to bring instructional aids into resource rooms and regular classrooms of community schools. This practice has created a number of service delivery alternatives for least restrictive placement. It has been customary to provide the following cascade system for placement of children with visual disabilities should be applied:

1. Regular class
2. Regular class with assistance by a vision consultant
3. Regular class with consultation and itinerant instruction (orientation and mobility training)
4. Adapted physical education conducted by a specialist; children attend part-time
5. Self-contained adapted physical education class
6. Residential schools for the blind

The itinerant teacher is a specialist who possesses specific skills to work with children of limited vision. This teacher teams with the regular classroom teacher.

MODIFICATIONS, ADAPTATIONS, AND INCLUSION TECHNIQUES

Special Devices, Aids, and Equipment

Distance in space for the visually limited is structured by auditory cues. Therefore, it is desirable to structure space with these cues. Equipment, aids, and devices that enhance the participation of the blind in physical activity should provide information about the environment.

Auditory aids can be built into equipment. *Audible balls* emit beeping sounds for easy location. They may be the size of a softball, soccer ball, or playground ball. The beep baseball is a regular softball with a battery-operated electronic beeping sound device. This special equipment tells the blind person where the ball is at all times because of continuous sound. A goal ball is constructed with bells inside it. When the ball moves, the bells help the players locate the ball. One of the skills of the game is to roll the ball smoothly to reduce auditory information (less sound from the bells) to make it more difficult for blind players to locate it. *Audible goal locators* are motor-driven noisemakers. They indicate the position of backboards in basketball, targets in archery, pins in bowling, and stakes in horseshoes. Audible bases, which are plastic cones 60 inches tall with a noise-maker inside are used in the game of beep baseball. Audible locators can also be used as boundaries or to identify dangerous objects in the environment.

The following activities can be conducted to develop space perception through the use of auditory aids in the environment:

1. Walk a straight line. Measure the distance of deviations over a specific distance. Use an audible device to provide initial assistance for direction and then fade the device.
2. Face sounds made at different positions. The intensity and duration of the sound can make the task more or less difficult.

3. Reproduce pathways and specific distances just taken with a partner.
4. Do not allow students with aphakia (absence of the natural lens of the eye, as when a cataract has been surgically removed), detached retina, or severe myopia to engage in high-impact activities such as jumping.[4]

Modifications

Some modifications that can be made to enable the participation of persons with visual limitations are detailed in Table 17-3.

Inclusion Techniques

The mission of physical education programs for blind persons is to enable these pupils to engage in independent recreational sport and physical activity in the community. To achieve this, it is usually necessary to move individuals from more restrictive to less restrictive training environments. Restrictiveness of an environment is determined by the amount of special support systems needed for an individual to participate or learn. Movement to less restrictive environments usually involves the withdrawal of support systems, so the individual gradually learns to function with greater independence. At least two considerations need to be studied for the placement of persons who are blind in integrated sport activity: (1) the question of whether it is possible to integrate an activity and (2) the need for support systems to enable integration.

Providing support systems for persons with visual limitations will enable them to participate in and enjoy group activities. These involve (1) the design of the game in which the nonsighted and sighted players play together (e.g., in beep ball, the pitcher and the catcher need to be sighted), (2) the

TABLE 17.3	Activity Modification for Students with Visual Impairments
Activity	**Modification**
Aerobic dance	Include verbal description of movement with demonstration.
Archery	Beeper is affixed to center of target.
Bicycling	Child assumes rear seat position on tandem bicycle with sighted partner in front seat.
Bowling	Beeper is attached above pins at end of lane.
Canoeing	Child assumes bow position, with sighted partner in stern.
Frisbee	A Frisbee has a beeper attached.
Horseshoes	Beeper is affixed to stake. Path to horseshoes pit is made of wood chips or sand.
Running	Ropes are used for guidance (guide wire).
Swimming	Lane lines designate the swimming lanes. Swimming pool has nonslip bottom. Pool decks have nonslip surface. Pool has a constant sound source for orientation. Small bells are suspended near gutters and are activated by waves as a person approaches the end of the pool.
Softball	Sand or wood chips are used for base paths. T-stand is used for batting, instead of batting from pitcher. Different texture of ground or floor is used when near a surface that could result in serious collision.
Weight training	Equipment and weights are put in the same place.
Class management	Environment is ordered and consistent. Reference points indicate the location of the child in the play area. Auditory cues identify obstacles in the environment. Tactile markings are on the floor. Boundaries of different textures are used.

use of peer tutors for activity play (allow the person to run or exercise with a partner), and (3) use a variety of environments in which support for integrated activity is gradually withdrawn, so the individual can eventually participate independently in recreational activity in the community. There are currently many educational integration models; however, in the last analysis, individuals with low vision must participate in the less restricted environment in the community. What are needed are educational models that match the activities available in the community. Songster and Doherty[21] have identified a formal process for the integration of individuals with disabilities, including blind players, into sport activity. The process involves (1) the selection of the activity around which the integration process will take place, (2) the development of a system of sequential supports in environments that enable greater independent functioning of the athletes among their normal peers, (3) the placement of the individuals in appropriate environments commensurate with their social and physical abilities, (4) the provision of needed supports to the individual, and (5) the fading of the individual's support systems through the less restrictive environments. Before the integration process is attempted, the sequential environments and support systems must be fully designed.

One of the purposes of physical education for students who have visual impairments is development of skills that can be used in interscholastic athletics, in intramurals, or for leisure in the community after formal schooling. Therefore, activity should be community-based. Clearly, according to the laws, there are to be equal opportunities for participation in extracurricular activities for individuals with and without disabilities. Therefore, opportunities for sports participation outside the schools should be integrally linked with the physical education program in the public schools. Such considerations for the extension of extracurricular activities to persons with limited vision involve the identification of activities that are available in the community.

COMMUNITY-BASED ACTIVITIES

Students with visual impairments who have had a positive physical education experience remain active after leaving school.[6] Activities and equipment that can be used to maintain the adult's physical and motor fitness include weight lifting, Universal gym equipment, isometric exercises, stationary running, the exercise bicycle, and the rowing machine. Instruction in proper technique and familiarity with community facilities that provide these types of equipment as part of the transition program will enhance the probability of continued participation after the school years. A growing number of sport activities are also available to the person with visual impairments. Goal ball and beep ball are two popular competitive sports for persons with visual impairments, and each can be modified to include players with sight. The United States Association for Blind Athletes (USABA) sponsor national competition in these sports yearly.

Goal Ball

Goal ball is a game that originated in Germany for blind veterans of World War II to provide gross motor movement cued by auditory stimuli (a bell ball). It is now played under the rules of the International Sports Organization for the Disabled.

The purpose of the game is for each team of three persons to roll the ball across the opponent's goal, which is 8.5 m (9 1/4 yards) wide for men and 7.5 m (about 8 yards) wide for women. A ball is rolled toward the opponent's goal. The entire team attempts to stop the ball before it reaches the goal by throwing the body into an elongated position. The ball is warded off with any part of or the whole body. Games last 10 minutes, with a 5-minute halftime. All players are blindfolded.

Many of the principles of accommodating persons with visual impairment have been incorporated into this game. Examples of the application of these principles follow:

- Instructional environment to accommodate the individual. The boundaries are made of rope so they can be detected by the players.

- Special aids and equipment. Elbow and knee pads are provided to the players so they are not hurt when the body hits the floor or lunges to stop the ball. Bells are placed in the ball so the rolling ball can be heard en route to the goal.
- Special instructional techniques. Kinesthetic movement of the body is required to instruct the players how to lunge to block the ball.
- Precautionary safety measures. Pads and mats can be placed at the end of the gym where the goals are. The sidelines should be clear of objects.
- Special feedback to facilitate learning. A piece of tin or materials that make sounds can be placed at the goal so players know when a goal has been scored rather than successfully defended.
- Seeing peers who assist instruction. Seeing persons can provide feedback as to whether the movements of the game have been successfully achieved.
- Players trained to understand the environment. The players should be trained to know where the goal ball training area is within the gym and how to enter and leave the gymnasium.

Beep Ball

Beep ball is a game, played throughout the United States, that is designed to encourage blind and sighted players to compete in softball. Each team has its own sighted pitcher and catcher. The catcher sets the target where the batter normally swings the bat, and the pitcher attempts to hit the target with the ball. Equipment required to play beep ball is available through the Telephone Pioneers of America. Equipment includes a buzzing base and a ball 16 inches in circumference with a battery-operated electronic sound device inside. The specifications of the equipment and playing area are (1) a regulation bat; (2) a beep ball; (3) 48-inch bases and pliable plastic cones with a 36-inch bottom and a 10-inch-long cylinder of foam-rubber top; (4) the bases placed 90 feet down respective lines and 5 feet off of the lines; and (5) sounding units that give off a buzzing sound when activated fixed 20 feet from the bases.

The specific rules of beep ball are as follows: (1) the umpire activates one of the bases when a ball is hit; (2) the runner must identify the correct base and run to it before a play is made by the defense; (3) a run is scored if the runner reaches the base before the fielder plays the ball and the beeper is turned off (there is no running from one base to another); (4) the batter is allowed five rather than the traditional three strikes (the fifth strike must be a total miss); (5) a hit ball must travel at least 40 feet to be considered fair (otherwise, it is considered foul); (6) games are six innings in duration, with three outs per inning. There is only a first and third base, which are 90 feet apart.[1] Teams are usually comprised of both males and females.

USABA Activities

The United States Association for Blind Athletes (USABA) sponsors national championships every year. Such high-level competition is an incentive for blind persons to engage in training regimens from which there are personal and physical benefits. Persons with visual impairments who participate in competitive activities such as those sponsored by the USABA may reach both sport and personal development goals.

To provide equity in competition, the classification of these competitors is based on the amount of sight. The USABA classification system of legally blind athletes is as follows:

> Class A—totally blind; possess light perception only, have no visual acuity or see less than 3 degrees in the visual field
>
> Class B—visual acuity no better than 20/400 or those with 3 to 10 degrees in the visual field; can see hand movement

TABLE 17.4	USABA Athletic Competition and Leisure Activities
Activity	**Skill**
Track running event	Physical fitness program
Cycling	Physical fitness and recreational program
Weight lifting	Physical fitness programs and body building
Sailing	Recreational aquatics
Crew rowing	Boat rowing for fishing and boat safety
Competitive diving	Recreational swimming and diving
Archery	Recreational shooting at archery ranges
Swimming	Recreational swimming in community pools
Downhill and cross-country skiing	Recreational skiing in selected communities where the resources are appropriate

Class C—visual acuity 20/399 through 20/299 or those with 10 to 20 degrees in the visual field

Several activities sponsored by the USABA are related to leisure activities. Thus, the competition can serve participants in two ways—for athletic competition and for participation in leisure activities in the community. Some of the activities that are a part of international competition and that can be expressed as a recreational skill in the community are listed in Table 17.4.

Other activities that are less community-based recreational activities but that provide opportunities to develop personal and social skills through participation are field events in track, wrestling, and gymnastics. Specific events in gymnastics and track and field are floor exercise; balance beam; uneven bars; vaulting; all-around competition; 60- and 100-meter dash; and 200-, 400-, 800-, 1500-, 3000-, and 10,000-meter runs.

SUMMARY

Children with visual impairments vary in functional ability to participate in physical activity. Persons classified as partially sighted have less than 20/70 acuity, and individuals are classified as blind if their acuity is 20/200 or less. *Low vision* is a term that is used when referring to individuals who have visual acuity of 20/70 or less when wearing their glasses. There are two basic categories of blindness: congenital blindness means that the person was born blind; adventitious blindness means the person was blinded after birth.

The underlying causes of visual loss are existing visual conditions, structural anomalies or injuries, and inefficient extraocular muscle control. Those associated with curvature of the light rays as they enter or pass through the eye are myopia, hyperopia, and astigmatism. Visual conditions include albinism, cataracts, glaucoma, retinitis pigmentosa, and retinopathy of prematurity. Nystagmus, suppression, and tropias are associated with difficulties in depth perception. Phorias are tendencies for the eyes to misalign.

Functional visual impairments may be identified by the Snellen test or with telebiopter visual screening tests. They also may be identified by observing abnormal eye conditions, movement patterns and preferences, and visual discrimination. Low-vision clinics offer comprehensive evaluations and assistance to individuals with visual disorders.

Vision loss has serious implications for motor, intellectual, psychological, and social development. Vision loss early in life may delay mastery of motor responses, which can affect other areas of development. Planned physical experiences will enhance physical and motor fitness and may counter maldevelopment in other areas.

Training programs in mobility increase the degree of independence of persons who are blind. Accompanying direct instruction to develop travel vision and motor skills are techniques for adaptation. This may be accomplished by modifying activity and instructional environments and introducing special aids, devices, or equipment.

Persons with visual disorders should be trained with self-help or recreational skills that can be used in the community. This may enable participation in some of the community sports programs for the blind and visually limited.

A process that will integrate players who are blind into inclusive physical activities involves the assessment of the social and physical skill level of the individual to assure success in the activity, appropriate placement in a continuum of environments with the appropriate sighted support systems, and sequential withdrawal of support systems and movement to less restrictive participation environments that are commensurate with improved motor and social skills.

REVIEW QUESTIONS

1. How do the movement capabilities of a child with slight loss of vision differ from that of a child who is totally blind?

2. What classification system for severity of blindness is used by the United States Association for Blind Athletes?

3. What are some causes of vision loss?

4. What are the general characteristics of persons with limited vision that impair physical performance of skills?

5. What social adjustment problems do students who are blind face when being included in the general physical education settings program?

6. What are five ways the physical education environment can be modified to include a student who is visually impaired?

7. What are the essential components for integrating players who are blind with sighted players in physical activity?

STUDENT ACTIVITIES

1. Working in small groups, devise a plan that would eventually enable Hosea to participate independently in community recreational activities.

2. There are several ways of adapting instruction and the environment to accommodate persons like Hosea. Select eight activities and indicate how you might modify the activity, environment, or equipment to enable him to participate with his sighted peers.

3. There are organizations designed to serve parents of children who are blind. Contact a local or a national organization to learn the purpose of these groups. What information do they provide? Do they serve as advocates for parents? What should physical education teachers know about these organizations?

REFERENCES

1. American Foundation for the Blind: *Creative recreation,* New York, 1988.

2. American Academy of Optometry and American Optometric Association: *Vision, learning and dyslexia: a joint organizational policy statement.* http://www.aaopt.org/JointStatement.html

3. Beers MH, Berkow R: *The Merk manual of diagnosis and therapy,* Whitehouse Station, NJ, 1999, Merck Research Laboratories.

4. Bloomquist, LE: Visual impairment. In Durstin JL, editor: *Exercise management for persons with chronic diseases and disabilities,* Champaign, IL, 1997, Human Kinetics.

5. Canadian Optometrists. http://www.optometrists.bc.ca/lowvision.html

6. Eichstaedt CB, Kalakian LH: *Developmental adapted physical education,* New York, 1987, Macmillan.

7. Fait H, Dunn J: *Special physical education,* Philadelphia, 1984, W. B. Saunders.

8. Goodman W: *Mobility training for people with disabilities,* Springfield, IL, 1989, Charles C Thomas.

9. Gordon B, Gavron SJ: A biomechanical analysis of the running pattern of blind athletes in the 100 meter dash, *Adapt Phys Act Q* 4:192–203, 1987.

10. Hughes M, Dote-Kwan J, Dolendo J: A close look at the cognitive play of preschoolers with visual impairments in the home, *Exceptional Children* 64: 451–462, 1998.

11. Kleeman M, Rimmer, JH: Relationship between fitness levels and attitudes toward physical education in a visually impaired population, *Clinical Kinesiology* Summer:29–32, 1994.

12. Lieberman L, Lepore, M: Camp abilities: a developmental sports camp for youths who are visually impaired, *Palaestra* Winter:28–31, 46, 1998.

13. Luria A: *Higher cortical functions in man,* ed. 2, New York, 1980, Basic Books.

14. Mastro JV, Canabal MY, French R: Psychological mood profiles of sighted and unsighted beep baseball players, *Res Q Ex Sport* 59:262–264, 1988.

15. McGuffin K, French R, Mastro J: Comparison of three techniques for sprinting by visually impaired adults, *Clin Kines* 44:97–99, 1990.

16. McHugh BE, Pyfer J: The development of rocking among children who are blind, *J of Visual Impairment & Blindness* 38:78–83, 1999.

17. NICHCY: *General information about visual impairments,* Fact sheet #13, 1997. http://Kidsource.com/nichcy/visual.html

18. Ribadi H, Rider RA, Toole T: A comparison of static and dynamic balance and congenitally blind and sighted blindfolded adolescents, *Adapt Phys Act Q* 4:220–225, 1987.

19. Richardson MJ, Mastro JV: So I can't see, I can play and I can learn, *Palaestra* 3:23–32, 1987.

20. Rouse M: Management of binocular anomalies: efficiency of visual therapy, *Am J Optom Physio Optics* 64:391–392, 1987.

21. Songster T, Doherty B: The Special Olympics integration process, Washington, DC, 1990, Special Olympics International Research Monograph.

22. Stanley SM, Kindig EE: Improvisations for blind bowlers, *Palaestra* 2:38–39, 1986.

23. Visual Fitness Institute: *Symptoms of visual skill disorders.* http://visualfitness.com/symptoms.html

Suggested Readings

Buell C: *Physical education for blind children,* ed. 2, Springfield, IL, 1984, Charles C Thomas.

Lieberman LJ, Cowart JF: *Games for people with sensory impairments,* Champaign, IL, 1996, Human Kinetics.

Recommended Websites

Please note that these recommendations are being made in the fall of 1999. It is possible the websites have moved or do not exist at the time you read this.

American Council of the Blind
http://www.acb.org

National Federation of the Blind
http://www.nfb.org/

Vision Impairments
http://web.lwc.edu/staff/rbeaudet/Blind.html

Recommended Videos

In the Eyes of the Beholder
color, 21 minutes, $195 purchase price
Aquarius Health Care Videos
5 Powerhouse Lane
PO Box 1159
Sherborn, MA 01770

Portraits of Possibility
color, 20 minutes, $189 purchase price

Insight Media
2162 Broadway
New York, NY 10024-0621

Out of Left Field
color, 7 minutes, $149 purchase price
Insight Media
2162 Broadway
New York, NY 10024-0621

CHAPTER

18

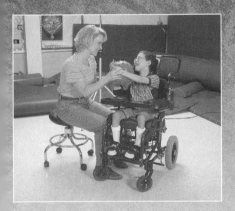

Specialized equipment provides
multisensory stimulation.
Courtesy Sportime, Atlanta, GA.

Other Health Impairments

The federal laws that have been passed in the United States during the past twenty-five years virtually ensure a free and appropriate public education to every individual who has a real or perceived impairment that limits major life activities. Other health
impairment, by federal definition, means that a child has limited
strength and vitality or alertness with respect to the environment that
is due to chronic or acute health problems, such as asthma, attention
deficit disorders, diabetes, epilepsy, a heart condition, hemophilia,
lead poisoning, leukemia, nephritis, rheumatic fever, and sickle cell
anemia, that adversely affect a child's educational performance. In
addition to the major health impairments identified in the federal

definition of IDEA, acquired immune deficiency syndrome (AIDS), anemia, childhood cancer, cystic fibrosis, diabetes, Prader-Willi syndrome, premenstrual syndrome and dysmenorrhea, and Tourette syndrome will also be addressed in this chapter.

When children with health impairments improve their motor performance, they also benefit socially and psychologically. Physical education programs that increase exercise tolerance and recreational sport skills may also improve self-care and social competence. Improved physical performance capability usually gives the student a great psychological boost. Involving students in skill and physical development activity programs often helps break a cycle of passive, debilitating physical and social lifestyles.

Most of the conditions discussed in this chapter require medical attention. When this is the case, it is advisable to request permission of the parents to consult with the student's physician to ensure that the type of exercises and activities selected for the student will not aggravate the condition. When the physical educator notices the symptoms that are described in this chapter being demonstrated by a student who is not diagnosed as having a health impairment, the child should be referred to the school nurse for additional evaluation.

ATTENTION DEFICIT DISORDER

Over the years, many terms have been used to describe inattentive and impulsive behaviors demonstrated by some children. Although this continuum of behaviors was originally identified in the 1930s,[69] research did not focus on it until the 1960s,[64] when the term *hyperkinetic impulse disorder* surfaced.[43] This was replaced by the term *hyperactive child syndrome* in the 1970s and by *attention deficit disorder (ADD)* in the 1980s.[65]

Individuals with ADD have difficulty attending in school, work, and social situations. They are easily distracted and frequently make careless mistakes because they rush through tasks without thinking. They have difficulty organizing their schoolwork and other responsibilities. They often appear to be daydreaming and/or not listening.

CASE STUDY

Roshard

Roshard is a high school freshman with a medical diagnosis of attention deficit disorder (ADD). Roshard has a long school history of difficulty. Roshard's parents have refused to give him medication to control his ADD because they believe the medication causes him to lose his intellectual edge. Being forced to learn in a traditional school environment which focuses on paper-and-pencil activities is very frustrating for Roshard. He acts out some of this frustration in his physical education class. He has temper tantrums if he loses. He becomes very sarcastic with his peers and, occasionally, the teacher. He appears to gain control if he is allowed to run or engage in other vigorous aerobic activity.

APPLICATION TASK

What could the general physical educator do to help Roshard manage his behavior in the physical education class? Are there any suggestions the general physical educator could make to Roshard's parents about activities they could do at home to help Roshard manage his ADD-associated behaviors?

When they do attempt tasks, their work is usually very messy and only partially completed. These individuals typically make every effort to avoid activities that demand sustained self-application, mental effort, and/or close concentration. They also have difficulty "reading" social situations and, as a result, make comments out of turn, initiate conversations at inappropriate times, and intrude on others. They are often judged by others to be lazy, uncaring, and unreliable when in reality they simply cannot focus their attention for any length of time.

Definition

ADD is a chronic disorder made up of heterogeneous groups who demonstrate a range of cognitive, behavioral, and social deficits.[20] The IDEA

Amendments of 1999 included attention deficit disorder and attention deficit hyperactivity disorder in the list of conditions that could render a child eligible for special services under the category of "other health impaired."[66] Three distinct forms of ADD have been identified: (1) attention deficit disorder with hyperactivity (ADHD), (2) attention deficit disorder without hyperactivity (ADD-WO), and (3) attention deficit disorder-residual (ADD-R).[32]

Incidence

Estimates of the incidence of attention deficit disorder range from 3 to 11 percent of the population. Males are diagnosed four times as frequently as females. The diagnosis can be made as early as three years, but more frequently it is not made until after a child enters school.[83]

Causes

The cause of the heterogeneous disorder of ADD is unknown. There is some evidence that there are abnormalities in the frontal portion of the brain that controls attention and motor intentional behavior.[68] When higher control centers such as these are involved, inhibition and executive functions are compromised.[6] Many studies also offer support for the idea that the disorder is genetic.[83]

Characteristics

The characteristics associated with each type of ADD appear in Figure 18-1.

Special Considerations

The management of ADD has received considerable study. The combination of drug therapy and psychological therapy shows the greatest promise for improving behavior and academic performance. Drug therapy most frequently is used with individuals who demonstrate ADHD. The two most common drugs prescribed are methylphenidate (Ritalin) and dextroamphetamine (Dexedrine), both of which are central nervous system stimulants. The use of these

Figure 18-1   Characteristics of the Types of Attention Deficit Disorder

ADHD—Short attention span, easily distractable, difficulty following rules, poor peer relations, low school achievement, poor listening skills,[60] incompleted tasks, impulsive, restless, aggressive, and high incidence of oppositional defiant order (60 percent);[28] over half have learning disabilities, conduct disorders, poor coordination, and obsessive-compulsive disorders[28]

ADD-WO—Loss of thought patterns, prone to daydreaming, deficits in focused attention, socially withdrawn, and symptoms of depression and anxiety;[52] at significant risk for academic failure because of depressed math, spelling, and reading performance; high (85.7 percent) incidence of diagnosed learning disability[39]

ADD-R—Identifies the adolescent child or young adult who has not outgrown the syndrome; approximately 30 to 60 percent of all ADD/HD individuals do not outgrow the syndrome[8]

drugs usually results in dramatic improvement in behavior. Interpersonal interaction improvements result in less conflict with parents, peers, and teachers. Improvements in attentiveness, information processing, and short-term memory result in academic performance gains.[20]

The psychosocial therapies most frequently used are behavior modification, cognitive-behavior therapy, and family therapy.[28] Behavior modification includes daily reporting about the frequency of problem behaviors, with positive reinforcement for compliance. Cognitive-behavior therapy involves focusing on demonstrated academic deficits and making accommodations for those deficits. Family therapy entails working with the family in counseling sessions and/or through support groups.[83]

Testing

The heterogeneous nature of the ADD group makes it difficult to generalize about testing needs. A recent study indicated that, as a group, individuals between the ages of seven and twelve years with ADHD demonstrated below-average fitness, fundamental gross motor skills, locomotor skills, and object-control skills.[26] It has been reported that, when individuals are involved in drug therapy, although motor performance is not improved, attention and concentration do improve. At the same time, aggressiveness is reduced.[28]

Physical and motor tests should be administered to determine the functioning levels of the youngster with ADD. Particular attention should be paid to evaluating the status of the neurological building blocks, as well as the integration processes of the individual under twelve years of age. The Bruininks-Oseretsky Test of Motor Proficiency augmented by visual screening should provide a wide range of information for the physical educator. After age twelve years, focus should be placed on evaluating the components of the types of activities that can be accessed in the community that the family can participate in.

Teaching Strategies

The decision of which teaching strategy to use depends on the age and needs of the student. The bottom-up teaching approach using group games for elementary-age children and stations for middle school students can be used to address underlying neurological building block deficits. After age twelve years, a top-down, task-specific approach is best. General points to keep in mind when working with these students are presented in Figure 18-2.

The Physical Education Program

Because of the physical and motor deficits many of these students demonstrate, whenever possible games and activities that limit competition should be stressed. Students with ADD do not need to participate in activities they have little hope of succeeding in. To require them to do so sets them up for failure and contributes to poor self-esteem. The more activities that use an individualized approach and allow the students to work at their own level, the better the chance the students have at succeeding.

Figure 18-2   Tips for Teaching Students with Attention Deficit Disorder
• Change activities frequently to accommodate the short attention span. • Use a positive behavior modification program to keep the student on task. • Incorporate 3 to 5 minutes of conscious relaxation at the end of the physical education period. • Give brief instructions. • Use activities that promote cooperation among all students (e.g., new games).

Community-Based Opportunities

Individuals who do not grow out of their attention deficit disorder frequently experience great difficulty completing school and taking a position in the community that is commensurate with their intelligence. These individuals often do not complete high school, usually take lower-status jobs, and have higher rates of antisocial personality. In addition, adolescents and young adults with ADD have a greater frequency of substance abuse than those individuals without ADD.[20] All of these prognoses make it crucial that the youngster with ADD be given every opportunity to learn and access activities that involve the entire family, so that family-centered recreation will contribute to the youngster's self-esteem and will promote the skills needed for establishing and maintaining a healthy lifestyle.

AIDS

Acquired immune deficiency syndrome (AIDS) has swept a deadly path throughout the world. Although AIDS was not recognized as a disease entity until 1981, by 1996, 10 million cases had been reported worldwide.[7]

Definition

AIDS is the development of opportunistic infections and/or certain secondary cancers known to be

CASE STUDY

Jimmy

Jimmy is a seven-year-old who was born HIV-positive because his mother had unknowingly been infected with HIV from a blood transfusion she received when she was a young girl. At this point, Jimmy, who is enrolled in the regular second-grade class, does not demonstrate any HIV/AIDS symptoms; however, his mother has alerted the school of his condition.

APPLICATION TASK
What precautions should the elementary physical education teacher take with Jimmy and his class?

associated with human immunodeficiency virus (HIV) infection. HIV disease (all stages of infection before the development of AIDS) is a progressive disease that is a result of the virus's infecting the CD_4 cells of the immune system. As HIV disease progresses, eventually all of the CD_4 cells in the body are depleted, which results in the suppression of the immune system.[34] AIDS is the final stage of a series of diseases caused by HIV infection.

Incidence

AIDS is clearly one of the most serious health problems confronting the United States. As of 1997, there were approximately 581,000 cases of AIDS reported in the United States, and 60 percent of those patients had died.[7] In America, the incidence of AIDS in women has increased rapidly; as of 1997, 20 percent of the reported cases were women.[7] One study reported that 97 percent of the children who test HIV-positive are healthy enough to attend school, and the number of children with HIV infections reaching school age will continue to grow.[14]

Causes

The HIV virus is spread from one person to another via body fluids. The primary transmission fluids are blood and blood products, semen, vaginal secretion, breast milk, and amniotic fluid.[61] In the United States, the high-risk categories for receiving and transmitting the virus are homosexual or bisexual males (58 percent of cases), intravenous drug abusers (23 percent of cases), prostitutes and those who frequent them, transfusion recipients and hemophiliacs (particularly those who received transfusions before 1985), and those who have sexual contact with any of these groups. Worldwide, 75 percent of AIDS cases are a result of heterosexual transmission.[61] A child can get the HIV virus from the mother during pregnancy, childbirth, and breastfeeding.

Characteristics

HIV infection causes a wide range of symptoms ranging from flulike symptoms to full-blown AIDS. There are three recognized stages of development. During stage 1, the person tests positive for HIV, but no symptoms are present. This stage can last as long as ten years. During stage 2, there is severe weight loss and wasting, chronic diarrhea, nonproductive cough with shortness of breath, dementia, fevers of unknown origin, chronic fatigue, swollen lymph glands, and decreased food consumption. With appropriate drug intervention, this stage can last several years. In stage 3, fully developed AIDS is apparent, which puts the individual at risk for infection and malignancy. However, once again, thanks to the advances in the development of antiviral agents and adjunct therapies during the mid 1990s, a relatively high quality of life can be enjoyed for many years.[34]

Special Considerations

Because of the manner in which the virus is spread, caution should be exercised if the child with HIV/AIDS becomes injured and there is blood loss. Although the risk of contracting HIV/AIDS through providing first-aid assistance is minimal, the Universal Precautions to protect against all infectious diseases should be followed. Those precautions state that staff must routinely use appropriate barrier precautions to prevent skin and mucous membrane exposure to blood and body fluids containing visible blood in the following ways:

1. Whenever possible, wear disposable plastic or latex gloves. Use towels or cloth between yourself and blood or body fluids when gloves are not available.
2. Gloves must always be worn whenever you are in contact with blood, body fluids, diapering, or invasive procedures if you have an open wound or lesion.
3. Toys should be cleansed by immersing them in a germicidal solution and rinsed thoroughly after use each day.
4. Cleaning up spills of body fluids requires the use of gloves. All surfaces should be cleansed with a germicide solution and rinsed, then air dried.
5. Soiled cloths and diapers should be placed in a plastic bag and given to the parent to clean at home.
6. Trash should be placed in a plastic bag and tied securely for removal.
7. All staff must use hand-washing techniques between handling each child during feedings, diapers, and nose cleaning.[50]

Athletic governing bodies are becoming more aware of the risks associated with the HIV virus. Rather than ban players known to be HIV-positive from competition, caution should be exercised.[46] Commonsense techniques that can prevent transmission include covering open wounds before competition and removing bleeding players from competition until wounds can be covered. In sports carrying a high risk for bleeding, such as wrestling and hockey, athletes should be encouraged to submit to voluntary testing to determine their HIV status.[63] It is not permissible to exclude individuals who are HIV-positive from activities, even high-risk ones, without supporting medical justification.[46]

Teaching Strategies

All schools should require that HIV infection, HIV diseases, and AIDS information be included in the school curriculum; however, increasingly in the United States sex-related topics are being removed from health education content. To deny a teacher the right to share information critical to a student's health and welfare seems shortsighted and contrary to good educational practice; however, teachers must follow administration policies or risk dismissal. In schools where these topics cannot be included in the curriculum, the school administration should be encouraged to allow medical resources in the community to provide this vital information and to solicit parental support for accessing those professionals.

A student who is HIV-positive can be included in the physical education program without the teacher's being aware of the condition. A physician may not disclose the status of a child's health to a third party without parental consent; however, in many states public health laws require the reporting of HIV cases to a state agency.[46] This information may, or may not, be shared with the school. If the teacher is aware of a student with an HIV condition, precaution should be taken to avoid an injury that leads to bleeding. Most schools have developed policies to follow should such injuries occur. Ways to prevent the possibility of contamination through contact with blood should be part of those policies, and they should be followed to the letter.

If the other students in the class are aware of the presence of a student who is HIV-positive and the school administration and the student approve, a frank discussion with the class should allay fears of the infection's being spread to classmates. Students should understand the condition, as well as the necessary precautions.

As is always the case, a sensitive, knowledgeable teacher who treats all students with respect and courtesy can make a tremendous difference in the quality of interaction that occurs in a class. Teachers must set the pace for the class by always presenting themselves as accepting, caring individuals who value all students. McHugh[41] provides several suggestions of ways teachers can address students' social needs in the physical education setting. The ideas she presents could be incorporated into any physical education class but would be particularly effective in a class where one or more students were differently abled. Those suggestions include (1) naming a most valuable person each day in physical education class (chosen alphabetically) and honor that person throughout the day; and (2) send home a Sunshine Gram once a month acknowledging children's positive qualities.

The Physical Education Program

Children in the public school who are HIV-positive should have an individual education program (IEP) commensurate with their needs. Because exercise has shown to be helpful in delaying the progress of the disease, physical activities are recommended.[80] The physical education teacher should consult with each student's physician to determine activity levels. Because of the progressive nature of HIV diseases, students' levels of physical and motor performance should be assessed frequently and their program modified to accommodate their levels of function. Surburg[71] has suggested that procedures to follow when implementing physical education programs for high school students with HIV/AIDS should include

providing appropriate rest periods, monitoring pulse rate, generally increasing the intensity level of exercise, and reducing activity in hot and/or humid conditions. However, for children who are rapidly deteriorating physically, it may be realistic to develop a program that will promote the maintenance of existing skills and capabilities. Each child with HIV/AIDS is different because of the many different forms of the illness; however, the ultimate goal should always be to include the student in as many activities as possible. The limitations to expect during physical activity (including testing) and the effects of exercise on individuals with HIV/AIDS are presented in Figure 18-3.

Modifications, Adaptations, and Inclusion Techniques

Although some lower federal courts have ordered HIV-positive youth not to participate in school-sponsored contact sports, that position conflicts with U.S. Supreme Court authority.[46] The teacher cannot arbitrarily exclude a student from an activity without supporting medical justification. Rather, if the student who is HIV-positive has been identified, and his or her physician contacted for

Figure 18-3   Limitations and Results of Exercise on Individuals with Various Stages of HIV Infection

Stage	Limitations	Results of exercise
1	No limitations for most	Increase in CD_4 cells Possible delay in onset of symptoms Increase in muscle function and size
2	Reduced exercise capacity Reduced VO_2 max Reduced heart rate and breathing reserve	Increase in CD_4 cells Possible diminished severity of symptoms
3	Dramatically reduced exercise capacity More severe VO_2 limitations than in Stage 2	Effects on CD_4 cells are unknown. Effects on symptoms are inclusive.

Modified from LaPerriere A, Klimas N, Major P, Perry A: Acquired immune deficiency syndrome. In Durstine JL, editor: *Exercise management for persons with chronic diseases and disabilities,* Champaign, IL, 1997, Human Kinetics.

program suggestions, modifications, and limitations, the teacher should discuss the content of the student's physical education program with the student. It is critical that the student understand the potential for injury in the various activities included in the program and be given the option to participate or select an alternative. Should the student decide to engage in all the class activities, the teacher is responsible for keeping the potential for injury to a minimum.

Community-Based Opportunities

The Americans with Disabilities Act of 1990 prohibits unjustified discrimination against all persons with disabling conditions.[46] All members of the community should have an opportunity to select the types of leisure activities they enjoy and can afford. It should be no different for the individual who is HIV-positive. In most of the larger communities in the United States, support groups for individuals who are HIV-positive have been formed and are available for the asking. Individuals who make up these support groups should encourage the person who is HIV-positive to enjoy those activities for which he or she has the interest and strength. As is always the case, precautions should be taken should an injury occur that results in bleeding.

ANEMIA

Definition

Anemia is a condition of the blood in which there is a deficiency of red cells or hemoglobin (a molecule in red blood cells that carries oxygen) in circulation.[7] There are several forms of anemia, which are classified as either acquired or congenital.[5] Examples of each are presented in Figure 18-4.

Anemia requires medical intervention for management. The usual treatment involves nutritional supplements and/or transfusion. Anemia caused by disease is addressed by treatment of the disease.

Iron deficiency is commonly seen in teenage girls and especially so in those who are active in sports. Care must be taken that nonanemic iron deficiency does not lead to anemic iron deficiency.

Figure 18-4   Types of Anemia

Acquired

- Nutritional, such as iron, B_{12}, or folic acid deficiency
- Acute or chronic blood loss, as from a peptic ulcer or hemorrhoids
- A result of disease, such as leukemia, juvenile rheumatoid arthritis, destruction of red cells by abnormal antibodies formed in a disease state

Congenital

- Sickle cell
- Sperocytosis (abnormal red cell membranes)

CASE STUDY

Sharone

Sharone is a ten-year-old boy with sickle cell anemia. Sharone loves physical education and dreams of playing professional football. However, he tires very quickly when he is involved in active play. He is very defensive about his anemia and tends to become disruptive in class rather than admit that he needs to stop and rest. In response to frustration if he cannot complete a task, he has occasionally become verbally and physically aggressive.

His object-control skills are excellent. He has acquired and uses, with ease, all of the basic locomotor skills: walk, run, gallop, jump, hop, and skip. His physical fitness scores are, however, below average. He can complete only four full push-ups in 1 minute. He is able to do nine abdominal curls in 1 minute. He is able to walk one-half mile in 18 minutes.

APPLICATION TASK
What can the physical educator do to help Sharone manage his behavior in the gymnasium?

Sickle cell anemia, one of the most well-known forms of anemia, is an inherited disorder. In this form of anemia, not all of the person's hemoglobin works correctly. Some of the hemoglobin forms rodlike structures that cause the blood cells to be sickle-shaped and stiff. These cells clog small blood vessels and prevent some tissues and organs from receiving adequate amounts of oxygen. When this occurs, severe pain results, and damage to organs and tissues frequently occurs.[30] Specific sites of the body that are most commonly affected by sickle cell anemia are the bones (usually the hands and feet in young children), intestines, spleen, gallbladder, brain, and lungs. Chronic ankle ulcers are a recurrent problem. Episodes of severe abdominal pain with vomiting may simulate severe abdominal disorders. Such painful crises usually are associated with back and joint pain. Sickle cell anemia affects only individuals of African descent.[7] Individuals from Mediterranean, Middle Eastern, and Indian ancestry have a similar form of anemia, which results from unbalanced hemoglobin synthesis.[7]

Sports anemia afflicts athletes with low values of red blood cells or hemoglobin. These athletes may range from fit individuals performing daily submaximum exercise to individuals participating in prolonged severe exercise and strenuous endurance training. Sports anemia is a consequence of physical activity and is only marginal.[12]

Incidence

The prevalence of iron deficiency anemia for adolescent girls and adult women in the United States is 2 percent and 5 percent, respectively; the reported incidence in high school and college female athletes ranges as high as 19 percent. In the United States, estimates of nonanemic iron deficiency, which can, if uncorrected, lead to iron deficiency anemia, are 11 percent for adult women and 9 percent for adolescent girls.[38] The sickle cell anemia trait is carried by about 8 percent of African Americans and over 17 percent of black Africans.[19] Over 100,000 babies are born each year with sickle cell disease.[7]

Causes

There are many causes of anemia, which can be categorized as either congenital or acquired. The congenital form is present at birth. An example of this form is sickle cell anemia. The acquired form may occur at any time during one's life and persist or move into remission. Some of the specific causes of anemia are as follows:

- Iron deficiencies in the diet
- Inadequate or abnormal utilization of iron in the blood
- Menstrual loss (a primary source of iron loss in females)
- Chronic posthemorrhaging when there is prolonged moderate blood loss, such as that caused by a peptic ulcer
- Acute posthemorrhaging caused by a massive hemorrhage, such as a ruptured artery
- Decreased production of bone marrow
- Vitamin B_{12} deficiency
- Deficiency in folic acid, which is destroyed in long-term cooking
- Mechanical injury or trauma that impacts blood circulation
- Gastrointestinal loss, common in runners
- Urinary loss in the presence of urinary tract trauma
- Sweat loss when exercise is prolonged
- Disorders of red blood cell metabolism
- Defective hemoglobin synthesis[7,25,44]

Primary diseases that give rise to anemia as a secondary condition include malaria, septic infections, and cirrhosis. In addition, poisons such as lead, insecticides, intestinal parasites, and arsenobenzene may contribute to anemia. Diseases associated with endocrine and vitamin deficiencies, such as chronic dysentery and intestinal parasites, can also cause anemia.

Characteristics

The physical education teacher should be aware of the characteristics that anemic persons display. Some of the symptoms that signify anemia are an increased rate of breathing, a bluish tinge of the lips and nails (because the blood is not as red), headache, nausea, faintness, weakness, and fatigue. Severe anemia results in vertigo (dizziness),

Figure 18-5   Performance Effect of Iron
Deficiency Anemia

Diminished VO_2 max
Decreased physical work capacity
Lowered endurance
Increased lactic acidosis
Increased fatigue

tinnitus (ringing in the ears), spots before the eyes, drowsiness, irritability, and bizarre behavior.[7] The performance effects of iron deficiency anemia are presented in Figure 18-5.

Testing

The student with anemia should be tested to determine the present level of physical fitness. Any standardized test may be used, as long as the teacher shortens the performance time during cardiovascular endurance activities. Selby[61] recommends using a 6-minute walk for testing CV endurance. Motor skills can be evaluated using the TGMD for elementary children and the OSU-Sigma for middle and high school students.

Special Considerations

Anemia is symptomatic of a disturbance that in many cases can be remedied. Persons who have anemia because of a disease process have different medical needs than athletes with sports anemia who are apparently healthy. The school nurse should be alerted if a student is suspected of being anemic. The nurse will be able to recommend specific medical intervention to enable treatment to be determined and initiated. Inasmuch as there are several varieties of anemia, the method of treatment depends on the type of anemia present. Treatment of iron deficiency anemia usually involves physician-directed iron supplementation. Physicians usually prescribe several months of iron therapy coupled with supplements of vitamin C for individuals who are nonanemic iron deficient.[25]

Aplastic anemia may be corrected by transplantation of bone marrow from healthy persons and by use of the male hormone testosterone, which is known to stimulate the production of cells by the bone marrow if enough red marrow is present for the hormone to act on. Vitamin B_{12} is stored in the liver and is released as required for the formation of red blood cells in the bone marrow.

There is no drug therapy for sickle cell anemia. The symptoms are treated as they appear. The initial symptoms of overexertion are headache or dizziness, leg cramps, chest pain, and/or left upper quadrant pain.[19] Continuing exercise under those conditions can lead to coma and/or death. Individuals with sickle cell anemia should avoid maximum effort exercise when unconditioned, in hot weather, or when new to a high altitude.[19] Coaches are advised that during preseason conditioning all athletes should train wisely, stay hydrated, heed environmental stress, and be alert to reactions to heat.[19]

Teaching Strategies

The alert physical educator should be able to assist in the identification of anemia and thus refer the student to medical authorities. Undiagnosed anemia may curtail motor skill and physical development and thus may set the child apart from peers in social experiences. The student who has been identified as having anemia should be evaluated to determine physical fitness and motor skill development levels, so that an appropriate intervention program can be started.

The primary difficulty the student will experience is lowered stamina. Both the teacher and the student must be sensitive to the need to curtail activity levels, so that the student does not overexert during the physical education class period. Indications that the student is reaching a point of fatigue include loss of body control (e.g., running into other players, stumbling or falling frequently), irritability, loss of temper, breathlessness, and an unwillingness to continue to participate. Should any of these behaviors appear, if the student does not ask to sit out, the teacher should insist on an immediate rest period. The student will be the best judge of when to return to activity. In the meantime, the teacher should offer encouragement and be supportive.

The Physical Education Program

The final decision regarding the nature of physical education activities for a student with anemia should be made by medical personnel. A well-conceived and supervised physical education program can be of great value because exercise stimulates the production of red blood cells through the increased demand for oxygen. However, to be beneficial, an activity must be planned qualitatively with regard to the specific anemic condition. It is not uncommon for children who have anemia to be delayed in the development of physical strength and endurance.

Modifications, Adaptations, and Inclusion Techniques

For the most part, students with anemia can participate in physical activities in the regular program; however, they should be closely monitored. Appropriate activities include modified (if needed) activities and prerequisite activities such as balance, eye-hand coordination, gross body coordination, and agility, as well as physical fitness components such as strength, endurance, and flexibility. Experiences that minimize access to a ready supply of oxygen, such as underwater swimming where students may be required to hold their breath for prolonged periods, should be avoided.[18]

Community-Based Opportunities

Individuals who have been provided with information about the impact of anemia on physical performance and stamina while in school will be alert to signs and symptoms that emerge after the school years. Medical advice should always be sought because most types of anemia can be treated and physical fitness levels restored. However, adults with anemia should participate in physically demanding activities only under the supervision of a physician or physical therapist.

ASTHMA

Definition

Asthma is a pulmonary disease characterized by reversible airway obstruction, airway inflammation, and increased airway responsiveness to a variety of stimuli.[7]

Incidence

There are approximately 12 million persons with asthma in the United States,[7] 13 percent of whom

---

CASE STUDY

Anna

Anna is a ten-year-old girl attending a rural elementary school within 15 miles of a major industrial city. Anna has asthma, complicated by allergies to ragweed and cedar elm. Her asthma symptoms increase dramatically on days on which the pollution count is particularly high and becomes very ill on days on which there is an ozone alert.

Anna's mother has been very overprotective. She provides countless physician's excuses so that Anna is not able to participate regularly in her school's physical education program. Her lack of activity has contributed to obesity, which has created a vicious cycle; it is difficult for her to move, so she doesn't move, so she becomes more obese, and her asthma symptoms increase in severity.

APPLICATION TASK

With a partner, role play. One person is the physical educator trying to convince the mother to allow Anna to participate in physical education. The partner is the mother trying to explain why she doesn't.

are under the age of seventeen years.[47] It is more common in males than in females (3 : 2 ratio). Asthma is the number one chronic condition causing school absenteeism.[7]

Causes

The disease is a result of the body's reaction to an allergen such as animal dander, mold spores, pollens, or house dust mites or to a nonallergenic stimulus such as cold air or exercise. The airways become obstructed because of a combination of factors, including a spasm of smooth muscle in the airways, edema of mucosa in the airways, increased mucus secretion, infiltration of the cells in the airway walls, and eventual permanent damage to the lining of the airways.[7] Asthma can be controlled by medications; however, nonadherence by children with asthma ranges from 17 to 90 percent.[17]

Characteristics

The symptoms of asthma vary widely. Some asthmatics just wheeze and have a dry cough. Others have a tight chest, wheeze and cough frequently, and have increased difficulty breathing following exposure to allergens, viral infections, and exercise.[7] An attack usually begins with an irritating cough, and the student complains of a tightness in the chest and difficulty breathing, especially during inspiration. The severity of the attack can be measured by the symptoms (see Figure 18-6). The early warning signs of an asthmatic attack are (1) a feeling of pressure on the chest, (2) chronic, persistent cough, (3) shortness of breath, (4) exercise intolerance, (5) sore throat, (6) restlessness, (7) headache, (8) runny nose, (9) clipped speech, (10) changes in breathing patterns, and (11) change in face color.[2]

Exercise-induced asthma (EIA) is acute airway narrowing after strenuous exertion.[72] The symptoms include chest tightness, shortness of breath, coughing, wheezing, fatigue, and prolonged recovery time.[59] The reaction begins after exercise, the reaction peaks in 8 to 15 minutes, and recovery usually occurs spontaneously in about 60 minutes after exercise. A second reaction 3 to 9 hours after

Figure 18-6   Levels of Severity of an Asthma Attack[7]

Stage	Symptoms and signs
I: Mild	Adequate air exchange, mild shortness of breath, diffuse wheezing
II: Moderate	Respiratory distress at rest, marked wheezing, use of accessory muscles to breathe, difficulty breathing
III: Severe	Marked respiratory distress, cyanosis, inability to speak more than a few words, marked wheezing, and use of accessory muscles to breathe
IV: Respiratory failure	Severe respiratory distress, lethargy, confusion, marked use of accessory muscles to breathe

exercising also can occur. About 50 percent of asthmatics have a refractory period of 2 to 4 hours after ceasing to exercise. During the refractory period, their airways respond to a second bout of exercise 50 percent better than during the initial exercise period.[59] EIA affects 12 to 15 percent of the population.[59]

Testing

The medical history of the student with asthma should always be reviewed before testing.[70] Particular attention should be paid to whether the student has EIA, what medications are being taken, and the student's normal activity level. No modifications of test procedures are necessary unless indicated in the medical history; however, cardiovascular endurance tests should not be given when the student is experiencing any upper respiratory distress, either as a result of a cold or in response to pollen, mold, dust, or dry, cold air. The student with asthma should be monitored during testing for signs of distress and allowed to determine the need to discontinue. If a fitness test is being used to measure cardiovascular endurance, a 10-minute gradual warm-up should take place.[72] The test should start slowly until the target heart rate is reached and then should continue for 8 to 10 minutes.[15] Strength testing or training that involves lifting heavy weights while holding the breath or sustaining forced expiration should be avoided.[47]

Special Considerations

Most individuals with asthma who are under a physician's care take either oral or inhaled medication to control their condition. The use of medication before exercise will allow most individuals with asthma to perform to the level of their nonasthmatic peers. Two categories of medications are used to reverse or prevent airflow obstruction for both acute and chronic asthma: anti-inflammatory agents and bronchodilators.[9] Corticosteroids (taken orally, intravenously, or as an inhalant) and nonsteroidal inhalants such as cromolyn sodium are used to control inflammation. Bronchodilators include beta2-agonists and methylxanthines such as theophylline.[9] Beta2-agonists are the most effective bronchodilators to prevent and reverse EIA. One or two doses just before exercise will greatly enhance the student's ability to persist with an exercise bout. Those who do not benefit from beta2-agonist inhalants frequently use the nonsteroidal inhalant cromolyn sodium because it blocks the postexercise bronchoconstriction that occurs several hours after exercise.[4] The usual respiratory medications are not effective in preventing or reducing ozone-induced pulmonary effects.[28]

Teaching Strategies

It is important for individuals with asthma to participate in the regular physical education class because of the physical and psychological benefits of exercise and the opportunities to socialize with classmates. Individual attention should be provided when needed to give the student the opportunity to develop sport skills to gain greater status and recognition by others.[47] As is always the case, an understanding and sensitive teacher can make the difference between an outstanding experience and a devastating one. The teacher must be aware of the student's condition, limitations, and anxieties in order to adjust the activity demands on the student and to foster understanding among other students in the class. A moderate or severe asthma attack can be very frightening to the child who is having the attack, as well as to the classmates who observe it. The teacher should request permission from the parents and the child who has asthma to provide information about asthma to the entire class.

The Physical Education Program

Inasmuch as children with asthma vary in their capabilities to participate in intense activity, each student's physical education program should be individualized as much as possible. This is not to say the program should be watered down for these students. Clearly, many persons with asthma are world-class athletes. In fact, 10 to 15 percent of Olympic athletes have exercise-induced asthma.[70] Thus, assumptions should not be made about the physical capabilities of students with asthma. For the most part, students with asthma can participate in the regular program without modification; however, environmental controls, special instruction in breathing and conscious relaxation, and a carefully controlled progressive exercise program are critical for these students.

The person with asthma must be selective about when and where to exercise. Gong and Krishnareddy[22] recommend limiting outdoor exercise to early morning or evening to avoid peak airborne allergen levels. Also, whenever possible, exercising in cold and dry environments, as well as outside on high-ozone- and/or allergen-level days, should be avoided.[21] Swimming in a heated pool and walking indoors are the least reaction-provoking activities; however, scuba diving is contraindicated for this population.[47]

All students should be taught to breathe through the nose and be given training in abdominal breathing. Breathing through the nose allows the air to warm as it enters the body and controls the rate of expiration. Conscious relaxation and abdominal breathing are recommended as part of the cooldown to reduce postexercise reactions.[47] Abdominal (deep) breathing can be accomplished by having the students lie on their backs on the floor and place one or both hands on their abdomens as they proceed with the following instructions:

1. Inhale slowly and naturally through the nose deep enough to push the diaphragm down (which will cause the hands on the abdomen to rise).
2. Exhale slowly against pursed lips to keep the small airways open.
3. Pause without holding the breath and count to self 1,001, 1,002. During this pause, allow the exhalation to come to a natural, unforced conclusion.
4. Repeat the first three steps for several minutes.

Abdominal breathing exercises will increase the strength and endurance of the respiratory muscles and will allow greater amounts of air to be inhaled and to be made available for exercise. Students with asthma should be cautioned that breathing in this manner may initially increase their phlegm and cause them to cough and wheeze. After extended training, those reactions will be greatly reduced.

At the elementary school level, every class should end with 3 to 4 minutes of relaxation techniques. At the middle and high school levels, relaxation sessions should be included at the end of any class using high-cardiovascular endurance activities. Training in relaxation is particularly critical for the individual with asthma because the practice can be used to lower the impact of anxiety on the body. When an individual's anxiety level is lowered, the tendency to cough and wheeze is also reduced. Several relaxation techniques are described in Appendix A.

Progressive exercise programs are a must for the individual with compromised endurance, whether it be a result of asthma, a sedentary lifestyle, or some other reason. Regular exercise that is gradu-

ally increased in frequency and intensity will improve respiration, circulation, physical functioning, and muscle strength.[67] Training outcomes for the student with asthma will include (1) increased physical exercise capacity at which one can exercise before lactate begins to accumulate in the blood, (2) reduced residual volume of the lungs due to less air being trapped in the lungs, (3) a more efficient pattern of respiration due to slower and deeper breathing, and (4) increased maximal attainable rate of ventilation due to less air being needed to perform submaximal work.[47] Elementary school children will benefit from a movement education program that is essentially self-paced; older students require an ongoing physical fitness program that is designed to meet their specific needs. Specific exercise guidelines are presented in Figure 18-7. See Chapter 8 for information on developing physical fitness programs.

Modifications, Adaptations, and Inclusion Techniques

Unless a physician indicates otherwise, no special modifications other than allowing the student to

Figure 18-7   Exercise Guidelines for Individuals with Asthma
1. Choose exercises that can be performed in a warm, humid environment, such as a pool. 2. If exercising outside in cold weather, wear a scarf or mask over the mouth to limit exposure to cold and pollutants. 3. Breathe through the nose whenever possible to warm and humidify inspired air. 4. Work out inside when pollutant or allergen levels are high outside. 5. Do 5 to 10 minutes of stretching and breathing exercises before a high-intensity workout. 6. Work out slowly for the first few minutes after warm-up. 7. Do a 10- to 20-minute cooldown after a workout.

From Gong H, Krishnareddy S: *Physician Sportsmed* 23(7): 35–42, 1995.

reduce his or her activity level and rest when needed are required for the student with asthma. However, until the student has developed skills and fitness levels commensurate with his or her peers, the student's progress should be carefully monitored to ensure ease of participation and continual improvement. The student should be given responsibility for taking the appropriate dosage of medication before exercise and regulating his or her exercise pace. To keep the student's anxiety about the possibility of an asthma attack to a minimum, the teacher should ensure that the appropriate program is followed, should be attentive to the status of the student, and should provide needed encouragement. If a student experiences an asthmatic attack, the procedure presented in Figure 18-8 is recommended.

Community-Based Opportunities

Adults with asthma should be given every opportunity to participate in ongoing exercise programs of their choice. Students who have been carefully taught about healthful exercise practices will continue to accrue benefits from regular exercise during their adult years. Adults who have not received appropriate instruction during their school years should seek out a health club or a university that employs a certified exercise physiologist who will provide the needed testing and exercising information.

Figure 18-8	Intervention for an Asthma Attack

1. Remove the person from the group to reduce anxiety.
2. Encourage the person to breathe deeply and slowly.
3. Use a beta2 aerosol, preferably albuterol.
4. Have the person get into a comfortable position.
5. Encourage the person to spit if needed to get rid of any mucus plugs.

Modified from Rimmer JH: *Fitness and rehabilitation programs for special populations,* Madison, WI, 1994, Brown & Benchmark.

CHILDHOOD CANCER

Definition

Cancer is a cellular malignancy whose unique characteristic is a loss of normal cell control. The body literally loses control of its cells' growth and the distribution of cells by function. There is a lack of differentiation of cells; the cells tend not to assume a particular function in the body. In addition, these unique, apparently random cells have the ability to invade local, healthy tissues and to metastasize (spread), destroying the healthy cells.[7]

CASE STUDY

Jonathan

Jonathan is a five-year-old boy who was diagnosed with leukemia at age three. After innumerable hospital stays, rounds of chemotherapy, and then, eventually, a bone marrow transplant, John is in a significant period of remission. His parents report that his prognosis is good.

Because Jonathan has spent so little time playing with other children his own age—in actuality, little time playing at all—he has developed no cooperative play skills. Jonathan engages in "onlooker" behavior, watching the other children play.

His leukemia, at this crucial stage in his development, has caused significant motor delays as well. He is able to walk, contralaterally. He can walk up and down stairs but uses a marked-time pattern. He can broad jump 6 inches but is unable to gallop, hop, or skip. He is unable to demonstrate age-appropriate object-control skills.

APPLICATION TASK
Describe some of the strategies the general physical educator might use to help Jonathan learn more age-appropriate play and motor skills. Briefly explain the type of activities that should be avoided during this critical phase of his development.

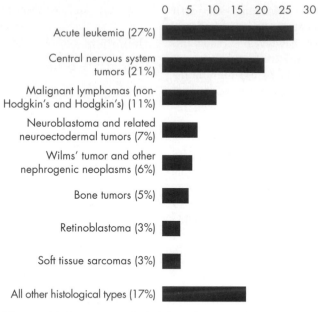

Figure 18-9   Types of Childhood Cancers by Percentage

Data from Gurney GG et al.: *Cancer* 75:2186–2195, 1995.

Incidence

Childhood cancer, a devastating childhood disease, is the major cause of death by disease in children between the ages of one and nineteen years.[23] One in every 330 children in the United States will get cancer before the age of nineteen years.[23] Leukemia accounts for 27 percent, brain tumors 23 percent, lymphomas 11 percent, and all other types 36 percent of all childhood cancers in children under the age of fifteen years.[23]

Causes

The onset of childhood cancer appears to be related to the relationship between the child's genetic/familial endowment and the child's environment. If the child has a chromosomal aberration, as is seen in Down syndrome, trisomy G, and Klinefelter's syndrome, the child is more likely than another to develop childhood cancer.[24] Chromosomal instability also is related to the development of childhood cancers, as are inherited traits

for immunodeficiency. The best example of this is the child born with AIDS; that child is highly likely to develop AIDS-related cancers.

The transformation of a cell from normalcy to malignancy is thought to occur in one cell through a series of two or more steps. The development of cancer cells, or malignancies, is initiated by a cell that is affected by an event. This cell then becomes an "initiated" cell. If this cell is further stimulated by an event, the cell may become precancerous. Any subsequent conversion or modification of this cell causes it to become malignant. Then the malignant cell "clones" itself. It appears that most tumors are clonal expansions of cells that grow unchecked because of acquired changes in the genes that regularly control the growth and development of cells.[79]

Common cancer-causing environmental substances include soot and mineral oil, arsenic, asbestos, hair dyes, painting materials, and lead.[7] If an infant is exposed to a large dose of lead, one of the child's cells may become an initiated cell. If that cell is subsequently exposed to additional large doses of lead, precancerous cell growth may be promoted. Any further modification of the cell may cause it to become malignant and then clone itself, metastasizing into other healthy tissues.[27]

Characteristics

The general symptoms of childhood cancer include the following

- Fatigue
- Weight loss
- Cough
- Changes in blood composition
- Changes in bowel activity
- Persistent pain
- Skeletal pain
- Fever
- Sweating[7]

Types of Childhood Cancers
Leukemia

Leukemia is a condition in which malignant neoplasms (tumors) have a significant negative impact on the blood-forming tissues of the body.[7] The factors that predispose a child to the development of leukemia are the same as those that predispose a child to the development of other forms of childhood cancer. These include the Epstein-Barr virus, the human T-cell lymphotrophic virus, exposure to ionizing radiation, genetic defects (such as Down syndrome), and familial disorders (Fanconi's anemia).[7] Acute leukemia is the most common form of malignancy in childhood.[23] There are two major forms: acute lymphoblastic leukemia (ALL) and acute nonlymphoblastic leukemia (ANLL).

Central Nervous System Tumors

The most common primary childhood brain tumors are astrocytomas, medulloblastomas, and brainstem gliomas.[23] These primary childhood tumors tend to remain confined to tissues within the central nervous system but are devastating in their impact on the total human being. Most of the general signs and symptoms of brain tumors are significantly related to elevated levels of intracranial pressure caused by the presence of abnormal tissue growth.[7,16]

Hodgkin's Disease

Hodgkin's disease in childhood is similar to the Hodgkin's disease that affects adults. About 15 percent of those affected by Hodgkin's disease are younger than fifteen years of age. It is a chronic condition in which large multinucleated reticulum cells (Reed-Sternberg cells) are present in lymph node tissue or in other nonreticular formation sites. The presence of these cells causes lesions. The primary lesions are located in the lymph nodes, spleen, and bone marrow.

Neuroblastoma

A neuroblastoma is a common solid tumor of childhood of the embryonal neural crest of the sympathetic nervous system. One in 7,000 children under the age of five years is affected. Approximately 75 percent of the cases are found in children under the age of five years.[7,77]

Wilms' Tumor

Wilms' tumor is a malignant embryonal tumor of the kidney. It usually occurs in children under the age of five years, but occasionally in older children. A genetic effect has been identified in some cases.[7]

Soft Tissue Tumors

One of the more common forms of soft tissue tumors in children is rhabdomyosarcoma, representing approximately 65 percent of childhood soft tissue sarcomas.[16] This malignancy affects the muscle tissue. In fact, the malignant cells arise from progenitor cells of the striated muscles.

Bone Tumors

The two best known childhood bone malignancies are Ewing's sarcoma and osteosarcoma. Ewing's sarcoma is the second most common form of malignant primary bone tumor of childhood.[29] It is a round cell bone tumor of childhood. The primary bone tumor usually appears in the extremities and most commonly metastasizes to the lungs and bone marrow. Osteosarcoma is a form of childhood bone cancer that appears between the ages of ten and twenty years. Pain and a noticeable mass are the usual symptoms. It is most common in the knee joint and is highly malignant.

Retinoblastoma

A retinoblastoma is a malignant tumor that arises from the immature retina. The disease may be inherited and has been traced to an autosomal dominant trait.[7] It has a significant negative impact on the child's vision.

Testing

The young child who is just beginning school may be developmentally delayed because of limited opportunities to run and play. An evaluation of basic locomotor and object-control skills, such as the Test of Gross Motor Development, should be administered to identify the level of development. Also, if structural deviations such as functional scoliosis are suspected, a postural examination should be conducted.

No special testing modifications are required for students who have or are recovering from cancer; however, their tolerance for exercise may be considerably lower than that of their classmates. Individuals undergoing chemotherapy or radiation therapy are easily fatigued, however, strength and flexibility testing as well as cardiorespiratory endurance testing are recommended.[62]

When the cardiorespiratory endurance of students who have had cancer is being evaluated, it is recommended that a test requiring minimal endurance be used. A walk/run or a step test should be administered, and the student should be permitted to cease exercising should fatigue set in.

Special Considerations

New and innovative treatments of childhood cancer have increased the likelihood that children who are diagnosed early will have a chance of survival. The remarkable advances in medicine have made it possible for so many to survive that 1 in every 1,000 young adults is a survivor of childhood cancer. Many of these survivors return to school and attempt to restore relative normalcy to their lives. The teacher must be aware of the side effects of the cancer and its treatment and be sensitive to the psychosocial needs of the student.

The side effects of the childhood cancers and their treatments include

- Retardation of growth
- Impaired fertility
- Scoliosis or other skeletal impairments
- Impaired renal, pulmonary, hepatic, and/or cardiac function
- Neuropsychological deficits
- Psychosocial deficits in some cases, including vastly affected peer relationships[33,42,54]

Teaching Strategies

The teacher needs to be sensitive to the physical deficits and needs of the child survivor of cancer and work in close cooperation with the child's physician, rehabilitation therapist, and parents in the development of a program that addresses the unique health needs of the student. In addition, the teacher must be aware of the significant psychosocial effects that a life-threatening illness has on the child, the parents and siblings, members of the extended family, and friends. The child who is able to return to school, to move from the more restricted hospital/homebound education program to the less restricted public school program, will face peers with a history of markedly different experiences. It is frequently difficult for the child to make the transition from a life-and-death situation to a life of play, games, and sports. However, play, games, and sports often serve as a vital link to normalcy for the child.

The Physical Education Program

The physical education program for students recovering from cancer should be designed to meet demonstrated specific needs. If the child's physical development lags behind his or her peers, opportunities should be provided to promote development in the needed area. In elementary schools where a movement education program is in place, it is relatively easy to provide for individual differences. In more structured educational settings, care must be taken not to place the child in a game or play situation beyond his or her capabilities. These children should be assigned less active roles that will enable them to participate as they gain the needed skills and performance levels of their classmates. Highly competitive activities should be avoided, so that these students are not placed in a situation where the level of play creates a potential for injury, or where their need to restrict their all-out efforts results in negative reactions from teammates. Physical fitness regimens should begin at the student's present level of performance and slowly build toward higher levels of fitness. Children who have been cured of leukemia frequently have cardiovascular limitations; therefore, their aerobic exercise should be at submaximal levels.[62] Also, if a postural deviation is identified during testing, a corrective program should be initiated (see Appendix A).

Modifications, Adaptations, and Inclusion Techniques

When a child returns to school after an extended absence because of cancer, special efforts should be made to help the child feel as one with his or her peers. Integration into educational settings could be aided by assigning buddies to interact with the student in various settings (e.g., lunch, physical education, art, field trips). The activity level the student is capable of maintaining is usually low because of the period of inactivity, as well as the therapeutic intervention. Regardless of the student's age, he or she must always be given the responsibility for self-regulating involvement in activity and determining when a rest period is needed.

Community-Based Opportunities

The student who has been given appropriate instruction in developing and maintaining a healthy lifestyle should continue to do so after leaving the school setting. The student who has been instructed in a variety of activities that are available in most communities will have the skills he or she needs to select from a variety of options.

CYSTIC FIBROSIS

Definition

Cystic fibrosis is a disease of the exocrine glands primarily affecting the gastrointestinal and respiratory systems.[7] The primary organs affected are the lungs, pancreas, intestines, and sweat glands.[13]

Incidence

The disease affects 1 in every 3,300 Caucasian births, 1 in every 15,300 African American births,

---

CASE STUDY

Pat

Pat is a third-grader with cystic fibrosis. An excellent student, she tires easily and resents time she needs to miss class for therapeutic treatments in the school nurse's office. She is acutely aware of the prognosis associated with cystic fibrosis. A gutsy little girl, she wants to make the most of every day.

Because of frequent and extended hospital stays, and periods of time when difficulty breathing has compromised her ability to participate in general physical education, her gross motor skills are typical of a younger child age five years. She is unable to participate in any vigorous aerobic activity—running, bicycling, and so on.

APPLICATION TASK
Describe some activities typically associated with the third-grade curriculum—jumping rope, tumbling, low-organized games, lead-up games to team sports—and explain how the general physical education teacher can involve Pat.

and 1 in every 32,000 Asian American births.[7] During the past 50 years the median life span of individuals with cystic fibrosis has improved from 4.5 to 31 years.[7] Survival prospects are significantly better in patients without pancreatic insufficiency.

Causes

Cystic fibrosis is an inherited disorder that is generally fatal. It is the most common life-shortening genetic disease in the Caucasian population.

Characteristics

The disease is characterized by the production of abnormally thick mucus, impaired absorption of fat and protein, a high concentration of sodium and chloride in the sweat, and progressive lung damage. As the disease progresses, pulmonary function deteriorates, and exercise tolerance diminishes.[49]

The symptoms and severity of cystic fibrosis vary from apparently normal to markedly impaired health. Nearly all of the exocrine glands are affected to some degree. The lungs appear normal at birth, but thick mucus secretions eventually clog the bronchial tubes and impair breathing.[7] There is usually continuing destruction of pancreatic tissue. Older children may also have diabetes. There is considerable variance in the physical capabilities among children with cystic fibrosis.

Testing

Each program should be tailored to the individual's physical capability. Any standard motor development or motor proficiency test can be administered to students with cystic fibrosis. However, if a cardiovascular endurance test is going to be administered to determine exercise tolerance and maximum heart rate, the student's physician must be contacted to provide pulmonary function advice and clearance. Regardless of how the cardiovascular endurance measure is made, the initial pace should be slow and the increment gradual. Heart rate should be monitored constantly. Because individuals with cystic fibrosis have limited ventilation capacity, they may have to cease

exercise before their maximum heart rate is reached.[49] If a treadmill or bicycle ergometer protocol is used, steady state can be assumed to have been reached between 4 and 5 minutes after the start of the exercise.[13] When measuring CV endurance, a self-paced 6-minute walk test is recommended.[49] Should the individual show signs of pallor and/or breathlessness at any time, testing should be discontinued.

Special Considerations

Increased understanding about cystic fibrosis and the value of aggressive intervention programs has resulted in improved prognosis over the past fifty years. Successful intervention includes a special diet, control of infection, pulmonary therapy, and physical exercise.

Diet

To offset the undernourishment that results from underabsorption of fat and protein, additions to the diet and supplements are used. The recommended special diet includes an intake of calories and protein that exceeds the Recommended Dietary Allowance (RDA) by 30 to 50 percent and a normal-to-high total fat intake. Twice the recommended daily allowance of multivitamins and supplemental vitamin E in water-miscible form are used to strengthen the immune system. Salt supplements during periods of exposure to high temperature and sweating reduces the chances of heat-associated illnesses.[7]

Control of Infection

A high incidence of pulmonary infections requires intermediate to long-term use of antibiotics, depending on the individual. The use of ibuprofen has been shown to slow the rate of pulmonary function decline in children five to thirteen years of age.[7] Vitamin K supplements are recommended for individuals receiving long-term antibiotic therapy and/or individuals with liver involvement.[7] Immunizations against whooping cough, measles, and flu are routine.

Pulmonary Therapy

Progressive bronchiolar and bronchial obstruction leads to infection of the bronchi and breakdown of lung tissue. Every effort is made to clear the bronchi of thick mucus that accumulates continually. Pulmonary involvement leads to death in over 90 percent of individuals with cystic fibrosis. Pulmonary therapy to lessen the accumulation of mucus consists of postural drainage, percussion, vibration, and assistance with coughing on indication of pulmonary involvement. Oral and aerosol bronchodilators are also used to reverse airway obstruction.[7] In severe cases, the constant use of supplemental oxygen is necessary.

Teaching Strategies

It may be helpful for physical education teachers to understand the behavior and medical treatments of individuals with cystic fibrosis. Some common behaviors and/or needs they demonstrate include

- They need to cough out the mucus in their lungs. Therefore, they should be encouraged to do so. Other students in the class need to understand that cystic fibrosis is not a communicable disease.
- The student's diet may be different from the norm; as such, the child may need to make frequent trips to the restroom.
- Although individuals with cystic fibrosis may have less stamina than others, it is important that they participate in modified physical activity commensurate with their abilities.
- Some may be on medication for both pancreatic and lung involvement and may subsequently need to take medication during physical education class.
- Some individuals may also demonstrate asthma or exercise-induced asthma and will require the use of bronchodilator therapy prior to physical activities.[49] Aerosol bronchodilator drugs are helpful in some cases and may need to be administered in class.
- Precautions should be taken to minimize the probability of respiratory infections.
- Teenagers frequently demonstrate a declining tolerance for exercise. Their physical education activity should be modified accordingly.

The Physical Education Program

Studies have demonstrated that individuals who have cystic fibrosis can benefit greatly from participating in regular exercise. Ongoing exercise programs have been shown to improve the flow of mucus from the lungs, build endurance of the breathing muscles, and improve the clinical status, sense of well-being, overall morale, and independence.[49] The primary aim of exercise should be to improve aerobic fitness. Twenty to thirty minutes of continuous aerobic exercise at a moderate intensity is recommended.[49]

The physical education program for young children with cystic fibrosis should not differ from that of their classmates. Students at the middle and high school levels should be encouraged to participate within their own limitations. They should be discouraged from engaging in highly competitive sports where there are pressures to exercise beyond what is a safe level for the individual.[13] Their individual physical fitness program should begin with low-intensity exercise and gradually increase to a target intensity of 50 to 70 percent of maximum heart rate for 20 to 30 minutes per session.[13] Three to five times weekly is recommended, unless the person has severe dysfunction, in which case days of rest must be interspersed with exercise days.[13] The types of exercise programs that have been shown to benefit the individual with cystic fibrosis include running, swimming, bicycling, and active play. Neither sky diving nor water diving is recommended for the person who has cystic fibrosis.[13]

Modifications, Adaptations, and Inclusion Techniques

To offset the boredom that can come from participating in repetitious activities involving large groups, it is recommended that individuals be given the opportunity to select from a variety of activities that interest and appeal to them. The greater the amount of selection available to the high school student, the greater their interest and compliance over time.

Community-Based Opportunities

Exercising with others should be promoted. Individuals are more inclined to exercise regularly if they have a friend or family member to share an activity they enjoy. Public and private health clubs in the community can increase interest and participation by offering special exercise opportunities in addition to their usual exercise fare.

DIABETES

Definition

Diabetes is a general term referring to a variety of disorders that are primarily divided into two groups: diabetes mellitus and diabetes insipidus.[8] Diabetes mellitus is a group of diseases characterized by hyperglycemia resulting from defects in insulin secretion, insulin action, or both.[45] Diabetes insipidus results from an inability to concentrate urine in the kidneys. There are two types of diabetes insipidus: pituitary and nephrogenic.

At the recommendation of a committee sponsored by the American Diabetes Association, since 1997 diabetes mellitus, which is the most common form of diabetes, has been divided into the following four classifications:

- Type 1—diabetes mellitus, formerly called insulin-dependent diabetes—IDD or juvenile
- Type 2—diabetes mellitus, formerly called noninsulin-dependent diabetes—NIDD
- Type 3—other specific types of diabetes mellitus
- Type 4—gestational diabetes mellitus[45]

Incidence

Diabetes is reported to be the most complicated disease managed in primary care in the United States.[31] About 14 million Americans are estimated to have diabetes mellitus, with 80 percent diagnosed as having Type 2 diabetes mellitus and 10 percent having Type 1 diabetes mellitus.[37] The incidence of diabetes insipidus is much less prevalent.

Causes

Diabetes mellitus has diverse genetic, environmental, and pathogenic origins.[7] Type 1 results in beta cell destruction, which usually leads to absolute insulin deficiency. Type 2 is characterized by insulin resistance in peripheral tissue and/or insulin secretory defects in a beta cell. Type 3 includes genetic defects of beta cell function, diseases of the exocrine pancreas, genetic defects in insulin action, endocrinopathies, and drug- or chemical-induced diabetes. Type 4, gestational diabetes, is a form of diabetes mellitus that is brought on by the metabolic stress of pregnancy; a genetic basis has not been confirmed.[40]

Both pituitary and nephrogenic diabetes insipidus have genetic bases. Pituitary diabetes in-

---

CASE STUDY

Kaneisha

Kaneisha is a fourteen-year-old girl who has been diagnosed with Type 2 diabetes. Kaneisha and her mother are working with a physician at a local clinic to help her lose weight, manage and control her diet, and increase her exercise and energy expenditure. This is complicated by the fact that Kaneisha is obese and very unfit.

APPLICATION TASK
The physician has recommended that Kaneisha participate in a carefully controlled walking program in general physical education. At the beginning of the semester, Kaneisha was able to walk only 3 minutes without stopping for rest. Her resting pulse was 105 beats per minute; at the end of her 3-minute walk, her pulse was 120 beats per minute. After a 2-minute rest period, her pulse was still 120 beats per minute.

Describe the specific strategies the physical educator would use to increase her aerobic fitness and energy expenditure.

sipidus results from damage to the pituitary and/or hypothalamus, which leads to a deficiency of the antidiuretic hormone (ADH); it can be inherited or acquired. Nephrogenic diabetes insipidus is a genetic disorder that is caused by a lack of response of resorption of the renal tubules. Because fluids are not resorbed in the kidneys, urine is excreted frequently in a nonconcentrated form. The recommended treatment is adequate and ongoing water intake.[7]

Characteristics

In diabetes mellitus, the body is unable to burn up its intake of carbohydrates because of a lack of production of insulin by the pancreas. The lack of insulin in the blood prevents the storage of glucose in the cells of the liver. Consequently, blood sugar accumulates in the bloodstream in greater than usual amounts (hyperglycemia). The chronic hyperglycemia of diabetes mellitus results in long-term damage to, dysfunction of, and failure of various organs, especially the eyes, kidneys, nerves, heart, and blood vessels.

Type 1 diabetes mellitus accounts for 10 to 15 percent of all diabetes mellitus. It must be controlled with insulin. An equal number of males and females are afflicted with the condition. The amount of insulin needed by these individuals varies widely. The biggest risk with this group is to take in more insulin than can be utilized, which will result in a hypoglycemic coma. Although insulin-dependent mellitus can occur at any age, it is usually acquired before age thirty.[7] It is the form that is most prevalent in school-age children. The onset is acute (sudden), and early symptoms include weight loss despite normal or increased dietary intake, frequent urination, and fatigue.[7] Persons with Type 1 diabetes may lower their need for insulin by exercising; however, they must monitor their carbohydrate intake before exercise and their blood sugar before, during, and after exercise, modifying their short-acting insulin injections accordingly.[74]

Type 2 diabetes mellitus is also characterized by hyperglycemia, but, because individuals with this disease usually retain some insulin secretion capability, ongoing insulin therapy is usually not necessary. Its onset is gradual and for years it has been reported that it does not usually occur until after thirty years of age; however, recent studies have documented a rising number of cases being identified in individuals under the age of twenty.[51,57] A far greater number of females than males are afflicted with this form of diabetes. Obesity, a sedentary lifestyle, and a family history of diabetes characterize Type 2 diabetes mellitus. Like Type 1, common symptoms include fatigue; weakness; thirst; frequent urination; lethargy; dry, hot skin; lack of hunger; fruity or winelike odor; heavy, labored breathing; and eventual stupor or unconsciousness.[58]

Type 3, other specific types of diabetes mellitus, results from conditions and syndromes that impact glucose tolerance, such as cystic fibrosis, organ transplants, acromegaly, renal dialysis, and drugs and chemical agents.[7] Care of the person with Type 3 diabetes is tied directly to the primary condition or syndrome.

Type 4, gestational diabetes mellitus, is usually not identified until a woman becomes pregnant. All pregnant women should be screened for this type of diabetes because untreated gestational carbohydrate intolerance results in increased fetal and neonatal loss. The problem occurs in 1 to 3 percent of all pregnancies; however, the incidence is higher in Mexican Americans, Indians, Asians, and Pacific Islanders.[7] Pregnant women with Type 4 diabetes frequently must take insulin during their pregnancy; however, diet modification, moderate exercise, maintenance of normal body weight, and weekly monitoring of glucose levels will also aid in controlling the condition.

Testing

Recommendations for physical fitness testing depend on the person's age, the duration of the diabetes, and existing complications.[1] Because of the impact exercise has on blood glucose levels, the student's physician should be contacted before stressful testing, particularly cardiovascular endurance and/or resistive exercise testing. The testing demands should be discussed with the physician to ensure that the exercise stress levels are within the student's workload capacity. In addition to medical guidance, the physical educator should discuss the type of testing that will be administered with the student before the testing sessions. Every effort should be made to balance the type of testing being done, so that the workload is consistent from one period to the next. Equalizing the workload demands will enable the student to determine appropriate levels of carbohydrate intake, blood glucose levels, and insulin dosage before the exercise period. Adequate amounts of water, and in some cases carbohydrates, must always be available to the student.

Special Considerations

Individuals with diabetes mellitus should be encouraged to exercise because regular, long-term exercise provides many benefits that contribute to control of the disease. However, unless strict food and insulin guidelines are followed, a single exercise bout can lead to negative reactions. Three negative exercise reactions that can occur but are avoidable are hypoglycemia (abnormally low blood sugar level), hyperglycemia (an excess amount of blood sugar), and ketoacidosis.

Hypoglycemia

Hypoglycemia is the greatest concern of the individual who has Type 1 diabetes mellitus. Signs of hypoglycemia include double vision, fatigue, excessive hunger, increased heart rate, nervousness, headache, numbness, palpitations, slurred speech, excessive sweating, and tremor.[74] Taunton and McCargar[73] caution that hypoglycemia can occur during exercise because of the following:

- A greater and often unpredictable amount of glucose is used during exercise.
- Insulin efficiency is enhanced with exercise to an unpredictable extent.
- Counterregulatory hormonal mechanisms are often somewhat impaired during exercise, which may limit glucose release from the liver.

- People often exercise to lose or control weight and are hesitant to eat extra food before exercising.

Because school-age children who are diabetic most frequently have Type 1 diabetes, if they have a negative reaction to exercise, it will probably be in the form of hypoglycemia. Hypoglycemic reactions can occur because of an error in insulin dosage, a missed meal, unplanned exercise, or no apparent cause.[7] A hypoglycemic reaction should be suspected when a student who has Type 1 diabetes mellitus demonstrates any or all of the following symptoms:

> Confusion
> Inappropriate behavior
> Visual disturbance
> Stupor
> Seizures

Should a student have a hypoglycemic reaction in class, the intervention presented in Figure 18-10 should be performed.

Hypoglycemic reactions can be prevented by decreasing insulin or increasing carbohydrate-consumption before, during, and after exercise.

Figure 18-10   Intervention to Counter a Hypoglycemic Reaction

1. Give some form of sugar immediately (improvement should be evident within a few minutes). Use fast-acting sugar in the form of a small box of raisins, 4 ounces of regular (not diet) cola or fruit juice, five small sugar cubes, six or seven life savers, or 1–2 teaspoons of honey.[55]
2. When improvement occurs, give additional food and then have the child resume normal activities.
3. If the child does not improve after sugar intake, call parents, the physician, and emergency medical assistance.
4. If the student becomes unconscious or is unable to take the sugar, immediately call for medical assistance.

There are formulas for determining how much short-acting insulin can be reduced (never change the dosage of long-acting insulin); also, alternate injection sites should be selected (e.g., inject into the abdomen or a limb not used during exercise).

Hyperglycemia

Hyperglycemia is also a problem for the active individual with either Type 1 or Type 2 diabetes mellitus. Hyperglycemia results when daily exercise volume is suddenly reduced without increasing insulin or any oral agents being used to control glucose levels.[73] The symptoms of hyperglycemia are increased thirst and increased urination.

Ketoacidosis

Ketoacidosis is a violent reaction to lack of circulating insulin. It is caused by the failure to take an appropriate dose of insulin or by an acute infection or trauma that requires additional insulin.[7] Students who forget to take their insulin or experience an acute infection or trauma may have a keto-acidotic reaction. Symptoms include

- Abdominal pain
- Dehydration caused by excessive urination
- Drowsiness
- Fruity-smelling breath
- Nausea
- Glucose and ketones in the urine

This condition requires immediate treatment with insulin, fluids, and electrolytes.[73] Delayed intervention can cause lethargy, which may lead to a coma.[7]

Teaching Strategies

The physical educator should be aware of students' individual needs. The school nurse can be very helpful in providing information about students who have existing medical conditions. After students with medical conditions are identified, programs of exercise should be established (with medical counsel) according to the needs of each student. The limits to the activity each diabetic child can perform vary; therefore, it is important that the physical educator be clear about the status of each child.

Information should be gathered from the primary physician, the student, and the student's caregivers. Awareness of the knowledge and attitudes of the student and his or her parents concerning the benefits of physical activity, the extent to which the student is able to monitor his or her own blood sugar levels, and the student's understanding of the condition all impact the type of physical education program the teacher recommends for the student. In addition, once a program of activity is initiated, the teacher has the responsibility for carefully monitoring the student's progress.

Every year more studies validate the roles of exercise and proper diet in the management of diabetes. As this knowledge reaches primary care physicians, they are better able to counsel individuals with diabetes and their caregivers about the importance of maintaining ongoing regimens of appropriate exercise and diet. The knowledgeable physician is the conscientious physical educator's best ally. The physical educator should seek both cooperation and advice from the physician. Information gathered should include the type of diabetes, the type of diet and therapeutic intervention, the knowledge level of the student and the student's parents or caregivers, recommendations of desirable activity levels, and contraindications.

Successful management of diabetes requires that the student participate in a regimen of care. Noncompliance with health practices related to diabetes can have serious short- and long-term effects. In general, a student with Type 1 or Type 2 diabetes mellitus should have the information presented in Figure 18-11.

The Physical Education Program

Regular exercise programs are of value to all individuals with diabetes, and it is particularly important that the child with diabetes be provided proper instruction that can be used throughout life. Exercise is an essential component of an effective treatment program for many diabetics. An

Figure 18-11   Required Practices of Students with Type 1 or Type 2 Diabetes Mellitus

1. Blood sugar levels should be monitored before, during, and after workouts, and the diet should be adjusted to make up for energy lost during exercise. If the blood sugar is less than 100 mg/dl, a snack should be eaten that contains at least 15 to 30 grams of carbohydrate (e.g., a slice of bread or 60 to 120 calories of fruit or crackers).
2. Always eat something 2 to 3 hours before and after exercise.
3. Prevent dehydration by drinking 2 cups of water 2 hours before exercise, 1 to 2 cups 30 minutes before, 1/2 a cup every 15 minutes during exercise, and enough afterward to regain any weight lost during the workout.
4. Spend 5 to 10 minutes warming up before exercising and cooling down after exercising with stretching and slow large muscle activity (e.g., walking, jogging).
5. Exercise with a buddy who knows the signs of hypoglycemia, hyperglycemia, and ketoacidosis.
6. Wear appropriate, well-fitting shoes for the activity (soft leather with few seams are best), and check feet regularly for infected blisters, scratches, or open wounds. Don't ever burst a blister.
7. Carry insulin, oral drugs, or hard candy with you.
8. Wear identification that gives your name, address, parents' home and work phone numbers, physician's name and phone number, and type of diabetes.
9. In addition, a student with type I diabetes should
    a. Keep a logbook to record levels of blood sugar, dosage of insulin, amount and type of food eaten, and type and intensity of exercise. That information will help the student establish the relationship among those factors and be better able to adjust for low and high levels of blood sugar.
    b. Review the effect frequent use of short-acting insulin has on blood sugar levels before, during, and after exercise.
    c. Not exercise if the blood sugar reading is less than 60 mg/dl.
    d. Time exercise to miss the peak period of administered insulin. Begin exercising no earlier than 1 hour after taking the insulin.
    e. Choose insulin administration sites away from actively exercising muscle groups.
    f. Take a high-carbohydrate snack, such as fruit juice, bread, or plain cookies, before exercise. Eat about 15 grams of carbohydrate or more if needed.
    g. For moderate bouts of exercise, reduce the dose of short-acting insulin by 10 percent. For vigorous bouts of exercise, reduce the dose of short-acting insulin by up to 50 percent.
    h. If using only intermediate-acting insulin, reduce the morning dose by 30 to 40 percent for moderate to vigorous exercise in the morning, midday, or early afternoon.
    i. Prevent nighttime hypoglycemia by exercising earlier in the day and by reducing insulin dosages in the evening after exercising. If hypoglycemia persists, monitor blood sugar levels at night and take additional carbohydrates before sleep.

    The teacher may want to develop a checklist with all of this information for the student. Until the routine becomes habitual, the student can refer to the checklist daily and occasionally share the results with the teacher.

Data from Taunton JE, McCargar L: *Physician Sportsmed* 23(3): 55–56, 1995.

exercise program may be helpful in the following ways:

1. It may improve diabetic control by decreasing the insulin requirements for insulin-dependent diabetics.[1,36]
2. Strengthening of skeletal muscles can make a significant contribution to the control of diabetes.[36]
3. It reduces the risk of coronary heart disease by controlling risk factors such as overweight.[1,36]
4. It provides increased stamina and physical functioning to improve work capacity.
5. It provides a sense of well-being and self-confidence.
6. It improves serum lipid levels.[1]
7. It reduces stress.[1]

8. It controls weight.[81]
9. It increases VO2 max.[81]
10. It increases insulin sensitivity.[81]
11. It increases muscular strength.[10,48]

The child with diabetes can and should participate, in general, in the activities of the unrestricted class. However, many diabetic patients are more susceptible to fatigue than are their nondiabetic peers. Therefore, the physical educator should be understanding in the event that the diabetic student cannot withstand prolonged bouts of more strenuous exercise.

The intensity of aerobic activities will be determined by the present levels of performance determined through testing. Individuals who have been sedentary and have not been able to develop adequate physical fitness levels should begin slowly and progress at a rate commensurate with their capability. The student's reactions during and after exercise will dictate the intensity, duration, and frequency levels. Individuals with either Type 1 or Type 2 diabetes mellitus should eventually participate in aerobic activity three to five times weekly for 30 minutes at 50 to 70 percent of maximal oxygen uptake.[72] To sustain that percentage, a heart rate between 100 and 160 should be maintained. Albright[1] suggests a workout should include large-muscle aerobic activities, strength training, stretching, and activity-specific exercise.

Modifications, Adaptations, and Inclusion Techniques

As indicated earlier in this section, it is recommended that the student with diabetes mellitus be included in the regular physical education program but be given the opportunity to rest when needed. To aid the teacher in monitoring student status, a buddy who has been trained to recognize the previously described adverse reactions to exercise should be assigned to exercise with the student with diabetes.

In developing an exercise program, it is desirable to provide activity that meets the student's interests and needs and still uses the large muscles of the body. Sport activity and aerobic exercise, such as walking, jogging, cycling, swimming, and cross-country skiing, are particularly desirable. Adults with Type 1 or Type 2 diabetes mellitus should avoid activities that would place them or others at significant risk of injury, such as scuba diving, hang gliding, parachuting, and automobile racing. Also, individuals with diabetes who develop autonomic neuropathy may bicycle and swim but should probably avoid running and hiking. Should retinopathy develop, activities that cause sudden increases in blood pressure, such as weight lifting, sprints, and other intense exercise, should be avoided.[73]

Community-Based Opportunities

Individuals who have grown up with diabetes and have been provided an appropriate physical education should reach adulthood with all the information necessary to maintain a healthy lifestyle. They should use the public and private recreational facilities of their choice with proper precautions, including alerting supervisory personnel of their condition and wearing identification with diabetic information and the emergency procedure that should be followed if a negative reaction to exercise occurs. If they decide to participate in training regimens for participation in sports, athletes with either Type 1 or Type 2 diabetes should maintain a diet similar to that of nondiabetic athletes. Their diets should be 55 to 65 percent carbohydrate, 10 to 15 percent protein, and 25 to 30 percent fat. Energy and water requirements of these athletes are greater than those of nonaffected athletes.[74]

PRADER-WILLI SYNDROME

Definition

Prader-Willi syndrome is a group of symptoms that begins with hypotonia, a weak cry, and feeding difficulty in infancy. An insatiable appetite and pica behavior (eating indiscriminately—dirt, crayons, paste, paper, etc.), which leads to obesity, begins between two and five years of age and persists throughout life.[53]

CASE STUDY

Bobby

Bobby is a nine-year-old boy with Prader-Willi Syndrome. He is receiving the majority of his educational services in a self-contained classroom for children who have intellectual deficits. Bobby has been tested, on several occasions, and his IQ composite scores range from 58 to 68.

Bobby was tested by an adapted physical education specialist. His scores on the Test of Gross Motor Development showed a significant delay. In fact, his gross motor performance is more typical of a five-year-old than a nine-year-old.

His gross motor performance and his health are seriously compromised by his high body fat percentage. At his last clinical evaluation, Bobby's total body fat percentage was in excess of 35 percent.

He has few friends, even in his self-contained classroom.

APPLICATION TASK

Can Bobby be successful in a general physical education curriculum? If so, what accommodations will the teacher need to make to ensure his success? If not, what can be done for Bobby in a separate adapted physical education class?

Incidence

The incidence of the condition is reported to be 1 in every 12,000 to 15,000 births. Both genders and all races are affected equally.[53]

Causes

The cause of Prader-Willi syndrome is a deletion of portions of, or absence of, the paternally contributed chromosome 15.[76]

Characteristics

Children and adults are short and have small hands and feet, almond-shaped eyes, a triangular-shaped mouth, a prominent nasal bridge, and underdeveloped gonads. Behavior difficulties, including temper tantrums, stubbornness, noncompliance and resistance to change, begin early in childhood and persist throughout adulthood.[53] As a group, individuals with Prader-Willi syndrome are very heterogeneous, with IQs ranging from less than 20 to 100. Individuals with intelligence in the normal range frequently have learning disabilities but demonstrate strong visual-spatial perception.[78]

Testing

A self-testing program in which the learner is actively involved in the evaluation process is best for the student with Prader-Willi syndrome. As with any obese learner, he or she will experience considerable failure and embarrassment if asked to participate, for example, in mass fitness testing. A time should be selected when the teacher can work one-on-one with the student, or the student's movements should be observed during routine class activities.

Special Considerations

The physical educator or adapted physical educator must work closely with the learner's parents. In addition to the physical education program at school, it is vital that the parents engage the child in regular exercise in the home. The physical educator can help the parents develop a home walking program, for example, that includes all family members. In addition to ongoing communication with the parents, it is vital that the school nurse be involved in the development of the IEP and be an active participant in the IEP meeting. The school nurse should schedule regular check-ups in which the learner's height/weight, heart rate, and blood pressure are monitored.

Teaching Strategies

Developing strategies for externally motivating the student with Prader-Willi syndrome is a vital and integral part of teaching. As is typical of most obese children, the student with Prader-Willi syndrome tends to fall into a vicious cycle in which he or she avoids activity because of a history of failure—gaining more weight and fatty tissue—which makes movement yet more difficult, increases the likelihood of failure, and encourages the student to avoid activity all the more. To provide motivation so that the child with Prader-Willi syndrome will persist, the use of a reward/encouragement system is usually critical. Rewards that may be particularly helpful in reinforcing interest in play, games, and leisure, recreation, and sport activities include baseball cards, five minutes to "shoot hoops" one-on-one with the teacher before or after school, and passes to sporting events. When behavior-modification programs are used to motivate students with Prader-Willi syndrome, food should never be used as a reinforcer.

The Physical Education Program

Because of the characteristic obesity, precautions must be taken to avoid overtaxing the cardiovascular system. It is crucial that these individuals participate in calorie-burning activities—activities that will elevate the body's metabolism. These individuals should participate in activities commensurate with their abilities; however, heart rate and blood pressure should be routinely monitored. In addition, it is vital that these individuals learn the skills necessary to participate in leisure and recreation activities. This is a better alternative than sedentary activities, which tend to be the choice of obese individuals.

A program with a wide range of activities, particularly individual leisure and recreation activities in which the learner has some choice in selection, is useful for the learner with Prader-Willi syndrome. Having the opportunity to select Frisbee golf, rather than vaulting in a gymnastics unit, will free the learner to develop a sense of competency in activity. In programs in which such choices are limited by necessity because of staff and facility limitations, a station approach to intervention may be helpful. For example, in a physical fitness unit, the learner may be given the opportunity to move to a station in which he or she plays catch with a medicine ball rather than trying to climb a sus-

pended rope. Once again, if the learner is given a choice, he or she may experience success—and then be more likely to seek, rather than avoid, movement.

Modifications, Adaptations, and Inclusion Techniques

Children and young adults with Prader-Willi syndrome are discriminated against more because of their obesity than because of their potentially limited intelligence. Under no circumstances should a learner with Prader-Willi syndrome be required to use a group shower; this is particularly crucial for an adolescent because embarrassment about the reduced size of genitalia may be devastating at this vulnerable developmental stage. In addition, if aquatics are part of the curriculum, the learner and the parents should discuss participation, and the learner should be given the opportunity to choose not to participate. If the learner chooses to participate, an individual dressing area is crucial, and the learner should be allowed to wear a T-shirt over his or her swimming suit.

A buddy system may be particularly helpful for the learner with Prader-Willi syndrome. The teacher must enlist the help of a caring and nurturing peer who will be a buddy to the learner during class and who will interact with the learner at lunch, during recess, and before or after school.

Community-Based Opportunities

The learner with Prader-Willi syndrome may experience success in a number of leisure and recreation activities. These community-based opportunities include but are not limited to

Bowling
Frisbee and Frisbee golf
Miniature golf
Archery
Riflery
Camping
Walking/hiking

It is important for the physical educator or adapted physical educator to discuss neighborhood leisure and recreation choices with the student and his or her family to identify common interests. The student with Prader-Willi syndrome, for example, may experience great success in bowling, but, if no one in the family and/or neighborhood bowls, it is unlikely the learner will use the skills within the community. Selecting activities that some or all of the family enjoy will increase the likelihood that the student will pursue opportunities to participate in the activity after the school years.

PREMENSTRUAL SYNDROME AND DYSMENORRHEA

Premenstrual syndrome and dysmenorrhea, though not conditions covered under the laws, are widespread conditions that affect many females. The conditions impact teenage girls' participation in physical education. Menstruation is a complex process that involves the endocrine glands, uterus, and ovaries. The average menstrual cycle lasts twenty-eight days; however, each girl or woman has her own rhythmic cycle of menstrual function. The cycle periods usually range from twenty-one to thirty-five days, but they may be longer or shorter and still fall within the range of normal.

The average total amount of blood lost during the normal menstrual period is 3 ounces; however, from 1 1/2 to 5 ounces may be lost. This blood is replaced by the active formation of blood cells in bone marrow and, consequently, does not cause anemia. On occasion, some girls or women may have excessive menstrual flow, and in this event a physician should be consulted. The average menstrual period lasts 3 to 5 days, but 2 to 7 days may be considered normal. The average age of onset of menstruation is 12.5 years, although the range of onset is from 9 to 18 years. Premenstrual syndrome (PMS) and/or dysmenorrhea is associated with most females' menstrual cycle.

Definitions

PMS is a condition that occurs during the seven to ten days before menstruation and usually disap-

---

CASE STUDY

Linda

Linda is a fifteen-year-old sophomore in high school who experiences severe low abdominal pain, headaches, and irritability during the first two days of her menstrual flow. Linda is somewhat overweight and does not enjoy physical activity, particularly vigorous activity. Every month when Linda starts her menstrual flow she brings a note from her mother asking to be excused from physical education class for two or three days. Her high school has a rule that requires all absences from physical education be made up in the after-school intramural activity program within six weeks of the absence. Linda rides the school bus home because both of her parents work until 6:00 P.M. during the week. There is public transportation available in her town.

APPLICATION TASK

How could a physical educator accommodate Linda without alienating her any further from physical activity?

---

pears a few hours after the onset of menstrual flow; however, it may persist throughout the menses.[7] Dysmenorrhea is cyclic pain that usually starts just before or with menses, peaks in twenty-four hours, and subsides after two days.[7]

Incidence

Significant functional dysmenorrhea is more common in the teenage years and tends to diminish after a woman gives birth, whereas PMS frequently begins in the twenties and increases with age.[8] These two conditions are the leading cause of females' absenteeism from work, school, and other activities.[82]

Causes

PMS seems to be related to estrogen and progesterone imbalances; however, carbohydrate metabolic changes, retention of sodium and water by the kidneys, and psychogenic factors have also been implicated. Primary dysmenorrhea is functional, meaning that it results from how the body functions. In recent years, it has been learned that an excess buildup of a natural hormone prostaglandins, that is found in the cells of the uterine lining is related to painful menstruation. During menstrual flow, when the uterine lining is shed, this hormone is released in large amounts.[82] Why discomfort results is not known. Approximately 30 percent of the cases are classified as secondary meaning they are caused by a physical condition such as endrometriosis, fibroids, or infections.[7]

Characteristics

PMS is characterized by nervousness, irritability, lack of control, agitation, anger, insomnia, depression, and severe fatigue. Fluid retention causes short-term weight gain and breast fullness and pain. Dysmenorrhea is low abdominal pain that may be crampy or a dull, constant ache that frequently radiates to the lower back and down the legs. Headache, nausea, constipation or diarrhea, dizziness, vomiting, and a feeling of tenseness are classic symptoms of dysmenorrhea. Significant dysmenorrhea is common among teenage girls and women in their early twenties who have never had a baby.[82]

Testing

These two conditions have a significant impact on a teenager's attitude. It is difficult to concentrate and put forth one's best effort when one is not feeling well. Thus, when motor or fitness testing is being conducted, it is recommended that the teenager who is experiencing PMS or dysmenorrhea be given the option of being tested during the scheduled time or delaying until she feels better.

Special Considerations

Many girls and women are unaware of the effects dietary habits can have on their degree of comfort before and during their menstrual flow. During this age of fast foods saturated with salt, the modern girl or woman needs to understand how her diet choices can influence her comfort during the menstrual cycle. With such knowledge, it is possible to reduce the painful discomfort of functional dysmenorrhea. Reduction of pain is directly associated with the amount of salt stored in the body.

Approximately one week before the onset of the menstrual period, the body begins storing sodium chloride. When this storing process begins, the girl or woman craves salt. If she yields to the craving for salt at that time in her cycle, a whole series of events occurs that results in abdominal bloating, which increases the pain associated with the first two days of the menstrual flow. What occurs is that, when salt intake is increased, the salt tends to move into and be held by the body tissues. The salt stored in the body tissues draws water toward those tissues, thereby upsetting the osmotic balance in the body. Much of the water that is drawn into the tissues is pulled from fecal matter moving through the large intestine. When large amounts of water are removed from the fecal mass, the mass begins to harden and its progress is slowed. Thus, the net result of increasing salt intake one week before the onset of the menstrual period is bloating from stored water and accumulating fecal material. This increased congestion presses against nerves in the abdominal and lower back area and causes pain.

The entire chain of events can be avoided (or markedly reduced) if, one week before the onset of her menstrual flow, the girl or woman decreases (or at least does not increase) salt intake and, at the same time, increases water and roughage (raw celery, carrots, apples) intake. By following these simple guidelines, she can preserve the osmotic balance of water in the body, and the softness and progression of the fecal mass through the large intestine can be maintained. Regular movement of the fecal mass results in reduction of the amount of bloating associated with the menstrual period. Reduced bloating and faithful adherence to the exercises described later in this chapter will relieve most of the pain associated with menstruation.

Teaching Strategies

The sensitive teacher will recognize the signs of PMS and dysmenorrhea. When normally high-spirited or easy-going teenage girls become irritable and moody, the menstrual cycle is frequently at fault. Encouraging the student to dress out, but allowing her to sit and observe the class if she chooses to do so, is recommended. Requiring that the student dress for class sends the message that the girl is experiencing a condition, not a sickness. Giving permission to sit out implies that the person experiencing the discomfort is in the best position to determine whether or not she should participate. In these cases, when the person who is not participating observes her classmates enjoying class activities, it is not uncommon for her to choose to join in some parts of the activity.

The Physical Education Program

There have been questions raised about the desirability of young women participating in physical education and exercise during the menstrual period. There is a perception among some that exercise during a period of discomfort is undesirable and that young women during this period should be excused from physical education classes. Young women have varying experiences as they pass through the menstrual cycle. Thus, judgments about physical exercise during menstruation should be made on an individual basis. However, there is evidence that there are benefits from physical exercise as it relates to physical fitness and postural efficiency in lessening the pain associated with menstruation.

The consensus among physicians and gynecologists is that restriction from participation in vigorous physical activity, intensive sports competition, and swimming during all phases of the menstrual period is unwarranted for those who are free of menstrual disturbances. However, with regard to the first half of the menstrual period, some physicians advise moderation with limited participation in intensive sports competition. The reason for moderation during the first half of the menstrual period is that the flow is heavier during

the first two or three days and some girls and women experience abdominal cramping during this time.

Modifications, Adaptations, and Inclusion Techniques

Regular exercise has been shown to relieve the symptoms of PMS and functional dysmenorrhea. Exercise reduces stress and provides relief of congestion in the abdominal cavity caused by gravity, poor posture, poor circulation, and/or poor abdominal muscle tone. Physical activity also helps relieve leg and back pain by stretching lumbar and pelvic ligaments in the fascia to minimize pressure on spinal nerves. Undue muscular tension also may have a bearing on painful menstruation; therefore, relaxation techniques and positioning of the body, accompanied by heat from a heating pad on the lower back area, may relax tensions and consequently lessen the pain. Other relaxation techniques and exercises also may be used to reduce tension in the body (see Appendix B).

Girls and women who suffer from dysmenorrhea may benefit from a daily exercise program designed to alleviate this condition. The exercises should provide for the improvement of posture (especially lordosis), the stimulation of circulation, and the stretching of tight fascia and ligaments. The exercises discussed here are suggested to alleviate the symptoms of dysmenorrhea.

Fascial Stretch

The purpose of fascial exercise is to stretch the shortened fascial ligamentous bands that extend between the lower back and the anterior aspect of the pelvis and legs. These shortened bands may result in increased pelvic tilt, which may irritate peripheral nerves passing through or near the fascia. The irritation of these nerves may be the cause of the pain. This exercise produces a stretching effect on the hip flexors and increases mobility of the hip joint (see Figure 18-12). To perform the exercise, the girl or woman should stand erect, with the left side of her body about the distance of the bent elbow from a wall; the feet should be together, with

Figure 18-13   Abdominal Pumping

Figure 18-14   Pelvic Tilt with Abdominal Pumping

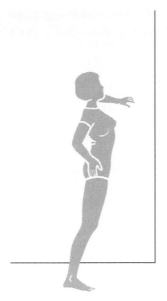

Figure 18-12   Fascial Stretch

the left forearm and palm against the wall, the elbow at shoulder height, and the heel of the other hand placed against the posterior aspect of the hollow portion of the right hip. From this position, abdominal and gluteal muscles should be contracted strongly to tilt the pelvis backward. The hips should slowly be pushed forward and diagonally toward the wall, and pressure should be applied with the right hand. This position should be held for a few counts; then a slow return should be made to the starting position. The stretch should be performed three times on each side of the body. The exercise should be continued even after relief has been obtained from dysmenorrhea. It has been suggested that the exercise be performed three times daily. To increase motivation, the girl or woman should record the number of days and times she performs the exercise.

Abdominal Pumping

The purpose of abdominal pumping is to increase circulation of the blood throughout the pelvic region. The exercise is performed by assuming a hook-lying position, placing the hands lightly on the abdomen, slowly and smoothly distending the abdomen on the count of one, then retracting the abdomen on the count of two, and relaxing (see Figure 18-13). The exercise should be repeated eight to ten times.

Pelvic Tilt with Abdominal Pumping

The purpose of the pelvic tilt with abdominal pumping is to increase the tone of the abdominal muscles. In a hook-lying position, with the feet and knees together, heels 1 inch apart and hands on the abdomen, the abdominal and gluteal muscles are contracted. The pelvis is rotated so that the tip of the coccyx comes forward and upward and the hips are slightly raised from the floor. The abdomen is distended and retracted. The hips are lowered slowly, vertebra by vertebra, until the original starting position is attained (see Figure 18-14). The exercise should be repeated eight to ten times.

Knee-Chest Position

The purpose of the knee-chest exercise is to stretch the extensors of the lumbar spine and strengthen the abdominal muscles. The exercise is performed by bending forward at the hips and placing the hands and arms on a mat. The chest is lowered toward the mat, in a knee-chest position, and held as close to the mat as possible for 3 to 5 minutes (see Figure 18-15). This exercise should be performed once or twice a day.

Figure 18-15   Knee-Chest Position

Community-Based Opportunities

The teenager who has been taught how to control PMS and functional dysmenorrhea through diet and exercise will have the knowledge she needs to continue to maintain a healthy and active lifestyle into her adult years.

TOURETTE SYNDROME

Definition

Tourette syndrome (TS) is a genetic disorder that results in multiple motor tics and one or more vocal tics.[3] The tics often begin in early childhood but are usually dismissed by parents as nervous mannerisms.[7] Often the tics are dramatically reduced or disappear between the ages of twenty and twenty-four years.[75]

Incidence

The prevalence rate is estimated to be 1 in 1,000 in children[75] but as little as 2.5 per 10,000 in young adults.[35] The condition is three times more common in males than in females.[7]

Causes

TS is an inherited neurological disorder with some associated symptoms that affect behavior.

Characteristics

The characteristics of individuals with this syndrome include involuntary motor and vocal tics and symptoms that come and go and change over time.[11] A tic is a sudden, rapid, recurrent, non-

---

CASE STUDY

Charlie

Charlie is an eighteen-year-old student with Tourette syndrome. Initially misdiagnosed, Charlie has struggled for years in a school system in which he was perceived to be a "troublemaker who used offensive language." Charlie, a very bright and sensitive young man, has been unable to control facial tics, inappropriate language, and finger tapping.

Charlie has often been placed in time-out, school-based suspension, and on several occasions was expelled before a formal diagnosis of Tourette syndrome was finally made. As a result, he has missed a great deal of physical education and lacks confidence in his basic skills.

APPLICATION TASK

What steps might the physical educator take to help Charlie develop confidence in his basic motor skills? Within the high school curriculum, what activities would help encourage the development of basic motor skills? Within that curriculum, what activities would only make Charlie feel less confident?

---

rhythmic, stereotyped movement or vocalization.[3] The motor tics that may be seen include sudden twitches of the entire body, shoulders, or head; eyeblinks or rolling of the head; repetitive tapping, drumming, or touching behaviors; and grimacing. The vocal tics are involuntary utterings of noises, words, or phrases, including sniffing, throat clearing, and repeated coughing, exhibiting coprolalia (saying socially inappropriate words), laughing involuntarily, uttering a variety of sounds or yells, barking, grunting, and exhibiting echolalia (repeating what others or oneself has just said).[11] Sometimes the symptoms are very frequent, but sometimes the child does not demonstrate them at all. Also, the symptoms change from one year to the next.

A high percentage of children with TS also have problems with attention, activity, and impulse control; learning disabilities; and visual-motor integration problems.[10] Some also demonstrate obsessive-compulsive behaviors and/or an inability to inhibit aggression.[56]

Diagnostic criteria developed by the American Psychiatric Association[3] are

- Both multiple motor tics and one or more vocal tics have been present for some time during the illness, although not necessarily concurrently.
- The tics occur many times a day (usually in bouts) nearly every day or have occurred intermittently throughout a period of more than one year, and during this period there was never a tic-free period of more than three consecutive months.
- The disturbance causes marked distress or significant impairment in social, occupational, or other important areas of functioning.
- The onset is before age eighteen.
- The disturbance is not due to the direct physiological effects of a substance (e.g., stimulants) or a general medical condition (e.g., Huntington's chorea or postviral encephalitis).

Testing

No adjustments in testing are required for the student with TS; however, allowances must be made for motor tics that are severe enough to interfere with voluntary motor control. If the student also has a specific learning disability, the testing procedures and interpretations provided in Chapter 13 are recommended.

Special Considerations

Students with learning disabilities and those with impulse-control difficulties represent a special challenge to a teacher. When a learning disability is present, the mode of presenting information to the student may have to be altered to accommodate his or her method of processing information. Some students learn better visually, others learn better auditorily, and some need a combination of techniques to comprehend new information. To determine how the student learns best, the teacher is advised to consult with the school counselor or other resource personnel who have access to the student's academic and cognitive test results.

When impulse control creates acting-out problems in class, the teacher must have a strategy for intervening, always keeping in mind that the student's behavior is involuntary. When possible and feasible, the teacher and the student should discuss anticipated problems early in the school year and agree on a procedure to follow should impulse control become a major problem.

The student may wish to have the option to time-out himself or herself or may prefer that the teacher intervene if the behavior interferes with other students' benefits from the class. Also, with the student and the student's parents' permission, the teacher or another representative of the school should share information about the condition with the student's classmates, so they will understand that the unusual behaviors are not under voluntary control.

Teaching Strategy

Because the median age of onset for motor tics is seven years,[3] the teacher of the child with TS may be the first to become aware of the emergence of the symptoms. Other than learning to tolerate the student's involuntary tics, the physical educator's primary concerns will probably be with fostering acceptance in the class and addressing the student's learning disabilities, impulse control, and visual-motor problems.

The Physical Education Program

Individuals with TS have a variety of visual-motor integration problems. These include alternating visual suppression (using each eye independently of the other), one or both eyes sitting in misalignment, and mild depth-perception difficulties. If an individual is suppressing one eye or if the eyes are misaligned, the individual's motor performance will suffer. Performance clues include poor striking success, inability to catch a thrown ball, avoidance of climbing apparatus, and/or the descent of stairs one step at a time. Should a student demonstrate any of these difficulties, the child should be referred for an orthoptic visual examination and remediation (see Chapter 17) before a physical education program is designed. If the student does not have visual-motor integration problems that interfere with movement efficiency, no modifications in the activity program are needed, except for those addressed under the text head "Special Considerations."

Modifications, Adaptations, and Inclusion Techniques

As the individual in charge, the teacher is responsible for establishing and maintaining a learning environment that will provide all students with the opportunity to learn and grow. A teacher is expected to make needed modifications and adaptations to enhance a student's potential to learn. Teachers can offer alternative strategies to individual students when they possess the needed information and have a class size that permits individual attention. The presence of a student with a potentially disabling condition provides a special learning opportunity for everyone in the class. Knowledge about an existing condition, acceptance of the situation, realistic expectations, and cooperation are prerequisites for a positive learning environment for all members of the class. Students with TS can easily become alienated from other students in the class because of their uncontrollable, unique behaviors. However, when the teacher and other students in the class understand the condition, know what to expect, and know what outcomes will result, opportunities will be enhanced and difficulties reduced to a minimum for the student with TS. The sensitive teacher will take the responsibility for ensuring that all members of the class are treated with fairness and respect.

Community-Based Opportunities

Adults with TS can participate in any public or private recreational activities where they feel comfortable. Their involuntary tics may, however, be met with ridicule, fear, or hostility by individuals who do not know them or understand the condition. As noted earlier in this section, an identifying characteristic of TS is that it "causes marked distress or significant impairment in social, occupational, or other important areas of functioning."[3] Attempts must be made to educate individuals who work and play in settings that the person with TS may frequent. A support group of friends and family members can provide others with information about the condition and perhaps facilitate understanding and acceptance.   ☙

SUMMARY

Other health impairment, by federal definition, means that a child has limited strength and vitality or alertness due to chronic or acute health problems. In addition to health impairments listed in the federal definition of the IDEA, other impairments that might limit a student's participation in physical education include AIDS, anemia, childhood cancer, cystic fibrosis, Prader-Willi syndrome, premenstrual syndrome and dysmenorrhea, and Tourette syndrome. The physical educator should understand the nature of each of these conditions, how the conditions can affect a student's performance capabilities, and the types of program modifications that best meet the needs of each student.

Most of the conditions discussed in this chapter require medical attention. When this is the case, it is advisable to request permission of the parents to consult with the student's physician to ensure that the type of exercises and activities selected for the student will not aggravate the condition. In most situations, mild exercise will benefit the student. However, in the case of the diabetic student, the type of diabetes must be known before specific exercise programs can be developed.

REVIEW QUESTIONS

1. What techniques can a physical education teacher use to keep a student with an attention deficit disorder on task?

2. How should persons with Type 1 diabetes adjust their insulin levels to accommodate increased exercise?

3. How should the physical education program be modified for students with asthma?

4. Summarize the Universal Precautions to protect against all infectious disease. Which are most pertinent to physical education?

5. What are the characteristics of a person with anemia?

6. What precautions must be used in developing an individual exercise program for a child with cystic fibrosis?

7. How do the emergency treatment procedures for hypoglycemia and hyperglycemia differ?

8. What is the primary characteristic of the child with Tourette syndrome? How does this interfere with the child's psychosocial development?

9. What is the major characteristic of a child with Prader-Willi syndrome? What precautions must be taken in the development of an exercise program for children with Prader-Willi syndrome?

STUDENT ACTIVITIES

1. Have the class break into small groups and share the application tasks developed for at least three of the conditions presented in this chapter. Have each group select one of the conditions and present its agreed-upon application for that condition.

2. Look through six recent issues of the *Journal of the American Medical Association*. List the articles that relate to the conditions described in this chapter. Read through some of the articles to see if exercise is mentioned as a possible way to relieve the condition.

3. Interview a person with diabetes. Find out what type of medication the person takes and how often it must be taken. Ask if the person ever failed to take the medication and how he or she felt because of missing the dosage.

4. Interview a school nurse. Find out what percentage of the students in the nurse's school have the conditions discussed in this chapter.

5. Contact an organization that advocates for children with the health impairments discussed in this chapter and study its literature. Identify the information that is relevant to conducting a physical education program for individuals with these health impairments.

6. Identify an athlete who is or was afflicted with one of the health impairments discussed in this chapter. Write a paper on accommodations that had to be made for the athlete.

REFERENCES

1. Albright AL: Diabetes. In Durstine JL, editor: *Exercise management for persons with chronic diseases and disabilities,* Champaign, IL, 1997, Human Kinetics.

2. American Lung Association: *Childhood asthma,* New York, 1994, Author.

3. American Psychiatric Association: *Diagnostic and statistical manual of mental disorders (DSM-IV),* Washington, DC, 1994, Author.

4. Anderson SD: Exercise-induced asthma. In Middleton E et al., editors: *Allergy: principles and practice,* ed. 4, St. Louis, 1993, Mosby.

5. Anemia. http://www.sleeptight.com/EncyMaster/A/anemia

6. Barkley RA: The North American perspective on attention deficit hyperactivity disorder, *Aust Educ Dev Psych* 13:2–23, 1996.

7. Beers MH, Berkow R, editors: *The Merck manual of diagnosis and therapy,* ed. 17, Rahway, NJ, 1999, Merck Research Laboratories.

8. Biederman J et al.: Gender differences in a sample of adults with attention deficit hyperactivity disorder, *Psychiatry Res* 53:13–29, 1994.

9. Borkgren MW, Gronkiewicz CA: Update your asthma care from hospital to home, *Am J Nurs* January: 26–34, 1995.

10. Brandon LJ, Boyette LW, Lloyd A, Gaasch DA: Effects of training on strength and floor rise ability in older diabetic adults, *Medicine and Science in Exercise and Sport,* Supplement No. 5, 31(suppl 5):S116, 1998.

11. Bronheim S: *An educator's guide to Tourette syndrome,* Bayside, NY, 1990, Tourette Syndrome Association.

12. Carlson DL, Mawdsley RH: Sports anemia: a review of the literature, *Am J Sports Med* 14:109–122, 1986.

13. Cerny F, Orenstein D: Cystic fibrosis. In Skinner JS, editor: *Exercise testing and exercise prescription for special cases,* Philadelphia, 1993, Lea & Febiger.

14. Cohen J, Reddington C, Jacobs D, Meade R, Picard D, Singleton K, Smith D, Caldwell MB, DeMaria A, Hsu H: School related issues among HIV-infected children, *Pediatrics* 100:126, 1997.

15. Cooper CB: Pulmonary disease. In Durstine JL, editor: *Exercise management for persons with chronic diseases and disabilities,* Champaign, IL, 1997, Human Kinetics.

16. Crist WM, Kun LE: Common solid tumors of childhood, *N Engl J Med* 324:461–471, 1991.

17. daCosta IG, Paroff MA, Lemanek K, Goldstein GL: Improving adherence to medication regimens for children with asthma and its effects on clinical outcome, *J of Applied Behavioral Analysis* 30:687–691, 1997.

18. Dunn JM, Fait H: *Special physical education,* Dubuque, IA, 1989, Wm. C. Brown.

19. Eichner ER: Sickle cell trait, heroic exercise, and fatal collapse, *Physician Sportsmed* 21(7):51–61, 1993.

20. Elia J, Ambrosini PJ, Rapoport JL: Treatment of attention-deficit-hyperactivity disorder, *N Eng J of Med* 340:780–788, 1999.

21. Gong H, Krishnareddy S: How pollution and airborne allergens affect exercise, *Physician Sportsmed* 23(7):35–42, 1995.

22. Gong H, Linn W: Health effects of criteria air pollutants. In Tierney DF, editor: *Current pulmonology,* vol. 15, St. Louis, 1994, Mosby.

23. Grovas A, Femgen A, Rauck A, Ruymann FB, Hutchinson CL, Winchester DP, Menck HR: The national cancer data base report on patterns of childhood cancers in the United States, *Cancer* 80:2321–2332, 1997.

24. Gurney GG et al.: Incidence of cancer in children in the United States, *Cancer* 75:2186–2195, 1995.

25. Harris SS, Tanner S: Helping active women avoid anemia, *Physician Sportsmed* 23:35–47, 1995.

26. Harvey WJ, Reid G: Motor performance of children with attention deficit hyperactivity disorder: a preliminary investigation, *Adapt Phys Activ Q* 14:189–202, 1997.

27. Helman LJ, Thiele CJ: New insights into the causes of cancer, *Pediatr Clin North Am* 38:201–221, 1991.

28. Hickey G, Fricker P: Attention deficit hyperactivity disorder, CNS stimulants and sport, *Sports Medicine* 27:11–21, 1999.

29. Horowitz ME, Neff JR, Kun LE: Ewing's sarcoma: radiotherapy versus surgery for local control, *Pediatr Clin North Am* 38:365–380, 1991.

30. JAMA Patient Page: Sickle cell anemia, *JAMA* 281:1768, 1999.

31. Kerr CP: Improving outcomes in diabetes: a review of the outpatient care of NIDDM patients, *J Fam Pract* 40:63–75, 1995.

32. King KJ: The attention deficit disorder (ADD) child, *KAPPAN* December:22–26, 1989.

33. Lansky SB: Management of stressful periods in childhood cancer, *Pediatr Clin North Am* 32:625–632, 1985.

34. LaPerriere A, Klimas N, Major P, Perry A: Acquired immune deficiency syndrome. In Durstine JL, editor: *Exercise management for persons with chronic diseases and disabilities,* Champaign, IL, 1997, Human Kinetics.

35. Leckman JF, Zhang H, Vitale A, Lahnin F, Lynch K, Bondi C, Kim Y, Peterson BS: Course of tic severity

in Tourette syndrome: the first two decades, *Pediatrics* 102:14–19, 1998.

36. Leon AS: Diabetes. In Skinner JS, editor: *Exercise testing and exercise prescription for special cases,* Philadelphia, 1993, Lea & Febiger.

37. Libman I, Arslanian SA: Type 2 diabetes: no longer just an adult disease, *Pediatric Annals* 28:589–593, 1999.

38. Looker AC, Dallman PR, Carrol, MD, Johnson CL: Prevalence of iron deficiency in the United States, *JAMA* 277:973–976, 1997.

39. Marshall RM, Hynd GW, Handwerk MJ, Hall J: Academic underachievement in ADHD subtypes, *J of Learning Dis* 30:635–642, 1997.

40. Mayfield J: Diagnosis and classification of diabetes mellitus: new criteria, *American Family Physician* October:1103–1113, 1998.

41. McHugh E: Going "beyond the physical": social skills and physical education, *J Phys Educ Rec Dance* 66(4):18–21, 1995.

42. Meadows AT, Krejimas NL, Belasco JB: The medical cost of cure: sequelae in survivors of childhood cancer. In van Eys J, Sullivan MP, editors: *Status of curability of childhood cancers,* New York, 1980, Raven Press.

43. Menkes M, Rowe J, Menkes J: A twenty-five year follow-up study on the hyperkinetic child with minimal brain dysfunction, *Pediatrics* 39:393–399, 1967.

44. Miller J, Keane RR: *Encyclopedia and dictionary of medicine, nursing, and allied health,* Philadelphia, 1987, W.B. Saunders.

45. Misben R: Report on the expert committee on the diagnosis and classification of diabetes mellitus, *Diabetes-Care* 20:1183–1190, 1997.

46. Mitten MJ: HIV-positive athletes: when medicine meets the law, *Physician Sportsmed* 22(10):63–68, 1994.

47. Morton AR, Fitch KD: Asthma. In Skinner JS, editor: *Exercise testing and exercise prescription for special cases,* Philadelphia, 1993, Lea & Febiger.

48. Mosher PE, Nash MS, Perry AC, LaPerriere AR, Goldberg RB: Aerobic circuit exercise training: effects on adolescents with well-controlled insulin-dependent diabetes mellitus, *Arch Phys Med Reh,* 79:652–657, 1998.

49. Nixon PA: Cystic fibrosis. In Durstine LD, editor: *Exercise management for persons with chronic*

diseases and disabilities, Champaign, IL, 1997, Human Kinetics.

50. Payton B: *Health and safety,* Dallas, 1994, Dallas Independent School District.

51. Pihoker C, Scott CR, Lensing Sy, Cradock MM, Smith J: Non-insulin dependent diabetes mellitus in African-American youths of Arkansas, *Clin Pediatr* 37:97–102, 1998.

52. Power TJ, DuPaul GJ: Attention-deficit hyperactivity disorder; the reemergence of subtypes, *School Psychology Review* 25:284–296, 1996.

53. Prader-Willi Syndrome Association, USA: *Prader-Willi syndrome basic facts.* http://www.pwsausa.org/basicfac.htm

54. Pratt CB: Some aspects of childhood cancer epidemiology, *Pediatr Clin North Am* 32:541–556, 1985.

55. Rimmer JH: *Fitness and rehabilitation programs for special populations,* Madison, WI, 1994, Brown & Benchmark.

56. Rosen AR: Tourette's syndrome: the school experience, *Clin Pediatr* 35:467–469, 1996.

57. Rosenbloom AL, House DV, Winter WE: Non-insulin dependent diabetes mellitus in minority youth; research priorities and needs, *Pediatr* 37:143–152, 1998.

58. Rosenthal-Malek A, Greenspan W: The student with diabetes in my class, *Teaching Exceptional Children,* January/February:38–43, 1999.

59. Rupp NT: Diagnosis and management of exercise-induced asthma, *Physician Sportsmed* 24:77–87, 1996.

60. Saunders B, Chambers SM: A review of the literature on attention-deficit hyperactivity disorder children: peer interactions and collaborative learning, *Psychology in the Schools* 33:333–340, 1996.

61. Selby G: Anemia. In Durstine LD, editor: *Exercise management for persons with chronic diseases and disabilities,* Champaign, IL, 1997, Human Kinetics.

62. Selby G: Cancer. In Durstine LD, editor: *Exercise management for persons with chronic diseases and disabilities,* Champaign, IL, 1997, Human Kinetics.

63. Seltzer DG: Educating athletes on HIV disease and AIDS, *Physician Sportsmed* 21(1):109–115, 1993.

64. Shaywitz SE, Shaywitz BA: Attention deficit disorder; current perspectives, *Pediat Neurol* 3:129–135, 1987.

65. Shaywitz SE, Shaywitz BA: Introduction to the special series on attention deficit disorder, *J Learning Disabil* 24:68–74, 1991.

66. Silverstein R: *A user's guide to the 1999 IDEA regulations,* 1999, ERIC Clearinghouse. Washington, D.C.

67. Simonsen JC, Simmons DJ, Zaccaro WF, Rejeski WJ, Berry MJ: Exercise and health related quality of life in male and female chronic obstructive pulmonary disease patients, *Med Sci Exer Spt,* 31 (suppl 5):S361, 1998.

68. Spencer T, Biederman J, Wilens T: Growth deficits in children with attention deficit hyperactivity disorder, *Pediatrics,* 102:501–506, 1998.

69. Stewart M et al.: The hyperactive child syndrome, *Am J Orthopsychiatry* 35:861–867, 1996.

70. Stormes WW: Exercise-induced asthma: diagnosis and treatment for the recreation or elite athlete, *Med Sci Exer Spt,* Supplement No. 1, 32:S33–S38, 1999.

71. Surburg PR: Are adapted physical educators ready for the students with AIDS? *Adapt Phys Ed Q* 5:259–263, 1988.

72. Tan RA, Spector SL: Exercise-induced asthma, *Sports Medicine* 25:1–6, 1998.

73. Taunton JE, McCargar L: Managing activity in patients who have diabetes, *Physician Sportsmed* 23(3):41–52, 1995.

74. Taunton JE, McCargar L: Staying active with diabetes, *Physician Sportsmed* 23(3):55–56, 1995.

75. Tourette Syndrome Association.http://neuro-www2.mgn.harvard.edu/tsa/tsamain.mclk

76. Trembath RC: Genetic mechanisms and mental retardation, *J R Coll Physicians Lond* 28(2):121–125, 1994.

77. Tuchman M et al.: Screening for neuroblastoma at 3 weeks of age: methods and preliminary results from the Quebec Neuroblastoma Screening Project, *Pediatrics* 86:765–773, 1990.

78. Waters J, Clarke DJ, Corbett JA: Educational and occupational outcome in Prader-Willi syndrome, *Child Care Health Dev* 16:271–282, 1990.

79. Weinberg RA: Oncogenes, antioncogenes and the molecular bases of multistep carcinogenesis, *Cancer Res* 49:3713–3721, 1989.

80. Werner T: Effects of exercise on an HIV-positive patient: a case study, *Clinical Kinesiology* 51:86–87, 1997/98.

81. White RD, Sherman C: Exercise in diabetes management, *Physician Sportsmed* 27:63–78, 1999.

82. Women's Health Interactive.http://www.womens-health.com/gym_health/gyn_md.html

83. Zametkin AJ, Ernst M: Problems in the management of attention-deficit-hyperactivity disorder, *New England J of Medicine* 340:40–46, 1999.

Suggested Readings

Conti SF, Chaytor ER: Steps to healthy feet for active people with diabetes, *Physician Sportsmed* 23(6): 71–72, 1995.

Durstine JL, editor: *Exercise management for persons with chronic diseases and disabilities,* Champaign, IL, 1997, Human Kinetics.

Harris SS, Tanner S: Give yourself the iron advantage, *Physician Sportsmed* 23(5):44, 1995.

Recommended Websites

Please note that these websites are being recommended in the summer and early fall of 1999. By the time you read this text, the websites may no longer exist or may be at a different URL.

Attention Deficit Disorder
   http://h2.interconnect.com:80/oneaddplace/

Attention Deficit Disorder WWW Archive
   http://homepage.seas.upenn.edu/~mengwong/add/

AIDS Clinical Trials Information Service
http://actis.org

AIDS Education Global Information System (AEGIS)
http://www.aegis.com

CDC National Prevention Information Network
http://www.cdcpin.org

Clinical Care Options for HIV
http://www.healthcg.com/hiv

Encyclopedia Main Index
http://www.sleeptight.com/EncyMaster/
A/anemia.html

Comprehensive List of Disability-Related Websites
http://www.icdi.wvu.edu/Others.htm

National Childhood Cancer Foundation
http://www.nccf.org/Menuframe.htm

Women's Health Interactive
http://www.womens-health.com/gym_health/
gyn_md.html

Prader-Willi Syndrome Association (USA)
http://www.pwsausa.org/basicfac.htm

Tourette Syndrome Association
http://www.mentalhealth.com/

RECOMMENDED VIDEOS

The Diagnosis and Treatment of Attention Deficit
Disorder in Children
27 minutes, color, $149 purchase price, $75 rental
Films for the Humanities & Sciences
PO Box 2053
Princeton, NJ 08543-2053

Coping with Attention Deficit Disorder in Children
24 minutes, color, $149 purchase price, $75 rental
Films for the Humanities & Sciences
PO Box 2053
Princeton, NJ 08543-2053

Aquarius Health Care Videos
5 Powderhouse Lane
PO Box 1159
Sherborn, MA 01770

AIDS: The Heart of the Matter
31 minutes, color, 1996, $150 purchase price

Angels Watch over Me
52 minutes, color, 1995, $110 purchase price

Before It's Too Late
19 minutes, color, 1998, $125 purchase price

Bigger Than This Manhattan
15 minutes, color, 1999, $99 purchase price

Living with Aids
28 minutes, color, 1996, $149 purchase price

Breathless: Living with Severe Asthma
51 minutes, color, $129 purchase price, $75 rental
Films for the Humanities & Sciences
PO Box 2053
Princeton, NJ 08543-2053

John's Not Mad: Tourette's Syndrome
30 minutes, color, $89.95 purchase price
Films for the Humanities & Sciences
PO Box 2053
Princeton, NJ 08543-2053

GLOSSARY

A

abdominal strength   Muscular strength of the abdominal muscles.

abduction   Away from the midline of the body.

abortive poliomyelitis   An acute viral infection that causes a headache, sore throat, mild fever, and nausea.

accessibility   The extent to which an environment can be used by all persons.

accommodation   Tailoring an educational program to a student's abilities and severity of disability.

accountability   Evidence that students with disabilities have received appropriate education services.

acquired anemia   Anemia that begins sometime during one's life.

acquired immune deficiency syndrome (AIDS)   The development of opportunistic infections and/or certain secondary cancers known to be associated with HIV infection.

Adam test   Position to determine the extent to which a scoliosis is structural.

Adapted Physical Activity Council (APAC)   A unit within the American Association of Active Lifestyles and Fitness of the American Alliance for Health, Physical Education, Recreation and Dance whose mission is to promote quality movement experiences for individuals with disabilities through research, advocacy, publications, programs at conventions and workshops, position statements, standards of practice, and cooperation with other organizations committed to people with disabilities.

adapted physical education   The art and science of developing, implementing, and monitoring a carefully designed physical education instructional program for a learner with a disability, based on a comprehensive assessment, to give the individual the skills necessary for a lifetime of rich leisure, recreation, and sport experiences to enhance physical fitness and wellness.

adapted physical education national standards (APENS)   Comprehensive national criteria detailing the professional preparation standards expected of adapted physical educators who seek accreditation.

adapted physical educator   A physical educator with highly specialized training in the assessment and evaluation of motor competency, physical fitness, play, and leisure, recreation, and sport skills.

adaptive skill areas   Communication, home living, community use, health and safety, leisure, self-care, social skills, self-direction, functional academics, and work.

adduction   Toward the midline of the body.

administrative feasibility   The extent to which it is practical to use a given test.

admission   An indicator that a student qualifies for special services because of an identifiable disability that interferes with educational progress.

adolescent scoliosis   Scoliosis that develops between the ages of three and twelve years in females and ages three and fourteen years in males.

adventitious   Acquired after birth.

affective function   Emotions resulting from experiences, beliefs, values, and predispositions.

agility   The ability to change direction while moving.

air conduction hearing aid   A hearing aid that is hooked to receivers located in the outer ear canal.

albinism   Lack of pigment in the eyes.

alternate-form reliability   The degree to which scores from two different tests purported to measure the same things agree when administered to two different groups.

alternator   A person who visually suppresses images received by one eye and then the other eye.

amblyopia   Cortical suppression of visual images received by one or both eyes.

ambulatory   Able to walk.

Americans with Disabilities Act of 1990 (ADA)   P.L. 101-336, which widened civil rights protections for persons with disabilities to all public accommodations and addressed private discrimination.

amputation   Missing part or all of a limb.

amyotrophic lateral sclerosis (ALS)   A progressive neurological disorder that results in degeneration of the muscular system; also known as Lou Gehrig disease.

anemia   Condition of the blood in which there is a deficiency of red (oxygen-carrying) cells or hemoglobin in cirulation.

ankle pronation   Abnormal turning of the ankle downward and medially (eversion and abduction).

ankylosed   Pertaining to the immobility of a joint resulting from pathological changes in the joint or in adjacent tissues.

ankylosing spondylitis   A gradual thickening of the axial skeleton and large peripheral joints of the body, which causes back pain and early morning stiffness.

annual goals   Statements that describe in measurable terms what a specific learner with a disability should be able to accomplish in a given year.

anorexia nervosa   A condition in which the person stops eating.

anxiety disorder   Intense feeling of anxiety and tension when there is no real danger.

Apgar scores   Numerical indicators of an infant's status immediately after birth.

aphasia   An impairment of language that affects the production or comprehension of speech and the ability to read or write.

aplastic anemia   A form of anemia in which the red bone marrow that forms blood cells is replaced by fatty marrow.

applied behavioral analysis   A style of teaching used with learners who have autism that involves a series of trails to shape a desired behavior or response; also known as the Lovaas approach.

arthritis   Inflammation of a joint.

arthrogryposis   A congenital condition that results in flexure or contracture of joints.

articulation disorder   Difficulty using some speech sounds.

asana   Muscle-stretching exercises used in hatha-yoga.

Asperger's disorder   A condition, known as "high-level autism," that shares many of the same symptoms as classic autism but that also includes motor clumsiness and a family history of Asperger traits.

assessment   A problem-solving process that involves gathering information from a variety of sources.

assistive technology   A piece of equipment or product system that increases, maintains, or improves the functional capabilities of persons with disabilities.

assistive technology service   Any service that directly assists an individual with a disability in the selection, acquisition, or use of an assistive technology device.

asthma   A pulmonary disease characterized by reversible airway obstruction, airway inflammation, and increased airway responsiveness to a variety of stimuli.

astigmatism   Refractive error caused by an irregularity in the curvature of the cornea of the lens; vision may become blurred.

asymmetrical tonic neck reflex   A reflex that causes extension of the arm on the face side and flexion of the arm on the posterior skull side when the head is turned.

at risk   Refers to individuals whose development is jeopardized by factors that include poverty, homelessness, prenatal and postnatal maternal neglect, environmental deprivation, child abuse, violence, drug abuse, and racism.

ataxia   A disturbance of equilibrium that results from the involvement of the cerebellum or its pathways.

athetosis   Clinical type of cerebral palsy that is characterized by uncoordinated movements of the voluntary muscles, often accompanied by impaired muscle control of the hands and impaired speech and swallowing.

atlantoaxial instability   Greater than normal mobility of the two upper cervical vertebrae.

atrophy   Wasting away of muscular tissue.

audible ball   A ball that emits a beeping sound for easy location by a person with limited vision.

audible goal locator   Motor driven noisemakers that enable a person with limited vision to identify placement of a base or boundary.

audiologist   A specially trained professional who can provide comprehensive evaluations of individuals' hearing capabilities.

audition   Pertaining to the sense of hearing and the hearing organs involved.

autism   One of five disorders included under the umbrella of pervasive developmental disorders. See *classic autism*.

autogenic training   Teaching a person to use mind images to promote a relaxed state.

autonomic neuropathy   A complication resulting from long-standing diabetes that leads to poor vascular supply and lack of sweating of the feet.

B

backward chaining   The last of a series of steps is taught first.

balance   The ability to maintain equilibrium in a held (static) or moving (dynamic) position.

basic neurological building blocks   Sensory input systems, including primitive reflexes, the vestibular system, refractive and orthoptic vision, audition, the tactile and kinesthetic systems, and equilibrium reflexes.

Becker muscular dystrophy   A disease of the muscular system very similar to Duchenne muscular dystrophy except that it progresses more slowly.

behavior disorder   A condition in which the behavioral response of a student is so different from generally accepted, age-appropriate, ethnic, or cultural norms as to result in significant impairment in self-care, social relationships, educational progress, classroom behavior, work adjustment, or personal happiness.

behavior modification (behavior therapy)   The changing of behavioral characteristics through the application of learning principles.

behavior-management strategies   Techniques for structuring the environment to produce changes in behavior.

benchmarks   Standards of performance for each grade level set at the local, district, or state level.

bio-underclass   Infants who are destined to fail to develop normally because of physical and chemical damage to their brains as a result of the mothers' use of drugs and/or malnutrition during the fetal period.

blindisms   Self-stimulatory behaviors, such as rocking the body or head, placing fingers or fists into the eyes, or flicking fingers in front of the face.

body awareness   How a person pictures his or her body and his or her attitude toward and knowledge of his or her bodily capabilities and limitations.

body composition   The percentage of body fat in relation to lean tissue in the body.

body image   System of ideas and feelings that a person has about his or her structure.

body righting reflex   Reflex that enables segmental rotation of the trunk and hips when the head is turned.

body-state regulation   The ability of the body to maintain homeostasis.

bone conduction hearing aid   A hearing aid that is placed in contact with the mastoid bone.

bottom-up strategy   Process whereby the sensory input system is evaluated and then ability tests are used to determine which deficits are in evidence.

bulimia   A condition wherein the person overeats and then purges the body of the intake.

C

campus-based decision-making committees   Groups of individuals who contribute to site-based management policies and procedures.

cancer   A cellular malignancy resulting in loss of normal cell function and uncontrolled cell growth.

cardiovascular/cardiorespiratory endurance   The ability of the heart, lungs, and blood vessels to direct needed oxygen to the muscles.

cataract   A condition in which the normally transparent lens of the eye becomes opaque.

center of gravity   A point in the human body where the pull of gravity on one side is equal to the pull of gravity on the other side.

central auditory processing problems   Deafness resulting from damage to the brainstem or in the cortex.

cerebral palsy   A lifelong condition resulting from a nonprogressive lesion of the brain before, during, or soon after birth (before age five years) that impairs voluntary movement.

certified adapted physical educator (C.A.P.E.)   An indicator that an individual has demonstrated knowledge of adapted physical education by passing the Adapted Physical Education National Standards test.

chaining   Leading a person through a series of teachable components of a motor task.

checklist   A screening instrument used to delineate critical aspects of movements.

child abuse and neglect   Physical or mental injury, sexual abuse, negligent treatment, or maltreatment of a child under eighteen years of age by a person who is responsible for the child, resulting in harm to the child's health or welfare.

Child Find   A national effort to identify children who have developmental disabilities or are at risk for developmental delays.

childhood disintegrative disorder (CDD)   A condition that presents itself between the ages of two and ten years that results in a regression in many areas, including movement, social and language skills, and bladder and bowel control; also known as Heller's syndrome.

chlorosis   Iron deficiency anemia that is characterized by a reduced amount of hemoglobin in the corpuscles.

choice making   A teaching strategy that provides persons with autism opportunities to make choices.

chromosomal abnormalities   Deviations in the structure of the chromosome.

chronic sorrow syndrome   A theory that proposes that the family members of a child with a disability can cope with the day-to-day requirements of providing support for the child with a disability; however, their underlying emotions include sadness, fear, anger, and guilt.

circuit training   Exercising at a series of stations with different types of activities at each station.

classic autism   A disorder originally known as Kanner's syndrome. Characteristics include global language disorder, abnormal (bizarre) behavior patterns, social isolation, and usually, but not always, mental retardation.

classroom conduct problems   Behaviors children demonstrate that interfere with instruction, impede social interaction, or endanger others.

cochlear implant   An electronic device that is surgically implanted into a bone in the skull that stimulates the remaining fibers of the auditory division of the eighth cranial nerve and enables persons who are profoundly deaf to hear and distinguish environmental sounds and warning signals.

cognitive behavioral methods   Intervention strategies designed to teach learners with autism to monitor their own behavior and provide self-reinforcement.

cognitive function   Ability to organize, reorganize, and contemplate information in the brain.

collaboration   A process in which two or more professionals share ideas and responsibilities.

communicative disorders   Conditions that interfere with one's ability to understand or be understood.

community-based assessment   Assessment that focuses on skills needed to live independently in the community.

community-based resources   Recreation, sport, and leisure agencies and facilities located in the community.

component model of functional routines   Breaking down a person's daily sport and other physical activities into a series of routines that are composed of several skills.

concentric muscular contraction   The amount of tension in the muscle is greater than the amount of applied resistance, so that the muscle shortens and movement results.

concussion   Impaired functioning of an organ, especially the brain, as a result of a violent blow or impact.

condition shifting   Program in which several conditions of behavioral objectives are altered to produce activities that are sequenced from lesser to greater difficulty.

conditions   A description of how the learner is to perform an objective.

conduct disorder   Specific actions, or failures to act, that cause a student to be in trouble within the home, school, or community.

conductive hearing impairment   Condition in which the intensity of sound is reduced before reaching the inner ear, where the auditory nerve begins.

congenital   Present at birth.

construct validity   The degree to which a test measures what its author claims it measures.

content analysis   Breaking down discrete or continuous tasks into parts or components.

content-referenced   Components of a task or steps in a sequence of tasks.

content-related validity   The degree to which the contents of the test represent an identified body of knowledge.

contingency contracting   An agreement between the student and the teacher that indicates what the student must do to earn a specific reward.

continuous reinforcement schedule   Reinforcing a behavior every time it is demonstrated.

contraindicated exercise   Activities that are to be avoided because of their potential for harm.

convergence   The ability to turn the eyes inward (medially) while visually tracking an object moving toward the body.

corrective physical education   Activity designed to habilitate or rehabilitate deficiencies in posture or mechanical alignment of the body.

counselor   Professional trained to facilitate students' affective development.

coxa plana   A vascular, necrotic flattening of the head of the femur; also known as Legg-Calvé-Perthes disease.

coxa valga   Increase in the angle of the neck of the head of the femur to less than 120 degrees.

coxa vara   Decrease in the angle of the neck of the head of the femur to less than 120 degrees.

criteria for eligibility   Requirements for being qualified to receive special educational services mandated by law.

criterion for mastery   Stated level of performance indicating attainment of an objective.

criterion shifting   Programs in which the level of mastery (number of repetitions, distance traveled, speed, or range of motion) is modified to make the task easier or more difficult.

criterion-referenced   Measurement against a predetermined level of mastery.

criterion-related validity   The degree to which a test compares with another acceptable standard of the same performance.

cross-lateral   Coordination of both sides of the body.

cross-pattern creep   Coordinating movements of legs and arms on opposite sides of the body while supporting the body on hands and knees.

cues and correction procedures   Techniques used to increase the probability that a skill learned in one setting will be demonstrated in a different setting.

cystic fibrosis   An inherited disease of the exocrine glands primarily affecting the gastrointestinal and respiratory systems.

D

de facto integration   Placing students in educational settings without concern for their individual needs.

deaf   A hearing impairment which is so severe that the person is impaired in processing linguistic information through hearing, with or without amplification, which adversely affects educational performance.

deaf-blind   Loss of both hearing and vision.

debilitating conditions   Physiological situations that progressively weaken individuals.

depth perception   The ability to visually determine the position of objects in space by comparing the images entering each eye with each other.

developmental approach   A bottom-up teaching strategy that addresses the lowest levels of motor development found to be deficient.

developmental delay   Retarded or arrested stages of performance, which hinder a child's ability to be successful at a task.

developmental disabilities   A term to describe all disabilities collectively.

developmentally appropriate learning environment   A learning situation that is sensitive and responsive to the unique needs of children.

developmentally appropriate movement experience   Play and movement opportunities, based on individual need, that allow a child to choose to participate in play and movement activities with success.

developmentally appropriate movement/play assessment   Observing and recording children's cognitive, social-emotional, communication and language, and sensory-motor development as they interact with their environment.

diabetes   A chronic metabolic disorder in which the cells cannot use glucose.

diabetes insipidus   A condition that results from an inability to concentrate urine in the kidneys.

diabetes mellitus   A group of diseases characterized by hyperglycemia resulting from defects in insulin secretion, insulin action, or both.

diplegia   A neurological condition involving both the arms and the legs, with the most involvement in the legs.

direct appeal to value areas   Controlling behavior by calling on values children have internalized.

direct services   Those professions identified by law with responsibility for providing educational services to students with disabilities (e.g., classroom teachers and physical educators).

directionality   Perception of direction in space.

disability   An obstacle.

disabled   An individual with physical, social, or psychological variations that significantly interfere with normal growth and development.

disciplinary review   A meeting between parents and educational professionals to discuss a student's disruptive behavior and develop a behavior-management strategy or plan.

disorder   General mental, physical, or psychological malfunction of the processes.

dissociative disorder   A condition characterized by an inability to integrate memories, perceptions, identity, or consciousness normally.

divergence   The ability to turn the eyes outward (laterally) while visually tracking an object moving away from the body.

dominant stage theory   A theory that proposes that the parent or sibling of a child with a disability experiences emotions and reactions that are identical to those experienced by an individual facing the death of a loved one or facing a terminal illness.

dorsiflexion   The act of bending the foot upward (flexion).

dorsoflexion of the head   Extending the head toward the back of the body.

drug therapy   The use of prescribed medications to relieve symptoms and to control unusual aggressive behaviors and other types of behaviors that interfere with learning.

Duchenne muscular dystrophy (pseudohypertrophic)   A disease of the muscular system characterized by progressive weakness and atrophy of the pelvic girdle followed by the shoulder girdle muscles.

due process   The procedure to be followed to determine the extent to which an individual's constitutional rights have been made available.

duration recording   Noting the length of time a behavior occurs.

dysmenorrhea   Cyclic pain that usually starts just before or with menses, peaks in twenty-four hours, and subsides after two days.

dysplasia   Separation of the hip joint.

E

early childhood intervention (ECI)   Providing developmentally appropriate programs for infants and toddlers ages birth to three years.

early childhood intervention (ECI) natural settings initiative   Educating infants and toddlers ages birth to three years in their most natural environments.

eccentric muscular contraction   The resistance is greater than the tension in the muscle, so that the muscle gradually lengthens without relaxing.

ecological inventory   A checklist of behaviors needed to function in a given environment.

educational accountability   A particular educational program, method, or intervention can be demonstrated to cause a significant positive change in one or more behaviors.

educational classification   The educational status of a student that has been determined by testing.

educational services   The curricula, programs, accommodations, placements, behavior-management plans, and personnel available to students.

emotional disturbance   A condition resulting in exhibiting over a long period of time or to a marked degree behaviors that adversely affect a student's educational performance that cannot be explained by intellectual, sensory, or health factors.

empathy experiences   Attempting to get the "feel" of having a disability by participating in activities while having a sensory or motor limitation placed on oneself (e.g., being blindfolded, ambulating in a wheelchair, wearing ear covers).

epilepsy   A disturbance resulting from abnormal electrical activity of the brain which briefly alters consciousness, motor activity, sensory phenomena, or behavior.

equilibrium dysfunction   Inability to maintain static and/or dynamic balance.

equilibrium reflexes   A reflex that helps a person maintain an upright position when the center of gravity is suddenly moved beyond the base of support.

esotropia   A condition in which the eyes turn inward, such as cross-eyes.

event recording   Noting the number of times a specifically defined behavior occurs within a time interval.

eversion   Lifting the outer border of the foot upward.

Ewing's sarcoma   A round cell bone tumor of childhood.

exclusionary time-out   Removing a student from the immediate environment to eliminate the possibility of the student's disrupting the class through inappropriate behavior.

exercise-induced asthma (EIA)   An acute airway narrowing after strenuous exertion.

exertion level   Amount of effort required for a task.

exotropia   A condition wherein an eye deviates laterally away from the nose.

expressive language   Ability to communicate feeling, emotions, needs, and thoughts through speaking and gesturing (facial or manual).

extinction   Removal of reinforcers that previously followed the behavior.

extraocular muscles of the eyes   The six pairs of muscles attached to the eye that permit movement of the eyes.

F

facilitated communication   The practice of using a helper to support the hand, wrist, or shoulder of a person with autism to enable that learner to make selections on a communication device such as a keyboard.

facioscapulohumeral muscular dystrophy (Landouzy-Dejerine)   A disease of the muscular system characterized by weakness of the facial muscles and shoulder girdles.

fading   Gradually withdrawing help from a task.

fatiguability   Easily tired.

fetal alcohol syndrome   Severe mental retardation because of impaired brain development as a result of maternal use of alcohol during pregnancy.

fixed-interval ratio reinforcement schedule   Reinforcing the occurrence of a desirable behavior demonstrated a set number of times according to a predetermined schedule (e.g., one reinforcer for every three instances of desired behavior).

flexibility   Range of motion available at any one or a combination of joints.

floor time   A systematic approach incorporating developmentally appropriate activities for the purpose of improving human interaction skills of persons with autism.

focal seizure   A seizure that involves loss of body tone and collapse while remaining conscious.

formal tests   Tests that have been developed for a specific purpose and have been standardized.

forward chaining   The first step of a series of tasks is taught first.

fragile X syndrome   An abnormality of the X chromosome, which results in a folic acid deficiency and leads to learning disabilities or mild to severe mental retardation.

free appropriate public education (FAPE)   Entitlement of all children to an education, without charge, that meets their specific needs.

full inclusion   Educating all children in supported, heterogeneous, age-appropriate, natural, child-focused classroom, school, and community environments.

full-service schools   Schools that include the educational, social, human, and health services to enable families to access on one site benefits available though local, state, and federal agencies.

functional adaptations   Modifications by using assistive devices or by changing the demands of a task to permit participation.

functional postural deficiencies   Postural imbalances that result from asymmetrical muscle development.

functional skills   Movements that can be used for a variety of tasks.

G

gait training   Teaching or reteaching an individual to ambulate by walking.

general curriculum   The educational offerings that are available to children without disabilities.

general metatarsalgia   Pain in the foot caused by undue pressure exerted on the plantar surface.

general physical education   Physical and motor instruction available to students from kindergraten through high school.

generalization   The transfer of abilities and skills from the training environment to nontraining environments.

gentle teaching   A learning environment that is created for persons with autism that is characterized by warmth and caring and is designed to reduce the potential for failure.

genu valgum   Knock-knee.

genu varum   Bowleg.

glaucoma   A condition in which the pressure of the fluid inside the eye is too high, causing loss of vision.

Gowers' sign   Moving from a hands and knees kneeling position to an upright position by pushing the hands against the legs in a climbing pattern.

grand mal seizure   Seizure that involves severe convulsions accompanied by stiffening, twisting, alternating contractions and relaxations, and unconsciousness.

guide runner   A person with vision who runs alongside a runner who is visually impaired and verbally describes the distance to the finish or touches the elbow of the runner to indicate any lateral off-step.

guide wire   Ropes or heavy string stretched 36 inches above lane makers that help runners with limited vision feel the perimeters of the lanes.

H

habilitation   An educational term that indicates that the person with a disability is to be taught basic skills needed for independence.

hallux valgus   Displacement of the great toe toward the other toes, such as occurs with a bunion.

hammer toe   The proximal phalanx (first joint) of the toe is hyperextended, the second phalanx (second joint) is flexed, and the distal phalanx (third joint) is flexed or extended.

hanging (posture) test   Visually assessing the alignment of the spine as the person being evaluated hangs by the hands from a horizontal support.

hard-of-hearing   A hearing impairment, whether permanent or fluctuating, which adversely affects a person's educational performance but which is not included under the category of deaf.

health-related fitness   Components of physiological functioning that are believed to offer protection against degenerative diseases.

health-related tests   Assessment instruments that include measures of cardiovascular endurance, muscular strength, percentage of body fat, and flexibility.

hemiplegia   A neurological condition involving both limbs on one side, with the arm being more affected than the leg.

heterogeneous groupings   Amassing students with different levels of abilities together.

heterophoria   Tendency toward visual malalignment.

heterotropia   Malalignments of the eyes in which one or both eyes consistently deviate from the central axis.

hierarchical order   A continuum of ordered activities in which a task of lower order and lesser difficulty is prerequisite to a related task of greater difficulty.

high rates of inappropriate behavior   Demonstrated behaviors that interfere with appropriate behavior and that occur frequently or for long periods of time.

Hodgkin's disease   A chronic condition in which large, multinucleated reticulum cells are present in lymph node tissue or in other nonreticular formation sites.

holding therapy   An intervention strategy, used with individuals who have autism, that involves physically holding or remaining in close physical proximity to the learner.

Homeless Assistance Act   A federal law passed in 1987 and amended in 1990 that mandates that all children, including homeless children, have a right to access a free, appropriate public education.

homeostasis   The human body's attempt to keep itself in a state of balance.

homogeneous grouping   Amassing students with similar levels of abilities together.

human immunodeficiency virus (HIV) infection   Infection caused by a retrovirus, resulting in a wide range of clinical manifestations varying from asymptomatic carrier states (HIV positive) to severely debilitating and fatal disorders related to defective cell-mediated immunity.

hurdle lesson   Structuring a task in which a child can be successful to boost self-confidence and discourage the possibility of disruptive, avoidance behaviors.

hydrocephalic   Refers to an abnormal condition that results when cerebral spinal fluid is not reabsorbed properly, thus collecting around the brain.

hyperglycemia   A condition that results in too much blood sugar.

hyperopia   A condition in which the light rays focus behind the retina, causing an unclear image of objects closer than 20 feet from the eye.

hypertropia A condition in which one or both eyes swing upward.

hypoglycemia A condition that results in too little blood sugar.

hypotropia A condition in which one or both eyes turn downward.

I

IDEA Individuals with Disabilities Education Act of 1990; P.L. 101-476.

illumination experience Exposing a person without a disability to a highly skilled person with a disability.

impulse control The ability to resist an impulse, a drive, or a temptation to perform a harmful, disruptive, or inappropriate behavior.

inappropriate reflex behavior Persistence of primitive reflexes beyond age one year and/or failure to demonstrate all of the equilibrium reflexes after the first year of life.

incest A sexual act on a child by an adult who is biologically related to the child.

incidental learning Learning that is unplanned.

inclusion Serving all students in the general education program.

inclusive environment An environment designed to accommodate a variety of learners regardless of functional abilities.

indirect services Services provided by related service personnel to enable a student with a disability to function more fully.

individual education program (IEP) Specially designed instruction to meet the unique needs of a person for self-sufficient living.

individual education program (IEP) document An individual student's formal IEP report, which must be approved by parents/guardians and educational professionals.

individual education program (IEP) meeting A formally scheduled gathering of parents and educational professionals to discuss a student's present level of educational performance, goals, and educational alternatives.

individual education program (IEP) process The procedure followed to develop an appropriate educational experience.

individual family service plan (IFSP) A family-centered plan for assessing and prioritizing needs and programming and for providing services for at-risk children under the age of three years.

individual motor education plan (IMEP) A substitute name for the individual physical education plan (IPEP).

individual physical education plan (IPEP) That portion of the IEP that addresses the physical and motor needs of the student.

individual transition plan (ITP) The specific strategies needed to move a child with a disability smoothly from home to preschool, preschool to school, or school to community.

individualized physical education program An activity program developed from assessment information to meet the unique needs of an individual with a disability.

Individuals with Disabilities Education Act of 1990 (IDEA) Federal legislation that replaced the term *handicapped* with *disability* and expanded on the types of services offered to persons with disabilities and types of conditions covered in the law.

infantile scoliosis Scoliosis that develops during the first three years of life.

informal tests Tests that have been developed for a general purpose and have not been standardized.

inner language process Ability to transform experience into symbols.

insight-oriented therapy Relieving symptoms by treating causes of behavior.

instructional environment A setting designed for the education of students.

integration Placement of students with disabilities in environments with nondisabled students.

integration processes Perceptual-motor, physical fitnesss, and motor fitness.

interest boosting Involving a child in an activity to engage his or her interest in positive behaviors.

interval recording Counting the occurrence or nonoccurrence of a behavior within a specified time interval.

intervention strategies Techniques for weakening or eliminating disruptive behaviors or reinforcing desirable behaviors or practices.

inversion Turning upward of the medial border of the foot.

isokinetic exercises Exercises that provide resistance through the entire range of movement, either by pushing one limb against the other or by using an exercise machine that provides resistance equal to the amount of pull throughout the range of motion.

isometric (static) muscular contraction   The amount of tension in the muscle equals the amount of applied resistance, so that no movement occurs.

isotonic exercises   Exercises using progressive resistance using free weights or a machine using stacked weights.

J

jacksonian focal seizure   A seizure that involves localized twitching of muscles in the extremities.

Jacobson relaxation techniques   Consciously relaxing voluntary skeletal muscles by stiffening and relaxing each body part in sequence.

juvenile arthritis (Still's disease)   A form of rheumatoid arthritis that afflicts children before the age of seven years.

K

Kaposi's sarcoma   An AIDS-related condition that manifests itself as a malignant tumor.

ketoacidosis   A violent reaction to lack of circulating insulin.

kinesthetic guidance   Manually moving a student through the correct movement pattern, so that the individual can get the "feel" of the motion.

kinesthetic system   Muscles, tendons, joints, and other body parts that help control and coordinate activities such as walking and talking.

kypholordosis   Exaggerated thoracic and lumbar spinal curves (round swayback).

kyphosis   Exaggerated thoracic spinal curve (humpback).

L

labyrinthine portion of inner ear   That part of the inner ear located in the vestibule that responds to movements of the head against gravity.

labyrinthine righting reaction   An equilibrium reflex that causes the head to move to an upright position when the head is suddenly tipped while the eyes are closed.

language disorder   An impairment in the ability to understand and/or use words in context, both verbally and nonverbally.

laterality   An awareness of the difference between both sides of the body.

least restrictive environment   The setting that enables an individual with disabilities to function to the fullest of his or her capability.

legally blind   Visual acuity of 20/20 or less in the better eye after maximum correction or having a visual field that subtends an angle of 20 degrees or less.

leukemia   A type of cancer that negatively affects the body's blood-forming tissues.

levels of motor function   Basic neurological building blocks, integration processes, functional motor skills, and sport and recreational skills.

local education agency (LEA)   The school district or education cooperative responsible for implementing state policy and interpreting that policy to meet the needs of learners within the district or cooperative.

locus of control   The extent to which behavior is determined from within oneself or is dependent on others.

lordosis   Exaggerated lumbar vertebral curve (swayback).

low rates of appropriate behavior   Inability to remain on task for a prolonged time in familiar or unfamiliar settings.

low vision   A severe visual impairment, not necessarily limited to distance vision.

low vitality   A generalized long-lasting feeling of lack of energy.

M

mainstreaming   Placement of children with disabilities in regular class, based on an IEP.

maintenance   The perpetuation of a trained behavior after all formal intervention has ceased.

malleolus   Ankle bone.

malnutrition   Faulty or inadequate nourishment resulting from an improper diet.

manual communication system   Techniques for communicating, including Pidgin Sign Language, American Sign Language, Manually Coded English, and fingerspelling.

manual guidance   Physically moving a person through a movement.

manual muscle testing   Evaluating the strength of a muscle by having an individual attempt to move a limb while the evaluator physically resists the movement.

mastoiditis   Infection of the air cells of the mastoid process.

mediation   A primary process used to resolve conflicts.

medical diagnostic service personnel   Medical personnel who provide diagnostic services to children with disabilities and verify the disability status of individuals.

medically fragile   Children with special health-management needs who require technology, special services, or some form of ongoing medical support for survival.

meditation   The art and technique of blocking out thoughts that create tension and refocusing attention and energy on soothing, quieting mental activity.

meningocele   A protruding sac containing the lining of the spinal column.

menstruation   The monthly loss of blood in mature females in response to hormonal cues.

mental retardation   Significantly subaverage general intellectual functioning existing concurrently with deficits in adaptive behavior, manifesting before age eighteen years.

metatarsal arch   The transverse arch of the foot, which runs across the ball of the foot.

metatarsalgia   Also known as Morton's toe; severe pain or cramp in the metatarsus in the region of the fourth toe.

midline problem   The inability to coordinate limbs on opposite sides of the body.

mobility training   An adaptive technique that is applied to the blind and enhances the ability to travel.

modeling   Demonstration of a task by the teacher or reinforcement by another student who performs a desirable behavior in the presence of the targeted student.

momentary time sampling   Noting whether a behavior is occurring at the end of specified time intervals.

monoplegia   A neurological condition involving a single limb.

mood disorders   A group of heterogeneous, typically recurrent illnesses that are characterized by pervasive mood disturbances, psychomotor dysfunction, and vegetative symptoms.

Morton's toe   See *metatarsalgia*.

motor coordination   The ability to use the muscles of the body to efficiently produce complex movement.

motor development lag   See *developmental delay*.

motor fitness   Agility, power, speed, and coordination.

motor milestones   Significant movement patterns and skills that emerge at predictable times during the life of a typically developing child.

motor neuropathy   A complication, resulting from long-standing diabetes, that causes an imbalance between the intrinsic and extrinsic muscles and contributes to deformities of the foot, change in gait pattern, and ulceration.

motor tics   Sudden twitches of the entire body, shoulders, and/or head; eyeblinks or rolling of the head; repetitive tapping, drumming, or touching behaviors; or grimacing.

motor-planning deficit   Inability to determine and execute a sequence of tasks needed to achieve a goal.

multiculturalism   A movement to make society a place in which people from all cultures have equal respect and equal influence in shaping larger community values.

multidisciplinary motor team   A group of direct service and related service providers who cooperate to determine and provide for students' physical and movement needs.

multiple sclerosis   A chronic degenerative neurological disease primarily affecting older adolescents and adults.

muscle tension recognition and release   Tensing and relaxing muscle groups at will; also known as differential relaxation.

muscular dystrophy   A group of inherited, progressive muscle disorders that differ according to which muscles are affected and that result in deterioration of muscle strength, power, and endurance.

muscular endurance   The ability of a muscle to contract repetitively.

mycobacterial infections   An AIDS-related condition that causes severe diseases localized in the lung or lymph nodes.

myelomeningocele   A protruding sac that contains the spinal cord and the lining of the spinal column.

myopia   A refractive condition in which the rays of light focus in front of the retina when a person views an object 20 feet away or more.

N

National Center on Physical Activity and Disability (NCPAD)   A project funded by the Centers for Disease Control and Prevention for the purpose of providing a clearinghouse for research and practice information to promote healthy lifestyles for persons with disabilities.

National Consortium for Physical Education and Recreation for Individuals with Disabilities (NCPERID)   An organization formed in 1973 to promote, stimulate, and encourage significant service delivery, quality professional preparation, and meaningful research in physical education and recreation for individuals with disabilities.

natural environment   Community settings where individuals function.

negative practice or satiation   Constantly acknowledging a behavior for the purpose of discouraging demonstration of the behavior.

negative support reflex   A reflex in which there is flexion of the knees when pressure is removed from the feet.

neuroblastoma   A solid tumor of the embryonal neural crest of the sympathetic nervous system.

neurological components   Sensory input systems and perceptual processes that underlie movement patterns and skills and affective and cognitive functioning.

neurological disability   Chronic debilitating conditions resulting from impairments of the central nervous system.

neurological validity   The extent to which a test item truly measures central nervous system function.

neuromuscular re-education   Exercises performed through a muscle's current range of motion to stimulate proprioceptors and enable greater functional use.

neurophysiological differences   Pertaining to structural and/or functional changes to the central nervous system.

nonexclusionary time-out   Removing the student from an activity but allowing the student to remain in the vicinity of the class.

nonparalytic poliomyelitis   An acute viral infection that involves the central nervous system but does not damage the motor cells of the spinal cord.

nonsequential stage theory   A theory that proposes that the parents, siblings, or extended family members of a child with a disability may experience some or all of the stages of grief described by Kübler-Ross, but not necessarily in predictable stages.

normalization   Making available to disabled individuals patterns and conditions of everyday life that are as close as possible to the norms and patterns of the mainstream of society.

normative-referenced test   A test that measures an individual in comparison with others of the same age. Comparison standards are reported in percentiles, age equivalencies, and/or stanines.

nystagmus   Rapid movement of the eyes from side to side, up and down, in a rotary motion, or in a combination of these movements.

O

obesity   Pathological overweight in which a person is 20 percent or more above the normal weight (compare with *overweight*).

occupational therapist   Professional who improves functional living and employment skills.

ocular-motor control   The ability to fixate visually on objects and track their movement.

oculomotor defects   Difficulty coordinating the movement of both eyes, resulting in depth perception deficits.

Office of Special Education and Rehabilitative Services (OSERS)   The unit within the Department of Education that has responsibility for setting the agenda and providing direction regarding the delivery of educational services for students with disabilities.

oppositional-defiant disorder   An antisocial behavior characterized by extreme disobedience, aggression, loss of temper, and arguments with adults and others in authority.

optical righting reaction   An equilibrium reflex that causes the head to move to the upright position when the body is suddenly tipped and the eyes are open.

options approach   A comprehensive program for persons with autism that is designed to enhance human performance and potential.

oral communication method   Hearing-impaired persons are provided amplification of sound and are taught through speech reading (lipreading).

orientation and mobility   Services provided to students who are blind or visually impaired to enable them to systematically use skills to orient them within their environments in schools, at home, and in the community.

orthopedic conditions   Deformities, diseases, and injuries of the bones and joints.

orthoptic vision   The ability to use the extraocular muscles of the eyes in unison.

orthoptics   The science of correcting deviations of the visual axis of the eye.

Osgood-Schlatter condition   Epiphysitis of the tibial tubercle.

osteoarthritis   A disorder of the hyaline cartilage primarily in the weight-bearing joints resulting from trauma or repeated use.

osteogenesis imperfecta (brittle bone disease)   A condition marked by both weak bones and elasticity of the joints, ligaments, and skin.

osteomyelitis   Inflammation of a bone and its medullary cavity; sometimes referred to as myelitis.

osteosarcoma   A form of childhood bone cancer.

other health impairment   Limitations in strength and vitality or alertness with respect to the environment that is a result of chronic or acute health problems such as asthma, attention deficit disorders, diabetes, epilepsy, a heart condition, hemophilia, lead poisoning, leukemia, nephritis, rheumatic fever, and sickle cell anemia that adversely affect a child's educational performance.

otitis media   Infection of the middle ear.

overcorrection   Repeated practice of an appropriate behavior whenever an inappropriate behavior is demonstrated.

overload principle   Improving muscular strength by gradually increasing the resistance used over time (days or months).

overweight   Any deviation of 10 percent or more above the ideal weight for a person (compare with *obesity*).

P

panic disorder   A sudden onset of uncomfortable symptoms associated with real or perceived fears.

paralytic poliomyelitis   An acute viral infection that involves the central nervous system and interferes with voluntary and involuntary muscle function.

paraplegia   A neurological condition involving both legs with little or no involvement of the arms.

parent counselors and trainers   Specially trained professionals who provide education and support services to parents of children with disabilities.

Parkinson's disease   A progressive disease that results in tremor of the resting muscles, a slowing of voluntary movements, muscular weakness, abnormal gait, and postural instability.

partial-interval time sampling   Noting whether a behavior was demonstrated any time during given periods of time.

partially sighted   Having less than 20/70 visual acuity in the better eye after correction, having a progressive eye disorder that will probably reduce vision below 20/70, or having peripheral vision that subtends an angle less than 20 degrees.

patella   Knee cap.

peer tutor   Same-age or cross-age (older) students who assist other students.

percentage of body fat   The amount of body fat in relation to muscle, bone, and other elements in the body.

perceptual function   Ability to integrate sensory input information into constructs in the central nervous system.

perceptual-motor abilities   Balance, cross-lateral integration, body image, spatial awareness, laterality, and directionality.

perinatal   During the birth process.

peripheral vascular disease   Insufficient blood flow to blood vessels of the extremities.

permanent product recording   Counting the actual products or behaviors that are demonstrated.

pernicious anemia   An anemia caused by a decrease in the number of red corpuscles in the blood.

personal futures planning (PFP) A proactive strategy for identifying resources within and without the school that will provide ongoing support to a student with a disability.

personality disorders Pervasive, inflexible, and stable personality traits that deviate from cultural norms and cause distress or functional impairment.

pervasive developmental disorder (PDD) Severe impairment in several areas of development. Types include autistic disorder, Asperger's disorder, Rett's disorder, childhood disintegrative disorder, and pervasive developmental disorder–not otherwise specified.

pervasive developmental disorder–not otherwise specified A condition in which the learner exhibits some, but not all, of the traits commonly associated with autism and/or pervasive developmental disorder.

pes cavus Exaggerated height of the longitudinal arch of the foot (hollow arch).

pes planus Extreme flatness of the longitudinal arch of the foot.

petit mal seizure Nonconvulsive seizure in which consciousness is lost for a few seconds.

phobia A significant, persistent, yet unrealistic and often debilitating fear of an event, a person, an activity, or an animal/insect.

physical fitness A physical state of well-being that allows people to perform daily activities with vigor, reduce their risk of health problems related to lack of exercise, and establish a fitness base for participation in a variety of activities; also refers to physical properties of muscular activity, such as strength, flexibility, endurance, and cardiovascular endurance.

physical lag A deficit in physical fitness components or function of a specific body part.

physical priming Physically holding and moving the body parts of the learner through the activity.

physical restraint Holding students to prevent them from physically harming themselves or someone else.

physical therapist A professional who evaluates and treats physical impairments through the use of various physical modalities.

placement Alternative educational environments available to students with disabilities.

planned ignoring Choosing not to react to a behavior to avoid reinforcing the behavior.

plantar flexion Moving the foot toward its plantar surface at the ankle joint (extension).

play therapy A type of intervention used with emotionally disturbed children that involves using play to provide insight into emotional problems.

plumb line (posture) test Comparing body landmarks with a gravity line to assess posture.

pneumocystis carinii pneumonia An AIDS-related condition that is a form of pneumonia caused by reactivation of chronic latent infections.

poliomyelitis (polio) An acute viral infection that may or may not lead to paralysis.

poly drugs More than one type of drug.

portfolio assessment process Using a variety of techniques to gather ongoing information about a child's developmental progress.

positive reinforcement A pleasing consequence that follows an action.

positive support reflex A reflex that causes the legs to extend and the feet to plantar flex when one is standing.

postnatal After birth.

postpoliomyelitis syndrome A condition that occurs many years after a paralytic poliomyelitis attack that results in muscle fatigue and decreased endurance, accompanied by weakness and atrophy in selected muscles.

posttraumatic stress disorder A recurring intense fear, helplessness, or horror as a result of direct or indirect personal experience of an event that involves actual or threatened death, serious injury, or threat to personal integrity.

posture screen Comparing body landmarks with a grid of vertical and horizontal lines to evaluate all segments of the body in relationship to each other.

Prader-Willi syndrome A condition characterized by neonatal hypotonia and feeding difficulty followed by excessive appetite, pica behavior, and obesity starting in early childhood.

premenstrual syndrome (PMS) A condition that occurs in some females seven to ten days before menstruation and usually persists until the menstrual flow begins and that is characterized by nervousness, irritability, agitation, anger, insomnia, depression, severe fatigue, and fluid retention.

prenatal During the pregnancy.

present level of educational performance   The skills, behaviors, and patterns an individual can demonstrate at any given time.

primitive reflexes   Automatic reactions that should appear in an infant's movement repertoire during the first six months of life.

principle of normalization   Routines of life that are typical for individuals without disabilities.

problem-oriented exercise management   Developing a therapeutic exercise plan based on assessment of subjective and objective data.

programmed instruction   An instructional strategy to promote students' abilities to direct their own learning.

progressive relaxation   Consciously releasing tension in specific muscle groups.

progressive resistive exercise   Systematically adding resistance to an exercise to place additional demand on a muscle for the purpose of increasing strength.

prompting   Physically holding and moving the body parts of the learner through an activity.

pronated feet   A combination of tipping of the outer border of the foot and toeing out.

pronation   Rotation of the palm of the hand downward or eversion and abduction of the foot.

prone lying test   Visually assessing the alignment of the spine as the person being evaluated lies prone.

proprioceptive facilitation   Exercises designed to excite motor units of a muscle to overcome paralysis.

proprioceptors   Sensory receptors, located in the muscles, joints, tendons, deep tissues, and vestibular portion of the inner ear, that respond to movement.

protective extensor thrust reflex   A reflex that causes immediate extension of the arms when the head and upper body are tipped suddenly forward.

proximity control   Positioning oneself close to a child to encourage on-task behavior.

psychiatrist   A physician with specialized training in the study and treatment of disorders of the mind.

psychologist   A licensed professional who measures the cognitive, affective, and/or social status of a child with a disability and recommends intervention strategies.

psychomotor seizure   Uncontrollable atypical social-motor behavior, including temper tantrums, hand clapping, spitting, swearing, and shouting for one or two minutes.

psychosocial competence   Sense of self-confidence necessary to participate in successful interpersonal relationships.

psychosocial development   The level of one's psychosocial competence.

ptosis   Weakness and prolapse of an organ (e.g., prominent abdomen).

Q

quadriplegia (tetraplegia)   A neurological condition involving all of the limbs to a similar degree.

R

rape   A sexual act involving penetration by an adult who is unrelated to the victim.

reasonable accommodation   Modification of policies, practices, and/or procedures, including provision of auxiliary aids and/or services to enable a person with disabilities to use a facility.

receptive language   Ability to comprehend meaning associated with language.

reciprocal exercises   Exercises to stimulate and strengthen a muscle's agonist (protagonist).

recreation therapist   Professional who works with physical and adapted physical educators and who provides information for individuals with disabilities to help them in making wise decisions in the use of leisure time.

reduction of tension through humor   Using amusing comments or behaviors to reduce anxiety-producing situations.

refractive vision   The process by which light rays are bent as they enter the eyes.

regular education initiative (REI)   A federally endorsed effort to return children with disabilities to regular education programs to receive the majority of services regardless of the child's unique needs.

regular education program   Routine educational services available to students without disabilities.

rehabilitation counselor   Specially trained person who provides services that focus specifically on career development, employment preparation, and the achievement of independence and integration in the work place and community.

reinforcement of appropriate target behavior
Rewarding a student for demonstrating a prespecified target behavior.

reinforcement of behavior other than target behavior
Rewarding a student for not demonstrating a prespecified misbehavior during a predetermined time limit.

reinforcement of incompatible behavior   Rewarding a student for demonstrating a behavior that is incompatible with the target misbehavior (e.g., rewarding a student for assisting rather than fighting with a peer).

reinforcement schedule   The frequency with which reinforcers are given.

related services   Services that help a person with disabilities benefit from direct services.

relaxation therapy   Teaching a person to achieve a state of both muscular and mental tension reduction by the systematic use of environmental cues.

reliability   Consistency.

remedial physical education   Activity designed to habilitate or rehabilitate functional motor movements and develop physical and motor prerequisites for functional skills.

removal of seductive objects   Controlling behavior by eliminating from view equipment children are attracted to.

repetition   The number of times the work interval is repeated under identical conditions.

reprimand   A form of punishment that involves verbally chastising a student for inappropriately exhibiting a target behavior.

resistance training   The use of isotonic or isokinetic exercise to improve musculoskeletal strength.

response generalization   Changes in behavior that were not specifically targeted for change.

response maintenance generalization   Changes in behavior that continue to be demonstrated after reinforcement has stopped.

restructure of classroom program   Modifying a class routine to control student behavior.

retinitis pigmentosa   Degeneration of the retina that produces gradual loss of peripheral vision.

retinoblastoma   A malignant tumor that arises from the immature retina.

retinopathy   A complication resulting from long-standing diabetes that is characterized by blurred vision, sudden loss of vision in one or both eyes, and/or black spots or flashing lights in the field of vision.

retinopathy of prematurity   A visual impairment caused by excess oxygen during incubation of premature infants.

Rett's disorder   A neurological disorder characterized by normal development during the first six months of life, followed by loss of acquired fine motor skills and development of impaired language skills, gait apraxia, and stereotypical hand movements.

reverse mainstreaming   The infusion of individuals without disabilities into educational and recreational settings to interact with persons with disabilities.

rheumatoid arthritis   A systemic disease that causes inflammation, and eventual thickening, of the synovial tissue that surrounds joints.

S

scaffolding   Providing an educational environment/support system that allows a child to move forward and continue to build new competencies.

schizophrenia   Abnormal behavior patterns and personality disorganization accompanied by less than adequate contact with reality.

school health service personnel   School staff, usually registered nurses, who monitor student health records, administer medicine, and provide other prescribed medical services.

school reform initiatives   Alterations in the structure, curriculum, and management of schools to improve the effectiveness of the learning environment.

schoolwide behavior-management system   A systematic, collaborative strategy to prevent and manage students' behavior in a positive fashion that involves teachers, staff, parents, and students.

scoliosis   Lateral and rotational deviation of the vertebral column.

self-correct   The ability to think about and modify one's own behavior.

self-management   Shifting responsibility for behavior from the teacher or parent to the student.

self-management practice   The ability to control one's own behavior.

sensorineural hearing impairment   A loss of hearing caused by absence or malfunction of the cochlea or eighth cranial nerve.

sensory input system dysfunction Failure of a sensory system to function because of a delay in development or neurological impairment.

sensory integration deficit Failure to process sensory information at the central nervous system level.

sensory neuropathy A complication, resulting from long-standing diabetes, that is characterized by loss of the senses of pain, light touch, and heat.

serious emotional disturbance A condition exhibiting one or more of the following characteristics over a long period of time and to a marked degree that adversely affects educational performance: (1) inability to learn that cannot be explained in other ways, (2) inability to maintain or build satisfactory interpersonal relationships, (3) inappropriate types of behavior or feelings, (4) general pervasive mood of unhappiness or depression, and (5) tendency to develop physical symptoms or fears associated with personal or school problems.

shaken baby syndrome Brain damage resulting from being violently shaken during infancy.

shaping Reinforcement of small, progressive steps that lead toward a desired behavior.

shortened gestation In utero life of less than thirty-six weeks. Gestations of less than twenty-seven weeks result in at-risk infants.

short-term instructional objectives Measurable intermediate steps that lead from the present level of performance to an annual goal.

shunt A drainage tube that is inserted to drain cerebral spinal fluid that is not being reabsorbed properly.

sickle cell anemia An inherited form of anemia that affects the bones, intestines, spleen, gallbladder, brain, and lungs.

signal interference Providing the student with a visible sign that a behavior is undesirable.

simulated training environment A teaching situation with task demands similar to those in the natural environment.

site-based management Local control of a school by a committee that includes the principal, teachers, parents, students, and community members.

situation or setting generalization Changes in behavior that occur from one environment to another and/or from one person to another.

skill problems Behaviors that interfere with a student's motor performance learning or efficiency.

skills The use of abilities to perform complex tasks competently as a result of reinforced practice.

social toxins Factors such as violence, poverty, hunger, homelessness, inadequate parenting, abuse and neglect, racism, and classism that seriously compromise the quality of life of children.

social worker A professional who provides individual and group counseling/assistance to children and their families.

socially aberrant behaviors Acting-out behaviors that are contrary to societal norms.

somatosensory strip in cerebral cortex The section of the cortex, just posterior to the central sulcus, that serves as a repository for incoming sensory information.

spasticity Clinical type of cerebral palsy characterized by muscle contractures and jerky, uncertain movements of the muscles.

spatial awareness The ability to replicate space in the "mind's eye" without visual input.

spatial relations The position of objects in space, particularly as the objects relate to the position of the body.

special physical education Another term used to describe adapted physical education.

specific learning disability A disorder in one or more of the basic psychological processes involved in understanding or in using language, spoken or written, which may manifest itself in the imperfect ability to listen, speak, read, write, spell, or do mathematical calculations.

speech disorder Difficulties producing speech sounds or problems with voice quality that interfere with an individual's ability to communicate effectively.

speech therapist A professional who evaluates children with speech and language deficits and provides intervention programs.

spina bifida Congenital separation or lack of union of the vertebral arches.

spina bifida cystica Congenital separation of the vertebral arches, resulting in a completely open spine with a protruding sac.

spina bifida occulta Congenital separation of the vertebral arches with no distension of the spinal cord lining or of the cord itself.

splinter skill   Particular perceptual or motor act that is performed in isolation and that does not generalize to other areas of performance.

split-half reliability   The degree to which scores from two halves of the same test agree when administered to one group.

spondylolisthesis   Congenital malformation of one or both of the neural arches of the fifth lumbar vertebra and anterior displacement on the sacrum.

spondylolysis   Congenital malformation of one or both of the neural arches of the fourth (rare) or fifth lumbar vertebra.

sports anemia   A form of anemia that afflicts athletes with low values of red blood cells or hemoglobin.

sports conditioning   An exercise program designed to promote general physical status as well as activities that maximize transfer to improved performance in competition.

sport-specific skills   Movements that are used to perform sport activities.

standardized test   A test that has been administered to a large group of persons under the same conditions to determine whether or not the test discriminates among ages and populations.

static stretching   Maintaining a muscle stretch for 30 to 60 seconds.

status epilepticus   A continual series of grand mal seizures with no letup.

stimulus change   Modifying the environment to discourage the expression of an undesirable behavior.

strabismus   Crossed eyes resulting from inability of the eye muscles to coordinate.

strength   The ability of a muscle to contract against resistance.

stress-coping training   Teaching a person to identify tension-producing situations and practice relaxation before or when confronted with those situations.

structural postural deficiencies   Postural imbalances that involve abnormalities in the bones and joints.

supination   Rotation of the palm of the hand upward, or abduction and inversion of the foot.

support from routine   Creating a highly structured program to enable insecure and/or emotionally disturbed children to function more effectively.

support personnel   Individuals who assist the direct service provider in enabling students with disabilities to function in the least restrictive environment.

symmetrical tonic neck reflex   A reflex in which the upper limbs tend to flex and the lower limbs extend when ventroflexing the head. If the head is dorsiflexed, the upper limbs extend and the lower limbs flex.

T

tactile defensive   An aversion to touch and other tactile stimulation.

tactile system   Knowledge of where the body ends and space begins and the ability to discriminate among pressure, texture, and size.

task analysis   Breaking a task into parts to determine which motor components are present.

task signals   Indicators that provide structure to the instructional environment.

task-specific approach   Teaching a skill directly and generalizing it to a variety of environments. If the skill cannot be learned, the prerequisites are taught.

TEACCH   A unique teaching strategy designed specifically for learners with autism that involves using an individual's daily routines to facilitate learning, particularly communication skills.

teaching style   The instructional approach used by the teacher.

tenotomy   Surgery on the tendons.

test objectivity   Freedom from bias and subjectivity.

test reliability   A measure of a test instrument's consistency.

test standardization   Administering an evaluation instrument to a large group of persons under the same conditions to determine whether the instrument discriminates among the group members.

test validity   How truthful a test is.

test-retest reliability   The degree to which scores agree when the same test is administered twice to the same persons.

tetraplegia (quadriplegia)   Involvement of all of the limbs to a similar degree.

three-year comprehensive re-evaluation   Laws require that every student with a disability who qualifies for special education services must receive a full re-evaluation at least every three years.

tibial torsion   Medial twisting of the lower leg on its long axis.

tic   A sudden, rapid, recurrent, nonrhythmic, stereotyped movement or vocalization.

tinnitus   Ringing in one or both ears in the absence of external stimuli.

token economy   A form of contingency management in which tokens are earned for desirable behavior.

tonic exercises   Passive movements of a muscle group to reduce the possibility of atrophy and/or to maintain organic efficiency.

tonic labyrinthine reflexes   Reflexes that are present when one maintains trunk extension when supine and trunk flexion when prone.

torticollis   Involuntary muscle contraction in the neck, causing the head to be twisted; wryneck.

total communication method   The hearing-impaired person elects to communicate through speech, signs, gesture, or writing.

total quality management (TQM)   A philosophy that promotes the practice of helping educators view themselves as supporters rather than judges; as mentors and coaches rather than lecturers; and as partners with parents, students, administrators, teachers, businesses, and entire communities rather than isolated workers within the walls of a classroom.

Tourette syndrome   A genetic disorder that results in multiple motor tics and one or more vocal tics.

toxoplasmic encephalitis   An AIDS-related condition that results in headaches, lethargy, confusion, seizures, and ring-enhancing lesions.

transdisciplinary   Representing different professions or disciplines.

transdisciplinary, play-based assessment (TPBA)   Two or more professionals sharing information about children they have observed in structured and unstructured play situations for the purpose of determining levels of functioning.

transition   Changing from one situation to another (e.g., from home to a school setting or from the school setting to a community environment).

transition service personnel   Specially trained professionals who provide the expertise to ensure that individuals with disabilities have the skills needed to work and function in the community.

transition services   Services available to facilitate the process of a child with a disability first entering public school, moving from a preschool to a school program, or moving from the school setting to a community setting.

transportation specialists   Individuals who assist in ensuring that disabled students are provided appropriate and timely transportation services.

traumatic brain injury (TBI)   Blows to the head that result in minor to serious brain damage.

traumatic conditions   Conditions resulting in damage to muscles, ligaments, tendons, or the nervous system as a result of a blow to the body.

travel vision   Residual vision in the blind that enables travel.

Trendelenburg test   A test for hip dislocation that is performed by standing on one leg.

type 1, insulin-dependent diabetes mellitus   A form of diabetes that is characterized by hyperglycemia and must be controlled with insulin therapy.

type 2, noninsulin-dependent diabetes mellitus   A form of diabetes that is characterized by hyperglycemia, but for which ongoing insulin therapy is usually not necessary.

type 3, other specific types of diabetes mellitus   Forms of diabetes that result from conditions and syndromes that impact glucose tolerance.

type 4, gestational carbohydrate intolerance diabetes mellitus   A form of diabetes that occurs in some pregnant women.

U

undernutrition   Insufficient nourishment, resulting in detriments to health and growth.

V

validity   Truthfulness.

Values clarification   A process of identifying and clarifying prejudices, attitudes, and notions.

variable-interval ratio reinforcement schedule   Modifying the number of behaviors reinforced according to a predetermined schedule (e.g., one reinforcer for every three instances followed by one reinforcer for every five instances of desirable behavior).

ventroflexion of the head   Flexing the head toward the front of the body.

vestibular sense   Response to balance.

vestibular system   The inner ear structures that are associated with balance and position in space.

vision specialist   A specially trained professional who evaluates the extent of visual disabilities and designs intervention programs that make possible a successful educational experience.

visual behavioral specialist (visual development specialist)   An optometrist or ophthalmologist who has specialized training in assessing and remediating misalignments of the eyes.

visual disability   Having a classification as partially sighted or blind.

vocal tics   Involuntary uttering of noises, words, or phrases, including sniffing, throat clearing, repeated coughing, coprolalia, laughing involuntarily, uttering a variety of sounds or yells, barking, grunting, and echolalia.

W

whole-interval time sampling   Noting whether a behavior occurred throughout an entire interval.

Wilms' tumor   A lethal tumor that is a form of nephroblastoma or renal embryoma.

winged scapula   Vertebral borders of the scapula project outward because of weakness of the serratus anterior of the middle and lower trapezius muscles.

Z

zero tolerance   A school policy to expel students from school or to place them in an alternative educational environment if they engage in specified disruptive behaviors.

Index

A

J

K

N

O

X

Y

Z